THE PAPERS OF

THOMAS JEFFERSON

RETIREMENT SERIES

THE PAPERS OF
Thomas Jefferson

RETIREMENT SERIES

Volume 8
1 October 1814 to 31 August 1815

J. JEFFERSON LOONEY, EDITOR

ROBERT F. HAGGARD, SENIOR ASSOCIATE EDITOR

JULIE L. LAUTENSCHLAGER, ASSOCIATE EDITOR

ELLEN C. HICKMAN AND CHRISTINE STERNBERG PATRICK,
ASSISTANT EDITORS

LISA A. FRANCAVILLA, MANAGING EDITOR

ANDREA R. GRAY AND PAULA VITERBO, EDITORIAL ASSISTANTS

CATHERINE COINER CRITTENDEN AND SUSAN SPENGLER,
SENIOR DIGITAL TECHNICIANS

PRINCETON AND OXFORD

PRINCETON UNIVERSITY PRESS

2011

Copyright © 2011 by Princeton University Press

Published by Princeton University Press, 41 William Street,

Princeton, New Jersey 08540

IN THE UNITED KINGDOM:

Princeton University Press, 6 Oxford Street,

Woodford, Oxfordshire OX20 1TW

Library of Congress Cataloging-in-Publication Data

Jefferson, Thomas, 1743–1826

The papers of Thomas Jefferson. Retirement series / J. Jefferson Looney, editor . . .

[et al.] p. cm.

Includes bibliographical references and index.

Contents: v. 1. 4 March to 15 November 1809—[etc.]—

v. 8. 1 October 1814 to 31 August 1815

ISBN 978-0-691-15318-6 (cloth: v. 8: alk. paper)

1. Jefferson, Thomas, 1743–1826—Archives. 2. Jefferson, Thomas, 1743–1826—

Correspondence. 3. Presidents—United States—Archives.

4. Presidents—United States—Correspondence. 5. United States—

Politics and government—1809–1817—Sources. 6. United States—Politics

and government—1817–1825—Sources. I. Looney, J. Jefferson.

II. Title. III. Title: Retirement series.

E302.J442 2004b

973.4'6'092—dc22   2004048327

This book has been composed in Monticello

Princeton University Press books are printed on
acid-free paper and meet the guidelines for permanence
and durability of the Committee on Production
Guidelines for Book Longevity of the
Council on Library Resources

Printed in the United States of America

DEDICATED TO THE MEMORY OF

ADOLPH S. OCHS

PUBLISHER OF THE NEW YORK TIMES

1896–1935

WHO BY THE EXAMPLE OF A RESPONSIBLE

PRESS ENLARGED AND FORTIFIED

THE JEFFERSONIAN CONCEPT

OF A FREE PRESS

THIS EDITION was made possible by a founding grant from The New York Times Company to Princeton University.

The Retirement Series is sponsored by the Thomas Jefferson Foundation, Inc., of Charlottesville, Virginia. It was created with a six-year founding grant from The Pew Charitable Trusts to the Foundation and to Princeton University, enabling the former to take over responsibility for the volumes associated with this period. Leading gifts from Richard Gilder, Mrs. Martin S. Davis, and Thomas A. Saunders III have assured the continuation of the Retirement Series. For these essential donations, and for other indispensable aid generously given by librarians, archivists, scholars, and collectors of manuscripts, the Editors record their sincere gratitude.

FOREWORD

THE 591 DOCUMENTS in this volume cover the period from 1 October 1814 to 31 August 1815. As usual, Thomas Jefferson both followed closely the events of the day and attended diligently to the needs of his farms, friends, and family. He was overjoyed by American victories on land and at sea during the last year of the War of 1812, optimistic about the nation's prospects, and highly interested in the negotiations leading to the Treaty of Ghent that closed the contest. Napoleon's return to power in France early in 1815 and defeat at the Battle of Waterloo in June were also a source of much reflection. Jefferson resigned the presidency of the American Philosophical Society in November 1814, continued to circulate his ideas about finance, supported David Bailie Warden's consular pretensions, and occasionally provided recommendations for federal employment. Most of his time, however, was spent on issues a bit closer to home.

Following Congress's decision to purchase Jefferson's library in January 1815, he oversaw the counting, packing, and transportation of his books to Washington, D.C. He used most of the funds from the sale to pay old debts. Famously remarking to John Adams that "I cannot live without books," Jefferson also spent some of the proceeds from his library acquiring replacement titles, both in the United States and Europe. In preparation for the payment of his wartime taxes, he drew up extensive lists of his possessions: real estate, manufactories, slaves, and household furnishings, among other items. Inventions and literary matters were still a source of diversion and, occasionally, exasperation. Jefferson engaged in the controversy over the originality of Walter Janes's loom, complained about patent abuses, corresponded with Horatio G. Spafford about his improved wheel-carriage, and received information from William Thornton about lining cisterns and a new type of filter. He continued to be stymied in his attempt to secure the early publication of a manuscript by Destutt de Tracy, revised draft chapters of Louis H. Girardin's continuation of John Daly Burk's and Skelton Jones's *History of Virginia*, and provided information to William Wirt on Virginia's and Rhode Island's Stamp Act resolutions. Of particular interest is Jefferson's vindication in a letter to Girardin of the bill of attainder he drew up in 1778 against the renegade Josiah Philips.

The third president's religious beliefs remained a topic of interest to many of his contemporaries. Several writers questioned him on the subject, his friend Charles Clay worried that he intended to publish his ideas, and Jefferson himself drafted but then drastically abridged a long letter to Peter H. Wendover criticizing the discussion of politics from the pulpit. Nor did the ex-president's regard for education wane. Toward the end of 1814 Jefferson drew up a detailed estimate of the cost of constructing an education pavilion and twenty dormitory rooms. He also drafted a bill to transform Albemarle Academy into Central College and offered to help tutor his grandson Francis Eppes in French and Latin.

As had hitherto been the case, visitors flocked to Monticello. Francis W. Gilmer, Francis C. Gray, and George Ticknor all left long descriptions of the mountaintop and its inhabitants, and Gray's visit led to an exchange about how many generations of white interbreeding it took to clear Negro blood. When the French philosophe Jean Baptiste Say expressed a desire to relocate to Albemarle County, Jefferson provided him with a comprehensive analysis of the local climate, agriculture, economy, society, and land values. Family also remained a primary focus. Although both his nephew Peter Carr and brother Randolph died in 1815 and ill-health beset other members of the family at various times, the marriage on 6 March 1815 of his grandson Thomas Jefferson Randolph to the daughter of his friend Wilson Cary Nicholas was a source of happiness. Jefferson also helped to oversee the conveyance of a tract of land to trustees as a way to protect his granddaughter Ann C. Bankhead and her children from the difficulties arising out of her husband's descent into alcoholism.

Two last documents deserve special mention. This volume begins with an extended satirical piece addressed to Jefferson and published in a Federalist newspaper that lampooned the sale of his library to the nation. Second, John Strachan's 30 January 1815 letter, which was published in the *Montreal Herald* and responds directly to Jefferson's missive of the preceding September offering his books to Congress, argues that the burning of the American capital in August 1814 was a justifiable retaliation for similar depredations committed by United States forces in Canada. Although Jefferson probably saw neither document, their intrinsic interest is so great that they are both printed below in full.

ACKNOWLEDGMENTS

MANY INDIVIDUALS and institutions provided aid and encourage-ment during the preparation of this volume. Those who helped us to locate and acquire primary and secondary sources and answered our research questions include our colleagues at the Thomas Jefferson Foundation, especially Anna Berkes, Eric D. M. Johnson, Jack Robertson, and Endrina Tay of the Jefferson Library, and Elizabeth Chew of the curatorial department; Robert Bean at the Albemarle Charlottesville Historical Society; Roy E. Goodman, Charles B. Greifenstein, and Valerie-Anne Lutz from the American Philosophical Society; Kimberly Reynolds of the Boston Public Library; Thomas P. Saine at the University of California at Irvine; Dayle Dooley of the Congressional Cemetery in Washington, D.C.; Joshua A. Lascell from Dartmouth College; Janie Morris of Duke University; Clark Muenzer at the Goethe Society of North America; Robert G. Hickman and Elizabeth W. Hickman from Houston, Texas; Woodrow C. Harper of the Hollywood Cemetery in Richmond; our friends at the Library of Congress's Manuscripts Division; Richard B. Meixsel from James Madison University; Irmgard Wagner of George Mason University; Emiko Hastings at the University of Michigan; Jessica Kratz from the National Archives; Timothy Connelly of the National Historical Publications and Records Commission; Michael J. North at the National Library of Medicine in Bethesda, Maryland; David Haugaard, Steve Smith, and Elsa Varela at the Historical Society of Pennsylvania; Chris Raible from Creemore, Ontario; Joseph B. Ringland of Oswego, New York; Anthony R. Morton of the Royal Military Academy at Sandhurst, England; Charlotte Craig from Rutgers University; Robert D. Schwarz from Philadelphia; Alison M. Foley at Saint Mary's Seminary and University in Baltimore; Laura Keim at Stenton, George Logan's home in Philadelphia; Thomas M. Whitehead of Temple University; Brent Tarter and his coworkers at the Library of Virginia; Paul D. Halliday of the University of Virginia; Anne Benham and Lewis Purifoy at the University of Virginia's Alderman Library and their colleagues at the Albert and Shirley Small Special Collections Library; Richard Block from the University of Washington in Seattle; and Joanne Yeck of Kettering, Ohio. As always, we received advice, assistance, and encouragement from a large number of our fellow documentary editors, including Margaret Hogan and Sara Georgini of the Adams Papers; Ellen R. Cohn and Adrina Garbooshian of the Papers of Benjamin Franklin; Daniel Preston from the Papers of

ACKNOWLEDGMENTS

James Monroe; Martha J. King, John Little, James P. McClure, Linda Monaco, Barbara B. Oberg, and Elaine Weber Pascu at the Papers of Thomas Jefferson at Princeton University; and Mary A. Hackett, Angela Kreider, David B. Mattern, and John C. A. Stagg from the Papers of James Madison. Genevieve Moene and Roland H. Simon transcribed and translated the French letters included in this volume, while John F. Miller assisted us with Latin quotations. The maps of Jefferson's Virginia and Albemarle County were created by Rick Britton. The other illustrations that appear in this volume were assembled with the assistance of Rebecca Fawcett of Dartmouth College; Bonnie Coles and Julie Miller at the Library of Congress; Peter Drummey and Elaine Grublin from the Massachusetts Historical Society; John Powell of the Newberry Library in Chicago; Alessandra Merrill, Marilyn Palmeri, and Robert Parks at the Pierpont Morgan Library and Museum in New York; Nick Homenda and Richard A. Workman from the University of Texas at Austin; Leah Stearns and Chad Wollerton of the Thomas Jefferson Foundation; Christina Deane, Edward Gaynor, Margaret Hrabe, and Regina Rush at the University of Virginia; and Susan A. Riggs from the College of William and Mary. Stephen Perkins of Dataformat.com continued to assist us in all things digital. Finally, we would like to acknowledge the efforts of the able staff at Princeton University Press, including Dimitri Karetnikov and Jan Lilly, and our production editor and special friend, Linny Schenck.

EDITORIAL METHOD AND APPARATUS

1. RENDERING THE TEXT

From its inception *The Papers of Thomas Jefferson* has insisted on high standards of accuracy in rendering text, but modifications in textual policy and editorial apparatus have been implemented as different approaches have become accepted in the field or as a more faithful rendering has become technically feasible. Prior discussions of textual policy appeared in Vols. 1:xxix–xxxiv, 22:vii–xi, 24:vii–viii, and 30:xiii–xiv of the First Series.

The textual method of the Retirement Series will adhere to the more literal approach adopted in Volume 30 of the parent edition. Original spelling, capitalization, and punctuation are retained as written. Such idiosyncrasies as Jefferson's failure to capitalize the beginnings of most of his sentences and abbreviations like "mr" are preserved, as are his preference for "it's" to "its" and his characteristic spellings of "knolege," "paiment," and "recieve." Modern usage is adopted in cases where intent is impossible to determine, an issue that arises most often in the context of capitalization. Some so-called slips of the pen are corrected, but the original reading is recorded in a subjoined textual note. Jefferson and others sometimes signaled a change in thought within a paragraph with extra horizontal space, and this is rendered by a three-em space. Blanks left for words and not subsequently filled by the authors are represented by a space approximating the length of the blank. Gaps, doubtful readings of illegible or damaged text, and wording supplied from other versions or by editorial conjecture are explained in the source note or in numbered textual notes. Foreign-language documents, the vast majority of which are in French during the retirement period, are transcribed in full as faithfully as possible and followed by a full translation.

Two modifications from past practice bring this series still closer to the original manuscripts. Underscored text is presented as such rather than being converted to italics. Superscripts are also preserved rather than being lowered to the baseline. In most cases of superscripting, the punctuation that is below or next to the superscripted letters is dropped, since it is virtually impossible to determine what is a period or dash as opposed to a flourish under, over, or adjacent to superscripted letters.

Limits to the more literal method are still recognized, however, and readability and consistency with past volumes are prime considerations. In keeping with the basic design implemented in the first volume of the Papers, salutations and signatures continue to display in large and small capitals rather than upper- and lowercase letters. Expansion marks over abbreviations are silently omitted. With very rare exceptions, deleted text and information on which words were added during the process of composition is not displayed within the document transcription. Based on the Editors' judgment of their significance, such emendations are either described in numbered textual notes or ignored. Datelines for letters are consistently printed at the head of the text, with a comment in the descriptive note when they have been moved. Address information, endorsements, and dockets are quoted or described in the source note rather than reproduced in the document proper.

2. TEXTUAL DEVICES

The following devices are employed throughout the work to clarify the presentation of the text.

[...]   Text missing and not conjecturable. The size of gaps longer than a word or two is estimated in annotation.

[   ]   Number or part of number missing or illegible.

[roman]   Conjectural reading for missing or illegible matter. A question mark follows when the reading is doubtful.

[*italic*] Editorial comment inserted in the text.

<*italic*> Matter deleted in the manuscript but restored in our text.

3. DESCRIPTIVE SYMBOLS

The following symbols are employed throughout the work to describe the various kinds of manuscript originals. When a series of versions is included, the first to be recorded is the version used for the printed text.

Dft   draft (usually a composition or rough draft; multiple drafts, when identifiable as such, are designated "2d Dft," etc.)

Dupl   duplicate

MS   manuscript (arbitrarily applied to most documents other than letters)

PoC polygraph copy
PrC press copy
RC recipient's copy
SC stylograph copy

All manuscripts of the above types are assumed to be in the hand of the author of the document to which the descriptive symbol pertains. If not, that fact is stated. On the other hand, the following types of manuscripts are assumed not to be in the hand of the author, and exceptions will be noted:

FC file copy (applied to all contemporary copies retained by the author or his agents)

Tr transcript (applied to all contemporary and later copies except file copies; period of transcription, unless clear by implication, will be given when known)

4. LOCATION SYMBOLS

The locations of documents printed in this edition from originals in private hands and from printed sources are recorded in self-explanatory form in the descriptive note following each document. The locations of documents printed or referenced from originals held by public and private institutions in the United States are recorded by means of the symbols used in the *MARC Code List for Organizations* (2000) maintained by the Library of Congress. The symbols DLC and MHi by themselves stand for the collections of Jefferson Papers proper in these repositories. When texts are drawn from other collections held by these two institutions, the names of those collections are added. Location symbols for documents held by institutions outside the United States are given in a subjoined list. The lists of symbols are limited to the institutions represented by documents printed or referred to in this volume.

CSmH Huntington Library, San Marino, California
     JF Jefferson File
     JF-BA Jefferson File, Bixby Acquisition
CtSoP Pequot Library Association, Southport, Connecticut
CtY Yale University, New Haven, Connecticut
DeGH Hagley Museum and Library, Greenville, Delaware
DGU Georgetown University, Washington, D.C.

DLC   Library of Congress, Washington, D.C.
             TJ Papers   Thomas Jefferson Papers (this is
             assumed if not stated, but also given as indicated
             to furnish the precise location of an undated,
             misdated, or otherwise problematic document,
             thus "DLC: TJ Papers, 213:38071–2" represents
             volume 213, folios 38071 and 38072 as the collec-
             tion was arranged at the time the first microfilm
             edition was made in 1944–45. Access to the
             microfilm edition of the collection as it was
             rearranged under the Library's Presidential
             Papers Program is provided by the *Index to
             the Thomas Jefferson Papers* [1976])

DNA   National Archives, Washington, D.C., with
             identifications of series (preceded by record
             group number) as follows:
             CS   Census Schedules
             CTSLO   Central Treasury and State Loan
                         Office Records Relating to the 6-
                         Percent Converted Stock of 1807
             DD   Diplomatic Dispatches
             GRMLO   General Records of the Missouri
                         Land Offices
             LAR   Letters of Application and
                         Recommendation
             LRAG   Letters Received by the Adjutant
                         General
             LRSCW   Letters Received and Drafts of Let-
                         ters Sent by the Superintendent
                         of the City of Washington
             LRSW   Letters Received by the Secretary
                         of War
             MTA   Miscellaneous Treasury Accounts
             NPEDP   Naturalization Petitions to the
                         United States Circuit and District
                         Courts for the Eastern District of
                         Pennsylvania

GU   University of Georgia, Athens
ICHi   Chicago Historical Society, Chicago, Illinois
ICN   Newberry Library, Chicago, Illinois
InU   Indiana University, Bloomington

LNT	Tulane University, New Orleans, Louisiana
MBPLi	Boston Public Library, Boston, Massachusetts
MdBS	Saint Mary's Seminary and University, Baltimore, Maryland
MdHi	Maryland Historical Society, Baltimore
MeHi	Maine Historical Society, Portland
MH	Harvard University, Cambridge, Massachusetts
MHi	Massachusetts Historical Society, Boston
MiU-C	Clements Library, University of Michigan, Ann Arbor
MoSHi	Missouri History Museum, Saint Louis
TJC-BC	Thomas Jefferson Collection, text formerly in Bixby Collection
MoSW	Washington University, Saint Louis, Missouri
MoSW-M	Washington University Medical School, Saint Louis, Missouri
NcD	Duke University, Durham, North Carolina
NcU	University of North Carolina, Chapel Hill
NPT	Southern Historical Collection, Nicholas Philip Trist Papers
NHi	New-York Historical Society, New York City
NjMoHP	Morristown National Historical Park, Morristown, New Jersey
NjP	Princeton University, Princeton, New Jersey
NN	New York Public Library, New York City
NNC	Columbia University, New York City
NNGL	Gilder Lehrman Collection, New York City
NNPM	Pierpont Morgan Library, New York City
OCU	University of Cincinnati, Cincinnati, Ohio
PHi	Historical Society of Pennsylvania, Philadelphia
PPAmP	American Philosophical Society, Philadelphia, Pennsylvania
PPAN	Academy of Natural Sciences, Philadelphia, Pennsylvania
PPGi	Girard College, Philadelphia, Pennsylvania
PPL	Library Company of Philadelphia, Philadelphia, Pennsylvania
PWacD	David Library of the American Revolution, Washington Crossing, Pennsylvania
RHi	Rhode Island Historical Society, Providence
Sc	South Carolina State Library, Columbia

T	Tennessee State Library and Archives, Nashville	
TxU	University of Texas, Austin	
Vi	Library of Virginia, Richmond	
ViCAHi	Albemarle Charlottesville Historical Society, Charlottesville, Virginia	
ViCMRL	Jefferson Library, Thomas Jefferson Foundation, Inc., Charlottesville, Virginia	
ViFreJM	James Monroe Museum and Memorial Library, Fredericksburg, Virginia	
ViHi	Virginia Historical Society, Richmond	
ViU	University of Virginia, Charlottesville	
	GT	George Tucker transcripts of Thomas Jefferson letters
	TJP	Thomas Jefferson Papers
	TJP-AR	Thomas Jefferson Papers, text formerly in Alexander Rives Papers
	TJP-CC	Thomas Jefferson Papers, text formerly in Carr-Cary Papers
	TJP-ER	Thomas Jefferson Papers, text formerly in Edgehill-Randolph Papers
	TJP-LBJM	Thomas Jefferson Papers, Thomas Jefferson's Legal Brief in *Jefferson v. Michie*, 1804–15, deposited by Mrs. Augustina David Carr Mills
	TJP-PC	Thomas Jefferson Papers, text formerly in Philip B. Campbell Deposit
ViW	College of William and Mary, Williamsburg, Virginia	
	TC-JP	Jefferson Papers, Tucker-Coleman Collection
	TJP	Thomas Jefferson Papers

The following symbols represent repositories located outside of the United States:

FrM	Archives Municipales de Marseille, France
OONL	Library and Archives Canada, Ottawa, Ontario
Uk	British Library, London, United Kingdom

5. *OTHER ABBREVIATIONS AND SYMBOLS*

The following abbreviations and symbols are commonly employed in the annotation throughout the work.

Lb   Letterbook (used to indicate texts copied or assembled into bound volumes)

RG   Record Group (used in designating the location of documents in the Library of Virginia and the National Archives)

SJL   Jefferson's "Summary Journal of Letters" written and received for the period 11 Nov. 1783 to 25 June 1826 (in DLC: TJ Papers). This epistolary record, kept in Jefferson's hand, has been checked against the TJ Editorial Files. It is to be assumed that all outgoing letters are recorded in SJL unless there is a note to the contrary. When the date of receipt of an incoming letter is recorded in SJL, it is incorporated in the notes. Information and discrepancies revealed in SJL but not found in the letter itself are also noted. Missing letters recorded in SJL are accounted for in the notes to documents mentioning them, in related documents, or in an appendix

TJ   Thomas Jefferson

TJ Editorial Files   Photoduplicates and other editorial materials in the office of the Papers of Thomas Jefferson: Retirement Series, Jefferson Library, Thomas Jefferson Foundation, Inc., Charlottesville

d   Penny or denier

f   Florin

£   Pound sterling or livre, depending upon context (in doubtful cases, a clarifying note will be given)

s   Shilling or sou (also expressed as /)

₶   Livre Tournois

℈   Per (occasionally used for pro, pre)

6. *SHORT TITLES*

The following list includes short titles of works cited frequently in this edition. Since it is impossible to anticipate all the works to be cited in abbreviated form, the list is revised from volume to volume.

Acts of Assembly   *Acts of the General Assembly of Virginia* (cited by session; title varies over time)

ANB   John A. Garraty and Mark C. Carnes, eds., *American National Biography*, 1999, 24 vols.

Annals   *Annals of the Congress of the United States: The Debates and Proceedings in the Congress of the United States . . . Compiled from Authentic Materials*, Washington, D.C., Gales & Seaton, 1834–56, 42 vols. (All editions are undependable and pagination varies from one printing to another. Citations given below are to the edition mounted on the American Memory website of the Library of Congress and give the date of the debate as well as page numbers)

APS   American Philosophical Society

ASP   *American State Papers: Documents, Legislative and Executive, of the Congress of the United States*, 1832–61, 38 vols.

Axelson, *Virginia Postmasters*   Edith F. Axelson, *Virginia Postmasters and Post Offices, 1789–1832*, 1991

Banner, *Hartford Convention*   James M. Banner Jr., *To the Hartford Convention: The Federalists and the Origins of Party Politics in Massachusetts, 1789–1815*, 1970

BDSCHR   Walter B. Edgar and others, eds., *Biographical Directory of the South Carolina House of Representatives*, 1974– , 5 vols.

Betts, *Farm Book*   Edwin M. Betts, ed., *Thomas Jefferson's Farm Book*, 1953 (in two separately paginated sections; unless otherwise specified, references are to the second section)

Betts, *Garden Book*   Edwin M. Betts, ed., *Thomas Jefferson's Garden Book, 1766–1824*, 1944

Biog. Dir. Cong.   *Biographical Directory of the United States Congress, 1774–1989*, 1989

Biographie universelle   *Biographie universelle, ancienne et moderne*, new ed., 1843–65, 45 vols.

Black's Law Dictionary   Bryan A. Garner and others, eds., *Black's Law Dictionary*, 7th ed., 1999

Brant, *Madison*   Irving Brant, *James Madison*, 1941–61, 6 vols.

Brigham, *American Newspapers*   Clarence S. Brigham, *History and Bibliography of American Newspapers, 1690–1820*, 1947, 2 vols.

Bruce, *University*   Philip Alexander Bruce, *History of the University of Virginia 1819–1919: The Lengthened Shadow of One Man*, 1920–22, 5 vols.

Burk, Jones, and Girardin, *History of Virginia*   John Daly Burk, Skelton Jones, and Louis H. Girardin, *The History of Virginia, from its First Settlement to the Present Day*, 4 vols., Petersburg, 1804–16; Sowerby, no. 464; Poor, *Jefferson's Library*, 4 (no. 127)

Bush, *Life Portraits*   Alfred L. Bush, *The Life Portraits of Thomas Jefferson*, rev. ed., 1987

Callahan, *U.S. Navy*   Edward W. Callahan, *List of Officers of the Navy of the United States and of the Marine Corps from 1775 to 1900*, 1901, repr. 1969

Chambers, *Poplar Forest*   S. Allen Chambers, *Poplar Forest & Thomas Jefferson*, 1993

Clay, *Papers*   James F. Hopkins and others, eds., *The Papers of Henry Clay*, 1959–1992, 11 vols.

Connelly, *Napoleonic France*   Owen Connelly and others, eds., *Historical Dictionary of Napoleonic France, 1799–1815*, 1985

CVSP   William P. Palmer and others, eds., *Calendar of Virginia State Papers . . . Preserved in the Capitol at Richmond*, 1875–93, 11 vols.

DAB   Allen Johnson and Dumas Malone, eds., *Dictionary of American Biography*, 1928–36, 20 vols.

Dallas, *Exposition*   Alexander J. Dallas, *An Exposition of the Causes and Character of the War*, Washington, 1815, reprinted in various places with slightly variant titles

DBF   *Dictionnaire de biographie française*, 1933– , 19 vols.

Delaplaine's Repository   *Delaplaine's Repository of the Lives and Portraits of Distinguished Americans*, Philadelphia, 1816–18, 2 vols.; Poor, *Jefferson's Library*, 4 (no. 139)

Destutt de Tracy, *Commentary and Review of Montesquieu's Spirit of Laws*   Antoine Louis Claude Destutt de Tracy, *A Commentary and Review of Montesquieu's Spirit of Laws. prepared for press from the Original Manuscript, in the hands of the publisher. To which are annexed, Observations on the Thirty-First Book, by the late M. Condorcet: and Two Letters of Helvetius, on the merits of the same work*, Philadelphia, 1811; Sowerby, no. 2327; Poor, *Jefferson's Library*, 10 (no. 623)

Dolley Madison, *Selected Letters*   David B. Mattern and Holly C. Shulman, eds., *The Selected Letters of Dolley Payne Madison*, 2003

Doyle, *French Revolution*   William Doyle, *The Oxford History of the French Revolution*, 1989

DSB   Charles C. Gillispie, ed., *Dictionary of Scientific Biography*, 1970–80, 16 vols.

DVB   John T. Kneebone and others, eds., *Dictionary of Virginia Biography*, 1998– , 3 vols.

EG   Dickinson W. Adams and Ruth W. Lester, eds., *Jefferson's*

Extracts from the Gospels, 1983, *The Papers of Thomas Jefferson*, Second Series

Fairclough, *Horace: Satires, Epistles and Ars Poetica*   H. Rushton Fairclough, trans., *Horace: Satires, Epistles and Ars Poetica*, Loeb Classical Library, 1926, repr. 2005

Fairclough, *Virgil*   H. Rushton Fairclough, trans., *Virgil*, Loeb Classical Library, 1916–18, rev. by G. P. Goold, 1999–2000, repr. 2002–06, 2 vols.

First Federal Congress   Linda Grant De Pauw and others, eds., *Documentary History of the First Federal Congress*, 1972– , 17 vols.

Ford   Paul Leicester Ford, ed., *The Writings of Thomas Jefferson*, Letterpress Edition, 1892–99, 10 vols.

Haggard, "Henderson Heirs"   Robert F. Haggard, "Thomas Jefferson v. The Heirs of Bennett Henderson, 1795–1818: A Case Study in Caveat Emptor," *MACH*, 63 (2005): 1–29

Hansard, *Parliamentary Debates*   Thomas C. Hansard, ed., *The Parliamentary Debates*, 1st ser., London, 1812–20, 20 vols.

Harvard Catalogue   *Harvard University Quinquennial Catalogue of the Officers and Graduates, 1636–1925*, 1925

HAW   Henry A. Washington, ed., *The Writings of Thomas Jefferson*, 1853–54, 9 vols.

Heitman, *Continental Army*   Francis B. Heitman, comp., *Historical Register of Officers of the Continental Army during the War of the Revolution, April, 1775, to December, 1783*, rev. ed., 1914

Heitman, *U.S. Army*   Francis B. Heitman, comp., *Historical Register and Dictionary of the United States Army*, 1903, 2 vols.

Hening   William Waller Hening, ed., *The Statutes at Large; being a Collection of all the Laws of Virginia*, Richmond, 1809–23, 13 vols.; Sowerby, no. 1863; Poor, *Jefferson's Library*, 10 (no. 573)

Hoefer, *Nouv. biog. générale*   J. C. F. Hoefer, *Nouvelle biographie générale depuis les temps les plus reculés jusqu'a nos jours*, 1852–83, 46 vols.

Hortus Third   Liberty Hyde Bailey, Ethel Zoe Bailey, and the staff of the Liberty Hyde Bailey Hortorium, Cornell University, *Hortus Third: A Concise Dictionary of Plants Cultivated in the United States and Canada*, 1976

Jackson, *Papers*   Sam B. Smith, Harold D. Moser, Daniel Feller, and others, eds., *The Papers of Andrew Jackson*, 1980– , 7 vols.

Jefferson Correspondence, Bixby   Worthington C. Ford, ed., *Thomas Jefferson Correspondence Printed from the Originals in the Collections of William K. Bixby*, 1916

JEP   *Journal of the Executive Proceedings of the Senate of the United States*

JHD   *Journal of the House of Delegates of the Commonwealth of Virginia*

JHR   *Journal of the House of Representatives of the United States*

JS   *Journal of the Senate of the United States*

JSV   *Journal of the Senate of Virginia*

Kimball, *Jefferson, Architect*   Fiske Kimball, *Thomas Jefferson, Architect*, 1916

L & B   Andrew A. Lipscomb and Albert E. Bergh, eds., *The Writings of Thomas Jefferson*, Library Edition, 1903–04, 20 vols.

Latrobe, *Papers*   John C. Van Horne and others, eds., *The Correspondence and Miscellaneous Papers of Benjamin Henry Latrobe*, 1984–88, 3 vols.

Lay, *Architecture*   K. Edward Lay, *The Architecture of Jefferson Country: Charlottesville and Albemarle County, Virginia*, 2000

LCB   Douglas L. Wilson, ed., *Jefferson's Literary Commonplace Book*, 1989, *The Papers of Thomas Jefferson*, Second Series

Leavitt, *Poplar Forest*   Messrs. Leavitt, *Catalogue of a Private Library . . . Also, The Remaining Portion of the Library of the Late Thomas Jefferson . . . offered by his grandson, Francis Eppes, of Poplar Forest, Va.*, 1873

Leonard, *General Assembly*   Cynthia Miller Leonard, comp., *The General Assembly of Virginia, July 30, 1619–January 11, 1978: A Bicentennial Register of Members*, 1978

List of Patents   *A List of Patents granted by the United States from April 10, 1790, to December 31, 1836*, 1872

Longworth's New York Directory   *Longworth's American Almanac, New-York Register, and City Directory*, New York, 1796–1842 (title varies; cited by year of publication)

MACH   *Magazine of Albemarle County History*, 1940– (title varies: issued until 1951 as *Papers of the Albemarle County Historical Society*)

Madison, *Papers*   William T. Hutchinson, Robert A. Rutland, John C. A. Stagg, and others, eds., *The Papers of James Madison*, 1962– , 32 vols.

　　　Congress. Ser., 17 vols.

　　　Pres. Ser., 6 vols.

　　　Retirement Ser., 1 vol.

　　　Sec. of State Ser., 8 vols.

Malcomson, *Historical Dictionary*   Robert Malcomson, *Historical Dictionary of the War of 1812*, 2006

Malone, *Jefferson*   Dumas Malone, *Jefferson and his Time*, 1948–81, 6 vols.

Marshall, *Papers*   Herbert A. Johnson, Charles T. Cullen, Charles F. Hobson, and others, eds., *The Papers of John Marshall*, 1974–2006, 12 vols.

Mazzei, *Writings*   Margherita Marchione and others, eds., *Philip Mazzei: Selected Writings and Correspondence*, 1983, 3 vols.

MB   James A. Bear Jr. and Lucia C. Stanton, eds., *Jefferson's Memorandum Books: Accounts, with Legal Records and Miscellany, 1767–1826*, 1997, *The Papers of Thomas Jefferson*, Second Series

Notes, ed. Peden   Thomas Jefferson, *Notes on the State of Virginia*, ed. William Peden, 1955

OCD   Simon Hornblower and Antony Spawforth, eds., *The Oxford Classical Dictionary*, 2003

ODNB   H. C. G. Matthew and Brian Harrison, eds., *Oxford Dictionary of National Biography*, 2004, 60 vols.

OED   James A. H. Murray, J. A. Simpson, E. S. C. Weiner, and others, eds., *The Oxford English Dictionary*, 2d ed., 1989, 20 vols.

Papenfuse, *Maryland Public Officials*   Edward C. Papenfuse and others, eds., *An Historical List of Public Officials of Maryland*, 1990– , 1 vol.

Peale, *Papers*   Lillian B. Miller and others, eds., *The Selected Papers of Charles Willson Peale and His Family*, 1983– , 5 vols. in 6

PMHB   *Pennsylvania Magazine of History and Biography*, 1877–

Poor, *Jefferson's Library*   Nathaniel P. Poor, *Catalogue. President Jefferson's Library*, 1829

Princetonians   James McLachlan and others, eds., *Princetonians: A Biographical Dictionary*, 1976–90, 5 vols.

PTJ   Julian P. Boyd, Charles T. Cullen, John Catanzariti, Barbara B. Oberg, and others, eds., *The Papers of Thomas Jefferson*, 1950– , 37 vols.

PW   Wilbur S. Howell, ed., *Jefferson's Parliamentary Writings*, 1988, *The Papers of Thomas Jefferson*, Second Series

Randall, *Life*   Henry S. Randall, *The Life of Thomas Jefferson*, 1858, 3 vols.

Randolph, *Domestic Life*   Sarah N. Randolph, *The Domestic Life of Thomas Jefferson, Compiled from Family Letters and Reminiscences by His Great-Granddaughter*, 1871

Shackelford, *Descendants*   George Green Shackelford, ed., *Col-*

lected Papers of the Monticello Association of the Descendants of Thomas Jefferson, 1965–84, 2 vols.

Sibley's Harvard Graduates   John L. Sibley and others, eds., *Sibley's Harvard Graduates*, 1873– , 18 vols.

Sowerby   E. Millicent Sowerby, comp., *Catalogue of the Library of Thomas Jefferson*, 1952–59, 5 vols.

Spafford, *Wheel-Carriages*   Horatio Gates Spafford, *Some Cursory Observations on the Ordinary Construction of Wheel-Carriages: with an attempt to point out their defects, and to show How They May Be Improved; whereby a saving may be made in the power applied, the motion be rendered more uniform and easy, and the danger of upsetting most effectually prevented. With appropriate Engravings*, Albany, 1815

Sprague, *American Pulpit*   William B. Sprague, *Annals of the American Pulpit*, 1857–69, 9 vols.

Stagg, *Madison's War*   John C. A. Stagg, *Mr. Madison's War: Politics, Diplomacy, and Warfare in the Early American Republic, 1783–1830*, 1983

Stein, *Worlds*   Susan R. Stein, *The Worlds of Thomas Jefferson at Monticello*, 1993

Terr. Papers   Clarence E. Carter and John Porter Bloom, eds., *The Territorial Papers of the United States*, 1934–75, 28 vols.

TJR   Thomas Jefferson Randolph, ed., *Memoir, Correspondence, and Miscellanies, from the Papers of Thomas Jefferson*, 1829, 4 vols.

True, "Agricultural Society"   Rodney H. True, "Minute Book of the Agricultural Society of Albemarle," *Annual Report of the American Historical Association for the Year 1918* (1921), 1:261–349

U.S. Reports   Cases Argued and Decided in the Supreme Court of the United States, 1790– (title varies; originally issued in distinct editions of separately numbered volumes with *U.S. Reports* volume numbers retroactively assigned; original volume numbers here given parenthetically)

U.S. Statutes at Large   Richard Peters, ed., *The Public Statutes at Large of the United States . . . 1789 to March 3, 1845*, 1845–67, 8 vols.

Va. Reports   Reports of Cases Argued and Adjudged in the Court of Appeals of Virginia, 1798– (title varies; originally issued in distinct editions of separately numbered volumes with *Va. Reports* volume numbers retroactively assigned; original volume numbers here given parenthetically)

VMHB   *Virginia Magazine of History and Biography*, 1893–

Washington, *Papers*   W. W. Abbot, Dorothy Twohig, Philander D. Chase, Theodore J. Crackel, and others, eds., *The Papers of George Washington*, 1983– , 55 vols.

  Colonial Ser., 10 vols.
  Confederation Ser., 6 vols.
  Pres. Ser., 15 vols.
  Retirement Ser., 4 vols.
  Rev. War Ser., 20 vols.

William and Mary Provisional List   *A Provisional List of Alumni, Grammar School Students, Members of the Faculty, and Members of the Board of Visitors of the College of William and Mary in Virginia. From 1693 to 1888*, 1941

WMQ   *William and Mary Quarterly*, 1892–

Woods, *Albemarle*   Edgar Woods, *Albemarle County in Virginia*, 1901, repr. 1991

CONTENTS

·《❴ 1814 ❵》·

CONTENTS

CONTENTS

CONTENTS

CONTENTS

·《 **1 8 1 5** 》·

CONTENTS

CONTENTS

CONTENTS

CONTENTS

CONTENTS

CONTENTS

CONTENTS

CONTENTS

CONTENTS

CONTENTS

MAPS

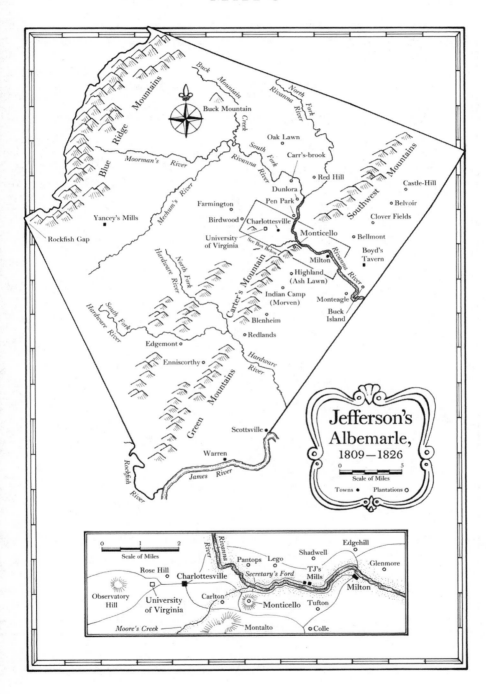

Jefferson's
Albemarle,
1809–1826

0   5
Scale of Miles

Towns •   Plantations ◦

Blue Ridge Mountains

Buck Mountain

Buck Mountain Creek

North Fork Rivanna River

South Fork Rivanna River

Moorman's River

Mechum's River

Oak Lawn

Carr's-brook

Red Hill

Dunlora

Pen Park

Southwest Mountains

Castle-Hill

Belvoir

Clover Fields

Farmington

Birdwood

Charlottesville

See Box Below

University of Virginia

Monticello

Bellmont

Boyd's Tavern

Milton

Rivanna River

Highland (Ash Lawn)

Carter's Mountain

Indian Camp (Morven)

Monteagle

Buck Island

Blenheim

Redlands

Yancey's Mills

Rockfish Gap

North Fork Hardware River

South Fork Hardware River

Hardware River

Edgemont

Ennliscorthy

Green Mountains

Scottsville

Warren

James River

Rockfish River

Lower inset map

0   1   2
Scale of Miles

Rivanna River

Rose Hill

Charlottesville

Pantops

Lego

Secretary's Ford

Shadwell

Edgehill

Glenmore

TJ's Mills

Observatory Hill

University of Virginia

Carlton

Monticello

Tufton

Milton

Moore's Creek

Montalto

Colle

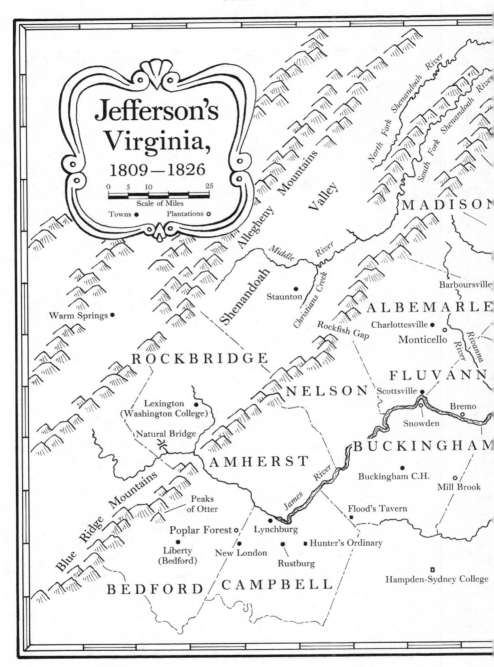

Jefferson's
Virginia,
1809—1826

0 5 10 25
Scale of Miles
Towns ● Plantations ○

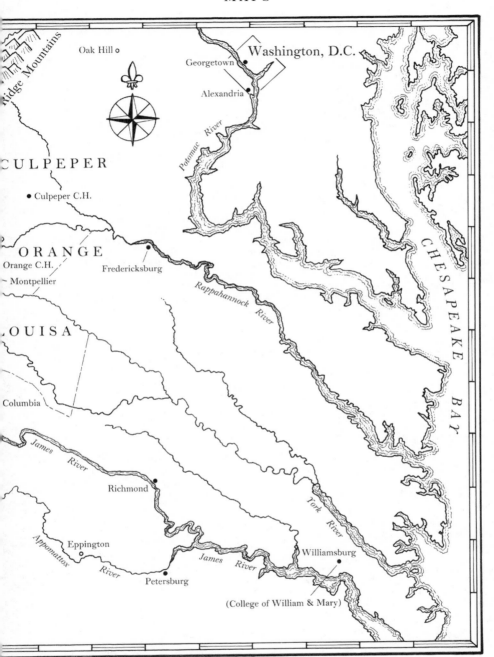

ILLUSTRATIONS

Following page 272

SAMUEL HARRISON SMITH

Newspaper editor, bank president, sometime public servant, and longtime friend and political ally of Thomas Jefferson, Samuel Harrison Smith (1772–1845) was federal commissioner of revenue when he played an instrumental role in the 1814–15 negotiations leading to the sale to the nation of the former president's large, personal library. The drawing of a bespectacled, middle-aged Smith was taken from a currently unlocated, 30-by-25-inch portrait executed in 1829 by the noted American artist Charles Bird King (*PTJ*, 32:31–2n; note to TJ to Smith, 6 Mar. 1809; Editorial Note and group of documents on The Sale of Thomas Jefferson's Library to Congress, at 21 Sept. 1814; Andrew J. Cosentino, *The Paintings of Charles Bird King [1785–1862]* [1977], 157).

Image from Gaillard Hunt, *The First Forty Years of Washington Society, Portrayed by the Family Letters of Mrs. Samuel Harrison Smith* (1906), opp. p. 40.

NOTES ON THOMAS JEFFERSON'S LIBRARY AT THE TIME OF SALE

Jefferson sold his library to Congress in the aftermath of the burning of the public buildings in Washington in August 1814. In order to document his claim for final payment, he checked the total number of books against his catalogue, arranged by size, and listed the ones that were missing and the ones he owned but had failed to list. Both pages of this document are pictured below. The manuscript is summarized under the above title at 18 Apr. 1815, and it will be printed in full or otherwise dealt with in an upcoming volume concerning Jefferson's libraries in the *Papers of Thomas Jefferson*, Second Series.

Courtesy of the Library of Congress.

MONTICELLO BOOKCASES

The bookcases that housed Jefferson's library prior to its dispatch to Washington by wagon in the spring of 1815 were manufactured locally out of pine, had backs, stood nine feet tall, and were arranged in three tiers in order to facilitate the storage of books of various sizes. The smallest volumes, duodecimos, sat on the top, octavos resided on the middle, and quartos and folios were placed on the lower shelves. According to Jefferson the books took up 855 square feet of wall space, from which it would follow that the walls of his private suite of rooms at Monticello were literally filled with books from floor to ceiling. After wrapping the best bindings, inserting slips before and after each volume, stuffing waste paper between the books and shelves, and spreading sheets of stationery over the face of each shelf, Jefferson had boards nailed onto the front of the bookcases in preparation for their journey north. His expectation was that the cases would continue to be used after their arrival in the capital, perhaps with the addition of "sash doors," which could "be made there at little expence." Although none of the original bookcases have survived, late in the 1950s the Thomas Jefferson Foundation commissioned six replicas from the well-known local architect Milton Grigg. These reproductions, one of which is depicted here, are now on display at Monticello (TJ's Observations on the Transportation of the Monticello Library, [ca. 27 Feb. 1815]; TJ to Joseph Milligan, 28 Mar. 1815; research report on "Bookcases" [ViCMRL]).

Courtesy of the Thomas Jefferson Foundation, Inc. Photograph by Bill Moretz.

"I CANNOT LIVE WITHOUT BOOKS"

Jefferson's sale of his library to Congress in 1815 "to replace the devastations of British Vandalism at Washington" in no way signaled a declining interest in bookish matters. In the letter depicted he made perhaps his most famous declaration of his love for literature, and in fact the ex-president remained an unrepentant bibliophile until the end of his days. The wagons carrying his "literary treasures" northward had hardly left Monticello before he began arranging for the acquisition of replacement copies of his favorite books and new titles that attracted his attention. During the decade left to him, Jefferson acquired another 1,600 volumes, many of them, as his retirement library was intended for "amusement, and not use," drawn from the fields of history, literature, philosophy, politics, and religion (Douglas L. Wilson, *Jefferson's Books* [1996], 45–9; Poor, *Jefferson's Library*).

Jefferson to John Adams, 10 June 1815, *Courtesy of the Massachusetts Historical Society.*

OWNERSHIP MARKS ON JEFFERSON'S BOOKS

Prior to the destruction by fire of the bulk of his library at Shadwell in 1770, Jefferson sometimes wrote "Ex Libris Thomæ Iefferson" ("From the library of Thomas Jefferson") on the title pages of the works he owned. Thereafter, he used a different way to signify ownership, an interesting technique but one that he did not originate. Printers at that time commonly assigned a letter of the Latin alphabet (which omits the English letters j, v, and w) to each quire of typeset pages included in the books they published. In his Great Library, which Jefferson assembled over nearly half a century and sold to the nation in 1815, he often placed a cursive "T." in front of the printed letter at the start of each "I" quire and an "I." after the printed letter at the beginning of each "T" quire. Although systematic in many things, he was not rigorously consistent in this practice. Some books bear no handwritten identifiers at all; sometimes only the first of multivolume works are marked; and occasionally only the "T" or "I" quires (or the first "T" or "I" quire) carry Jefferson's initials. The books in his post-1815 retirement library are denoted in the same manner—and with similar omissions and inconsistencies—except that he appears to have consciously used block, instead of cursive, lettering when marking the books he acquired late in life (James A. Bear Jr., *Thomas Jefferson's Book-Marks* [1958; repr. 1993]).

The Book of Common Prayer (Oxford, 1752; Poor, *Jefferson's Library,*

9 [no. 514]). *Courtesy of the Albert and Shirley Small Special Collections Library, University of Virginia.*
Richard François Philippe Brunck, ed., *Ηθικη Ποιησις: Sive Gnomici Poetæ Græci* (Strasbourg, 1784; Sowerby, no. 4466; Poor, *Jefferson's Library*, 12 [no. 780]). *Courtesy of the Thomas Jefferson Foundation, Inc.*

DINING ROOM AT MONTICELLO

Monticello's dining room, which was used for everything from quiet, family gatherings to crowded, noisy affairs when large numbers of guests invaded Jefferson's mountaintop home, is an eighteen-foot cubical chamber located on the northern side of the house. Adjoining the entrance hall, parlor, and a small, unheated tea room, it boasts one of the mansion's many skylights, a mantelpiece that the third president kept stocked with books, dumbwaiters built into the fireplace for the conveyance of bottles from the wine cellar, and a large window looking out on the gardens in the rear of the house. The walls, which were painted a chrome yellow during Jefferson's retirement, were hung with artworks of various sizes. The upper tier held roughly a dozen oil paintings, with their subjects drawn from both the Bible and classical antiquity. Those at eye level concentrated on specifically American topics: its natural wonders, impressive man-made structures, and important personalities. Here depictions of Natural Bridge and Niagara Falls vied for attention with representations of the President's House and New Orleans and a likeness of George Washington. The furnishings and tableware were chosen with the same exacting care. Instead of one long dining table, Jefferson relied on a number of smaller ones that could be pushed together. Sections not in use could be folded up and placed against the wall. Chairs, a large sideboard, and several stand-alone dumbwaiters completed the complement of furniture. Meals at Monticello were served twice a day: a modest breakfast at nine in the morning and a multicourse dinner at four in the afternoon. Tablecloths and floorcloths were commonly used at mealtime to protect against damaging spills, and the table was adorned with an assortment of porcelain, creamware, and eating utensils manufactured in China, England, France, and the United States (Stein, *Worlds*, 79–87; Damon Lee Fowler, ed., *Dining at Monticello* [2005], 71–8; Margaret Bayard Smith's Account of a Visit to Monticello, [29 July–2 Aug. 1809]; George Ticknor's Account of a Visit to Monticello, [4–7 Feb. 1815]).
Courtesy of the Thomas Jefferson Foundation, Inc. Photograph by Philip Beaurline.

JEFFERSON'S NOTES ON HOUSEHOLD CONSUMPTION

Jefferson went to great lengths to document his expenditures, log his correspondence, record weather readings, catalogue his libraries and works of art, and keep track of his farmwork and garden plantings. His meticulous record keeping also extended to household consumption of beef, firewood, and various luxury foods and beverages. In this document, which is printed below in full at 16 Oct. 1814, Jefferson details the use of such domestic items as coffee, white sugar, brown sugar, tea, brandy, whiskey, and cotton between 29 Jan. 1813 and 16 Oct. 1814 and estimates his needs with regard to the first four items. The manuscript is part of a grouping of notes of this type drawn up by Jefferson between 1797 and 1816 and now in the Jefferson Papers at the Massachusetts Historical Society. All such texts composed after he left the presidency in March 1809 are being included in the Retirement Series. In addition to the above document, see TJ's Notes on Household Consumption, 3 June 1809–23 Oct. 1811 (printed at the later date), and 21 Feb. 1815; Notes on Bottle and Beverage Supplies, [6 Oct. 1814–Feb. 1816] (printed at the earlier date); and Notes on Wine Consumption, 15 Feb.–21 July 1816 (printed at the later date).

Courtesy of the Massachusetts Historical Society.

GEORGE TICKNOR

Before he achieved lasting fame with his pioneering history of Spanish literature, the scholar and educator George Ticknor (1791–1871) visited Jefferson at Monticello in 1815 and again in 1824. He was a thirty-nine-year-old professor at Harvard University when he commissioned the famed American portraitist Thomas Sully to take his likeness. The resulting 36-by-28-inch, oil-on-canvas artwork was completed late in August 1831. It shows Ticknor at half-length, sitting comfortably on a sofa with a manuscript in his left hand. Although a copy of this painting was given by his daughter Anna E. Ticknor to the Boston Public Library during the mid-1890s, the family retained the original until 1943, when it was donated to Ticknor's alma mater, Dartmouth College (*DAB*; *Annual Report of the Trustees of the Public Library of the City of Boston* 44 [1896]: 23; 45 [1897]: 20; Edward Biddle and Mantle Fielding, *The Life and Works of Thomas Sully [1783–1872]* [1921], 296).

Courtesy of the Hood Museum of Art, Dartmouth College, Hanover, New Hampshire; gift of Constance V. R. White, Nathaniel T. Dexter, Philip Dexter, and Mary Ann Streeter.

Volume 8

1 October 1814 to 31 August 1815

JEFFERSON CHRONOLOGY
1743 · 1826

1743	Born at Shadwell, 13 April (New Style).
1760–1762	Studies at the College of William and Mary.
1762–1767	Self-education and preparation for law.
1769–1774	Albemarle delegate to House of Burgesses.
1772	Marries Martha Wayles Skelton, 1 January.
1775–1776	In Continental Congress.
1776	Drafts Declaration of Independence.
1776–1779	In Virginia House of Delegates.
1779	Submits Bill for Establishing Religious Freedom.
1779–1781	Governor of Virginia.
1782	Martha Wayles Skelton Jefferson dies, 6 September.
1783–1784	In Continental Congress.
1784–1789	In France on commission to negotiate commercial treaties and then as minister plenipotentiary at Versailles.
1790–1793	Secretary of State of the United States.
1797–1801	Vice President of the United States.
1801–1809	President of the United States.

RETIREMENT

1809	Attends James Madison's inauguration, 4 March.
	Arrives at Monticello, 15 March.
1810	Completes legal brief on New Orleans batture case, 31 July.
1811	Batture case dismissed, 5 December.
1812	Correspondence with John Adams resumed, 1 January.
	Batture pamphlet preface completed, 25 February; printed by 21 March.
1814	Named a trustee of Albemarle Academy, 25 March.
	Resigns presidency of American Philosophical Society, 23 November.
1815	Sells personal library to Congress.
1816	Writes introduction and revises translation of Destutt de Tracy, *A Treatise on Political Economy* [1818].
	Named a visitor of Central College, 18 October.
1818	Attends Rockfish Gap conference to choose location of proposed University of Virginia, 1–4 August.
	Visits Warm Springs, 7–27 August.
1819	University of Virginia chartered, 25 January; named to Board of Visitors, 13 February; elected rector, 29 March.
	Debts greatly increased by bankruptcy of Wilson Cary Nicholas.
1820	Likens debate over slavery and Missouri statehood to "a fire bell in the night," 22 April.
1821	Writes memoirs, 6 January–29 July.
1823	Visits Poplar Forest for last time, 16–25 May.
1824	Lafayette visits Monticello, 4–15 November.
1825	University of Virginia opens, 7 March.
1826	Writes will, 16–17 March.
	Last recorded letter, 25 June.
	Dies at Monticello, 4 July.

THE PAPERS OF
THOMAS JEFFERSON

·‹ ═══════ ›·

From "Johannes Vonderpuff"

DEAR SIR—   *Missouri, October* 1, 1814.

I have a library of books which I should be glad to sell. It consists
of about 5000 volumes, selected with care and caution. Various projects had occured to me to effect this object, but none has appeared
free of objection. One feels awkwardly[1] to be hawking his commodities about streets, and to send such a quantity of books to auction and
hire a master of the arts, which there succeed to puff them off with
the prevalent common-place slang, seems not quite consistent with
those delicate feelings which should govern high-minded men. At
the same time, the object is interesting, and if an old man can turn his
old books into cash, just as he has done with them and the world, at
a good price, and especially if a *great portion of them were presents
to him*, (which, *inter nos*, you know is the fact with yours and mine),
it would be quite a handsome speculation, and save his executors
much trouble.

Observing that you have, in one of your lucky moments, (and I
never knew a man who has had more such moments) hit upon a project entirely new, and seeing that it is very popular, I wish to know if
you cannot, in a second application to Congress, through some republican friend, aid me.

My grand father, my father and my self, have employed much
time in the last century and in this, in making the collection, so that
it may be considered as the acquisition of nearly one hundred years
labour. Many of my books are rare, most of them elegant and all
inestimable.

A considerable part of the works are in the Sanscrit, Coptic, Celtic
and Arabic tongues. These can be translated, if it is thought proper,
at little expence, though I should prefer that they should remain as
written, and would respectfully recommend that Congress should
immediately employ a competent number of Professors to teach the
members of that honorable body those languages. I am aware that

[3]

there is not now so *much "surplus revenue"* as there was under your glorious administration (owing[2] to the war which the "vandalism" of Great Britain has produced,) yet stock may be created sufficient for their salaries and *contingent* funds. I hope I shall not be tho't, by this, to wish to see the "undefined field of contingencies" opened again, *if they have ever been closed.*

My grand father was a dutch merchant, and spent all his time, while resident in Amsterdam, except what was employed in *smoaking,* in the "principal book marts," laying aside all the works of genius and taste which that country produced. The treatises there obtained are chiefly devoted to music, painting and poetry. My father and I have passed much time in both the Indies, and have occasionally visited almost all the enlightened parts of each. Our intercourse was not confined to those regions, but has been extended from Kamschatka to Buenos Ayres. A propensity for curious books, in every science, being incident to the family, it will not be thought vain in me to declare that this library is exceeded only by yours.

Being now nearly eighty years of age, and having no children, *to whom my estate can descend,* and not finding much time for reading, I should be much pleased to turn these books into cash. A few of them however, I wish to retain for my own use after they shall be sold, taking care to see, *after I am dead,* that they be safely transmitted to Washington. Those of this description are Vanderhuyden's poetical works, in 16 volumes, with notes, critical and explanatory, by Mynheer Van Tromp, dedicated to Admiral Ruyter, who went up the English channel, as mentioned in your letter. Also, a new edition, greatly enlarged, of Robinson Crusoe, in 7 volumes, bound in calf, containing full length portraits of that great traveller and his man Friday, with exact drawings of their working tools and other implements, with *facsimiles* of their handwriting.[3] Also, the whole works of Thomas Paine, your old friend, "who has already received his reward in the thankfulness of nations," consisting of his invaluable discoveries in moral, political and theological science. Those copies, (I believe I have only thirty different editions) with those included in your proposals, and the various editions of Hobbes and Spinosa, those learned and virtuous men, will be sufficient, in that peculiarly *charming* part of theology, for the Congressional library.

As to the price, I shall leave it entirely to the liberality of congress, not wishing to be my own judge, and believing, *inter nos,* that by thus reposing on their generosity, the books will sell at from 50 to 100 per cent, higher than in any other conceivable mode.

To promote the bargain, I wish you to suggest, at the outset of your letter, that I hate, abhor and detest with all my soul, strength and understanding, the whole British nation; that I consider every Englishman, except those who have been naturalized, here (and them, I sincerely love) a thief, liar, poltroon, robber, murderer, assassin, traitor, and that every man, woman and child ought to be hung, imbowelled, impaled, or broken on a wheel. In fine, that the character of that people is justly pourtrayed in a late Washington City Gazette, a paper which is second only to the National Intelligencer, and Binns's Democratic Press, for truth and wisdom; I am aware that such an introduction to a letter, proposing, merely to *sell* books is rather unusual, but I see you have resorted to it, and I think very wisely. People are to be treated according to their prejudices and partialities, and I have witnessed your success with them, by those means, in your splendid career from your inaugural address, through dry docks, gun boats, and salt mountains down to that most *august* measure, *the Embargo.*

I intended to have furnished you with an elegant catalogue of my library, that it might have been open to inspection; but am now wholly occupied in furnishing a drawing of the Capitol and President's House, while on fire, with Mr. M. mounted on a fleet charger, and in full speed flying to a place of safety, from the "vandalism" of the enemy, and capt. Jones, with a boatswain's whistle, calling all hands to burn the Navy Yard, and the frigate on the stocks to prevent them from being carried away by the *Cossacks.*

I will however, mention a few of the great number of books, and give you a sketch of the character of the whole.

There are entire sets of the works of all the atheistical writers in every age and nation and tongue, superbly bound and lettered. Forty different editions of the Bible, thirty nine of which are in the Arabic, and one in the Hebrew Idiom; these are as good as when they came from the hands of the book binder. A very learned treatise in ten volumes quarto, on the nature, properties, and uses of the animal called *tad-pole*, stiled vulgarly, *Polly-wangs*, with an appendix in three volumes; on the toad of Caffrania. The whole of these, I have caused to be translated into six different languages. There is also an elaborate and voluminous account of the *terrapin*, some times called *mud-turtle*, written by the author of sundry ingenious disquisitions on gun boats and dry docks, in modern French—An essay on "free trade and sailors' rights," by a citizen of Algiers, bound in morocco with a copious appendix on allegiance. In this will be found a great part of the instructions given to the American ministers at Petersburgh and at Ghent. It is embellished with striking likenesses of John Henry and the Duke de Crillon. Also, a new edition in seven volumes folio, on the Russian climate, and its effect on Frenchmen, French horses and American politics, with very learned notes by his Excellency Jonathan Russell, late charge de affaires at the Court of St. James, now minister Plenipotentiary at London, Envoy Extraordinary at Gottenburgh and Ghent, otherwise called Jonathan Russell, Esq. of Providence, Trader.—This book is dedicated to Napoleon Bonaparte living at Elba, it went thro' six editions at Ghent in 4 months. A treatise on Treasury notes, Banks and paper money, bound in *calf*, with a splendid title page, by Jacob Barker, superintendant general of the Finances of the United States and first Lord of the Treasury. A work of great worth, written in Persian, on the *grass hopper* of the east, delineating, with entire accuracy, the size of his legs in different regions of that extensive country, with a copious appendix containing the whole learning on the subject of that highly curious animal called the *weasel*.

A complete system of Ornithology, giving an account of every flying creature, from the insect of a day to the *whip poor-will*, the night hawk and the crane, in blank verse, by Inchiquin, translated from the Italian into the Sclavonic, by a learned foreigner, comprized in 13 volumes folio.

Of the whole collection, I take the liberty of saying, that it has been made with a particular view to the promotion of genuine republicanism, and the true orthodoxy in matters of faith of regenerated France, as set forth by those great Apostles, Diderot,[4] De Lambre, Paine and Godwin. The books are in excellent order, many of them truly elegant. Not a syllable could be taken from them without prejudice to the rest, as all the arts and sciences have a certain natural connection. I cannot consent to see my library *gerry-mandered*, for though such procedures are proper to promote *democracy*, which you know is the "chief end of man," yet they are not admissible in cases like the present. I must sell the whole or none. Ten waggons would carry the whole from my residence, which is only 200 miles up the Missouri, in the vicinity of our *red brethren, the allies of England*, to Washington, in a short space of time.

If it should be objected, that four-fifths of this library are in foreign languages, and of course, unintelligible by nine-tenths of the members of congress, I would reply that such an objection can come only from short-sighted men. The enlightened philosopher looks to the present war, which we have so wisely and righteously waged, as terminating not only in the everlasting establishment upon an eternal basis of "free trade and sailors' rights," *(and if it should not so issue, we can make another war at any time)* but also in the conquest of immeasurable regions to the north west and south, and to the day when the representatives of this country, will be composed "of all people, nations & languages under the whole Heavens." Accept the assurances of my high consideration. JOHANNES VONDERPUFF.

Printed in the Georgetown *Federal Republican*, 18 Oct. 1814; at head of text: "TO THOMAS JEFFERSON, ESQ. *Late President of the United States*"; dateline at foot of text.

The pseudonymous Vonderpuff's satirical communication was probably created solely for journalistic purposes. It is not recorded in SJL and may never have been seen by TJ. The piece is framed as a direct response to TJ's much-publicized second letter to Samuel H. Smith of 21 Sept. 1814, wherein the ex-president comments on British VANDALISM, mentions his search for titles in all the "principal book marts" of Europe, expresses the desire that he be allowed to retain a portion of his library even after its sale, refers to Dutch admiral Michiel Adriaanszoon de Ruyter's 1667 voyage up the Thames River, requests that Congress set the price for the books, and insists that his library be purchased in toto or not at all. TJ remarks on the UNDEFINED FIELD OF CONTINGENCIES in his 8 Dec. 1801 annual message to Congress (*PTJ*, 36:52–67, quote on p. 61). Vonderpuff's revelation that he had NO CHILDREN, TO WHOM MY ESTATE CAN DESCEND, is perhaps an allusion to TJ's reputed children by his slave Sally Hemings. MYNHEER is a Dutch title of respect meaning "Sir" or "Mr." TJ included a variant of the phrase WHO HAS ALREADY RECEIVED HIS REWARD IN THE THANKFULNESS OF NATIONS in his letter to Thomas Paine of 18 Mar. 1801 (*PTJ*, 33:358–9). His first INAUGURAL ADDRESS is printed in *PTJ*, 33:134–52.

The reference to SALT MOUNTAINS is explained in note to TJ to Benjamin Waterhouse, 9 Mar. 1813. MR. M. was President James Madison, while CAPT. JONES was Secretary of the Navy William Jones. Kaffraria (CAFFRANIA) is in the present-day Republic of South Africa. The popular slogan FREE TRADE AND SAILORS' RIGHTS was often used by those supporting the war against Great Britain (Malcomson, *Historical Dictionary*, 194).
The RUSSIAN CLIMATE helped defeat Napoleon's *Grande Armée* in 1812 (David G. Chandler, *The Campaigns of Napoleon* [1966], 858–9). Following his fall from power in April 1814, Napoleon was exiled to the Mediterranean island of ELBA (Felix Markham, *Napoleon* [1963], 217). The question "What is the CHIEF END OF MAN?" had long been a part of the standard Anglican catechism (*The Humble Advice Of the Assembly of Divines, Now by Authority of Parliament sitting at Westminster, Concerning A Larger Catechism* [London, 1647], 3; *The Shorter Catcehism, composed by the Assembly of Divines at Westminster* [Philadelphia, 1814], 11). OF ALL PEOPLE, NATIONS & LANGUAGES UNDER THE WHOLE HEAVENS combines phrases found in various books of the Bible (see, for instance, Genesis 7.19, Daniel 7.14, 27, Revelation 10.11).

¹ Printed text: "aukwardly."
² Printed text: "owning."
³ Printed text: "hands writing."
⁴ Printed text: "Diduot."

From Joseph Delaplaine

DEAR SIR,   Philadelphia October 3ᵈ 1814

I duly received your favour of the 28ʰ of August, enclosing your outline of the engraved portrait of Columbus [in the?] work of De Bry.

I beg you to accept my sincere thanks for your kindness in giving me such satisfactory information respecting the authenticity of the Portraits of Columbus. I will avail myself of it & when an opportunity occurs will cause a drawing to be taken from the picture in your possession.

I would have had the pleasure of replying to your favour earlier, but I have been waiting for a reply to my letter to Mʳ Stuart on the subject of your portrait, in the hope of giving you a favourable account of the result of our respective applications to him. I am sorry, very sorry, to inform you that he has not even noticed my letter.

I am anxious to have an engraving of your portrait, & I beg of you to consider what steps you will take for the accomplishment of this object.

Others, it is well known, have been treated by Mʳ Stuart precisely in the same manner, and many gentlemen are impressed with a perfect belief that neither you nor myself, will ever be able to prevail upon him to place in your hands that which is your own & which it is so unjust to with-hold.

I should greatly regret to be compelled to suspend my work, in consequence of not receiving your portrait, and I therefore take the liberty of knowing from you whether you will authorize me by power of Attorney to obtain it.

I enclose you an engraved portrait of the President & request your opinion of it.

Hoping to receive an early answer, I remain

Dear sir, with great regard your very obed. sevᵗ

JOSEPH DELAPLAINE

RC (DLC); torn at seal; endorsed by TJ as received 12 Oct. 1814 and so recorded in SJL. RC (NHi: Thomas Jefferson Papers); address cover only; with PoC of TJ to Patrick Gibson, 25 Oct. 1814, on verso; addressed: "Thomas Jefferson Esqʳ Monticello Virginia"; franked; postmarked Philadelphia, 5 Oct.

Despite several APPLICATIONS to the artist, Delaplaine ultimately failed in his attempt to obtain Gilbert Stuart's 1805 "Edgehill Portrait" of TJ for use in his *Repository of the Lives and Portraits of Distinguished Americans* (note to TJ to Delaplaine, 30 May 1813; TJ to Stuart, 9 Aug. 1814). The enclosure was apparently an early state of the stipple en-graving of PRESIDENT James Madison (entitled *James Madison Esq* [Philadelphia, 1814]) executed for Delaplaine by William R. Jones from Stuart's 1804 life portrait (Theodore Bolton, "The Life Portraits of James Madison," *WMQ*, 3d ser., 8 [1951]: 30–1, 39, 41–2).

From Gabriel Penn

DEAR SIR   Portsmouth N.H. Octr 3rd 1814

Although not having the pleasure of your personal acquaintance I presume you will pass over the liberty I have taken of writing to you when you know the object. It has long been my desire to enter the service of my country and for that end went to sea in the merchant service since the war I have been in an armed Vessel. The object of this letter is to solicit your Friendship in procuring for me an appointment in the Navy. I have written to my Father James Penn of New London whose estate joins the Poplar Forest and with whom I presume you are acquainted for some letters of recommen to the secretary of the Navy. but as there are a number of applications I was fearfull that I should meet with some difficulty unless I could have the good will of some person who was acquainted with me and at the Navy department. As it is presumed that every young man who makes an application will not[1] receive an warrant for the greater part are quite young some mere boys: I have been to Sea for three years and think I am[2] of a proper age to go in the Navy I am twenty years of age and am vain enough to think Myself capable of the duties of a Midshipman I first went to sea with the intention of entering the Navy but not wishing to enter a Novice have endeavored to inprov myself and become capable of the duties of that station.

We are now engaged in a war that is to establish our liberty on the sea and as I am deeply interested in the welfare of my country. our little Navy increasing and will of course want young officers, a desire to serve my country[3] has prompte me to take the liberty of writing to you Soliciting your interest in procuring a warrant for me in the Navy and I trust never shall disgrace you or my country.—

Virginia has fewer officers than any other State in the Navy and as I presume you wish to see them in the list of Naval officers as soon as any other Men Request your Patronage and hope one day to make myself worthy it.

I arrived in this place from sea and as it is a long distance home and should I obtain my wish my services[4] will be better here than on any other station. Although not in the Navy I am[5] not Idle having a station in Fort Constitution and should an opportunity offer shall enderivor to do my duty.—

Should you condescend to answr this letter it will meet with the highest marks of respect from your Most Obt Serv[t]

GABRIEL PENN

RC (DLC); addressed: "Thomas Jefferson Eq[r] Charlottsvill Virginia"; franked; postmarked Portsmouth, N.H., 11 Oct.; endorsed by TJ as received 19 Oct. 1814 and so recorded in SJL.

Gabriel Penn (b. ca. 1794) received no commission in the United States Navy. TJ did not write on his behalf, although he had dined at his grandfather Gabriel Penn's Amherst County ordinary and done legal work for the elder Penn prior to the Revolutionary War (Lee Forney Crawford, *William Webb Crawford, Dean of Birmingham Bankers, and Family Sketches, Genealogies* [1958], 35–6; *Raleigh Register, and North-Carolina Gazette*, 17 Dec. 1813; *MB*, 1:40, 319).

[1] Preceding two words interlined in place of "to."
[2] Manuscript: "an."
[3] Manuscript: "county."
[4] Manuscript: "serrces."
[5] Manuscript: "an."

To Jeremiah A. Goodman

DEAR SIR   Monticello Oct. 4. 14.

I wrote you Sep. 27. since that your brother has been taken ill, and is in such a situation in point of health as to render it certain he cannot go to Bedford. consequently the job of covering the offices must lie over till the spring. my affairs here too are such as to render the time of my being with you extremely uncertain. with the hope always of going in 10. days or a fortnight, I am still totally unable to say when I can come. in the mean time I hope your letter is on the way informing me of the amount of my taxes, in order that I may send the sheriff a draught for it, and at the same time write to mr Gibson directly to pay it on application, should the sheriff go before my draught gets to you.   Another most important object is the getting in the crop of wheat at both places. 4. ploughs at the least at each place should be running from this time, to get it in by the middle of November. whatever then is wanting, with the horses remaining and oxen, must be bought. let the horses you buy be good able horses. stout chunky built are the most serviceable, large enough for the waggon, & let them be tolerably young. obtain credit till May that I may have full time to sell my crop. lose not a moment in procuring them so as to have all the ploughs agoing. I shall be with you the mo-

ment it is in my power; but put off nothing for that, the time is so uncertain. accept my best wishes.   TH: JEFFERSON

RC (DLC: TJ Papers, ser. 9); addressed: "Mr Jeremiah A. Goodman
Poplar Forest near Lynchburg"; franked;
postmarked Charlottesville, 7 Oct.

TJ's letter to Goodman of SEP. 27 is
recorded in SJL but has not been found.

BOTH PLACES: TJ's Bear Creek and
Tomahawk plantations at Poplar Forest.
Missing letters from Goodman of 18
July, 1 Aug., and 20 Sept. 1814 are
recorded in SJL as received from Poplar
Forest on 22 July, 10 Aug., and 26 Sept.
1814, respectively.

From James Monroe

DEAR SIR   washington octr 4. 1814
    I have had the pleasure to receive your favor of the 24th of sep^r, to
which I shall pay particular attention, and on which I will write you
again soon.
    Nothing but the disasters here, and the duties which have devolvd
on me, in consequence, the most burthensome that I have ever en-
counterd, would have prevented my writing you long since, as well as
more recently. I had devoted this morning to a full communication to
you, but have been pressd by committees, on military topics, till the
period has passed. You Shall hear from me again in a few days. with
great respect
    & esteem y^r friend   JA^s MONROE

RC (DLC); endorsed by TJ as received
7 Oct. 1814 and so recorded in SJL.

The office of secretary of war had recently DEVOLVD on Monroe, who also
continued as secretary of state (note to
James W. Wallace to TJ, 29 Aug. 1814).

Notes on Bottle and Beverage Supplies

[6 Oct. 1814–Feb. 1816]

Juggs rec^d from R: Randolph

1814	large	small	
in Summer	12	6^1	
Oct. 6.	84	33	

1815. Dec. 24. Census of bottles.	glass quart bottles	950
	quart jugs	50
	pottle jugs	105 1210 q^{ts}

1816. Feb.   rec^d from Capt Peyton   540

Ale. brewed.   7 casks of   30. gall^s = 210
                1. d°   60   60
        still to brew 10. b. malt 70   70
                                              340. gall^s

        cyder. bot of Massie   143. gall^s
            of mrs Brand. Crab   44   187
            of d°   common   93
                                               280

MS (MHi); written entirely in TJ's hand at multiple sittings on one side of a single sheet; partially dated.

B.: barrels. TJ paid Charles MASSIE $25 and Fanny BRAND $28.50 for the abovementioned cider on 22 and 24 Dec. 1815, respectively (*MB*, 2:1317).

[1] The entry relating to the receipt of 126 jugs from Richard Randolph was apparently added at some point after 6 Oct. 1814.

To Thomas Cooper

DEAR SIR   Monticello Oct. 7. 14.

Your several favors of Sep. 15. 21. 22. came all together by our last mail. I have given to that of the 15th a single reading only, because the handwriting (not your own) is microscopic & difficult, and because I shall have an opportunity of studying it in the Portfolio in print. according to your request I return it for that publication, where it will do a great deal of good. it will give our young men some idea of what constitutes a well educated man: that Caesar and Virgil, & a few books of Euclid do not really contain the sum of all human knolege, nor give to a man figure in the ranks of science. your letter will be a valuable source of consultation for us in our Collegiate courses when, and if ever, we advance to that stage of our establishment.

I agree with yours of the 22^d that a professorship of Theology should have no place in our institution. but we cannot always do what is absolutely best. those with whom we act, entertaining different views, have the power and the right of carrying them into practice. truth advances, & error recedes step by step only; and to do to our fellow-men the most good in our power, we must lead where we can, follow where we cannot, and still go with them, watching always the favorable moment for helping them to another step. perhaps I should concur with you also in excluding the Theory [not the Practice] of medecine. this is the Charlatanerie of the body, as the other is of the mind. for Classical learning I have ever been a zealous advocate: and in this, as in his theory of bleeding, and mercury, I was ever opposed to my friend Rush, whom I greatly loved; but who has done much harm, in the sincerest persuasion that he was preserving life and happiness to all around him. I have not however carried so far as you do my ideas of the importance of a hypercritical knolege of the Latin & Greek languages. I have believed it sufficient to possess a substantial understanding of their authors.   In the exclusion of Anatomy and Botany from the II^d grade of education, which is that of the man of independant fortune, we separate in opinion. in my view, no knolege can be more satisfactory to a man than that of his own frame, it's parts, their functions & actions. and Botany I rank with the most[1] valuable sciences, whether we consider it's subjects as furnishing the principal subsistence of life to man & beast, delicious varieties for our tables, refreshments from our orchards, the adornments of our flower-borders, shade and perfume of our groves, materials for our buildings, or medicaments for our bodies. to the gentleman it is certainly more interesting than Mineralogy (which I by no means however undervalue) and is more at hand for his amusement. and to a country family it constitutes a great portion of their social entertainment. no country gentleman should be without what amuses every step he takes into his fields.

I am sorry to learn the fate of your Emporium. it was adding fast to our useful knolege. our Artists particularly & our Statesmen will have cause to regret it. but my hope is that it's suspension will be temporary only; and that as soon as we get over the crisis of our disordered circulation, your publishers will resume it among their first enterprises.   Accept my thanks for the benefit of your ideas to our scheme of education, and the assurance of my constant esteem and respect.   TH: JEFFERSON

PoC (DLC); brackets in original; at foot of first page: "Thomas Cooper esq."; endorsed by TJ. Enclosure: Cooper to TJ, 15 Sept. 1814. Enclosed in TJ to Joseph C. Cabell, 5 Jan. 1815.

[1] Reworked from "more."

From Samuel H. Smith

DEAR SIR   Washington Oct. 7. 1814

It gives me great pleasure to acknowledge the receipt of Your favor of the ult. w^{ich} from some casualty did not reach me until the 2^d Instant. It is impossible to repress indignant feeling at the barbarism of our enemy, wch would have cast a shade over the remote ages when civilisation had scarcely dawned on mankind. Instead, however, at present resting in the indulgence of such feeling, it is infinitely better to deal back the blow, thus in some degree drawing good out of evil. To retrieve also the injury done as speedily as we can, is equally the dictate of wisdom.

The Library, that is lost, was valuable and was the commencement of an Institution fitted in its maturity to be the pride and ornament of our Country. But valuable as it was, if replaced by Your collection the loss will be more than supplied. Being somewhat of an enthusiast as to the benefits that arise from such institutions I cordially hail the prospect of seeing so broad a foundation laid for a national one on a scale of expanding grandeur.

I submitted, without delay, Your letter and catalogue to the Library Committees of the two Houses of Congress. That of the Senate consists of Mesrs Goldsborough, Tait & Fromentine, and that of the Representatives of Mesrs Seybert, Lowndes & Gaston. The tender was respectfully received by both Committees, with the assurance that no time should be lost in acting upon it. They each expressed the opinion that the Committees could not go further than to recommend to their Houses such steps as they should on consultation consider advisable, and promised to inform me of the course determined on. I have made several other members acquainted with the offer made by you, and have been happy to find that it is highly appreciated by them and will receive their warm support.

I perceive no obstacle to its acceptance but the pending proposition to remove the seat of government. I fear that many of those who are interested in this measure will consider the possession of such a library as depriving them of a strong argument in favor of removal, and will thence be apt by delay or evasion to keep back its consideration. Should this prove to be the case I submit to You the policy of permitting a publication of Your letters

In the hope that You continue to enjoy health & happiness, I am with sentiments of great & unabated respect and regard

SA H SMITH

I am just advised by m^r Goldsborough that the joint Com^e have reported a resolution empowering[1] them to contract for the purchase of the Library

RC (DLC); postscript written perpendicularly in left margin; at foot of text: "Thomas Jefferson Esquire"; endorsed by TJ as received 12 Oct. 1814 and so recorded in SJL.

For YOUR FAVOR OF THE ULT. see TJ's two letters to Smith of 21 Sept. 1814. Early in the autumn of 1814 the United States House of Representatives hotly debated a proposal TO REMOVE THE SEAT

OF GOVERNMENT from Washington for the duration of the war with Great Britain. A bill to that effect was introduced on 13 Oct. 1814 but voted down two days later (*Annals*, 13th Cong., 3d sess., esp. 311–2, 387–8, 394–6 [26 Sept., 13, 15 Oct. 1814]).

¹ Manuscript: "empowerig."

From Thomas Ritchie

SIR   Richmond, Oct. 9. 1814.

I have the honor to enclose you the letters of Dʳ Mease & Mʳ Greer, which you were so kind as to forward me some time since. The interest excited by the fall of Washington, the events which have since transpired, and the military duresse to which I have been subjected, have drawn off my attention too much from other objects. Let this plead my Apology for the delay!

These letters have answered the purpose for which they were transmitted, without my having made any public use of them. The day I recᵈ them, I made it a point to see Mʳ Clopper, and very frankly informed him of my Intention to state on the ensuing Morning the facts which had been disclosed to me. Mʳ C. was evidently alarmed, and begged me to suspend the article until he could see me again in the Evening. He was punctual to his appointment, and the conference ended in a solemn pledge on his part, that he would not sell any patent right in Vᵃ for more than $20. nor would he sell out on shares, to any association of persons, without informing them of the current price in Baltimore at $20.—I also made it a point to see Mʳ Harris, and acquaint him with the same circumstances. He has since joined an Association of Gentlemen, who have bought of Mʳ Clopper on shares. What part they mean to play, and what price to ask for their patent, I have not understood—but it will be time to act, when their schemes shall have been developed.

I profoundly regret, Sir, that it is out of my power to edit at this moment the interesting Work of m. de Tracy. I had some hopes of being able to make an Arrangement for this purpose; but th[e] call of the Legislature, the military duties to which my hands are subjected, and other circumstances which it is useless to specify, have compleatly prevented me.—It would not be in my power to strike upon it, until the Spring—but the delay which has already taken place in the publication, makes you, I presume, solicitous to have it out as soon as possible.—Your friendly proposition to myself, Sir, can never be forgotten.

Such works, as M. Tracy's, are too scarce in the world, and a fortiori too slightly studied in this world of ours. We want financiers to extract and to economise our resources. We have <u>men</u>, and <u>munitions</u> enough—the great want at present is <u>money</u>—not gold & silver merely, but some representative of the credit & resources of the nation.—I had the honor of seeing, some short time past, some M.S. letters of yours on Finances and Bank Paper. It is, I suppose, useless to intreat you to give them to your Country. Their speculations were bold & original—and I could not but wish that the pleasure which they gave <u>me</u>, should be made a common property.

I sincerely wish that M. de Tracy's 12th Chap. "On the Revenues & Expences of Government and of their debts"—was at this moment before us. Mr Campbell's last Report on our Finances seems to argue a want of this species of information.—<u>His</u> Report has set every thing afloat—The Com: of Ways & Means ought to come out with some vigorous Projet, to anchor the public mind.

I am, Sir,

With the highest Respect, Y^{rs}   THOMAS RITCHIE.

RC (DLC); edge chipped; dateline at foot of text; addressed: "Thomas Jefferson Esq^e Monticello"; franked; postmarked Richmond, 9 and 12 Oct.; endorsed by TJ as received 14 Oct. 1814 and so recorded in SJL. Enclosures: enclosures to TJ to Ritchie, 15 Aug. 1814.

Ritchie's MILITARY DURESSE arose out of his brief service during the waning days of the War of 1812 (*DAB*). The INTERESTING WORK was the as-yet-unpublished fourth volume of Destutt de Tracy's *Élémens d'Idéologie*. For TJ's FRIENDLY PROPOSITION that Ritchie publish this manuscript, see TJ to Ritchie, 27 Sept. 1814. For former treasury secretary George W. Campbell's LAST REPORT ON OUR FINANCES, see *ASP, Finance*, 2:840–53.

From James Madison

DEAR SIR   Washington Oc^r 10. 1814

Your favor of the 24th ult: came duly to hand. I learn that the Library Com^e will report favorably on your proposition to supply the loss of books by Cong^s. It will prove a gain to them, if they have the wisdom to replace it by such a Collection as yours. Mr Smith will doubtless write you on the subject.

I have not yet read your last comunication to Mr Monroe on the subject of finance. It seems clear, according to your reasoning in the preceding one, that a circulating medium, to take the place of a bank or metallic medium, may be created by law and made to answer the purpose of a loan, or rather anticipation of a tax; but as the resource can not be extended beyond the amount of a <u>sufficient</u> medium, and of course can not be <u>continued</u> but by successive re-emissions & re-demptions by taxes, resort must eventually be had to loans, of the usual sort, or an[1] augmentation of taxes, according to the public exi-gences: I say augmentations of taxes, because these absorbing a larger sum into circulation, will admit an enlargement of the medium employed for the purpose. In England where the paper medium, is a legal tender in paying a hundred millions of taxes, thirty millions of interest to the public creditors &c &c, and in private debts, so as to stay a final recovery, we have Seen what a mass of paper has been kept afloat with little if any depreciation. That the difference in value between[2] the circulating[3] notes and the metals proceeded rather from the rise in the latter than from the depreciation of the former, is now proved by the fact, that the notes are, notwithstanding a late increase of their quantity, rising towards a par with the metals, in conse-quence of a favorable balance of trade which diminishes the demand of them for foreign markets.

We have just rec[d] despatches from Ghent, which I shall lay before Cong[s] today. The British sine qua non, excluded us from fishing within the soverignty attached to her shores, and from using these in curing fish—required a Cession of as much of Maine as w[d] remove[4] the obstruction to a <u>direct</u> communication between Quebec & Hali-fax, confirmed to her the Passamaquoddy Islands as always hers of right—included in the pacification the Indian Allies, with a boundary for them,[5] (such as that of the Treaty of[6] Greenville) ag[st] the U.S. mutually guaranteed, and the Indians restrained from selling their lands to either party, but free to sell them to a <u>third</u> party—prohibited the U.S. from having an armed force on the Lakes or forts on their shores, the British prohibited as to neither—and substituted for the present N.W. limit of the U.S. a line running direct from the W. end of L. Superior to the Mississippi, with a right of G.B. to the naviga-tion of this river. our ministers were all present & in perfect harmony of opinion on the arrogance of such demands. They w[d] probably leav[e] Ghent shortly after the sailing of the vessel just arrived. Noth-ing can prevent it, but a sudden change in the B. Cabinet not likely to happen, tho' it might be somewhat favored by an indignant rup-ture of the negociation, as well as by the intelligence from this Coun-try, and the fermentations taking place in Europe.

I intended to have said something on the changes in the Cabinet, involving in one instance, circumstances of which the public can as yet very little judge, but cannot do it now.

The situation of Sacketts Harbour is very critical. I hope for the best, but have serious apprehensions.

With truest affection always y^{rs}　　　　　JAMES MADISON

RC (DLC: Madison Papers); edge trimmed; at foot of text: "Thomas Jefferson"; endorsed by TJ as received 12 Oct. 1814 and so recorded in SJL.

For the August 1814 DESPATCHES FROM GHENT, see *ASP, Foreign Relations*, 3:695, 705–10. For the 1795 TREATY OF GREENVILLE between the United States and various Northwest Indian nations, see *U.S. Statutes at Large*, 7:49–54. THE LAKES: the Great Lakes. In the most recent reorganization of the CABINET, James Monroe took over for John Armstrong at the War Department

and Alexander J. Dallas replaced George W. Campbell at the Treasury Department (*JEP*, 2:530, 533 [26, 27 Sept., 5, 6 Oct. 1814]). Reports of an imminent British attack on the American post at SACKETTS HARBOUR proved to be unfounded (Washington *Daily National Intelligencer*, 10 Oct., 10 Nov. 1814).

¹ Preceding six words interlined.
² Manuscript: "betwen."
³ Word interlined in place of "paper."
⁴ Word interlined in place of "allow."
⁵ Preceding two words interlined.
⁶ Preceding three words interlined.

From James Monroe

DEAR SIR　　　　　　　　　　washington. oct^r 10th 1814

The suspension of payments in specie by the banks is undoubtedly a species of insolvency. At this time, the foundation of their credit with the public, in a principal degree, at least, is the stock of the u states in their possession. On it they issue their paper, for which they obtain an interest of about 7 p^r cent. The u States pay them that interest on advances, on the credit of their own funds. The demonstration is complete, that having better credit than any bank, or than all the banks together, the gov^t might issue a paper, which would circulate without their aid, throughout the U States, and on much better terms to the public. Your letters I shall take the liberty of shewing to mr Dallas, who is expected here in a day or two. They were put up with my papers on the late occurrence, and are not yet unpack,d, being sent to Lee'sbg.

I shall be happy to promote the disposition of your library in the manner your propose, tho' I regret that you are to be deprivd of such a resource & consolation in your retirement.

Letters were rec^d yesterday from our ministers at Ghent, which announce the approaching termination of the negotiation, without any hope of peace. They will probably return in less than a month. The demands of G Britain, corresponding with what the papers had before given us, have renderd all accomodation impracticable. The President will communicate these despatches to Congress to day, so that you may probably receive them by this mail. very respectfully your friend

& servant   JAˢ MONROE

RC (DLC); endorsed by TJ as received 12 Oct. 1814 and so recorded in SJL.

The letters on finance that Monroe intended to show Treasury Secretary Alexander J. DALLAS were TJ to John Wayles Eppes, 24 June, 11 Sept., 6 Nov.

1813, TJ to Joseph C. Cabell, 17 Jan. 1814, and possibly also TJ to Cabell, 23 Sept. 1814. The LATE OCCURRENCE was the government's evacuation of Washington following the American defeat at Bladensburg on 24 Aug. 1814.

From John Barnes

DEAR SIR—   Ge[orge] Town 11ᵗʰ Octʳ 1814—

Your favʳ 30ᵗʰ Ultᵒ reached me last Evening, Covering five dollar Alexᵃ Bank Note. they pass Currᵗ with us. and I trust will continue so to do—

and I regret to perceive they're refused in exchange even for Virgᵃ paper,—Not to Accomodate with so near a Neighbour—whose late Misfortunes Shᵈ rather excite Compassion—and Assistance—then fear of their not being able to repair their unavoidable losses—,—the[1] present distresses of our Banks' Circulation—Arises chiefly between the Northern[2] and Southern Banks. the latter being all indebted to the former—The Philadᵃ and N York merchᵗˢ having been Accustomed to forward their Customers Notes of hand made payable at the place of their Residence—viz Geo Town Alexᵃ Richmond, & Petersburg—to the Cashiers of those several Banks untill they were obliged from necessity to refuse Collecting them—it is however presumed some Accomodation will soon take place between Certain of the Northern & southern Cashiers—in Order to Accomodate each Other—at this distressing time in Bank Circulation—and thereby prevent the fatal consequences[3] which might Otherwise follow.— the best Established Banks—will I trust stand their ground—at a depreciated Value—as to Stock—and dividend. the Others of less Stability will risque perhaps—their existance—those Banks who have already Subscribed to the loans—has so far reduced their Capital—which they cannot now replace—but at very considerable loss.— wil[l ne]vertheless recive a hansome Interest—and thereby be inabled to pay a Reasonable dividend.

the failure in the late Loan—is of all—the most unfortunate at this Crisis of our Public Affairs—and some effectual Remedy must— and I trust—will soon be Applied—the present good spirits of the Army and Navy must be incouraged & supported—their Continued successes are beyond our most sanguin expectations—to damp their Ardor for the want of Resources would be fatal—in the extreme—More especially—as we are now freed from a lingering Suspense,—more dangerous in its Consequences—then a determined Resolution—(however to be dreaded.) by either—to abide—and to be decided—by the length of the Sword,—all party disputes We may now expect to be buried—and with one United Voice and Arm to Resist—rather then submit to such degrading Ignominous terms, and Conditions—as proposed (Knowing they could not[4] be Assented to,)—Our Invoys, will I hope be soon hailed—on their[5] safe Arrival, with repeated Acclamations of Joy and triumph,—the Resources of the Country are more then sufficient[6]—for the Occasion—and I trust will be[7] drawn forth, and Acquiesce in, with Cheerfullness and full Confidince as to the Result—Another successfull Campaign, will have—I expect the like effect of that in which—(you will Recollect) when Doct[r] Franklin and if I mistake not M[r] Adams met the Admiral and his Bro[r] Gen[l] How—at Staten Island [in] 1776—

Excuse my hasty involuntary Ideas. they press upon me irresistably[8]—that I cannot restrain myself—from expressing them—

Yours most sincerely & obed[t]   JOHN BARNES,

PS. it is with equal sentiments of Congratulation—at the fortunate Circumstance of my being inabled to close the good Gen[l] K— Bank stock at so adventageous a Crisis and transpose the proceeds in the late Loan—on the like adventageous terms—but not yet particularly[9] adjusted—

RC (ViU: TJP-ER); torn at seal; at foot of text: "Thomas Jefferson Esq[r] Monticello"; endorsed by TJ as received 14 Oct. 1814 and so recorded in SJL.

Since the outbreak of the War of 1812, Congress had authorized LOANS for up to $48.5 million (*U.S. Statutes at Large*, 2:798–9, 3:75–7, 111–2 [8 Feb., 2 Aug. 1813, 24 Mar. 1814]). Treasury Secretary George W. Campbell effectively conceded the FAILURE IN THE LATE LOAN by reporting to the United States Senate late in September that only $4.3 million had been raised out of $25 million in borrowing authorized on 24 Mar. 1814 (*ASP, Finance*, 2:841–2). A committee of the Continental Congress composed of Benjamin Franklin, John Adams, and Edward Rutledge adamantly refused to reconsider the issue of America's independence from Great Britain during a meeting with Admiral Richard Howe (General William Howe being absent) on STATEN ISLAND in September 1776 (Leonard W. Labaree and others, eds., *The Papers of Benjamin Franklin* [1959–], 22:598–605). GEN[L] K—: Tadeusz Kosciuszko.

[1] Manuscript: "thee."
[2] Manuscript: "Northen."
[3] Manuscript: "consiquences."
[4] Word interlined.
[5] Manuscript: "they."
[6] Manuscript: "suffient."
[7] Manuscript: "and will I trust will be."
[8] Manuscript: "irrestably."
[9] Manuscript: "particular."

From Isaac A. Coles

Dᴿ Sɪʀ,   Enniscorthy Oct: 11ᵗʰ 1814.

I send you by the Bearer the <u>wild</u> Orange of South Carolina—It grows in the middle & upper parts of the State, is Said to be a very hardy tree, & one of the Most beautiful in the world—I am induced to beleive from the account I have received of it, that it will do well in our climate—.

mʳˢ Singleton from whom I received it, is very desirous of getting a few plants of the Marseilles Fig to Carry back with her to Carolina, where it is not known at all, & where the climate will Suit it So well— you will oblige me much by sending a few Plants[1] by the Servant—

The Enemy having left the Chesapeake I propose to Spend a week with my friends, & mean to visit Monticello before my return—with Sincere respectful attachment

I am ever yʳ obᵈᵗ Servᵗ   I. A. Coʟᴇs

RC (DLC); at foot of text: "Thoˢ Jefferson"; endorsed by TJ as received 11 Oct. 1814 and so recorded in SJL.

Mᴿˢ Sɪɴɢʟᴇᴛᴏɴ was probably Coles's sister Rebecca Coles Singleton (William B. Coles, *The Coles Family of Virginia* [1931], 52, 111).

[1] Word interlined.

From James Oldham

Dᴇᴀʀᴇ Sɪʀ   Richmond October 11ᵗʰ 1814.

youre Letter of the 27 Ultimo was duly Received. I have examened Richmond thruoute and there is not A Pane of glass lerger than 9 I. by 11 I in the Town. understanding there was A Probebility of Some in Peters-burge, I rote to Mʳ Frederick Y. Roddy who Informs me there is none to be Purchas'd A Mʳ Foulke of Richmond sets oute for Baltimore this day and is well acquanted with the manegers of the Glass-workes there, has Promised me to have the Glass cut and Sent on to Richmond by the first convayance; I consulted Mʳ Gibson and he wos of the opinion that it wos the only way to get it.

With Grate Respect I am Sir your Obᵗ Sevᵗ   J, Oʟᴅʜᴀᴍ

RC (MHi); at foot of text: "Thoˢ Jefferson Esqʳ"; endorsed by TJ as received 17 Oct. 1814 and so recorded in SJL.

To Samuel H. Smith

DEAR SIR   Monticello Oct. 11. 14.

In the letter which accompanied my catalogue I promised an Alphabetical Index of Author's names referring to the chapters of the catalogue in which the titles of their works would be found at large. I have just finished & now inclose it. mr Millegan will be so good as to stitch it in at the end of the catalogue, the paper being of the same format.

My affairs at a distant possession (in Bedford) call me thither urgently and would require a considerable stay there. but if the library committee contemplate, in your opinion, an acceptance of the offer of the library I will so arrange my journey as to occasion as little delay as possible, supposing that many members would find, in it's early possession, a considerable alleviation of their vacant hours. if you will be so good as to drop me a line immediately expressing your expectations on this subject, it may be recieved before my departure, and will serve to govern the time and term of my journey. Accept assurances of my great esteem & respect.   TH: JEFFERSON

RC (Charles M. Storey, Boston, 1958); adjacent to signature: "Saml H. Smith esq."; notation by Smith at foot of text: "Answ^d Oct. 14. 1814." PoC (DLC); endorsed by TJ. Enclosure not found.

From Joseph Milligan

DEAR SIR   Georgetown Oct 12th 1814
By this days Stage I have sent you a Box containing
    7th & 8th Ornithology
    6 Jeffersons Manual
    1 Herodotus 4 vols
    1 Southeys Life of Nelson
    and
    Sundries for Mrs Randolph and Children
The Box is sent to the care of William F Gray Bookseller of Fredericksburg via[1]
    With Respect   JOSEPH MILLIGAN

RC (DLC); at foot of text: "Th^{os} Jefferson Esqr"; endorsed by TJ as received 14 Oct. 1814 and so recorded in SJL.

ORNITHOLOGY: TJ sold all nine volumes of Alexander Wilson's *American Ornithology; or, The Natural History of the Birds of the United States* (Philadelphia, 1808–14; Sowerby, no. 1022) to Congress. However, he retained William Beloe's annotated English translation of *The History of Herodotus*, 4 vols. (London, 1791, and later eds.; Poor, *Jefferson's Library*, 3 [no. 6]) and Robert Southey's *The Life of Nelson* (London, 1813, and later eds.; Poor, *Jefferson's Library*, 4 [no. 110]).

¹ Abbreviation for "Virginia."

To James Madison

DEAR SIR   Monticello Oct. 13. 14.

It seems as if we should never find men for our public agencies with mind enough to rise above the little motives of pride & jealousy, & to do their duties in harmony, as the good of their country, & their own happiness would require. poor Warden, I find, has been thought an object of jealousy to Crawford, and the scenes of Dʳ Franklin and mr Adams, Dʳ Franklin & Lee, Dʳ Franklin and Izard (si magnis componere parva licebit) are to be acted over again in Crawford & Warden. I inclose you a letter from the latter, which seems so simple a narrative as to carry truth on it's face. Warden has science enough, with his modest manners, to have gained the affections & society of the literati, and even those of the high circles of the place. Crawford has sound sense, but no science, speaks not a word of the language, and has not the easy manners which open the doors of the polite circle. his functions are limited by insuperable barriers to a formal correspondence, <u>by letter</u>, with the minister. it is natural that in this situation he should be uneasy & discontented, and easy for him to mistake the objects on which it should be manifested. I have no doubt, from what I learn through other channels, that Warden renders us an essential service, which mere superiority of office does not put in the power of the other, of keeping the public there truly informed of the events of the war here. I have as little doubt that if Crawford could suppress the little pride & jealousy which are beneath him, he might often make Warden the entering wedge for accomplishing with that government, what will be totally beyond his own faculties. I fear his experience has not yet taught him the lesson, indispensable in the practical business of life, to consider men, as other machines, to be used¹ for what they are fitted; that a razor should be employed to shave our beards, and an axe to cut our wood, and that we should not throw away the axe because it will not shave us, nor the razor because it will not cut our wood. it is true that on the subject of the letter inclosed, I have heard not a tittle from any other source. to you, who have doubtless recieved the doleances of Crawford, I have thought it would be satisfactory audire alteram partem; and the rather as he has perhaps unbosomed himself to a private individual more unreservedly than he would in a formal defence addressed to yourself. ever affectionately & respectfully yours.

TH: JEFFERSON

RC (DLC). PoC (DLC); at foot of first page: "The President of the US."; endorsed by TJ. Enclosure: David Bailie Warden to TJ, 25 July [1814]. Enclosed in Madison to TJ, 23 Oct. 1814 (second letter).

SI MAGNIS COMPONERE PARVA LICEBIT is a change in word order but not in meaning from "si parva licet componere magnis" ("if we may compare small things with great"), in Virgil, *Georgics*, 4.176 (Fairclough, *Virgil*, 1:230–1). DOLEANCES: "complaints" (*OED*). AUDIRE ALTERAM PARTEM: "to hear the other side."

[1] Preceding three words interlined.

From John L. E. W. Shecut

ESTEEMED SIR   Charleston S° Car° Oct 13. 1814

Your very obliging letter of the 25. Ult, has been received and I cannot but be grateful for the friendly interest you take for the success of my proposed Publication, as also for the advice afforded[1] me towards applying for Some Vacancy under Government. Previous to entering on any other subject I beg leave to Say, that I exceedingly regret, the evident changes in your health as mentioned in your letter, and to express my Sincerest wishes for the prolongation of a life, dear to every genuine American. And that you may live to See these United States rais'd to the Scale highest in the rank of Nations, and enjoying all those blessings which cannot fail to spring from that Constitution, which owes So much of its excellence to your head and heart. That time I hope is certainly approaching And I look forward to share, at least a Small Portion of its blessings with you.

I have addressed a Letter to the Speaker of the House, being formerly intimately acquainted with him. The other Honble Members from S° Carolina, I have not had the pleasure of a Personal acquaintance, I doubt not however that Mr Cheves will oblige me by interesting them in my Favour.

My esteemed Friend Doctor Ramsay, has been also good enough to mention to Mr Cheves, "I have read the Manuscript Copy of the work referred to in this Letter and am of opinion that it is executed with great industry, ingenuity and ability and promises to do honor to the author and to be well worth the purchase and perusal of Numerous readers."—

In my application, I have given a Preference to an appointment to France, but leave it in the power of my Friends to place me either there or at or near the Government. I feel perfectly assured, that shoud it be in your power to aid to the Success of my application, in any manner consistent with those rules that you have laid down for yourself, that you will most cordially do So without further solicitation.

Permit me to offer you the renewed assurances of grateful esteem accompanied with my best wishes for the restoration of your health and every other blessing. Dear Sir with Sincere respect

Yours most Obed^t   J L E W SHECUT

RC (DLC); at foot of text: "His Excellency Thomas Jefferson"; endorsed by TJ as received 24 Oct. 1814 and so recorded in SJL.

In his APPLICATION of about this date for a secretaryship, Shecut advised President James Madison that he would "prefer being Sent to France" (RC in DNA: RG 59, LAR, 1809–17; dateline frayed).

[1] Manuscript: "affirded."

From William F. Gray

SIR,   Fredericksburg Oct. 14. 1814

Mr Joseph Milligan of Geo. Town has requested me to take charge of any little Packets that may be forwarded to this place for you; and by his desire I acquaint you of my willingness to do so. Any thing that may be committed to my care for you, be assured shall be promptly[1] attended to.

If, Sir, I can serve you in the line of my business, be pleased to command me.

Yours &c   W^M F. GRAY

RC (DLC); endorsed by TJ as received 19 Oct. 1814 and so recorded in SJL.

[1] Manuscript: "promply."

From Samuel H. Smith

DEAR SIR   Washington Oct. 14. 1814

I had this day the pleasure of receiving[1] Your favor of the 11ᵗʰ Inst. with the Alphabetical Index of Authors Names &c.

As You will have seen by the Newspapers the Library Comᵉ of the Senate reported with great promptness a resolution to authorise them to contract for the library, and in terms worthy of the object, wᶜʰ the Senate as promptly adopted.

A similar recommendation having subsequently gone to the House from their committee was discussed on Tuesday. I understand, from the indication of sentiment, furnished by this discission,[2] as well as from conversation with a number of members, that a decided majority are in favor of the offer; the opposition made was from the federal side of the House, and was rather incidental than direct. I entertain scarcely a doubt of the eventual adoption of the resolution, and that, probably, within a few days. You are, however perfectly acquainted with the mode of transacting business in a large deliberate-body, and know how difficult it is to make any accurate calculation of the period within wᶜʰ any pending measure will be drawn to a close. Should a determination take place I will not fail to advise You of it without delay, directing[3] to Monticello, until otherwise desired.

Be pleased to give our best remembrances to Mʳ & Mʳˢ Randolph with the other members of Your family, and [ac]cept my assurances of high and unequivocal respect & regard.   SA H SMITH

RC (DLC); torn at seal; addressed: "Thomas Jefferson Esquire Monticello Virgᵃ"; franked; postmarked Washington, 15 Oct.; endorsed by TJ as received 19 Oct. 1814 and so recorded in SJL.

On Tuesday, 11 Oct. 1814, Jotham Post of the FEDERAL SIDE of the United States House of Representatives unsuccessfully proposed that it "re-consider the vote giving leave to the committeee of the Whole House to sit again on the resolution aforesaid" (*JHR*, 9:472).

[1] Manuscript: "receivig."
[2] Thus in manuscript, intending either "decision" or "discussion."
[3] Manuscript: "directig."

To James Madison

DEAR SIR   Monticello Oct. 15. 14.

I thank you for the information of your letter of the 10ᵗʰ. it gives at length a fixed character to our prospects. the war undertaken, on both sides, to settle the questions of impressment & the Orders of

Council, now that these are done away by events, is declared by Great Britain to have changed it's object, and to have become a war of Conquest, to be waged until she conquers from us our fisheries, the province of Maine, the lakes, states & territories North of the Ohio, and the Navigation of the Missisipi; in other words, till she reduces us to unconditional submission. on our part then we ought to propose, as a counterchange of object, the establishment of the meridian of the mouth of Sorel Northwardly[1] as the Western boundary of all her possessions. two measures will enable us to effect it; and, without these, we cannot even defend ourselves. 1. to organize the militia into classes, as you have recommended in your message;[2] abolishing by a Declaratory law the doubts which abstract scruples in some, and cowardice & treachery in others[3] have conjured up about passing imaginary lines, & limiting, at the same time, their services to the contiguous provinces of the enemy. the 2^d is the Ways and Means. you have seen my ideas on this subject; and I shall add nothing but a rectification of what either I have ill expressed, or you have misapprehended. if I have used any expression restraining the emissions of Treasury notes to a sufficient medium, as your letter seems to imply, I have done it inadvertently, and under the impression then possessing me, that the war would be very short. a sufficient medium would not, on the principles of any writer, exceed 30. Millions of Dollars, & on those of some not 10. millions. our experience has proved it may be run up to 2. or 300.M. without more than doubling what would be the prices of things under a sufficient medium, or say a Metallic one, which would always keep itself at the sufficient point: and if the rise to this term, and descent from it, be gradual, it would not produce sensible revolutions in private fortunes. I shall be able to[4] explain my views more definitely by the use of numbers. suppose we require, to carry on the war, an annual loan of 20.M. then I propose that in the 1st year you shall lay a tax of 2. Millions, and emit 20.M. of Treasury notes, of a size proper for circulation, & bearing no interest, to the redemption of which the proceeds of that tax shall be inviolably pledged & applied by recalling annually their amount of the identical bills funded on them. the 2^d year lay another tax of 2.M. and emit 20.M. more. the 3^d year the same, and so on, until you reach the Maximum of taxes which ought to be imposed. let me suppose this Maximum to be 1.D. a head, or 10.M. of Dollars; merely as an exemplification more familiar than would be the Algebraical symbols x. or y. you would reach this in 5. years. the 6th year then, still emit 20.M. of treasury notes, and continue all the taxes 2. years longer. the 7th

year 20.M. more & continue the whole taxes another two years; and so on.   Observe that altho' you emit 20.M. a year, you call in 10.M. and consequently add but 10.M. annually to the circulation. it would be in 30. years then, primâ facie, that you would reach the present circulation of 300.M. or the ultimate term to which we might adventure. but observe also that in that time we shall have become 30.M. of people, to whom 300.M. of D.[5] would be no more than 100.M. to us now, which sum would probably not have raised prices more than 50. p.c. [on][6] what may be deemed the standard or Metallic[7] prices. this increased population and consumption, while it would be increasing the proceeds of the redemption-tax, and lessening the balance annually thrown into circulation, would also absorb, without saturation, more of the surplus medium, and enable us to push the same process to a much higher term, to one which we might safely call indefinite, because extending so far beyond the limits, either in time or expence, of any supposable war. all we should have to do would be, when the war should be ended, to leave the gradual extinction of these notes to the operation of the taxes pledged for their redemption, not to suffer a dollar of paper to be emitted either by public or private authority, but let the metallic medium flow back into the channels of circulation, and occupy them until another war should oblige us to recur for it's support, to the same resource, & the same process on the circulating medium.

The citizens of a country like ours, will never have unemployed capital. too many enterprises are open, offering high profits, to permit them to lend their capitals on a regular and moderate interest. they are too enterprising and sanguine themselves not to believe they can do better with it. I never did believe you could have gone beyond a 1st or at most a 2d loan: not from a want of confidence[8] in the public faith, which is perfectly sound, but from a want of disposable funds in individuals. the circulating fund is the only one we can ever command with certainty. it is sufficient for all our wants; and the impossibility of even defending the country without it's aid as a borrowing fund, renders indispensable that the nation should take and keep it in their own hands, as their exclusive resource.

I have trespassed on your time so far for explanation only: I will do it no further than by adding the assurances of my affectionate & respectful attachment.   TH: JEFFERSON

A tabular statement of the amount of emissions taxes, redemptions, and balances left in circulation, every year, on the plan above sketched.

years	emissions	taxes and redemptions	balances in circuln at end of year	years	taxes and redemptions	balancs in circuln at end of year.
1815	20. Millions	2. Millions	18. Millions	1822.	10. Millions	80. Millions
1816	20.	4.	34	1823	10.	70
1817	20.	6.	48	1824.	10.	60.
1818	20.	8.	60	1825	10.	50.
1819.	20.	10.	70.	1826	10.	40.
1820	20.	10.	80	1827.	10.	30.
1821	20. 140.	10.[9]	90.[10]	1828.	10.	20.
				1829	10.	10.
				1830.	10.	0.
					140.	

Suppose the war to terminate here, to wit, at the end of 7. years. then the reductions will proceed as follows.

RC (DLC: Madison Papers); signature and paragraph preceding it, clipped, supplied from PoC. PoC (NN: James Monroe Papers); mistakenly endorsed by Monroe as a letter of 1816. FC (DLC); entirely in TJ's hand. Tr (ViU: TJP); in Joseph C. Cabell's hand; endorsed by Cabell: "Copy of a Letter from Mr Jefferson to a friend, 15. Oct: 1814. enclosed in Mr J's letter to Jos: C: Cabell of 16 Oct: 1814." Enclosed in TJ to Monroe, 16 Oct. 1814, TJ to Cabell, 16 Oct. 1814, and Cabell to TJ, 27 Dec. 1814.

The SOREL is an obsolete name for the Richelieu River in Quebec, Canada (*A Gazetteer of the World, or Dictionary of Geographical Knowledge* [1850–56], 6:671). For President Madison's 20 Sept.

1814 MESSAGE to Congress, see *JHR*, 9:449–52, esp. 451.

[1] Word interlined.
[2] TJ here canceled "2." Preceding seven words replaced in FC and Tr by "assigning to each class the duties for which it is fitted (which, had it been done when proposed years ago, would have prevented all our misfortunes)."
[3] Reworked from "which cowardice & treachery."
[4] Preceding three words interlined.
[5] Preceding two words interlined.
[6] TJ here canceled "<of> upon." Omitted word supplied from FC and Tr.
[7] Preceding two words interlined.
[8] Word interlined in place of "credit."
[9] Number not in Tr.
[10] Number not in Tr.

To Joseph C. Cabell

DEAR SIR   Monticello Oct. 16. 14.

Either inaccurate expression in myself, or the misapprehension[1] of a friend to whom I had communicated my former letters on our finances, having obliged me to write another in explanation, I inclose you a copy of it because you had taken the trouble to read the others. I should wish this to be seen by those to whom you had communicated the former, lest they also should have misapprehended me, taking care only to keep it out of the public papers and to return it when done with.[2] I am aware of the nest of hornets it would raise upon me and am too old to court controversy. 40. years ago I might have indulged the spirit of proselytism; but at present I seek not to disturb the opinions of others. Accept the assurance of my friendly & respectful attachment   TH: JEFFERSON

RC (ViU: TJP); addressed: "Joseph C. Cabell of the Senate of Virginia now at Richmond"; franked; postmarked Milton, 19 Oct.; endorsed by Cabell as answered 27 Dec. 1814. PoC (DLC); endorsed by TJ. Enclosure: TJ to James Madison, 15 Oct. 1814.

The FORMER LETTERS ON OUR FINANCES included TJ to John Wayles Eppes, 24 June, 11 Sept., and 6 Nov. 1813, and TJ to Cabell, 23 Sept. 1814.

[1] Manuscript: "misappehension."
[2] Preceding seven words interlined.

Notes on Household Consumption

[ca. 16 Oct. 1814]

estimate

1. ℔. coffee ⎫
1. ℔ wh. sugar ⎬ daily.   1. ℔ tea in 3. weeks.
2. ℔ brown d° ⎭

	coffee	wh. sug.	brown d°	tea	brandy	whiskey	Cotton
1813. Jan. 29.	10.		20				
Feb. 3		30 ℔		2 lb.			
18	25	15¼	26	2			
Apr. 3.	15	20.	30	2			
19				2			
20	15	20	30				
June 14		25	50	2			
July 1.		25	50	2			
21		25	50	2			
26			25				
31			25				
Aug. 3		12[1]					
4		24					
17	4½		280				
18	25.						
Sep. 15				2			
Oct 1				2			
16					1. canteen		
Dec. 18	25	2 loaves		2			
1814. Jan. 3		2 loaves		2			
6					1 canteen		
18		2 loaves					

Feb. 18		2 loave		2		
28	20.					1. cant.[2]
Mar. 9					2 canteens	
10		2.		2		
19			15.[3]			
Apr. 1		2	50			
May 6.			20	2		
9.	30	4.				
July		2. loaves		2		
Aug.		2. loaves[4]	50.			50.℔
Oct. 5.			15[5]			
16	25	4[6] loaves		2[7]		

MS (MHi); written entirely in TJ's hand on one side of a single sheet; undated. An image of this manuscript is reproduced elsewhere in this volume.

[1] Reworked from "24."
[2] Preceding two words repeated but canceled in preceding column.
[3] Reworked from "30."
[4] Preceding two words written over "50 lb," erased.
[5] Reworked from "150."
[6] Reworked from "2."
[7] TJ deleted "50" from the preceding column.

To James Monroe

DEAR SIR   Monticello Oct. 16. 14.

Your letter of the 10th has been duly recieved. the objects of our contest being thus entirely changed by England, we must prepare for interminable war. to this end we should put our house in order, by providing men and money to indefinite extent. the former may be done by classing our militia, and assigning each class to the description of duties for which it is fit. it is nonsense to talk of regulars. they are not to be had among a people so easy and happy at home as ours. we might as well rely on calling down an army of angels from heaven. I trust it is now seen that the refusal to class the militia, when proposed years ago, is the real source of all our misfortunes in this war.   the other great and indispensable object is to enter on such a system of finance, as can be permanently pursued to any length of time whatever. let us be allured by no projects of banks, public or private, or ephemeral expedients, which enabling us to gasp and flounder a little longer, only increase, by protracting, the agonies of death.

Percieving, in a letter from the President, that either I had ill expressed my ideas on a particular part of this subject, in the letters I sent you, or that he had misapprehended them, I wrote him yesterday an explanation; and as you have thought the other letters worth a perusal, and a communication to the Secretary of the treasury, I inclose you a copy of this, lest I should be misunderstood by others also. only be so good as to return me the whole, when done with, as I have no other copies.   Since writing the letter now inclosed, I have seen the Report of the Committee of finance, proposing taxes to the amount of 20. Millions. this is a dashing proposition. but if Congress pass it, I shall consider it sufficient evidence that their constituents generally can pay the tax. no man has greater confidence, than I have, in the spirit of our people, to a rational extent. whatever they can, they will. but without either market or medium, I know not how it is to be done. all markets abroad, and all at home, are shut to us; so that we have been feeding our horses on wheat. before the day of collection bank notes will be but as oak leaves: and of specie there is not within all the US. one half of the proposed amount of the taxes. I had thought myself as bold as was safe in contemplating as possible an annual taxation of ten millions as a fund for emissions of treasury notes, and when further emissions should be necessary, that it would be better to enlarge the time, than the tax for redemption. our position with respect to our enemy, & our markets distinguishes us from all other nations; inasmuch as a state of war, with us, annihilates in an instant all our surplus produce; that on which we depended for many comforts of life. this renders peculiarly expedient the throwing a part of the burthens of war on times of peace & commerce. still however my hope is that others see resources, which in my abstraction from the world, are unseen by me; that there will be both market and medium to meet these taxes, and that there are circumstances which render it wiser to levy 20. Millions at once on the people, than to obtain the same sum on a tenth of the tax.

I inclose you a letter from Col° James Lewis, now of Tennissee, who wishes to be appointed Indian agent; and I do it lest he should have relied solely on this channel of communication. you know him better than I do, as he was long your agent. I have always believed him an honest man, and very good-humored and accomodating. of his other qualifications for the office you are the best judge.—Believe me to be ever affectionately yours.   Th: Jefferson

RC (DLC: Monroe Papers); endorsed by Monroe. PoC (DLC); at foot of first page: "James Monroe." Enclosures: (1) TJ to James Madison, 15 Oct. 1814. (2) James Lewis to TJ, 17 Sept. 1814, not found, but recorded in SJL as received 5

Oct. 1814 from "near Winchester" in Franklin County, Tennessee.

For the letters on finance that Monroe thought worthy of A PERUSAL, AND A COMMUNICATION TO THE SECRETARY OF THE TREASURY, see note to Monroe to TJ, 10 Oct. 1814. The REPORT of the Ways and Means Committee of the United States House of Representatives of 10 Oct. 1814 proposed that taxes be more than doubled, from $10.8 to $22.4 million (*ASP, Finance*, 2:854–5).

To Joseph Milligan

DEAR SIR   Monticello Oct. 17. 14.

Your two letters of Sep. 24. & Oct. 12. have been duly recieved. the packet of books will probably come on by the next stage. by the present one I send to the care of mr Gray of Fredericksbg a packet of 6. vols, which though made up of 4. different works, I wish to have bound as one work in 6. vols, to be labelled on the back 'the Book of Kings.' the 1ˢᵗ & 2ᵈ vols will be composed of the Memoirs of Bareuth, the binding to remain as it is, only changing the label. the Memoirs of Madᵉ La Motte will make the 3ᵈ & 4.ᵗʰ vols, pared down to the size of the first & bound uniform with them. Mʳˢ Clarke's will be the 5ᵗʰ vol. pared & bound as before, and 'the Book' will make the 6ᵗʰ which to be uniform in size with the rest must perhaps be left with it's present rough edges. pray do it immediately and return it by the stage that they may be replaced on their shelves should Congress take my library, the proposition for which is before them. I mentioned to you the work on political economy by Tracy which had been translated by Genˡ Duane, but could not be printed by him. I then wrote & offered it to mr Ritchie, from whom I had not recieved an answer when you were here, and I consulted you as to the allowance which ought to be made by Ritchie to Duane. Ritchie declines printing it, and I now inclose you a copy of my letter to him, which I will pray you to consider as now addressed to yourself, but to be returned to me, as I have no other copy. I shall be very glad if you will undertake the printing it, and I think it the best work ever written on the subject, and that you might count on a great sale of it to the members of Congress. answer me as soon as you can if you please, because I have not yet answered Duane's letter. the moment you say you will undertake it & specify the allowance for translating, I will have the MSS. brought on, I will correct the translation here and forward it to you sheet by sheet. when Congress return my Catalogue I will send that also to you to be printed. Accept assurances of my esteem & respect.

                                                    TH: JEFFERSON

PoC (DLC); at foot of text: "Mr Joseph Milligan"; endorsed by TJ. Enclosure: TJ to Thomas Ritchie, 19 Aug. 1814 (see TJ to Ritchie, 27 Sept. 1814, and note).

MEMOIRS OF MAD^E LA MOTTE: the autobiographical *Vie de Jeanne de St. Remy de Valois, ci-devant Comtesse de La Motte* (Paris, 1792; Sowerby, nos. 227, 411).

To Joseph Delaplaine

SIR   Monticello Oct. 18. 14.

Your letter of the 3^d is at hand. I have little doubt that I shall recieve an answer from mr Stewart, either yielding to my request, or stating the reasons why he may wish to retain the portrait longer in his possession. whatever these may be, I should not refuse him, nor indeed in any case press a compliance beyond the request I have made. I will inform you of his answer whenever it shall be recieved. in the mean time accept my thanks for the print of the President which you have been so kind as to send me, and the assurances of my esteem & respect.   TH: JEFFERSON

RC (LNT: George H. and Katherine M. Davis Collection); addressed: "Mr Joseph Delaplaine Philadelphia"; franked; postmarked Milton, 19 Oct.; endorsed by Delaplaine. PoC (DLC); endorsed by TJ.

To Andrew Moore

DEAR SIR   Monticello Oct. 18. 14.

Capt Miller's longer stay in Norfolk than he had proposed when he left this neighborhood in the spring, and the daily expectation of a hostile army in that quarter made it a duty in me to place his case under your attention in my letter of July 21. and the rather as I had sollicited the indulgence of that visit. about the same time, the same considerations occurred to himself, and to prevent all suspicion he returned of himself to his station at Charlottesville. his conduct here ever since, his candor, and unquestionably friendly dispositions, have removed from every mind the doubts which nothing but his protracted stay below had excited with some of our neighbors. his property all remaining in this state, his purpose of remaining in it permanently himself, and the lucrative business of brewing in which he is so succesfully engaged, are all pledges of his fidelity; and I am so satisfied of the integrity of his character and that his free residence in Norfolk, with his property and business, may be safely permitted, that I should have no hesitation in being held personally responsible for him. the enemy being no longer in force in our waters, & the season for brewing being now arrived, he is about setting out for Norfolk under the protection of your former license, and of the passport from the deputy marshal permitting his late tour to this neighborhood & back again. his partner, I understand, has laid in from 5. to 10,000. bushels of grain for malting, and depends on his skill solely for the operations, he being I believe the best brewer we have ever had in this country. the fear that an abridgment of his permission to remain there, might break up his business, and with the loss of their stock of materials, produce their ruin, has given him some anxiety. I have taken the liberty therefore of troubling you once more on his account, & of solliciting the continuance of his permission to remain there, confident as I am that the fidelity of[1] his demeanor will ever meet your approbation. in the mean time he has been taking measures for establishing his rights as a native. Accept the assurance of my constant esteem and respect.   TH: JEFFERSON

PoC (DLC); at foot of text: "General Moore"; endorsed by TJ.

The DEPUTY MARSHAL for the Virginia District was William Mann. Joseph Miller's PARTNER was Joseph Hayes.

[1] Preceding three words interlined.

From Joseph C. Cabell

DEAR SIR,   Richmond. 19 Octr 1814.

Your favor of 23^d Sepr reached me before I left home: that of 30th since I came to this place. I have already given & shall continue to give to those letters the fullest consideration in my power. We have as yet settled upon no plan of finance or defence: & are waiting to hear the plans of congress. Our difficulties are great & encreasing. Your idea of issuing state certificates ought, & I trust, will be adopted, at least so far as to support the public credit of the state, when the Treasury may happen to be empty. I was the only person in the Senate who voted ag^t the Bill which has this day passed authorizing the two Banks in this city to issue notes under five dollars. I should be extremely thankful for any further communications you may at any time be pleased to make me: feeling myself always highly gratified & instructed by any views which you take of any subject.   I am dear Sir, most respectfully & sincerely yours

JOS: C: CABELL

RC (ViU: TJP-PC); endorsed by TJ as received 21 Oct. 1814 and so recorded in SJL.

On this day the Virginia General Assembly passed "An Act concerning the Bank of Virginia and Farmers' Bank of Virginia," which allowed those institutions to issue $1, $2, and $3 NOTES until six months following the termination of the current war with Great Britain (*Acts of Assembly* [1814–15 sess.], 65–6).

From Samuel H. Smith

DEAR SIR   Washington[1] Oct. 19. 1814

I have the pleasure to inform You that the H. of R. this day concurred by a great majority in the resolution of the Senate authorising the Library Com^e to contract for the purchase of Your Library, after so amending it as to reserve to Congress the definitive ratification of the contract. That they will[2] ratify the agreement that shall be made by the Com^e there can be no doubt. As I calculate upon the prompt attention of the Com^e to the conclusion of the business, I submit to you the propriety of communicating without delay any further suggestions wch You may wish to make as to the terms and mode of disposition.

With a tender of my invariable[3] wishes for your happiness, I am with great respect   SA H SMITH

RC (DLC); endorsed by TJ as received 26 Oct. 1814 and so recorded in SJL.

[1] Manuscript: "Washigton."
[2] Word interlined.
[3] Manuscript: "invariabl."

From David Bailie Warden

DEAR SIR,   Paris, 20 october, 1814.

mr. mazzei has sent me the inclosed letter, with a request to forward it to you by a safe channel of conveyance, which I now find by a french[1] flag-vessel bound to new york.

I had the honor of writing to you in may last, and of sending, for your acceptance, a copy of my "Essay on Consular Establishments" and brochures by mr. Corran—In June last, I sent to the care of mr. Shaler, at Ghent, a trunk containing several volumes and brochures to your address, which he promised to forward by the <u>John Adams</u>, and to have it delivered to mr. Short, to whom mr. Rochon has written on this subject.

In my letter, of the 5th of may last, forwarded by mr. Corran, I informed you of the delivery of the letters, which you were pleased to

Send to my care. I lately wrote to you by mr. Todd, son of mrs. madison, and took the liberty of informing you of the suspension of my Consular powers, inclosing at the same time, a copy of my justification on the two points of accusation which mr. Crawford states as the ground of this suspension. With regard to the first—my conduct in relation to the prizes of Commodore Rodgers—I have proven by strong testimony that my opinion was correct; namely, that the Commodore had a right to the consignment of his prize; and, that I, as his legal consignee, was authorised to direct, and manage the sale and proceeds. mr. Crawford, on his arrival in France, gave a different opinion, and in favor of mr. Lees' pretentions, to which I immediately submitted, as the ministers' interference freed me from that responsability to which I was liable in virtue of the Commodore's powers. In this affair, as in all others relating to my office, I had no personal interest:[2] I acted from motives of duty having solely at heart the interests of my Government, and those of Commodore Rodgers.—I beg leave to inclose a copy of a letter from the Prince of Benevent, minister of foreign affairs, which justifies my conduct concerning the correspondence with the french Government after mr. Barlows' death, and untill the time when mr. Crawford delivered his letters of credence.—I have been informed, that this correspondence was the only cause of the Presidents' displeasure,[3] and the reason for granting to mr. Crawford large discretionary powers.—The intended appointment of the nephew of mr. Barlow as Secretary of Legation was entirely unknown to me. my Correspondence with mr. Crawford shews, that I submitted every[4] affair to his direction, or decision, except the Legalisation of documents[5]—I never gave him cause of displeasure— It is my wish to be employed by the Government, and if the President would reinstate me, or give me some appointment as <u>chargé d'affaire</u>, he will find me faithful, and active in the discharge of my duties—I wait here his further orders.—

The depredations of the English[6] have excited a general indignation throughout france, which is strengthened by a knowledge of the commercial projects of England in relation to this Country. The productions of the islands ceded to France have been purchased in advance for the two ensuing years by British agents, who have also bought up the raw materials for manufactures in France, which they have actually transported to England, for the purpose of sending them back to the former Country in a manufactured state.[7] But all this will be of little[8] avail[9]—The manufactures of france, for general consumption, have been carried to a high degree of improvement during the last fifteen years, and cannot be destroyed except by very impolitic measures of this Government, which, I do not think can be adopted, for reasons well known to all.

Professor Leslie of Edinborough, who lately visited Paris, made much enquiry concerning mr Randolph and family, and expressed a great desire to hear from him.

mr. De Tracy is anxious to know whether the translation of a certain work has yet appeared.

I have some pamphlets for you which I shall forward by the first opportunity. I am, dear Sir, with great respect, your very obliged Servant.   DAVID BAILIE WARDEN

RC (DLC); at foot of text: "Thomas Jefferson Esquire, monticello"; endorsed by TJ as received 15 July 1815 and so recorded in SJL. Dft (MdHi: Warden Papers); incomplete. Enclosures: (1) Philip Mazzei to TJ, 24 Sept. 1814. (2) Talleyrand to Warden, Paris, 29 Aug. 1814, indicating as requested by Warden that after William H. Crawford presented his letters of credence, the French foreign ministry discontinued the correspondence it had kept up with Warden following the death in 1812 of Joel Barlow, but that this change came as a matter of course, in order to streamline the conduct of its affairs, and not because of any actions taken by Warden (Tr in DLC: TJ Papers, 202:35939, entirely in Warden's hand and attested by him: "the above is a true copy of the original," above attestation: "mr. Warden, Rue St Dominique D'Enfer, no. 18"; Tr in DLC: TJ Papers, 202:35934, attested "a true copy of the original" by Warden; Tr in DLC: TJ Papers, 202:35938, attested "a true copy" by Warden; Tr in DLC: TJ Papers, 202:35935; all Trs are in French).

Warden's letter to TJ was dated 6 May 1814, not THE 5TH OF MAY. The letter he sent to TJ through John Payne TODD was dated 18 June 1814. Under the Treaty of Paris of 30 May 1814, Great Britain agreed to return to France most of the colonies it had captured during the conflict, including THE ISLANDS of Guadeloupe, Martinique, and Réunion (Lawrence James, *The Rise and Fall of the British Empire* [1994], 154, 165; Connelly, *Napoleonic France*, 382).

[1] Word interlined in Dft.
[2] Preceding nine words interlined in Dft.
[3] Remainder of sentence not in Dft.
[4] Dft here adds "important."
[5] Preceding five words not in Dft.
[6] Dft here adds "in the U.S."
[7] In Dft, sentence reads "The agents of the former have purchased for the three ensuing years, the productions of the Islands lately ceded to England: they have also bought the raw materials for french manufactures."
[8] RC: "litle." Dft: "no."
[9] Dft ends here with "Yours &c."

From William C. C. Claiborne

DEAR SIR,   New-Orleans October 21st 1814

Mr Dorsey a worthy Citizen, and a very respectable Merchant of New-Orleans, designing on his way to Baltimore, to pass by the way of Charlottsville, I have taken the liberty to introduce him to the honor of your Acquaintance.—Mr Dorsey can satisfy all your Enquiries as to the State of things in this Section of the Union;—he will inform you of the exertions we are making to give the Enemy a warm reception, should he hazard an attack on this Capital, and how much our Strength has been encreased by the union and the zeal which at the present moment, pervade the State.

I have the honor to be with the greatest Respect Your faithful friend   WILLIAM C. C. CLAIBORNE

RC (DLC); at foot of text: "Mr Thomas Jefferson Monticello Virginia"; endorsed by TJ as received 20 Dec. 1814 and so recorded in SJL. Enclosed in Greenberry Dorsey to TJ, 13 Dec. 1814.

From Samuel H. Smith

DEAR SIR   Wash Oct. 21. 1814

I was this day invited by the Library Com to a conference with them.

They represented that in consequence of the amendment to their report, it became necessary to ascertain the value of the library & to obtain an authority from the two Houses to pay it, to enable them to do wch they enquired of me whether I could specify the sum that would be received for it. I replied that I was unable to state its value, and that I was certain that it would be much more agreeable to You that this should be done either by the come themselves or by disinterested persons; that I was persuaded that you would feel some delicacy, if not repugnance, to setting a value on Your own property, & that You might in forming the estimate from obvious motives[1] be driven to the alternative of either depreciating its value, or of laying yourself open to the imputation of extravagance. I therefore proposed another course. That the Library should be estimated by some one sent for that purpose, or, wch I considered most advisable, that it should be brought to this place without delay, valued by the Committee, or by persons named by the Come, or by the Come & myself, that this valuation should be submitted to the Come, and if agreed to by them that[2] a correspondent report & contract should be made to Congress, of whose approbation I did not entertain a doubt; that should, however, a different result ensue I would take the responsibility on myself.

To this the Come answered that they did not consider themselves authorised to take the proposed steps, & that having agreed to receive the library, even provisionally, Congress might be considered as committed in regard to a definitive agreement. They added that in ascertaining[3] its value they did not wish any estimate, as made by you, to be submitted to them; that the information I might obtain would be entirely private & confidential; and that <u>my proposition</u>, that a certain sum would be received for it, wch sum they did not mean should be computed with close precision, would be accepted as the basis of a contract.

Our conversation conclusively exhibited their purpose not to proceed without a proposition analogous to that desired.

Upon the whole, although not insensible to the delicacy of the step, I would recommend that you authorise me to state that a sum not exceeding a specified amount will be received, & that to guard against any unjust imputation such sum within that amount will be taken as shall be the result of a valuation to be made after the library is on the spot.

Our political movements here, although as usual tardy, presage uncommon harmony.

I am, with great & sincere respect & esteem.   SA H SMITH

RC (DLC); at foot of text: "Thomas Jefferson Esq."; endorsed by TJ as received 26 Oct. 1814 and so recorded in SJL. FC (DLC: J. Henley Smith Papers); internally addressed, initialed, and described as a "Copy" by Smith.

The AMENDMENT to the draft resolution proposed by the congressional Joint Library Committee required final approval by the TWO HOUSES of Congress of the contract for the purchase of TJ's library (editorial headnote on The Sale of Thomas Jefferson's Library to Congress, printed above at 21 Sept. 1814).

[1] Preceding three words interlined.
[2] Preceding six words interlined.
[3] RC: "ascertainig." FC: "ascertaining."

From Jonathan Williams

DEAR SIR   Philosophical Hall. Friday Even^g Octo^r 21. 1814.

After the Society was adjourned a number of members (all your particular Friends) were conversing on various subjects when the proposed sale of your Library to Congress was mentioned.

It can hardly be supposed, that in this Room surrounded by a Library consisting almost wholly[1] of donations, with your almost animated Bust[2] looking full in our faces, we could avoid expressing our regret that the rich collection of so many years of scientific research should be devoted to a political Body, where it cannot produce any benefit to them or to the World.—Works of History, Law, Government Finance, political Œconomy, and general Information,[3] may with propriety be so deposited; but such Books as would adorn our Library[4] and aid this Society in "the promotion of useful knowledge" must there become motheaten upon the Shelves.

I cannot resist an impulse which induces me to communicate this sentiment of regret to you, especially as your own reccollection will assist me in the beleif, that when you were a resident among us, you encouraged the expectation that your last Will would contain a handsome[5] increase of our Stock of Science.

If this Letter should offend you I shall be sorry, but I shall console myself in the reflection that it is the effect of an honest zeal, which under opposite circumstances would not offend me.

I am with great respect[6] Dear Sir Your obedient Servant

JON WILLIAMS

RC (MHi); at foot of text: "Thomas Jefferson Esq[r] President of the American Philosophical Society"; endorsed by TJ as received 15 Nov. 1814 and so recorded in SJL, which mistakenly dates it 28 Oct. 1814. Dft (InU: Williams Papers); endorsed by Williams, in part: "Copy to M[r] Jefferson about the sale of his Library to Congress."

The American Philosophical Society had ADJOURNED a meeting on this day (APS, Minutes [MS at PPAmP]). It acquired a copy of Jean Antoine Houdon's ALMOST ANIMATED BUST of TJ in 1811 (APS, Minutes, 5 Apr., 20 Sept. 1811; *PTJ*, 25:31n; Bush, *Life Portraits*, 11, 13). The society's full name was the American Philosophical Society held at Philadelphia for promoting USEFUL KNOWLEGE.

THIS LETTER may have inspired a critique published the following year: "Mr. Jefferson, of whose hypocrisy science itself has been the dupe, having declared his intention to bestow a portion, at least, of his books on the American Philosophical Society, of which he was President; — when the proposal to sell his Library to Congress was made public, a letter was addressed to Mr. Jefferson, reminding him of his promise in behalf of the Society, and his Philosophical Highness, with a generosity worthy of himself, sent the Society—*his resignation!*" (*Salem* [Mass.] *Gazette*, 9 June 1815).

[1] Preceding two words canceled in Dft.
[2] Reworked in Dft from "Donations, and observed by your <*Bust*> almost animated resemblance."
[3] Word inserted in place of "Knowledge," erased, and added in margin of Dft in place of "<*Science*> Knowledge."
[4] Preceding two words interlined in Dft.
[5] RC: "a handsome a handsome." In Dft Williams here canceled "Legacy to."
[6] Dft here adds "& Esteem."

To John H. Cocke

DEAR SIR   Monticello Oct. 23. 14.

I am thankful for the indulgence of your kind letter of Aug. 27. and happy in being now able to forward you an order on my correspondents in Richmond for the price of the horse you were so good as to let me have. I find him really valuable, and in the carriage particularly excellent, so as to be entirely contented with him.

Our intelligence from abroad gives us reason to expect a long state of warfare. regular forces being unobtainable in a country whose inhabitants are so happily situated as ours are at home our reliance must be on Militia: and if these be put into the effective form which has been so often pressed on Congress, we have nothing to fear but the creation of debt. this I hope, with economy, and a good system of finance, may be kept within moderate and safe bounds. when the issue of the present campaign shall be known in England, if ever it shall be truly known there, I think they will regret the exorbitance of pretensions to which their inflated arrogance has led them. it falls to our lot to convince them that there are limits to their power & successes, and I have no fear but that we shall do it.   I am in hopes the active part you are taking in this great concern has been favorable to your health, and that the usual influence of the autumnal season in the country where you are has not reached yourself. Accept the assurance of my great esteem and respect.   TH: JEFFERSON

RC (ViU: TJP); addressed: "Gen¹ John Hartwell Cocke"; franked; postmarked Milton, 26 Oct.; endorsed by Cocke. PoC (DLC); on verso of reused address cover of Patrick Gibson to TJ, 30 Sept. 1814; mutilated at seal, with lost text interlined by TJ; endorsed by TJ.

The enclosed ORDER on Gibson & Jefferson, TJ's CORRESPONDENTS IN RICHMOND, not found, was "for 167.D. in favr. John H. Cocke in payment for a horse" named Bremo (*MB*, 2:1299, 1304; see also TJ to Cocke, 19 Apr. 1814, and note). At this time Cocke and the Virginia militia units under his command were encamped at Camp Carter in THE COUNTRY a dozen miles below Richmond (Stuart L. Butler, "Gen. John Hartwell Cocke in the War of 1812," *MACH* 65 [2007]: 29, 32).

From James Cutbush

SIR   Norfolk Oct* 23ᵈ 1814

There is an improvement in agriculture, in the planting of corn, which a gentleman, who has been here, has introduced; but with what effect I know not. As he has obtained, among many other respectable certificates,[1] one from you, as to his character &c. I am anxious to know whether you have made the experiment, and found it to answer. The reason I make the enquiry is, that I gave him letters to several gentlemen in Philadᵃ (as I am lately from that city) among whom to judge Peters and Mʳ Vaughan, in order that they might have his "<u>apparatus</u>" tried in that state. As a member of the American Philosophical and Agricultural Societies, I was anxious that, if it should be an improvement, its introduction into general use might be facilitated through the medium of these respectable bodies.

In consequence of these certificates,[2] principally, he has made already a considerable[3] sum; his price being $10, down, and $20 if they <u>succeeded</u>. Mʳ Tazewell of this place granted him a certificate, and bought a right, altogether upon the respectable authority of its recommenders: Mr T. I know has not tried the experiment, and therefore is unable to say from experience, any thing of its merits.

Mr James Hall is the person to whom I allude, and with whom I became acquainted very accidentally. His character, from some of his certificates stands fair: but it is surprising, that without performing[4] his <u>process</u>, shewing his <u>apparatus</u>, or any thing of this kind, he has been able to make some days $120 on the terms before mentioned.—

If You are acquainted with any of his improvements in agriculture, and especially his plan of planting corn, by which from "2 to 10 negroes can do the work of 100," or that of "sowing an acre sooner than a man could walk over it," according to his expression; you would confer a particular favour on a member of Your society by communicating it to him.

I hope you have, ere this, received Your copy of the Artists manual, from Philad^a

I have just heard from our friend <u>James Sloan</u> of New Jersey: I am informed, that in consequence of his late establishment at his mineral Spring (which I examined for him some time since) producing Considerable embarassments, without Conducting the establishment to meet the views of <u>gentlemen epicures</u> &[c] (for Mr S. would <u>make</u> them conform to <u>his</u> habits) he has failed, and lost every thing. The case is indeed hard, for a gentleman of his years. In every company he was affable and free, and whenever politics came up, he invariably quoted You as an example of political science and of virtue.

I am, Sir, Very respectfully, Your friend & humble Servt

JA^s CUTBUSH

U.S. Ass: Apothecary General 5th Mil. D^t—

RC (DLC); torn at seal; addressed to "Thomas Jefferson Esquire Monticello. Virginia" from the "Ass: Apothecary Gen^{ls} office 5th Mil. D^t"; franked; postmarked; endorsed by TJ as received 15 Nov. 1814 and so recorded in SJL.

A copy of James Hall's 19 Nov. 1814 patent and specification for his IMPROVEMENT IN AGRICULTURE, wherein he described simple machinery and techniques that he claimed would yield much more efficient ways to plow, plant, and enrich the earth, later made its way into TJ's papers (printed text in DLC: TJ Papers, 202:36053; endorsed by TJ: "Agriculture. Indian corn Hall's patent method";

List of Patents, 143). The AGRICULTURAL society to which Cutbush belonged was the Philadelphia Society for Promoting Agriculture (Laws of the Philadelphia Society for Promoting Agriculture [Philadelphia, 1812], 5). YOUR SOCIETY: presumably the American Philosophical Society. ARTISTS MANUAL: Cutbush, The American Artist's Manual, 2 vols. (Philadelphia, 1814; Poor, Jefferson's Library, 6 [no. 221]).

[1] Manuscript: "cirtificates."
[2] Manuscript: "cirtificates."
[3] Manuscript: "considerabl."
[4] Manuscript: "performing."

From James Madison

Dear Sir   Washington Oc[r] 23. 1814

I have rec[d] yours of the 15: and attended to your remarks on "ways & means." I find that the variance in our ideas relates 1. to the probable quantity of circulating medium: 2. to the effect of an annual augmentation of it. I cannot persuade myself that in the present[1] stagnation of private dealings, & the proposed limitation of taxes, the two great absorbents of money, the circulating sum would amount even to 20 mill[s]. But be this amount what it may, every emission beyond it, must either enter into circulation and depreciate[2] the whole mass; or it must be locked up. If it bear an interest it may be locked up for the sake of the interest, in which case it is a loan, both in substance & in form, and implies a capacity to lend, in other words a disposable capital, in the Country. If it does not bear an interest, it could not be locked up, but on the supposition that the terms on which it is rec[d] are such as to promise indemnity at least, for the intermediate loss of interest, by its value at a future day: but this both involves the Substance of[3] a loan, to the amount of the value locked up: and implies a depreciation differing only from the career of the old Continental currency, by a gradual return from a certain point of depression, to its original level. If this view of the Subject be in any measure correct, I am aware of the gloomy inferences from it. I trust however that our case is not altogether without remedy. To a certain extent paper in some form or other, will, as a circulating medium, answer the purpose your plan contemplates.[4] The increase of taxes will have the double operation of widening the channel of circulation, and of pumping the medium out of it. And I cannot but think that domestic capital existing under various shapes, and disposeable to the public, may still[5] be obtained on terms tho' hard, not intolerable; and that it will not be very long before the money market abroad, will not be entirely shut ag[st] us: a market, however ineligible in some respects, not to be declined under our circumstances.

We hear nothing from our Envoys since the despatches now in print; nor any thing else of importance from abroad.[6] We continue anxious for the situation of Sackett's Harbour. Izard has joined Brown on the Canada side of the Straight; and offered battle to Drummond, which he does not accept, and which it seems can not be forced on him with[t] risk from re-enforcements now transportable to him. The most that can fairly be hoped for by us now, is that the campaign may end where it is.   Be assured always of my most affec[e] respects   JAMES MADISON

RC (DLC: Madison Papers); at foot of text: "Mr Jefferson"; endorsed by TJ as received 26 Oct. 1814 and so recorded in SJL.

The American generals George Izard and Jacob Brown had recently joined forces on the Niagara River (THE STRAIGHT) near Buffalo, New York. Although they marched into Canada and OFFERED BATTLE, Gordon Drummond, the British general opposing them, successfully avoided a general engagement. An artillery duel on 16 Oct. 1814 and an inconclusive skirmish three days later at Cook's Mills, Upper Canada, ended the CAMPAIGN on the Niagara Peninsula (Malcomson, *Historical Dictionary*, 118–9).

[1] Word interlined.
[2] Manuscript: "depeciate."
[3] Preceding two words interlined in place of "idea of."
[4] Preceding five words interlined in place of "present purposes."
[5] Word interlined.
[6] Manuscript: "abrod."

From James Madison

DEAR SIR   Washington Oc^r 23. 1814.

I have rec^d yours of Oc^r . with that inclosed from Warden. His tale is plausibly told but entitled to little confidence. Be assured he is not the man he passed for with all of us originally. His apparent modesty & suavity cover ambition vanity avidity (from poverty at least) & intrigue. These traits began to betray themselves before he last left the U.S. on his arrival in Paris with his office confirmed by the Senate, they rapidly disclosed themselves. And on the death of Barlow, & the scuffle for the Charge of our affairs, the mask fell off entirely. He behaved badly to Mrs Barlow, and having made himself acceptable to the French Gov^{t1} thro' his intimacy with subalterns, he seized, with its concurrence, the station for which he had as little of qualifications as of pretensions. Crawford carried with him our view of W's character, and his experience in Paris has greatly strengthened it. He states circumstances convicting W. of equal impudence & mendacity. The friends of the latter there consist of the Irish, and persons of rank & Science to whom he has paid his court, and passed himself for the favorite of certain[2] individuals here as well as of the Gov^t. Crawford is a man of strong intellect & sound integrity: but of a temper not perhaps sufficiently pliant, or manners sufficiently polished for diplomatic life. These however will improve, whilst[3] he remains abroad, I cannot believe that his high tone of mind would have permitted him to be jealous of a man whom he must justly regard[4] as so infinitely below him. I return you Wardens letter; & that, if you chuse you may prevent the possibility of future publicity to yours to me, I inclose yours with it, and keep no copy of this.

Affec^{ly} yours   J. M.

RC (DLC: Madison Papers); endorsed by TJ as received 26 Oct. 1814 and so recorded in SJL. Enclosures: (1) David Bailie Warden to TJ, 25 July [1814]. (2) TJ to Madison, 13 Oct. 1814.

Warden LAST LEFT THE U.S. in August 1811 to become America's consul at Paris (*Alexandria Daily Gazette, Commercial & Political*, 7 Aug. 1811; *JEP*, 2:173, 174–5 [1, 3 Mar. 1811]). William H. Crawford,

the United States minister plenipotentiary to France, accused Warden of IMPUDENCE & MENDACITY in his letters to James Monroe of 20, 22 Sept. 1813, and 16 Jan. 1814 (DNA: RG 59, DD, France).

[1] Word interlined.
[2] Word interlined.
[3] Word interlined in place of "and."
[4] Reworked from "he justly regards."

From Charles Yancey

DᴿSIR,   Richmond 23ʳᵈ October 1814

an apology is due to you, as I promised to write you, while in Service; a sick family, caused by an unusual fever, has caused me to lose about $2000 worth of property: on Receiving this information from home, I left camp for 8 days, & went home; this prevented my communication with friends in the manner I wished. I am Now in the legislature, & hope in any situation, I Shall Never forget that attention which is So Justly due to you, On accᵗ of Services already Rendered. we have Several Important Resolutions &ᶜ before us, one of which was to appoint a Joint Committee, to repair to washington, to confer with the General Government, on the best possible means of defending this State during the war with G.B.—to this I gave my decided Negative, as it appeared to assume a Dictatorial tone, & an exclusive previledge, which I thought we were not intitled to, having by Solemn compact, long ago, given to the Federal Government, the Sole power, of defending &ᶜ &ᶜ. this resolution, however, has been So Amended, as to Cause a Communication to be open'd by the Executive of V.A. with the General[1] government, respecting this states Quota of Men &ᶜ, to Carry on the War: we have also a bill before us, to suspend the exⁿ law, deeds of trust &ᶜ which I expect with Some Modification, will pass into a law. a Committee[2] have reported a bill appropriating $200.000 for paying troops &ᶜ. a committee is appointed to Organize the Militia System of this state, on the plan of the U.S. also a committee[3] to Revise & amend the laws, Respecting public Roa[ds], all parties[4] Seem to agree that we ought now to Join in defending &ᶜ but the Same old Spirit, of blaming the Jeffersonian policy, Seems to prevail among the Federalists, & I am doubtfull they are Aiming to degrade the Genˡ Government: they Seem to be inclined to avail themselves of the embarrased Situation of the country, to get a Majority, & office Hunters seem to Join with them, too Much. the common cant among us for several days has been, who is to be the Next Governor & Senator? for the former I have heard Named, W. C. Nicholas, T. M. Randolph, Hugh Nelson, A. Mason, J. W. Epps & A Stevenson. I am inclined to think our county will furnish a Governor, the 3 Gentlemen being all equally friendly, & Men of talents having all Just claims, Make it disagreeable to the representatives from the county, but I hope men voting from proper Motives, will Never incur the displeasure of good men: for the latter office, the Now Governor, Senator Brent, J. W. Epps, & Mason, are talked of: our taxes will be Raised. this you know, the Soldier must be paid; cant you drop me a hint as to public Roads? with all sincere Regard your friend & Mo. ob. S^t   CHARLES YANCEY

RC (DLC); edge frayed; addressed: "Thomas Jefferson Esqr late president of the u.S. Monticello"; franked; postmarked Richmond, 26 Oct.; endorsed by TJ as received 15 Nov. 1814 and so recorded in SJL.

The SOLEMN COMPACT was the United States Constitution. The EX^N LAW was suspended until 1 Mar. 1816 by the 25 Nov. 1814 "Act concerning Executions, and for other purposes" (*Acts of Assembly* [1814–15 sess.], 68–75). The 3 GENTLEMEN from Albemarle County named as

possible gubernatorial candidates were Wilson Cary Nicholas, Thomas Mann Randolph, and Hugh Nelson. The NOW GOVERNOR was James Barbour. The Virginia General Assembly elected Nicholas governor shortly thereafter and sent Barbour to the United States Senate early the following year (*Petersburg Daily Courier*, 12 Nov. 1814, 7 Jan. 1815).

[1] Manuscript: "Genearl."
[2] Manuscript: "Committe."
[3] Manuscript: "comittee."
[4] Manuscript: "partiies."

To Patrick Gibson

DEAR SIR   Monticello Oct. 25. 14.

Your's of Sep. 30. has been recieved, informing me of the enlargement of my note in the bank. three days before that date I had drawn on you in favor of Clifton Harris sheriff of Albemarle for 230.32 D the amount of my taxes E^tc in this county, and on the 11th inst. I drew in favor of the same person for 150.D. for so much cash recieved here in exchange. Genl Cocke will also present you a draught for 167.D. of the 23^d inst. I have been expecting the Sheriff of Bedford would have notified to me the amount of my taxes in that county, but I have not heard from him. I shall set out in a few days for that county and shall probably have to draw from thence for his demand & perhaps others.

we are grinding our wheat altho' under a poor prospect as to price. Accept the assurance of my great esteem & respect.

TH: JEFFERSON

PoC (NHi: Thomas Jefferson Papers); on verso of reused address cover of Joseph Delaplaine to TJ, 3 Oct. 1814; at foot of text: "Mr Gibson"; endorsed by TJ.

Clifton Harris was deputy sheriff rather than SHERIFF OF ALBEMARLE County.

To William F. Gray

SIR   Monticello Oct. 25. 14

I thank you for the kind letter recieved of Oct. 14. before the reciept of that I had taken the liberty of sending a package of books to mr Millegan addressed to your care, which I had done on the authority of his assurance that you would be so kind as to see that they were forwarded. in a letter to me of the 12th he mentions having forwarded a package to me, which I presume is some where on the way—all charges of transportation of things for me to Milton will be paid to the Stage-driver by mr Higgenbotham at that place. mr Millegan will pay those to Georgetown. should there however happen to be occasion at any time for any payment at Fredericks^bg, on a note from you of the amount it shall always be rep[aid] by return of mail. Accept the assurance of my thankf[ulness] and respect.   TH: JEFFERSON

PoC (DLC); on verso of reused address cover to TJ; mutilated at seal; at foot of text: "Mr Wm F. Gray"; endorsed by TJ.

A letter from Gray to TJ of 13 Apr. 1815, not found, is recorded in SJL as received 19 Apr. 1815 from Fredericksburg.

From James Leitch

SIR,   Charlottesville October 26th 1814

For Several weeks I have contemplated on Calling on you, & presenting your Account as requested—being So much engaged about my Building &c I have found it very Inconvenient to Spare the time & now enclose your Acc^t which I am in hopes you will find Correct Should any Error appear be So good as to Inform me of it—: yours with respect   JA^s LEITCH

RC (MHi); at foot of text: "Thos Jefferson Esqr"; endorsed by TJ as received 26 Oct. 1814 and so recorded in SJL. Enclosure not found.

From Patrick Gibson

SIR   Richmond 27ᵗʰ Octʳ 1814—

Your note at bank falling due on the 11ᵗʰ Prox°¹ I take the liberty of enclosing you one for its renewal, and as I think it probable from your last letter, that you may still be in Bedford, I shall forward a Copy of this to that place under cover to Mʳ samˡ J: Harrison I am respectfully

Your obᵗ Servᵗ   PATRICK GIBSON

Your favor of the 25ᵗʰ is just received
the several dfts you mention shall be paid on presentation

RC (ViU: TJP-ER); postscript adjacent to signature; between dateline and salutation: "Thomas Jefferson Esqʳᵉ"; at foot of text: "Monticello"; endorsed by TJ as received 15 Nov. 1814 and so recorded in SJL. Dupl (ViU: TJP-ER); lacks postscript; at foot of text: "Bedford"; endorsed by TJ as received 2 Nov. 1814 and so recorded in SJL. Enclosure not found.

¹ Reworked from "Inᵗ."

From John Adams

DEAR SIR   Quincy Oct° 28. 14

I¹ have great pleasure in giving this² Letter to the Gentleman who requests it. The Revᵈ Edward³ Everett, the Successor of Mʳ Buckminster and Thatcher and Cooper in the politest Congregation in Boston, and probably the first litterary Character of his Age and State, is very desirous of Seeing Mʳ Jefferson. I hope he will arrive before your Library is translated to Washington.

By the Way I envy you that immortal honour: but I cannot enter into competition with you for my books are not half the number of yours: and moreover, I have Shaftesbury, Bolingbroke, Hume Gibbon and Raynal, as well as Voltaire.

Mʳ Everet is respectable in every View; in Family fortune Station Genius Learning and Character. What more ought to be Said to Thomas Jefferson by   JOHN ADAMS

RC (MHi: Edward Everett Papers); at foot of text: "President Jefferson." FC (Lb in MHi: Adams Papers). Not recorded in SJL and probably never received by TJ.

Edward Everett (1794–1865), Unitarian clergyman, public official, and orator, was born in Dorchester, Massachusetts, and received an A.B. from Harvard University in 1811 and a Ph.D. from Göttingen University six years later. He was minister of the Unitarian Brattle Street Church in Boston, 1814–15, editor for a time of the *North American Review*, and served Harvard as a professor of Greek literature, 1815–26, and president, 1846–49. Although the two men never met, Everett exchanged more than a dozen letters with TJ during the 1820s. He also sat in the United States House of Representatives, 1825–35, and served as governor of Massachusetts, 1836–40, envoy extraordinary and minister plenipotentiary to Great Britain, 1841–45, United States secretary of state, 1852–53, and part of one term in the United States Senate, 1853–54. Everett supported industrialization, education reform, protectionism, the Bank of the United States, and the preservation of the Union. At the November 1863 dedication of the national cemetery at Gettysburg, he delivered the two-hour speech immediately preceding Abraham Lincoln's more memorable closing remarks. Everett died in Boston (*ANB*; *DAB*; Ronald F. Reid, *Edward*

Everett: Unionist Orator [1990]; MHi: Everett Papers; *Harvard Catalogue*, 63, 188; *Boston Daily Advertiser*, 16 Jan. 1865).

Joseph Stevens BUCKMINSTER, William Cooper, Samuel Cooper, and Peter Thacher (THATCHER) were ministers at the Brattle Street Church from 1805–12, 1716–43, 1746–83, and 1785–1802, respectively (Samuel Kirkland Lothrop, *A History of the Church in Brattle Street, Boston* [1851], 77, 125, 140, 159; *The Manifesto Church: Records of the Church in Brattle Square Boston* [1902], viii–x).

[1] "I have received" is canceled above the opening paragraph in FC.
[2] Word interlined in place of "you a" in FC.
[3] Given name interlined in place of "David."

From William Short

DEAR SIR   Philadelphia Oct. 28.—14

Your favor of the 20th of August followed me in my summer's tour & overtook me whilst on the road—I postponed therefore acknowledging it until my return to winter quarters—I have been not the less grateful for your kindness & the trouble you are taking to bring to a happy conclusion the disputed limits between Monroe & myself—If his presence should be really necessary, or even his personal agency be made by him a sine quan non I fear these limits will remain as long unsettled as those brought forward at Ghent are likely to be—I have always known Monroe to be dilatory, always behind his business, always hurried & of course unable to attend to any but those calls which are most[1] imperious & force his mind—Now in the midst of so many other louder & more imperious calls furnished by the duties of his public & double offices I have little hope that this little microscopic & silent object which has been allowed to sleep for so many years, can now make itself to be either seen or heard—And the more so, as its result at best might only be to awaken an old & silent debt, instead of adding to the extent of his territory. I believe I mentioned to you that M[r] Carter had been here & told me what had passed on this subject—On hearing of this claim of Monroe it awakened on his side a claim which he had also against him for the land he had sold him—He said the balance due was about equal to the land claimed by Monroe, & he had proposed to him, I think, to set off one against the other as the easiest & best mode of terminating the business, if Monroes claim should prove to be founded—But this mode of paying old debts did not probably meet Monroes' approbation, as nothing further has been done on the subject.—For myself I feel a great desire to have it settled in one way or other, not so much from the value of the subject as from an inherent aversion which I feel to leaving things in an unsettled state.— You mentioned, as the call of Congress would render Monroes attendance impossible, you would endeavor to prevail on him to appoint some one to act for him, so as to finish the affair—I suppose he has not done this & I regret it—for as to his acting or attending in person I consider it out of the question—And if he does not substitute some one the thing must go on without end.

I think with you on the subject of the downfall of Bonaparté. I believe however that as our war was begun & carried on, his continuance in power would not have given us peace—The war to be sure, could not have been carried on against us by our enemy with the same violence, nor would his terms have been so outrageous—but yet many causes of war would have existed which have ceased by the peace of Europe—& I am persuaded our Western statesmen would have remained too sensitive on the rights of sailors to have admitted of a return to the ways of peace in defiance of John Bulls prejudices— There is always more difficulty in resuming peace than in avoiding war—Of this our great statesmen do not seem to have been aware— At present it is useless to look back—Either by our own follies, or by the follies & ignorance of our leaders we are at sea—& the only thing to be enquired into, is the best or least bad manner of getting again into port—For my part however who am never sanguine, all my hopes are gone—I have no doubt that the soil & men will remain unconquerable—& that the deadly hatred will increase against an enemy which makes us suffer so much & will make us suffer so much more—For I have no doubt the war will continue, & continuing will change our mode of existence not only in a private but political sense—And when once we enter on that kind of ocean I see no hand able to guide us—I have certainly none of those party prejudices against our leaders which are felt by so many—If there be a man in the country who is impartial & who allows his mind coolly & dispassionately to examine the measures of government I think I may say I am that man—I have nothing to hope or fear from them so as to have my judgment biassed—I try indeed to hope for the best—I have need of that kind of consolation—but the effects of their measures or their madness (for I do them the justice to believe they wish well to their country) have been long staring me too full in the face to admit of my being blind to them notwithstanding my real desire to be so—"Delirant reges plectuntur Achivi"—I have had too many occasions to see that a nations sufferings may come from other leaders as well as Kings, & may be carried as far—

I have been more than once astonished to find myself on the verge of taking up my pen to address the public—I have never yet appeared in that character & nothing but indignation could make me assume it—I have been checked perhaps as much as by any thing else, by the want of some chanel—for the newspapers are all so completely of one or the other color, that whatever appears in them loses its natural tone & is considered as belonging to one or other of the sides of party spirit, & of course would be recieved or rejected according to the passion of the reader & could answer no good purpose—Although it would be indignation which would make me write, yet it would be with the hope or the view of being useful.

It often occurs to me to repass in my mind your manner of viewing political subjects. I remember that you are less than any one apt to despond—It would be a relief to me if I were so near you as to hear your sentiments—This might perhaps restore hope to me—At present I really have none—The continuance of the war appears to me inevitable—Our enemy is resolved on it most unquestionably—& without his consent we cannot have peace, as it requires both parties to get out of a war although one is sufficient to get into it—One of the attendants here on war, must be a paper money—It may be called by some other name & will be attempted to be disguised in various ways—but come it must, or the wheels of government must stop notwithstanding the great financial talents of the ingenious & dexterous new secretary.—I had a right to hope that my situation was a secure one—my fortune was clear & ample—it had grown gradually & was therefore the more solid—It was never exposed to speculation of any kind in order to increase it—So far as my own acts were concerned it could not be exposed—but against the acts of government I have no means of securing myself—The men & the soil will not be conquered by the enemy—but they may be conquered by ruin & will then be ready for any change—We need not go beyond modern history & modern dates to see what changes may be effected in men's minds by a change of circumstances.— A person who is not on the spot to examine can form no idea of the mass of distress & ruin which exists already or threatens to exist—If by a mere reform of expences this could be met, it would be supportable—but it bears on that class which had no reform to make—The rich are beginning to prepare for misfortune—I might be considered among the most rich, in comparing my revenue to my moderate wants—and yet I see I shall be obliged to draw still further on that source, the moderation of my wants—In addition to all this should Lord Hill make his appearance the distress would be encreased to an hundredfold degree—As it is, thousands of the best men of the place, most of them with families & many with families dependent on their labor or their industry are now in camp & have been since the invasion of Washington—How unequal the conflict, in the eye of a real statesman, between such men as these & the ragamuffin of Europe bought at a few pence a day & whose loss is only felt in their regiment, & repaired by a new recruit, whilst on our side the loss is felt throughout a whole family wch remains behind—It will not bear reflecting on—I will fly to a more agreeable subject, that of assuring you of the sincere & invariable sentiments with which I am bound to you most affectionately

W SHORT

Is Correa still with you? We long to have him here but I fear he will soon fly from us & since the downfall of Bonaparte, I feel growing in me a desire wch was dead, that of returning to France.

RC (MHi); postscript adjacent to signature; endorsed by TJ as received 15 Nov. 1814 and so recorded in SJL.

James Monroe's DOUBLE OFFICES were concurrent leadership of the State and War departments. On 20 Sept. 1793 William Champe Carter SOLD Monroe a 1,000-acre tract adjacent to Monticello, a property which Monroe later dubbed his "Highland" estate (Albemarle Co. Deed Book, 11:163–5; Harry Ammon, *James Monroe: The Quest For National Identity* [1971], 163). Quidquid DELIRANT REGES PLECTUNTUR ACHIVI: "Whatever folly the kings commit, the Achaeans pay the penalty" (Horace, *Epistles*, 1.2.14, in Fairclough, *Horace: Satires, Epistles and Ars Poetica*, 262–3). The INGENIOUS & DEXTEROUS NEW SECRETARY of the Treasury was Alexander J. Dallas. Unfounded rumors circulating at this time alleged that a large expedition headed by the British general Rowland, Lord HILL, was en route to North America (Philadelphia *Poulson's American Daily Advertiser*, 11, 19, 24 Oct. 1814; *ODNB*).

[1] Word interlined.

To Joseph Milligan

DEAR SIR   Monticello Oct. 29. 14.

I wrote you on the 17ᵗʰ to which I presume I shall recieve an answer in due time. the packet of books mentioned in yours of the 12ᵗʰ is not yet heard of. I mentioned this to mr Gray in a letter of the 25ᵗʰ so that I suppose it will be forwarded, if it's loitering is at Fredericksburg.   The Library committee requires a proposition on my part as to the price of my library, & as a ground of negociation. in making such a proposition I could take no ground but from the number of vols, their sizes, & average value. but having sent them my catalogue, I have no means of coming at the¹ numbers: for the conjecture I had formerly made was on counting a few pages only, taking an average of them, and multiplying by the number of pages. in this way I guessed the whole number to be about 9000. but more accuracy is now requisite. I have ventured to say, in a letter to mr Smith, that I thought you would be so good as to take the trouble of actually counting the numbers of every page of the Catalogue, distinguishing separately the folios, 4ᵗᵒˢ 8ᵛᵒˢ and 12ᵐᵒˢ so as to inform him how many there are of each format, which would enable him to set a value on the whole, & to propose it to the Committee: and this favor I have to sollicit from you, & further that you will be so good as to call on him and to inform him as to the character of the bindings generally, and state of preservation in which you saw them here. I have tried a rough method of coming at their numbers, by taking the running measure of each format as they stand on their shelves, and counting a few shelves for an average. then estimating these conjectural numbers at what I thought a moderate price, the average price of the whole per volume came out almost exactly what you had conjectured when here, to wit, 3.D. a volume. I imagine mr Smith will adopt some such method of estimate, by the sizes and numbers you will be so good as to furnish him. this mode of guessing at the number of volumes made it less than the former estimate. when this proposition of a sum shall have been made, I have asked the favor of the return of the catalogue, and as soon as I can correct that by an actual review of the library, which will be a work of a week or 10. days, I will begin to send you sheets of the catalogue for printing. I set out tomorrow for Bedford & shall return by the 15ᵗʰ of October. Accept assurances

of my great esteem & respect.   TH: JEFFERSON

PoC (DLC); on reused address cover of letter from James Leitch to TJ; at foot of first page: "Mr Joseph Millegan"; endorsed by TJ.

TJ arrived back at Monticello from Poplar Forest on 15 Nov., not in OCTOBER (*MB*, 2:1304; SJL).

¹ TJ here canceled "value."

To Samuel H. Smith

DEAR SIR   Monticello Oct. 29. 14.

Your favors of the 19th and 21st were recieved by our mail of the day before yesterday. presuming that the proposition in my letter of Sep. 21. was not sufficiently explained, I will state more particularly the course I had supposed the transaction would have taken.   the proposition was that the books should be valued by persons named by the committee themselves, and the payment made in whatever form, and at such distant time as they might think accomodated to the circumstances of the times. I supposed they would send one or two persons here, acquainted with the subject, perhaps booksellers, to value the books either singly, or by an average deduced from their sizes and numbers. this valuation I expected to be binding on me, while I had, and have no objection to a right of rejection either in the Committee or in Congress. if the valuation were accepted by them, I supposed they would send on some person to see to the exact delivery of the books, and to their safe conveyance. they are arranged at present in plain pine cases, close in the back, but open in front, & so compact that they might go as they stand on their shelves, the fronts only being nailed up, and be ready to set up in any room, in perfect order. having no anxiety about the sum or mode of valuation, but wishing the collection secured to the public, and at the moment of the recent loss rather than any other, I supposed a valuation by persons of their own choice the most unexceptionable ground I could propose to the committee: but persevering in the same object, I will acquiesce in any other which they shall prefer, except that of proposing a value myself, for which I really am not qualified by a sufficient familiarity with prices, nor willing to trust myself in a case where motives of interest might subject me to bias, & certainly to the suspicion of it. I cannot propose to you the trouble of making an estimate, of which no one would be more capable: but the labor of counting in every page of the catalogue the number of folios, 4^tos 8^vos & 12^mos and summing all these, might be performed by another, and

[55]

might furnish you ground, by an average of numbers & size, to name to the Committee a sum which you would deem reasonable: and whatever sum you should name shall be binding on me as a maximum, subject to be reduced, but not enlarged by actual valuation by any persons the committee shall think proper to appoint. in all this I wish myself to be entirely passive, and to abide absolutely by the estimate thus formed.   as the condition of the books must enter of course, as an element, into their valuation, mr Millegan, bookseller of Georgetown, who has lately had an opportunity of seeing them, can give you information on that head; and I have written to ask the favor of him to take the trouble of numbering them in the catalogue, & of reporting the sizes and numbers to you, from which you could readily deduce an estimate of the total, to be proposed as a maximum.   mr Millegan had asked permission of me to print the catalogue on his own account, as a book of sale. you must still be aware that some of the books entered in the catalogue will doubtless be missing. the collection has not been revised since my return from Europe. during my absences from home it has been open to limited uses, and I have occasionally found books missing. some of these may be only misplaced, but some are probably lost. I should mention also that there are two entered in the catalogue which I did not possess, but meaning to import them immediately, I entered them while writing the catalogue; the war however supervening prevented my importing them. these are the Geoponics, Gr. Lat. & an English translation of them lately published.

I had expressed in my letter a wish to keep some of the books during my life, not to be paid for of course until delivered; but that I should retire from the wish if at all unacceptable. I must of course replace many by new purchases. but, among my classics particularly, there are some special editions which could not now be replaced; & some mathematical books which I should unwillingly be without until peace shall open the means of getting them from Europe. the number I might wish to retain, for awhile at least, would be between one and two hundred volumes. but I repeat my willingness to let all go at once if preferred by the committee.

I shall set out tomorrow on a journey which will occasion an absence of about a fortnight. the return of the Catalogue by that term, if the Committee shall have no further[1] use for it would be desirable; because I would then begin the general review of the library, the restoring to their proper places the volumes which have been misplaced, and the ascertaining such as may have been lost. this would be a work of several days, and it would only be after that operation that the valuation could take place, if that idea be accepted by the committee. I tender you with great sincerity the assurances of my esteem & respect. TH: JEFFERSON

RC (DLC: J. Henley Smith Papers); at foot of first page: "Samuel H. Smith esq:." PoC (DLC); endorsed by TJ.

THE COMMITTEE was the congressional Joint Library Committee. An image of a replica of one of TJ's PLAIN PINE CASES is reproduced elsewhere in this volume, as is a likeness of Smith. TJ's RETURN FROM EUROPE took place in 1789. Thomas Owen's two-volume translation of Cassianus Bassus's GEOPONICS was published in London, 1805–06.

[1] Word interlined.

From Thomas A. Pellet

SIR, Boston 31st Octr 1814

I perceive by the letter in which you offer your Library to Congress, you have indulged yourself in a <u>tirade</u> against the "Vandalism" of the British, in burning the public buildings at Washington.—I think with you, that it was a shameful proceeding—but please to look at the enclosed <u>official</u> statement (publish'd in the Boston Daily Advertiser of the 29th Inst) and I am sure you will agree with me, that the conduct of <u>our</u> Officers towards the innocent inhabitants of Canada, has been most shameful.— THOs A PELLET

RC (MHi); addressed: "Thomas Jefferson, Esquire Late President of the U.S. <u>Monticello</u> Virginia"; franked; postmarked Boston, 2 Nov.; endorsed by TJ as received 15 Nov. 1814 from "Oellet Thos A." and so recorded in SJL.

TJ offered his LIBRARY TO CONGRESS in his second letter to Samuel H. Smith of 21 Sept. 1814. On 29 Oct. 1814 the BOSTON DAILY ADVERTISER reprinted several pieces from the 8 Oct. issue of the *Montreal Herald* denouncing the burning of Canadian towns and villages by United States forces; commenting that, "having reduced Fire and Pillage into a uniform practice, on such a variety of occasions, it is adding insult to injury to pretend, that those cruelties were perpetrated without or against orders"; questioning whether President James Madison had the right to complain about the recent destruction of the public buildings at Washington; and calling that act "a most hallowed retaliation."

Notes on the Peacock Plow

Smallest Peacock plough.
beam. 4 f–5.I long, breadth vertical 3.I $\frac{1}{4}$
thickness horizontal 2$\frac{1}{2}$
height of beam from ground behind 12$\frac{1}{4}$
before 15$\frac{1}{2}$ I.

length of handles 4.f.
their opening at top 21.I.[1]
angle of their elevation from the horizontal line 33°

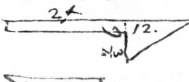

thickness of iron mould board $\frac{3}{8} + \frac{1}{16}$
share & bar

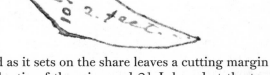

mould board

the mould board as it sets on the share leaves a cutting margin of 3.I.
behind, i.e. at the tip of the wing and $2\frac{1}{2}$ I. broad at the toe of the
mould board of course the block of which it is formed is but $6\frac{3}{4}$ wide
at bottom. it is 2 f long & 10.I. high. and must be 11 I. wide at top. the
 heel of the mould board is $8\frac{3}{4}$ from the left side of the
bar, it's hinder and upper tip is 13 I. from the perpend.
of the left side of the bar. it's cast therefore is $4\frac{1}{4}$

1814. Oct. these mould boards cast for me at Richmond weigh 18 ℔ 2.oz.

MS (ICN); entirely in TJ's hand; written on a scrap in two sittings, with the
first entry undated and the second partially dated.

For the twenty-four moldboards cast
for TJ AT RICHMOND, see TJ to John
Staples, 4 May 1814, and note to TJ to
Patrick Gibson, 15 Aug. 1814.

[1] Line interlined.

From Francis W. Gilmer

Dear Sir.   Richmond 1st Novr 1814
My inclination to visit Philadelphia with Mr Correa which has
been strengthened by every days acquaintance with h[im] has finally
determined me to do so; and I must beg of you the favor which you
were so kind as to promise, in giving me a letter to Doctr. Wistar. I

am sensible, of the obligation which such a recommendation as yours will imp[ose] upon me of deserving it, & will promise my endeavours to do so. I am sensible too of the personal obligation which I owe to you for such a mark of your good opinion.

Mr Correa joins me in wishing you a long continuance of health & happiness

very sincerely yours &c   F. W. GILMER

P:S: a letter will reach me in Washington within a fortnight of th[is] time, and at Philadelphia afterwards.

RC (MoSHi: Gilmer Papers); edge frayed, with missing text supplied from Richard Beale Davis, ed., *Correspondence of Thomas Jefferson and Francis Walker Gilmer 1814–1826* (1946), 31; at foot of text: "Thomas Jefferson esqr"; endorsed by TJ as received 3 Dec. 1814 and so recorded in SJL.

Francis Walker Gilmer (1790–1826), attorney, author, and educational emissary, was born at Pen Park in Albemarle County. Orphaned by the age of ten, he was taught French by TJ's daughter Martha Jefferson Randolph, attended a school in Georgetown, 1808–09, and graduated from the College of William and Mary in 1810. Gilmer then studied law under William Wirt in Richmond, served briefly in an artillery regiment during the War of 1812, and established a law office in Winchester. In 1818 he moved his practice to Richmond. Gilmer was keenly interested in a wide variety of topics. His publications included *Sketches of American Orators* (Baltimore, 1816), *A Vindication of the Laws, Limiting the Rate of Interest on Loans* (Richmond, 1820; Poor, *Jefferson's Library*, 11 [no. 676]), and one volume of the *Va. Reports* (Poor, *Jefferson's Library*, 10 [no. 584]). At TJ's request, in 1824 Gilmer sailed to Great Britain to hire professors and buy books and equipment for the newly created University of Virginia. He succeeded in that endeavor, but the trip undermined his already fragile health. Although he accepted the university's law professorship in the autumn of 1825, Gilmer died before he could take up his duties (*ANB*; *DAB*; Richard Beale Davis, *Francis Walker Gilmer: Life and Learning in Jefferson's Virginia* [1939]; Malone, *Jefferson*, 6:397–402, 409–10, 469; TJ to Gilmer, 11 Oct. 1825; *Richmond Enquirer*, 28 Feb. 1826; Albemarle Co. Will Book, 8:179–80).

From Leonard Sargent

SIR   Manchester (Vermont) 1st Nov 1814

Since the publication [of]¹ your Letter of the 21st Sept last to the Honᵉ S. H. Smith relative to the disposal of your Library: it has become a theme of much conversation in this part of our Country of what this vast number of Books can consist; Could you Sir without much inconvenience to yourself forward to this place a Catalogue of sᵈ Library you would not only confer a great favor on many citizens in this quarter[,] but it would Doubtless be of material service to the

Heads of our Literary Institutions in assisting them to make proper selections for their use

I am Sir with high Consideration your obt S^{vt}

LEONARD SARGENT

RC (DLC); mutilated at seal; addressed: "Hon^e Thos Jefferson Monticello Virginia"; franked; endorsed by TJ as received 24 Nov. 1814 and so recorded in SJL, which mistakenly describes it as a letter of 14 Nov. 1814.

Leonard Sargent (1793–1880), attorney and public official, was a native of Dorset, Vermont. He trained as a lawyer and worked briefly in Pawlet before relocating his practice to Manchester. His account of an 1819 murder case in which he was involved was used by the British novelist Wilkie Collins as the basis for his 1874 tale *The Dead Alive.* During his long legal career, Sargent served at various times as a postmaster, justice of the peace, state attorney, member of both houses of the Vermont legislature, probate judge and, for many years, on the council of censors. Beginning politically as a Republican, he was a Whig when he served as lieutenant governor, 1846–48. Sargent died at the home of his daughter in Johns-town, Pennsylvania (John S. Sargent and Aaron Sargent, *Sargent Genealogy* [1895], 69; Hiel Hollister, *Pawlet for One Hundred Years* [1867], 102; Leonard Sargent, *The Trial, Confessions and Conviction of Jesse and Stephen Boorn, for the murder of Russell Colvin, and the return of the man supposed to have been murdered* [1873]; Wilkie Collins, *The Dead Alive* [1874], 157; Burlington *Northern Sentinel,* 3 Sept. 1819; Bennington *Vermont Gazette,* 30 Jan. 1821, 15 Dec. 1829; *Journal of the House of Representatives of the State of Vermont* [1836], 3; New London, Ct., *Morning News,* 16 July 1847; Edward Conant, *Vermont Historical Reader* [1907], 166; Montpelier *Vermont Patriot & State Gazette,* 29 Sept. 1854; *Journal of the Council of Censors of the State of Vermont* [1862], 3, 4; Marcus D. Gilman, *The Bibliography of Vermont* [1897], 242).

[1] Omitted word editorially supplied.

List of Slaves at Poplar Forest

[ca. 2–13 Nov. 1814]

1743. Jame Hubbard.
  47. Cate.
       Bess.
  49. Betty. isl^d
  53. Will. Smith.
       Abby.
  66. Dinah.
  67. Dick.
       Hal. smith. Bess's
  70. Hanah. Cate's.
  71. Armistead.
  72. Jesse.
  73. Nace.

74. Caesar. Bess's
75. Austin. isl^d Betty's
76. Maria.
77. Sal. Will's
78. Nanny. Phill's.
    Gawen. isl^d Betty's.
83. Flora. Will's.
86. Phill Hub^d
88. Cate. Betty's
    Cate. Suck's.
    Fanny. Will's.
    Sally. Cate's.
89. Aggy. Dinah's.
90 Daniel. Bess's.
91. Lucinda. Hanah's.
92. Mary. isl^d Betty's.
    Edy. Will's.
93. Reuben. Hanah's.
94. Manuel. Will's.
    Stephen. Suck's.
    Evans. Dinah's
    Hercules. isl^d Betty's
96. Hanah. Dinah's.
97. Amy. Will's
    Milly. Sal's[1]
    [Cate. Rachael's.]
[98.] Maria. Nannys
    Sally. Hanah's.
99. Ambrose. Suck's
    Lucy. Dinah's.
    Billy. Hanah's.
    Nisy. Maria's.
01. Betty. Sal's.
    Phill. Nanny's
02. Jamy. Dinah's.
04. Prince. Suck's.
    Gawen. Flora's.
    Johnny. Maria's.
    Abby. Sall's.
[0]5. Jamey. Hanah's.
    Briley. Dinah's
06. Joe. Suck's.

Milley. Nanny's.
Davy. Suck's.
Edy. Sall's.
Aleck. Flora's.

[0]7. Rachael. Fanny's

[0]8. Billy. Sally's.
George Dennis. Nanny's.
Phill. Hanah's
Billy. Flora's.

[0]9. Martin. Sall's.
Shepherd. Suck's.
Melinda. Lucinda's.
Edmund. Hanah's.
Isaac. Maria's

10. Anderson. Sally's.
Anderson. Nanny's.

11. Moses. Sal's (Will's)
John. Cate's. (Suck's)
Rhody. Fanny's.
Boston. Flora's.

[12.] Nancy. Edy's.
George Welsh. Hanah's.[2]
[Janetta. Nanny's]
[Dolly. Maria's]
Rebecca. Lucinda's
Mary Anne. Sal's. (Will')
Henry. Sal's. Cate's.
Sally. Aggy's.

13. Zacharias. Fanny's.
Sandy. Milly's.

14. Solomon. Cate's (Suck's)
Ellen. Nanny's.
Gabriel. Mary's (Betty's)

MS (ViFreJM); written entirely in TJ's hand on both sides of a single sheet; edges chipped, with missing text supplied from Betts, *Farm Book*, pt. 1, 130–1; with left column of first page consisting of the following conclusion, mistakenly omitted by the Editors, of TJ's List of Landholdings and Monticello Slaves, [ca. 1811–1812] (with the last two bracketed names below supplied from *Farm Book* to fill blanks left by TJ in manuscript):

[10.] [Tucker. Mary's]
Patsy. Edy's.
Jordan. Bagw's.
Polly. Aggy's.
Washington B. Rachael's.

11. Lucy. Lilly's.
Cornelius. Ursula's
Jamey.   Scilla's.
[Matilda.] Cretia's.
Jenny.   Fanny's.
[Robert.] Virginia's.

The above list of Poplar Forest slaves was most likely prepared by TJ during his autumn trip to Bedford County in order to assess his 1814 tax liability.

[1] Recto ends here.
[2] First column of verso ends here.

To Patrick Gibson

DEAR SIR   Poplar forest Nov. 3.[1] 14.

I arrived here yesterday evening and find your's of Oct. 27. covering a blank note for renewal in the bank, and hasten to sign and commit it to the post office of Lynchburg that it may be recieved in time. I draw on you this day for 75. Dollars in favor of Reuben Perry. the sheriff of this county has not yet called on me. his demand for taxes is, I am told, about 113.D. I learn here that salt is sold in Lynchburg for 5.D. a bushel, cash. if so, I shall procure my winter's stock (about 20. bushels) and draw on you for the amount.

Accept the assurances of my esteem and respect.

TH: JEFFERSON

PoC (NHi: Thomas Jefferson Papers); at foot of text: "Mr Gibson"; endorsed by TJ. Enclosure not found.

In his account book TJ indicated that a day later, on 4 Nov. 1814, he signed the

BLANK NOTE (postdated to 11 Nov.) and drew on Gibson & Jefferson IN FAVOR OF REUBEN PERRY (*MB*, 2:1304).

[1] Reworked from "4."

To Reuben Perry

DEAR SIR   Poplar Forest Nov. 3. 14.

I am glad to have it now in my power to give you a draught on Richmond for 75.D. which overpays our former balance of 67.48 and it's interest. if any merchant in Lynchburg should want money in Richmond you may perhaps exchange it for cash. otherwise if you inclose it to mr Gibson he will forward the money to you by mail: or if you prefer returning me the note, I will write to mr Gibson to inclose you the money by mail. I shall endeavor to see mr Adkinson and press him to compleat my bill of scantling. Accept my best wishes

TH: JEFFERSON

PoC (ViW: TC-JP); at foot of text: "Mr Reuben Perry"; endorsed by TJ. Enclosure not found.

From William C. C. Claiborne

VERY D^R SIR,   New-Orleans Novr 4^h 1814.

By Mr Dorsey, a very respectable Citizen of this place, I took the liberty a short time since to address You, and to refer you to him for the news in this quarter.—The Louisianians continue to manifest the most patriotic disposition, and we have arrayed, as great a portion of the local Militia, as our population will well admit of:—But unless soon reinforced by the militia from the Western States; (which is expected) this State if attacked with a Considerable force, cannot be defended. The Gallant General Jackson continues with a respectable Army, (say 4–5000 Men Militia included) near Mobile, & if the Enemy, should advance in that quarter, a good account will be given of him;—If he takes the direct route by way of the Missippi, all my means will be exerted to resist him, and if his force be not an overwhelming one, you need be under no apprehensions for our Safety;— We however look with great Confidence to our Western Brethren for succour.

Mr Livingston has seized upon this perilous moment, when all hearts Should be united, again[1] to stir the question of the Batture, and the inclosed handbill will shew You the light in which this subject is still[2] viewed by the City Council.

I am Dr Sir with sentiments of[3] the greatest Respect Your faithful friend   WILLIAM C. C. CLAIBORNE

RC (DLC); at foot of text: "Mr Thomas Jefferson Monticello Virginia"; endorsed by TJ as received 1 Dec. 1814 and so recorded in SJL. Enclosure: Resolutions of the New Orleans City Council, approved 2 Nov. 1814 and signed by both Felix Arnaud, the recorder, and Nicolas Girod, the mayor, reporting that "Edward Livingston resorts to every means and intricacy of chicanery to wrest the Batture fronting the suburb St. Mary from the public," including a recent attempt to obtain a declaration from a jury that "a new dyke or levee nearer to the river than that now existing . . . could be erected"; repeating its determination "to support with all their means and power" the public's right to the batture and to protect the citizens of Louisiana and other states from any prosecution by Livingston that would "hinder them from taking earth from the said Batture or from any other legal enjoyment of that public property"; and resolving that "the present deliberation" be sent to Claiborne, the judge of Orleans Parish, and every nearby planter, be reprinted in both French and English in the local newspapers, and be posted as necessary (printed broadside in CtY: Beinecke Rare Book and Manuscript Library; in French and English; docketed as filed 4 June 1818 by Martin Gordon, clerk of the United States District Court in New Orleans).

[1] Word interlined.
[2] Manuscript: "stil."
[3] Manuscript: "of of."

From Enoch Jones

Sir   Norfolk Nov 5th 1814.

It may appear a little singular to you to receive a letter from one of whom you have never heard, but as you have evidenced an unusual mind and as my scituation and attempts have not been of the most common kind I believe no apology requisite for my writing—I have ever since I knew of you had much desire to see and converse with one whom I conceived to be so great a phylosopher as you are, but it has never been in my power to visit you.

My mind and circunstances have always been such as have caused me to encounter some difficulties which but few are in the habit of brooking—I had always a great desire to be a schollar, but unfortunately was curtaled in my education in consequence of the great number of children my parents had together with the smallness of their estate.

My mother has had fourteen children to live until old enough to attend school, thirteen of whome are now living and in the Indiany teritory. I am the oldest of all—. My mind inclined to the study of medicine, but I have been oblieged to support myself by teaching school and other means during my acquirement of anatomical and medical knowledge. I married when young and as my father in law could not understand my designs he has withholden all aid saying if he gave me any thing that before I could get into practice I should spend it, but I have persevered until after a sattisfactory examination I have been imployed as surgeons mate in the Navy on this station, but have not yet received a commition tho' I have served more than twelve months—As I have not been able to attend the lectures at Philidelphia, If I could gain a patron so as to enable me to attend there the next course to me it would be all important.

If you are so good as to answer these lines any communication will be thankfully received by sir
   your obedient humble servant   ENOCH JONES

RC (MHi); addressed: "Thomas Jefferson Esqʳ Monticello V.a."; franked; postmarked Norfolk, 8 Nov.; endorsed by TJ as received 15 Nov. 1814 and so recorded in SJL.

Enoch Jones (b. 1785), physician, was the son of Ebenezer Jones and Mary Jones, of Delaware. Later in the 1780s he moved to North Carolina, and in 1808 he married Nancy Swain, the daughter of Eleazer Swain, of that state's Washington County. Jones was commissioned as a surgeon's mate in the United States Navy on 10 Dec. 1814, but he resigned on 2 Mar. of the following year. By 1818 he was living in Posey County, Indiana, where he established a medical practice. Jones moved his family to Mississippi in the 1820s and to the Republic of Texas by the end of the following decade. Census records describe him as a dentist in 1850 and a farmer in 1860. In his later years Jones owned real estate valued at $480 and personal property worth $200 (Gilbert X. Drendel Jr., *Footprints on the Frontier: The Ebenezer and Mary Jones Family* [2008], 6, 7, 132–8; *Edenton Gazette, and North Carolina Advertiser*, 11 Nov. 1808; *JEP*, 2:588, 591 [1, 10 Dec. 1814]; Callahan, *U.S. Navy*, 301; DNA: RG 29, CS, Ind., Posey Co., 1820, Tex., Grimes Co., 1850, Dewitt Co., 1860).

From John H. Cocke

DEAR SIR,   Camp Carters Nov[r] 6. 1814

I have to acknowledge the rec[t] of your letter of the 23[d] Octo: with an order on your correspondents in Richmond, for the price of the Horse I sold you. I am glad to hear he turns out to your satisfaction.

Since the late intelligence from abroad leaving us no alternative, but national disgrace & infamy or a continuation of the war, I have been looking with great anxiety to Congress for some plan by which the strength of the Country may be drawn forth & directed with effect against the Enemy.

The scheme which seems to be relied upon by the Secretary of War, I trust will be found practicable & judicious, to recruit the ranks of the U.S. Army.

For the defence of the States, I shou'd prefer some efficient organization of the militia to a dependence on regulars, even if they cou'd be obtain'd. A free people shou'd be taught to rely only upon themselves for the defence of their territory against invaders.—A fatal consequence of relying upon regular Armies wou'd be a neglect of the use of Arms; and the noble & manly determination to encounter every hardship & privation in defence of our birthrights, wou'd give place to the mean, calculating, commercial spirit which wou'd look only to buying off the resentment of our Enemies.—Destroy the national sentiment that the people are able to defend the Country against its Enemies, & we are at once reduced[1] to a situation that a single battle might lose us our liberties.—whereas if an improved militia system is adopted, diffusing military information, & correct notions of military subordination thro' the mass of our population we shall, at least, be render'd invincible at home.

The classification of the militia, & calling out the younger part of the population woud be placing the burthen of service where it cou'd be easiest borne & using the materials most susceptible of being wrought upon. A twelve months, or two years tour wou'd be sufficient to establish discipline and this of itself wou'd produce the doubly happy effect of getting rid of the incompetent militia officers &

bringing into command the men of respectability & intelligence & public spirit thro' out the Country.—Under our deplorable existing system every man of common reflection at once sees the impossibility of being able to do anything either useful for the Country or creditable to himself. Shou'd any change take place promising a more favourable result to the efforts of those engaged in the public service, I wou'd gladly devote my best exertions to the State during the War.—

My health has never been as [good?] in my life as since I have been in Camp—May you long continue in the full enjoyment of this first of earthly blessings

Yours with the highest respect & Esteem   JN⁰ H. COCKE

RC (DLC); torn at seal; addressed: "Mʳ Jefferson Monticello"; franked; postmarked Richmond, 9 Nov.; endorsed by TJ as received 15 Nov. 1814 and so recorded in SJL.

On 17 Oct. 1814 Secretary of War James Monroe sent the United States Senate's military affairs committee his plan for expanding the RANKS OF THE U.S. ARMY by some 40,000 troops. Although he proposed several methods of accomplishing this goal, he preferred to "Let the free male population of the United States, between eighteen and forty-five years, be formed into classes of one hundred men each," with property holdings distributed equally among the classes, and to "let each class furnish four men for the war, within thirty days after the classification, and replace them in the event of casualty." Cocke favored the second of Monroe's four options, which called for dividing the militia into age groups and extending the term of service to two years (ASP, Military Affairs, 1:514–7).

[1] Manuscript: "reduceed."

To Andrew Jamieson

SIR   Poplar Forest Nov 7.[1] 14.

Mʳ Goodman my manager here informs me you will furnish me 20. bushels of salt at 5.½ D. taking a draught on Messʳˢ Gibson and Jefferson, my correspondents at Richmond. I now inclose you a draught on them for 110. Dollars, which you can have remitted by mail before it will be convenient for me to send for the salt, the greater part of which I have to send for from Albemarle. Accept the assurances of my respect   TH: JEFFERSON

PoC (MHi); at foot of text: "Mʳ Jamieson"; endorsed by TJ. Enclosure not found.

Andrew Jamieson (d. 1821), a merchant in Lynchburg, was a native of Scotland. In 1814 he became one of the directors of his adopted city's branch of the Farmers Bank of Virginia. Jamieson died after returning to the land of his birth (William Asbury Christian, Lynchburg and Its People [1900; repr. 1967], 53; Lynchburg Press, 23 Nov. 1821).

[1] Reworked from "8."

From Abram R. North
(for Andrew Jamieson)

DEAR SIR   Lynchbg. Novemb. 7ᵗʰ 1814

Yours by your boy is duly to hand, inclosing us a draft on Messʳˢ Gibson & Jefferson for One hundred and Ten dollars, for which we will deliver you; or to your Order Twenty Bushels Salt on application at any time betwen this and the Twentyfifth day of Decemb next—we will be thankful in furnishing any kind of goods in our line at any time you may want, we have an extensive assortment of Negroe Cloathing Particular Negroe or say Napt Cotton & Blankets &c I am
Yr most obᵗ   for A. JAMIESON
                                                                              ABRAM R NORTH

RC (MHi); addressed: "Mr Thomas Jefferson Bedford"; endorsed by TJ as a letter from Jamieson received 7 Nov. 1814 and so recorded in SJL.

Abram R. North (ca. 1792–1837) operated a bookstore in Lynchburg for at least a decade prior to his death. He conducted book auctions in a number of southern states, joined a committee soliciting contributions to pay off TJ's debts in 1826, supported Andrew Jackson politically in 1828, and served as a militia colonel during the 1830s. North died during a visit to Vicksburg, Mississippi, leaving an estate valued at just over $2,000 (Vi: Abram R. North Business Records, 1827–36; William Asbury Christian, *Lynchburg and Its People* [1900; repr. 1967], 83–4; Margaret Anthony Cabell, *Sketches and Recollections of Lynchburg by the Oldest Inhabitant (Mrs. Cabell) 1858* [1858; repr. with additional material by Louise A. Blunt, 1974], suppl., 55; *Richmond Enquirer*, 19 Jan. 1828, 22 June 1832; Lynchburg Hustings and Corporation Court Will Book, B:322–3; Jackson *Mississippian*, 21 Apr. 1837; *Lynchburg Virginian*, 4 May 1837).

To Francis Eppes

MY DEAR FRANCIS   Poplar Forest Nov. 11.[1] 14.

I arrived here a few days ago, and sent for you immediately and did not learn till the return of the messenger that your school had separated, and would not reassemble until after Christmas. as your father will probably be from home all that time, would it not be better that you should pass it at Monticello. in two month[s] we can advance you so much in French that you would be able to pursue it by yourself afterwards, and especially when aided by our occasional meetings at this place. on this subject consult with your Mama who will decide for you what is best, and to whom present my friendly respects. in the hope she will conclude in favor of your visit to Monticello I give you[2] here the assurances of my love.   TH: JEFFERSON

PoC (CSmH: JF); edge trimmed; endorsed by TJ. Not recorded in SJL.

¹ Reworked from "12."
² Word interlined.

YOUR MAMA: Francis Eppes's stepmother, Martha Burke Jones Eppes.

From William & Reuben Mitchell

Lynchburg Nov. 11ᵗʰ 1814

Mʳ Thomas Jefferson

1814	In a/c with W. &. R. Mitchell	D
June 4ᵗʰ	To Balance ℔ a/c Rendered	$226.92
14	To 1 Barrel Sfine flour ℔ Order	5.00
		$231.92

W. &. R. Mitchell Presents their respects to Mʳ Jefferson and will thank him to send by Mʳ C. Mitchell the above balance—if it suits Mʳ Jeffersons Convenience better to draw on Richmond, it will be no inconveniance to W. &. R. M—

RC (ViU: TJP-ER); dateline at foot of text; in the hand of a representative of William & Reuben Mitchell; endorsed by TJ: "Mitchell W. & R."

TJ's 14 June 1814 purchase from the firm of 1 BARREL SFINE (superfine) flour for $5.00 "℔ negro Jesse" is also documented in a separate receipt for this transaction (MS in ViU: TJP-ER; written on a scrap in the hand of the same representative of William & Reuben Mitchell).

Instructions for
Poplar Forest Management

1814. Nov. 11. Poplar Forest.

The crop here for 1815. is to be as follows

Corn in Early's field. 80: acres.

Wheat in McDaniel's, in the corn field & the oldest tobacco ground South of South Tomahawk, & in as much of the Fork field as can now be sowed.

Oats in such parts of the Fork field as cannot be sown in wheat; and if these be not enough, some may be sowed in the best spots of the Tomahawk field. but

Peas must be put into the main body of Tomahawk field.

Clover to be sown in the Fork field.

The Ridge & Belted fields to rest. and the old straw to be carted on the galled & poorest parts of the ridge field. the cart should not be idle from this a single day, when not necessarily otherwise employed.

Tobacco in last year's clearing, and in such new clearings as can be made this winter. the clearing is to be of meadow on the upper part of South Tomahawk, and of the highland between Perry's and South Tomahawk, and on the Western side so as to bring it up conveniently to make a part of McDaniel's field. aim at 80,000. hills.

let all the Corn be measured, & write me at Christmas how much.

As soon as you finish sowing wheat, begin to carry the crop of wheat to the mills, that this may be finished before the roads get bad. a cart with 2 oxen & a horse, will do as much at this as a waggon. all the hauling force possible should be mustered up for this.

The first winter's job must be the finishing the Bear creek road, doing every thing compleat before you quit it.

then mend up all the negro's houses, & finish Hanah's. on no accounts must these houses go another winter as they are.

put the Corn-field fence (Early's) into compleat repair, so that it may continue good the 6. years it will remain before it comes into corn again; running the dividing fence between that & the Belted field, to wit, along Early's branch; and clear up all the branches within it, and the patches left uncleared; this being to be done always in the field which is to go into corn.

Mend up the yard fence compleat, & let no animal of any kind ever enter it. more than half my trees are already[1] destroyed by them. continue the yard-fence from it's South West corner due Westwardly to the next fence; and sow oats & clover in the lot it will inclose adjacent to the yard, to prepare it for an orchard;[2] & finish placing the fences of the curtilage exactly on Capt Slaughter's lines.

Inclose & clean up the meadow ground at the foot of the hill near where they distill. if not too wet, pumpkins may be tended there next year to prepare it for timothy.

I think it will be well to send 25. bushels of rye & wheat to get whiskey distilled for the harvest.

The tobacco made this year should be prepared as fast as you can, to be prized & kept in the tob° house until I can see what is best to be done with it.

As fast as the flour is got ready at the mill, it must be sent to Richmond to Gibson & Jefferson, who will pay the carriage. one barrel of the very best must be brought here for my use. mr Mitchell must pay himself out of this wheat the balance due on last year's.

9. pots must be bought at the iron-works, or elsewhere, and given to Fanny, Suck's Cate, Lucinda, Edy, Aggy, Flora, Maria, Milly, &

Betty's Mary. if you cannot otherwise pay for them, let me know the amount & I will provide it. a sifter must be got for every woman living in a house to themselves. I give none to men having no wives here.

4. horses must be bought on credit till May. let them be young and able to do work in the waggon.

The Chickasaw colt to be sent to Monticello at Christmas.

Sow from half an acre to an acre of hemp, & 4. acres of pumpkins. more than half the fattening of the hogs may be on pumpkins

Cotton must be bought at Lynchburg, for which I will always order money to be remitted to you from Richmond, on your giving me notice.

Mr Adkinson is to get the rest of the scantling immediately after Christmas. let it be hauled in, & properly piled as fast as he gets it.

beds of good hempen rolls are to be got for Bess, Cate's Sally, Fanny & Suck's Cate.

have the peach trees beyond S. Tomahawk trimmed up.

The sheep should be brought up to their pen every night & counted. this should be done thro' the whole year, except in the great heats of summer, when they only feed through the night. they must be regularly fed through the months of December, January, February & March with corn meal, allowing a pint a day to every sheep, & a bundle of blades to every two sheep. there should be a particular person charged with counting & feeding them. the ewes near yeaning should be put by themselves at night.[3] the patch where the burnet and oatgrass are would be a good place. after the lamb is 3. or 4. days old the ewe may join the flock.

Our sufferings and losses this last year by depending solely on a crop of corn for the support of the plantations ought to be a lesson to us not to risque so much again on the failure of that crop. had the peafield of 80. acres at each place been planted the last year, well cultivated, & carefully gathered & preserved, the plantations would have been in affluence notwithstanding the short crop of corn. the 80. acres would have given 800. bushels at each place. this is counting on only the half of the common crop where peas are cultivated, & but the half of what I have made through large fields in Albemarle. 300. bushels of these would have fattened all the hogs, after a beginning of pumpkins, and the remaining 500 would have abundantly fed 8. horses. we should not then have lost 6. horses from diseases produced by poverty & labor, nor consequently the sowing 100. acres of wheat, as we now shall, and which will be a loss of 800. bushels of wheat in the next crop. if we added to this, as we might do, large supplies of hay[4] from clean & well kept meadows, our oxen would be kept in order to do double work, cows give 3. or 4 times the milk, & every thing be fat, without opening the corn house door for a single animal. we could never fail to make corn enough to feed the people. 300. barrels would feed[5] all at both places. these considerations are mentioned in order to urge an attention to the peafields and meadows, as a supplement to the cornfield. while we depend on corn alone, we shall never see any thing but poverty and misery and dying animals on the plantations.

Of the 21. hogs put up here, 7 must be kept for my use, & for the workmen who will come up in the spring, $12\frac{1}{2}$ will be necessary to give half a hog apiece to each of the grown people, of whom there are 25, as may be seen by the list of them on another paper, and there will remain $1\frac{1}{2}$ towards mr Goodman's quantity, which must be made up by taking some from Bear creek.

Of the 34. hogs at Bear creek, $8\frac{1}{2}$ will be necessary to give half a hog to each of the 17. grown people there, 1. to be given to Jame Hubbard, & supposing 9. or 10. will make up mr Goodman's complement and mr Darnell's allowance, there will remain about 15. to be driven to Monticello at Christmas. in giving the half hogs to the people, arrange the sizes of the hogs according to the sizes of the families, giving the largest to those who have the largest families. I suppose the offal will last them a month or two.

Keep 5 bushels of the salt bought at Lynchburg to salt the hogs here, and have the other 15. bushels packed in flour barrels headed close, ready when I shall send for them to Albemarle.

I should be glad mr Goodman would write to me once a month, stating how things are, & always looking over this memorandum & saying what [par]ts of it are executed.

MS (NjP: Andre deCoppet Collection); entirely in TJ's hand; last page's (mostly blank) lower right quarter torn away.

TJ probably prepared this memorandum to guide the work of Jeremiah A. Goodman, his overseer in charge at Poplar Forest.

By HERE TJ means his Tomahawk plantation. For CAP[T] SLAUGHTER'S LINES, see Joseph Slaughter's Survey of the Poplar Forest Curtilage, 5 Dec. 1812. BOTH PLACES: TJ's Poplar Forest plantations, Bear Creek and Tomahawk. The list of slaves written ON ANOTHER PAPER has not been found.

[1] Manuscript: "alread."
[2] Remainder of sentence interlined.
[3] Preceding two words interlined.
[4] Preceding two words interlined.
[5] Reworked from "feel."

To Archibald Robertson

DEAR SIR   Poplar forest Nov. 11.[1] 14.

The sheriff of Bedford called on me yesterday for the first time to inform me of the amount of my taxes, and that he must recieve them at the ensuing Bedford court. being to leave this place the day after tomorrow I am obliged to ask your assistance to draw from Richmond the amount of the inclosed draught on Gibson & Jefferson which may be recieved by mail before Bedford court, where I promised the sheriff, mr Claytor, he would recieve it through the hands of mr Garland.   I will thank you to forward to me to Monticello by mail, the sequel of my account from the date to which it was furnished last. desperate as the times are for paying money from the ordinary means, I have a prospect of another resource, altho' not yet absolutely certain of doing something in this case. Accept the assurance of my esteem and respect   TH: JEFFERSON

PoC (ViU: TJP); at foot of text: "Mr Archibald Robertson"; endorsed by TJ.

The INCLOSED DRAUGHT, not found, was "for 129.23 in favr. of Arch. Robertson to be pd. to Clayton Sheriff of Bedford for my taxes in Bedford & Campbell this year" (*MB*, 2:1304). The current sheriff of Bedford County was Isaac Otey, not his predecessor, John CLAYTOR (Bedford Co. Deed Book, 14:2, 191–2).

[1] Reworked from "12."

From Archibald Robertson

DEAR SIR   Lynchburg 11th novr 1814

Your favor of this date have recd enclosing a dft on mr P. Gibson which shall be attended to, and the amount paid mr Claytor at Bedford Court—

I am glad to hear that you have a prospect of receiving money, other than from the ordinary sources, in that case hope it will be in your power to aid us, nothing but absolute necessity would induce us to apply to our customers for money in these difficult times,

We have received a small assortment of Fall Goods & will be glad to furnish what you may have to purchase,

Respectfully Your ob St   A. ROBERTSON

PS Enclosed you have a copy of your acct to 31 augt which hope on examination will be found correct—   A.R

RC (ViU: TJP); endorsed by TJ as received 11 (reworked from 12) Nov. 1814 and so recorded in SJL. Enclosure not found.

From Thomas Jefferson Abbott

state of ohio Ros County Living on the North
Fork of paint Creek seven miles from
SIR   Chillicothe[1] November 12[the] AD 1814

we are all tolerable well At present Exept my father who is Down with the Rhuematick pains & has been Subject to it this six years & I hope these Lines will find you & yours Enjoying your healths And I, am named after you sir and was Born Just Eight days Before you took your Seat as late president of unighted states of America—and I shal beg leave of you to Ask of You a small Complement or Gift, Which If granted I Shall bee most Gratefuly & humble Obliged to you for it and sir y[ou m]ust pleas To Excuse, for my writing as I never had more Than Ninty Days schoolling & my mother has Had twins three times & has had Ten 10 Children[2]

your most obedient serv[t]   THOMAS JEFFERSON ABBOTT
                                    AD 1814

RC (MHi); mutilated at seal; addressed (trimmed): "To the honorable Thomas Jeferson secrty [...]"; franked; endorsed by TJ as received 14 Dec. 1814 from Chillicothe and so recorded in SJL.

[1] Remainder of dateline between body of letter and closing.

[2] Abbott here canceled "As follows."

To Charles Clay

TH:J TO MR CLAY   Pop. For. Nov. 12. 14.

I propose to set out tomorrow if ready, or certainly next day, and therefore send the bearer for the Cape of my coat.

I recollect an opportunity I shall have of sending for your spectacles by a gentleman going to Philadelphia. I charge myself therefore with that commission. perhaps by writing myself to M[c]Alister he may pay more attention to the quality.

The wild-rye seed you gave me before was sowed in a place to which the sheep had access & they destroyed it. if you will give me some now I will sow it within an inclosure, as I am desirous of trying it. the bearer brings a small bag.[1] health and happiness to you.

RC (on deposit ViHi); dateline at foot of text. Not recorded in SJL.

The GENTLEMAN GOING TO PHILADELPHIA was probably Francis W.

Gilmer. For the gift of WILD-RYE SEED, see Clay to TJ, 5 Sept. 1810.

[1] Sentence interlined, with caret mistakenly placed in front of the period at the close of the preceding sentence.

From William Fleming

DEAR SIR, Richmond 12th November 1814.

DEAR SIR, Richmond 12th November 1814.

I beg leave to recommend to your notice and good offices, the bearer of this letter, my young friend, m^r Colin Clarke, son of col^o James Clarke of Powhatan county, with whom you are acquainted: — He is at present a practitioner of the law; but wishes to serve his country, at this crisis, in a military capacity, and solicits, from you, a letter in his favour to the secretary of war. — I have been well acquainted with him from his early infancy, and know him to be a young gentleman of respectable talents, active, and spirited; and of great sobriety & steady habits. — The principles of his whole family are truly republican.

I have the honour to be, dear sir,
Your respectful friend & obed^t servant   W^M FLEMING.

RC (MHi); endorsed by TJ as received 4 (reworked from 3) Dec. 1814. Recorded in SJL as received 3 (reworked from 4) Dec. 1814.

Colin Clarke (1792–1865), attorney and plantation owner, studied at James Ogilvie's school near Milton, attended the College of William and Mary in 1811, and later served on the latter institution's board of visitors. He did not receive a military appointment at this time. Clarke represented his native Powhatan County in the Virginia House of Delegates, 1816–19, and sat for Chesterfield County, 1826–28. He moved to Chesterfield County by 1820, and in 1834 he pur-

chased an estate in Gloucester County, where he lived thereafter. In 1860 Clarke owned real estate worth $35,000 and personal property valued at $55,400, including eighty-one slaves (G. Brown Goode, *Virginia Cousins: A Study of the Ancestry and Posterity of John Goode of Whitby* [1887], 229–30; Vi: Clarke Family Papers; Ogilvie to TJ, Nov. [1814]; *William and Mary Provisional List*, 13, 52; Leonard, *General Assembly*, 287, 291, 295, 333, 338; DNA: RG 29, CS, Chesterfield Co., 1820, Richmond, 1830, Gloucester Co., 1860; L. Roane Hunt, ed., *Death Records of Gloucester County, Virginia 1865–1890* [2000], 30; Gloucester Co. Will Book, A:16–7).

From John Melish

DEAR SIR   Philadelphia 12 Nov <u>1814</u>

Considering the late pretensions set up by the British at Ghent, to be of such a nature as to set aside all the ordinary principles of reasoning, I was of opinion that the best mode of exhibiting their nature and tendency was to publish a map representing the proposed Boundary, which I have the honour to enclose accompanied by the Documents relative to the negotiation, and remarks on the extent of the British pretensions, and the effect they would produce if acceded to. —

Mr Monroes instructions to the Plenipotentiaries, N 1, is an admirable production; and the whole of the Documents are an excellent Commentary on the State of the relations between this Country and Britain,—too valuable to be laid aside Among the mass of matter in the newspapers. The remarks will I hope meet your approbation

The Juvenile Atlas would have been Sent long ago, but being in folio I could not get it forwarded through the medium of the post office. It is now forwarded to my friend m^r Thomas Richie of Richmond, who will send it to you.—

Some time ago I published a description of the Roads in the United States, of which I would have Sent you a Copy; but I am preparing a short Geographical description of the United States with some local maps to Accompany it[1] when it will be published Anew under the title of "A Travelling Directory" As soon as it is ready I shall forward it.

Having devoted my time almost exclusively to the study of American Geography, and of promulgating Valuable matter regarding it, I am very desirous of seeing Authentic maps & Descriptions of the Various States. I had in connection with some of the principal Artists here made preparations for publishing a General American Atlas, upon the plan exhibited in the enclosed prospectus, and Circular; but in consequence of the general pressure of the times we have suspended the publication; but not abandoned it. A number of the General maps are nearly engraved, and we will resume the subject as soon as it appears there will be a sufficient demand for the Work to defray the expence. In the meantime I would wish to promote the promulgation of the Geography of the Country by States—keeping in view that any maps to be delineated for that purpose shall in size & execution comport with the plan of the General Atlas, of which they may eventually form a part. In turning this subject in my mind it has occurred to me that A new Edition of Your notes on Virginia accompanied by A map of the kind alluded to would be an excellent subject to begin with. The estimation in which I hold this work is well known, and it would give me real pleasure to Contribute my aid in bringing forward a new Edition of it embracing a view of the present State of Virginia. I hope I will not be deemed presumtuous in suggesting this subject for consideration. In doing so I am solely Actuated by a desire to see a work reissued in a new dress, which I think would be honourable to the State of Virginia, and valuable to the American Community. In case you should think favourably of the suggestion my own services are offered because I think that my Arrangements are such that I can do more justice in the editorial department of a Geographical & Statistical work than Any other publisher in this Country.

With perfect respect & esteem I am Dear Sir Your obd—

JOHN MELISH

RC (DLC); addressed: "Thomas Jefferson Esq Monticello"; endorsed by TJ as received 24 Nov. 1814 and so recorded in SJL. Enclosures: (1) Melish, *The Sine Qua Non: A Map of the United States, shewing the boundary line proposed by the British commissioners at Ghent, with the documents relative to the negotiations* (Philadelphia, 1814), including Secretary of State James Monroe's instructions of 15 Apr. 1813 to the American treaty commissioners (pp. 3–21) and Melish's 8 Nov. 1814 "Remarks on the extent of the British pretensions, and the Effect they would produce if acceded to," which concluded that the British were demanding American territory totaling "Above 165 millions of acres," worth "Nearly 125 millions of dollars," and peopled by "128 thousand inhabitants" (pp. 57–63, quotations on p. 63). (2) Melish's "Prospectus of an American General Atlas," criticizing previously published atlases; hailing "the improved state of geographical science in the United States"; listing the work's projected thirty-six maps (two in two sheets and one in four sheets), to consist of the earth as a whole, the five most heavily populated continents, Canada, Mexico, the West Indies, the United States, and all twenty-three of its states and territories; vowing that the maps will be detailed and accurate; announcing his business arrangement with three noted engravers, George Murray, Henry Schenck Tanner, and John Vallance; stating that the publication will consist of forty-one 22-by-20-inch sheets, on "paper of the best quality" and "handsomely coloured," and be published in ten numbers at two-month intervals at a total cost of fifty dollars; and offering a free copy to those who obtain seven subscriptions and collect the money (DLC: TJ Papers, 201:36041–2; printed text with handwritten correction by Melish of his Philadelphia address from 209 Chesnut Street to 330 Market Street; undated). (3) Circular letter by Melish, Philadelphia, 18 July 1814, declaring his intention to publish henceforth "*maps, charts*, and *geographical works* generally"; explaining that under his new arrangement, he will be in charge of the "geographical department," Tanner and Vallance will oversee the engraving of the maps, and Murray will be in charge of "vignette and ornamental engraving"; remarking that his earlier publications have been received favorably; hoping that he will secure "public patronage"; advertising the *American General Atlas* and indicating that "specimens of the work so far as executed, are to be seen at the Map Store" at 330 Market Street; commenting on the difficulty and high cost of producing state and local "*maps from actual survey*," but promising to execute works of that nature "free of such expence, and with a degree of celerity hitherto unknown"; with an annexed "List of Works Lately Published," consisting of fifteen numbered items, including Melish's "Travels in the United States," a "Description of Florida," a "Plan of Quebec," documents relating to the British takeover of Canada in 1759–60, a "Statistical Account of the United States," the *New Juvenile Atlas* described below, and maps of "the Seat of War in North America," the United States, the coastline from Norfolk, Virginia, to Newport, Rhode Island, the Chesapeake and Delaware bays, New York Harbor, Long Island Sound, the Detroit River, Ohio, "the Seat of War in Europe," and Wayne and Pike counties in Pennsylvania; and also announcing that Melish, "A Description of the Roads in the United States," and Miguel Ramos Arizpe, "Memorial on the Natural, Political, and Civil State of the Provinces of Cohauila [Coahuila], Texas, &c. in the Kingdom of Mexico," are both "In the press and will speedily be published" (DLC: TJ Papers, 201:36043; printed text with handwritten correction by Melish of his address as in preceding enclosure; with "List of Works" on verso).

The JUVENILE ATLAS was the first American edition of Robert Laurie and James Whittle's *A New Juvenile Atlas, and familiar introduction to the use of maps* (Philadelphia, 1814). On this date Melish wrote President James Madison a very similar letter enclosing a copy of *The Sine Qua Non* (DLC: Madison Papers).

[1] Preceding three words interlined.

From Francis W. Gilmer

DEAR SIR.   Washington Nov. 13th 1814.

I wrote to you from Richmond, soliciting a compliance with the promise which you were so kind as to make of a letter to D[r] Wistar. The apprehension that my letter may not have reache[d] you, and the desire of making my visit to Philadelphia as pleasing, and as instructive as possible induce me to renew my applicatio[n] To which permit me to add, that nothing will give me more pleasure, than to be able to serve you in any manner whateve[r;] either during my journey with mr. Correa, or during my longer journey thro' life. you have grown old in active service among men, & perhaps have found little to make you desirous of contracting new friendships; to me will belong hardly any thing else, than to reverence your memory, & be grateful for your past services. I wish that I may ever be able, to add any thing to your present happiness, or your future glory.

yours sincerely &c.   F. W. GILMER

RC (MoSHi: Gilmer Papers); edge frayed, with missing text supplied from Richard Beale Davis, ed., *Correspondence of Thomas Jefferson and Francis Walker Gilmer 1814–1826* (1946), 32; endorsed by TJ as received 19 Nov. 1814 and so recorded in SJL. RC (MoSW-M); address cover only; with PoC of TJ to John McAllister (1753–1830), 24 Dec. 1814, on verso; addressed: "Thomas Jefferson esq[r] Monticello, near Milton Virginia" by "mail"; franked; postmarked Washington, 14 Nov.

To Jeremiah A. Goodman

DEAR SIR   Maj[r] Flood's Nov. 14. 1814

I forgot to take a note of the debt due for corn about Christmas; also the debts for the two horses. be so good as to let me know by mail, how much they are, to whom due, & when to be paid. I forgot also[1] to desire a clover lot to be made at Bear creek where we proposed.—with respect to the Asparagus bed, of which I spoke to mrs Goodman, make them mow off the stalks and lay them one side, then cover the bed with 2. inches of dung, and then lay on the stalks again to shade the manure from the sun.

Burwell went to Lynchburg on Friday and I gave him a 5. dollar note to get changed that I might have it on the road. he bought $2\frac{1}{2}$ dollars worth of something in mr Benjamin Perkins's store and the young gentleman in the store gave him in change a silver half dollar & the two dollar bill now inclosed, which Burwell gave me with other change for my five dollars. I never looked at the bill till I went to pay for some oats at Hunter's & found it to be a South Carolina bill which nobody will recieve. I suppose it has been given by the young gentleman thro' inadvertence and the servant not being able to read, took it without knowing it to be not current here. I presume it will be taken back on your application: but if there is any hesitation, just throw it in the fire, as the sum is too insignificant to make any difficulty about, only that one does not like to give five dollars for three. accept my best wishes,

TH: JEFFERSON

RC (NNGL, on deposit NHi); at foot of text: "Mr Jeremiah A. Goodman." Not recorded in SJL.

On 14 Feb. 1815 TJ asked Patrick Gibson to send Goodman $60 so that he could pay for the HORSES "bought

payable Mar. 1" (*MB*, 2:1306). On the day before the above letter was written, TJ purchased SOME OATS for seventy-five cents at Robert Hunter's ordinary in Campbell County (*MB*, 2:1304).

¹ Word interlined.

From Joseph Miller

HONRD FRIND   Norfolk Novr 14th 1814—

I take the liberty of informing you that this Day I have Shiped for you one Cask of ___ on Board the Slope Eliza-Ann Josiah [Allven?] Capt which I hope will Come Safe to hand hoping you will Wright Merss Gibson Jefferson C^o to forward it to you for been Rather Perishable and to be Keept Dry you will Open the End your name is on as it Contains 3 Diff^r Sorts—
I have Commence^d Malting and has Ventured 1000 Dol in a ship bound for France with Tobacco which if arives Safe will Pay Good I have Inshured
hoping to heare from you when you Rec^d
my well wishing to you and Famuly
I Rem your Hum Servent   JOSEPH MELLER
Drec^t me at Mr Joseph¹ Hayes

RC (DLC); one word illegible; at head of text: "Mr Jefferson"; endorsed by TJ as received 19 Nov. 1814 and so recorded in SJL.

¹ Given name interlined.

From Charles Willson Peale

DEAR SIR   Belfield Novr 14th 1814.

When we beleive that we have made any discovery that offers somthing for the benefit of man, no time should be lost to communicate it to our friends, that they may give it to others if the communication will be of any importance.

some time past I had a well dug in a situation to give Water to my Cattle &c The Ingenious Isaih Lukens made me a small brass cylender and Boxes to form a pump and also frixion wheels &c to turn sails to the wind, my wind-mill pumped the Water up in a satisfactory manner, but it was blown down several times, and I make some improvments that prevented the like accidents. my next difficulty was to prevent it from going too fast when the wind blew a gale, after I had made several experiments with springs to make the sails yield to the wind as I heard had been done, I found such difficulties that I had almost given it up as a bad job. my experiments however[1] shewed me what were the causes of my failure—my plan then was to make the

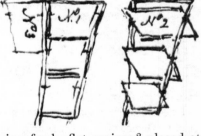

centrefugal force & the pressure of the air to check the velocity of the sails in a storm of wind. a loose sketch will give you my Invention:

The four arms placed in an angle of about 45 degree's, with frames within them to moove on pivots $\frac{1}{3}$ from the top, $\frac{2}{3}$ to be pressed out by the Wind blowing fresh. flat springs[2] placed at each joint of the several sails these springs[3] are made of such force as will be just sufficient to keep the sail flat to the frame in a very light breese, the point of the spring presses on a pin a little above the joint of the sail, but when the sail is brought to a right angle, then the point of the spring bears on another pin a little higher up, and further back, as the[4] two indicates—If one spring is found too weak a second or third may be screwed on them, I first put 12 sails and finding the principle good I added 4 more of a little larger size, as the sketch shews, so that with a gentle breese the mill works and in a high wind it mooves moderately, and, is not acccellerated by a storm of wind—for as soon as the motion becomes quick the Centrefugal force throws out the Sails & the mooving power is taken off. one other improvement I invented to lighten the labour of the

N° 3 is one of the additional Sails mentioned or the other Side.

N° 1 is an Arm with the Sails flat to the frame & N° 2. an arm to Shew them blown open &

[80]

mill: a double crank, I put a pole to the opposite  crank of equal weight to that lifting the Pistern, having a ring to embrace it, and one pole thus steadies the other.

In a large Mill a number of Cranks to work several Pumps, some mooving up while others are decending &c By my small Wind mill, which is not 7 feet spand, I know that an immence quantity of Water may be raised by this mode of Sails. And where there is water & convenient Banks[5] to make resevoirs of water, a great many manufactories may be erected to advantage, The demand for Mill seats are numerous of late. It is not difficult to work Pumps in any direction, if the perpendicular direction cannot be had.

The City of Philad[a] expends with each Steam Engine between 3 & 4 Cord of Wood [per][r] day, besides the[6] Wages of a number of men employed night & day. a few Wind mills might save much, if not the whole of that expence, and the Cost of Mills would be of small account—Each of their Steam Engines now to be erected at the new Bason will cost 20,000$

I have addressed the Corporation by letter, inviting them to appoint a committee to view my Wind mill and they have instructed their watering committee[7] to wait on me. I cannot expect that those who have interest in the construction of Steam Engines will be disposed to make any experiments to obtain the power of the Winds.   one remark more on this subject, If the sails of Wind mills are made of canvis, the linnen may be preservd by dissolving Bee's Wax in spirits of turpentine & coating the linnen with it, the turpentine will evaporate, & the wax having penetrated into the threads will preserve it. But the sails may be made of thin boards or sheet Iron—if the weight is not objectionable.

I have long wanted to resume my Pensil to execute some works which might be more valuable to the Museum & my family than my present labours, but perhaps it is better as it is, a sendentary life might injure my health, & at present I enjoy good health. my labour is of various kinds, Carpenters work; turning; making machinery in the Mill to save various labours of the Farm; Masonry and sometimes diging or remooving Earth &c—My Thorn fences are improoving fast, and from experiance I find that they must be cut at least twice in the year, perhaps 3 or 4 times would be better to make them grow thicker. planting them on the sides of banks is not so good, as on flats, If put on the sides of Banks, flats should be made to retain the moisture.

Your favorite persuit, Gardening, I have extended, but in these times especially, Gardiners good for real[8] service, cannot be had for any wages. I am heartily sick of employing them, rare and curious vegetables must be dispenced with, and various fruits be substituted—Currants may be cultivated[9] to considerable profits in making wines.

At one time I thought of sending Garden truck to market the cost of Carriage with little dependance of getting an honest return, discourages[10] the attempt, to put the Garden on shares multiplies the cares & would have a tendency to discontent if I gave to my Children or friends part of the produce, and therefore my present prospect is to do occasionally what I can myself with the aid of a man I shall keep to go on arrants & extra labour independant of the farmers work—

My wishes now are to live as quiet and easey as I can consistant with the necessary labour to ensure health, for without labour I cannot believe any Person can enjoy perfect health, as by experience I often have found when the Body is in some degree uneasey, whether it may something[11] of that inexplicable disease, Gout or Reumatism, some active labour, such as[12] plainning a board or diging in the Ground, to produce a gentle perspiration,[13] generally performs the cure. I made Doct[r] Wistar laugh, when I told him that I knew the cure for a Cough—By running up & down a steep hill with an open mouth, thus inhallling the oxogen or pure air.

My scrole is lenthy enough, without I could give you more intertaining Matter, I see too much of Egotism in it. I wish to hear of your enjoying a good share of health, and also, I desire to be informed how your Grandson Tho[s] Jefferson spends his time, I hope he will be a comfort to you when old age creeps on.

Accept my best wishes for your happiness and Beleive me with much esteem your friend   C W PEALE

RC (DLC); at foot of text: "The Honble Thomas Jefferson Esq[r]"; endorsed by TJ as received 26 Nov. 1814 and so recorded in SJL. PoC (PPAmP: Peale Letterbook).

The NEW BASON is apparently a reference to Philadelphia's Fairmount reservoir and pumping station, facilities constructed between 1812 and 1815 (John F. Watson, *Annals of Philadelphia, and Pennsylvania, in the olden time* [1899], 3:397). Peale wrote the CORPORATION of Philadelphia on 18 Oct. 1814. After viewing his windmill at Belfield, the WATERING COMMITTEE reported in January 1815 that the shore of the Schuylkill River could not accommodate the twenty or more windmills necessary to replace the steam engine already in use (Peale, *Papers*, 3:272n). TJ's GRANDSON was Thomas Jefferson Randolph.

[1] Word interlined.
[2] Manuscript: "spings."
[3] Manuscript: "spings."
[4] Manuscript: "the the."
[5] Manuscript: "convenient Banks convenient."
[6] Manuscript: "the the."
[7] Manuscript: "committe."
[8] Word interlined.

⁹ Manuscript: "cutivated."
¹⁰ Manuscript: "discorouges."
¹¹ Thus in manuscript.

¹² Manuscript: "a."
¹³ Manuscript: "sperspiration."

From Joseph Milligan

DEAR SIR   Georgetown November 16ᵗʰ 1814

I have run through the Catalogue & find that the amount of Volumes if we include[1] the Edinburg review will amount[2] to Say 6500 which agreeable to the Rule which I have laid down Viz

for a folio ten dollars
for a Quarto Six Dollars
for an Octavo Three Dollars
for[3] a Duodecimo one Dollar.

will Amount to a trifle over $24000
I have not Counted the Edinburg Review in the Number as the Number of Volumes were blank there are a few other lines that I could not make out Most of them I marked * except a few that were [thus] Supposed them to be included in other works
I will undertake to print the Manuscript by Tracy and If I can dispose of 500 Copies I will allow 50 Copies in boards for the Translation and If I can dispose of 1000 Copies[4] I will allow 100[5] Copies for Translation but Suppose it may Sell 750 in that Case 75 copies[6] for the Translation

With Great Respct yours   JOSEPH MILLIGAN

P.S. I will call on Mʳ Smith this day with the result of my Counting I will furnish him with a Copy of Enclosed Statement of the Number of Books with the Calculations of Value on a separate paper

RC (DLC); brackets in original; with postscript written perpendicularly along the left margin; at foot of text: "Thos Jefferson Esqr Monticello virginia"; endorsed by TJ as received 19 Nov. 1814 and so recorded in SJL. Enclosure not found.

[1] Thus in manuscript, but given what follows Milligan presumably meant "exclude."
[2] Manuscript: "amont."
[3] Manuscript: "fo."
[4] Manuscript: "Copes."
[5] Reworked from "1000."
[6] Manuscript: "copes."

From Elizabeth Trist

My Worthy and Dear friend   Henry Cᵗʸ Nov 17ᵗʰ 1814

I have long wish'd to address you but have been deter'd, from a fear of being troublesome, I want to know what you think of the state of our Country at present, The disasters at Washington has been a mortifying and distressing event, but when I had Reason to think that it woud be productive of good in[1] the end, by rousing the people from the torpid State which they were beguiled into, by the expectation of peace, and that party cabals wou'd give place to resentment for the injury and insult which had been perpetrated by a set of barbarians on our Country[2] but I fear the worst has not yet happend the yankies seem determined on making a Seperate peace with England and if we do not make such concessions as they may think fit to impose, such as turning out the President &a the Union will be destroy'd a civil war will ensue and God only knows where or when it will end. poor Mʳ Madison with all his caution and conciliatory disposition can not Steer clear of abuse Good Heavens! who wou'd ever wish to fill that Office, can happiness ever attend it? I have often rejoiced that you had quited the Helm before the storm got to its height—our finances Seem desperate, the Taxes contemplated, will I fear produce discontent, but that I dont mind if we were only united we cou'd repel our foes with ease and insure to our Country an honorable peace I never suffer myself to despair nor shall I ever do so, while our army and Navy perform such noble achievements as have occurd on the Niagra, at plattsburg on Champlain and Mobile, it is a great sourse of exultation to every true American if only in disappointing the English in their expectation of humbling us, the Goverment of England will find that every campaign will obscure the Glory of their veteran Troops, our little Navy on the Ocean have lately done their best to humble the pride of that insolent nation, the action which took place between the Reindeer and wasp, has terminated to the honor of our flag I feel more perhaps, from my Nephew being a partaker in the Glory which they have achieved he was a midshipman on board the wasp and in the list of the kill'd and wounded his name is not inserted—I have also to be glad and truly thankful for the success of our arms against that Band of pirates on Barataria the Safety of Orleans will be Secure at least for a time I heard that Colonel Randolph had again enterd on a Military career for the preservation of his native State I am under no apprehension of our Troops being in danger from the enemy, for they seldom go where they are prepared to receive them, but those Station'd below Richmond suffer much from sickness the mortality which has taken place at Norfolk Since the war has exceeded Six thousand beside those who die in consiquence of the sickness they generate in that low country after they leave it—I wish some other plan coud be[3] fallen upon than drawing men from this upper Country to dig their own Graves I dont believe there exists more patriotism than among the people of this District, but I am told they begin to murmur at being sent to Norfolk any where else where they cou'd have a chance of meeting an honorable death—I observe that you have disposed of your Library hope they have given you the full value I seldom have a chance of hearing from Albemarle my friends are not interested enough in my happiness to induce them to write to me but I shall never cease to love and respect them I hope My Dear Patsy enjoys good health and spirits her children all well and happy and that your own health is in perfect repair, this tenement of Clay that I inhabit will not stand many years longer every year makes me feel its decline but I am not dismay'd by the thoughts of quitting a situation that can afford little but mournful regrets

M[r] Gilmer and my neice unite with me in love to the family and every good wish for yours and their happiness that God may bless and preserve you long is the constant prayer of your obliged and sincere friend   E. TRIST

RC (MHi); addressed: "Thomas Jefferson Esq[r] Monticello Albemarle"; stamped; postmarked Martinsville, 22 Nov., and Charlottesville, 11 Dec.; endorsed by TJ as received 14 Dec. 1814 and so recorded in SJL.

Trist's NEPHEW William S. House seems to have survived the 28 June 1814 engagement in the English Channel with HMS *Reindeer*, but if so he perished when his sloop, the USS *Wasp*, went down with all hands in the North Atlantic that October (Malcomson, *Historical Dictionary*, 598, 599; Callahan, *U.S. Navy*, 277). Although the United States military had recently dispersed the BAND OF PIRATES ON BARATARIA Island near New Orleans, Governor William C. C. Clai-

borne invited them to join in the defense of the city in December. President James Madison later pardoned them as a reward for their role in repelling the British invasion (Dunbar Rowland, ed., *Official Letter Books of W. C. C. Claiborne, 1801–1816* [1917; repr. 1972], 6:291, 324, 338; *Annals*, 13th Cong., 3d sess., 1829–30 [6 Feb. 1815]). PATSY: Martha Jefferson Randolph. The English poet John Dryden included the phrase TENEMENT OF CLAY in his long allegorical poem *Absalom and Achitophel* (pt. 1, line 158). MY NEICE: Mary House Gilmer.

[1] Manuscript: "in in."
[2] Preceding three words interlined.
[3] Trist here canceled "addopted."

Estimate and Plans for Albemarle Academy/Central College

[ca. 18 Nov. 1814]

The walls of the Pavilion are 116.f. running measure.

Cellar 2. bricks thick, 10 f. high. 24. bricks to a square foot.

24 × 10 × 116 amount to	27,840. bricks	27[84]0

Upper walls 23.[1] f. high,

$1\frac{1}{2}$ brick thick. 18. bricks to a

square foot. 18 × 23 × 116	48,024	say	53360
the chimney	4,752		4752
6. pilasters	1134.		1134
	81,750. bricks		87,086

the necessary Appendix, passage

E[t]c[2] (61.f. runn[g] measure,

9 f. high. 1. brick thick)	6,588

each Chamber has 36.f. of wall, running measure.

if 10.f. high & 1. brick thick,

10 × 12 × 36. amount to	4320. bricks.

one half of the chimney (one

chimney serving 2. chambers)	656
2. pilasters	270
	5246.

but if the walls be $1\frac{1}{2}$ br. thick

there must be added	2160
	7406[3]

20. chambers to each pavilion

therefore will require	104,920. bricks or 148,120

And a Pavilion with it's 20.

chambers will take	192,258[4]	or 235,[2]06[5]

The method of making a rough estimate, in Philadelphia, of the cost of a brick dwelling house, finished in a plain way, is to reckon the Carpenter's <u>work</u> equal to the cost of the brick walls, and the Carpenter's <u>materials</u> and the ironmongery equal also to the cost of the brickwalls. but in the present case the carpenter's materials, (timber) will either be given, or cost very little, and the ironmongery will be little; I believe therefore the cost of the Carpenter's materials & ironmongery need not be stated at more than half the cost of the brickwalls. reckoning brickwork therefore at 10.D. the thousand, the cost may be roughly estimated as follows.

Pavilion. walls 817. D 50 C Carpenter's work

        817. D 50 C Carpenter's materials &   D   C

        ironmongery 408. D 75 C =   20[4]3.[75]

Appendix. on the same principles   164.70

Chambers. each on the same principles costing

        131. D 15 C, 20 chambers will cost   2623.

        the establishment of a Pavilion &   ―――――

        20. Chambers for each professorship

        will cost therefore   4831.45

but if the brickwork costs 13.D. & the other work in proportion a pavilion & 20 Dormitories [will cost 6280.89][6]

The estimate above is made on the supposition that each Professor, with his pupils (suppose 20) shall have a separate Pavilion of 26. by 34.f. outside, & 24. by 32.f. inside measure: in which the ground-floor (of 12.f. pitch clear) is to be the schoolroom, and 2. rooms above (10.[7] f. pitch clear) and a kitchen & cellar below (7.f. pitch clear) for the use of the Professor. on each side of the Pavilion are to be 10. chambers, 10. by 14.f. in the clear & 8.f. pitch, with a fireplace in each, for the students. the whole to communicate by a colonnade of 8.f. width in the clear. the pilasters, of brick generally $5\frac{1}{2}$ f. apart from center to center.

The kitchen will be 24. by 14. on the back of the building adjacent to the chimney, with 2. windows looking back. the cellar 24. by 10. also, on the front side, with 2. windows looking into the colonnade. the Pavilions fronting South should have their stair-case on the East; those fronting East or West should have the stairs at the North end of the building, that the windows may open to the pleasantest breezes.

Back-yards, gardens, stables, horselots E[t]c to be in the grounds adjacent to the Square, on the outside.

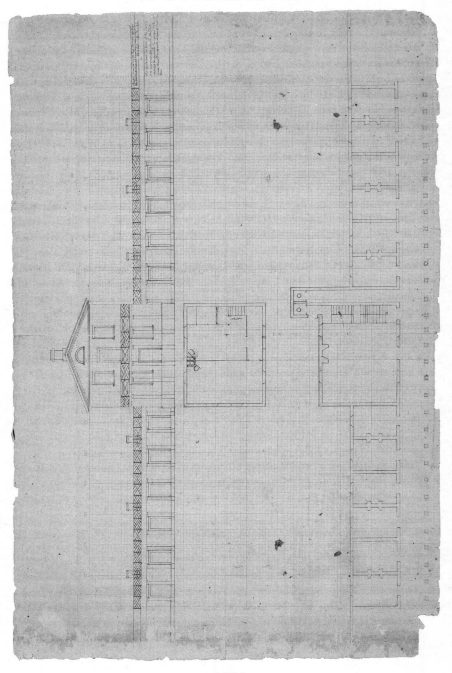

[In TJ's hand to right of preceding drawing:]
there is an error in this Chinese railing the pannels should have been from pilaster to pilaster as is seen in the Pavilion.
the pilasters in front of the Pavili[on] are erroneously placed. the two outer should be opposite the corners & the [four] inner should be equally distanced betw[een] them.

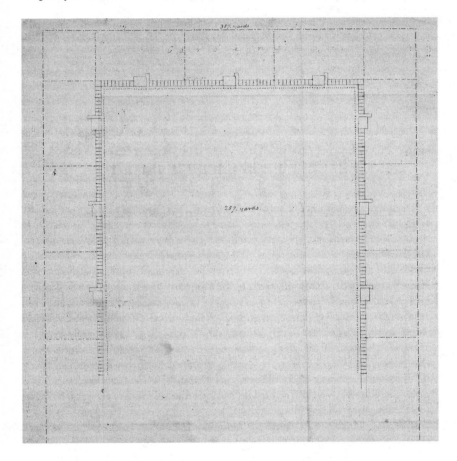

MS (ViU: TJP); written entirely in TJ's hand on 21-by-13½-inch sheet of brown, single-sided, engraved, coordinate paper folded in half to form four pages, with cost estimates on p. 1, first drawing on pp. 2–3, and second drawing on p. 4; undated, with some words and numbers faint.

For the dating of this document, see the Minutes of the Albemarle Academy Board of Trustees, 25 Mar. 1814, with editorial headnote on The Founding of the University of Virginia: Albemarle Academy, 1803–1816, and TJ to Benjamin Henry Latrobe, 3 Aug. 1817. The elevation has sometimes been identified as an early study for Pavilion VII, the first building constructed at the University of Virginia (Frederick Doveton Nichols, *Thomas Jefferson's Architectural Drawings* [1960; repr. 1995], 40 [no. 309]).

In making the ESTIMATE ABOVE, TJ utilized the left-hand column, which required fewer bricks. If he had used the one on the right and included the missing bricks for the "Appendix, passage Eᵗc" (see note 5 below), the cost to construct a pavilion and twenty student rooms would have been $6,044.85 at $10 per thousand bricks and $7,858.31 at $13 per thousand. Horse lots (HORSELOTS)

are plots of land on which horses are pastured (*OED*).

[1] TJ wrote "26" above this number, which would make the figure in the far right column 54,288, not 53,360.

[2] TJ here canceled "will take."

[3] Preceding two lines interlined.

[4] Correct sum is 193,258.

[5] TJ neglected to add the 6,588 bricks for the "Appendix, passage Eᵗc" to this column. Had he done so, the total would have come to 241,794.

[6] Line added by TJ in pencil.

[7] TJ wrote "13." above this number.

Draft Bill to Create Central College and Amend the 1796 Public Schools Act

[ca. 18 Nov. 1814]

An Act for establishing a College in the county of Albemarle and for amending the act for establishing public schools.

Be it enacted by the General assembly that there shall be established in the county of Albemarle, at the place which has been, or shall be selected[1] by the trustees of Albemarle Academy, and in lieu of such academy, an institution for the education of youth, to be called the Central College, which shall be constituted,[2] governed and administered as follows.

The Governor of this Commonwealth for the time being shall be the Patron of the said College, and shall have power to appoint the Visitors thereof in the first instance, and to fill up such vacancies in the Board of Visitors as may exist afterwards from time to time.

There shall be six Visitors, who shall hold their offices each for the term of three years,[3] if he shall so long demean himself well, of which the Chancellor of the District shall be the competent judge.

The sd Board of Visitors shall have two stated meetings in every year, in the sd College, to wit on the[4]   of
                    and   and such[5] occasional meetings as may be called from time to time by any three members, giving effectual and timely notice to the others.[6]

They, or a Majority of them shall have power
to appoint a Treasurer and Proctor.[7]
to establish professorships, appoint professors,[8] prescribe their
    duties, & the course of education to be pursued, determine the

salaries & accomodations they shall recieve from the College, & the perquisites from their pupils:

to lay down rules for the government and discipline of the Students, for their subsistence, board, & accomodation, & the charges to which they shall be subject for these & for tuition.

to prescribe and controul the duties and proceedings of all officers, servants & others with respect to the buildings, lands & other property of the college, & to the providing subsistence, board, accomodations, and all necessaries for the Students & others appurtaining to the same, and to fix the allowance & emoluments for their services:[9]

and, in general to direct and do[10] all other matters and things which to them shall seem best for promoting the purposes of the institution, and for securing, improving, and employing it's property, which several functions may be exercised by them in the form of Bye-laws, rules, orders, instructions, or otherwise as they shall deem proper.

There shall be a Treasurer, to be appointed by the Visitors, to hold his office during their pleasure; whose duty it shall be to recieve all monies which shall become due, or accrue to the College, to pay all monies which shall be due from it, according to such directions, general or special, as shall be given by the board of Visitors, and to render his accounts at such times, in such forms, and to such persons, as they shall require, or to themselves.

There shall be a Proctor,[11] to be appointed by the Visitors, to hold his office during their pleasure. in him, in trust for the College, shall be vested, transmissible to his successors, the legal estate in all property of the College, whether in possession, in interest, or in action; and he shall have authority to maintain the same in all suits, as plaintiff or defendant, which suits shall not abate by the determination of his office, but shall stand revived in the name of his successor. he shall be capable in law, and in trust for the College, of recieving subscriptions and donations real & personal, of purchasing, recieving & holding, transmissible to his successors, all property, real or personal, in possession, interest or action.

It shall be his duty to superintend, manage, preserve, & improve all the property of the College, in possession, interest, or action:

to erect, preserve, & repair the buildings, improvements & possessions:

to provide subsistence & other necessaries, and to direct and controul the due and economical dispensation of them:

to employ and controul all agents, servants, & others necessary for the works or the services, praedial or menial of the institution. and in all these functions he shall act conformably with the provisions and principles established by the Visitors, of whose laws regulations and orders he shall have the general execution, when not addressed to any other person.

And for the preservation of the peace and good behavior within the College and the buildings and grounds appurtenant thereto, in cases beyond the ordinary Authority of the professors, and within the cognisance of the laws of the land, the sd Proctor shall be invested with all the powers and authorities of a justice of the peace, exercisable within the College only, or the buildings and grounds appurtenant thereto, and for cases only arising within the same. and for the due exercise of such authority, according to the laws of the land, he shall take before the court of the county the oaths of a justice of the peace, limited to that local precinct. and to his precepts the Jailer of the county shall yield obedience as to those of any other justice. but if a Student be the offender, he may be confined in any apartment in, or appurtaining to the said College, or, by a Mandate addressed to himself he may be restrained to such apartment, on pain of being committed to the common jail of the county.[12]

And be it further enacted that the rights and claims now existing in the said Albemarle academy and it's trustees, shall by this act become vested in the sd Central college, and it's proper officers, so soon as they shall be appointed: and that, in aid of the subscriptions and donations obtained, and to be obtained, and of the proceeds of the lottery authorised by the act for establishing the Albemarle academy, the said College shall, by it's proper officers, when appointed, be authorised to demand & recieve the monies which arose from the sales of the glebe lands of the parishes of St Ann & Fredericksville in the said county of Albemarle,[13] in whatsoever hands they may be, to be employed for the purposes of the sd College;[14] and also to demand and recieve from the President and Directors of the literary fund, annually, a dividend of the interest or profits of that fund in the same proportion which the contributions of the sd county bore to those of the rest of the state in the preceding year, to be applied annually for the benefit of the said College.

And with a view to the extension of a competent education to the children of the citizens of the sd county of Albemarle generally, by a division of the county into sections, or wards, and the establishment, in every ward, of a School for their education, as provided in the act for establishing public schools, passed on the 22^d day of Dec. 1796.

Be it enacted that the determination of the time when the sd act shall be carried into execution in the said county[15] shall be vested in the Visitors of the sd College exclusively; and that in addition to the powers given by the sd act to the Aldermen, they shall be authorised to require from the parents and guardians of such children attending the Ward-schools as are able, a reasonable compensation for their tuition, to be applied in payment of the stipends to the tutors of the several Wards.[16]

And be it further enacted that the act passed in 1803. for establishing the sd Albemarle academy, that of the same year amending the said act, and all other provisions of other acts contrary to the purview of this act shall be repealed from and after the appointment of Visitors as therein provided.[17]

FC (DLC: TJ Papers, 202:35951–2); entirely in TJ's hand; undated. Dft (ViU: TJP, TB [Thurlow-Berkeley] no. 1386); entirely in TJ's hand, with subsequent alterations by him to reflect the final wording of the bill; portions faint; undated; notation in left margin: "Note the words or erasures underscored are alterations made by the legislature on passing the bill"; endorsed by TJ: "Central College." The bill in its final form, which passed on 14 Feb. 1816, is printed in *Acts of Assembly* [1815–16 sess.], 191–3, with numbered sections, and with only the most significant variations noted below. Enclosed in TJ to Joseph C. Cabell, 5 Jan. 1815.

For the background to and dating of this document, see Minutes of the Albemarle Academy Board of Trustees, 25 Mar. 1814, with editorial headnote on The Founding of the University of Virginia: Albemarle Academy, 1803–1816. The CHANCELLOR OF THE DISTRICT including Albemarle County was John Brown (1762–1826), who presided over the Superior Court of Chancery held in Staunton. A 14 Dec. 1815 report from the Committee of Propositions and Grievances of the Virginia House of Delegates recommended against vesting Albemarle County's share of the state's LITERARY FUND "in the said Trustees for the use of the said Academy" (*JHD* [1815–16 sess.], 38). The legislation OF THE SAME YEAR

AMENDING THE SAID ACT, "An Act to amend the act, intituled, 'an act to establish an academy in the county of Albemarle, and for other purposes,'" which appointed additional trustees, actually passed on 20 Jan. 1804 (*Acts of Assembly* [1803–04 sess.], 50).

[1] Reworked from "established." *Acts of Assembly*: "elected."

[2] *Acts of Assembly*: "established."

[3] In Dft TJ here canceled "from the date of his appointment."

[4] In the *Acts of Assembly*, the blanks that follow are filled in with "day of the commencement of the Spring term of the Albemarle Circuit Court; and on the day of the commencement of the Fall term of the said Circuit Court."

[5] Reworked from "and so many."

[6] *Acts of Assembly* here adds "and if, from any cause, the said visitors do not attend the said stated meetings, or such occasional meetings as may be called from time to time, the said meetings may be adjourned from day to day, until a general meeting shall be had."

[7] Word inserted in Dft in place of "Director."

[8] Preceding two words not in *Acts of Assembly*.

[9] *Acts of Assembly*: "salaries."

[10] Preceding two words interlined.

[11] Word interlined in Dft in place of "Director."

[12] Paragraph not in *Acts of Assembly*.

¹³ *Acts of Assembly* here adds "or such part thereof as belongs to the county of Albemarle or its citizens."

¹⁴ Remainder of this and the following paragraph not in *Acts of Assembly.*

¹⁵ Preceding four words interlined.

¹⁶ Paragraph inserted in Dft above, to left of, and below the text that follows.

¹⁷ *Acts of Assembly* here adds "11. This act shall commence and be in force from and after the passing thereof."

From Anonymous

SIR, [received 19 Nov. 1814]

I have looked to your Library as a source from whence the late national loss might be nearly, perhaps fully, supplied with many valuable works not elswhere to be found; permit me to say therefore, that I shall exceedingly regret to hear that it is, <u>at</u> <u>present</u>, placed any nearer within the reach of those modern vandals, who are the enemies of Literature, the Arts and Sciences.

Will a remark from a stranger on the political affairs of our country at this solemn crisis be displeasing to you? if so, be pleased to close this letter here.

We are at war with a nation, at this time from a combination of circumstances, powerful in the means of anoyance, and hostile to our commercial prosperity and free institutions.

A powerful opposition to this war exists in the bosom of our country; while perhaps, our enemy were never more unanimous in the prosecution of a contest.

Permit me to ask, Sir, would not a manifesto in the name of the American government, or in the name of the American people seting forth in a plain, but expressive and pointed manner the causes which led to this war, and the terms on which our govern^t is willing to terminate it, have a Salutary effect on the public mind?

Particularly, would not such a manifesto, shewing the terms on which our government is willing to terminate the contest, have a salutary effect, as respects us, on the public mind of G. Britain.—

Our gover^t is a govern^t resting on public opinion. This public opinion must therefore be enlightened and informed not outraged or abused, not flattered or deceived.

You can be no stranger to the continual efforts made to mislead and deceive the public mind; nor can you wonder at the success with which these efforts are attended.

For myself I am well perswaded Sir, that the most beneficial effects would result from a well-executed manifesto upon the plan I have suggested.

All that would be required could be comprized in an Octv° of plain print, not to exceed 200 pages.

Its language should be forcible, commanding, expressive and pointed. It should State facts of importance only, and support them by referance to, or quotations from authentic documents.

Its subject should be the wrongs we have sustained from G. Britain; their hostile bearing upon our commercial prosperity and upon our sovereignty; and the many fruitless efforts we have made to obtain redress.

A work upon the plan I have suggested, should be published by the Nat^l Gov^t; not less than 20. or 30 thousand Copies, and distributed over the United States, and particularly in those states where the public opinion is adverse to the administration.

I address you Sir, only with the view of calling your attention to, and procuring your support of measures essential to the public good. My name could add no weight to the correctness of my reasoning, therefore it is not subscribed.—

RC (DLC: TJ Papers, 202:36051–2); undated; at head of text: "To Thomas Jefferson, late President of the United States"; endorsed by TJ as an "Anon. Political" letter received 19 Nov. 1814 and so recorded in SJL.

To David Higginbotham

Saturday. Nov. 19. 14.

Th:J. will be obliged to mr Higginbotham for the loan of 30.D. in as small bills as convenient, especially Dollar bills if he has them, and some small silver, which shall be soon replaced.   also a bushel of salt by the bearer.

if mr & mrs Higginbotham can take a neighborly dinner with us tomorrow we shall be glad, as at all times to see them.

RC (ViCMRL); written on a small scrap; dateline at foot of text; addressed: "Mr Higgenbotham"; endorsed by Higginbotham. Not recorded in SJL.

TJ repaid the LOAN "About the 15th" of Dec. 1814, when he "gave D. Higginbotham an ord. on Gibson & Jeff. for 50.D. to cover the 30.D. ante Nov. 18.,"

asking Higginbotham at the same time to "let Carden have a bushel of salt out of it, which I am to charge to Carden, the balance on acct." (*MB*, 2:1305).

SJL records missing letters from Higginbotham to TJ of 9 Dec. 1814 and 1 Jan. 1815 as received 9 Dec. 1814 and 5 Jan. 1815, respectively, with the latter having been sent from Milton.

From Philip Thornton

Dᴿ Sɪʀ   Richmond, November 19ᵗʰ 1814

I have made a contract for all the lead at the mines, and all that they can make, so that I shall have the exclusive buisness of making shot, I am willing to close the contract you propose, to give you one hundred and fifty dollars per year for a lease on the Natural Ridge and the tract of land appertaining thereto for seven years if the lease is not renewed the Improvements to be paid for by the proprietor at Valuation,   Yours Respectfˡʸ   Pʜɪʟɪᴘ Tʜᴏʀɴᴛᴏɴ

NB An answer is requird by the return post as I shall leave town.

P.T.

RC (MHi); endorsed by TJ as received 3 Dec. 1814 and so recorded in SJL.

Philip Thornton (1788–1853), physician, received training at the Pennsylvania Hospital, 1806–08, and then returned to his native Virginia to set up a medical practice. He lived in Richmond until 1819 and on an estate thereafter in the portion of Culpeper County that became Rappahannock County. Thornton successively represented Culpeper and Rappahannock counties in the Virginia House of Delegates, 1832–33, and 1833–35. He left personal property valued at $15,100, including thirty-seven slaves (Caspar Wistar to TJ, 28 Nov. 1808 [DLC]; J. Forsyth Meigs, *A History of the First Quarter of the Second Century of the Pennsylvania Hospital* [1877], 96; "Autobiography of Mrs. Caroline Homassel Thornton [1795–1875]," *MACH* 6 [1945/46]: 22, 36–7, 39–40; *The Richmond Directory, Register and Almanac for the Year 1819* [Richmond, 1819], 71; DNA: RG 29, CS,

Culpeper Co., 1820; Leonard, *General Assembly*, 363, 369, 373; Rappahannock Co. Will Book, C:342–3, 362–3; Washington *Daily National Intelligencer*, 5 Mar. 1853; gravestone inscription in Fairview Cemetery, Culpeper).

During a visit by Thornton to Monticello late in October 1814, TJ almost certainly discussed the terms of ᴛʜᴇ ᴄᴏɴᴛʀᴀᴄᴛ with which he soon leased his land at Natural Bridge for use in manufacturing shot (Agreement to Lease Natural Bridge to Philip Thornton, 2 Dec. 1814). In a letter written from Monticello on 30 Oct., Ellen W. Randolph (Coolidge) reported to her sister Virginia J. Randolph (Trist) that "Doctor Philip Thornton called on us the other day on his way to Wythe County, he says that Papa [Thomas Mann Randolph] is talked of for the next Governor, and it is generally thought that if he will accept of the office, he will certainly be elected" (NcU: NPT).

To Patrick Gibson

Dᴇᴀʀ Sɪʀ   Monticello Nov. 21. 14.

I inclose you a note of mr John Harvie for 176.90 which has been due since the 1ˢᵗ of March & had escaped my notice. he informed me Dʳ Brokenborough was his agent in this state and would pay these notes as they should become due. will you be so good as to make the application? another will be due in about 3. months.   I must ask the favor of you to send me 75.D. in single Dollar bills by my grandson the bearer of this, and who will stay but a few hours in Richmond. few of these have reached us yet and[1] we are totally without change[2] as since the stoppage of issues of[3] cash by the banks, nobody will give silver in change. I must also request you to send me by Johnson's boat a bale of about 300.℔ of cotton. we use about 3 such bales a year here and 2 in Bedford, which last however we get at Lynchbg where it is generally[4] as cheap as in Richmond. Capt Miller of Norfolk informs me he has sent a cask for me to your address; which also I would wish to be trusted to Johnson only.[5]   I have directed my tob° in Bedf^d to be prized but not sent away till further order, being much at a loss what to do with it. of peace there is no prospect till another campaign. but if it be true that the neutral vessels have been discharged at Halifax, it would seem that the <u>neutrals are respected by England</u> and that a neutral demand may arise. I shall be glad of your advices from time to time. Your's with great respect & esteem   Th:J

Dft (NHi: Thomas Jefferson Papers); on verso of reused address cover of Edward Coles to TJ, 26 Sept. 1814; at foot of text: "Mr Gibson"; endorsed by TJ. Enclosure not found.

TJ's GRANDSON Thomas Jefferson Randolph was the BEARER. American newspapers began reporting late in October 1814 that in HALIFAX "an order had been received . . . permitting the neutral vessels which have been sent in there and not adjudicated, to sail for their original ports of destination in the United States, not known to them to be blockaded at the time they commenced their voyages, and

to return with cargoes" (Boston *New-England Palladium*, 28 Oct. 1814). This announcement was soon determined to be unfounded (Providence *Rhode-Island American, and General Advertiser*, 15 Nov. 1814).

[1] Preceding eight words interlined, with the first word reworked from "none."
[2] TJ here canceled "in this neighborhood."
[3] Preceding two words interlined in place of "paying."
[4] Preceding four words interlined.
[5] Sentence interlined.

From William Caruthers

D^R SIR   Lexington 22nd Novr 1814
    haveing Just Got home from the Tour I Was on to the North, when I had the Pleasure of Seeing you at Monticello,[1] When you Was So Good as to Grant me the Previledge of using the Natural Bridge in this county for makeing Shot. In conformity to your recommendation, I called to See Doc^t Bruff in the City, also a M^r

Williamson in Boltimore Both their inventions I think Display[2] Great ingenuity But I doubt in practice they Will not be found to Succeed Well, especially for Small Shot M[r] Williamsons[3] I think a preferable plan to the Doctors

Therefore if you Will please to Send me Such Authority as Will Secure to me the use of the Bridge for Such time as you may Judge Right (make it Ten years if you please, as I Shall have to be at Some considerable expence in fixing, in Which I Shall be carefull as you Observed Not to injure the Natural curiosity) (indeed I think it May add to its Beauty)—If it is found Necessary to enclose[4] a funnel (as I incline to think it Will from the Best information I could collect) it Shall be a light frame planked & painted White Without Breaking the Rock at all or in any Way injuring the Appearance of the Bridge as a Natural Curiossity Which I think ought[5] to be particularly Attended to.

While on to the North I procured Such of the materials for the Machenery, & Arsncik, as could Not be procured here & Wish to proceed to make the fix for commencing[6] Soon as I hear from you and hope to be ready to make in time for the Spring demand   I am Verry Respectfully Y[r] Ob[t] Hu[l] Ser[t]   W[M] CARUTHERS

NB If you think it Necessary I Will Wait On You at Monticello, but if Not Would be Glad to close the Business in this Way—Any restrictions[7] you think proper to make either as to the erection of the Works Or use of timber if you Will Signify them by letter I Will be Bound by them

RC (DLC); between dateline and salutation: "Honb[l] Thomas Jefferson"; with postscript written perpendicularly along the left margin; endorsed by TJ as received 3 Dec. 1814 and so recorded in SJL.

In 1813 Thomas BRUFF, of Washington, D.C., and Peregrine WILLIAMSON, of Baltimore, each patented improvements in the manufacture of shot and bullets (*List of Patents*, 125, 126). Arsenic (AR-SNCIK) was used to harden lead and make balls of shot more spherical (John Percy, *The Metallurgy of Lead* [1870], 71).

[1] Manuscript: "Montcello."
[2] Manuscript: "Dispay."
[3] Manuscript: "Williansons."
[4] Manuscript: "encolse."
[5] Manuscript: "ough."
[6] Manuscript: "commening."
[7] Manuscript: "restrictictions."

From Edward Coles

Wednesday 12 oclock Nov. 23ᵈ '14

Edward Coles is desired by the President to send Mʳ Jefferson the enclosed papers; and to inform him of the sudden death of the Vice President, who expired after a few moments illness, with a kind of paralytick fit, about one hour since

RC (DLC); dateline at foot of text; endorsed by TJ as received 26 Nov. 1814 from Washington and so recorded in SJL. Enclosures not found.

VICE PRESIDENT Elbridge Gerry died within twenty minutes after suffering a hemorrhage of the lungs on his way to the United States Senate on the morning of 23 Nov. 1814 (*DAB*).

From William Duane

RESPECTED SIR,   Philᵃ 23ᵈ Novr 1814

I enclose you one of 12 copies of another of my humble efforts to give <u>direction to the minds</u> of <u>Congress</u> towards their danger and their Salvation.

It behoves every man to employ his whole influence and mind to stimulate Congress in time to provide against the Spring A <u>mighty effort</u> can be accomplished if the members of Congress can but be brought to perceive the danger; and the war may be terminated before the middle of July by the utter expulsion of the enemy from Canada; any thing short of that will be doing nothing or worse. Driven out of that our whole disposable force would be adequate to meet the Enemy at any point on the Seaboard. And the regular force might be if necessary reduced to one half.

With the greatest respect & Esteem Your friend   Wᴹ DUANE

RC (DLC); endorsed by TJ as received 3 Dec. 1814 and so recorded in SJL. Enclosure not found.

From Francis Eppes

DEAR GRANDPAPA   Millbrook Nov 23ᵈ 1814

I wish to see you very much. I have not been able to go to School this Session. I cannot Come to Monticello Christmas for I expect my Father Home. give my love to Aunt Randolph and all of my[1] Cousins. belive me to be Your most Affectionate Grandson

FRANCIS EPPES

RC (ViU: TJP-ER); addressed: "Mr Thomas Jefferson Monticello by Martin"; endorsed by TJ as received 25 Nov. 1814 and so recorded in SJL.

On 26 Oct. 1814 Eppes's FATHER, John Wayles Eppes, wrote his son from Washington, D.C., that he planned to come home for "five or six days" during the Christmas holidays (NcD: John Wayles Eppes Papers).

[1] Reworked from "the."

From Patrick Gibson

SIR   Richmond 23ᵈ Novemʳ 1814

Mʳ Randolph deliver'd me your favor of the 21ˢᵗ inclosing Mʳ John Harvie's note for $176.90, his agent Doctor Brockenbrough is not at present in town, I shall apply to him on his return when I have no doubt it will be paid In consequence of his absence and the great demand here for small notes I have only been able to pick up $45 in 1 & 2$ notes which you will receive inclosed—I shall send the Cotton as desired by Johnson as well as the Cask from Norfolk which was received a few days ago The neutral vessels sent into Halifax have been discharged, that is allowed to proceed to the West Indies or elsewhere, but not to enter any of our ports—I have no expectation that neutrals will be respected by England under the existing state of affairs in Europe, and do not calculate upon an encreased demand for our produce from that cause—another circumstance however has given a stir to our Tobᵒ market the prices in England have risen to such a pitch say 4/6 & 5/. that considerable shipments are now making to profit by the first favorable opportunity to run out, to some port in France, or indeed the first they can make on the Continent should these prove successful we may calculate upon obtaining good prices for Tobᵒ the risk however of getting out is so great that I should prefer seizing the present opportunity and therefore regret yours is not here, as, if fine, it would sell wel[l]

With great regard & respect I am
Your obᵗ Servᵗ   PATRICK GIBSON

RC (MHi); edge frayed; between dateline and salutation: "Thomas Jefferson Esqʳᵉ"; endorsed by TJ as received 25 Nov. 1814 and so recorded in SJL.

To Francis W. Gilmer

DEAR SIR   Monticello Nov. 23. 14.

Your favor of Nov. 13. from Washington was brought by our last mail. that said to have been written before is not recieved. I now inclose you a letter to Dr Wistar. after your feast of science in Philadelphia I am happy to learn we shall still have attractions worthy of drawing & retaining you here, permanently as it is hoped. the position is a good one, whatever line of life you propose to pursue. you will enter on it with the high prospects which worth, talent, and science present, and public opinion hails. there would be nothing you might not promise yourself, were the state of education with us what we could wish. but the present confidence of our youth in innate knolege, their disinclination to waste time on enquiries into the progress which science has already made, or to avail themselves of the labors of the industrious ages preceding them, leave you without rivals on the theatre of public life. I wish you all you can wish for yourself, convinced you will employ it for the good of our country, and, with thanks for your kind tender of services which I will always ask when occasion offers, I salute you with sincere affection & respect.   TH: JEFFERSON

RC (ViU: TJP); at foot of text: "Francis Gilmer esq." PoC (MHi); endorsed by TJ. Enclosure: TJ to Caspar Wistar, 23 Nov. 1814.

To Robert Patterson

DEAR SIR   Monticello Nov. 23. 14.

I have heretofore confided to you my wishes to retire from the chair of the Philosophical society, which however under the influence of your recommendations I have hitherto deferred. I have never however ceased from the purpose; and from every thing I can observe or learn at this distance, I suppose that a new choice can now be made with as much harmony as may be expected at any future time. I send therefore by this mail my resignation, with such entreaties to be omitted at the ensuing election as I must hope will be yielded to: for in truth I cannot be easy in holding as a sinecure an honor so justly due to the talents and services of others. I pray your friendly assistance in assuring the society of the sentiments of affectionate respect & gratitude with which I retire from the high and honorable relation in which I have stood with them, & that you will believe me to be ever and affectionately your's   TH: JEFFERSON

RC (ViU: TJP); at foot of text: "Dʳ Robert Patterson." PoC (DLC).   PHILOSOPHICAL SOCIETY: American Philosophical Society.

To Robert M. Patterson

SIR   Monticello Nov. 23. 14.

I sollicited on a former occasion permission from the American Philosophical society to retire from the honor of their chair, under a consciousness that distance as well as other circumstances denied me the power of executing the duties of the station, and that those on whom they devolved were best entitled to the honors they confer. it was the pleasure of the society at that time that I should remain in their service, and they have continued since to renew the same marks of their partiality. of these I have been ever duly sensible, and now beg leave to return my thanks for them with humble gratitude. still I have never ceased, nor can I cease to feel that I am holding honors without yielding requital, and justly belonging to others. as the period of election is now therefore[1] approaching, I take the occasion of begging to be withdrawn from the attention of the society at their ensuing choice, and to be permitted now to resign the office of President into their hands, which I hereby do. I shall consider myself sufficiently honored in remaining a private member of their body, and shall ever avail myself with zeal of every occasion which may occur of being useful to them, retaining indelibly a profound sense of their past favors.[2]

I avail myself of the channel thro' which the last notification of the pleasure of the society was conveyed to me, to make this communication; and with the greater satisfaction, as it gratifies me with the occasion of assuring you personally of my high respect for yourself, and of the interest I shall ever take in learning that your worth and talents secure to you the successes they merit.   TH: JEFFERSON

RC (PPAmP: APS Archives); addressed: "Robert M. Patterson Secretary of the Am. Phil. society Philadelphia"; franked; postmarked Milton, 24 Nov.; endorsed in an unidentified hand as "offering his resignation of the Presidency of the Society" and stating that TJ was "Informed by the Secʸ that it could not be acted upon before the Anˡ Meeting Janʸ 1815." PoC (DLC). Tr (APS, Minutes, 2 Dec. 1814 [MS in PPAmP]).

TJ had tried in both 1800 and 1808 to RESIGN THE OFFICE OF PRESIDENT of the American Philosophical Society (*PTJ*, 32:298; TJ to the Vice Presidents of the American Philosophical Society [Benjamin Smith Barton, Robert Patterson, and Caspar Wistar], 30 Nov. 1808 [PPAmP: APS Archives]). The most recent NOTIFICATION of his reelection to this post is in Robert M. Patterson to TJ, 7 Jan. 1814.

¹ Word interlined.
² Tr here ends "I avail myself—&c. &c. (Signed) Th. Jefferson."

To Caspar Wistar

DEAR SIR   Monticello. Nov. 23. 14.

I am glad of opportunities of recalling myself to your recollection altho' it should even be when I am to give you some trouble. mr Francis Gilmer a young neighbor of mine; is about to visit Philadelphia, & wishes the honor of being presented to you. altho his being with mr Correa would be a passport for him to every friend of science, I should not fulfil my duties to his deceased father, my friend and neighbor Dʳ Gilmer, nor to his own merit, were I to omit my testimony in his favor. in the vast dearth of scientific education in our state he presents almost the solitary object, known to me as eminent in genius, in science, in industry & excellent dispositions. he is well deserving your notice, and I wish it were in my power to present to you more such specimens and to say they were fair ones of the youth of our state. Truth however obliges me to say we have nothing better, and little as good.

I forward, by this mail, my resignation of the chair of the A. P. Society. I have long been conscious it was the right of others, and been kept in it by a respect for the will of the society, and a desire to give time for their opinions to ripen & concur in the just choice of a successor. I hope that period is now at maturity, and that there will be little difficulty in concentrating their choice; and I ask your friendly aid in satisfying the society of the sentiments of affectionate respect & gratitude with which I resign the high & honorable relation with them in which it has been their pleasure so long to continue me.

Be so good as to present me affectionately to M. Correa, to whom I shall take other occasions of writing, and be assured yourself of my constant friendship & respect.   TH: JEFFERSON

PoC (DLC); at foot of text: "Doctʳ Wistar." Enclosed in TJ to Francis W. Gilmer, 23 Nov. 1814.

A. P. SOCIETY: American Philosophical Society.

To James Cutbush

SIR   Monticello Nov. 24. 14.

A long absence from home occasions this late acknolegement of your favor of Oct. 23. the mention of a certificate from me in favor of mr Hall's method of making corn hills or tob° hills excites my curiosity. I remember his calling on me at Washington, with recommendations of his method from some gentlemen of character in Maryland, & particularly of mr Carrol of Carrolton in whose service he had been. I think too he explained to me his process, not to be by raising the hills, but by depressing[1] the intervals by a roller. but I never saw his machine, nor it's work. I do not recollect giving him any certificate, yet this is no proof I did not, for my memory is not to be trusted. I ask myself on what could I give a certificate? of the performance of the machine? I never saw it. of my opinion of it? I am so poor a judge in questions of agriculture that I could scarcely offer that. I have been always scrupulous in my certificates, stating their matter all in my own handwriting, & not subscribing to what others had written. if you can furnish me the purport of the one I am supposed to have given mr Hall, I shall be gratified.

I am sorry for mr Sloane's misfortunes. he got out of temper with his old friends because they would not let him move the capitol to Philadelphia, and joined himself to those to whom he had always been opposed. this I presume produced the loss of his seat in Congress. since that I had never heard any thing of him till the reciept of your letter. altho I disapproved of his change of sides I always wished him personally well.   be pleased to accept the assurance of my great esteem and respect   TH: JEFFERSON

PoC (DLC); at foot of text: "Dr Cutbush"; endorsed by TJ.

James Hall visited TJ AT WASHINGTON in March 1807 (Hall to TJ, 23 Mar., 11 Dec. 1807 [DLC]).

Early in February 1808 New Jersey congressman James Sloan proposed moving the United States CAPITOL from Washington to Philadelphia. The latter, he contended, was more conducive to good health, more centrally located with respect to population, and easier to defend against its enemies. In addition, unlike the current capital, Philadelphia was "surrounded with a rich country, thick settled with industrious free citizens,"

and it did not require the construction of costly public residences, offices, and other facilities, the building of which encouraged fraud and made the executive branch of government too powerful (Sloan, *Reasons Offered to the Consideration of the Citizens of the United States, In Favor of the Removal of the Seat of Government, from Washington City, to Philadelphia* [n.p., 1808]). Sloan, who changed SIDES in 1808 by supporting George Clinton rather than James Madison for president, did not stand for reelection that year (New Haven *Connecticut Herald*, 3 May 1808; *Biog. Dir. Cong.*).

[1] Reworked from "compressing."

To William Duane

Monticello Nov. 24. 14.

On reciept of your letter of Aug. 11. informing me you could not undertake the publication of the work of Tracy, I considered it a duty to get it effected by some other. I applied to mr Ritchie, and while he had the proposition under consideration I happened to see mr Milligan of George town & asked his opinion (for my own information) as to the allowance which mr Ritchie might afford to make for the translation, if done to his hand: he judged that 50. copies for an impression of 500. and in proportion for a larger, & for every subsequent impression would be a fair allowance. mr Ritchie in the end answered that he could not undertake the work earlier than the spring. I then proposed it to mr Milligan, who answers me that he will undertake it immediately and 'if he can dispose of 500. copies he will allow 50. copies in boards for translation; if he can dispose of 1000 copies, he will allow 100. but suppose it may sell 750, in that case 75. copies for the translation.' these are the words of his letter. I must now therefore ask the favor of you to return me the original French manuscript; and either to send on the translation with it, if you approve of mr Millegan's proposition, or dispose of it as you think best. I think it a duty to Tracy, and indeed to the public to get it published & without delay.

We are laboring as in the former war for men & money. men I am in hopes the present Congress will find means of providing: but I do not like their course of finance. expedients & projects will not carry us through; and I dread a tax of 21. million on a people who cannot get half a dollar a bushel for their wheat, & pay 12.D. a bushel for salt. the taxgatherer too will be in the height of his collection while the election of a new President will be going on. however if we hold together nothing can hurt us. I salute you with constant esteem & respect TH: JEFFERSON

PoC (DLC); at foot of text: "General Duane."

On 19 Aug. 1814 TJ asked Thomas Ritchie to UNDERTAKE THE PUBLICA-TION of a translation of the as-yet-unpublished fourth volume of Destutt de Tracy's *Élémens d'Idéologie* (see TJ to Ritchie, 27 Sept. 1814). The FORMER WAR was the Revolutionary War.

To Joseph Milligan

DEAR SIR   Monticello Nov. 24. 14.

Your favor of the 16th was recieved on the 19th and I thank you for the trouble you have taken with my catalogue, and I have no doubt your enumeration is right, mine having been estimated by counting a few pages & taking them for an average. I am contented also with your estimate of price, if the committee should be so, or that they should send on valuers, fixing on your estimate as a maximum.

I write by this mail to Genl Duane for Tracy's work

The box of books arrived two days ago in good order, and I am charged with the thanks of all the members of the family to you. Accept the assurance of my esteem & respect   TH: JEFFERSON

PoC (DLC); at foot of text: "Mr Millegan"; endorsed by TJ.

From Horatio G. Spafford

RESPECTED FRIEND—   Washington City, 11 Mo. 25, 1814.

At length I have arrived in this city, exhausted with fatigue, having been travelling near 5 weeks. It is about 6 weeks since I crossed the St. Lawrence, on my return from Upper Canada, & I only rested one week at Albany. Under these circumstances, I regret to learn that it [is]¹ much further than I had supposed, to Monticello. The winter is also approaching, & I feel in haste to return to the north. My wife writes me that on the 19th, it Snowed hard all day at Albany; & on the 20th was very cold. Still, could I know of thy being at home, & willing to spare some time for me, I could hardly persuade myself to return without seeing thee. Should it be so, please inform me, & to direct the best route & method of going to Monticello. My good friend the Vice President, is much missed by me. I have just returned from the Presidents'—he is unwell, confined to his room. I saw him, however, & he recieved me with kindness. I should like to belong to the number of his friends in this city, & the scanty number of those who cherish the interests of the country, with a good, hearty, old fashioned zeal. And I have the vanity to suppose I could do considerable toward promoting its cause. On this subject, I want to converse freely with thee. Pray have the goodness to let me hear from thee, as soon as may be practicable; & accept the assurances of my high esteem.

HORATIO GATES SPAFFORD.

RC (MHi); at foot of text: "Thomas Jefferson, Esq."; endorsed by TJ as received 3 Dec. 1814 and so recorded in SJL.

VICE PRESIDENT Elbridge Gerry had passed away two days earlier.

[1] Omitted word editorially supplied.

To William Short

DEAR SIR   Monticello Nov. 28. 14.

Yours of Oct. 28. came to hand on the 15th inst. only. the settlement of your boundary with Col° Monroe is protracted by circumstances which seem foreign to it. one would hardly have expected that the hostile expedition to Washington could have had any connection with an operation 100. miles distant. yet, preventing his attendance, nothing could be done. I am satisfied there is no unwillingness on his part, but on the contrary a desire to have it settled; and therefore, if he should think it indispensable to be present at the investigation, as is possible, the very first time he comes here, I will press him to give a day to the decision, without regarding mr Carter's absence. such an occasion must certainly offer soon after the 4th of March, when Congress rises of necessity, and be assured I will not lose one possible moment in effecting it.

Altho' withdrawn from all anxious[1] attention to political concerns yet I will state my impressions as to the present war, because your letter leads to the subject. the essential grounds of the war were 1. the orders of council, & 2. the impressment of our citizens; (for I put out of sight, from the love of peace, the multiplied insults on our government, and aggressions on our commerce, with which our pouch, like the Indian's, had long been filled to the mouth) what immediately produced the Declaration was 1. the Proclamation of the prince regent that he would never repeal the orders of council as to us until Bonaparte should have revoked his Decrees as to all other nations as well as ours; and 2. the declaration of his minister to ours that no arrangement whatever could be devised, admissible in lieu of impressment. it was certainly a misfortune that they did not know themselves at the date of this silly and insolent proclamation, that within one month they would repeal the Orders, and that we, at the Date of our Declaration, could not know of the repeal which was then going on, 1000 leagues distant. their determinations, as declared by themselves, could alone guide us, and they shut the door on all further negociation, throwing down to us the gauntlet of war or submission as the only alternatives. we cannot blame the government for chusing that of war, because certainly the great majority of the nation thought it ought to be chosen. not that they were to gain by it in Dollars and cents: all men know that War is a losing game to both parties. but they know also that if they do not resist encroachment at some point, all will be taken from them, and that more would then be lost even in Dollars and cents, by submission than by resistance. it is the case of giving a part to save the whole, a limb to save life. it is the melancholy law of human societies to be compelled sometimes to chuse a great evil, in order to ward off a greater; to deter their neighbors from rapine by making it cost them more than honest gains. the enemy are accordingly now disgorging what they had so ravenously swallowed. the orders of council had taken from us near 1000. vessels. our list of captures from them is now at 1300. and, just become sensible that it is small, & not large ships which gall them most, we shall probably add 1000 prizes a year to their past losses.   again, supposing that, according to the confession of their own minister in parliament, the Americans they had impressed were something short of 2000. the war against us alone cannot cost them less than 20. millions of Dollars a year, so that each American impressed has already cost them 10,000 D. and every year will add 5000.D. more to his price. we, I suppose, expend more; but had we adopted the other alternative of submission no mortal can tell what the cost would have been. I consider the war then as entirely justifiable on our part, altho' I am still sensible it is a deplorable misfortune to us. it has arrested the course of the most remarkable tide of prosperity any nation ever experienced, and has closed such prospects of future improvement as were never before in the view of any people. farewell all hope of extinguishing public debt! farewell all visions of applying surpluses of revenue to the improvements of peace rather than the ravages of war. our enemy has indeed the consolation of Satan on removing our first parents from Paradise; from a peaceable and agricultural nation he[2] makes us a military & manufacturing one. we shall indeed survive the conflict. breeders enough will remain to carry on population. we shall retain our country, and rapid advances in the art of war will soon enable us to beat our enemy, & probably drive him from the continent. we have men enough, and I am in hopes the present session of Congress will provide the means of commanding their services. but I wish I could see them get into a better train of finance. their banking projects are like dosing dropsy with more water. if any thing could revolt our citizens against the war it would be the extravagance with which they are about to be taxed. it is strange indeed that at this day, and in a country where English proceedings are so familiar, the principles and advantages of funding, should be neglected, and expedients resorted to. their new bank, if not abortive at it's birth, will not last thro' one campaign; and the taxes proposed cannot be paid. how can a people who cannot get 50. cents a bushel for their wheat, while they pay 12.D. a bushel for their salt, pay five times the amount of taxes they ever paid before? yet that will be the case in all the states South of the Patomac. our resources are competent to the maintenance of the war if duly economised & skilfully employed in the way of anticipation.—however, we must suffer, I suppose, from our ignorance in funding, as we did from that of fighting, until necessity teaches us both; and fortunately our stamina are so vigorous as to rise superior to great mismanagement. this year I think we shall have learnt how to call forth our force, and by the next I hope our funds: and even if the state of Europe should not by that time give the enemy[3] employment enough nearer home, we shall leave him nothing to fight for here.—These are my views of the war. they embrace a great deal of sufferance, trying privations, and no benefit but that of teaching our enemy that he is never to gain by wanton injuries on us. to me this state of things brings a sacrifice of all tranquility & comfort through the residue of life. for altho' the debility of age disables me from the services & the sufferings of the field, yet, by the total annihilation in value of the produce which was to give me subsistence and independance, I shall be like Tantalus, up to the shoulders in water, yet dying with thirst. we can make indeed enough to eat drink & clothe ourselves; but nothing for our salt, iron, groceries, & taxes, which must be paid in money. for what can we raise for market? wheat? we can only give it to our horses, as we have been doing ever since harvest. tobacco? it is not worth the pipe it is smoked in. some say Whiskey; but all mankind must become drunkards to consume it. but altho' we feel, we shall not flinch. we must consider now, as in the revolutionary war, that altho' the evils of resistance are great, those of submission would be greater. we must meet therefore the former as the casualties of tempests and earthquakes, & like them[4] necessarily resulting from the constitution of the world.—your situation, my dear friend, is much better. for altho' I do not know with certainty the nature of your investments, yet I presume they are not in banks, insurance companies, or any other of those gossamer castles. if in ground-rents, they are solid: if in stock of the US. they are equally so. I once thought that in the event of war we should be obliged to suspend paying the interest of the public debt. but a dozen years more of experience and observation on our people and government have satisfied me it will never be done. the sense of the necessity of public credit is so universal & so deeply rooted, that no other necessity will prevail against it. and I am glad to see that while the former 8. millions are stedfastly applied to the sinking of the old debt, the Senate have lately insisted on a sinking fund for the new. this is the dawn of that improvement in the management of our finances which I look to for salvation; and I trust that the light will continue to advance & point out their way to our legislators. they will soon see that instead of taxes for the whole years expences, which the people cannot pay, a tax to the amount of the interest & a reasonable portion of the principal will command the whole sum, and throw a part of the burthens of war on times of peace and prosperity. a sacred payment of interest is the only way to make the most of their resources, and a sense of that renders your income from our funds more certain than mine from lands. some apprehend danger from the defection of Massachusets. it is a disagreeable circumstance, but not a dangerous one. if they become neutral, we are sufficient for our enemy without them. and in fact we get no aid from them now. if their administration determines to join the enemy, their force will be annihilated by equality of division among themselves. their federalists will then call in the English army, the republicans ours, and it will only be a transfer of the scene of war from Canada to Massachusets; and we can get ten men to go to Massachusets for one who will go to Canada. every one too must know that we can at any moment make peace with England at the expence of the navigation and fisheries of Massachusets. but it will not come to this. their own people will put down these factionists as soon as they see the real object of their opposition. and of this Vermont, N. Hampshire & even Connecticut itself furnish proofs.

You intimate a possibility of your return to France, now that Bonaparte is put down. I do not wonder at it. France, freed from that monster, must again become the most agreeable country on earth. it would be the 2^d choice of all whose ties of family & fortune give a preference to some other one, and the 1st of all not under those ties. yet I doubt if the tranquility of France is entirely settled. if her Pretorian bands are not furnished with employment on her external enemies, I fear they will recall the old, or set up some new Caesar.—God bless you and preserve you in bodily health. tranquility of mind depends much on ourselves, and greatly on due reflection 'how much pain have cost us the evils which have never happened.' affectionately Adieu. TH: JEFFERSON

RC (DLC: Short Papers); edge torn and trimmed, with missing text supplied from PoC; at foot of first page: "W. Short esquire"; endorsed by Short as received 5 Dec. 1814. PoC (DLC).

For the PROCLAMATION by the prince regent (later George IV) and the DECLARATION by Lord Castlereagh, see note to TJ to Madame de Staël Holstein, 28 May 1813. The United States Senate's insistence that a permanent SINKING FUND, "gradually to reduce and eventually to extinguish the public debt, contracted and to be contracted during the present war . . . be established during the present session of Congress" ultimately made its way into the 15 Nov. 1814 "Act to authorize a loan for a sum not exceeding

three millions of dollars" (*JS*, 5:551; *U.S. Statutes at Large*, 3:144–5). CONNECTICUT declined to issue the first call for a convention in Hartford, while New Hampshire and Vermont refused to send official delegations to the gathering (Banner, *Hartford Convention*, 328–9). The aphorism HOW MUCH PAIN HAVE COST US THE EVILS WHICH HAVE NEVER HAPPENED appears in TJ's "canons of conduct," which he sent to friends and family at various times (enclosure to TJ to Charles Clay, 12 July 1817; TJ to Thomas Jefferson Smith, 21 Feb. 1825).

[1] TJ here canceled "concern."
[2] Reworked from "she."
[3] Reworked from "give them."
[4] Preceding two words interlined.

From Jason Chamberlain

HONᴰ SIR,   Burlington, Vermont, Nov. 30, 1814,

I feel myself highly flattered by the notice you were pleased to take of my Oration, in your letter of July last. Your speculations, on the study of the Classicks, meet my own views on that subject; and the method, you recommend, is exactly the one I adopted. I have seen many an ingenious young man, after a course of Classical reading in the manner you propose, become well versed in most of the studies, taught by the other Professors.

Inter arma, Musæ silent. Our College Edifice is leased to the Government, for the accomodation of the Army; and our Collegiate exercises are suspended. Meanwhile, I have resorted to the practice of the Law, in order to obtain a reputable support. There are other situations, here, which would be more congenial to my feelings, but would not afford a good living. I receive a handsome income from my practice, and cheerfully submit to my destiny. Though anxious to obtain general information, and to visit other countries, I shall probably spend my days in this place.

We all of us turned out in Sept. last, to expel the Invader from our shores, and the result must be grateful to the feelings of every friend of his country. The aged forgot their decripitude, and vied with the young, in repairing to the scene of action, and in the active contest. All ranks and all ages took their rifles, and with no other uniform, than a sprig of Ever green from their native mountains, sought the enemy, and fought with enthusiasm. The days of the wildest chivalry, furnish not a scene, in which so much ardour and spirit pervaded every class of people. The Lake was alive with our hardy Mountaineers, whom the oars and winds could not propel with the speed of their wishes.

With sentiments of great respect, I am your most obedient,

JASON CHAMBERLAIN.

RC (MHi); addressed: "The Hon. Thomas Jefferson, Late President of the United States. Monticello, Virginia"; franked; endorsed by TJ as received 16 Dec. 1814 from Jason "Chamberlayne" and so recorded in SJL.

INTER ARMA, MUSÆ SILENT ("During wartime, the muses are silent") is a variant of Cicero's famous phrase "silent enim leges inter arma" ("When arms speak, the laws are silent") (Cicero, *Pro T. Annio*

Milone, 4.11, in *Cicero: Pro Milone . . . Pro Rege Deiotaro*, trans. Nevile H. Watts, Loeb Classical Library [1931; rev. ed. 1953], 16–7). OUR COLLEGE: the University of Vermont. Late in the summer of 1814 roughly 2,500 Vermont militia crossed to the western shore of LAKE Champlain and joined in the successful defense of Plattsburgh, New York, against a British force under the command of Sir George Prevost (Malcomson, *Historical Dictionary*, 442–5).

From James Monroe

DEAR SIR   Washington nov[r] 30. 1814

Despatches are rec[d] from our ministers as late of[1] the 31. ult[o], at which time the negotiation was depending. On paper, serious difficulties seem to be remov'd, and few only to remain, the principal one of which is however important. Impressment is laid aside, for the reason urgd in the instructions to our ministers, which is strengthend, by being us'd as an argument on the part of the British ministers. The Indian boundary is given up by them, with the claim to the exclusive command of the lakes, & occupancy of our Shore, for military purposes. A stipulation of peace for the tribes fighting on their side, to be reciprocal is all that is desird, on that point[2] & to that our ministers have assented. In this stage, the uti possidetis was proposed, as the basis, of the treaty relating to limits, & was suggested by intelligence that British troops had taken possession of certain parts of M[ain]e, which was rejected by our gent[n]. Thus it appears that the principal obstacle to accomodation, is the desire of the British gov[t] to hold a part of massachussetts, to retain which the war goes on. our gentl[n] think that if this difficulty was settled[3] another would arise, believing that they are gaining time only, to see the result of negotiations at Vienna, which is very uncertain, but more likely to preserve peace, than produce war[.] The communication will go to Congress to day but presuming that it will not be in time for the mail—I indeavour to give you an idea of the contents—

with great respect your friend & servant   JAˢ MONROE

RC (DLC); torn at fold and edge trimmed, with missing text supplied from Stanislaus Murray Hamilton, ed., *The Writings of James Monroe* (1898–1903), 5:300–1; endorsed by TJ as received 7 Dec. 1814 and so recorded in SJL.

For the DESPATCHES from the United States diplomats at Ghent, see *ASP, Foreign Relations*, 3:710–26. On 25 June 1814 Monroe issued INSTRUCTIONS allowing the American negotiators to set aside the question of impressment: "The United States having resisted by war the practice of impressment, and continued the war until that practice had ceased by a peace in Europe, their object has been essentially obtained for the present." The BRITISH MINISTERS agreed to omit the subject from the treaty ending the War of 1812 on the same practical grounds (*ASP, Foreign Relations*, 3:704, 725). THE LAKES: the Great Lakes.

The legal principle of UTI POSSIDETIS required that the borders of newly independent states be established (or, in the case of the current conflict, reestablished) in accordance with the old administrative boundaries (*Black's Law Dictionary*). At the Congress of VIENNA, September 1814–June 1815, representatives from the various European nations redrew boundaries, settled outstanding differences, and promoted international stability in the wake of the Revolutionary and Napoleonic wars (Connelly, *Napoleonic France*, 486–8). The recently received diplomatic correspondence was submitted to CONGRESS on 1 Dec. 1814, not the date of this letter (*JHR*, 9:559).

[1] Thus in manuscript.
[2] Previous three words interlined.
[3] Manuscript: "setlted."

From James Ogilvie

MY DEAR SIR,   Richmond Novʳ—

The young gentleman, Mʳ Colin Clark, who will present this letter was formerly a pupil of mine; his academical proficiency & good conduct, gave him a solid claim to my confidence & affection: of the sincerity of these sentiments I afford him an unequivocal evidence, by making him known to you.—

I can scarcely indulge the hope of seeing you again, but assuredly, wherever hereafter, my uncertain & romantic destiny may lead me & whatever may be the vicissitudes of that destiny, I never can retrace the hours I have spent in your society, or the happy days I have passed under your hospitable roof & in the circle[1] of that family of love, with which you are surrounded, without sentiments of the most respectful & affectionate recollection.—

After my arrival in Britain, I will trouble you with a letter occasionally & few circumstances could afford me greater pleasure than to be instrumental in executing any command with which you may honor me, during my residence in London: with kindest & most respectful regards to all around you believe me to be,

my dear Sir yours truly   JAMES OGILVIE

RC (MHi); partially dated; addressed: "Thomas Jefferson Esq' Monticello"; endorsed by TJ as received 4 (reworked from 3) Dec. 1814. Recorded in SJL as an

undated letter received 3 (reworked from 4) Dec. 1814.

[1] Word interlined in place of "bosom."

From John Wilson

SIR,   Washington City November   1814.

It is painful, to know we live in such an age, that the most laudable sentiments which can emanate from the mind of man, if they come not from the highest & as it may be called, disinterested source, lose much of the influence they would otherwise acquire. It is a knowledge of that frailty, which has determined me to lay before you, a sketch, of the doctrine & discipline, which at present prevails, in regard to a very important subject, that of

National Clerks.

I shall endeavor to exhibit, some of the leading consequences of the system, &, to point out the road to reformation; not doubting, that in the course of the discussion, you will sanction the plan in the tenor of your correspondence.

I have been a Clerk in the Accountant's Office W.D. nearly ten years; I have been an attentive witness to the mode & effects of employing & paying the Clks in various Departments & Offices, resulting from the present organization of the rewards & rewarded, the employer & employed. My subject very much concerns the disparity of Clerks' Salaries. Would you believe that I have heard the exclamation from those having a mediocrity of Salary "It is not the amount of Salary I care for, it is the inevitable degradation; & I would rather even get 200 or 300$ less than I do, provided an equalization could be effected, that all should be on an equal footing." Mark, in the narrative, what the term all indicates.

Were I guided altogether by Self interest, I might have contented myself with a private communication to my own employer, of the Sentiments avowed; but wishing for a general & Speedy reformation, I shall not be ashamed to pursue & to support the discussion in a more public manner. It is one of the few blessings resulting from the evils of war, that it teaches us "the greatest knowledge is ourselves to know;" it shews us the dependance on each other and disposes the heart to the cultivation of friendship with all classes. Having premised thus much my motive is first to procure justice to the community of Clerks.

It is a matter of notoriety, that, on an average, the disbursement for living is double what has hitherto been the maximum; from this I am unable any longer to repress such facts & declarations, as may induce the proper authority to provide for inadequate Salaries. If the Records of Salaries are examined, it will be found that they have been augmented in the war, State & navy Departments, in a ratio of equalization & justice, more consonant to the emergency of the times & to the equitable nature of our excellent government, upon which they were, at first, founded. I say at first, because in the infancy of those institutions of the government, (when there were but few gentlemen in an office) Congress considered, that none but discreet, respectable, experienced men of business, should be employed as national Clerks; men possessing the ground work for acquiring the official duties in all their mysterious ramifications. They knew what compensation was adequate to such qualifications, and appropriated a like Sum for each, upon the Same principle, that they now appropriate a like sum, annually, for the Head of an Office which they have created; it makes no odds who succeeds to this office, they give them all alike. Not because a man who just comes into office, knows as much, the nature of official transactions as a nine years incumbent; no, no, but on the presumption that every successor possesses the ground work, & makes up in attention, what his predecessor was worth by practice. By that equalization, the Same respectability was attached to one branch of business & to one clerk, as another; precisely as the Same respectability attaches to the Sucessor as to the predecessor of an office. In those days, so jealous were legislatures of improper partiality, or improper prejudice to any one Clerk; so cautious were they of not interrupting that harmony which the law of equal Salary is calculated to promote, that an appropriation even for extra Services could not be paid to a person <u>already</u> employed. This is now the case with the Clerks to the Sec^y of the Senate & those to the Clerk of the H of Representatives. Congress gives them all the Same Salary which they have generously encreased Since the war from 1000 to 1250$, but <u>they</u> can receive nothing for extra Service; because it is considered, this would interfere or interrupt the regular process of business; whereas an equal Salary would only prevent a man from endeavouring to do too much, by which he must ultimately become unable to do enough. This is a Salutary regulation, inasmuch, as it would banish that most unblushing manoeuvre of lighting up the offices, or writing by candlelight during the session of Congress, just for <u>So long</u> as business is neglected in the day time & the official hours. an admirable method, upon my word, to reward for <u>extra Services</u> & to bestow the <u>surplus</u> as the Clerks term it!

It were to be wished that the Head of every department & office, Stimulated by a noble emulation, would follow the course with Clerks, which was adopted in early times, as well as that which is pursued at present, by Some of the official employers, & by Congress in regard to their Engrossing clerks, of equalizing & increasing the Salaries of those who have not been hitherto favoured. What can be more just at least, than to give the Clerks in the accountant's Office (principally examining Clerks) as much as those in any other Department or Office, & to place them more upon an equal footing? Their duties are without question the most arduous, the most intricate of any under the government. What is more difficult than the investigation, the tracing, retracing, discovering differences, & settlement of such voluminous masses of accounts as they have, with the notations, correspondence; & dissections in those settlements 10 to 20 times over, into the specific appropriations!

How absurd the idea of giving one successor to the same office more than another, yet not more so than the practice of allowing each Clerk, selected & employed on the like business, 20, 10, 5, 3, 2, nay I dare say even 1 dollar more than the other! I say nothing of the disparity with respect to minors; where they are employed in Offices, the distinction in their Salary[1] is proper, until they arrive at maturity.

Nothing herein contained is designed to impair the system of pre-eminent or principal & subordinate Clerks; I would only inculcate, that each denomination should be perfectly coordinate & receive a coequal Salary, distinguishing between <u>principal</u> Clerks & <u>Clerks</u>. This I think the most effectual means to banish every thing <u>inordinate</u>. An equal participation in the <u>Public bounty</u> is the <u>true</u> way to excite that ingenuousness & uniform diligence amongst the Clerks which is necessary to the due performance of the national business.

I come now more particularly to notice that odious distribution of the Salary appropriation which withholds from one coordinate clerk 5 & 600$ more than another; a disparity I will venture to affirm, which, considering the equality of services rendered, no other government has exceeded. Four or 5 grades of Clerks we have, yes, and perhaps 20 gradations in their emoluments, does it comport with the dignity of this government? Does not every one who gets 10$ more than another think himself that much a better Clerk? You might with the same impropriety give to one Capt[n] 200$ more than another Captain, or to one private of the Same Company 50$ more than another.

Only see the analogy, is there more reason for one, than the other distinction? Say, let me ask, is this the way to put all the wheels of office in motion, is this the way that justice is to be done, either to the nation or to the individuals concerned? The beautiful theory of our Republican institutions & the Spirit of our constitution indeed, is but a shadow, if we permit such a custom to usurp the dictates of our understanding. By this, do we not revive the execrable System of Lords & vassals, Patricians & Plebians, with all the trans atlantic distinctions or orders of persons & things which are perfectly assimilated? Is A to languish in obscurity & receive less for his <u>clerical</u> than B for his <u>miscellaneous</u> services, because A brings not with him in office all the advantage of intimate acquaintance with the employer, or a <u>mass</u> of recommendations equal to those of a more fortunate fellow citizen?

I understand the Clerks are called by the Honerable Congressmen, <u>bloodsuckers</u> but let those gentlemen take the pains to consult the Register of Clerks Salaries & they will find, that such a <u>sanguinary</u> epithet does not apply to the majority. Certain it is that some of them do not get <u>as much</u> as they deserve, but it is not certain that any of them get <u>more</u> than they deserve.

The <u>apportionment</u> of Salary, I should suppose, is one of the most unpleasant tasks which falls to the lot of Heads of dep^{ts} or offices. It cannot be agreeable to them, tho' Custom has sanctioned it, to permit such a disparity in the Salaries, when they know, that if they do not encourage a Clerk he must often become a kind of vassal; a being more dependant than the most menial Servants of our Metropolis; who, if they have reason to be dissatisfied can easily find other employers. It is not so with an unfavoured Clerk, he is <u>even</u> deprived of that little gratification. The longer he remains in this situation, the more difficult it is to effect his promotion; for no other person will listen to his application without a recommendation from him by whom he is employed. But what chance, think you has a clerk in such a predicament, of an efficient recommendation, or how will his feelings permit him to ask it?

Necessity induces many to enter an office with a Salary of 5 or 600$ & when once a man perceives no chance of promotion, it must abstract his mind, if he have any merit, if he have any regard for his family, to other views & pursuits. Yet, unfortunately, when his mind is so abstracted, he cannot take a pride in the business of his employer, which is necessary to constitute what we call a good Clerk. Hence the chance of promotion in the line of his employ, is still more distant, & the uncharitable idea, is, if he gets no more, he is worth no more! Should he not succeed in his prospects, it operates as a libel on his capacity, perhaps he becomes a victim to disappointment, or his degradation is sealed forever!

What a picture am I drawing for the public eye, it is one which my pen blushes to present, but it is nevertheless a faithful Representation.

From the proofs I have already received of your disposition I flatter myself that you will feel no hesitation in investigating whatever may be projected for the benefit of the public and the community who are most interested. I therefore beg the favor of your correspondence & the most Strict examination of the subject proposed, herein, in order if I cannot obviate any objections you may suggest that I may abandon the effort.

Yours very respectfully   JNⁿ WILSON

RC (CSmH: JF-BA); partially dated; endorsed by TJ as a letter of Nov. 1814 received 3 Dec. 1814 and so recorded in SJL.

w. d.: the United States War Department. THE GREATEST KNOWLEDGE IS

OURSELVES TO KNOW: "And all our *Knowledge* is, *Ourselves to know*" (Alexander Pope, *An Essay on Man. In Epistles to a Friend. Epistle IV*, line 393 [London, 1734], 18).

[1] Preceding three words interlined.

To Joseph Milligan

1814. Dec. 1. wrote to mr Millegan to procure me
Garnet's Naut. Almanac 15. to be forwarded by mail.
& his dⁿ for subseqᵗ years.
Blount's Naut. Alm. for 1815 & subsequent
Stewart's elements of the Philos. of the human mind. 8ᵛⁿ

FC (DLC); abstract in TJ's hand; on verso of portion of reused address cover to TJ; endorsed by TJ.

TJ was subscribing to John Garnett's (GARNET'S) and Edmund M. Blunt's (BLOUNT'S) nautical almanacs.

William Mitchell's Agreement to Grind Wheat

Lynchburg Decʳ 2ⁿᵈ 1814

I am willing to grind Mʳ Thomas Jefferson,s present[1] Crop of wheat on the following terms VIZ, I will give a Bble of fine flour for every five & half bushells wheat. Or I will give a Bble Superfine flour for every Six bushells wheat or fifty Cents Extra on every Bble Sfine flour which ever Mr Jefferson may perfer

[...]

W^M MITCHELL

🙰 JNO. M^cALLISTER JR

MS (ViU: TJP-ER); in McAllister's hand, with lower left portion of page torn away, presumably to cancel the agreement through the removal of TJ's signature; endorsed by TJ: "Mitchell Wm Lynchbg Dec. 14. 14."

John McAllister, the namesake son of a Revolutionary War veteran, worked for a time as a clerk at the Lynchburg firm of William & Reuben Mitchell. Having served as a private in the Virginia militia during the War of 1812, he was promoted to lieutenant in 1817. McAllister became an attorney and migrated successively to Indiana and Illinois (John Meriwether McAllister and Lura Boulton Tandy, eds., *Genealogies of the Lewis and Kindred Families* [1906], 333; Ruth H. Early, *Campbell Chronicles and Family Sketches Embracing the History of Campbell County, Virginia, 1782–1926* [1927], 280; Campbell Co. Will Book, 4:314–6; Campbell Co. Order Book, 12:194).

[1] Word interlined.

Agreement to Lease Natural Bridge to Philip Thornton

Memorandum of an agreement entered into on the 2^d Day of December 1814. between Thomas Jefferson of Monticello in the county of Albemarle on the one part and Philip Thornton of Richmond in the county of Henrico on the other part.

The sd Thomas agrees to lease to the sd Philip for the term of five years from the date hereof, & does hereby lease accordingly, a site for a manufacture of leaden shot to be placed either on or near to the Natural bridge in the county of Rockbridge (being the property of the sd Thomas) wheresoever on the sd property of the sd Thomas the sd Philip shall chuse, with leave to erect thereon, at the expence of the sd Philip, the buildings and works he shall deem necessary; as also to lease to him for the same term a site for a dwelling house or houses & gardens to be laid off in a square of two acres wheresoever near the sd bridge he shall chuse, with all conveniences & ways of communication between the several buildings, and also a right to the use of the water of the stream over which the bridge is, to erect dams & ponds on the same for the purposes of his manufactory aforesaid, with ways to & from them: reserving out of the same to the sd Thomas & his heirs the yearly rent of one hundred and fifty dollars to be paid to him on the last day of every year of the said five years, with a right of distress for the same on failure of paiment and grants to the sd Philip also the right to cut any timber on his lands necessary for erecting or repairing his buildings, inclosures or works, gratis and a right to cut firewood on the sd lands paying for the same a reasonable price by the cord as shall be agreed by themselves or settled by arbitration.

The sd Philip covenants on his part that he will pay the sd annual rent as reserved to the sd Thomas & his heirs, that he will make no erection or do any other thing which shall disfigure the sd bridge as a natural curiosity; that he will commit no waste or destruction on the said bridge or lands, on pain of an immediate right of reentry by the sd Thomas if the sd waste, destruction or disfiguration be committed on the said bridge, but that he will to the best of his power preserve the sd bridge in it's perfect natural and uninjured form; and that he will keep a fair & just account of the firewood cut and account for the same as before provided.

And to the execution of these articles of agreement both parties hereby bind themselves, their heirs, executors, administrators & assigns respectively, and in testimony of the whole, hereto set their hands & seals on the day and year first abovementioned

Signed, sealed & delivered   TH: JEFFERSON
in presence of   PHILIP THORNTON
TH: J. RANDOLPH

MS (MHi); in TJ's hand, signed by TJ, Thornton, and Randolph; sealed by TJ and Thornton; endorsed by TJ: "Jefferson with Thornton} Mem° of Agreement."

To William Caruthers

SIR   Monticello Dec. 3 14.

Your letter of Nov. 22. came to hand yesterday afternoon only: and I sincerely regret it had not been a single day earlier. a few days after you called on me on your way to the North Dr Thornton came and proposed to lease the Natural bridge for the purpose of establishing a shot manufactory. I told him at once you had applied for it for the same purpose a few days before, & must have a preference. he expressed much concern at the disappointment, being then on his way to the lead mines to contract for lead. I at length agreed if he could find a secondary situation on the bank, I would lease it to him: but that you must have the bridge, if you chose it on your return, as you were not entirely decided when you passed on. I then had occasion for the first time to turn my mind to the principles on which a rent should be fixed, and we agreed that he should pay 150.D. a year for a site. he went on to the mines and contracted for the whole lead which could be furnished there in one year. he called on me again the evening before last, and still pressed for the bridge. I considered that when you went Northwardly you were undecided, that you were to let me know on your return, that you had been back some time, & I had heard nothing from you, and Dr Thornton informed me he had spoken with a person in Richmond who he understood was to have had some concern with you in the enterprise, who told him you had been returned some time, had got no workmen, & that it seemed the speculation would not answer & must be abandoned. he told me also it was his purpose to propose to you a part in the concern, if you chose it. under these circumstances I really supposed the thing abandoned by you, & that I ought not to lose a certain offer. I therefore executed a lease for 5. years to the Doctor, with which he had left me about 6. hours when your letter came to hand.—this, Sir, is an exact statement of what has passed on this occasion, and I sincerely regret that I did not recieve your letter a few hours only sooner; as it was my desire and purpose to have given you a preference to any other applicant whatever. and I shall be gratified if your taking part in a joint concern should be more eligible to you than one in rivalship, and especially after you had been forestalled in the produce of the mines, which of itself excluded every rival.—I hope you will find in these circumstances my excuse for acting on the belief that you had abandoned your views on this object, and that you will accept the assurance of my great esteem and respect.   TH: JEFFERSON

PoC (DLC); at foot of first page: "Mr Carutthers"; endorsed by TJ.

To Louis H. Girardin

Monticello Dec. 3. 14.

Th: Jefferson returns his thanks to mr Girardin for the two plants of Cape Jessamine which are very acceptable, and will hold himself accountable for the price. he returns the copy of Tacitus having precisely the same edition in his petit-format library in Bedford, and if mr Girardin thinks it can go safely by post to mr Anderson, he will cover it by his frank. he has the Iliad¹ also in 12mo but proposes to get a compleat edition of both the Iliad & Odyssey of which he has heard. Th:J. will without delay look over Skelton's MS. he apprehends mr Girardin supposes his own MS. left with him, which he believes very certainly was not the case, but will be ready to look over it whenever mr Girardin shall afford him that pleasure. he sends the Journal desired. he always understood, altho' he knows not from what source, that mr Henry was the person in view for the Dictator & he believes this understanding was general & notorious; but of the particular anecdote respecting Archibald Carey he does not recollect to have heard before; yet it is so like the firm resolution of the man that he is ready to believe it. of the particulars of the intrigue as to the Dictatorship Th:J. has been but very imperfectly informed.—he is sorry to hear of the indisposition of mr Girardin, hopes it will soon pass off, and that he shall soon have the pleasure of seeing him at Monticello. he salutes him with esteem & respect.

RC (PPAmP: Thomas Jefferson Papers); dateline at foot of text; addressed: "Mr Girardin Glenmore." Not recorded in SJL. Enclosures not found.

TJ offered to examine WITHOUT DELAY the manuscript constituting part of vol. 4 of Burk, Jones, and Girardin, *History of Virginia*. In the ANECDOTE, the speaker of the Senate of Virginia, Archibald Cary, threatened to assassinate Patrick Henry if he was chosen to be dictator: "the day of his appointment shall be the day of his death—for he shall feel my dagger in his heart before the sunset of that day" (William Wirt, *Sketches of the Life and Character of Patrick Henry*

[Philadelphia, 1817; Poor, *Jefferson's Library*, 4 (no. 131)], 205). Although Jones and Girardin failed to include the story in their completion of Burk's *History of Virginia*, they commended Cary for his "bold, impassioned, and energetic temper" during the crisis and stated that his staunch opposition to the idea "places him by the side of Cato, or even Brutus" (4:190).

A missing letter from Girardin to TJ of this date is recorded in SJL as received 3 (reworked from 4) Dec. 1814 from Glenmore.

[1] Reworked from "he has the identical edition also of the Iliad by."

From Robert M. Patterson

SIR,   Philadelphia, December 3d., 1814.

I had the honor to receive your letter, of the 24th of last month, in which you decline a reelection as president of the American philosophical Society. This letter was laid before the Society, at their meeting last evening, and excited a general regret among the members: no particular order, however, was taken on it; the Society choosing to adopt, in this particular, the Same course which was pursued, on a Similar occasion, in the year 1809.

It would be improper for me, in the present letter, to express my private feelings, on the Subject of your communication; but it gives me great Satisfaction to be able to offer you my grateful thanks for your kind and flattering wishes, and to assure you of my warm admiration and devoted attachment.   R. M. PATTERSON.

RC (MHi); endorsed by TJ as received 16 Dec. 1814 and so recorded in SJL. RC (DLC); address cover only; with PoC of TJ to John Vaughan, 1 Mar. 1815, on verso; addressed: "Thomas Jefferson, Late President of the United States, Monticello"; franked; postmarked Philadelphia, 5 Dec.

TJ's letter to Patterson declining re-election as American Philosophical Society president was dated 23 Nov. 1814, not THE 24TH. At its recent meeting the society had resolved that TJ's letter be transcribed into the minutes, but "declined taking any particular order on it; thus adopting the Same course which was pursued, on a Similar occasion, in decemʳ 1808" (APS, Minutes, 16 Dec. 1808, 2 Dec. 1814 [MS at PPAmP]).

To Philip Thornton

DEAR SIR   Monticello Dec. 3. 14.

In the evening of the day on which you left me, I recieved a letter of Nov. 22. from mr Caruthers, desiring a conclusion on his proposition to lease the Natural bridge. you know how sincerely I had meant to give him a preference as the first applicant, & the circumstances which induced me to suppose he had declined it, and therefore to execute the lease to you. I have explained these to him and referred to you for their confirmation; and am in hopes that by the partnership you suggested, his views may be answered, & especially as he could no otherwise procure the material for a separate concern.

I had paid to mr Wilson sheriff of Rockbridge, the taxes for 1811. and 1812. those for 13–14. are I believe unpaid. they were about 67. cents a year, and I will request you to pay them now & at all times during the lease, on my account.   mr Bankhead & family arrived the afternoon you left us, having left Dʳ Bankhead & family well. Accept the assurance of my great esteem & respect.

TH: JEFFERSON

PoC (MHi); at foot of text: "Dʳ Thornton"; endorsed by TJ.

On 21 Oct. 1812 TJ PAID John Wilson, the sheriff of Rockbridge County, "2.D.

being 3 years taxes for my lands at the Natural bridge, to wit for the years 1811. 1812. & the next year 1813. He says he recieved them up to 1810. inclusive from Mr. Caruthers" (MB, 2:1283).

To John Wilson

SIR   Monticello Dec. 4. 14.

The subject of your letter of Nov.   is entirely unknown to me[.] I only know in general that the heads of departments had been authorised by law to apportion the sum allowed for salaries to their clerks at their discretion. no duty I presume could be more embarrassing to those gentlemen. but of the particular graduation of the salaries I never heard, nor enquired, the subject having been entirely out of the line of my cognisance. at present especially it would be as useless as intrusive for me to express an opinion on it, had I the materials. but, to my total ignorance of the objects and scale of that distribution, is added a due sense of the impropriety of my entertaining the subject at all. I have ever considered those clerkships as unfortunate baits to young men who are at all capable of doing any thing for themselves. in these they can never look beyond a bare and barren subsistance. whereas in a country like ours, so many pursuits offer themselves, that those of the least talent & enterprise cannot fail to advance themselves to situations of greater comfort & independance. Accept the assurance of my respect. Th: Jefferson

PoC (CSmH: JF-BA); edge trimmed, with missing punctuation supplied from *Jefferson Correspondence*, Bixby, 217; at foot of text: "M[r] John Wilson"; endorsed by TJ.

From John H. Carr

Sir, Port Gibson Miss: Territory Dec[r] 5th 1814

I presume once more to solicit your aid in forwarding my views which I hope will not be refused when they are to be exercised in the prosecution of that which calls for the assistance of the American youth: Permit me to remind you of the letter which you wrote to Philip Grymes Esquire Attorney General at New Orleans, by which I met with every attention which M[r] Grymes could bestow. The present letter is written to request your aid in procuring me a Lieutenancy in the Army of the United States. My request is founded upon a wish to enter into the service of the United States to which the attention of every young man should be turned. You are no doubt acquainted with my Father, and the connection generally I hope, Sir, that this considiration will induce you to assist me. With the hope that you will befriend me I shall conclude by subscribing myself

D[r] Sir Your Ob[t] H[bl] Serv[t] John H. Carr

RC (DLC); at foot of text: "Tho[s] Jefferson Esq"; endorsed by TJ as received 5 Jan. 1815 and so recorded in SJL.

John H. Carr (d. ca. 1823) was the son of John Carr, an Albemarle County district and circuit court clerk. Having studied law under Dabney Carr, he moved to Mississippi Territory by 1811. Carr failed to secure a military appointment. He returned to Albemarle County by the autumn of 1816 and became a deputy circuit court clerk, but he evidently spent some of his last years in Kentucky (Woods, *Albemarle*, 159, 401; TJ to Philip Grymes, 3 Mar. 1810; *Terr. Papers*, 6:227; Albemarle Co. Law Order Book [1809–21], 255; DNA: RG 29, CS, Ky., Mount Sterling, 1820; Albemarle Co. Will Book, 7:258, 325).

TJ wrote to PHILIP GRYMES on Carr's behalf on 3 Mar. 1810, where the Editors erroneously identified the man introduced there as Lewis Carr. On 5 Dec. 1814 John H. Carr also asked James Monroe for an appointment in the ARMY OF THE UNITED STATES (DNA: RG 94, LRAG).

From John Barnes

DEAR SIR—   George Town Coᵃ 6ᵗʰ Decʳ 1814—

I have great pleasure—inclosing you the above Copy—least you should not have received any advices of the like tenor—Your last favʳ was of the 10ʰ Sepʳ—replied to 11ᵗʰ Octʳ—very Uncertain as to the final events—in Europe—as well at Washington. We may at least be permitted to Hope! something may yet be effected to Uphold—the National Credit—at this Eventfull Crisis—

most Respectfully, I am Dear Sir Your Obedᵗ servant.

JOHN BARNES.

PS. no adjustmᵗˢ has yet transpired at Bank of Colᵃ respecting the late Loan Subscriptions—

RC (ViU: TJP-ER); subjoined to enclosure; endorsed by TJ as received 13 Dec. 1814, but recorded in SJL as received a day later. RC (DLC); address cover only; with PoC of TJ to James Monroe, 21 Jan. 1815, on verso; addressed: "Thomas Jefferson Esqʳ Monticello—Virginia"; franked; postmarked Georgetown, 7 Dec.

TJ's most recent letter to Barnes was dated 30 Sept. 1814, not THE 10ᴴ SEPᴿ.

ENCLOSURE

Baring Brothers & Company to John Barnes

SIR,   London 20ᵗʰ Octʳ 1814—

We have in course, your Esteemed favor of the 22ᵈ June with a Remittance inclosed for Account of Genˡ Kosciusko, for £400. sterling a 60 days—on William Murdock—which was duly Accepted—and for which, We shall Understand, with said Gentleman to whom—We have forwarded your letter.— and have the Honor to be—

Sir—Your most Obed Humˡ servᵗ

(signed) BARING BROTHERS & Cᵒ

Tr (ViU: TJP-ER); entirely in Barnes's hand; adjacent to signature: "To John Barnes, George Town Coᵃ"; with covering letter subjoined.

To Alexander J. Dallas

DEAR SIR   Monticello Dec. 7.[1] 14.

I tender my sincere congratulations on the occasion of your counsel and services being engaged for the public, and trust they will feel their benefit. the department[2] to which you are called is the most arduous now in our government, and is that on which every other depends for it's motion. were our commerce open, no degree of contribution would be felt; but shut up as it is, the call on the people for taxes is truly a call for bricks without straw: in this state especially where we are feeding our horses with wheat as the cheapest forage; 50 cents being it's price thro' the middle country.

On the adoption of the land tax of the last year, an office of Assessor was established in every district, with power to determine what every land owner should pay, by his own judgment & without appeal. this important power could not fail to interest us highly in the choice of the person vested with it. on a consultation with most of the principal persons in our quarter, there was but one opinion as to the fittest man in our district. all agreed that in the hands of a mr Peter Minor they would be safe, his ability, his judgment & independance being a sufficient security. I took the liberty therefore of writing to the President and to mr Campbell recommending this appointment. we were told soon after that it had been given to a mr Armstead of a neighboring county. this was given out by himself and mr Garland (formerly a member of Congress) whose protegé Armstead is. the Assumption of the land tax by the state prevented further interest in the case. we now learn he had not the appointment and is now going on for it. if there be a better man than Minor we wish his appointment, but as to mr Armstead all agree he is the weakest & laziest man that could be found. some believe him honest, others very openly deny it. of his character however I know nothing personally, stating what I do from the information of others. Col° Monroe, I think, knows Minor personally, & the President knows his family, it's standing & character. he is nephew to Gen[l] Minor of Fredericksburg. the Collector being of this county (Albemarle) the principle of distribution might be supposed to require the Assessor from a different one. this principle may weigh between candidates of equal merit: but it cannot make the worse the better man, nor remedy the evils of an incorrect agent. the importance of this appointment towards a just apportionment of the public burthens, & one which will probably be permanent, will I hope excuse my expressing to the government my own sense of it, and that of the most respectable persons of our quarter, with an assurance nevertheless of our entire confidence that whatever appointment the government shall make will be founded in the best motives: and I avail myself of this occasion of assuring you of my great esteem & respect.   TH: JEFFERSON

RC (NNGL, on deposit NHi); addressed: "Alexander Dallas esq. Secretary of the Treasury Washington"; endorsed by Dallas. PoC (DLC); endorsed by TJ.

Alexander James Dallas (1759–1817), attorney, court reporter, and public official, was born in Jamaica and educated in Edinburgh. After briefly working as a clerk and accountant in London, he returned to the island of his birth in 1781 and became a lawyer. Two years later Dallas immigrated to the United States. Having established a legal practice in Philadelphia in 1785, he served as secretary of the commonwealth of Pennsylvania, 1791–1801. During this period Dallas was elected to the American Philosophical Society (1791), earned a reputation as a leading Republican in his state, and attracted notice as one of the first reporters of United States Supreme Court decisions and as the compiler of the *Laws of the Commonwealth of Pennsylvania*, 4 vols. (Philadelphia and Lancaster, 1793–1801). TJ appointed him United States attorney for the Eastern District of Pennsylvania in 1801, and he was still in that office when James Madison selected him in 1814 to become secretary of the treasury. While at the Treasury Department, Dallas supported increasing taxes to pay for the War of 1812, reviving the national bank and, after the conclusion of hostilities, erecting a system of protective tariffs. In addition to his other duties, he was acting secretary of war for much of 1815, and in the same year he acted briefly

as secretary of state. In October 1816 Dallas resigned from the government and returned to private practice. He died in Philadelphia (*ANB*; *DAB*; *PTJ*, 26:467–8; Raymond Walters Jr., *Alexander James Dallas: Lawyer—Politician—Financier, 1759–1817* [1943]; APS, Minutes, 21 Oct. 1791 [MS in PPAmP]; *JEP*, 1:402, 405, 2:533 [6, 26 Jan. 1802, 5, 6 Oct. 1814]; Philadelphia *Poulson's American Daily Advertiser*, 17 Jan. 1817; *Port Folio*, 4th ser., 3 [1817]: 181–6).

Pharaoh commanded the Israelites to make BRICKS WITHOUT STRAW in the Bible (Exodus 5). Colloquially, the phrase refers to an attempt to do something without the proper materials (E. Cobham Brewer, *Dictionary of Phrase and Fable* [1898], 796). Although TJ wrote James Madison on Minor's behalf on 23 Aug. 1813, no letter of recommendation has been found to Dallas's predecessor, George W. CAMPBELL. William Armistead (ARMSTEAD) hailed from the NEIGHBORING COUNTY of Amherst. For the ASSUMPTION OF THE LAND TAX BY THE STATE of Virginia on 7 Jan. 1814, see *Acts of Assembly* (1814–15 sess.), 61. TJ's grandson Thomas Jefferson Randolph was the revenue COLLECTOR for the 19th Collection District at this time.

A missing letter from Congressman David S. Garland to TJ of 1 May 1810 is noted in SJL as received from Washington eight days later.

[1] Reworked from "8."
[2] Word interlined in place of "post."

From Patrick Gibson

SIR   Richmond 7th Decr 1814

I presented to Doctor Brockenborough who return'd the day before yesterday, Mr John Harvie's note enclosed in yours of the 21st Ulto, he regrets that it was not sooner forwarded, as just before leaving town he remitted to Mr Harvie, all the funds he had in his hands about £1000. he informs me that he is not certain of receiving any money on M^r H'^{s} account until the 1st of March next, but that if he can collect any either on M^r H'^{s} or his own account sooner he will take up the note, be pleased to say if I shall retain or return it to you

I have not yet been able to obtain the money from O. Philpots for the 4 Hhd^s Tob^o sold him in 1812—altho suit was brought immediately. I am inform'd he has property but it is difficult getting at it— Some Sales of prime Tobacco have been made as high as $8—

With great respect I am Your Ob Servt PATRICK GIBSON

Flour $4 dull—

RC (ViU: TJP-ER); between dateline and salutation: "Thomas Jefferson Esqre"; endorsed by TJ as received 9 Dec. 1814 and so recorded in SJL.

To James Monroe

DEAR SIR   Monticello Dec. 7. 14.

A most important appointment for the landholders of our part of the country is now about to be made, that of the Assessor of the land tax, who is to decide what portion of the aggregate sum assessed on our district shall be paid by each individual. such a man should be enlightened, judicious, firm and independant. on consultation with our best men, I the last year recommended to the President & Secretary of the Treasury, Peter Minor, a nephew of Genl John Minor of Fredsbg, settled near Charlottesville. I think you must know his character and probably his person. every one who has been spoken to considers him as the most unexceptionable & perfect character for the office in the district, and the one in whose hands they should think themselves the most secure in the repartition now to be made, & which probably will be permanent. there is no appeal from his sentence. however we were told the last year that a mr Armstead of an upper county of the district had obtained[1] the appointment. this was given out by himself, & by Garland (former member of Congress) who was his intercessor, and who is as unscrupulous in the means of fabricating an interest as in the use he makes of it, insomuch that tho elected by hook & by crook for the <u>district</u> before, he was rejected by his <u>county</u> at their last election of a delegate to the state legislature. it is now affirmed that no appointment was made the last year, and that Armstead is now going on to sollicit it. I know nothing of him personally, but all who have spoken of him to me agree that he is the

[128]

weakest and laziest man in the district: some think him honest, others deny it. I have written to mr Dallas on this occasion, as I did to the President on the former, and sollicit your testimony as to the character of Minor.

A mr Clarke applied to me a few days ago to write on his behalf to you for a military commission, which I declined on the general determination never[2] to take any part in these sollicitations. Minor's is not in that case, for he did not know of our wish to get him appointed. his recommendation was on our own motion.   Clarke is the son of a most worthy father, Col° John Clarke of Powhatan, probably known to you.

I am a good deal pressed to get the question of boundary between you & mr Short settled. I know it has been impossible for you to attend; and suppose it could not be well settled without your presence or that of mr Carter. the last is entirely desperate. as you will probably come up immediately after the 4th of March, I will pray you without regarding mr Carter's attendance, to give a day to it, let us take some neighbors and settle & be done with it. — our prospects here are woful. where a few bushels of wheat can be sold at all it is for 50. cents only. some feed their horses with it, & spare their corn as it will keep better. I dread the coincidence of the taxgatherer's progress the next year with the Presidential elections. ever affectionately yours.

Th: Jefferson

RC (DLC: Monroe Papers); endorsed by Monroe. PoC (DLC); at foot of first page: "Col° Monroe"; endorsed by TJ.

JOHN CLARKE: James Clarke. As the 13th Congress was to come to a close on 3

Mar. 1815, TJ expected that Monroe would be able to leave the capital on or shortly after THE 4TH of that month.

[1] Word interlined.
[2] Reworked from "not."

To Thomas Taylor

SIR   Monticello Dec. 7. 14.

In the Enquirer of Nov. 29. I see an advertisement with your name to it as acting for mr Thos Wilson & offering a place for sale called Westham. whether by this appellation Beverley town is meant to be included, I do not know, but lest it should I think it a duty to give notice that I own 4. or 5. lots in that town, one of which is the ferry lot established by act of assembly, & to which I attach considerable value, notwithstanding it's present disuse. I had heard that somebody had inclosed the town, but considered the public property in the streets against which no limitation of time could run, as protecting the lots they inclose, and the whole site of the town. as I never saw the advertisement till this morning, & the sale is for the 15ᵗʰ the information which you may be so kind as to give me whether my lots are to be included in this transaction, may come too late for me to notify the bidders either personally or publicly. in that case I would hope you would think it necessary to inform them of it. if the town be not included, I have then to ask your pardon for this intrusion on your time & to pray you to accept the assurance of my great esteem & respect.   Tʜ: Jᴇꜰꜰᴇʀsᴏɴ

PoC (MHi); at foot of text: "Thomas Taylor esq."; endorsed by TJ.

Thomas Taylor (1767–1832), Richmond commission merchant and auctioneer, partnered with John Satchell until 1805, when he joined with James Brown Jr. to form the firm of Taylor & Brown. He assigned his property to creditors in 1824. Taylor was a friend of John Randolph of Roanoke, one of the securities for Aaron Burr during his 1807 treason trial, a commissioner charged with arranging the repair of the Virginia state capitol in 1812 and, in 1831, an opponent of Andrew Jackson's reelection. He died in Richmond (Fillmore Norfleet, *Saint-Mémin in Virginia: Portraits and Biographies* [1942], 212; Richmond *Enquirer*, 11 Oct. 1805; David Robertson, *Reports of the Trials of Colonel Aaron Burr* [Philadelphia, 1808], 1:106; *Acts of Assembly* [1811–12 sess.], 4; *Richmond Enquirer*, 2 Apr. 1824, 9 Sept. 1831, 23 Mar.

1832; gravestone inscription in Hollywood Cemetery, Richmond).

Taylor's ᴀᴅᴠᴇʀᴛɪsᴇᴍᴇɴᴛ, dated 26 Nov., provided for the auction on 15 Dec. or the next seasonable day thereafter of "that valuable farm upon James River, called *Westham*, which contains 250 Acres," to be "sold in Lotts of about 50 or 60 acres each, extending from the river out. Each Lott will partake of a due portion of low-grounds and wood-land" (Richmond *Enquirer*, 26 Nov. 1814). The unbuilt town of ʙᴇᴠᴇʀʟᴇʏ was located on the James River some six miles upstream from Richmond (*MB*, 2:1326n). TJ owned four, not 5. ʟᴏᴛs there (Betts, *Farm Book,* pt. 1, 127; George Jefferson to TJ, 1 Aug. 1811). On 26 Dec. 1792 the Virginia legislature passed an act requiring that a ꜰᴇʀʀʏ be maintained at "the upper landing in Beverley town" (*Acts of Assembly* [1792–93 sess.], 87–93, esp. 90).

From José Corrêa da Serra

Sɪʀ   Philadelphia 9 Decʳ 1814.
I am in Philadelphia returned again to my old train of Life, that is reading and walking. From the inclosed you will see that i have not forgotten the cement for your cisterns. That alone would have occasioned this Letter, but i have matter of much more importance to communicate to you. The Last arrivals have brought english and french papers, pamphlets and Letters which i wish i could put under your eyes, to give you a just idea of what is going in Europe. No

favourable result is to be expected from Vienna; war is adjourned. So far you know already and from better sources, but what is very important and remarkable, and which only an attentive Lectures of a great number of the above materials can show, is that the only ally that you have now in Europe, and a powerful one, if properly seconded, is public opinion, which has sprung again in Europe immediately after the pressure of circumstances has disappeared, wishing for rest and deprecating ambition. Your enemies with their papers and pamphlets strive to persuade Europe that this country is the nest of antimonarchical jacobinism and this government the tail of Bonaparte, to be severely chastised and crushed Like him. It seems as if they wished to raise a crusade against this country. The papers of the continent sympathize with you, and consider you as a nation wronged by a piratical and ungenerous mode of warfare. The british government writers speak of american <u>insolence</u> the necessity of punishing this country, and the <u>interest of Monarchs</u>. The continental papers seem far from partaking this opinion, and even in England i see from the opposition papers many people do not partake it. As you are remained alone on the theatre all the eyes are turned on you and your contest. A dignified resistance without imitating what the continent highly disapproves in them, and causes their feelings to be on your side is the only means to conserve this advantage of public opinion, which is in this case what the weather gage is in naval combats. Such line of conduct and pinching trade are the only means of bringing honorable peace.

You intended to write to the President on an object which was incidental in a conversation. I earnestly entreat you now to employ all your influence to suspend it. In the present moment it must have a deleterious effect instead of doing good, it could serve to excite the fellow feelings of many powerful people, and give pretext to excite an ill will where it does not exist. The same capital employed on the trade would be more profitable and without inconvenient. I know at present from good authority that the two points in question have not been neglected in the Last obstinate Law suit as they were before, but for personal reasons have been much contemplated. This is so natural, that i wonder the possibility of it did not occur to the gentleman that mentioned them, together with the natural reflection that sixteen years might bring very material changes. All this i submit to your wisdom, i dare not give advices to such a man as you, but i make just and friendly representations.   Most sincerely yours

J. CORRÈA DE SERRA

RC (DLC); endorsed by TJ as received 18 Dec. 1814 and so recorded in SJL. Enclosure not found.

LECTURES (lecture): "reading; perusal" (*OED*). To have THE WEATHER GAGE is to be windward of another vessel, which provided a major tactical advantage in NAVAL COMBATS (*OED*).

To Jeremiah A. Goodman

DEAR SIR   Monticello Dec. 10. 14.

I now send James with a small cart and 2. mules for the salt, which I am in hopes you have had packed in strong barrels, or such as can be well strengthened. I do not think he can bring more than 10. bushels, which with their barrels will weigh 700.℔. the rest of the salt (5. bushels) and the butter must come by the waggon at Christmas. 2. men & a boy from here will pay a visit to their friends at Poplar forest at Christmas & assist in bringing the hogs & beef. I send a plough by James, and shall send more of the same kind by the waggon. I promised Rachael's Cate she might come at Christmas to see her mother. let her now come by the cart and she will return with the waggon, which will give a few days more for her visit. James brings 22. blankets to be given according to the written directions I left.   he also brings some trees E^tc which please to have planted immediately in the Nursery behind the stable 12. Inches apart. the three boxes he brings may be set away in one of the rooms of the house. I am satisfied there will be peace this winter. hasten therefore the getting the tobacco ready & sending it off to Richmond with all possible speed, never losing a moment when it can be handled. the great prices will be for that at market the moment peace opens the bay. the wheat should also be got to the mill & the flour forwarded to Richmond as fast as you can.   I inclose you a statement of the cash and orders not entered on our last account, as they stand in my book. I am not certain whether the order for 50.D. in favor of mr Darnell should be charged to you, not knowing whether that money past thro' your hands or not. I delivered the order to mr Darnell himself and it was drawn payable to himself.—I shall be glad to know if he is returned and how you go on with the road. send me also the accounts I wrote for in my letter from Flood's the day I left you. it will be well for you to accompany James to Lynchburg & see the salt put on board. he may rest a day at Poplar Forest.

Dec. 11. the snow of yesterday prevented James's setting off till to-day. Accept best wishes   TH: JEFFERSON

RC (CtY: Franklin Collection); addressed from "Th: Jefferson" to "Mr Jeremiah A. Goodman Poplar Forest Bedford by James and Billy."

Neither the WRITTEN DIRECTIONS TJ left at Poplar Forest concerning the distribution of blankets to his slaves nor the enclosed STATEMENT of cash and orders have been found.

An undated letter from Goodman to TJ, not found, is recorded in SJL as received 3 Dec. 1814.

To John Melish

DEAR SIR   Monticello Dec. 10. 14.

I thank you for your favor of the map of the Sine quâ non, inclosed in your letter of Nov. 12. it was an excellent idea; and if, with the Documents distributed by Congress, copies of these had been sent to be posted up in every street, on every Town-house and Court-house, it would have painted to the eyes of those who cannot read, and of those also who read without reflecting, that reconquest is the ultimate object of Britain. the first step towards this is to set a limit to their expansion by taking from them that noble country which the foresight of their fathers provided for their multiplying and needy offspring: to be followed up by the compression, land-board and sea-board, of that omnipotence which the English fancy themselves now to possess. a vain & foolish imagination! instead of fearing and endeavoring to crush our prosperity, had they cultivated it in friendship, it might have become a bulwark instead of a breaker to them. there has never been an administration in this country which would not gladly have met them more than half way on the road to an equal, a just, & solid connection of friendship and intercourse. and as to repressing our growth, they might as well attempt to repress the waves of the ocean.

Your American Atlas is an useful undertaking for those who will live to see and to use it. to me every mail, in the departure of some Cotemporary, brings warning to be in readiness my self also and to cease from new engagements.[1] it is a warning of no alarm.   when faculty after faculty is retiring from us, and all the avenues to chearful sensation closing, sight failing now, hearing next, then memory, debility of body, habetude of mind, nothing remaining but a sickly vegetation, with scarcely the relief of a little loco-motion, the last cannot be but a coup de grace.

You propose to me the preparation of a new edition of the Notes on Virginia. I formerly entertained the idea, and from time to time noted some new [ma]tter, which I thought I would arrange at leisure for a posthumous edition. [but I?] begin to see that it is impracticable for me. nearly forty years of addi[tional experie]nce in the affairs of mankind would lead me into dilatations ending I know not where. that experience indeed has not altered a single principle. but it has furnished matter of abundant developement. every moment too, which I have to spare from my daily exercise and affairs is engrossed by a correspondence, the result of the extensive relations which my course of life has necessarily occasioned. and now the act of writing itself is becoming slow, laborious and irksome. I consider therefore the idea of preparing a new copy of that work as no more to be entertained. the work itself indeed is nothing more than the measure of a shadow, never stationary, but lengthening as the sun advances, and to be taken anew from hour to hour. it must remain therefore for some other hand to sketch it's appearance at another epoch, to furnish another element for calculating the course and motion of this member of our federal system. for this every day is adding new matter, & strange matter. that of reducing, by impulse instead of attraction, a sister planet into it's orbit, will be as new in our political, as in the planetary system. the operation however will be painful rather than difficult. the sound part of our wandering star will probably, by it's own internal energies, keep the unsound within it's course: or, if a foreign power is called in, we shall have to meet it but so much the nearer, and with a more overwhelming force. it will probably shorten the war. for I think it probable that the Sine quâ non was designedly put into an impossible form to give time for the developement of their plots & concerts with the factionists of Boston, and that they are holding off to see the issue, not of the Congress of Vienna, but of that of Hartford. this will begin a new chapter in our history, and with a wish that you may live in health to see it's easy close, I tender you the assurance of my great esteem & respect.

Th: Jefferson

PoC (DLC); lower left corner of recto torn away.

Virginia's SISTER PLANET was Massachusetts. The HARTFORD Convention, which met between 15 Dec. 1814 and 5 Jan. 1815, brought together representatives from the five New England states to discuss their grievances against the federal government and its mismanagement of the war. Far from advocating secession, the body's final report merely chastised Washington officials for failing to defend the region adequately, repeated long-standing complaints about embargoes, slave representation, western expansion, and the admission of new states, proposed constitutional amendments to address these problems, and recommended that a suitable portion of the federal tax revenue be set aside for the defense of states threatened during wartime (Banner,

Hartford Convention; Malcomson, *Historical Dictionary*, 239–40; Stagg, *Madison's War*, 479, 482).

[1] Preceding six words interlined, with redundant period at end of insertion editorially omitted.

From John Adams

DEAR SIR   Quincy December 11. 1814

The Bearer of this Letter, after an Education at our Cambridge, travelled with J.Q.A. to Russia, Spent two years in looking at parts of Europe, returned to Boston, read Law with one of our first Professors in Boston, is admitted to the Bar, and now Wishes to have the honour of Seeing Montecello and paying his respects to President Jefferson. His Name is Francis C. Gray a Son of our Lt Governor Gray.

If he can explain to you the incomprehensible Politicks of New England, he can do more than I Shall or can pretend to do.

Paine Lovel and Gerry are gone and I am left alone. Gerry is happy in his Death; for what horrors of Calumny has he not escaped in the Electioneering campaigne of next Summer? But what is to be the destiny of an amiable Widow and nine Children all as amiable as they are destitute?   JOHN ADAMS

RC (DLC); at foot of text: "President Jefferson"; endorsed by TJ as received 4 Feb. 1815 from "mr Gray" and so recorded in SJL. FC (Lb in MHi: Adams Papers).

J.Q.A.: John Quincy Adams. Francis C. Gray had studied law with ONE OF OUR FIRST PROFESSORS IN BOSTON, William

Prescott (Marjorie B. Cohn, *Francis Calley Gray and Art Collecting for America* [1986], 38). Three of Adams's Massachusetts colleagues at the Continental Congress had died during the preceding six months, Robert Treat PAINE, James Lovell (LOVEL), and Elbridge GERRY (*ANB*).

From William Thornton

DEAR SIR   City of Washington 11th Dec[r] 1814 —

I have long owed you a Letter, relative to Clopper's Looms: but I wished to see him or hear from him before I should write again. I wrote but received from him no Answer. I wrote to his Brother to enquire where he was, & the proprietor of the Patent right called on me. I said so much to him on the Subject, that he[1] acknowledged he had done wrong in hold[g] his rights in Virg[a] at such a price: but he seemed not much disposed to alter now, his mode of vending them, which was by Counties. He told me he had corresponded with you, and I think he said he had seen you.—A manufactury is now establishing here, at the mill Seat in Virgᵃ just over the little Falls Bridge to which I shall pay some attention, and inform you how it progresses. It belongs to Charles Goldsborough & Cᵒ—

I saw, since I wrote last, the proprietor of the Patent Loom for Baltimore County. He was here, & told me he had written & promised you a compleat loom.—

What dreadful scenes we have witnessed here! but all may be repair'd, and in some respects we shall be benefitted: for if the Buildings should be repair'd, we shall never hear any more of the removal of Congress: and I have congratulated the members on the loss of their Library, since you offered yours on such generous Terms.—I advised them to offer you $50,000 at once: for I had seen the Books, & knew them to be very valuable: that they ought not therefore to value them as Books in a common Library; for, beside the learning & ability it would require to select the Books, they were not to be obtained but at very great trouble, great expense, great risk, & many of them not to be had at all: but I fear they will not give half the value.—

I have a very great favor to ask of you.—Stewart (the Painter) painted a very beautiful Bust of you, on a blue ground—in Chiaroscuro. He offered to paint my portrait in the same manner; but I did not sit. I wish much to copy your Head, and also the Piece painted for you by mʳ West.—If packed up in a small well made Box, and covered with silk paper, before they be pressed down, so as not to rub; or put first into a port folio, they would come safely, and might be sent with the Books. I would take of them the utmost care, and return them in the safest manner, as soon as I had copied them; and I would not keep them long.—I admired them both, and if you would grant me this favor I should be very much obliged.—The Piece of West's to which I allude, is Hector taking leave of Andromache, in Chiaroscuro.[2]

I am, dear Sir, with the highest respect & consideration Yʳˢ

WILLIAM THORNTON—

RC (DLC); endorsed by TJ as received 16 Dec. 1814 and so recorded in SJL. RC (DLC); address cover only; with PoC of TJ to John Garnett, 4 Jan. 1815, on verso; addressed: "Honorable Thomas Jefferson—Monticello"; franked; postmarked Washington, 12 Dec.

No retirement-era correspondence has been found between TJ and Francis C. Clopper, the PROPRIETOR OF THE PATENT RIGHT in Virginia for Walter Janes's loom. The LITTLE FALLS BRIDGE was located on the Potomac River a few miles upstream from Georgetown (*Balti-*

more Patriot & Evening Advertiser, 8 May 1816). George Greer, the PROPRIETOR OF THE PATENT LOOM FOR BALTIMORE COUNTY, wrote TJ on 9 Aug. 1814. After receiving Gilbert Stuart's 1805 medallion-style BUST from TJ, Thornton made at least three copies, one of which he presented to the Library of Congress in 1816 (Bush, *Life Portraits*, 62–3). In June 1797 Benjamin West had given Tadeusz Kosciuszko his drawing of

The Fright of Astyanax, which is also known as HECTOR TAKING LEAVE OF ANDROMACHE. TJ received this artwork from Kosciuszko prior to the latter's departure for Europe in the spring of the following year (Stein, *Worlds*, 150–1; *PTJ*, 30:xli–xlii).

[1] Reworked from "I."
[2] Manuscript: "Chiarosuro."

From William H. Crawford

MY DEAR SIR   Paris. 12th Dec[r] 1814.

I have just been informed that our Envoys at Ghent are about to dispatch a fast Sailing vessel from Amsterdam with dispatches. I have only time to Scribble you a few lines. Indeed I have but little to communicate in addition to my former letter. The Congress at Vienna proceeds much slower than had been anticipated. It is uncertain whether they have Settled any one point of importance. I am however Still of opinion, that an amicable arrangement will be effected, or to speak more Correctly, that they will be so arranged as to avoid an immediate war. This would be impossible if France was in a situation to Second the efforts of her ministers, with a powerful army. This is not her situation, and a considerable time is likely to pass away, before mutual Confidence will be Restored between the King, & people, if it ever happens. The representations given in the Gazettes, of the extreme Popularity of the King, and of the happiness of the People, are entitled to the same Credit that Representations of the Same character were entitled to, twelve months ago, and no more. Indeed I believe the latter were less false than the former. The Nation has been Relieved from the conscription, and exempted from the positive evils of war. This was sensibly felt, and Reconciled the people[1] to the change which had just taken place. These benefits are already forgotten. The peace has not brought them Commerce, it has checked their manufactures, it has added fifty Per cent to their impositions, but what is of more importance, it has in the estimation of the nation degraded, and humiliated France. No King can long be popular, who Suffers the Nation to be degraded in the eyes of the people. A few days ago a general alarm Prevailed at the palace; the King & other members of the family, together with the Garrison, were up the whole night. The Next day the minister of War was Removed, & the director of the Police was translated into the marine department, and a man less Scrupulous, placed at the head of the police. An impression Prevails to a Considerable extent, even in Paris, that the Royal family will be expelled in the Course of the winter. None of them, however, have any distinct idea, of the manner, in which this is to be effected. Notwithstanding the measures of the gov^t add daily to the Number of the malcontents, yet still I am inclined to believe that the Revolution will be Permanent. The gov^t however has a crisis yet to pass: A sense of the degradation into which France has fallen, and a belief that the King has contributed to that degradation, is a maddening Reflexion for the great mass of Frenchmen—it is Rendered Still more irritating by the impression that the King is friendly to England. To Relieve the nation from these Painful and humiliating Sensations, a war with England, & also with Austria is almost indispensable[.] But a war must necessarily assemble a large army, & this army may overturn the throne. This is the dilemma in which the King is placed. I believe the boldest course is the best. At least the Suspense in which the parties are held, would be Sooner terminated. I think it highly probable that exertions will be made to Remove the Emperor from the ile of Elba, by his Consent, if it can be obtained. This is not Probable. He has fortified the Island So that he Can defend himself against a powerful army. Should they break their engagements with him, they incur great risks, from the State of Public feeling in Italy and in France. If he was to Shew himself in Italy at the head of a Small body of men I am by no means Certain that he would not be able to expel the Austrian and Sardinian troops before they could be re-inforced. In this event France must remain Perfectly Still. To march an army into the South East of the Kingdom, would only invite him into France. In every part of the Continent, except Russia, public feeling is extremely favorable to adventurous enterprize: In Spain, the King must be dethroned, or the Nation must be enslaved. I am fearful that the latter alternative will be effected.

Our negociations at Ghent are Still carried on. The prospect is more favorable now than in the three first months. Here nothing can be Relied upon in Relation to us. The man who directs the foreign Relations of France, is according to the opinion of his friends, governed Solely by his Pecuniary interest. The interest of the Nation is not considered—Under such an administration, the interests of our enemy must Prevail, because, after bribing all Europe for so many years, they[2] will Not grudge what will be necessary to bribe a minister who is notoriously venal.

I am dear Sir with Sentiments of the highest Consideration your most ob^t & Very humb^l Servt   W^M H CRAWFORD

PS. Knowing that you felt some interest in the reinstatement of Mr Warden in 1810–11. & understanding that he would endeavor to engage your influence in Restoring him again, I have felt it to be My duty to Send you two letters which he has written Since his Removal. They bear instrinsic evidence of his total want of veracity. I am Sorry to add that his official acts are indelibly impressed with the Same character. Upon those the gov^t has decided his Removal. I have no right to disclose them. He continues to Represent his Removal as an arbitrary act of mine, when he Knows it to be the act of the gov^t. By means of this misrepresentation, he has obtained many letters, from very respectable men Recommending his reinstatement. To this I can have no objection, if it is made with a full Knowledge of the case.   WHC

RC (DLC); edge trimmed; with canceled "(Duplicate)" at head of text, keyed to deleted note written perpendicularly in left margin of first page: "The original was [. . .] to the Sec^y of the French legation Mr Roth. It is [. . .] partly in cypher"; adjacent to signature: "Thos Jefferson late President of the U.S."; endorsed by TJ as received 7 June 1816 and so recorded in SJL. Enclosed in Crawford to TJ, 31 May 1816.

A little over a week earlier, Louis XVIII had replaced his MINISTER OF WAR, Pierre Dupont de l'Etang, and the DIRECTOR OF THE POLICE, Jacques Claude Beugnot, with Nicolas Jean de Dieu Soult, duc de Dalmatie, and Antoine Balthazar Joseph d'André, respectively (Jacques Victor Albert, duc de Broglie, ed., *Memoirs of the Prince of Talleyrand* [1891–92], 2:350; Connelly, *Napoleonic France*, 69, 159, 449). The EMPEROR was Napoleon. Talleyrand directed the FOREIGN RELATIONS OF FRANCE. The TWO LETTERS by David Bailie Warden, not found, were originally enclosed with this letter, but they were removed over a year later by Crawford when he redirected it to TJ and thus were not seen by him (Crawford to TJ, 31 May 1816).

[1] Word interlined in place of "nation."
[2] Manuscript: "thay."

From Greenberry Dorsey

SIR   Grenville V^a Decem^r 13th 1814

Previous to my departure from new orleans, I contemplated having the Honor of visiting you personally, but in Consequence of the excessive bad state of the Roads, and my business requiring[1] my attention in Balt° as early as possible, I have been obliged to pass by winchester—I have therefore taken the liberty of enclosing the letter Governor[2] Claiborne was good enough to give me, presuming it may Contain something interesting to you respecting the situation of the State of Louisiana.

Permit me Sir to present to you through[3] this channel the respects of Benj Morgan Esq, and Joseph Saul Esqr, the former of whom was also so obliging as to give a letter to you, and believe me

to be sir, your very ob hu[1] Ser[t]   G[R] DORSEY

RC (MHi); at foot of text: "Thomas Jefferson Esqr Charlottsville"; endorsed by TJ as received 20 Dec. 1814 and so recorded in SJL. Enclosure: William C. C. Claiborne to TJ, 21 Oct. 1814.

Greenberry Dorsey (ca. 1787–1869), merchant and public official, was a native of Baltimore who moved permanently to New Orleans in about 1812. He served as a director of the Bank of Louisiana and of the local branch of the Bank of the United States, a War Department pension agent, and a federal receiver of public monies. President John Tyler nominated him in 1844 as a federal customs collector, but the Senate rejected this appointment. In 1850 Dorsey owned real estate valued at $800. He died of pneumonia (*Dorsey et al. v. Olive Sternenberg & Company et al.*,

Court of Civil Appeals of Texas, 11 Apr. 1906, *The Southwestern Reporter*, 1st ser. [1886–1928], 94:413–4; *JEP*, 6:191–2, 231, 249 [3 Mar. 1843, 6 Feb., 21 Mar. 1844]; *Register of all Officers and Agents, civil, military, and naval, in the Service of the United States, on the thirtieth September, 1847* [1847], 139; DNA: RG 29, CS, La., New Orleans, 1850–60, 1870 mortality schedules; *New-Orleans Times*, 12 Nov. 1866).

Greenville (GRENVILLE) is in Augusta County. The letter to TJ from Benjamin MORGAN, not recorded in SJL and not found, was presumably another introduction of Dorsey that the latter retained.

[1] Manuscript: "requing."
[2] Manuscript: "Govenor."
[3] Manuscript: "though."

To Louis H. Girardin

Dec. 13. 14.

Th: Jefferson must apologise to mr Girardin for not sending an answer to his note of the day before yesterday, which was occasioned by his servant's departure while he was writing it. he now sends him Jones's MS. and Mellish's travells. the copy of the British spy which he possesses belongs to his petit format library in Bedford, where it now is. he has made a few unimportant notes with the pencil on mr Jones's work; he will go over mr Girardin's with pleasure & attention, and will freely make any remarks which he may think would be useful. from what he has already gone over he thinks there will be little room for any observation.—after mr Girardin left him the other day, he recollected that mr Wirt had requested information from him as to the proposition for a dictator, & that on that occasion he ransacked his papers & his memory, and wrote mr Wirt the result, which was almost nothing. he now sends mr Girardin a copy of what he wrote to mr Wirt on that occasion. he thinks with mr G. that Henry's foibles should be lightly touched. it is not easy indeed to say whether his scheme of a dictator proceeded from ambition of which he had a

great deal, or want of judgment, of which he had little. he was profoundly acquainted with mankind, particularly the lower order, &
knew well how to lead them, towards which his unparalleled eloquence furnished an irresistable instrument. he salutes mr Girardin
with friendship & respect.

RC (PPAmP: Thomas Jefferson Pa-
pers); dateline at foot of text; addressed:
"Mʳ Girardin Glenmore." Enclosures:
(1) manuscript, not found, of a portion of
vol. 4 of Burk, Jones, and Girardin, *History of Virginia*. (2) John Melish, *Travels
in the United States of America, in the
Years 1806 & 1807, and 1809, 1810, &
1811*, 2 vols. (Philadelphia, 1812; Sower-

by, no. 4034). (3) extract from TJ to
William Wirt, 14 Aug. 1814.

Missing letters from Girardin to TJ of
THE DAY BEFORE YESTERDAY and 13
Dec. 1814 are recorded in SJL as received
the days they were written. THE BRITISH
SPY: Wirt, *The Letters of the British Spy*
(Baltimore, 1811, and other eds.; Leavitt,
Poplar Forest, 40 [no. 670]).

From Alexander J. Dallas

SIR.   Treasury Department 14 Dec. 1814.

On recieving your letter of the 7ʰ instant, I ascertained that
William Armstead had been appointed the Principal Assessor, for the
19ᵗʰ Collection District of Virginia, with the consent of the Senate, on
the 23ᵈ of December 1813; and that he had signified his acceptance of
the office, on the 7ᵗʰ of February following. If, under these circumstances, it is your wish, that any measure should be adopted, on the
subject of your letter, I will chearfully attend to it.

Accept, Sir, my best thanks for your personal kindness. I shall
endeavour to merit your good opinion; for, I am confident, that
whatever may be the issue of a very arduous undertaking, your
approbation rests upon considerations, which do not render success
indispensable.

I have the honor to be, with perfect respect, Sir, Your most obed
Serv   A. J. DALLAS

RC (DLC); endorsed by TJ as received
21 Dec. 1814 and so recorded in SJL. RC
(ViU: TJP); address cover only; with
PoC of TJ to Patrick Gibson, 7 Jan. 1815,
on verso; addressed from "Treasury De-

partment. A. J. Dallas" to "Thomas
Jefferson Esqʳ Monticello Virginia";
franked; postmarked Washington, 16
Dec.

From Patrick Gibson

SIR   Richmond 14th Decem^r 1814—

I wrote you by last mail to which I beg leave to refer you and have now solely to inform you that I have received of Mr Jacquelin Harvie the amount of his brother's note with $8.24 Interest say $185.14 at your credit—With great respect

I am   Your ob^t Servt   PATRICK GIBSON

RC (ViU: TJP-ER); endorsed by TJ as received 16 Dec. 1814 and so recorded in SJL. RC (CSmH: JF); address cover only; with PoC of TJ to William Short, 25 Mar. 1815, on verso; addressed: "Thomas Jefferson Esqr Monticello"; franked; postmarked Richmond, 14 Dec.

From Joseph Milligan

DR SIR.   George Town December 14th 1814

your Note of the 1st Postmarked 7th reached me on monday the 12th I have Ordered the Nautical Almanacs both from Philadelphia and New york to be Sent to you by Mail.

By a Calculation that I have made of the weight of the Monticello Library Ten Waggons to Carry 2500 lbs each will be Sufficient for Transporting it to washington If you have not a person Skilled in packing Books they are Liable to great Injury by land Carriage as I have Experienced Since the war If you Should want a person to as-sist in packing I can Send a young man that has had Experience in that way

Yours with respect   JOSEPH MILLIGAN

RC (DLC); at foot of text: "Thos Jefferson Esqr Monticello"; endorsed by TJ as received 21 Dec. 1814 and so recorded in SJL.

From James Oldham

DEARE SIR   Richmond December 14th 1814.

I informed you on the 11th of October of Mr Foulke Promissing me to have youre memorandum of glass put up at the Glassworks in bal-timore and forworded on to richmond, he rites me that the Glass workes is not in operation and have not bin for Some time and Such Sizes of Glass cannot be Got in Baltimore.

the agent for the boston company has ritten for it and informs me this morning that I may have it in 24 or 25 days. the moment it comes to hand I Shol inform you.

With Grate Respect I have the Hon^r to be Sir your Ob^t Sev^t

J. OLDHAM

RC (MHi); at foot of text: "Thos Jefferson Esqr"; endorsed by TJ as received 16 Dec. 1814 and so recorded in SJL.

To Horatio G. Spafford

DEAR SIR   Monticello Dec. 16. 14.

By the condition of the roads and repeated abandonments of the mail by the way your favor of Nov. 25. did not come to hand until it was certain from it's contents, you had left Washington. I have delayed acknoleging it therefore till you might have reached Albany, and indeed the only object of doing it thus late is to express my regret at not having had the pleasure of recieving you here, which would have been a gratification. for as to public affairs I am entirely withdrawn from every degree of intermedling with them, and almost of reading or thinking of them. my confidence in those at the helm is so entire, as to satisfy me without enquiry that they are going right; and I prefer reading the histories of other times, which furnish amusement without anxiety. writing too is becoming laborious to me & irksome so that I go to the writing table with reluctance. retaining however my esteem and gratitude for those whose good will has been so kindly bestowed upon me, I acknolege yours particularly and tender you my best prayers for your health & prosperity

TH: JEFFERSON

RC (NjMoHP: Lloyd W. Smith Collection); signature, clipped, supplied from PoC, with adjacent note initialed by Spafford on RC: "I permitted J Cook to cut out this Name, as he wished to preserve a specimen of the Autography"; addressed: "Mr Horatio G. Spafford, Albany"; franked; postmarked Milton, 25 Dec.; with notes by Spafford on address cover giving, presumably, the date that this letter was received, 5 Jan. 1815, the dates of two of Spafford's later letters to TJ, 23 Jan. and 15 Feb. 1815, the cryptic notation "2 W.C." [Wheel Carriages?], and his calculation that Samuel Williams was seventy years old (see Spafford to TJ, 24 Feb. 1815). PoC (MHi); on verso of reused address cover to TJ; endorsed by TJ. Mistakenly recorded in SJL as a letter of 10 Dec. 1814.

From John Garnett

S<small>IR</small>   N. Brunswick. N.J. 17 December 1814

I take the liberty to inclose a new method of reducing the "Moon's distance" which I flatter myself is more simple and uniform than any hitherto used.

Having conducted the American Edition of the Nautical Almanac from its beginning in 1803 at a considerable pecuniary loss, besides the great attention it necessarily takes, M[r] Patterson the Professor at Philadelphia has recommended it to published[1] in future by subscription, from the present situation of Commerce, and the Necessity of its being continued for its great use in the Navy of the United States:

If at your suggestion the Secretary of the Navy would so far promote it by takeing a Certain number yearly, it would assist me essentialy; a former Secretary took 150 Copies for the use of the Navy but it was not continued for more than that year. Your well known attachment to Science and the kind attention shewn me when I was introduced to you at Washington, and in your correspondence with the late General Gates which he shew'd me, has encouraged me to make this application

I am with the greatest Respect Sir Your obliged Serv[t]

J<small>OHN</small> G<small>ARNETT</small>

PS. I am going in a short time to pay a farewell visit to <u>England</u>, if there are any late publications or any thing you wish to procure, it would give me great pleasure to be of the least use to you—

The N. Almanac of 1815 is now published. of 1816 I have y[. . .]

RC (DLC); lacking final page; dateline adjacent to closing; endorsed by TJ as received 30 Dec. 1814 and so recorded in SJL. Enclosure not found.

John Garnett (ca. 1750–1820), a native of England and cousin of the Revolutionary War general Horatio Gates, immigrated late in the 1790s to the United States and in 1798 purchased a farm near New Brunswick, New Jersey. For about a decade he edited an American edition of the *Nautical Almanac and Astronomical Ephemeris*, and he published similar scientific works, several of which TJ owned. Garnett was also an avid

agriculturist and a member of both the American Academy of Arts and Sciences and the American Philosophical Society. He died of apoplexy at his New Jersey home (*PTJ*, 30:110, 36:50–1; New Jersey Historical Society, *Proceedings*, new ser., 6 [1921]: 17–20; Sowerby, nos. 3807, 3809–10, 3778; American Academy of Arts and Sciences, *Memoirs*, new ser., 11 [1882]: 40; APS, Minutes, 16 July 1802 [MS in PPAmP]; New York *American*, 19 May 1820).

Garnett met TJ early in 1803 during what Gates called Garnett's "Vissit of Curiosity to W<small>ASHINGTON</small>" (Madison, *Papers, Sec. of State Ser.*, 4:295; TJ to Meriwether Lewis, 30 Apr., 16 May 1803, and TJ to James Cheetham, 17 June 1803 [all DLC]). The United States Navy, under the direction of FORMER SECRETARY Paul Hamilton, used Garnett's edition of

the *Nautical Almanac* in 1811 (Edmund M. Blunt to TJ, 28 June 1811).

[1] Thus in manuscript.

From John Barnes

DEAR SIR— [Geor]ge Town 18th Decr 1814.—

My last Respects, was of the 6th Inst since when—your Scrip Certificate for $10.000—has been left with Mr Nourse to be Consolidated in the Amot of $12,500—6 ₱Ct stock, at the Rate—of 80$ advance for $100 stock—in your Name—of course, it will require your Genl Power of Atty to receive the Int. due the 1h Jany—as well every succeeding Quarterly—payment,

I am most Respectfully—Your Obedt servant

JOHN BARNES.

RC (ViU: TJP-ER); torn at seal; at foot of text: "Thomas Jefferson Esqr Monticello Virgaⁿ"; endorsed by TJ as received 27 Dec. 1814 and so recorded in SJL.

Joseph NOURSE served for decades as register of the United States Treasury

(*JEP*, 1:26, 4:56 [12 Sept. 1789, 10 Feb. 1830]). Tadeusz Kosciuszko's CONSOLIDATED six-percent government stock had been entered in the Treasury ledger on the preceding day, 17 Dec. 1814 (DNA: RG 53, CTSLO, Central Treasury Records Ledger, 65:65).

From Thomas Taylor

SIR, Richmond 19th December 1814.—

I duly received your letter dated the 7th Inst and immediately informed mr Wilson of your claim to 4 or 5 lots of ground in Beverley Town, which is certainly the very center of the little Tract of land he Contemplated selling on the 15th—Mr Wilson is of opinion that the Right to lots in that Town, Reverted to the original proprietors.—from whom he says he purchased, and they having Conveyed to him a general Warrantee—does not seem disposed to admit Your Claim—we did not offer the land for sale, or I shou'd have made Known (Publicly) Your Claim—You will see in the Enquirer, the land, immediately opposite, and on the Chesterfield side of the River, advertized to be sold in the first week in January next—this Tract, I beleive includes the Ferry landing on that side of the River—I have been appointed to make sale of this land altho' I have not seen either of the Gentlemen whose names appear to the advertizement—beleiving it to be as much my duty to protect the purchaser, as it is to procure the best price for the seller—I will esteem it a favour Sir, to Know from You; if Your interest in the Ferry extends to the South side of the River, or if it is Your opinion, the Ferry can be now Established at this place against the wishes of the present incumbents.—I shall with great pleasure do any thing in my power to serve You—.

I am Sir, with Very great respect Your Ob^t Servt

THOS TAYLOR

P.S. m^r Wilson admits that our much respected, and departed friend George Jefferson had notified him of Your claim, but thinks he Claimed only one lot.

RC (MHi); postscript adjacent to signature; at foot of text: "Thos Jefferson Esqr"; endorsed by TJ as received 27 Dec. 1814 and so recorded in SJL.

According to the newspaper ADVERTIZEMENT, on 2 Jan. 1815 Taylor was to auction off 400 acres in Chesterfield County fronting on the James River and belonging to John H. Smith, Peter F. Smith, William Watts, and Jordan Smith (Richmond *Enquirer*, 17 Dec. 1814). TJ had evidently NOTIFIED Thomas Wilson of his claim to lots in Beverley through George Jefferson in 1811 (Jefferson to TJ, 1 Aug. 1811).

From Samuel Thurber

SIR,   Providence RI. 19th Decr 1814—

I presume you will consider it reather as novel to receive an address from a stranger on a subject that he knows not that you ever in the least interested your self in,—The subject is that of Manufactureing of Cotton, a business that is well known to be carried on extensively in the N E States, A business for which I have lately exchanged the Manufactureing of Paper and that which I wish to carrey into one of the Middle States,—As I am a stranger beyond R Island, I know not to whom to apply, from whom to expect more than from one of the Fathers of our country,—I therefore presume to make known to you Sir, That I am anxious to remoove from this, to one of the Southern or Western States, where prospects are better, and where the chance for a rappedly increasing Family is greater than here, To one where the opposers to the best Government in the World have less influence then they have in N England, My mind hath long been in Pennsylvania, Virginia or more West, as I might find most convenant for warter privileges,—The business hath been extreemly lucrative, it is now reather on the decline, and will with all other business in NE. be rewined[1] if the present ungrateful management towards the Southern States continues to be persisted in,—I should preveous to this, have been looking for a place in the Southern or Western States, had I not been opposed by my Family, all of whom are tolerably conversent in the business; They, as they increas and consider, begin to think with me, Therefore I can at a short notice remoove with three Sons, the eldest a natural Mechanic, is now an Agent in a Factory, the Sec^d hath the indoore charge, the Third, a first workeman in the same, a Wife and two Daughters who well know how to handle yarn, these togeather with such other assistants as will be needed, with, say from 8 to 10,000 Dol^s after selling our interests, to put with you, or some other good man, to that purpose, should the idea meet your consideration, you will undoubtedly want something more than my mear say so, I expect to procure such credentials as will be perfectly satisfactory,

Altho Mr Richd Jackson, in Congress is oppos^d in political sentements, I shall not hisetate to resk my reputation with him, M^r J B Howell, in the Senate, is tolerably acquainted with my family, reputation and circumstances, it may not be dificult to obtain further reputable advice,—The Manufactureing of Cotton on a moderate profitable scale will require a Capital of from 30 to 50,000 Dol^s something depending on the situation, 50,000, would be the utmost that I should wish to begin with, 30,000 in a real convenant situation will be entirely sufficient,—I should not engage with any one unless my family could be interested to the amount of about one half, what we did not advance, to have credit for untell we could worke it out by Labour and Profits,

Altho it is probable that you may feel indisposed to trouble yourself with business of the kind, still I think it not improbable but that you may be desirous it should be further extended in your vicinity than it now is, and may have knowledge of some respectable Gentlemen who are desireous of an interest in such an establishment, In case of incouragement I should be highly gratefyed in knowing it, in order that I may speedely see the situation, I verely believe, indeed I know the business may be managed to very great public, as well as private advantage,

The expence of transportation &c of the Cotton and the Goods as at this time, which if saved would be a very handsom income, from a well managed capital of say 30,000 Dol^s—Virginia will in my oppinion ever have a preference of at least 5 ℗ʳCᵗ from Manufactury equally as well managed there—

With Sentements of the highest respect. Sir your Very Humbˡ Sarvᵗ   SAMᴸ THURBER—

RC (RHi); at foot of text: "Thoˢ Jefferson Esqʳ"; endorsed by TJ as received 30 Dec. 1814 and so recorded in SJL.

Samuel Thurber (1757–1839), merchant and manufacturer, was a lifelong resident of Providence, Rhode Island. After serving as a soldier and commissary officer during the American Revolution, he joined his father and two siblings in 1780 to establish a paper mill in the northern part of town, near the family's gristmill. Thurber also operated a store selling paper products in Providence and, late in life, did some farming. He was a justice of the peace during the 1790s and treasurer for nearly thirty years of the local mechanics' and manufacturers' association. Thurber requested information from George Washington in 1788 about starting up a paper mill in Virginia and unsuccessfully sought a government appointment from TJ in 1801 (Richard M. Bayles, ed., *History of Providence County, Rhode Island* [1891], 1:589, 601; Washington, *Papers, Confederation Ser.,* 6:508–9; *PTJ,* 33:187–8, 35:752; *Providence Gazette and Country Journal,* 12 May 1792; *Providence Journal and Town and Country Advertiser,* 10 Apr. 1799; *Providence Gazette,* 4 Apr. 1801; Newport *Rhode-Island Republican,* 12 Apr. 1815; Thurber to TJ, 15 Sept. 1820; *Providence Patriot,* 16 Apr. 1825; gravestone inscription at North Burial Ground, Providence; *Newport Mercury,* 9 Nov. 1839).

[1] Thus in manuscript, presumably meaning "ruined."

From John Adams

DEAR SIR   Quincy December 20. 1814

The most exalted of our young Genius's in Boston have an Ambition to See Montecello, its Library and its Sage. I lately gave a Line of Introduction to Mʳ Everett, our most celebrated Youth: But his Calls at home, forced him back from Washington.

George Ticknor Esquire who will have the Honour to present this to you, has a reputation here, equal to the Character given him in the enclosed Letter from my Nephew, our Athenæum Man, whom you know.

As you are all Heluones Librorum I think you ought to have a Sympathy for each other.

I gave a Letter to Francis Gray a Son of our great Merchant and Patriot which I hope he will have the Honor to present[1] in due time.

The Gentleman you recommended to me, to my great regret has not arrived. I hope no Misfortune has befallen him.

Paine, Lovell and Gerry are gone and left alone

JOHN ADAMS

RC (DLC); at foot of text: "President Jefferson"; endorsed by TJ as received 4 Feb. 1815 via "mr Ticknor" and so recorded in SJL. RC (DLC); address cover only; in same hand as FC; with PoC of TJ to Charles W. Goldsborough, 9 Feb. 1815, on verso; addressed: "His Excellency Thomas Jefferson. Monticello. Virginia. Favor'd by George Ticknor Esquire." FC (Lb in MHi: Adams Papers). Enclosure: William S. Shaw to Adams, Boston, 19 Dec. 1814, apologizing for his inability to introduce Ticknor in person; indicating that he is the son of Elisha Ticknor; describing him as an industrious, studious, well-educated lawyer; commending him for his mastery of Greek, Latin, German, Italian, Spanish, and French; explaining that, prior to pursuing his studies in Europe, he desires to visit various parts of the United States, including "Monticello and the great philosopher there and the great library &c"; and asking Adams to write a letter introducing Ticknor to TJ (RC in DLC; addressed: "The Hon John Adams Esqr. Quincy Favored by George Tickenor Esqr.").

HELUONES LIBRORUM: "gluttons for books." TJ had RECOMMENDED William C. Rives to Adams.

[1] FC: "deliver."

From Charles Clay

C. CLAY TO M[R] JEFFERSON   Dec. 20. 1814.

Reflecting on an expression of yours Relative to an Idea Sometimes entertained by you of Compresing the Moral doctrines taught by Jesus of Nazareth in the Gospels, divested of all other Matters into a small and Regular system of the purest morality ever taught to Mankind, & meritting the highest praise, & most worthy the Strictest attention &c &c. however laudable may be your View & meritorious your intentions in Such a [new?][1] & Critical (delicate) undertaking, I cannot help entertaining doubts & fears for the final issue, how it may effect your future character & Reputation on the page of history as a Patriot, legislator & sound Philosopher, The Metaphysical sophystry of the Day have drawn its adepts into Such a Variety of strange whims & Vagaries, such nicities & Refinements of Reasoning & diction, & such amazing strange, novel, & paradoxical results from such premises, that I feel sensibly for the final event, should you be induced to permit yourself to Send forth Such a piece to the public, lest they might not sufficiently appreciate your good intentions, but ascribe it to Views as inimical to the christian Religion in particular, & eventually to all Religion from divine Authority,—which I am persuaded you Can have no intention of doing, for when we Consider that whatever may occasionally have been its excesses, extravagances, or abusives, it is by far better to be as it is, than[2] be altogether without any,—& that no System of morality however pure it might be, yet without the Santion of, divine authority stampt upon it, would have

[149]

sufficient weight on Vulgar minds to ensure an Observance internal and external,—notwithstanding the excellent beauty of Holiness, & the inticing Charms of Virtue all lovely as she might appear to noble minds when fairly exhibitted in her pure simple & natural form, divested of all insignia.—my fears are, that should your performance not exactly meet the approbation of the public, (both now & hereafter), that your Name will be degraded from the Venerable Council of true, genuine, Useful Philosophy; & Condemned to be Ranked[3] with the wild Sophisters of Jacobinsm the Theosophies of Masonry, With Martinists, Swedenborgers, & Rosecrusians, with the Epopts & Magi of Illuminism &c. which Phantastic kind of beings, future Historians will most assuredly denominate by Some opprobious epithet, as the maniacs of Philosophy &c—And it certainly may be expected that the whole of your numerous Enimies in the Northern[4] & eastern parts of the U.S. with all their Friends, Disciples, followers & associates through out America; (& who it must be Confessed possess Considerable influence in the public education & Consequently in forming the Opinion of the Rising generation) should the performance not exactly Coincide with their Ideas & meet their entire approbation, even in the minutiæ of diction (which it is highly probable it would not) they would greedily Seize the Occasion, & Raise the hue & Cry after you through the world, & all the Canaille of America & Europe would[5] be found barking at your heels!

accept[6] assurances of Respect & esteem   C. CLAY

RC (MHi); dateline at foot of text; endorsed by TJ as received 16 Jan. 1815 and so recorded in SJL. RC (DLC); address cover only; with FC of TJ to Josiah Meigs, 16 Mar. 1815, on verso; addressed: "Tho Jefferson Esqʳ of Monticello Albemarle"; franked; postmarked Lynchburg, 4 Jan., and Charlottesville, 8 Jan.

MARTINISTS adhered to a brand of mystical, cabalistic, and pantheistic gnos-

ticism, while EPOPTS had been fully initiated into the religious mysteries celebrated at ancient Eleusis (*OED*).

[1] Word, illegible, evidently reworked from "nice," or vice versa.
[2] Manuscript: "that."
[3] Manuscript: "Rankled."
[4] Manuscript: "Nothern."
[5] Manuscript: "wuld."
[6] Manuscript: "except."

From William Lee

RESPECTED & VERY DEAR SIR   Bordeaux Decr 20 1814

I take the liberty to send you a copy of a work which I have published here with a view to enlighten the people of France on the motives of our War and to help our good cause. I beg you will read it with indulgence particularly that part relating to the Bourbons which the authorities here insisted on my inserting before they would permit me to print it. It is very imperfect for want of documents but I trust you will pardon its faults and consider it as a mite in support of an administration which has contributed so much to the honor & Glory of our dear Country

It would give me great pleasure to be useful to you here—I have not forgotten how much I owe to the confidence you honord me with and regret I have never had it in my power to prove to you my sincere gratitude—I have named a darling son after you who is now seven years old and promises well

With high respect & venerration I am my very dear Sir Your obliged & obedient Servant   Wᴹ Lᴇᴇ

RC (DLC); at foot of text: "Mʳ Jefferson"; endorsed by TJ as received 22 July 1815 and so recorded in SJL. Enclosure: Lee, *Les États-Unis et L'Angleterre* (Bordeaux, 1814; Poor, *Jefferson's Library*, 11 [no. 684]).

In pp. 343–4 of the enclosed book, Lee portrays ᴛʜᴇ ʙᴏᴜʀʙᴏɴs as a noble family; speaks of America's affection for Louis XVI and its happiness that his successor, Louis XVIII, has reascended the throne of his ancestors; describes the current king of France as generous and wise; and comments that, unlike the autocratic Napoleon, he prefers to rule through kindness.

From John B. Colvin

Sɪʀ,   City of Washington, Decʳ 21. 1814.

In compiling a new edition of the laws of the United States, on which work I am now employed, by appointment from the Secretary of State, I have been at some loss concerning the orthography of names in the Indian treaties. Those state papers, however well framed as to the objects for which they were intended, have, in many cases, evidently been written by illiterate persons, and the spelling of some of the names varies almost in every different treaty; and, sometimes, in the same treaty. I do not mean the name of each Indian, whose ✕ and description appear to the treaties in question; but the names of the nations or tribes; as, for example, the Pattawatimas, Shawanees, &c. frequently spelt Putawatimies, Shawanoese, &c. The orthography, I presume, has, in general, been according to the judgment of the several writers when applying their own conceptions of the established powers of the letters of our alphabet to fix the various sounds of the Indian dialects. I should be thankful for your opinion on the subject; and, from your researches and knowledge, I have no doubt it would be acceptable to your fellow citizens at large.

I have the honor to be, Sir, very respectfully,

your mo. ob. ser.   J. B. COLVIN.

RC (DLC); at foot of text: "His excellency Thomas Jefferson." Recorded in SJL as received 30 Dec. 1814.

On 18 Apr. 1814 Congress passed "An Act authorizing a subscription for the laws of the United States, and for the distribution thereof," which empowered SECRETARY OF STATE James Monroe "to

appoint a competent person" to edit the proposed work. Monroe assigned the task to Colvin on 13 June. The resulting publication was the *Laws of the United States of America, from the 4th of March, 1789, to the 4th of March, 1815*, 5 vols. (Philadelphia and Washington, 1815) (*U.S. Statutes at Large*, 3:129–30; *Laws of the United States of America*, 1:vii).

To Louis H. Girardin

TH: JEFFERSON TO MR GIRARDIN.   Monticello Dec. 21. 14.

I thank you for the gazettes, review, & Cootes's history, all of which I have read, except the last, which I have sufficiently examined to see that it is valuable as a repertory only, without any particular merit. on your mention of Mellish's opinion of the tenets which distinguish the two political parties of this country, I recollected I had written him a letter on the subject of that opinion, and was searching for it to shew it to you when you took your leave. I now send it for your perusal. you will percieve that I analyse the federalists into 3. sections. 1. the Essex junto who are Anglomen, Monarchists, & Separatists. 2. the Hamiltonians, who are Anglomen & Monarchists, but not Separatists. 3. the common mass of federalists who are Anglomen, but neither Monarchists nor Seperatists. the return of this letter with that to mr Adams when perused to satisfaction is requested. I salute you with esteem & respect.

RC (PPAmP: Thomas Jefferson Papers); dateline at foot of text. Enclosure: TJ to John Melish, 13 Jan. 1813.

COOTES'S HISTORY: Charles Coote, *The History of Modern Europe; and a view of the Progress of Society, from the Peace of Paris, in 1763, to the Treaty of Amiens, in*

1802. being a Continuation of Dr. Russell's History (Philadelphia, 1811).

SJL records missing letters from Girardin to TJ of 20 and 21 Dec. 1814, both received from Glenmore on the latter date, and from TJ to Girardin of 25 Dec. 1814.

From James Monroe

Dear Sir   Washington Dec[r] 21. 1814

On enquiry I found that major Armstead had been regularly appointed principal assessor for our district by the advice of the senate & been furnishd with his commission. It had been intended, as I understood, to appt M[r] Minor, but the office of Collector, having been disposed of in our county, it was decided on the distributive principle to confer the other office on some person in another county. The functions of the assessor having hitherto been suspended[1] led to the mistake that the office had not been disposed of.

I have never been in a situation of so much difficulty & embarrassment as that in which I find myself.[2] I came into it not as a volunteer. This city might[3] have been savd, had the measures proposed by the President to the heads of dep[ts] on the 1st of july, and advised by them, and order'd by him,[4] been carried into effect. For this there was full time before the attack was made. whatever may be the merits of general winder, who is undoubtedly intelligent & brave, an infatuation seemed to have taken possession of Gen[l] armstrong, relative to the[5] danger of this place. He could never be made to believe that it was in any danger. The representations of corporate bodies, committees of citizens &ca, were slighted & derided both before & after the first of July. As late as the 23 of aug[t], when the enemy were within 10 miles, by a direct route & marching against it, he treated the idea with contempt altho there was no serious impediment in their way, for[6] the force intended for its defense, was then to be collected at the places of rendevouz & formed into an army.[7] The battle of the next day gave the city to the enemy. The consternation attending in alex[a] & the neighbring country need not be describd. The President, M[r] Rush & I return'd on the 27th. The squadron of the enemy was then before[8] fort washington. Alex[a] had capitulated; this city was prepar'd to[9] surrender a second time, & Georgetown, was ready to capitulate. The infection ran along the coast. Baltimore totter'd, as did other places,[10] all of which were unprepard to resist an immediate attack Armstrong was at Frederick town & winder at Baltimore. no time could be spar'd.[11] The President requested me to act in their stead, which I did as well as I could. The citizens cooperated with me. In two or three days the Secr[ry] of war returnd, but all confidence in him[12] was gone. I observd to the President that the Secr[y] having returnd my functions must cease: that the delicate[13] relations subsisting between the heads of depts renderd it improper for me to act while he was here, without his knowledge & consent.[14] The President saw the justice of the remark. He had an immediate[15] interview, with the secr[y], the consequence of which was the departure of the latter for his home next morning. Such was the state of affairs, and their evident tendency, that no time could be spard for corresponding with any one at a distance to take the office. The pressure on Alex[a], and approaching attack on Bal: with other dangers and in many quarters[16] allowed not a moment of respite for the dep[t]. 24 hours of inaction was sure to produce serious[17] mischief. Those considerations inducd me to retain the office & to incur a labour, & expose[18] myself to a[19] responsibility, the nature & extent[20] of which I well understood, & whose weight has already[21] almost borne me down.

Our finances are in a deplorable state. With a country consisting of the best materials[22] in the world; whose people are patriotic & virtuous, & willing to support the war; whose resources are greater than those of any other country; & whose means have scarcely yet been touchd, we have neither money in the treasury or credit. my opinion always was that a paper medium supported by taxes, to be funded[23] at proper times would answer the public exigencies, with a great saving to the Treasury.[24] Your plan with some modifications, appeard to me to be admirably well adapted to the object.[25] M[r] Dallas had decided on another,[26] which he reported to the committee immediately after his arrival. As soon as I obtaind my papers from Leesburg, I put your remarks on the subject into his hands. He spoke highly of them, but adherd to his own plan, & such is the pressure of difficulties, and the danger attending it;[27] that I have been willing to adopt almost any plan, rather than encounter the risk, of the overthrow of our whole system, which has been so obvious & iminent.[28] secy Dallas is still in possession of your remarks, but I will obtain & send them to you in a few days.[29]

Of the[30] Hartford convention we have yet no intelligence. These gentry, will I suspect, find that they have overacted their part. They cannot dismember the union, or league with the enemy, as I trust[31] & believe,[32] & they cannot now retreat without disgrace. I hope that the leaders, will soon take rank in society with Burr & others of that stamp. with great respect &

esteem I am dear Sir your friend & servant   JA[s] MONROE

RC (DLC); endorsed by TJ as received 27 Dec. 1814 and so recorded in SJL. Dft (DLC: Monroe Papers); lacks closing and signature; endorsed by Monroe, in part, as "relating to the capture of the city."

President James Madison had appointed TJ's son-in-law Thomas Mann Randolph, of Albemarle County, to the OFFICE OF COLLECTOR (*JEP*, 2:456, 461 [18, 21 Jan. 1814]). The FUNCTIONS OF THE ASSESSOR had been suspended in

Virginia as a result of the commonwealth's decision, on 7 Jan. 1814, to pay its portion of the land tax out of its own funds (*Acts of Assembly* [1813–14 sess.], 61). In his memorandum of a 1 July 1814 meeting with the HEADS OF DEP^TS, Madison noted agreement on the need for a "Survey of the grounds" near Washington, the bringing forward of "Arms & Camp Equipage," and the massing of 13,140 troops for the protection of the United States capital (DLC: Madison Papers). British forces captured Washington following their victory over the Americans at the BATTLE of Bladensburg.

In his 17 Oct. 1814 report to the Ways and Means COMMITTEE of the United States House of Representatives, Secretary of the Treasury Alexander J. Dallas called for both sizable tax increases and the "establishment of a national institution, operating upon credit combined with capital, and regulated by prudence and good faith," which he believed to be "the only efficient remedy for the disordered condition of our circulating medium" (*ASP, Finance*, 2:866–9). For the REMARKS ON THE SUBJECT of finance shown to Dallas, see note to Monroe to TJ, 10 Oct. 1814.

[1] Reworked in Dft from "The law imposing the tax having been suspended last year."
[2] Preceding seven words interlined in Dft in place of "attendd with such weight of labour, as at present."
[3] Word interlined in Dft in place of "ought to."
[4] Preceding four words interlined in Dft.
[5] In Dft Monroe here canceled "probable."
[6] In Dft Monroe here canceled "at that time winder."
[7] In Dft Monroe here canceled "winder

had under him, here, abt 2300 men; Stansbury had just reached Bladensbg with abt 2,200."
[8] Dft: "then approaching."
[9] In Dft Monroe here canceled "effect another."
[10] Remainder of sentence interlined in Dft.
[11] Word interlined in Dft in place of "lost."
[12] Dft here adds "if any had before existed."
[13] Word interlined in Dft.
[14] In Dft Monroe here canceled "that altho I had thought it the duty of every man to put his shoulder to the wheel, in the embarrassd state in which We had found aff^rs on our return to the city."
[15] Word interlined in Dft.
[16] Preceding seven words interlined in Dft.
[17] Reworked in Dft from "to be felt seriously."
[18] RC: "expose expose."
[19] Preceding four words interlined in Dft.
[20] Preceding two words interlined in Dft.
[21] Word interlined in Dft.
[22] Reworked in Dft from "population."
[23] In Dft Monroe here canceled "annually, or a pledge for it."
[24] Dft: "public treasury."
[25] Preceding eleven words interlined in Dft in place of "had my approbation."
[26] In Dft Monroe here canceled "& digested it."
[27] Preceding five words not in Dft.
[28] Reworked in Dft from "which was imminent."
[29] Sentence not in Dft.
[30] Dft here adds "proceedings of the."
[31] Dft: "hope."
[32] Remainder of sentence interlined in Dft, which also gives the sentences of this paragraph in a different sequence.

From James Savage

Boston 21 Decr. 1814

by the hands of my friend, Geo: Ticknor Esqr. who is honoured with letters of introduction to you, I have the pleasure of forwarding the first volume of State Papers, published by Thos: B. Wait & sons. Those gentlemen, having engaged me to assist their publication, have desired me to acknowledge with due respect the letter of 25 Septr. last, in which you kindly communicated the information and advice, of which they were in want.

On examination of the volume, I think your Excellency will observe that a very large part of its contents are not contained in the pages of the National Intelligencer. Much difficulty occurred in the search for some of the papers; and of one, the message of 6 Decr. 1805, referred to in p. 268 the copy could not be obtained until last week. It will appear in the Second volume, which will be ready for delivery in a fortnight. Of that and the Succeeding volumes a copy will, with your permission, be forwarded, as they successively issue from the press.

With sentiments of high respect, I remain,

Sir, your obedient servant   JAMES SAVAGE

RC (DLC); at head of text: "Thos. Jefferson Esqr."; endorsed by TJ as received 4 Feb. 1815 and so recorded in SJL. Enclosure: *State Papers and Publick Documents of the United States from the accession of Thomas Jefferson to the presidency, exhibiting a complete view of our foreign relations since that time,* 5 vols. (Boston, 1814–15; Poor, *Jefferson's Library,* 11 [no. 659]), vol. 1.

James Savage (1784–1873) was a life-long resident of Boston who graduated from Harvard University in 1803, studied law, and was admitted to the Massachusetts bar four years later. He made his mark, however, as an antiquarian and public servant. During his long career Savage compiled and edited numerous legal, historical, and genealogical works, including *A Genealogical Dictionary of the First Settlers of New England,* 4 vols. (1860–62), and two editions of John Winthrop, *The History of New England from 1630 to 1649* (Boston, 1825–26 and 1853). He also helped to establish public

elementary schools in his hometown, one of the country's first savings banks, and the Boston Athenæum, and he was a member of the local school committee. Savage served several terms in the Massachusetts legislature during the 1820s and was a delegate to his state's 1820 constitutional convention. He sat on Harvard's board of overseers, 1838–53, belonged to the Massachusetts Historical Society for sixty years, 1813–73, and was president of the latter organization, 1841–55 (*DAB; Tribute of the Massachusetts Historical Society to the memory of their Late Senior Member and Former President, the Hon. James Savage, LL.D.* [1873], esp. 4–5, 19–20; *Harvard Catalogue,* 112, 184; Boston *New-England Palladium,* 20 Jan. 1807; Boston *Repertory,* 17 Oct. 1820; Salem *Essex Register,* 16 May 1821, 14 May 1827; Boston *Columbian Centinel,* 11 May 1825; *Boston Daily Advertiser,* 10 Mar. 1873).

TJ's MESSAGE OF 6 DECR. 1805 to Congress discussed the hostile attitude of the Spanish court toward the United

States. The first volume of the *State Papers and Publick Documents* wrongly suggested that it "probably consisted of but few words," while the next volume printed the document in full (1:268, 2:4–6).

To Patrick Gibson

SIR   Monticello. Dec. 23. 14.

Since mine of Nov. 21. I have recieved yours of Nov. 23. Dec. 7. & 14. in that of[1] Nov. 23. came the 45.D. small bills, and in the last a notice of mr Harvie's payment. I regret much my tobacco is not at market, and am pressing my manager to hurry it. we are but just now beginning to grind our wheat, which will go down as fast as it is ground. I think the remaining[2] fibre of difference between the negociators at Ghent is so slender, & that too on the principle of uti possidetis which the English will find to be against them, that peace cannot fail to follow.

if you have obtained a judgment against Philpot, there should be no hesitation at issuing an execution against his body. we have nothing to do with hunting out his fraudulent concealments of property. when committed to jail he must either lie there, swear out, or pay the money. be so good then as to take this step immediately. I did not know the paiment was still deferred.   I must ask the favor of you to inclose 130.D. to Jeremiah A. Goodman at Poplar Forest near Lynchburg by the first mail to that place. Accept the assurance of my great esteem & respect   TH: JEFFERSON

PoC (Sheldon Vanauken, Lynchburg, 1958, on deposit ViU: TJP); on verso of reused address cover to TJ; torn at seal, with missing word recopied by TJ above the line; at foot of text: "Mr Gibson"; endorsed by TJ.

TJ's MANAGER at Poplar Forest was Jeremiah A. Goodman. For the legal PRINCIPLE OF UTI POSSIDETIS, see note to James Monroe to TJ, 30 Nov. 1814.

[1] TJ here canceled "the 7th."
[2] Word interlined.

To Jeremiah A. Goodman

D^R SIR   Monticello Dec. 23. 14

James arrived last night with your letter of the 19th. that of the 8th had been rec^d a day or two before, and that [of][1] the 3^d about a week. I will by our next mail desire mr Gibson to inclose you 130.D. for mr Poindexter by mail, which I suppose you will recieve in a fortnight. I have a letter from mr Radford desiring the road thro' his land may not be opened until the court establishes it, assuring me he will make no opposition. we must let that part lie then, & finish the rest. the account of your wheat crop is really disheartening. after taking out the seed sown, it does not give 2. for 1. the corn too is short. but it is sufficient if dealt out economically. by which I do not mean that any thing is to be under-fed. I know that neither people nor horses can work unless well fed, nor can hogs or sheep be raised. but full experience here has proved that 12. barrels for every laborer will carry the year through if kept under lock & key. we have tried this year the grinding the corn for the fattening hogs, & boiling the meal into mush. it is surprising how much sooner they have fattened. we think we have saved one half. the same saving might be made by grinding the corn for your horses and mixing the meal with chopped straw. the sending only 20. blankets was a mistake of mrs Randolph's. the other 2. shall go by the waggon. I hope you are hurrying the tobacco. Davy, Bartlet, Nace & Eve set out this morning for Poplar Forest. let them start on their return with the hogs the day after your holidays end, which I suppose will be on Wednesday night, so that they may set out Thursday morning. caution them against whipping the hogs. the last year there was one so bruised all over, that not a single piece of it could be used, & several were so injured that many pieces of them were lost. I am very glad to learn that the negroes have recieved their clothes. Accept my best wishes   TH: JEFFERSON

RC (NN: George Arents Tobacco Collection); addressed from "Th: Jefferson" to "Mr Jeremiah A. Goodman Poplar Forest Bedford by Davy, Bartlet Nace & Eve."

Missing letters from Goodman to TJ of 3, 8, 19, and 21 Dec. 1814 are recorded in SJL as received 14, 20, 22 Dec. 1814, and 7 Jan. 1815, respectively, with the last three letters described as coming from Poplar Forest.

On 29 July 1814 Goodman had mutually bound himself and TJ to pay Dabney POINDEXTER £39 by Christmas Day "for value received." Goodman made a partial payment of $100 for TJ on 11 Jan. 1815, an additional payment of £8.16 on an unspecified date, and a final payment of 4 shillings "in full of the within bond" on 29 July 1815 (MS in CSmH: JF; in Goodman's hand and signed by him "for thos jefferson"; witnessed by Samuel Poindexter; signed receipts on verso in Dabney Poindexter's hand, with the first one witnessed by James Poindexter; endorsed by Dabney Poindexter: "Bond of Jeremiah A. Goodman & Thomas Jefferson"; endorsed by TJ: "Poindexter Dabney 1814. Dec. 25.").

The letter from William Radford to TJ concerning THE ROAD THRO' HIS LAND is presumably that of 8 Dec. 1814, not found, which is recorded in SJL as received 20 Dec. 1814 from Lynchburg. SJL also records missing letters from TJ to Radford, 24 Dec. 1814, and Radford to TJ, 7 Jan. 1815, with the latter received 18 Jan. 1815 from Poplar Forest.

TJ expected the Christmas HOLIDAYS at Poplar Forest to end on Wednesday, 28 Dec. 1814.

[1] Omitted word editorially supplied.

To John McAllister (1753–1830)

SIR   Mon[t]i[c]ello Dec. 24. 14.

I inclose you a pr of spectacle frames with their compleat set of glasses, which is one of 3. or 4. sets you were so kind as to furnish me with several years ago. it is lately only that I have called them into use. I found the glasses actually in them render a perfect vision: but on changing them for any of the other numbers, the object is entirely confused. I know I have not mismatched the other numbers because, for fear of that, I have made it a point never to take out two numbers at the same time, but always to put up one pair before I took out another. I am obliged therefore to ask your rectifying hand to them, and when you shall have put them to rights, to return them to me by mail, by which conveyance I send them to you. I occasionally have to remit small sums to Philadelphia for books, newspapers E&c. and will take care to add your bill to my first remittance. Accept the assurance of my esteem & respect   TH: JEFFERSON

PoC (MoSW-M: Bernard Becker Medical Library); on verso of reused address cover of Francis W. Gilmer to TJ, 13 Nov. 1814; dateline faint; at foot of text: "Mr John McAlister"; endorsed by TJ.

John McAllister (1753–1830), optician and craftsman, was born in Glasgow and apprenticed there as a turner, spinning-wheel maker, carpenter, and joiner. He immigrated to America in 1775 and worked in New York City until 1781, when he moved to Philadelphia. During the decades that followed, McAllister specialized in the production of walking sticks, riding whips, and spectacles. TJ purchased glasses from him, both for himself and others, in 1800, 1804, 1806, and 1808. After partnering briefly with James Matthews, 1800–03, McAllister operated on his own until he brought his namesake son into the firm in 1811. John McAllister & Son remained in business until the elder McAllister's death, when its name changed to John McAllister, Jr., & Company. The younger John McAllister (1786–1877), who had graduated from the University of Pennsylvania in 1803, retired in 1836 and spent the rest of his life pursuing various historical and literary interests and amassing a thirty-thousand-volume personal library (Henry Simpson, *The Lives of Eminent Philadelphians* [1859], 731–3; *Association of Centenary Firms and Corporations of the United States* [1916], 71–2; *General Alumni Catalogue of the University of Pennsylvania* [1917], 25; *MB*, 2:1017, 1193; TJ to McAllister, 5 June 1804 [MHi]; McAllister to TJ, 25 Nov. 1808 [DLC]; Philadelphia *Poulson's American Daily Advertiser*, 17 May 1803, 8 Apr. 1811, 20 May 1830; *Philadelphia Inquirer*, 18 Dec. 1877; Philadelphia *North American*, 19 Dec. 1877).

To William Thornton

Your letter of the 11th is duly recieved, and the two drawings you desire shall be immediately packed. the difficulty of finding a conveyance may occasion delay. that which you propose with the books is uncertain; but I will be on the watch for a passenger in the stage to Washington, who will take care of the box to give it an inside passage.[1] the painting of Hector & Andromache had been made by West for his own purposes, & was given by him to Genl Kosciuzko when he was in London recieving the compliments, addresses, services of plate E^{t}c which he had so well merited. on his leaving this country he gave it to me. Clopper exhibited his loom at the court of our county, and might on that day have contracted for 20 or 30. single looms at the Connecticut or Baltimore prices; but asking 100.D. for a loom, and 50.D. for the patent right of a single one, he contracted for not a single one, and never will here. for the people on reflection asked why give 100.D. to let the left hand & both feet be idle? if I could employ them on some thing else while the right hand is doing their work, it might be worth while. mr Cooper too in his last Emporium has brought the originality of the invention into doubt. he supposes the machinery taken from that of the water, steam & horse looms which have been many years introduced into England & France, & some here. the price of a loom in Connecticut is 40.D. in Baltimore 50.D. the patent price of a single one 20.D. the patentee at Baltimore very kindly wrote to me in consequence of your letter to him, and offered to make me one for 50.D. but as I dare not use it here without paying 50.D. more for a patent right, I have deferred answering him until I could negociate with the patentee here. the law I think should not permit sales by geographical districts. every man should be free to use any where what he can lawfully buy any where. this abuse with the plagiarisms committed & imposed on us renders the advantage of the patent law problematical. I wish it were a rule for you to report to Congress annually the titles of the patents granted in the year. I have your report of 1811. if there have been any others, one of the supernumerary copies would be very acceptable.—your trials in Washington have been severe. but they have done us double good by rousing our people and loading our enemies with eternal disgrace. I hope the public buildings will be repaired, without regard to expence. that of their library will be more than repaired should they conclude to take mine. the rarity of many of the books and choice of editions of the greater part render the collection really valuable. present my respects to the ladies & accept the assurance of my great esteem

TH: JEFFERSON

RC (DLC: Thornton Papers); addressed: "Doct" William Thornton Washington. Col."; franked; postmarked Milton, 28 Dec. PoC (DLC); endorsed by TJ.

After mentioning Walter Janes's patent, Thomas Cooper commented in his EMPORIUM that "It seems to me a kind of speculation in the Eastern states . . . to take out patents for English inventions, and sell the patent rights to the more careless and credulous manufacturers in the Southern states. But I wish it were recol-

lected, that by the laws of the United States, no patent can be legally obtained for an invention already invented: no man can legally obtain a patent under our federal laws, for merely introducing a process or machine invented elsewhere" (*Emporium of Arts & Sciences*, new ser., 3 [1814]: 458–9). The PATENTEE AT BALTIMORE of Janes's loom, George Greer, had written TJ on 9 Aug. 1814. The PATENTEE HERE in Virginia was Francis C. Clopper.

¹ Reworked from "package."

From Thomas Appleton

Paris 26 December 1814.

I believe, Sir, that the last time I had the honor of addressing you, it was on the Subject of the bust of General Washington modell'd by Cerracchi. I had, in vain, long sought this bust at your Request, when finally I discover'd that m^r Lee, Consul at Bordeaux was the owner of it; at which place Cerracchi disembark'd from America, previous to his fatal journey to Paris.—In compliance with my advice m^r Lee has forwarded it to me in Italy, and I have Confided it with a friend at Carrara.—All those Americans who have Seen it, and among the number is our friend m^r mazzei, universally pronounce it an incomparable likeness; and I have had already copied various busts in marble by a Sculptor in that City and who in this branch of the art, is perhaps little inferior to Canova of Rome.—Should the government, as I have been inform'd, be desirous of a Statue or a bust, it Can be executed at Carrara on very moderate terms, & Superior in Stile to any other spot in Europe.—As our Commerce became totally anihilated in the mediterranean, I Came to this City a few months since to terminate Some Small unadjusted Concerns, when the Consulate of this place became vacant by the dismissal of m^r Warden.—Mr Barnet now officiates, but only provisionally, as he is Consul for Havre, and will very shortly repair to his consulate on the Re-opening of trade, a period, it seems, from the Conclusion of peace, very near approaching.—I am, Sir, for various Reasons after having fill'd the Consulate of Leghorn for Seventeen years, now desirous to obtain an exchange in that of the Consulate, and agency of Paris, and to which end I have written to the government, as likewise, has m^r Crawford interested himself to obtain for me this nomination.—I have particularisd "and agency," for you are Sensible, Sir, that the Consulate of this City, tho' it is attended with considerable occupation, it is unaccompanied with any pecuniary emoluments, unless the form of agency is annex'd to it; it is for this reason, the government has Connected them together, and Affix'd the Salary of 2000– Dollars—may I then request, Sir, your generous mediation in my behalf, should it not be inconsistent with those rules which govern you on Similar Applications.—

I beg, Sir, you will Accept, the most unfeign'd expressions of my unalterable respect—

TH: APPLETON
Consul for U.S.A
Leghorn.

RC (DLC); at foot of text: "Th. Jefferson Esqr monticello"; endorsed by TJ as received 22 Mar. 1815 and so recorded in SJL.

Thomas Appleton (1763–1840), the son of a merchant in Boston, traveled to France in 1786 bearing a letter of introduction to TJ. Over the course of the next few years he was involved in supplying oil to Paris. Appleton attempted unsuccessfully to secure the United States consulship at Lisbon early in the 1790s. In 1798 President John Adams appointed him consul at Leghorn (Livorno), and he held that position until his death. During his long tenure Appleton procured wine and marble for TJ and corresponded with the former president about Philip Mazzei and his relations, the settlement of Mazzei's estate, the execution of work in marble for the University of Virginia, and other matters (Isaac Appleton Jewett, comp., *Memorial of Samuel Appleton, of Ipswich, Massachusetts* [1850], 36; *PTJ*, 10:160, 14:60, 18:152, 358–9; Washington, *Papers, Pres. Ser.*, 9:246–7; *JEP*, 1:260, 5:290 [7, 8 Feb. 1798, 15 June 1840]; Philipp Fehl, "The Account Book

of Thomas Appleton of Livorno: A Document in the History of American Art, 1802–1825," *Winterthur Portfolio* 9 [1974]: 123–51; *MB*, 2:1116, 1318, 1362, 1406–7; Appleton to TJ, 25 Oct. 1815, 18 Mar. 1820, 8 May 1825).

TJ first wrote Appleton about Giuseppe Ceracchi's BUST OF GENERAL WASHINGTON on 5 July 1803. The consul's most recent letter to TJ, which also dealt with the procurement of the sculpture, was dated 26 Nov. 1808 (both DLC). The Metropolitan Museum of Art in New York City owns a marble version of this bust (Washington, *Papers, Pres. Ser.*, 9:132–5). Ceracchi's FATAL JOURNEY TO PARIS ended in January 1801 with his execution for his alleged participation in a plot to assassinate Napoleon (*PTJ*, 32:62n).

Appleton requested a transfer to the consulate in Paris in letters to Secretary of State James Monroe and President James Madison of 15 Aug. and 26 Dec. 1814, respectively (DNA: RG 59, LAR, 1809–17). Both letters claimed the support of William H. CRAWFORD, United States minister plenipotentiary to France.

To Elizabeth Trist

MY GOOD FRIEND   Monticello Dec. 26.

The mail between us passes very slowly. your letter of Nov. 17. reached this place on the 14th inst only. I think while you were writing it the candles must have burnt blue, and that a priest or some other Conjurer should have been called in to exorcise your room. — to be serious however, your view of things is more gloomy than necessary. true, we are at war; that that war was unsuccesful by land the first year, but honorable the same year by sea, and equally by sea and land ever since. our resources, both of men and money are abundant, if wisely called forth & administered. I acknolege that experience does not as yet seem to have led our legislatures into the best course of either. the plan of Colo Monroe both as to regulars & militia, was marked with the stamp of perfect wisdom. but it seems to have been overruled, and the projects for raising money by establishing more banks, is like the dropsical man aiming at a cure by additional potations of water. I am afraid therefore it will require another year of distress for men & money, to bring us up to the military establishment we have rejected, and to the system of funding on special hypothecations of taxes, which the experience of the whole world has proved the only practicable method of anticipating, during a war, the resources of peace. — but we are strong. we can bear a great deal of suffering and still beat our enemy in the end.   I think however there will be peace. the Negociators at Ghent are agreed in every thing except as to a rag of Maine which we cannot[1] yield, nor they seriously care about. but it serves them to hold by until they can hear what the Convention of Hartford will do. when they shall see, as they will see, that nothing is done there, they will let go their hold, and we shall have peace, on the status ante bellum.

you have seen that New Hampshire & Vermont refuse to join the mutineers, and Connecticut does it with a 'saving of her duty to the federal[2] Constitution.' do you believe that Massachusets, on the good faith and aid of little Rhode-island will undertake a war against the rest of the Union & the one half of herself certainly never. — so much for politics. — we are all well, little and big, young & old. mr & mrs Divers enjoy very so so health, but keep about. mr Randolph had the command of a select corps during summer; but that has been discharged some time. we are feeding horses with our wheat, and looking at the taxes coming on us, as an approaching wave in a storm. still I think we shall live as long, eat as much, & drink as much, as if the wave had already glided under our ship. some how or other these things find their way out as they come in, & so I suppose they will now. God bless you and give you health, happiness & hope the real comforters of this netherworld. TH: JEFFERSON

PoC (MHi); partially dated; at foot of first page: "Mrs Trist"; endorsed by TJ as a letter of 26 Dec. 1814 and so recorded in SJL.

NEW HAMPSHIRE & VERMONT refused to send official delegations to the Hartford Convention, although several predominantly Federalist counties in these states dispatched representatives (Banner, *Hartford Convention*, 328–9). SAV-ING OF HER DUTY TO THE FEDERAL CONSTITUTION: Connecticut's legislature instructed its convention delegates to devise and recommend only "such measures for the safety and welfare of these States, as may consist with our obligations as members of the national Union" (New Haven *Connecticut Journal*, 7 Nov. 1814).

[1] TJ here canceled "give."
[2] Word interlined.

From Joseph C. Cabell

DEAR SIR   Richmond. 27 Decr 1814.

The enclosed letter, which I received under cover of your favor of 16th Oct. having remained a sufficient length of time in my hands, I now return it agreeably to your desire, & beg you to receive my sincere thanks for the communication. I have taken the liberty to keep a copy of it, for my own gratification & instruction & for the occasional perusal of such friends as may be desirous to obtain information. It shall neither go into the papers, nor be indiscreetly used. Should you continue your researches upon finance, or any of the Branches of political economy, you would gratify me extremely by affording me a perusal of your papers. Mr Ritchie has shewn me your Letter on the subject of Tracy's work on Political economy. This was the first intelligence I have received of that work: & from the manner in which you speak of it, as well as from the high reputation of that illustrious senator, it must be a very interesting production. I therefore entreat the favor of you, in the event of Col: Duane's not publishing his translation, & of your recovering the French Copy, to give me an opportunity of perusing the latter. I would take particular care of it, & return it safely into your hands in the course of a month or six months: so that none of your other friends who might sollicit a similar favor, sh^d be disappointed from neglect or tardiness on my part.

The Session will terminate about the end of this or the middle of next week. Our revenue will be swelled by the new taxes we have imposed to a million of Dollars. The Farmer's Bank have already advanced the sum of $200,000; & are now in treaty with us to advance the[1] sum of $800,000—in anticipation of the Revenue. In addition to this, a Loan for a million of Dollars will be attempted, probably on the terms stated in the report of the Committee of Finance of the H. of Delegates, which you have seen in the papers. Constitutional[2] difficulties deter many of the members from the idea[3] of issuing treasury notes by the State, on the plan of the notes issued at Washington. Auditor's warrants or certificates, founded on real antecedent transactions between the state & its citizens, bearing 6 p^r cent interest, will probably be authorized: & a further authority to fund these certificates at 8 p^r cent will probably be given to the Treasurer. In the course of a few days these measures will be decided on. From the commencement of the session, I have entertained doubts whether a million could be borrowed at 8 p^r cent: & the money being clearly necessary to prepare the state for defence during the next campaign, I should have been willing & indeed have been desirous to ensure the Loan, by making a contract with the Virginia Bank, on such a scheme of borrowing as w^d not have augmented the Currency of bank paper, & yet w^d have procured for the state the am^t wanted. But the officers of that institution, after first favoring the plan, suddenly tacked about, and put a stop to all ideas of the kind, by demanding such terms as no one can think of granting. We are thrown back on the scheme of a Loan from Individuals at 8 p^r cent—which I should greatly prefer, were such a Loan practicable. In order to obtain the funds requisite for the use of the State, we have to wade with patience thro' the difficulties resulting from diversity of views & opinions in the Houses of assembly, & conflicting, antisocial interests in society. I still hope, however, that we shall provide the sums necessary for the defence of the State, whatever want of system or consistency may appear on the face of our measures. The defence Bill, or Bill for classing the militia is still before the House of Delegates. It will probably be rejected.

Col: Yancey in the course of this session has shewn me a petition Signed by Col: Randolph, the object of which was to obtain the passage of a law authorizing him to open the mountain falls above milton, & to receive a toll on vessels & produce passing the same. I observed to Col: Y. that the object of that petition appeared to m[e in?] conflict with the Charter of the Company with which you have had [so?] much trouble, and advised him to procure from Col: R. an explanatory statement of the reasons that induced the petition: for without shewing that the Company have forfeited their Charter I do not see how we could transfer the powers & rights of the company to an Individual. Perhaps I do not understand Col: R's views on this subject. Col: Y. has determined to lay over the petition till another

Session. A Bill has passed authorizing Wm Wood to open the River from Milton down to Columbia: but in this case, it is understood that the company authorized by a former law has never been formed, & that the law is a dead letter. I need not observe that it would give me great pleasure to serve Col: Randolph—& that I remain

most faithfully & sincerely y^r friend   JOSEPH C. CABELL.

RC (ViU: TJP-PC); damaged at seal; addressed: "Thomas Jefferson esq. Monticello"; franked; postmarked Richmond, 28 Dec.; endorsed by TJ as received 30 Dec. 1814 and so recorded in SJL; with notation by TJ on address cover pertaining to his 5 Jan. 1815 reply to Cabell: "must go further wrong before we shall get right. Tracy's work Say Auditor's notes Col° R." Enclosure: TJ to James Madison, 15 Oct. 1814.

TJ's 19 Aug. 1814 letter concerning Destutt de Tracy's WORK ON POLITICAL ECONOMY is noted at TJ to Thomas Ritchie, 27 Sept. 1814. The session of the Virginia General Assembly ended on 19 Jan. 1815 instead of the END OF THIS OR THE MIDDLE OF NEXT WEEK (Leonard, General Assembly, 277). The General Assembly passed legislation allowing the governor of Virginia to borrow $200,000 and up to $800,000 from the FARMER'S BANK on 18 Nov. and 29 Dec. 1814, respectively (Acts of Assembly [1814–15 sess.], 56–7). On 10 Jan. 1815 the legislature authorized a loan of a little more than A MILLION OF DOLLARS, repayable

through the redemption of certificates carrying an interest rate of up to 8 percent (Acts of Assembly, 58–9). The DEFENCE BILL, OR BILL FOR CLASSING THE MILITIA, did pass into law on 18 Jan. 1815 as "An Act authorizing a Regular Force for the Defence of the Commonwealth" (Acts of Assembly, 40–52).

No petition written or signed by Thomas Mann Randolph regarding the opening of the MOUNTAIN FALLS ABOVE MILTON has been found. The Rivanna Company had sporadically caused TJ MUCH TROUBLE. The FORMER LAW of 29 Jan. 1811 created the Rivanna River Company and authorized it to improve navigation "from the town of Columbia, in the county of Fluvanna, to the town of Milton, in the county of Albemarle" (Acts of Assembly [1810–11 sess.], 42–5; see also Petition of Thomas Jefferson and Others to the Virginia General Assembly, [before 13 Dec. 1810]).

[1] Manuscript: "the the."
[2] Cabell here canceled "scrup."
[3] Word interlined in place of "plan."

To José Corrêa da Serra

DEAR SIR   Monticello Dec. 27. 14.

Yours of the 9th has been duly recieved, & I thank you for the Recipe for imitating Puzzolane; which I shall certainly try on my cisterns the ensuing summer. the making them impermeable to water is of great consequence to me. that one chemical subject may follow another, I inclose you two morsels of ore found in this neighborhood, & supposed to be of Antimony. I am not certain, but I believe both are from the same peice: and altho' the very spot where that was found is not known, yet it is known to be within a certain space not too large to be minutely examined, if the material be worth it. this you can have ascertained in Philadelphia, where it is best known to the artists how great a desideratum antimony is with them.

You will have seen that I resigned the chair of the American Philosophical society, not awaiting your further information as to the settlement of the general opinion on a successor, without schism. I did it because the term of election was too near to admit further delay.

On the subject which entered incidentally into our conversation while you were here, when I came to reflect maturely, I concluded to be silent. to do wrong is a melancholy resource. even where retaliation renders it indispensably necessary. it is better to suffer much from the scalpings, the conflagrations,[1] the rapes and rapine of savages, than to countenance and strengthen such barbarisms by retortion. I have ever deemed it more honorable, & more profitable too, to set a good example than to follow a bad one. the good opinion of mankind, like the lever of Archimedes, with the given fulcrum, moves the world. I therefore have never proposed or mentioned the subject to any one.

I have recieved a letter from mr Say, in which he expresses a thought of removing to this country, having discontinued the manufactory in which he was engaged; and he asks information from me of the prices of land, labor, produce E^{t}c. in the neighborhood of Charlottesville, on which he has cast his eye. it's neighborhood has certainly the advantages of good soil, fine climate, navigation to market, and rational and republican society. it would be a good enough position too for the reestablishment of his cotton works, on a moderate scale, and combined with the small plan of agriculture, to which he seems solely to look. but when called on to name prices, what is to be said? we have no fixed prices now. our dropsical medium is long since divested of the quality of a measure of value; nor can I find any other. in most countries a fixed quantity of wheat is perhaps the best permanent standard. but here the blockade of our whole coast preventing all access to a market, has depressed the price of that, and exalted that of other things, in opposite directions, and, combined with the effects of the paper deluge, leaves really no common measure of values to be resorted to. this paper too, recieved now without confidence & for momentary purposes only, may, in a moment, be worth nothing. I shall think further on the subject, and give to mr Say the best information in my power. to myself such an addition to our rural society would be inestimable; and I can readily concieve that it may be for the benefit of his children & their descendants to remove to a country where, for enterprise & talents, so many avenues are open to fortune and fame. but whether, at his time of life, & with habits

formed on the state of society in France, a change for one so entirely
different will be for his personal happiness you can better judge than
myself.

Mᵣ Say will be surprised to find that 40. years after the developement of sound financial principles by Adam Smith and the Economists, and a dozen years after he has given them to us in a corrected,
dense & lucid form, there should be so much ignorance of them in
our country: that instead of funding issues of paper on the hypothe-
cation of specific redeeming taxes, (the only method of anticipating,
in a time of war, the resources of times of peace, tested by the experience of nations,) we are trusting to tricks of jugglers on the cards, to
the illusions of banking schemes for the resources of the war, and for
the cure of colic to inflations of more wind. the wise proposition of the
Secretary at war too for filling our ranks with regulars, and putting
our militia into an effective form, seems to be laid aside. I fear therefore that, if the war continues, it will require another year of sufferance for men and money to lead our legislators into such a military
and financial regimen as may carry us thro' a war of any length. but
my hope is in peace. the Negociators at Ghent are agreed now on
every point save one, the demand and cession of a portion of Maine.
this, it is well known, cannot be yielded by us, nor deemed by them
an object for continuing a war so expensive, so injurious to their commerce & manufactures, & so odious in the eyes of the world. but it is
a thread to hold by until they can hear the result, not of the Congress
of Vienna, but of Hartford. when they shall know, as they will know,
that nothing will be done there, they will let go their hold, and complete the peace of the world, by agreeing to the status ante bellum. indemnity for the past, and security for the future, which was our motto
at the beginning of this war, must be adjourned to another, when,
disarmed & bankrupt, our enemy shall be less able to insult and plunder the world with impunity. this will be after my time. one war, such
as that of our revolution, is enough for one life. mine has been too
much prolonged to make me the witness of a second, & I hope for a
coup de grace before a third shall come upon us. if indeed Europe has
matters to settle which may reduce this hostis humani generis to a
state of peace and moral order, I shall see that with pleasure, and then
sing, with old Simeon, nunc dimittas Domine. for yourself cura ut
valeas, et me, ut amaris, ama.   Tʜ: Jᴇғғᴇʀsᴏɴ

PoC (DLC); at foot of first page: "M.
Correa de Serra."

ᴘᴜᴢᴢᴏʟᴀɴᴇ is a variant spelling of
"pozzolana," a volcanic ash used to make
waterproof cement (*OED*). Frank Carr
had sent TJ the enclosed specimens of
what he thought to be ᴀɴᴛɪᴍᴏɴʏ in his

letter of 26 June 1813. Jean Baptiste Say published his *Traité d'Economie Politique* (Paris, 1803; Sowerby, no. 3547; Poor, *Jefferson's Library*, 11 [no. 697]) about A DOZEN YEARS previously. HOSTIS HUMANI GENERIS: "enemy of the human race" (*Black's Law Dictionary*). CURA UT VALEAS, ET ME, UT AMARIS, AMA: "take care that you fare well, and love me as you are loved."

¹ Word interlined in place of "incensions," an obsolete synonym for "burnings" or "conflagrations" (*OED*).

From Charles Yancey

DR SIR.   Richmond 27th decr 1814

Inclosed is a Copy of the Subjects of Taxation, for the next year. time, will not allow me to attend to you, as I wish to do. I ho[pe] You will excuse, Yours Respectfully   C YANCEY

PS please to let my friend Peter Carr Esqr & Neighbors See it

RC (DLC); torn at seal; addressed: "Thos Jefferson Esqr Albemarle va near Charlottesville" by "mail"; stamped; postmarked Charlottesville, 1 Jan.; endorsed by TJ as received 5 Jan. 1815 and so recorded in SJL.

The enclosure listing the SUBJECTS OF TAXATION was probably the 21 Dec. 1814 Virginia Act Imposing Taxes for the Support of Government (broadside at MoSHi: TJC-BC; containing underscoring, probably by TJ; endorsed by TJ: "Taxes. State. 1815"; repr. in *Acts of Assembly* [1814–15 sess.], 3–8).

To Thomas Taylor

SIR   Monticello Dec. 28. 14.

I recieved yesterday evening your favor of the 19th & answer it without delay, that no laches may be imputed as to notice of my right, & that of others interested in the lots & streets of the town of Beverley. I do not comprehend what mr Wilson understands by saying that 'the right to lots in that town reverted to the original <u>proprietors,</u> from whom he purchased, and they having conveyed to him a general warranty, he does not admit my claim.' here seems to be error both of law and fact. of law, because, by that, in no event could these lots revert to the original proprietor. of fact, because the late Colo Byrd, or rather his father, was the original proprietor, and I am confident that Colo Byrd never sold the site of Beverley town to mr Wilson, or any other than the purchasers of the lots. mr Wilson may have purchased of the original <u>trespassor,</u> who inclosed the whole town I believe about 10. or a dozen years ago, whose general warranty may bind his own lands to mr Wilson, but not those of others.

The town of Beverley was laid off on the 6th of June 1751. under an act of assembly then recently passed. the original[1] plan of the town, signed by Peter Randolph as Commissioner or Trustee, and by Peter Jefferson (my father) who surveyed, and marked the lots and streets by metes & bounds, was recorded in Henrico court, & the N° of every lot, and name of the purchaser written within the lot. of this I have a copy with the following authentication. 'a copy from the plan of the town of Beverley now remaining in the office of Henrico county court, test J. Beckley D. clk for Thomas Adams Clk.' if the original was among the records destroyed by the British, still, my copy, being an authentic one, is sufficient evidence of the titles. the lots I hold there are by the double right of descent & devise from my father.[2] I was a boy of about 8. years age, living with my father at Tuckahoe, when this transaction took place, and well remember his going to Westham to lay off the town, and his mentioning the price at which the lots were sold, which was a doubloon (£4–6) apiece the purchasers drawing their numbers (if I recollect) by lot, and not chusing them. Westham was then the landing for all the produce coming down James river; and was therefore expected to become a place of consequence, & the lots were chiefly bought by the landholders above, with a view to providing some cover there for their tobacco; the annual loss on which was considerable from it's lying exposed on the bank, until it could be waggoned away. a ferry was established from the uppermost lot on the river N° 151. to the lands of one Britton on the opposite side who, on his own right on that side, kept the ferry till after the revolution, for I remember crossing there during that. whether he paid any rent to my father for the use of the landing on the ferry lot on this side, I do not know. I never recieved nor required any from him. the opening the James river canal put an end to the value of lots in this town as a depot, except the ferry lot, which must in time become of value, because the falls render any other ferry impracticable from thence to Richm^d. the sense of duty which you express of protecting the purchaser against a false title, as well as of procuring the best price for the seller is perfectly just and honorable; and it is to enable you to do that that I trouble you with this letter, to which, on behalf of the other claimants, I will subjoin a list of the original purchasers, and of the lots now claimable under them. considering the continuance of that town as without an object at present, I shall have no objection, in conjunction with as many of the other claimants as can be found, to consent to the passage of an act of assembly repealing the former one, and ordering a sale of the whole site, lots and streets, for the benefit of the owners of the lots, so as to restore the ground to agriculture, for which alone it is fit; but, mr Wilson's justice will say, let this be done <u>by law</u>, & for the benefit of the owners who paid upwards of 1500.D. for the lots & streets 63. years ago, and not for that of the intruder, or to exonerate him of his warranty to those claiming under him, and saving also the ferry lot & road to it, which is the only one now having any value but merely as ground for cultivation. the original purchasers having been almost entirely landholders on James river, most of their families still remain and can be brought forward to act in conjunction by the newspapers. or if any more practicable or reasonable proposition can be made, I shall not obstruct it. Accept the assurance of my great esteem and respect.

Th: Jefferson

PoC (MHi); at foot of first page: "Mr Thomas Taylor"; written on one sheet folded to form four pages, with letter on pp. 1–2 and enclosure described below on pp. 3–4; endorsed by TJ on p. 4.

The act establishing the town of Beverley became law in February 1752, and so it was most likely LAID OFF in June of that year rather than in 1751 as indicated above (Hening, 6:273–4). The COPY FROM THE PLAN OF THE TOWN, which is indeed dated 6 June 1751, is in ViU: TJP-ER. Just prior to the American Revolution, John James Beckley spent some time as the deputy clerk (D. CLK) of Henrico County under Thomas Adams (*DVB*). The extension of the JAMES RIVER CANAL past the falls above Richmond in 1800 greatly reduced the value of Beverley's lots (*MB*, 2:1326n).

The alphabetical LIST of the original seventy-eight purchasers was most likely drawn from the above plan of Beverley. It identifies the purchasers and their lots and, more often than not, provides additional data about the buyers, such as "the former inspector, or perhaps his father," "of Richmond presumably," "English merchant," "has descendants in Buckingham," and "this [John Roberts] might be the steward of old Colo J. Bolling at Licking hole." Peter Jefferson is shown to have acquired lots 57, 107–8, and 151, with the last being the ferry lot. Other purchasers of note and relatives and acquaintances of TJ include Peter Jeffer-

son's surveying colleagues William Cabell (lots 6, 18, 31, 51, 87, 100) and Joshua Fry (lots 83, 117–8); John Bolling ("of Cobbs in Chesterfield, grand father of it's present proprietor"; lots 49, 95); Carter Braxton, a signer of the Declaration of Independence ("of York river"; lots 105–6, 154–6); John Fleming ("father of the judge, or brother"; lot 20); TJ's guardian John Harvie (1706–67; "father of the late Colo John Harvey of Richmond"; lot 27); James Skelton ("owner of Elk island"; lot 21); William Stith ("Presidt of W. M. College"; lot 77); John Woodson ("known by the name of Courthouse John"; lot 5); and John Woodson ("known by the name of Sheriff John"; lot 2). In a box in the lower right corner of the final page, TJ provides general information about the property: "156. lots of half an acre each.

40. of them are blank, probably Colo Byrds, to wit, Nos 46. 101–104. 111.–106. [i.e. 116] 121.–129. 131–150.

poles
width of the town on the river about 104½
extent from the river, medium abt 181½
contents about 115. acres.
the ferry lot is 18. poles on the river, abt 3. po. wide
each lot with it's proportion of street is abt ¾ acre" (PoC in MHi; entirely in TJ's hand; undated; subjoined to PoC of covering letter).

¹ Word interlined.
² Preceding three words interlined.

To John Barnes

Dear Sir   Monticello Dec. 29. 14.

Your letters of Dec. 6. & 18. have been recieved. the last came to hand yesterday evening only. we have two mails a week between this & Washington, which come in the evenings of Wednesday & Friday, & go out the mornings of Wednesday & Thursday. they are therefore little better than one: yours of the 18th recieved last night (Wednesday)[1] could not be answered in time for the mail which went out this morning and will therefore lie in our post office till next Wednesday, which must account for your late reciept of this. I inclose you a power of attorney for recieving the payments of interest on Kosciuzko's 12,500.D. which is made in my own name, because you say in your's of the 18th that the Certificate is in my name. if purely so, this power will do: but if the Certificate is in my name as Atty, or Trustee for Kosciuzko, the power inclosed ought to be the same. in that case, if you will return it to me, I will send another, as I will also if this be defective in any thing which the forms of the treasury require. hoping always that you retain your health & spirits I tender you the assurance of my constant esteem & respect.   Th: Jefferson

PoC (DLC); on verso of reused address cover to TJ; torn at seal, with missing text supplied by TJ above the line; at foot of text: "Mr Barnes"; endorsed by TJ.

[1] Word interlined.

ENCLOSURE

Power of Attorney to John Barnes

Know all men by these presents that I Thomas Jefferson of Monticello in Virginia do hereby constitute and appoint John Barnes of George town in the territory of Columbia my Attorney in fact for the purpose of recieving from the Treasury of the United States all sums of interest due or to become due on any stock standing in my name in the books or funds of the United States: and I do hereby give to the said John Barnes full power and authority to recieve all such sums of interest as are now due, and from time to time such other sums as may hereafter become due, and for the same to give discharges and acquittances, which shall be equally valid, and are hereby confirmed, as if given by myself. Witness my hand and seal at Monticello aforesd this 29th day of December 1814.

Witness   Th: Jefferson

PoC (DLC); on verso of reused address cover to TJ; endorsed by TJ: "Barnes John. copy Power of atty."

From Randolph Jefferson

DEAR BROTHER Decemr 29: 14

I would be greatly oblige to you if mr Randolph has reternd home from Richmond if you will be so good as to ask him to send old Stephen[1] over with my watch as I am at the greatest loss in the world for the want of her and at the same time would take it a great favour of you to send the bitch by him that you were so good as to give me when I was over as I have a great desire to see her I have waited with all the patience I am master of expecting Stephen over for three weaks and he has not come yet and I suppose it is on account of mr Randolphs not reterning home from Richmond yet if mr Randolph has not reternd Stephen may wait and as soon as he gits back you will be pleased to send Stephen over with my watch & bitch as it is out of my power to leave home at this time we are all well heare at present my wife Joins me in love to you and family.

I am your most affectionattely RH: JEFFERSON

RC (ViU: TJP-CC); dateline at foot of text; with unrelated calculations by TJ on verso; endorsed by TJ as received 31 Dec. 1814 and so recorded in SJL.

[1] Manuscript: "Stphen."

From Jeremiah A. Goodman

DR SIR desember 30 day 1814

this mornning friday dick starts to mounticello with 15 hougs one beaf about fourehundread & Eighteen Bu^s of wheat is deliver to the mill this is all except the sowed, 18 for my self six to M^r darneel as for mind I will write to m^r Clarkson Let you have the same there I Should be Glad to know the price m^r mitchell is to give for the wheat per Bu^s I expect fill hubbard is gon to mounticello but the Cause I do not know for why only from dick he says he belives him & hanner was ingage to be marrid at Crismas and in the Crismas I Slap hanner three or foure times for some words she had bin making use of not thinking of her and fill in that way this mout ofened her and She possiable give him a deniel dick tell me that fill was Like a mad man and Said he would not stay here[1] I am very sawry to hear[2] it for I nover had a better hand but if fill will Come back & wants a wife I will try and selistit hanner to have him for I have don nothing to him but when I heard of it I told him that if him & hanner did mak up a match I would give them pot & house but had aggey a hous bilt and give

[173]

them one end of dicks hous I have bought two more horsis one at 55 dollars 8 years old from Lewis[3] Brown pay first of may one at 60 dollars 6 years old baught of m[r] Cob: pay April next[4] I Shall write to M[r] Clarkson[5] to Let dick bring up the beast I have Charge them not to whip the hogs the beaf is very fat I am in hops you have received my Last Letter about the wool as the wants 40 wts Sir the statments above is that I judge which made fill go off but this is no Cause if fill had Come to me and I had said he Should not have the girl it would of Altered the Case or that any person had heard me say so but I was willing for it to be he has went off in drunking madness to me I had put him to take Ceare of the stock at the barn this Conduck I Can not santion and with your approbation after vewing the Case I shall Let him know he is not to do so I do not know the tale may be told to you by him but I am willing to meat him on any ground that I have not done any thing amiss to him, I have sent the butter Also the salt I have Company the waggon to the reaver and send them over safe

JEREMIAH A GOODMAN

RC (ViU: TJP-ER); with notes by TJ, detailed below, in margin of first page and on address cover; addressed: "To M[r] Th[s] Jefferson Albemarle Mounticello by dick & people"; endorsed by TJ as received 4 Jan. 1815 and so recorded in SJL.

In the left margin of the first page, TJ tabulated the BU[s] (bushels) of wheat grown at Poplar Forest and the farm products sent to Monticello:
"418
  18
   6
 442
 215 sown
 130. eaten
 787
 418. B. Corn
 958. ℔ pork to Mont°."
On the address cover TJ inserted a

mathematical computation apparently related to the above table.

M[R] CLARKSON: probably Goodman's father-in-law, Manoah Clarkson, a former Monticello overseer and longtime resident of Albemarle County (*MB*, 2:912; Woods, *Albemarle*, 168). On the address cover TJ noted the prices of the two horses purchased by Goodman and the dates on which payment was to be made to Lewis Brown and Mr. Cobb (COB). Goodman's LAST LETTER was dated 21 Dec. 1814 (see note to TJ to Goodman, 23 Dec. 1814).

[1] Manuscript: "her."
[2] Manuscript: "her."
[3] Given name repeated by TJ in left margin for clarity.
[4] Preceding three words interlined.
[5] Manuscript: "Carkson."

From William Plumer

SIR   Epping (N.H.) December 30. 1814

Having been sometime engaged in writing the history of the United States, & the biography of some of its most eminent citizens; & knowing, from the acquaintance I had with you at Washington[1] during the five years I was a member of the Senate, of your extensive knowledge of historical facts not only relating to this country but of the world in general, I am induced to take the liberty of enquiring, whether in the course of your reading you recollect of any country, or even considerable island, that at the time when it was first discovered was uninhabited by human beings? This appears to me an enquiry of some importance as connected with the history of the Indians of our own country. I have recently received President Adams's answer to the same enquiry, which is in the negative.

I have recently met with some extracts from a work, entitled "A summary view of the rights of British America—by Th: Jefferson, 1774—" but the pamphlet itself I have not been able to obtain. If you have a spare copy on hand, will you have the goodness to transmit me one under your frank?

I have obtained the first volume of Henning's Virginia statutes at large up to 1660; did he continue the work, & of how many volumes does it consist? A knowledge of the laws of the several States appears to me essentially necessary to a full history of the nation. A history written without a thorough knowledge of the laws & customs of a people, cannot develope their character, or explain their conduct on many important transactions.

I have written the three first chapters of my[2] history; & hope in the course of the next year to have the first volume ready for the press. I shall not however be in haste to publish it; as I wish to render it as perfect as I am able. Any communication relating to my undertaking will be gratefully acknowledged.

The united & unremitted opposition of the Congregational & presbyterian clergy of New England, to all the leading measures of the[3] general government, induced me to examine their conduct. In doing this I endeavored to meet & answer them upon their own principles. The result of this examination was first published in one of our most respectable republican journals, & since has been reprinted. Will you do me the favor to accept of one of the pamphlets herewith enclosed.

We are in the eastern States threatened with insurrection & rebellion by the Hartford convention now in session. It portends much evil & no good to our country; but I trust will terminate in fumo. A great portion of the people contemn them—yet an enemy despised may prove formidable. Their object is dismemberment—which will injure the south, but ruin the north: Your flour, rice, tobacco & cotton are necessary to us—without them our commerce cannot subsist.

I am with sentiments of much respect & esteem,
Sir, Your most obedient humble servant   WILLIAM PLUMER

RC (ViW: TC-JP); at foot of text: "Hon. Thomas Jefferson Monticello Virginia"; endorsed by TJ as received 16 Jan. 1815 and so recorded in SJL. FC (Lb in DLC: Plumer Papers); in Plumer's hand. Enclosure: "A Layman" [Plumer], *Address to the Clergy of New-England, on Their Opposition to the Rulers of the United States* (Concord, N.H., 1814), consisting of articles published under the same nom de plume in the Concord *New-Hampshire Patriot*, 14 Dec. 1813–12 Apr. 1814.

Plumer completed neither his HISTORY

OF THE UNITED STATES nor a collection of biographies of SOME OF ITS MOST EMINENT CITIZENS (Lynn W. Turner, *William Plumer of New Hampshire, 1759–1850* [1962], 201, 336–7). John Adams commented in his RECENTLY RECEIVED letter of 4 Dec. 1814 that he knew of "no Island, discovered, without human Inhabitants Except Robinson crusoes" (RC in MBPLi: Chamberlain Collection). FUMO: "smoke."

[1] Preceding two words not in FC.
[2] Reworked from "a."
[3] FC: "our."

To James Monroe

DEAR SIR   Monticello Jan. 1. 15.

Your letters of Nov. 30. & Dec. 21. have been recieved with great pleasure. a truth now and then projecting into the ocean of Newspaper lies, serves like headlands to correct our course. indeed my scepticism as to every thing I see in a newspaper makes me indifferent whether I ever see one. the embarrasments at Washington in August last, I expected would be great in any state of things; but they proved greater than expected. I never doubted that the plans of the President were wise and sufficient. their failure we all impute 1. to the insubordinate temper of Armstrong: 2. & to the indecision of Winder. however, it ends well. it mortifies ourselves, and so may check perhaps the silly boasting spirit of our newspapers, and it enlists the feelings of the world on our side; and the advantage of public opinion, is like that of the weather gage in a naval action. in Europe, the transient possession of our capital can be no disgrace. nearly every capital there was in possession of it's enemy; some often, & long. but diabolical as they paint that enemy, he burnt neither public edifices nor private dwellings. it was reserved for England to shew that Bonaparte in atrocity was an infant to their ministers and their generals. they are taking his place in the eyes of Europe, and have turned into our channel all it's good will. this will be worth the million of Dollars the repairs of their conflagrations will cost us. I hope that to preserve this weather-gage of public opinion, & to counteract the slanders & falsehoods disseminated by the English papers, the government will make it a standing instruction to their ministers at foreign courts to keep Europe truly informed of occurrences here, by publishing in their papers the naked truth always, whether favorable or unfavorable. for they will believe the good if we candidly tell them the bad also.

But you have two more serious causes of uneasiness; the want of men & money. for the former nothing more wise, nor efficient could have been imagined than what you proposed. it would have filled our ranks with regulars, & that too by throwing a just share of the bur-then on the purses of those whose persons are exempt either by age or office; and it would have rendered our militia, like those of the Greeks & Romans, a nation of warriors. but the go-by seems to have been given to your proposition, and longer sufferance is necessary to force us to what is best.—we seem equally incorrigible in our finan-cial course. altho' a century of British experience has proved to what a wonderful extent the funding on specific redeeming taxes enables a nation to anticipate in war the resources of peace, and altho' the other nations of Europe have tried and trodden every path of force or folly in fruitless quest of the same object, yet <u>we</u> still expect to find in jug-gling tricks and banking dreams, that money can be made out of nothing, and in sufficient quantity to meet the expences of a heavy war by sea and land.   it is said indeed that money cannot be borrowed from our merchants as from those of England. but it can be borrowed from our[1] people. they will give you all the necessaries of war they produce, if, instead of the bankrupt trash they now are obliged to recieve for want of any other, you will give them a paper promise funded on a specific pledge, and of a size for common circu-lation. but you say the merchants will not take this paper. what the people take the merchants must take, or sell nothing. all these doubts & fears prove only the extent of the dominion which the banking in-stitutions have obtained over the minds of our citizens, and especially of those inhabiting cities, or other banking places: and this dominion must be broken, or it will break us. but here, as in the other case, we must make up our mind to suffer yet longer before we can get right. the misfortune is that in the mean time we shall plunge ourselves into inextinguishable debt, and entail on our posterity an inheritance of eternal taxes, which will bring our government & people into the con-dition of those of England, a nation of pikes & gudgeons, the latter bred merely as food for the former.—but however these two difficul-ties of men & money may be disposed of, it is fortunate that neither of them will affect our war by sea. privateers will find their own men & money. let nothing be spared to encourage them. they are the dag-ger which strikes at the heart of the enemy, their commerce. frigates and 74^s are a sacrifice we must make, heavy as it is, to the prejudices of a part of our citizens. they have indeed rendered a great moral service, which has delighted me as much as any one in the US. but they have had no physical effect sensible to the enemy; and now, while we must fortify them in our harbors, and keep armies to defend them, our <u>privateers</u> are bearding and blockading the enemy in their own seaports. encourage them to burn all their prizes, & let the public pay for them. they will cheat us enormously. no matter; they will make their merchants feel, and squeal, & cry out for peace.

I much regretted your acceptance of the war department. not that I knew a person who I think would better conduct it. but, conduct it ever so wisely, it will be a sacrifice of yourself. were an angel from heaven to undertake that office, all our[2] miscarriages would be ascribed to him. raw troops, no troops, insubordinate militia, want of arms, want of money, want of provisions, all will be charged to want of management in you. I speak from experience when I was governor of Virginia. without a regular in the state, and scarcely a musket to put into the hands of the militia, invaded by two armies, Arnold's from the sea-bord, & Cornwallis's from the Southward, when we were driven from Richmond & Charlottesville, and every member of my council fled to their homes, it was not the total destitution of means, but the mismanagement of them which, in the querulous voice of the public, caused all our misfortunes. it ended indeed in the capture of the whole hostile force, but not till means were brought us by Gen[l] Washington's army, & the French fleet and army. and altho' the Legislature, who were personally intimate with both the means and measures, acquitted me with justice and thanks, yet the lying Lee has put all those imputations among the romances of his historical Novel, for the amusement of credulous & uninquisitive readers. — not that I have seen the least disposition to censure you. on the contrary, your conduct on the attack of Washington has met the praises of every one, and your plan for regulars and militia, their approbation. but no campaign is as yet opened. no generals have yet an interest in shifting their own incompetence on you, no army agents their rogueries. I sincerely pray you may never meet censure where you will deserve most praise, and that your own happiness & prosperity may be the result of your patriotic services. ever & affectionately yours   TH: JEFFERSON

P.S. I shall be glad to recieve my papers as soon as convenient.

RC (DLC: Monroe Papers); endorsed by Monroe. PoC (DLC); edge torn; at foot of first page: "Colo Monroe."

The WEATHER GAGE is defined in note to José Corrêa da Serra to TJ, 9 Dec. 1814. 74[s] were ships of the line that carried seventy-four guns (*OED*). The WHOLE HOSTILE FORCE was captured at the Battle of Yorktown in October 1781.

In mid-December 1781 the Virginia General Assembly acquitted TJ WITH JUSTICE AND THANKS of the criticisms leveled against him as a result of his conduct during the recent British invasion of Virginia (*PTJ*, 6:135–7). Henry LEE accused the former governor, however, of failing to prepare the state's defenses adequately in his *Memoirs of the War in the Southern* *Department of the United States* (Philadelphia, 1812; Sowerby, no. 533), 2:3, 13. For the papers on finance to be returned AS SOON AS CONVENIENT, see Monroe to TJ, 10 Oct., and TJ to Monroe, 16 Oct. 1814.

¹ Word interlined in place of "the."
² Word interlined in place of "it's."

To John B. Colvin

SIR   Monticello Jan. 2. 15.

Your favor of Dec. 21. is just recieved. with respect to the orthography of the Indian names of individuals & tribes, it seems as yet to be unfixed, their names having but rarely occurred. it is the same as yet in many instances which are familiar. the mode of spelling the name of the Patowmack, Potomack, Potomac, Potomak, is not yet settled. the last perhaps is gaining an ascendancy. I imagine the first step is to find the true native pronuntiation of the names, and then to represent these sounds according to the power of the letters of our Alphabet, in their most usual employment. I am glad this question has attracted your notice, because I am sure you will make the best of it you can, and the orthography you employ in an edition of the laws will probably be adopted & appealed to as authentic. testifying my satisfaction that this task has fallen into so good hands I tender you the assurance of my esteem & respect   TH: JEFFERSON

PoC (DLC); on verso of reused address cover to TJ; at foot of text: "Mʳ Colvin"; endorsed by TJ.

To Samuel Thurber

SIR   Monticello Jan. 2. 15.

Your favor of Dec. 19. was recieved on the 30ᵗʰ of that month only. it could not have been addressed to one less capable of answering your enquiries. I live very far from the sea-coast, up among the mountains. I have no doubt that Richmond is the best place within this state for the establishment of a cotton manufactory. Washington & Alexandria might compete with it in some important circumstances; but the very superior advantages of Richmond in the command of water and abundance of fuel, might give it a preference. but altho I once lived there and knew nearly every body in it, yet I have been there but twice or thric[e][1] within the last 30. years, and think there is not a single person living there now who was an inhabitant when I was. I cannot therefore address you to any one. nor do I think you ought to adventure on a removal but after your own personal examination. should you come there, you could not consult[2] with a person of better information than mr Ritchie, editor of the Enquirer, who, on your presenting him this letter, would kindly consider it as a request from me[3] to put you into good hands for[4] satisfying the enquiries interesting to you. Accept my best wishes for your success & the assurances of my respect   TH: JEFFERSON

PoC (MoSHi: TJC-BC); on verso of reused address cover from Samuel H. Smith to TJ; edge cut off; at foot of text: "Mr Samuel Thurber"; endorsed by TJ.

[1] Preceding two words interlined.
[2] Reworked from "I do not think you could consult."
[3] Preceding two words interlined.
[4] TJ here canceled "making."

From Patrick Gibson

SIR   Richmond 3^d January 1815
    In consequence of a violent rheumatic attack in the right shoulder I have been unable sooner to reply to your favor of the 23^d—Mr Hay who has obtaind the judgement ag^t Philpot, has promised me that every step shall be taken to force him to the paym^t of the debt—I have remitted Mr Goodman the $130 directed in yours of the 23^d and now inclose you $100 including as many small notes as I[1] have been able to pick up, neither of the Banks having any at this time— I also inclose you a blank note for your signature to renew yours in bank due 10/13th Ins^t which I will thank you to return me in course— with great respect I am
    Your ob^t Servt   PATRICK GIBSON

RC (MHi); between dateline and salutation: "Thomas Jefferson Esqre"; endorsed by TJ as received 7 Jan. 1815 and so recorded in SJL. Enclosure not found.

Despite the JUDGEMENT in his favor, TJ seems never to have been paid for the four hogsheads of tobacco he sold Oakley Philpotts in 1812. Although Gibson stated that he was enclosing $100 in SMALL

NOTES in his letters to TJ of both this and the following day, TJ recorded the receipt of only $100 from Gibson at this time, on 7 Jan. 1815 (*MB*, 2:1306). The bills almost certainly accompanied the latter letter, James Ligon (for Gibson) to TJ, 4 Jan. 1815.

[1] Reworked from "we."

To John Garnett

SIR   Monticello Jan. 4. 15.

Your favor of Dec. 17. was recieved on the 30th with the copy of your new method of correcting the Moon's apparent distance which you were so kind as to inclose. every thing which can facilitate to the mariner the ascertainment of his place at sea is a valuable present to him. I had written some days ago to mr Millegan, my corresponding bookseller at George town, to procure me your Nautical Almanac for this year, & am in the daily expectation of recieving it. as you propose to publish it in future by subscription, I shall gladly become a sub-scriber, the copy to be always forwarded to mr Millegan whose cor-respondence in the book-line in Philadelphia will render the payment for it more easy.—I have no acquaintance with the new Secretary of the Treasury, having never either seen him or had any communica-tion with him. I do not therefore feel myself free to undertake to recommend to him what his duty will of course suggest, to wit, to subscribe for as many of your almanacs as may be requisite annually for the navy. but I have no question he will do it and especially if you forward the subscription paper to him. it is possible that Blount's edi-tion of N. York may enter into competition with yours, especially with those who, habituated to the English edition, shrink from every alteration altho' for the better. I thank you for your kind offer of ser-vice in your visit to England, but at present have nothing with which I would wish to trouble you there. wishing you every success here or there, and a happy voyage, I tender you the assurance of my great esteem & respect.   TH: JEFFERSON

PoC (DLC); on verso of reused ad-dress cover of William Thornton to TJ, 11 Dec. 1814; at foot of text: "Mr Garnett"; endorsed by TJ.

TJ had recently exchanged letters with Alexander J. Dallas, the NEW SECRETARY OF THE TREASURY. Instead of Dallas he probably meant Benjamin W. Crownin-shield, the new secretary of the navy and the man with whom Garnett had actually asked him to intercede. BLOUNT'S: Ed-mund M. Blunt's.

From James Ligon
(for Patrick Gibson)

SIR   Richmond 4ʰ Janʸ 1815

I send you inclosed as directed in yours of the 31ˢᵗ ultᵒ $100, (25$ in 1 & 2$ notes & the Balance in 5$ notes) I¹ could not obtain any more Small notes as the Banks here are without them

respectfully yr ob Servᵗ   PATRICK GIBSON
                                            P. Js LIGON

RC (MHi); entirely in Ligon's hand; endorsed by TJ as received 7 Jan. 1815 and so recorded in SJL.

TJ's missing letter to Gibson of THE 31ˢᵀ ULTᵒ is recorded in SJL and described in Goodspeed's Book Shop's August 1963 newsletter, the *Flying Quill*, item 66-A, as a small, one-page letter in

TJ's hand containing the following text: "it did not occur that executions were now suspended by law . . . send me by mail 100 D. with a tolerable supply of Dollar, and 2 D. bills among them for change."

¹ Reworked from "we."

To Joseph C. Cabell

DEAR SIR   Monticello Jan. 5. 15.

Your favor of Dec. 27. with the letter inclosed, has been recieved. knowing well that the bank-mania still possesses the great body of our countrymen, it was not expected that any radical cure of that could be at once effected. we must go further wrong, probably to a ne plus ultra before we shall be forced into what is right. something will be obtained however, if we can excite, in those who think, doubt first, reflexion next, and conviction at last. the constitution too presents difficulties here with which the general government is not embarrassed. if your Auditor's notes are made payable to bearer, and of sizes suitable for circulation, they will find their way into circulation, as well as into the hoards of the thrifty. especially in important payments for land Eᵗc which are to lie on hand some time waiting for employment. a bank-note is now recieved only as a 'Robin's-alive.'

On mr Ritchie's declining the publication of Tracy's work, I proposed it to a mr Millegan of George town who undertakes it. I had therefore written to Genˡ Duane to forward it to him; so that it will not be in my possession until it is published. have you seen the Review of Montesquieu by an anonymous author? the ablest work of the age. it was translated and published by Duane about 3. years ago. in giving the most correct analysis of the principles of political association which has yet been offered, he states, in the branch of political economy particularly, altho' much in brief, some of the soundest and most profound views we have ever had on those subjects.—I have lately recieved a letter from Say. he has in contemplation to remove to this country, and to this neighborhood particularly; and asks from me answers to some enquiries he makes. could the petition which the Albemarle academy addressed to our legislature have succeeded at the late session, a little aid additional to the objects of that would have enabled us to have here immediately the best seminary of the US. I do not know to whom P. Carr (President of the board of trustees) committed the petition and papers; but I have seen no trace of their having been offered. thinking it possible you may not have seen them, I send for your perusal the copies I retained for my own use. they consist 1. of a letter to him, sketching at the request of the trustees, a plan for the institution. 2. one to Judge Cooper in answer to some observations he had favored me with, on the plan. 3. a copy of the petition of the trustees. 4. a copy of the act we wished from the legislature. they are long. but, as we always counted on you as the main pillar of their support, and we shall probably return to the charge at the next session, the trouble of reading them will come upon you, and as well now as then. the lottery allowed by the former act, the proceeds of our two glebes, and our dividend of the literary fund, with the reorganisation of the institution are what was asked in that petition. in addition to this if we could obtain a loan, for 4. or 5. years, only, of 7. or 8000 D. I think I have it now in my power to obtain three of the ablest characters in the world to fill the higher professorships of what in the plan is called the II^d or General grade of education; three such characters as are not in a single university of Europe: and for those of languages & Mathematics, a part of the same grade, able professors doubtless could also be readily obtained. with these characters, I should not be afraid to say that the circle of the sciences composing that 2^d or General grade, would be more profoundly taught here than in any institution in the US. and I might go farther.   The I^{st} or Elementary grade of education is not developed in this plan; an authority only being asked to it's Visitors for putting into motion a former proposition for that object. for an explanation of this therefore, I am obliged to add to these papers a letter I wrote some time since to mr Adams, in which I had occasion to give some account of what had been proposed here for culling from every condition of our people the natural aristocracy of talents & virtue, and of preparing it by education, at the public expence, for the care of the public concerns. this letter will present to you some measures still requisite to compleat & secure our republican edifice, and which remain in charge for our younger statesmen. on yourself, mr Rives, mr Gilmer, when they shall enter the public councils, I rest my hopes for this great accomplishment, and doubtless you will have other able coadjutors not known to me.

Col⁰ Randolph having gone to Richmond before the rising of the legislature, you will have had an opportunity of explaining to him personally the part of your letter respecting his petition for opening the Milton falls, which his departure prevented my communicating to him. I had not heard him speak of it, and had been glad, as to myself, by the act recently passed, to have saved our own rights in the defensive war with the Rivanna company, and should not have advised the renewing and carrying the war into the enemy's country.   Be so good as to return all the inclosed papers after perusal, and to accept assurances of my great esteem & respect.

Th: Jefferson

RC (ViU: TJP); at foot of first page: "Joseph C. Cabell esq."; endorsed by Cabell as answered 5 Mar. 1815. PoC (DLC); endorsed by TJ. Enclosures: (1) TJ to Peter Carr, 7 Sept. 1814. (2) TJ to Thomas Cooper, 7 Oct. 1814. (3) Draft Bill to Create Central College and Amend the 1796 Public Schools Act, [ca. 18 Nov. 1814]. (4) TJ to John Adams, 28 Oct. 1813. Other enclosure not found, but for information about the Albemarle Academy Board of Trustees' petition, see the editorial headnote to the Minutes of the Albemarle Academy Board of Trustees, 25 Mar. 1814, and *JHD* (1815–16 sess.), 23, 38 (7, 14 Dec. 1814).

In the game of ROBIN'S-ALIVE a burning object is passed quickly from person to person (William Wells Newell, *Games and Songs of American Children* [1883], 135–6). The FORMER ACT was the Virginia General Assembly's 12 Jan. 1803 "Act to establish an academy in the county of Albemarle, and for other purposes" (*Acts of Assembly* [1802–03 sess.], 23–4). The ACT RECENTLY PASSED was the 22 Dec. 1814 "Act authorizing William Wood of the County of Albemarle, to open and improve the navigation of the Rivannah River, and for other purposes" (*Acts of Assembly* [1814–15 sess.], 113–5).

An undated letter from Thomas Mann RANDOLPH to TJ, not found, is recorded in SJL as received 7 Mar. 1815 from Richmond.

To Jeremiah A. Goodman

DEAR SIR   Monticello Jan. 6. 15.

Dick arrived here on the 4.ᵗʰ with the butter, salt, beef & hogs. one he said had been left at Lynchburg, one tired and was killed on the road, the other 13. have been killed here. their weights were 101. 99. 91. 91. 80. 76. 67. 67. 67. 61. 56. 55. 47. as they would not make bacon at all, being so small they would dry up to nothing, we shall try to make them up into salt pork, in which way they may do for the peo-

ple. but such a supply of pork, and 14. bushels of wheat[1] a hand carried to market are very damping circumstances. Dick carries with
him a pair of the Guinea breed of hogs, of the same which I sent formerly, but which seem to have had no effect. we killed hogs of this
breed here this year, not 18. months old weighing 200.℔. and a great
part of them 150. & all under that age. yours average $73\frac{3}{4}$.

I send by Dick 4. ploughs, which with the one sent by James, and a
Peacock plough sent formerly, allows three for each place.   he
brings 2. barrels containing bottled beer, to be put into the cellar, and
2. barrels containing 40.℔ of wool. we can very illy spare it, not having enough for our people here, but we will try a mixture of hemp &
cotton for the negro children here, in order to help out for your people. it is indispensably necessary that you take as much care of the
lambs &[2] sheep as if they were children. we feel now the misfortune
of the loss of so many last year as well as mr Darnell's trespass.[3] the
wool sent is half blooded Merino, and very difficult to make any thing
of for coarse cloth. you can do nothing with it with wool-cards. it
must either be carded with fine cotton cards, or carded at some of the
carding machines. it would be better indeed if you could exchange it
for common wool with some of the neighbors who want to make fine
cloth for their own use. I expected to have recieved by Dick a list of
the stock, and now send you blank lists for each place, which I will be
glad to have filled up and returned to me by the mail. I must get you
to speak to mr Watkins and let him know I depend on his promise to
come and make a wheat machine for me. the stuff has been all ready
this twelvemonth. if he can make his arrangements to come about the
middle of April, it would be in time. I should have an opportunity of
seeing him at Poplar Forest the 1st week in April, when I shall be
there.   Phill Hubard arrived here the 2d day after Christmas.
his subject of complaint is exactly what you supposed. he says that he
and Dick's Hanah had become husband & wife, but that you drove
him repeatedly from her father's house and would not let him go
there, punishing her, as he supposes, for recieving him. certainly
there is nothing I desire so much as that all the young people in the
estate should intermarry with one another and stay at home. they are
worth a great deal more in that case than when they have husbands
and wives abroad. Phill has been long petitioning me to let him go to
Bearcreek to live with his family. and Nanny has been as long at me
to let her come to the Poplar forest. we may therefore now gratify
both, by sending Phill & his wife to Bear creek, and bringing Nanny
and any one of the single men from there, that is to say Reuben,
Daniel, or Stephen. no new house will be wanting because Phill can

take the house Nanny leaves, and Nanny may take the house which Cate's Hanah leaves. I would wish you to give to Dick's Hanah a pot, and a bed, which I always promise them when they take husbands at home, and I shall be very glad to hear that others of the young people follow their example. a crocus bed may be got from mr Robertson. I would by no means have Phill punished for what he has done; for altho I had let them all know that their runnings away should be punished, yet Phill's character is not that of a runaway. I have known him from a boy and that he has not come off to sculk from his work.—mr Mitchell will take his debt out of the wheat, at the price he pays to others, and the rest must be ground & sent immediately to Richmond. I hope you are getting on with the tobacco. it is very pressing to have that at Richmond. Dick carries the two blankets which were short of the number intended to have been sent by James. let the beer be put into the cellar immediately, for fear of it's freezing, setting the proper head of the barrels uppermost, that the bottles in them may stand with the corks up. Accept my best wishes.

Th: Jefferson

RC (NNGL, on deposit NHi); addressed: "Mr Jeremiah A. Goodman Poplar Forest"; frank erased; with Goodman's computation on address cover of the number of bushels of wheat due him as overseer (see Goodman to TJ, 30 Dec. 1814, and note). Enclosure not found.

EACH PLACE: TJ's Poplar Forest plantations, Tomahawk (also known as Poplar Forest) and Bear Creek. A CRO-

CUS BED is a bed covered with coarse sacking material (Betts, *Farm Book*, 512).

Goodman's reply to TJ of 12 Jan. 1815, not found, is recorded in SJL as received 26 Jan. 1815.

[1] Manuscript: "bushels a wheat."
[2] TJ here canceled "children."
[3] Preceding six words interlined, with redundant terminal punctuation editorially omitted.

To Patrick Gibson

DEAR SIR   Monticello Jan. 7. 14. [15]

On the 31st Ult. I asked the favor of you to inclose me by mail 100.D. which I presume to be now on the way. in the mean time another call has come on me which obliges me to draw on you in favor of my grandson Th: J. Randolph for 120.D. I shall have one more of about the same amount in the course of this month which will I believe close my wants until the spring by which time my flour & tobo may be down, and perhaps disposed of. before that time I hope we may hear that the British do not think their prospect of obtaining a slice of the province of Maine worth the continuance of the war, for that I believe is the only article which at present both parties have not agreed to. Accept the assurance of my great esteem & respect.

TH: JEFFERSON

PoC (ViU: TJP); on verso of reused address cover of Alexander J. Dallas to TJ, 14 Dec. 1814; misdated; at foot of text: "Mr Gibson"; endorsed by TJ as a letter of 7 Jan. 1815 and so recorded in SJL.

On the following day Thomas Jefferson RANDOLPH repaid TJ "for the sd draught 120.D." (*MB*, 2:1306).

SJL records a missing letter from TJ to Gibson of 8 Jan. 1815, which presumably covered a signed note authorizing the renewal of his loan at the Bank of Virginia (see Gibson to TJ, 3 Jan. 1815).

From Abraham O. Stansbury

DEAR SIR   New york January 7th 1815

It is one of the characteristics of our free government, that the humblest individual in Society may address without fear of repulse the most exalted, and even calculate upon a favourable reception— Your example Sir, as the most elevated in office and distinguished in Science & literature in condescending to reply to the letter of an obscure individual is an admirable comment upon our Republican Institutions & calculated to encourage that spirit of free inquiry which is the best guardian of Truth whether Religious Moral or Political. These remarks are prompted by seeing in the Evg Post printed here a communication addressed to you by one of the Society of friends together with your reply and though I greatly disapprove of such a correspondence getting into the public prints & consider it a flagrant breach of private confidence, yet since it has been made public I hope to be excused for making it the occasion of addressing you. The sentiments there advocated are such as I once held, & with the celebrated Pope I once agreed that whether as Jehovah of the Israelites, Jove of the pagans, or Lord of Christians there was no difference in the worship of the "Great first Cause." I hope therefore to be viewed as exempt from fanaticism & as a candid advocate when I solicit your attention to a few points in your Letter which appear to merit your serious reconsideration.

That the subject itself has engaged your attention you freely acknowlege and truly it is one of all others the most momentous—We find ourselves possessed of an intelligent nature & feel that we are responsible Creatures we know that very shortly we must die, & what is to be the issue of the dissolution—into what State our intelligent nature shall enter when separated from the body in which it has hitherto dwelt is a question the most interesting & which has agitated the hearts of all reflecting men in every age of the world: to affect indifference on this subject is not a proof of Philosophy but insanity, not of a liberal mind, but of a depraved heart. Nothing so powerfully disinclines to the investigation of truth as the dread that its discovery will disclose our own condemnation, and it is this which has ever opposed the strongest obstacle to the reception of the doctrines of the Bible—professing to come from God & to be a revelation to man of the will of his maker, it teaches him that he is the subject of his just displeasure—that he has forfeited the favour of God by his sins and represents that God as infinitely holy—as a consuming fire, with whom iniquity cannot dwell—The Bible & that alone, makes known a State of blessedness after death, but it bars admission to all but the holy—The man who is conscious that this is not his character goes away offended and either openly rejects the system or endeavours to mould it to suit his own views—selecting certain parts & passing over others till he has formed such a set of notions as allow him to cherish hope beyond the grave The character of a Sinner exposes him to punishment & that character his conscience testifies is his—how then shall he meet his Judge? The Scriptures are express on this point but here too something occurs to be modified—instead of a sacrifice for Sin by which the obligation to punishment is taken away: instead of the doctrine of substitution by which the righteousness of the head covers & extends to all the members—instead of the principle of faith embracing & resting on this sacrifice & this righteousness—some other way is sought & the performance of something acceptable in its nature to the revealed character of God offers the readiest expedient for securing his favour. thus while men profess to receive the Bible as a revelation from heaven they act the inconsistent part of rejecting its principal requisitions & endeavour to satisfy their conscience by substituting what they imagine ought to be required—That this is the true reason why the doctrines of the Gospel are not more cordially embraced is certain from the experience of many who have long practised deceptions on their understandings but who recovering from the delusion & honestly embracing the truth, have confessed their former disingenuousness. But I am detaining you with digressions, to return therefore to your Letter;—the first thing that struck my attention was your expressions on the subject of moral obligation as learned from "all the beings around us" & their prescribing the course we should observe.—that any standard of duty is to be learned from all the beings around us which can regulate our conduct towards God & restore us to his favour appears so inconsistent with the tenor of the New testament that I am at a loss to reconcile such expressions with your subsequent declarations & you evidently refer to the Scripture in speaking of admission into Heaven; the point to be determined seems then to be on what ground the hope of Heaven may be built; & here you cordially coincide with the preacher that "good men" will all be regarded "as children & brethren of the same family." what constitutes this[1] character you do not say, but it is conveyed in that general expression "the moral precepts in which all religions concur" as distinguished from & opposed to, "the dogmas in which all differ" & more fully explained in "the principles which are in concert with the supreme mind"—observance of these moral precepts & this conformity constitute the good man, & whether he be with Aristides a pagan idolater, & Cato an advocate of self destruction, or Penn the denyer of the atonement, or Tillotson the advocate of Christian truth & ordinances it makes no difference in your estimate—still you profess your preference for the System of Morality "of Jesus" over every other that has come under your observation.—What more, may it be asked could any Christian ask than such an avowal—is it not liberal, can any but a bigot object? You seem yourself amply satisfied, & conclude there is no ground for uneasiness though all that marks Christianity as differing from mere systems of moral obligation be disregarded. all this you term subtlety & mystery erected on the doctrines of Jesus & mere unessentials—Now Sir I would beg leave to call your serious attention to this point—Is Christianity then no more than the morality of Jesus?—If so I would ask what sort of morality was that he taught when he assumed to himself what would be considered intolerable arrogance in any Man who should use the same expressions in our day—When he declared "before Abraham was I am." "I & the Father are one" "except ye eat my flesh & drink my blood ye have no life in you" "I go to prepar[e] a place for you that where I am ye may be also" "If[2] I go away I will send the Comforter the Holy Spirit who shall be in you &c" "I have power to lay down my life & I have power to take it again" "I am the resurrection and the life he that beleiveth in me shall never die"—"I[3] lay down my life for my Sheep" "I[4] give unto them eternal life and they shall never perish!"—listen to him at the well instructing the woman of Samaria—& promising what none but God had power to bestow—mark his reply to the question what shall we do that we might work the works of God? "this is the work of God, that ye beleive on him whom he hath sent" and in all his discourses making use of language utterly irreconcileable with the idea of his being a simple teacher of morality—the enumeration were almost endless As a teacher he professed to have power never arrogated by man—power to raise the dead from their[5] graves—declaring that the time should come when all that were in their graves should hear his voice and come forth As a teacher he claimed the prerogative of pardoning Sin—As a teacher he commanded the wind & the Sea—what other teacher ever taught thus? And is all this indeed no more than the morality of Jesus? What was it that excited the rage of the Jewish doctors against him but such claims as they well observed belonged to none but God—did he deny the charge did he not admit it? and wherefore was he crucified? because he made himself "equal with God" it was this that roused their resentment he came as the Lord of the Temple—He came "the messenger of the Covenant" But I forbear—I have already greatly trespassed on your patience and have to apologize for so far exceeding the limits I had prescribed to myself The importance of the subject must plead my excuse—I am a stranger to you Sir, & may be thought impertinent; but as one who had long wandered in the darkness of unbelief upon the Son of God and in that dread uncertainty as to a future state which nothing but the Gospel can remove—as one too who by the grace of God has been brought out of that darkness & uncertainty into the blessed light of divine truth, and been made a partaker of the consolations which result from believing on him who is the Lord our Righteousness our strength & our Saviour from the wrath to come resting on his faithful word & looking up to him for grace to walk worthy of the profession of his holy name—commemorating his death with tender gratitude & waiting until the hour of my dissolution shall introduce me to his Kingdom to behold his glory, I feel an interest in all who yet remain strangers to his love—secure in a fancied conformity to the divine Will while they reject that revelation of divine mercy in the atonement of Christ which alone can take away their guilt and restore them to the favour of God.—You speak Sir,[6] of your age—let me entreat you then as the term of life draws to a close, and the realities of eternity are near at hand to consider Christ Jesus as revealed in the Gospel not only the preeminent teacher but as Paul considered him "the apostle & high priest of our profession" the Sent of God the sacrifice for Sin—the Lamb of God—predicted by the prophets typified in the Sacrifices of the Law, testified by the apostles, ascended to that glory which he had with the father, & ever living to make intercession for his people—as the head of all things to his Church & to use his own words "the way the truth and the Life no man coming to the Father but by me." And may he grant that the eyes of your understanding being enlightened you may be enabled to perceive with all Saints what is the breadth and length & depth and height and to know the love of Christ which passeth knowlege that you may be filled with all the fulness of God & I would conclude with his apostle's benediction to the Ephesians—To Him that is able to do exceedingly abundantly above all that we ask or think according to the power that worketh in us To Him be glory in the Church by Christ Jesus throughout all ages world without end

I am Sir, with great consideration Your hble Servant

A. O. STANSB[URY]

RC (DLC); edge trimmed, torn at seal; addressed: "Thomas Jefferson Esqr Monticello Virginia"; franked; postmarked New York, 12 Jan.; mistakenly endorsed by TJ as a letter of 7 Jan. 1814 received 20 Jan. Recorded in SJL as received 20 Jan. 1815.

Abraham Ogier Stansbury (1776–1829), merchant, publisher, inventor, educator, and Presbyterian minister, was born in Philadelphia and moved to New York City by 1800. He received patents for an Egyptian lock and an improved printing press in 1807 and 1821, respectively, and was the superintendent of a school for the deaf and dumb late in the 1810s. A member of the New-York Missionary Society, Stansbury published a short work entitled Considerations on the Lawfulness of Lotteries, and the propriety of Christians holding tickets (New York, 1813). He died in the town of Southeast, Putnam County, New York (Stephen O. Saxe, American Iron Hand Presses [1992], 29–33; DNA: RG 29, CS, N.Y., New York, 1800; Longworth's New York Directory [1801]: 323; [1803]: 269; New York Chronicle Express, 11 July 1803; List of Patents, 58, 225; New York National Advocate, 4 May 1818; Albany Argus, 12 Jan. 1819; Hartford Connecticut Courant, 19 May 1829; Quarterly Register and Journal of the American Education Society 2 [Aug. 1829]: 54; New York Genealogical and Biographical Record 33 [1902]: 140–1).

Two days earlier the New-York Evening Post (EV^G POST) had published William Canby's letter to TJ of 27 Aug. 1813 and TJ's reply of 18 Sept. 1813. The

first five lines of "The Universal Prayer" by Alexander POPE read: "Father of All! in every Age,/ In every Clime ador'd,/ By Saint, by Savage, and by Sage,/ Jehovah, Jove, or Lord/ Thou Great First Cause, least understood!"

The following biblical quotes are all from the book of John: BEFORE ABRAHAM WAS I AM (8.58); I & THE FATHER ARE ONE (10.30); EXCEPT YE EAT . . . NO LIFE IN YOU (6.53); I GO TO PREPARE . . . YE MAY BE ALSO (14.3); IF I GO AWAY . . . SHALL BE IN YOU (16.7); I HAVE POWER . . . TAKE IT AGAIN (10.18); I AM THE RESURRECTION . . . SHALL NEVER DIE (11.25); I LAY DOWN MY LIFE FOR MY SHEEP (10.15); I GIVE UNTO THEM . . . SHALL NEVER PERISH (10.28).

The conversation between Jesus and THE WOMAN OF SAMARIA appears in John 4.7–29. The question WHAT SHALL WE DO THAT WE MIGHT WORK THE WORKS OF GOD and Jesus's reply are in John 6.28–9. Jesus asserts that those IN THEIR GRAVES SHOULD HEAR HIS VOICE AND COME FORTH in John 5.28–9. In the New Testament Jesus spends time PARDONING SIN (Mark 2.5), commanding THE WIND & THE SEA (Mark 4.39), and making himself EQUAL WITH GOD (John 5.18). God promises to dispatch the MESSENGER OF THE COVENANT in Malachi 3.1. In Hebrews 3.1, Jesus is described as the APOSTLE & HIGH PRIEST OF OUR PROFESSION, while THE WAY THE TRUTH AND THE LIFE . . . BY ME is from John 14.6. Paul's benediction TO HIM THAT IS ABLE . . . WORLD WITHOUT END is in Ephesians 3.20–1.

[1] Stansbury here canceled "modified."
[2] Omitted opening quotation mark editorially supplied.
[3] Omitted opening quotation mark editorially supplied.

[4] Omitted opening quotation mark editorially supplied.
[5] Manuscript: "thein."
[6] Reworked from "Sin."

From John McAllister & Son

SIR   Philad[a] Jany 9th 1815[1]

Your letter of 24th Ulto with a pair of Spectacles and their Set of Glasses was duly rec[d] by mail—

The reason that [the] Glasses rendered indistinct vision and confused obje[cts] was, that the Centre of Convexity was not in the Centre of the Glass—at the time they were fitted up we were not fully aware of the necessity of having them so, and the workman who fitted them to the frames had Cut them down too much on one side—we herewith send in lieu of them others which you will find to be free of that fault.—Those in the frames are 16 Inches Focus—you will know the Focus of the others by the marks on their respective envelopes—

There is no charge for what we have done, and we regret that our former Error has deprived you of the use of the Glasses and given you the trouble of Sending them—

with sentiments of respect   JOHN M[c]ALLISTER & SON

RC (MoSHi: TJC-BC); hole in manuscript; in a clerk's hand; at foot of text: "Thomas Jefferson Esq Monticello"; endorsed by TJ as received 20 Jan. 1815 and so recorded in SJL.

Filed with the RC of this letter, but possibly not originally enclosed with it, is a printed sheet headed "John M[c]Allister and Son, Spectacle Manufacturers, No. 43, Chesnut Street, *Philadelphia*," which the firm used when shipping a pair of spectacles and three sets of extra lenses, with blanks to be filled in with the focal distance of each set of lenses and instructions that as one's vision worsened new lenses could be substituted for those in the frame "by unscrewing the small screws near the ends of the Front"; stating also that the firm sells glasses "in Gold, Silver, Tortoise-Shell, Plated, or Steel Frames, with Convex, Concave or

Green Glasses, suitable for various eyes, and various sights," with a variety of spectacle cases; that the lenses are carefully fitted to the individual, "as many injure their eyes by using glasses of an improper focus"; that customers ordering from a distance should send a sample of the lens worn most recently, "as *the age* does not afford a rule for judging of the sight"; that spectacles are supplied in assortments by the dozen to country storekeepers; and that, for customers ordering from a distance, "we have adopted the mode of fitting them up with several sets of extra glasses, comprising a variety of sights, from which a pair can be selected by the person for whom they are intended" (broadside in MoSHi: TJC-BC; undated; blanks not filled in; endorsed by TJ: "M[c]Allister John & Son").

[1] Reworked from "1814."

From John Vaughan

DEAR SIR   Philad. Jan.ʸ 9. 1815

Notwithstanding the previous communications of Mʳ Correa, & your positive letter of resignation, very great difficulty occurred in prevailing upon the members of the American Philos. Society to accede to your wishes—It was at last Generally understood, amongst them, that Your name was to be withdrawn,—leaving however the whole open by not formally acting upon your letter. On the Day of the Election, An idea had suggested itself to some, that notwithstanding the letter—some misconstruction might, by design or otherwise, be put by our Papers on the motives of the Change, & an opinion was Circulated, that, to prevent it, you should still be elected; & that then if you could not be prevailed upon to serve Again—The Act of Resignation would be <u>your own</u> & a <u>public</u> one.—Could this have been generally Communicated, the measure would generally have been adopted—It was too late, & Dʳ Wistar was elected to succeed you, altho' he was of those who earnestly desired the former Course to be pursued.—Our friend Correa would no Doubt have done the same; but there was no oppʸ of Communicating to him or others, the change proposed in the plan—. It was suggested by those who acted upon it, that if your Determination was not to be shaken, Wistar would come in probably by an Unanimous Vote; as he had been V-P. 5 yˢ before Mʳ Patterson, & 7 Yˢ before Dʳ Barton—In announcing the Election, we did not think it proper to publish to the world the whole of Your letter; which might have been occasionally detatched from the publication;—but prefered interweaving the <u>Fact</u> with it;— in the manner you will have seen.—But for your peremptory letter, supported by Your private Communications to M Correa—Your name <u>could not have been withdrawn</u>; It had served us too well, to be Easily relinquished—

You will shortly have a Visit from a Young man of distinguished learning & Talents, a Mʳ George Ticknor of Boston he carries Letters from Mʳ Adams & Dʳ Wistar—his career will be the Law, but his fortune admitting it, he means to pass Some time in Europe, with a View of enlarging his Knowledge before he establishes himself at home— previous to his Tour he visits our Cities as far as Washington & in his way to pay his respects to you—such young men, appearing as Travellers will do credit to the Country[1]—I have brought him acquainted with Mʳ Gilmor with whom, he is much pleased, & thinks of him more highly than of any Young Man he has seen since he left home— I believe Mʳ G is equally pleased with him—M Correa will give Mʳ T.

letters for Europe—& if from the State of Europe M^r C puts in Execution his favorite project of returning to Paris I shall try to arrange the plan for their going together—Mr T. will be happy to be honored with your Commands—Wishing You many happy returns of the Season   I remain Your sincere friend   J^no VAUGHAN

P.S:

I do not Know whether you possess any part of Michaux's Am^n Forest Trees—The 2^d & 3^d Vol. are here The first Vol. consists of the Pines & Noyers.—some persons who had taken this being removed from the Country,[2] these two last Vol. can be procured—but not I believe the whole Work—It is much appreciated & I could very readily dispose of Several complete Copies if I had them—

RC (MHi); at head of text: "Thomas Jefferson Esqr Monticello"; adjacent to signature: "P.T.O" (that is, "Please Turn Over") for postscript on verso; mistakenly endorsed by TJ as a letter of 4 Jan. 1815 received 30 Jan. 1815 and so recorded in SJL.

The LETTER OF RESIGNATION is TJ to Robert M. Patterson, 23 Nov. 1814. Caspar Wistar was ELECTED TO SUCCEED TJ as president of the American Philosophical Society on 6 Jan. 1815. He had served as a vice president (V-P.) since 1795, while Robert Patterson and

Benjamin Smith Barton had only held that office since 1799 and 1802, respectively (APS, Minutes, 2 Jan. 1795, 4 Jan. 1799, 1 Jan. 1802, 6 Jan. 1815 [MS in PPAmP]). In ANNOUNCING THE ELECTION results, the society explained that Wistar was chosen only after TJ "formally resigned, and expressly declined a reelection to this office, which he had held eighteen years" (Philadelphia *Poulson's American Daily Advertiser*, 9 Jan. 1815). NOYERS: walnut trees.

[1] Reworked from "County."
[2] Reworked from "County."

From John Barnes

DEAR SIR—   George Town 10th Jany 1815.

Your fav^r 29th Ult^o recd the 5th Covered, your Genl power of Att^y—in my fav^r—the Accruing Int (Averaged.) from 10^h July—to 31st Decr Am^t 358\frac{32}{100}$ I recd the 7^h and passed, to the Credit of Genl K^s a/c—The two Certificates[1] of said Stock—recites the following

viz—for $11,363$\frac{63}{100}$ Thomas Jefferson of Virginia—or, his Assigns bearing Int 6 p Ct per Ann^m from 10th July 1814. inclusively pay^ble Quarter Yearly. being stock Created p act of Congres[s] for a Loan of 25 Millions of Doll^s passed the 24th March 1814. Redeemable at the pleasur[e] of Congress at any time After Decr 1825—

N° 10.

Nº 10 Also for $1136\frac{36}{100}$ Same Time & date for the 10 ℗Ct advance—
$$\overline{12,499\frac{99}{100}}\qquad\text{Equal to 80 for 100—say \$12,500}$$

The above recited Certificates—are lodged—in safe Custerdy—in the
Customhouse Iron chest. Subject—to your Order—
and, am, most Respectfully—
Dear Sir—   Your obed^t servant.   JOHN BARNES.

RC (ViU: TJP-ER); edge frayed; endorsed by TJ as received 16 Jan. 1815 and
so recorded in SJL. RC (CSmH: JF); address cover only; with PoC of TJ to
Thomas Munroe, 4 Mar. 1815, on verso;
addressed: "Thomas Jefferson Esquire
Monticello—Virginia"; franked; postmarked Georgetown, 11 Jan.

GEN^L K^S: Tadeusz Kosciuszko's. According to the United States "act to
authorize a loan for a sum not exceeding twenty-five millions of dollars," the
monies borrowed were to become RE-
DEEMABLE after the last day of December
1826, not 1825 (U.S. Statutes at Large,
3:111–2).

[1] Manuscript: "Certifiates."

From William Thornton

DEAR SIR   City of Washington 11th Jany 1815—
I am very much obliged by the kind promise you have been so good
as to make me, of the loan of the two paintings; of which I shall take
great care.—
A few Days ago a Mr Crossbie, formerly from England, called at
my Office, and asserts that m^r Janes, who took out the Patent for the
Loom, obtained the same from one that he (Crossbie) had invented,
& had then in operation. He means to proceed against Janes, with an
intention to set aside his Patent. Crossbie is a very ingenious man, &
liberal in his conduct. I wish to examine his plans, and, when satisfied
of their goodness, shall endeavour to obtain from him such proposals
for you and the Gentlemen of your neighbourhood as may serve you
all.—
I have at length found a Copy of the Patents issued in 1812 which
with 1813 I have the pleasure of inclosing for you. I send also a short
account of Steam-boats.—
As soon as the List of Patents for 1814 shall have been published I
shall not fail to send one.—
I have seen in the Artist's manual a machine for raising Water
which is so simple in its construction, that it would answer admirably
at monticello. Thinking you may not have a copy of this work (in 2
Vol: 8vo published in Phila^a—Author, James Cutbush) I have drawn
it and now inclose the same.—

Wishing you the Complim^{ts} of the Season, with every blessing—I am dear Sir Yours very sincerely   WILLIAM THORNTON—

If the Bucket of a machine on the principle of the one I have drawn, were to be much larger, & the stroke of the Piston also longer, by allowing the Bucket a greater fall, you might raise a large quantity of water to the top of your elevated Situation, and water your Gardens & grounds round it.—I have contrived a very cheap and effectual Filter for Water Cyder &c &c, which operates well, and without any trouble. If you wish it I will send a description of it.—

   Y^{rs} &c   W.T.

RC (DLC); above postscript: "Honorable Thomas Jefferson"; endorsed by TJ as received 20 Jan. 1815 and so recorded in SJL. Enclosures: (1) *Letter from the Secretary of State, transmitting A List of the Names of Persons to whom Patents have been Issued . . . from January 1, 1812, to January 1, 1813* (Washington, 1813). (2) *Letter from the Secretary of State, transmitting A List of the Names of Persons to whom Patents have been Issued . . . from January 1st, 1813, to January 1st, 1814* (Washington, 1814). (3) Thornton, *Short Account of the Origin of Steam Boats* (Washington, 1814).

The enclosed drawing and description of a MACHINE FOR RAISING WATER reproduces portions of two 1801 letters from Henry Sarjeant, of Whitehaven, England, to the Society for the Encouragement of Arts, Manufactures, and Commerce, wherein he describes the device used by him at Irton Hall to pump water up an ascent of about sixty feet to the main house, compares the apparatus to one used formerly by James Spedding at a lead mine near Keswick, England, and claims that the "only Artists employed, except the plumber, were a country Blacksmith & Carpenter; & the whole cost, exclusive of the pump & pipes, did not amount to five pounds"; and quotes Thomas Green Fessenden's observation in *The Register of Arts, or a compendious view of some of the most useful modern discoveries and inventions* (Philadelphia, 1808), 9, that "the simplicity of construction, and the cheapness of this machine, must render it worthy of attention, not only for raising Water for domestic purposes, but in many cases it might be turned to account in Agriculture" (Tr in DLC: TJ Papers, 203:36117–8; entirely in Thornton's hand; undated; endorsed by TJ: "Machine to raise water. voce [i.e., 'under the heading,' *OED*] 'Engine' 1st Cutbush"; copied from James Cutbush, *The American Artist's Manual* [Philadelphia, 1814; Poor, *Jefferson's Library*, 6 (no. 221)], vol. 1, section on "Engines").

From John Seabrook

DEAR SIR,   Richmond Jany 12, 1815[1]

   The appearance of a letter in the public prints ascribed to you, in which you deny the authenticity of the Gospel, and ridicule the idea of its containing a Divine revelation, induces me to Send you the enclosed book: with an earnest & respectful request that you will read it with candor and attention. And should you possess the magnanimous condescension to be entreated by an obscure fellow citizen to review with renewed attention the important subject of religion, notwithstanding you had long ago made up your mind thereon;—it may be, that it may please the Almighty in his infinite goodness & mercy to remove from your mind that cloud of prejudice and super-stition, which has heretofore obscured your intellectual vision. But here let me declare that I mean no disparagement; I am sensible of your vast superiority in literary attainments, and intellectual endow-ments; nor have I the least wish to tarnish the celebrity you have ac-quired as a Statesman[2] & Philosopher: Yet I am confidently of opinion that in relation to the all important matter of religion, your mind is under the influence of prejudice and Superstition; otherwise you Could not withstand the proofs adduced in confirmation of the Authenticity of the Gospel, which have satisfied So many learned and wise men—

I acknowledge that this language may appear harsh and opprobri-ous, but when you are apprized of my reasons for using it, you will I trust be disposed to excuse it—they are these—I am persuaded the letter in question will do, nay has already done, great and irreparable mischief to my beloved Country: inasmuch, as in my opinion, it is eminently Calculated to relax, nay, to dissolve every Obligation to moral rectitude, and thus to introduce in our land every Species of vice, and thus consequently to subvert our happy republican institu-tions:—That it is calculated to do the more and greater mischief, par-ticularly in this my native State, because very many persons hold the author of it in high estimation, and deem him qualified to judge and decide correctly on every subject.

And that at this time it is Calculated to spread its baneful influence to a greater extent, by the co-operation of the demoralizing effects of a State of war—

I will not multiply reasons, because I presume that if you will give me Credit for but a Small portion of patriotism, you will allow these[3] to be Sufficient, at least, to excuse, if not to justify what I have done and said—

And now I pray the Most High & Merciful God, in Christs name, and for his sake, to dispose you to re-examine the evidences of the Christian religion: that he will liberate your mind from the Shackles of prejudice and superstition: that he will enlighten it, to perceive the truth and the excellency of the Gospel dispensation, and that he will prepare your <u>heart</u> by the renovating influences of his blessed Spirit to receive it in the love of it—Amen. Should my prayer be answered, I have not the least doubt, but you will then feel the greatest Solici-tude to make all the reparation in your power for the injury, which you will then perceive, the promulgation of your infidel opinions has been long inflicting on your fellow Citizens & on Your Country.

JOHN SEABROOK.

RC (MHi); addressed: "Thomas Jefferson Esquire Monticello Virginia"; endorsed by TJ as received 16 Jan. 1815 and so recorded in SJL. Enclosure not found.

John Seabrook (ca. 1768–1844), a native of Portsmouth, was a longtime resident of Richmond. When Richmond's Presbyterians formed a congregation in 1812, he was ordained an elder, and in the same year he became librarian of the city's new Christian Library. Seven years later a city directory listed Seabrook as a collector. He eventually moved to nearby Hanover County, where he owned six slaves a few years before his death (William Henry Foote, *Sketches of Virginia, Historical and Biographical*, 2d ser. [1855], 325; Richmond *Enquirer*, 30 Oct.

1812; *The Richmond Directory, Register and Almanac, for the Year 1819* [Richmond, 1819], 68; DNA: RG 29, CS, Richmond, 1810, Henrico Co., 1820, Hanover Co., 1840; *Richmond Whig and Public Advertiser*, 26 Sept. 1844).

TJ's 18 Sept. 1813 letter to William Canby on religion appeared in a number of PUBLIC PRINTS in Virginia, including the *Petersburg Daily Courier*, 21 Nov. 1814, the *Alexandria Gazette, Commercial and Political*, 22 Nov. 1814, and the Richmond *Enquirer*, 24 Nov. 1814.

[1] Reworked from "1814."
[2] Manuscript: "Stateeman."
[3] Manuscript: "thise," reworked from "this."

From Mathew Carey

SIR   Philad[a] Jan. 14. 1815

By this day's mail I send you a copy of the Olive Branch, of which I request Your acceptance, & am,

Your ob[t] h[ble] serv[t]   MATHEW CAREY

RC (MHi); dateline at foot of text; at head of text: "Hon. Thomas Jefferson, Esq[r]"; endorsed by TJ as received 30 Jan. 1815 and so recorded in SJL.

The work sent to TJ BY THIS DAY'S MAIL was probably the 9 Jan. 1815 sec-

ond edition of Carey's *The Olive Branch: or Faults on Both Sides, Federal and Democratic. A Serious Appeal on the Necessity of Mutual Forgiveness and Harmony, to save Our Common Country from Ruin* (Philadelphia, 1815; Sowerby, no. 3539).

From Lancelot Minor

DEAR SIR   Louisa Jan[y] 14 1815

Diffident of Judging of the qualifications of my Son I have called upon some of my friends, Who have had it more in their power; and better able to Judge Impartially of his merits their Certificates I inclose.—

From the youthfull age and Inexperience of Wm T. Minor I do not suppose that he ought to look higher than a Lieutenants or Ensigns commission. Either of which Grade I hope he will fill with honor and propriety The prospect of Raising state troops seems to be done away but should a state army be Raised, he, as well as myself have an objection to his Joining that, for this Reason; that I suppose if the state troops are Raised they will be confined principally to Garrison duty. It is my wish if my Son Joins the army that he shall be where there is active duty—

I will therefore ask that you will be so good as to endeavour to procure for him in the U States army a Lieutenants or Ensigns Commission—I feel particularly anxious that if he Joins the Army that it Could be assertained shortly the prospect of entering the army has in a great measure Suspended his Medical persuits and I fear will continue to do So untill it is determined

acept Dear Sir my best wishes for your happiness

LAN MINOR

RC (DLC: James Monroe Papers); addressed in the unidentified hand that copied the enclosures below: "Thomas Jefferson Esquire Monticello"; franked; postmarked "Mitchells Store V^a," 14 Jan. 1815; endorsed by TJ as received 20 Jan. 1815 and so recorded in SJL. Enclosures: (1) Recommendation of William T. Minor by Lieutenant Colonel Henry Timberlake, Camp Carter, 7 Dec. 1814, stating that if the younger Minor obtains a commission, he will discharge his duties honorably; and adding that Minor joined the Virginia militia as a volunteer in August 1814, when he was under the age of eighteen, and that he is still in service (Tr in DLC: Monroe Papers). (2) Recommendation of Minor by George W. Trueheart and Andrew Kean, Louisa County, 8 Jan. 1805 [1815], remarking that they have known him for many years and can testify to his probity and good character; and commenting that they are "anxious to see in the Military service of our Country at this Crisis a young Man on whose virtuous principles, correct habits, promising talents, & republican [republican] devotion we can implicitly confide, for an able and zealous discharge of any trust reposed in him" (Tr in DLC: Monroe Papers; subjoined to preceding enclosure). Enclosed in TJ to James Monroe, 21 Jan. 1815.

William Tompkins Minor (1797–1854), physician and eldest son of Lancelot Minor, was born in Caroline County. Despite his wartime service in the Virginia militia and his father's best efforts, he never obtained a military commission. The younger Minor did receive a medical degree from the University of Pennsylvania in 1818 and moved shortly thereafter to Alabama, where he lived for the remainder of his life. In 1850 he owned twenty-three slaves (John B. Minor, *The Minor Family of Virginia* [1923], 20–1; *General Alumni Catalogue of the University of Pennsylvania* [1917], 579; DNA: RG 29, CS, Ala., Morgan Co., 1850 slave schedules; gravestone in Minor family cemetery, Morgan Co., Ala.).

SJL records missing letters from Lancelot Minor to TJ, 8 Dec. 1814, received from Louisa County the day after it was written, and from TJ to Minor, 9 Dec. 1814 and 21 Jan. 1815.

To Louis H. Girardin

Monticello Jan. 15. 15.

I have no document respecting Clarke's expedition except the letters of which you are in possession, one of which I believe gives some account of it; nor do I possess Imlay's history of Kentucky.

Of mr Wythe's early history I scarcely know any thing, except that he was self-taught; & perhaps this might not have been as to the Latin language. Dr Small was his bosom friend, and to me as a father. to his enlightened & affectionate guidance of my studies while at College I am indebted for every thing.

he was professor of Mathematics at W. & M. & for some time was in the philosophical chair. he first introduced into both schools rational & elevated courses of study, and from an extraordinary conjunction of eloquence & logic was enabled to communicate them to the students with great effect. he procured for me the patronage of mr Wythe, & both of them, the attentions of Governor Fauquier, the ablest man who ever filled the chair of government here. they were inseparable friends, and at their frequent dinners with the Governor (after his family had returned to England) he admitted me always to make it a partie quarreé. at these dinners I have heard more good sense, more rational & philosophical conversations than in all my life besides. they were truly Attic societies. the Governor was musical also & a good performer and associated me with 2. or 3. other amateurs in his weekly concerts. he merits honorable mention in your history, if any proper occasion for it offers. so also does Dabney Carr, father of Peter Carr, mover of the proposition of Mar. 1773. for Commees of correspondence, the first fruit of which was the Call of an American Congress: I return your two pamphlets with thanks & salute you with esteem & respect

RC (DLC); dateline at foot of text. Not recorded in SJL. Enclosures not found.

George Rogers Clark's (CLARKE'S) Revolutionary War campaigns culminated in the conquest of the region later known as the Northwest Territory (DVB). Gilbert Imlay's HISTORY OF KENTUCKY was entitled *A Topographical Description of the Western Territory of North America; containing a Succinct Account of its Climate, Natural History, Population, Agriculture, Manners and Customs . . . to which is annexed, a Delineation of the* *Laws and Government of the State of Kentucky* (London, 1792).

During the colonial period the College of William and Mary (W. & M.) had both a collegiate department and a grammar school. As a member of the Board of Visitors, in 1779 TJ championed the elimination of the latter, although it was later revived (Susan H. Godson and others, *The College of William and Mary: A History* [1993], esp. 1:29–30, 130–4, 173; *PTJ*, 2:535–43). PARTIE QUARREÉ (partie carrée): "foursome."

On 12 Mar. 1773 TJ's brother-in-law

Dabney Carr (1743–73) presented a series of resolutions according to which the Virginia House of Burgesses would establish a committee of CORRESPONDENCE charged with establishing better communications with its counterparts in the other British colonies. They were unanimously adopted that same day (William J. Van Schreeven, Robert L.

Scribner, and Brent Tarter, eds., *Revolutionary Virginia, the Road to Independence: A Documentary Record* [1973–83], 1:89–92).

Missing letters from Girardin to TJ of 26 Dec. 1814, 6, 15, and 16 Jan. 1815, the first and last of which are described as sent from Glenmore, are recorded in SJL as received the days they were written.

From Charles W. Goldsborough

SIR,   Georgetown Jan[y] 19th 1815

Understanding that you have it in contemplation to establish a few of the most approved patented looms, I beg leave to call your attention to my advertisement in the "Federal Republican" & "National Intelligencer" upon the subject of Patented Looms—I do this for two reasons—1st because I believe I can establish, by competent testimony, that the essential principles of Jane's loom, which I am told you highly approve, have been taken from a Loom invented & patented by M[r] Richard Crosbie a considerable time before M[r] Janes took out his Patent for his improved Loom—& 2nd to afford you an opportunity of procuring, should You desire it, the right of using Looms which without question are preferable to any now in use.

In a short time I shall have a Loom for exhibition in this place—& shall be happy to shew it in operation to any gentleman whom you may wish to see it, & whose opinion as to it's merits you might desire.—I will here only observe that, in addition to all the improvements in Jane's Loom, it may be put in operation by elementary power, & will work with infinite ease & celerity.—

When you shall be satisfied as to the merit of M[r] Crosbie's Loom, I would dispose of to <u>you</u> the right of using any number, on terms probably as moderate as you would desire.

I am with great respect
sir y[r] ob s[t]   CH: W: GOLDSBOROUGH

RC (DLC); endorsed by TJ as received 30 Jan. 1815 and so recorded in SJL.

Charles Washington Goldsborough (1777–1843), public official and merchant, was born in Cambridge, Maryland, joined the Navy Department in 1798, and served as its chief clerk, 1802–13. He operated a store in George-

town for a number of years and was a director of the Farmers and Mechanics' National Bank in that city, a member of the District of Columbia's city council in 1808, and sat on the Board of Aldermen, 1821–24 and 1832–41 (with service as president, 1835–41). Goldsborough returned to the Navy Department as a clerk of the Navy Board in 1815, served as the board's secretary, 1823–42, and was chief of the naval Bureau of Provisions and Clothing, 1842–43. He published *An Original and Correct List of the United States Navy* (Washington, 1800) and *The United States' Naval Chronicle* (Washington, 1824). Goldsborough died in Washington (Christopher McKee, *A Gentlemanly and Honorable Profession: The Creation of the U.S. Naval Officer Corps, 1794–1815* [1991], 15, 17; Allan B. Slauson, ed., *A History of the City of Washington: Its Men and Institutions* [1903], 177; Wilhelmus B. Bryan, *Forms of Local Government in the District of Columbia* [1903], 31, 34–5, 37–9; *A Naval Encyclopædia* [1881], 314; Callahan, *U.S. Navy*, 2, 5; Georgetown *Federal Republican, and Commercial Gazette*, 30 Aug. 1813; Washington *Daily National Intelligencer*, 26 Apr. 1815, 7 Aug. 1818, 16, 29 Dec. 1843, 3 Apr. 1844; gravestone inscription in Congressional Cemetery, Washington, D.C.).

In an ADVERTISEMENT that he published as "Sole Agent of Richard Crosbie," Goldsborough warned against the purchase "of any Patented Loom without first ascertaining that the improvements thereon have not been taken from Mr. Crosbie; and such as may have purchased the right of using Looms improved upon his principles, are admonished to desist from the further use thereof. The date of his Patent is 6th January, 1812; but his legal right extends back to the date of his inventions, and he claims accordingly" (Georgetown *Federal Republican*, 17 Jan. 1815; Washington *Daily National Intelligencer*, 23 Jan. 1815).

From the American Philosophical Society

SIR,   Hall of the Am. Ph. Soc., January 20., 1815.

The American Philosophical Society, after having, at Several periods, withstood your Solicitations to be withdrawn from their presidency, have at length, with great reluctance, felt themselves obliged to yield to the decided resignation expressed[1] in your letter of the 23d. of november last, and have, accordingly, elected doctor Caspar[2] Wistar to that office.

The important connection which has Subsisted, between yourself and the Society, for eighteen years, being thus dissolved, the Society avail themselves of the opportunity of expressing[3] to you their warmest thanks for the very valuable Services which you have rendered them, and of Soliciting the continuance of the friendly attentions which you have always shown to their interests.

The Society add the expressions of their attachment and respect, and their Sincerest wishes for your happiness.

Communicated, by order of the Society.   R. M. PATTERSON.
                                                     Secretary.

RC (MHi); in Robert M. Patterson's hand; at head of text: "To Thomas Jefferson"; dateline at foot of text; endorsed by TJ as a letter from Patterson at the "Philos. Soc^ty" received 1 Feb. 1815 and so recorded in SJL. FC (APS, Minutes,

20 Jan. 1815 [MS in PPAmP]); in Patterson's hand. Enclosed in Patterson to TJ, 21 Jan. 1815.

[1] RC: "expessed." FC: "expressed."
[2] RC: "Casper." FC: "Caspar."
[3] RC: "of expressing of expressing." FC: "of expressing."

To Louis H. Girardin

TH: JEFFERSON TO MR GIRARDIN   Monticello Jan. 20. 15.

I return your cahier, with[1] about half a dozen unimportant alterations only. three or four of these are foreignisms (if I may coin a word where the language gives none) indeed I have wondered that you could have so perfectly possessed yourself of the idiom and spirit of the English language, as not to write it correctly merely, but so often elegantly. permit me to suggest a single doubt on the matter of this Cahier. in giving an account of some of the legislative acts, do you not descend more into detail than will be acceptable to common readers? the general substance of a law divested of the technical terms & tautologies of the profession, & omitting it's minute provisions, seems to satisfy best the functions of history. and of this you have given perfect models in your account of some of the laws. this suggestion however is made merely to bring the matter under your own reflection, which I know will suffice to produce the most correct result. I salute you with great esteem and respect.

RC (PPAmP: Thomas Jefferson Papers). Enclosure: manuscript, not found, of a portion of Burk, Jones, and Girardin, *History of Virginia*, vol. 4.

According to SJL, Girardin sent TJ a letter dated 21 Jan. 1815, not found, which is inconsistently recorded as received 20 Jan. 1815 from Glenmore.

TJ's is, indeed, the earliest documented use of the word FOREIGNISMS (*OED*).

[1] Reworked from "without."

To William P. Newby

SIR   Monticello Jan. 20. 15.

In a letter to my grandson the last summer[1] you expressed a willingness to return to my employment; but at that time I had no place vacant, and the one particularly at which you had lived was then, & still is occupied by a person who gives entire satisfaction. in Bedford I have two plantations, adjoining, of 16. hands each, uplands of the first quality where I cultivate both tobacco & wheat. in point of soil, climate, and a substantial thrifty & good neighborhood I think it the

[203]

finest part of Virginia. my wages there are 200.D. something less than the place here, where the business is much more multiplied & troublesome. indeed the times require a general reduction of wages, as nothing can be sold for the expence of making it. one of these places will be vacant the next year, & I make you the first offer of it. if you chuse to undertake it, and will so inform me by answer, it is at your command. the house is uncomfortable, being a single room [and?] a loft above. but I wish to add to it & make it comfortable.— another room with a passage between, can quickly be added, of hewen logs as is usual in that country, plaistered, with windows, stone chimney E^{t}c and as this would take but a very short time, I would rather leave it to be done by yourself, immediately on your arrival, that you might do it to please yourself. the place is 10. miles from Lynchburg, the second town of the state as to the quantity of business, and the most thriving one in the state. I write to you thus early as if you accept it, it will be satisfactory to us both to be at rest on that point, and if not, that I may have the more time to look about me. your answer therefore is requested as soon as you can make up your mind on it. accept my best wishes & respects

TH: JEFFERSON

P.S. whether you accept or not, I shall be glad to have nothing said about it till midsummer, as it might be injurious to the present service of the place.

PoC (DLC); on verso of reused address cover to TJ; torn at seal; postscript adjacent to signature; at foot of text: "Mr Wm P. Newby"; endorsed by TJ. Enclosed in TJ to Benjamin Shackelford, [ca. 20 Jan. 1815], which is not recorded in SJL and has not been found (see Shackelford to TJ, 16 Mar. 1815).

Newby had written to Thomas Jefferson Randolph, TJ's GRANDSON. He had previously served as overseer at TJ's Tufton estate, a position which was now held by William Ballard, WHO GIVES ENTIRE SATISFACTION.

[1] Word interlined in place of "winter."

To Thomas Eston Randolph

DEAR SIR   Monticello Jan. 20. 15

As mr Randolph and yourself have the Shadwell mill in partnership this year and the details of it's business, on account of his absences, will chiefly fall on you, I submit to you the following considerations as to the rent. while Shoemaker held the mill the rent was fixed in money at 1280.D. a year payable quarterly. when mr Randolph and M^{c}kinney took it they wished it to be fixed in flour

@ 6.D. a barrel, to which I consented and it was settled at 213⅓ Barrels of flour payable quarterly. flour getting afterwards to 10. & 12.D. a barrel, and this being thought to make the rent too high, I consented to change it back again to money at the old rate, and so it now stands. but flour, instead of double price as before, is now at half price only, so that to pay the rent in money now would take a double quantity of flour. I propose therefore to leave to yourselves now to say whether the rent shall be fixed in future in money or flour, and to remain unalterably in whichever article is now determined on. I think myself that flour is the safest, because it's value is so much more fluctuating than that of money, and it is the sole article on which the mill is employed. if the rent be payable in that, both owner & tenant bear proportionably the loss of low prices and reap[1] the gain of high ones. and it is the sharing in both of these which alone can give to either a proper average of value. however I leave the election between the two articles entirely to yourselves. by a special agreement between mr Randolph and myself, the year begins always the 1st of July, so that whatever you determine will have retrospect to that date. accept the assurance of my great friendship and respect.   TH: JEFFERSON

PoC (MHi); at foot of text: "Thomas E. Randolph esq."; endorsed by TJ.

Randolph had entered into a PARTNERSHIP with Thomas Mann Randolph to lease the Shadwell mills in 1814 (note to Thomas Eston Randolph to TJ, 3 Sept. 1809). Jonathan & Isaac SHOEMAKER rented the mills from TJ from 1807–11

(Account with Jonathan & Isaac Shoemaker, 15 Jan., 8 June 1811). Their successors, Thomas Mann Randolph and James McKinney, apparently began paying their rent in money AT THE OLD RATE in 1812 (TJ to Nathaniel H. Hooe, 6 Oct. 1811, TJ to William Short, 17 Oct. 1812).

[1] Word interlined.

To James Monroe

DEAR SIR   Monticello. Jan. 21. 15.
    When I retired from the government, I yielded with too much facility, first to the importunities of my friends to aid them in getting commands in the army and navy, next of mere acquaintances, and lastly of those also of whom I knew nothing. the business became laborious and irksome to myself, and, as I was sufficiently sensible, embarrassing and unpleasant to the government. determined at length to reliev[e] both them & myself, I availed myself of the simultaneous change in both departments to put an end to it; and to subsequent applications I answered by making known my determination to withdraw from those sollicitations; as I accordingly have done since

Armstrong & Jones entered on those offices. it is impossible however that some cases should not now and then occur in which duty as well as inclination require compliance. such a case now occurs. Col° Lancelot Minor, brother of our friend Col° John Minor, wishes a commission in the army for his son. I apprised him he could only enter in the lowest grade, and he is satisfied with that. I do not know the young man, but have known many of the name, and never knew one who did not possess worth and good sense. the papers I inclose you will speak of him more particularly, and it will be a great gratification to me, as well as to his most worthy father if he can obtain a command, and as early as propriety will admit The President also knows the family[1]—for fear the multiplicity of your business should put the return of my letters to mr Eppes E^tc. out of recollection, I remind you of their return, and assure you of my affectionate esteem & respect.   TH: JEFFERSON

PoC (DLC); on verso of reused address cover of John Barnes to TJ, 6 Dec. 1814; edge trimmed; at foot of text: "Col° Monroe"; endorsed by TJ. Enclosures: Lancelot Minor to TJ, 14 Jan. 1815, and enclosures.

The SIMULTANEOUS CHANGE occurred when President James Madison selected John Armstrong and William Jones to head the recently vacated War and Navy departments, respectively, on 8 Jan. 1813. The appointments were confirmed by the United States Senate on 12 and 13 Jan. 1813 (*JEP*, 2:315, 316). For the LETTERS still in Monroe's possession, see note to Monroe to TJ, 10 Oct. 1814.

[1] Preceding six words interlined.

From Robert M. Patterson

SIR,   Philadelphia, Jan. 21. 1815.

I have the honor to forward, in this enclosure, a letter addressed to you by the American Philosophical Society, on the occasion of your having withdrawn from their presidency. It was adopted at a meeting held last evening;—the first meeting after the election,—and was accompanied[1] with observations, from all the members of Standing, which were highly gratifying to your personal friends.

Permit me, Sir, to join the voice of the Society in expressing my Sincere regret at your having left its chair, and in assuring[2] you of my warm attachment and high respect.   R. M. PATTERSON.

RC (MHi); endorsed by TJ as received 1 Feb. 1815 and so recorded in SJL. RC (MHi); address cover only; with PoC of TJ to John Bankhead, 20 Feb. 1815, on recto and verso; addressed: "Thomas Jefferson Montecello"; franked; postmarked Philadelphia, 21 Jan. Enclosure: American Philosophical Society to TJ, 20 Jan. 1815.

[1] Manuscript: "accompanid."
[2] Manuscript: "assuing."

From Thomas Eston Randolph

DEAR SIR   Shadwell Mill, Saturday 21st Jan[y] 1815

I expect to go to Richmond tomorrow, and as soon as I see M[r] Randolph, I will communicate to him the contents of your letter of yesterday—

The proposition to pay the Rent of Shadwell Mill in Flour, in lieu of money, will be very agreable to me, and probably will be equally so to M[r] Randolph,—under any possible arrangement we must sustain a considerable loss this year—at the present money Rent, certainly not less than $600,—the quantity of wheat which will be received is inconsiderable and that generally so very indifferent that we are obliged to grind higher than usual to make the quality of the Flour even what it is,—It cannot I conceive be improper to state to you, that in consequence of a considerable loan from me to M[r] Randolph, and his retaining so much of the interest arising therefrom as will be equal to my moiety of the rent, it is understood[1] that he is responsible to you for the whole rent as usual.—So soon as I return I will inform you the result of my consultation with M[r] Randolph—with assurance of very affectionate regards I am yr: friend, &—

THO[s] ESTON RANDOLPH

RC (MHi); dateline at foot of text; endorsed by TJ as received 24 Jan. 1815 and so recorded in SJL.

[1] Randolph interlined "agreed" above this word.

From Samuel M. Burnside

SIR,   Worcester Mass. Jan[y] 23[d] 1815—

Your letter of the 8th of August last, addressed to me as recording Secretary of the A. A. Society was laid before them at their last meeting, and I am directed by them to tender You their thanks for the interesting and valuable manuscript, which accompanied it.—The Society, Sir, feel highly gratified, that you have consented to be enrolled Among its members.

Indeed they have ever been encouraged to hope, that he, who had become old in public Service, and had lived to See his Country ranked as independent among the nations of the world, would not[1] withhold the benefit of his name and personal influence from an infant Institution, whose object is to give a literary Character to that Country, to whose political existence You have So long contributed.—Any Communications Sir, which You may be able to make to the Society to facilitate the progress of its enquiries will be always most gratefully received.—We wish it to be universally understood, that the Society is not local.—Had Congress been thought to be vested with powers to incorporate a Society like this, application would doubtless have been made there for an act for this purpose.— But although[2] it derives its legal existence from the laws of a State, it is intended to be a <u>national</u> institution. As Such, we ask for its advancement, the aid of the learned and liberal throughout our extensive Country. The war, in which we are engaged presents a formidable obstacle to our pursuits.—It may with truth be said, that <u>Literæ, sicut, leges, silent inter arma.</u>—We indulge a hope however, that the present embarrassments of our Country will Soon be Succeeded by an era, in which Science and the useful arts will again add lustre to the American Name.—

With much respect, I subscribe myself Sir, Your obed^t Servt

S M BURNSIDE

RC (DLC); endorsed by TJ as received 5 Feb. 1815 and so recorded in SJL. RC (ViW: TC-JP); address cover only; with PoC of TJ to James Savage, 9 Feb. 1815, on verso; addressed: "Hon. Thomas Jefferson Esqr Monticello.—Virginia"; franked; postmarked.

The American Antiquarian Society (A. A. SOCIETY) derived its LEGAL EXISTENCE from an act of incorporation passed by the Massachusetts legislature (*An Account of the American Antiquarian Society, incorporated, October 24th, 1812*

[Boston, 1813], 14–7). LITERÆ, SICUT, LEGES, SILENT INTER ARMA ("During wartime, learning, like the law, is silent") is a variant of Cicero's famous phrase "silent enim leges inter arma" ("When arms speak, the laws are silent") (Cicero, *Pro T. Annio Milone*, 4.11, in *Cicero: Pro Milone . . . Pro Rege Deiotaro*, trans. Nevile H. Watts, Loeb Classical Library [1931; rev. ed. 1953], 16–7).

[1] Word interlined.
[2] Manuscript: "althoug."

From Horatio G. Spafford

ESTEEMED FRIEND,   [A]lbany, 1 Mo. 23, 1815.
I was duly honored w[...] a late date; and as I am always happy to have [...] thy health remains good, so I always esteem it [...] favor to receive thy Letters.

The within will [...]ow I am busying myself this Winter, & I expec[t] [...] a pretty respectable Collection. I am, besid[es] [...] printing a small pamphlet, a copy of whi[ch I d]esign for thee; & I am in [hopes][1] it may amuse thee for a few hours. I wish I had permission [to de]dicate it to thee. The title is

"Some Curs[ory Observatio]ns on the ordinary construction of wheel-carriage[s: with an attempt] to Show how they may be improved;—where[by a saving may be] made in the power applied, & the danger of [upsetting most effe]ctually prevented." I have Patented the i[...].

In a Letter f[rom] [...] [Preside]nt Adams, of the 2ᵈ inst., he enquires, "Did you [see Mr. Jefferson on] your late tour, & how does he do?" I also [...] his Son, by the late dispatches from our M[inisters] [...] [fer]vent prayers for the long continuance of thy [...] I tender thee assurances of my gratitude & [...]

HORATIO G. SPAFFORD.

RC (DLC); mutilated, with loss of most of center third of text; some words supplied from title page of Spafford, *Wheel-Carriages*, and John Adams to Spafford, 2 Jan. 1815 (Lb in MHi: Adams Papers); addressed: "Hon. Thomas Jefferson, LL. D. Monticello, Virginia"; franked; postmarked; endorsed by TJ on verso of enclosure as received 5 Feb. 1815 and so recorded in SJL. Enclosure: Spafford's circular letter to prospective assistants, Albany, 1 Jan. 1815, declaring his intention to assemble a collection of "all the valuable Ores, Minerals, and Fossils" found in the state of New York; requesting that samples be sent to him "accompanied with some information of the place, and local situation where it was found, together with the known or supposed quantity thereof"; referring those assisting him to his *Gazetteer of the State of New-York* for a list of minerals; singling out iron, lead, copper, silver, lime, marble, and gypsum for particular attention; reporting that contributors will be recognized in a projected catalogue; offering to sell them copies of that work at half price; and announcing in a postscript dated 19 Hamilton Street, Albany, 1 Jan. 1815, that he will shortly have available copies of the *Gazetteer* bound "with neat engravings of Lake George, and the Falls of Niagara" (broadside in DLC: TJ Papers, 203:36125, at head of text, in parentheses: "CIRCULAR," with address cover of covering letter on verso; broadside in DLC: TJ Papers, 203:36147, with canceled circular of 15 Apr. 1813 [see note to Spafford to TJ, 2 Aug. 1813] on verso).

Spafford PATENTED his improvement in wheel carriages on 25 Nov. 1814 (*List of Patents*, 143).

[1] Omitted word editorially supplied.

From John B. Spargella

SIR!   Philadelphia. 24ʰ Januar 1815

I beg leave in addressing You to present Six copies of an allegorical engraving, I have had executed, which is intended to transmit to

posterity the eminent Services You have rendered your Contry, before presenting the Same to the public, with the most lively acknowledgements, I Should hear this small token of my respect has met your
Approbation.

I have the honour to be with much respect and regard.

Sir!

Your M° Obt humble Ser^t J. B. SPARGELLA:

143. S. 5^h Street

RC (CSmH: JF-BA); at foot of text: "Thomas Jefferson Esqu^{re}"; endorsed by TJ as received 5 Feb. 1815 and so recorded in SJL. Enclosure not found.

John Baptiste Spargella (1761–1828), merchant, was a native of Vigevano in northern Italy who immigrated to the United States by way of France in 1813. He petitioned for American citizenship late in 1817 and operated a dry-goods store on North Second Street in Philadelphia thereafter. An 1828 city directory describes Spargella as a gentleman at New Street (Spargella's naturalization records, 21, 28 Nov. 1817 [DNA: RG 21, NPEDP]; Edward Dawes, *The Philadelphia Directory, for 1817* [Philadelphia, 1817?], 337; Thomas Wilson, ed., *The Philadelphia Directory and Stranger's Guide, for 1825* [Philadelphia, 1825], 132; *Desilver's Philadelphia Directory and Stranger's Guide, for 1828* [1828], 77; Philadelphia *Poulson's American Daily Advertiser*, 10 Apr. 1828).

From James Cutbush

SIR   Philad^a Jany 28th 1815.

At the time I wrote you from Norfolk, I was taken with the disease
so common at that place and Neighborhood; and after recovery, I
proceeded to Washington, and was transferred to this district.

I received, however, your letter in reply to mine, on the subject of
Mr Halls improvement, as it is termed, in Agriculture; but not recollecting the particulars, of the certificate I mentioned to you in my letter, I am unable to satisfy your enquiries. Since I arrived here, I find
that Mr H. changed his tack, and never Came on; but Dr Mease tells
me that he, Mr H. has published a pamphlet on his improvement
which I have not seen, a copy however he sent the Doctor. Mr H. then
must be in Virginia.—

An American edition of Gregory's Cyclopedia has just made its appearance. I. Peirce, publisher, Philad^a. The work I have seen; it is altogether, or at least for the major part, a work of science;—with many
plates. It appears in numbers, and when finished will comprehend
but two folia volumes.—

I am now enjoying the comforts of a domestic life, with my family, after an absence of some time; but privations must be endured for the public good.—

I am D^r sir, very sincerely, & respectfully;—Your very humble Servt   JA^s CUTBUSH

RC (DLC); endorsed by TJ as received 14 Feb. 1815 and so recorded in SJL. RC (DLC: TJ Papers, 203:36168); address cover only; with Dft of TJ's Observations on the Transportation of the Monticello Library, [ca. 27 Feb. 1815], on verso; addressed: "Thomas Jefferson Esquire. Monticello, Virginia"; franked; postmarked Philadelphia, 30 Jan.

From Horatio G. Spafford

ESTEEMED FRIEND—   Albany, 1 Mo. 28, 1815.

I send, herewith, the little pamphlet I mentioned in my Letter a few days since. I am in hopes it may amuse thee a few hours, & that thou wilt favor me with thy opinion of the principles I have laid down, & of the utility of my invention. The numerous & expensive experiments which I have made on this subject, shall be, in due time, detailed for some Literary or philosophical Society. I have a high opinion of this invention—& so confident am I of its ingenuity & usefulness, that I almost, persuaded myself to presume on dedicating the pamphlet to my Hon^d Friend, the late President Jefferson.   If I had done so, should I have done wrong? Or would my venerrable friend have objected to it? Please distribute the spare copies, at thy discretion. I much regret that I could not have seen thee; & I hope thy goodness will excuse me, if I ask; should I never see thee, some small trifle as a memento. With the most cordial & respectful esteem, thy grateful, obliged

  friend,   H. G. SPAFFORD.

RC (MHi); at foot of text: "Hon. T. Jefferson"; endorsed by TJ as received 17 Feb. 1815 and so recorded in SJL. Enclosure: multiple copies of Spafford, *Wheel-Carriages*.

To Charles Clay

DEAR SIR   Monticello Jan. 29. 15.

Your letter of Dec. 20. was 4. weeks on it's way to me. I thank you for it: for altho founded on a misconception, it is evidence of that friendly concern for my peace and welfare which I have ever believed you to feel. of publishing a book on religion, my dear Sir, I never had an idea. I should as soon think of writing for the reformation of Bedlam, as of the world of religious sects. of these there must be at least ten thousand, every individual of every one of which believes all are wrong but his own. to undertake to bring them all right, would be like undertaking, single handed, to fell the forests of America. probably you have heard me say I had taken the four evangelists, had cut out from them every text they had recorded of the moral precepts of Jesus, and arranged them in a certain order, and altho' they appeared but as fragments, yet fragments of the most sublime edifice of morality which had ever been exhibited to man. this I have probably mentioned to you, because it is true; and the idea of it's publication may have suggested itself as an inference of your own mind. I not only write nothing on religion but rarely permit myself to speak on it, and never but in a reasonable society. I have probably said more to you than to any other person, because we have had more hours of conversation in duetto in our meetings at the Forest. I abuse the priests indeed, who have so much abused the pure and holy doctrines of their master, and who have laid me under no obligations of reticence as to the tricks of their trade. the genuine system of Jesus, and the artificial structures they have erected to make him[1] the instrument of wealth, power, and preeminence to themselves are as distinct things in my view as light and darkness: and, while I have classed them with soothsayers and necromancers, I place him among the greatest of the reformers of morals, and scourges of priest-craft, that have ever existed. they felt him as such, and never rested till they silenced him by death. but his heresies against Judaism prevailing in the long run, the priests have tacked about, and rebuilt upon them the temple which he destroyed, as splendid, as profitable, and as imposing as that.

Government, as well as religion, has furnished it's schisms, it's persecutions, and it's devices for fattening idleness on the earnings of the people. it has it's hierarchy of emperors, kings, princes & nobles, as that has of popes, cardinals, archbishops, bishops, and priests. in short, Cannibals are not to be found in the wilds of America only, but are revelling on the blood of every living people.   turning then from this loathsome combination of church and state, and weeping over the follies of our fellow-men, who yield themselves the willing dupes & drudges of these Mountebanks, I consider reformation and redress as desperate, & abandon them to the Quixotism of more enthusiastic minds.

I have recieved from Philadelphia by mail, the spectacles you had desired, and now forward them by the same conveyance, as equally safe and more in time, than were they to await my own going. in a separate case is a compleat set of glasses from early use to old age. I think the pair now in the frames will suit your eyes, but should they not, you will easily change them by the screws. I believe the largest numbers are the smallest magnifiers, but am not certain. trial will readily ascertain it. you must do me the favor to accept them as a token of my friendship & with them the assurance of my great esteem & respect.   TH: JEFFERSON

PoC (DLC); at foot of first page: "Charles Clay esq."

TO: "together." Poplar Forest was THE FOREST.

For TJ's compilations of the MORAL PRECEPTS OF JESUS, see EG. IN DUET-

[1] Reworked from "them."

To Samuel H. Smith

DEAR SIR   Monticello Jan. 30. 15.

Presuming that my Catalogue has by this time answered all the purposes of information as to the contents of my library, and needing it almost daily myself, I will ask the favor of it's return; but only in the case of it's being no longer useful to the Committee. I propose, on recieving it, to commence the task of reducing the whole mass exactly to the arrangement of the Catalogue, some volumes and parts of which have become misplaced[1] by removals & by neglect. this is necessary even for my own use of it.

Not having heard from you since yours of Oct. 21. I should be gratified to learn in what position the business now stands; and the rather as the time is near at hand when Congress will not be able to give their attention to any but matters of the most indispensable pressure. Accept the assurance of my great esteem & respect

TH: JEFFERSON

PoC (DLC); at foot of text: "Sam¹ H. Smith esq."; endorsed by TJ. RC (DLC: J. Henley Smith Papers); address cover only; addressed: "Samuel H. Smith esquire Washington Col."; franked; endorsed by Smith, in part, as "respᵍ Library."

The COMMITTEE was the congressional Joint Library Committee. TJ worried that Congress would only have time for MATTERS OF THE MOST INDISPENSABLE PRESSURE as its session drew to a close.

[1] Manuscript: "miplaced."

From Samuel H. Smith

DEAR SIR   Jan. 30. 1815.

I am happy to advise You that the bill authorising[1] the purchase of Your Library has passed the two houses of Congress. I enclose for Your satisfaction a copy of the bill. It now rests with the Library committee to make the final agreement. The sum stipulated is precisely that estimated by Mr Milligan. I shall, doubtless, in a few days hear from the Committee, when I will again write You.

We have had a most rigid spell of weather. The mercury in my thermometer was yesterday morning[2] one degree below zero, and the ice in our streams is already a foot thick. The cold and storm without have probably driven you into the retirement of Your closet, where You must experience a fine contrast to the roaring[3] winds without. It is on such occasions that man feels the reason he has to exult in his civilisation & philosophy.

I am with great & sincere respect & regard   SA H SMITH

RC (DLC); endorsed by TJ as received 5 Feb. 1815 and so recorded in SJL. Enclosure: "An Act to authorize the purchase of the library of Thomas Jefferson, late President of the United States," 30 Jan. 1815 (*U.S. Statutes at Large*, 3:195).

RIGID in this context means "severe" (*OED*).

[1] Manuscript: "authorisig."
[2] Manuscript: "mornig."
[3] Manuscript: "roarig."

From John Strachan

SIR,—   York, 30th Jan'y. 1815.

In your letter to a member of Congress recently published respecting the sale of your library,* I perceive by the extract thereof underneath that you are angry with the British, for the destruction of the public buildings at Washington, and attempt with your accustomed candour to compare that transaction to the devastations committed by the barbarians in the middle ages. As you are not ignorant of the mode of carrying on the war, adopted by your friends, you must have known that this was a small retaliation after redress had been refused

(* *Note.*) *Monticello, 21st Sept.* 1814.

DEAR SIR, "—I learn from the newspapers that the vandalism of our enemy has triumphed at Washington over science as well as the arts, by the destruction of the public library with the noble edifice in which it was deposited. Of this transaction, as that of Copenhagen, the world will entertain but one sentiment. They will see a nation suddenly withdrawn from a great war, full armed and full handed, taking advantage of another, whom they had recently forced into it; unarmed, and unprepared to indulge themselves in acts of barbarism which do not belong to a civilized age."

for burnings and depredations not only of public but private property committed by them in Canada; but we are too well acquainted with your hatred to Great Britain to look for truth or candour in any statement of yours, where *she* is concerned. It is not for your information, therefore, that I relate in this letter, those acts of the army of the United States in the Canadas, which provoked the conflagration of the public buildings at Washington, because you are well acquainted with them already; but to shew the world that to the United States and not to Great Britain must be charged all the miseries attending a mode of warfare, originating with them, and unprecedented in modern times.

A stranger to the history of the last three years, on reading this part of your letter would naturally suppose that Great Britain in the pride of power had taken advantage of the weak and defenceless situation of the United States to wreak her vengeance upon them. But what would be his astonishment when told that the nation said to be unarmed and unprepared, had provoked and first declared the war, and carried it on offensively for two years, with a ferocity unexampled before the British had the means of making effectual resistance.—War was declared against Great Britain by the United States of America in June 1812. Washington was taken in August 1814. Let us see in what spirit your countrymen carried on the war during this interval.

In July 1812, General Hull invaded the British province of Upper Canada, and took possession of the Town of Sandwich. He threatened (by a proclamation) to exterminate the inhabitants, if they made any resistance; he plundered those, with whom he had been in habits of intimacy for years before the war. Their plate and linen were found in his possession after his *surrender to General Brock*. He marked out the Loyal subjects of the King, as objects of peculiar resentment, and consigned their property to pillage and conflagration. In autumn 1812 some thousand barns were burnt[1] by the American forces near Fort Erie in Upper Canada.

In April 1813; the public buildings at York, the capital of Upper Canada, were burnt by the troops of the United States, contrary to the articles of capitulation. They consisted of two elegant Halls with convenient offices, for the accommodation of the Legislature, & of the Courts of Justice. The library and all the papers and records belonging to these institutions were consumed at the same time the Church was robbed, and the Town Library totally pillaged. Commodore Chauncey, who has generally behaved honourably, was so ashamed of this last transaction, that he endeavoured to collect the books belonging to the Public Library, and actually sent back two boxes filled with them, but hardly any were complete. Much private property was plundered, and several houses left in a state of ruin; can you tell me, sir, the reason why the public buildings and library at Washington, should be held more sacred than those at York? A false and ridiculous story is told of a scalp having been found above the Speakers Chair intended as an ornament.

In June 1813, Newark came into the possession of your army (after the capture of Fort George) and its inhabitants were repeatedly promised protection to themselves and property, both by General Dearborn and General Boyd[.] In the midst of these professions, the most respectable of them altho' non combattants, were made prisoners, and sent into the United States. The two churches were burnt to the ground; detachments were sent under the direction of British traitors to pillage the Loyal Inhabitants in the neighborhood, and to carry them away captive. Many farm houses were burnt during the summer, and at length to fill up the measure of iniquity, the whole of the beautiful village of Newark, with so short a previous intimation as to amount to none was consigned to the Flames. The wretched inhabitants had scarcely time to save themselves, much less any of their property. More than four hundred Women and Children were exposed without shelter on the night of the tenth of December, to the intense cold of a Canadian winter, and great numbers must have perished, had not the flight of your troops after perpetrating this ferocious act, enabled the inhabitants of the country to come in to their relief.

Your friend Mr. Madison has attempted to justify this cruel deed, on the plea that it was necessary for the defence of Fort George. Nothing can be more false. The village was some distance from the Fort; and instead of thinking to defend it, General M'Clure was actually retreating to his own shore, when he caused Newark to be burnt. This officer says that he acted in conformity with the orders of his government; the government finding their justification useless disavow his conduct; M'Clure appears to be the fit agent of such a government. He not only complies with his instructions but refines upon them by choosing a day of intense frost, giving the inhabitants almost no warning till the fire began, and commencing the conflagration in the night as above mentioned.

In Nov. 1813, the army of your friend General Wilkinson committed great depredations in its progress through the eastern district of Upper Canada, and was proceeding to systematic pillage, when the commander got frightened, and fled to his own shore, on finding the population in that district inveterately hostile.

The history of the two first campaigns prove beyond dispute, that you had reduced fire and pillage to a regular system. It was hoped, that the severe retaliation taken for the burning of Newark, would have put a stop to a practice so repugnant to the manners and habits of a civilized age; but so far was this from being the case, that the third campaign exhibits equal enormities. Gen. Brown laid waste the country between Chippawa and Fort Erie,[2] burning mills and private houses and rendering those not consumed by fire uninhabitable. The pleasant village of St. David, was burnt by his army when about to retreat.

On the 15th May, a detachment of the American army, under Colonel Campbell, landed at Long Point, district of London, Upper Canada and on that and the following day, pillaged and laid waste as much of the adjacent country as they could reach. They burnt the village of Dover, with the mills, and all the mills, stores, distilleries, and dwelling houses in the vicinity, carrying away such property as was portable, and killing the cattle. The property taken and destroyed on this occasion, was estimated at fifty thousand dollars.

On the 16th of August, some American troops and Indians from Detroit, surprised the settlement of Port Talbot, where they committed the most atrocious[3] acts of violence, leaving upwards of 234 men, women, and children, in a state of nakedness and want.

On the 20th of September, a second excursion was made by the garrison of Detroit, spreading fire and pillage through the settlements in the Western district of Upper Canada. Twenty seven families were reduced on this occasion to the greatest distress. . . . . Early in Nov. Gen. McArthur, with a large body of mounted Kentuckians and Indians, made a rapid march through the Western, & part of the London districts, burning all the mills, and destroying provisions, and living upon the inhabitants. If there was less private plunder than usual, it was, because the invaders had no means of carrying it away.

On our part, sir, the war has been carried on in the most forbearing manner. During the two first campaigns, we abstained from any acts of retaliation, notwithstanding the great enormities which we have mentioned. It was not till the horrible destruction of Newark, attended with so many acts of atrocity, that we burnt the villages of Lewiston, Buffaloe, and Black Rock. At this our Commander paused. He pledged himself to proceed no farther, on the condition of your returning to the rules of legitimate warfare. Finding you pursuing the same system this last campaign, instead of destroying the towns and villages within his reach, to which he had conditionally extended his protection, he applied to Admiral Cochrane to make *retaliation* upon the coast. The Admiral informed Mr Monroe of the nature of this application, and his determination to comply, unless compensation was made for the private property wantonly destroyed in Upper Canada. No answer was returned for several weeks, during which time Washington was taken. At length, a letter purporting to be an answer, arrived, in which the Secretary dwells, with much lamentation, on the destruction of the public buildings at Washington; which notwithstanding the destruction of the same kind of buildings at the capital of Upper Canada, he affects to consider without a parallel in modern times. So little regard has he for truth, that at the very moment of his speaking of the honor and generosity practised by his government in conducting the war, General McArthur was directed by the President to proceed upon his burning excursion.

Perhaps you will bring forward the report of the Committee appointed by Congress to inquire into British cruelties, and to class them under the heads furnished by Mr Madison, as an offset for the facts that have been mentioned. The committee must have found the subject extremely barren, as only one report has seen the light: but since the articles of accusation are before the public, and have been quoted by the enemies of England, as capable of ample proof, let us give them a brief examination.

1st. Ill treatment of American prisoners.

2d. Detention of American prisoners as British subjects, under the pretext of their being born on British territory, or of naturalization.

3d. Detention of sailors as prisoners, because they were in England when war was declared.

4th. Forced service of American sailors, pressed on board English men of war.

5th. Violence of flags of truce.

6th. Ransom of American prisoners taken by the savages in the service of England.

7th. Pillage and destruction of private property in the bay of Chesapeake, and the neighbouring country.

8th. Massacre of American prisoners surrendered to the officers of Great Britain, by the savages engaged in its service. Abandoning to the savages the corpses of American prisoners killed by the English, into whose hands they had been surrendered; pillage and murder of American citizens, who had repaired to the English under the assurance of their protection; the burning of their houses.

9th. Cruelties exercised at Hampton in Virginia.

1st. *Ill treatment of American prisoners.*

General Brock sent all the militia taken at Detroit home on their parole, accompanied by a guard to protect them from the Indians, detaining only the regulars, whom he sent to Quebec, where they met with the most liberal treatment, as the honest among them have frequently confessed. General Sheaffe acted in the same manner after the battle of Queenston, keeping the regulars & dismissing the militia on their parole. Nor was the liberal course departed from, till the gross misconduct of the American government, in liberating, without exchange, those so sent home, and in carrying away non-combatants, and seizing the whole inhabitants of the districts, which they invaded, rendered it absolutely necessary.

When they were not able to take all the unarmed inhabitants away they made those they left sign a parole, a conduct never known in the annals of war, the conditions of which not only precluded them from afterwards bearing arms, but from giving in any manner their *services to government*. The farmers were dragged out of their houses and carried into the States. Clergymen were forced to give their parole, in fine it appeared to make no difference, whether a man was in arms or not, he was sure to experience the same treatment.

Many people, when prisoners, have been treated in the most infamous manner. Officers, tho' sick and wounded have been forced to march on foot through the country, while American officers taken by us were conveyed in boats or carriages to the place of destination.

Our captured troops have been marched as spectacles through the towns, altho' you affect to complain of Hull's and other prisoners being marched publicly into Montreal. The officers of the 41st regt. were confined in the Penetentiary at Kentucky among Felons of the most infamous description. They were treated with harshness; often with cruelty, and persons, who wished to be kind to them, were insulted by the populace.

Even the stipulations, respecting Prisoners, agreed to by the American Government, have been most shamefully broken. Sir George Prevost and Mr. Madison agreed that all prisoners taken before the 15th day of April 1814 should be exchanged on or before the 15th day of May last to be conveyed into their respective countries by the nearest routes. On that day the Governor in Chief faithful to his engagements, sent home every American prisoner; but the Government of the United States seemed for a long time to have totally forgotten the stipulation. A few Prisoners were sent back in June, but many of the officers and all the soldiers of the 41st Regiment were detained till towards the end of October. To the soldiers of this Regiment (as indeed to all others) every temptation had been presented to induce them to desert and enlist in their service by money, land &c. After it was found impossible to persuade any number of them to do so, the American government encamped them for nearly two months in a pestilential marsh near Sandusky without any covering. There having neither shelter nor the necessary quantity of provisions, they all got sick, many died, and in October, the remainder were sent to Long Point, sick, naked and miserable. From this place they could not be conveyed, till clothes had been sent to cover their nakedness; great numbers sunk under their calamities and the utmost care and attention were required to save any of them alive. Such an accumulation of cruelty was never exhibited before.

The government of the United States assumed the prerogative of relieving officers from parole without exchanging them, and even Commodore Rodgers took twelve seamen out of a cartel, as it was proceeding to Boston Bay and was justified for this outrage by his government.

2d. Detention of American Prisoners as British Subjects.

It is notorious that a great many of the American army have been British subjects since the commencement of the war, and had we determined to punish these traitors with death, if found invading our territories, and after giving them warning, acted up to such a determination, it would have been strictly right and in such case very few would have entered Canada. While these persons act merely as Militia defending their adopted country against invasion, some lenity might be shewn them; but when they march into the British Provinces for the sake of conquest, they ought to be considered Traitors to their King and Country and treated accordingly.

3d.—Detention of Sailors as Prisoners, because they were in England when war was declared.

This accusation is ridiculous, as sailors are always considered in the first class of combatants, but it comes with an ill grace from those who have detained peaceable British subjects engaged in civil life, and banished fifteen miles from the coast, those of them who happened to be in America at the declaration of war, and treated them almost in every respect like Prisoners of war, according to Bonaparte's example.

4. Forced service of American Sailors pressed on board of English Men of war.

This accusation has been often made, but never coupled with the offer of Mr. Foster to discharge every American so detained on being furnished with the list. The list was never furnished.

5. *Violence of Flags of Truce.*

This accusation of Mr. Madison contains about as much truth as those that have been already examined. We shall give two exampl[es] of the treatment experienced by the Bearers of Flags of Truce from the British Army.

Major Fulton, Aid-de-Camp to General Sir George Prevost, was stopped by Major Forsyth of the United States army at the outposts, who insulted him most grossly, endeavored to seize his despatches and threatened to put him to death. So much ashamed were Forsyths superiors at this outrage, that he was sent for a short time, to the rear.

General Proctor sent Lieut. Le Breton to General Harrison after the battle of Moravian Town to ascertain our loss of officers and men; but instead of sending him back, General Harrison detained him many weeks, took him round the Lake; and after all did not furnish him with the required information, which had been otherwise procured in the mean time.

6. *Ransom of American prisoners taken by the savages in the service of England.*

Some nations of the Natives were at war with the Americans, long before hostilities commenced against England, many others not. When attempts were made to conquer the Canadas, the Indians beyond our territories, part by choice and part by solicitation came and joined us as Allies, while those within the Provinces, had as great an interest in defending them, as the other proprietors of the soil. To mitigate as much as possible the horrors of war, it was expressly and repeatedly told the Indians that scalping the dead & killing Prisoners or unresisting enemies, were practices extremely repugnant to our feelings, and no presents would be given them, but for Prisoners. This, therefore instead of becoming an article of accusation ought to have excited their gratitude, for the presence and authority of a British force uniformly tended to secure the lives of all who were defenceless, and[4] all who surrendered—It almost without exception saved the lives of our enemies, yet the American government brand us as worse than savages, for fighting by the sides of Indians, and at first threatened our extermination if we did so, altho' they employed all the Indians they could. Many individuals have acknowledged their obligation to us for having been saved by the benevolent & humane exertions of our officers & troops, but no officer of rank ever had the justice to make a public acknowledgment. The eighth accusation is much the same as this, and must have been seperated in order to multiply the number of articles. It is notorious that some British soldiers have been killed by the Indians, protecting their prisoners. This was the case at General Winchester's defeat and at General Clay's. The grossest exaggerations have been published. General Winchester was declared in all the American papers to have been scalped, and mangled in the most horrid manner, when he was i[n his] quarters at Quebec. In a General Order dated Kingston 26th July, 1813, among other things respecting Indians, it is said that the head money for the Prisoners of War, brought in by the Indian warriors is to be immediately paid by the Commissariat, upon the certificate of the General officer commanding the division with which they are acting at the time. Let us now see how the poor Indians are treated by the Americans, after promising that they have done their utmost to employ as many Indians as possible against us. It is a fact that the first scalp taken this war was by the Americans at the river Canard between Sandwich and Amherstburgh. At this place an Indian was killed by the advance of General Hull's army, and immediately scalped.*

At the skirmish of Brownston several Indians fell and were scalped by the American troops.

The Kentuckians are commonly armed with a Tomahawk and long scalping knife, and burnt Indians as a pastime.

At the river Au Raisin, Capt. Caldwell of the Indian department, saved an American officer from the Indians, and as he was leading him off, the ungrateful monster stabbed him in the neck, on which he was killed by Captain Caldwell's friends.

The American troops under General Winchester killed an Indian in a skirmish near the river Au Raisin, on the 18th January 1813, and tore him litera[l]ly into pieces, which so exasperated the Indians that they refused burial to the Americans killed on the 22d.—The Indian Hero Tecumseth after being killed was literally flayed in part by the Americans and his skin carried off as a trophy.

Twenty Indian women and children of the Kickapoo nation were inhumanly put to death by the Americans a short time ago near Prairie on the Illinois river, after dri[v]ing their husbands into a morass where they perished with cold and hunger. Indian towns were burnt as an amusement or common place practice. All this how-

[(No]te)* An Indian never scalps his enemy un[til after] he is dead, and does so to preserve a proof [or token] of his victory.

ever is nothing compared to the recent massacre of the Creeks. General Coffee in his letter to General Jackson dated 4th November 1813, informs him that he surrounded the Indian Towns at Tullushatches in the night with nine hundred men. That about an hour after sunrise, he was discovered by the enemy, who endeavored tho' taken by surprise to make some resistance[.] In a few minutes the last warrior[5] of them was killed. He mentions the number of warriors seen dead to be 186 and supposes as many among the weeds as would make them up two hundred. He confesses that some of the women and children were killed, owing to the warriors mixing with their families. He men[ti]ons taking only 84 Prisoners of Women and Chil[dr]en. Now it is evident that in a village containing [two] hundred warriors, there must have been nearly [as m]any women and men perhaps more; and un[quest]ionably the number of children exceeded the men and women together; what then became of all [t]hese[.] Neither does General Coffee mention the old men. Such things speak for themselves. The poor Indians fought it appears, with bows and arrows, and were able only to kill five Americans. Their situation was too remote for them to receive assistance from the British. Their lands were wanted and they must be exterminated. Since this period, the greater part of the nation has been massacred by General Jackson, who destroyed them wantonly in cold blood. There was no resistance, if we except individual ebullition of despair, when it was found that there was no mercy. Jackson mentions exultingly that the morning after he had destroyed a whole village, sixteen Indians were discovered, hid under the bank of the river, who were dragged out and murdered; upon these inhuman exploits President Madison only remarks to Congress that the Creeks had received a salutary chastisement which would make a lasting impression upon their fears. The cruelties exercised against these wretched nations are without a parallel except the coldness and apathy with which they are glossed over by the President. Such is the conduct of the humane government of the United States, which is incessantly employed as they pretend in civilizing the Indians; but it is time to finish this horrid detail we shall therefore conclude with a short extract of a letter from the Spanish Governor of East Florida, Benigno Garzia, to Mr. Mitchell Governor of the State of Georgia to show that the policy of the Government of the United States in regard to the Indians is now generally known.

"The Province of East Florida may be invaded in time of profound peace, the planters ruined, and the population of the capital starved, and according to your doctrine all is fair; they are a set of outlaws if they resist. The Indians are to be insulted threatened & driven from their lands; if they resist, nothing less than extermination is to be their fate."

7th & *9th.—Pillage and destruction of private property in the Bay of Chesapeake and the neighboring country, and cruelties exercised in Hampton in Virginia.*

It required astonishing effrontery to make these articles of accusation, after the depredations and cruelties committed by the army of the United States in the Canadas.

In the attack upon Craney Island, some boats in the service of Great Britain ran aground. In this situation they made signals of surrender, but the Americans continued to fire upon them from the shore. Many jumped into the water and swam towards land, but they were shot, as they approached, without mercy. A few days after, Hampton was taken and some depredations were committing by the Foreign troops, who had seen some of their comrades so cruelly massacred, but before any material damage was done, they were remanded on board. Several letters from Hampton mention the behaviour of the British, while there, as highly meritorious, and contradict the vile calumnies of the Democratic prints, which Mr. Madison copies in his Message to Congress.

This brief account of the conduct of your Govt. and army since the commencement of hostilities (which might have been greatly extended) will fill the world with astonishment at the forbearance of Great Britain in suffering so many enormities and such a determined departure from the laws of civilized warfare, to pass so long without signal punishment.

Before finishing this letter, permit me, Sir, to remark that the destruction of the public buildings at Washington, entitled the British to your gratitude and praise by affording you a noble opportunity of proving your devotion to your country. In former times, when you spoke of the magnitude of your services and the fervor of your patriotism, your political enemies were apt to mention your elevated situation, and the greatness of your salary. But by presenting your library a freewill offering to the nation at this moment of uncommon pressure, when the Treasury is empty, and every help to the acquisition of knowledge is so very necessary to keep the government from sinking, you would have astonished the world, with one solitary action in your political life, worthy of commendation.

Nor are your obligations to the British army unimportant, tho' you have not aspired to generous praise. An opportunity has been given you of disposing of a library at your own price, which if sold volume by volume, would have fetched nothing, You have no doubt seen that old libraries do not sell well, after the death of the proprietor, and with a lively attention to your own interest, you take advantage of the times. I am, Sir, with due consideration, &c.

JOHN STRACHAN, D. D.
Treasurer of the Loyal and Patriotic
Society of Upper-Canada.

POSTSCRIPT.— From General M'Arthur's official account of his predatory excursion, I make the following extract to prove his extraordinary veracity

"We were thus enabled to arrive at the town of Oxford, one hundred and fifty miles distant from Detroit, before the inhabitants knew that a force was approaching. They were promised protection to their persons and property, upon the condition that they remained peaceably at their respective homes; otherwise, they were assurred, that their property would be destroyed.

However, notwithstanding this injunction, and the sacred obligation of a previous parole, two of the inhabitants escaped to Burford with the intelligence of our arrival. Their property consisting of two dwelling houses, two barns, and one shop, were instantly consumed."

George Nichol and Jacob Wood, are the persons here alluded to, both of whom applied to the Loyal and Patriotic Society of Upper Canada for relief. The former had returned home before General M'Arthur's report to the Secretary at War appeared in the Newspapers: but the latter was at York after that publication. "At a meeting of the Directors of the Loyal and Patriotic Society holden at York on the 21st of January 1815, appeared Jacob Wood, from the County of Oxford, and produced a certificate from Major Bowen, stating that he accompanied George Nichol from Oxford to Burford to give information of the advance of the American army, and in consequence of which his House, Furniture, Barn, Hay, Grain, Joiner's shop and Tools were destroyed by the enemy.

Jacob Wood was interrogated by the Society, whether he or George Nichol were paroled by General M'Arthur, previous to their giving the British warning of the approach of the American army. In answer, he stated, that he and George Nichol had left their homes on hearing of the approach of the enemy, and were so far from giving their parole that they never were in the power of General M'Arthur, or his Army.

The Directors put this question to Jacob Wood, because General M'Arthur, in his official report, states it as his reason for burning the houses, and destroying every thing belonging to these two men, that they had broken their parole."

General M'Arthur had some reputation to lose, and ought to have known that such a gross departure from truth was not the way to preserve it. The courage and zeal of Nichol and Wood, instead of punishment, deserved and would have obtained the respect of a gallant and generous enemy. But on all occasions, the loyal inhabitants of this Province have been selected by your Generals as the objects of their peculiar hatred.

To pass rapidly, with a large body of cavalry, through a country thinly inhabited, and without the means of resistance, to feed upon the defenceless inhabitants; to burn the mills, none of which belonged to Government, and to destroy the provisions and the whole property of respectable men of principle; and then to run away, at the first symptom of serious opposition; is no great exploit. General M'Arthur has been the Author of much distress to the defenceless inhabitants; many of whom have now One Hundred and Twenty Miles to go to mill, but in a military point of view he has done nothing. It is for the people of the United States to reflect seriously upon this mode of carrying on the war; and it is your interest, Sir, to advise a return to humanity, lest Monticello should share the fate of hundreds of Farms in Upper Canada.   I am, &c.   J. S.

Printed in the *Montreal Herald*, 15 Apr. 1815; copy at OONL damaged, with losses supplied from the version printed in *The Report of the Loyal and Patriotic Society of Upper Canada* (Montreal, 1817), 398–413; ellipsis in original; at head of text: "*To Thomas Jefferson Esquire of Monticello, Ex-President of the United States of America*"; dateline above postscript; beneath postscript: "THOS. JEFFERSON, *Esqr.*" Not recorded in SJL and probably never seen by TJ.

The editor of the *Montreal Herald*, Mungo Kay, prefaced Stachan's letter thus: "*The following letter was received by the Editor of the Herald before the Treaty of Peace with the United States was known here, but prevented from publication, by the pressure of other matter at the time. The change of circumstances since, would have been an inducement to with hold it from the public, had it not been perceived, that the opposition in the Imperial Parliament, have made a handle of the destruction of the public buildings at Washington, as if a wanton and unprecedented act of desolation. Such a statement being calculated to*

impose upon the world, it becomes material that some document in proof of the causes which led to that destruction should be in possession of the public, that the real authors of those calamities may be known; and as the British or Provincial Government has not seen fit (excepting in the case of Newark) to publish an official detail of the numerous acts of departure from the practice of civilized warfare by the troops of the United States in the late contest; it becomes necessary to take the next most authentic source of information thereon.—Such is the following, being from a man of high private character and intelligence, who scruples not to put his name thereto. The Editor therefore disavowing all hostile motives, still sees strong reasons for publishing the same upon public grounds, as a justification of those meritorious British Officers, who resorted to a necessary, but tardy retaliation upon the enemy, for the miseries inflicted by them upon British subjects."

John Strachan (1778–1867), educator and Anglican clergyman, was born in Aberdeen, Scotland, and graduated from the university there in 1797. After teaching at a parish school, he immigrated to Canada in 1799. Although Strachan continued to teach until 1823 and espoused the expansion and reform of education throughout his long life, within a few years of his arrival in North America he had redirected his primary focus to religion. Having been ordained a deacon in the Church of England in 1803 and a priest the following year, he served as rector of Cornwall, Upper Canada, 1803–12, rector of York (later Toronto), 1812–47, archdeacon of York, 1827–47, and bishop of Toronto, 1839–67. A political and social conservative, Strachan was also active in Canadian politics. He was a founder, president, and treasurer of the Loyal and Patriotic Society of Upper Canada during the War of 1812. Strachan sat on the province's executive council, 1815–36, and served in its legislative council, 1820–41. He died in Toronto (*ODNB*; George W. Brown and others, eds., *Dictionary of Canadian Biography* [1966–   ], 9:751–66; David Flint, *John Strachan: Pastor and Politician* [1971]; Toronto *Globe*, 2, 6 Nov. 1867).

Strachan was responding to TJ's second letter of 21 Sept. 1814 to Samuel H. Smith, who was not A MEMBER OF CONGRESS. General William Hull's 13 July 1812 PROCLAMATION to the inhabitants of Canada states that "If contrary to your own interest, and the just expectations of my country, you should take a part in the approaching contest, you will be considered as enemies, and the horrours and calamities of war will stalk before you. If the barbarous and savage policy of Great Britain be pursued, and the savages be let loose to murder our citizens and butcher our women and children, this war will be a war of extermination" (Hull, *Memoirs of the Campaign of the North Western Army of the United States, A.D. 1812* [Boston, 1824], 45–6; Madison, *Papers, Pres. Ser.*, 5:198n). General Henry Dearborn's STORY that a "scalp was found in the executive and legislative chamber, suspended near the speaker's chair, in company with the mace and other emblems of royalty" was picked up by the American press and frequently repeated during the spring of 1813 (Dearborn to

John Armstrong, 3 May 1813 [*ASP, Military Affairs*, 1:444]; Washington *Daily National Intelligencer*, 18 May 1813, and elsewhere). The Upper Canada town of Niagara (now Niagara-on-the-Lake, Ontario), was formerly known as NEWARK.

OUR COMMANDER: Sir George Prevost, governor general of British North America. For Admiral Alexander Cochrane's letter to Secretary of State James Monroe of 18 Aug. 1814 and Monroe's LAMENTATION of 6 Sept., see *ASP, Foreign Relations*, 3:693–4. The committee of the United States House of Representatives charged with investigating BRITISH CRUELTIES issued its report on 31 July 1813 (*ASP, Military Affairs*, 1:339–82). For the 1814 convention regulating the exchange of ALL PRISONERS TAKEN BEFORE THE 15TH DAY OF APRIL 1814, which was negotiated by the representatives of Governor Prevost and Secretary of State Monroe, not President James Madison, see *ASP, Foreign Relations*, 3:728.

Commodore John Rodgers removed a dozen British sailors from A CARTEL in September 1812. Monroe later justified the action on the grounds of retaliation (*ASP, Foreign Relations*, 3:598, 633). The British diplomat Augustus John Foster requested that he be FURNISHED WITH THE LIST of impressed American seamen in his letter to Monroe of 15 Apr. 1812 (*ASP, Foreign Relations*, 3:454). The Battle of the Thames (BATTLE OF MORAVIAN TOWN) was fought in Canada a few miles from Lake Erie (THE LAKE). General Green CLAY's defeat occurred early in May 1813 during the siege of Fort Meigs, Ohio (Malcomson, *Historical Dictionary*, 329–30).

In February 1813 General James Winchester was incorrectly reported in ALL THE AMERICAN PAPERS to have been "killed, scalped, and shockingly mangled" (Georgetown *Federal Republican, and Commercial Gazette*, 10 Feb. 1813, and elsewhere; *DAB*). The SKIRMISH OF BROWNSTON (Brownstown, Michigan) took place on 5 Aug. 1812 (Malcomson, *Historical Dictionary*, 65). For John Coffee's letter to Andrew Jackson DATED 4TH NOVEMBER 1813, see Jackson, *Papers*, 2:592; Richmond *Enquirer*, 23 Nov.

1813, and elsewhere. Jackson mentions the killing of the SIXTEEN INDIANS in his 28 Mar. 1814 report on the Battle of Horseshoe Bend (Jackson, *Papers*, 3:52–4; Washington *Daily National Intelligencer*, 18 Apr. 1814, and elsewhere). Madison's REMARKS TO CONGRESS of 7 Dec. 1813 expressed the hope that the United States "might not only chastise the savages into present peace, but make a lasting impression on their fears" (*JS*, 5:388–92, quotation on p. 389). The 12 Dec. 1812 LETTER FROM THE SPANISH GOVERNOR OF EAST FLORIDA was printed in the Philadelphia *Poulson's American Daily Advertiser*, 12 Jan. 1813, and elsewhere. The unsuccessful British ATTACK UPON CRANEY ISLAND near Portsmouth, Virginia, took place on 22 June 1813 (Malcomson, *Historical Dictionary*, 124–6). General Duncan McArthur submitted his OFFICIAL ACCOUNT in an 18 Nov. 1814 letter to Secretary of War Monroe (DNA: RG 107, LRSW; Washington *Daily National Intelligencer*, 22 Dec. 1814, and elsewhere).

[1] Preceding five words corrected to "a number of houses and barns burnt" in the *Montreal Herald*, 22 Apr. 1815. *Report of the Loyal and Patriotic Society*: "some houses and barns were burnt."

[2] *Montreal Herald*: "Erio." *Report of the Loyal and Patriotic Society*: "Erie."

[3] *Montreal Herald*: "atrocieus." *Report of the Loyal and Patriotic Society*: "atrocious."

[4] *Montreal Herald*: "and and." *Report of the Loyal and Patriotic Society*: "and."

[5] *Montreal Herald*: "warior." *Report of the Loyal and Patriotic Society*: "warrior."

From Peter H. Wendover

RESPECTED SIR   New York January 30th 1815

Permit me to apologize to you for what might by some be deemed an intrusion, while I venture to solicit your friendly reception of a small volume, the contents of which I recently heard from the pulpit, and which sentiments I consider of great importance to our beloved Country, particularly at this momentous Crisis—

The author though an adopted Citizen, I esteem as one of the best friends of mankind; a zealous advocate for the Liberties of the United States; and a firm supporter of Republican Institutions—he is acknowledged to be a man of sound mind and great abilities—

Should you disapprove of the liberty I have taken in troubling you with it, I only have to plead that nothing but the great esteem in which I hold the name, and virtues of a Jefferson could have prompted me to it—

With my best wishes for your personal Health, and Happiness, I have the Honor to be Sir your very Hum[b] Serv[t]

P[R] H: WENDOVER

RC (MoSHi: TJC-BC); dateline adjacent to signature; at foot of text: "Thomas Jefferson Esquire"; endorsed by TJ as received 17 Feb. 1815 and so recorded in SJL. Enclosure: Alexander McLeod, *A Scriptural View of the Character, Causes, and Ends of the Present War* (New York, 1815).

Peter Hercules Wendover (1768–1834), sailmaker and public official, held several local offices in New York City and was a delegate to the state constitutional conventions of 1801 and 1821. He served in the New York legislature in 1804 and in the United States House of Representatives, 1815–21, where he led a successful effort to alter the nation's flag to its current design of thirteen stripes and a star for each state. Wendover was also sheriff of New York County for four years during the 1820s, a founder of the American Colonization Society, and a member of the Dutch Reformed Church. He died at his home in Greenwich, New York (*Biog. Dir. Cong.*; *History of the School of the Collegiate Reformed Dutch Church in the City of New York from 1633 to 1883*, 2d

ed. [1883], 101; Charles Z. Lincoln, *The Constitutional History of New York* [1906], 1:609, 631; Edgar L. Murlin, *The New York Red Book* [1913], 393; Marc Leepson, *Flag: An American Biography* [2005], 77–83; Henry Noble Sherwood, "The Formation of the American Colonization Society," *Journal of Negro History* 2 [1917]: 227; New York *Daily Advertiser*, 10 Sept. 1791; New York *Evening Post*, 24 Sept. 1834).

The author of the enclosed defense of the administration's war policy, an ADOPTED CITIZEN who had emigrated from the Scottish island of Mull in 1792, was pastor of the First Reformed Presbyterian Church in New York City (*DAB*).

To William Plumer

DEAR SIR   Monticello Jan. 31. 15.

Your favor of Dec. 30. has been recieved. in answer to your question whether, in the course of my reading, I have ever found that any country, or even considerable island was without inhabitants when first discovered? I must answer, with mr Adams, in the negative. altho' the fact is curious, it had never before struck my attention. some small islands have been found, and are at this day, without inhabitants. but this is easily accounted for. Man, being a gregarious animal, will not remain but where there can be a sufficient herd of his own kind to satisfy his social propensities. add to this, that insulated settlements, if small, would be liable to extirpations by occasional epidemics.

I thank you for the pamphlet you have been so kind as to send me, and have read it with much satisfaction. but with those to whom it is addressed Moses and the prophets have no authority but when administering to their worldly gain. the paradox with me is how any friend to the union of our country can, in conscience, contribute a cent to the maintenance of any one who perverts the sanctity of his desk to the open inculcation of rebellion, civil war, dissolution of government, and the miseries of anarchy.[1] when England took alarm lest France, become republican, should recover energies dangerous to her, she employed emissaries with means to engage incendiaries and anarchists in the disorganisation of all government there. these assuming exaggerated zeal for republican government, and the rights of the people, crowded their inscriptions into the Jacobin societies, and, overwhelming by their majorities the honest & enlightened patriots of the original institution, distorted it's objects, pursued it's genuine founders, under the name of Brissotines & Girondists, unto death, intrigued themselves into the municipality of Paris, controuled by terrorism the proceedings of the legislature, in which they were faithfully aided by their co-stipendiaries there, the Dantons and Marats of the Mountain, murdered their king Septembrized the nation, and thus accomplished their stipulated task of demolishing liberty, and government with it.   England now fears the rising force of this republican nation, and, by the same means, is endeavoring to effect the same course of miseries and destruction here. it is impossible, where one sees like courses of events commence, not to ascribe them to like causes. we know that[2] the government of England, maintaining itself by corruption at home, uses the same means in other countries of which she has any jealousy, by subsidizing agitators and traitors among themselves, to distract and parylize them. she sufficiently manifests that she has no disposition to spare ours. we see, in the proceedings of Massachusets, symptoms which plainly indicate such a cause; and we know, as far as such practices can ever be dragged into light, that she has practised, and with success, on leading individuals of that state. nay further, we see those individuals acting on the very plan which our information had warned us was settled between the parties. these elements of explanation history cannot fail of putting together in recording the crime of combining with the oppressors of the earth to extinguish the last spark of human hope, that here, at length, will be preserved a model of government, securing to man his rights and the fruits of his labor, by an organization constantly subject to his own will. the crime indeed, if accomplished, would immortalize it's perpetrators, and their names would descend in history, with those of Robespierre & his associates, as the guardian genii of despotism, and daemons of human liberty.—I do not mean to say that all who are acting with these men are under the same motives. I know some of them personally to be incapable of it. nor was that the case with the disorganizers and assassins of Paris. delusions there, and party perversions here furnish unconscious assistants to the hired actors in these atrocious scenes.   but I have never entertained one moment's fear on this subject. the people of this country enjoy too much happiness to risk it for nothing; and I have never doubted that whenever the incendiaries of Massachusets should venture openly to raise the standard of Separation, it's citizens would rise in mass, and do justice themselves on their own parricides.

I am glad to learn that you persevere in your historical work. I am sure it will be executed in sound principles of Americanism: and I hope your opportunities will enable you to make the abortive crimes of the present, useful as a lesson for future times.

In aid of your general work I possess no materials whatever, or they should be entirely at your service: and I am sorry that I have not a single copy of the pamphlet you ask, entitled 'a Summary view of the rights of British America.' it was the draught of an Instruction which I had meant to propose for our Delegates to the first Congress. being prevented by sickness from attending our Convention, I sent it to them, and they printed without adopting it, in the hope that conciliation was not yet desperate. it's only merit was in being the first publication which carried the claim of our rights their whole length, and asserted that there was no rightful link of connection between us and England but that of being under the same king.—Hening's collection of our statutes is published, I know, as far as to the 3^d volume, bringing them down to 1710. and I rather believe a 4th has appeared. one more will probably compleat the work to the revolution, and will be to us an inestimable treasure as being the only collection of^3 all the acts of our legislatures now extant in print or Manuscript.

Accept the assurance of my great esteem and respect.

Th: Jefferson

RC (MBPLi); at foot of first page: "Governor Plumer." PoC (DLC). Tr (ViU: TJP); extract; posthumous copy.

The GIRONDISTS (also known as Brissotins) and Montagnards (the MOUNTAIN) were competing political factions in France's national legislature during the early years of the French Revolution (D. M. G. Sutherland, *The French Revolution and Empire* [2003], 147–51). SEPTEMBRIZED THE NATION: made murder for political reasons the order of the day (*OED*).

^{1} Tr, which consists of preceding three sentences, ends here.
^{2} TJ here canceled "England."
^{3} Manuscript: "of of."

From Thomas Law

D^R sir—   [ca. Jan. 1815]

I have the pleasure to enclose a Letter written currente Calamo—
I remain with unfeigned Esteem & regard Y^r m^t ob^t st

Thos Law—

RC (DLC: TJ Papers, 203:36110); undated; addressed: "To Thomas Jefferson Esqr Montecello"; endorsed by TJ as received 5 Jan. 1815, but recorded in SJL as received 5 Feb. 1815. Enclosure not found.

CURRENTE CALAMO: "rapidly; offhand; without premeditation."

From Peter Carr

MY DEAR SIR   Carr's brook. Feb 2ᵈ 15—

My inexorable rheumatism still confines me, and has for the last three weeks bound me hand and foot. A violent ague and fever superadded, has reduced me to a state of debility never before experienced. I am beginning today to take the warm bath, from which I hope for beneficial effects. If I weather this storm, I must endeavour to spend the next winter, in some milder climate. my Phisician recommends some tonic remedies—sound port or claret, or wine of that character. I have sent to Richmond for some, which has not yet arrived—if you have any such, I should in the mean time be much obliged by the favor of a couple of bottles. With the warmest affection.

Yʳˢ

Pᴿ CARR

RC (ViU: TJP-CC); addressed: "Mʳ Jefferson Monticello"; endorsed by TJ as received 2 Feb. 1815 and so recorded in SJL.

Carr failed to WEATHER THIS STORM, dying at his Carr's-brook home on 17 Feb. 1815 (DVB).

Francis C. Gray's Account of a Visit to Monticello

[4–7 Feb. 1815]

on Thursday the 2d of Febʸ Mr. T & myself at half after 3 o'clock[1] with each a small bundle left Richmond in the Stage coach for Charlottesville[2] in the county of Albemarle, in order to pay a visit to Mr. Jefferson to whom we both had letters from Mr. Adams. At 12 miles from town we passed Tuckahoe creek & soon after reached our breakfasting house, where for the first time in my life, I sat down to table with the Landlord & his wife, and we continued to do so during the whole ride to Charlotte. we were here told that all the people east of the mountains call those on the west cohees, and are called by them Tuckahoes. The first is Irish, from which nation the valley was first settled, & the latter the Indian name of a vegetable growing in the

Southern & Eastern parts of Virginia eaten by the hogs & perhaps formerly by the inhabitants. (This vegetable I once supposed to be the truffle but find from mr. Jeff. that it certainly is not so.) On leaving our breakfasting house we rode for 16 miles through a fine country along the Northern bank of James River, Soon quitting the country of coal in the center of which is situated the inn at which we had breakfasted 14 miles from Rich. In several of the houses at which we stopped the whiskey drunk by the passengers did not form an item in the bill as they were private not public houses ie. they had no license. At 45 miles from Richmond according to the regular course of the stage we slept the first night. On the next day we passed through a miserable barren country covered with pines & found a ford at junk creek half frozen over & in quite as bad a State as the Matawomin. But our white[3] driver with a spirit & industry far superior to that of the Maryland black, broke the ice before his horses & carried them through without difficulty (a dead horse was lying on the farther bank, who had been drowned in attempting to pass.) We overtook particularly on the first day many soldiers of the militia who had been in the service of the U.S 6 months at Norfolk without winter clothing, exposed to three epidemics which desolated their camp, The ague & fever, the Typhus, and the Throat distemper, & were now discharged without pay, many of them had not sufficient money to procure food & some as we were told, had eaten nothing for 30 hours—

The country constantly ascended as we proceeded west & on Friday soon after noon, we crossed the North River at the Ford near Milton & soon reached Monticello between which & another mountain belonging to Mr. Jefferson, passed our road to Charlottesville, at which town we dined there.[4] It contains a few brick houses a court house very large & a stone goal, the basement story of which is occupied as shops by a couple of Sadlers. This town though the largest in this part of the country contains no meeting house, nor is there any within 7 miles, but divine service is performed here in the court house every other Sunday—On Saturday it rained & at 12. O'clock we went from our tavern in a hack to monticello three miles east of Charlottesville on the same road we had passed the day before Our road passed between monticello & the S.W mountain which is much higher & along whose side runs the narrow path which led us between these hills to the gate on the S.E side of monticello. The Sides of both these hills & the valley between them are covered with a noble forest of oaks in all stages of growth & of decay. Their trunks straight & tall put forth no branches till they reach a height almost equal to the Summits of our loftiest trees in New England. Those which were rooted in the valley, in the richest soil overtopped many which sprung from spots far above them on the side of the mountain. The forest had evidently been abandoned to nature, some of the trees were decaying from age, some were blasted, some uprooted by the wind & some appeared even to have been twisted from their trunks by the violence of a hurricane. They rendered the approach to the house even at this season of the year extremely grand & impos- ing. On reaching the house we found no bell nor knocker & entering through the hall the parlour saw a Gentleman (Col. Randolph) who took our letters to Mr. Jefferson.

Mr. Jefferson soon made his appearance he is quite tall, 6 feet one or two inches, face streaked & speckled with red, light grey eyes, white hair, dressed in shoes of very thin soft leather with pointed toes & heels ascending in a peak behind, with very short quarters grey worsted stockings, corderoy small clothes blue waistcoat & coat, of stiff, thick cloth made of the wool of his own merinos & badly manu- factured, the buttons of his coat & small clothes of horn, & an under waistcoat flanel bound with red velvet—His figure bony, long[5] with broad shoulders, a true Virginian. He begged he might put up our carriage, send for our baggage & keep us with him some time. We as- sented & he left the room to give the necessary directions, sending as we requested the carriage back to Charlottesville.[6] On looking round the room in which we sat the first thing which attracted our attention was the state of the chairs. They had leather bottoms stuffed with hair, but the bottoms were completely worn through & the hair stick- ing out in all directions, on the mantle piece which was large & of marble were many books of all kinds Livy, Orosius, Edinburg review, 1 vol. of Edgeworths moral tales &c. &c. There were many miserable prints & some fine pictures hung round the room, among them two plans for[7] the completion of the Capitol at washington one of them very elegant. A Harpsichord stood in one corner of the room. There were four double[8] windows from the wall to the floor of fine large glass & a recess in one side of the apartment. This was the Break- fasting room. after half an hours conversation with Mr. Jeff. & Col. Randolph we were invited into the parlour where a fire was just kin- dled & a servant occupied in substituting a wooden pannel for a square of glass, which had been broken in one of the folding doors opening on the lawn. Mr. J. had procured the glass for his house in Bohemia, where the price is so much the square foot whatever be the size of the glass purchased, & these panes were so large that unable to replace the square in this part of the country, he had been obliged to send to Boston to have some glass made of sufficient size to replace that broken, & this had not yet been received. We passed the whole forenoon, which was rainy, in conversation with Mr. Jeff & Mr. Randolph & at 4 o'clock toddy was brought us, which neither of us took & which was never after handed again, & we were ushered back into the breakfast room to dinner, where we were introduced to Mrs. Randolph Miss Randolph, & Mr. T. J. Randolph. The rest of the family at table[9] were mrs. Marks a sister of mr. Jefferson & 2 other daughters of Col. Randolph The drinking cups were of silver marked G.W. to T.J— the table liquors were beer & cider & after dinner wine. In the same room we took tea & at ten in the evening retired—Fires were lighted in our bed rooms & again in the morning before we rose—the beds were all in recesses—At 15 minutes after 8. we heard the first breakfast bell & at 9. the second, whose sound assembled us in the breakfast room—We sat an hour after breakfast chatting with the Ladies & then adjourned to the parlour, Mr. Jefferson gave us the catalogue of his books to examine & soon after conducted us to his library, & passed an hour there in pointing out to us its principal treasures. His collection of ancient classics was complete as to the authors but very careless in the editions. They[10] were generally interleaved with the best English Translations. The Ancient English authors were also all here & some very rare editions of them. a black letter Chaucer & the first of milton's Paradise Lost divided into ten books were the most remarkable. A considerable number of books valuable to the Biblical critic were here, & various ancient editions of all[11] the genuine & apocryphal books Erasmus' edition &c. Many of the most valuable works on the civil and maritime law & on diplomacy, together with a complete collection of the Laws of the different states, those of Virginia in manuscript, & all the old elementary writers & reporters of England formed the legal library. The ancient and most distinguished modern historians render this department nearly complete, & the histories & descriptions of the kingdoms of Asia were remarkably numerous Rapin was here in French though very rare in that language, mr. Jeff. said that after all it was still the best history of England, for Hume's tory principles are to him insupportable. The best mode of counteracting their effect is, he thinks, to publish an Edition of Hume expunging all those reflections & reasonings, whose influence is so injurious, this has been attempted by[12] Baxter, but he has injured the work by making other material abridgements. D'Avila was there in Italian in mr J's opinion one of the most entertaining books he ever read—I was surprised to find here two little volumes on Chronology by Count Potocki of St. Petersburg. Mr. J has also a fine collection of Saxon & mœso Gothic books, among them Alfred's translations of Orosius & Boethius—& shewed[13] us some attempts he had made at facilitating the study of this language. He thought the singularity of the letters one of the greatest difficulties & proposed publishing the Saxon books in four columns the first to contain the Saxon, the second the same in Roman characters, the third a strictly verbal translation & the fourth a free one. Mr. J. said the French Dict[y] of Trevoux was better than that of the Academy, thought Charron de la Sagesse an excellent work & brought us a commentary & review on Montesquieu published by Duane the translator from the French M.S. which he called the best book on politics which had been published for a century, & agreed with its author in his opinion of Montesquieu—

Of all branches of learning however that relating to the[14] History of North & South America is the most perfectly displayed in this library. The collection on this subject is without a question the most valuable[15] in the world. Here are the works of all the Spanish travellers in America & the great work of De Brie in which he has collected latin translations of the smaller works published by the earliest visitors of America whose original publications are now lost. It is finely printed & adorned with many plates. Here also is a copy of the letters of Hernando[16] Cortes in Spanish, one of a small edition, & the copy retained by the Editor the Cardinal Archbishop of Toledo for himself, but given by him to the American Consul for mr. Jefferson. This work contains the official letters of Cortes to his court his maps of the country & plates representing the dresses, armour & other contents of the treasury of the Mexican Sovereigns—We saw here also some beautiful modern M.S.S. one of [a][17] work which had been suppressed in France, Most of the greek Romances—Mr. Jeff took us from his library into his bed chamber where on a table before the fire stood a polygraph with which he said he always wrote.[18] Mr. Jefferson took his accustomed ride before dinner & on his return told us that the ice was crowded & thick on the banks of the Rivanna & had carried away 30 feet of his mill dam; this was all he said on the subject, & from his manner I supposed his loss was probably about one or two hundred dollars, but on our ride back to Richmond we heard it every where spoken of as a serious loss & the countrymen some of them even estimated it at 30000$. this to be sure must [have been][19] a most wonderful miscalculation, but no doubt the loss was serious.

MS (NcD: Gray Diary, 1811–15); with emendations in an unidentified hand, including notation at foot of text: "Dept Monticello, Tuesday, Feb. 7. 1815."

Francis Calley Gray (1790–1856), attorney, public official, and man of letters, was born in Salem, Massachusetts, and graduated from Harvard University in 1809. He spent four years in Russia as a secretary to United States minister plenipotentiary John Quincy Adams, 1809–13. Thereafter Gray lived in Boston and was admitted to the Massachusetts bar in 1814, although he never practiced law. An author of some note, he published pieces on a host of historical, antiquarian, and legal topics, including penal reform. Gray served as a fellow at Harvard, 1826–36, as vice president and president of the Boston Athenæum, 1826–32 and 1833–36, respectively, and as a member of the state legislature, principally during the 1820s. He died in Boston. A lifelong bachelor, Gray left a fine collection of engravings to his alma mater along with a large portion of his estate to endow the collection and establish a museum of comparative zoology (*DAB*; Marjorie B. Cohn, *Francis Calley Gray and Art Collecting for America* [1986]; *Harvard Catalogue*, 71, 187; *The Athenæum Centenary: The Influence and History of the Boston Athenæum from 1807 to 1907* [1907], 115, 116; Boston *Columbian Centinel*, 16 May 1821, 14 May 1823; *Pittsfield Sun*, 21 Apr. 1825; *Boston Daily Advertiser*, 30 Dec. 1856).

MR. T: George Ticknor. MATAWOMIN: Mattawoman Creek. NORTH RIVER: Rivanna River. ANOTHER MOUNTAIN owned by TJ was Montalto. GOAL: "jail." MISS RANDOLPH was the Randolphs' eldest unmarried daughter, TJ's granddaughter Ellen W. Randolph (Coolidge). For TJ's silver DRINKING CUPS, see TJ to John Le Tellier, 27 Mar. 1810. D'AVILA: Enrico Caterino Davila, *Istoria delle guerre civili di Francia* (Venice, 1741; Sowerby, no. 198; Poor, *Jefferson's Library*, 4 [no. 73]). ALFRED'S TRANSLATIONS OF OROSIUS & BOETHIUS were *The Anglo-Saxon Version, From the Historian Orosius. By Ælfred the Great. Together with an English Translation from the Anglo-Saxon* (London, 1773; Sowerby, no. 4868), and *Consolationis Philosophiæ Libri V. Anglo-Saxonice Redditi ab Alfredo, Inclyto Anglo-Saxonum Rege* (Oxford, 1698; Sowerby, no. 4867; Poor, *Jefferson's Library*, 14 [no. 907]). TJ also proposed the publication of SAXON BOOKS IN FOUR COLUMNS in an essay on the study of the Anglo-Saxon language that he prepared for the University of Virginia late in life (Stanley R. Hauer, "Thomas Jefferson and the Anglo-Saxon Language," *Publications of the Modern Language Association of America* 98 [1983]: 879–98, esp. 889).

The DICT^Y OF TREVOUX was the *Dictionnaire Universel François et Latin, vulgairement appelé Dictionnaire de Trévoux* (Paris, 1771; Sowerby, no. 4824). For the GREAT WORK OF DE BRIE (Theodor de Bry), see Sowerby, nos. 3973–83. For TJ's acquisition of the LETTERS OF HERNANDO CORTES, which was edited by Archbishop Francisco Antonio Lorenzana y Butrón and published as the *Historia de Nueva-España, escrita por su esclarecido conquistador Hernan Cortes, aumentada con otros documentos, y notas* (Mexico, 1770; Sowerby, no. 4120), see *PTJ*, 20:210–1, 28:381–3. Lorenzana had provided the AMERICAN CONSUL William Carmichael (actually chargé d'affaires and treaty commissioner) with a copy for transmittal to TJ.

[1] An unidentified person here interlined "a.m."
[2] Manuscript: "Charlotteville."
[3] Word interlined.
[4] Gray here canceled "friday."
[5] Gray here canceled "& sharp."
[6] Manuscript: "Charlotteville."
[7] Reworked from "two projects of."
[8] Word interlined.
[9] Preceding two words interlined.
[10] Reworked from "The greek classics."
[11] Word interlined.
[12] Gray here canceled "Baker."
[13] Manuscript: "shew."

14 Gray here canceled "Ancient."
15 Word interlined in place of "per-fect."
16 Manuscript: "Fernando."

17 Omitted word editorially supplied.
18 Gray here canceled "We dined."
19 Preceding two words interlined in an unidentified hand.

George Ticknor's Account of a Visit to Monticello

[4–7 Feb. 1815]

We left Charlottesville on Saturday morning, the 4th of February, for Mr. Jefferson's. He lives, you know, on a mountain, which he has named Monticello, and which, perhaps you do not know, is a synonyme for Carter's mountain. The ascent of this steep, savage hill, was as pensive and slow as Satan's ascent to Paradise. We were obliged to wind two thirds round its sides before we reached the artificial lawn on which the house stands; and, when we had arrived there, we were about six hundred feet, I understand, above the stream which flows at its foot. It is an abrupt mountain. The fine growth of ancient forest-trees conceals its sides and shades part of its summit. The prospect is admirable. . . . . The lawn on the top, as I hinted, was artificially formed by cutting down the peak of the height. In its centre, and facing the southeast, Mr. Jefferson has placed his house, which is of brick, two stories high in the wings, with a piazza in front of a receding centre. It is built, I suppose, in the French style. You enter, by a glass folding-door, into a hall which reminds you of Fielding's "Man of the Mountain," by the strange furniture of its walls. On one side hang the head and horns of an elk, a deer, and a buffalo; another is covered with curiosities which Lewis and Clarke found in their wild and perilous expedition. On the third, among many other striking matters, was the head of a mammoth, or, as Cuvier calls it, a mastodon, containing the only *os frontis*, Mr. Jefferson tells me, that has yet been found. On the fourth side, in odd union with a fine painting of the Repentance of Saint Peter, is an Indian map on leather, of the southern waters of the Missouri, and an Indian representation of a bloody battle, handed down in their traditions.

Through this hall—or rather museum—we passed to the dining-room, and sent our letters to Mr. Jefferson, who was of course in his study. Here again we found ourselves surrounded with paintings that seemed good.

We had hardly time to glance at the pictures before Mr. Jefferson entered; and if I was astonished to find Mr. Madison short and somewhat awkward, I was doubly astonished to find Mr. Jefferson, whom I had always supposed to be a small man, more than six feet high, with dignity in his appearance, and ease and graciousness in his manners. . . . . He rang, and sent to Charlottesville for our baggage, and, as dinner approached, took us to the drawing-room,—a large and rather elegant room, twenty or thirty feet high,—which, with the hall I have described, composed the whole centre of the house, from top to bottom. The floor of this room is tessellated. It is formed of alternate diamonds of cherry and beech, and kept polished as highly as if it were of fine mahogany.

Here are the best pictures of the collection. Over the fireplace is the Laughing and Weeping Philosophers, dividing the world between them; on its right, the earliest navigators to America,—Columbus, Americus Vespuccius, Magellan, etc.,—copied, Mr. Jefferson said, from originals in the Florence Gallery. Farther round, Mr. Madison in the plain, Quaker-like dress of his youth, Lafayette in his Revolutionary uniform, and Franklin in the dress in which we always see him. There were other pictures, and a copy of Raphael's Transfiguration.

We conversed on various subjects until dinner-time, and at dinner were introduced to the grown members of his family. These are his only remaining child, Mrs. Randolph, her husband, Colonel Randolph, and the two oldest of their unmarried children, Thomas Jefferson and Ellen; and I assure you I have seldom met a pleasanter party.

The evening passed away pleasantly in general conversation, of which Mr. Jefferson was necessarily the leader. I shall probably surprise you by saying that, in conversation, he reminded me of Dr. Freeman. He has the same discursive manner and love of paradox, with the same appearance of sobriety and cool reason. He seems equally fond of American antiquities, and especially the antiquities of his native State, and talks of them with freedom and, I suppose, accuracy. He has, too, the appearance of that fairness and simplicity which Dr. Freeman has; and, if the parallel holds no further here, they will again meet on the ground of their love of old books and young society.

On Sunday morning, after breakfast, Mr. Jefferson asked me into his library, and there I spent the forenoon of that day as I had that of yesterday. This collection of books, now so much talked about, consists of about seven thousand volumes, contained in a suite of fine rooms, and is arranged in the catalogue, and on the shelves, according to the divisions and subdivisions of human learning by Lord Bacon. In so short a time I could not, of course, estimate its value, even if I had been competent to do so.

Perhaps the most curious single specimen—or, at least, the most characteristic of the man and expressive of his hatred of royalty—was a collection which he had bound up in six volumes, and lettered "The Book of Kings," consisting of the "Memoires de la Princesse de Bareith," two volumes; "Les Memoires de la Comtesse de la Motte," two volumes; the "Trial of the Duke of York," one volume; and *The Book,*" one volume. These documents of regal scandal seemed to be favorites with the philosopher, who pointed them out to me with a satisfaction somewhat inconsistent with the measured gravity he claims in relation to such subjects generally.

On Monday morning I spent a couple of hours with him in his study. He gave me there an account of the manner in which he passed the portion of his time in Europe which he could rescue from public business; told me that while he was in France he had formed a plan of going to Italy, Sicily, and Greece, and that he should have executed it, if he had not left Europe in the full conviction that he should immediately return there, and find a better opportunity. He spoke of my intention to go, and, without my even hinting any purpose to ask him for letters, told me that he was now seventy-two years old, and that most of his friends and correspondents in Europe had died in the course of the twenty-seven years since he left France, but that he would gladly furnish me with the means of becoming acquainted with some of the remainder, if I would give him a month's notice, and regretted that their number was so reduced.

The afternoon and evening passed as on the two days previous; for everything is done with such regularity, that when you know how one day is filled, I suppose you know how it is with the others. At eight o'clock the first bell is rung in the great hall, and at nine the second summons you to the breakfast-room, where you find everything ready. After breakfast every one goes, as inclination leads him, to his chamber, the drawing-room, or the library. The children retire to their school-room with their mother, Mr. Jefferson rides to his mills on the Rivanna, and returns at about twelve. At half past three the great bell rings, and those who are disposed resort to the drawing-room, and the rest go to the dining-room at the second call of the bell, which is at four o'clock. The dinner was always choice, and served in the French style; but no wine was set on the table till the cloth was removed. The ladies sat until about six, then retired, but returned with the tea-tray a little before seven, and spent the evening with the gentlemen; which was always pleasant, for they are obviously accustomed to join in the conversation, however high the topic may be. At about half past ten, which seemed to be their usual hour of retiring, I went to my chamber, found there a fire, candle, and a servant in waiting to receive my orders for the morning, and in the morning was waked by his return to build the fire.

To-day, Tuesday, we told Mr. Jefferson that we should leave Monticello in the afternoon. He seemed much surprised, and said as much as politeness would permit on the badness of the roads and the prospect of bad weather, to induce us to remain longer. It was evident, I thought, that they had calculated on our staying a week. At dinner, Mr. Jefferson again urged us to stay, not in an oppressive way, but with kind politeness; and when the horses were at the door, asked if he should not send them away; but, as he found us resolved on going, he bade us farewell in the heartiest style of Southern hospitality, after thrice reminding me that I must write to him for letters to his friends in Europe. I came away almost regretting that the coach returned so soon, and thinking, with General Hamilton, that he was a perfect gentleman in his own house.

Two little incidents which occurred while we were at Monticello should not be passed by. The night before we left, young Randolph came up late from Charlottesville, and brought the astounding news that the English had been defeated before New Orleans by General Jackson. Mr. Jefferson had made up his mind that the city would fall, and told me that the English would hold it permanently—or for some time—by a force of Sepoys from the East Indies. He had gone to bed, like the rest of us; but of course his grandson went to his chamber with the paper containing the news. But the old philosopher refused to open his door, saying he could wait till the morning; and when we met at breakfast I found he had not yet seen it.

One morning, when he came back from his ride, he told Mr. Randolph, very quietly, that the dam had been carried away the night before. From his manner, I supposed it an affair of small consequence, but at Charlottesville, on my way to Richmond, I found the country ringing with it. Mr. Jefferson's great dam was gone, and it would cost $30,000 to rebuild it.

There is a breathing of notional philosophy in Mr. Jefferson,—in his dress, his house, his conversation. His setness, for instance, in wearing very sharp toed shoes, corduroy small-clothes, and red plush waistcoat, which have been laughed at till he might perhaps wisely have dismissed them.

So, though he told me he thought Charron, "De la Sagesse," the best treatise on moral philosophy ever written, and an obscure Review of Montesquieu, by Dupont de Nemours, the best political work that had been printed for fifty years,—though he talked very freely of the natural impossibility that one generation should bind another to pay a public debt, and of the expediency of vesting all the legislative authority of a State in one branch, and the executive authority in another, and leaving them to govern it by joint discretion,—I considered such opinions simply as curious *indicia* of an extraordinary character.

Printed in George S. Hillard, ed., *Life, Letters, and Journals of George Ticknor* (1876), 1:34–8, where it is described as part of a letter to the author's father, Elisha Ticknor, dated Charlottesville, 7 Feb. 1815; ellipses in original.

George Ticknor (1791–1871), educator and scholar, was born in Boston and graduated from Dartmouth College in 1807. Although he was trained in the law and admitted to the Massachusetts bar in 1813, he practiced for just one year. After visiting TJ at Monticello, Ticknor sailed to Europe to further his literary studies. During the four years that followed, he toured much of the continent, procured books for the ex-president, met many of the literati of the day, and attended lectures at the University of Göttingen. Ticknor then returned to America and served as professor of French and Spanish literature and of belles lettres at Harvard University, 1819–35. In 1824 he traveled to Monticello a second time, and four years later he became a member of the American Philosophical Society. Ticknor revisited Europe, 1835–38, and spent the following decade researching and writing his magnum opus, a multivolume *History of Spanish Literature*, which was published to great critical acclaim in 1849, went through several editions, and was quickly translated into French, German, and Spanish. In addition he is counted among the founders of the Boston Public Library in 1852, an institution that he

helped to administer until 1866 and to which he donated almost four thousand books. Ticknor helped supervise the activities of local banks, hospitals, insurance companies, and schools. He died in Boston (*ANB*; *DAB*; Hillard, ed., *Life of Ticknor*; David B. Tyack, *George Ticknor and the Boston Brahmins* [1967]; *General Catalogue of Dartmouth College and the Associated Schools, 1769–1925* [1925], 115; *Harvard Catalogue*, 122; Ticknor's Account of a Visit to Monticello, [ca. 14–19 Dec. 1824]; APS, Minutes, 18 July 1828 [MS in PPAmP]; Boston Public Library, *Bulletin*, 4th ser., 3 [1921]: 304; *Boston Daily Advertiser*, 27 Jan. 1871). A likeness of Ticknor and a photograph of the Monticello dining room he describes above are reproduced elsewhere in this volume.

The Man of the Hill (MAN OF THE MOUNTAIN) appears in the eighth and ninth books of Henry Fielding, *The History of Tom Jones, a Foundling* (London, 1749). OS FRONTIS: "frontal bone; forehead" (*OED*). For the FINE PAINTING in the Entrance Hall and the BEST PICTURES OF THE COLLECTION, see Stein, *Worlds*, 70, 128–9, 132–7, 144. The TRIAL OF THE DUKE OF YORK was Gwyllym L. Wardle, *A Circumstantial Report of the Evidence and Proceedings upon the Charges preferred against His Royal Highness the Duke of York* (London, 1809; Sowerby, no. 409). The REVIEW OF MONTESQUIEU was by Destutt de Tracy, not Pierre Samuel Du Pont de Nemours.

For a wholly fictional account by a former slave of his visit to Monticello that supposedly took place in July 1815, see Jabez D. Hammond, *Life and Opinions of Julius Melbourn; with sketches of the lives and characters of Thomas Jefferson, John Quincy Adams, John Randolph, and several other eminent American statesmen* (1847; 2d ed., 1851), 63–78.

From Caspar Wistar

Dᴿ Sɪʀ   [received 4 Feb. 1815]

In a day or two I shall reply to your very interesting letter. The object of this note is to present to you the Bearer, Mʳ Ticknor of Boston, a young gentleman who intends to visit Europe for the purpose of acquiring information. Before he leaves his native Country he wishes to See Some of the States to the South of this, & to pay his respects to you—In a letter from Dʳ Warren of Boston Mʳ Ticknor is mentioned in the most respectful terms, & Several Gentlemen of that place, who are now here, unite in describing him as a young gentleman of very uncommon merit. Any assistance you may afford him, by advice or letters, will add one more to the many kind services you have rendered

to your much obliged friend   C. Wɪsᴛᴀʀ

Mʳ Gilmer remains with us, & answers fully to your description—He thinks of visiting Europe with Mʳ Correa.

RC (DLC: TJ Papers, 203:36132); undated; endorsed by TJ as received 4 Feb. 1815 "by mr Ticknor" and so recorded in SJL.   ʜᴇʀᴇ: Philadelphia.

From Caspar Wistar

Mʏ Dᴇᴀʀ Sɪʀ   Sunday Febʸ 5. 1815

I believe that I have never been So much in arrears in my epistolary account with you & certainly I never felt more disposed to discharge my debts. In a few days I hope to Send you a short account of an ineffectual[1] effort to improve our plan of Education, in which Dʳ Franklin took a part, & also an account of a Mammoths Head which was in existence three years ago, & probably now exists.

At present I detain Mʳ Gilmer while I tell you that we have been much pleased with him & feel Sincere Regret at his departure—He has fully Justified your account of him—

[243]

My determination to write again in three or four days allows me now to Conclude without saying more
than that I am most Sincerely
your highly obliged friend   C. WISTAR

RC (DLC); dateline at foot of text; en-   [1] Word interlined.
dorsed by TJ as received 24 Mar. 1815
from Philadelphia and so recorded in
SJL.

From David Bailie Warden

DEAR SIR,   Paris 7 february, 1815.[1]
    I am informed that you have been pleased to write to the President of the united States in my behalf. I feel deeply grateful for this favor; and beg leave to send you the inclosed copy of a letter addressed to me by the <u>Prince of Benevent</u>, which completely justifies me[2] on the only point of accusation against me renewed by mr. Crawford. I wait with great anxiety the decision of the Government—your interference is a Source of consolation—
    I beg leave to inclose a copy of observations on the English doctrine of allegiance as applied to citizens of the united states: it was written, and printed when there was no prospect of a speedy peace— I find that several tracts have been lately published in England; of which one is[3] by mr. Reeves, formerly of the alien-office "to shew that americans born before the Independence are, by the Law of England, not aliens" and "that mr. Jefferson might have the benefit of his american citizenship in perfect compatibility with the claims upon him from British allegiance."
    The french Government is preparing an Expedition for the Western coast of <u>Africa</u>, which will Sail in the course of a few weeks under the command of Capt. Baudoin for the purpose of scientific researches, and the establishment of a free Colony between the 8° and 16°. Twenty seven scientific Men will accompany this expedition— their place of rendezvous will be at <u>cape Vert</u>—The new establishment is to serve as a Botany-Bay for France—[4]
    Professor Leslie of Edinburgh, who was lately, at Paris, bid me recall him to the remembrance of mr. Randolph—for whom he has a great esteem. He asked a thousand questions concerning your family—   Through him I have been requested to furnish the <u>article america</u>, and others for the supplement to the[5] <u>Encyclopedia Brittanica</u>—

I sent you Some volumes in a case addressed to mr. shaler, at ghent, which unfortunately was left there—and I wait for an opportunity of forwarding it from some neighbouring port.

I have been obliged to undergo a Surgical operation for an inflammation of the eye which prevents me from having the pleasure of communicating to you other information on subjects in which you are interested—   wishing you to present my respects to mr. and mrs. Randolph—with great respect I am, dear Sir, your very obed^t Servant   D. B. WARDEN—

RC (DLC); at foot of text: "Thomas Jefferson Esquire"; endorsed by TJ as received 20 June 1815 and so recorded in SJL. FC (MdHi: Warden Letterbook); in Warden's hand; incomplete. Enclosure: second enclosure to Warden to TJ, 20 Oct. 1814. Other enclosure not found.

John REEVES claimed that "Mr. Jefferson might have the benefit of his American citizenship, in perfect compatibility with the claims upon him from British allegiance" in his *Two Tracts shewing, that Americans, born before the Independence,* *are, by the law of England, not aliens* (London, 1814; 2d ed., London, 1816), 16. A BOTANY-BAY is a colony peopled by convicts (*OED*).

[1] Reworked from "1814."
[2] Remainder of paragraph in FC reads "concerning my correspondence with this Government."
[3] Preceding four words in FC read "and particularly one."
[4] FC ends here.
[5] Preceding three words interlined.

From Charles Clay

DEAR SIR   Bedford Feb. 8.—15

I am pleased to find you viewed my letter in the light it was intended,—a Real Concern for your present peace & future Reputation alone dictated it, & Strongly impressed my mind to draw your attention to the probable Consequences Should your ultimate Views have been publication; in the[1] brokn form of fragments & which must have been conected perhaps by some observations, or explanations, to preserve a concatination of Ideas, in these lay the difficulties & dangers I was apprehensive of;—& altho every one may, & every one has an undoubted Right to amuse himself sometimes, & even be playful in his Closet on any Subject,—yet an Idea Suggested itself, most possibly it might not be for yourself only the time was Spent, & from hence the inference of probable publication naturally occured.—I sincerely will your name may Remain in the Annals of America as the Cedar of Libanus, or the live Oak of America, & if any thing has escaped from me that would imply the Contrary, my Dear Sir Correct it, & make it Speak better things your letter of the 29 ult. I Recieved yesterday with the packet &c but I apprehend you made a small mistake in putting them up & Sent your Own spectacles[2] in place of the frames[3] that Came with the glasses,—the glasses in the package papers, are Considerably too Small for their place in the frames[4] Sent, & the glass in the Rims are quite too Young for my Eyes please inform me if you made no mistake in the frames sent, I am quite at a loss what to do with them till I hear from you.—and if you insist on my taking them on the terms mentioned in your letter it must be so, but it will opperate as a ban against my ever Soliciting your aid in procuring me any particular Hobby in future

   accept assurance of profound Respect & high esteem

C. CLAY

RC (MHi); endorsed by TJ as received 20 Feb. 1815 and so recorded in SJL. RC (DLC); address cover only; with PoC of TJ to Joseph Dougherty, 27 Feb. 1815, on verso; addressed: "Tho. Jefferson Esquire of Monticello Albemarle"; franked; postmarked Lynchburg, 11 Feb., and Charlottesville, 19 Feb.

In the Bible the cedar of Lebanon (LIBANUS) symbolizes strength, power, prosperity, and majesty (Ezekiel 31.5–9, Psalms 92.12, 104.16–7).

[1] Manuscript: "in the in the."
[2] Manuscript: "spectatles."
[3] Manuscript: "fraims."
[4] Manuscript: "fraims."

To Robert M. Patterson

SIR   Monticello Feb. 8. 15.

   I am honored with your letter of Jan. 20. conveying to me the flattering[1] sentiments which the American Philosophical Society have condescended,[2] through you to express on my resignation of the office of President, in which they had been pleased so long to continue me. I recieve them with equal sensibility and gratitude. the motives for withdrawing from a station the duties of which could not, in my situation, be fulfilled, were truly expressed in my letter of Nov. 23. they had been conscientiously felt when, on a former occasion, I asked a like permission, and so continued to be: and I trust it is seen that I have rendered a service in giving occasion for the choice of a successor so eminently meriting the honor, so fully equal to it's duties, and in place to perform them. in retaining still the character of a member of the society, I am gratified by the idea of a continued fellowship with them, and shall never be more so than on occasions of being useful to them.

   Praying you to present them the homage of my dutiful respects, permit me also to add my obligations to yourself personally for the friendly terms in which you are pleased to make their communication, and accept the assurance of my great consideration and esteem.

TH: JEFFERSON

RC (PPAmP: APS Archives); at foot of text: "D[r] R. M. Patterson"; endorsed by John Vaughan, in part, as TJ's "answer to the Letter of Sec[y] R: M Patterson relative to the accept[e] of his resignation as President, Copied into Minutes 3 March 1815." PoC (DLC). Tr (APS, Minutes, 3 Mar. 1815 [MS at PPAmP]); in Patterson's hand.

TJ's SUCCESSOR as American Philosophical Society president was Caspar Wistar.

[1] TJ here canceled "expressions."
[2] Word interlined in place of "been pleased."

To John Vaughan

DEAR SIR   Monticello Feb. 8. 15.

Your very friendly letter of Jan. 4. is but just recieved, and I am much gratified by the interest taken by yourself, and others of my collegues of the Philosophical Society, in what concerned myself on withdrawing from the presidency of the society. my desire to do so had been so long known to every member, and the continuance of it to some, that I do not suppose it can be misunderstood by the public. setting aside the consideration of distance, which must be obvious to all, nothing is more incumbent on the old than to know when they should get out of the way, and relinquish to younger successors the honors they can no longer earn, and the duties they can no longer perform. I rejoice in the election of D[r] Wistar, and trust that his senior standing in the society will have been considered as a fair motive of preference by those whose merits, standing alone, would have justly entitled them to the honor, and who as juniors, according to the course of nature, may still expect their turn.

I have recieved with very great pleasure the visit of mr Ticknor, and find him highly distinguished[1] by science and good sense. he was accompanied by mr Gray, son of the late L[t] Gov[r] of Massachusets, of great information and promise also. it gives me ineffable comfort to see such subjects coming forward to take charge of the political & civil rights the establishment of which has cost us such sacrifices. mr Ticknor will be fortunate if he can get under the wing of mr Correa: and if the happiness of mr Correa requires (as I suppose it does) his return to Europe we must sacrifice to it that which his residence here would have given us, and acquiesce under the regrets which our transient acquaintance with his worth cannot fail to embody with our future recollections of him.—of Michaux's work I possess 3. vols, or rather Cahiers, one on Oaks, another Beeches & Birches, and a third on Pines.

I salute you with great friendship and respect.

TH: JEFFERSON

RC (PPAmP: Thomas Jefferson Papers); at foot of text: "John Vaughan esq." PoC (DLC).

Vaughan's VERY FRIENDLY LETTER was dated 9 Jan. 1815, not JAN. 4. François André Michaux's WORK on oak, beech, birch, and pine trees was his *Histoire des Arbres Forestiers de l'Amérique Septentrionale* (Paris, 1810–13; Sowerby, no. 1083).

[1] Word interlined in place of "qualified."

To Mathew Carey

SIR   Monticello Feb. 9. 15.

I thank you for the copy of the Olive branch you have been so kind as to send me. many extracts from it which I had seen in the newspapers had excited a wish to procure it, but the effecting this had been prevented by the difficulty of making small or fractional remittances to Philadelphia and especially since the bank bills of the different states have ceased to be recievable in all others. a cursory view over the work has confirmed the expectation excited by the extracts, that it will do great good. faults have doubtless been committed on both sides, and most, probably, by those who have the oftenest been obliged to decide which branch of a dilemma should be pursued. a more serious perusal[1] of the book which I shall immediately undertake will, I doubt not, confirm the good opinion formed of it. Accept the assurance of my great esteem and respect.

TH: JEFFERSON

RC (NjMoHP: Lloyd W. Smith Collection); addressed: "Mr Matthew Carey Philadelphia"; franked; postmarked Charlottesville, 15 Feb. PoC (DLC); on verso of reused address cover to TJ; endorsed by TJ. Carey printed an extract from the above letter, consisting of the dateline and the first, opening portion of the second, and third sentences, in the unpaginated frontmatter to the 6th and later editions of *The Olive Branch*.

[1] Word interlined in place of "examination."

To Charles W. Goldsborough

Sir   Monticello Feb. 9. 15.

I thank you for the information of your letter of Jan. 19. on the subject of the newly improved looms; but the extent of my manufactures is merely the cloathing my family which employs two common looms with the flying shuttle. I had indeed been much pleased with the beauty of the operation of Janes's loom, which was exhibited, by the purchaser of his patent right for this state, at our Courthouse in Charlottesville. had he offered them at the price asked by the patentee in Connecticut (40.D.) he might have sold 30. or 40. that day; but asking 80. or 100.D. he did not sell a single one, nor will he as many, I think, in the whole state for after all, it only gives a useless holliday to one hand and both feet. Cooper's Emporium suggested the first doubt that it was no invention of Janes, and a letter from Dr Thornton mentioned mr Crosbie's claim to it, which is more specifically stated in yours. the litigious state of the invention renders the use of it under either claimant a little hazardous at present. whenever that [shall][1] be acknoleged, an[d] the machine at a price which my little manufactory might justify I should certainly be disposed to get one, and to encourage my county to do the same. any future information as to these points which you may be so kind as to favor me with will be recieved with interest & thankfulness. Accept the assurance of [my] great respect.   TH: JEFFERSON

PoC (DLC); on verso of reused address cover of John Adams to TJ, 20 Dec. 1814; mutilated at seal, with missing text recopied by TJ above the line; hole in manuscript and ink stained; at foot of text: "Ch. W. Gouldsborough esq."; endorsed by TJ.

Francis C. Clopper purchased Walter Janes's PATENT RIGHT FOR THIS STATE. For Thomas Cooper's DOUBT about the novelty of Janes's patent, see note to TJ to William Thornton, 24 Dec. 1814.

[1] Word faint.

From Francis De Masson

Sir,   Paris, Rue neuve de Luxembourg N° 20, 9 February 1815

In the second year of your first Presidency you were pleased to appoint me a member of the Corps of Engineers, in which capacity I was stationed for nine years at the Military Academy at West Point. That my services have not been totally useless I am inclined to believe from the repeated approbation[1] and long friendship with which I was honored from that highly distinguished officer, Gen. Jon. Williams, who, during that period, commanded the Engineers, and from the gratifying observation that, in the late contest with England, every military man who formerly belonged to the institution at West Point, has made himself deservedly conspicuous. Nor have my leisure hours been entirely unemployed. Among several works of mine intended for the Military Philosophical Society to which I was recording secretary, one on the Military Constitution of Nations, was so particularly honored with your approbation that you deigned to have it printed and distributed among the members of Congress. To these pleasing recollections I must add that when I first set out from France to America, your sainted friend, the immortal M^r De Malesherbes, gave me for you the warmest letter of introduction, recommendation and credit. I transmitted to you this letter only seven years ago under cover to Gen. Jon. Williams; through some unaccountable accident[2] it was lost at the Post office, but you were pleased to assure Gen. Williams of your wish to show your regard for M^r De Malesherbes by your readiness in obliging his friend whenever an opportunity would offer. After a stay of more than twenty years in the United States, a natural desire of seeing again my native country and friends has[3] called me back to France, but even here I cannot forget the ties which, for so long a time, have bound me to America. I wish I could have it in my power to serve the American Government in Europe. Under that impression, emboldened by the circumstances above related, having long been a naturalized citizen of the United States, and married to an American lady,[4] I take the liberty of applying to you, Sir, for an appointment either to any part of the American legation in Paris, or to the Consulate of the United States at Nantes.[5] However, although one of these two appointments would be most agreeable, if they were already disposed of, any other of the same kind in one of the principal places[6] either in France, England or Italy, would be gratefully received. My past services, the esteem I have long had the happiness of enjoying from Gen. Williams, Macomb, Swift, and many other distinguished characters[7] in America, and the inclosed letter of recommendation from the Marquis De la Fayette,[8] are pledges of the constant zeal with which I shall discharge the duties of those offices.

Be assured, Sir, of the gratitude which I shall always feel for your protection, and please to receive the homage of the profound respect with which I have the honor to be,

Sir, Your most obedient and most humble servant

FRANCIS DE MASSON

Dupl (DLC: James Madison Papers); dateline beneath signature; at foot of text: "Th. Jefferson Esquire"; endorsed by TJ as received 11 May 1815 and so recorded in SJL; enclosed in TJ to Madison, 12 May 1815. RC (DNA: RG 59, LAR, 1809–17); dated 10 Jan. 1815; at foot of text: "Thomas Jefferson Esq." The RC was apparently sent to Washington under the mistaken belief that TJ was secretary of state and never seen by its intended recipient (Masson to William H. Crawford, 20 Apr. 1816 [DNA: RG 59, LAR, 1809–17]). Enclosure: Lafayette's Recommendation of Masson, La Grange, 11 Feb. 1815, which supports Masson's candidacy for a consular appointment in France on the basis of his tenure at the United States Military Academy at West Point, his martial merits, and the respectability of his French relations (DLC: Madison Papers).

Francis De Masson (b. ca. 1774), a native of France whose family had moved to Saint Domingue, immigrated to the United States by 1792. He settled first in New York and then relocated to New Jersey. TJ selected Masson to teach French at the United States Military Academy at West Point in 1803, an appointment which was submitted to and confirmed by the United States Senate the following year. During his tenure he also taught drawing and the art of fortification, wrote a number of articles, and was the recording secretary of the United States Military Philosophical Society. Masson returned to Europe on furlough in 1810 and resigned his post two years later. His bid for an American consulship failed, but he served as master of fortification at England's Royal Military College at Sandhurst, 1815–34 (George W. Cullum, *Biographical Register of the Officers and Graduates of the U. S. Military Academy at West Point, N. Y.*, 3d ed. [1891], 3:494–5, 516, 520, 529; Heitman, *U.S. Army*, 1:696; *JEP*, 1:467, 468 [24, 26 Mar. 1804]; *PTJ*, 24:267–8; Madison, *Papers, Pres. Ser.*, 2:177; Arthur P. Wade, "A Military Offspring of the American Philosophical Society," *Military Affairs* 38 [1974]: 105; Roswell Park, *A Sketch of the History and Topography of West Point and the U. S. Military Academy* [1840], 54; Royal Military College Staff Register [Royal Military Academy, Sandhurst, U.K.: Sandhurst Collection]).

Masson's essay on the military constitution of nations was published anonymously both in the *National Intelligencer & Washington Advertiser* on 18 Nov. 1808 and, shortly thereafter, as a stand-alone monograph. After discussing the dangers of relying on either a professional standing army or a poorly trained militia, he proposed a compromise: "All the young men from eighteen to twenty-five years of age, with a few peculiar exceptions, should be divided into four classes, each of which would by turns spend three months dispersed in the different camps of instruction. Each class during its stay in the camps would form the standing army of the country, and as such receive the stated pay of the line. So that the permanent standing army would never amount to more than one-fourth of the youth between eighteen and twenty-five years of age, and every young man during the three-fourths of the year, would be enabled to follow his own particular avocations." Men over the age of twenty-five were to be discharged from the service and embodied into the militia.

The letter of introduction, recommendation and credit by Malesherbes was dated 30 July 1792 and miscarried seven years ago on its way to TJ (*PTJ*, 24:267–8; Jonathan Williams to TJ, 20 Sept. 1808, and TJ to Williams, 28 Oct. 1808 [both DLC]).

¹ Dupl: "appobation." RC: "approbation."
² RC: "inconceivable misfortune."
³ RC here adds "lately."
⁴ Preceding six words not in RC.
⁵ Dupl: "Nantz." RC: "Nantes."
⁶ Preceding six words not in RC.
⁷ Dupl: "caracters." RC: "characters."
⁸ Preceding twelve words not in RC.

To James Savage

SIR   Monticello Feb. 9. 15.

I thank you for the volume of American State papers you have been so kind as to send me. the Collection certainly will be a very useful one. the messages of the Presidents giving to Congress a state of the nation regularly once a year, with the documents supporting it, do in fact amount to a history of the nation, with the advantage of being authentic. the message of Dec. 6. 1805. was not printed at the time because it was confidential, which was the case also of some of the document[s] particularly the letters of our ministers. nor am I quite certain that the National Intelligencer always published all the documents. they might sometimes perhaps omit those they thought uninteresting. the loose sheets printed daily for the use of the members would be most to be depended on, if a copy has been preserved by any of your members. Accept the a[ssurances] of my great respect.

                                             TH JEFFERSON

PoC (ViW: TC-JP); on verso of reused address cover of Samuel M. Burnside to TJ, 23 Jan. 1815; edge chipped, mutilated at seal; at foot of text: "Mr James Savage"; endorsed by TJ.

To William Thornton

DEAR SIR   Monticello Feb. 9. 15.

I have to thank you for the drawing of the beautiful hydraulic machine with which you favored me in yours of Jan. 11. in simplicity and effect it promises to go far beyond Montgolfier's hydraulic ram. I have endeavored to constitute a supply of water at Monticello by cisterns for recieving and preserving the rain water falling on my buildings. these would furnish me 600. galls of water a day, if I could by cement or plaister make them hold water. but this I have not been able to do as yet. they are of brick, 4. in number[1] being cubes of 8.f. sunk in the ground.

I did not, till your letter, know of mr Crosbie's claim to Janes's loom. my own manufactory is for my family only, & employs but two looms. the ingenuity of Janes's would have induced me to try one of his, if his patentee would have taken Janes's price (40.D.) but his demand of 100.D. has revolted every one, and I have never yet heard of a single one sold. Crosbie's claim will compleatly prevent their sale.

[252]

whenever a settlement of the right shall render the use safe, and the price become reasonable, I shall be glad to procure one for myself, and to recommend them to my neighbors. mr Gouldsborough has favored me with a letter on Crosbie's claim.

I thank you for the list of patents, as I also shall for your filter for water, cyder E⁺c. my expectation is that my cistern water may be made potable, which will add much to their value. I salute you with great esteem and respect.   TH: JEFFERSON

RC (PPAmP: Thomas Jefferson Papers); addressed: "Doct⁷ William Thornton Washington Col."; franked; postmarked Charlottesville, 15 Feb.; with unrelated drawing of a scorpion in an unidentified hand and notes by Thornton relating to his 3 Apr. 1815 reply to TJ on address cover: "Good mortar 2 or 3 of Sand to one of lime—This is suffered to stand until hard—It is then broken down again, and mixed with molasses, wᶜʰ would not take a quart to a Bushell. This

is to be <*laid on*> immediately, plastered on in a thin coat, & when sufficiently dry lay on another thin coat which will fill up all the cracks." PoC (MHi); on verso of reused address cover to TJ; endorsed by TJ.

Walter Janes's PATENTEE was Francis C. Clopper.

¹ TJ here canceled "holding."

To William Duane

DEAR SIR   Monticello Feb. 10. 15.

I wrote to you on the 24ᵗʰ of Nov. on the subject of mr Tracy's book. a mr Ticknor from Massachusets was lately with me, and being to proceed to Paris within about four weeks offers so safe a conveyance for my letters that I cannot avoid writing to mr Tracy. I have hoped that the delay of your answer was occasioned by some prospect of publishing the work yourself, or of getting it published to your own mind, either of which I should prefer. if that be the case, only be so good as to let me know what I may with certainty say to mr Tracy. if it be not the case, I must renew my request for the return of the MS. either with or without the translation, as you think best, that I may be enabled to discharge the trust reposed in me by mr Tracy.

Our late news from New Orleans is enlivening. the personal interest which British ministers find in a state of war, rather than of peace, in riding the various contractors, and other douceurs, on such enormous expenditures of money, and recruiting their broken fortunes, or making new ones forbids the hope of peace as long as, by any delusions, they can keep the temper of the nation up to the war-point. but their disasters of the last campaign on the Northern frontier, their recent discomfiture at N. Orleans, especially if it should end in the capture of their army, the evaporation of their hopes at Hartford,[1] and the reprobation of their conduct by all Europe, may excite a clamor productive of peace. I suppose Cobbet will not let these things be unknown to the nation. still the best stimulus to peace is an effective provision of men and money for war. I do not much attend to the proceedings of Congress: but as far as I have noted them, I am not over-confident in the means proposed for either. experience however of what will not do, will lead them to what will, and, with their good intentions, all will come right. Accept the assurance of my great esteem & respect.

TH: JEFFERSON

RC (NjP: Andre deCoppet Collection); addressed: "Gen[l] William Duane Philadelphia"; franked; postmarked Charlottesville, 15 Feb.; mistakenly endorsed by Duane as a letter of 15 Feb.

1815. PoC (DLC); on verso of reused address cover to TJ; endorsed by TJ.

[1] Manuscript: "Harford."

To John B. Spargella

Monticello Feb. 10. 15.

Th: Jefferson presents his compliments to mr Spargella, and his thanks for the elegant engravings of which he has been so kind as to send him half a dozen copies. he fears it will be to the design and execution, more than to the choice of subject they may owe their success. he tenders nevertheless his acknolegements to mr Spargella[1] for his partiality in the selection of a subject for the manifestation of talent, and with his best wishes for his success, he salutes him with great consideration.

PoC (CSmH: JF-BA); dateline at foot of text; endorsed by TJ.

[1] Manuscript: "Spargetta."

Statement of Bedford and Campbell County Property Subject to Federal Tax

Property in Bedford and Campbell taxed by the general government.

ages.
- 71. Jame Hubbard.
- 67. Cate
- Bess.
- 65. Betty island.
- 61. Will. smith.
- Abby (age unknown)
- 48. Dinah.
- 47. Dick.
- Hal.
- 44. Hanah. Cate's
- 43. Armistead.
- 42. Jesse.
- 41. Nace
- 40. Caesar
- Austin.
- 38. Maria. Cate's
- 37. Sal. Will's
- 36. Nanny
- Gawen
- 31. Flora.
- 26. Cate. Betty's
- Cate. Suck's
- Fanny. Will's
- Sally. Cate's
- 25. Aggy. Dinah's
- 24. Daniel.
- 23. Lucinda.
- 22. Mary. Betty's
- Edy.
- 21. Reuben
- 20. Manuel.
- Stephen
- Evans.
- Hercules
- 18. Hanah. Dinah's

ages
- 17. Amy. Will's
- Milly Sall's.
- Cate. Rachael's
- 16. Maria. Nanny's
- Sally. Hanah's
- 15. Ambrose. Suck's
- Lucy. Dinah's
- Nisy. Maria's
- 13. Betty Sall's
- Phill. Nanny's
- 12. Jamy. Dinah's
- 10. Prince.
- Gawen.
- Johnny. Maria's
- Abby. Sall's
- 9. Jamy. Hanah's
- Briley. Dinah's
- 8. Joe. Suck's
- Milly. Nanny's
- Davy Cate's
- Edy. Sall's
- Aleck. Flora's
- 7. Rachael. Fanny's
- 6. Billy. Sally's
- George Dennis
- Phill. Hanah's
- Billy. Flora's
- 5. Martin. Sall's
- Shepherd. Suck's
- Melinda. Lucinda's
- Edmund. Hanah's
- Isaac. Maria's
- 4. Anderson. Sally's
- Anderson. Nanny's

ages
- 3. Moses. Sal's
- John. Cate's
- Rhody. Fanny's
- Boston. Flora's
- 2. Nancy. Edy's
- George Welsh.
- Janetta. Nanny's
- Rebecca. Lucinda's
- Mary-Anne. Sall's
- Henry. Sally's
- Sally. Aggy's
- 1. Zacharias. Fanny's
- Sandy. Milly's
- 0. Solomon. Cate's
- Ellen. Nanney's
- Gabriel. Mary's

Land. 2184. a^s of Poplar forest.

214.	Dan. Robinson's patent.
29.	from Ben Johnson
380.	Callaway's patent.
183.	John Robinson's patent.
800.	on Buffalo waters.
3790.	acres in Bedford & Campbell

Furniture tax. I have not seen the law of Congress imposing this. according to the newspaper statement beds, bedding & kitchen furniture is exempt, & where the rest of the furniture of a house does not exceed 200.D. it pays nothing. I consider my furniture at Poplar forest as under that value. but of this the Assessor will judge for himself on an examination[1] of the furniture.

TH: JEFFERSON
Monticello Feb. 11. 1815.

MS (Christie's, New York City, 2004); entirely in TJ's hand; with TJ's Statement of Bedford and Campbell County Property Subject to State Tax, 11 Feb. 1815, on other side of sheet.

The FURNITURE TAX was the 18 Jan. 1815 "Act to provide additional revenues for defraying the expenses of government, and maintaining the public credit, by laying duties on household furniture, and on gold and silver watches" (*U.S. Statutes at Large*, 3:186–92).

A month later TJ paid the direct tax on Poplar Forest in full and duly obtained a receipt for $189.40 dated 14 Mar. 1815 (MS in ViU: TJP; on a small scrap; entirely in Deputy Sheriff William Salmon's hand and signed by him for Thomas B. Greer; endorsed by TJ: "Sheriff Bedford").

[1] Manuscript: "examinetion."

Statement of Bedford and Campbell County Property Subject to State Tax

Property in Bedford and Campbell taxed by the State.

		D C
46. slaves of 12. years old & upwards.	@ 80. cents	36.80
of 9. years and under 12.	@ 50	19.50[1]
12. horses and colts	@ 21.	2.52
39. cattle	@ 3.	1.17
4. bookcases with mahogany sashes	@ 50.	2.
3. parts of Dining tables mahogany	@ 25.	.75
4. Pembroke tables, say tea tables.[2] mahogany	@ 25.	1.
		63.74

3790. acres of land @ 85. cents on the 100.D. value
a Dwelling house (of more than 500.D. value)

TH: JEFFERSON
Monticello Feb. 11. 15.

MS (Christie's, New York City, 2004); entirely in TJ's hand; with TJ's Statement of Bedford and Campbell County Property Subject to Federal Tax, 11 Feb. 1815, on other side of sheet.

[1] TJ calculated this entry as if all thirty-nine of his Bedford and Campbell County slaves under the age of twelve were between nine and eleven years old.
[2] Manuscript: "teatables."

To William Caruthers

Monticello Feb. 11. 15.

Th: Jefferson presents his compliments to mr Caruthers and asks the favor of him to have the inclosed letter delivered to the officer to whom it is addressed, as the name is unknown to him. he has left it unsealed for mr Caruther's perusal, as he may be able to explain it to the Assessor & Collector. he salutes him with great esteem & respect.

RC (ViU: TJP); dateline at foot of text; addressed: "William Caruthers esq. Lexington Virginia"; franked; postmarked Charlottesville, 15 Feb.; endorsed by Caruthers. Not recorded in SJL. Enclosure: TJ to the Federal Assessor for Rockbridge County, 11 Feb. 1815.

To the Federal Assessor for Rockbridge County

SIR   Monticello Feb. 11. 15.

I own a tract of land of 157. acres in the county of Rockbridge including the Natural bridge, which being liable to the tax laid by Congress it is my duty to give you notice of it. I have[1] leased to Dr William Thornton of Richmond a site on it for a shot manufactory, and nothing being provided in the lease as to taxes, I propose to pay those on the land, as he will of whatever improvements he makes on it. I therefore ask the favor of you to make the assessments distinct that each of us may know our separate part altho' he will in the first instance pay the whole.

Accept the assurance of my respect   TH: JEFFERSON

PoC (MHi); on verso of reused address cover to TJ; at foot of text (mutilated): "Th[e] Assessor for the county of Rockbridge"; endorsed by TJ, with his notes above and below endorsement: "Taxes" and "inclosed under cover to Wm Caruthers." Enclosed in TJ to William Caruthers, 11 Feb. 1815.

The assessor for ROCKBRIDGE and Augusta counties was William Abney (U.S. Statutes at Large, 3:24 [22 July 1813]; JEP, 2:439, 440 [13, 20 Dec. 1813]). Thornton's first name was Philip, not WILLIAM.

[1] Preceding two words interlined in place of "it is."

From Randolph Jefferson

DEAR BROTHER. —   Snowden February 13: 1815

I have concluded to send over Squire, after the bitch that you was so good to give me, when I was over as I should be extreemly happy[1] to get her, if she has not pupt, or if she has and he can make out to bring her and some of the pupies. I can send over for the rest at Easter,[2] without mr Randolph will let old Stephen come over and bring the rest for me. if the bitch has no[3] more then too Squire can bring them him self, I have waited expecting to see stephen[4] every day, but the reason I suppose his not coming is that mr Randolph has not reternd yet from below. as for my watch I have bin without her so long that I am intirely weand from her, however if mr Randolph should of reternd and brought her, I should be extreemly happy once more to receive her agane. I would be extreemly oblige to you for a few scions,[5] of your good fruit, of apple & cherry. if it should not be too late to moove them now, or any other fruit that you would oblige me with, that you have to spare also a few cabbage seed and ice[6] lettuce seed. if it is but one half spoon full provided you have as many to spare without disfernishing yourself. I expect I shall be summonsed over to march court on account of Randolph & Craven patons sute in albemarle court. I am at the greatest loss immagenable for the want of my watch. if mr Randolph has not reternd yet I shall be oblige to send down to verino but I am still in hopes there will not be any occasion to do that, as he must certainly have reternd long before this time. my wife Joins me in love and respect to you and family. I am your most[7] affectionately.— RH; JEFFERSON

do pray Sir give Squire such derections in respect to the bitch as you think most necessary. and you will very much oblige[8]
    your most affectionately. RH: JEFFERSON

RC (ViU: TJP-CC); mistakenly endorsed by TJ as a letter of 15 Feb. 1815 received that same day and so recorded in SJL; notation at foot of text by TJ: "apples cherries cabbage ice lettuce."

Craven Peyton's (PATONS) lawsuit against Randolph Jefferson's son Isham Randolph Jefferson concerned the payment of a debt (Albemarle Co. Order Book [1813–15], 460–1). Varina (VERI-NO) was Thomas Mann Randolph's estate in Henrico County.

[1] Manuscript: "hapy."
[2] Manuscript: "Esther."
[3] Word interlined.
[4] Manuscript: "stphen."
[5] Manuscript: "science."
[6] Word interlined.
[7] Word interlined.
[8] Jefferson here canceled "me."

To William H. Crawford

DEAR SIR   Monticello Feb. 14.[1] 15.

I have to thank you for your letter of June 16. it presents those special views of the state of things in Europe, for which we look in vain into newspapers. they tell us only of the downfall of Bonaparte, but nothing of the temper, the views, and secret workings of the high agents in these transactions. altho' we neither expected, nor wished any act of friendship from Bonaparte, and always detested him as a tyrant, yet he gave emplo[y]ment to much of the force of the nation who was our common enemy. so far his downfall was illy timed for us. it gave to England an opportunity to turn full handed on us, when we were unprepared.   no matter. we can beat her on our own soil, leaving the laws of the ocean to be settled by the maritime powers of Europe, who are equally oppressed & insulted by the usurpations of England on that element. our particular and separate grievance is only the impressment of our citizens. we must sacrifice the last dollar and drop of blood to rid us of that badge of slavery; and it must rest with England alone to say whether it is worth eternal war, for eternal it must be if she holds to the wrong. she will probably find that the 6000. citizens she took from us by impressment have already cost her ten thousand guineas a man, and will cost her in addition the half of that annually, during the continuance of the war, besides the captures on the ocean, & the loss of our commerce. she might certainly find cheaper means of manning her fleet, or, if to be manned at this ex- pence, her fleet will break her down. the 1st year of our warfare by land was disastrous. Detroit, Queen's town, French town, & Bever- dam witness that. but the 2d was generally succesful, and the 3d en- tirely so, both by sea and land, for I set down the coup de main at Washington as more disgraceful to England than to us. the victories of the last year at Chippeway, Niagara, Fort Erie, Plattsburg, and New Orleans, the capture of their two fleets on Lakes Erie and Champlain, and repeated triumphs of our frigates over hers, when- ever engaging with equal force, shew that we have officers now be- coming prominent, and capable of making them feel the superiority of our means, in a war on our own soil.   our means are abun- dant both as to men and money, wanting only skilful arrangement, and experience alone brings skill. as to men, nothing wiser can be de- vised than what the Secretary at war (Monroe) proposed in his Re- port at the commencement of Congress. it would have kept our regular army always[2] of necessity full, and by classing our militia ac- cording to ages,[3] would have put them into a form ready for whatever service, distant or at home, should require them. Congress have not adopted it, but their next experiment will lead to it. our financial sys- tem is least arranged. the fatal possession of the whole circulating medium by our banks, the excess of those institutions, and their present discredit, cause all our difficulties. treasury notes of small as well as high denomination, bottomed on a tax which would redeem them in 10. years, would place at our disposal the whole circulating medium of the US. a fund of credit sufficient to carry us thro' any probable length of war. a small issue of such paper is now commencing. it will immediately supersede the bank paper; nobody recieving that now but for the purposes of the day, and never in payments which are to lie by for any time. in fact, all the banks having declared they will not give cash in exchange for their own notes, these circulate merely because there is no other medium of exchange. as soon as the Treasury notes get into circulation, the others will cease to hold any competition with them. I trust that another year will confirm this experiment, and restore this fund to the public, who ought never more to permit it's being filched from them by private speculators and disorganisers of the circulation.

Do they send you from Washington the Historical Register of the US? it is published there annually, and gives a succinct and judicious history of the events of the war, not too long to be inserted in the European newspapers and would keep the European public truly informed, by correcting the lying statements of the British papers. it gives too all public documents of any value. Niles's Weekly Register is also an excellent repository of facts & documents and has the advantage of coming out weekly, whereas the other is yearly.

This will be handed you by mr Ticknor, a young gentleman of Boston, of high education, and great promise. after going thro' his studies here, he goes to Europe to finish them, and to see what is to be seen there. he brought me high recommendations from mr Adams and others, and from a stay of some days with me, I was persuaded he merited them, as he will whatever attentions you will be so good as to shew him. I pray you to accept the assurance of my great esteem and respect.   TH: JEFFERSON

P.S. Feb. 26. On the day of the date of this letter the news of peace reached Washington, and this place two days after.[4] I am glad of it, altho', no provision being made against the impressment of our seamen, it is in fact but an Armistice, to be terminated by the first act of impressment committed on an American citizen. it may be thought that useless blood was spilt at New Orleans, after the treaty of peace had been actually signed and ratified. I think it had many valuable uses. it proved the fidelity of the Orleanese to the US. it proved that New Orleans can be defended both by land & water; that the Western country will fly to it's relief (of which ourselves had doubted before) that our militia are heroes when they have heroes to lead them on; and that when unembarrassed by field evolutions, which they do not understand, their skill in the fire-arm, and deadly aim, give them great advantages over regulars. What nonsense for the manakin prince regent to talk of their conquest of the country East of the Penobscot river! then, as in the revolutionary war, their conquests were never more than of the spot on which their army stood, never extended beyond the range of their cannon shot. if England is now wise or just enough to settle peaceably the question of impressment, the late treaty may become one of peace, and of long peace. we owe to their past follies and wrongs the incalculable advantage of being made independant of them for every material manufacture. these have taken such root, in our private families especially, that nothing now can ever extirpate them.

PoC (DLC); edge trimmed. Tr (MHi); fragment; posthumous copy. Enclosed in George Ticknor to TJ, 21 Mar. 1815, TJ to John Graham, 14 May 1815, and probably also in TJ to Ticknor, 3 Mar. 1815 (see note to TJ to Ticknor, 19 Mar. 1815).

Colonel Charles Boerstler surrendered the United States Army detachment under his command at the Battle of Beaver Dams (BEVERDAM), which took place on 24 June 1813 a few miles outside of Fort George, Canada (Malcomson, *Historical Dictionary*, 31–2). In his speech of 8 Nov. 1814 at the opening of the British parliament, the PRINCE RE-GENT George claimed that "The expedition directed from Halifax to the northern coast of the United States . . . has been followed by the immediate submission of the extensive and important district, east of the Penobscot river" in Maine (Hansard, *Parliamentary Debates*, 29:1–4, quote on p. 2).

[1] Reworked from what appears to be "26."
[2] Word interlined.
[3] Final letter of this word repeated due to polygraph malfunction.
[4] Tr begins here and continues to end of text.

To Lafayette

MY DEAR FRIEND   Monticello Feb. 14. 15.

Your letter of Aug. 14. has been recieved and read again & again with extraordinary pleasure. it is the first glimpse which has been furnished me of the interior workings of the late unexpected, but fortunate revolution of your country. the newspapers told us only that the great beast was fallen; but what part in this the patriots acted, and what the egoists, whether the former slept while the latter were awake to their own interests only, the hireling scribblers of the English press said little, and knew less. I see now the mortifying alternative under which the patriot there is placed, of being either silent, or disgraced by an association in opposition with the remains of Bonapartyism. a full measure of liberty is not now perhaps to be expected by your nation; nor am I confident they are prepared to preserve it. more than a generation will be requisite, under the administration of reasonable laws favoring the progress of knolege in the general mass of the people, and their habituation to an independant security of person and property, before they will be capable of estimating the value of freedom, and the necessity of a sacred adherence to the principles on which it rests for preservation. instead of that liberty which takes root and growth in the progress of reason, if recovered by mere force or accident, it becomes, with an unprepared people, a tyranny still, of the many, the few, or the one.   possibly you may remember, at the date of the jeu de paume, how earnestly I urged yourself, and the patriots of my acquaintance, to enter then into a compact with the king, securing freedom of religion, freedom of the press, trial by jury, Habeas corpus, & a national legislature, all of which it was known he would then yield; to go home, and let these work on the amelioration of the condition of the people, until they should have rendered them capable of more, when occasions would not fail to arise for communicating to them more. this was as much as I then thought them able to bear soberly & usefully for themselves. you thought otherwise, and that the dose might still be larger. and I found you were right; for subsequent events proved they were equal to the constitution of 1791. unfortunately some of the most honest and enlightened of our patriotic friends, (but closet politicians merely, unpracticed in the knolege of man) thought more could still be obtained & borne. they did not weigh the hazards of a transition from one form of government to another, the value of what they had already rescued from those hazards, and might hold in security if they pleased, nor the imprudence of giving up the certainty of such a degree of liberty, under a limited monarch, for the uncertainty of a little more under the form of a republic. you differed from them. you were for stopping there, and for securing the constitution which the National Assembly had obtained. here too you were right; and from this fatal error of the republicans, from their separation from yourself & the Constitutionalists in their councils, flowed all the subsequent sufferings and crimes of the French nation. the hazards of a second change fell upon them by the way. the foreigner gained time to anarchize by gold the government he could not overthrow by arms, to crush in their own councils the genuine republicans, by the fraternal embraces of exaggerated and hired pretenders, and to turn the machine of jacobinism from the change, to the destruction, of order: and, in the end, the limited monarchy they had secured was exchanged for the unprincipled and bloody tyranny of Robespierre, and the equally unprincipled and maniac tyranny of Bonaparte. you are now rid of him, and I sincerely wish you may continue so. but this may depend on the wisdom & moderation of the restored dynasty. it is for them now to read a lesson in the fatal errors of the republicans; to be contented with a certain portion of power, secured by formal compact with the nation, rather than, grasping at more, hazard all upon uncertainty, and risk meeting the fate of their predecessor, or a renewal of their own exile. we are just informed too of an example which merits, if true, their most profound contemplation. the gazettes say that Ferdinand of Spain is dethroned, and his father reestablished on the basis of their new constitution. this order of magistrates must therefore see that altho' the attempts at reformation have not succeeded in their whole length, and some recession from the ultimate point has taken place, yet that men have by no means fallen back to their former passiveness, but, on the contrary, that a sense of their rights, and a restlessness to obtain them, remain deeply impressed on every mind, and, if not quieted by reasonable relaxations of power, will break out like a volcano on the first occasion and overwhelm every thing again in it's way. I always thought the present king an honest and moderate man: and, having no issue, he is under a motive the less for yielding to personal considerations. I cannot therefore but hope that the patriots in and out of your legislature, acting in phalanx, but temperately and wisely, pressing unremittingly the principles omitted in the late capitulation of the king, and watching the occasions which the course of events will create, may get those principles engrafted into it, and sanctioned by the solemnity of a national act.

With us the affairs of war have taken the more favorable turn which was to be expected. our 30. years of peace had taken off, or superannuated, all our revolutionary officers of experience and grade; and our first draught in the lottery of untried characters had been most unfortunate. the delivery of the fort and army of Detroit by the traitor Hull, the disgrace at Queen's-town under Van Renslaer, the massacre at Frenchtown under Winchester, and surrender of Boerstler in an open field to one third of his own numbers, were the inauspicious beginnings of the first year of our warfare. the second witnessed but the single miscarriage occasioned by the disagreement of Wilkinson and Hampton, mentioned in my letter to you of Nov. 30. 13. while it gave us the capture of York by Dearborn and Pike, the capture of Fort George by Dearborn also, the capture of Proctor's army on the Thames by Harrison, Shelby and Johnson, and that of the whole British fleet on Lake Erie by Perry. the 3^d year has been a continued series of victories. to wit of Brown and Scott at

Chippeway, of the same at Niagara, of Gaines over Drummond at Fort Erie that of Brown over Drummond at the same place[1] the capture of another fleet on Lake Champlain by McDonough, the entire defeat of their army under Prevost, on the same day by McComb, and now recently their defeats at New Orleans by Jackson, Coffee and Carroll, with the loss of 4000. men out of 9600, with their two Generals Packingham and Gibbs killed and a third Keane wounded, mortally as is said. this series of successes has been tarnished only by the conflagrations at Washington, a coup de main differing from that at Richmond, which you remember, in the revolutionary war, in the circumstance only that we had in that case but 48. hours notice that an enemy had arrived within our Capes; whereas at Washington there was abundant previous notice. the force designated by the President was the double of what was necessary; but failed, as is the general opinion, through the insubordination of Armstrong, who would never believe the attack intended until it was actually made, and the sluggishness of Winder before the occasion, and his indecision during it. still, in the end, the transaction has helped rather than hurt us, by arrousing the general indignation of our country, and by marking to the world of Europe the Vandalism and brutal character of the English government: it has merely served to immortalize their infamy.[2] and add further that, thro' the whole period of the war, we have beaten them single-handed at sea, and so thoroughly established our superiority over them with equal force, that they retire from that kind of contest, and never suffer their frigates to cruize singly. the Endymion would never have engaged the frigate[3] President but knowing herself backed by three frigates & a Razée,[4] who though somewhat slower sailors, would get up before she could be taken. the disclosure to the world of the fatal secret that they can be beaten at sea with an equal force, the evidence furnished by the military operations of the last year that experience is rearing us officers who, when our means shall be fully under way, will plant our standard on the walls of Quebec and Halifax, their recent and signal disaster at New Orleans, & the evaporation of their hopes from the Hartford convention, will probably raise a clamor in the British nation which will force their ministry into peace. I say force them; because, willingly, they would never be at peace. the British ministers find, in a state of war rather than of peace, by riding the various contractors, and recieving douceurs on the vast expenditures of the war-supplies, that they recruit their broken fortunes, or make new ones, and therefore will not make peace, as long as, by any delusions they can keep the temper of the nation up to the war-point.　　they found some hopes on the state of our finances. it is true that the excess of our banking institutions, and their present discredit, has shut us out from the best source of credit we could ever command with certainty. but the foundations of credit still remain to us, and need but skill, which experience will soon produce, to marshal them into an order which may carry us thro' any length of war. but they have hoped more in their Hartford convention. their fears of republican France being now done away, they are directed to republican America, and they are playing the same game for disorganization here which they played in your country. the Marats, the Dantons & Robespierres of Massachusets are in the same pay, under the same orders, and making the same efforts to anarchize us, as their prototypes in France were. I do not say that all who met at Hartford were under the same motives of money: nor were those of France. some of them are Outs, and wish to be Ins; some the mere dupes of the Agitators, or of their own party passions; while the Maratists alone are in the real secret. but they have very different materials to work on. the yeomanry of the US. are not the Canaille of Paris. we might safely give them leave to go thro' the US. recruiting their ranks, and I am satisfied they could not raise one single regiment (gambling merchants and silk stocking clerks excepted) who would support them in any effort to separate from the union. the cement of this union is in the heart blood of every American. I do not believe there is on earth a government established on so immovable a basis. let them, in any state, even in Massachusets itself, raise the standard of[5] Separation, and it's citizens will rise in mass, and do justice themselves on their own incendiaries. if they could have induced the government to some effort of suppression, or even to enter into discussion with them, it would have given them some importance, have brought them into some notice. but they have not been able to make themselves even a subject of conversation, either of public or private societies. a silent contempt has been the sole notice they could excite; consoled indeed, some of them, by the <u>palpable</u> favors of Philip.　　have then no fears for us, my friend. the grounds of these exist only in English newspapers, credited or endowed by the Castlereaghs or the Cannings, or some other such models of pure & uncorrupted virtue. their military heroes by land and sea, may sink our oyster boats, rob our henroosts, burn our negro huts and run off. but a campaign or two more will relieve them from further trouble or expence in defending their American possessions.

you once gave me a copy of the journal of your campaign in Virginia in 1781, which I must have lent to some one of the undertakers to write the history of the revolutionary war, and forgot to reclaim. I conclude this because it is no longer among my papers, which I have very diligently searched for it, but in vain. an author of real ability is now writing that part of the history of Virginia. he does it in my neighborhood, and I lay open to him all my papers. but I possess none, nor has he any which can enable him to do justice to your faithful and able services in that campaign. if you could be so good as to send me another copy, by the very first vessel bound to any port of the US. it might be here in time; for altho' he expects to begin to print within a month or two, yet you know the delays of these undertakings. at any rate it might be got in as a supplement. the old C^t Rochambeau gave me also his Memoire of the operations at York, which is gone the same way, and I have no means of applying to his family for it. perhaps you could render them as well as us the service of procuring another copy.

I learn with real sorrow the deaths of M. and M^{de} de Tessé. they made an interesting part in the idle reveries, in which I have sometimes indulged myself, of seeing all my friends at Paris once more, for a month or two; a thing impossible, which however I never permitted myself to despair of. the regrets however of 73. at the loss of friends may be the less, as the time is shorter within which we are to meet again, according to the creed of our education.

I shall write to M. Tracy, and wait, in order to do it, only for an answer from the person who undertook the translation and printing the work he last sent me. I have been very ill used by this person. flattered from time to time by his assurances of progress, which still, like my shadow walked before me, when pressed for a conclusion the last autumn, he informed me his translation was compleat, but he believed he must decline the printing. I immediately applied elsewhere, and procured an undertaker to publish it, on which, by a first letter I requested the original to be returned to me. that being unanswered I repeated the request by a second letter, the answer to which is what I now await to enable me to write on full information to mr Tracy. the distance of 300. miles between this and Philadelphia increases difficulties. on reciept of his answer I will do whatever is necessary, and make it the subject of a letter to M. Tracy, which I trust will be in time for this conveyance.   This letter will be handed you by mr Ticknor a young gentleman of Boston of great erudition, indefatigable industry and preparation for a life of distinction in his own country. he passed a few days with me here, brought high recommendation from mr Adams and others, & appeared in every respect to merit them. he is well worthy of those attentions which you so kindly bestow on our countrymen, and for those he may recieve I shall join him in acknoleging personal obligations. I salute you with assurances of my constant and affectionate friendship & respect.

TH: JEFFERSON

P.S. Feb. 26. 15. my letter had not yet been sealed when I recieved news of our peace. I am glad of it, and especially that we closed our war, with the eclat of the action at New Orleans. but I consider it as an armistice only, because no security is provided against the impressment of our seamen. while this is unsettled we are in hostility of mind with England, altho actual deeds of arms may be suspended by a truce. if she thinks the exercise of this outrage is worth eternal war, eternal war it must be, or extermination of the one or the other party. the first act of impressment she commits on an American will be answered by reprisal, or by a declaration of war here, and the interval must be merely a state of preparation for it. in this we have much to do, in further fortifying our seaport towns, providing military stores, classing and disciplining our militia, arranging our financial system, and above all pushing our domestic manufactures, which have taken such root as never again can be shaken. once more god bless you.

RC (NjMoHP: Lloyd W. Smith Collection); at foot of first page: "M. de la Fayette." PoC (DLC). Probably enclosed in TJ to George Ticknor, 3 Mar. 1815, for which see note to TJ to Ticknor, 19 Mar. 1815.

At a celebrated 20 June 1789 meeting at an indoor tennis court (the JEU DE PAUME), the deputies of the third estate declared that they would not disband until they had provided France with a constitution (William Doyle, *Origins of the French Revolution*, 2d ed. [1988], 174). Ferdinand VII of Spain had not, in fact, been replaced by HIS FATHER, the former king Charles IV. The LATE CAPITULATION of Louis XVIII, the so-called "Charter of 1814," established a bicameral legislature in France, with the lower house to be elected by limited male suffrage, and a bill of rights to preserve freedom of religion, speech, and the press (Connelly, *Napoleonic France*, 107).

The engagement AT NIAGARA was the 25 July 1814 Battle of Lundy's Lane. During the siege of FORT ERIE, General Edward Gaines repulsed an attempt by British commander Gordon Drummond to take the stronghold by storm on 15 Aug. 1814, and General Jacob Brown launched a sortie on 17 Sept. that was followed, a few days later, by a British withdrawal (Malcomson, *Historical Dictionary*, 169–71, 172–4, 298–300). TJ greatly exaggerated the losses suffered by the British under General Edward Pakenham (PACKINGHAM) at the Battle of New Orleans (Stagg, *Madison's War*, 498). The USS PRESIDENT was captured on 15 Jan. 1815 by a British squadron that included HMS *Endymion* (Malcomson, *Historical Dictionary*, 315).

The FAVORS OF PHILIP of Macedon were bribes (see "philippize," *OED*). The AUTHOR OF REAL ABILITY was Louis H. Girardin. TJ considered himself to have been VERY ILL USED by William Duane.

The new UNDERTAKER TJ had found to publish Destutt de Tracy's manuscript was Joseph Milligan.

[1] Preceding nine words interlined.
[2] Preceding eight words interlined,

with the caret mistakenly placed in front of the colon.
[3] Word interlined.
[4] RC: "Raseé." PoC corrected by TJ to "Razée."
[5] Manuscript: "of of."

From Joseph Dougherty

DEAR SIR.   Washington City Feb. 15th 1815

Thinking that I might profit by being employ[d] to superintend the[1] bringing your library to Washington: I offered my Services to the library committe—who asked me what I would ask to bring it—to which I could not give a satisfactory answer before I heard from you.

will you Sir do me the favour to Say; how many waggons in your opinion would be required to bring the books—whether any waggons could be procured in your neighbourhood—whether boxes: or plank to make box[s] can be had there—how many days a waggon could travel it in—and how many boxes; and what the probable cost.

waggoners ask 8 dollars per day.

As the library committe, as also myself, will be guided by the contents of your letter to me: will you please Sir to write me as Soon as you can make it convenient.

I am Sir your Humble Serv[t]   JO[s] DOUGHERTY

The treaty of piece betwen the U.S & G.B. was laid befor the Senate to day.

The Senate adj[2] before they acted on it. It is generally Supposed that it will be confirm[d]   J. D.

RC (DLC); endorsed by TJ as received 23 Feb. 1815 and so recorded in SJL. RC (DLC); address cover only; with PoC of TJ to Joseph Milligan, 27 Feb. 1815, on verso; addressed: "Tho[s] Jefferson Esq[r] Late President of the U.S. Monticello"; franked; postmarked Washington, 15 Feb.

On hearing that President James Madison had approved $4 per day to cover Dougherty's expenditures in BRINGING TJ's library to Washington, D.C., Dougherty submitted an estimate of his daily "traveling expences": hiring of horses, $1.25; breakfast, 50 cents; dinner, 75 cents; supper and lodging, 75 cents;

and four gallons of oats and hay, $87\frac{1}{2}$ cents, for a total of 4.12\frac{1}{2}$ per day. He added that "To go the upper road to monticello—being a Country rout; the above charges would, perhaps, be considerably lessened" (Dougherty to Samuel H. Smith, 28 Mar. 1815 [DLC: J. Henley Smith Papers]). Madison agreed to a per diem of $5 in light of Dougherty's estimate, although he considered it too high. If Dougherty asked for still more, Madison suggested that someone else could probably be hired, but added that if no one suitable could be found for $5 he would go as high as $6 for Dougherty, to whom he was inclined to give "the preference" (Madison to Smith, 8 Apr. 1815

[NNGL, on deposit NHi]). Dougherty accepted the offer of $5 per day (Dougherty's Note on the Transportation of TJ's Library, 11 Apr. 1815 [DLC: J. Henley Smith Papers]).

Madison submitted the TREATY ending the War of 1812 to the United States Senate on 15 Feb. 1815, but it adjourned (ADJ) for the day with the matter still under consideration. The upper house unanimously ratified the treaty on the following day (*JEP*, 2:618–20).

[1] Manuscript: "the the."
[2] Dougherty here canceled "without."

From James Monroe

DEAR SIR   washington Feby 15. 1815

It is with infinite satisfaction that I inform you of the arrival of mr Carroll yesterday from Ghent, with a treaty of peace between the U States & G. Britain which was concluded on the 24. of Decr last. It is in all respects honorable to our country. no concession is made of any kind. Boundaries are to be trac'd on the principles of the treaty of 1783. by Com^{rs}, whose difference, should they disagree, is to be left to the decision of[1] a friendly power. It is evident that this treaty has been extorted from the British ministry. The late victory at New orleans, terminates this contest, with peculiar advantage, & even splendour, to the U States.

The treaty will be submitted to the senate, today, & I presume approved, without opposition. a Sketch will be in the intelligencer of this date.

my late severe indisposition prevented my writing you of late. the business which accumulated[2] the week, that I was[3] ill, has since borne heavily on me.

with great respect & esteem your friend   JA^s MONROE

RC (DLC); endorsed by TJ as received 17 Feb. 1815 and so recorded in SJL, which adds "peace" in square brackets. RC (DLC); address cover only; with PoC of TJ to George Hay, 26 Feb. 1815, on verso; addressed: "Thomas Jefferson Monticello"; franked; postmarked Washington, 15 Feb.

The Paris peace TREATY OF 1783 ended the Revolutionary War and established the boundaries between Great Britain and its former colonies in North America. A brief SKETCH of the 1814 treaty did appear on this date in the Washington *Daily National Intelligencer*.

[1] Preceding three words interlined.
[2] Manuscript: "accumuted."
[3] Manuscript: "will."

From Samuel H. Smith

DEAR SIR   Washington,[1] Feb. 15. 1815.

I tender you my cordial felicitations on the returning blessings of peace, the value of wch will be more sensibly realised by a people who have borne with fortitude the privations and met with courage the perils of war,—blessings to wch they have always had a moral right, and wch they now hold by[2] the tenure of physical power. How inestimable the benefits that have flowed from the possession of New Orleans! and how ridiculous the prophecies, that it would weaken, if not destroy the union! Its annexation to our territories saved us from[3] war: its brave defence has[4] insured us a lasting and honorable peace. May these precious consolations, unalloyed, descend with you to the grave!

Agreeably to the law lately passed, the Library Committee have desired the Secretary of the Treasury to issue, payable to your order, Treasury Notes to the amount of 23,950 dollars, this being the exact amount at wch the Library was valued by Mr Milligan. Will you advise me how these Notes shall be filled? If with your name, they must be sent to you for your endorsement before they can be transferred to another. If you wish to appropriate them here or elsewhere to any immediate purpose, a letter from you, desiring them to be filled with the name of any one, will be a sufficient warrant to the Secretary. I have requested that they be not made out until your answer is received. The Chairman of the Com^e has promised a return of the Catalogue, wch shall, as soon as received, be forwarded to you.[5]

The Committee, not considering themselves authorised to take any steps for the transportation of the Library, purpose to obtain a power from Congress to act on this point.

I am, with invariable sentiments of the highest regard & respect.

SA H SMITH

RC (DLC); at foot of text: "Thomas Jefferson Esquire"; endorsed by TJ as received 23 Feb. 1815 and so recorded in SJL. Dft (DLC: J. Henley Smith Papers); endorsed by Smith, in part, as "Respecti[n]g Library, &c."

The United States's ANNEXATION of Louisiana had helped to prevent a war with France. On 20 Feb. 1815 the CHAIRMAN of the congressional Joint Library Committee, Senator Robert H. Goldsborough, reported "a bill to provide a library room, and for transporting the library lately purchased from Thomas Jefferson, Esquire, to the city of Washington" (JS, 5:652).

[1] RC and Dft: "Washigton."
[2] Word interlined in Dft in place of "under."
[3] In Dft Smith here canceled "one."
[4] In Dft Smith here canceled "snatched."
[5] Sentence set as its own paragraph in Dft.

From Horatio G. Spafford

IF MY HON^D & ESTEEMED FRIEND   Albany, 2 Mo. 15, 1815.

Could be apprized how often the enquiry is made, "what does Mr Jefferson think of your improvement in Wheel Carriages;?" & did he know my own anxiety to learn, his goodness would certainly excuse my impatience. For myself, I am perfectly satisfied; but the public thinks little of my opinion, & much of thine. Thy bitterest foes allow thee the highest rank in science, & philosophy. I therefore want to know thy opinion, that I may anticipate the public opinion; & I pray thee to favor me with it, as soon as may be convenient to thyself. Did I not feel a far greater anxiety than could be supposed for this little thing, I would hardly have troubled thee about it. But, I have, in reserve, a grand disclosure relative to the laws of mechanics, for which this is merely preparatory.

I should esteem it an honor to present to thee my Certificate No. 1, for a Right to use my improvement; & if it will be accepted for use, I will gladly send it. The advertisement on the back of my pamphlet, is designed to extend a knowledge of my invention, & to announce my intention to defend my Right. Have the principles of my Patent ever been applied in this way before, in any age or Country? I write in haste, from a sick Room, devoted to the care of a most excellent Wife, & rely on thy indulgence. With gratitude & esteem, thy obliged friend,   H. G. SPAFFORD.

Permit me to congratulate thee on the news of peace. Although we do not know the conditions of the treaty; yet my confidence in our Ministers & our Government, assure my hopes.

RC (DLC); postscript written perpendicularly in left margin; addressed: "Hon. Thomas Jefferson, LL.D. Monticello, Virginia"; endorsed by TJ as received 23 Feb. 1815 and so recorded in SJL; written on a sheet folded to form four pages, with letter on p. 1, address on p. 2, canceled Spafford circular of 15 Apr. 1813 (see note to Spafford to TJ, 2 Aug. 1813) on p. 3, and endorsement on p. 4, which also has a copy of the enclosure to Spafford to TJ, 23 Jan. 1815.

At the back of Spafford, *Wheel-Carriages*, was an unpaginated ADVERTISEMENT dated Albany, 8 Feb. 1815, announcing that Spafford had received a United States patent for his improved carriage; naming the terms for obtaining the right to use the invention, including a base price of $5 per patent right, the granting of special privileges to "The first applicants in every considerable City or Town," and discounts to cartmen; and asserting that he would "vigilantly . . . protect and guard it against every infringement."

To Randolph Jefferson

DEAR BROTHER   Monticello Feb. 16. 15

After several disappointments in getting your watch from Richmond, I recieved[1] her a week ago. I sent for Stephen, who came to me and pretended to be sick. finding he did not mean to go to Snowden I had concluded to send her to you in a day or two, when Squire arrived. she appears to have gone well since I have had her, except a little too fast. with respect to Stephen mr Randolph got rid of him long ago. I am told he stays now at North Milton or somewhere there. he talks of going down the country to live. I send you some green curled Savoy cabbage seed. I have no ice lettuce, but send you what I think better the white loaf lettuce. the ice lettuce does not do well in a dry season. I send you also some sprout kale, the finest winter vegetable we have. sow it and plant it as cabbage, but let it stand out all winter. it will give you sprouts from the first of December to April. the bitch I had given you was caught in the very act of eating a sheep which she had killed. she was immediately hung, and as we had a fine litter at the same time from another bitch, I preserved one of them for you, which Squire is now gone for and will carry over to you.—I have for some years so entirely neglected my fruit trees that I have nothing in my nursery but refuse stuff, unknown & of no value.—there is a rumor here of peace; but that we shall have peace in the spring I have little doubt. I hold up my flour therefore till May. present my compliments to my sister and be assured of my sincere affections.

TH: JEFFERSON

Feb. 17. the news of peace is confirmed since yesterday so that I have little doubt of it. wheat and tob° will be immediately at a good price. corn which was at 27/ at Richmond will tumble down instantly, because their supplies which are always from the great corn country of Rappahanoc will come round by water now freely & immediately.

PoC (ViU: TJP-CC); above postscript: "mr Randolph Jefferson"; endorsed by TJ.

MY SISTER: TJ's sister-in-law, Mitchie B. Pryor Jefferson.

[1] Manuscript: "reciever."

Samuel Harrison Smith

Notes on Thomas Jefferson's Library at the Time of Sale (*page 1*)

Notes on Thomas Jefferson's Library at the Time of Sale (*page 2*)

Monticello Bookcases

I have ~~borrow~~ met with, and very kindly and opportunely offered me the means of reprocuring some part of the literary treasures which I have ceded to Congress to replace the devastation of British Vanda-lism at Washington. I cannot live without books: but fewer will suffice where amusement, and not use, is the only future object. I am about sending him a catalogue to which less than his criti-cal knolege of books would hardly be adequate. present my high respects to mrs Adams, and accept yourself the assurances of my affectionate attachment.

Th: Jefferson

"I cannot live without books"

T.I.

Ownership Marks on Jefferson's Books

Dining Room at Monticello

estimate
1. ℔. coffee
1. ℔ wh. sugar } daily.
2. ℔ brown do.

1. ℔ tea in 3. weeks.

1813.	coffee	wh. sug.	brown do	tea	brandy	whiskey	Cotton
Jan. 29.	10.			20			
Feb. 3	- - -	30℔	- - -	20	2 ℔.		
18	25	15¼	26	2			
Apr. 3.	15	20.	30				
19	-	-	-	2			
20	15	20	30				
June 14	- - -	25	50	2			
July 1.	- -	25	50	2			
21	- - -	25	50	2			
26	- - -		25	- -			
31			25				
Aug. 3	- - -	22					
4	- -	24					
17	4½	- - - -	280				
18	25.						
Sep. 15	- -	-	-	2			
Oct. 1	-	-	-	- -	2	1. canteen	
16	-	-		- -	2		
Dec. 18	25	2 loaves	- -	2			
1814. Jan. 3		2 loaves	- -	2		1 canteen	
6	-			- -			
18		2 loaves					
Feb. 18		2 loaves		2			
28	20.	- -	- - -			1. cant.	
Mar. 9	.		- - -		2 canteens		
10	- -	2.		2			
19	- -		15.				
Apr. 1	- -	2	50				
May 6.	-	-	20	2			
9.	30	4.					
July		2 loaves		2			:50.℔
Aug.		2 loaves	50,				
Oct. 5.	- -	- - -	15℔				
16	25	4 loaves	50,	2			

Jefferson's Notes on Household Consumption

George Ticknor

From Josiah Meigs

MY RESPECTED FRIEND   Washington City Feb. 16. 1815
I cannot resist an impulse which all good men must feel. With the multitude of my Brethren of the United States, I congratulate you on the astonishing events of which we have received information within a very short period.

Next to that Good Being who has kindly guided this great people to their present happy state, I feel an emotion of Gratitude to Mr Jefferson which I have not language to express.

Your evening of life will be calm, serene[1] & glorious.

I promise myself the pleasure of paying you my respects[2] personally in the course of the approaching summer—

I ask no excuse for this Note—It certainly needs none—

I am, very respectfully

Your

                              JOSIAH MEIGS.

RC (DLC); at foot of text: "Thomas Jefferson Esq"; endorsed by TJ as received 23 Feb. 1815 and so recorded in SJL, which mistakenly dates the letter 15 Feb. 1815.

[1] Manuscript: "serenee."
[2] Manuscript: "respcts."

From Horatio G. Spafford

HOND & ESTEEMED FRIEND—   Albany, 2 Mo. 18, 1815.
Having sent thee my little pamphlet on Wheel-Carriages, & being anxious to have the principles of my invention fairly tested, I now send thee a Certificate of a single Right to use my improvement. The Certificate is the first I have filled; & I have pleasure in presenting it to the Man, who, of all others, I deem the best qualified to understand the principles of my Patent, & whose favorable opinion would best recommend it to public attention. I hope thou wilt immediately put it to actual use. Thy mind will instantly determine the degree of utility, which this application promises; but most men[1] can only conceive it by mechanical demonstration. To afford opportunity for that, I have widely distributed my pamphlet; & I shall send some few Certificates[2] to distinguished characters, & some of my Correspondents in several States.

I shall wait with some impatience to hear from thee, & remain, with great esteem & respect, thy friend,

                          HORATIO GATES SPAFFORD.

RC (MHi); at foot of text: "Hon. Thomas Jefferson"; endorsed by TJ as received 3 Mar. 1815 and so recorded in SJL. Enclosure: Spafford's license to use his improved carriage patent, Albany, 18 Feb. 1815, priced at "$*10*" and numbered "*one*," granting "a single Right" to use his improvement "in any kind of Carriage having *four* wheels, and in any part of the United States, from this date to 11 Mo. 1, 1828"; stating that the certificate was transferable; and declaring that it could be used for a carriage either constructed on or adapted to these principles, and might be replaced when it wore out (printed form in MHi; with blanks filled in by Spafford rendered above in italics; signed and dated by Spafford).

[1] Word interlined.
[2] Manuscript: "Cirtificates."

From Benjamin Smith Barton

DEAR SIR,   Philadelphia, Feb. 19. 1815.

In about 3 weeks, perhaps less, I shall sail for Europe. I shall visit France; the borders at least of Italy; & England (for a short time) on my return. my first & great object is the recovery of my health, which has suffered most severely this winter: indeed, a few days ago, I was so ill, that I hardly hoped to be able to take the voyage.—Besides my health, I have some favourite schemes in science in view. I shall not go wholly a stranger; but I still know, that letters from you, to any of your Europpean friends,[1] especially the men of science & letters, will be eminently acceptable to me or any thing in a general way.—I am unacquainted with Mr Monroe, our Secretary. But you best know what would[2] be useful to me.

Can I be of any service to you in Europe? I hope to visit Florence, where I may pick up something[3] curious, relative to our country. Can you point out any objects for my inquiry? where do you think, Sir, I may chance to pass my summer, most agreeably to my health? Great heat is distressing to me.

whatever letters you may think proper to give me, I shall be happy to receive as early as you can: as I shall sail by the first good conveyance: to a French port, if I can.

I feel as though I stand, as an American,[4] upon higher ground now in Europe, than before the war. We can hardly have fallen in the estimation of Europe.—

I beg you to present my best respects to Col. Randolpth & all your family: & be assured, that I am, with very high respect, Dear Sir,

Your very obedient servant, &c., &c.,   B. S. BARTON.

RC (DLC); dateline at foot of text; endorsed by TJ as received 1 Mar. 1815 and so recorded in SJL.

[1] Manuscript: "frieds."

[2] Manuscript: "woul."
[3] Manuscript: "somethig."
[4] Manuscript: "stand, as an American, stand."

From Caesar A. Rodney

HONORED & DEAR SIR,   Wilmington Feb[y] 19. 1815.

It has been so long since I had the pleasure of hearing from you, that I feel anxious to know whether in the tranquil scenes of retirement you continue to enjoy your usual good health, for I know you must enjoy, unclouded, except by sickness, that serenity of mind, which is the constant companion of a pure conscience: The diadem of a man, who can repeat with truth, the sentiment of the Latin Lyric bard

"Integer vitæ, scelerisque purus."

And who can say with justice, to an enemy,

"Hic murus ahæneus esto Nil conscire sibi, nulla palescere culpa."

Tho' you can not have been, since you left Washington, without solicitude for the welfare of the Republic, you have been releived from that burthen of cares, necessarily incident, to the high office you, filled with so much dignity, & executed with such exalted integrity, directed by the most enlightened understanding, that you gained the affections of the people at large, & the warm attachment of every individual, capable of attachment, who had the honor of being more intimately connected with you, by the ties of friendship, or the relations of office. Fidelity & frankness to your friends was the unerring & undeviating maxim of your public life. And I shall never forget, your last advice, your parental legacy & injunction, to those you left behind, on going out of office, "To love one another as you had loved them." But I have often regretted, that I did not adhere rigidly, to the resolution I had formed, of retiring with you, from the post you had spontaniously bestowed, unsought, unsolicited & unexpected, on me, & which I accepted with a heart over flowing with gratitude. Your successor, however, intreated, and persuaded me to continue, & I remained until a just sense of honor & of character, compelled me to resign.

Since that time I have devoted myself to my profession, to improve my fortune, too much neglected & empaired by public life. For in the wreck, alone, of my furniture library &c on their passage to Washington in 1810 I sustained a loss of more than $5,000 besides being deprived of many book & articles not to be replaced. And you will recollect[1] the sacrifice I made, when at your solicitation, I was drawn from my practice, my only dependence, at an important period of life, to deprive of his seat in congress, one of our present ministers in Europe, who had been very violent & virulent against the Republican Chief magistrate & the Republican cause. My situation was the more delicate, because, tho we had been always opposed in public, we have been uniformly on the most intimate terms, in private life.

The war which I am happy to add, tho' a sincere advocate for it, is now ended, initiated me into the elements of the military science, of which I blush to own I was before ignorant, by inducing me to raise a company of artillery for the protection of our country against a cruel & vindictive enemy. My ambition prompted me, to qualify myself for the task of disciplining & commanding them.

The contest with England also dragged me into the Senate of this State with the veiw of urging the legislature to provide the means of defence within thier proper sphere, & this object was partially accomplished.

With these exceptions I have confined myself exclusively to the practice of the law.

Since we last parted what wonderful revolutions & changes have taken place at home & abroad. "Tempora mutantur," & some men have changed with the times. But I will not descant on this subject, when it shall be in my power to visit you I may. This pleasure & satisfaction, I anticipate before a very[2] long time. I have a great desire to spend a few days with the best of men, in his retreat of whom some future historian will say with more propriety, than it was said of Scipio in ancient or, Scarborough in modern times

"Nil non laudændum, aut fecit, aut dixit, aut sensit"

With every sentiment of esteem, of gratitude & affection I remain Dr Sir, Your Most Sincerely & Truly   C A. RODNEY

RC (DLC); endorsed by TJ as received 3 Mar. 1815 and so recorded in SJL.

INTEGER VITÆ, SCELERISQUE PURUS: "The man of unblemished life who is unstained by crime" (Horace, *Odes*, 1.22.1, in *Horace: Odes and Epodes*, trans. Niall Rudd, Loeb Classical Library [2004], 66–7). HIC MURUS AHÆNEUS . . . CULPA ("hic murus aeneus esto, nil conscire sibi, nulla pallescere culpa"): "Be this our wall of bronze, to have no guilt at heart, no wrongdoing to turn us pale," from Horace, *Epistles*, 1.1.60–1 (Fairclough, *Horace: Satires, Epistles and Ars Poetica*, 254–5). TO LOVE ONE ANOTHER AS YOU HAD LOVED THEM is a reworking of Jesus's admonition in the Bible to "love one another; as I have loved you" (John 13.34). In 1802 Rodney won his seat in the United States House of Representatives by defeating James A. Bayard, ONE OF OUR PRESENT MINISTERS IN EUROPE. TEMPORA MUTANTUR: "times change."

NIL NON LAUDÆNDUM . . . SENSIT ("nisi laudandum aut fectit aut dixit ac sensit"): "guilty of no act, word, or thought that was not praiseworthy" (Velleius Paterculus, *Historiae Romanae*, 1.12.3, in *Velleius Paterculus: Compendium of Roman History Res Gestae Divi Augusti*, trans. Frederick W. Shipley, Loeb Classical Library [1924; repr. 1961], 30–1). Philip Dormer Stanhope, 4th Earl of Chesterfield, included this quote in his 1759 sketch of Richard Lumley, 2d Earl of Scarborough (*Characters by Lord Chesterfield contrasted with Characters of the same Great Personages by other respectable Writers* [London, 1778], 41–4, quote on p. 42).

[1] Manuscript: "rcollect."
[2] Manuscript: "very a very."

To John Bankhead

DEAR SIR   Monticello Feb. 20. 15.

I take the liberty of writing to you on a subject of great interest and tender concern to our family, and equally so, I am sure, to yours, inasmuch as it relates to the future well-being of mr Bankhead your son, his wife and children, towards whom we have all the same affectionate feelings.

I understand it is decided, and with your approbation, that their Tract of land adjoining us shall be sold, the proceeds to be applied in the first instance to the payment of his debts, and the residue to be invested in lands somewhere else. it is on the latter part of this proposition I would sollicit your reconsideration. he is offered by mr Kelly, as I am told, 25.D. an acre for the lands above the road from Moor's creek to Charlottesville, supposed 300. acres, amounting of course to 7500.D. which is something more than would pay his debts as they are understood to be. he would then have remaining about 500. a[s], nearly every foot arable, and of first rate quality where then could the surplus money be better invested than in this, either as to soil, climate, convenience to navigation, or society? add to this what is surely a matter of consideration, their vicinity to us, which ensures the care of themselves & their children under all circumstances which might befall either of them. this question is therefore what we submit to yourself and mrs Bankhead, ready to acquiesce in your decision, whatever it may be. as a further provision to place them still in ease and competence, if it shall be determined to reserve the lands as proposed, I will add to their farm somewhere between 150. and 200. acres of my lands adjoining to it, lying over the road in front of their house on the side of the High-mountain, as rich lands, a considerable part of them, as any I own, on a slope so gentle as to be forever preserved by our horizontal method of ploughing, and abounding in the best timber, which will go downhill to every part almost of his farm. to this however I should annex a condition, intended solely for their own good, and that of their children, that not only what I convey, but Anne's moiety also of the present tract shall be located adjacent to this and including the house, and shall be vested in trustees, without whose assent her's shall not be sufficient to authorize a sale of the land. nothing else could ensure the family against the hazard of it's being lost to them or render this provision more secure than the first. the trustees shall be named by yourself. if you approve of these propositions, nothing less than your influence probably would prevail on mr Bankhead to concur in them: and should you think them not advisable, I should wish them to remain known to mrs Bankhead and yourself only, as they are here to mr and mrs Randolph alone, being unwilling to give umbrage to mr Bankhead by appearing to intermeddle in his affairs. he is restless to change his residence, and go to the Western country, not aware that the causes of his unhappiness are within himself, and will of course attend him to every other situation. pardon this observation. it should not have been suggested but that the grounds of it are partly known to yourself, and ought to enter into the consideration of whatever you may contemplate, advise, or do, for his good and that of his children.

I pray you to be assured of my sincere esteem & high respect for mrs Bankhead and yourself.   TH: JEFFERSON

PoC (MHi); on reused address cover of Robert M. Patterson to TJ, 21 Jan. 1815; mutilated at seal, with missing text recopied by TJ above the line; at foot of first page: "Doct' Bankhead"; endorsed by TJ.

John Bankhead (ca. 1760–1836), physician, was a native of Westmoreland County, friend of TJ, and cousin of James Monroe. He was educated at the College of William and Mary, 1775–76, and studied medicine at the University of Edinburgh during the ensuing decade. Bankhead lived thereafter in Caroline County, where he owned fifty-three slaves in 1810 and seventy-nine twenty years later. TJ's surviving retirement-era correspondence with Bankhead centers around the descent into alcoholism of the latter's

son Charles L. Bankhead and the attempt to shield those closest to him, including his wife, TJ's granddaughter Ann C. Bankhead, from the worst consequences of that disease (J. E. Warren, "Bankhead Family," *WMQ*, 2d ser., 9 [1929]: 310; Wyndham B. Blanton, *Medicine in Virginia in the Eighteenth Century* [1931], 75, 87, 384; *William and Mary Provisional List*, 6; Merrow Egerton Sorley, *Lewis of Warner Hall: The History of a Family* [1935; repr. 1979], 282; DNA: RG 29, CS, Caroline Co., 1810–30; TJ to Bankhead, 28 Oct. 1815, 14 Oct. 1816; Bankhead's will, 13 Mar. 1830, admitted to probate 13 June 1836, in papers for *Thomas Hord and wife v. Bailey Macrae and wife etc.*, Fauquier Co. Chancery Records, case ended 1846).

The TRACT OF LAND was Carlton (*MB*,

2:1269–70n; Albemarle Co. Deed Book, 18:27–9). The HIGH-MOUNTAIN was Montalto.

Bankhead's reply to TJ of 15 Mar. 1815, not found, is recorded in SJL as received 22 Mar. 1815.

To Charles Clay

DEAR SIR   Monticello Feb. 21. 15.

I recieved last night your favor of the 8th and find on examination that I have committed exactly the mistake you conjectured. McAllister had made me a pair of spectacles in 1804. by a drawing I had sent him, & believing they were of the size you would like best, I directed him to make the new ones like them. when they came I took out mine to compare them, and in packing up yours again, I put up the paper of spare glasses which belonged to mine by mistake for yours. so that it is not the frames, but the spare glasses which have been sent wrong. I now inclose you the right ones, and you can return me the spare glasses I sent you which belong to my frames.

You say that if I insist on your acceptance of them gratis it must operate as a bar against your availing yourself in future of my aid. how so? you do me a great many acts of neighborly kindness. must I refuse them hereafter because done gratis? I cannot return them in the same way, may I not do it therefore in my own way? in administering to your convenience in ways which are open to me, but not to you? where friendships are reciprocal each party must be permitted to offer manifestations of it in the way most in his power.

I congratulate you on peace, and especially that we closed the war with the whorra! of New Orleans. I salute you with friendship and respect.   TH: JEFFERSON

RC (ViU: TJP); chipped at creases and along right margin, with missing text supplied from PoC; at foot of text: "Mr Clay." PoC (DLC); endorsed by TJ.

TJ ordered a PAIR OF SPECTACLES from John McAllister in a letter dated 5 June 1804 (MHi). WHORRA!: "hurrah!"

From Alexander J. Dallas

SIR   Treasury Department 21. February 1815.

I have the honor to inform you, that, under the authority of an Act of Congress, I am ready to issue Treasury Notes, for the Sum of Twenty three thousand, nine hundred, and fifty dollars, in your favor: on account of the purchase of your Library, for the use of the Government. Be so good as to state, to whom the Notes shall be made payable, at what place, and of what denominations, the issues being for 1000, 100, and 20 Dollars.

I am, with sincere respect and esteem, Sir, Y^r mo. obed^t Servt

A. J. DALLAS

RC (DLC); endorsed by TJ as received 1 Mar. 1815 and so recorded in SJL. RC (DLC); address cover only; with PoC of TJ to William W. Hening, 11 Mar. 1815, on verso; addressed: "Thomas Jefferson Esq. Monticello Virginia"; franked and postmarked.

Notes on Household Consumption

1815. Feb. 21. a very large stalled beef killed Feb. 7. lasts till now, to wit, a fortnight.

MS (MHi); entirely in TJ's hand; subjoined to his Notes on Household Consumption, 3 June 1809–23 Oct. 1811, printed above at the latter date.

STALLED: confined or fattened in a stall (*OED*).

To Horatio G. Spafford

DEAR SIR   Monticello Feb. 21. 15.

Your favor of Jan. 28. was three weeks on it's passage to this place. I thank you for the copies of the pamphlet you have been so good as to send me. I have read it with pleasure and observe the ingenuity of the idea. having however been myself very much of a projector in mechanics, and often disappointed in my theoretical combinations, I have learnt neither to form, nor to trust any opinion on these conceptions, until confirmed by experiment. I understand from the pamphlet, and still more distinctly from your letter, that you have verified the improvement by numerous experiments, and this silences all doubt. but on this authority, I should not have expected that shifting the center of gravity of the load backward or forward from the axle would relieve the power; nor, (distinguishing between the direct line of traction from the power to the weight, and the indirect ones formed by shafts, traces E^{t}c. and in your case by the shaft and crank) that the indirect lines of traction p.a.w. p.b.w. p.c.w. would have any advantage over the direct line p.w. into which, I had supposed, all would resolve themselves. but doubt must yield to fact, and experiment controul opinion. I sincerely wish success to your invention, as well for your own benefit as that of the public.

Since you are so kind as to wish it, I take the liberty of inclosing a trifle as a memento of my respect. it is a profile, engraved by Edwin, from an original drawn by Stewart, and deemed the best which has been taken of me. it's chief value however is in the function it performs of gratifying your wish, and with it I pray you to accept the assurance of my great esteem and respect.　　　Tн: Jefferson

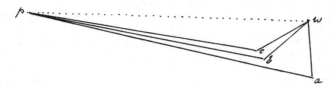

RC (NjMoHP: Lloyd W. Smith Collection); between signature and drawing: "Mr Spafford"; endorsed by Spafford, in part, as received 2 Mar. 1815 and as "enclosed, with his profile bust." PoC (MHi); endorsed by TJ. Enclosure: enclosure to William Birch to TJ, 8 July 1812, which was based on a profile drawn by Gilbert Stuart.

From William Caruthers

Dʀ Sɪʀ　　　　　　　　　　　　　Lexington 22ⁿᵈ Febʸ 1815

I have now to Acknowledge the recpᵗ of Two favours from you, the One in Answer to mine respecting[1] the N Bridge,[2] and the Other covering yourˢ to the Assessor Which Shall be handed to him as you direct Soon as One is Appointed for this County—of Which appointment (if any is made) I have not yet heard—As to the Other the reasons you Suggest Were certainly Sifficient to Warrant your closing with the Doctor I have only to regret the delay of my letter which Occasioned it As it compelled me to change the Arrangements I had made and make others that at the time did not feell so agreeable But may perhaps eventuate as Well—

The late pleasant change in our National affairs Will effect our establishment at the Bridge so materially, that (if We determine on continuing the Business) it may be Necessary to Add Some farther improvements than Was contemplated, as the Sales of Shot Will be so much limited by the change, that it may be Necessary[3] to Add Some other Branches of the plumbery Business to it to make it Worth prosecuting—in Which case it may be Necessary to change Or alter in Some Way the Agreement With you—for the improvement

Necessary[4] might be too expensive to put On land Leased Without a provision for allowance Therefor at the end of The Term—And to understand your Idias on this Subject Would Better enable us to Determine What course Would be Our interest to persue[5]—If you Would Sell at a fair Value Or One that We could think it Worth— That Way Would leave us at perfect liberty to choose On the Subject of improvements

Soon as I Get the Shot makeing a little more perfected I Will Send you a Sample to Amuse yourself With

Accept my best Respects[6]   Wᴹ Caruthers

As far as I am acquainted With the Tract the land is of Verry little Value for cultivation   W C

RC (DLC); between dateline and salutation: "Thoˢ Jefferson Esqʳ"; postscript written perpendicularly in left margin; endorsed by TJ as received 1 Mar. 1815 and so recorded in SJL.

ɴ ʙʀɪᴅɢᴇ: Natural Bridge. The ᴅᴏᴄᴛᴏʀ was Philip Thornton. The ʟᴀᴛᴇ ᴘʟᴇᴀꜱᴀɴᴛ ᴄʜᴀɴɢᴇ ɪɴ ᴏᴜʀ ɴᴀᴛɪᴏɴᴀʟ ᴀꜰꜰᴀɪʀꜱ was the the end of the War of 1812. ᴘʟᴜᴍʙᴇʀʏ is the trade or workshop of a plumber, in this context meaning "lead-working" (*OED*).

[1] Manuscript: "respeting."
[2] Manuscript: "Bride."
[3] Manuscript: "Necessarry."
[4] Manuscript: "Necssary."
[5] Manuscript: "pesue."
[6] Manuscript: "Respets."

From Hugh Nelson

City of Washington Feᵇʸ 22

Hugh Nelson takes the liberty to enclose to Mʳ Jefferson, a copy of the treaty of Peace; and with pride and with pleasure to tender to him his congratulations on the return of this happy state of things—

RC (DLC: TJ Papers, 203:36159); dateline at foot of text; partially dated; endorsed by TJ as a letter of 22 Feb. 1815 received 1 Mar. 1815 and so recorded in SJL. Enclosure: copy of the Treaty of Ghent ending the War of 1812, signed 24 Dec. 1814 (Hunter Miller, ed., *Treaties and other International Acts of the United States of America* [1931–48], 2:574–84).

From Horatio G. Spafford

Esteemed Friend—   Albany, 2 Mo. 24, 1815.

My attention is called, by an old man of about 70 years, to a wish of his that 2 volumes of his writings may be submitted to thy examination. Doct. Williams has written the History of Vermont, in 2 8vo.

volumes, & very naturally thinks that he has written very well. He is anxious to learn thy opinion of that Work; or at least to have it read by thee. The Doctor writes & thinks & feels like an American; a 'Sect' of which he esteems thee a principal patron! The Work sells at 5 dolls., but I am directed to send thee a Copy from the Author, who by-the-by is a very poor old man. If thou hast not read his Work, please inform me. The Doctor was my early Preceptor; & he was the Preceptor and generous friend of Benjamin Thompson, whom he educated at his own expense. If I am correctly informed, (for the Doct. will not say much about it,) Count Rumford was very ungrateful to his patron. The Doct. was formerly Professor of Math. et Nat. Philosophy in the university[1] of Cambridge, Massachusetts, & always[2] a distinguished Republican. Benj. Thompson, by becoming a Royalist, was Knighted in England, & became in time Count Rumford; but all the while neglected to reward the Man who, from a poor dependant orphan, had raised his promising talents in youth to notice, & taught him to become a man. I have just announced to the Society of Arts, my intention to write the Count's Life, & it seems to be well received. I studied under the Doctor's instruction, & well know his reverence & respect for thee. I hope my former Letters have duly reached thee, & that thou wilt excuse my troubling thee so often. With much respect,

H. G. SPAFFORD.

The return of peace, seems to please almost every body here, & we will soon forget the evils that we complained of in the time of War.

RC (MHi); postscript written perpendicularly in left margin; endorsed by TJ as received 8 Mar. 1815 and so recorded in SJL. RC (ViU: TJP-ER); address cover only; with PoC of TJ to Thomas Jefferson Randolph, 31 Mar. 1815, on verso; addressed: "Hon. Thomas Jefferson, LL.D., Monticello, Virginia"; franked; postmarked Albany, 24 Feb.

Samuel WILLIAMS was the author of *The Natural and Civil History of Vermont* (Walpole, N.H., 1794; Sowerby, no. 457;

2d ed., Burlington, Vt., 1809, 2 vols.). He was on the Harvard University faculty, 1780–88 (*Harvard Catalogue*, 132). ET: "and." By the SOCIETY OF ARTS, Spafford probably means New York's Society for the Promotion of Useful Arts, of which he had been an officer since 1813 (*Transactions of the Society for the Promotion of Useful Arts, in the State of New-York* 3 [1814]: n.p.; 4, pt.1 [1816]: n.p.).

[1] Manuscript: "univesity."
[2] Word interlined.

To Patrick Gibson

DEAR SIR   Mont[icello] Feb. 25. 15.

Nobody rejoices more sincerely than myself at the return of peace, nor could the season for it's being made known be better timed. I shall get down the rest of my flour as fast as possible. my crop was a poor one here, and still worse in Bedford. it will be under 100. Barrels of flour there. here the crop will furnish about 300. Barrels and 150. Bar. rent from my mill, in all something over 500. Bar. and probably about 20,000 ℔ tobᵒ from Bedford. I should be glad to keep off the sale of my flour until a sufficient concourse of vessels shall produce an animated demand and fair price. for the price we get depends on the demand <u>here</u>. in order to give time I shall avoid drawing as much as possible. nor do I know of any call impending but one of[1] about 100.D. and that perhaps may be some time yet. I expect that April will be the season of highest price: but on these views I leave both time and price to your discretion; so also as to that of my tobacco when you shall have recieved it.—I am happy to inform you that I shall be able to pay off the whole of my note in bank towards the end of March. this will be from a distinct source. Accept the assurance of my great esteem and respect.   TH: JEFFERSON

PoC (MH); on verso of reused address cover to TJ; dateline faint; mutilated at seal, with missing text supplied by TJ above the line; at foot of text: "Mʳ Gibson"; endorsed by TJ.

SJL records missing letters from TJ to Gibson of 14 Feb. 1815 and from Gibson to TJ of 18 Feb. 1815, with the latter having been received from Richmond two days after it was written.

[1] Manuscript: "off."

To Benjamin Smith Barton

DEAR SIR   Monticello Feb. 26. 15.

Congress having concluded to replace by my library the one which they lost by British Vandalism, it is now become their property and of course my duty to collect and put in place whatever stood in the Catalogue by which they purchased. this renders it necessary for me to request the return of Persoon's Botanical work of which you asked the use some time ago. I am in hopes you will have been able to make it answer the purposes for which you wished it's use. if well enveloped in strong paper it will come safely by mail.

I congratulate you on the happy event of peace and the great action of eclat at N. Orleans by which the war was closed. I hope the legislature will take care of your city, now become of so much greater importance by it's manufactures. I have come to a resolution my self as I hope every good citizen will, [never ag]ain to purchase any article of foreign manufacture which can be had of American make, be the difference of price what it may. the greatest obstacle I apprehend to our manufactures is our slavish obsequiousness to British fashions. the British stuffs in fashion will be sent to us, and while our workmen are preparing to imitate them the fashion will have vanished, and our belles and beaux be drawn off to something newer. this is a great evil, but I fear an irremediable one. it is the particular domain in which the fools have usurped dominion over the wise, and as they are a majority they hold to the fundamental law of the majority.

Accept the assurance of my constant esteem & respect.

TH: JEFFERSON

PoC (DLC); on recto of reused address cover to TJ; mutilated at seal; at foot of text: "Doctʳ Barton"; endorsed by TJ.

In his letter to TJ of 16 Oct. 1810, Barton had asked for Christiaan Hendrik

PERSOON'S *Synopsis Plantarum, seu Enchiridium Botanicum*, 2 vols. (Paris, 1805–07; Sowerby, no. 1073; Poor, *Jefferson's Library*, 6 [no. 277]). YOUR CITY: Philadelphia.

To George Hay

DEAR SIR   Monticello Feb. 26. 15.

Congress having concluded to replace by my library the one which they lost by British Vandalism, it is now become their property, and of course my duty to collect and put in place whatever belongs to it. this obliges me to ask of you the return of Reyneval's law of nature and nations of which you asked the reading some time ago. if well wrapped up in paper it will come safely by the mail.

Am I rid of old Scott's suit, or when shall I be? to quiet the purchaser I gave him a mortgage on another piece of land as a security [for] the title, which I wish to relieve from the mortgage. Accept the assurance of my great esteem and respect.   TH: JEFFERSON

PoC (DLC); on verso of reused address cover of James Monroe to TJ, 15 Feb. 1815; ink stained; at foot of text: "George Hay esq."; endorsed by TJ.

TJ sought the RETURN of Joseph Matthias Gérard de Rayneval, *Institu-*

tions du Droit de la Nature et des Gens (Paris, 1803; Sowerby, no. 1444). For the agreement TJ made TO QUIET THE PURCHASER, see Mortgage of Campbell County Land to Samuel J. Harrison, 18 May 1812.

From Henry Dearborn

Dear Sir   Troy February 27ᵗʰ 1815

It is with peculier satisfaction that I can congratulate you on the happy and honorable termination of a war, that was forced upon our Country, by the impolitic and unjust measures of the British Government. but while I rejoice at the close of the war & at the glorious events which terminated our Military conflicts, I feel the most severe mortification & depression, as a Citizen of Massachusetts. our State has been most retchedly humbled & degraded, by an unprinciple'd and Treacherous faction. I cannot but hope that their shamefull race is nearly run, and that on cool reflection, the great body of the Citizens will spurn such men from power & influence. — the extraordinery & unparelleld victory at New Orlians, when concidered with all its bearings, on the Enimy and on that Country, including the whole western States & Territories, is really a most wonderfull event. A formidable veteran Army, defeated and almost destroy'd by a body of Militia assembled principly from near one thousand miles distance, and on very short notice. we may search history in vain for a parellel case. especially when the disproportion of killed and wounded in the two Armies, is taken into the account. — I shall now retire from the service of my Country, and spend¹ the remainder of my life in the character of a private Citizen, and I anticipate the pleasure of once more seing you at Monticello. be assured Sir, there is no other man on earth that I so much desire to see. in the mean time, that you may be as happy as the lot of humanity permits, is the sincere wish of your
    unshaken friend.   H. Dearborn

P.S. Mrˢ Dearborn desires me to presint to you her most respectfull compliments.

———

The present Mrˢ D. was Mrˢ Bowdoin.

RC (DLC); above postscript: "Honᵇˡ Thomas Jefferson"; endorsed by TJ as received 11 Mar. 1815 and so recorded in SJL.

The DISPROPORTION OF KILLED AND WOUNDED at the Battle of New Orleans of 8 Jan. 1815 was, indeed, great. The British army suffered 2,037 casualties, while General Andrew Jackson reported his losses as around twenty, with an additional fifteen to thirty servicemen captured (Malcomson, *Historical Dictionary*, 369; Jackson, *Papers*, 3:239–41).

¹ Manuscript: "spnd."

To Joseph Dougherty

DEAR SIR   Monticello Feb. 27.

Your letter of the 15th was eight days on the road, and I answer it by the first return of our mail. I had prepared for mr Smith some notes on the transportation of the library, and as they give exactly all the information you desire, I send you a copy of them on the next leaf. they will inform you of the price of waggonage here, the number which will be requisite, the distance, and best roads, and that I shall send the books in the cases as they stand. I am now preparing and jointing boards to cover the cases and my own workmen will do whatever is wanting in their line without any additional charge. wishing every thing which may promote your interest I salute you with my best wishes.   TH: JEFFERSON

PoC (DLC: TJ Papers, 203:36165); on verso of reused address cover of Charles Clay to TJ, 8 Feb. 1815; partially dated; at foot of text: "M[r] Joseph Dougherty"; endorsed by TJ as a letter of 27 Feb. 1815 and so recorded in SJL. Enclosure: TJ's Observations on the Transportation of the Monticello Library, [ca. 27 Feb. 1815].

To Joseph Milligan

DEAR SIR   Monticello Feb. 27. 15.

The library committee of Congress having concluded to take my library without further[1] valuation, at the amount of your estimate, I shall on reciept of the catalogue proceed to review it, arrange and number all the books according as they stand in the catalogue. as on this review many will doubtless be found missing & irrecoverable, deductions proportioned to their size and number must of course be made from the amount of compensation. besides this there should be some one skilled in packing to attend to that and see that the fine bindings should not[2] be destroyed by the joultings of the waggons. you were so kind, in one of your letters, as to say you would come and see to this. I have therefore proposed to mr Smith to have you authorized by the committee as their agent, and I hope if it meets their approbation that yours will not be wanting. when I have finished the review I am to give him[3] notice that all is ready. I have mentioned to him too that waggons can be had here at 4.D. to take 2500.℔ each, and an accurate estimate makes 11. such waggon loads. but I have suggested to him the necessity of sending on a waggon load of bookbinders paper-parings and waste paper, the former to fill the interstices between the books and shelves, the latter to wrap the best bindings, and for slips between all the books. I should be very sorry to have them injured by the way. I suppose the review will employ me near a fortnight, and immediately after that and before the possibility of any new derangement I should be anxious to have the delivery made. if these propositions should be accepted I hope your concurrence will not be wanting, and that we shall have the pleasure of recieving you here in the course of the next month. Accept the assurance of my great esteem and respect. TH: JEFFERSON

RC (DLC: TJ Papers, ser. 10); at foot of text: "Mʳ Millegan." PoC (DLC); on verso of reused address cover of Joseph Dougherty to TJ, 15 Feb. 1815; torn at seal; endorsed by TJ.

In his letter of 14 Dec. 1814 Milligan

offered to "Send a young man" to assist in the packing of TJ's library, not to COME AND SEE TO THIS himself.

¹ Word interlined.
² Word interlined.
³ Word interlined.

To Samuel H. Smith

DEAR SIR   Monticello Feb. 27. 15.

Your favor of the 15ᵗʰ¹ was 8. days on it's way, and this goes by the first return mail. with respect to the Treasury notes, they of course should not be made out until the library is delivered, or ready to be delivered. when this takes place, I will take the liberty of specifying my wishes as to the notes. as soon as I recieve the Catalogue, I will set about revising and arranging the books. this can be done only by myself, and admits of no help. in doing it I must be constantly on my legs, and I must ask indulgence therefore to proceed only as my strength will admit. I count on it's taking me many days, perhaps a fortnight. as soon as all are in their places, and numbered, I will give you notice. I am now calling in all which have been lent out as far as noted, but there will doubtless be many irrecoverably lost. as these must be struck off the catalogue, and deductions accordingly be made from the amount of compensation, it would be not only very desirable to me, but entirely proper to have some agent of the Committee here² to see what are delivered and adjust the deductions, as well as to superintend the packing & perhaps the transportation. it would be a great pity to have the fine bindings destroyed for want of this small additional expence.³ mr Millegan, in a former letter to me, expressed his willingness to come and see to the packing & whatever else might be necessary, and no one would be more competent to the whole business. however he, or any other person whom the committee shall appoint will be acceptable to me. I send you on the next leaf some notes which may be useful towards arranging the transportation. the compensation embracing the whole of the catalogue, I shall not retain a single one, the only modification to be made being a deduction from the compensation in proportion to the size and number of the books which on the review shall appear to have been lost. Accept the assurance of my great esteem and respect.

TH: JEFFERSON

RC (DLC: J. Henley Smith Papers); addressed: "Samuel H. Smith esq. Washington. Col."; franked; endorsed by Smith as answered 11 Mar. 1815 and with his notation: "Library." PoC (DLC); endorsed by TJ. Enclosure: TJ's Observations on the Transportation of the Monticello Library, [ca. 27 Feb. 1815].

The COMMITTEE was Congress's Joint Library Committee.

[1] Reworked from "14th."
[2] Word interlined separately in RC and PoC.
[3] Sentence interlined separately in RC and PoC, with caret in RC incorrectly placed before the period at the end of the preceding sentence.

Observations on the Transportation of the Monticello Library

[ca. 27 Feb. 1815]

Observations on the transportation[1] of the Monticello library.

The books stand at present in pine cases with backs and shelves, without fronts. the Cases are generally of three tier, one upon another, about 9. feet high in the whole.[2] the lowest case is generally[3] 13. Inches deep, the 2^d $6\frac{3}{4}$ I.[4] and the uppermost $5\frac{3}{4}$ I. averaging together $8\frac{1}{2}$ I. to which add $\frac{3}{4}$[5] I. for the front of boards[6] to be nailed on, and it makes an average depth of $9\frac{1}{4}$ I.[7] I have measured the surface of wall which these cases cover, and find it to be 855. square feet, which multiplied by $9\frac{1}{4}$ I. give 676.[8] cubic feet. of these 232. cub. f. would be the wood of the cases, and 444. cub. feet the books. I find a cubical foot of books to weigh 40. ℔. and as this is the weight of dry pine also, we need not distinguish between the weight of the wood and the books, but say the whole 676. cub. f at 40. ℔ makes 27,040. ℔, or[9] 11. waggon loads of 2458. ℔. each.

It is said[10] that waggon hire at Washington is 8.D. a day, finding themselves. here it is exactly half that price, and a half dozen of waggons can be got here at 4.D. who will undertake to carry 2500. ℔ each. I think it would be better therefore to employ the waggons of this neighborhood, and let them make two trips. but, as[11] the interstices between the books and shelves (which however are very small) will require a certain quantity of book binders paper parings, a great many elegant bindings will require to be wrapped in waste paper and all should have slips of paper between them,[12] which cannot be had here, would it not be necessary to send on a waggon load from Washington to be deposited here before the books are packed? it might take a return load of the books.[13] the books should go in their cases, every one in it's station, so that the cases, on their arrival,[14] need only be set up on end, and they will be arranged exactly as they stand in the Catalogue. I will have the fronts closed with boards for the journey,[15] which being taken off on their arrival at Washington, sash doors may be made there at little expence.[16] but the books will require careful and skilful packing, to prevent their being rubbed in so long and rough a journey, by the joultings of the waggons.

The best road by far for waggons, at this season, is from Monticello by Orange Court House, Culpeper C.H. Fauquier C.H. Ewell's mill, Songster's, Lane's, and George town ferry, 125. miles,[17] because it is along crossroads nearly the whole way, which are very little travelled by waggons. the road by Fredericksburg is considerably further, and deeply cut thro' the whole. that by Stephensburg is[18] the shortest and levellest of all, but being generally a deep, livery clay, is absolutely impassable from November to May. the worst circumstance of the road by the Courthouses is that two branches of Rappahanoc, and three of Occoquan are to be forded, and they are liable to sudden[19] swells. I presume a waggon will go loaded in 7. days, return empty in 6. and allowing one for loading and accidents, the trip will be of a fortnight, and come to 56.D. I will have the waggons engaged, if it is desired, to attend on any day which may be named.

MS (DLC: J. Henley Smith Papers); entirely in TJ's hand; undated. Dft (DLC: TJ Papers, 203:36168); on verso of reused address cover of James Cutbush to TJ, 28 Jan. 1815. Enclosed in TJ to Joseph Dougherty and TJ to Samuel H. Smith, both 27 Feb. 1815.

LIVERY: "heavy" (*OED*). TJ had recommended the ROAD BY THE COURTHOUSES on many occasions. He used it for his return home to Monticello at the conclusion of his presidency in March 1809 (TJ to Edmund Bacon, 27 Feb. 1809 [CSmH: JF]; *MB*, 2:1243). At 56.D. per wagon, the total cost of shipping TJ's library to Washington would be $616.

[1] Word interlined in Dft in place of "removal."
[2] Preceding three words interlined in Dft.
[3] Preceding two words interlined in Dft in place of "being."
[4] Preceding two words interlined in Dft in place of "8.I."
[5] In Dft TJ reworked this number to "1.I" and back again.
[6] Preceding three words interlined in Dft in place of "facing."
[7] Dft: "it makes <$9\frac{1}{2}$> $9\frac{1}{4}$ I. depth."

8 Correct figure is 659.
9 In Dft TJ here canceled "nearly."
10 Preceding three words interlined in Dft in place of "<*We could pro*> I learn."
11 In Dft TJ here canceled "there will want a good deal of waste."
12 Preceding nine words interlined in Dft.
13 Sentence interlined in Dft.
14 Preceding three words interlined in Dft.

15 Preceding four words interlined in Dft in place of "plank."
16 Reworked in Dft from "being taken off the cases may have their fronts closed with sash doors at little expence."
17 Preceding two words not in Dft.
18 In Dft TJ here canceled "something."
19 Word interlined in Dft.

To David Bailie Warden

DEAR SIR   Monticello Feb. 27. 15.

My last to you was of Dec. 29. 13. since which I have recieved[1] your's of May 5. and July 25. with P.S.S. of June 18. & Aug. 1. these gave me the first information of your being under any difficulty with our government, and I lost no time in writing to the President & Sec^y of State, sending the statement you inclosed. the plain and direct narrative of this paper I did not doubt would impress their minds, as it had done mine; and remove all difficulties. mr Correa was here at the time. I communicated to him what I was doing, and engaged him on his return to Washington, which was to take place in a few days, to cooperate with me verbally. I recieved no answer from the President, nor could I, according to usage or propriety, expect one. his answers, in such cases, being only to be read in his acts.[2] nor have I heard from Mr Correa on the subject, nor indeed in any way learned what has been decided or done. this renders me entirely uncertain whether this letter will find you at Paris, or whether you may not be on your way to Washington, according to an idea expressed in your P.S. of Aug. 1.   the books and brochures from the Abbé Rochon, addressed[3] thro' mr Short, are not yet recieved, probably not come to his hands, or he would have noticed them to me. according to your request, I send you a copy of my Parliamentary Manual, and am to acknolege the reciept of Toulongeon, whom I have read with great satisfaction and information. he has given me the first luminous[4] view of the course of the French revolution to the death of Robespierre, of which till then my ideas had been entirely chaotic. he has solved to me the riddle of the Jacobins. many of the earlier set of them had been personally known to me, and altho' I knew them disposed to establish a republic on the ruins of the constitution of 91. yet

I could never recognize them in the anarchical proceedings which overthrew all government. a history of that club would be curious, & valuable. but what we now want especially is a history of the Directory, and one of Bonaparte. I hope some well informed, candid, plain narrator is engaged in it. no one would do it better than M. Toulongeon.—On the conflagration of the Capitol at Washington, and of the public[5] library, I thought it a duty to offer mine, and to relinquish the barren use and amusement I might have derived from it the few years I have remaining, for the more important purposes it may answer in their hands. Congress has accepted it, and I have now to make up again a collection for my self of such as may amuse my hours of reading. I should have trespassed on your goodness as to the part of the catalogue which must come from Paris, but for the uncertainty of your being there. I believe I shall trouble mr Ticknor with it, who is the bearer of this letter, and who is himself a well informed bibliograph. should he find you at Paris, I recommend him to you as an excellently educated young man, candid, amiable and worthy of every attention you can shew him. he is from Massachusets, proposes to pass two or three years in Europe, and then to take a stand at the bar of his own state; and I have no doubt will afterwards go far in the career of public honors and employments, should he embrace a political life.

We have recently heard that peace is concluded. it is well; because peace is better than war for every body. but we were just getting forward a set of officers, who having already redeemed the honor we lost under the traitors cowards and fools of the first year, would very soon have planted our banners on the walls of Quebec and Halifax. I pray you to accept the assurance of my great esteem and respect.

Th: Jefferson

RC (MdHi: Warden Papers); addressed: "Mʳ David B. Warden Consul of the United States at Paris"; notation by TJ at foot of address cover: "with a book"; endorsed by Warden adjacent to dateline: "from mr. Jefferson recd by mr Ticknor may 1817." PoC (DLC); on reused address cover from Randolph Jefferson to TJ; torn at seal, with missing text recopied by TJ above the line; endorsed by TJ. Tr (PHi: Joel R. Poinsett Papers); extract in Warden's hand in his 1 Nov. 1827 letter to Poinsett. Enclosure: TJ, *A Manual of Parliamentary Practice. For the Use of the Senate of the United States* (Washington, 1801; 2d ed., Philadelphia, 1812; Poor, *Jefferson's Library*, 11 [no. 687]; repr. in *PW*). Probably enclosed in TJ to George Ticknor, 3 Mar. 1815, for which see note to TJ to Ticknor, 19 Mar. 1815.

Warden's letter to TJ of MAY 5. is printed above at 6 May 1814, the date of the RC. His P.S.S. OF JUNE 18. & AUG. 1. are printed as separate letters to TJ at their respective dates. No correspondence from TJ to SECʸ OF STATE James Monroe on Warden's behalf has been found. Instead of NO ANSWER FROM THE PRESI-

DENT to his letter in support of Warden, TJ had in a fact received a strongly worded rejection of Warden's defense (TJ to James Madison, 13 Oct. 1814; Madison to TJ, 23 Oct. 1814 [second letter]).

[1] Tr begins here with "yours of 25 July & 18 June gave me the first information."
[2] Tr ends here.
[3] Manuscript: "addresdressed."
[4] TJ here canceled "ideas."
[5] Word interlined.

To Pierre Samuel Du Pont de Nemours

MY DEAR AND RESPECTED FRIEND   Monticello Feb. 28. 15.

My last to you was of Nov. 29. & Dec. 14. 13. since which I have recieved your's of July 14. I have to congratulate you, which I do sincerely on having got back from Robespierre and Bonaparte, to your ante-revolutionary condition. you are now nearly where you were at the Jeu de paume on the 20th of June 1789. the king would then have yielded by convention freedom of religion, freedom of the press, trial by jury, Habeas corpus, and a representative legislature. these I consider as the essentials constituting free government, and that the organization of the Executive is interesting, as it may ensure wisdom and integrity in the first place, but next as it may favor or endanger the preservation of these fundamentals. altho' I do not think the late Capitulation of the king quite[1] equal to all this, yet believing his dispositions to be moderate and friendly to the happiness of the people, and seeing that he is without the bias of issue, I am in hopes your patriots may, by constant and prudent pressure, obtain from him what is still wanting to give you a temperate degree of freedom and security. should this not be done, I should really apprehend a relapse into discontents, which might again let in Bonaparte.

Here, at length, we have peace. but I view it as an Armistice only, because no provision is made against the practice of impressment. as this then will revive in the first moment of a war in Europe, it's revival will be a declaration of war here. our whole business, in the mean time ought to be a sedulous preparation for it, fortifying our seaports, filling our magazines, classing and disciplining our militia, forming officers, and above all establishing a sound system of finance. you will see by the want of system in this last department, and even the want of principles, how much we are in arrears in that science. with sufficient means in the hands of our citizens, and sufficient will to bestow them on the government, we are floundering in expedients equally unproductive and ruinous; and proving how little are understood here those sound principles of political economy first developed by the[2] Economists, since commented & dilated by Smith, Say, yourself, and the luminous Reviewer of Montesquieu. I have been endeavoring to get the able paper on this subject, which you addressed to me in July 1810, and enlarged in a copy recieved the last year, translated & printed here, in order to draw the attention of our citizens to this subject; but have not as yet succeeded. our printers are enterprizing only in novels and light reading. the readers of works of science, altho' in considerable number, are so sparse in their situations, that such works are of slow circulation. but I shall persevere.

This letter will be delivered you by mr Ticknor, a young gentleman from Massachusets of much erudition, and great merit. he has compleated his course of law reading, and, before entering on the practice, proposes to pass two or three years in seeing Europe, and adding to his stores of knolege what he can acquire there. should he enter the career of politics in his own country he will go far in obtaining it's honors and powers. he is worthy of any friendly offices you may be so good as to render him, and to his acknolegements of them will be added my own. by him I send you a copy of the Review of Montesquieu, from my own shelf, the impression being, I believe, exhausted by the late President of the college of Williamsburg having adopted it as the elementary book there. I am persuading the author to permit me to give his name to the public, and to permit the original to be printed in Paris. altho' your presses, I observe, are put under the leading strings of your government, yet this is such a work as would have been licensed at any period, early or late, of the reign of Louis XVI. Surely the present government will not expect to repress the progress of the public mind farther back than that. I salute you with all veneration and affection.   TH: JEFFERSON

RC (DeGH: Pierre Samuel Du Pont de Nemours Papers, Winterthur Manuscripts); at foot of first page: "M. Dupont de Nemours." PoC (DLC). Tr (MHi); posthumous copy. For the return to TJ of the as-yet-undelivered RC, see George Ticknor to TJ, 25 Nov. 1815, and note. Enclosure: Destutt de Tracy, *Commentary and Review of Montesquieu's Spirit of Laws.* Probably enclosed in TJ to George Ticknor, 3 Mar. 1815, for which see note to TJ to Ticknor, 19 Mar. 1815.

Du Pont's communication to TJ OF JULY 14, not found, is recorded in SJL as a letter dated only "July" and received 14

Oct. 1814 from Paris. It presumably covered an expanded version of Du Pont's treatise on political economy, which is printed in this edition at 28 July 1810. For the meeting at the JEU DE PAUME, see note to TJ to Lafayette, 14 Feb. 1815. Independently of TJ's efforts, the lengthy July 1810 Du Pont letter was TRANSLATED & PRINTED in the Philadelphia *Aurora General Advertiser* between 4 and 27 Nov. 1815, and elsewhere. The LATE PRESIDENT OF THE COLLEGE of William and Mary was Bishop James Madison.

[1] Word not in Tr.
[2] Word not in Tr.

From Elizabeth Trist

MY EVER RESPECTED FRIEND   Bird wood Henry 28th Feb^y—15

I can not deny my self the pleasure of addressing you on this joyful occasion tho I expect you will be borne down with congratulations, mine may mingle with the more important as no one can feel more than I do the happy termination of the war, and the victory we obtaind at New Orleans one of the most singular and Glorious that the Annals of our country can furnish, and will establishs our national character for courage and abilities that may insure Us greater security than we ever enjoy'd, the more I reflect on it, the more wonderful it appears to me that so much was effected with so little loss on our side, the unanimity and spirit which the Inhabitants of that Country display'd on this occasion will insure to them the Confidence and esteem of their sister States as doubts had always been entertaind of their stability and Attachment to our Goverment, but they have evinced as much patriotism and firmness as any of the States have or cou'd have done and a great deel more then her jealous elder sisters have perform'd, they will now be convinced of the great advantage of that Country to us, tho they derided you for having purchased it. They only wanted a Man of firmness and decision to command them and General Jackson seems to have been ordain'd by Heaven for the purpose, he was of no party listend to none of their cabals yet insured the confidence of every body by his manly and upright deportment all were call'd upon to perform their duty and all willingly complied. my friend Mrs Ross sent me a diary of the transactions from the first of their landing till they disimbark'd¹ their Troops again, an awful perid and which will never be forgotten by the Women and children for all had some dear connection or friend combating the enemy the roar of the cannon and the bursting of the bombs convulsed the earth, one peice of intelligence that I am indebted to her for, is this anecdote which I think shews the character of Jackson at once He appointed Livingstone and Duncan the Lawyer his aids, neither very partial to each other Duncan is detested by the french of course they were not pleased at his having the appointment but little was said about it, as the enemy approach'd Duncan told the General that the Legeslative Counsel had it in² contemplation to offer to capitulate on certain terms I believe it was after the engagement that took place on the 23th Dec the General immediatily sent to the Governor to order a Guard to be placed at the door of the Principal and to blow them up Skipwith who is President of the Legeslative counsel observed in Company with Mrs Ross that the Gene^l had not taken three breaths before he repented having given the order blow them up, but the messenger[3] was gone Skipwith dont spare Duncan and says that at a proper time, it shall be laid before the public that their lives were not safe while such reports were going about and they call Duncan the intriguer I have not a doubt but he wou'd have brought it about if he cou'd and mention'd it, just to feel the Generals pulse upon the subject, I cou'd Say a great deel about the fellow but I despise him and in charity to you conclude after presenting M[r] and M[rs] Gilmers respectful Compliments and wishes for your health and happiness and that God may preserve you many years is my constant[4] prayer

E. TRIST

PS
I shall take the liberty to enclose a letter to M[rs] Randolph in this

RC (MHi); endorsed by TJ as received 28 Mar. 1815 and so recorded in SJL. Enclosure not found, but the reply, Martha Jefferson Randolph to Trist, 31 May 1815 (typescript in ViHi: Trist Papers), dwells at length on family news, including the bankruptcy of Richard Hackley and the quarrel between John Randolph of Roanoke and Ann Cary Randolph Morris in connection with the 1792–93 Bizarre Scandal.

During the engagement that took place on 28 Dec. 1814, not THE 23TH, General Andrew Jackson was informed by his aide Abner L. Duncan that he had received a report that the state legislature intended to surrender Louisiana to the British. Although Jackson apparently disbelieved the rumor, he desired GOVERNOR William C. C. Claiborne "to make strict enquiry into the subject; and if true, to blow them up." On receiving Jackson's message Claiborne directed that the statehouse doors be locked, but he revoked this order that same evening (Jackson, *Papers*, 3:226–7; *Report of the Committee of Inquiry, on the Military Measures Executed Against the Legislature of the State of Louisiana, the 28th of December 1814* [New Orleans, 1815; repr. in *Louisiana Historical Quarterly* 9 (1926): 223–80, esp. 252–3]).

[1] Thus in manuscript, with "imbark'd" probably intended.
[2] Manuscript: "had in in."
[3] Reworked from "blow them up, call'd to the messenger but he."
[4] Manuscript: "contant."

Francis W. Gilmer's Description of Thomas Jefferson and Monticello

[ca. Feb. 1815]

. . . For first of our state and second only to Washington of our nation is a venerable Patriot & statesman, whose evening ray still gilds the summit of our mountains. His greatness has not the dazzling luster of military glory and we must pause & consider it with calmness & attention.

In his person he is above the ordinary height, with large bones

& prominent muscles. His face bears an expression of benevolence mixed with an air of contemplation, dignity & elevation which is captivating & imposing in its effect. His motions are not graceful, but an universal, habitual politeness & delicate, nay even flattering attention to all around him impart an amenity to his manners beyond the graces of courts. His conversation is light & attic, having sometimes the agreable levity of the French, at others the graver instruction of a philosopher, but always the simplicity & pleasantry which are among the characteristics of greatness. His mind must have been by nature one of uncommon capaciousness and retention, of wonderful clearness, and as rapid as is consistent with accurate thought. His application from very early youth has not only been intense but unremitted. When young he adopted a system, perhaps an entire plan of life from which neither the exigencies of business nor the allurements of pleasure could drive or seduce him. Much of his success is to be ascribed to methodical industry. Even when at school he used to be seen with his Greek Grammar in his hand while his comrades were enjoying relaxation in the interval of school hours. He had constant access to the most extensive libraries, & the best informed society of our country. you may imagine then how rich, how vast, how accurately arranged, how carefully digested, the knowledge of such a mind so aided, must be after 60 years application. Tho' now in his 73^d year age appears neither to have "dim^d the discernment, nor enfeebled the fancy nor narrowed the range of his mind." on a very recent occasion when the public thought he had retired for ever to that repose which they imagined to be most grateful to a very old man grown gray in public service, he buckled on his armour & burst forth like a Giant joyful for the field. He appears to have done more nearly every thing which his natural advantages enabled him to do than any man I have known or of whom after Cicero I have even heard. He has enjoyed every honor his country could confer upon him. He has directed the course of its future policy as a nation. He is ranked amongst the learned of most of the polite nations of Europe. His agreable manners & personal address have always secured him the esteem & admiration of those with whom he is in any way connected. and with a good share of health[1] remaining he adorns the evening of his life with communion with books and philosophers, & the yet sweeter society of his descendants who look up to him with the reverence & love which the children of our primitive parents felt towards the patriarchs of those simple times. at his beautiful residence called monticello.

This place is itself a monument of his taste, & will in after times be identified with his glory. It stands on a mountain elevated to the height of 500 feet. at its base flows the Rivanna river. The prospect to the north, north east & West, is bounded by the blue ridge. The manner in which the view terminates to the North East is singularly beautiful. The mountains which are no where entirely interrupted become more and more dim as they recede from the eye, until finally the struggling vision doubts whether they have sunk beneath the horizon or faded before the sight. they mingle their azure summits with the clouds or sky & disappear. The tumult of this stormy scene whose awful[2] sublimity & grandeur is softened by distance into the beautiful, is finely contrasted with the opposite horizon. There a uniform plane, 'a boundless contiguity of shade' stills the agitation into which the chaos of mountains has thrown you; and the eye is relieved by its level hardly broken by the small mountain to the S. West which has been often mentioned as exhibiting the phenomenon known to sailors by the name of looming. The difficulty which mr. Jefferson[3] finds in accounting for this natural appearance on any principles of refraction does not really exist. He considers the different densities of the atmosphere at different heights as the only irregularity which occurs. But besides this there are many inequalities of density[4] at the same height arising from moisture temperature &c. It is some of these which produces the phenomenon of looming as an uneven piece of glass will distort the images of things into every variety of form.

The prospect from Monticello is most interesting[5] on a summers night. The elevation prevents or at least very much diminishes the descent of dews, & you walk with impunity at all hours on the lawn or terrace. The distant summits reflecting the silvery light, the moon beams floating on the mists below, the pale clouds hanging lightly on the declivities of the mountains, the motionless leaf, the softly murmuring wave, the glittering tapers in the surrounding vale, altogether remind one of that beautiful description of night in the Iliad.

as when the moon, refulgent lamp of night:
o'er heaven's clear azure spreads her sacred light,
when not a breath disturbs the deep serene
and not a cloud o'ercasts the solemn scene;
around her throne the vivid planets roll
and stars unnumbered gild the glowing pole.
o'er the dark trees a yellower verdure shed
and tipt with silver ev'ry mountains head
Then, shine the vales, the rocks in prospect rise
a flood of glory bursts from all the skies

His universal learning refutes the general opinion that excellence in many things is unattainable[6] In this brief sketch I have forborn to say any thing of the political life of mr. J—n. which will constitute his chief claim to the admiration of posterity. Upon that we are not likely to agree.

[*Extract from section on James Monroe, which follows a discussion of James Madison:*]
Mr Jefferson . . . in his practice of law, his diplomatic correspondence, his character as secretary of state was perpetually required to decide correctly & to fortify his opinions with all the muniments of reason & logic. He had also drunk deeper of the fountain of science & learning and acquired a passion for reading in his youth, which he indulged in his closet without the interruptions of the camp.

[*Extract from conclusion of section on Monroe:*]
mr. Jeffersons mind is the most capacious, madisons the most rapid, monroes the most sure. One has most learning, another most brilliancy, a third most judgement. Mr. Jefferson surpasses in the management of bodies of men, & monroe of individuals. We adore Mr Jefferson, admire Mr. Madison & esteem Mr Monroe.

MS (ViU: Gilmer Notebook, 1815); entirely in Gilmer's hand; containing the manuscript of his anonymously published *Sketches of American Orators* (Baltimore, 1816), which was "written in Washington Feb. 1815," followed by an unpaginated, undated, and ultimately unpublished essay entitled "Sketches of American Statesmen," from which the above extracts are taken.

The assertion that age had neither DIM^D THE DISCERNMENT, NOR ENFEEBLED THE FANCY NOR NARROWED THE RANGE OF HIS MIND is adapted from James Mackintosh, *Vindiciæ Gallicæ. Defence of the French Revolution and its English admirers against the accusations of the Right Hon. Edmund Burke* (London, 1791; Sowerby, no. 2545), iv. In a much-publicized letter to Samuel H. Smith of 21 Sept. 1814, TJ BUCKLED ON HIS ARMOUR by castigating the British for their destruction of the public buildings at Washington, D.C., and offering to sell his personal library to the nation. William Cowper used the phrase a BOUNDLESS CONTIGUITY OF SHADE in *The Task, a Poem* (London, 1785), book 2, line 2. The SMALL MOUNTAIN TO THE S. WEST was Willis's Mountain. TJ discusses the PHENOMENON OF LOOMING at some length in his *Notes on the State of Virginia* (*Notes*, ed. Peden, 80–1). The quote from Alexander Pope's translation of Homer's ILIAD is from book 8, lines 687–96 (*The Iliad of Homer* [London, 1759, and other eds.; Sowerby, no. 4264], 2:152).

[1] Gilmer here either reworked or canceled the word "still."
[2] Word interlined.
[3] Gilmer here canceled "mentions."
[4] Gilmer here canceled "even."
[5] Word interlined in place of "beautiful."
[6] Gilmer here adds a bracketed note to himself to "expand this idea."

To Tadeusz Kosciuszko

My dear friend and General   Monticello Mar. 1. 15.

We at length it seems have peace; but of what duration is uncertain, because, no arrangement being made against the impressment of American citizens, the first act of that character will be a declaration of war. the mean time should therefore be considered merely as an armistice, and employed on our part in fortifying our seaports, providing military stores, classing & disciplining the militia, and arranging our finances. while engaged in this we may also be endeavoring to prevent the occasion for them by a convention against impressment. you will have heard of the brilliant transactions at New Orleans which closed our war. of 9600 men which they landed, 4000 were killed or taken on different days, their 1st and 2^{d} generals killed, & the 3^{d} wounded, mortally as is said. indeed in every action of the last campaign, we proved the superiority of both our regulars & militia, when well commanded, to the regulars of the enemy. the coup de main at Washington would have been nothing without the burning the government house, Capitol and library, and that has only served to immortalize their infamy. we have at length some officers becoming prominent, and such as, had the war gone on, would have planted our standard on the walls of Quebec in the first campaign, & on those of Halifax in the second.

My last to you was of June 28. yours since recieved have been of May 15. & July 14. I informed you in mine of the operation by which we had saved your capital by a timely withdrawing of it from the banks, before their failure. every bank in the US. has since stopped payment. they promise indeed they will resume as soon as cash can be obtained. perhaps some of them may be able; but most of them are irrecoverably gone, and in the mean time their stock is become an absolute zero at market. I informed you also that by the sale of your bank stock before the alarm had depreciated it, and by the bonuses offered in a loan proposed by the US. we had been able to turn your capital of 8000.D. into one of 11,363. D 63 C at an interest of 6. per cent.   but more favorable terms having been obtained in the same loan by some later offers, the government very justly extended the same advantages by retrospect to those who had been more prompt in their offers of aid; by which an additional allowance of 1136. D 36 C has been made to you, which has raised that portion of your capital to 12,500.D. bearing interest at 6. per cent.   on the other portion of your funds, to wit, the 4500.D. in my hands, your income will be somewhat lessened. this sum you know had been repaid to mr Barnes by the treasury, and happened not yet to be rein-vested, when, on my winding up at Washington, finding myself in ar-rears there, I availed my self of the use of this sum before I could have time to consult you. as bank stock then yielded a profit of 8. p. cent while legal interest was but at 6. and this money might have been reinvested for you in bank stock, I thought it just that I should pay you 8. p. cent, which I have done ever since. it is now in my power to replace the sum I had borrowed, and the banks being down we have no safe investment of it but in the Treasury notes of the US. these bear an interest of $5\frac{2}{3}$ p. cent. I shall accordingly, in the ensuing month deposit with the Treasury of the US. 4500.D. in their notes; thus placing your whole capital of 17,000.D. in their hands; the in-terest of which will be 1005.D. a year. I hope that in all this I shall meet your approbation, and am bound at the same time to ex-press to you my great thankfulness for the accomodation I recieved from your funds, in a moment of great need, and for the time with which I have been indulged to replace them. I expected sooner to have been enabled to do it, but I am not a strict manager in the economies of my house or farms, and the war was an immediate and total suspension of profits by shutting up our produce to rot on our hands. I salute you with affectionate and unchangeable friendship and respect   TH: JEFFERSON

RC (ICN); ink stained, with obscured letter supplied from PoC; at foot of first page: "Gen¹ Kosciuzko." PoC (MHi); en-dorsed by TJ.

TJ accurately reported the British loss at the Battle of New Orleans of THEIR 1ST AND 2D GENERALS, Edward Pakenham and Samuel Gibbs. A third, John Keane, was seriously wounded, though not MOR-TALLY (Malcomson, *Historical Dictio-nary*, 214–5, 271, 369, 405–6).

To John Vaughan

DEAR SIR   Monticello Mar. 1. 15.

On the destruction of the Capitol and library at Washington, I offered to Congress my library to replace that which they had lost. it was peculiarly a library for American statesmen, and, in that way, a collection invaluable to the US. the divisions of Classics, Politics, Law, Geography & history, and American history and geography es-pecially, constituted it's principal mass. having been for 40. years my-self abstracted by other duties from the Mathematical and Physical sciences, I had added little in those classes to my early stock. Con-gress has accepted the offer, and I have now to reprocure for myself very many of the books yielded to them. I must do this chiefly by importations from Paris and London, at each of which places of course I must make deposits of money, perhaps of 500.D. at each the first year. at the latter place this will be at the disposal of my antient friend and class-mate, James Maury, our Consul at Liverpool. but at Paris I have no correspondent in the mercantile or banking way. does mr Girard retain connections of business there, and would he consent to[1] be the medium for my little concerns? or can you advise me to any other? I should also have to ask the favor of you to procure me bills to the amount of what I shall remit you when my catalogue & funds shall be ready. the readiest remittance to you would be in Treasury bills of the emission under the law of Mar. 4. 14. which are payable in one year from their date with $5\frac{2}{3}$ p.c. interest, this being the medium I am to recieve for my books. will this sell at par, or at what price, with you? if below par, I must defer my proceedings until a concourse of vessels and of demand at our market for tobacco and flour will enable me to sell mine to advantage, which will probably not be till May. I must place with you at the same time some additional funds to answer the purchase of such books as I may get in Philadelphia. will you be so good as to advise me of the price of such stock, and of bills on London, Liverpool or Paris for my government? I believe this application to you is in the regular line of your business, altho' I am not certainly informed as to that. if so, consider it as made from a preference of your agency to that of any other; if not, indulge it on the ground of friendship, & to one who would otherwise be at a loss from whom to ask such information. I salute you with friendship and respect.

TH: JEFFERSON

RC (PPAmP: Vaughan Papers); addressed: "John Vaughan esquire Philadelphia"; franked; postmarked Milton, 2 Mar. PoC (DLC); on reused address cover of Robert M. Patterson to TJ, 3 Dec. 1814; endorsed by TJ.

Under the provisions of the 30 Jan. 1815 legislation authorizing the purchase of TJ's library, the former president was to be paid in bills issued under the LAW OF MAR. 4. 14, "An act to authorize the issuing of treasury notes for the service of the year one thousand eight hundred and fourteen" (*U.S. Statutes at Large*, 3:100–2, 195).

[1] Preceding two words interlined separately in RC and PoC.

To Jean Baptiste Say

DEAR SIR   Monticello Mar. 2. 15.

Your letter of June 15. came to hand in December, and it is not till the ratification of our peace that a safe conveyance for an answer could be obtained. I thank you for the copy of the new edition of your work which accompanied your letter. I had considered it in it's first form as superceding all other works on that subject and shall set proportional value on any improvement of it.   I should have been happy to have recieved your son here, as expected from your letter, on his passage thro' this state; and to have given proofs thro' him of my respect for you. but I live far from the great stage road which forms the communication of our states from North to South, and such a deviation was probably not admitted by his business.   The question proposed in my letter of Feb. 1. 1804 has since become quite a 'question oiseuse.' I had then persuaded myself that a nation, distant as we are from the contentions of Europe, avoiding all offence to other powers, and not over-hasty in resenting offence from them, doing justice to all, faithfully fulfilling the duties of neutrality, performing all offices of amity, and administering to their[1] interests by the benefits of our[2] commerce, that such a nation, I say, might expect to live in peace, and to consider itself merely as a member of the great family of mankind; that in such case it might devote itself to whatever it could best produce, secure of a peaceable exchange of surplus for what could be more advantageously furnished by others, as takes place between one county and another of France. but experience has shewn that continued peace depends not merely on our own justice & prudence but on that of others also: that, when forced into war, the interception of exchanges which must be made across a wide ocean, becomes a powerful weapon in the hands of an enemy domineering over that element, and to the other distresses of war adds the want of all those necessaries for which we have permitted ourselves to be dependant on others, even arms and clothing. this fact therefore solves the question by reducing it to it's ultimate form, Whether profit or preservation is the first interest of a state? we are consequently become manufacturers to a degree incredible to those who do not see it, and who only consider the short period of time during which we have been driven to them, by the suicidal policy of England. the prohibitory duties we lay on all articles of foreign[3] manufacture which prudence requires us to establish at home with the patriotic determination of every good citizen to use no foreign article which can be made within ourselves, without regard to difference of price, secures us against a relapse into foreign dependancy. and this circumstance may be worthy of your consideration, should you continue in the disposition to emigrate to this country. your manufactory of cotton, on a moderate scale combined with a farm, might be preferable to either singly, and the one or the other might become principal as experience should recommend. cotton, ready spun is in ready[4] demand, and if woven, still more so.

I will proceed now to answer the enquiries which respect your views of removal; and I am glad that, in looking over our map, your eye has been attracted by the village of Charlottesville, because I am better acquainted with that than any other portion of the US. being within 3. or 4. miles of the place of my birth & residence. it is a portion of country which certainly possesses great advantages. it's soil is equal in natural fertility to any high lands I have ever seen; it is red and hilly, very like much of the country of Champagne and Burgundy, on the route of Sens, Vermanton, Vitteaux, Dijon, and along the Cote to Chagny, excellently adapted to wheat, maize, and clover. like all mountainous countries it is perfectly healthy, liable to no agues and fevers, or to any particular epidemic, as is evidenced by the robust constitution of it's inhabitants, and their numerous families. as many instances of Nonagenaires exist habitually in this neighborhood as in the same degree of population anywhere. it's temperature may be considered as a medium of that of the US. the extreme of cold in ordinary winters being about 7° of Reaumur below zero,[5] and in the severest −12.°[6] while the ordinary mornings are above zero. the maximum of heat in summer is 28.°[7] of which we have one or two instances in a summer for a few hours. about 10 or 12. days in July and August the thermometer rises for 2. or 3. hours to about 23.°[8] while the ordinary mid-day heat of those months is about 21.°[9] the mercury continuing at that 2. or 3. hours, and falling in the evening to about 17°.[10] white frosts commence about the middle of October, and tender vegetables are in danger from them till nearly the middle of April. the Mercury begins about the middle of November, to be occasionally at the freezing point, and ceases to be so about the middle of March. we have of freezing[11] nights about 50. in the course of the winter, but not more than 10. days in which the mercury does not rise above the freezing point. fire is desirable even in close apartments whenever the outward air is below 10° (= 55° Farenheit) and that is the case with us thro' the day 132. days in the year, and on mornings and evenings 68. days more. so that we have constant fires 5 months, and a little over 2. months more on mornings and evenings. observations made at York town in the lower country shew that they need 7. days less of constant fires and 38. less of mornings and evenings.[12] on an average of 7. years I have found our snows amount in the whole to 15. Inches depth, and to cover the ground 15. days. these, with the rains give us 4. feet of water in the year. the garden pea, which we are now sowing, comes to table about the 12th of May; strawberries & cherries about the same time; Asparagus the 1st of April. the artichoke stands the winter without cover; lettuce and endive with a slight one of bushes, and often without any; and the fig, protected by a little straw, begins to ripen in July, if unprotected, not till the 1st of September.   There is navigation for boats of 6. tons from Charlottesville to Richmond, the nearest tide water, and principal market for our produce. the country[13] is what we call well-inhabited, there being in our county, Albemarle, of about 750. square miles, about 20,000. inhabitants, or 27. to a square mile; of whom however one half are people of colour either slaves or free. the society is much better than is common in country situations; perhaps there is not a better <u>country</u> society in the US. but do not imagine this a Parisian or an Academical society. it consists of plain, honest and rational neighbors, some of them well informed, and men of reading, all superintending their farms, hospitable, and friendly, and speaking nothing but English. the manners of every nation are the standard of orthodoxy within itself. but these standards being arbitrary, reasonable people in all allow free toleration for the manners, as for the religion of others.   Our culture is of wheat for market, and of maize, oats, peas and clover for the support of the farm. we reckon it a good distribution to divide a farm into three fields, putting one into wheat, half a one into maize, the other half into oats or pease, and the third into clover, and to tend the fields successively in this rotation. some woodland in addition is always necessary to furnish fuel fences, and timber for constructions. our best farmers (such as mr Randolph my son in law) get from 10. to 20. bushels of wheat to the acre; our worst (such as myself) from 6. to 10. with little or no manuring. the bushel of wheat is worth in common times about 1. Dollar. the common produce of maize is from 10. to 20. bushels, worth half a dollar the bushel,[14] which is of a cubic foot & a quarter, or, more exactly, of 2178. cubic inches. from these data you may judge best for yourself of the size of the farm which would suit your family; bearing in mind that while you can be furnished by the farm itself for consumption, with every article it is adapted to produce, the sale of your wheat at market is to furnish the fund for all other necessary articles.   I will add that both soil and climate are admirably adapted to the vine, which is the abundant natural production of our forests, and that you cannot bring a more valuable laborer than one acquainted with both it's culture, and manipulation into wine.

Your only enquiry now unanswered is the price of these lands? to answer that with precision[15] would require details too long for a letter; the fact being that we have no metallic measure of values at present, while we are overwhelmed with bank paper. the depreciation of this swells nominal prices, without furnishing any stable index of real value. I will endeavor briefly to give you an idea of this state of things by an outline of it's history.

Dol.

in 1781. we had 1. bank, it's capital	1,000,000	and at this time
1791.	6.	13,135,000	we have probably
1794.	17.	18,642,000	100. banks, with
1796.	24.	20,472,000	capitals amount-
1803.	34.	29,112,000	ing to 100. mil-
1804.	66 their am^t of capital not known		lions of Dollars,

on which they are authorized by law to issue notes to three times that amount. so that our circulating medium may now be estimated at from two to three hundred millions of Dollars on a population of 8½ millions. the banks were able for a while to keep this trash at a par with metallic money, or rather to depreciate the metals to a par with their paper, by keeping deposits of cash sufficient to exchange for such of their notes as they were called on to pay in cash. but the circumstances of the war draining away all our specie, all these banks have stopped payment, but with a promise to resume specie[16] exchanges whenever circumstances shall produce a return of the metals. some of the most prudent and honest will possibly do this; but the mass of them never will nor can. yet, having no other medium, we take their paper of necessity for purposes of the instant, but never to lay by us. the government is now issuing treasury notes for circulation, bottomed on solid funds, and bearing interest. the banking confederacy (and the merchants bound to them by their debts) will endeavor to crush the credit of these notes: but the country is eager for them, as something they can trust to, and so soon as a competent quantity of them can get into circulation, the bank notes die. you may judge that, in this state of things, the holders of bank notes will give free prices for lands, and that were I to tell you simply the present prices of lands in this medium, it would give you no idea on which you could calculate. but I will state to you the progressive prices which have been paid for particular parcels of land for some years back, which may enable you to distinguish between the real increase of value, regularly produced by our advancement in population, wealth and skill, and the bloated value arising from the present disordered and dropsical state of our medium. there are two tracts of land adjoining me, and another not far off, all of excellent quality, which happen to have been sold at different epochs as follows.

			D		D
one was sold in 1793. for 4.D. an acre;	in 1812.[17] at 10. & is now rated	16
the 2^d	in 1786. for 5$\frac{1}{3}$ D.	in 1803.[18] at 10.	now	20.
the 3^d	1797. for 7.	in 1811. at 16.	now	20.

on the whole however I suppose we may estimate that the steady annual rise of our lands is in a geometrical ratio of 5. per cent: that were our medium now in a wholsome state, they might be estimated at from 12. to 15. Dollars the acre; and I may add, I believe with correctness that there is not any part of the Atlantic states where lands of equal quality and advantages can be had as cheap. when sold with a dwelling house on them little additional is generally asked for the house. these buildings indeed are generally of wooden materials, and of indifferent structure and accomodation.   most of the hired labor here is of people of color, either slaves or free. an able bodied man has 60.D. a year and is clothed and fed by the employer; a woman half that. white laborers may be had, but they are less subordinate, their wages higher, and their nourishment much more expensive.   a good horse for the plough costs 50. or 60.D. a draught ox 20. to 25. a milch cow 15. to 18. a sheep 2.D. beef is about[19] 5. Cents, mutton & pork 7. cents the pound. a turkey or goose 50. cents apiece, a chicken 8$\frac{1}{3}$. cents, a dozen eggs the same, fresh butter 20. to 25. cents the pound; and to render as full as I can the information which may enable you to calculate for yourself, I inclose you a Philadelphia Price current, giving the prices in regular times of most of the articles of produce or manufacture foreign and domestic.

That it may be for the benefit of your children and their descendants to remove to a country where, for enterprize and talents, so many avenues are open to fortune and fame, I have little doubt. but I should be afraid to affirm that at your time of life, and with habits formed on the state of society in France, a change for one so entirely different would be for your personal happiness. fearful therefore to persuade I shall add with sincere truth that I shall very highly estimate the addition of such a neighbor to our society, and that there is no service in my power which I shall not render with pleasure and promptitude. with this assurance be pleased to accept that of my great esteem & respect.   Th: Jefferson

P.S. this letter will be handed you by mr Ticknor, a young gentleman of Massachusets, of great erudition and worth, and who will be gratified by the occasion of being presented to the author of the Traité d'Economie Politique.

PoC (DLC); at foot of first page: "Jean Batiste Say." Tr (MHi); posthumous copy. Enclosed in TJ to George Ticknor, 3 Mar. 1815 (see note to TJ to Ticknor, 19 Mar. 1815), and TJ to José Corrêa da Serra, 6 Mar. 1815.

In his letter to Say of 1 Feb. 1804 (DLC), TJ posed the QUESTION OISEUSE ("idle question") whether "all our laborers should be employed in Agriculture?" COTE: Côte d'Or.

On this date Albemarle County clerk Alexander Garrett sent TJ a memorandum summarizing from the Albemarle County Deed Book a series of sales of Viewmont, an estate located NOT FAR OFF from Monticello. The estate had been sold in 1786, 1798, 1801, 1802 (twice), and 1803, with the principals being Joshua Fry, Edmund Randolph, William Champe Carter, Edward H. Carter, Whitaker Carter, Tucker M. Woodson, and John Harris (MS in MHi; in Garrett's hand and signed by him; with notes and calculations by TJ to the right of each line converting pounds into dollars; addressed: "Mr Jefferson"). TJ used the information in that document for THE 2D line of his table demonstrating the increase in land prices. THE 3D seemingly refers to Carlton, an 800-acre farm adjacent to Monticello that had been pur-

chased by Charles L. Bankhead and Ann C. Bankhead early in 1812 (Albemarle Co. Deed Book, 18:27–9; Elizabeth Trist to Catharine Wistar Bache, 7 May 1811 [PPAmP: Bache Papers]).

The enclosed PHILADELPHIA PRICE CURRENT was probably an unidentified issue of *Hope's Philadelphia Price-Current, and Commercial Record*.

[1] PoC: "theirs." Tr: "their."
[2] Word interlined in place of "their."
[3] TJ here canceled "produce."
[4] Word interlined in place of "great."
[5] In right margin TJ wrote "= 16° Farenh."
[6] In right margin TJ wrote "= 5°."
[7] In right margin TJ wrote "= 96°."
[8] In right margin TJ wrote "= 84°."
[9] In right margin TJ wrote "= 80°."
[10] In right margin TJ wrote "= 70°."
[11] PoC: "freezings." Tr: "freezing."
[12] Preceding three sentences interlined and in right margin.
[13] Tr: "county."
[14] Preceding six words not in Tr.
[15] Preceding two words interlined.
[16] Word not in Tr.
[17] Preceding two words recopied above the line by TJ for clarity.
[18] Tr: "1810."
[19] Preceding two words not in Tr.

From William Caruthers

DR SIR   Lexington 4th March 1815

I Took the liberty a few days ago of addressing a few lines to you respecting Our Shot establishment at the Natural Bridge— In addition to the effect that the late peace Will have on it, Since I Wrote you we had the missfortune to have a part of the fix consumed[1] by accidental fire—Which Will make it the More Doubtfull Whether it Will be our interest Now to continue the establishment—The present[2] is therefore to enquire On What Terms you

Will cancil the lease in case We Should be enclined to Drop the Shot makeing—

I am not instructed by Doc[t] Thornton to make this enquiry but haveing Taken an interest With him & M[r] Brown Both of Whom are in Richmond and haveing Written them On the Subject of determining What is to be done With the Shot factory I am desirouse of being able to lay the matter fairly before them in every point of View is the reason in addition to the Accident above mentioned that I Trouble you again On the Subject.

To be explicit as far as my own Opinion Goes I am Still in favour of continuing the establishment—provided you Are disposed to Sell to us at a fair price, So that We can Safely make Such farther improvements as Will in time of peace make it a Business worth parsuing, the Shot alone I think Would Not, the Sales Will be so much Limitted by other establishments—Soon as you can Spare the time I hope you Will favour us With a reply—in m[n]time

Accep[t] My Best Respects[3]   W[M] CARUTHERS

RC (DLC); endorsed by TJ without date of receipt, but recorded in SJL as received 8 Mar. 1815. RC (DLC); address cover only; with PoC of TJ to Joseph Milligan, 28 Mar. 1815, on recto and verso; addressed: "Thomas Jefferson Esqr Montecello Milton post Office"; franked; postmarked Lexington, 6 Mar.

FIX is material used to line puddling-furnaces (*OED*).

[1] Manuscript: "comsumed."
[2] Manuscript: "pesent."
[3] Manuscript: "Respcts."

To Louis H. Girardin

TH:J. TO MR GIRARDIN.   Monticello Mar. 4. 15.

I will with pleasure examine the Cahiers you have sent me. I send you Ramsay's revoln, La Motte, 1st Toulongeon and the last Nat[l] Intelligencer, and am sorry that the use of these and all other resources for you[1] from my library are likely to be abridged so much. within 3. weeks from this time I expect waggons will be on from Washington to recieve the library, and before that date I shall be obliged to have every book in it's place, arranged and numbered correspondingly with the catalogue for the inspection & reciept of the agent which shall come on from the Commee. I mention this that you may consider how to make the greatest advantage of this short interval.—on the three[2] desiderata mentioned in your note, I can offer nothing new. I think you told me you had sent Bezout to mr Garnet forgetting I had bespoke it. if so, I would rather not deprive him of it. I am making out a catalogue for Paris which I shall be able to recieve this summer, and I would rather send for a new edition in which I see that his Course for the Artillery is embodied with that of Navigation[3] in 5. vols, & the whole for 20. francs.

RC (PPAmP: Thomas Jefferson Papers); written on a small sheet; dateline at foot of text; addressed: "Mr Girardin Glenmore." Not recorded in SJL.

The CAHIERS contained the manuscript, not found, of a portion of Burk, Jones, and Girardin, *History of Virginia*, vol. 4. The publications enclosed with this letter included either David RAMSAY's history of the American Revolution or his history of the same period in South Carolina (Sowerby, nos. 488, 490); one of several works on a scandal just prior to the French Revolution involving Jeanne de Saint Remy de Valois, comtesse de LA MOTTE (Sowerby, nos. 227, 2228, 2229);

François Emmanuel, vicomte de TOULONGEON, *Histoire de France, depuis la Révolution de 1789* (Paris, 1801–06; Sowerby, no. 240; Poor, *Jefferson's Library*, 4 [no. 88]), 1st of 2 vols. as bound by TJ; and an unidentified issue of the Washington NAT^L INTELLIGENCER. The agent of the congressional Joint Library Committee (THE COMMEE) coming to Monticello was Joseph Milligan. Girardin's NOTE, not found, is most likely the letter to TJ recorded in SJL as having been written and received on this date.

[1] Preceding two words interlined.
[2] TJ here canceled "subjects."
[3] Preceding two words interlined.

To Francis C. Gray

DEAR SIR   Monticello Mar. 4. 15.

Dispatching to mr Ticknor my packet of letters for Paris, it occurs to me that I committed an error in a matter of information which you asked of me while here. it is indeed of little importance, yet as well corrected as otherwise; and the rather as it gives me an occasion of renewing my respects to you. you asked me in conversation what constituted a mulatto by our law? and I believe I told you 4 crossings with the whites. I looked afterwards into our law, and found it to be in these words. 'every person, other than a negro, of whose grandfathers or grandmothers any one shall have been a negro, shall be deemed a mulatto, and so every such person who shall have one fourth part or more of negro blood; shall in like manner be deemed a mulatto.' L. Virga. 1792. Dec. 17 the case put in the first member of this paragraph of the law is exempli gratiâ. the latter contains the true Canon, which is that $\frac{1}{4}$ of negro blood, mixed with any portion of white, constitutes the mulatto. as the issue has one half of the blood of each parent, and the blood of each of these may be made up of a variety of fractional mixtures, the estimate of their compound, in some cases, may be[1] intricate. it becomes a Mathematical problem of the same class with those on the mixtures of different liquors or different metals. as in these therefore, the Algebraical notation[2] is the most convenient & intelligible. let us express the pure blood of the white in the capital letters of the printed[3] alphabet, the pure blood of the negro in the small letters of the printed alphabet, and any given mixture of either, by way of abridgment in MS. letters.

let the 1st crossing be of **a**, pure negro, with **A**. pure white. the Unit of blood of the issue being composed of the half of that of each parent, will be $\frac{a}{2} + \frac{A}{2}$ call it, for abbreviation, h (half-blood)

let the 2^d crossing be of h. and **B**. the blood of the issue will be $\frac{h}{2} + \frac{B}{2}$, or substituting for $\frac{h}{2}$ it's equivalent, it will be $\frac{a}{4} + \frac{A}{4} + \frac{B}{2}$. call it q (quarteroon) being $\frac{1}{4}$ negro blood

let the 3^d crossing be of q. and **C**. their offspring will be $\frac{q}{2} + \frac{C}{2} = \frac{a}{8} + \frac{A}{8} + \frac{B}{4} + \frac{C}{2}$. call this e. (eighth) who having less than $\frac{1}{4}$ of **a**. or of pure negro blood, to wit $\frac{1}{8}$ only, is no longer a mulatto. so that a 3^d cross clears the blood.

from these elements let us examine other compounds.

for example, let h. and q. cohabit. their issue will be $\frac{h}{2} + \frac{q}{2} = \frac{a}{4} + \frac{A}{4} + \frac{a}{8} + \frac{A}{8} + \frac{B}{4} = \frac{3a}{8} + \frac{3A}{8} + \frac{B}{4}$ wherein we find $\frac{3}{8}$ of **a**. or of negro blood.

let h. and e. cohabit. their issue will be $\frac{h}{2} + \frac{e}{2} = \frac{a}{4} + \frac{A}{4} + \frac{a}{16} + \frac{A}{16} + \frac{B}{8} + \frac{C}{4} = \frac{5a}{16} + \frac{5A}{16} + \frac{B}{8} + \frac{C}{4}$ wherein $\frac{5}{16}$ **a**. makes still a mulatto.

let q. and e. cohabit. the half of the blood of each will be $\frac{q}{2} + \frac{e}{2} = \frac{a}{8} + \frac{A}{8} + \frac{B}{4} + \frac{a}{16} + \frac{A}{16} + \frac{B}{8} + \frac{C}{4} = \frac{3a}{16} + \frac{3A}{16} + \frac{3B}{8} + \frac{C}{4}$ wherein $\frac{3}{16}$ of **a** is no longer mulatto.

and thus may every compound be noted & summed, the sum of the fractions composing the blood of the issue being always equal to Unit.   it is understood in Natural history that a 4th cross of one race of animals with another gives an issue equivalent for all sensible purposes to the original blood. thus a Merino ram being crossed 1st with a country ewe, 2dly with this daughter, 3dly with this grandaughter, and 4^{thly} with the great grandaughter, the last issue is deemed pure Merino, having in fact but $\frac{1}{16}$ of the country blood. our Canon considers 2. crosses with the pure white, and a 3^d with any degree of mixture, however small, as clearing the issue of the negro blood. but observe that this does not reestablish freedom, which depends on the condition of the mother, the principle of the civil law, partus sequitur ventrem, being adopted here. but if e. be emancipated, he becomes a free <u>white</u> man, and a citizen[4] of the US. to all intents and purposes— so much for this trifle, by way of correction.

I sincerely congratulate you on the peace, and more especially on the close of our war with so much eclat. our 2^d and 3^d campaigns have, I trust, more than redeemed the disgraces of the 1st and proved that altho a republican[5] government is slow to move, yet, when once in motion, it's momentum becomes irresistable, and I am persuaded it would have been found so in the late war, had it continued. experience had just begun to elicit those among our officers who had talents for war, and under the guidance of these one campaign would have planted our standard on the walls of Quebec, and another on those of Halifax. but peace is better for us all, and if it could be followed by a cordial conciliation between us and England it would ensure the happiness and prosperity of both. the bag of wind however on which they are now riding must be suffered to blow out, before they will be able soberly to settle on their true bottom. if they adopt a course of friendship with us, the commerce of 100. millions of people, which some now born will live to see here, will maintain them for ever as a great Unit of the European family. but if they go on checking, irritating, injuring, and hostilizing us, they will force on us the motto 'Carthago delenda est.' and some Scipio Americanus will leave to posterity the problem of conjecturing where stood once the antient and splendid city of London? nothing more simple or certain than the elements of this calculation. I hope the good sense of both parties will concur in travelling rather the paths of peace, of affection and reciprocations of interests.   I salute you with sincere and friendly esteem, and if the homage offered to the virtues of your father can be acceptable to him, place mine at his feet.

TH: JEFFERSON

PoC (DLC); composed in at least two sittings, with final paragraph in a different ink; at foot of first page: "Francis C. Gray esq." Tr (MHi); incomplete; posthumous copy.

In 1810 TJ had calculated how to obtain PURE MERINO sheep through the breeding of mixed stock (TJ to James Madison, 13 May 1810, and enclosure). PARTUS SEQUITUR VENTREM: "The offspring follows the condition of the mother" (A Dictionary of Select and Popular Quotations, which are in daily use [1828], 203). If TJ had a liaison with his slave Sally Hemings and if she was a quadroon, according to these calculations their offspring would have been legally white and entitled to citizenship if they were EMANCIPATED. The Roman senator Marcus Cato supposedly exclaimed CARTHAGO DELENDA EST ("Carthage must be destroyed") each time he voted (Plutarch, Cato, book 27, in Plutarch's Lives, trans. Bernadotte Perrin, Loeb Classical Library [1914–26; repr. 1968], 2:382–3; Charles E. Little, "The Authenticity and Form of Cato's Saying 'Carthago Delenda Est,'" Classical Journal 29 [1934]: 429–35).

[1] Reworked from "become."
[2] Word interlined in place of "method of solution."
[3] Word interlined.
[4] Tr begins with the last syllable of this word and continues to end of letter.
[5] PoC: "republian." Tr: "republican."

To Benjamin Jones

SIR   Monticello Mar. 4. 15.

The war has so long interrupted ordinary intercourse that it's reestablishment is like a new work. I do not know whether you continue the same business of ironmongery, but presuming you do I take the liberty of addressing you, as I shall be glad to renew my dealings with you, not on so large a scale as I have given over manufacturing nails but for my self. I will thank you to send me by the first vessel from your port to Richmond the articles below written, to be addressed to Messrs Gibson and Jefferson there as formerly. favor me at the same time with a bill of the amount, and it shall be punctually remitted within our former usual term of 90. days. Accept the renewed assurances of my esteem and respect.   TH: JEFFERSON

1. ~~Cwt~~ of 4^d hoop iron
2.[1] ~~Cwt~~ of 30^d nail rod
7.[2] ~~Cwt~~ of rods assorted in equal quantities for all sized nails from 6^d to 20^d
a quarter ton of bar iron, assorted of tire-bars, those proper for axes, mattocks, horseshoeing & some inch bars of the toughest quality

PoC (MHi); on verso of reused address cover to TJ; above postscript: "Mr Benjamin Jones"; endorsed by TJ.

YOUR PORT: Philadelphia. TIRE-BARS (tire-iron) were turned into the curved pieces of plate used to shoe cart and carriage wheels (*OED*).

[1] Reworked from "1."
[2] Reworked from "8."

To Thomas Munroe

DEAR SIR   Monticello Mar. 4. 15.

I observe the bill has past for repairing the public buildings in Washington, at which I am sincerely rejoiced, and trust it will for ever silence the question of a removal of the seat of government. you will have much to do for the accomodation of Congress & the government and it will be required in the least time possible. you will therefore I presume be glad of the offer of good workmen from every quarter. two such propose to offer themselves from hence, James Dinsmore and John Nielson. the former I brought from Philadelphia in 1798. and he lived with me 10. years. a more faithful, sober, discreet, honest and respectable man I have never known. he is at present half owner of a valuable manufacturing mill in this neighborhood. Nielson I also got from Philadelphia in 1804. and he lived with me 4. years, and I have found him also, an honest sober, and excellent man. both are house joiners of the first order. they have done the whole of that work in my house, to which I can affirm there is nothing superior in the US. after they had finished with me they worked 2. or 3. year's for the President, to whom therefore they are well known. mr Mills knows them also personally and their works. Doct^r Thornton knows their works, perhaps their persons.[1] whatever they will undertake with you, you may be assured they will perform and in the best and most faithful manner. the most difficult job you have is the dome of the Representatives, and I doubt if there be any men more equal to it than these. Dinsmore built the one to my house, which tho' much smaller, is precisely on the same principles, to wit those of the dome of the meal market of Paris. I strongly recommend these men to you, and if you employ them I shall have the double gratification of having served men worthy of trust, and of putting a public trust into worthy hands. — I am still further gratified by the occasion it has furnished me of addressing you after a long intermission of intercourse between us, and of assuring you that I retain the same sentiments of esteem for you, with which your long & faithful services under my eye inspired me, and the same wishes for your welfare & happiness; with these I pray you to accept my friendly salutations.

Th: Jefferson

PoC (CSmH: JF); on verso of reused address cover of John Barnes to TJ, 10 Jan. 1815; at foot of text: "Mr Thomas Munro"; endorsed by TJ. Tr (DNA: RG 42, LRSCW); at foot of text: "True Copy of the original"; addressed: "Mr Thomas Munroe Washington"; endorsed by the transcriber as "Mr Jeffersons recomendation of J. Dinsmore & J. Neilson as Joiners and Architects 4 March 1815"; notation at foot of address cover in a different hand: "address to either J. Dinsmore J. Neilson or Mr Jefferson"; filed with docket slip.

Thomas Munroe (1771–1852), public official, belonged to a prominent family of merchants in Annapolis. He moved to Washington by the middle of the 1790s and became clerk of the commissioners of the Federal District. Munroe served as the postmaster of Washington, 1799–1829, and as the city's superintendent

from the creation of the post in 1802 until 1816. He was also a director of the local branch of the Bank of the United States, a trustee of the public schools, and a founder of the Columbia Manufacturing Company, which made cotton fabric (*Records of the Columbia Historical Society* 6 [1903]: 156–70; Wilhelmus Bogart Bryan, *A History of the National Capital* [1914–16], 1:478–9; *Centinel of Liberty and George-Town Advertiser*, 24 June 1796; *Washington Federalist*, 7 June 1802; Munroe to TJ, 19 June 1802 [DLC]; *Message from the President of the United States, transmitting a Report of the Secretary of the Treasury of Certain Expenses which have been incurred for public edifices and improvements in the City of Washington* [Washington, 1816]; *Washington City Weekly Gazette*, 4 May 1816, 1 Feb. 1817; Washington *Daily National Intelligencer*, 15 Apr. 1852).

The 13 Feb. 1815 "Act making appropriations for repairing or rebuilding" Washington's PUBLIC BUILDINGS authorized a loan of $500,000 at 6 percent interest for this purpose (*U.S. Statutes at Large*, 3:205). While he was minister plenipotentiary to France, TJ met Maria Cosway in and drew architectural inspira-

tion from the famed MEAL MARKET OF PARIS (La Halle au Blé) (*PTJ*, 10:444–5, 454n).

¹ Sentence interlined, with omitted period preceding caret supplied from Tr.

From the Seventy-Six Association

SIR   [after 4 Mar. 1815]

In obedience to the direction of the 76 association we transmit to you a copy of Mr White's oration as an evidence of their continued esteem for your efforts in supporting the principles of the Republic With the highest respect your obd^t serv^ts

J JERVEY
W^M YEADON
BENJ^N ELLIOTT   } COMMITTEE
R. Y. HAYNE

RC (ViU); written entirely in an unidentified hand on verso of title page of TJ's copy of enclosure; undated; at foot of text: "Hon: Thos Jefferson." Enclosure: John Blake White, *An Oration, Delivered in the Third Episcopal Church, before the Inhabitants of Charleston, South-Carolina, On the 4th March, 1815, in commemoration of the adoption of the Federal Constitution, By appointment of The '76 Association, And published at the request of that Society* (Charleston, 1815; Poor, *Jefferson's Library*, 13 [no. 818]), extolling the adoption of the United States Constitution, the bounty of the nation's farmers, the richness and vastness of America's lands and rivers, the separation of powers established in the Constitution, the freedoms guaranteed by the Bill of Rights, and the proposition that "*all men are created equal*," which is the "adamant key-stone of our Constitution" (p. 11); and encouraging all Americans to learn the principles of the Constitution, to which all must "resort for the '*security of life, Liberty, and the pursuit of happiness*'" (p. 8).

William Yeadon (1777–1849), attorney and public official, served as sheriff

of Charleston, 1813–23, and keeper of the state arsenal, 1823–49. He was a longtime artillery officer in the state militia, including service during the War of 1812 (Thomas Smyth, *A Pattern of Mercy and of Holiness, exhibited in the Conversion and Subsequent Character of Col. William Yeadon, Ruling Elder in the Second Presbyterian Church, Charleston, S.C.* [1849]; *Hoff's Agricultural & Commercial Almanac, calculated for the states of Georgia and the Carolinas; For . . . 1815* [Charleston, 1814], 43; DNA: RG 29, CS, S.C., Charleston, 1810–40; *Charleston Courier*, 13 Nov. 1849).

Benjamin Elliott (ca. 1787–1836), attorney and author, graduated from the College of New Jersey (later Princeton University) in 1806, was admitted to the South Carolina bar in 1810, and thereafter practiced law and resided in his native Charleston. He served in the South Carolina House of Representatives, 1814–15, and rose from register to master in equity of the Court of Equity for the Charleston District between 1815 and his death. Elliott belonged to the Charleston Library Society, the Literary and Philosophical Society of South-Carolina, and the Seventy-Six Association, serving as president of the last in 1821. He was a zealous defender of states' rights, Nullification, and the institution of slavery. Elliott's writings included a letter "To Our Northern Brethren" in Edwin C. Holland, *A Refutation of the Calumnies circulated against The Southern & Western States, respecting the institution and existence of Slavery among them* (Charleston, 1822), 79–82, and reputedly *Debates Which Arose in the House of Representatives of South-Carolina, on the Constitution framed for the United States* (1831). He spoke regularly in public forums, and the Seventy-Six Association published

two of his orations and sent them to TJ (*DAB; BDSCHR,* 4:182–3; *General Catalogue of Princeton University 1746–1906* [1908], 118; Lester D. Stephens, "The Literary and Philosophical Society of South Carolina: A Forum for Intellectual Progress in Antebellum Charleston," *South Carolina Historical Magazine* 104 [2003]: 156, 159–60, 162; Seventy-Six Association to TJ, 26 Apr. 1813, 15 July 1817; Charleston *City Gazette and Commercial Daily Advertiser,* 7 July 1821; Charleston Death Register, 11–18 Sept. 1836 [Sc]; *Charleston Mercury,* 27 Sept. 1836).

From Joseph C. Cabell

DEAR SIR,   Warminster. 5 March. 1815.

After a long detention on the road by the deep snow that fell in the latter part of the month of January I arrived here on 5th ult, since which I have had the pleasure to receive your favor of 5th Jan: together with the papers enclosed. you have imposed on me new obligations by this communication. The particular posture of my domestic affairs at the time I reached home, and the new arrangements in regard to my property demanded by the return of peace, have not permitted me to go over these interesting papers as often, nor to consider their contents as fully & maturely as I could desire. I have read them several times, and bestowed a good deal of reflection on them; but I will beg the favor of another reading towards the end of the year & immediately previous to the meeting of the Assembly. In the interval I shall make a visit to Albemarle, when I should be happy to converse with you and to express more fully than I can at present my views of this subject. Why the petition was not presented I cannot inform you. The papers[1] were never shewn to me, nor did I ever hear of them but incidentally, and I believe[2] after it had been determined not to bring them to the view of the Assembly. Col: Yancey generally consulted with me on the business from Albemarle, and once observed that certain papers relative to an Academy proposed to be established in Charlottesville had been sent down: that they were drawn by yourself, and were so finished off and complete, that the Delegates had only to determine on the expediency of presenting them. I collected from him, that they were in the hands of some of the members of the House of Delegates who would consider & exercise a discretion on the question of their presentment. Being a member of the upper House, I waited of course for the petition to make its appearance in the lower House before I could take up the subject; which at that time I supposed was one of a much more local & confined nature, than I find it really is. Subsequently to this conversation with Col: yancey, I was accidentally a witness to a small part of a conversation between Doctor Carr & Mr Wirt upon the subject of these papers, when Doctor Carr remarked that they had been sent by Mr Peter Carr to Mr David Watson of Louisa, who had determined from some cause or other that they should not be presented at the Last session. I have the highest respect & friendship for Mr Watson, & concluded that the reasons which had decided his mind, were solid & sufficient. This is the amount of the knowledge I then had on the subject. I assure you I had no hint from any quarter that I was expected to bestow particular care on[3] this business, or I should have paid to it the greatest attention imaginable, & done any thing in the compass of my feeble abilities to promote your views. I confess I see nothing at this time that ought to impede the passage of your Bill thro' the Assembly; nor can I conceive from what quarter objections could[4] arise, unless from some of the people of Albemarle, who might not wish to appropriate the proceeds of the sales of the glebes to the establishment of an academy at Charlottesville, or from certain members of the Assembly, who might have other views of the ultimate destination of the Literary[5] fund, or from certain Delegates from the Lower counties who might have fears for William & Mary, or from a certain class of members who might not wish to lend the am^t prayed to be loaned. I hope there would be no other effect produced by the plan upon W^m & Mary than that necessarily resulting from another College in the State. Having had a considerable share in getting Mr Smith to take the Presidency, I should feel somewhat delicately situated in regard to that Seminary. I should be much pleased if such men as M^r say, could find it their interest to reside in Virginia. I have the Commentary on Montesquieu of which you speak, & have commenced its perusal. It is to be inferred from your Letters, I think, that Mr Tracy is the author. His political economy, I will purchase on Sight.

The honorable acquittal of my friend Coles gives me great pleasure. I leave this in a few days for the lower country, to make some new arrangements with my property in Lancaster. If Cockburn has not sent my negroes out of the U. States, I ought to have them again. But I presume they are now making Sugar in the West Indies, and if they have not left the limits of the U. States, I imagine the British will now as formerly disregard the treaty.[6] The negroes from Corrottoman were carried to Tangier Island—From what I have heard, I am led to believe the enemy some time since broke up their establishment on that Island.

I am, d[r] Sir, with great respect y[r] friend   JOSEPH C. CABELL.

RC (ViU: TJP-PC); addressed: "M[r] Jefferson Monticello"; endorsed by TJ as received 10 Mar. 1815 and so recorded in SJL.

TJ's Draft Bill to Create Central College and Amend the 1796 Public Schools Act, [ca. 18 Nov. 1814], does not ask for any money to BE LOANED to the school by the Virginia General Assembly, but TJ mentioned the possibility in his 5 Jan. 1815 letter to Cabell. For the charges against Colonel Isaac A. Coles and his HONORABLE ACQUITTAL, see TJ to Coles, 27 Aug. 1814, and note. In the spring of 1814 British admiral George COCKBURN selected Tangier Island as a refuge for the American slaves liberated by his forces during his campaigns in the Chesapeake Bay and began to organize a company of colonial marines made up of freed bondsmen (Malcomson, *Historical Dictionary*, 107). Cabell owned a large estate called Corotoman (CORROTTOMAN) in Lancaster County (*DVB*).

[1] Reworked from "They."
[2] Preceding two words interlined.
[3] Word interlined in place of "& attention to."
[4] Cabell here canceled "fairly."
[5] Manuscript: "Letirary."
[6] Cabell here canceled "My negroes."

To Thomas Appleton

DEAR SIR   Monticello Mar. 6. 15.

My friend Doct[r] Barton proposes, for the benefit of his health, to try a sea voyage and the air of Europe. he will certainly visit Florence, and not improbably Leghorn. he is one of the Vice presidents of the American Philosophical society, and of the Professors of the University of Philadelphia, distinguished by his writings in the physical sciences. should he visit Leghorn, I ask for him your civilities and good offices, of which, as a distinguished citizen of the United States he is fully worthy, and to his acknolegements will be added mine. I avail myself of this occasion of assuring you of the continuance of my sincere esteem and respect.   TH: JEFFERSON

RC (MBPLi); at foot of text: "M[r] Appleton." PoC (DLC); endorsed by TJ. Recorded in SJL as sent to Leghorn "by D[r] Barton." Enclosed in TJ to Benjamin Smith Barton, 7 Mar. 1815.

From Benjamin Smith Barton

DEAR SIR,   March 6. 1815.
I return one of the vols. of Persoon. The other shall follow in a few days. I greatly regret the long keeping. an unpleasant accident, which it is unnecessary to mention particularly, was the cause of my so long depriving you of these books. It will be very grateful to me to learn, from you, in any way you please, of the safe return of these[1] vols. For the loan of them, I am very much obligd to you;
    I am, Dear Sir, with very great respect, yours, &c.,

B. S. BARTON.

RC (DLC); dateline at foot of text; addressed: "To Thomas Jefferson, Esq., Monticello, Virginia"; franked; postmarked Philadelphia, 7 Mar.; endorsed by TJ as received 16 Mar. 1815 from Philadelphia and so recorded in SJL. Enclosure: Christiaan Hendrik Persoon, *Synopsis Plantarum, seu Enchiridium Botanicum* (Paris, 1805–07; Sowerby, no. 1073; Poor, *Jefferson's Library*, 6 [no. 277]), vol. 2.

[1] Barton here canceled "books."

To Stephen Cathalan

MY GOOD AND MUCH
ESTEEMED FRIEND   Monticello Mar. 6. 1815.
    I am much gratified by the opportunity of recalling myself to your recollection by this letter which will be handed you by my friend Doctor Barton. he is one of the Vice presidents of the American Philosophical society, and of the Professors of the University of Philadelphia, distinguished by his writings in the Physical sciences. he tries a sea-voyage and the air of Europe for the benefit of his health, and will surely visit Marseilles in his route. recieve him as my friend and add this to former testimonies that my respect for you has been thought worthy of a friendly reciprocation. Accept the assurance of my constant and sincere esteem and respect.

TH: JEFFERSON

RC (MBPLi); at foot of text: "M. Cathalan." PoC (PPAmP: Benjamin Smith Barton Papers); endorsed by TJ. Recorded in SJL as sent to Marseilles "by Dr Barton." Enclosed in TJ to Benjamin Smith Barton, 7 Mar. 1815.

To José Corrêa da Serra

DEAR SIR   Monticello Mar. 6. 15.

I mentioned to you in a former letter that mr Say had asked of me information relative to the price of lands E.^tc. in the neighborhood of Charlottesville with a view to the removal of his family to this country. in the inclosed letter I have given him the best and fullest information I could, of every circumstance which might influence his judgment and final determination. altho' I have endeavored to confine myself rigorously t[o] matters of fact, yet aware of our natural partiality to our own country, and even our own neighborhood, I am afraid I may have given an aspect influenced by that. of this a foreigner would be a better judge than a native, and none better than yourself. I have therefore left the letter open, and request you to peruse it, and if you find any thing which ought to be corrected, that you will be so good as to note it in a letter to mr Say with whom I believe you are particularly acquainted. when perused be so good as to stick a wafer in it, and also in the envelope to mr Ticknor, and commit it to the mail, with as little delay as you can, as mr Ticknor will sail for Europe very soon.

We all rejoice at the peace, and most especially as we closed the war with such a sample to England of our character as an enemy, in proportion as we advance in the exercises of war. yet it is but a truce, unless in the interval of general peace, she settles amicably the business of impressment. the first American citizen she impresses will be a declaration of war. I am not without apprehensions that the late change in the condition of Europe may tempt you to leave us. if this be necessary for your happiness, as is but too probable, our friendship for you[1] would require us to submit to the sacrifice. if you continue with us a while longer, I shall hope for your passing at Monticello as much of the summer as you can. the cession of my library to Congress will have left you that resource the less for your amusement with us. but the season for botanizing will in some measure supply it. Accept my affectionate and respectful salutations.

TH: JEFFERSON

PoC (DLC); one word faint; at foot of text: "M. Correa de Serra"; endorsed by TJ. Enclosure: TJ to Jean Baptiste Say, 2 Mar. 1815.

The ENVELOPE TO MR TICKNOR covered the enclosed letter to Say (see TJ to George Ticknor, 19 Mar. 1815).

[1] Preceding two words interlined.

To William H. Crawford

DEAR SIR   Monticello Mar. 6. 15.

This will be handed you by my friend Dr Barton, one of the Vice-presidents of the American Philosophical society, a professor in the University of Philadelphia and distinguished by his writings in the Physical sciences. he proposes for the benefit of his health to take a voyage across the Atlantic and to try the air of Europe for a while — if not personally known to you, I am sure he is sufficiently so by character, to ensure to him all the good offices and civilities you will be so kind as to shew him, and he will be especially thankful for any introductions you can procure him into the literary circles of Paris. I am happy in this as in every other occasion of assuring you of my high respect and great esteem.   TH: JEFFERSON

RC (MBPLi); at foot of text: "His Excellency Mr Crawford." PoC (DLC); endorsed by TJ. Recorded in SJL as sent to Paris "by Dr Barton." Enclosed in TJ to Benjamin Smith Barton, 7 Mar. 1815.

To Adamo Fabbroni, Antoine Gouan, Lacépède, Marc Auguste Pictet, and André Thoüin

SIR[1]   Monticello in Virginia. Mar. 6. 1815.

Doct^r Barton, my friend, proposing, for the benefit of his health, a voyage across the Atlantic, and a trial of the air of Europe,[2] will probably visit[3] Florence in the course of his travels. he is one of the Vice presidents of the American Philosophical society, Professor of Natural history, Botany, Materia Medica, and of the Institutes and Clinical practice of Medecine in the University of Philadelphia, and distinguished by his writings in the Physical sciences. I have thought I should render a service acceptable to yourself as well as to him, and perhaps to Science itself, by procuring a personal acquaintance between two of her sons[4] laboring in their different hemispheres for the instruction of man. I have therefore requested Dr Barton to present to you himself this letter, which, while it conveys to you the assurances of my high esteem and respect, may gratify me with new testimonies of a continuance of yours, in the attentions and civilities you may be so kind as to shew to my learned friend. I perform this office with the greater pleasure as it furnishes me a new occasion of tendering you the tribute of my high respect and consideration.   TH: JEFFERSON

RC (PPAN: John Torrey Letters); addressed: "Al Signior Addamo Fabbroni Socio corrispondente della Reale Accademia economica della Toscana à Firenze." Dft (MHi); on verso of reused address cover to TJ; unsigned; at foot of text: "C^t de Lacepede M. Thouin Pictet Fabbroni Gouan"; with list on verso containing both the names of the ten men TJ wrote this day on Benjamin Smith Barton's behalf and four others: Destutt de Tracy, Pierre Samuel Du Pont de Nemours, Alexander von Humboldt, and Alexis Marie Rochon, with check marks by the five names covered by the circular letter above and the remaining names canceled; endorsed by TJ as a letter to Lacépède, Thoüin, Gouan, Pictet, and Fabbroni. Recorded in SJL as five separate letters to be delivered "by Dr Barton" to Lacépède and Thoüin in Paris, Gouan in Montpellier, Pictet in Geneva, and Fabbroni in Florence. Enclosed in TJ to Barton, 7 Mar. 1815.

Adamo Fabbroni (1748–1816) was born in Florence and studied and lived in various parts of the Italian peninsula before returning to his hometown in 1787. He was a member of the Florentine Academy and a host of other learned societies, the editor for several years of an agricultural journal, and the author of many scholarly publications, five of which TJ received during the 1780s from Fabbroni's brother Giovanni. In addition to his more general agricultural works, Fabbroni published monographs on a wide range of topics, including archaeology, sculpture, silkworms, the valuation of land, and the manufacture of wine (*Dizionario Biografico degli Italiani* [1960–], 43:669–73; Giuseppe Sarchiani, "Elogio d'Adamo Fabbroni," *Continuazione degli Atti dell'Imp. e Reale Accademia Economico-Agraria dei Georgofili di Firenze* [Florence, 1818], 1:197–206; *PTJ*, 10:155–6, 14:701, 27:754–5; Sowerby, nos. 119, 120, 770, 816, 1210).

Antoine Gouan (1733–1821), botanist and zoologist, was born in Montpellier, France, and received his medical degree from the University of Montpellier in 1752. He was appointed professor of botany at his alma mater late in the 1760s and was the director of Montpellier's botanical garden for many years. A friend and follower of Carolus Linnaeus, Gouan wrote prolifically on plants, fish, and insects. TJ met the Frenchman while on his 1787 tour of southern France, received seeds from him during his presidency, and owned a work by him explaining the Linnaean botanical system. Gouan was a member of the Institut de France and the Légion d'honneur and served as a physician in the French army, 1793–94. He retired from teaching in 1802 due to illness, became blind during the last decade of his life, and died in his hometown (*Biographie universelle*, 17:223–5; M. Amoreux, "Notice Historique Sur Antoine Gouan, professeur de botanique à l'Ecole de Médecine de Montpellier," *Mémoires de la Société Linnéenne de Paris* 1 [1822]: 656–82; *PTJ*, 11:444; Sowerby, no. 1079; Gouan to TJ, 28 Oct. 1804 [DLC]; "Portraits of Botanists," *Taxon* 21 [1972]: 302).

Marc Auguste Pictet (1752–1825), educator and scientist, was born and educated in Geneva, Switzerland. Although originally trained as an attorney, he turned to science while still in his twenties. Pictet was professor of natural philosophy at the Academy of Geneva, 1786–1825, director of the local observatory, 1790–1819, and a member of both the Institut de France and the Royal Society of London. In 1790 he published an important work on heat, and six years later he helped found a journal, the *Bibliothèque Britannique*, to disseminate British scientific and technological discoveries. Although Pictet's diverse scholarly interests included astronomy, geology, and meteorology, TJ only owned two of his works, a compilation of letters written in 1801 during a tour of the British Isles and an 1803 discourse on customs duties. A frequent visitor to Paris during the Consulate and Empire, he joined Napoleon's Tribunate in 1802 and was an inspector of France's Université Impériale for a number of years. After the emperor's downfall, Pictet returned to Geneva and continued his studies there until his death (*DSB*; *PTJ*, 28:239–40; Jean Rilliet and Jean Cassaigneau, *Marc-Auguste Pictet ou le rendez-vous de l'Europe universelle, 1752–1825* [1995]; Hoefer, *Nouv. biog. générale*, 39:91–2; *Dictionnaire historique de la Suisse* [2002–   ]; Sowerby, nos. 2859, 3867).

[1] Dft: "Dr Sir."
[2] In Dft TJ here canceled "for some time."
[3] In Dft remainder of sentence reads "Paris on his route Southwardly."
[4] Preceding four words interlined in Dft in place of "sçavants" ("scholars").

From Patrick Gibson

SIR   Richmond 6th March 1815

Your favor of the 25th ult[o] is received I should be much pleased to find your opinion to be correct, with regard to a rise in the price of flour in April, we know at present nothing of the markets in Europe on which to form a correct judgement, but my present impression is that they will not justify higher prices, and the quantity required in the West Indies (together with our own consumpt) is too small to make much impression upon that on hand—it is now very dull, a few sales were on the first news of peace made at 7$ Cash, & subsequently on time, it continues to be the <u>asking price</u>, but there are no purchasers, nor do I think 6½$ could be obtain'd—. Tobacco continues to be very brisk at from 8 to 13$ and in few instances 14$—   Your note in bank becoming due in a few days I inclose you a blank for your signature—With great regard

I am Your ob[t] Serv[t]   PATRICK GIBSON

RC (MHi); between dateline and salutation: "Thomas Jefferson Esq[re]"; endorsed by TJ as received 7 Mar. 1815 and so recorded in SJL. Enclosure not found.

TJ's reply to Gibson of 8 Mar. 1815, not found, is recorded in SJL. He indicated in his financial records for that date that he had "Renewed my note in bank" (*MB*, 2:1306).

To Philip Mazzei

DEAR SIR   Monticello Mar. 6. 15.

My friend D[r] Barton proposing for the benefit of his health a voyage across the Atlantic, and a trial of the air of Europe, intends to visit Florence and Pisa in the course of his travels. he is a Vice president of the American Philosophical society, Professor of Natural history, Botany, Materia Medica, and of the Institutes and Clinical practice of Medicine in the University of Philadelphia. knowing your devotion to this, your, as well as our country, and the pleasure with which you recieve all it's citizens, I have requested Dr Barton to deliver you this letter himself. he will be able to communicate to you the events of our late war, and the present state of things here in all the details in which I know you are ever anxious to learn him.[1] I wrote you on the 29th of Dec. 1813. an interesting letter on your affairs here, which I hope you recieved and shall very soon write you another, in the mean time I am anxious to hear from you. be so good as to recieve Dr Barton as my friend, procure him such literary acquaintance as you may conveniently and he may wish and be assured of my constant and affectionate friendship   TH: JEFFERSON

RC (NNGL, on deposit NHi); addressed: "Mr Philip Mazzei at Pisa." PoC (DLC); endorsed by TJ. Recorded in SJL as sent to Pisa "by Dr Barton." Enclosed in TJ to Benjamin Smith Barton, 7 Mar. 1815.

[1] Thus in manuscript.

To John A. Morton

DEAR SIR   Monticello Mar. 6. 15.

My friend Dr Barton for the benefit of his health proposes a voyage across the Atlantic, and a trial of the air of Europe. his route on the continent not being fixed, he may possibly visit Bordeaux. in that case I ask for him your civilities and good offices. he is one of the Vice presidents of the American Philosophical society, and of the Professors of the University of Philadelphia, and well known by his writings in the Physical sciences. should he make any stay with you, as the fine temperature of your city might invite, you will oblige me by procuring for him an acquaintance with some of the persons of science in your city; and I am happy in this occasion of assuring you of my great esteem and respect.   TH: JEFFERSON

PoC (MHi); at foot of text: "Mr Moreton"; endorsed by TJ. Recorded in SJL as sent to Bordeaux "by Dr Barton." Enclosed in TJ to Benjamin Smith Barton, 7 Mar. 1815.

From George Ticknor

DEAR SIR,   Philadelphia March 6. 1815.

In consequence of letters, which I have this morning and, in fact, this moment received from Boston, giving me notice of the intention of several of my nearest friends to embark for Europe in some of the earliest vessels, I have determined to hasten home & avail myself of an opportunity, which, on every account will be so grateful to me. I take, therefore, the liberty you allowed me, of writing to you and asking you to do me the favour to forward to my address in Boston the letters to your friends in Europe, which your politeness offered me, and any commands in relation to collecting a library or any other business, wh. it may suit your convenience to entrust to me. If to these, you will have the goodness to add a letter to Mr. Gallatin, to whom, I believe, nobody in N. England is competent to introduce me, & on whom as an American citizen, I suppose, I have some indefinite claims, you will add much to the favour which your kindness has already promised me.

I cannot suffer this opportunity to pass, without repeating my acknowledgements, for the advice & instruction I received from you in relation to my projected voyage & visit to Europe; and all the various kindness and hospitality which I found under your roof & amidst your family. I beg you to present my regards to Col. Randolph, & his lady and to those of your grandchildren with whom I had the pleasure of becoming acquainted, & to permit me to hope, that, if I am so fortunate as to be remembered[1] in the happy circle which philosophy & affection have gathered, round your fire-side, it may be as your

Most obliged & obedient friend GEORGE TICKNOR.

RC (MHi); at foot of text: "Mr. Jefferson, Monticello"; endorsed by TJ as received 16 Mar. 1815 and so recorded in SJL.

[1] Manuscript: "rememembered."

To Benjamin Smith Barton

DEAR SIR Monticello Mar. 7. 15.

Your letter of Feb. 19. was ten days on it's passage to me, and this followed by an interval of six days between the arrival & departure of our mail, leaves but 6. days for this to reach you within the three weeks limited for your departure. I am sorry to learn that the state of your health is such as to oblige you to seek it's repair in other countries, and with pleasure furnish you such letters as may assist in alleviating your peregrinations. supposing the National Museum, and National garden at Paris would be the most interesting objects for you, I inclose a letter for the Count de Lacepede at the head of the former, and M. Thouin who has the direction of the latter. I have not added letters for Dupont and Humboldt, because I am sure you are personally acquainted with them, and they can make you known to such of the literary circle as you may chuse. mr Crawford, even without a letter, would have been your patron ex officio. you ask my opinion of the best summering place. Geneva is that of the English, and affords very learned society. I inclose a letter to mr Pictet whose eminence is known to you. I do not know him personally, and altho' our correspondence was only in the exchange of a letter or two, yet it was on a matter interesting to him, and I am sure he will recieve the letter I address to him with attention. but I should prefer Montpellier for the summer; for altho' in a Southern part of France it is very elevated in it's situation, open to all the winds, has a beautiful and extensive public garden, bowers, baths, and a good literary society. I give you a letter to Dr Gouan the patriarch of the literati there, and of the place, and who does it's honors to strangers with great kindness. he has written in Botany and Medecine.[1] on your way Southwardly you will visit Marseilles of course, a delightful residence and affording good society in science. my old friend Cathalan is but a merchant, but he knows every body and can make you known to them.

for Florence where you propose to make some stay, I give you a letter to Mr Fabbroni, well known to the men of science of Europe. he is of an Agricultural society of Florence, and has written in that line; he is also at the head of the public library there. you will surely from thence visit Pisa, celebrated for it's fine situation, salubrity, for it's academy and learned society. there my friend Mazzei (if alive, for he is upwards of 80.) will make you known. he is a furious republican, affectionately attached to America, and will be delighted with what you will tell him of the successes of our two last campaigns. he is author of the Recherches politiques et historiques des E.U. d'Amerique.[2] should you visit Leghorn also from Florence the letter to Appleton will be of service.—I will add an observation worthy the notice of every traveller. when one has to go from one place to another at a distance, never think of the direct road, which generally leads on the ridges and barrenest parts between river & river, but make directly for a river and take the road along that, which always leads thro' the richest country, the best cultivated & most populous. thus in going from Paris to Marseilles ascend the Seine to Dijon then fall in upon the Saone at Chalons and descend that and the Rhone to Arles, & then across to Marseilles. so from Paris to Amsterdam ascend the Seine & Marne to Vitry, cross over to Nancy and direct to Strasburg, and thence along the Rhine E^tc.

If you should be at Leisure to write from any of your stations, I shall always be happy to recieve a line from you, altho I should not be able to return it unless I could shoot flying. I think it possible you may find some of my friends to whom I inclose letters, dead, as several are old, and I have not heard from them for some time. wishing you all the delights the journey is calculated to afford, and all the benefits of health you wish from it, I tender you the assurances of my great esteem & respect.   TH: JEFFERSON

P.S. altho' you speak of going no further than Florence, as you may be tempted to visit Rome, I have added a letter to Cardinal Dugnani, an excellent man with whom I was much acquainted at Paris during our residence there.

RC (MBPLi); at foot of first page: "Doct^r Barton." PoC (DLC); endorsed by TJ. Enclosures: (1) TJ to Thomas Appleton, 6 Mar. 1815. (2) TJ to Stephen Cathalan, 6 Mar. 1815. (3) TJ to William H. Crawford, 6 Mar. 1815. (4–8) TJ to Adamo Fabbroni, Antoine Gouan, Lacépède, Marc Auguste Pictet, and André Thoüin, 6 Mar. 1815. (9) TJ to Philip Mazzei, 6 Mar. 1815. (10) TJ to John A. Morton, 6 Mar. 1815. (11) TJ to Antonio Dugnani, 7 Mar. 1815.

In 1795 Pictet and TJ exchanged letters on A MATTER INTERESTING TO HIM, Pictet's proposed immigration to the United States (*PTJ*, 28:239–40, 505, 34:152–4).

[1] Sentence interlined.
[2] Sentence interlined.

To Antonio Dugnani

Monticello in Virginia Mar. 7. 15

MY DEAR AND EXCELLENT CARDINAL.

My friend Doct^r Barton proposing, for the benefit of his health, a voyage across the Atlantic, and a trial of the air of Europe, will probably be tempted to visit the classical and Splendid city of Rome. he is one of the Vice presidents of the American Philosophical society, Professor of Natural history, Botany, Materia Medica, and of the Institutes and Clinical practice of medecine in the University of Philadelphia, and distinguished by his writings in the physical sciences. your known and kind patronage to American citizens visiting Rome gives me confidence that the worth of Doct^r Barton will ensure it's benefit to him. in requesting my learned friend to present to you this letter himself, I am much gratified by the occasion it[1] affords me of recalling myself to your recollection, and of renewing to you this testimony of my high respect. during so much revolution every where it has been a subject of anxiety to me to learn how you have steered through it. Accept, I pray you, the assurances of my constant and great esteem and consideration.   TH: JEFFERSON

PoC (MHi); at foot of text: "His Excellency Cardinal Dugnani"; endorsed by TJ. Recorded in SJL as sent to Rome "by D[r] Barton." Enclosed in TJ to Benjamin Smith Barton, 7 Mar. 1815.

Antonio Dugnani (1748–1818), a native of Milan, was educated in that city and at the University of Pavia, where he received a doctorate in canon and civil law. Having moved to Rome to pursue an ecclesiastical career, he became a personal secretary to Pope Clement XIV in 1770 and was ordained a priest the following year. After serving for over a decade as a papal lawyer and auditor, Dugnani was elevated to archbishop in 1785. He was dispatched to France as apostolic nuncio in 1787 and struck up a friendship with TJ in Paris. When the French Revolution began Dugnani was unable to prevent the confiscation of church property and the reorganization of the French clergy to the Vatican's detriment. He left the French capital in 1791. Raised to cardinal in 1794, Dugnani labored as a papal legate, adviser, and prefect of justice during the years that followed. He died in Rome (*Dizionario Biografico degli Italiani* [1960–]; *PTJ*, 13:339, 346–7, 29:370, 31:559–60; TJ to Dugnani, 14 Feb. 1818).

[1] Manuscript: "if."

From George Hay

SIR   Richmond. March 8. 1815

I ought to ask your pardon and I do ask it, for not having returned long ago, the book which you were so good as to lend me. M. Rayneval has been of Service to me, on more occasions than one: he has more liberality than Some of his predecessors: but the Science of public law appears to me to be far, very far from that point, to which Some very obvious principles are capable of conducting it.

Scotts bill was dismissed in June last, and the Execution for the Costs was delivered in October to M[r] Wirt. I did believe until the receipt of your late letter that I had duly informed you of the decision.

I have Some rough notes on the Subject of party Spirit. My object is to trace it step by step to its real origin in the human heart. Humes essay on parties in general is unworthy of the subject and of himself. I think that I may venture, tho' I know not exactly when, to publish my reflections on this very interesting topic, about which however I have no books to consult. If you recollect any, from which you conceive any aid can be derived, I should deem[1] myself honored & obliged, by your taking the trouble to point them out.

I am with great respect y[r] mo. ob. Se.   GEO: HAY.

RC (DLC); endorsed by TJ as received 10 Mar. 1815 and so recorded in SJL.

For the work by Joseph Matthias Gérard de RAYNEVAL probably enclosed herein, see note to TJ to Hay, 26 Feb. 1815.

David Hume's ESSAY ON PARTIES IN GENERAL first appeared in his *Essays, Moral and Political* (Edinburgh, 1741), 105–18. In it he argues that the founders of sects and factions ought "to be detested and hated; because the Influence of Factions is directly contrary to that of

Laws. Factions subvert Government; render Laws impotent, and beget the fiercest Animosities among Men of the same Nation"; contends that parties "rise more easily, and propagate themselves faster in free Governments"; posits that they may be divided into two categories, the personal and those based "on some real Difference of Sentiment or Interest"; states that within the latter, those concerned with "abstract speculative Principles" are particularly dangerous to the body politic; gives as an example the often bloody disputes over theology; and accuses religious parties of being "more furious and enrag'd than the most cruel Factions, that ever arose from Interest or Ambition."

[1] Manuscript: "deemed."

From John Rhea

9th March 1815 Washington—

With the expression of sincere esteem John Rhea of Tennessee has the honor to present the inclosed Copy of a Circular letter to Thomas Jefferson late President of the United States.

RC (MHi); dateline at foot of text; endorsed by TJ as received 16 Mar. 1815 and so recorded in SJL. Enclosure: Rhea to his constituents, Washington, D.C., 27 Feb. 1815, contending that the peace negotiations at Ghent had been delayed by the British government's claim to "a large part of the district of Maine; the absolute dominion of all the great lakes, and fortified positions on their shores . . . a large part of the state of Ohio; the Michigan, Indiana, Illinois, and western territories . . . together with the free navigation of the Mississippi" River; explaining the content and necessity of the taxes passed by Congress to meet America's wartime needs and keep the public credit on a proper footing; hailing the peace treaties signed with Great Britain and her Indian allies; justifying the 1812 declaration of war by the United States; describing America's successes on land and sea during the conflict, with particular emphasis on General Andrew Jackson's decisive victories, first over the Creek Indians and then over the British at the Battle of New Orleans; stating that with the return of peace the "honor, rights, liberties, sovereignty, and independence, of this nation, are preserved and confirmed, and will be transmitted pure to posterity"; and asking his fellow citizens to join him in thanking "the Almighty Being, who holds in his power the destinies of men and of nations!" (printed circular in DLC: Printed Ephemera Collection; reprinted in Noble E. Cunningham Jr., ed., *Circular Letters of Congressmen to Their Constituents, 1789–1829* [1978], 2:921–7).

To William W. Hening

DEAR SIR   Monticello Mar. 11. 15.

Congress having concluded to replace by my library the one which they lost by British Vandalism, it is now become their property, and of course my duty to collect and put in place whatever belongs to it. this obliges me to request of you the return of the Vth vol. of my Collection of the Virginia laws, being that in which the Sessions acts were bound together. should there be in the volume any acts not yet published nor copied, you could perhaps have them copied within the time the library will still remain here, which will probably be yet two or three weeks. I had always expected that the library would have been valued volume by volume, in which case I meant to reserve these acts and journals of the legislature of Virginia: but instead of that they took it in a lump as it stood on the catalogue at a sum in gross, so that I cannot retain a single volume. be so good as to have it well packed and addressed to me by the mail stage to Milton.   It would gratify me to learn how far you have got in the actual publication of the laws, how many more volumes there will be, and when you expect to compleat the whole publication. Accept the assurance of my esteem & respect.   Th: Jefferson

PoC (DLC); on verso of reused address cover of Alexander J. Dallas to TJ, 21 Feb. 1815; at foot of text: "Mʳ Hening"; endorsed by TJ.

From William Short

Dear sir   Philadelphia March 11—15

Your kind & friendly letter of Nov. 28. gave me not the less pleasure for having remained so long unacknowleged—The cause of my silence has been an affliction[1] in the eyes so highly inflamatory as to preclude me from the use of my pen & my books—The disorder seems now to have left me, but I am not yet placed in the <u>statu quo ante</u>, & am obliged to use my eyes sparingly. I cannot however longer postpone thanking you for all the details of your letter & particularly for one phrase which was of great use & comfort to me during that dark & to me desponding period—I frequently recurred to the letter to read over again the sentence "tranquillity of mind depends much on ourselves & greatly on due reflection 'how much pain have cost us the evils which have never happened'"[2]—   I little then expected how soon this would be verified in an event which all human reason forbad us to look for—the restoration of peace—I hail it as the salvation of our country & as a new proof how inscrutable are the ways of Providence.

As to the war I have always thought that both France & England gave us sufficient cause to declare it against either at any time from the commencement of theirs—It was the expediency of declaring it that I denied—& the stupid manner in which it was conducted that I blamed—I was disgusted also to see with so many persons who were called Americans that an injury or insult offered to America was considered so only according to the country from which it came—Some were English some French & none Americans—From many of those who were now all alive to national honor as regarded England & ready to throw down the gauntlet, I remembered when in Europe to have read speeches at the time of the French war all pacific & making calculations to shew how many more dollars one campaign would cost us than all the vessels & cargoes that France could take from us. Mr Madison I recollect when first I met him at Monticello went into an argument with me by way of interrogations, the whole marrow of which was to shew, (& shewed that he thought) the Directory a set of good honest souls who never would have thought of plundering or injuring us in any way if we[3] had been kind & shewn affection to them &c. &c. I could not help smiling in his face at so much simplicity or so much ignorance—& assured him they were a pack of the most worthless scoundrels that chance had ever put at the head of a government—& that they plundered us for the real love of plunder & want of employment for some of their dependents—that if we were nearer to them & more in their power they would plunder us so much the more—as they had done to those powers or rather those people who had always shewn the greatest possible affection for them—I could not restrain myself & probably showed a contempt of his fine system which has never I believe been forgiven me—He knit his brow & never again interrogated me as to France—Acting on this as all those fretful & obstinate men who do not enquire in order really to obtain information, but to obtain answers confirming their own systems & ideas.—However peace be to him—Providence has favored him & drawn him out of a situation which otherwise would have placed him in a point of view truly ridiculous in history—I congratulate him on his happy escape, because we are saved with him.

It gave me great pleasure to see that your valuable Library was to be secured & forever kept together—It would have been much to be regretted that it should have been exposed after you to be divided & separated. This would unavoidably have been the case in a few generations if left to private hands—The fate of that of Westover was a sufficient warning—It was scattered in the winds—& separate volumes are every now & then to be found in the booksales here.   I suppose of course you will be paid for it in Treasury notes—These are yet at a small depreciation I have thought it probable that that might prevent you from offering them to me—I hope that will not be the case & to prevent it I now mention to you that they will suit me perfectly, & if I were to have them soon I could make an arrangement by which they would answer me perfectly as bank-notes, without the smallest loss.

This is about the time you expected Co^lo Monroe to be in Albe-marle—I hope he will now terminate our affair—particularly as he seems to think his personal presence necessary. The appearances are now I am told all in favor of his being the next President. He will then be less capable of attending to such a microscopic object as this.   Correa however who has travelled & observed a great deal says the next President will be from N. York—& he has fixed on Tomkins for that office—For my part I hope now our destiny will be a happy one, whoever may be the President, & feeling myself person-ally dead as to all such matters I take very little interest in them.

I have been endeavoring all the winter to reason away my antipa-thy to the sea in order to avail myself of a very favorable occasion I now have of passing it—but I have a kind of thalassophobia that re-sists all kind of argument—It is like the antipathy which some people have to rats or cats & I fear will be with me unconquerable until I shall feel myself too old to make it worthwhile to take the trouble—I do not like my poor vegetating situation which I hold here—but I do not know how to change it for the better—My friends all advise me to marry—but my taste is too fastidious I believe—& my chance is worse every year—for old bachelors grow difficult in proportion as they are older & have less right to chuse—

God bless you my dear sir—May you long live to enjoy your sound philosophy—& be happy—Believe me your respectful & your affec-tionate friend   W Short

RC (MHi); endorsed by TJ as received 17 Mar. 1815 and so recorded in SJL. RC (MHi); address cover only; with PoC of TJ to John Watts, 25 Mar. 1815, on verso; addressed: "Thomas Jefferson Monticello mail to Milton, Virginia"; franked; postmarked Philadelphia, 11 Mar.

The FRENCH WAR is a reference to America's so-called "Quasi-War" with France late in the 1790s. Short and James Madison apparently disagreed over the merits of the French DIRECTORY during their visit to Monticello in September 1802 (Madison, *Papers, Sec. of State Ser.*, 3:578, 582; Short to TJ, 7 May 1816). TJ himself owned a number of titles from the dispersed library amassed by William Byrd (1674–1744) at his WESTOVER es-tate (*MB*, 1:327; Sowerby; Kevin J. Hayes, *The Library of William Byrd of Westover* [1997]). Daniel D. Tompkins (TOMKINS) was governor of New York at this time and served as vice president of the United States, 1817–25. THALASSO-PHOBIA: "a morbid dread of the sea" (*OED*).

[1] Manuscript: "affiction."
[2] Omitted closing double quotation mark editorially supplied.
[3] Word interlined in place of "they."

From Samuel H. Smith

DEAR SIR   Washington[1] Mar. 11. 1815

I have the pleasure of acknowledging[2] the receipt of your favor of the 27th ult.

Congress having on the last day of their sitting modified the pending bill for the transportation of the Library so to leave the necessary dispositions to the President of the U.S. I yesterday consulted with him on the subject. He considers it advisable to postpone its transportation until some time in May, and that it be transported by land in such way as shall be most agreeable to you. For this purpose it is contemplated to employ Joseph Dougherty. I forward to you in a distinct packet the Catalogue. If then, you will be pleased, when the Library shall be in a condition for transportation, to drop me a line, with any further suggestions that may occur to you, arrangements shall be immediately made for closing[3] the business.

I am, with great respect & regard,
    Yo. ob^t s^t   SA H SMITH

RC (DLC); endorsed by TJ as received 16 Mar. 1815 and so recorded in SJL. FC (DLC: J. Henley Smith Papers); in Smith's hand and endorsed by him.

The 3 Mar. 1815 "Act to provide a library room, and for transporting the library lately purchased" to the nation's capital gave PRESIDENT James Madison the authority to accomplish both goals "during the ensuing recess of Congress" (*U.S. Statutes at Large*, 3:225–6).

[1] Manuscript: "Washigton."
[2] Manuscript: "acknowledgig."
[3] Manuscript: "closig."

To William Wirt

                                        Monticello Mar. 11. 15.

Th: Jefferson presents his compliments to mr Wirt, and on enquiry what had been done in Scott's suit against him he learns that it was dismissed in June last, and that the execution for the costs has been delivered to mr Wirt. he asks the favor of it's being forwarded to him and salutes him with assurances of his great esteem and respect.

PoC (MHi); dateline at foot of text; on verso of reused address cover from Hugh Nelson to TJ; endorsed by TJ.

To Louis H. Girardin

Th: Jefferson to mr Girardin   Monticello Mar. 12. 15.

I return the three Cahiers, which I have perused with the usual satisfaction. you will find a few pencilled notes, merely verbal.

But in one place I have taken a greater liberty than I ever took before, or ever indeed had occasion to take. it is in the case of Josiah[1] Philips, which I find strangely represented by judge Tucker and mr Edmund Randolph, and very negligently vindicated by mr Henry. that case is personally known to me, because I was of the legislature at the time, was one of those consulted by mr Henry, and had my share in the passage of the bill. I never before saw the observations of those gentlemen, which you quote on this case, and will now therefore briefly make some strictures on them.

Judge Tucker, instead of a definition[2] of the functions of bills of attainder, has given a diatribe against their abuse. the occasion and proper[3] office of a bill of attainder is this. when a person, charged with a crime, withdraws from justice, or resists it by force, either in his own or a foreign country, no other means of bringing him to trial or punishment being practicable, a special act is passed by the legislature, adapted to the particular case. this prescribes to him a sufficient term to appear and submit to a trial by his peers; declares that his refusal to appear shall be taken as a confession of guilt, as in the ordinary case of an offender at the bar refusing to plead, and pronounces the sentence which would have been rendered on his confession or conviction in a court of law. no doubt that these acts of attainder have been abused in England, as instruments of vengeance, by a succesful over a defeated party. but what institution is insusceptible of abuse in wicked hands?

Again the judge says, 'the court refused to pass sentence of execution pursuant to the directions of the act.' the court could not refuse this, because it was never proposed to them; and my authority for this assertion shall be presently given.

For the perversion of a fact so intimately known to himself mr Randolph can be excused only by our indulgence for orators who, pressed by a powerful adversary, lose sight, in the ardor of conflict, of the rigorous accuracies of fact, and permit their imagination to distort and colour them to the views of the moment. he was Attorney General at the time, and told me himself, the first time I saw him after the trial of Philips, that when taken & delivered up to justice, he had thought it best to make no use of the act of attainder, and to take no measure under it; that he had indicted him at the Common law either for murder or robbery (I forget which & whether for both) that he was tried on this indictment in the ordinary way, found guilty by the jury, sentenced and executed under the common law; a course which every one approved, because the first object of the act of attainder was to bring him to fair trial. whether mr Randolph was right in this information to me, or when in the debate with mr Henry, he represents this atrocious offender as sentenced and executed under the act of attainder, let the record of the case decide.

'without being confronted with his accusers and witnesses, without the privilege of calling for evidence in his behalf, he was sentenced to death, and afterwards actually executed.' I appeal to the universe to produce one single instance from the first establishment of government in this state to the present day, where, in a trial at bar, a criminal has been refused confrontation with his accusers and witnesses, or denied the privilege of calling for evidence in his behalf. had it been done in this case, I would have asked of the Attorney General why he proposed or permitted it? but, without having seen the record, I will venture, on the character of our courts, to deny that it was done. but if mr Randolph meant only that Philips had not these advantages on the passage of the bill of Attainder, how idle to charge the legislature with omitting to confront the culprit with his witnesses, when he was standing out in arms, and in defiance of their authority, and their sentence was to take effect only on his own refusal to come in and be confronted. we must either therefore consider this as a mere hyperbolism of imagination in the heat of debate, or what I should rather believe, a defective statement by the Reporter of mr Randolph's argument. I suspect this last the rather because this point in the charge of mr Randolph is equally omitted in the defence of mr Henry. this gentleman must have known that Philips was tried and executed under the Common law, and yet, according to this report, he rests his defence on a justification of the attainder only. but all who knew mr Henry know that when at ease in argument, he was sometimes careless, not giving himself the trouble of ransacking either his memory or imagination for all the topics of his subject, or his audience that of hearing them. no man on earth knew better when he had said enough for his hearers.

Mr Randolph charges us with having read the bill three times in the same day. I do not remember the fact, nor whether this was enforced on us by the urgency of the ravages of Philips, or of the time at which the bill was introduced. I have some idea it was at or near the close of the session. the journals, which I have not, will ascertain this fact.

After these particular strictures I will proceed to propose 1. that

the word 'substantially' pa. 92. 1. 6 be changed for 'which has been*
charged with' [subjoining a note of reference *1. Tucker's Blackst.
Append. 292. Debates of Virginia convent.]

2. that the whole of the quotations from Tucker, Randolph and
Henry be struck out, and instead of the text beginning pa. 92. 1. 12.
with the words 'Bills of attainder'[4] E[t]c to the words 'so often merited'
pa. 95. 1. 4. be inserted the following, to wit.[5]

'this was passed on the following occasion. A certain Josiah Philips,
laborer, of the parish of Lynhaven in the county of Princess Anne, a
man of daring & ferocious disposition, associating with other individuals of a similar cast, spread terror and desolation thro' the lower
country, committing murders, burning houses, wasting farms, and
perpetrating other enormities, at the bare mention of which humanity shudders. every effort to apprehend him had proved abortive.
strong in the number of his ruffian associates, or where force would
have failed resorting to stratagem and ambush; striking the deadly
blow, or applying the fatal torch at the midnight hour and in those
places which their insulated situation left almost unprotected, he retired with impunity to his secret haunts, reeking with blood, and
loaded with plunder. [so far the text of mr Girardin is preserved.] the
inhabitants of the counties which were the theatre of his crimes,
never secure a moment by day or by night, in their fields or their
beds, sent representations of their distresses to the governor, claiming the public protection. he consulted with some members of the
legislature, then sitting, on the best method of proceeding against
this atrocious offender. too powerful to be arrested by the sheriff and
his posse comitatus, it was not doubted but an armed force might be
sent to hunt and destroy him and his accomplices, in their morasses
and fastnesses wherever found. but the proceeding concluded to be
most consonant with the forms and principles of our government,
was that the legislature should pass an act giving him a reasonable
but limited day to surrender himself to justice, and to submit to a trial
by his peers, according to the laws of the land;[6] to consider a refusal
as a confession of guilt, and, divesting him as an Outlaw of the character of citizen, to pass on him the sentence prescribed by the law;
and, the public officer being defied, to make every one his deputy, and
especially those whose safety hourly depended on his destruction. the
case was laid before the legislature, the proofs were ample, his outrages as notorious as those of the public enemy, and well known to
the members of both houses from those counties. no one pretended
then that the perpetrator of crimes who could succesfully resist the

officers of justice, should be protected in the continuance of them by the privileges of his citizenship, and that baffling ordinary process, nothing extraordinary could be rightfully adopted to protect the citizens against him. no one doubted that society had a right to erase from the roll of it's members any one who rendered his own existence inconsistent with theirs, to withdraw from him the protection of their laws, and to remove him from among them by exile, or even by death if necessary. an enemy in lawful war putting to death, in cold blood, the prisoner he has taken, authorizes retaliation, which would be inflicted with peculiar justice on the individual guilty of the deed, were it to happen that he should be taken. and could the murders and robberies of a pyrate or Outlaw entitle him to more tenderness? they passed the law therefore, and without opposition. he did not come in before the day prescribed, continued his lawless outrages, was afterwards taken in arms, but delivered over to the ordinary justice of the country. the Attorney General for the Commonwealth, the immediate agent of the government, waiving all appeal to the act of attainder, indicted him at the Common law as a murderer & robber. he was arraigned on that indictment in the usual forms, before a jury of his vicinage, and no use whatever made of the act of attainder in any part of the proceedings. he pleaded that he was a British subject, authorized to bear arms by a Commission from Ld Dunmore, that he was therefore a mere prisoner of war, and under the protection of the law of nations. the court being of opinion that a commission from an enemy could not protect a citizen in deeds of murder and robbery, overruled his plea; he was found guilty by his jury, sentenced by the court, and executed by the ordinary officer of justice and all according to the forms and rules of the Common law.'

I recommend an examination of the records for ascertaining the facts of this case; for altho' my memory assures me of the leading ones, I am not so certain in my recollection of the details. I am not sure of the character of the particular crimes committed by Philips, or charged in his indictment, whether his plea of alien enemy was formally put in and overruled, what were the specific provisions of the act of attainder, the urgency which caused it to be read three times in one day, if the fact were so E^{t}c.

RC (PPAmP: Thomas Jefferson Papers); brackets in original; addressed: "Mr Girardin Glenmore." PoC (DLC). Tr (MHi); posthumous copy. Extract, not found, enclosed in TJ to William Wirt, 12 May 1815. Enclosure: manuscript, not found, of a portion of Burk, Jones, and Girardin, *History of Virginia*, vol. 4.

For an extended discussion of the 1778 CASE OF JOSIAH PHILIPS and TJ's draft of the bill of attainder against him and his associates, see *PTJ*, 2:189–93. TJ thought the matter was STRANGELY REPRESENTED by St. George Tucker in his edition of *Blackstone's Commentaries* (Philadelphia, 1803; Sowerby, no. 1807), 1:292–3, and by Edmund Randolph in a 6 June 1788 speech before the Virginia ratification convention (Merrill Jensen, John P. Kaminski, and others, eds., *The Documentary History of the Ratification of the Constitution* [1976–], 9:972; see also Sowerby, no. 3011).

Patrick Henry, who had been Virginia's governor in 1778, VERY NEGLIGENTLY VINDICATED the government's case in his 7 June 1788 rebuttal to Randolph at the convention: "He [Philips] was not executed according to those beautiful legal ceremonies which are pointed out by the laws, in criminal cases. The enormity of his crimes did not entitle him to it. I am truly a friend to legal forms and methods; but, Sir, the occasion warranted the measure. A pirate, an out-law, or a common enemy to all mankind, may be put to death at any time. It is justified by the laws of nature and nations" (Jensen, *Ratification*, 9:1038). WITHOUT BEING CONFRONTED . . . AFTERWARDS ACTUALLY EXECUTED comes from Randolph's convention speech. With only minor variations, Girardin did replace the QUOTATIONS BY TUCKER, RANDOLPH AND HENRY with the text supplied by TJ (Burk, Jones, and Girardin, *History of Virginia*, 4:305–6).

[1] Tr: "Joseph."
[2] Reworked from "the definitions."
[3] Word interlined.
[4] Omitted closing quotation mark editorially supplied.
[5] TJ began a new page at this point.
[6] Tr adds "to refuse" in front of the semicolon.

From James Madison

DEAR SIR   Washington Mar. 12. 1815

It was long desireable that an Exposé of the causes and character of the War between the U.S. & G.B. should remedy the mischief produced by the Declaration of the Prince Regent & other mistatements which had poisoned the opinion of the World on the subject. Since the pacification in Europe & the effect of that and other occurrences in turning the attention of that quarter of the World towards the U.S. the antidote became at once more necessary & more hopeful. It was accordingly determined soon after the meeting of Cong[s] that a correct & full view of the War should be prepared & made public in the usual demi Official form. The commencement of it was however Somewhat delayed by the probability of an early termination of the negotiations at Ghent, either, in a peace, or in a new epoch particularly inviting a new appeal to the neutral public. The long suspension of intelligence from our Envoys, & the critical state of our affairs at home, as well as abroad, finally overruled this delay, and the execution of the task was committed to M[r] Dallas. Altho' he hastened it as much as the nature of it, and his other laborious attentions admitted, it was not finished in time for publication before the news of peace arrived. The latter pages had not even been struck off at the press. Under these circumstances, it became a question whether it should be published with a prefatory notice that it was written before the cessation of hostilities, and thence derived its spirit & language; or should be suppressed; or written over with a view to preserve the Substantial vindication of our Country agst prevailing calumnies, and avoid asperities of every Sort unbecoming the change in the relations of the two Countries. This last course, tho' not a little difficult might have been best in itself, but it required a time & labor not to be spared for it. And the suppression was preferred to the first course, which w^d have been liable to misconstructions of an injurious tendency. The printed copies however amounting to several hundred are not destroyed, and will hereafter contribute materials for a historical review of the period which the document embraces. I have thought a perusal of it might amuse an hour of your leisure; requesting only that as it is to be guarded agst publication, you will be so good as either to return the Copy, or to place it where it will be in no danger of escaping. You will observe, from the plan & cast of the Work, that it was meant for the eye of the British people, and of our own, as well as for that of the Neutral world. This threefold object increased the labor not a little, and gives the composition some features not otherwise to be explained.

The dispatch Vessel with the peace via France has just arrived. It brings little more than duplicates of what was rec^d via England. The Affairs at Vienna remain in a fog, which rather thickens than disperses. The situation of France also has yet it would seem to pass Some clearing up Shower. The peace between this Country & G.B. gives sincere pleasure there,[1] as releiving the Gov^t and the Nation, from the dilemma, of humiliating Submissions to the antineutral measures of G. Britain, or of a premature contest with her. In Spain, every thing suffers under the phrenzy of the Throne, and the fanaticism of the people. But for our peace with England, it is not impossible, that a new War from that quarter would have been opened upon us. The affair at New Orleans will perhaps be a still better Guarantee agst such an event.

Mr Smith will have communicated to you the result of our consultation on the transportation of the Library.

We are indulging hopes of paying a trip soon to our farm; and shall not fail, if it be practicable, to add to it the pleasure of a visit to Monticello.

Always & with sincerest[2] affection Y^{rs} JAMES MADISON

[339]

RC (DLC: Madison Papers); at foot of text: "M*r* Jefferson"; endorsed by TJ as received 16 Mar. 1815 and so recorded in SJL. Enclosure: a prepublication copy of Dallas, *Exposition*.

The MEETING, or opening, of the third session of the 13th Congress took place on 19 Sept. 1814. A PREFATORY NOTICE was indeed attached to the Washington edition of the above work stating that it had been "prepared and committed to the press" prior to the conclusion of the War of 1812; that it "would have been difficult, even if it were desirable, to withold" it from the public; and that a refutation of the accusations brought against the United States government was "necessary, in

peace as much as in war . . . lest those charges should obtain credit with the present generation; or pass, for truth, into the history of the times, upon the evidence of a silent acquiescence." On 3 Mar. 1815 the United States DISPATCH VESSEL *Transit* arrived from France in New London, Connecticut (New Haven *Connecticut Journal*, 6 Mar. 1815). PHRENZY OF THE THRONE: Ferdinand VII renounced the liberal constitution of 1812 and persecuted Spanish progressives following his return to power in 1814 (Connelly, *Napoleonic France*, 176).

[1] Word interlined.
[2] Manuscript: "sincerst."

Jefferson's Letter to Peter H. Wendover

I. THOMAS JEFFERSON TO PETER H. WENDOVER (DRAFT), 13 MAR. 1815

II. THOMAS JEFFERSON TO PETER H. WENDOVER (FINAL STATE), 13 MAR. 1815

EDITORIAL NOTE

In composing his response to Peter H. Wendover's letter of 30 Jan. 1815, Jefferson completed a draft that criticized the discussion of public affairs from the pulpit by religious leaders. Realizing the controversial nature of what he had written and being unable to count on the discretion of its intended recipient, with whom he had not corresponded previously, Jefferson wrote a briefer and much less revealing version. After mailing the latter to Wendover, he took the comparatively unusual step of retaining both copies among his papers. Their intrinsic interest is so great that both the draft and the final version are printed in full below.

I. Thomas Jefferson to Peter H. Wendover (Draft)

SIR   Monticello Mar. 13. 15.

Your favor of Jan. 30. was recieved after long delay on the road, and I have to thank you for the volume of discourses which you have been so kind as to send me. I have gone over them with great satisfaction, and concur with the able preacher in his estimate of the character of the belligerents in our late war, and lawfulness of defensive war. I consider the war, with him, as 'made on good advice,' that is, for just causes, and it's dispensation as providential, inasmuch as it has exercised our patriotism and submission to order, has planted and invigorated among us arts of urgent necessity, has manifested the strong and the weak parts of our republican institutions, and the excellence of a representative democracy compared with the misrule of kings; has rallied the opinions of mankind to the natural right of expatriation, and of a common property in the ocean, and raised us to that grade in the scale of nations which the bravery and liberality of our citizen-souldiers, by land and by sea, the wisdom of our institutions and their observance of justice entitled us to in the eyes of the world. all this mr M^cleod has well proved, and from those sources of argument particularly which belong to his profession. on one question only I differ from him, and it is that which constitutes the subject of his first discourse, the right of discussing public affairs in¹ the pulpit. I add the last words because I admit the right in general conversation, and in writing; in which last form it has been exercised in the valuable book you have now favored me with.

The mass of human concerns, moral and physical, is so vast, the field of the knolege requisite for man to conduct them to best advantage is so extensive, that no human being can acquire the whole himself, and much less in that degree necessary for the instruction of others. it has of necessity then been distributed into different departments, each of which singly may give occupation enough to the whole time and attention of a single individual. thus we have teachers of languages, teachers of mathematics, of Natural philosophy, of chemistry, of medecine, of law, of history, of government E^tc. religion too is a separate department, and happens to be the only one deemed requisite for all men, however high or low. collections of men associate together, under the name of congregations, and employ a religious teacher, of the particular sect of opinions of which they happen to be, and contribute to make up a stipend as a compensation for the trouble of delivering them, at such periods as they agree on, lessons in the religion they profess. if they want instruction in other sciences or arts, they apply to other instructors, and this is generally the business of early life. but I suppose there is not an instance of a single congregation which has employed their preacher for the mixt purposes of lecturing them from the pulpit, in chemistry, in medecine, in law, in the science and principles of government, or in any thing but religion exclusively. whenever therefore preachers, instead of a lesson in religion, put them off with a discourse on the Copernican system, on chemical affinities, on the construction of government, or the characters or conduct of those administering it, it is a breach of contract, depriving their audience of the kind of service for which they are salaried, and giving them, instead of it, what they did not want, or, if wanted, would rather seek from better sources in that particular art or science. in chusing our pastor we look to his religious qualifications, without enquiring into his physical or political dogmas, with which we mean to have nothing to do. I am aware that arguments may be found which may twist a thread of politics into the cord of religious duties. so may they for every other branch of human art or science. thus, for example, it is a religious duty to obey the laws of our country. the teacher of religion therefore must instruct us in those laws, that we may know how to obey them. it is a religious duty to assist our sick neighbors: the preacher must therefore teach us medecine, that we may do it understandingly. it is a religious duty to preserve our own health: our religious teacher then must tell us what dishes are wholsome, and give us recipes in cookery, that we may learn how to prepare them. and so ingenuity, by generalising more and more, may amalgamate all the branches of science into any one of them, and the physician who is paid to visit the sick, may give a sermon instead of medecine; and the merchant to whom money is sent for a hat, may send a handkerchief instead of it. but notwithstanding this possible confusion of all sciences into one, common sense draws lines between them sufficiently distinct for the general purposes of life, and no one is at a loss to understand that a recipe in medecine or cookery, or a demonstration in geometry, is not a lesson in religion.   I do not deny but that a congregation may, if they please, agree with their preacher that he shall instruct them in medecine also, or law, or politics. then lectures in these, from the pulpit, become not only a matter of right, but of duty also. but this must be with the consent of every individual; because the association being voluntary, the mere majority has no right to apply the contributions of the minority to purposes unspecified in the agreement of the congregation. I agree too that on all other occasions the preacher has the right, equally with every other citizen, to express his sentiments, in speaking or writing, on the subjects of medecine, law, politics, E'c his leisure time being his own, and his congregation not obliged to listen to his conversation, or to read his writings; and no one would have regretted more than myself, had any scruple as to this right witheld from us the valuable discourses which have led to the expression of an opinion as to the true limits of the right. I feel my portion of indebtment to the reverend author, for the distinguished learning, the logic and the eloquence with which he has proved that religion, as well as reason, confirms the soundness of those principles on which our government has been founded and it's rights asserted.

These are my views of this question. they are in opposition to those of the highly respected and able preacher, and are therefore the more doubtingly offered. difference of opinion leads to enquiry, and enquiry to truth; and that, I am sure, is the ultimate and sincere object of us both. we both value too much the freedom of opinion sanctioned by our constitution, not to cherish[2] it's exercise even where in opposition to ourselves.

Unaccustomed to reserve or mystery in the expression of my opinions, I have opened myself frankly on a question suggested by your letter and present. and altho' I have not the honor of your acquaintance, this mark of attention, and still more the sentiments of esteem so kindly expressed in your letter, are entitled to a confidence that observations not intended for the public will not be ushered to their notice, as has happened to me sometimes. tranquility, at my age, is the balm of life. while I know I am safe in the honor & charity of a M^cleod, I do not wish to be cast forth to the Marats, the Dantons, & the Robespierres of the priesthood: I mean the Parishes, the Ogdens, and the Gardiners of Massachusets.

I pray you to accept the assurances of my esteem & respect

TH: JEFFERSON

[*Note by TJ at foot of text:*] On further consideration, this letter was not sent, mr Wendover's character & calling being entirely unknown. instead of it, the following was sent.

Dft (DLC); at foot of first page: "Mr Wendover"; with PoC of final state of letter on verso of last page.

MADE ON GOOD ADVICE is a variant of the biblical phrase "with good advice make war" (Proverbs 20.18). Alexander McLeod quotes the expression at the head of the third and fourth sermons printed in *A Scriptural View of the Character, Causes, and Ends of the Present War* (New York, 1815), 101, 149. By the OGDENS TJ may actually be alluding to David Osgood, a prominent Federalist pastor living in Medford, Massachusetts (Aaron Hill to TJ, 24 May 1810; TJ's Explanations of the Three Volumes Bound in Marbled Paper, 4 Feb. 1818).

[1] Word interlined in place of "from."
[2] Word interlined in place of "think."

II. Thomas Jefferson to Peter H. Wendover (Final State)

Monticello Mar. 13. 15.

Th: Jefferson presents his compliments to mr Wendover and his thanks for the volume of mr M^cleod's discourses which he has been so kind as to send him. he has seen with great satisfaction the able proofs adduced by the eloquent author from Scriptural sources, in justification of a war so palpably supported by reason. he supposes indeed that true religion and well informed reason will ever be in unison in the hands of candid interpretation and that in the impassioned endeavors to place these two great authorities at variance, on so important a question, the Eastern clergy have not deserved well either of their religion or their country. he renders deserved honor to mr M^cleod for the piety and patriotism of his discourses, and salutes mr Wendover with respect and esteem.

PoC (DLC); on verso of final page of TJ's Dft of this letter; dateline at foot of text. Tr (ViU: GT); posthumous copy.

From Tadeusz Kosciuszko

MON CHER AMI   [14 Mars 1815.]

Les Grands et les petits les riches et les pauvres de notre Hemisphere admirent le devoument qui vous a porté à accepter la place de secretaire d'État, afin d'etre utile a votre Patrie, par vos connoissances parfaites du Pays, du courage du Peuple, de vos[1] résources et de la Politique Européenne, qui n'est que l'art de mieux tromper. Comme je suis dans la classe des pauvres et que je ne veux rien accepter ni aller dans mon Pays jusqu'a ce quil ne soit pas rétablit en entier avec une Constitution liberale, je vous prierai bien et avec empressement de m'envoyer incessament mes interets et même Le fond de mon Capital après La ratification de votre paix avec l'Angleterre pourvue que je ne perd pas beaucoup[2] car je n'ai plus[3] rien pour mon entretien.

Agréez l'assurance de mon Estime de mon admiration et de ma Sincere[4] amitié.   T KOSCIUSZKO

PS: Souvenez vous d'etablir une grande École Civile et Militaire en même temps pour vos jeunes Gens de chaque provinces Sans en omêttre aucune, et Sous La Garde et l'inspection immediate du Congres; car il faut toujours entretenir l'Esprit Republicain, avec les moeurs et les connoissances necessaires Seule base solide d'un État libre[5]—.

EDITORS' TRANSLATION

MY DEAR FRIEND   [14 March 1815.]
The great, the small, the rich, and the poor of our hemisphere admire the devotion that moved you to accept the position of secretary of state in order to be useful to your native land through your perfect knowledge of the country, its people's courage, your resources, and European politics, which is nothing but the art of deception. As I am counted among the poor and wish to accept nothing nor return to my country until it has been completely restored with a liberal constitution, I earnestly beg you to send me my interest and even the principal of my capital after the ratification of peace with England, so long as I do not lose very much, because I no longer have anything to live on.

Accept the assurance of my esteem, admiration, and sincere friendship.

T KOSCIUSZKO

PS: Remember to establish for your young men a large civil and military school in each state, without exception, and place it under the jurisdiction and immediate supervision of Congress, because one must always nurture the republican spirit with moral values and knowledge, which are the only solid foundation of a free state—.

RC (ViU: TJP); undated, with date supplied from Dupl; endorsed by TJ as received 11 May 1815 and so recorded in SJL. RC (DLC); address cover only; with PoC of TJ to Hezekiah Niles, 26 June 1815, on verso; addressed in unidentified hands: "Hon. Th. Jefferson <Secretary of State Washington City> Monticello"; franked; postmarked Washington City, 6 May. Dupl (MHi); fully dated beneath signature; postscript on verso; endorsed by TJ; recorded in SJL as received 3 Oct. 1815. Translation by Dr. Genevieve Moene.

TJ was the United States SECRETAIRE D'ÉTAT ("secretary of state"), 1790–93, but he accepted no public office after leaving the presidency in 1809.

[1] Dupl here adds "grands" ("abundant").

[2] RC: "beacoup." Dupl: "beaucoup," followed by "ce pour cela je joins ici ma procuration d'agire comme vous voudrez" ("for this reason I hereby enclose my power of attorney for you to use as you see fit").

[3] Word not in Dupl.

[4] RC: "Sincerre." Dupl: "Sincere."

[5] Dupl here adds "comme le votre" ("such as yours").

Power of Attorney from Tadeusz Kosciuszko

Know all Men by these presents That I Thadeus Kosciuszko do make ordain constitute and appoint Thomas Jefferson of Monticello in the State of Virginia my true and lawful Attorney for me and in my name, and on my behalf, to sell assign and transfer, unto any person or persons whatsoever, and for such price or consideration as my said Attorney shall think fit all or any part of the sum of

of the funded Six per Cent Stock of the United States of America to me belonging, which Stock was purchased for my account by order of the said Thomas Jefferson and is standing in my name in the Books of the United States
being the amount of   Certificate

and also for me and in my name, to make and execute all necessary acts of Assignment and transfers, to receive and give receipts, acquittances and discharges for the consideration money arising from the sale thereof; And also for me and in my name, and on my behalf, to receive all Interest and Dividends now due, or that may or shall hereafter become due on the said Capital Stock, until the transfer thereof, and to give receipts, acquittances and discharges for the same, and further to do, execute, perform and finish all and singular acts, matters and things, which shall be expedient and necessary touching and concerning the premises as fully and effectually to all intents and purposes whatsoever as I the said General Kosciuszko, might or could do in and about the same, if personally present; and also with power to my said Attorney, to substitute an Attorney or Attornies under him for all or any of the purposes aforesaid, and to do all lawful acts requisite for effecting the premises, hereby ratifying and confirming all that my said Attorney or his Substitute or Substitutes shall do therein by Virtue of these presents—

In Witness whereof I have hereunto set my hand and seal at Paris this Thirteenth day of March in the Year of Our Lord One thousand eight hundred and fifteen—   THAD: KOSCIUSZKO
Signed Sealed and acknowledged in the presence of
J B. MÉLON
A STYLES

MS (MHi); in a clerk's hand; signed by Kosciuszko, Mélon, and Styles; with Kosciuszko's seal; subjoined to attestation in the same clerk's hand on letterhead beginning with an engraving of the American eagle and signed by Isaac Cox Barnet: "Consulate of the United States. Be it known that on this Thirteenth day of March in the Year One thousand eight hundred and fifteen, and of the Independence of the United States the 39th, before me Isaac Cox Barnet Consul of the said States for Paris and the Departments of Normandy Agent of Prize causes, Came General Kosciuszko and did sign and execute the within Power of Attorney, and acknowledge the same to be his act and deed—In Testimony whereof I have hereunto set my Hand and affixed my Seal of Office the day and Year above written."

To William Caruthers

SIR   Monticello Mar. 15. 15.

Your favors of Feb. 22. and Mar. 4. have been both recieved. the
lease at[1] the Natural bridge having been made to D[r] Thornton, if the
change of circumstances which has intervened should make him apprehensive of loss, I should let him off without asking any consideration. but I have heard nothing from him on the subject. in your letter
of Feb. 22. you suppose it may be necessary to extend your views to
some other branches of the plumbing business, which would require
improvements too expensive to put on leased land without a provision for allowance at the end of the term, and ask my ideas on the
subject. for any permanent improvements immediately pertinent to
the plumbing business & not exceeding what would be the amount of
the rents to be recieved in the course of the lease, such as[2] a successor to the business might fairly be expected to pay additional rent for,
I should be willing to allow what they should be worth at the end of
the term. I have no idea of selling the land. I view it in some degree
as a public trust, and would on no consideration permit the bridge[3]
to be injured, defaced or masked from the public view. I propose to
visit it in the course of the ensuing summer and shall then be much
better qualified to go into details on the subject. Accept the assurance
of my great esteem & respect.   TH:J.

Dft (DLC); on verso of reused address
cover from James Ligon (for Patrick Gibson) to TJ; at foot of text: "William
Caruthers esq. Lexington"; endorsed by
TJ.

[1] Word interlined in place of "of."
[2] Reworked from "not exceeding the
amount of the rents recieved, such as."
[3] Preceding two words added in mar-
gins in place of "it."

The CHANGE OF CIRCUMSTANCES was
the end of the War of 1812.

To DeWitt Clinton

                                              Monticello. Mar. 15. 15.

Th: Jefferson presents his compliments to mr Clinton, and his
thanks for the copy he has been so kind as to send him of his
Introductory discourse to the Literary and Philosophical society of
New York. the field which he has therein spread before the lovers
of science offers ample room for their cultivation. and he is happy
to observe that New York is so fast advancing to the work. she is
certainly much favored by circumstances which lead to eminence[1]

in that career.   he congratulates mr Clinton on the event of peace, and especially on the splendid events in the South which so honorably closed the war. and he salutes him with high respect and consideration.

RC (NNC: Clinton Papers); dateline at foot of text; addressed: "Dewitt Clinton esquire New York"; frank clipped; postmarked Milton, 22 Mar.; at head of text in Clinton's hand: "15"; endorsed by Clinton. FC (DLC); entirely in TJ's hand and endorsed by him.

DeWitt Clinton (1769–1828), public official, was born in Orange County, New York, graduated from Columbia College (later Columbia University) in 1786, and was subsequently admitted to the bar. During a long and important public career that began with service as private secretary to his uncle, New York governor George Clinton, the younger Clinton began as a states'-rights Republican, successively opposed Federalist leader John Jay and the Tammany wing of his own party, ran for president in 1812 with strong Federalist support and captured most of New England's electoral votes, and supported Andrew Jackson's presidential aspirations. Clinton sat in the New York Assembly, 1797–98, the New York Senate, 1798–1802, and the United States Senate, 1802–03. He had a long period of service as mayor of New York City, 1803–07, 1808–10, and 1811–15, and was sometimes concurrently a member of the state senate and lieutenant governor, holding the former post from 1806–11 and the latter from 1811–13. As governor of New York, 1817–23 and 1825–28, Clinton championed and ultimately saw to completion the Erie and Champlain canals, which connected these lakes to the Hudson River and thus brought much of the trade of the West to New York City. His long career was also marked by an intense interest in public education, antiquities, and historical, literary, and scientific investigation (*ANB*; *DAB*; *PTJ*, 35:283–4; Milton Halsey Thomas, *Columbia University Officers and Alumni 1754–1857* [1936], 111; *Daily Albany Argus*, 12 Feb. 1828).

TJ had recently received a COPY of Clinton, *An Introductory Discourse, delivered before the Literary and Philosophical Society of New-York, on the Fourth of May, 1814* (New York, 1815; Poor, *Jefferson's Library*, 7 [no. 304]; TJ's copy, inscribed "With Mr Clinton's Compliments," is at MiU-C). Clinton was a founder and first president of this society. His extensive review at its inaugural meeting of scientific education, research, and knowledge in the United States drew on both TJ's *Notes on the State of Virginia* and his work on the megalonyx, an extinct species of sloth.

[1] FC: "distinction."

From William W. Hening

DEAR SIR,   Richmond 15th March 1815

Previously to the receipt of your letter of the 11th Inst I had carefully packed up all your M.S.S. with a view to return them to you by the first safe conveyance. —The Vth Vol. containing the sessions acts was all that I meant to retain; and that only, till I could complete the publication of that part. I had finished the 5th Vol. of the Statutes at Large; and had made considerable progress in the 6th (bringing down the sessions acts to about the middle of your Vth vol.) when the late War commenced.—The interruptions unavoidable, from the state of the country, in the first instance, and lastly from the death of Mr Pleasants, the publisher, has so far suspended the work, that it has been absolutely impossible to print off the whole of the matter contained in your V. Volume.—From the year 1771, to the present time, I have a complete collection of the Acts of the General Assembly, and Ordinances of the convention, during the interregnum. But, deprived of your Vth Vol. I cannot possibly complete the work.—To transcribe what remains of the 5th Vol. would not only be a very laborious and expensive undertaking, but I could not vouch for the accuracy of the impression, unless it could be examined by the original.—Indeed, I do not know, how the Examiners could certify the edition to have been published agreeably to law, unless they could compare it with the printed copy.—Under these circumstances I should presume, Congress could have no difficulty in your retaining the 5th Vol, until the matter now remaining, can be transferred to the Statutes at Large.—The 5th Vol. of this work, will very shortly be published; and not a moment will be lost, in completing the entire edition;—but it is really difficult to say, to what number of volumes, it will extend.—The Ordinances of Convention, & acts of the legislature during the Revolutionary war, are so very important, that not one can be omitted.

If, from this candid representation of facts, you deem it indispensible, that I should send you, the Vth vol. of your sessions acts, I will certainly comply with your request;[1] on receiving an intimation, to that effect.

I am respy Yrs

W^M W: HENING

RC (DLC); endorsed by TJ as received 17 Mar. 1815 and so recorded in SJL.

The ordinances enacted by the Virginia conventions held during the 1775–76 INTERREGNUM were printed in 1821 in the ninth volume of Hening. According to the 5 Feb. 1808 Virginia "Act authorising William Waller Hening to Publish an Edition of certain Laws of this Commonwealth, and for other purposes," once the EXAMINERS, William Munford, Creed Taylor, and William Wirt, stated "that they had carefully compared the edition of the acts so to be published, with the original laws, and found them to be truly and accurately printed, they shall be received and considered of equal authority in the courts of this commonwealth, as the originals, from which they are taken" (*Acts of Assembly* [1807–08 sess.], 24). Although Hening hoped that the fifth volume would VERY SHORTLY BE PUBLISHED, it did not actually appear until 1819.

[1] Manuscript: "requet."

To Horatio G. Spafford

DEAR SIR   Monticello Mar. 15. 15.

Your favors of Feb. 15. 18. and 24. have all been recieved, and you could not even at the date of the last have recieved mine of Feb. 21. on the subject of your improvement in wheel carriages. I have now to thank you for the certificate of a right to employ it in a carriage. it will be some time before I can avail myself[1] of it. I have been obliged latterly[2] to relinquish the use of the gigg in travelling on account of fatigue, for that of a 4 wheeled carriage to which your improvement cannot be adapted: and our carts having been always made with wooden axles, we have no works in our neighborhood where so massive an axle of iron can be made as would be necessary for a cart. I shall therefore have to apply to some distant work for one. in the mean time I should be glad to learn how it answers on trial for actual business.[3]

With Doct[r] Williams's Natural and Civil history of Vermont I have been long acquainted. it was printed in a single vol. 8[vo] at Walpole in N.H. in 1794. I procured it as soon as it appeared, read it with great pleasure and consider it among the very[4] best of the accounts which have been published of our different states. it now makes a part of the library I have lately ceded to Congress on the loss of theirs. if the history[5] which you mention be a different work, it is unknown to me, and I shall be very glad to recieve it and to remit the price, which I can do to Philada, where I have dealings, but not so easily to Vermont or even New York, unless Congress should emit treasury bills of low denomination which may have a general currency, no bank bills being recieved here but of our own state. be so good as to present my respects to D[r] Williams whom I find by your account[6] to be within 3. years of my own age, and to accept yourself the assurances of my esteem & best wishes   TH: JEFFERSON

FC (MHi); in TJ's hand; on verso of reused address cover in James Ligon's hand (writing for Patrick Gibson); at foot of text: "Horatio G. Spafford Albany"; endorsed by TJ.

Samuel Williams was, indeed, close in AGE, having been born in the same month and year as TJ (*Sibley's Harvard Graduates*, 15:134).

[1] Preceding two words interlined in place of "make use."

[2] Word interlined.

[3] Sentence interlined, with the insertion mark mistakenly placed after the ninth word of the following paragraph.

[4] Word interlined.

[5] Word interlined in place of "work."

[6] TJ here canceled "of his age that to be nearly."

From William Wirt

DEAR SIR.   Richmond. March 15. 1815.

The clerk of the court of chancery has, this day, for the first time put into my hands the fi: fa. in your case with Scott which I hasten to enclose to you—and beg you to believe me as ever

your devoted serv[t]   W[M] WIRT

RC (MHi); endorsed by TJ as received 17 Mar. 1815 and so recorded in SJL. RC (DLC); address cover only; with PoC of TJ to James Madison, 25 Mar. 1815, on verso; addressed: "Thomas Jefferson esq[r] Monticello" by "mail"; franked; postmarked Richmond, 15 Mar. Enclosure: statement of account with the Superior Court of Chancery for the Richmond District, [ca. 15 Mar. 1815], showing that TJ is owed $23.08 from the fieri facias in *Scott v. Jefferson and Harrison*, deducting $3.03 for his 1815 Campbell County land tax, and leaving a balance due TJ of $20.05 (MS in ViU: TJP; written on a scrap in an unidentified hand; undated; endorsed by TJ: "Scott Samuel"; with notation in a different hand: "February 26th 1816 Received").

William W. Hening was the CLERK of the Superior Court of Chancery for the Richmond District.

To Josiah Meigs

D[R] SIR   Monticello Mar. 16. 15.

Your favor of Feb. 15. has been recieved and I cordially reciprocate your congratulns on the great events which have taken place in the South, and the peace which has followed them. the latter, altho' desired is rendered[1] infinitely more acceptable by the former, which indeed was necessary to impress on both parties a just idea of the bravery of both: but most especially to let England see she can gain nothing of us by war. I hope her government will now have the wisdom as well as justice, by a satisfactory provision against the impressment of our citizens, to convert into a permanent peace what is really but a truce without that provision. still her loss by the war will be incalculable, as it has planted all the important manufactures so firmly in our soil as never again to be eradicated. I am confident that two thirds of the articles we formerly took from England, will now be furnished among ourselves. we shall hardly again send our cotton to England to be spun, woven & returned for our own wearing.

I am particularly to thank you for the kind expressions of your letter towards myself[2] and for the opportunity it gives me of assuring you of the friendly interest I take in your happiness and success. this pleasure will be greatly increased if an opportunity should be afforded me of doing it in person should your passage thro' this part of our country permit me to see you here in the course of the ensuing summer as your letter flatters me. with this assurance be pleased to accept that of my friendly esteem & respect   TH: JEFFERSON

FC (DLC); in TJ's hand; on verso of reused address cover of Charles Clay to TJ, 20 Dec. 1814; at foot of text: "Mr Josiah Meigs"; endorsed by TJ. Enclosed in TJ to Return J. Meigs, 16 Mar. 1815.

Meigs's FAVOR to TJ was actually dated 16 Feb. 1815.

¹ Word interlined.
² Preceding two words interlined.

To Return J. Meigs

Monticello Mar. 16. 15.

Th: Jefferson presents his compliments to mr Meigs, and having recieved a letter from mr Josiah Meigs dated at Washington, and not knowing to what place to address the answer he has taken the liberty of putting it under cover, and of asking the favor of mr Meigs to superscribe the proper direction of place. he salutes him at the same time with great esteem & respect.

RC (Nancy McGlashan, Queens, New York, 1998); dateline at foot of text; addressed: "R. J. Meigs esquire Post master Genl Washington"; franked. Enclosure: TJ to Josiah Meigs, 16 Mar. 1815.

Return Jonathan Meigs (ca. 1765–1825), attorney and public official, was born in Middletown, Connecticut, the son of Return Jonathan Meigs (1740–1823), a prominent Continental army officer and Indian agent, and the nephew of Josiah Meigs. He graduated from Yale College (now University) in 1785 and was admitted to the bar in 1788. In the latter year Meigs moved to Marietta in the Northwest Territory, where he was a postmaster, territorial judge and legislator, and chief justice of the new state of Ohio's supreme court, 1803–04. After brief stints as a judge in the Louisiana and Michigan territories, he returned to Ohio and served in the United States Senate, 1808–10, and as governor, 1810–14. Meigs was a conservative Republican whose strong support of the War of 1812 helped him to his appointment as United States postmaster general in 1814. He resigned this post in 1823, citing ill health, and retired to Marietta, where he died (ANB; DAB; Franklin Bowditch Dexter, Biographical Sketches of the Graduates of Yale College [1885–1912], 4:428–30; JEP, 1:261, 2:8, 13, 511, 3:343 [9, 12 Feb. 1798, 20 Dec. 1805, 3 Jan. 1806, 17 Mar. 1814, 8 Dec. 1823]; PTJ, 36:470n; Washington Daily National Intelligencer, 11, 18 Apr. 1825; tombstone inscription in Mound Cemetery, Marietta).

From James Ogilvie

DEAR SIR,   Columbia March 16th 1815—

I take the liberty to enclose a printed paper containing a brief outline of a literary enterprise, on the execution of which I have entered, in the College of Columbia.—It would I trust be quite impertinent to Say how gratifying and acceptable to me, the communication of any idea that may occur to you during its perusal, will be:—You will particularly oblige me, by mentioning the French authors not generally known[1] who have illustrated the principles of Rhetoric.—

The object of my lecture will be an analysis of what may be stiled the Philosophy of Oratory: For such an analysis the speculations of Philologists & Rhetoricians have prepared the way.

The circumstances in which I make my first effort in this way are as propitious, as I can well desire.—

On opening my design, to the Trustees & the Faculty of the College of Columbia, it was not only unanimously but cordially approved: On the evening of the day[2] after it was made known to the students, the college & the House of the President were illuminated: In making up my classes, the only difficulty arose from the limitation of the number of members which each was to include: unable to agree about the selection, the students unanimously devolved that thankless office, on the President, who altho' he has made the selection, (so far as I can judge) with impartiality & discrimination, has not escaped giving offense to more than one.—As to pecuniary compensation, its amount being left exclusively to myself, & every disposition manifested to pay liberally, I deemed it on every account most proper in the first instance, if I erred at all, to err on the side of moderation.—

should my exhibition & examination at the close of the course, produce the public impression which I am willing to hope it may, I can readily raise the fee should I repeat the course.—

The expectation which you seemd confidently to entertain that peace would be speedily reestablished betwixt G. Britain & the U.S. has at length been realisd, & the event[3] has I doubt not been hailed, by the most virtuous & enlightened inhabitants of both countries, with heart-felt & diffusive joy.

You will now, I trust be able to carry into effect your plan for the establishiment of a college in Albemarle:—I am very anxious to learn what progress h[as] been made in the business since I left Virginia.—D[r] Blackburn (with whose[4] character & mathematical attainments you are I presume acquaintd) is about to leave the College of Columbia in a few months & would I am sure ceteris paribus prefer a professorship in the Institution you contemplate, to any other that could be offered to him.—

Believe me to be,

Dear Sir, with profound respect & sincere affection your oblig[d] & ob[t] serv[t]   JAMES OGILVIE

RC (MHi); mutilated at seal; addressed: "Thomas Jefferson Esqr Monticello—Albemarle V^a"; stamped; postmarked Columbia, S.C., 25 Mar.; endorsed by TJ as received 4 Apr. 1815 and so recorded in SJL.

The enclosed PRINTED PAPER has not been found, but a version of it was appended to Ogilvie's *Philosophical Essays; to which are subjoined, Copious Notes, Critical and Explanatory, and A Supplementary Narrative; with An Appendix* (Philadelphia, 1816). Addressed "To Students of the Senior and Junior Classes, in the College of Columbia," it emphasized the importance of training in elocution; noted that when he arrived at South Carolina College (later the University of South Carolina), no "distinct professorship of oratory and rhetoric" existed at any college or seminary in the United States; explained his proposal to offer a course of "Lectures on Rhetoric,

and Exercises in Elocution, Criticism, and Composition"; stressed that it would not interfere with the school's existing instruction and exercises and that it was offered with the full approval of Jonathan Maxcy, the college's PRESIDENT; and specified that a class for from twelve to twenty seniors and another for from twenty to fifty juniors would meet twice a week for four months at a cost of $12 per senior and $6 per junior. The appendix to *Philosophical Essays* also included Ogilvie's advertisement for the public EXHIBITION & EXAMINATION given at the termination of the same course and subsequent enthusiastic testimonials from faculty, trustees, and others.

¹ Preceding three words interlined.
² Reworked from "On the <*day*> night when I."
³ Preceding two words interlined.
⁴ Manuscript: "who."

To Caesar A. Rodney

My DEAR FRIEND &
ANTIENT COLLEAGUE   Monticello. Mar. 16. 15.

Your letter of Feb. 19. has been recieved with very sincere pleasure. it recalls to memory the sociability, the friendship, and harmony of action which united personal happiness with public duties, during the portion of our lives in which we acted together. indeed the affectionate harmony of our Cabinet is among the sweetest of my recollections. I have just recieved a letter of friendship from Genl Dearborne. he writes me that he is now retiring from every species of public occupation, to pass the remainder of life as a private citizen; and he promises me a visit in the course of the summer. as you hold out a hope of the same gratification, if chance or purpose could time your visits together it would make it a real jubilee. but come as you will, or as you can, it will always be joy enough to me. only you must give me a month's notice; because I go three or four times a year to a possession 90 miles Southwestward, and am absent a month at a time, and the mortification would be indelible of losing such a visit by a mistimed absence. you will find me in habitual good health, great contentedness, enfeebled in body, impaired in memory, but without decay in my friendships.

Great indeed have been the revolutions in the world, since you & I have had any thing to do with it. to me they have been like the howlings of the winter-storm, over the battlements, while warm in my bed. the unprincipled tyrant of the land is fallen, his power reduced to it's original nothingness, his person, only not yet, in the Madhouse, where it ought always to have been. his equally unprincipled competitor, the tyrant of the ocean, in the Mad-house indeed in person, but his power still stalking over the deep. 'quem deus vult perdere, prius dementat.' the madness is acknoleged; the perdition of course impending. are we to be the instruments? a friendly, a just, and a reasonable conduct on their part, might make us the main pillar of their prosperity and existence. but their deep-rooted hatred to us seems to be the means which providence permits to lead them to their final catastrophe. 'nullam enim in terris gentem esse, nullum infestiorem populum, nomini Romano,' said the general who erased Capua from the list of powers. what nourishment and support would not England recieve from an hundred millions of industrious[1] descendants whom some of her people now born will live to see here. what their energies are she has lately tried. and what has she not to fear from an hundred millions of such men, if she continues her maniac course of hatred & hostility to them. I hope in god she will change. there is not a nation on the globe with whom I have more earnestly wished a friendly intercourse on equal conditions. on no other would I hold out the hand of friendship to any. I know that their creatures represent me as personally an enemy to England. but fools only can believe this, or those who think me a fool. I am an enemy to her insults and injuries. I am an enemy to the flagitious principles of her administration, and to those which govern her conduct towards other nations. but would she give to morality some place in her political code, and especially would she exercise decency, and at least neutral passions towards us, there is not, I repeat it, a people on earth with whom I would sacrifice so much to be in friendship. they can do us, as enemies, more harm than any other nation; and in peace and in war they have more means of disturbing us internally. their merchants established among us, the bonds by which our own are chained to their feet, and the banking combinations interwoven with the whole, have shewn the extent of their controul even during a war with her. they are the workers of all the embarasments our finances have experienced during the war. declaring themselves bankrupt, they have been able still to chain the government to a dependance on them; and had the war continued, they would have reduced us to the inability to command a single dollar. they dared to proclaim that they would not pay their own paper obligations, yet our government could not venture to avail themselves of this opportunity of sweeping their paper from the circulation, and substituting their own notes bottomed on specific taxes for redemption, which every one would have eagerly taken and trusted, rather than the baseless trash of bankrupt companies; our government, I say, have still been overawed from a contest with them, and has even countenanced and strengthened their influence, by proposing new establishments with authority to swindle yet greater sums from our citizens. this is the British influence to which I am an enemy, and which we must subject to our government, or it will subject us to that of Britain. towards relieving us from our commercial dependance much was done by the embargo & non importation laws; and still more by the war. these have permanently planted manufactures among us. the cities, I suppose, will still affect English fashions, & of course English manufactures. but the cities are not the people of America. the country will be clothed in homespun; and what we shall take from England, hereafter, will be as nothing to what we took before the embargo. when you come to see us, you will find our spinning jennies & looms in full activity, never more to be laid aside. of a population of 20,000. people in the county I live in, I do not believe 20. will evermore be clothed from England. and what is true of this county, is equally so of nearly every other in the state. come however and see that we are an industrious, plain, hospitable and honest, altho' not a psalm-singing, people. and especially come & gratify by seeing you once more, a friend who assures you with sincerity of his constant and affectionate attachment and respect. TH: JEFFERSON

RC (NjP: Andre deCoppet Collection, 1955); edge trimmed, with missing text supplied from PoC. PoC (DLC); at foot of first page: "Caesar A. Rodney."

The UNPRINCIPLED TYRANT OF THE LAND was Napoleon, while the TYRANT OF THE OCEAN was George III, whose delusions and diminished mental abilities led to the establishment on 7 Feb. 1811 of a regency that lasted until his death in 1820 (*ODNB*). QUEM DEUS . . . DEMENTAT: "the one whom a god wishes to destroy he first drives mad." NULLAM ENIM . . . NOMINI ROMANO ("For no nation, no people in the world was more hostile to the Roman people") was uttered by Quintus Fulvius Flaccus after the fall of Capua in 211 B.C. (Livy, *Ab Urbe Condita*, 26.27.12, in *Livy with an English Translation*, trans. Benjamin O. Foster, Frank Gardner Moore, and others, Loeb Classical Library [1919–59], 7:106–7; *OCD*, 289, 614).

[1] TJ here canceled "friends."

From Benjamin Shackelford

Culpeper Co House March 16. 1815

Benj. Shackelford presents his sincere respects to Thomas Jefferson Esq[r] and acknowledges the receipt of his Letter enclosing one for M[r] W[m] P Newby which wou'd have been conveyed to him without delay had he been at Home, but being informed by his friends at this place that he was gone to the lower parts of this State & thought it most adviseable to hold the Letter untill he returned, but yesterday the enclosed letter was recieved from m[r] Newby requesting the letter to be forwarded[1] to him which has been complyed with.
he salutes him with due esteem & respect

RC (MHi); dateline at foot of text; endorsed by TJ as received 31 Mar. 1815 and so recorded in SJL. Enclosure: William P. Newby to Shackelford, Lancaster County, 11 Mar. 1815, requesting that TJ's letter to him [of 20 Jan.] be forwarded "by my Servant" and asking Shackelford to inform TJ that he would see him early in April on a matter "of considerable importance to me" (RC in MHi; addressed: "Capt Benjamin Shackleford Fairfax By Jacob").

[1] Manuscript: "forwared."

To Henry Dearborn

MY DEAR GENERAL, FRIEND &
ANTIENT COLLEAGUE.   Monticello Mar. 17. 15.

I have recieved your favor of Feb. 27. with very great pleasure, and sincerely reciprocate congratulations on the late events. peace was indeed desirable; yet it would not have been as welcome without the successes of New Orleans. these last have established truths too important not to be valued: that the people of Louisiana are sincerely attached to the union: that their city can be defended: that the Western states make it's defence their peculiar concern: that the militia are brave: that their deadly aim countervails the maneuvering skill of their enemy: that we have officers of natural genius now starting forward from the mass; and that, putting together all our conflicts, we can beat the British, by sea and by land, with equal numbers. all this being now proved, I am glad of the pacification of Ghent, and shall still be more[1] so, if by a reasonable arrangement against impressment, they will make it truly a treaty of peace, and not a mere truce, as we must all consider it, until the principle of the war is settled. nor among the incidents of the war will we forget your services. after the disasters produced by the treason or the cowardice, or both, of Hull, and the follies of some others, your capture of York and Fort George first turned the tide of success in our favor; and the subsequent campaigns sufficiently wiped away the disgraces of the first. if it were justifiable to look to your own happiness only, your resolution to retire from all public business could not but be approved. but you are too young to ask a discharge as yet; and the public councils too much needing the wisdom of it's ablest citizens to relinquish their claim on you. and surely none needs your aid more than your own state. Oh! Massachusets! how have I lamented the degradation of your apostacy! Massachusetts, with whom I went with pride in 76. whose vote was my vote on every public question, and whose principles were then the standard of whatever was free or fearless. but then she was under the counsels of the two Adamses; while Strong, her present leader, was promoting petitions for submission to British power and British usurpation. while under her present councils she must be contented to be nothing: as having a vote indeed to be counted, but not respected. but should the state once more buckle on her republican harness, we shall recieve her again as a sister, and recollect her wanderings among the crimes only of the parricide party which would have basely sold what their fathers so bravely won from the same enemy. let us look forward then to the act of repentance, which, by dismissing her venal traitors, shall be the signal of return to the bosom and to the principles of her brethren: and if her late humiliation can just give her modesty enough to suppose that her Southern brethren are somewhat on a par with her in wisdom, in information, in patriotism, in bravery, and even in honesty altho' not in psalm-singing, she will more justly estimate her own relative momentum in the union. with her antient principles she would really be great if she did not think herself the whole. I should be pleased to hear that you go into her councils, and assist in bringing her back to those principles and to a sober satisfaction with her proportionable share in the direction of our affairs.

What most affects me in your letter is the hope it excites of once more seeing you, and, at Monticello. 'Oh welcome hour whenever.' you do not say whether the curiosity of mrs Dearborne excites no inclination on her part to come and see her Southern friends, the Hottentots of Doctors Morse, and Parish, and Ogden, and Gardener Eᵗc. Eᵗc. Eᵗc. and yet she would be recieved by them with cordiality and distinction, and no where more affectionately than at Monticello. I have just recieved a letter of friendship from Caesar Rodney who flatters me with a like hope of a visit this summer. and I have written to him that if chance or purpose could time your visits together, it would make it a real jubilee; and that if your time should happen to be his, you will pick him up by the way. but come as you will, or as you can, it will make me supremely happy. only you must give me a month's notice, because I am subject three or four times a year to absences of a month at a very distant possession in the South, which however with notice, are entirely at my command. it would be mortification indelible to lose such a visit by a mistimed absence. be so good as to lay my homage at the feet of mrs Dearborne, and to be assured that I am ever and affectionately your friend. TH: JEFFERSON

RC (photocopy in ViU: TJP); endorsed by Dearborn. PoC (DLC); at head of text in an unidentified hand: "Gen¹ Dearborne."

OH WELCOME HOUR WHENEVER is in John Milton, *Paradise Lost*, 10.771. HOTTENTOTS: persons of inferior intellect or culture (*OED*). Jedidiah MORSE, Elijah PARISH, David Osgood (OGDEN), and John Sylvester John GARDINER were prominent clergymen and authors from the northeastern states.

¹ Reworked from "mores." PoC: "mores."

To Louis H. Girardin

TH:J. TO MR GIRARDIN. Monticello. Mar. 18. 15.

Your messenger finds me to the elbows in the dust of my bookshelves. I recieved my Catalogue, last night, and have begun the revisal of the shelves to-day. from this small specimen it seems as if it would take me three weeks very laborious work.—I send you 2ᵈ Toulongeon, and return your Cahier, with approbation of every thing except as to the detention of the Convention troops, where altho' I am on your side, yet I think the grounds of the conduct of Congress should be stated. I have not time now to explain, and we must do it vivâ voce. come when it suits you, all days being equal with me; the most convenient hour that of dinner. with respect to whatever I furnish written or verbal, it is my wish you should use it entirely as your own, either verbatim or modified as you please, and without naming me at all, unless for any fact which you think absolutely requires it.— I will search as to the bill for dividing the counties into wards. Accept my friendly salutations.

RC (PPAmP: Thomas Jefferson Papers); dateline at foot of text; addressed: "Mʳ Girardin Glenmore." Enclosures: (1) François Emmanuel, vicomte de Toulongeon, *Histoire de France, depuis la Révolution de 1789* (Paris, 1801–06; Sowerby, no. 240; 2d of 2 vols. as bound by TJ). See also TJ's other copy at MoSW (Poor, *Jefferson's Library*, 4 [no. 88]). (2) manuscript, not found, of a portion of Burk, Jones, and Girardin, *History of Virginia*, vol. 4.

The British and Hessian soldiers who surrendered on 17 Oct. 1777 at the Battle of Saratoga were known as CONVENTION

TROOPS, and under the terms of surrender they were to be returned to Britain after promising that they would not serve in America during the remainder of the Revolutionary War (Philander D. Chase, "'Years of Hardships and Revelations': The Convention Army at the Albemarle Barracks, 1779–1781," *MACH* 41 [1983]: 9–53, esp. 12–5). In the concluding volume of Burk, Jones, and Girardin, *History of Virginia*, Girardin explains the decision of the Continental CONGRESS to detain these prisoners in the vicinity of Charlottesville; uses TJ's own papers as source material; and quotes TJ's correspondence with some of the imprisoned officers (4:245–6, 323–8, 421–2). TJ included a proposal for DIVIDING THE COUNTIES INTO WARDS or hundreds in his 1778 Bill for the More General Diffusion of Knowledge (*PTJ*, 2:527–8).

Missing letters from Girardin to TJ of 13 and 18 Mar. 1815 are recorded in SJL as having been received from Glenmore on the days on which they were written.

To Albert Gallatin

DEAR SIR   Monticello Mar. 19. 15.

This letter will be presented to you by mr George Ticknor, a young gentleman of Boston. he favored me with a visit here and brought high recommendations from mr Adams and others, and during a stay of several days with us, I found he merited every thing which had been said of him. he has been excellently educated, is learned, industrious eager after knolege, and as far as his stay with us could enable us to judge, he is amiable, modest, and correct in his deportment. he had prepared himself for the bar, but, before engaging in business he proposes to pass two or three years in Europe to see and to learn what can be seen and learnt there. should he on his return, enter the political line, he will go far in that career. every American considers his minister at Paris as his natural patron: but knowing how acceptable it is in your station to be informed who are worthy of your particular attentions, I write this letter for your sake as well as his. I had given him one to mr Crawford, not then knowing your appointment. I sincerely congratulate you on it, knowing you will do much good there, as you would have done here also, had you returned. how much have we wanted you! in fighting we have done well. we have good officers at length coming forward from the mass, who would soon have planted our standard on the walls of Quebec & Halifax. our men were always good; and after the affair of N. Orleans, theirs would never have faced ours again. and it is long since they have ceased to trust their frigates to sail alone. but in finance we have suffered cruelly. with a revenue which all acknolege will bring us in 35. millions this year, we are begging daily bread at the doors of our bankrupt banks. but this letter is not for public subjects. I shall write to you soon, glad you are there, wishing for you here, knowing your value every where, and being every where and always your affectionate friend

TH: JEFFERSON

RC (NHi: Gallatin Papers); addressed: "His Excellency Albert Gallatin Min. Plenipot. of the US. at Paris favored by mr Ticknor"; endorsed by Gallatin. PoC (DLC). Enclosed in TJ to George Ticknor, 19 Mar. 1815.

TJ's letter to William H. Crawford of 14 Feb., with a 26 Feb. 1815 postscript, was completed prior to the United States Senate's approval on 28 Feb. of Gallatin's APPOINTMENT as the new envoy extraordinary and minister plenipotentiary to France (JEP, 2:623, 624 [27, 28 Feb. 1815]).

To George Ticknor

DEAR SIR   Monticello Mar. 19. 15.

Your letter of the 6th is recieved. mine of the 3rd had gone on and will probably be in Boston as soon as you will. in addition to the letters then inclosed, I put another under your cover a day or two after, addressed to mr Say, author of the ablest work which has ever been written on Political Economy. I did not then know of the appointment of mr Gallatin, but now inclose the letter to him which you ask.

You will have seen by my former letter to you that I meant to avail myself of the kind offer you had made, and which you are so good as to repeat, of your aid in making the little collection of books necessary for my future amusement. but it will be some time before I shall be able to make out my list and it's accompaniments. I shall forward it to you within a month or two through the Secretary of state's office. in the mean time I have thought it best to put into your hands while here a catalogue to which I shall often refer in my list. it was furnished me, while in Europe, by Koenigh bookseller of Strasburg, in whose store I found the greatest collection of Classics, and of the finest editions, I met with in Europe. I bought much of him on the spot, and much afterwards as long as I staid at Paris. it was as easy to drop him an order for a book, and it was sent by the Diligence as quick as I could get it almost from a bookstore of Paris. his prices were much lower, & his own arrangements with the Diligence took all expence and trouble off of the hands of his customer. it is possible that in procuring books for yourself you may find it convenient to correspond with him, if living, for he was then (25. years ago) below middle age, a faithful diligent man; and should it be necessary to apply to him for any part of my catalogue, it is possible that the recollection of an old customer, applying to him after such an interval may animate his attentions. after all it is to be considered whether the opportunity of examining the condition, the bindings E^tc of different copies in a bookstore of Paris may not be more than equivalent to the advance of the Paris bookseller on Koenig's prices, and these last are doubtless sensibly advanced since the date of the inclosed catalogue. I asked information of you of the time of your actual departure, which I shall still be glad to recieve, and after fulfilling the request of our fireside to convey to you the assurances of their esteem and respect, I pray you to accept mine, with my best wishes for a safe and pleasant voyage, an agreeable tour & residence on the other continent, and a happy return to your friends.   TH: JEFFERSON

PoC (MHi); at foot of first page: "Mr Ticknor"; endorsed by TJ. Enclosures: (1) TJ to Albert Gallatin, 19 Mar. 1815. (2) Amand Koenig, *Catalogus auctorum classicorum tam graecorum quam, latinorum, et qui iis adnumerantur, sparsis hic et illic annotatiunculis litterariis, qui venales extant Argentorati in officina libraria Amandi Koenigii* (Strasbourg, 1789).

TJ's letter to Ticknor of THE 3RD is recorded in SJL but has not been found.

Jean Baptiste SAY was the author of the two-volume *Traité d'Économie Politique.* TJ owned both the first edition (Paris, 1803; Sowerby, no. 3547) and the second edition (Paris, 1814; Poor, *Jefferson's Library,* 11 [no. 697]; Say to TJ, 15 June 1814). TJ discovered the Strasbourg bookstore of Koenig (KOENIGH) while touring the Rhine River valley in 1788. In June of the following year he received the enclosed CATALOGUE (*PTJ,* 13:xxviii, 26, 15:223–4).

From John Vaughan

D SIR   Philad. 19 March 1815

Your favors, of Feb^y & of 1 March were recieved—To the last I would have given immediate reply, but I wanted to fix a Credit in France, which I have not yet done to my Satisfaction—This however upon reflection has nothing to do with the Agency for the Purchase of Books—This I would recommend to be committed To <u>F. A. Michaux. Botanist Paris</u>, He has been an indefatigable agent for our Society, & in return I recieve his Books & works & dispose of them free of any Charge He will feel himself honord by your Commands will execute them with zeal—He is always on the best footing with our functionaries & makes use of public Vessels or private opportunities, as may most conveniently be embraced—When your orders are made out, let it be by duplicate, put one under an unsealed cover adressed to Robt Dickey New York—Put that & your Duplicate both under Cover to me—I will accompany each with a letter from myself to Michaux, & point out the arrangement—Should the Vessel be a publick Vessel & go to any other port than Philad[a] you can Designate your own friends—or mine, these are, Rob. Dickey New York, Moses Myers & Son Norfolk Hugh Thompson Baltimore—when I recieve your letters, I will either (as I may be directed) purchase a Bill or procure a Credit, & If I cannot get the latter, I will give Mich[x] a Credit on Bordeaux, which may answer the purpose 'till remittance can be made. Treasury notes are about 3 or $3\frac{1}{2}$ Discount, but may probably grow better—I would not however delay making my Catalogue & Sending it, as some time must necessarily elapse, before its Execution Upon this or any other occasion where my services can be made Useful, it will give me pleasure to find myself called upon by you—

A line to our Public Characters to assist M[r] M[x] when public opportunities offer may confirm the disposition to facilitate; I must Say that they have been remarkably accomodating to our Society—I ask for Duplicates—which I will forward by private Vessels—You can Send a third by the Channel of the Department of State & I can Send a letter to Michaux to accompany it—

I believe I can furnish all you want to Complete Michaux Work

Vol 1	{	You have the Pines—which form	1. 2 Livr[es]	
	{	I can furnish Noyaux	3. 4	4$
Vol 2	{	You have the oaks	5 a 8	
	{	Also—Birches	9: 10	
	{	I can furnish—Maples	11. 12	} 24$
Vol. 3	{	which Closes the Work	13 a 24	

These have been Sold by me for Michaux at 4$ Noyaux & 24$ for maples & 3[d] Vol—

I have disposed of about 20 Sets & shall hope soon to hear whether you wish these Sent to you—We are very anxious to get when Convenient a Catalogue of your Library however rough it may be, altho' I hope a regular & full one will be published by Congress.—

I remain sincerely[1] Yours &c   JN VAUGHAN

Very Good opportunities are now offering to france.

RC (MHi); at head of text: "Thomas Jefferson—Monticello"; postscript on verso of last page; endorsed by TJ as received 24 Mar. 1815 and so recorded in SJL.

Vaughan, TJ, and François André MICHAUX were members of the American Philosophical SOCIETY. Michaux's WORK was *Histoire des Arbres Forestiers de l'Amérique Septentrionale*, 3 vols. (Paris, 1810–13; Sowerby, no. 1083). LIVR[ES]: a livraison is a part, number, or fascicle of a work published by installments (*OED*). NOYAUX is French for "fruits with pits"; Vaughan presumably intended "noyers," for "walnut trees."

[1] Manuscript: "sincerly."

From David Barrow

Montgomery Kentucky, Near Mountsterling,
March 20th 1815.

VERY DEAR SIR.

From whatever Motives it may have arisen, I have for many Years wished a personal Acquaintance with you: but as that is impracticable under existing Circumstances, I take the Liberty of addressing a few Lines to you. In doing which, I shall not let the Fear of being considered a Flatterer, or of doing you an Injury by letting you know my entire Approbation of the Spirit that breathes in your Writings[1] & your public Conduct while you filled the highest Office in the Nation.[2] These Considerations have endeared your Name & Character to me, & I feel it a Tribute justly due, from to you an unknown Individual to pay it, however small it may appear[3] in the Aggregate. I congratulate you in that Repose, I trust you are enjoying in your Retirement from ardent public Labours, & on the Exhibition of the olive Branch of Peace; and I hope that the Sweets of those Reflections & Sensations will be greatly hightned in an [o]ld & trusty Servant, by the bright Prospects & comfortable Assurances of a blessed Immortality flowing through Jesus Christ our Lord. I trust that Bigotry, that tarnishes the Aspects & sours the Tempers of so many of the Professors of Christianity, has never influenced your Prejudice so as to bias your Judgment, relative to the great Subject of Religion: and I live under flattering Expectations that the Tolerance of our Government, will ultimately have the goodly Effect to remove[4] those Animosities[5] & party Spirit, that is too visible among the different Christian Sects, and that they will be[6] led under the Influence of that "Charity that never fails"[7] to meet & embrace one another upon pure[8] Apostolic Grounds, and thereby manifest to an admiring World, the native Beauty and Utility of the Doctrines & Morality of the Lord Jesus.

The enclosed Scraps will furnish you with a more[9] general Idea, of some Things that have been agitated in this Quarter, than I have Time or Room at present to insert.—I forward them with a Hope, that at some leisure Hour, you may find Freedom to drop me some Hints, that your Knowledge, Feelings & Observations on the Subjects of Slavery & emancipation[10] may dictate, which may be helpful to us in our present Struggles.

And now Dear Sir, I most sincerely pray, that after a Life of public Toil & Usefulness[11] you may through Divine Grace,[12] be found among the heavenly Songsters rendering "Blessing, and Honour, and Glory, and Power unto him who sitteth upon the Throne, and unto the Lamb, for ever and ever."

I remain honored Sir, with every Sentiment of Esteem, yours to serve &c. &c.   DAVID BARROW.

RC (MHi); edge frayed, with missing text supplied from Dft; endorsed by TJ as received from Mount Sterling on 13 Apr. 1815 and so recorded in SJL. Dft (OCU: John Day Caldwell Collection); dated 9 Mar. 1815; endorsed by Barrow: "Copy of a Letter to the Honourable Thoˢ Jefferson Esqʳ Monticello Virginia."

David Barrow (1753–1819), Baptist minister and abolitionist, was a native of Brunswick County. He joined the Baptist Church about 1770, was ordained around 1772, and served as a minister in Isle of Wight County, 1774–97. Barrow freed both of his slaves in 1784 and often spoke out thereafter about the evils of slavery. After two preliminary trips to Kentucky, he moved there permanently in 1798. In a letter he published that year, Barrow explained that he left Virginia partly because he could not prosper there without slaves. His support for emancipation led to several church schisms after his arrival in Kentucky, but he continued to preach. In 1808 Barrow published an important antislavery tract and helped to organize the Kentucky Abolition Society. As president of the society, in October 1815 he unsuccessfully petitioned Congress to set aside some public land for freed slaves. Barrow died at his home in Montgomery County, Kentucky (*DVB*; John H. Spencer, *A History of Kentucky Baptists* [1886], 1:192–7; Carlos R. Allen Jr., "David Barrow's *Circular Letter* of 1798," *WMQ*, 3d ser., 20 [1963]: 440–51; *ASP, Miscellaneous*, 2:278–9).

Barrow may have been inspired to write this letter after receiving one dated 27 Dec. 1814 from his congressman, James Clark, in which Clark forwarded copies of William Canby to TJ, 27 Aug. 1813, and TJ to Canby, 18 Sept. 1813, both of which had recently appeared in the newspapers. Clark commented that he sent Barrow the exchange "under a supposition that everything from the pen of so distinguished a citizen as mʳ Jeffer-

son and particularly upon the subject of religion will be gratifying" (OCU: John Day Caldwell Collection).

The CHARITY THAT NEVER FAILS is from the Bible, 1 Corinthians 13.8. The ENCLOSED SCRAPS probably included the *Minutes of the Kentucky Abolition Society, met at George Smith's, in Franklin County, on the 19th of October, 1814, and continued until the evening of the following day* (Winchester, Ky., 1814; probably Poor, *Jefferson's Library*, 10 [no. 546]), which contained a circular letter and a society constitution each issued under Barrow's signature as president; and possibly also Barrow's *Involuntary, Unmerited, Perpetual, Absolute, Hereditary Slavery, Examined; on the Principles of Nature, Reason, Justice, Policy, and Scripture* (Lexington, Ky., 1808; probably Poor, *Jefferson's Library*, 10 [no. 546]). The biblical tribute rendered by the HEAVENLY SONGSTERS is in Revelation 5.13.

[1] Reworked in Dft from "Approbation of your Writings," with "Spirit" inadvertently omitted from the interlined addition.

[2] Preceding two words interlined in Dft in place of "our great Republic."

[3] Preceding two words interlined in Dft in place of "is."

[4] Word interlined in Dft in place of "destroy."

[5] RC: "Animosties." Dft: "Animosities."

[6] Dft here adds "finally."

[7] RC: "failes." Dft: "fails."

[8] Word interlined in Dft in place of "old."

[9] Preceding two words interlined in Dft in place of "a."

[10] Preceding eight words interlined in Dft in place of "long Experience," with last two words also interlined in RC.

[11] Preceding two words interlined in Dft.

[12] Reworked in Dft from "through the Grace, of our Lord Jesus Christ."

From Joseph Milligan

DEAR SIR Georgetown March 20th 1815

Your Esteemed favour of the 27th u[lt] post marked Milton March 8th reached me last week

When you have compleated the review of the library I am ready to come & pack the Books. I will have the paper-shavings and wrapping paper ready that they may be Sent on as Soon as I hear that you are Ready—

It will be necessary to have the packing cases that Each may Contain about 300 w[t] (but they need not be Made until I come) So that they be made of Such Size that each wagon will hold Eight Cases

With Great respect[1] yours JOSEPH MILLIGAN

RC (DLC: James Madison Papers); at foot of text: "Thos Jefferson Esqr Monticello"; endorsed by TJ as received 22 Mar. 1815 and so recorded in SJL. Enclosed in TJ to James Madison, 23 Mar.

1815, and enclosed with that in TJ to Madison, 24 Mar. 1815.

[1] Manuscript: "respct."

To Charles Willson Peale

DEAR SIR Monticello Mar. 21. 15.

I have been long your debtor in our epistolary account. a farmer being privileged to write only on rainy Sundays, his pen-work is apt to accumulate and get into arrears. in so hard a winter too as we have had, one could not but yield to the pleasure of hovering over a fire with a book, rather than go to the writing table. we have indeed had a hard winter. our average of snow in a common winter is 15.I. which cover the ground 15. days in the whole. this winter we have had $29\frac{1}{2}$ I. of snow which covered the ground 39. days. in general we have 4. ploughing days in the week, taking the winter through. I do not think we have had 3. a week this winter; so that we have much ploughing still to do for our oats and corn. but we have had a method of planting corn suggested by a mr Hall which dispenses with the plough entirely. he marks the ground off in squares of 10.f. by a coulter, or an iron pin. at each crossing of the lines he digs 2 f 3 I. square (equal nearly to 5.[1] square feet) as deep as the mattock will go. this little square is manured as you would have manured the whole ground, taking consequently but $\frac{1}{20}$ of the manure; a grain of corn is planted within 6.I. of each corner, so as to produce 4. stalks about 15.I. apart; this is to be kept clean of weeds either by the hoe, or by covering it with straw so deep as to smother weeds, when the plant is 12.I. high. he asks but 2. laborers to make 2500. bushels of corn. he has taken a patent for his process, and has given me a right to use it, for I certainly should not have thought the right worth 50.D. the price of a license. I am about trying one acre. I have lately had my mould board cast in iron, very thin, for a furrow of 9.I. wide & 6.I. deep, and fitted to a plough, so light that two small horses or mules draw it with less labor than I have ever before seen necessary. it does beautiful work and is approved by every one. I will have one made and send it to you now that the sea is open. I think your farming friends will adopt it.

I am much gratified by your account of various mechanical improvements by yourself and others. your method of regulating the motion of windmills, if it answers finally, will be valuable. it has long been a desideratum. the question is whether your regulating springs are practicable on a large scale. I wish the machine for cleaning clover seed, on the principle of the coffee mill may be found effectual. I have had & tried the Corn sheller of a single cylinder studded with iron pins, & turning within a quadrantal case studded also: but it cannot be made to adapt itself to all sizes of the ears of corn. if that which you mention with a large & a small cylinder answers perfectly, I should be very glad to know it, as it would be valuable with us. we cut our straw with the simplest of all things. we make a bench with a mortise thus ⬚ thro' that mortise we put an old scythe blade with the point broken off and the handle, of the size of that of a reap hook, bent at a right angle. this moving[2] freely in the mortise without any fixture,[3] & fed with straw by the left hand works easier obliquely[4] with the motion of a saw, than the direct cut of the common cutting knives. I think your neighbor who has spent so many thousands to employ the pendulum as a power, will be totally disappointed. the pendulum like the fly wheel is a regulator of power & motion, but also a consumer of it, requiring some additional power to renew it's own motion perpetually, as in the case of the clock. an ingenious friend at Albany supposes he has greatly improved two-wheeled carriages[5] by a cranked axle thus ⌐⌐ fastening his shafts at a.a. by rings so that the crank moves freely from the vertical to the horizontal line. he supposes he may use wheels of any height, without danger of oversetting. but whenever the force of the draught draws the crank into a horizontal position, this danger recurs. I have fixed my homony beater differently from yours. I make the saw-gate of my saw mill move a lever, to the other end of which is suspended a wooden pestle falling into a common homony morter made of a block. all our homony is beaten by this. I make the same[6] saw-gate move another lever at the other end of which is suspended the upper head-block of a common hemp break (but much heavier than common) the break is ranged under that arm of the lever, in the same plane, and the center of it's motion as nearly as may be under that of the lever. while two persons feed the break with the hempstalks, a third holds the hemp already beaten & formed into a twist, under the head block, which beats it most perfectly: but as one beater is not enough for 2. break-ers, I lengthen that arm of the lever 3 f. beyond the point of suspen-sion of the head block, and at the end suspend a pestle, which falling on a block under it, presents a 2[d] beater. to make this work true, a section of a circle (like the felloe of a cart wheel, but shorter) is mor-tised on the end of the lever, with a groove in it for the suspending chain to lie in. the following is a coarse side view of the whole.

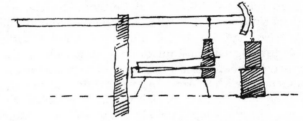

two breakers & 2. beaters will compleatly break and beat 400.℔ in a day, & they need not be men. a patent has been obtained for fixing the upper swords to the underside of the saw gate, and placing the bench & lower swords under it, and the patentee gave me leave to use it; but that place being wet and inconvenient, I thought it better to remove the action by a lever to a drier & more convenient spot, outside of the mill. I wish to make the same agent work an apparatus for fulling our homespun; but have not yet attempted it, tho' we need it much, as we clothe ourselves chiefly, & our laborers entirely in what we spin and weave in our family. for this I find the old spinning Jenny far simpler and preferable to Arkwright's clock[7] work machines. of threshing machines we have thousands in this state, no farmer who can raise 100.D. being without one. we have also abundance of patents for im-provements on them, not one of which is worth a copper. the bands are fallacious and troublesome. the original Scotch machine with it's geer is best. the best of these machines I have ever seen is double-geered only, and with 2. horses at their ease gets out 130. bushels of wheat a day. it differs from the Scotch construction only in having spurs, instead of face wheels & wallowers, except the horse wheel.

most of our other machines take 4. and 6. horses, and do little more work, perhaps half as much more.—my grandson after whom you kindly enquire, and who retains a just sense and gratitude for your friendship to him, was married a few days ago to a daughter of mr Nicholas our present governor. he is becoming one of our best farmers. Accept the assurances of my constant friendship & respect.

Th: Jefferson

RC (PPAmP: Peale-Sellers Papers). PoC (DLC); at foot of first page: "Charles W. Peale." Tr (MHi); posthumous copy; incomplete.

For TJ's copy of James Hall's 19 Nov. 1814 patent and specification for improvements in crop cultivation, including a new method of PLANTING CORN, see note to James Cutbush to TJ, 23 Oct. 1814. TJ's INGENIOUS FRIEND was Horatio G. Spafford. A SAW-GATE is a rectangular frame in which a mill's saw is placed, while a FELLOE is a curved piece of wood that, when joined with others, forms the circular rim of a wheel (OED). By ORIGINAL SCOTCH MACHINE TJ probably means the threshing machine invented by Andrew Meikle and George Meikle, of Scotland (ODNB). FACE WHEELS are cogwheels with teeth set at right angles to their plane and placed on an axis perpendicular to the axes of WALLOWERS, which are cogwheels in the shape of a cylinder in which the top and bottom plates are connected by staves that serve as teeth (OED). TJ's GRANDSON Thomas Jefferson Randolph married Jane Hollins Nicholas on 6 Mar. 1815 (Shackelford, Descendants, 1:77).

[1] Word interlined in place of "10."
[2] Word interlined in place of "working."
[3] Preceding three words interlined.
[4] Word interlined.
[5] Tr begins here.
[6] TJ here canceled "lever."
[7] Tr: "dock."

From Samuel H. Smith

Dear Sir   March 21. 1815

I drop you a line to advise you that the President has had a conversation with Mʳ Milligan on aiding you in the arrangement & packing[1] the Library, in wᶜʰ the latter has been requested to comply fully with your wishes on this head. He will, accordingly, repair to Monticello whenever you shall wish him, & will take such steps as to a supply of wrapping[2] paper, as you or he may consider necessary.

I am, with respectful consideration   Sa H Smith

RC (DLC); endorsed by TJ as received 24 Mar. 1815 and so recorded in SJL. FC (DLC: J. Henley Smith Papers); entirely in Smith's hand; lacks closing; endorsed by Smith, in part: "Library."

[1] Manuscript: "packig."
[2] Manuscript: "wrappig."

From George Ticknor

I reached home yesterday morning, after a tedious and indeed a perilous journey, and found that your kindness had anticipated the request I sent you from Philadelphia. I need not tell you how much I am indebted to you for the signal favour you have done me by giving me the means of becoming acquainted with men so distinguished and so entirely of the class I should be most ambitious to know.

You judged rightly, when you conjectured, that the peace might first lead me to England. If I were to be governed only by my own inclinations, I should undoubted[ly] go first to Paris—the great mart of the science & literature of the world—but, three friends who are nearer to me than all the world besides, except my own family, are going to London & I cannot resist the affectionate kindness, which led them before I had returned & without consulting me, to bespeak my passage in the same ship with themselves. I shall, however, remain there but a short time, and then cross over to the continent. In this way, I imagine, I can be more useful to you than on my original plan. I shall be long enough in London to purchase such books as can be best obtained there, and yet soon enough in Paris to purchase the remainder. On this subject, however, I shall wait your instructions. We shall leave this port about the 12th proximo &, of course, a letter from Monticello will have full time to reach me before I sail; and even if it should arrive after I am gone, my father will immediately forward it to me in some one of the numerous vessels, which will leave here in the course of April & May.—

I shall observe your directions, in relation to the letters, which you have confided to me. As soon after I reach England, as a suitable opportunity occurs, I will send them to France—probably to our minister there—reserving to myself as a lawyer would say—a lien on their introduc[tory] contents and a consequent claim to become acquainted with the persons to whom they are addressed.

As occasions or subjects may offer, I shall not fail to take advantage of the permission you have given me of keeping for myself a place in your memory by addressing a few lines to you from amidst the literary society of Europe, and shall consider myself singularly fortunate, if, by giving you early[1] notice of the advance of science there, I may be able in any imperfect degree to express my gratitude for all the kindness you have shown me.—

I cannot close a letter addressed to Monticello without recollecting & again acknowledging the hospitality I received there and asking you to do me the favour to remember me particularly to all its inhabitants.

Your's very respectfully,[2]   GEO: TICKNOR.

N.B. My father's address is—Mr. Elisha Ticknor Boston—and any letters, which you may do me the favour to send to me either before I sail, or after I am gone, will, if directed to him, reach me by the first opportunity, through Mr. Adams our minister in Lond.

I enclose you the letter to Mr. Crawford, who, as you of course, know is on his return.—

RC (MHi); torn at seal; addressed: "Thomas Jefferson Esqr. Monticello, Albermarle county, Virginia"; franked; postmarked Boston, 23 Mar.; endorsed by TJ as received 30 Mar. 1815 and so recorded in SJL. Enclosure: TJ to William H. Crawford, 14 Feb. 1815.

ton Haven, and Samuel G. Perkins (George S. Hillard, ed., *Life, Letters, and Journals of George Ticknor* [1876], 1:49; Ticknor, *The Remains of Nathaniel Appleton Haven. With a Memoir of His Life* [1827], xxiv; Boston *Columbian Centinel*, 15 Apr. 1815).

The THREE FRIENDS who accompanied Ticknor aboard the *New-Packet* were Edward Everett, Nathaniel Apple-

[1] Word interlined.
[2] Manuscript: "recpectfully."

To James Madison

DEAR SIR   Monticello Mar. 23. 15.

I duly recieved your favor of the 12th and with it the pamphlet on the causes and conduct of the war, which I now return. I have read it with great pleasure, but with irresistable desire that it should be published. the reasons in favor of this are so strong, and those against it are so easily gotten over, that there appears to me no balance between them. 1. we need it in Europe. they have totally mistaken our character. accustomed to rise at a feather themselves, and to be always fighting, they will see in our conduct, fairly stated, that acquiescence under wrong, to a certain degree, is wisdom & not pusillanimity, and that peace and happiness are preferable to that false honor which, by eternal wars, keeps their people in eternal labor, want and wretchedness. 2. it is necessary for the people of England, who have been decieved as to the causes and conduct of the war, and do not entertain a doubt that it was entirely wanton & wicked on our part, and under the order of Bonaparte. by rectifying their ideas, it will tend to that conciliation which is absolutely necessary to the peace and prosperity of both nations. 3. it is necessary for our own people, who, altho' they have known the details as they went along, yet have been so plied with false facts and false views by the federalists, that some impression has been left that all has not been right. it may be said that it will be thought unfriendly. but truths necessary for our own character must not be suppressed out of tenderness to it's calumniators. altho written generally with great moderation, there may be some things in the pamphlet which may perhaps irritate. the characterizing every act, for example, by it's appropriate epithet is not necessary to shew it's deformity to an intelligent reader. the naked narrative will present it truly to his mind, and the more strongly, from it's moderation, as he will percieve that no exaggeration is aimed at. rubbing down these roughnesses, and they are neither many nor prominent, and preserving the original date might I think remove all the offensiveness, and give more effect to the publication. indeed I think that a soothing Postscript, addressed to the interests, the prospects & the sober reason of both nations, would make it acceptable to both. the trifling expence of reprinting it ought not to be considered a moment. mr Gallatin could have it translated into French, and suffer it to get abroad in Europe without either avowal or disavowal. but it would be useful to print some copies of an Appendix containing all the documents referred to, to be preserved in libraries, and to facilitate to the present and future writers of history the acquisition of the materials which test the truths it contains.

I sincerely congratulate you on the peace; and more especially on the eclat with which the war was closed. the affair of N. Orleans was fraught with useful lessons to ourselves, our enemies, and our friends, and will powerfully influence our future relations with the nations of Europe. it will shew them we mean to take no part in their wars, and count no odds when engaged in our own. I presume that, having spared to the pride of England her formal[1] acknolegement of the atrocity of impressment in an article of the treaty, she will concur in a convention for relinquishing it. without this she must understand that the present is but a truce, determinable on the first act of impressment of an American citizen committed by any officer of hers. would it not be better that this Convention should be a separate act, unconnected with any treaty of commerce, and made an indispensable preliminary to all other treaty? if blended with a treaty of commerce, she will make it the price of injurious concessions. indeed we are infinitely better without such treaties with any nation. we cannot too distinctly detach ourselves from the European system, which is essentially belligerent, nor too sedulously cultivate an American system, essentially pacific. but if we go into commercial treaties at all, they should be with all at the same time with whom we have important commercial relations. France, Spain, Portugal, Holland, Denmark, Sweden, Russia, all should proceed pari passu. our ministers marching in phalanx on the same line, and inter-communicating freely, each will be supported by the weight of the whole mass, and the facility with which the other nations will agree to equal terms of intercourse, will discountenance the selfish hig-glings of England, or justify our rejection of them. perhaps with all of them it would be best to have but the single article gentis ami-cissimae, leaving every thing else to the usages & courtesies of civi-lized nations. but all these things will occur to yourself, with their counter-considerations.

Mr Smith wrote to me on the transportation of the library, and par-ticularly that it is submitted to your direction. he mentioned also that Dougherty would be engaged to superintend it. no one will more carefully & faithfully execute all those duties which would belong to a waggon master. but it requires a character acquainted with books to recieve the library. I am now employing as many hours of every day as my strength will permit, in arranging the books, and putting every one in it's place on the shelves corresponding with it's order in the Catalogue, and shall have them numbered correspondently. this op-eration will employ me a considerable time yet. then I should wish a competent agent to attend, and, with the catalogue in his hand, see that every book is on the shelves, and have their lids nailed on, one by one, as he proceeds. this would take such a person about two days, after which Dougherty's business would be the mere mechanical re-moval at convenience. I inclose you a letter from Mr Millegan offer-ing his service, which would not cost more than 8. or 10. days reasonable compensation. this is necessary for my safety and your sat-isfaction as a just caution for the public. you know there are persons both in and out of the public councils, who will seize every occasion of imputation on either of us, the more difficult to be repelled in this case in which a negative could not be proved. if you approve of it therefore, as soon as I am thro' the review, I will give notice to mr Millegan, or any other person whom you will name, to come on im-mediately. indeed it would be well worth while to add to his duty that of^2 covering the books with a little paper (the good bindings at least) and filling the vacancies of the presses with paper parings, to be brought from Washington. this would add little more to the time, as he could carry on both operations at once. Accept the assurances of my constant & affectionate friendship & respect.

Th: Jefferson

RC (DLC: Madison Papers); endorsed by Madison. PoC (DLC); at foot of first page: "Madison President." Enclosures: (1) enclosure to Madison to TJ, 12 Mar. 1815. (2) Joseph Milligan to TJ, 20 Mar. 1815. Enclosed in TJ to Madison, 24 Mar. 1815.

GENTIS AMICISSIMAE: "of the most favored nation."

[1] Word interlined.
[2] TJ here canceled "packing."

From Francis C. Gray

Dear Sir,   Boston 24. March 1815

On my return to Boston on the 20th instant, I had the honour of receiving your letter of the 4th. for which & for the information it contains I must add new thanks to those which I already owed you. My enquiries on the subject, which you have so kindly and perfectly explained, were more particular, because the word mulatto in the Statutes of Massachusetts received a very singular definition in the Supreme court of the State in the year 1810, a period when the bench was occupied by some of the most distinguished Lawyers, whom our State has ever produced. The question before the Court was whether the offspring of a half-blood & a white is a mulatto within the Statute of marriages passed in 1786. The Court decided that it is not so; & stated it as their "unanimous opinion that a mulatto is a person begotten between a white & a black." As the Statute recognizes no fourth class, it must be concluded that the person then before the court was considered a white, & by analogy that the offspring of a mulatto & a black is considered a black. The general rule thus laid down by the Court leads to the strange conclusion, that three persons, who have the same proportions of black & white blood, may be, one a white man, one a negro & one a mulatto, as is easily proved by the method you have adopted to explain the mixtures of white & negro blood.

Let the small letters w. b express the white & black blood, the capitals W. B. the white man & negro, & M the mulatto; And let the varieties of each be denoted by the addition of the Arabic numerals.

Admitting then that the offspring of a white & black is a mulatto, of a mulatto & white, a white; of a mulatto & black, a black; let the 1st crossing be of a pure negro **B.** and a pure white **W.** the issue will be **M.** whose blood is $\frac{w}{2} + \frac{b}{2}$.

the 2d crossing of **M.** & **B.** the issue will be **B2.** whose blood is $\frac{w}{4} + \frac{3b}{4}$

the 3d	of **B2** & **W.**	**M2**	$\frac{5w}{8} + \frac{3b}{8}$
the 4th.	of **M2** & **B2**	**B3**	$\frac{7w}{16} + \frac{9b}{16}$
the 5th	of **B3** & **W.**	**M3**	$\frac{23w}{32} + \frac{9b}{32}$
the 6th.	of **M3** & **B3**	**B4**	$\frac{37w}{64} + \frac{27b}{64}$.

A negro the larger portion of whose blood is white—Without tracing the descent from the pure blood, assume **B5**[1] whose blood is $\frac{5w}{32} + \frac{27b}{32}$. A crossing of **B5** & **W.** will produce **M4** whose blood is $\frac{37w}{64} + \frac{27b}{64}$ the same as that of **B4.**

In the same manner assume **W2** whose blood is $\frac{21w}{32} + \frac{11b}{32}$. A crossing of **W2** & **M.** will produce **W3** whose blood is $\frac{37w}{64} + \frac{27b}{64}$ the same as that of **B4** & **M4.**

It follows also from the strict letter of the definition given by the Court that even the offspring of two Mulattoes is not a mulatto. Should the question again arise in this State, it is probable that a different rule would be laid down, but, as in this instance it is peculiarly true that if a definite signification be affixed to the word it is of little importance what that signification is, it may be expected that this case will be considered an authority as to the point decided, & that no person will be considered a Mulatto within the meaning of our Statutes, who has not more than one fourth of each blood.

I sincerely reciprocate your congratulations on the peace; it is certainly an immediate & important benefit; though neither the friendship nor hostility of any foreign powers can much affect the prosperity of this country. Its true sources are beyond their reach; they cannot diminish the fertility of the soil, nor stifle the enterprise of its inhabitants. Mr. Corea states that 70.000 persons from the Atlantic States annually cross the Allegany, & there increase with a rapidity almost as disproportionate to ours, as ours is to the slow advances of the European nations. This increase of population has sometimes been expected to lead to the establishment of independent & dissimilar governments in different parts of the country. I hope unreasonably. In the present state of society the tendency of small states to coalesce into great nations is peculiarly strong, & its operation is now evident & extensive even in Europe, where it is counteracted by the diversity of language, institutions & manners; all which form in this country new bonds of connexion. As the population increases, the means of intercourse & the motives to it will multiply, we shall become better acquainted & more closely connected with each other, interwoven by innumerable ramifications, which could be severed only by some great moral convulsion, such as cannot be an object of calculation. The improvement of the roads alone will produce an effect on the character of the nation, which we should almost blush to owe to such a cause; & perhaps before many years that western country, whose rapid advances have excited the apprehensions & jealousy of the Eastern States, will become the very knot of the Union; its ornament & security. These are high hopes; but there are causes now in operation adequate to their fulfillment, & it is probable that the result will rather exceed than disappoint them. Permit me Sir to present my best wishes & grateful remembrance to your family, & to join with my father in offering you the assurance of the highest respect.

I have the honour to remain your Most humble & Obed. Servt.

FRANCIS C. GRAY.

RC (DLC); addressed: "Thomas Jefferson Late President of the United States. Monticello"; franked; postmarked Boston, 25 Mar.; endorsed by TJ as received 8 Apr. 1815 and so recorded in SJL.

The SINGULAR DEFINITION of a mulatto as "a person begotten between a white and a black" was established in *Medway v. Natick* during the October 1810 term of the Supreme Judicial Court of Massachusetts. The DISTINGUISHED LAWYERS on the court were Theophilus Parsons, Theodore Sedgwick, Samuel Sewall, and Isaac Parker. A 22 June 1786 Massachusetts STATUTE "for the orderly Solemnization of Marriages" prohibited unions between whites and mulattoes (Dudley Atkins Tyng, *Reports of Cases Argued and Determined in the Supreme Judicial Court of the Commonwealth of Massachusetts* [1853], 7:87–8; *Laws of the Commonwealth of Massachusetts, From November 28, 1780 to February 28, 1807* [Boston, 1807], 1:321–4).

[1] Gray here interlined and then canceled "a negro."

To James Madison

DEAR SIR   Monticello Mar. 24. 15.

I had written the inclosed letter but had not yet sent it to the post office when mr Nelson calling, informed me you were to leave Washington on Tuesday last (the 20th) I have thought it better therefore to inclose it to you at Montpelier. I am laboriously employed in arranging the library, to be ready for it's delivery. and as soon as I can name the day on which I shall have finished I will give notice to the person whom you may appoint to verify the catalogue. on this subject I shall be glad to hear from you as soon as possible; but this will be retarded by the unlucky arrangement of our mails; for altho' we have two departures in the week for Washington, yet they are on Wednesday & Thursday, leaving intervals of 24. hours, or of 6. days. this letter therefore will lie 5. days in our office before it's departure. I wish much to see you, and if the arrangement of the library should give me any interval during your stay, and the roads permit, I will try to pay you a visit. I say, if the roads permit; for increasing feebleness obliges me now to be driven by others, and consequently to the use of heavier carriages. a visit by mrs Madison and yourself altho' always desired, it would be unreasonable to expect out of the short time you are permitted to stay & after so long an absence. but if you can afford it, I should recieve it as a deodand. Adieu affectionately.

TH: JEFFERSON

RC (DLC: Madison Papers); at foot of text: "The President of the US."; endorsed by Madison. PoC (DLC); endorsed by TJ. Enclosure: TJ to Madison, 23 Mar. 1815, and enclosures.

TUESDAY LAST was actually 21 Mar. 1815. DEODAND: "something forfeited or given to God," especially property ceded to the Crown and applied to pious uses such as a distribution of alms (*OED*).

From John Vaughan

DR SIR   Philad. March 24. 1815

I have Seen Mr Girard—who will lodge the necessary directions with Mess Perregaux & Lafitte Banquiers at Paris to supply to the extent of 500$ as Called Upon by Your Agent for purchases.—When therefore you Send your orders to me send therewith your Directions to your purchasing agent to call on these Gentlemen for funds as wanted, & write a letter to Perregaux & Lafitte to furnish the money on the Call of the Agent—If Michaux is the Person he will call for 50 or 100$ & when that is laid out a further sum, & furnish you an exact accot of Expenditures—When it becomes convenient You can furnish the funds, & I will then see Mr Girard & either pay him or remit to his Bankers as he may choose—Send Duplicates or I will have duplicates made of the list here, the letters had better be your own—or even triplicates which I shall carefully forward—Exchange on France is about 1$ for 5 fs on England 3 p % below par, So that Treasury notes which are at 3 p % would purchase a Sterling Bill at Par—Any purchases to be[1] made here I shall chearfully attend to—Your directions must be particular as to Editions &c We are rather bare of good English Editions, but if I have your list you Shall be speedily informed—Any purchases here may be made on a Credit to suit your Convenience altho' abatemt in price is the result of Cash—

I shall most chearfully either here or thro' the medium of my friends in Europe do every thing in my power to assist you in your object I have a Brother William Vaughan, who will be equally desirous of being made Serviceable

M Alex Everitt who goes Sec^y with D Eustis is here, he is Brother to the Minister at Boston lately appointed Greek Prof at Cambridge this gentleman A. E. was with M Adams 18 m^s at Petersburg; he will do us Credit abroad M Correa Well, desires respects & is anxiously waiting the Settling of the troubled[2] Waters in Europe, in order to adjourn to Paris—We shall miss him much

    I remain with respect Your friend & sert   J N VAUGHAN

RC (MHi); endorsed by TJ as received 30 Mar. 1815 and so recorded in SJL.

Alexander H. Everett (EVERITT) and William EUSTIS, the newly appointed envoy extraordinary and minister plenipotentiary to the Netherlands, sailed from Boston on 8 June. Edward Everett was appointed professor of GREEK literature at Harvard University in 1815 (*Boston Patriot*, 10 June 1815; *New-Bedford Mercury*, 16 June 1815; *Harvard Catalogue*, 63).

[1] Preceding two words interlined.

[2] Word interlined.

From Elizabeth Patterson Bonaparte

SIR   Baltimore march 25. 1815

    I allow myself a great liberty in thus addressing you on a subject entirely personal. My health obliges me to go to Europe & I shall embark with m^r & m^rs Eustis for Holland on my way to France. If you, Sir, will have the goodness to give me letters of recommendation; my admittance into the first Circles of Paris will be secured, as the respect & admiration with which you are considered in Europe must attract attention to the Person, who has the honour of being introduced under your Auspices. Should I be happy enough to succeed in obtaining Letters from you, Sir, I will thank you to have the goodness to mention me as m^rs Patterson; since I am informed by letters from Paris that my retaining there[1] the name of Bonaparte, could be only prejudicial. Letters for me, enclosed to m^r Eustis minister to Holland, at Boston, would reach me there; or in the event of our having sailed, would be sent after us.

    I have the honour to remain, Sir, with the highest respect your ob^t hb^le &c. &c.   E BONAPARTE.

RC (DLC); endorsed by TJ as received 31 Mar. 1815 and so recorded in SJL. RC (DLC); address cover only; with PoC of TJ to Bonaparte, 24 Apr. 1815, on verso; addressed: "Thomas Jefferson Esqr Charlottsville Virginia"; stamped; postmarked Baltimore, 25 Mar., and Charlottesville, 30 Mar.

Elizabeth Patterson Bonaparte (1785–1879), the daughter of a wealthy Baltimore shipping and real-estate magnate, married Napoleon's youngest brother, Jerome Bonaparte, in Baltimore in 1803. The French ruler, however, had other matrimonial plans for his sibling and ordered him back to France, refused to recognize the marriage and, when unable to procure a papal annulment, had the union disavowed by a French ecclesiastical court in 1806. Bonaparte accompanied her husband to Europe, but they separated permanently even before she bore him a son in England in the summer of 1805 and returned to the United States. Although Napoleon later granted her an annual pension, she sought and obtained a divorce from the Maryland legislature in 1813. During the two decades following Napoleon's downfall, Bonaparte traveled extensively in Europe. Her father left her very little when he died in 1834. Bonaparte's astute business sense and frugal lifestyle, however, allowed her to leave a large estate when she died in Baltimore (*ANB*; *DAB*; Connelly, *Napoleonic France*, 77–8; Charlene Boyer Lewis, "Elizabeth Patterson Bonaparte: A Woman between Two Worlds," in Leonard J. Sadosky and others, eds., *Old World, New World: America and Europe in the Age of Jefferson* [2010], 247–75; *New-York Tribune*, 5 Apr. 1879).

William Eustis and his entourage SAILED from Boston on 8 June (*Boston Patriot*, 10 June 1815).

[1] Word interlined.

To William W. Hening

DEAR SIR   Monticello Mar. 25. 15.

I would do any thing rather than defeat the invaluable collection you are making of our statutes and will therefore undertake to apologize to the library committee of Congress for the detention of the Vth volume of the laws, and it's safe delivery in time. but I must pray you to send off the rest without delay, as within 10. days or a fortnight an agent will be on from Washington to recieve the library. if very well packed to secure them against rubbing, they will come safest and quickest by the conveyance of the Stage to Milton[1] the expence of which I would gladly pay rather than wait for any other. but unless you will be so good as to see them set off yourself, they will as likely lie at the stage office 6. months as not.

It was never my intention to have included this collection of our laws in the sale to Congress, and in my original offer I reserved a right to retain some books. but they have lumped the transaction in such a manner as that I am not able to retain a single volume, which became known to me so late that no time was left to get a change made before Congress rose. Accept the assurance of my esteem and respect.   TH: JEFFERSON

PoC (DLC); on verso of reused address cover to TJ; at foot of text: "M[r] Hening"; endorsed by TJ.

The AGENT was Joseph Dougherty.

[1] Preceding five words interlined.

From Benjamin Jones

RESPECTED FRIEND   Philadel[a] 25th March 1815
I reced your favor of 4[h] Int and was glad to recognise your well
known hand once more and I now Send you the articles order'd remarking at the Same time that Iron had become very Scarce and the
price very high previous to the news of peace. it has fall[n] A little but
is Still high compared with former times. A few months I hope will
regulate these things.   I send you now

16 Bars of Iron assorted w[t] 5.0. 7 at 8.50 p w[t] $43.04
18 Bundles rod Iron   9.0 0 at 10.   90.00
 1 Bundle 4[d] hoop Iron   3.11 at 11   9.35
                                                142.39
                              portage   37½
                                              $142.76½

the vessel was to have Loaded Some days ago but did not get ready
till this day. She will Sail in 2 or 3 day
      I am with much Respect yours   BENJ[N] JONES

RC (MHi); numerous superfluous periods editorially omitted; between dateline and
salutation: "Thomas Jefferson Esq[r]"; endorsed by TJ as received 31 Mar. 1815 and so
recorded in SJL.

To James Leitch

Mar. 25. 15.
any clothing which the bearer Burwell may chuse for himself
                                              TH:J.

RC (MdHi: Vertical Files); dateline beneath signature; written on a small scrap; at
foot of text: "M[r] Leitch." Not recorded in SJL.

From George Logan

DEAR SIR   Stenton March 25th 1815
I sincerely congratulate you on the restoration of peace to our
beloved country. Nothwithstanding the cavils of a few individuals; I
assure you the event gives universal satisfaction to the citizens of
Pennsylvania. As to sailors rights, it is a subject that may be amicably adjusted between the two governments, in a treaty of friendship
and commerce. I have written on these subjects to my friends Lord

Sidmouth, Sir John Sinclaire, Henry Bathurst Bishop of Norwich, and Mr Wilberforce. To all of whom I have expressed an anxious desire that in the event of a treaty of commerce[1] taking place between Great Britain and the U states: the negotiation will not be tarnished by temporary expedients, or mere local considerations, injurious to the general interest. But that a spirit of magnanimity will prevail; as the soundest policy, to insure the peace and future prosperity of both countries

Accept assurances of my friendship   GEO LOGAN

RC (DLC); endorsed by TJ as received 31 Mar. 1815 and so recorded in SJL. RC (DLC); address cover only; with PoC of TJ to John Hollins, 22 Apr. 1815, on verso; addressed: "Thomas Jefferson Esqr Monticello virginia"; franked; postmarked Philadelphia, 25 Mar.

[1] Manuscript: "commere."

To James Madison

DEAR SIR   Monticello Mar. 25. 15.

After I had sent my letters of yesterday and the day before to the post office the return of the messenger brought me a letter from Saml H. Smith informing me you had directed Milligan to come on whenever I should call for him. I mention this to save you the trouble of further writing on that subject.   the same mail brought me the Aurora, beginning the publication of the Causes and Conduct of the war, which settles the question of publication. I still think however it would be worth while for the government to smooth & reprint it. if done instantly it will get to Europe before the newspaper details, and at any rate may be declared to be the genuine edition as pub-lished by the government, and may be with truth so declared in a conciliatory P.S.   ever and affectionately Yours

TH: JEFFERSON

RC (DLC: Madison Papers); at foot of text: "The President of the US."; endorsed by Madison. PoC (DLC); on verso of reused address cover of William Wirt to TJ, 15 Mar. 1815; endorsed by TJ.

The Philadelphia *Aurora General Advertiser* began serial PUBLICATION of Dallas, *Exposition*, on 17 Mar. 1815 and finished it six days later.

To William Short

DEAR SIR   Monticello Mar. 25. 15.

I was waiting to write to you on the subject of my bonds only until I could recieve an answer to a letter I had written enquiring the footing on which treasury notes could be recieved. here they are eagerly recieved at par and the interest, while no one will recieve a bank note but for the purposes of the moment. I speak of the country people, and not of the banking cabals. your letter removing all doubt, as soon as my library can be delivered, and the notes for it recieved I shall pay off the two bonds due, & probably all. this cannot be till April, and may not till May. but it shall[1] not be delayed one moment which I can prevent. in the mean time inform me whether you would prefer notes payable at Washington or Philadelphia, and whether in a single large note, or in those of 1000. 100. 50. or 20.D indeed I am not certain that they will issue any larger than 1000.

There is reason to expect Col° Monroe here shortly. if he will give me a single day your affair shall be settled.

I do not wonder at your wish to return to France. were it not for my family and possessions here, I should prefer that residence to any other. Paris is the only place where a man who is not obliged to do any thing will always find something amusing to do. here the man who has nothing to do is the prey of ennui.

'Life's cares are comforts, such by heav'n designed:
    He that has none, must make them or be wretched.'
in this country a family for leisure moments, and a farm or profession for those of employment[2] are indispensable for happiness. these mixed with books, a little letter writing, and neighborly and friendly society constitute a plenum of occupation and of happiness which leaves no wish for the noisy & barren amusements and distractions of a city.—God bless the peace! no man in the US. wished for it more than myself. yet without the 'sauce à l'Orleans' the dish would not have been so highly palatable. I salute you with constant & affectionate friendship   TH: JEFFERSON

P.S. I forget whether you returned Dupont on education. I wish much to read Grimm, but he is too bulky for the mail.

RC (ViW: TJP); postscript written perpendicularly in left margin; addressed: "William Short esquire Philadelphia"; franked; postmarked Charlottesville, 29 Mar.; endorsed by Short as received 2 Apr. 1815. PoC (CSmH: JF); on verso of reused address cover of Patrick Gibson to TJ, 14 Dec. 1814; postscript added separately in left margin; endorsed by TJ.

The ANSWER to the enquiry about treasury notes was John Vaughan to TJ, 24 Mar. 1815. LIFE'S CARES ARE COMFORTS . . . OR BE WRETCHED comes from Edward Young's poem, "Night the Second. on Time, Death, Friendship" (Young, *The Works of the Author of the Night-Thoughts* [London, 1762], 3:26; Sowerby, no. 4548; *LCB*, 100). SAUCE À L'ORLEANS ("Orleans sauce") refers to the recent American victory at the Battle of New Orleans.

In a letter dated 3 Mar. 1814, Short had returned Pierre Samuel DUPONT de Nemours, *Sur l'éducation nationale dans les États-Unis d'Amérique* (Paris, 1812; Poor, *Jefferson's Library*, 5 [nos. 207, 209–10]). In 1818 TJ acquired the first sixteen volumes (out of seventeen) of Friedrich Melchior, Freiherr von GRIMM, *Correspondance Littéraire, Philosophique et Critique* (Paris, 1812–14; Poor, *Jefferson's Library*, 14 [no. 918]) (Robert Walsh to TJ, 27 Jan. 1818; Joseph Milligan to TJ, 6 Feb. 1818).

[1] Manuscript: "shell."
[2] Preceding four words interlined.

To John Watts

DEAR SIR   Monticello Mar. 25. 15.

I have the pleasure to inform you that I shall be able with certainty to pay off the two bonds of mine to Griffin in your hands, in the course of the spring, perhaps in April, but more probably in May. I mention this thus early that you may be enabled with confidence to make any arrangements which may suit you on that ground. I expect to be in Bedford in two or three weeks. I sincerely congratulate you on the peace which may once more enable us to count on the engagements we make or recieve. Accept the assurance of my great esteem and respect.   TH: JEFFERSON

PoC (MHi); on verso of reused address cover of William Short to TJ, 11 Mar. 1815; at foot of text: "Col° Watts"; mistakenly endorsed by TJ as a letter to "Watts Wᵐ" and so recorded in SJL.

From John M. Carter

SIR,   Georgetown, D.C. March 27. 1815.—

Without having the honor of an acquaintance with you I have presumed to obtrude myself upon your attention—in the presentation of Arator, by Colᴵ John Taylor of your State—This being the second edition of that work, the author has avowed himself, which he did not do in the first[1] edition.—I have taken this liberty with you, as the publisher of Arator, merely from the Strictures contained in it, upon your "notes on Virginia," which, coming from so distinguished a citizen as Colᴵ Taylor, I supposed you would wish to see.—From which circumstance, Sir, I trust you will not attribute to me any sort of offence, as intended.

With the most respectful considerations, Sir, I am your very ob^t serv^t JNO. M. CARTER

RC (MHi); endorsed by TJ as received 31 Mar. 1815 and so recorded in SJL. RC (DLC); address cover only; with PoC of TJ to Albert Gallatin, 24 Apr. 1815 (second letter), on verso; addressed: "The Honorable Thos Jefferson, Monticello, Virginia"; franked; postmarked Georgetown, 29 Mar. Enclosure: John Taylor of Caroline, *Arator; being a series of Agricultural Essays, Practical & Political*, 2d ed. (Georgetown, 1814; Poor, *Jefferson's Library*, 6 [no. 255]).

John M. Carter, printer, was one of the proprietors of the semiweekly District of Columbia newspaper, *The Spirit of 'Seventy-Six*, 1810–14. The first of John Taylor of Caroline's "Arator" essays appeared in that newspaper on 25 Dec. 1810. Carter published editions of *Arator*

in Georgetown in 1813 and 1814, in Baltimore in 1817, and in Petersburg in 1818, each with additional material (Brigham, *American Newspapers*, 1:94, 106; Washington *Spirit of 'Seventy-Six*, 18 Dec. 1810; Georgetown *Federal Republican, and Commercial Gazette*, 17 Nov. 1813; Freda F. Stohrer, "Arator: A Publishing History," *VMHB* 88 [1980]: 442–5).

On pp. 61–7 of the enclosed second edition of *Arator*, in essay "Number 14. Slavery, Continued," Taylor included STRICTURES defending the institution of slavery from the critical remarks in TJ's *Notes on the State of Virginia*. The first edition of *Arator* (Georgetown, 1813) contained the same passage on pp. 67–74.

^{1} Word interlined in place of "second."

To Louis H. Girardin

TH: JEFFERSON TO MR GIRARDIN.   Monticello Mar. 27. 15.

I return your 14th Chapter with only 2. or 3. unimportant alterations as usual, and with a note suggested, of doubtful admissibility. I believe it would be acceptable to the reader of every nation except England, and I do not suppose that, even without it, your book will be a popular one there. however you will decide for yourself.

As to what is to be said of myself, I of course am not the judge. but my sincere wish is that the faithful historian, like the able Surgeon, would consider me in his hands, while living, as a dead subject: that the same judgment may now be expressed which will be rendered hereafter, so far as my small agency in human affairs may attract future notice: & I would of choice now stand as at the bar of posterity 'Cum semel occideris, et de te ultima Minos Fecerit arbitria.' the only exact testimony of a man is his actions, leaving the reader to pronounce on them his own judgment. in anticipating this, too little is safer than too much; and I sincerely assure you that you will please me most by a rigorous suppression of all friendly partialities. this candid expression of sentiment once delivered, passive silence becomes the future duty.

It is with real regret I inform you that the day of delivering the library is close at hand. a letter by last mail informs me that mr Millegan is ordered to come on the instant I am ready to deliver. I shall compleat the arrangement of the books on Saturday. there will then remain only to paste on them their numbers which will be begun on Sunday. of this mr Millegan[1] has notice and may be expected every hour after Monday next. he will examine the books by the catalogue, and nail up the presses, one by one, as he gets thro' them. but it is indispensable for me to have all the books in their places when we begin to number them, and it would be a great convenience to have all you can do without now, to put them into the places they should occupy. Antient history is numbered. Modern history comes next. the bearer carries a basket to recieve what he can bring of those you are done with. I salute you with friendship and respect.

RC (PPAmP: Thomas Jefferson Papers); dateline at foot of text. PoC (DLC). Tr (Arthur M. Schlesinger, Cambridge, Mass., 1945); posthumous copy. Enclosure: manuscript, not found, of chap. 14 of Burk, Jones, and Girardin, *History of Virginia*, vol. 4.

The NOTE SUGGESTED by TJ for Burk, Jones, and Girardin, *History of Virginia*, was probably the one on 4:328 concerning the invasion and occupation of Georgia by the British in 1779: "The British principle, here avowed by the Ministers and Commissioners of that nation, was not new. It was long before that of the Carthagenians, a people in whose political code morality had no chapter, and with whom, in every transaction, the only question was, what was best for themselves? Observe their conduct towards those friends in Italy, whom they had alienated. 'Præceps in avaritiam et crudelitatem animus, ad spolianda quæ tueri nequibat, *ut vastata hosti relinquer-entur*, inclinavit Fædum consilium quum incepto, tum exitu, fuit. Neque enim indigna patientium modo abalienabantur animi, sed cæterorum etiam Quippe ad plures exemplum, quam calamatas pertinebat'— Liv. 26, 28." This passage, which TJ cited incorrectly, translates as

"Naturally inclined to greed and cruelty, his temperament favoured despoiling what he was unable to protect, in order to leave desolated lands to the enemy. That policy was shameful in the beginning, and especially so in the outcome. For not only were those who suffered undeserved treatment alienated, but all the rest as well; for the lesson reached larger numbers than did the suffering" (Livy, *Ab Urbe Condita*, 26.38.3–5, in *Livy with an English Translation*, trans. Benjamin O. Foster, Frank Gardner Moore, and others, Loeb Classical Library [1919–59], 7:140–3). Readers in ENGLAND would also have been displeased by Girardin's accounts on 4:314–7 of "ruthless incursions" committed by Native Americans who had been "stimulated by the corrupting liberality and insidious promises of British emissaries" and by the description on 4:334–5 of British troops as "*devils incarnate*" who displayed "savage barbarity" and who, by committing "murder, rapine, rape, violence, fill up the dark catalogue of their detestable transactions" in Virginia in 1779.

Another note in the *History of Virginia* that probably reflects TJ's input is that on 4:349–50, which describes legislation drafted by TJ that would "divide every county into wards of 5 or 6 miles square.—To establish in each ward a free school for reading, writing, and common arithmetic—to provide for the annual selection of the best subjects from these schools, who might receive at the public expence a higher degree of education at a district school—and from these district schools, to select a certain number of the most promising subjects, to be completed at an university, where all the useful sciences should be taught, worth and genius would thus be sought out of every condition of life, and completely prepared by education for defeating the competition of wealth and birth for public trusts. Had this bill been adopted, we have understood that Mr. Jefferson had in contemplation a further object; It was to impart to the wards or Townships those portions of self government for which they are best qualified, by confiding to them the care of their poor, their roads, police, elections, the nomination of jurors, administration of justice in small cases, elementary exercise of militia; in short, to have made them little republics with a warden at the head of each, for all those concerns which, being under their eye, they would better manage than the larger republics of the country or State. A general call of ward-meetings by their wardens on the same day, through the State, would, at any time, produce the genuine sense of the people on any required point, and would enable the State to act in a mass, as is done in some other States." For TJ's original proposal, see "A Bill for the More General Diffusion of Knowledge," *PTJ*, 2:526–35.

The phrase CUM SEMEL OCCIDERIS, ET DE TE ULTIMA MINOS FECERIT ARBI-TRIA is from Horace, *Odes*, 4.7.21–4, and continues with "non, Torquate, genus, non te facundia, non te restituet pietas": "Once you have died and Minos has pronounced his solemn verdict, neither high birth, nor eloquence, Torquatus, nor piety will bring you back" (*Horace: Odes and Epodes*, trans. Niall Rudd, Loeb Classical Library [2004], 240–1).

Girardin's FRIENDLY PARTIALITIES are evident in a number of places in the *History of Virginia*, including 4:352, where he notes that the "virtues, abilities, and services" of TJ made him an obvious choice for governor in 1779, as did "his early and efficient attachment to the cause of America.—We have seen his name gloriously connected with the most important revolutionary transactions—especially, with the declaration of Independence." Although TJ "did not aspire to the eminence and pomp of office" and preferred "a more tranquil sphere of usefulness, in which the labours of the statesman were occasionally intermingled with the pursuits of the philosopher, and the pleasures of domestic retirement," he nevertheless accepted the call to serve his country, relying in part on "the purity and zeal of his own bosom, for the successful discharge of his new duties."

The letter in the LAST MAIL, which arrived 24 Mar., was Samuel H. Smith to TJ, 21 Mar. 1815. TJ expected to finish arranging his books on SATURDAY, 1 Apr. 1815.

Missing letters from Girardin to TJ of 20 and 27 Mar. 1815 are recorded in SJL as received from Glenmore on 21 and 27 Mar. 1815, respectively.

[1] TJ here canceled "will."

To Joseph Milligan

DR SIR   Monticello Mar. 28. 15.

By a letter from Mr Saml H. Smith I am informed that the President had engaged you to come on here as soon as I should be ready to examine and pack the library, and that mr Dougherty was to superintend the transportation. I have been a fortnight laboriously engaged in revising the books, & placing them on their shelves every one in the place and order in which it stands in the Catalogue. this I shall finish the next Saturday (Apr. 1.) we shall then have only to paste the numbers on the books corresponding with the catalogue, which will be a work of 3. or 4. days say to Apr. 5. or 6[th][1] and I should be glad if you could be here as soon as that is done, say in the latter half of the ensuing week. there can be no better packing boxes than the pine cases in which they stand. not a book need be moved. only a leaf of paper be put between every 2. volumes, paper parings stuffed in the interval between the tops of the books and shelf above, and sheets of waste paper spread over the whole face of the press over which the lid is to be nailed. the presses are of the proper size to lay in a waggon, except 2. or 3. which we can easily cut. you must bring the waste paper and paper parings, as they cannot be had here, and as I presume a waggon must come on with them, we can load her back with books, now ready. for carrying the rest of the library I have recommended to take the waggons of this neighborhood, which can be had for 4.D. a day.—The library not having been revised for 20. years before, I expected great losses. they are not less than expected. some can be recovered, some replaced, and the rest more than countervailed by the many books which had by accident been omitted to be catalogued. when the President, while Secretary of state, was engaged in writing on Neutral rights, I lent him Wynne's life of Jenkins, 2. large folios, and a work in Latin entitled 'Scriptores de jure maritimo, sc. Stypmannus, Kuricke, Loccenius, et Heineccius.' 4[to]. they were never returned, and are now probably with the books in the office of state, if they were saved from conflagration. will you be so good as to enquire, and if there, have them brought on with the waggon? many of those wanting I think you can procure in Wash[n] & George town at my cost, and have them brought on also. the waggon should arrive here the day after you. I am very anxious to get thro your part of this business, the packing and nailing up, because my affairs in Bedford call for me distressingly, & I shall set out the moment you are done. Dougherty may then take off the presses at his leisure. I state below the books I wish you to try to get & bring on. Accept the assurances of my esteem and respect

TH: JEFFERSON

RC (NjP: John Story Gulick Collection of American Statesmen); with MS of enclosure subjoined. PoC (DLC); on reused address cover of William Caruthers to TJ, 4 Mar. 1815; with PoC of enclosure subjoined; at foot of first page: "M[r] Milligan"; endorsed by TJ.

James Madison borrowed William WYNNE's *The Life of Sir Leoline Jenkins,* 2 vols. (London, 1724; Sowerby, no. 374), and the SCRIPTORES entitled *Scriptorum de Jure Nautico et Maritimo Fasciculus* (Halle an der Saale, 1740; Sowerby, no. 2122), consisting of works by Franz

Stypmann, Reinhold Kuricke, Johannes Loccenius, and Johann Gottlieb Heineccius. Madison cited these publications in his *An Examination of the British Doctrine, which subjects to capture a Neutral* *Trade, not open in Time of Peace* (1806; Sowerby, no. 2116), 117–9, 180.

¹ Preceding six words interlined.

E N C L O S U R E

List of Books to be Acquired by Joseph Milligan

[ca. 28 Mar. 1815]

Impartial history of the Revolution in France. 1. v. 8ᵛᵒ
Ray's American tars in Tripoli. 12ᵐᵒ printed in the US.
Sampson's memoirs. 8ᵛᵒ
Hepburn's book of gardening. 12ᵐᵒ printed at Washington.
Bracken's pocket farrier. 12ᵐᵒ
Fulton on canals. a thin 4ᵗᵒ
Duane's Handbook for infantry 8ᵛᵒ
White on bees.
Jeffery's narrative of 2. aerial voyages. a pamphlet 4ᵗᵒ
Smith's Distillery. 8ᵛᵒ printed in Phila.
Harris's three treatises. 8ᵛᵒ
the Book of Common prayer. an 8ᵛᵒ edition.
the power of religion on the mind by Lindlay Murray. 12ᵐᵒ
Sterne's sermons. a 12ᵐᵒ edition of preference.
Harrison's Chancery practice 2. v. 8ᵛᵒ
Beccaria on crimes & punishments. either in Italian or Eng.
Beverley's hist. of Virginia
Young's farmer's guide. 8ᵛᵒ
Young's Rural Socrates. 8ᵛᵒ [this is sometimes bound up with the former]
Young's Physiology. printed somewhere in New England. 8ᵛᵒ
Burkhard's elements of the philosophy of nature by Smith. 12ᵐᵒ
Wise's Young man's companion. 12ᵐᵒ

MS (NjP: John Story Gulick Collection of American Statesmen); entirely in TJ's hand; subjoined to RC of covering letter; undated; brackets in original; with text obscured by tape supplied from PoC. PoC (DLC: TJ Papers, 203:36216); subjoined to PoC of covering letter.

From Joseph Delaplaine

DEAR SIR,   Philadᵃ March 29ᵗʰ 1815

I am compelled, from necessity, to resort to London for my Portraits. Mʳ Edwin, on whom my principal reliance was placed, has been unabled for a long time, by an affection of the gout in his head, to execute any portraits for me.

Our eminent portrait painter Mr Wood is engaged in making copies from original pictures of revolutionary[1] characters, which, together with original portraits of living men, I shall soon send by a friend of mine about to visit London.

I am sorry sir, we cannot prevail upon Mr Stuart to do his duty by yielding to your request in placing your portrait into my hands.

The President's picture* is still in my hands, & is to be copied by Mr Wood next week. If I had Stuart's <u>orig^l</u> picture of you I would also have that copied to be sent to London.

My friend John Winthrop Esqr of Boston is now here. He is a connoiseur in the fine Arts & knows Mr Stuart well. Mr Winthrop says he will be happy to receive your order in <u>his name</u>, on Mr Stuart for the picture, which he considers, under existing circumstances, the best means to obtain it.

I pledge to you my honor sir, that Mr Winthrop is a gentleman of the first standing in society, & of the first family in the New England States.

Be pleased sir, to drop me a letter & enclose the order, which I will present to Mr Winthrop on its arrival.

Hoping to hear from you soon,

I remain with great respect Your obed. hum^e s^t

JOSEPH DELAPLAINE

P.S. When your picture arrives here, if Mr Edwin should be well enough to engrave it, I shall offer him a high price to do it. If he should not be however, I shall then have the copy taken & sent to London.

*By Stuart

RC (DLC); dateline at foot of text; postscript between signature and dateline; at head of text: "Thomas Jefferson Esqr"; endorsed by TJ as received 8 Apr. 1815 and so recorded in SJL.

[1] Manuscript: "revolutionay."

From Patrick Gibson

SIR   Richmond 29th March 1815

I send you inclosed $70 in the manner requested in your favor of the 22nd Ins^t—Our flour market has, as I apprehended declined considerably, sales cannot now be made at $6, nor do I think our northern, nor the European markets (if accounts received from thence be correct) would justify a higher price, letters from the Havanna mention the arrival there of a ship from France with 5000 bls: which cost 5$ only, consequently shipments there the W.I:[1] would not answer at anything beyond our present prices, such are my impressions; they may however be incorrect and as I am much interrested in the event; you will greatly oblige me by informing me upon what you ground your expectations of a rise—257 bls: of your Shadwell flour have been received this season none as yet from Bedford, nor has your Tobacco yet come down—, this article still continues brisk at the prices formerly mentiond, in a few instances competition has carried it to 15 & in two instances to 4 Hhd[s] 2 Hhd[s]

16[5]/. & 16[15]/. $—With great respect I am Your ob[t] Serv

PATRICK GIBSON

RC (ViU: TJP-ER); between dateline and salutation: "Thomas Jefferson Esq[re]"; endorsed by TJ as received 4 Apr. 1815 and so recorded in SJL.

TJ's letter to Gibson of THE 22ND INS[T] is recorded in SJL but has not been found. w.i: West Indies.

[1] Preceding two words interlined.

To Thomas Jefferson Randolph

DEAR JEFFERSON   Monticello Mar. 31. 15.

Ellen's visit to Warren has been delayed by an unlucky accident. on Monday we heard that my brother was very sick. mrs Marks wishing to go & see him I sent her the next morning in the gig with a pair of my horses, counting on their return the next day so that Ellen & Cornelia might have gone on Thursday according to arrangement. after mrs Marks had got about 7. miles on her road, one of the horses (Bedford) was taken so ill that she thought it best to return. he died that night, and no pair of the remaining three could be trusted to draw a carriage. mrs Marks going off again to-day to Snowden, I make Wormley take Seelah, and direct him to return by Warren & exchange him with you for the mare Hyatilda. she is an excellent draught animal, and with a match I have for her at Tufton will carry the girls very well; only that as it is some time since she was in geer, it will be advisable to drive her in the waggon two or three days. in the mean time as your business will probably bring you to court the girls will have the benefit of your escort to Warren. this is the best arrangement it is in my power to make. Ellen is still unwell, and her face tied up, which however she would not have permitted to disappoint her visit. the family here wish to be presented with respect to mrs Nicholas and the family of Warren. to our new friend whom you have brought into so near relation with us, give assurances that we recieve her as a member of our family with very great pleasure and cordiality[1] and shall endeavor and hope to make this an acceptable home to you both. ever affectionately yours   TH: JEFFERSON

PoC (ViU: TJP-ER); on verso of reused address cover of Horatio G. Spafford to TJ, 24 Feb. 1815; at foot of text: "Th: J. Randolph"; endorsed by TJ.

COURT: Albemarle County Court. Although Ellen W. Randolph (Coolidge)'s face was TIED UP as a result of an illness that had temporarily paralyzed her jaw, she and her sister Cornelia intended to visit their brother and his bride (OUR NEW FRIEND), Jane Hollins Nicholas Randolph, whom he had married on 6 Mar. 1815 (Martha Jefferson Randolph to Thomas Jefferson Randolph, 14 Mar. 1815 [NcU: NPT]; Shackelford, *Descendants*, 1:77).

A missing letter from Randolph to TJ of 25 Mar. 1815 is recorded in SJL as received the next day from Carysbrook.

[1] Preceding two words interlined.

From William Wingate

DEAR SIR,   Haverhill[1] Mas, march 31. 1815.
    I consider you as my Safest confidential Friend,
I have taken the liberty for to Send to you a Book, Title—The American Olive Branch In Perpetual Blow, Founded on Wisdom, Justice, and Equity, God and Truth its only Director—Perpetual Union and Perfect Harmony, Between Each Individual Inhabitant, of the United States of America, The only object—
I wish you carefully to examine its contents, and let me know the candid result of your mind, whether it is possiable for to carry it into execution, I wrote it directly[2] into the Book, and have not retained a copy of no part of it—therefore must request you for to return the Same Book to me, perhaps in the course of three months, no Person has ever Seen a word it contains, except, the Honorable Benjamin Austin of Boston, He has read it, and gave me the Result of his mind, He tells me that He approves of it, and advised me for to Send it to you, He also mentioned m^r John Adams, which I told m^r Austin I could not concent to do—it being an object of the Greatest Importance[3] to our country—I cannot think but that all Those Persons I have named would readyly embrace its contents, unless they are determined on the distruction of our country—
I am Sensiable that it will require many alterations for the better—
I Sincerly wish your best assistance, as it would be the Salvation of our country—I think that it will appear So to you—not doubting but

that you will do me and our Bleeding country Strict Justice, Shall add no more—

Sir, Believe me to be with the highest Sentiments of Essteem and Respect, Your most obedient Humble Servant—

WILLIAM WINGATE

RC (MiU-C); at foot of text: "Honorable Thomas Jefferson Esquire"; endorsed by TJ as received 13 Apr. 1815 and so recorded in SJL. Enclosure not found.

William Wingate (1745–1821), the brother of former United States congressman Paine Wingate and a longtime resident of Haverhill, served briefly in the Massachusetts militia during the early days of the Revolutionary War and as a notary public and postmaster thereafter. A committed Republican, he blamed his financial difficulties on the machinations of his political opponents and complained that many of the federal officeholders in his state needed to be replaced. Although the increasingly destitute Wingate successively sought appointments from George Washington, TJ, and James Madison, he never secured one. The volume enclosed with this letter was not published, and Wingate's manuscript of the following year charting Napoleon's career in the biblical book of Revelation

met the same fate. During the last decade of his life Wingate circulated between the district of Maine, Massachusetts, and New Hampshire. He died in Stratham, New Hampshire (Charles E. L. Wingate, *History of the Wingate Family in England and in America* [1886], 158–65; George Wingate Chase, *The History of Haverhill, Massachusetts* [1861], 384; Washington, *Papers, Pres. Ser.*, 7:382; *Fleet's Pocket Almanack For the Year of our Lord 1797* [Boston, 1796?], 43; *PTJ*, 35:754; Wingate to TJ, 7 Feb. 1803, 15 Feb. 1804 [DNA: RG 59, LAR, 1801–09]; DNA: RG 29, CS, Maine, New Sharon, 1810; Madison, *Papers, Pres. Ser.*, 5:540–4; Wingate to TJ, 8 Apr. 1816; TJ to Wingate, 4 May 1816; Portsmouth *New-Hampshire Gazette*, 4 Dec. 1821).

[1] Above this word Wingate canceled "Boston."

[2] Manuscript: "direcly."

[3] Manuscript: "Importane."

Statement of Albemarle County Property Subject to State Tax

A list of the taxable property of the subscriber in Albemarle Mar. 1815.

5640. acres of land (including 400. a^s on Hardware held jointly with Hudson & others) @ .85

	rate	amount
90. slaves of or above the age of 12. years	@ .80	72:
12. d° of 9. and under 12. years of age	.50	6.
73. head of cattle	.03	2.19
27. horses, mares, mules & colts	.21	5.67
1. Ice house	5.	5.
1. gigg & harness		

1.	4-wheeled carriage (Landau)		
	House		
4	clocks		
1.	Bureau or Secretary. mahogany	.50	.50
2.	book cases d⁰	.50	1.
4.	chests of drawers d⁰	.25	1.
1.	Side board with doors & drawers. mahogany		
8.	separate parts of Dining tables. d⁰	.25	2.
13.	tea and card tables d⁰	.25	3.25
6.	Sophas with gold leaf	.22¼	1.33½
36.	Chairs. mahogany	.06¼	2.25
44.	d⁰ gold leaf	.03	1.32
11.	pr window curtains. foreign	.10	1.10
16.	portraits in oil	.25	4.
1.	d⁰ Crayon	.12½	.12½
64.	picture, prints & engravings with frames		
	more than 12.I.	.15	9.60
39.	d⁰ under 12.I. with gilt frames	.10	3.90
3.	looking glasses 5.f. long	5.	15.
3.	d⁰ 4.f. and not 5.f.	3.	9.
1.	d⁰ 3.f. and not 4 f.	2.	2.
2.	d⁰ 2 f. and not 3.f.	1.	2.
1.	harpsichord[1]		
2.	silver watches	.50	1.
2.	silver coffee pots	.50	1.
3.	plated urns & coffee pots	.10	.30
13.	plated candlesticks	.05	.65
4.	cut glass decanters	.05	.20
10.	silver cups	.10	1.
1.	manufacturing mill renting at 1280.D. @ 2¾ p.c.		
1.	toll grist mill		
1.	saw-mill		

TH: JEFFERSON

MS (MHi); entirely in TJ's hand; partially dated; endorsed by TJ: "Taxable property Feb. 1815."

TJ, Christopher HUDSON, and Mary Stith held shares in a 400-acre tract known as the Limestone Survey and situated along the Hardware River in Albemarle County (TJ to Stith, 7 Mar. 1811; TJ's List of Landholdings and Monticello Slaves, [ca. 1811–1812]; TJ to Robert Anderson, 13 June 1819).

TJ also prepared an undated summary of state and federal tax rates for 1815, with the former based explicitly on the Richmond *Enquirer*'s 24 Dec. 1814 printing of the 21 Dec. Virginia "Act imposing Taxes for the Support of Government" (*Acts of*

Assembly [1814–15 sess.], 3–8) and the latter limited to taxes on carriages and furniture (MS in MoSHi: TJC-BC; written entirely in TJ's hand on a small scrap).

[1] TJ erased "1." from the amount column for this entry.

Conveyance of Carlton by Charles L. Bankhead and Ann C. Bankhead to their Trustees

This indenture made on the first day of April one thousand eight hundred and fifteen between Charles Lewis Bankhead and Anne Cary his wife of the county of Albemarle on the one part, and John Bankhead of the county of Caroline, father of the sd Charles L. Thomas Mann Randolph father of the sd Anne C., and Reuben Lindsay both of the same county of Albemarle, on the other part Witnesseth that the sd Charles L. and Anne C. in consideration of the sum of twelve hundred pounds lawful money of Virginia assumed by the said John to be paid to the creditors of the sd Charles L. as herein after specified, and of the further sum of nine hundred and four pounds of like money assumed by the sd John and Thomas Mann to be paid in like manner to the creditors of the sd Charles L. as herein after also specified, to wit to John Kelly one thousand and twelve pounds, to James Overton four hundred and thirty two pounds, to John J. Taylor the sum of five hundred and ten pounds, to James Leitch the sum of one hundred and fifty pounds, all of like money, and to any other persons such other sums as shall be proved to the satisfaction of the said John, Thomas M. and Reuben to be lawfully due at this time from the said Charles L. to the same persons for property actually and bonâ fide delivered, or for services performed, of which the judgment is referred and reserved to the sd John, Thomas M. and Reuben exclusively, ultimately, and without appeal; and in further consideration of the sum of one dollar to them the said Charles L. and Anne C. now in hand paid, have given, granted, bargained and sold to the said John Bankhead, Thomas Mann Randolph and Reuben Lindsay the tract of land called Carlton in the same county of Albemarle, whereon the sd Charles L. and Anne C. now live, lying on both sides of Moore's creek, and on the Rivanna river, adjoining the lands of Molly Lewis, Thomas Jefferson, and Robert Sthreshly, and containing by estimation eight hundred acres, be the same more or less, as also the following slaves, to wit, old Robin, little Robin, Nelson, Jerry, Frederic, Peter Green, William Green, Billy Stewart, big Billy, little Billy, little William, George, Jack, Scilla, Letty, Lucy big Nancy, Nancy Green, Violet, Jane, Jenney, Amy, Fanny, Priscilla, Spencer, Henry, Washington, Abigail, Davy, Susan, Sally, Lucy, Jane, Sarah, Luberta, Hilliard and Patty, being thirty seven in all, together with nine horses, fourteen head of cattle, six head of sheep, fifty head of hogs, now on or belonging to the said lands, and all the furniture now in the dwelling house or outhouses on the said lands, the plantation utensils on the same or belonging thereto, and all debts now due to the sd Charles L. to have and to hold the said property real and personal to them the sd John Bankhead, Thomas Mann Randolph and Reuben Lindsay, their heirs, executors, administrators and assigns, to and for the Uses & Trusts following, that is to say, to reimburse to the sd John & Thomas Mann in the first place the said sum of nine hundred and four pounds assumed by them jointly to be paid as aforesaid for specified debts, and also the amount of unspecified debts which they shall pay; and afterwards the said property real and personal, and the profits and proceeds thereof, to be held, possessed, employed, alienated, and applied at the discretion and absolute will of the said John, Thomas M. & Reuben, (free from all right, claim, controul, or interference of the sd Charles L. & Anne C. or either of them, and from all liability for any debts or contracts, past or future, of the sd Charles L. or Anne C. or either of them, other than those before described & assumed) to the maintenance of the sd Charles L. and Anne C. and of the children and other descendants of them or either of them, to the education of the sd children & other descendants, and to their advancement in life, in such portions of principal or profits as they the said John, Thomas M. and Reuben, in their discretion, shall think just, retaining always what they shall deem sufficient to maintain comfortably the sd Charles L. and Anne C. during their lives, and the life of the survivor. and the sd Charles L. and Anne C. reserve the reversion in whatever may remain of the sd property real and personal, after the compleat execution of the sd trusts, and after the possibility of their compleat execution may have become extinct (should that happen) to themselves severally, and their several heirs, each the exact parts, and portions of their original and respective rights in the sd property, as they would have existed had this deed never been made: and they covenant that themselves, their heirs, executors, and administrators, all the property and rights real and personal hereby conveyed to the sd John Bankhead, Thomas M. Randolph and Reuben Lindsay and their heirs will for ever warrant and defend against themselves the sd Charles L. and Anne C. their heirs, executors and administrators, and all other persons claiming from or under them. and the sd John Bankhead & Thomas Mann Randolph, on their part, covenant with the sd Charles L. and Anne C. that they will pay the debts herein before specified to the persons lawfully entitled to recieve them;[1] that is to say, the sd John to the amount of the sd sum of twelve hundred pounds, and the sd John & Thomas M. to the further amount of the sd sum of nine hundred and four pounds, as above assumed, and thereof do, and forever will exonerate & acquit the persons of the sd Charles L. and Anne C. his wife, and warrant them from all damage and injury on account of the sd debts so specifically assumed. In witness whereof the several parties have hereto set their hands and seals on the day & year above written.

Signed, sealed, and delivered by   CHAS: L BANKHEAD
Charles L. Bankhead, Anne C.
Bankhead & John Bankhead the 7th
line from the bottom being previously
obliterated in presence of   ANN C BANKHEAD
EDMUND BACON
W BALLARD   1 May 1815   J. BANKHEAD
ROLIN GOODMAN
Signed, sealed and delivered by
Thomas M. Randolph and Reuben
Lindsay in presence of   TH M: RANDOLPH
EDMUND BACON
ROLIN GOODMAN
TH: J. RANDOLPH   RN LINDSAY—

MS (ViU: TJP-AR); on indented paper; in TJ's hand except for signatures and attestations; sealed by Charles L. Bankhead, John Bankhead, Thomas Mann Randolph, and Lindsay, with Ann C. Bankhead's seal torn away; endorsed by TJ: "Bankhead et ux. to Bankhead et al } Deed"; with Albemarle County clerk Alexander Garrett's four attestations (all but the second being signed) on verso of last page: (1) "1st May 1815 proved before me in my office, by Wm Ballard"; (2) "1st May 1815 fully proved by Edmd Bacon, & Rolin Goodman, and ordered to be recorded"; (3) "In the Office of the County Court of Albemarle 1st May 1815 This Indenture was proved before me in my Office by the oath of William Ballard a witness thereto And at a Court held for Albemarle County 1st May 1815 This Indenture was produced into Court & fully proved by the oaths of Edmund Bacon & Rolin Goodman two other witnesses thereto and ordered to be recorded"; (4) "At A court held for Albemarle county the 5th day of August 1822 This Indenture was again produced into court and further and fully proved by the oath of William Ballard a subscribing witness thereto and ordered to be recorded. and on motion of the trustees within mentioned, It is ordered by the court that the same be certified to the county court of Caroline for record"; under Garrett's second attestation is one signed by Caroline County clerk John L. Pendleton: "In Caroline County Court August 12ʰ 1822. This Deed was this day Presented in Court & having been heretofore admitted to Record in the Clerks office of Albemarle County Court is Ordered to be Recorded in this Court." Tr (Albemarle Co. Deed Book, 19:318–9); in Garrett's hand; lacking first, second, and fourth attestations.

Reuben Lindsay (1747–1831), planter, came to Albemarle County from Westmoreland County by 1775. He was a volunteer in the local militia in that year, a lieutenant colonel, 1781–82, and a member of the Albemarle County Court. Lindsay was a longtime friend of TJ, who often stopped at Springfield Farm, Lindsay's estate in northeastern Albemarle County. After TJ's death, Lindsay was among those who appraised his estate. In 1828 he was a political supporter of Andrew Jackson. Lindsay left a personal estate valued at $13,556, including forty-eight slaves (Margaret Isabella Lindsay, *The Lindsays of America: A Genealogical Narrative, and Family Record* [1889], 241; Woods, *Albemarle*, 257, 364, 368,

376; *VMHB* 10 [1902–03]: 96–7, 203, 310–1; 11 [1903]: 101–2; Fillmore Norfleet, *Saint-Mémin in Virginia: Portraits and Biographies* [1942], 115, 186; Albemarle Co. Deed Book, 6:529; *PTJ*, 5:468–9, 554–5; *MB*, esp. 1:292; Lay, *Architecture*, 142; Appraisal and Inventory of TJ's Albemarle County Estate by Lindsay, John H. Craven, and Martin Dawson, 4 Oct. 1826, and Appraisal and Inventory of Tufton and Lego by John H. Craven, John M. Perry, and Lindsay, 11 Jan. 1827 [ViU: TJP]; *Richmond Enquirer*, 19 Jan. 1828; Albemarle Co. Will Book, 10:311, 11:109–10; Washington *Daily National Intelligencer*, 19 Oct. 1831).

The CHILDREN of Charles L. Bankhead and Ann C. Bankhead at this time were John Warner Bankhead, Thomas Mann Randolph Bankhead, and Ellen Monroe Bankhead (Carter). Their son William Stuart Bankhead was born in 1826 (Shackelford, *Descendants*, 2:33, 48).

¹ TJ here canceled the "7ᵗʰ line from the bottom" as mentioned above: "that they do hereby assume, and make themselves responsible for the amounts the sd persons."

Conveyance of Land Adjoining Carlton by Thomas Jefferson to Trustees of Charles L. Bankhead and Ann C. Bankhead

This indenture tripartite made on the first day of April one thousand eight hundred and fifteen between Thomas Jefferson of the county of Albemarle of the first part, Anne Cary¹ Bankhead wife of Charles L. Bankhead and granddaughter of the sd Thomas, of the county of Albemarle also, on the second part, and John Bankhead of the county of Caroline, Thomas Mann Randolph and Reuben Lindsay both of the same county of Albemarle on the third part witnesseth that the said Thomas, in consideration of the natural affection which he beareth to his sd granddaughter Anne Cary Bankhead, and for her advancement and better support in life, and for the further consideration of one Dollar to him in hand paid, hath given granted bargained and sold to the sd John Bankhead, Thomas Mann Randolph, & Reuben Lindsay the following parcels of land in the sd county of Albemarle, lying on the North side of the High mountain adjacent to the lands whereon the sd Charles L. and Anne C. his wife now live, and to those of Robert Sthreshly, to wit, one parcel of forty acres purchased by the sd Thomas of Thomas Wells, one other parcel of sixty one & a quarter acres purchased of Benjamin Brown, and one other parcel adjoining this last, being parcel of a larger tract purchased of Edward Carter deceased, and to be divided from the residue of the sd lands purchased from Carter by a line to begin on the public road leading from the Thorough-fare towards Charlottesville where the lands of the said Charles L. & Anne his wife and those of the sd Thomas corner together on the said road near a large rock adjacent to the sd road, and running thence up the sd High mountain in a direct line which by protraction is South 48. degrees West one hundred and six and a quarter poles to a corner of the sd parcel purchased from Benjamin Brown formed by the meeting of two lines running from the sd corner, the one due North and the other due West, which parcel of the larger tract purchased from Carter contains by protraction twenty nine acres, making the whole of what is now meant to be conveyed about one hundred and thirty acres be the same more or less: to have and to hold the sd tract or parcel of one hundred and thirty acres of land more or less to the sd John Bankhead, Thomas Mann Randolph, & Reuben Lindsay and their heirs for the Uses and Trusts following, that is to say, to be held, possessed, employed, and applied at the discretion and absolute will of the sd John, Thomas M. and Reuben (free from all right of possession, claim, controul or interference of the sd Charles L. or Anne C. or either of them, and from all liability for any debts or contracts past or future of the sd Charles L. or Anne C. or either of them) to the maintenance of the sd Charles L. and Anne C., and the maintenance & education of their children, born or to be born, and, after the death of the sd Anne to convey the same, by way of advancement to such of her children as the sd John, Thomas M. and Reuben shall deem best according to circumstances, and in default of such conveyance, then to remain over to the heirs of the sd Anne Cary in fee simple. and the sd Thomas Jefferson and his heirs the said tract of land hereby conveyed to the sd John Bankhead, Thomas Mann Randolph and Reuben Lindsay and their heirs, for the uses and trusts beforementioned will warrant & defend against all persons claiming from or under him. In witness whereof the said Thomas hath hereto set his hand and seal on the day & year above written.

Signed sealed ⎱
and delivered ⎬
in presence of ⎰

Rolin Goodman
Edmund Bacon
W Ballard

TH: JEFFERSON

MS (ViU: TJP-AR); on indented paper; in TJ's hand, signed by TJ, Goodman, Bacon, and Ballard; with TJ's seal adjacent to his signature and signed attestation by Albemarle County clerk Alexander Garrett at foot of text: "In the Office of the County Court of Albemarle 1ˢᵗ May 1815 This Indenture was acknowledged before me in my office by Thomas Jefferson party thereto & admitted to record according to Law"; endorsed by TJ: "Jefferson to Bankhead et al.} Deed"; beneath endorsement in Garrett's hand and signed by him: "1ˢᵗ May 1815 acknowledged before me in my office the date above." Tr (Albemarle Co. Deed Book, 19:322–4); in Garrett's hand and including his 1 May 1815 attestation.

The tract of land on HIGH MOUNTAIN, also called Montalto, was ADJACENT TO the Bankheads' Carlton estate. TJ's Montalto property included 483 acres PURCHASED OF EDWARD CARTER in 1777 (Albemarle Co. Deed Book, 7:132–3; MB, esp. 1:452; Betts, Farm Book, pt. 1, p. 32). Property is said to REMAIN when it is "granted to a person as a remainder" (OED).

[1] Word interlined.

From William W. Hening

Dear Sir,   Richmond 1ˢᵗ April 1815

I have this moment placed in the hands of the stage-driver from this to Charlottesville, your M.S. laws of Virginia, and paid him not only <u>his</u> price, for transportation, but that of the driver who succeeds him, at Tinsley's, in Goochland:—They are made up in three parcels, each parcel securely packed, under three courses of strong wrapping paper, which, by being more elastic, the driver supposed would render them less liable to injury, than by being placed in a box:—He has promised to carry them in the <u>inner</u> box of the stage, and thinks that from the manner they were put up, it is impossible they can be injured.—

Measures are now in a train, by the representative of the late Mʳ Pleasants, to complete the publication of the Statutes at Large, with all possible expedition.—As soon as I come down to the Sessions acts of 1769,[1] from which date my own collection is complete, I will advise you,[2] and will either send your 5ᵗʰ Volume to Monticello, or to the City of Washington as shall be most agreeable to yourself.

I am respʸ yrs   Wᴹ W: Hening

RC (DLC); endorsed by TJ as received 8 Apr. 1815 and so recorded in SJL.

[1] Reworked from "1771."
[2] Word interlined, with superfluous preceding comma editorially omitted.

From Randolph Jefferson

Dear brother   april 2: 15

my sister marks arrived heare very safe on friday Evening, but was verry much fatigued after her Jorney. I have got pritty well a gane, but Extreemly week at this time, Scarce able to walk. I am exceedingly oblige to you for the things you sent me, I have Just sold to charles A: Scott, 70 acres of my low grounds, at a hundred dollers pr acre, for which he is to make the first payment a bout the twelth of this month, which will take me out of debt with every[1] man that I am involved with and which will enable me to keep all my Slaves as long as I live. the next payment he is to make me this time twelve months. I will try and take a ride over some time this summer if my health will permit. the river is so high that they cant put in the sane to fish, but as soon as the river gits down so as they ketch any we will immidiately send you over a parcel by Squire. my wife Joins me in love and affection to you and family.—I am you most affectionately

RH; JEFFERSON

ps Jefferson & young Wilson Nicholas took a ride to see me on saterday but made no stay of account with us for the first time.—

RC (ViU: TJP-CC); endorsed by TJ as received 3 Apr. 1815 from Snowden and so recorded in SJL.

SANE: "seine." JEFFERSON: Thomas Jefferson Randolph.

[1] Manuscript: "ev every."

From George N. Ralls

Dear sir   Washington Culpeper V[a] 2nd April 1815.

Can I flatter myself you,ll have the goodness to pardon the liberty I have thus taken? Altho I have not the pleasure of your acquaintance still your love of natural history, and the progress you have made, in this most interesting science, is not unknown to me. Finding no mention made in your "Notes on Virginia," of a certain discription of Flint Stones found in various parts of the state, and being very anxious to have your opinion respecting their formation &ca[1] I have been induced to request you,ll gratify me the first oportunity which your convenience may point out.—The Stones I make no doubt have excited your attention, they are generally composed of the most transparent flint, and have to every appearance once passed thro the hands of some skillful <u>lapidist</u>, the one I have now before me is cut in part, beautifully smooth, is of a hexigon figure. **A**.—The part **B** is rough and unpolished, to break them I dont discover any thing like a continuation, or layers of the same regularity, or smoothness within, which I think, would be the case if they were the works of nature.—

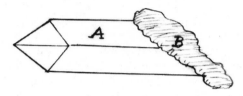

But how to account for their use, or, for the great variety in figure, as well as size (<u>no two</u> being alike, or of the same dimensions) is beyonnd my reach—

I trust sir, you,ll pardon me, and have the goodness to let me have the pleasure of hearing from you very shortly—Wishing you every possible happiness,

I am dear sir,

Very Sincerely yr friend

Geo: N: Ralls.

RC (ViW: TC-JP); at foot of text: "Thomas Jefferson Esqʳ Monticello Vᵃⁿ"; endorsed by TJ as a letter from "Ralls, or Kalls, Geo. N." received 8 May 1815 and so recorded in SJL.

George N. Ralls (d. 1822) was a native of Alexandria. He served as secretary of the city's Masonic lodge, 1812–13. Ralls moved to Culpeper County in about 1814, and he was soundly defeated in the 1820 election to represent that county in the Virginia House of Delegates. At the time of his death he was the vice commercial agent for the United States at Havana (*Alexandria Gazette, Commercial and Political*, 30 Dec. 1812, 25 May 1813; Franklin L. Brockett, *The Lodge of Washington. A History of the Alexandria Washington Lodge, No. 22, A. F. and A. M. of Alexandria, Va., 1783–1876* [1876], 32–3; Vi: RG 48, Personal Property Tax Returns, Culpeper Co., 1814–20; Fredericksburg *Virginia Herald*, 22 Apr. 1820; Washington *Daily National Intelligencer*, 16 July 1822).

The FLINT STONES were probably crystals of quartz (silicon dioxide), which often appear as colorless, hexagonal prisms (Gustav B. Baetcke, *Identification Guide to Common Minerals and Rocks of Virginia* [1961], 17, 25, 47).

[1] Preceding four words interlined.

From William Thornton

DEAR SIR   City of Washington 3ᵈ April 1815.—

I should before now have answered your esteemed favor of the 9ᵗʰ Febʸ last, but I wished to communicate something relative to the Looms: I find nothing yet worthy of your attention.—

I have made several Enquiries relative to the mode of lining the Cisterns for Water. In the West Indies where Pouzzolane abounds, they plaster them in the inside with this Substance mixed with lime & sand, and it has the peculiar quality of becoming as hard as stone by Water: so that immediately after lining them they may be filled with water, and the iron which is contained in the pouzzolane, by the action of the Water forms a perfect stone, impermeable to water, and there seems to be no end to its duration. The Roman Baths are made in this way, & were found to be as perfect after the lapse of centuries as when first made.—If the turnings of the Cannon, obtainable here from Foxall's Foundary were to be mixed in a small quantity with mortar I am confident that the decomposition in consequence of its contact with water would produce as perfect a cement as could well be formed; and when the waggons or Carts come with the library I can send you some. It will not take much to line your cisterns. But I have heard also of another cement, that is said to answer perfectly, and it may be immediately tried.—I have such evidence of its answering that I cannot doubt it. Let good mortar be made of two or three parts of sand to one of good stone Lime. Let it stand in a heap till hard; then break it down again, and let it be well beaten with molasses, of which it will not take a quart to a Bushell. This is to be plastered on immediately, & it will be stiff enough to make a good plaster; but it must be laid on in a <u>thin coat</u>, which must be suffered to dry sufficiently to lay on another coat which will fill up every small crack or fissure in the first, and it will make a firm and solid piece of work.—The Molasses becomes a kind of resin, being compleatly changed in its nature, and sometimes it has been used for plastering the outside of buildings, giving a yellowish warm hue when mixed in the proportion of about one gallon to 30 of white wash or the water wᵗʰ which rough-cast is formed.—

I shall now describe the filtre.—I invented it above twenty Years ago.—I had purchased some very fine rich Cyder, & being advised to filter it through Sand, I put the Cyder through a Cloth, & let it fall gently on Sand, put on Straw, to keep the bottom holes of the Vessel open. In a very short time I found that the mucus contained in the

Cyder, filled up the interstices of the Grains of sand, & the Cyder instead of filtering through stood on the Surface. To prevent this, I contrived a Cask, filled, within some Inches of the top, with Strata of rough pebbles, finer gravel, rough & fine Sand, the roughest at the bottom, and gradually increasing in fineness to the top.—Over this Cask or Vessel on an inside rim, I place another Cask covered with fine netting, or Haircloth, such as is used for Sieves, to prevent the gross impurities, or the pomice of Cyder &c to pass, & a Tube carries the Liquor from the bottom of the upper Vessel, to the bottom of the lower Vessel, which Tube enters between the bottom of the lower Vessel & a false bottom pierced full of holes.—The Cyder or Liquor being put into the upper Vessel enters between the true & false bottoms of the lower Vessel, & rising through the different Strata of Gravel & Sand, runs off, pure, through a cock placed some distance from the top of the Sand, & with the velocity of a descent of Water falling from the upper Vessel through a Tube whose exit would be as much below the upper Vessel as the Cock is placed. Care must be taken that this Cock be wide enough to carry off the liquor as fast as it rises.—If the Sand should boil up the Cock should be placed further from it, or a Hair-Sieve may be put immediately on the Sand. To render the Water perfectly sweet it may be passed through a Vessel filled with fresh[1] Charcoal, and to render it perfectly cool, it may be let down from the filtering Vessel into a Well or Cistern and remain there in a vessel of Tin, or Earthen Ware with an inverted Syphon to draw it off when wanted. On the next page I will explain the whole by a drawing.—

I am dear Sir with the highest respect Yours &c

W. Thornton.—

RC (DLC); at foot of text: "Hon: Thomas Jefferson"; with enclosure on verso of last page; endorsed by TJ as received 8 Apr. 1815 and so recorded in SJL.

POUZZOLANE: pozzolana.

[1] Word interlined.

William Thornton's Drawing and Description
of a Water and Cider Filter

[ca. 3 Apr. 1815]

Filtering Machine;—which filters per assensum.—

A. Under Vessel

B. Upper vessel

C. Netting or Hair-Cloth when Cyder is to be filtered.—

D. Tube of Wood or metal leading from **B** to **A.**—

E. False bottom full of holes

F. Lower Cock, to be opened only to let out Water that has stood long or hot Water poured on the top after removing the Vessel **B** that all the impurities may be washed out.—

G. Upper Cock to draw off fine Water. &c.—

H. If the Water should require to be as cold as spring Water it may be let down this Tube into

I. A Reservoir, in a Well of common Water, or in a deep dry well, covered over the Reservoir some feet with Earth, & the well tightly closed—It is obvious that as long as this is supplied with Water it will rise up the Tube

K. which delivers it as pure as Spring Water by the Cock **L.**—This inverted Syphon may however be dispensed with:—but would be very convenient to cool rain Water in Wells of bad Water.—

MS (DLC: TJ Papers, 203:36219); text and drawing entirely in Thornton's hand; undated; on verso of last page of covering letter.

PER ASSENSUM [ascensum]: "by means of ascent."

From William Wingate

MY DEAR FRIEND. Haverhill April 3ᵈ 1815.

I was at Boston on march 31. I then wrote you in Great haste, Also Sent to you the Book I mentioned in my Letter, I hope you will receive them all Safe—I now find it necessary for to write you more particular on the Subject—Firstly Shall observe, that it was God that compelled me for to write the Book, and as He directed me, all the Praise must be given to God, I am confident that God will Appear in Your Heart and direct You what to do with it, Without Him We can do nothing, Our cause is perfectly Just, it being founded on Wisdom, Justice, and Equity, Therefore We may rest fully Assured, That God will Support us and His cause, We may Justly consider ourselves as Gods Stewards, and that we are accountable to God for all we do, God is now declaring to me that we are the only ones He can Trust with the care of His American Vineyard—Sir, I feel it to be a Solem and Important undertaking, no less than the Political and Future Salvation of ourselves and our common country, our Good old Friend Washington considered it as Such, Witness His Farewell Address, and that God was with Him when He wrote it down, and directed Him what to write, it apparently Appears that God then told the good old Man, all that would come to pass, which We have found to be True, and now behold with our own eyes—My Friend if Such Stubborn facts are not Sufficient for to convince you and me, and every Individual in America, nothing Short of our being distroyed as a Nation as Sodom was, will convince us, and then it will be too late for us to repent and esscape the Just vengence of God, I am Sensiable that we can do no more than God Shall command and enable us to do, I am feelingly Sensiable that I am incapable of doing any thing in and of myself—So must you do, if our Hearts are only Sincere, God has Solemly promised us Both in His Holy Word that He will Support us and maintain His cause, God never once failed nor never will fail of fulfilling all His Promises, but God will require of us that our Faith be pure and unwavering as was good old Jacobs of old, God then Saved His Son, We are now dealing with the Same God, and He will Save us and our country, when Sinking, in as miraculous a manner as He did Issaac—for my own part, I feel it, I can now Se it, but not as man Seeth, I hope Sir that God will Shew it to You, as He has done to Washington and me—I am Sensiable that the ground I have Selected out is the roughest and most Stubborn ground in America for us to fallow up and to cultivate, So as to make it Yeild good Fruit, which must be done, God will draw the Plow for us and direct us how to proceed, and will Supply us with as much good Seed as will cover all the ground over as We go along, We cannot ask or reasonably wish for any more help from God—God is now telling me how We must proceed, I will here pen it down As it is delivered to me,—God requires our whole Hearts, and that Wisdom Justice and Equity be our only motive and object, and trust Him for to reward us for all we do—The American Olive Branch is to be our Plow, God will require of You that You carefully examine every part of the Plow, And that you repair it in every part thereof agreeable to Wisdom, Justice and Equity, it must consist of nothing else, Sir, you now have liberty from me to do it agreeable to your own best Judgment, and to take your own time for to do it in—It will require us both for to hold the Plow, I must be with you, besides you will need my advice, and before we begin, it will be necessary for us, for to provide ourselves with as many Branches as will enable us for to give one to each of Those Persons I proposed to apply too, if They all Should approve of it, the rest of our work would be certain and light to us, Sir, What a glorious Harvest would America Produce, it must asstonish all Europe, and more than probable would Soon cover the whole Earth— Which now Bares nothing but Tares, I am Sensiable that the Hearts of all Men are naturally prone to evil and are now desperately Wicked, I am also Sensiable that God can do all things, and that He will do what is right, it is evident to me that this is the only favorable time we shall ever live to Se, for to Rebuild the American Goverment on So good a¹ foundation as the one I have now offered—not doubting but that God will direct you in all I have or may require of you to do, I will here proceed for to direct you how to proceed—

As Soon as you get the Plow ready—Firstly, Shew it to m^r Maddison, if He approves of the Measure—next Shew it to one of your best Friends of the Senate, if He approves of the measure, next Shew it to one of your next Safest and best Friends of the Senate, and So proceed in course with all your Friends of the Senate, when this is done and They all Should approve of the measure, you will now form a Society, and Select out one of its least Enemies in the Senate and Shew it to Him, if He approves of the measure, then proceed in the Same manner one by one to Each of the Senate, and with all others—it can-not be done in no other Way, You must begin with one Spark and So collect one Spark after another untill you collect the whole number we may Se fit to offer it too—my Friend keep Sacred these last lines, our Success and the Salvation of our country wholly depends on this proceedure—

otherwise one misstept may extinguish all the Sparks we have collected,

Great care must be taken that each Member Solemly keep Secret, the contents of the American Olive Branch, The Printer of the copies must be Sworn to keep Secret its contents untill the whole business is completed, otherwise one drop of water may possiably put out the whole, but after we have Secured all Those Persons I have proposed, we may then defy the whole world to Stop its progress throughout America,—

Sir I positively know that you will have to encounter Wolves in Sheep cloathing, you will Soon discover who they are, you must man-age These wisely and cautiously, They must be Subdued, never leave Such Men untill they approve of the measure, Shall here observe, that I found that m^r Austin had given the Loan office more of his Heart, than he had given to his country, Such my Friend is the de-pravity of humane nature, and I may Justly add of our foremost Re-publican Friends, what will not a Small office or a Small Sum of money do with Such as are governed by Selfish motives, but Such In-stances must not deter us, the Rougher the Ground we turn up, the greater will be the increase, and our reward—if we have but God on our Side and to draw the Plow we have nothing to fear, but if either of us Should now look back, Remember the fate of Lotts Wife—

Sir, I am a poor man, made So by a combination of the Essex Junto, who have robbed me out of a handsome property, If you Should find it necessa[ry] that I Should come to Washington for to assist you or others in carrying this business into execution, it will be necessary that you procure for me as much money as to bare my expences, and in case I Should ever obtain any money for my Services I would repay it, with interest,[2] otherwise it will be out of my power even to pay the postage of a Single letter—Such Sir, is my present unfortunate[3] Sit-uation, for myself and our country[4] I was in hopes that m^r Maddison would have appointed me Inspector at Newbury port, instead of an undeserving Man who now holds it, as I have not received any an-swer, have concluded that he will not appoint me—one of my Sons would have assisted me in doing the business—

Sir, Believe me to be with the Highest Sentiments of Essteem and Respect, your most obedient Humble Serv[t]

WILLIAM WINGATE

P.S

whatever you write me Shall die in my own Breast—

Sir, I Solemly warn you not to admit, or Shew it but to one new member at a time untill you collect the whole, this is Wisdom, Justice and Equity—

RC (DLC); mutilated at seal; with second postscript written perpendicularly in left margin of last page; addressed: "Honorable Thomas Jefferson Esquire Monticello Virginia"; endorsed by TJ as received 15 Apr. 1815 and so recorded in SJL.

George Washington's FAREWELL ADDRESS first appeared in the Philadelphia *Claypoole's American Daily Advertiser,* 19 Sept. 1796. The biblical reference to GOOD FRUIT is in Matthew 12.33; the parable of the GOOD SEED, which mentions the growth of TARES, is in Matthew 13.24–30; and Jesus compares false prophets to WOLVES IN SHEEP CLOATHING in Matthew 7.15. TJ appointed Benjamin AUSTIN commissioner of loans for Massachusetts in 1804 (*JEP,* 1:476, 477 [30 Nov., 11 Dec. 1804]). In 1811 James Madison appointed William Cross INSPECTOR of the revenue at Newburyport, Massachusetts, and Cross held this position until his death in 1832 (*JEP,* 2:188, 189, 4:239 [13, 15 Nov. 1811, 14 Apr. 1832]).

[1] Manuscript: "a a."
[2] Preceding two words interlined.
[3] Word interlined.
[4] Preceding five words interlined.

From William Thornton

City of Washington 4th April 1815.

W: Thornton's respects to the Hon[ble] Thomas Jefferson, and, according to promise, sends a Copy of the List of Patents for the last Year: he has also the honor of presenting a Copy of the Piece he wrote some years ago, and incloses one for the Hon: Colonel Randolph.—

W.T. has this Day seen a model of a machine which prepares Cotton for spinning without Carding. It is a very simple machine, and the inclosed was spun from Cotton thus prepared.—

RC (MHi); dateline at foot of text; endorsed by TJ as received 8 Apr. 1815 and so recorded in SJL. Enclosure: *Letter from the Secretary of State, transmitting A List of Persons who Have Made Any New and Useful Invention, and for which Patents Have Been Obtained, from thirty-first December, 1813, to the first January, 1815* (Washington, 1815; Poor, *Jefferson's Library,* 6 [no. 224]). Other enclosure not found.

From DeWitt Clinton

DEAR SIR   New York 6 April 1815

Knowing the deep interest you take in the promotion of useful knowledge, I enclose a circular letter and Report of our Literary & Philosophical[1] Society, formed and distributed in order to obtain an accurate statistical account of this State. Similar attempts, if crowned with success, in other places, would greatly tend to advance the prosperity of our Country.

Under an impression that you will not consider it improper in me to propose you as an <u>honorary member</u> of that Society, I shall take the liberty of doing it at their next meeting: It will, I am persuaded, be received by all the members with the highest satisfaction.

It will be often in my power to transmit to you new publications without the least inconvenience to myself and which I should do with pleasure, but I am not certain whether your priveleges at the post-office extend to cases of this Nature

With great respect I am Your most Obed^t serv^t

DEWITT CLINTON

RC (DLC); adjacent to closing: "T. Jefferson Esqr"; endorsed by TJ as received 13 Apr. 1815 and so recorded in SJL. FC (Lb in NNC: Clinton Papers); in Clinton's hand; lacks closing and signature. Enclosure: *Circular Letter of the Literary and Philosophical Society, of New-York; on the Subject of a Statistical Account of the State of New-York* (New York, 1815; signed by Clinton as society president), asking selected residents of every town and county in the state to provide data on the subjects suggested in twenty-eight categories, plus any miscellaneous information not otherwise requested and "Specimens of Minerals, and other subjects of Natural History."

TJ was duly selected as an HONORARY MEMBER (Literary and Philosophical Society of New-York, *Transactions* [1815]: xvi). He received franking PRIVELEGES for mail sent him "after the expiration of his term of office and during his life" under "An Act freeing from postage all letters and packets to Thomas Jefferson" (*U.S. Statutes at Large*, 2:526 [28 Feb. 1809]).

[1] RC: "L. & P." FC: "Literary & Philosophical."

From Joseph Coppinger

SIR   New York 6th April 1815.

It is now about fifteen years ago, since I did myself the honor of Addressing you on the subject of naturalization being then only Just arrived in this Country from England. you then occupied the Presidential chair and notwithstanding your eminent station you were pleased to answer my letter with a politeness, and condescension that I shall always gratefully remember, and is now my principal inducement for laying before you a subject that I conceive to be essentially connected with the best Interests of this Country. If so it needs no other recommendation to insure your active support and consequent success The object is a subscription Brewery proposed to be established at Washington with a moderate Capital for the purpose of improving, encouraging, and extending the brewing trade of America in a way well calculated to insure this result and whilst engaged in effecting this great National purpose the experiment could not fail (under proper management) of handsomely repaying its patriotick supporters See the outlines of the Plan inclosed

You will also find the copy of a preface proposed to be annexed to a small practical treatise on Brewing & Malting which I have now nearly ready for the press to be entitled the American brewer In contra-distinction to the work entitled the American Distiller If it only meet a like Encouragem^t I will not be without Some reward for my trouble although I can with truth declare pecuniary considerations are not exclusively my object: but principally an earnest desire to improve and encourage the Brewing trade of America, which If my view of its importance be correct whether considered in a National, commercial, or agricultural point of view, most certainly deserves the encouragement of all classes of our population, Independent of its great influence on their health and Morals— Some of the new and most useful processes intended to be given in this work are the following

A new and better mode of Malting Indian corn by which this grain now principally devoted to the destructive purposes of the Distillery can be converted into good Malt and made a valuable addition to Brewing materials. Another is a simple, and easy process of making beer, only a week brewed, assume all the appearances of age, possessing transparency flavour, and above all the preserving quality so essential to good beer. A third process is mak^g a good and preserving beer from bran and Shorts without Malt, this Process in many situations Where Malt is not easily procured will be found useful.[1] A fourth process peculiarly adapted to Gentlemen, farmers, and house-Keepers, as economical, and giving but little trouble is a method of brewing, and fermenting beer by close fermentation: suffering neither yeast nor feculencies to escape at the bung hole. this simple and easy process makes a transparent pungent beer, which seems to improve whilst any remains in the Cask and by no means subject to turn sour, or flat as is common with other beer. There are many other matters that I trust will be found new and useful in a work of this Kind. by the notice proposed to be given with the preface you will perceive it is contemplated to add an Acco^t of wine making and Tanning on an improved plan as is now practiced in France. The work will be printed with large tipe and on good Paper Price to subscribers \$2.— in boards this is half the price that is asked for Morrises Small work on brewing which I trust in point of usefulness, will not bear a comparisson with the one I am now about to present the Publick. If you permit me I will have the honor of putting down your name as a Subscriber but whether permitted or not believe me with sentiments of high respect and regard

Sir Your most Ob^t Hb^e Servt JOSEPH COPPINGER
198 Duane S^t
New York

P.S living somewhat out of the City compells me to have my letters Addressed to the house of a friend—

RC (DLC); at foot of text: "Thomas Jefferson Esqr"; endorsed by TJ as received 13 Apr. 1815 and so recorded in SJL. Enclosure: Preface to Coppinger's publication on brewing, which expounds on the merits of brewing beer, citing the £7.5 million in tax revenue generated annually in England; the "immense fortunes" made by brewers in England, Ireland, and Scotland; the good health enjoyed by consumers of beer; the economic benefit to the farmer who "can raise no crop that will pay better than hops," from which in a good year he can clear \$100 per acre, and for whom barley is also a valuable crop; and the financial profit to the merchant who exports beer to the East and West Indies, South America, and especially to Russia, where "good beer is in great demand"; and commending the recent improvement by brewers in New York, who may eventually be able to produce a malt wine (Tr in DLC: TJ Papers, 201:35882–3, in Coppinger's hand, dated New York, 15 Aug. 1814, at head of text: "Preface"; printed without the concluding five sentences in Coppinger, *The American Practical Brewer and Tanner* [New York, 1815], v–vii). Other enclosure printed below.

Joseph Coppinger (d. ca. 1825), brewer and inventor, immigrated to the United States in 1802 from Midleton, county Cork, Ireland. After a brief stay in New York City, he moved to Pittsburgh, where he used his twelve years of experience in the craft to run the Point Brewery. Disagreements with his financial partners led to a move within a year to Lexington, Kentucky. Coppinger was peripatetic thereafter, hailing from Saint Louis in 1807, from Washington and Baltimore in 1809, and from South Carolina, Georgia, and New York City in 1810. In the last year he attempted to enlist President James Madison's support for a national brewery to be located in Washington. Coppinger finally settled by 1817 in New York City, where he initially kept a clothing store and wrote *On the Construction of Flat Roofed Buildings, Whether of Stone, Brick, or Wood, and the Mode of Rendering Them Fire Proof* (New York, 1819) and, with coauthors Alden Spooner and William Higgins, *Catholic Doctrines and Catholic Principles Explained* (New York, 1817; Poor, *Jefferson's Library*, 9 [no. 523]). He held United States patents for machines to split shingles, plane wood, thresh and clean grain, flail rice, and drive a whipsaw, and for methods to distill in cast iron and preserve food (John Burke, *A Genealogical and Heraldic History of the Commoners of Great Britain and Ireland* [1835], 2:328; *Journal of the Cork Historical & Archæological Society*, 2d. ser., 8 [1902]: 149; William Coppinger to Bishop John Carroll, 22 Apr. 1802, 3 Jan. 1803, and Joseph Coppinger to Carroll, 12 Mar. 1803 [MdBS: Archdiocese of Baltimore Archives, Carroll Papers]; Gregg Smith, *Beer in America: The Early Years—1587–1840* [1998], 134–7; Coppinger to TJ, 17 Oct. 1802 [DLC]; Philadelphia *Gazette of the United States*, 10 May 1803; Coppinger to Benjamin Rush, 18 Aug. 1807 [PPL: Rush Correspondence]; Lexington *Kentucky Gazette and General Advertiser*, 13 Mar. 1809; *National Intelligencer & Washington Advertiser*, 3 July, 25 Sept. 1809; Madison, *Papers, Pres. Ser.*, 3:71, 79; *Longworth's New York Directory* [1817]: 139; [1825]: 131; DNA: RG 29, CS, N.Y., New York, 1820; *List of Patents*, 76–7, 80).

Coppinger corresponded with TJ on the SUBJECT OF NATURALIZATION be-cause he needed to become a citizen of the United States in order to patent an invention there (Coppinger to TJ, 17 Oct. 1802, 3 Jan., 18 Feb. 1803, and TJ to Coppinger, 23 Oct. 1802 [all in DLC]). Coppinger published his TREATISE as *The American Practical Brewer and Tanner* (New York, 1815). In response to an 1813 advertisement, TJ had already expressed a desire to purchase this work when it was published (TJ to Nicolas G. Dufief, [18] Sept. 1813). Coppinger wrote in CONTRA-DISTINCTION to Michael Krafft, *The American Distiller; or, the Theory and Practice of Distilling, According to the Latest Discoveries and Improvements, Including the Most Improved Methods of Constructing Stills, and of Rectification* (Philadelphia, 1804; Sowerby, no. 1208). MORRISES SMALL WORK ON BREWING: Alexander Morrice, *A Treatise on Brewing*, 2d ed. (London, 1802), which was in its fifth edition by 1815.

[1] Manuscript: "uself."

ENCLOSURE

Joseph Coppinger's Plan for a Brewing Company

[ca. 6 Apr. 1815]

Brewing Company

At a time that companies of every description are establishing in almost every section of the Union, I would beg leave to recommend, one that seems to have been overlooked, and that too perhaps not the least important I mean a Brewing Company to be established in Washington principally with a view to improve the quality of American Malt liquors, and at the same time give every Possible encouragement to the extension of the Brewing trade, as an object of great National importance intimately connected with the health and Morals of our population. And as such worthy the attention of every true Patriot and friend to his Country. The Capital optional, say from 25 to 100000 Dollars to be subscribed for in such sums as may be thought most convenient the scale to be exactly Proportioned to the Capital and one half only to be allowed to the purchase of ground permanent buildings utensils &ᶜ—the remaining half to be employed in the active Capital of the Company. The establishment to be made in Washington or its immediate neighbourhood preferably to any other situation, as affording every member of both houses of Congress an easy opportunity of inspecting the works obtaining Plans &c—And thereby induce and enable them To encourage similar establishments on a smaller scale in their own districts. The company to be incorporated by the general Government on the express condition of not applying to their own use or Account more than 20 ℔ Cᵗ of the annual Profit accruing on their Capital for a certain number of years as may be agreed on. the surplus profit to form an accumulating fund to enable the company to give premiums to the best brewer and the best Malster to be found in a given section of every state in the Union who may Produce the best Malt and the best beer within that district or section, which should be satisfactorily ascertained to the Company who may further advantageously publish every Six or twelve months one Vᵐ of Reports: giving an account of the new establishments formed in the Brewing line intimations of which could easily be procured, through the agency of the Several members of Congress, whose cooperation and assistance might be reasonably counted on for so laudable a Purpose: in the same Vᵐ should be given the most useful processes for making every Kind of Malt liquor as well as Malt itself which Instructions would have A general circulation and a consequent happy effect in improving the quality of Malt liquors generally. foreign improvements may occasionally be added, as they could without difficulty be easily procured by the Companies committee of correspondance. By some it may be thought hard that the Company shou'd not divide their full Profites for a certain number [of]¹ years. But when it is recollected that this small sacrifice is made to promote a great National good it most certainly follows that every liberal and well minded Stock holder will have no objection to it: The more as it is acknowledged that 20 ℔ Cᵗ is a handsome profit in any trade, and aught to satisfy any reasonable Man, when we see the holders of Bank Stock satisfied with an Interest of 9 ℔ Cᵗ and that arrising on a Capital which has been bought in 40 ℔ Cᵗ above par which is exactly the case of many of the New York Bank Stock holders² at this Day. However to Plan is one thing, to execute another, it only remains for me to leave it in your hands praying you to give it that attention you think it deserves—And If it is not too great a favor will thank you for your opinion of its merites and probable success should it in your estimation appear to have any. here I must acknowledge I am apt to be too sanguine in wishing to see accomplished what I conceive to be a Publick good the more when no individual loss need be apprehended to arrise—

MS (DLC: TJ Papers, 201:35880–1);   ¹ Omitted word editorially supplied.
in Coppinger's hand; undated.   ² Word interlined.

From Horatio G. Spafford

RESPECTED FRIEND—   Albany, 4 Mo. 6, 1815.

    The work of Dr. Williams, of which I spoke, is a Second edition of that which thou hast seen, published in 1809, at Burlington Vt., in 2 8vo volumes, containing about 1000 pages. Much of it is written anew, & the additions are extensive & valuable. I know the Doctor would be highly gratified to have it read & applauded by thee. He prides himself on his Republican Sentiments, particularly in the 2^d vol. of this edition.

Gen. S. Van Rensselaer, the proprietor of the Manor of Rensselaer Wyck,[1] has a Chaise nearly finished, on my plan. The proportions as I propose. It will be in motion next week, when I shall close my Letter with an account of its success. Except to myself, the sight will be novel in Albany, & hundreds are curious & waiting to try it. I know that in overcoming a 6 inch obstacle, with a load of 500 pounds, at a standing draught, the wheel of 7 feet will effect an advantage, equal to 96 pounds, when compared with the wheel of 4 feet 8 inches: & I also know that on the crooked axle, the same power, that is, 250 pounds, carries the same load, with the same results, also at a standing draught. But, giving the impulse of motion, by permitting the wheels to roll a short distance before they meet the obstacle, there is also a gain in the cranked, over the straight axle, which is very considerable. I let the power fall over a pulley, in the above experiments. To carry the wheels of 4 feet 8 inches over the same obstacle, with the same load, I have to increase the power, (or weight over the pulley,) by the addition of 96 pounds to the power. The small wheels that I used, are a trifle short of 4 feet 8 inches diameter.

When the load & power are thus tried, first on the small, & then on the large wheels; first with straight & then with cranked axles; standing, & then in motion, when they meet the obstacle, I have a most complete series of experiments for demonstration: And such were the facts, on which my reasoning was founded.

When the wheels, loaded upon the straight axle, meet the obstacle, it is by a sudden stroke, which deadens the impulse; &, if they mount it, they do so by a joult as sudden;—when, on the contrary, the load is on the cranked axle, & the wheels meet the obstacle, the Shock is less violent, & the impulse acts with greater power, by a kind of es-lastic effort: Nor is the joult near so great, in passing over.

The above experiments show that there is no loss of power, in employing the cranked axle, in order to reduce the height of the load, & the line of draught, raised too high by employing large wheels. And if this occasions no loss, it must effect a great gain;—by enabling me to employ large wheels, & by bringing the load nearer to the point of contact, the actual centre of motion: as well as by equalizing the draught, & the motion of the load. Every inequality of motion, increases the friction, & that in a greater degree than seems to have been considered.

Stages, which employ Jacks, (as they are called here by the Coach-Makers,) on which to fasten the leathers on which the body rests, have their loads from 2 to 3 feet above the centre of the wheels; & these of course are but low. The consequence of which is, a great disadvantage in the application of the power of the horses, and a loss of the power of at least one in five when passing over rough or uneven roads, by the increased friction occasioned by the position of the load. These Stages so frequently upset, that travelling in them excites general terror. At least 20 lives have been lost in this way, within the United States, during the last year. Were these vehicles constructed with wheels of 6 & 7 feet diameter, & their axles cranked to the ordinary or best line of draught for the horses, there would be little danger of upsetting, & I am confident the 4th or 5th horse might be spared from the team. A Stage proprietor here, proposes to make trial of my method. If my reasoning is correct, & my inferences fair, from numerous experiments, this subject well merits the attention of the Post-Master General. That Officer ought to, & probably would, consider the saving of lives deserving his[2] attention; & he is the proper organ to foster such an improvement, as important to considerations of political economy. And if travelling in[3] Stages were considered less tedious & tiresome, & more safe & free from danger, the travelling by them[4] would increase, & the government would be enabled to make contracts for carrying the mails on better terms. I hope this subject may engage the attention of the intelligent Gentleman who conducts the concerns of the Post Office Department. Were he to encourage a fair trial on Some principal route, I am fully persuaded he would essentially contribute to the public interest. Between Washington & Baltimore, I found the roads excedingly bad; & there would be a good place to try improved Stages. Or, between this City & Schenectady;—if he would encourage the Contractors to try it, I would give the Right, & superintend the construction of a Carriage. The only objection to my construction, would be, that the Carriage would not turn on so little ground. Stages are made to go forward, & turning short, is but a little part of the object for which they are employed. A mason I once employed, objected to connecting the brick-work of my chimney back, in the fire place, by laying some of the bricks transversely, because of the difficulty of detaching the back end, when the back should need repairs: & when I persisted, proposed to use, for that purpose, Soft bricks!

4 Mo. 12, 1815.

The Chaise has been now, 3 days in motion, hundreds have been to examine it—& many have rode in it. I rode with the owner a few miles, today, on muddy & dry, rough & smooth, level & uneven roads, & the motion, & apparent ease to the horse fully satisfied us that the principles are correctly [...] in my pamphlet. We have no hesitation, nor do I believe any one has who has tried it, in believing that it effects a saving of full one quarter. The ease and uniformity of its motion, are truly astonishing. It sinks far less into the mud, raises less on the wheel, & throws very little. When the road would admit of it, we drove very fast, & immediately after passing through deep & soft mud: the top was turned back, & we concluded it did not throw So much mud as an ordinary wheel. The timber should be good for the Spokes, & they should preserve their width, pretty fully, down to the felloes. I wish some person in Virginia would try it immediately: & if any person would try it in a Stage, I would willingly give the Right. In deep roads, it will make a Saving of near one half. To a Stage Proprietor in V^a who first tries it in a Stage, I will give Rights to the amount of the expense of altering his vehicle to this plan. With offering an apology, for so long a Letter, I conclude, by renewed assurances of my esteem & respect.

HORATIO GATES SPAFFORD.

RC (MHi); one word illegible; endorsed by TJ as received 19 Apr. 1815 and so recorded in SJL. RC (DLC); address cover only; with PoC of TJ to Nathaniel Bowditch, 2 May 1815, on verso; addressed: "Hon. Thomas Jefferson, late President of the United States, Monticello, Virginia"; franked; postmarked Albany, 12 Apr.

[1] Spafford here left a blank and above it interlined "V. the Gazetteer of N.Y.," with "V." presumably an abbreviation for "vide" ("see"). Spafford wrote on Rensselaerwyck Manor in his *Gazetteer of the State of New-York* (Albany, 1813; Sowerby, no. 4172), esp. 96–7, 116.

[2] Word interlined.

[3] Preceding two words interlined.

[4] Preceding two words interlined.

From Joseph Dougherty

DEAR SIR   Washington City Ap^l 7th —15

your letter of the 27th Feb. came duly to hand. The number of wagons wanted to bring the library will be "eleven, and six of that number can be got in your neighbourhood, at four dollars per day"—it should be understood that those waggons[1] are verry well covred—and indeed it would be necessary that they should have double covers; the better to guard against heavy rains, which might hapen on the road. please sir, let me know if more than Six waggons can be got there.

I have for a long time back been verry[2] anxious to get a favourable oppertunity to go to monticello—and thinking the present, the most favourable one that might offer; I cheerfully embraced it—and while amusing myself in thinking what[3] happiness I should have in seeing you once more; and perhaps for the last time—I saw your letter to M[r] Millegan; stating that, "as soon as the books were packed, you would go to Bedford"—this at once, blasted all my cheering prospects—and am now careless about the journey—knowing that at the time that I would be there, you would be absent.

as it remains altogether[4] with you & me, what time the books may be brought—I will abide by your instructions; only arange it so, that, you will be at Monticello[5] when I go there. I am ready to start in 3. day warning.

I am Sir, your Humble Serv[t]   JO[s] DOUGHERTY

RC (DLC); addressed: "Tho[s] Jefferson Esq[r] Late President of the U. States Monticello"; franked; postmarked Washington City, 10 Apr.; endorsed by TJ as received 13 Apr. 1815 and so recorded in SJL.

[1] Word interlined.
[2] Manuscript: "vrry."
[3] Dougherty here canceled "a consolation."
[4] Manuscript: "altogethe."
[5] Manuscript: "Monticcello."

From Jeremiah A. Goodman

DR SR   April the 7 day 1815

received your Letter & has put the execution against scott in the hands of the sheriff, I expect your tobacco is at richmond Seven hogsheads, there[1] is one more Light & part stem part Leaf which I Shall try to sell at Lynchburg as for the wheat, you dessired me to Let M[r] mitchell pay him self out of the wheat & send the ballance off, his debt was $244,56 foure hundred & nineteen Bu[s] of wheat at the price wheat has bin Selling at heare I beleave would not more then pay the debt therefore I wated expecting better times and never sittle'd with him untill I received your Last Letter I tryed very hard to git six Shillings pe[r] Bu[s] but could not M[r] mitchell give me choises say take 4[s]/6[d] pe[r] Bu[s] or send it to richmond by Counsell I exceptd 4[s]/6[d] which Leaves ninety odd Bu[s] in your favoure

JEREMIAH A GOODMAN

RC (ViU: TJP-ER); at foot of text: "M^r jefferson"; endorsed by TJ as received 18 Apr. 1815 from Poplar Forest and so recorded in SJL.

The missing LETTER was probably TJ to Goodman, 22 Mar. 1815. This and an earlier letter from TJ to Goodman of 11 Feb. 1815 are recorded in SJL but not found. The EXECUTION against Samuel Scott for court costs resulted from the dismissal of *Scott v. Jefferson and Harrison* (George Hay to TJ, 8 Mar. 1815).

[1] Manuscript: "the."

To William W. Hening

DEAR SIR   Monticello Apr. 8. 15.

I have duly recieved the MS. volumes which were forwarded by the stage, and in good condition. these were as follows

one marked ⟨43⟩ of laws from 1629. to 1633.

one marked **F.**   laws from 1639 to 1667.

MS. copies by myself from Mercer's MS of the laws of 1661.

the Charles city MS. laws from 1661 to 1702

the 2^d Charles city MS. laws of 1705.

the Rosewell MS. laws of 1705. to 1711.

Besides these there remain two others of those I lent you which I have no doubt you have overlooked in the mass of those you have, or not recollected from whom they came. these are

a MS. marked **A.** containing the laws of 1623/4 Mar. 5. in 35. acts. it is a very thin vol. indeed, bound new in white calf opening at the end, and not at the side of the volume, given me by Peyton Randolph from among the Collection of materials by Sr John Randolph when about to write the history of Virginia. it is the only copy extant of those laws.

Another MS. marked **D.** of laws from 1642/3 to 1661/2

As you have long ago passed the period of those volumes I will ask their return by the same mode of conveyance as the former. if sent by the first Milton stage, they may still be in time to be packed with the others. these two volumes were on my Catalogue, and as the sale of the library was by the Catalogue, as it stood, they go. but a very antient volume of records too tender to be sent you with the others, was not on the catalogue, and so does not go. when you have brought your work to the revolution, this might furnish matter for a valuable supplementary Appendix, as it contains some laws interspersed in it, which perhaps were in none of the others. it shall be at your service. I hope you will push your valuable publication with urgency to it's conclusion. Accept the assurances of my [e]steem and respect   TH: JEFFERSON

PoC (DLC); lower corner torn away; at foot of text: "Mr Hening"; endorsed by TJ.

TJ had the manuscript VOLUMES mentioned here, now in DLC: TJ Papers, ser. 8 (see Sowerby, nos. 1822–7, 1829–30), bound in 1796 at the same time as other "Volumes of the Laws of Virginia, Manu-

script and Printed" then in his possession (*PTJ*, 28:581–91). The VERY ANTIENT VOLUME OF RECORDS not included in the 1815 sale to Congress has not been identified but was probably among the "Old Records of Virginia" (Poor, *Jefferson's Library*, 4 [no. 122]) acquired by DLC shortly after TJ's death and now also in its TJ Papers, ser. 8.

From Benjamin Galloway

SIR   Hagers Town April 9th 1815.

I now contemplate to leave my residence for Monticello on or about the fifth of next month; and shall be glad to be informed, whether you will be at home, when I propose to make my appearance there— Tomorrow I commence a Journey to the lower part of our State; and shall be gone about a fortnight. I understand, that Mr Munroe and Lady are on a visit to some part of your Commonwealth; I hope, I shall find them at the Cottage in your vicinity—After labour; Refreshment is both necessary and agreeable. and will no doubt must be So to him—The public voice here and hereabouts is loud in praise of his activity and judgment whilst he was engaged last year in the office of Secretary of War pro temp—The feds in general are warm in their commendations of his late conduct; and profess to have no wish to disappoint or obstruct the efforts of his political friends in their attempt to place him at the next election in the presidential chair—how far, some of them, may be sincere in their professions, quoad hoc; I will not undertake to say; but, I verily believe, that the major part of them in our district, are disposed to coalesce with the friends to the powers that are: the present administration: and, if they do not openly support M^r M—s Election: I verily believe, they will be content to lay on their Oars, and quietly suffer the political vessell, without opposition on their part, to take the course which the republicans wish and design it to do—

The Anglo Feds, here, and hereabouts, appear to be chop-fallens. since the Treaty of peace was ratified by the United States: and, if a certain cast of politicians will govern their angry passions, and only exercise a due discretion, by displaying that sort of temper, moderation and <u>firmness</u>, which is so needfull; and more especially <u>adviseable</u>: to be practiced <u>at this time</u>; The Opposition, in our district, will <u>dissolve</u>, in <u>its own</u> imbecillity

please to favour me with an answer to this; which I could wish to receive at the city of washington, if it can reach that place before the 22^d instant, to be directed to care of my nephew Tench Ringgold Esqr Washington—As I shall travel to Monti Cello on Horseback; and as I am a total Stranger to the Road I shall be obliged to you for such instructions as you may think will facilitate my Journey.—

Compliments to M^{rs} and Mr Munroe, should they be in your vicinity—I enclose this to the Post Master at Milton—

I am Sir with Esteem and Regard Y^{rs} Respectfully

BENJAMIN GALLOWAY

RC (DLC); endorsed by TJ as received 22 Apr. 1815 and so recorded in SJL.

CHOP-FALLENS: "those with the lower jaw fallen; dispirited persons" (*OED*). Charles Vest was the POST MASTER at Milton (Axelson, *Virginia Postmasters*, 5).

From David Bailie Warden

DEAR SIR,   Paris, 9 april, 1815.

I have forwarded to you, by mr. Deseaves, <u>via</u> Havre, a collection of seeds from mr. Thouin, which he promises to send to you from Baltimore, where he proposes to reside. The trunk containing Books and pamphlets for you and mr. Short, addressed to the care of mr. Shaler,[1] was unfortunately left at Ghent, where it still remains—I shall have it forwarded by the first vessel which sails from that quarter. I beg leave to inclose a copy of the letter addressed to me by the Prince of Benevento—my removal has excited the regret of liberal thinking men, and of the best friends of the liberties of America; and the reestablishment of the Emperor napoleon, and appointment of mr. Gallatin as minister to Paris, inspire Me, through your friendly intercession, with fresh hopes of success.[2]

Whatever be my fate my gratitude to you shall be as lasting as life.—I have nearly finished an[3] article on the progress of the U.S. during the last 15 years,[4] of which I propose to send you a copy. It is written for the Supplement[5] to the Encylopedia Brittanica at the request of Professor Leslie & Editor[6]—   I am, dear Sir, with great respect your most obed Sevant   D. B. WARDEN

[Postscript in Dupl only:]
P.S. I have sent you a copy of the <u>Journal</u> de <u>la Société D'Encouragement</u> for a year,[7] to the care of mr. Chambord, New york—who will forward it to monticello.

RC (DLC); at foot of text: "Thomas Jefferson Esquire"; endorsed by TJ as received 3 Oct. 1815 and so recorded in SJL. Dupl (DLC); differs substantially from RC, with only the most significant variations noted below; at head of text: "Dupliccate"; endorsed by TJ as received 15 Dec. 1815 and so recorded in SJL. Enclosure: second enclosure to Warden to TJ, 20 Oct. 1814. Enclosed in Albert Gallatin to TJ, 6 Sept. 1815.

[1] Preceding seven words not in Dupl.
[2] Dupl: "of being reestablished in office."
[3] Dupl: "a Statistical."
[4] Preceding five words replaced in Dupl by "since your first election."
[5] Dupl here adds "of six volumes."
[6] Preceding two words replaced in Dupl by "the former Preceptor of mr Randolph."
[7] Preceding three words added in margin.

From John Hollins

DEAR SIR   Baltimore 10th April 1815

At the request of my very particular friend, & next door neighbour, James A Buchanan Esqr I now address you, to solicit for his son W^m B: Buchanan, a young Gentleman of accomplishments, a letter or two to some of your friends in Europe, where he means to pass some time, in visiting different places, he is to embark with Doctor Eustis, & will continue in his family a while in Holland; sh^d you have occasion to have executed any commission in Europe, I am satisfied it will be most pleasing to M^r W: B: B, to see it properly executed; & as peace & quiet is again very happily restored, I hope soon to receive your orders for plaister of paris &c &c

M^{rs} H who joins me in best respects to your good self & family, were sorry to be informed of the death of our worthy friend p: Carr, he is however removed from a world of trouble & anxiety, & I have no doubt to a place of everlasting comfort & happiness

If your Grandson & his bride, be under your hospitable roof, I pray you to present our best wishes to them, for their health & happiness. —

Hoping you will excuse the freedom I use in asking for the letters for my young friend, I

Remain with very great respect & esteem
Dear sir   y^r fnd & Servt   JN° HOLLINS

RC (MHi); with unrelated calculation by TJ at foot of text; endorsed by TJ as received 15 Apr. 1815 and so recorded in SJL. RC (DLC); address cover only; with PoC of TJ to John Graham, 14 May 1815, on verso; addressed: "Thomas Jefferson Esq Monticello"; franked; postmarked Baltimore, 10 Apr.

Hollins and his NEIGHBOUR, the merchant James A. Buchanan, resided on Washington Square in Baltimore (James Lakin, *Baltimore Directory and Register, for 1814–15* [Baltimore, 1814], 48, 106). TJ's GRANDSON was Thomas Jefferson Randolph.

From Benjamin Smith Barton

DEAR SIR, March [Apr.] 13. 1815.

I acknowledge, with many thanks, the receipt of your package, which came safe to-day. The letters will, doubtless, be highly valuable to me. They contain every thing I could wish for.

I beg your acceptance of a few[1] small tracts in natural history. They may amuse you & our friend Mr Randolph, in a hour of leisure. Sickness stopped me short, in the progress of my publication of several other & more important essays, &c. These, with the return of health, I shall yet give to the public. The first number of my Archaeologia may, possibly, amuse you: the subsequent numbers will, I trust, be acceptable to the public.

I shall be very anxious to learn, that Persoon has come safe. Both vols. have been sent: the 2^d by the earlier mail.

I shall take great pleasure & pride in writing to you, from Europe. In the meanwhile, I remain, Sir, with very great respect, & with the sincerest wishes for your health & happiness, Your much obliged friend, &c., B. S. BARTON.

P.S. I beg you to present my compliments to all your[2] family, & especially to the head of the younger part of it, my respected friend, Colonel Th: M: Randolph.

RC (DLC: TJ Papers, 203:36190); misdated, with dateline beneath signature; addressed: "Mr Jeffeson, Monticello, Virginia"; franked; postmarked Philadelphia, 13 Apr.; endorsed by TJ as a letter of "March 13. 15. for April?" Recorded in SJL as a letter of "Mar. 13. [qu. Apr?]" received 19 Apr. 1815. Enclosure: Barton, *Archaeologiae Americanae Telluris Collectanea et Specimina. Or Collections, with Specimens, for a Series of Memoirs on certain Extinct Animals and Vegetables of North-America* (Philadelpia, 1814), pt. 1 (no more published).

The enclosed SMALL TRACTS may have included Barton's *Additional Facts, Observations, and Conjectures relative to the Generation of the Opossum of North-America* (Philadelphia, 1813) and *A Memoir concerning the Fascinating Faculty which has been Ascribed to Various Species of Serpents. A New Edition, Greatly Enlarged, and Embellished by a Plate*

(Philadelphia, 1814). The ESSAYS left unfinished at Barton's death on 19 Dec. 1815 included one on the life and writings of Joseph Priestley and another on the insects of the United States (Francis W. Pennell, "Benjamin Smith Barton as Naturalist," APS, *Proceedings* 86 [1942]: 120–1).

[1] Barton here canceled "(3)."
[2] Word interlined in place of "my."

To Louis H. Girardin

TH:J. TO MR GIRARDIN.   Mont° Apr. 14. 15.

Your servant finds us just setting down to table, so I can only scribble you a line. I will have one for mrs Lewis ready for you when you call; this being on your road to her house, I will then shew you also an honorable acknolegement of G. Nicholas on the subject of the enquiries into the conduct of the executive the letter as to Arnold was addressed to Gen¹ Muhlenbg, perhaps he might then be only a Colonel. I will read Adams's letter with pleasure & return it, with your 2. cahiers, my daily & nightly labor not having yet permitted me to read the first, and they will continue 2. or 3. days longer. strange that I do not hear a word from mr Millegan. I salute you with esteem & respect

RC (PPAmP: Thomas Jefferson Papers); dateline at foot of text; addressed: "Mʳ Girardin Glenmore." Not recorded in SJL.

In June 1781 George NICHOLAS introduced a resolution in the Virginia House of Delegates calling for an inquiry into TJ's conduct as governor. Later that year the House exonerated TJ (*PTJ*, 6:88–90, 97, 133–4, 135–7). Girardin's history noted that Nicholas "has since paid to him [TJ] an homage equally honourable to both" (Burk, Jones, and Girardin, *History of Virginia*, vol. 4, appendix, p. 12; see *PTJ*, 4:261–2, 268n,

for a similar claim by TJ and for the 1798 public statement by Nicholas on which he based it).

TJ laid out a plan to capture Benedict ARNOLD in a 31 Jan. 1781 letter to General John Peter Gabriel Muhlenberg (MUHLENBG) (*PTJ*, 4:487–8). This document was published in Burk, Jones, and Girardin, *History of Virginia*, 4:458.

A missing letter from Girardin to TJ of 1 Apr. 1815, received the same day from Glenmore, is recorded in SJL, which records receipt on 14 Apr. 1815 of an undated letter from Girardin, also not found.

From William Wingate

MY DEAR FRIEND.   Haverhill April 14. 1815.

I wrote you on the third instant—I now have enclosed one Sheet of The American Olive Branch, which I wish you for to put into the

Book I Sent you—firstly, it will be necessary that we arrange and complete the Book—and when you Shew the Book to any Person, it will be necessary that Such Person Should at the Same time give His approbation in <u>writing</u>, in order that each new Member may Se for himself who approves of the measure—it is true that the Book now contains what is intended for it not to contain—And that The covenant does not now contain but a garden Spot, compared to what I contemplate it to contain—I intend that it Shall be a Small Book after completed, but of incalculable consequences to America, and I confidentially hope to the World—I beg your Wisdom and Patience untill God Shall enable us, and Se fit for to Send it abroad—I cannot with propriety and consistantly with my Solem Trust add no more— I Shall wait patiently untill I hear from you—in the interim, I wish you for to consult your [ow]n best Judgment, and perhaps Mr Maddisons—if He Should not appear to be our Sincere Friend, I Shall be greatly deceived and as greatly disappointed—
Sir, Be assured that I am, and that I always Shall remain your un-shaken Friend, let what will take place, I feel forbid to Say any more at this time—
Yours Sincerely   WILLIAM WINGATE

RC (MoSHi: TJC-BC); torn at seal; at foot of text (torn): "Honorable [...]"; endorsed by TJ as received 26 Apr. 1815 and so recorded in SJL. Enclosure not found.

From William W. Hening

SIR,   Richmond 15th April 1815

I should have answered your letter of the 8th by the return of the mail, had I not found it necessary to occupy much time in searching for the two MS. Vol^s, which you say are still wanting.—
I have such a strong impression that the thin M:S, marked A. was put up between the two thin boards, sent up, that I cannot help thinking it may yet be found there.—I have made very diligent search among my books and papers, and have not been able to find it. The MS. marked **D**, containing the laws from 1642/3 to 1661/2 I certainly received from the late Edmund Randolph Esqr as <u>his prop-erty</u>; and, had he lived, I should as certainly have returned it to him.—I have several times offered it to his son Peyton, but he declined taking it.—It is now in my possession, & I have no doubt, that

it is <u>your property</u>:—for I discover, that it is, in fact, marked **D**,—a circumstance which never before arrested my attention.—

I had very carefully, as the printing progressed, packed away the M.S.S. received from you, and had it not been for a fire which happened within a few feet of my house, in May last, and which entirely consumed the adjacent building (tho' mine almost miraculously escaped), they would have been in the most perfect order.—On this occasion, my house was suddenly emptied of every article:—Your books were the <u>first</u> that I carried out:—all my books and papers were placed on a carpet, in the street, but the carpet being wanted, to cover the house, and protect it, from the approaching flames, was suddenly drawn, from under the books and papers, & they were left in the street.—From their deranged state, I have not yet been able to extricate them.—The frequent alarms from the enemy, during the last summer, and the scenes[1] acted at Washington, inducing us to expect nothing better from them, than the Goths & Vandals, rendered it expedient to keep all important books & papers, packed up, ready for removal, at the shortest notice.—Mine were not unpacked, until since the restoration of peace.

I will make another effort, to find the thin M.S. marked **A.**—& in any event, will send up that marked **D**, being well satisfied that it is your property.

I am Rep^{ly} Yrs   W^M W. HENING

RC (DLC); endorsed by TJ as received   [1] Manuscript: "scences."
24 Apr. 1815 and so recorded in SJL.

To John Barnes

DEAR SIR   Monticello Apr. 18. 15.

The departure of the mail and my distance from the office leave me barely time to inclose you an order on the Treasury for 4870.D. to wit 4500.D. the principal of Genl Kosciuzko's money in my hands, and 360.D. one years interest. the order is for 10.D. over to cover any fraction of interest. the high interest on this principal has made me anxious to get first rid of it, and I have informed Genl Kosciuzko that I should make this deposit for him in the treasury of the US. and that his annual interest would of course, as to that sum, be reduced from 8. to $5\frac{2}{3}$ p. cent. I think it probable that at the end of the year when the principal is payable, we may convert it into some government loan of higher interest. Accept the assurance of my best wishes for your health and of my constant & affectionate esteem & respect.

Th: Jefferson

PoC (DLC); at foot of text: "Mʳ Barnes"; endorsed by TJ.

The closest post OFFICE was in Milton.

ENCLOSURE

Order on United States Treasury

Apr. 18. 1815
          J. B.   4 870
    Pay to Wᵐ S. or order 10,500 D. in part of the sum of 23,950 D. appropᵈ by the act of Congr. for the purchase of my library as advised in my lre to the Secʸ of the Treasury[1] of this days date, to wit Apr. 18. 1815.   Th:J

Dft (DLC: TJ Papers, 203:36233); written entirely in TJ's hand on a scrap; subjoined to Dft of Receipt for Sale of TJ's Library, 23 Apr. 1815; on verso of Dft of TJ to Alexander J. Dallas, 18 Apr. 1815.

Individual versions of this order, not found, were enclosed in the above letter to John Barnes (J. B.) and in TJ's letter of this date to William Short (wᴹ s.).

[1] Preceding six words interlined.

To Alexander J. Dallas

Dear Sir   Monticello. Apr. 18. 1815.
    Your favor of Feb. 21. was recieved in due time. I thought it a duty to spare you the trouble of reading an useless answer, and have therefore delayed acknoleging it until now. not having revised the library for many years, I expected that books would be missing without being able to conjecture how many, and that in that case a deduction should be made for the deficient volumes. I have gone through a rigorous review of them, and find indeed some missing, which were on the Catalogue, on which[1] the estimate and purchase were made; but that considerably more both in number and value had been omitted by oversight in copying that catalogue from the original one which was done two years ago. I have not thought it right to withdraw these from the library, so that the whole delivered exceeds on the principles of the estimate, the sum appropriated, and of course there is no ground for any deduction. the books being now all ready for delivery,

[426]

and their removal actually commenced, I may with propriety now recieve the payment. entirely unacquainted as I am with the forms established at the treasury for the security of the public[2] I must only say
what I wish, and so far as it may be inconsistent with the necessary
forms, you will have the goodness to correct me and inform me what
is necessary. if my convenience can be so far consulted,[3] I would
request payments to be made

Dollars

to William Short
   of Philadelphia of 10,500   ⎫   in bills of such of the specified
to John Barnes   ⎬   d[e]nominations & places of paiment
   of George town of 4,870. ⎭   as they shall chuse
to myself   8,580   to be inclosed to me by mail in 82.
                        23,950

notes of 100.D. each and 19. of 20.D. each, payable in Richmond, for
which last sum I inclose my reciept, and I forward to mr Short and mr
Barnes orders on the Treasurer[4] for the sums to be paid them for
which they will give acquittals.[5] should these papers be deficient[6] in
form, I will, at a moment's warning send on any others in whatever
form shall be necessary. should it be requisite that the whole should be
payable at one and the same place, then Washington would be the
most convenient for the whole. as I wait only the completion of the delivery of all the books to set out on a journey of considerable absence
and urgency, it would be a great favor to me if the sum which I ask to
be remitted to myself, could be sent by as early a mail as the convenience of the Treasury will admit. I pray you to accept my friendly and
respectful salutations   TH: JEFFERSON

PoC (DLC); edge trimmed; at foot of
first page: "The Secretary of the Treasury"; endorsed by TJ. Dft (DLC: TJ
Papers, 203:36233); incomplete fragment; with Dfts of enclosure to TJ to
John Barnes, 18 Apr. 1815, and of Receipt
for Sale of TJ's Library, 23 Apr. 1815, on
verso. Enclosure: Receipt for Sale of TJ's
Library, 23 Apr. 1815.

[1] Dft begins here.
[2] Dft: "govmt."
[3] Dft: "can be indulged."
[4] Dft: "treasury."
[5] Dft: "reciepts."
[6] Dft ends here.

Notes on Thomas Jefferson's Library
at the Time of Sale

[*Ed. Note*: TJ probably began preparing these notes after receiving his library catalogue back from Samuel H. Smith on or about 16 Mar. 1815. Work on it was well advanced by 28 Mar., and he completed it no later than 18 Apr. 1815 (Smith to TJ, 11 Mar. 1815; TJ to Joseph Milligan, 28 Mar. 1815; TJ to Alexander J. Dallas, 18 Apr. 1815). The notes consist of four sections: (1) "Additions to the Catalogue of books <u>omitted</u> in copying it," which groups books by catalogue chapter; gives the identification number assigned to each book; cites the title, author, or both; and records the size and number of volumes for each book, for a total of $194\frac{1}{2}$ volumes that TJ valued at $513.50. (2) A chart of the forty-four chapters in the library catalogue, with the total number of folios, quartos, octavos, duodecimos, and pamphlets on each page. (3) A chart with the total folios, quartos, octavos, and pamphlets in each chapter. (4) "Books missing," which lists the catalogue chapter and title, author, or both of each book; gives the size and number of volumes for each book; has eight entries struck out; and contains 83 volumes, according to TJ's count, that are worth $211. TJ then subtracted the value of the missing books from that of the omitted books and arrived at a total of $202.50 in his favor. In a 2 Aug. 1815 letter Joseph Milligan advised TJ that he had erred in these calculations. A photograph of these notes is reproduced elsewhere in this volume.]

MS (DLC: TJ Papers, 209:37212); written in TJ's hand on both sides of a single sheet, with additions in red ink by Milligan; with section 1 at left margin of recto, section 2 spanning recto and verso, section 3 in middle of verso, and section 4 at right margin of verso; undated.

To William Short

DEAR SIR   Monticello Apr. 18. 15.

The departure of the post and my distance from the office leave me barely time to acknolege the reciept of your favor of the 4th inst. and to inclose you an order on the Treasury of the US. for 10,500 D. which, I believe, is a little over the amount of my three bonds with the interest. this however you will ascertain by calculation, and if there be a surplus, be so good as to put it into the hands of mr John Vaughan to whom I shall have occasion to make a remittance. the Treasury emits notes only of 1000, 100, & 20.D. each, so that you will have to chuse among them. I believe they will make them payable where you please.

Colo Monroe left Washington 3. or 4. weeks ago for Loudoun, but is not yet arrived here. he is expected daily, and I shall be attentive to your affair with him.—Dupont's book was recieved as I have found on examination. my messenger presses me to close here with assurances of my constant & affectionate friendship

TH: JEFFERSON

RC (ViW: TJP); at foot of text: "Mr Short." PoC (MHi); endorsed by T.J.

Short's letter OF THE 4TH INST., not found, is recorded in SJL as received 13 Apr. 1815 from Philadelphia. For the enclosed ORDER, see enclosure to TJ to John Barnes, 18 Apr. 1815.

From Louis H. Girardin

L. H. GIRARDIN TO MR JEFFERSON.   April 19. 1815.

I send to You, Dear & Respected Sir, some books of Mr Joseph Cabell's, which Col. Randolph tells me he would like to read—Perhaps, they may also amuse some of Your moments—I am sure Mr Cabell will be pleased with my leaving them at Monticello. Col. Randolph has promised to return them to Mr Cabell where and when he may chuse.—

I wish You complete relief from Your troublesome Bibliography— and Salute You with most affectionate Respect.

	The Books are		
	Journal de Physique	9 Cahiers	4to
	Anatomie Comparée de Cuvier	5 vol.	8vo
	Théorie de la terre—par La metherie	5. vol.	8vo
	Wildenow—Species plantarum	8 vol.	8vo
	Chemical Nomenclature	1 vol.	4^to1
	Helvetiens Flora	2 vol.	16mo
[(]with Col. Rand^h)	Murray's Linné	1 vol.	8vo
	Pestalozzi	1 vol.	8vo Boards.
	Des fontaines Tableau Botanique &.c	1 vol.	8vo—Dto—

P.S. I find, upon trying the trunk, that it will not contain all the books—I keep for another time
Lametherie—
Des fontaines—
H. Flora.
Journal de Physique.

RC (DLC); edge trimmed; endorsed by Thomas Mann Randolph.

Girardin's list included Georges CUVIER, *Leçons d'Anatomie Comparée*, 5 vols. (Paris, 1800–05; Sowerby, no. 999); Jean Claude de Lamétherie (LA METHERIE), *Théorie de La Terre* (Paris,

1795); and Karl Ludwig Willdenow (WILLDENOW), *Species Plantarum*, 5 vols. (Berlin, 1797–1810). The work on CHEMICAL NOMENCLATURE was George Pearson, *A Translation of the Table of Chemical Nomenclature, proposed by de Guyton, formerly de Morveau, Lavoisier, Bertholet and de Fourcroy, with additions and alterations* (London, 1794; 2d ed. London, 1799), and that on FLORA was Johann Rudolf Suter, *Flora Helvetica: Exhibens Plantas Helvetiae Indigenas Hallerianas, et Omnes quae Nuper Detec-* *tae sunt Ordine Linnaeano* (Zurich, 1802; Joseph C. Cabell's autographed copy is at ViU). The publication of LINNÉ was Johann Andreas Murray, ed., *Caroli a Linné . . . Systema Vegetabilium secundum Classes Ordines Genera Species cum Characteribus et Differentiis* (Göttingen, 1774). The TABLEAU was René Louiche Desfontaines, *Tableau de l'École de Botanique du Muséum d'Histoire Naturelle* (Paris, 1804).

[1] Word inserted in place of "fol°."

From John Barnes

DEAR SIR—   George Town 22[d] April 1815.

I am anxiously waiting to hear from the good Gen[l] on his receiving the proceeds of the £400 ster[g] remitted him July last on Mess[r] Baring Brothers & C[o] London—as well to renew a Remittance early in May for a like sum—I should prefer a Bill on London—in preferance to one on Paris even if the exchange should be on equal terms. the difference in Negotiation is made up—in point of security—being purchased here on the Spot—in Case of Accident for the Bills on Paris, are generally drawn by The French[1] Merch[ts] in Philad[a] and N York, with whom We are quite Unacquainted

I hope, by the time you receive this—you will be eased of the extra-trouble and fatigue—you must have gone thro with in Arranging—packing, and safe delivering your very extensive and Valuable Library—

Most Respectfully & very Sincerely your Obed[t] servant.

JOHN BARNES.

RC (ViU: TJP-ER); at foot of text: "Thomas Jefferson Esq[r] Monticello"; endorsed by TJ as received 3 May 1815 and so recorded in SJL.

The GEN[L] was Tadeusz Kosciuszko.

[1] Manuscript: "Frence."

To Louis H. Girardin

Th:J. to mr Girardin   Monticello Apr. 22. 15.

I return you the 15th 16th and 17th chapters which I have kept too long; but since mr Millegan's arrival I have scarcely had a moment at command. I have made a few verbal alterations only as usual, except in the 15th where I suggest an alteration giving a more precise explanation of the transaction it relates to than your text had done. but I observe an omission of one of the most interesting episodes of the war as to the bringing off the prisoners taken at King's mountain. it was a chase by a considerable British force sent to rescue those prisoners, after[1] a much inferior party bringing them off, continued some hundred miles with a rapidity on both sides unexampled, pushed far into Virginia, close upon the heels of the retiring party which was saved at last by some accident of a swoln river or something of that sort. the whole continent was under anxious alarm while this chase continued, and it ended only at Staunton. I do not remember the commander on either side. I suppose General Moore, or some of the Campbell family most likely to recollect particulars, the former from memory, the latter the tradition of their fathers. I can state no more than what I mention here. but it is strange if all our histories have omitted it. I salute you with esteem & respect.

RC (PPAmP: Thomas Jefferson Papers); dateline at foot of text; addressed: "Mr Girardin Glenmore." Not recorded in SJL. Enclosure: manuscript, not found, of chapters 15–7 of Burk, Jones, and Girardin, *History of Virginia*, vol. 4.

As published, chapter 16 of *History of Virginia*, 4:407–10, describes the events surrounding the American victory at KING'S MOUNTAIN on 7 Oct. 1780 and TJ's plans for the disposition of prisoners traveling to Virginia. His memory of a dramatic chase all the way to Staunton by a CONSIDERABLE BRITISH FORCE unsuccessfully seeking to free the prisoners taken at the battle is not repeated in *History of Virginia* and has not been confirmed. The captured Loyalists were in fact poorly guarded, and the vast majority escaped or were paroled within three months (Lyman C. Draper, *King's Mountain and Its Heroes* [1881], 358–60).

Missing letters from Girardin to TJ of 22 Apr. and 6 May 1815 are recorded in SJL as received the days they were written, with the former described as sent from Glenmore.

[1] Word interlined in place of "of."

To John Hollins

DEAR SIR   Monticello Apr. 22. 15.

The present arrangements of our post office put out of our power the answering our Northern letters under a week. your favor of the 10th has been that time in my hands, and this circumstance must account for the delay of my answer. I left Europe in 1789, the French revolution being then begun. in it's course, it swept off the far greater part of my friends, these and a lapse of 26. years has withdrawn the rest from life by it's ordinary occurrences. my present correspondence in France is with authors and men in the literary line, whose persons are unknown to me mostly, and whose pursuits would render them of little use to the young friend on whose behalf you ask letters of introduction from me. under this incapacity of serving him as I would, I inclose for him a letter to mr Gallat[in,] who can supply fully my deficiencies, and who, I am sure, will [do so.?]

Presuming that Mrs Bonaparte has left the co[ntine]nt, I take the liberty of putting under cover to you a letter for her, as I expect you will best know where and thro' what channel it will be most likely to find her. I sincerely reciprocate your congratulations on the return of peace, the more welcome after the specimen we gave them at Orleans of the enemy they will have to contend with if their future aggressions should again bring us into collision. Your friends at Warren, Carrsbrook & Monticello are all well. all feel the dreadful void which has been made among us by the late loss of our friend P. Carr. after those of his own house no one feels more indelible affliction from it than myself. I salute you, my dear Sir, with sincere esteem and respect.   TH: JEFFERSON

PoC (DLC); mutilated at seal; on verso of reused address cover of George Logan to TJ, 25 Mar. 1815; at foot of text: "John Hollins esq."; endorsed by TJ. Enclosures: (1) TJ to Elizabeth Patterson Bonaparte, 24 Apr. 1815, and enclosure. (2) TJ to Albert Gallatin, 24 Apr. 1815 (first letter).

From William P. Newby

DEAR SIR   Culpeper CtHouse 22nd April 15

It affords me grate pleasure to acknowledge the reciept of your lettar, I wish most earnestly that it was in my power to decide at this time whether it will be possible for me to engage in your business or not, Should you not hear from me by the 20th Augt it will be out of my power to Comply, my Farther died Some time in March and left me a very multiply,d estate to Settle there being Several very heavy Chancery Suits in which he was a party, and yet undetermin'd, I Should have answerd you before this, but the mortallity has been So greate in my family it really has never been in my power,

The prevelant Complaint is Still raging very much in this County, be assurd my anxiety is very greate to live with you, and Shall at all times consider my Self under many obligations to you for your attention to my Sitewation, be pleas,d to except my best wishes for your health & happiness,

I am dear Sir yours very Respectfully.   W^M P NEWBY

RC (DLC); endorsed by TJ as received 3 May 1815 and so recorded in SJL.

After the death of his father (FAR-THER), William Newby, the younger

Newby became a party in several SUITS, one of which was the *Administrators of Charles L. McTyre v. Administrators of William Newby* (Vi: Lancaster Co. Chancery Court Records, no. 1822-003).

To Benjamin Galloway

DEAR SIR   Monticello April 23. 15.

Your favor of the 9th did not come to hand until yesterday the very day on which you requested an answer might be lodged in Washington; add to this that our mail will not[1] depart until the 26th and the delay will be explained which necessarily attends your reciept of this. I have made an appointment to be in Bedford (90. miles Southward of this) the 1st or 2^d week of May, & shall hardly be returned till the 25th of that[2] month. I learn too that Col^o Monroe has been obliged to return to Washington by the serious illness of mrs Monroe, who was to come to Virginia with him. this circumstance will probably retard his return home, till my return from Bedford, and of course the pleasure of recieving here the visit with which you flatter us both. be assured that I shall take great pleasure in seeing you at Monticello, and in expressing to you vivâ voce my great esteem and respect.

TH: JEFFERSON

PoC (DLC); on verso of reused address cover to TJ; at foot of text: "Benjamin Galloway esq."; endorsed by TJ as a letter of 23 Mar. 1815 but recorded under its correct date in SJL.

[1] Preceding two words reworked from "will."

[2] Reworked from "this."

Receipt for Sale of Library

Recieved at the Treasury of the United States eight thousand five hundred and eighty Dollars, which with that of ten thousand five hundred Dollars ordered to be paid to William Short of Philadelphia, and four thousand eight hundred and seventy Dollars to John Barnes of George town will make up the full payment of the sum of twenty three thousand nine hundred and fifty Dollars appropriated by the act of Congress for the purchase of my library. Given under my hand this 23ᵈ day of April 1815.   TH: JEFFERSON

PoC (DLC); entirely in TJ's hand; with TJ's calculation at foot of text that the numbers in the receipt added up correctly. Dft (DLC: TJ Papers, 203:36233); written on a scrap; with subjoined Dft of enclosure to TJ to John Barnes, 18 Apr. 1815; on verso of Dft of TJ to Alexander J. Dallas, 18 Apr. 1815. Enclosed in TJ to Dallas, 18 Apr. 1815.

To Elizabeth Patterson Bonaparte

Monticello Apr.[1] 24. 15.

Your favor, Madam, of Mar. 23. from the usual difficulties of the roads in that season, was so long coming to me that there was no hope of an answer still finding you in America: a circumstance of the less importance as my power of being useful to you, in the way requested, falls so far short of my wishes to be so. the fact is that the persons of distinction with whom I had particular acquaintance while in France, and to whom it would have been a gratification to me, as well as yourself, to have made you known, were all swept off by the violences of the revolution, or have since been withdrawn from life by it's ordinary occurrences: for it is now 25. years since I left that country. my present correspondence there is merely with the literati, whose persons are mostly unknown to me, as having appeared on that theatre since I left it. under this inability to render you service I inclose you a letter to mr Gallatin, our minister there, merely as an evidence of what I would wish to do, could I do more; and I send it thro' the medium of your friends in Baltimore, as most likely to know where, and thro what channel it may reach you. you will have the goodness to accept it as the offering merely of my great respect and consideration   TH: JEFFERSON

RC (MdHi: Elizabeth Patterson Papers); addressed: "Mʳˢ Elizabeth Patterson recommended to the care of the Minister plenipotentiary of the United States of America at the Hague." PoC (DLC); on verso of reused address cover of Bonaparte to TJ, 25 Mar. 1815; endorsed by TJ. Enclosure: TJ to Albert Gallatin, 24 Apr. 1815 (second letter). Enclosed in TJ to John Hollins, 22 Apr. 1815.

Bonaparte's letter to TJ was dated 25 Mar. 1815, not MAR. 23.

[1] First letter reworked from "M."

To Joseph Delaplaine

SIR   Monticello Apr. 24. 15.

Occupations from which it was impossible to withdraw have occasioned the delay of acknoleging the receipt of your letter of Mar. 29. on the subject of my portrait in the hands of mr Stewart. I considered the delay as less important inasmuch as I could not avail my self of the opportunity you proposed of obtaining the portrait. I am unwilling to press mr Stewart unkindly to the delivery of it whenever his views respecting it are answered, I have no doubt he will attend to the justice of it's delivery to me. with my regrets therefore that I cannot procure you the use of it, accept the assurance of my esteem & respect.   TH: JEFFERSON

PoC (DLC); on verso of reused address cover to TJ; at foot of text: "Mr Delaplaine"; endorsed by TJ.

To Nicolas G. Dufief

DEAR SIR   Monticello April 24. 15.

Having occasion to make you a remittance in August last, I took the liberty of embodying with it certain sums which I owed to others in Philadelphia, and of asking the favor of you to pay them to the persons on their application. among these was a sum of 15.D. for the editor of the Aurora for 3. years of that paper. I have lately recieved his account by which it would seem either that he has not applied to you for the money, or has failed to give me credit for it. will you have the goodness to inform me on this subject?   in your catalogue of 1811. pages 9. 15. & 18. I see three books noted, which if still on hand I shall be glad to recieve.

Dictionnaire Espagnol et Français de Cormon. 2. v. 8vo
La Sagesse par Charron. 8vo
Correspondence de Fernand Cortez avec Charles V. 12mo

I shall be glad at the same time to recieve the state of my account the amount of which shall be remitted without delay. I salute you with great esteem and respect.   TH: JEFFERSON

P.S. in the same Catalogue pa. 32. I see Taylor's Demosthenes the edition of Cambridge Gr. Lat. 2. v. 8vo. is it still on hand? and what would be it's price?

PoC (DLC); on verso of reused address cover to TJ; adjacent to signature: "M. Dufief"; endorsed by TJ.

EDITOR William Duane's ACCOUNT appeared on an undated, printed form that listed the respective "Terms of Subscription" in one column, all payable in advance: the "Aurora, published daily" at $9, $5, and $3 for twelve, six, and three months; the "Country Aurora, published three times a week" at $5 and $3 for twelve and six months; and the "Weekly Aurora, published every Tuesday" at $3 and $2 for twelve and six months. It also announced the "Terms of Advertising" in a second column: 50 cents "per square each insertion in both City and Country papers"; 25 cents "per square each insertion after the first, in the City paper only"; and "All advertisements appear the first insertion in both papers." Beneath these columns a line indicated that TJ owed $15 for a "subscription to the Country Aurora, from 1 May 1812, to May 1815" (printed form in DLC: TJ Papers, 204:36296; undated; with blanks filled by an unidentified hand; endorsement by TJ [trimmed]: "[Newspapers?] Duane W^m"; with TJ's Notes on Newspaper Subscriptions, [ca. 23 Aug. 1817], on verso beneath endorsement).

On 26 Nov. 1811 Dufief sent TJ a CATALOGUE of books available at his bookstore.

To Albert Gallatin

DEAR SIR   Monticello Apr. 24. 15.

An American going to Paris considers you of course as his natural patron there; but still it is well you should know when worth presents itself, and is added to the claim of a fellow citizen on your good offices. the bearer mr William B. Buchanan is the son of James A. Buchanan esquire of Baltimore of great worth and respectability.[1] he embarks for Europe with Doct^r Eustis, and will continue some time in his family in Holland, after which he proposes to visit different parts of Europe and will take Paris in his tour. I am not personally acquainted with him but hear much good spoken of him by friends in whom I have confidence, and on whose authority I have no hesitation in recommending him to your notice while in Paris. I do it with the more pleasure as it furnishes me the occasion of renewing to you the assurances of my constant & affectionate esteem and respect.

TH: JEFFERSON

RC (NHi: Gallatin Papers); addressed: "His Excellency Albert Gallatin Min. Plenip^y of the United States at Paris favored by mr Buchanan"; endorsed by Gallatin. PoC (MHi); on verso of reused address cover to TJ; endorsed by TJ.

Recorded in SJL as to be carried "by Buchanan." Enclosed in TJ to John Hollins, 22 Apr. 1815.

[1] Manuscript: "respectabity."

To Albert Gallatin

Dear Sir   Monticello April 24. 15.

This letter will be handed you by mrs Patterson, daughter of mr Patterson of Baltimore, with whose high standing worth and patriotism you are well acquainted, and probably with his person. mrs Patterson, as a citizen of the United States, would naturally recieve your patronage and attentions, while at Paris; which with your knolege of her family would render unnecessary any recommendations of mine. the presenting her therefore to your civilities and good offices is merely an act of gratification to myself, as an acknolegement of my own high respect for herself & her family, and a desire to bear testimony to their worth on every occasion. and I avail my self of it with the greater pleasure as it gives me opportunity at the same time of repeating to you the assurances of my constant and affectionate esteem & respect.   Th: Jefferson

RC (NHi: Gallatin Papers); addressed: "His Excellency Albert Gallatin Minister Plenipotentiary of the United States at Paris. honored by mrs Patterson"; endorsed by Gallatin. PoC (DLC); on verso of reused address cover of John M. Carter to TJ, 27 Mar. 1815; endorsed by TJ. Recorded in SJL as to be carried "by mrs Patterson." Enclosed in TJ to John Hollins, 22 Apr. 1815, and TJ to Elizabeth Patterson Bonaparte, 24 Apr. 1815.

From John Barnes

Dear Sir—   George Town 25th April. 1815.

I had closed my letter of the 22d Saturdy (but not sealed it) when I was favrd with yours of the 18th Covering—Order on the Treasury of the U States, for, $4870. which I presented to Mr Shelden Yesterdy who asked of me—in what sums, I wished the Treasury Notes to be of,[1] in Order, that he might prepare the Warrant—to be drawn for them—they being of viz. 1000—100—and of $20—each. I prefer'd—viz.

4—of 1000 each is	$4000.	
8—of 100—do	800.	
3—of 20—do	60	
Bank Note for Residue	10	$4,870.

which in course of a day or two—when passed thro the several official[2] forms, will be ready for Receipting and delivery—in part of your $29,950.[3]—

The next question is, how to dispose of the $4,500. and $360—is

$4,860. on a/c of the good Gen[1] I purpose, to make, the Needfull inquiries—for the most eligable and Convenient Stock—for your Goverment, mean while—I am Anxious to secure a sett of exchange on London for £400 Ster[g] as I find to day, the Drawers are Unwilling to draw—at present, expecting a Rising market to the Eastward—at $2\frac{1}{2}$ ℔Ct above par, and Bills on Paris—at 3 and $3\frac{1}{2}$—you were perfectly Justified in disengaging your self from paying 8 ℔C[t] on so considerable a sum—which for these 6 Yrs passed Amo[t] to $2160—almost equal to a Moiety of the Principal:—for the Fractional part of the Int—being paid—Principal and Int. in the same M[o] (in conformity to Bank Usage) is not demandable,—

with great Esteem & Respect, Dear Sir—your most obed[t]

JOHN BARNES.

RC (ViU: TJP-ER); endorsed by TJ as received 3 May 1815 and so recorded in SJL. RC (DLC); address cover only; with PoC of TJ to James Madison, 15 June 1815, on verso; addressed: "Thomas Jefferson, Esquire, Monticello, Virginia"; franked; postmarked Georgetown, 26 Apr.

The GOOD GEN[L] was Tadeusz Kosciuszko. The ORDER ON THE TREASURY was presented to treasury clerk Daniel Shelden, who prepared WARRANT number 8585 for $4,870, dated 21 Apr., in partial payment for the purchase of TJ's

library (Alexander J. Dallas, *From the Secretary of the Treasury, accompanied With a Statement exhibiting the sums respectively paid to each clerk in the several offices attached to the Treasury Department, for Services Rendered in the Year 1814* [Washington, 1815], 2; *An Account of the Receipts and Expenditures of the United States. For the Year 1815* [Washington, 1816], 103).

[1] Manuscript: "off."
[2] Manuscript: "offical."
[3] The correct figure was $23,950.

To Joseph Coppinger

SIR   Monticello Apr. 25. 15.

I have to acknolege the reciept of your favor of the 6th. I have no doubt, either in a moral or economical view, of the desirableness to introduce a taste for malt liquors instead of that for ardent spirits. the difficulty is in changing the public taste & habit. the business of brewing is now so much introduced in every state, that it appears to me to need no other encouragement than to increase the number of consumers. I do not think it a case where a company need form itself on patriotic principles meerly, because there is a sufficiency of private capital which would embark itself in the business if there were a demand. but as to my self particularly I am too old & too fond of quiet to engage in new & distant undertakings. I am lately become a brewer for family use, having had the benefit of instruction to one of my people by an English brewer of the first order. I had noted the advertisement of your book in which the process of malting corn was promised & had engaged a bookseller to send it to me as soon as it should come out. we tried it here the last fall with perfect success, and I shall use it principally hereafter. during the revolutionary war, the brewers on James river used Indian corn almost exclusively of all other. in my family brewing I have used whea[t] also[1] as we do not raise barley. I shall still desire my bookseller to send me on your book when printed. Accept the assurance of my respect and best wishes for the extension of the use of malt liquors.　　　　Th: Jefferson

PoC (DLC); edge trimmed; at foot of text: "Mr Joseph Coppinger"; endorsed by TJ.

Joseph Miller was the BREWER who instructed TJ's slave Peter Hemmings in that art (TJ to William D. Meriwether, 17 Sept. 1813; TJ to Andrew Moore, 2 Oct. 1813; Miller to TJ, 1 Sept. 1815; Stanley Baron, *Brewed in America: A History of Beer and Ale in the United States* [1962], 137–43).

[1] Word added in margin.

To William W. Hening

Dear Sir　　　　　　　　　　　Monticello Apr. 25. 15.

Your favor of the 15th never came to hand till yesterday. you may be assured that the MS. **A.** is not here. every book in the library has past twice thro' my own hands, and twice more thro' the hands of the numberer and packer, and we all are confident this is not among them. it is exactly the one described in the 1st vol. of your statutes pa. 121.

With respect to the MS. **D.** your information gives me great joy, inasmuch as it's existence is established. I was wrong in saying it was sent with the others, and you are right in saying you recieved it from mr Randolph. the history of it is this. mr Randolph contemplating the writing a history of Virginia, borrowed all the MSS. from my library while I was in France. when he was to go on to[1] reside with the General govmt as Atty Gen. he sent his books (and these MS. with them) to N. York. on sending them back from there to Philadelphia the box containing these MS. was found missing, & no enquiry could discover what was become of them. he communicated it to me, and we both considered them as lost. but some 2. or 3. years afterwards, on removing a pile of hides in the warehouse where his books had been stored this box was found & sent to him. he returned to me the MSS. but on comparing those he sent me with my catalogue, one was missing, & exactly the one I had always deemed the most valuable as comprehending the greatest number of the laws. I have long believed & deplored the loss of this volume. but the MS. **D**. is the very one, was overlooked by mr Randolph when he returned me the others; and I have no doubt you recieved it from him. it escaped my memory, when I wrote you my last letter that this was the very volume which had never been returned to me, and whi[ch] I therefore imagined without sufficient reflection, I had sent you with the rest. I shall be happy therefore to recieve, and replace it with it's companions. Accept the assurance of my esteem & respect.   TH: JEFFERSON

PoC (DLC); edge trimmed; on verso of reused address cover to TJ; at foot of text: "Mr Hening"; endorsed by TJ.

Joseph Milligan was the PACKER.

Hening, 1:121, DESCRIBED the Virginia statutes of 5 Mar. 1624 (Sowerby, no. 1822), indicating that his edition was based on the handwritten copy in TJ's possession and quoting TJ's endorsement: "This was found among the manuscript papers of Sir John Randolph, and by the Honorable Peyton Randolph, Esqr. his son, was given to Thomas Jefferson." The missing manuscript **A** was recovered in 1820 and sent to the Li-brary of Congress (TJ to George Watterston, 1 Sept. 1820; TJ to Hening, 3 Sept. 1820).

In the spring of 1792 Edmund Randolph COMMUNICATED to TJ that the box holding manuscripts borrowed from TJ had not been found in the New York City warehouse where it had been stored (*PTJ*, 23:295, 27:817). TJ never did RE-CIEVE manuscript **D** (Sowerby, no. 1825) because Hening sent it directly to the Library of Congress by 1820 (Hening to TJ, 23 Sept. 1816, 19 Aug. 1820; TJ to Hening, 12 Oct. 1816).

¹ TJ here canceled "Phila."

From Thomas T. Tucker

TREASURY OF THE UNITED STATES,
SIR,   Washington, *April 25th 1815*

ENCLOSED you will find my draft No. *280*, on *Thos Nelson, C^r of Ls*—for, Dollars, *8.580*—the amount of warrant No. *95*—issued by the Secretary of *the Treasury*—on receipt whereof be pleased to favor me with an early acknowledgment, specifying the sum received, *in Treasury Notes—*

With *great respect*,¹ I am, Sir, Your obedient servant,
                                        TH: T. TUCKER
                                        Treasurer of the United States.

RC (DLC); printed form, with blanks filled in by a United States Treasury Department clerk, signed by Tucker; hand-written material presented above in italics; at foot of text in a clerk's hand: "Thomas Jefferson Esq"; endorsed by TJ as received 28 Apr. 1815. Enclosure: draft no. 280 on United States Treasury, Washington, 25 Apr. 1815, ordering that, pursuant to Treasury warrant no. 95, Nelson, commissioner of loans in Richmond, should "AT sight pay to *Thomas Jefferson Esq—Monticello—*or order, *Eight thousand five hundred & eighty—*Dollars, IN TREASURY NOTES, value received" (MS in DNA: RG 217, MTA; printed form, with blanks filled in by a Treasury clerk, signed by Tucker; handwritten material presented in italics; endorsement on verso, mutilated at seal, in James Ligon's hand except for signature by TJ: "Pay to Ja[mes Li]gon or order Th: Jefferson [Re]ceived payment 6 May 1815 James Ligon").

Thomas Tudor Tucker (1745–1828), physician and public official, was born and raised in Bermuda. He received a medical degree from the University of Edinburgh in 1770, and by 1771 he was practicing medicine in Charleston, South Carolina. Tucker served as a hospital physician and surgeon in the Continental army. In 1789 he helped found the South Carolina Medical Society. By 1799 Tucker owned thirty-one slaves and almost eight thousand acres of land in the Camden, Charleston, and Ninety-Six districts. He served in the South Carolina House of Representatives, 1782 and 1785–87, represented his state in the Confederation Congress, 1787–88, and was a strongly Republican supporter of states' rights in the United States House of Representatives, 1789–93. TJ appointed him United States treasurer in 1801, and Tucker held the position until his death (*BDSCHR*, 3:725–6; *First Federal Congress*, 14:857–63; Heitman, *Continental Army*, 550; *PTJ*, 35:530–1, 606; *JEP*, 1:400, 405 [6, 26 Jan. 1802]; Washington *Daily National Intelligencer*, 3 May 1828).

¹ Preceding two words interlined by Tucker in place of the printed words "due consideration."

To William Wingate

Sir   Monticello Apr. 25. 15.

I return you the volume you were pleased to send for my perusal. the piety and patriotism of your views merit high commendation, and I am sensible of the honor of your proposition that I should undertake a cooperation in them with you. but I am now too old to embark in new enterprizes, and particularly to undertake a journey to Washington to communicate it to the Senators. recommending therefore your associating some younger co-adjutor I beg you to accept my best wishes for your success in the endeavor to harmonize & conciliate our political schisms.   Th: Jefferson

PoC (MoSHi: TJC-BC); on verso of reused address cover to TJ; at foot of text: "Mʳ Wᵐ Wingate"; endorsed by TJ. Enclosure not found.

To John M. Carter

Monticello Apr. 26. 15.

Th: Jefferson presents his compliments to mr Carter and his thanks for the copy of Arator which he has been so kind as to send him. we are indebted to Col° Taylor for a great deal of valuable information given us in that volume on the subject of Agriculture; and whether we consider the question of slavery as a political or religious one, all differences of opinion are entitled to toleration, and he is confident of it's being fully & mutually indulged between Col° Taylor & himself.

PoC (DLC); on verso of reused address cover to TJ; dateline at foot of text; endorsed by TJ.

From James Monroe

DEAR SIR   washington april 26. 1815.

I expected to have had the pleasure of seeing you, more than a month past, and to have deliver'd to you the enclosed letters on finance in person, with a paper on the same subject, which was written in our revolution by the President & given to me for perusal, with a request that I would forward it to you for the same purpose. The ill health of Mrs Monroe, and more recently of our daughter, have detaind me here, and will do it a week or ten days longer. Prior to their indisposition I had suffer'd much from a very severe attack of the sciatick, or rather of the prevailing epidemick which seized on the weaker parts of the system. From this, I soon recoverd, so far as to attend to business, but have not yet regaind my strength, and am affected by cold & sometimes fever on the slightest exposure. ashamd at having so long retaind your letters, and uncertain when I may be able to present them myself, I forward them by the mail. I send also a copy of a report which I made, from the dept of war, on the causes of the differences between this govt & those of some Eastern States, relative to the power of the former over the militia. The letters of those govrs and the time & circumstances under which they were written, prove satisfactorily their object. Arrangments had been made, had the war continued, to organize a force in that quarter, which, had they succeeded, would have render'd the treasonable designs of these men abortive, of which I will give you a detail when we meet. Happily the peace has relievd the nation from all embarrassment on that, and very many other causes, that weighed heavily on the government. I hope you have considerd it, under all circumstances, an honorable one to the nation. If I can obtain a copy I will send it to you, of my report to the military committees, on the reduction of the army necessary to accomodate it to the peace establishment. Our friends pushed it beyond the limit which I proposed. By the last, two major Gen^ls, & 4. Brig^rs are to be retaind. Brown & Jackson were supposed, by service, to have the strongest claim to the first grade, and Scott, Gaines, McComb, & Ripley, to the second. This will discharge many having claims by long, in some instances very meritorious services, as well as, by age, & poverty. Employment will be given where it can, to these officers, in other lines, but I fear many will remain distressd and discontented.

In regard to our foreign affairs much is to be done. we have treaties with none, and not much kindness to be expected from any. The war, by the gallantry of our land & naval forces, has given us credit, and that may aid us in future arrangments, tho' in some quarters it will produce a different effect. on these subjects we will confer more fully when we meet.

I am dear Sir with great respect & esteem your friend & servant

JA^s MONROE

RC (DLC); endorsed by TJ as received 28 Apr. 1815. Enclosures: (1) TJ to John Wayles Eppes, 24 June, 11 Sept., 6 Nov. 1813. (2) TJ to Joseph C. Cabell, 17 Jan., 23 Sept. 1814. (3) James Madison, "Money," an essay written between Sept. 1779 and Mar. 1780, arguing that, contrary to popular opinion, "If the circulating medium be of universal value as specie, a local increase or decrease of its quantity, will not, whilst a communication subsists with other countries, produce a correspondent rise or fall in its value"; that paper money payable in specie on demand is superior to that payable at some future date, which depreciates; that "distrust of public credit" also leads to depreciation and has been "erroneously imputed to the quantity of money"; that neither monopolies, nor "misconduct in the purchasing departments," nor a "deficiency of imported commodities" affect the value of money; that from the previous principles, it can be concluded that "a loan-office certificate differs in nothing from a common bill of credit, except in its higher denomination, and in the interest allowed on it"; and thus that issuing such certificates yields no benefit and removes redemption to "a more distant day" (printed in the Philadelphia *National Gazette*, 19, 22 Dec. 1791; repr. in *Madison, Papers, Congress. Ser.*, 1:302–10). (4) Report by Monroe as secretary of war to William B. Giles, chair of the United States Senate's Committee on Military Affairs, on the relative powers of the federal and state governments over the militia, 11 Feb. 1815, suggesting that recent challenges by several state governors to the president's power to call out state militias and assign regular army officers to command them is "repugnant" to the principles of the United States Constitution and of "dangerous tendency"; that the "power which is thus given to Congress by the people of the United States, to provide for calling forth the milita, for purposes specified in the constitution, is unconditional"; that it was the "intention of the framers of the constitution, that these powers, vested in the General Government, should be independent of the States' authorities"; that Congress has the power to call forth the militia to "execute the laws of the Union," suppress insurrection, and "repel invasions"; that restraining the government's power over the militia would "force the United States to resort to standing armies for all national purposes"; that state authority over the militia ceases when it is called into national service; that "nothing in the constitution" requires the president to command the militia in person, as some governors have claimed; and that the president has the authority to appoint officers and organize the army into appropriate miltiary units; with appended letters from the governors of Massachusetts, Connecticut, Rhode Island, and New Jersey: Caleb Strong, John C. Smith, William Jones, and William Pennington, respectively (*ASP, Military Affairs*, 1:604–23).

Monroe submitted more than one report on the REDUCTION of the military through Giles to the Senate military affairs committee (Monroe to Giles, 22, 24 Feb. 1815 [DNA: RG 46, Senate Records, 13th Cong., 3d sess.]; the first is printed in Stanislaus Murray Hamilton, ed., *The Writings of James Monroe* [1898–1903], 5:321–7). Congress established the LIMIT of TWO MAJOR GEN^{LS} and four brigadier generals in a 3 Mar. 1815 "Act fixing the military peace establishment of the United States" (*U.S. Statutes at Large*, 3:224–5).

From George Watterston

SIR, City of Washington Ap^l 26th 1815.

You will excuse the liberty I take, as a stranger, in trespassing on your attention—The President has been pleased to appoint me Librarian to Congress. & consiquently superintendent of the books now in your possession. I am solicitous to obtain your opinion, as a gentleman of literary taste, on the subject of arrangement—Your long acquaintance with books & your literary habits have, doubtless, led you to the adoption of some plan of arrangement with respect to libraries, which I should be happy, if you would communicate—If you think the plan you have followed in the arrangement of the present library be the most judicious, you would oblige me, by having the books packed up in boxes, according to that arrangement I have long thought the arrangement of the old library was incorrect & injudicious—& must therefore, be avoided in the present which is considerably larger, & I presume much more select & valuable.

You would oblige me, by advising me, when you think the books will reach this place—I am preparing a room for their reception which I think will be completed in the course of a month—You will not neglect to forward a catalogue—if you have a spare copy as I wish to have it printed as early as possible. I fear the room selected is not quite large enough to contain the books—if so, I will have some artificial stands erected to receive them—

I have the honor to be very respectfully, Sir, Yr ob^t serv^t

GEO, WATTERSTON

RC (DLC); at foot of text: "Thos Jefferson Esq^e"; endorsed by TJ as received 3 May 1815 and so recorded in SJL.

George Watterston (1783–1854), author, journalist, and librarian of Congress, was born to Scottish immigrants on a ship at New York City. His family moved in 1791 to Washington, D.C. Watterston studied law after completing his studies at Charlotte Hall School, Saint Mary's County, Maryland. By 1808 he had set up practice in Hagerstown, Maryland. He soon published *The Lawyer, or Man as he ought not to be* (Pittsburgh, 1808), the first of his many novels, poems, newspaper articles, and nonfiction works. By 1811 Watterston had settled in Washington, and in 1814 he was the editor of the *Washington City Gazette*, a Republican newspaper. James Madison appointed him librarian of Congress in 1815, a position he held until Andrew Jackson dismissed him in 1829. Watterston was also a founder and longtime secretary of the Washington National Monument

Society, which was responsible for the initial phase of construction of the obelisk in the nation's capital dedicated to George Washington (*ANB*; *DAB*; William Matheson, "George Watterston: Advocate of the National Library," *Quarterly Journal of the Library of Congress* 32 [1975]: 370–88; Brigham, *American Newspapers*, 1:99; William Dawson Johnston, *History of the Library of Congress* [1904], 1:107–19, 189; Watterston to Madison, 25 Mar. 1815 [DLC: Madison Papers]; Rudolph De Zapp, *The Washington Monument* [1900], 7–8, 28; Washington *Daily National Intelligencer*, 6, 7 Feb. 1854).

Watterston was PREPARING A ROOM under the provisions of a 3 Mar. 1815 "Act to provide a library room, and for transporting the library lately purchased." The room was located in the post office building (formerly Blodget's Hotel) on the corner of Seventh and E Streets N.W., which served as the temporary home of Congress (*U.S. Statutes at Large*, 3:225–6; *ASP, Miscellaneous*, 2:279–80; Johnston, *Library of Congress*, 1:120–1).

From Caspar Wistar

MY DEAR SIR,   Philadelphia April 27–1815—

If I were not Conscious of the fact I should not think it possible to defer[1] long any thing which is So gratifying in itself as writing to you. Among many inducements to write there is one of great force, to thank you for ye many demonstrations of kindness which you have exhibited, & especially for the last, when you Retired from the Chair of our Society. I have allways Regarded the Circumstance which procured for me the honour of your acquaintance as one of the most happy events of my life & most ardently wish that the evening of your time may be as long and Serene as the noon day of it has been useful & brilliant. In your last letter you inquire respecting the mode of education followed in the University of Pennsylvania—There are but three Professors now in the Institution. One (the President) teaches Moral Philosophy, the operations of the human mind, & the various Subjects naturally Connected with these. Another has charge of the department of Physicks & Mathematics & the auxiliary branches[.] The third is the Professor of Languages & is principally occupied with teaching latin and greek—Our Institution has allways appeared more interesting to me for what it has attempted unsuccessfully, than for what it has performed.

An attempt was made in it to open the Schools of Science to Students who were only acquainted with their mother tongue. As there are many young men destined to Commercial and mechanical pursuits that Spend three or four years at School, to acquire useful knowledge, & learn nothing there but the languages, which they forget in less time than was necessary to acquire them. It was thought right to[2] make an attempt of this kind, but it was not successful. We had nearly lost by it the Study of the languages, without adding any thing to the knowledge of the English Scholars. While this attempt was making D[r] Franklin Returned from Europe & resumed his Seat among the Trustees of the University—He immediately declared in favour of the plan, & Said he had Several times before Engaged in Similar Schemes in New-Jersey & in Pennsylvania; but[3] Schools for the latin & greek languages were Connected with the establishments, & swallowed up all the other parts of the plan, in Consequence of the prejudices of the different parties concerned in favour of these languages. He thought that the treasures which were once locked up in these languages might now be obtained without them & one of the last instances of his pleasant mode of elucidation was exhibited on this occasion—He Compared the dead languages to the Chapeaux Bras of persons of high fashion which were Retained &[4] Carried about, when[5] heads were dressed in Such a way, that they Could not be Covered by hats. M[r] Hill who was Seated next to him had buttons on the cuffs of his coat Sleves. These buttons Said Franklin are "like the dead languages; I remember when the Cuffs were drawn over the hands to keep them warm when we went into the cold. Buttons were then necessary, to keep the cuffs in their places when they were turned back, while people were within door[s] but although Cuffs are fixed back permanently at the present time, you retain the buttons."

The subject was very Seriously discussed among the Trustees at large—One Gentleman observed that a man Could not be Completely acquainted with his own language without Studying another, that the latin language did not arrive at its perfection until the Romans Studied the greek—Another Gentleman Enquired of him what language was Studied by the Greeks—No answer was given to this—

An arrangement was made for trying the experiment, but the persons who were to act in it were all averse to the scheme; & the result was this the dead languages were studied negligently, & nothing better or Equally good was Substituted in their room—We have hardly recovered from the effects of this Speculation. It is however Certain that a large number of the young people who are occupied from 13 to 17 years of age with the languages & then enter into Compting Houses or engage in Similar pursuits forget very Soon what they have learned. Ought not Such persons to apply this time in question to learning Arithmetic Compleatly & extensively; Mathematics to a Certain extent—Physicks or Nat^l Phylosophy in the Same way—Natural History, Chemistry Geography & History—   I have heard that Some gentlemen have urged you to take up the investigation of Certain Subjects intimately Connected with the welfare of our Country—May I also offer a petition in favour of that portion of our young Country men who are destined to Commercial, Agricultural & Mechanical pursuits, & will not have leisure to Study after they leave their Schools or Colleges. I believe the subject was not sufficiently Studied by the Gentlemen who engaged in it here—In our Magazine for this month is a paper on University Education, which is So applicable to the present Subject that I Send it to you—It is evidently the production of Mr Thos Cooper who is unquestionably a man of most uncommon attainments—

At the Same time I beg leave to Send an Elementary Work on Anatomy in which I have been engaged a long time. In addition to the opportunity of expressing my regard, my particular object in begging your acceptance of it was to exhibit to you the Cause of my deferring so long the examination of the[6] bones which you sent to the Society. I cannot recommend to your perusal any part of the work[7] but the account of experiments on decapitated animals, in Vol: 2^d page. 80

In a short time I hope to Send you an account of two very Curious heads which I Selected from your Collection at Washington—One of them which is as large as the head of a Small Cow, & Resembles it very strongly at first view; when accurately examined, will be found to be more nearly allied to the Sheep & Goat—A Sheep or Goat of that Size must have been a very interesting animal, & if we Can procure a good engraving, it will interest the Scavans of Europe.

These Specimens did not escape the Sagacity of your friend Geo: Rogers Clarke. When I inquired of Wm Clarke where he had found them he observed that his brother George had been very attentive to them, & Said they were more like ye Deer & Sheep than the Cow—

The greatest desideratum for the history of the Sceleton of the Mammoth is the Cranium. This part has been found[8] so much decayed that it Could not be examined, in all the heads which I have heard of, except two—One of them was at Manscoes lick near Nashville in Tenessee, & was broken to pieces before they were aware of its existence. The other has lately been described to me by Dr Leander Sharp who lives in the South west part of Kentucky. He assures me that he Saw it about three years ago near Green River, in the Same part of the State; & that the whole head, of which it was a part, was intire. I assure you that I omitted nothing which I expected would excite Dr Sharp to attend to it. He promised to go, or Send, to the Gentleman who owned it, & to procure it for me—I have not yet heard from him, & begin to feel uneasy on that account. As I am not afraid of tiring you with this Subject I will mention that there Seems reason to believe that in Some of the Mammoths there were two Small tusks about an inch in diameter which projected forward from the Chin, or front part of the lower Jaw, of the Animal. I have been in possession for many years of a fragment of a lower Jaw in which there were Sockets for tusks of this kind—In your Collection there was a fragment of a Small tusk which Corresponded in Size to Such a Socket, upon exhibiting them to Genl Clarke I found he was acquainted with the Circumstance, & had Seen Such tusks in the Jaw, in their natural Situation.

I have within a few days been engaged in an attempt to make arrangements for procuring Sceletons of the Bear, Buffaloe Panther &^{ca} from the western Country; if I can effect this it will be a good beginning of a Museum of Comparative Anatomy—

I cannot Conclude this miscellaneous letter without attaching to it an expostulation with Col: Randolph on the subject of his passing through Philadelphia without making himself known to his friends in this place—I felt Sincere regard for him when he was a boy at Edinburgh, & upon this have been engrafted very grateful feelings for the kindness which he as well as the Rest of your family extended to my Sister. It would therefore have been a great gratification to me to

have Seen him—Please to assure his Son Jefferson of my kind remembrance & believe that my best wishes will ever attend you my
Dear Sir   C. WISTAR—

Ap^l 29th 10–a.m.

The extraordinary news from France is confirmed—It is said that
the Soldiers deserted the Generals who adhered to the Bourbons, &
joined Buonaparte in his march to Paris—A News Paper (the Moniteur) of the 23^d of March is Said to be received—

RC (DLC); edges chipped and trimmed; postscript on verso of address cover; addressed: "The Honble Thos Jefferson Monticello near Charlottesville Virginia"; franked; postmarked Philadelphia, 28 Apr.; endorsed by TJ as received 3 May 1815 and so recorded in SJL. Enclosures: (1) Port Folio, 3d ser., 5 (Apr. 1815), containing Thomas Cooper to TJ, 15 Sept. 1814. (2) Wistar, A System of Anatomy for the Use of Students of Medicine, 2 vols. (Philadelphia, 1811–14; Poor, Jefferson's Library, 5 [no. 179]).

TJ had inquired about the MODE OF EDUCATION at the University of Pennsylvania in his letter to Wistar of 25 Aug. 1814. The THREE PROFESSORS at that institution were Frederick Beasley, provost and professor of moral philosophy, 1813–28; Robert M. Patterson, who held the chair of natural philosophy and mathematics, 1814–28; and James G. Thomson, professor of Greek and Latin languages, 1802–28. Benjamin FRANKLIN returned from France in 1785, and he served as president of the board of trustees of the University of the State of Pennsylvania, 1789–90. Wistar was also a trustee, 1789–91 (University of Pennsylvania: Biographical Catalogue of the Matriculates of the College, 1749–1893 [1894], xii, xvii, xix, xxi). Franklin published SCHEMES for permitting students to avoid the study of Greek and Latin as early as 1749 and 1751 (Leonard W.

Labaree and others, eds., The Papers of Benjamin Franklin [1959–], 3:395–421, 4:101–8).

Small, three-cornered hats that could be carried under the arm, CHAPEAUX BRAS, were worn by gentlemen at court or in full dress (OED). In 1808 Wistar selected BONES from TJ's collection of fossils for presentation to the American Philosophical Society (TJ to Wistar, 24 Apr. 1808 [DLC]; TJ to Francis Adrian Van der Kemp, 17 Jan. 1813). SCAVANS (sçavants): savants (OED). Meriwether Lewis and William Clark obtained fossil SPECIMENS in 1803 for TJ from Big Bone Lick in Kentucky during their journey to the Pacific Northwest. They were lost in transit, but Clark acquired more for TJ on a separate trip to this fossil site in 1807 (Stein, Worlds, 400–3). Wistar's SISTER was Catharine Wistar Bache.

[1] Wistar here canceled "So."
[2] Wistar here canceled "arrange this mode of Education So that more English Students might attend the Schools."
[3] Wistar here canceled "they all failed in Consequence of the."
[4] Preceding two words interlined.
[5] Wistar here canceled "they Could no longer."
[6] Wistar here canceled "big bones from."
[7] Preceding three words interlined.
[8] Wistar here canceled "So much decayed as to be unfit."

From Thomas Branagan

DEAR SIR   Philad^a April 28: 1815

I take the Liberty to Solicit your Signature to this patriotic Work. Should you Condescend to Grant this humble request you Can Send this paper back by Post with your distinguished Signature to the proposal & I will endevour to forward you a handsome Copy by the first oppertunity from your Warm admirer & Sincre Well Wisher—

THO BRANAGAN
163 Green St Philad^a
auther of "Preliminary Essay"
& 16 Subsequent Works

☞ I open the letter to Suggest a thought that Strikes My Mind viz. Our ALMIGHTY benefactor has been Showering down upon you for near $\frac{3}{4}$ of a Century his choicest blessings. He has endowed you with a Capacious & comprehensive mind He has given you 10 Talants for to improve O My much Esteemed Sir prove gratefull for these distingushed favours improve these Shining talants. You & I See clearly that Slavery is now the bane & will hereafter be the destruction of our beloved country do therefore before you die address your Country men on this momentious Subject first liberating your own Slaves & your rewards will be Sure & great[1]

About 9 Year ago I Sent you my "penitential[2] Tyrant" Since Which I have often repented the liberty I took & I hope the above remark Will not offend you It comes from a heart that reverences you

RC (DLC: Printed Ephemera Collection); postscript on address cover; addressed: "The Hon Tho Jefferson Late president of the US Montecello"; franked; postmarked Philadelphia, 3 May; endorsed by TJ as a letter of 25 Apr. 1815 received 11 May 1815 and so recorded in SJL. Enclosure: prospectus and subscription list for publication by T. Boyle, of New York City, William Reynolds, of Philadelphia, and J. Campbell, of Baltimore, of *The pride of Britannia humbled; Or the Queen of the Ocean Unqueen'd*, indicating that the publication will include four letters from William Cobbett to Robert Banks Jenkinson, 2d Earl of Liverpool, on the War of 1812; that to this will be added a summary of American land and naval victories and a "persuasive to political moderation"; that the work is especially directed to "persons composing the two great parties in the United States, in general, and to the politicians of Connecticut and Massachusetts, in particular"; that it is intended to promote national prosperity, reduce "party rancour and political intolerance," inspire "an ardent love of virtue, liberty, and independence, and detestation of monarchy and aristocracy," and encourage gratitude toward God, the nation's "legitimate sovereign," to whose care the "honourable peace" can be attributed; and stating that the proposed publication will contain between two and three hundred duodecimo pages, "printed on good paper, and handsomely bound in boards," at a cost of $87\frac{1}{2}$ cents, with a free copy for anyone obtaining six subscriptions (undated broadside conjoined with RC of covering letter; with unused blanks at foot for subscribers' names, addresses, and number of copies ordered). The above publishers printed two editions of *The Pride of Britannia Humbled* in 1815 with no listed author.

Thomas Branagan (1774–1843), author and abolitionist, was born in Dublin. As a young man he worked in the African slave trade and then as overseer of a sugar plantation in Antigua. After experiencing a religious conversion and developing an abhorrence to slavery, Branagan immigrated to the United States about 1798 and settled in Philadelphia. Drawing on his own experience he published, in both prose and verse, some twenty-five antislavery and religious works between 1804 and 1839. In his latter years he became a watchman. Branagan sent some of his books to TJ, including his first publication, *A Preliminary Essay, on the Oppression of the Exiled Sons of Africa* (Philadelphia, 1804; Sowerby, no. 1394). Because of the politically sensitive themes of

Branagan's writings, TJ never replied to his letters, although in 1805 he asked George Logan to explain his silence verbally to Branagan. Nonetheless, Branagan claimed in 1839 that TJ had been his "most generous patron" (autobiographical front matter in Branagan, *The Penitential Tyrant* [Philadelphia, 1805; Sowerby, no. 4516], vii–xxxvii, and *The Guardian Genius of the Federal Union* [1839], 2–24, esp. 20; Lewis Leary, "Thomas Branagan: Republican Rhetoric and Romanticism in America," *PMHB* 77 [1953]: 332–52; Branagan to TJ, 7 May, 17 Nov. 1805, 27 Apr. 1806, and TJ to Logan, 11 May 1805 [all DLC]; Philadelphia city directories, 1809–33; *A. M'Elroy's Philadelphia Directory for 1837* [1837], 22; DNA: RG 29, CS, Pa., Philadelphia, 1840; Sowerby, nos. 1395, 4515; Poor, *Jefferson's Library*, 9 [no. 528]).

The biblical parable of the talents (TALANTS) is in Matthew 25.14–30.

[1] Preceding nine words interlined.
[2] Manuscript: "penilential."

From Alexander J. Dallas

SIR. Treasury Department 28 April 1815

I have the honor to acknowledge the receipt of your letter, dated the 18: instant, and to inform you, that measures were immediately[1] taken to comply with your request. Your draft in favor of M[r] Barnes has been paid. M[r] Short has been informed, that the draft in his favor will be paid, as soon as it is presented here. The Treasury Notes, to be paid on your own account, have been ordered to be sent, as soon as they can be signed at Philadelphia, to the Loan Officer at Richmond, who is instructed to forward them to you.

I have the honor to be, very respectfully, Sir, Y[r] mo. obed Serv

A. J. DALLAS.

RC (DLC); at foot of text: "Thomas Jefferson Esq."; endorsed by TJ as received 3 May 1815 from Washington and so recorded in SJL.

Thomas Nelson was the federal LOAN commissioner at Richmond.

[1] Manuscript: "imdiately."

From George P. Stevenson

DEAR SIR   Baltimore April 28ᵗʰ 1815—

Beleiving it may be pleasing to you to learn the passing events of the world, I take the liberty to subjoin copy of a letter received this morning by Express from my partner in New York—Wonders will never cease—; farther particulars may be expected tomorrow when I will forward them to you—

"New York April 26ᵗʰ 6 O.Clock P:M: I hasten to advise you for the information of our friends that the schooner Sîne-qua-non has just arrived here in 25 days from La Rochelle bringing the following important and wonderful tidings—

Buonaparte landed with 600 men at Frejus the last of February, was joined by Berthier with 20,000 men, & entered Paris on the 20ᵗʰ March at the head of 80,000 men.—Louis and his family had gone to England—. Buonaparte had issued his proclamation announcing his reascending the throne of France, & had order,d the sequestration of all British Property.—The captain of the Sîne-qua-non says that the tri-colored flag had been flying ten days at La Rochelle.—The schooner has brought Paris-papers detailing the wondrous story, & giving the names of the different Functionaries appointed by the Emperor, amongst the most conspicuous of whom are his old friends Bassano & Soult.

This no matter how strange and how unaccountable is nevertheless true"—

The world will probably undergo some material change upon this grand & sudden event—and I am much in hopes our late enemy may be the sufferer in the end—

With best respects to those around you, in which mʳˢ S— joins me—

I have the honor to be Yʳ Obed Servᵗ   GEO: P: STEVENSON

RC (DLC); endorsed by TJ. RC (MHi); address cover only; with PoC of TJ to Joel Yancey, 7 June 1815, on verso; addressed: "Thomas Jefferson Esqʳᵉ Monticello near Milton Vᵃ"; franked; postmarked Baltimore, 28 Apr. Recorded in SJL as received 3 May 1815.

Stevenson's PARTNER was his brother-in-law Thomas P. Goodwin (*New-York Evening Post*, 5 Nov. 1816; "The Goodwins of Baltimore, Maryland," *WMQ*, 1st ser., 8 [1899]: 110–1). The INFORMATION in Goodwin's letter came from Captain Pond of the *Sine Qua Non* and from the Paris *Moniteur*. The New York *National Advocate*, 27 Apr. 1815, quoted both sources.

From Joseph Dougherty

DEAR SIR   Washington City Ap^l 29th 1814 [1815]

I will Set out from here on Tuesday[1] next for monticello: on friday next I expects to arive there.[2] I depend altogether on getting waggons in your Neighbourhood witth the exception of one which I shall take from here.

It is probable that ere this reaches you—you will have heard of Bonapartes, having mounted the Throne of France on the 20th of March last—The account comes verry straight—and brings every appearance of truth with it.

I am Sir your Humble Servt   JOS. DOUGHERTY

RC (DLC: TJ Papers, 201:35752); misdated; at foot of text: "Mr Thos Jefferson"; endorsed by TJ as a letter of 29 Apr. 1815 received 3 May 1815 and so recorded in SJL.

[1] "Tusday" interlined in place of "monday."
[2] Manuscript: "ther."

From James Maury

MY DEAR SIR,   Liverpool 29th April 1815

I now resume the conveyance of public information to you in the old way, and will, from time to time, have that pleasure.

The peace appears to have given in the United States a more general satisfaction than in this country; where indeed it, at first, was by no means palatable to many; but now is, I believe, universally welcome: and I cannot help confidently hoping that, even should this country be again involved in war with France, the peace with the U.S.A. will not be disturbed, for I am strongly under the impression that the provocations which occasioned the late rupture will not be repeated.

The return of intercource has not yet introduced into this port as many cargoes of our produce as it was generally expected would have been before this time: those however which are arrived meet a good market. Tob°, for example, now is selling from 6^d a 21^d ℔ ℔. The Stocks of this article Cotton & some others had been nearly exhausted.

I have lately heard of the benefit you experience from a singular practice, I am told, you have of putting your legs into cold water every morning. Is it so? I have lately resumed a practice, perhaps as singular for the 70th year: namely plunging into a cold bath thrice a week during the whole winter: to which I attribute my having been freer of cold than during any one of the preceding twenty eight winters that I have been in this place.

Accept the sincere good wishes of
Your old obliged friend   JAMES MAURY

RC (DLC); at foot of text: "Thomas Jefferson &C &C Monticello"; endorsed by TJ as received 14 June 1815 and so recorded in SJL. Enclosures not found.

From George Divers

D^R SIR   Farmington 30th April 1815

We returnd home yesterday from a visit of several days and I did not examine into the state of our peas til late in the evening, when I found them quite ready, they have Suffer'd so much from the drought that they will last but a few days, we should be glad you will come up and partake of our first dish today & that Mr Maddison would come with you, with sincere respect

I am yr. friend & Servt   GEORGE DIVERS

RC (MHi); endorsed by TJ as received 30 Apr. 1815 and so recorded in SJL.

To David Barrow

SIR   Monticello May 1. 15.

I have duly recieved your favor of Mar. 20. and am truly thankful for the favorable sentiments expressed in it towards my self. if, in the course of my life, it has been in any degree useful to the cause of humanity, the fact itself bears it's full reward. the particular subject of the pamphlets you inclosed me was one of early and tender consideration with me, and had I continued in the councils of my own state, it should never have been out of sight. the only practicable plan I could ever devise is stated under the 14th quaere of the Notes on Virginia, and it is still the one most sound in my judgment. unhappily it is a case for which both parties require long and difficult preparation. the mind of the master is to be apprised by reflection, and strengthened by the energies of conscience, against the obstacles of self interest, to an acquiescence in the rights of others; that of the slave is to be prepared by instruction and habit for self-government and for the honest pursuits of industry and social duty. both of these courses of preparation require time, and the former must precede the latter. some progress is sensibly made in it; yet not so much as I had hoped and expected. but it will yield in time to temperate & steady pursuit, to the enlargement of the human mind, and it's advancement in science. we are not in a world ungoverned by the laws and the power of a superior agent. our efforts are in his hand, and directed by it; and he will give them their effect in his own time. where the disease is most deeply seated, there it will be slowest in eradication. in the Northern states it was merely superficial, & easily corrected. in the Southern it is incorporated with the whole system, and requires time, patience, and perseverance in the curative process. that it may finally be effected and it's[1] progress hastened will be the last and fondest prayer of him who now salutes you with respect & consideration.

TH: JEFFERSON

RC (OCU: John Day Caldwell Collection); addressed: "The rev^d David Barrow near Mount-Stirling Kentucky"; franked; postmarked Milton, 5 May. PoC (DLC).

In the chapter on "Laws," Query 14 in his *Notes on the State of Virginia*, TJ in-cluded his PLAN for the gradual emancipation of American slaves, according to which they were to be freed at birth, given vocational training at public expense, and sent abroad when they reached adulthood (*Notes*, ed. Peden, 137–8).

[1] TJ here canceled "durati."

To Nathaniel Bowditch

Monticello May 2. 15.

I thank you, Sir, for your highly scientific pamphlet on the motion of the Pendulum, and more particularly for that containing the deductions of longitudes of places in the United States, from the Solar eclipse of 1811. that of Monticello is especially acceptable, having too long lost familiarity with such operations to have undertaken it my self. mr Lambert of Washington had also favored me with his calculation, which varied minutely only from your's; he having, from the same elements, made the Longitude of Monticello 78°–50′–18.877″ W. from Greenwich. I am happy indeed to find that this most sublime of all sciences is so eminently cultivated by you, and that our Rittenhouse was not the only meteor of the hemisphere in which he lived.

Accept the homage due to your science from one who is only a dilettante, and sincere wishes for your health & happiness.

TH: JEFFERSON

RC (MBPLi: Bowditch Collection); at foot of text: "Mr Nathaniel Bowditch. Salem." PoC (DLC); on verso of reused address cover of Horatio G. Spafford to TJ, 6 Apr. 1815; endorsed by TJ.

Nathaniel Bowditch (1773–1838), astronomer, was a native of Salem, Massachusetts. He worked as a clerk in a ship-chandlery as an adolescent and took part in five lengthy sea voyages, 1795–1803, the last as master and supercargo. In 1804 Bowditch entered the business world, first as a fire and marine insurer in his native town and, from 1823, as actuary of the Massachusetts Hospital Life Insurance Company in Boston. He succeeded in these endeavors, but he made his biggest contribution as an independent scholar. Largely self-taught, Bowditch became a fellow of the American Academy of Arts and Sciences in 1799, published twenty-three papers in its *Memoirs* between 1804 and 1820, and served as its president from 1829 until his death. He also published in other journals, both in America and abroad. The subjects addressed ranged widely, from an 1807 meteor explosion in Connecticut to the movement of comets and motion of the pendulum. However, Bowditch is best known for his *New American Practical Navigator* (Newburyport, Mass., 1802, and many other editions) and his translation with extensive commentary, 1829–

39, of the first four volumes of Pierre Simon Laplace's *Mécanique Céleste*. He was elected to the American Philosophical Society in 1809 and the Royal Society of London in 1818. Having rejected an earlier faculty appointment at Harvard University, in the latter year Bowditch turned down TJ's offer of the professorship of mathematics at the University of Virginia. He died in Boston (*ANB; DAB; DSB;* APS, Minutes, 21 Apr. 1809 [MS in PPAmP]; Henry A. S. Dearborn to TJ, 14 Oct. 1811, and enclosure; TJ to Bowditch, 26 Oct. 1818; Bowditch to TJ, 4 Nov. 1818; *Boston Daily Advertiser,* 17 Mar. 1838; *Salem Gazette,* 20 Mar. 1838).

Both of Bowditch's HIGHLY SCIENTIFIC works, "On the Eclipse of the Sun of Sept. 17, 1811, with the longitudes of several places in this country, deduced from all the observations of the Eclipses of the Sun and Transits of Mercury and Venus" and "On the Motion of a Pendulum Suspended from Two Points," are printed in American Academy of Arts and Sciences, *Memoirs,* vol. 3, pt. 2 (1815): 255–304, 413–36. Bowditch concluded on pp. 268–9 of the former, on the basis of the SOLAR ECLIPSE OF 1811, that Monticello's longitude was "78° 47′ 36″ W from Greenwich." William Lambert sent TJ his CALCULATION of its longitude in a letter dated 8 Jan. 1812.

To DeWitt Clinton

DEAR SIR   Monticello May. 2. 15.

Your favor of Apr. 6. has been duly recieved, with the circular letter it inclosed from the Literary & Philosophical society of New York. the association you propose to me with that respectable body cannot but be honorable to me, altho' it must excite the regret of consciousness that I should be an unprofitable member. the hand of age has more than begun to press upon me, and with the diminished vigor of body the mind also has it's sympathy. ardor sensibly abates in those pursuits which were the delight of earlier years, and would have been their exclusive occupation, had the history of the times in which I have lived permitted it. but, in every capacity, associated or not, I honor & respect every literary society, and should be happy in any occasion of rendering them service. Accept the assurance of my great esteem & respect.   TH: JEFFERSON

RC (NNC: Clinton Papers); addressed: "DeWitt Clinton esq. New York"; franked; postmarked Milton, 10 May; endorsed by Clinton. PoC (DLC); endorsed by TJ.

From Charles Willson Peale

DEAR SIR   Belfield May 2ᵈ 1815.

Your favor of March 21ˢᵗ came in due time—and a rainy[1] day now[2] gives me leasure to write, to thank you for your interresting letter, abounding with useful information to the farmer and Mechannic. You observe that the winter has been hard.—the Spring appears to be backward, I hope it will be favorable to our fruits, the last year gave us but little. My small green House[3] accidently constructed keept the Plants during the severity of the winter remarkably well To trace a spring in my falling Garden, we had dug out a large hole in the Earth, this hole I thought if covered over might be useful to keep Turnips and other roots, therefore it was arched over, the tryal proved that it was too warm and moist, every thing of the vegetable for our tables, grew & were spoiled. I built a front, to the south, of Glass windows, in which front building are put the pots of Plants on shelves, no fire is necessary to keep Plants in such situation. The spring[4] is covered in the cave, and the water by a trunk carried to a bason below. I believe that the springs within the Earth are all seasons of equal temperature, that our feelings induce a belief that they are warm in winter & cool in summer; the same with sellers and Caves—Perhaps a Green-house of considerable size might in this manner be constructed to save all the expence of fuel; a great quantity of air keept from impression of the external air by a thick body of Earth, would mix with the air in the front of such cave, where the necessary light must be had for Plants, But to render such Green-house complete it might be necessary to have double windows, this of course[5] would be expensive, yet in the end a great saving, for as Doctʳ Franklin said, "it is cheaper to build two Chimnies than to keep one fire"—I do not think Mʳ Halls[6] invention will benifit the farmer, it is necessary to plow the land to put it [in][7] order for other crops, and it is also necessary to manure the whole land to fit it to nourish the long extending roots of Corn. Our land properly prepaired will produce fine Corn in rows 5 feet apart and two or 3 Grains at $2\frac{1}{2}$ feet distance, which were we to place the rows 6 feet apart I suppose is planting more corn on the acre, I have made no calculation on what the difference would be. Amongst a variety of cast mould boards, I could find none of the shape of that, your plan gives, and I had, some time past, meditated making some tryal at forming a patern to get some castings made, I could not determine on the material to make the patern—I was fearful of the warping of a thin patern of wood or pasteboard, but suppose there is no difficulty of casting from another casting,[8] If I have your permission when I receive your Plow, will get some cast by it, that others may be benefited by getting so perfect a form to so important an Utensil as the Plow. I have conversed with many engenious farmers who have thought that they knew how to make good forms to their mould boards, some have told me that after making their mould-boards to what they thought a good form and after plowing with them, that they observed at what points was most worn, that in such places they trimed off. my oppinion is that all the Mould boards I have seen, have hollows where they ought not to be, and such hollows brake the sods in the action of turning them over, thus increase[g] the labour of breaking a tough sward in addition to that of turning it over.

With respect to the springs for sails[9] of large wind-mills, I believe there will be no difficulty, or no more than in my small ones, they must be stronger in the proportion to their office—But in a large wind-mill I would not make each sail large, no wider than the common sheet Iron, prefer-ing such to canvis, and being painted would be very durable. The spring should be regulated by a Screw: thus  The end of spring with a link to connect to the staple in the sail, and this staple should be placed near to the joint of the sails motion, in order to obtain only a small motion of the spring. I have found that in my first plan of making[10] the spring work or pins, that the constant motion on the pins subjected them [to][11] be soon worn out, the joints of the link should be strong or with washers to prevent as little wear as possible. long and continued motion will undoubtably wear out by friction, therefore, in such parts as can be supplied with oil from resevoirs, should be adopted to save trouble and attention, such as the Boxes of the main shaft crank, and friction wheels.

The Corn shelling machine[12] with 2 cylinders is a good invention; and I believe will work well with a small crank receive[g] its motion from the foot of the person feeding it—mine is mooved by a band from a Drum in the mill—by the weight of a log of white oak 2 feet long & 20 Inches diameter, its motion from the foot with very little exertion will be powerful enough for the shelling, the young man who made that I have, told me of their working satisfactorlily where he made them (at Columbia)—I remember seeing a machine with a single Cylinder such as you describe at the Philosophical Society, exhibited if I remember right by the inventor, but I do not remember whether it was a solid or hollow cylinder? the objection of not adapting itself to the different sizes of Corn at the time, Struck me, and thinking to obviate this fault I thought of placing strong springs over the axis—and intending to make such a machine, I spoke of it to the young man who by chance had been employed in making those of 2 Cylinders and by his recomdation I was induced to employ him to make me one. If you wish to have one I will order one to be made. I admire the simplicity of your machine for cutting straw[13]—that I have made must have cost me near 20$, and it is like many other of my contrivances, costing much more than can be saved of labour in my time. the chief consolation I have that I am amused, and by that and much labour I am keept healthy and happy—To be sure, I now and then meet with a hard rub—such as no prudent man will be at the cost of making a thrashing machine, who has only a few acres of land—of making wind mills to pump water, when the common Pump and little labour of the men on a farm would give the necessary supply. &ᶜ &ᶜ. But I have the pleasure of at least believing that my exertions may benefit others. These are innocent amusements, provided no one suffers that is under my charge. With respect to the principle of the Coffee mill for getting out clover seed, that I have used is a perfect cylinder of 6 Inches diameter & 2 feet long, this had been bored out of large hard pine timber, then sawed through lengthways and ribs of wrought Iron nailed close togather round each side, and a turned shaft about $4\frac{1}{2}$ diameter, and on which is nailed ribs also of wrought Iron, in a spiral form, the clover[14] is put into a hopper on one side of the core or shaft at the top, an oblong hole below[15] $3\frac{1}{2}$ Inches long & one Inch wide, & a pin passes lengthways through this opening, which being pushed forward prevents the clover from coming out until it is ground sufficiently to free the seeds from the husks. From this it falls into a trough on the bottom is a wire sieve, this Trough is placed decending in an angle of 45° with a board mooving up and down by means of a crank, in order to rub the seed from the husks, the seed & its dust passing through the wire to fans below—I ground out a little more than 4 Bushels of clean seed, I choose to tend the mill myself, but I found it a very unhealthy work, inhaling so much fine dust, although I covered my head with fine silk gause I found my lunges was ingured—& I was glad to quit such work. Yet I intend to make one or two hours more of experiment to assertain whether the Machine will perfectly grind out all the seed in one operation—The work is not sufficiently expeditious in the size of my machine, I did not[16] get out one bushel ℘r day—but in a longer cylinder & suffered to deliver faster, it might be a substitute [for][17] grinding with Stones—But the getting out clover seed, unless it is carried into a seperate appartment for the fanning and riddling of it, is certainly a very unhealthy business, men who will work in clover-mills in Lancaster County, are paid double wages—I, at first thought, that I could make a considerable profit by selling the seed I might get from the farm; & if my clover mill could execute the work with greater speed, say 2 or 3 Bushels ℘r day, then with the labour of 2 men[18] one or two weeks, we might get from an 8 acre lot of 2d crop about $100. and the straw from the thrashing, add manure. Seed for our own use, may as well be sowed in the husk, and if we intend to sell, I have my doubts whether it will not be the better mode to send it 8 or 9 miles to a clover mill & pay the tole. I have a machine on the coffee-mill principle,[19] it is a strong tub 20 Ins diameter at top & 1 foot at bottom, this with the Nut has wrought Iron ribs nailed on.[20] I use it for braking corn cobs, unshelled corn put into it, shells & brakes the cobs to a size convenient for grinding with my Mill stones—some farmers say that the cobs is the better substitute for cut straw—and they send the corn to some farmers who have such mills but of Cast Iron, for grinding their bark and afterwards to be ground at grist mills. I grow no hemp,[21] but of flax we are progressing to make all our house-linnen, sheets, Table cloaths, Towels, some coarse linnen, & a piece of fine for my Shirts—And this year we have sown more flax seed than heretofore—I proposed to my farmer to fix a braker of flax to the Mill,[22] but he told me that an equal stroke would not answer the purpose, that the quality would require sometimes hard & at other times more gentle strokes, I suppose the treatment of Hemp may be very different, the pounding of it in the manner you describe must be very important.

My Son Franklin has commenced making Machinery for carrying on the Cotton Business, and employs his two brothers in the work. Linneus and Titian, they all possess talents for mechanic[23] labours— Franklin in one years practice, with Messrs Hodgson, English men bred to the machine manufactory, became one of their best hands.— The Youth was always emulous to execute his work in the neatest and best manner. Every machine they make use off, must be made by themselves, I cannot afford to purchace any thing more than the materials[24] for them to work on.

Franklin, not 21 years of age, has taken to himself a wife, perhaps he should have waited untill his manufactory had got into full opperation and some profits coming in from the labours, My life has been a continued exertions of all my powers in various imployments—and I have trusted to others to educate my Children, all that I have done was by my conversations to stimulate them to good actions, I have never used coehersive means, except in a very few instances with the youngest of them, and I beleive then very little good accrued. I have ten Children, five of them married. I am now in my 75th Year; and it is my wish to settle all my worldly affairs in the best manner I can— The Museum[25] must be sold, for if it is not disposed off, before my death, a division of it will be its distruction—when I applied to the Legeslature to grant me permission to extend it over the wings of the state-House, I then offered to secure its permanency[26] there, which would have given the state of Pennsylvania the honour of an important establishment without one cent of cost to her. The chief opposition came from some of our members of Philad[a] and its invirons, I became disgusted with their weak & illiberal conduct, & therefore determined never to trouble them more—a Senetor from the City, who always invied me the previledge I had of the use of the State-House, last winter[27] by his industry, got a Bill passed to make me pay $400 ⅌[r] year Rent—This I assented to, as the best mode for me at present—as the Museum in the last 7 years has continued to advance in its income, and by my Son Rubens talents and exertions render[g] it continually more and more interresting—in the City of Philad[a] it is worth from $120,000 to 130,000, and by an increase of inhabitants with care & good management its income may be increased. My present Idea is to dispose of it by Lot—The plan is now under consideration, I must enquire what will be the cost amongst those who are active in this kind of business, I have thought that when a certain number of Names have been, in Philad[a], subscribed, that then they should appoint a President and Directors to manage the business & see what is comprized in the Museum,[28] and guard against any part being taken from it, and every increase made as usial; that all the monies arising from the sale of tickets should be safely deposited in Banks, and not subject to my controle untill a transfer of the property is made. The Museum ought to belong to Government, yet it should be seen by a payment of a small sum, which would pay the expence, of attendants and support the institution in good order. An individual may do a great deal by industry for its improvement, yet legacies and donations would be more numerous & of greater value, when in the hands of the Public, and a great many more Persons would exert themselves to increase its stores. I will be much obliged to you for your sentiments on this subject, before I begin to act; I have yet to advise with my friends & the friends of the Museum—My Reasons independant of my fears of its being divided—or being the cause of strife amongst my Children in case of my departure, is, that I might give to such of them as now really want the aid of money to put them in a better way to make themselves independant. Aid in these moments will be infinitely more acceptable, than in times when they could do without it. My Son Rembrandt I fear has ventured on too great an undertaking in his Establishment of his Museum in Baltimore. He possesses great talents and is indefaticable in his labours, but his constitution is not strong, and he has a large family— but if he meets with great difficulties he is apt to dispond, or be dishartened.

There is no need for me to trouble you with details of the situation of my Children, some can do without my aid, yet to those most needy, I should wish to see how they would use what I should chuse to give them—as I deem it prudent "to keep the loaf in my own hands" and parting with a slice as occasion might require. And on my own account I might indulge in some improvments on the farm, and occasinally make some short excursons abroad.

At Present I have very little trouble in the Management of the farm, having two young men that take all that care & labour off my hands—my principle work is in the Garden, and to put my thorn Hedges in good order, and also to do what I find is necessary to Machinery at the Mill—I had forgot one other of my imployments, namely, to oblige some few friends by my giving them the means of masticating their food. I have for many years practiced the making of artificial Teeth[29] of a variety of Ivory & by my practice have acquired the knowledge of giving relief in some difficult cases—but as all sorts of Ivory, bones, and even shells are all subject to decay—I have lately been prepairing to make some essays at making them in Enamel—for the small quantity of work that I shall ever do, perhaps it is scarcely worth the trouble & expence of making a furnace & prepairing the Materials & then make many tryals before I can expect to succeed to my satisfaction. Yet if I am successfull in making a good Enamel I may give an important business to some ingenous Person who may relieve the distresses of many who want teeth for health as well as beauty. I am not unconcious that I have mispent much of my time, a steady habit to any one object perhaps would have been more advantagous, I can reconcile this conduct to myself, because it has constituted much of my happiness—but the judicious and prudent, will condemn me! It seems almost impossible to forbear putting my hands to execute what the fancy dictates, but having frequently trifled away my time I have of late paused, and turned over in my mind the means and the end, and sought advice from my friends. Yet at this moment I am doubtful whether my actions are governed by Wisdom—I frequently think that my Pensil ought not to lay Idle. I still fancy that I could produce things worthy of notice; more valuable than my mechanic labours, By a diversity of objects, times flies swiftly away like a dream.

I turn again to your interresting letter, and think how justly you describe the principle of the Pendulum's motion,[30] it induces a desire to see what the man has done with his Pendulum moovements. The "Ingenious friend at Albany,"[31] I think has not made any new discovry, Cranked axle-trees[32] have long been used to lower the Bodies of carriages, and indeed the weight being placed low, appears to be the chief principle to prevent oversetting. Turning to the copies of my letters, I find that I had described the Corn shelling Machine[33] in my letter of Dec:r 1813. By the use of it since that period I have found it very useful, and not much liable to derangement, the space between the large Roller & the frame where the Corn passes between the two rollers, must be small to prevent the cobs from getting in & breaking them. but truth in moovement & strength of parts in proportion to the power required, must always insure the just opperation of a Machine. I do not know that a log turned from the centre of its groath,[34] would in any sensible degree become untrue by shrinking—I know that the rolling-press for copper plate printing sometimes require turning anew—whether it is caused by the axis not being put in the Center of the commencement of the groath of tree, or that one side may be of a more porus substance than another and thus be a cause of becoming untrue, should that be the case I see no other resourse in the corn shelling Machine[35] but to fix a rest, and then drive the pins most projecting from the centre of Motion.

Since writing the above I have conversed with the Person who made my shelling Machine, and he says that Apple-Tree turned, in drying becomes oval, and Hickory next, but that white-oak scarcely alters in its form from true roundness by seasoning. He says that he has a good log, and he will make a Machine for me when I may give him notice. I have desired him to save the stuff until I can hear from you.

Weaving by water is carried on by my next neibour, they are weaving Muslin, and I suppose there is no difficulty in weaving other goods by the same means, each loom weaves 30 Yards p[r] day, they appear to work well, in a short view I took of them the other day. The owner[36] took a Patent for his improvements on the Machine, He had in hand a Machine for dressing, or rather for the sizing the thread, of his own invention, whether it is a good principle or not, I do not know. I believe that he permits the joiner who made his Machines, to sell weaving and dressing Machines when wanted, I cannot be certain at what price.   My Son Franklin has never seen the old spinning Jenney,[37] he thinks that the wheel machines works well, but I suppose much of the goodness of the work, will depend on the accuracy with which such Machines[38] are made. Franklin discourraged me from putting a p[r] of small fulling stocks[39] in my Mill where I had left a convenient[40] corner for them, his reasons were, that the repeated shocks of lifting the shaft, was cause of derangement to the Water wheel, that such wheels should be purposely constructed; of great strength, for a fulling mill.

What you remark on Patent improvements on thrashing Machines is verified in a Patent Machine, with a drum studded[41] with a great number of Iron pins, belonging to M[r] Johnson in the upper part of Germanton, M[r] Johnson tells me that it is out of order, and not worth the attempt of repair. I wish to know if the thrashing Machine[42] you approve of—will clean the wheat to be merchantable[43] in the same opperation of thrashing—Mine blows off the Husks, but carries too many long straws with the Grain, so that we are obliged to pass the wheat through the common Fan. Does the dashers on the Drum strike upwards or downwards?[44]—one Gentlman told me that a Machine he had seen, struck downwards and the grain went through a hollowed Grating, out of which the straw was thrown on the back or opposite[45] side, free of all grain; that the grating was near to the Drum & imbraced about half of it.   Your Grandson has fulfilded his duty to the community by taking to himself a wife, I wish him a great deal of happiness, numerous ofspring, and a long life—I offended him once or twice, highly, while[46] he was with me, by some severe remarks I made on the folly of dueling. I have always felt it my duty to speak on the motives which actuate men of that character, when in the company of Young men, and being fearful that young M[r] Jefferson might resent some of the foolish and Idle Chattering of a profligate set of young men, his companions attending the Medical Lectures, I found he took fire when he heard any illiberal remarks on his Grandfather, I endeavored to make him dispise and consider such offenders, as beneath his notice, much more his resentment. I was alarmed, as several duels had taken place amongst the Pupils— and uttered much contempt on Duellists, I did not know that Thomas's father had fought a Duel, untill he told it to me with some warmth. I loved him the more for his filial Affections, and, for his and friends benefit, my severity was directed against that greatest of follies, Duelling.

By keeping my letter open, and now & then taking up the pen, I have touched on a variety of subjects, and now think it time to conclude, well knowing that very little is worth your time of reading it, yet I am much interrested in getting an answer to some parts, especially about the final disposition of the Museum. In the last year, twice, I have been in danger by accidents, of sudden death, I promise myself in future to be cautious, in my labours, to avoid danger—But dangers may happen even with the most prudent; then how necessary it is to be always prepaired against what cannot be foreseen— The government of our Passions, and prudential care will make man last untill the machine is worn out by age; natural decay, as all nature testifies. May you my dear Sir, last untill you feel no pain in leaving this world, is the earnest prayer of

your obliged friend   C W PEALE

RC (DLC); edges chipped, with missing text supplied from PoC; with glosses added by TJ in left margin as noted below; endorsed by TJ as received 4 June 1815 and so recorded in SJL. RC (MHi); address cover only; with PoC of TJ to Stephen Girard, 10 July 1815, on verso; addressed: "The Honble Thomas Jefferson Esq' Monticella Virginia"; franked; postmarked Philadephia, 9 May. PoC (PPAmP: Peale Letterbook).

Benjamin FRANKLIN printed the adage "'tis easier to build two Chimnies than to keep one in Fuel" in *Poor Richard improved: Being An Almanack and Ephemeris . . . for the Year of our Lord 1758* (Philadelphia, 1757), 29. Peale APPLIED in February 1802 for public assistance in housing his museum, and on 17 Mar. of that year the state legislature granted the museum lodging in the statehouse in Philadelphia (later known as Independence Hall). State SENETOR

Nicholas Biddle had recently given Peale the option of continuing to use the space if he paid $400 in rent (Peale, *Papers*, vol. 2, pt. 1, 393–401; vol. 3:298–9; *Acts of the General Assembly of the Commonwealth of Pennsylvania* [1801–02 sess.]: 283–4; [1814–15 sess.]: 162–3).

[1] RC: "rainey." Corrected to "rainy" on PoC.

[2] Word interlined.

[3] In margin adjacent to line with this phrase in RC, TJ added the gloss "green house."

[4] Manuscript: "sping."

[5] Manuscript: "couse."

[6] In margin adjacent to line with this word in RC, TJ added the gloss "Hall's corn."

[7] Omitted word editorially supplied.

[8] In margin adjacent to line with this word in RC, TJ added the gloss "mould board."

[9] In margin adjacent to line with this

phrase in RC, TJ added the gloss "springs for sails."

[10] Manuscript: "makin."

[11] Omitted word editorially supplied.

[12] In margin adjacent to line with this phrase in RC, TJ added the gloss "Corn sheller."

[13] In margin adjacent to line with this phrase in RC, TJ added the gloss "straw cutter."

[14] In margin adjacent to line with this word in RC, TJ added the gloss "clover."

[15] Word interlined.

[16] Manuscript: "not not."

[17] Omitted word editorially supplied.

[18] Peale here interlined and then canceled "occasionally."

[19] In margin adjacent to line with this phrase in RC, TJ added the gloss "Cobcrusher."

[20] Preceding two words interlined.

[21] In margin adjacent to line with this phrase in RC, TJ added the gloss "hemp break."

[22] Preceding three words interlined.

[23] Manuscript: "mecanic."

[24] Manuscript: "meterials."

[25] In margin adjacent to line with this word in RC, TJ added the gloss "Museum."

[26] Manuscript: "permancy."

[27] Preceding two words interlined.

[28] Manuscript: "Museun."

[29] In margin adjacent to the start of this paragraph in RC, TJ added the gloss "artificial teeth."

[30] In margin adjacent to the start of this paragraph in RC, TJ added the gloss "pendulum."

[31] Manuscript: "Ingenous friend at Abany."

[32] In margin adjacent to line with this phrase in RC, TJ added the gloss "cranked axle."

[33] In margin adjacent to line with this phrase in RC, TJ added the gloss "corn sheller."

[34] In margin adjacent to line with this phrase in RC, TJ added the gloss "springing of wood."

[35] Preceding five words interlined.

[36] Manuscript: "ower."

[37] In margin adjacent to line with this phrase in RC, TJ added the gloss "spinning Jenny."

[38] Manuscript: "Machinces."

[39] In margin adjacent to line with this phrase in RC, TJ added the gloss "fulling."

[40] Manuscript: "convenint."

[41] Manuscript: "studied."

[42] In margin adjacent to line with this phrase in RC, TJ added the gloss "threshing & winnowing."

[43] Manuscript: "merchantale," reworked from "merchanable."

[44] In margin adjacent to line with this query in RC, TJ inserted a question mark.

[45] Preceding two words interlined.

[46] Manuscript: "white."

From Patrick Gibson

SIR   Richmond 3ᵈ May 1815

I wrote you on the 28ᵗʰ Ultº and have since received your favor of the 29ᵗʰ inclosing an order on the Commʳ of loans for $8580 payable in treasury notes, on application at the office I find that Mʳ Nelson has none on hand, but expects a supply shortly—With regard to the taking up your note with them I have only to repeat what I mention'd in my last, that it is not possible to do so except at a discount

Respectfully Yours   PATRICK GIBSON

RC (MHi); between dateline and salutation: "Thomas Jefferson Esqʳᵉ"; endorsed by TJ as received 6 May 1815 and so recorded in SJL.

Both Gibson's letter to TJ of THE 28ᵀᴴ ULTᵒ, which was received 3 May 1815 from Richmond, and TJ's FAVOR of 29 Apr. 1815 are recorded in SJL, but neither has been found except for the address cover of the former (RC in DLC; addressed: "Thomas Jefferson Esqʳᵉ Monticello"; franked; postmarked Richmond, 1 May; with PoC of TJ to John George Baxter, 16 July 1815, on verso).

To David Hosack

Monticello May 3. 15.

Th: Jefferson presents his compliments to Dʳ Hosack and his thanks for his very instructive pamphlet on yellow fever. without competence to decide the question which ha[s] so much divided the Medical faculty here, Whether that fever is produced by an atmosphere specially vitiated solely or with the aid of infection from a diseased body, in other word[s] whether it originates here, or is imported, Dʳ Hosack has undoubtedly thrown great light on the question by the facts he adduces and his reasonings on them. Th:J. salutes him with great respect & consideration.

PoC (DLC); dateline at foot of text; edge trimmed; on verso of reused address cover to TJ; endorsed by TJ.

David Hosack (1769–1835), physician, medical educator, and botanist, was a native of New York City who studied at Columbia College (later University) before receiving an A.B. degree from the College of New Jersey (later Princeton University) in 1789. He received an M.D. from the University of the State of Pennsylvania in 1791 and began a medical practice in Alexandria. From 1792–94 Hosack pursued further studies in medicine, botany, and mineralogy in Edinburgh and London. Thereafter he practiced medicine in New York City, where he numbered many prominent citizens among his patients. He was Alexander Hamilton's surgeon at the latter's fatal 1804 duel with Aaron Burr. Success in 1797 treating victims of a New York City yellow fever epidemic contributed greatly to Hosack's standing in the medical world. His theory that the disease was a contagious tropical import put him in direct opposition to his former teacher Benjamin Rush. Hosack's long and often contentious work as a medical educator included terms as professor of botany, 1795–1811, and materia medica, 1796–1811, at Columbia College; professor of botany and materia medica, 1807–08, and the theory and practice of physic, 1811–26, at the College of Physicians and Surgeons (later part of Columbia University); and service as president of Rutgers Medical College from its founding in 1826 until its dissolution in 1830. He was a founder of the *American Medical and Philosophical Register* and presented some of his publications on medical theory and practice to TJ. Hosack was also noted for his botanical expertise. He acquired duplicate specimens from Linnaeus's herbarium during his European sojourn, and in 1801 he founded the Elgin Botanic Garden in New York City, which he sold in 1810 to the state of New York with the ill-founded hope that it would endure as a public institution. Hosack's extensive involvement in scientific, civic, and cultural organizations included helping to found the New-York Historical Society in 1804, service as its president, 1820–28, and election to the American Philosophical Society in 1810 (*ANB*; *DAB*; *Princetonians, 1784–90*, pp. 402–12; Christine Chapman Robbins, *David Hosack: Citizen of New York* [1964]; Hosack to TJ, 10 Sept. 1806 [MHi], enclosing his *Catalogue of*

Plants Contained in the Botanic Garden at Elgin, in the Vicinity of New-York, Established in 1801 [New York, 1806]; Poor, *Jefferson's Library,* 5 [nos. 165, 173, 182, 190, 191, 199]; APS, Minutes, 20 July 1810 [MS in PPAmP]; Hosack, *A Statement of Facts Relative to the Establishment and Progress of the Elgin Botanical Garden* [New York, 1811]; New York *Herald,* 24 Dec. 1835; Washington *Daily National Intelligencer,* 28 Dec. 1835).

The INSTRUCTIVE PAMPHLET was Hosack's *Observations on the Laws Governing the Communication of Contagious Diseases, and the Means of Arresting Their Progress* (New York, 1815; Poor, *Jefferson's Library,* 7 [no. 304]).

From Nicolas G. Dufief

MONSIEUR,   A Philadelphie ce 4 mai 1815

C'est par la faute de Mr Duane que la quinze dollars n'ont point été passés à votre crédit sur ses livres. Le jour même que je reçus la lettre où vous m'annonciez que je devais recevoir la traite de 150^{dlls} de Mr P. Gibson, je vis ce Monsieur & voulus lui payer Les 15 dollars. Il refusa de recevoir cet argent comme il me devait beaucoup plus. Je l'en créditai & il oublia de vous en tenir compte Sur Ses livres: mais cet oubli est reparé par le reçu ci-Inclus

De tous les livres que vous me demandez, je ne puis vous procurer que la sagesse de charon, bonne edition en 2 vol 8vo prix cinq dollars cet ouvrage vous Sera envoyé de la manière que vous demandez Je me propose de partir dans quelque temps pour l'Europe, afin d'y faire un choix de livres mais je ne partirai certainement point, Sans avoir eu l'honneur de recevoir vos ordres à ce Sujet

Agreez les assurances du profond respect avec lequel

Je Suis inviolablement

votre très-dévoué Serviteur   N. G. DUFIEF

EDITORS' TRANSLATION

SIR,   Philadelphia 4 May 1815

Mr. Duane is to blame for failing to credit the fifteen dollars to your account on his books. The very same day I got the letter in which you announced to me that I would receive the draft for 150 dollars from Mr. P. Gibson, I saw this gentleman and tried to pay him the 15 dollars. He refused to accept the money, because he owed me a lot more than that. I credited his account with that sum, but he forgot to do likewise on his own books. The enclosed receipt repairs this oversight.

Of all the books you request, I can only get you Charron's *De La Sagesse*, a good edition in 2 octavo volumes, price five dollars. This work will be sent to you in the manner you desire. I plan to set out for Europe shortly in order to obtain a selection of books, but I will certainly not leave without receiving your orders on this subject

Accept the assurances of the profound respect with which

I am inviolably

your very devoted servant
N. G. DUFIEF

RC (DLC); endorsed by TJ as received 11 May 1815 and so recorded in SJL. RC (DLC); address cover only; with PoC of TJ to Joseph Milligan, 26 June 1815, on verso; addressed: "Thos Jefferson Esq. Monticello Va"; franked; postmarked Philadelphia, 4 May. Translation by Dr. Genevieve Moene. Enclosure: receipt from William Duane to Dufief, Philadelphia, 2 May 1815, for $15, "being so much paid by him on account of Thomas Jefferson late Prest of the United States in account with me" (MS in DLC; written on a small scrap by Duane and signed by him; endorsed by TJ: "Newspapers Duane Wm receipt to May 1. 1815").

In a LETTRE dated 16 Aug. 1814, TJ informed Dufief that he would receive a draft for $150.

Account with Nicolas G. Dufief

[ca. 4 May 1815]

Dr	Thos Jefferson Esq. In a/c with N. G. Dufief			Cr
	1814		1814	
Jany 13. To Balance due		4.93	Sep 5. By Cash	150.00
April 14 Newton's Principia		18 00		
Aug. 20 Dufief's Dicy		11.50		
24 History of the Shakers		1.00		
Sep 6 Paid Bradford & Inskeep		68 75		
" " John F. Watson		11 25		
22 Barton		18.00		
1815				
May 2. Paid Wm Duane		15 00		
4 To La Sagesse		5 00	Balance due N G. D	3.43
		153 43		153 43
1815				
May 4 Balance due		$ 3.43		

MS (DLC: TJ Papers, 204:36270); undated; entirely in Dufief's hand.

The HISTORY OF THE SHAKERS was Thomas Brown, *An Account of the People called Shakers: their Faith, Doctrines, and Practice* (Troy, N.Y., 1812; Sowerby, no. 1707). LA SAGESSE: TJ owned several editions of Pierre Charron, *De La Sagesse* (note to TJ to Louis H. Girardin, 7 July 1814).

From Horatio G. Spafford

Albany, 4 Mo. [May] 4, 1815.

I embrace every opportunity for presenting my respects, constantly wishing thee all possible health & happiness.

This Work has long been wanting, & for years I have been urged to undertake it. I am pretty well satisfied with the plan of it, & hope it may meet thy approbation. May I be permitted to solicit from thee something for it? It is designed for general circulation, & I shall spare no pains to make it worthy of it. If the Subscriptions fill as I expect, the first No. may appear the last of this month. Nothing from thy pen, could fail to be interesting.

The Carriage seems to make its way to the satisfaction of all who try it. My reasoning upon it, will bear the test of experience, & I think the plan must come into general use. I have sent the Pamphlets to England, France, & Russia.

What strange events in Europe! The Speculations of an old, experienced Statesman, on the present state of the World, would deeply interest every body. With esteem & respect; thy constant,

grateful friend,   H. G. Spafford.

RC (DLC: Printed Ephemera Collection); misdated; dateline beneath signature; written on verso of enclosure; addressed: "Thomas Jefferson, LL.D. Monticello, Virginia"; franked; postmarked Albany, 6 May; endorsed by TJ as a letter of 4 Apr. 1815 received 12 May 1815 and so recorded in SJL. Enclosure: prospectus by John Cook, of Albany, and Charles Holt, of New York, for the *American Magazine*, a "Monthly Miscellany" to be edited by Spafford, indicating that the contents will consist of "original and selected pieces on all subjects," with sections devoted to agriculture, mechanical arts, manufacturing, mercantile interests, and foreign history, events, and politics; an "American Register" that will present public documents and an "impartial abstract" of American news; occasional essays on United States politics, while insuring that "cunning and foul designs" will never "usurp the place or right of fair argument and sound reasoning"; a poetry department; reviews of new publications; notices of new works and publications; lists of marriages and deaths; brief biog-

raphies of "such persons as are, or may have been of distinguished fame"; and political, literary, scientific, moral, religious, and philosophical essays; with the whole thus providing "a useful and instructive companion for the leisure hours of all descriptions of people"; and adding that the proposed magazine will be published on the last Tuesday of every month; that it will contain at least thirty-six octavo pages per number and twelve numbers per volume of 432–500 pages, with a table of contents in each number and a cumulative index in the twelfth number; that many issues will include an "appropriate engraving"; that a year's subscription will cost $2.50 if paid in advance or on receipt of the first number and $3 if paid at the end of the year; and that orders should be sent to the publishers, to the printers E. & E. Hosford, or to Spafford, at Albany (broadside in DLC: Printed Ephemera Collection; dated Albany, 2 May 1815, with unused blanks at the foot for subscribers' names, addresses, and number of copies ordered, and with covering letter on verso; reprinted in part on pp. 5–6 of the first number of the *American Magazine*, which was dated June 1815 and no longer listed Cook and Holt among those associated with the publication).

To highlight the new CARRIAGE, an abridgement of Spafford, *Wheel-Carriages*, appeared in the *American Magazine* 1 (1815): 39–40, 70–2, and plate opp. 39.

From Patrick Gibson

SIR   Richmond 6th May 1815
I have received from the loan office the amount of the order enclosed in your last say $8580 in treasy notes, which being all made out in your name I now send you enclosed—With great respect
Your Obt Servt   PATRICK GIBSON

RC (MHi); between dateline and salutation: "Thomas Jefferson Esqre"; franked; endorsed by TJ as received 9 May 1815 and so recorded in SJL; with

TJ's calculation on verso allocating the $8,580 as enumerated in his 10 May 1815 reply to Gibson, for which see Gibson to TJ, 17 May 1815, and note.

From Joseph Milligan

RESPECTED[1] FRIEND   Fredericksburg May 6th 1815 Three O,clock
I have by the mail which will bring you this Sent you four Copies of the Exposition &c two are for yourself one for Col Randolph & one for Capt Carr   Capt Car will pay you for his Copy and I will charge it to your acccount
as ℔ invoice on the next page I have sent you the part of your order that I could procure in this place the rest will be sent from Georgetown
yesterday at one oclock I had the Seven wagons passed over the River Rappahannock which we Loaded on tuesday morning the one which we loaded on wednesday morning has not yet arrived here but as I have now waited until it is three o clock I will leave orders with Capt Wm F Gray for[2] him & set out
With Great respect[3] yours   JOSEPH MILLIGAN

RC (DLC); addressed: "Thomas Jefferson Esqr Monticello Milton Via [i.e., Virginia]"; franked; postmarked Fredericksburg, 9 May; endorsed by TJ as received 11 May and so recorded in SJL; with enclosure on verso of address leaf.

Milligan mailed FOUR COPIES of Dallas, *Exposition*. TUESDAY was 2 May 1815.

[1] Manuscript: "Respcted."
[2] Manuscript: "fro."
[3] Manuscript: "respct."

Joseph Milligan's Invoice for Books

Fred^g May 6th 1815

Mr Joseph Miligan
> Bot. of William F. Gray

1 Marshalls Life of Washington	$17.50
1 Stewart on the Mind	5.00
1 Coopers Justinian	6.00
1 Walkers Dictionary	3.50
1 Medical Companion	3.00
1 Thompsons Four Gospels	1.50
1 Priestley's Charts of Biography	2.00
1 Criminal Recorder	1.00
	$39.50
4 Exposition	50	2 00

MS (DLC); written in a clerk's hand on verso of address cover of covering letter.

The MEDICAL COMPANION was James Ewell, *The Planter's and Mariner's Medical Companion* (Philadelphia, 1807; Sowerby, no. 893; Poor, *Jefferson's Library*, 5 [no. 183]). The work containing the FOUR GOSPELS was Charles Thomson, *A Synopsis of the Four Evangelists: or, A Regular History of the Conception, Birth, Doctrine, Miracles, Death, Resurrection, and Ascension of Jesus Christ, in the Words of the Evangelists* (Philadelphia, 1815; Poor, *Jefferson's Library*, 9 [no. 509]).

To John Barnes

DEAR SIR   Monticello May 7. 15.

Your favors of Apr. 22. & 25. are at hand. you observe that the question is how to dispose of the 4500.D & the 360.D   the latter being interest, I supposed would be remitted to the General for use; and the 4500.D. principal being itself a stock bearing interest at $5\frac{2}{3}$ p.c. and payable at the end of one year, I had supposed it would be best to keep it in it's present form until payable, and then to be on the lookout for some other stock, of the US. bearing higher interest, if to be had at par, in lieu[1] of payment of the principal. I say stock of the US. for I would trust no other. that the banks will ever fully resume the payment of specie for their notes I do not believe. late experience has shewn they cannot be forced; and their paper now circulates only for want of any other medium, and not that the public have any confidence in it. we certainly therefore must not meddle with their stock. I some time ago gave the General notice of this defalcation in the amount of interest on this particular part of his capital. but the improvement in the other part will make it up. I have learnt with great pleasure from mr Millegan & Dougherty that your health continues good; and that it may so continue to the end is my sincere prayer

TH: JEFFERSON

PoC (DLC); at foot of text: "Mr Barnes"; endorsed by TJ.

THE GENERAL was Tadeusz Kosciuszko.

[1] Manuscript: "in-lieu," with the hyphen falling at the end of a line.

To George Watterston

SIR   Monticello May 7. 15.

I have duly recieved your favor of Apr. 26. in which you are pleased to ask my opinion on the subject of the arrangement of libraries. I shall communicate with pleasure what occurs to me on it. two methods offer themselves. the one Alphabetical, the other according to the subject of the book. the former is very unsatisfactory, because of the medley it presents to the mind, the difficulty sometimes of recollecting an author's name, and the greater difficulty, where the name is not given of selecting the word in the title which shall determine it's Alphabetical place. the arrangement according to subject is far preferable, altho' sometimes presenting difficulty also. for it is often doubtful to what particular subject a book should be ascribed. this is remarkably the case with books of travels, which often blend together the geography, natural history, civil history, agriculture, manufactures, commerce, arts, occupations, manners E^tc. of a country, so as to render it difficult to say to which they chiefly relate. others again are polygraphical in their nature, as Encyclopedias, Magazines E^tc. yet on the whole I have preferred arrangement according to subject; because of the peculiar satisfaction, when we wish to consider a particular one, of seeing at a glance the books which have been written on it, and selecting those from which we expect most readily the information we seek. on this principle the arrangement of my library was formed, and I took the basis of it's distribution from Ld Bacon's table of science, modifying it to the changes in scientific pursuits which have taken place since his time, and to the greater or less extent of reading in the several sciences which I proposed to myself. thus the law having been my profession, and politics the occupation to which the circumstances of the times in which I have lived called my particular attention, my provision of books in these lines, and in those most nearly connected with them, was more copious, and required in particular instances subdivisions into sections and paragraphs, while other subjects, of which general views only were contemplated, are thrown into masses.

a physician or theologist would have modified differently the chapters sections and paragraphs of a library adapted to their particular pursuits.

You will recieve my library arranged very perfectly in the order observed in the Catalogue, which I have sent with it. in placing the books on their shelves, I have generally, but not always, collocated distinctly the folios, 4^{tos} 8^{vos} & 12^{mos} placing with the last all smaller sizes. on every book is a label, indicating the chapter of the catalogue to which it belongs, and the order it holds among those of the same format. so that, altho' the N^{os} seem confused on the catalogue, they are consecutive on the volumes as they stand on their shelves & indicate at once the place they occupy there.   Mr Millegan, in packing them has preserved their arrangement so exactly, in their respective presses, that on setting the presses up on end, he will be able readily to replace them in the order corresponding with the catalogue, and thus save you the immense labor which their rearrangement would otherwise require.

To give to my catalogue the conveniences of the Alphabetical arrangement, I have made at the end an Alphabet of Authors' names, and have noted the chapter, or chapters, in which the name will be found. where it occurs several times in the same chapter it is indicated by one or more[1] perpendicular scores, thus | | | |. according to the number of times it will be found in the chapter. where a book bears no author's name, I have selected, in it's title, some leading word for denoting it Alphabetically. this member of the catalogue would be more perfect if, instead of the score, the number on the book were particularly noted. this could not be done when I made the catalogue, because no label of numbers had then been put on the books. that alteration can now be readily made, and would add greatly to the convenient use of the Catalogue. I gave to mr Millegan a note of three folio volumes of the laws of Virginia belonging to the library which being in known hands, will be certainly recovered, and shall be forwarded to you. one is a MS. volume from which a printed copy is now preparing for publication.

This statement meets, I believe, all the enquiries of your letter, and where it is not sufficiently minute, mr Millegan, from his necessary acquaintance with the arrangement, will be able to supply the smaller details. Accept the assurances of my respect and consideration.

TH: JEFFERSON

PoC (DLC); at foot of first page: "Mr Watterston"; endorsed by TJ as a letter to "Watterston P." and so recorded in SJL.

TJ based the organization of his library on a TABLE of "The Emanation of Sciences, from the Intellectual Faculties of Memory, Imagination, Reason," on p. 41 of Francis Bacon, *Of the Advancement and Proficiencie of Learning: or the Partitions of Sciences* (London, 1674; Sowerby, no. 4916). The CATALOGUE sent with TJ's library has not been found. Watterston modified and published it as a *Catalogue of the Library of the United States. To Which is Annexed, A Copious Index, Alphabetically Arranged* (Washington, 1815). A reconstruction of TJ's original catalogue prepared at his request by Nicholas P. Trist is at DLC: Rare Book and Special Collections (Trist to TJ, 18 Oct. 1823; James Gilreath and Douglas

L. Wilson, eds., *Thomas Jefferson's Library: A Catalog with the Entries in His Own Order* [1989]).

The THREE FOLIO VOLUMES consisted of laws and orders of the Virginia General Assembly, 5 Mar. 1624, marked A, and lent to William W. Hening; laws of the Virginia Council and General Assembly, 2 Mar. 1643–23 Mar. 1662, marked D; and sheets of printed laws, 1734–72, vol. 5 of TJ's 8-volume set of Virginia laws, which Hening used in PREPARING FOR PUBLICATION the eighth volume of his *Statutes at Large* (Sowerby, nos. 1822, 1825, 1841; TJ to Hening, 7 June 1808, and enclosed "Manuscripts of the laws sent to mr Hening June 1808" [DLC]; Hening to TJ, 15 Mar. 1815; TJ to Hening, 25 Mar., 8 Apr. 1815).

[1] Preceding three words interlined.

From Thomas Law

DEAR SIR   Washington May 8 1815—
    I have the pleasure to enclose observations on the proposed Bank—
The articles of association are printed in the National Intelligencer—
I remain With unfeigned esteem regard & respect

THOs LAW—

RC (DLC); endorsed by TJ as received 12 May 1815 and so recorded in SJL. RC (DLC); address cover only; with PoC of TJ to Wilson Cary Nicholas, 15 July 1815, on recto and verso; addressed: "To Thomas Jefferson, Esqr Monticello Virginia"; franked; postmarked Washington, 9 May.

The enclosed OBSERVATIONS on the proposed Patriotic Bank of Washington have not been found. Law was named one of thirteen commissioners charged with overseeing subscriptions to the new bank in the twenty-nine ARTICLES OF ASSOCIATION printed in the Washington *Daily National Intelligencer*, 2 May 1815.

To Samuel H. Smith

DEAR SIR   Monticello May 8. 15.

Our 10th and last waggon load of books goes off to-day. this closes the transaction here, and I cannot permit it to close without returning my thanks to you who began it. this I sincerely do for the trouble you have taken in it. when I first proposed to you to make the overture to the library committee, I thought that the only trouble you would have had, that they would have said yea, or nay directly, have appointed valuers, and spared you all further intermediation: and I saw with great regret this agency afterwards added to the heavy labors of your office.

it is done however, and an interesting treasure is added to your city, now become the depository of unquestionably the choicest collection of books in the US. and I hope it will not be without some general effect on the literature of our country.

When will the age of wonders cease in France! the first revolution was a wonder. the restitution of the Bourbons a wonder. the re-enthronement of Bonaparte as great as any. joy seems to have been manifested with us on this event; inspired I suppose by the pleasure of seeing the scourge again brandished over the back of England. but it's effect on us may be doubted. we stood on good ground before, but now on doubtful. the change cannot improve our situation, & may make it worse. if they have a general war we may be involved in it; if peace, we shall have the hostile and ignorant caprices of Bonaparte[1] to regulate our commerce with that country, instead of it's antient and regular course. but these considerations are for the young; I am done with them. present me affectionately to mrs Smith, with my wishes that you could make a visit to Monticello a respite to your labors, and the assurances of my friendship & respect   TH: JEFFERSON

RC (DLC: J. Henley Smith Papers).   [1] Preceding two words interlined.
PoC (DLC); at foot of text: "Mr Saml H.
Smith"; endorsed by TJ.

To George P. Stevenson

DEAR SIR   Monticello May 9. 15.

I thank you for the information contained in your lette[r] of Apr. 28. and in the paper accompanying it. that the whole army would join Bonaparte whenever he [c]ould[1] safely enter France, I never doubted; but I had not expected the people would have done so. the cause of this however is to be found in the return of the antient nobility to their former possessions, and reclamation of them and their antient rights. the people saw in Bonaparte their only protection against their former Seigneurs, and hailed him as their guardian angel. like most other worldly dispensations this is mixed of good and evil. I participate in the general satisfaction on two grounds. 1. the restoration of the Bourbons, after that of the Stuarts, would have produced a general belief and despair of the possibility of changing their antient dynasties. 2. I rejoice at seeing the cowhide once more brandished over the back of great Britain, and a barrier at length presented to her power. but these views of the subject have their counterpoise. if war arises in Europe, we shall certainly feel it's harrasments on the ocean, & possibly be involved in it. if peace continues, our commercial intercourse with France will be subject to the unfriendly and ignorant caprices of Bonaparte, instead of the antient regulations of the Bourbons which were tolerably favorable. add to this the doubt whether the people of France will gain by the exchange of their former government which had known limits to it's power, for a military despotism. but hope is always more comfortable than fear. let us therefore hope. your mother and friends in this quarter are well. accept the assurance of my great esteem & respect.

Th: Jeffer[so]n

PoC (DLC); edge trimmed; signature faint; at foot of text: "George Stevenson esq."; endorsed by TJ.

[1] Word partially illegible.

From Patrick Gibson

Sir   Richmond 10th May 1815

In the hurry of forwarding you the Treasury notes on Saturday last, I omitted sending you the small notes you had requested, which I now inclose—I have made sale of all the flour now down say 215 bls: Sf & 18 fine to Tarlton Saunders at 7$ on 60 d/− with interest added, as I am induced to believe I can get the note discounted you may consider the proceeds on hand—I have been endeavouring to dispose of your 6 hhds Tobacco at the price I stated them to be worth, namely $10. but as yet without success. the stemmd Hhd: I have sold at 5$—   With great respect I am

Your obt Servt   Patrick Gibson

RC (ViU: TJP-ER); between dateline and salutation: "Thomas Jefferson Esqre"; endorsed by TJ as received 12 May 1815 and so recorded in SJL.

The enclosed SMALL NOTES amounted to $50 (*MB*, 2:1308). SF: "superfine."

To Albert Gallatin

DEAR SIR   Monticello April[1] [May] 11. 15.

Mr Girardin, who will have the honor of presenting you this letter, revisits his native country after a residence of 20. years in this his country by adoption. he will consider this relation as placing him under your protection, of which he is entirely worthy. a residence of some years in my neighborhood enables me to assure you that he is a gentleman of science, of worth, and perfect correctness of conduct. he has just compleated a history of Virginia during the period of the revolution, which is now in the press, and both the matter and the manner of the execution, will ensure to the work a welcome acceptance, and to himself the honorable acknolegements of the public. I take the liberty of presenting him to you as worthy of any attentions you [shall?] be so good as to shew him, and add the assuran[ces of] my constant and affectionate friendship and respect.

TH: JEFFERSON

PoC (DLC: TJ Papers, 203:36229); on recto of reused address cover to TJ; misdated; mutilated at seal; at foot of text: "His Excellency Mr Gallatin"; endorsed by TJ as a letter of 11 May 1815 and so recorded in SJL, with the additional notation that it was to be delivered "by Girardin." Enclosed in TJ to Louis H. Girardin, 12 May 1815.

[1] Reworked from "Mar."

To Lafayette

MY DEAR FRIEND   Monticello May. 11. 15.

In my letter of Feb. 14. I mentioned to you that a well qualified author was writing, in my neighborhood, that part of the history of Virginia which embraced your campaign of 1781; and that I was so well satisfied with the ability with which he was executing the work, that I had laid open to him all my papers; and regretted that among them was no longer to be found the Memoir you were so kind as to give me of that campaign. it was regretted the more as no enquiries we could make enabled him to give a distinct statement of your operations. the writer of the work, mr Girardin, is the person who will have the honor of delivering you this letter. he is a native of France, but a citizen of the US. of 20. years adoption, and pays a visit to his native country on matters of business. to these however he adds the view of writing your history, which being a favorite theme in America, would be a work of much demand. his talents would enable him to maintain the interest of the subject, and his zeal for your character would ensure the full exertion of them. he writes the English not merely with purity & correctness, but possesses in a high degree the elegancies of the language. he sollicits your consent to his undertaking, and of course your aid as to the materials. in this I join him. which I certainly would not do, were not my confidence in his competence as entire as my affections to your virtues and fame are sincere. he is a gentleman of science of worth, & of perfect correctness of conduct, and as such I recommend him to your attentions, happy in every opportunity of renewing to you the assurances of my constant & affectionate friendship and respect.　　　　Th: Jefferson

PoC (DLC); at foot of text: "M. de la fayette"; endorsed by TJ. Recorded in SJL as to be delivered "by Girardin." Enclosed in TJ to Louis H. Girardin, 12 May 1815.

To Benjamin Henry Latrobe

Dear Sir　　　　　　　　　　　　Monticello May. 11. 15.

After expressing my satisfaction that the restoration of the Capitol is confided to you, which ensures it's being properly done, I have to offer you two house joiners of the very first order both in their knolege in Architecture, and their practical abilities. James Dinsmore, one of them, I brought from Philada in 1798. and he lived with me 10. years. a more faithful, sober, discreet, honest & respectable man I have never known. he is at present half owner of a valuable manufacturing mill in this neighborhood. John Nielson, the other one, I got also from Philadelphia in 1804. and he lived with me 4. years, and I have found him also an honest, sober, and excellent man. they have done the whole of the joiner's work of my house, to which I can affirm I have never seen any superior in the US. after they had finished with me they worked 2. or 3. years for the President, to whom therefore they are well known. mr Mills also knows them personally and their works. whatever they undertake you may be assured they will perform in the best & most faithful manner; and I shall be gratified if I shall have procured to you good men & to them good employment. Accept the assurance of my continued esteem & respect.　　　　Th: Jefferson

PoC (DLC); on verso of reused address cover to TJ; at foot of text: "B. H. Latrobe esq."; endorsed by TJ.

Latrobe received his commission to oversee the RESTORATION OF THE CAPITOL in the latter half of April (Latrobe, *Papers*, 3:626–30, 643–47).

To André Thoüin

MY DEAR AND ANTIENT FRIEND & COLLEAGUE   Monticello May. 11. 15.

The peace of Paris had given us the hope that wars had at length ceased, and the ocean become open to the intercourses of friendship and science. but we just now learn the great events of March last, and that France, and we may say the world, is again overshadowed with clouds; and of what is to follow we have no indications. in this uncertain state of things, mr Girardin, who will have the honor of presenting you this letter, undertakes a visit to his native country, from that which has been for 20. years his country of adoption. he is a gentleman of science, worth, and perfect correctness. among other views, he wishes to become an eye-witness of the wonderful progress of science in your country, and particularly in that of which you are at the head. well skilled in the earlier systems of Botany, he is qualified to do justice to the improvements made on them, and will sometimes ask the lights of your conversation. indulge him for my sake, and flatter me with this mark of regard for the high respect and affectionate esteem of which he furnishes me this opportunity of tendering the assurances.   TH: JEFFERSON

PoC (DLC); at foot of text: "M. Thoüin"; endorsed by TJ. Recorded in SJL as to be delivered "by Girardin." Enclosed in TJ to Louis H. Girardin, 12 May 1815.

The GREAT EVENTS OF MARCH LAST: Napoleon's second ascension to the throne of France.

To John Barnes

DEAR SIR   Monticello May 12. 15.

I have just recieved a letter from Genl Kosciuszko, desiring me to remit his whole principal to him in France. the letter is without date, and as I conjecture was not only before the late revolution, but before our peace. it seems to indicate a state of despair of recieving his remittances regularly, and his distresses for want of them. in consequence of these changes, however, as peace renders regular remittance practicable, and the revolution in France may render that place insecure for his property, I shall venture to suspend executing his request, until I can write and get[1] an answer. in the mean time I think it is best to keep his principal in it's present form I salute you with affection & respect. TH: JEFFERSON

P.S. I set out for Bedford in 3. days and shall be absent 3. weeks.

PoC (DLC); on verso of reused address cover to TJ; at foot of text: "Mr Barnes"; endorsed by TJ.

TJ correctly inferred that the letter from Tadeusz Kosciuszko, printed above at 14 Mar. 1815, was written BEFORE THE LATE REVOLUTION that put Napoleon back on the French throne and evidently also before word reached him of the United States Senate ratification on 16 Feb. 1815 of OUR PEACE, the Treaty of Ghent ending the War of 1812 (*JEP*, 2:620).

[1] Reworked from "give."

To Louis H. Girardin

DEAR SIR   Monticello May 12. 15.

The unfortunate error into which I led you in conversation by [a] lapse of my memory, having interwoven itself into your narrative, I found it necessary to remodel that, in order to present a distinct view of the movements of the enemy, & my own, day by day as they occurred during Arnold's excursion to Richmond. this is accordingly done now with an accuracy which you may rely on. this remodelling however rendered necessary some transpositions of the matter of your text, in order to connect every article with the fact to which it was adapted. but all is stated in your own words. so that altho' looking at the marks of the pencil from page 257. to 261. it would seem as if I proposed to omit 3. or 4. pages, yet in truth the whole is retained with some changes only of order. but all this is still submitted to your own judgment; one thing only I ask from a sentiment of feeling; that is, to suppress altogether the note respecting Trent & Tatham. it may give pain to the latter who is living, and to the numerous & respectable friends of the former who is dead. have you any where[1] mentioned the fact so honorable to Virginia that during an eight years revolutionary war, not a single person suffered by the sword of the law for treason?—I inclose you letters for Fayette, Thouin and Gallatin. Dupont is arrived in America. be so good as to let me know by return of the bearer the cost of the books you were so kind as to let me have that I may make provision on the subject before I set out to Bedford. lest you should have mislaid the list I will name them.

Tertullian. Charron. Virey. Greek & Ital. lexicon. Simson's mathematical exercises. Orations from Livy, Tacitus E^{t}c. Janua trilinguis, Mair's exercises. some others were noted, but had been otherwise disposed of. I salute you with esteem and respect

TH: JEFFERSON

RC (PPAmP: Thomas Jefferson Papers); one word faint; at foot of text: "Mr Girardin." Enclosures: (1) TJ to Lafayette, 11 May 1815. (2) TJ to André Thoüin, 11 May 1815. (3) TJ to Albert Gallatin, 11 [May] 1815.

Burk, Jones, and Girardin, *History of Virginia*, 4:452–70, contains a NARRATIVE of TJ's actions as governor during Benedict Arnold's invasion of Virginia, 1780–81. The volume does not refer to TRENT or William TATHAM. The lenient policy against traitors is mentioned on p. 461.

In a LIST in his letter to Girardin of 7 July 1814, TJ expressed his intention to purchase works by Tertullian, Pierre Charron, Julien Joseph Virey, and Thomas Simpson, as well as a modern Greek–Italian dictionary. He did not there include the other books mentioned here: Jean Baptiste Dumouchel and François Joseph Goffaux, *Narrationes excerptæ ex Latinis scriptoribus servato temporum ordine dispositæ; or, Select Narrations, taken from the best Latin authors, Justin, Quintus Curtius, Cæsar, Cicero, Titus Livius, Sallust, Suetonius, and Tacitus*, 1st American ed. (Philadelphia, 1810; Poor, *Jefferson's Library*, 3 [no.

16]); Jan Amos Komenský (Comenius), *Janua Linguarum Reserata*, Greek trans. Theodor Simon, French trans. Étienne de Courcelles (Amsterdam, 1643, and later eds.; Poor, *Jefferson's Library*, 13 [no. 843]); and John Mair, *An Introduction to Latin Syntax* (Edinburgh, 1755, and later eds.; Poor, *Jefferson's Library*, 13 [no. 871]).

Missing letters from Girardin to TJ of 12 May, 26 July, and 16 Aug. 1815 are recorded in SJL as received from Glenmore on 12 May, from Richmond on 3 Aug., and from Milton on 16 Aug. 1815, respectively. TJ's letter to Girardin of 2 July, not found, is also recorded in SJL. This last letter from TJ may be the one from which an extract appeared in the *Richmond Enquirer*, 26 Oct. 1816, in a publication announcement for Burk, Jones, and Girardin, *History of Virginia*, vol. 4: "Thomas Jefferson returns to Mr. Girardin his *M. S.* which he has read with great satisfaction. And must express with sincerely, his peculiar gratification on seeing this portion of American History, that of his native State, so ably recorded for posterity."

[1] TJ here canceled "omitted."

To James Madison

DEAR SIR   Monticello May 12. 15.

I have totally forgotten the writer of the letter I forward to you, and every circumstance of his case. I leave it therefore on his own letter and that of the Marquis de la Fayette to you, which came inclosed, and is now forwarded with the other.   I shall set out for Bedford within three days, and expect to be absent as many weeks. the newspapers have begun the war for the European powers; but if the people of France are as unanimous as they represent, I cannot believe that those powers will imagine they can force a sovereign on that nation, and therefore presume the Continental powers will prefer a compromise, and that the financial difficulties of England will deter her from the Quixotism of attempting it single-handed. present us all affectionately to mrs Madison and accept best wishes for your own health, quiet & happiness.   Th: Jefferson

RC (DLC: Madison Papers); addressed: "James Madison President of the US. Montpelier near Orange C.H"; franked; postmarked Milton, 17 May; endorsed by Madison. PoC (DLC); on verso of reused address cover of missing letter from William Short to TJ, 25 Apr. 1815 (see note to TJ to Short, 15 May 1815); endorsed by TJ. Enclosure: Francis De Masson to TJ, 9 Feb. 1815, and enclosure.

To Thomas T. Tucker

Dear Sir   Monticello May 12. 15.
    In compliance with the request of your letter of Apr. 28 I now acknolege the reciept of 8580. Dollars in treasury notes from the Commissioner of loans in Richmond; that I have also recieved mr Barnes's acknolegement of his receipt at Washington of 4,860. Dollars in Treasury notes, & 10.D in other paper for which I had given him an order. I am not informed of mr Short's receipt of the 10,500. Dollars for which he had an order, but I presume he has furnished it to you himself, and thus closed the paiment of the whole sum of 23,950 th[e a]mount of the appropriation for the purchase of my library. [Ac]cept the assurance of my great esteem & respect.   Th: Jefferson

PoC (DLC); on verso of reused address cover from William W. Hening to TJ; torn at seal; at foot of text: "Thomas T. Tucker esq."; endorsed by TJ.

The LETTER OF APR. 28 was actually dated 25 Apr. 1815. Thomas Nelson was the federal COMMISSIONER OF LOANS IN RICHMOND. The PAIMENT of these three orders was reported in *An Account of the Receipts and Expenditures of the United States. For the Year 1815* (Washington, 1816), 103.

To William Wirt

Dear Sir   Monticello May 12. 15.
    Among some queries you addressed to me some time ago, was one on the case of Josiah Philips, which happened early in the revolution. not aware that the propriety of the proceeding in that case had been questioned and reprehended, my answer was general on that

query. an application from another quarter having informed me of the doubts which have been expressed on it, I have bestowed more reflection on it, and I send you an extract from my answer, by way of supplement to what I said to you on the subject. I was then thoroughly persuaded of the correctness of the proceeding, and am more and more convinced by reflection. if I am in error, it is an error of principle. I know of no substitute for the process of outlawry, so familiar to our law, or to it's kindred process by act of attainder, duly applied, which could have reached the case of Josiah Phillips. one of these, or absolute impunity seems the only alternative. ever and affectionately

Your friend & serv^t Th: Jefferson

RC (ViU: TJP); addressed: "William Wirt esq. Richmond"; franked; postmarked Milton, 14 May. PoC (DLC); endorsed by TJ. Tr (MdHi: Wirt Papers).

The enclosed EXTRACT, not found, was taken from TJ to Louis H. Girardin, 12 Mar. 1815.

From Baring Brothers & Company

Sir London 13 May 1815

We received only a few days ago your much esteemed favor of the 28th of June last Year, but the Letter from Mr Barnes, with the original of the Bill of £400– on Wm Murdock, for account of General Kosciuzko at Paris, reached us in due Course, and the amount has been placed at the disposal of the General—. We beg you will be assured that we shall on all occasions have much pleasure in Rendering ourselves usefull to You or your friends, and that you will believe us, with the most perfect Regard

Sir Your most obedient & very humble Servants

Baring Brothers & Co

RC (DLC); in a clerk's hand, signed by a representative of the firm; at foot of text: "The Honble Thos Jefferson & & & Monticello Virginia"; endorsed by TJ as received 9 Aug. 1815 and so recorded in SJL.

John Barnes sent a LETTER to Baring Brothers & Company on or about 22 June 1814 with a remittance for Tadeusz Kosciuszko (see Barnes to TJ, 22 June 1814, and note).

Statement of Albemarle County
Property Subject to Federal Tax

A list of the property of the subscriber in the county of Albemarle liable to the taxes imposed by Congress at their session of 1814–15.

———

5640. acres of land, including 400. a[s] on Hardware[1] belonging to himself, Hudson & others.

      2. slaves above 60. years of age
      9. d⁰ between 50. & 60.
      9.[2] d⁰ between 40. & 50.
   16. d⁰ between 30. & 40.
   24. d⁰ between 20. & 30.
   29. d⁰ between 10. & 20.
   <u>43.</u> d⁰ under 10.
 132.

Houshold furniture.[3]

     4. clocks
     1. desk & bookcase
     2. book cases.
     4. chests of drawers
     1. sideboard
     5. single & 2. double[4] leaved dining tables[5]
   13. tea & card tables
   36. chairs
     1. Sopha.

Mahogany. (bracket spanning the above group)

     6. d⁰ with some gilding
     1.[6] d⁰ plain painted.
   44. chairs with some gilding
   11 d⁰ plain painted.
   11. window curtains
   80. pictures & prints above 12.I. wide
   39. smaller
     9. looking glasses above 2.f. long.
     4. smaller d⁰[7]
     1. harpsichord
     1. tea urn, coffee d⁰ beakers[8] & candlesticks
  752. oz. of plate Troy weight equal to 804.D.
     2. silver watches[9]

all which said houshold furniture the subscriber believes would not sell at public vendue for more than three thousand dollars.[10]

> TH: JEFFERSON
> May. 14. 1815.

MS (MHi); entirely in TJ's hand; endorsed by TJ: "taxes Albemarle 1815 for the Assessor." Dft (MHi); on verso of reused address cover to TJ.

TAXES on dwellings, land, and slaves were imposed by "An Act to provide additional revenues for defraying the expenses of government, and maintaining the public credit, by laying a direct tax upon the United States, and to provide for assessing and collecting the same," 9 Jan. 1815. Other taxes were collected under "An Act to provide additional revenues for defraying the expenses of government, and maintaining the public credit, by laying duties on household furniture, and on gold and silver watches," 18 Jan. 1815 (U.S. Statutes at Large, 3:164–80, 186–92).

[1] Preceding two words not in Dft.
[2] Reworked from "10" in Dft.
[3] Preceding two words interlined in Dft. TJ valued each of the following entries in pencil in a column in right margin of Dft. He valued his clocks at a total of $80, his combination desk and bookcase at $20, his bookcases at $20, his chests of drawers at $40, his sideboard at $20, his dining tables at $60, his tea and card tables at $78, his chairs and sofa without gilding at $90, his gilt and painted sofas at $54, his chairs with gilding at $110, his painted chairs at $20, his window curtains at $66, his larger pictures and prints at $240, his smaller pictures and prints at $39, his looking glasses at $95, his harpsichord at $100, his 752 troy ounces of "plate" (silver flatware and hollowware) at $804, and his plated tea and coffee urns, beakers, and candlesticks at $60. According to his calculations, the furniture was worth $1132 and the silver $864, for a total of $1996.

[4] Preceding three words interlined.
[5] Entry reworked in Dft from "[...] ding tables of 3 & 1. of 2. leaves."
[6] Dft: "2."
[7] Preceding three words interlined in Dft.
[8] MS: "bickers." Dft: "beakers."
[9] TJ placed a question mark to the left of this entry in Dft.
[10] Beneath this line in Dft TJ wrote in pencil: "not exceeding 2000. 10
            3000. 17."

From Joseph Cabell Breckinridge

DEAR SIR,   Lexington May 14. 1815.
The freedom I take in obtruding this letter upon you, needs an apology. I hope a sufficient one will be found in the following statement.

Doctor Buchanan, a native of this state—a gentleman of unusual talents—for several years past, distinguished as a metaphysician—and now the Editor of a patriotic Newspaper, in Frankfort, called the "Palladium"—is engaged in collecting materials for a Biographical work, to be confined in its selections to the western states. He has expressed a wish to include my Father—and requests my aid in procuring matter. I have written to several of the early friends and associates of my Father, from whom I expect to obtain such[1] information, touching the earlier incidents of his life, as is required for the satisfactory execution of the undertaking. But it will probably be on that portion of the narrative which includes his political exertions, that the writer will bestow most attention, and towards which the public curiosity will be most eagerly directed.—Have the feelings of a fond Son carried me too far in my solicitude for the memory of a beloved Father, in the appeal I am about to make? Who could know him better, than the man he respected most? Who better decide on the merits of his acts, than the great projector of that republican system of policy, which it was his unceasing aim to consummate?—Tho' lost to his country, his family, and his friends,—cut off from usefulness and increasing fame, there are those whose approbation can add a precious consolation to the bereaved, and an earnest to posterity of that excellence which an untimely death obscured! Relying then on the benevolent kindness of that disposition, which it was among the first lessons of my childhood to revere, I ask from you a communication on the subject of this memoir—Your compliance with this request will draw largely on the gratitude, but can add nothing to the respect of your

Admirer and Friend.   JOSEPH CABELL BRECKINRIDGE

RC (DLC); endorsed by TJ as received 6 June 1815 and so recorded in SJL.

Joseph Cabell Breckinridge (1788–1823) was a native of Virginia whose family moved to Kentucky in 1793. His father, John Breckinridge, served as attorney general in TJ's administration from 1805 until his death the following year. After graduating from the College of New Jersey (later Princeton University) in 1810, the younger Breckinridge studied law and opened a practice in Lexington. He represented Fayette County in the Kentucky House of Representatives, 1816–19, and was its Speaker, 1817–19. Breckinridge served as Kentucky's secretary of state from 1820 until his death. His son, John Cabell Breckinridge, was vice president of the United States, 1857–61 (James C. Klotter, *The Breckinridges of Kentucky, 1760–1981* [1986],

95–6, 110–2; *The Biographical Encyclopedia of Kentucky of the Dead and Living Men of the Nineteenth Century* [1878], 19; *Journal of the House of Representatives of the Commonwealth of Kentucky* [1816–17 sess.]: 47, 56; [1817–18 sess.]: 3, 4–5; [1818–19 sess.]: 3, 5; *PTJ*, 27:270–1; Clay, *Papers*, 3:493; *Louisville Public Advertiser*, 6 Sept. 1823).

Joseph BUCHANAN was a publisher of the Frankfort *Kentucky Palladium*. His BIOGRAPHICAL WORK was never published (*DAB*; Brigham, *American Newspapers*, 1:153–4). Wilson Cary Nicholas was among the EARLY FRIENDS AND ASSOCIATES to whom Breckinridge wrote (Breckinridge to Nicholas, 30 Apr. 1815, and Nicholas, biographical essay on John Breckinridge, [after 10 May 1815] [both MHi]).

[1] Word interlined.

To John Graham

DEAR SIR   Monticello May 14. 15.

The inclosed letter for mr Crawford was delivered to a gentleman who was going to France. hearing before his departure that mr Crawford was on his return, he sent the letter back to me. I am anxious however that Mr Crawford should recieve it, and as of the date it bears. will you have the goodness to let it lie in your office with such papers as may be destined for him, and to let him on his return recieve it with them, either at the office if he comes there, or otherwise by mail. Accept renewed assurances of my great esteem and respect.

                                                     TH: JEFFERSON

PoC (DLC); on verso of reused address cover of John Hollins to TJ, 10 Apr. 1815; at foot of text: "Mr Graham"; endorsed by TJ. Enclosure: TJ to William H. Crawford, 14 Feb. 1815.

George Ticknor was the GENTLEMAN bound for France.

To Horatio G. Spafford

DEAR SIR   Monticello May 14. 15.

Your favor of April 4. was not recieved till the day before yesterday. I subscribe with pleasure to your American magazine,[1] but hope you will have some agent in our state to recieve the annual subscription, nothing being so difficult as remittances to other states for want of some paper of general circulation. with respect to aiding it with materials for publication, I am become so averse to the labors of the writing table as to be always far behind in the most necessary and pressing business. I am glad to learn that your carriage succeeds. our reasoning on new machines is so often baffled by small circumstances which it is difficult to take into account, that I am always unwilling to rest on any thing but actual experience. Accept the assurance of my esteem and respect   TH: JEFFERSON

RC (NjMoHP: Lloyd W. Smith Collection); addressed: "Mr Horatio G. Spafford Albany"; franked; postmarked Charlottesville, 17 May; with Spafford's notes on address cover: "Subscription" and "5. 23, '15." PoC (MHi); on verso of reused address cover of missing letter from William Short to TJ, 4 Apr. 1815 (see note to TJ to Short, 18 Apr. 1815); endorsed by TJ.

Spafford's misdated FAVOR is printed above at 4 May 1815.

[1] In the RC, Spafford used a "+" symbol in the left margin to key the line ending with this word to a note at foot of text: "entered, 5. 23, '15."

To Pierre Samuel Du Pont de Nemours

MY DEAR FRIEND   Monticello. May 15. 15

The newspapers tell us you are arrived in the US. I congratulate my country on this as a manifestation that you consider it's civil advantages as more than equivalent to the physical comforts and social delights of a country which possesses both in the highest degree of any one on earth. you despair of your country, and so do I. a military despotism is now fixed upon it permanently, especially if the son of the tyrant should have virtues and talents. what a treat would it be to me, to be with you, and to learn from you all the intrigues, apostacies and treacheries which have produced this last death's blow to the hopes of France. for altho' not in the will, there was in the imbecility of the Bourbons a foundation of hope that the patriots of France might obtain a moderate representative government. here you will find rejoicings on this event, and by a strange qui pro quo[1] not by the party hostile to liberty, but by it's zealous friends. in this they see nothing but the scourge reproduced for the back of England. they do not permit themselves to see in it the blast of all the hopes of mankind, and that however it may jeopardize England, it gives to her self-defence the lying countenance[2] again of being the sole champion of the rights of man, to which, in all other nations she is most adverse. I wrote to you on the 28th of February, by a mr Ticknor, then proposing to sail for France: but the conclusion of peace induced him to go first to England. I hope he will keep my letter out of the post offices of France; for it was not written for the inspection of those now in power; You will now be a witness of our deplorable ignorance in finance and political economy generally. I mentioned in my letter of Feb. that I was endeavoring to get your memoir on that subject printed. I have not yet succeeded: I am just setting out to a distant possession of mine and shall be absent three weeks. God bless you.

TH: JEFFERSON

RC (DeGH: Pierre Samuel Du Pont de Nemours Papers, Winterthur Manuscripts); at foot of text: "M. Dupont de Nemours." PoC (DLC); endorsed by TJ.

Du Pont ARRIVED in the harbor of New York City on 1 May 1815 (*New-York Evening Post*, 2 May 1815; *Alexandria Gazette, Commercial and Political*, 5 May 1815). Napoleon Bonaparte abdicated on 22 June 1815 in favor of his namesake SON, titled the king of Rome, who died in 1832 without ascending to the French throne (Connelly, *Napoleonic France*, 356, 359).

[1] Preceding seven words interlined.
[2] Word interlined in place of "appearance of."

To William Short

DEAR SIR Monticello May. 15. 15.

Your favor of the 3ᵈ finds me just on my departure for Bedford, and I return you therefore the paper you inclosed me, without delay. to the fact of the want of time I will further add that no person on earth would more willingly than myself do whatever was within my power to reward with the honors they have merited our naval heroes, for the respect which their heroism has procured for our country, and for the humiliations they have inflicted on an insulting, a vindictive, and causeless enemy. but I never had that sort of poetical fancy which qualifies for allegorical devices, mottos Eᵗc. painters, poets, men of happy imagination can alone do these things with taste. I must therefore refer it back to you for some one who will do justice to the subject.   the re-revolution of France furnishes an additional element of calculation for the problem of your return to France. adversity may have taught Bonaparte moderation; but I apprehend that his temper & particular kink of insanity render him incapable of that. what a treat indeed would the conversation of Dupont be! he must totally despair for his country, as I do. a military despotism is now I fear fixed on it permanently. among the victims of his return to power, I contemplate but one with pleasure; that is the Pope. the insult which he and the bigot of Spain have offered to the lights of the 19ᵗʰ century by the reestablishment of the inquisition admits no forgiveness. how happily distant are we from the bedlam of Europe. affectionately Adieu.   TH: JEFFERSON

RC (PHi: Brinton Coxe Collection, George Harrison Correspondence); addressed: "William Short esquire Philadelphia"; franked; postmarked Charlottesville, 17 May. PoC (MHi); on verso of reused address cover to TJ; endorsed by TJ as a letter of 14 May 1815 but recorded under correct date in SJL. Enclosure not found.

On the verso of the address leaf of the RC is a note from Short to George Harrison, a Philadelphia naval agent: "Saturday—Dear sir I despatch to you just as I have recᵈ it the letter from the Gentleman who was as you see setting out on a journey, & disqualifies himself—I am sorry not to give you a better accᵗ of my negotiation—I send the letter that you may read & see it is not my fault. yʳˢ truˡʸ W Short" (RC in PHi: Brinton Coxe Collection, George Harrison Correspondence; partially dated; addressed: "Geo. Harrison Eqʳ 156 Chesnut Strʳ").

Missing letters from Short to TJ of 25 Apr. and of THE 3ᴰ and 9 May 1815 are recorded in SJL as received from Philadelphia on 3, 11 May, and 4 June 1815, respectively. TJ reused the address cover of the letter of 25 Apr. (addressed: "Thomas Jefferson Monticello Mail to Milton Virginia"; franked; postmarked Philadelphia, 25 Apr.) for the PoC of his letter to James Madison, 12 May 1815. He reused the address cover of the 3 May letter (addressed: "Thomas Jefferson Monticello Mail to Milton Vᵃ"; franked; postmarked Philadelphia, 3 May) for the PoC of his letter to Joseph Miller, 26 June 1815, and he reused the address cover of the 9 May letter (addressed: "Thomas Jefferson Monticello Mail to Milton Virginia"; franked; postmarked Philadelphia, 9 May) for the PoC of his letter to Elisha Ticknor, 5 July 1815.

Pius VII, the Catholic POPE, restored the Holy Office of the Inquisition in Rome and the Papal States in 1814, and in that year Ferdinand VII OF SPAIN did the same in his nation (James Mac-Caffrey, *History of the Catholic Church in the Nineteenth Century [1798–1908]*, 2d ed. [1910], 1:209–10; Juan Antonio Llorente, *The History of the Inquisition of Spain, from The Time of its Establishment to the Reign of Ferdinand VII* [1843], 204; *New-York Evening Post*, 4 Oct. 1814).

From Patrick Gibson

SIR   Richmond 17ᵗʰ May 1815

I have received your favor of the 10ᵗʰ Insᵗ inclosing $2940 in treasury notes, $2000 of which I shall hold subject to your order, as the balance together with the prds of your flour & Tobacco, will be sufficient to discharge the several sums mentioned in your letter of the 6ᵗʰ—I send you annexed account sales of your flour & Tobacco nᵗ prdˢ $2314.81 at your credit, nothing but the order and flavor of your Tobacco enabled me to get 10$ for it.

With great respect I am Your obᵗ Servᵗ   PATRICK GIBSON

P.S: On reflection I have consider'd that it would be better to pay off your note in bank with the treasury notes at the $1\frac{1}{2}$ pʳCᵗ than to let them lie idle and borrow the money at a discᵗ of the bank; and should it[1] be wanted here, have still to make that sacrifice—In case you should require any sum hereafter more than will arise from the sale of your flour yet to come down, you may calculate on my obtaining it from the bank upon your Sending me your note.—

RC (MHi); with enclosure conjoined; addressed, in James Ligon's hand: "Thomas Jefferson Esqʳ Monticello"; franked; postmarked Richmond, 31 May; with TJ's notations: "sales of tob° & flour"   "B
1814. Dec. 14.   24
1815. May 8.   233
                  257"; endorsed by TJ as received 4 June 1815 and so recorded in SJL.

Missing letters from TJ to Gibson of THE 10ᵀᴴ INSᵀ and THE 6ᵀᴴ are recorded in SJL. According to TJ's financial records, the letter of 6 May modified "my ord. to Gibson" of Apr. 29, while the letter of 10 May enclosed $2,940 in treasury notes and directed the allocation of $1,900 "for the bank"; $140 to pay Joseph Darmsdatt for fish; $100 for the use of TJ's granddaughter Ellen W. Randolph (Coolidge); and $800 "to cover his [Gibson's] advances for me" (*MB*, 2:1308).

Nᵀ PRDˢ: "net proceeds." When applied specifically to tobacco, ORDER means physical condition (*OED*).

On 6 June 1815 TJ recorded payment of his NOTE of $3,900 due to the BANK of Virginia in Richmond. He then BORROWED $1,000 from the bank, SENDING a note for that amount in a letter to Gibson of 6 June (see note to TJ to Benjamin Jones, 6 June 1815; *MB*, 2:1310).

[1] Word interlined in place of "the money."

ENCLOSURE

Account with Patrick Gibson for Flour and Tobacco Sales

Sales of 257 Bbls flour made on a/c of Thomas Jefferson Esq[r]

Dec[r] 1814	To Isaac White for Cash 24 Bbls Sup[r]fine			At $96.—	
May 8[th]	" Tarlton Saunders at				
1815	60[d]/ with In[t] added 215 " "	at 7$	1505.—		
	18 " fine	6½	117	1622 —	
	257 Bbls			$1718.—	

Charges

toll on 257 Bbls $26.77 Inspection 5.14		$31.91
freight 50 Bbls by W[m] Johnson	a 2/3	27. 8
Cooperage 2.12 Storage at 9[d] $32.12		34.24
Commission on $1718 at 2½ p Cent		42.95 136.18
		$1581.82

1815				
May 5th	To B. Stetson 1 Hhd			
	ref[d] Tob[o] Sh[o] 206.	1180 Stem[d] at 6$	70.80	
15	" D.W & C. Warwick			
	6 Hhds viz	640.142.1322		
		641.145.1040		
		642.140.1100		
		643.145.1190		
		644.148.1330		
		645.145.1210		
		7192[w]	a 10$	719.20
				$ 790.—

Charges

Freight 7 Hhds weighing 8372 at 2/ p 100	$27.92	
dray[e] d[o] 117 toll 292 Inspection 5.25	9.34	
Com[n] on $790 at 2½ p Cent	19.75	57: 1 $ 732.99
Nett proceeds 257 Bbls flour and 7 Hhds Tobacco		$2314:81

E. Excepted 17th May 1815—

PATRICK GIBSON

p JA[s] LIGON

MS (MHi); entirely in James Ligon's hand; conjoined with covering letter.

From Sackville King

SIR   Wards Road 6 miles from Lynchburg 17th may–15

I am inform'd that you are dissatisfied with the managment of your Bedford Estate & it is Say,d You have great reason to be so, that when you come up & now Expected, you mean[1] to employ new Overseers make new arangments &ca on your arival please inform me & I'll ride up & see you, for the purpose of aiding you in those arangments, & point out to you a man who Shall do more for you than any person ever has done, I Shall be glad if you—Shou'd think it worth your while to See me I Know it will Serve your Interest

I am Sir Y^r friend   SACKVILLE KING.

RC (MHi); dateline adjacent to signature; addressed: "Thomas Jefferson Esqr at his Bedford plantation"; endorsed by TJ as received 19 May 1815 and so recorded in SJL.

Sackville King (ca. 1748–1839), public official, was a native of Hanover County. He owned property in Louisa County in 1775. King served in the Fluvanna County militia during the Revolutionary War, rising from second lieutenant in 1781 to captain the following year. At that time he was residing on a 300-acre estate along Cary Creek in Fluvanna County, but by 1786 he was at the Oxford ironworks in Campbell County. King resided in Lynchburg for some time thereafter. In 1824 he started the community of Kingston on his Ward's Road land south of Lynchburg, and he served two terms as sheriff of Campbell County. TJ's acquaintance with him extended from at least 1792, when King owed him £99.5. At his death, King's personal estate was valued at only $15.50 (Ruth H. Early, *Campbell Chronicles and Family Sketches Embracing the History of Campbell County, Virginia, 1782–1926* [1927], 101–2; *VMHB* 6 [1899]: 315, 428; 13 [1905]: 47–8;

John H. Gwathmey, *Historical Register of Virginians in the Revolution: Soldiers, Sailors, Marines, 1775–1783* [1938], 447; Richmond *Virginia Gazette, or the American Advertiser*, 21 Jan. 1786; *PTJ*, 24:575; *Acts of Assembly* [1794 sess.], 17–8 [22 Dec. 1794]; Robert Enoch Withers, *Autobiography of an Octogenarian* [1907], 17–8; *JHD* [1824–25 sess.], 15, 21 [3, 7 Dec. 1824]; Campbell Co. Will Book, 8:256, 308; *Lynchburg Virginian*, 17 Jan. 1839).

TJ's dissatisfaction with the MANAGMENT of Poplar Forest, his BEDFORD County estate, led to the dismissal of overseers Jeremiah A. Goodman and Nimrod Darnil, the employment of Joel Yancey as superintendent, and the hiring as NEW OVERSEERS of William J. Miller at the Tomahawk plantation (sometimes also called Poplar Forest), on which TJ's house was located, and Robert Miller at the Bear Creek plantation north of it (TJ to Archibald Robertson, 1 June 1815; Goodman to TJ, 16 June 1815; TJ to William P. Newby, 21 June 1815; *MB*, 2:1317, 1332; Chambers, *Poplar Forest*, 88–90, 221).

[1] Manuscript: "meam."

From John Porter

I Am under the Necessity of applying to my friends for Some help
from a long Confinement Under the afflicting hand of god with the
Rhumatick Complaint is now about 29 years helpless in a Very great
measure and am become more So of late years with other Complaints
had an inflamation fell in my legs Nearly five years ago with a Braking out all over my legs with a Constant Runing no intermition and
Continues bad I believe my long Confinement proceeded from being
Exposed to the fatigues and hardships incident to a Soldiers life in
the old Revolutinary war was three years & a half in the Regular
Service and had the honour to bear my part in the memorable Battles
of Garman Town Brandywine and that Unfortunate defeat Under
Co^ln Bueford—from my long Confinement and Sufferings I have
been at a very great Expence on phisicions as well as many other
ways which has Caused my little fortune to be Consumed and am left
in Very indigent Circumstance therefore I hope Sir you will Consider
my long distress Situation and help your afflicted friend for which
will be Very acceptable and thankfully acknowledged and I hope you
will not loose your Reward Neither in time nor Eternity I Can assure
you it is my great necessity and Sufferings which Caused me to make
the application in hopes Sir you will Excuse my boldness in making
So free it is the rich people that I make application to those that god
has blesst with riches and honour Charrity is a great thing in the
Eyes of god and there is a great Blessing promis to those that walks
therein for it Covers a multitude of Sins—In hopes Sir you will Receive this letter as from a friend who is a Well Wisher to all people y^r
friend and fellow Citizen   JOHN PORTER

please to write me I live near the <u>Green Springs</u>

Sir

I have been Contending for a Claim for Services rendered in the
old Revolutinary war and was Rejected the last Session of Congress
a Juster Claim there is not against the United States I think it is a
Very hard thing that my Claim should be Rejected for my own personal Service which ought now to bring me in upwards of a thousand
dollars with principle and intrust but do not Expect to get a Cent
when I had Brought forward Every Necessary proof to Establish my
Claim it was thought by good Judges though Congress thinks other-
ways if it had been allowed it would been a great thing to me in my

Situation Sir I am Very thankful for the advice you give me on the Subject Several years ago is there no Remedy for me against the United States

please to inform me yrs

JP

RC (MHi); adjacent to full signature: "Mr Thos Jefferson"; endorsed by TJ as received 4 June 1815 and so recorded in SJL.

The 3d Virginia Regiment of the Continental army suffered an UNFORTUNATE DEFEAT under Colonel Abraham Buford on 29 May 1780 at Waxhaws, South Carolina (Mark M. Boatner III, *Encyclopedia of the American Revolution* [1994], 1173–5).

Porter's CLAIM was first presented to Congress on 12 Feb. 1808. It was referred to the Committee on Pensions and Revolutionary Claims on 10 Dec. 1814, during the 3d SESSION of the 13th Congress. This same petition was referred to committee once again on 23 Jan. 1818. Porter finally received an annual pension of $96,

commencing on 20 May 1818 and continuing until his death. He left an estate valued at $14.56 (*JHR*, 9:573, 11:172; *The Pension Roll of 1835* [1835; indexed ed., 1992], 3:716; Virgil D. White, *Genealogical Abstracts of Revolutionary War Pension Files* [1992], 3:2734; Porter C. Wright, "John Porter: An Old Revolutionary Soldier," *Louisa County Historical Magazine* 5, no. 2 [1973–74]: 22; Louisa Co. Will Book, 7:375, 377). TJ offered ADVICE on Porter's earlier attempt to obtain compensation in a letter of 2 Nov. 1809, where the Editors identified Porter with incorrect birth and death dates, which should be ca. 1756–1827.

[1] Reworked from "March."

From Daniel Brent

DEAR SIR,   Washington, Dep^t of State, May 20 1815.

your letter of the 14th Inst to Mr Graham, enclosing one for Mr Crawford, our Minister in France, has just been received at this office. Mr Graham being now, as he probably will be for some time to come, in the State of Kentuckey, I have taken charge of the Enclosure, and will forward it by the first opportunity to Mr Crawford, at Paris.

I have the Honor to remain, with perfect Respect, D^r sir, your Obed^t humble servant,   DANIEL BRENT.

RC (DLC); at foot of text: "Mr Jefferson"; endorsed by TJ as received 4 June 1815 and so recorded in SJL.

Daniel Brent (ca. 1774–1841) served as a clerk in the United States Treasury Department under Alexander Hamilton. He resigned early in 1794 to return to his native Virginia, where he represented Stafford County in the Virginia House of

Delegates in 1796. By 1801 Brent had resumed service in the federal government as a clerk in the State Department, with promotion to chief clerk early in the administration of James Monroe. Brent continued in that post until 1833, when Andrew Jackson appointed him United States consul at Paris, where he died (Harold C. Syrett and others, eds., *The Papers of Alexander Hamilton* [1961–87],

13:463, 15:592; Leonard, *General Assembly*, 205; *PTJ*, 17:354–5, 33:512–3, 36:312; Brent to TJ, 10 Aug. 1802 [DLC]; *JEP*, 3:119, 4:344, 348 [30 Jan. 1801, 21 Jan., 10 Feb. 1834]; Washington *Daily National Intelligencer*, 24 Sept. 1817, 15 July 1830, 26 Feb. 1841).

From Charles Clay

C. CLAY TO Mᴿ THO. JEFFERSON   may 23. 15
thro' forgetfulness inattention or Some other Cause I am unable to hint to Cap. Slaughter the precise nature of the Service for which he is wanted.—whether it is a Superintendance of the business in its present form, as inspector Genˡ or in a more particular & pointed manner, Such as I Suppose mʳ Goodman now Acts in—breviter is it to overlook the Overseers & people or the[1] people only

RC (MHi); dateline at foot of text; addressed: "Tho. Jefferson Esqʳᵉ Poplar Forest"; endorsed by TJ as received 23 May 1815 and so recorded in SJL.

BREVITER: "in short; briefly."

[1] Manuscript: "the the."

To Archibald Robertson

SIR   Poplar Forest May 23. 15.
On recurring[1] to my papers I found a memorandum[2] of the bond which I suppose mr Garland had left with me; but into which, as I was not ready to pay I imagine I did not look, not doubting that[3] the accounts he gave me, among which this was, were all right. among my papers at home I expect I shall find the accounts on which it was founded. my error had been in supposing that all had been carried forward into the accounts from year to year. Accept the assurance of my esteem and respect   TH: JEFFERSON

PoC (ViU: TJP); faint and overwritten by TJ, with resulting anomalies noted below; at foot of text: "Mʳ Robertson"; endorsed by TJ.

The MEMORANDUM by Lynchburg attorney Samuel GARLAND, not found, concerned TJ's unpaid bond of 1 Sept. 1807 to former Poplar Forest overseer Burgess Griffin in the amount of $779.19. TJ settled his ACCOUNTS with Robertson, up to 31 Aug. 1814, by paying $1,962.06 on 20 May 1815 (*MB*, 2:1309, 1362).

[1] Manuscript: "reecurring."
[2] Manuscript: "meorandum."
[3] Manuscript: "tha."

From Archibald Robertson

DEAR SIR   Lynchburg 23ʳᵈ may 1815

I am faverd with yours of yesterday & to days date & have furnishd mʳ Goodman with Sixty Dollars, the other sums you mention will be furnishd at any time they are wanted—

I am glad you have found a memᵒ of the bond executed by Griffin & hope on your return home you will find the accounts all right—

Respectfully Your mo ob Sᵗ   A. ROBERTSON

RC (ViU: TJP); endorsed by TJ as received 23 May 1815 and so recorded in SJL.

TJ's letter of YESTERDAY, 22 May 1815, is not recorded in SJL and has not been found. Jeremiah A. GOODMAN was to use the $60 to pay for a horse purchased from a Mr. Cobb (*MB*, 2:1309).

From John Barnes

DEAR SIR—   George Town. 25ᵗʰ May 1815.

Since my last respects of the 25ᵗʰ Ultᵒ I am Honor'd by your two favʳˢ of the 7ᵗʰ and 12ᵗʰ Insᵗ. Anxiously—wishing to furnish the good Genˡ K. with a Remittance,—and finding the market advancing in the ex for Bills on London and France, I determined instantly—without waiting the Return of your post and concluded the purchase of £400. Sterg ex a 2½ ℔Ct above par is $1822.22, of Messʳ Bowie & Kurtz—on Mʳ Wᵐ Murdock London—very fortunately—there were of theirs, at Alexandria two Vessels loaded & ready for sea. I therefore lost no time in inclosing a Sett by each to Messʳˢ Baring and Brothers—with particular request to do the Needfull, for the Use and Accoᵗ of Genˡ Kosciusko at Paris, and Messʳˢ B & K. took charge of them—and doubt not,[1] they are ere this in the hands of Messʳ Barings—

I also advised the Genˡ—and herewith inclose you Copy.—as well my 3 several statemᵗˢ of his Accoᵗ now depending with me—which at your leisure I pray you to examine, and if incorrect, to advise for my Govermᵗ

I do not wonder at the Genˡˢ impatience for the want of resourses, but—when the very & most extra Occurances that has of late transpired—on a Cool dispassionate Review—Will I doubt not suffer his funds to remain with you—

Exclusive of these impediments (and presuming the Genˡ possessed of the whole of them in France)—I should be Apprehensive—Thro the Various Unforeseen Events that may possibly—happen—and is yet to be dreaded.—they would be less—productive—and probably broke in Upon;—   This Counter Revolution—so unlooked for—has placed the Contest on the very same ground of the first:— but with many weighty Circumstances in Bona's favor—As the Acknowledged Sovereign[2] by each of the Contending Powers—And who can pretend to say—that Bona. is not deserving of a Crown?— in Preferance to most of his Mercenary and Rapacious Enemies.— Neither is it possible to conceive, from what has happened that France can ever be Governed by any Other so long as Bona. is in existance—or by some Other of like—Qualifications—for the very Opposition which has hitherto been made has been the Principle cause of his Advancem[t] to his present greatness—to Continue the Contest; After what has resently transpired—would be National Suicide Brutal, and inhuman,—to Compromise and Spare The Blood of Millions of Innocent individuals, who has no Other Interest to contend for, but to defend themselves & helpless families—would be the height of Beneficence and Godlike Attribute!—

but such are not likely to be the effects—to be produced from the Overbearing Powers,—The Pride—Ambition and dire revange of Emperors Kings, and Sovereign[3] Princes—alike subject to the Control of each Other as Occasion Offers—Miserable indeed must be the people—under—whose Control they are Subject,—the Contrast,[4] with this Goverment, how instructive—and Happy.—yet not Content,—such is the Unhappy depravity of Mankind generally—he is not [to][5] be Altogether happy—on this Terestrial Globe[6] of his Existance—but enough,—We are lost in Conjecture—as to what may be the Event without Star or Compass may not, One or Other of these Adventrous—Sovereigns Prince Regents &c be drifted—by the ebb & flow—of these Political tides, and adverse Winds—to some unknown & desolate Island, Other then Elba!

Excuse this Unavoidable degression—

and Beleive me to be Dear Sir—Your very Obed[t] servant

JOHN BARNES,

PS. be pleased to transmit one set of the within Statem[ts] to G K—in your next Communication to him—

RC (ViU: TJP-ER); at foot of text: "Thomas Jefferson Esq[r] Monticello— Virg[a]"; endorsed by TJ as received 4 June 1815 and so recorded in SJL. Enclosure: Barnes to Tadeusz Kosciuszko, Georgetown, 28 Apr. 1815, acknowledging that he has seen Kosciuszko to TJ, 24 Jan. 1814; noting that on "the 22[d] June 1814—I inclosed to you thro the hands, of Mess[r] Baring Brothers and Comp[y]—a sett of Exchange, Bowie & Kurtz on Wm Murdock in London for £400. Ster^g" to be paid to Kosciuszko in Paris; explaining that he has made a similar "remittance of £400. Sterling exchange at 2½ per Cent above par, the 24th Instant, equal to $1822.22, now risen to 4 ℔Ct and expected still to 7½ per Ct."; asking for his likeness, which he will keep with others "of my most Valued friends"; and promising to send his accounts, with duplicates to TJ, "at my better leisure" (Tr in ViU: TJP-ER; in Barnes's hand; at head of text: "Copy"). Other enclosures printed below.

[1] Word added in margin.
[2] Manuscript: "Sowereign."
[3] Manuscript: "Soverergn."
[4] Manuscript: "Contras."
[5] Omitted word editorially supplied.
[6] Manuscript: "Glope."

ENCLOSURES

I

John Barnes's Account with Tadeusz Kosciuszko

Genl Kosciusko[1] In a/c with John Barnes in a/ Sales of his Penn^a Bank Stock & Subscrip^n to the US. Loan of 25 Millions of Dollars—

1814.		Doll^s C^{ts}	
May 25th	To Wm Whann Cash^r Bank of Colum^a for my Subscrip^s—in Name of Thos Jefferson—to the loan of 25 Millions US. a 88 for 100.	$2,500	
June 25th	July 25. & Sepr 8th Each for $2,500	7.500	10,000
	To 1 per Cent on paym^{ts} made and disc^{ts} charged JB. at Bank on his Notes given		100
	To Bal^e due this Acco^t Car^d to former Acco^t		802
			10.902
	Per Contra—		
June 4th	By Sale made of G K. 20 shares of Penn^a Bank		
& 8th	stock of $400 each a 138 ℔C^t ad^{ce} on each share is equal to 552 ℔ share	11.040	
	deduct the Usual Brokerage & Merchantile ⎫ Commiss^{ns} a 1¼ per Cent ⎭	138	
			10.902

E E. George Town Co^a
25 June & 8 Sepr 1814.
JOHN BARNES.

MS (ViU: TJP-ER); in Barnes's hand; with horizontal and vertical rules in red ink; conjoined with third enclosure below.

E.E.: "errors excepted."

[1] Manuscript: "Kosciusk."

II

John Barnes's Account with Tadeusz Kosciuszko

John Barnes. George Town Co^a In a/c wth Genl Kosciusko in Paris

1814.		Dolls–Cents.	
May 12th to Sepr 8th	for Proceeds of $10,000, Subscribed to the US. Loan, of 25 Millions a 88 for $100 — liquidated a 80 for $100. of 6 ⅌Ct Stock of the US. bearing^1 Int of 6 ⅌Ct^2 pay^{ble} quarterly on	12.500	–
1815. Jany 8th	for proceeds of Int. Accruing on Average from 10th July to 31st Decr 1814. on the above Subscrip	358.32.	
	Negotiat^n on d^o	8.95.	
		349.37.	
April 8th	for 3 M^{os} Int. due the 1^h Ins^t on $12.500	187.50.	
	Nego^n	4.68.	182.82.
	Dollars,	$532.19.	

E E. George Town Co^a
8^h April 1815
JOHN BARNES,

MS (ViU: TJP-ER); in Barnes's hand; with horizontal and vertical rules in red ink.

^{1} Manuscript: "beaing."
^{2} Reworked from what appears to be "$5\frac{2}{5}$th."

III

John Barnes's Account with Tadeusz Kosciuszko

Genl Thad: Kosciusko in Paris In a/c wth John Barnes. Geo Town Co^a

1814		Doll^s & C^{ts}		
Sepr 2^d	By Amo^t of Acco^t rendered Bal^e due Genl K	755.88		
"	By Amo. of a/c Annexed for the proceeds of Penn^a B. Stock & Loan subscrip^n	802	1557	88.
1815 Apr^l 26.	By T. Jefferson for 12 M^{os} Int due 1^h Ins^t on $4500 a 8 per Cent	360		
	Nego^n	9	351	
			1908	88
	Payments			
Apr^l 24.	To Bowie & Kurtz for sett of Ex a 60 days on Wm Murdock London for £400 Sterling a 2½ ⅌Ct advance	1822.22.		
	Neg^n paying & remitting	36.44.		
	paid postage G. K. lett^r 1^h Decr 1813	22.	1858	88

"	26ʰ	By Balᶜᵉ due this Accoᵗ Carrᵈ to New Accᵗ	Dollˢ	50
	"	By this Principal sum Recd from		
		Mr Jeffersons order on the Treasury US.		
		in Treasury Notes, dated 21 Aprˡ and		
		payᵇˡᵉ 21 Apˡ 1816. wʰ Int 5⅖ʰ for		4,500*

*Deposited in Iron Chest with J Barnes—

E. E. George Town Coᵃ
26 April 1815
JOHN BARNES.

MS (ViU: TJP-ER); in Barnes's hand; with horizontal and vertical rules in red ink; conjoined with first enclosure printed above.

To Charles Clay

TH:J. TO MR CLAY.   May 25. 15.

On the subject which has been passing between us I have had an offer from a person who has many proper points in his character, and would see both my plantations every day. altho my inclinations are as they were before, yet there is ground for consultation with you on comparative merits. this suggests that while it is necessary to sound the dispositions of the party first thought of thoroughly, it is best to commit me as little as possible, until I can communicate with you on the subject of the second offer. ever affectionately yours.

RC (Christian S. Hutter Jr., Charlottesville, 1945; photostat in ViU: TJP); dateline at foot of text; addressed: "Mʳ Clay"; endorsed by Clay. Not recorded in SJL.

The recent OFFER came from Joel Yancey, whom TJ hired later this month as the manager of the Bear Creek and Tomahawk PLANTATIONS that comprised his Poplar Forest estate (TJ to Archibald Robertson, 1 June 1815).

From Pierre Samuel Du Pont de Nemours

TRÈS CHER ET TRÈS   Eleutherian Mill, near Wilmington
NOBLE AMI,   a delaware 26 may 1815.

J'avais compté vous porter moi même la nouvelle de mon arrivée en Amérique. Mais vos Journaux Sont des indiscrets, et je Suis resté chez mes Enfans, entouré de mes Petits-Enfans, plus longtems que je ne l'avais projetté.

L'Espoir de trouver à Mounticello un Frere en Economie politique, un Maitre en Philosophie, est fortement entré dans le choix de ma retraite, Si c'est une Retraite.

Je ne crois pas encore que c'en Soit une. Je ne regarde mon voyage et mon Séjour que comme l'acquisition d'un nouveau Cabinet plus paisible, où je pourrai travailler à me perfectionner, à murir mes idées, à les mieux lier, à les mettre avec plus d'ordre et de talent Sous les yeux des Hommes que <u>Dieu</u> appelle, ou appellera, à proposer et à rédiger des Constitutions et des Loix.

A peine m'est-il arrivé une couple de fois dans ma longue vie d'être à peu près content de mon ouvrage. Il m'a fallu occuper à la fois mes deux mains, mes deux yeux, les deux cotés de ma Tête à des choses tout-à-fait differentes, dont l'une nuisait toujours à l'autre. Les devoirs de l'Administrateur, et les affaires du Pere de Famille donnaient trop de distractions[1] au Philosophe.

Aujourd'hui, je Suis moralement Sur de mon diner.

Je n'ai pas d'inquiétude pour mes Enfans. Ils ont toujours été des hommes d'esprit de probité, et de courage. Ils peuvent servir utilement le Pays où j'ai cru devoir les placer. Ils ont acquit une capacité très distinguée. S'ils l'emploient à procurer à mes Petits-Enfans une existence absolument indépendante, ils pourront les laisser parmi les plus libres et les plus êclairés de leurs Concitoyens éclairés et libres.

Ils ont eu de belles et bonnes Femmes. Les hommes Se font comme les mérinos; et pour tous les Animaux qui naissent en nombre égal de chaque Sexe et[2] qui ont atteint leur plein développement Dieu a imaginé l'Amour, afin d'apparier les races. J'ai donc d'assez fortes raisons d'espérer que Sous un Gouvernement où la Noblesse n'est point héréditaire et n'influe pas Sur les mariages ma Famille deviendra illustre, méritera de l'être.

Je n'ai plus d'engagemens positifs avec aucun Etat politique.

Je n'ai à craindre ni d'être appelé à une Magistrature, ni d'en être expulsé.

Je n'aurai point à improviser des discours dans une Assemblée, ni à les écrire du Soir au lendemain pour un Conseil d'Etat ou pour un Comité de Législation.

J'aurai le tems de cultiver ce que Dieu a bien voulu m'accorder de raison, pour juger et contenir l'impétuosité naturelle qu'il m'avait aussi donnée.

Je n'ai encore êté qu'un jeune homme actif, avec de bons Sentimens.—Mes cheveux blancs me demandent et me commandent d'etre enfin quelque chose de plus.

Je pourrai consulter Jefferson et Corréa. Aucun Empereur n'a deux Conseillers de cette force.

Aussi ne travaillerons nous pas pour des Empires; mais pour le monde et pour les Siecles.

La conjoncture y est favorable.

Dix ou douze grandes Républiques Se forment Sur votre Continent. Elles S'y établiront et S'y consolideront quand même quelques unes d'entre elles pourraient être passagerement vaincues par la force ou la faiblesse de l'Espagne européenne.

Trois de ces Républiques déja unies m'ont fait l'honneur de me consulter.

Elles Se confédereront toutes, et aussi avec votre République victorieuse, qui leur donnera de bons exemples et pourra de même en recevoir.

Ces Confédérations, Si elles Sont bien conçues et Sagement Stipulées, pourront faire de l'Amérique une République immense, ayant deux mille lieues de long Sur cinq cent lieues de largeur moyenne.— Nous rirons alors de ceux qui ont cru Si longtems qu'on ne pouvait organiser[3] de République hors de l'enceinte d'une petite ville ou d'un petit canton.

Nous en rirons, mais avec une indulgente modération. Ils n'avaient point encore l'idée des <u>Gouvernemens représentatifs</u>, et ils avaient l'experience du danger des Assemblées tumultueuses.

Les Gouvernemens représentatifs commencés en Angleterre, et perfectionnés aux Etats unis par des Senats qui ne Sont point héréditaîres, n'ont encore nulle part atteint la perfection dont ils Sont Susceptibles. Il aurait fallu les commencer par le commencement, par une bonne constitution de Commune dont les principes même ne Sont encore posés en aucun Pays.

Mais dès qu'on Sera parvenu à former des Communes justes, raisonnables et bien Administrées, il n'y aura rien de plus facile que d'instituer avec un certain nombre de ces bonnes Communes de bons cantons, puis avec ces bons cantons de bons districts, avec les bons districts de bons Cercles, avec les bons Cercles d'excellentes Républiques, et avec Ces excellentes Republiques[4] de puissantes et paisibles Confédérations.

Le chaos[5] actuel de l'Amérique espagnole dont il faudra Sortir par des Gouvernemens, me Semble offrir plus de chances pour les avoir bons, que l'orage guerrier de l'Europe. Ma raison pour concevoir cette opinion et cette esperance est que l'Amérique n'a point encore de Princes, Si ce n'est un pauvre Roi de Portugal dont l'exemple n'est pas tentatif.

Les Généraux des Insurgés ne pourront pas aisément se faire Princes ni Rois. Ils Sont obligés d'armer leur Peuple pour l'<u>indépendance</u> Et vos Etats-unis quand ils ont eu conquis la leur n'ont pas couronné Washington: Les Secours qu'ils auront à donner en Armes et en munitions, ajouteront du poids à leur exemple Dès que la liberté Américaine Sera clairement assurée contre les absurdes et orgueilleuses et rapaces prétentions de l'Europe, les habitans de chaque division naturelle indiquée par les montagnes et les rivieres Songeront à Se donner une Patrie; et leurs Chefs Se trouveront heureux d'en être les Magistrats.

Ce Sera l'affaire[6] d'un très petit nombre d'années, pendant lesquelles la malheureuse Europe Sera livrée à une guerre affreuse; mais dont le dernier résultat ne Sera point aussi funeste que nous pourrions être portés à le croire.

Le despotisme militaire ne pourra pas Se Soutenir. Les Nations ne Suffiraient point aux Armées. Buonaparte et Son armée invoquent aujourd'hui des idées républicaines, ou même plus que Républicaines, des idées populaires, la haine contre les nobles, contre les Prêtres, contre les mauvais impôts. Il n'y a qu'un pas de cette disposition d'esprit à la révolte[7] contre les Rois. dans deux ans l'empereur Napoléon ne parviendra plus à Satisfaire à la fois Ses Troupes et Ses Sujets.[8] L'embarras où il Se trouvera conduirait plustot à une nouvelle Ochlocratie qu'à la continuation d'un Gouvernement arbitraire et absolu.

Vers le même tems l'Allemagne, l'Italie, l'Angleterre peut-être, S'ennuieront de combattre pour une Famille, qu'elles ne pourraient pas Soutenir Si leurs Soldats réussissaient la ramener en France, parce qu'on ne croirait plus à Ses promesses, et que la fierté nationale demeurerait trop offensée. La grande apparence est que l'Allemagne l'Italie, l'Angleterre même, renverront leurs Rois et renonceront non[9] Seulement leurs Rois, mais à la Royauté.

Aucun de ces Pays cependant ne voudra obeir à Buonaparte car Sa Royauté Serait fort dure dans ces Pays etrangers,[10] et il n'aura plus la force de les contraindre. Son Empire resterait-il Seul au milieu de toutes ces nouvelles Républiques? et celles-ci consentiront elles à de mauvaises constitutions, Si l'Amérique en a de bonnes? Nil desperandum

Je Suis très faché d'être vieux; bien plus encore que le passage aux Gouvernemens libres doive couter tant de Sang. On n'en aurait pas versé une goutte Si les détestables Lameth n'avaient pas Souillé la révolution française par les Séditions qu'eux et leurs Amis ont organisées.—Mais là dessus ce qui est fait est fait. Une partie de ce qui est à faire, en bien, en mal, est devenu inévitable. Tachons d'adoucir et d'abréger les calamités; c'est une très belle mission.

Bon Jefferson, ques vos lumieres y aident mon courage. Mes calculs Sur les diverses époques de ma vie me promettent encore environ huit ans. Vous en avez trois de moins que moi, et je crois votre Santé meilleure que la mienne.

Ne mourons pas Sans avoir placé le tems qui nous reste à grand profit.

Je vous embrasse avec tendresse et respect

DuPont (de nemours)

Ma Femme était malade lors de mon départ. Elle n'a pu me Suivre. Je l'attends dans quelques mois, ou au plus tard dans un an. Jusqu'à Son arrivée, je n'aurai que la moitié de mon esprit. Elle m'est d'un grand Secours: Sa tête et Son coeur Sont pleins de conseils excellens.

Mais je ne pouvais attendre à Paris l'arrivée de Buonaparte devenu hypocrite. Je Savais ce qu'il en a couté, même de gloire, à Cicéron pour avoir cru aux promesses d'Octave. Et ce que je puis encore faire de bon travail ne me permettait pas de m'exposer à mourir dans un cachot, par les refus qu'il m'aurait convenu de rendre très fiers.

Je compte aller avec Corréa passer quelques jours à Mounticello, quand nous Serons instruits que vous y Serez de retour.[11]

EDITORS' TRANSLATION

Eleutherian Mill, near Wilmington in
VERY DEAR AND NOBLE FRIEND,   delaware 26 may 1815.

I had intended to advise you of my arrival in America personally, but your newspapers are indiscreet, and I stayed longer than I had planned with my children, surrounded by my grandchildren.

The hope of finding at Monticello a brother in political economy and a master of philosophy entered very much into the choice of my retreat, if this is a retreat.

I still do not believe that it is one. I consider my trip and sojourn to be but the acquisition of a new, more tranquil study, where I will be able to work at perfecting myself, developing, linking, and better organizing my ideas under the eyes of men on whom God calls, or will call, to propose and draft constitutions and laws.

In my long life I have been satisfied with my work on only a couple of occasions. I have had to use both my hands, both my eyes, and both sides of my head simultaneously in order to take care of many quite different things, and one task was always interfering with the other. Administrative duties and paternal matters provided too many distractions to the philosopher.

Today, I am morally sure of my dinner.

I have no worries about my children. They have always been men of wit, integrity, and courage. They can usefully serve the country in which I thought it appropriate to place them. They have achieved a very distinguished position. If they use it to procure for my grandchildren an absolutely independent life, they will leave them among the most free and enlightened of their free and enlightened fellow citizens.

They have had beautiful and good wives. Men are made like merinos; for all the animals that are born with equal numbers of each sex, once they have reached their full development, God invented love in order to pair up the races. Therefore, I have good reasons to hope that under a government in which nobility is not hereditary and has no influence over marriage, my family will become illustrious and will deserve to be so.

I no longer have commitments to any political state.

I fear neither being called to office nor being expelled from it.

I will no longer have to improvise speeches in an assembly or write them overnight for a state council or legislative committee.

I will have time to cultivate what God was willing to grant me by way of reason in order to judge and restrain the natural impetuosity that he has also given me.

Until now I have only been an active young man full of good intentions. My white hair requests and commands me to be something more at last.

I will be able to consult Jefferson and Corrêa. No emperor has two such worthy counselors.

Also, we will not be working for empires, but for the world and the centuries to come.

The situation is favorable for it.

Ten or twelve large republics are being created on your continent. They will establish themselves and grow stronger, although a few might be temporarily vanquished by the strength or weakness of European Spain.

Three of these republics, which are already united, have done me the honor of consulting me.

They will all become confederations and will join your victorious republic, which will give them good examples to follow and will receive the same from them.

These confederations, if they are well conceived and wisely set up, will be able to make America into an immense republic two thousand leagues in length and, on average, five hundred in breadth. Then we will laugh at those who believed for so long that a republic could not be organized outside the limits of a small city or canton.

We will laugh about it, but with indulgent moderation. They had no idea yet about representative governments, and they had experienced the danger of tumultuous assemblies.

Representative governments, which started in England and were perfected by nonhereditary senates in the United States, have nowhere, as of yet, reached the perfection of which they are capable. They should have started from the beginning with a good communal constitution, the principles of which have not yet been formulated in any country.

But as soon as just, reasonable, well-administered communes have been formed, nothing will be easier than to take a certain number of the better ones and create good cantons with them. Then, with these good cantons form good districts; with good districts establish good circles; with good circles found excellent republics; and with these excellent republics produce powerful and peaceful confederations.

It seems to me that the current chaos in Spanish America, which will have to be overcome by its governments, still offers a better chance to form good ones, than the warlike storm of Europe. My reason for this opinion and hope is that America does not yet have princes, except a poor king of Portugal, whose example is not tempting.

The insurgent generals will not easily turn themselves into princes or kings. They have to arm their people for <u>independence</u>, and your United States, when they had won their independence, did not crown Washington; the aid they will have to give in arms and munitions will add weight to their example. As soon as American liberty will be clearly assured against the absurd, arrogant, and predatory pretensions of Europe, the inhabitants of each natural region defined by mountains and rivers will think of establishing a <u>Fatherland</u>; and their chiefs will be happy to be its magistrates.

It will be a matter of only a few years, during which unhappy Europe will fall into a dreadful war, but the final result will not be as fatal as we might be led to think.

Military despotism will be unable to sustain itself. Armies alone do not suffice for nations. Today, Bonaparte and his army put forth republican ideas, or even more than republican, popular ideas: hatred of the aristocracy, priests, and bad taxes. From this frame of mind it is only one step to a revolt against kings. In two years the Emperor Napoleon will no longer be able to satisfy both his troops and his subjects. The difficulty in which he will find himself would lead to a new ochlocracy rather than the continuation of an arbitrary and absolute government.

At about the same time, Germany, Italy, and perhaps England will tire of fighting for a family that they could not support even if their soldiers succeeded in bringing it back to France, because the people would no longer believe its promises and national pride would still be too offended. Germany, Italy, and even England will clearly get rid of their kings and renounce not only specific rulers, but monarchy as well.

None of these countries, however, will willingly obey Bonaparte, because his rule would be very harsh in these foreign countries, and he will no longer have the strength to force them to accept it. Would his empire be the only one remaining amidst all these new republics? And would these republics accept bad constitutions if America has good ones? <u>Nil desperandum</u>

I am very angry at being old; and even more for the fact that the transition to free governments would cost so much blood. Not a drop of it would have been spilled if the detestable Lameths had not defiled the French Revolution by seditions organized by them and their friends. But in this respect, what is done is done. Some portion of what remains to be accomplished, both good and ill, has become inevitable. Let us try to soften and shorten the calamities; it is a very important mission.

Good Jefferson, may your enlightenment increase my courage. My calculations of the various periods of my life promise me still about another eight years. You are three years younger than I am, and I believe your health is better than mine.

Let us not die without having put the time left to us to good use.

I embrace you with tenderness and respect

DuPont (de nemours)

My wife was sick when I left. She could not accompany me. I am expecting her in a few months or at most in a year. Until her arrival I will have only half of my intellect. She is of great help to me; her head and heart are full of excellent advice.

But I could not await in Paris the arrival of Bonaparte, who had turned into a hypocrite. I knew what it had cost Cicero, even in glory, after he believed Octavius's promises, and the good work that I am still able to do kept me from risking death in a prison cell because it would have suited me to make very arrogant refusals.

Corrêa and I intend to come and spend a few days at Monticello once we are told that you have returned.

RC (DLC); at head of text: "Mr Jefferson"; endorsed by TJ as received 4 June 1815 and so recorded in SJL. FC (DeGH: Pierre Samuel Du Pont de Nemours Papers, Winterthur Manuscripts). Translation by Dr. Genevieve Moene.

In 1814 the South American patriot Manuel Palacio-Fajardo was in Paris representing the state of New Granada, which was composed of TROIS DE CES RÉPUBLIQUES in rebellion against Spanish rule. While there, he apparently asked Du Pont to make recommendations and draw up model constitutions. The resulting unpublished work, Du Pont's "Mémoire aux républiques équinoxiales," which he sent to TJ and others over the course of the next several years, has not been found (Ambrose Saricks, *Pierre Samuel Du Pont de Nemours* [1965], 346–7; Du Pont to TJ, 20 Dec. 1815, 31 Mar. 1816). John, the prince regent of PORTUGAL from 1792 until his accession to the throne as John VI in 1816, was driven by the French in 1807 from Portugal to its colony of Brazil, which he elevated to a kingdom and united with the mother country in 1815. He did not return to Europe until 1821. UNE FAMILLE: the Bourbons.

The LAMETH brothers, Alexandre and Charles, were leaders of the Feuillants, a group of constitutional royalists who split off from the Jacobins early in the French Revolution (Doyle, *French Revolution*, 154). The Roman orator and politician Marcus Tullius Cicero (CICÉRON) received promises from Julius Caesar's grandnephew and heir, Gaius Octavius (OCTAVE), the future Emperor Augustus, that he would protect him in return for Cicero's political support during the power struggle that followed Caesar's assassination in 44 B.C. Cicero saw to it that the young man was made a consul the following year, but within a few months Octavius agreed to the execution of the elder statesman (Plutarch, *Cicero*, books 44, 46, in *Plutarch's Lives, with an English Translation*, trans. Bernadotte Perrin, Loeb Classical Library [1914–26; repr. 1994], 7:194–5, 200–1; Henry C. Boren, *Roman Society: A Social, Economic, and Cultural History* [1977], 120–1).

[1] RC: "distrations." FC: "distractions."
[2] Preceding nine words interlined.
[3] RC: "organiserser." FC: "organiser."
[4] Preceding five words not in FC.
[5] RC and FC: "cahos."
[6] Reworked from "l'emploi" ("the work").
[7] Word interlined in place of "haine" ("hatred").
[8] Remainder of paragraph interlined.
[9] Preceding two words interlined in place of "non pas" ("not").
[10] Preceding ten words interlined.
[11] Sentence not in FC.

From John Fowler

DEAR SIR, State of Kentucky Lexington 27. May 1815

Mr Thomas Smith now a resident (and has been for many years) of this place intends to visit the neighbourhood of Richmond (Virginia) some time this summer and wish's to pay his respects to you on his way thither. I beg leave to introduce him to your Acquaintance, He is an amiable intelligent Gentleman, Has been Uniformly a warm supporter of the Rights of our excellent Government, and will be proud to Acknowledge your civilities and attentions paid him
I have the Honor to be respectfully
Your Ob^t servant JOHN FOWLER

RC (MHi); endorsed by TJ as received 23 June 1815 and so recorded in SJL.

Thomas Smith (ca. 1792–1865), printer and merchant, was the publisher and editor of the Lexington *Kentucky Gazette,* 1809–12, and, after service in the War of 1812, of the Lexington *Kentucky Reporter,* 1816–32. He was a director in 1824 of the Transylvania Botanic Garden Company, and he served in 1836 both as a trustee of the Newcastle Female Academy and as a director of the Lexington Fire, Life and Marine Insurance Company. He married a niece of Henry Clay, and the latter entrusted Smith with the publication of his speeches, oversight of some of his

financial concerns, and promotion of his political career. By 1845 Smith moved to Louisville, where he was a partner in Kennedy, Smith & Company, an agency for selling rope and hemp bagging (George W. Ranck, *History of Lexington Kentucky: Its Early Annals and Recent Progress* [1872], 233–4, 247; Brigham, *American Newspapers,* 1:163, 166; *Cincinnati Literary Gazette,* 13 Mar. 1824; *Acts Passed at the First Session of the Forty-Fourth General Assembly of the Commonwealth of Kentucky* [1836], 463, 601; Clay, *Papers,* esp. 2:723–5, 6:1, 397, 1073, 8:206, 10:200–1; gravestone inscription, Lexington Cemetery).

To Archibald Robertson

DEAR SIR Poplar Forest May 27. 15.

I had to pay in this neighborhood a sum of between 13. and 1400 D. and came prepared to do it with Treasury bills; but the creditor refuses to recieve them without a discount of 3. per cent; this neither my principles as a citizen, nor my opinion of the comparative solidity of Treasury & bank bills permit me to yield to. I am informed there is a probability that there may be merchants in Lynchburg who would exchange for the Treasury bills at par, as being convenient for remittance to the North where our state bank bills will not be recieved, and I[1] have presumed on your goodness that you would make this enquiry for me and let me know by the return of the bearer whether it can be done. if it can, I will send mr Goodman tomorrow morning with the Treasury bills & to recieve the others, the person for whom they are intended proposing to set out on a journey the next day. the bearer will await and bring me the result of your enquiry. accept the assurance of my esteem and respect

TH: JEFFERSON

PoC (ViU: TJP); at foot of text: "Mr Robertson"; endorsed by TJ.

On 29 May 1815 TJ paid the SUM of $1,393.11 due on two notes he had given to his former overseer Burgess Griffin, which were now held by Bedford County resident John Watts, the CREDITOR (*MB*, 2:1282, 1309; TJ to Watts, 28 May 1815).

[1] Manuscript: "I I."

From James Penn
(for Archibald Robertson)

SIR,   Lynchburg, May 27th 1815

In the absence of Mr Robertson I have opended your Letter and made the enquiry requested. Fortunately I found a Gentleman in Town, who was going on to the north, with whom I have exchanged $1400 Treasury notes for bank bills, these you can have by Sending down Mr Goodman to morrow. In the exchange I was compeled to take Several notes which are not very current here, though very good, of this circumstance you will apprise Mr Goodman, or Probably he might not receive them.

very respectfully Yr Mo Obt srvt   J PENN

RC (ViU: TJP); endorsed by TJ as a letter from Archibald Robertson "by J. Penn" received 27 May 1815 and so recorded (with no mention of Penn) in SJL.

James Penn (1794–1870), clerk of the Lynchburg merchant Archibald Robertson, later became a member of that city's mercantile firm of Garland, Walton, & Penn. Financial difficulties prompted him to move in 1825 to Alabama. Penn settled in Huntsville, Madison County, which he represented in the state's House of Representatives, 1828–32, with service as Speaker, 1830–32. He was appointed cashier of the Huntsville branch of the Bank of the State of Alabama in 1835. Penn moved by 1850 to Memphis, Tennessee, where he served as cashier of the Planters' Bank Branch until 1856. The 1860 census valued his personal property at $10,000, including three slaves. Penn was a prominent Masonic leader in Virginia and other southern states (John H. Cowles, *The Supreme Council, 33°: Mother Council of the World Ancient and Accepted Scottish Rite of Freemasonry, Southern Jurisdiction, U.S.A.* [1931], vii, 195–6; *Lynchburg Virginian*, 8 Feb. 1830; *Va. Reports*, 32 [5 Leigh]: 65–6; Thomas McAdory Owen, *History of Alabama and Dictionary of Alabama Biography* [1921], 873, 926; *Daily Louisville Public Advertiser*, 2 Dec. 1830; Washington *Daily National Intelligencer*, 9 Dec. 1831; *Richmond Enquirer*, 28 Feb. 1835, 16 May 1837; Larry Schweikart, "Antebellum Southern Bankers: Origins and Mobility," *Business and Economic History*, 2d ser., 14 [1985]: 94; DNA: RG 29, CS, Tenn., Shelby Co., 1860; Little Rock *Daily Arkansas Gazette*, 23 July 1870).

To James Penn
(for Archibald Robertson)

SIR   Poplar Forest May 28. 15

I thank you for your kind attention to my request of yesterday, and mr Goodman now takes on 1400.D. of treasury notes to exchange for banknotes. but as the person for whom they are intended shews difficulty as to the kind of money he will recieve, should there be among those you will send me any which he will reject, I shall hope to be permitted to send them back tomorrow and to recieve in return either my treasury notes or banknotes of our state. Accept the assurances of my respect   TH: JEFFERSON

PoC (ViU: TJP); at foot of text: "Mr Penn for mr Robertson"; endorsed by TJ as a letter to Robertson and so recorded in SJL.

From James Penn

SIR,   Lynchburg, May the 28th 1815

I have received by mr Goodman your Treasury Notes and have sent you in return $1400 in bank bills. You will find nearly $1,000 in Va Notes the balance in Columbia, Alexandria and Some few others on different Banks. The Columbia & Alexandria notes pass very currently and the others are only refused by those planters, who have but few transactions in town.

Yrs mo Obtly   J PENN

RC (ViU: TJP); endorsed by TJ as a letter from Archibald Robertson "by J. Penn" received 28 May 1815 and so recorded (with no mention of Penn) in SJL.

To John Watts

SIR   Poplar forest May 28. 15

I have lost no time in endeavoring to get my Treasury bills exchanged for bank bills, and having learnt that the merchants in Lynchburg who deal to the Northward would willingly take treasury notes which served for remittances to other states in exchange for bank notes which would not be recieved there, I sent yesterday to mr Robertson to request him to procure me such an exchange. he answered by my messenger that I might count on the exchange & send on the Treasury bills. this I have done by mr Goodman this morning, and if he returns in time I will call on you in the evening with the bank bills he will bring, or if not in time, I will be with you after an early breakfast tomorrow morning. I have thought it a duty to give you this information as soon as I could get the business fixed lest doubt might delay your intended journey of tomorrow. Accept the assurances of my respect. TH: JEFFERSON

RC (Paul Francis Webster, Beverly Hills, Calif., 1972); at foot of text: "Col° Watts." PoC (MoSHi: TJC-BC); endorsed by TJ.

From John Watts

SIR   28th May 1815.

I am about to leave home this morning and it may so happen not return untill late in the evening and not wishing to give you any further trouble in the adjustment of the business on which you write, will wait on you in the morning on my [way?][1] to Lynchburg, respectfully

Your most obt ser   JOHN WATTS

RC (MoSHi: TJC-BC); dateline beneath signature; at foot of text: "Mr Jefferson"; endorsed by TJ as received 28 May 1815 and so recorded in SJL.

[1] Omitted word editorially supplied.

To Thomas A. Holcombe

DEAR SIR   Poplar Forest May 31. 15.

I am venturing on a measure with respect to my grandson Francis on which I would have consulted you had it occurred to me before I had the pleasure of recieving you here. I think however you will approve of it, as I am sure his father will, and I take on myself all the responsibility of it to him. French is now become an indispensable part in modern education. it is the only language in which a man of any country can be understood out of his own; and is now the preeminent depository of general science, every branch of which (medicine excepted) is better treated in books of that than of any other language in the world. the difficulty of getting instruction in it's true pronunciation had made me very anxious that Francis should have passed his last vacation at Monticello, where his aunt, who speaks it as a native, (having been from the age of 10. to 16. in a convent of Paris where nothing else was spoken) would in a short time have so advanced him that he could have gone on afterwards by himself. but my letter to him proposing this to his father miscarried. another vacation is now approa[ch]ing, and I feel such anxiety that he should avail himself of that for the same purpose, that having so convenient an opportunity of taking him on with me in the carriage, I have thought it best to anticipate the term of vacation, which indeed will not give him more than time enough to be thoroughly grounded. I will take care at the same time so to carry him on in his Latin that he shall not be behind his class in the knolege of that at the end of his vacation. hoping that you will concur with me in opinion that this measure will be for his advantage I tender you the assurance of my great esteem & respect.

TH: JEFFERSON

PoC (DLC); edge trimmed; at foot of text: "Mʳ Holcombe"; endorsed by TJ.

The CONVENT OF PARIS was the Abbaye Royale de Panthémont (*PTJ*, 7:576–7). TJ's LETTER to Francis Eppes of 9 Sept. 1814 MISCARRIED.

To John Wayles Eppes

DEAR SIR   Poplar Forest June 1. 15.

For want of time to consult you on it, I have taken a measure of great responsibility on my self as to Francis, for your pardon for which I must rely on the motives, and what I hope will be the effect of it. French is become the most indispensable[1] part of modern education. it is the only language in which a man of any country can be understood out of his own; and is now the preeminent depository of general science, every branch of which (Medecine excepted)[2] is better treated in books of that than of any other language in the world. the difficulty of getting instruction in it's true pronuntiation had made me very anxious that Francis should have passed his last vacation at Monticello, where his aunt, who speaks it as a native, & all his cousins who have got it well from her, could in a short time have so advanced him as to go on afterwards by himself. I wrote to him to propose this to you, and never knew, till he tells me, that he did not get the letter, which I lodged at Flood's for him, and which Flood assures him he forwarded. another vacation is now approaching, and I feel such anxiety that he should avail himself of that for the same purpose, that, having so convenient an opportunity of taking him on with me in the carriage, I venture to anticipate the term of vacation, and carry him with me. this will not give him more time than enough to ground him thoroughly in the language. it gives him 4. months to the end of the vacation, in which time we will ensure his reading French with perfect ease. and although while he must devote the main portion of the day to French, he cannot be expected to read <u>as much</u> Latin as in the whole day at school yet I will take on me to ensure that employing in it a couple of hours every day with my undivided attention and instruction, he shall, when he rejoins his class, have made more effectual progress than they, with the small portion of the attention which each of them can separately recieve from even the best teacher whose attention is divided among five and twenty. I have provided the necessary books for him, and shall furnish him with others as he advances. I will send him to visit you at any moment you shall desire it, and I hope you will approve of the disposition I have ventured to make, te inconsulto, of 4. months of his time: and that at the end of them you will be satisfied they have not been misemployed. my motives have been purely his good & your satisfaction, adding always the assurance of my constant and unchanged affections.   TH: JEFFERSON

PoC (CSmH: JF); at foot of first page: "John W. Eppes esq."; endorsed by TJ.

[1] Manuscript: "indispensablee."
[2] Parenthetical phrase interlined.

TE INCONSULTO: "without consulting you."

To Joseph Milligan

DEAR SIR   Poplar Forest June 1. 15.
    I keep at this place a small Polygraph which requir[es] paper exactly of the size of that now inclosed. I must ask the favor of you to send me a ream of that size. the quality too of the model is much liked, altho' perhaps we do not make any such. I shall be glad also of another ream of 4to letter paper for use at Monticello. that I now write on is about a good size. these may be packed and come on with the books you have to bind for me. send on at the same time if you please a copy of Dufief's French & English dictionary in 3. vols. I salute you with esteem and respect.   TH: JEFFERSON

PoC (DLC); edge trimmed; at foot of text: "Mr Joseph Millegan"; endorsed by TJ. Enclosure not found.

To Archibald Robertson

DEAR SIR   Poplar Forest June 1. 15.

According to your permission I have given mr Clay an order of this day on you for 55. Dollars, and I now inclose you a draught on Gibson and Jefferson for 138. Dollars to cover this and the two sums of 60.D. and 23.D. which you were so kind as to furnish mr Goodman with.

Having found it necessary to make a change in the management of my affairs here, I have engaged mr Joel Yancey to undertake the direction of them & superintendance of the overseers. and I have desired him to apply to your store for any necessaries which may be wanting for the people here or place. Accept the assurance of my great esteem & respect.   TH: JEFFERSON

PoC (ViU: TJP); at foot of text: "Mr Robertson"; endorsed by TJ. Enclosure not found.

TJ's order to Charles CLAY paid for a horse "bought of Brown." The SUMS given Jeremiah A. Goodman on 22 May 1815 included $23 to pay for 100 pounds of cotton (*MB*, 2:1309, 1310).

SJL records a missing letter from TJ to Joel Yancey of 30 May 1815.

From Archibald Robertson

DEAR SIR   Lynchburg 1 June 1815

Your favor of this date enclosing a dft on Gibson & Jefferson for $138, have received—your order in favor of m^r Clay will be duly honor'd—

I am much pleased to hear that you have been fortunate enough to get m^r Yancey to superintend your business in Bedford, there is no man in whom I should place more confidence than him, & think the more you are acquainted, the better you will be pleased with him—I remain—

Very Respectfully Your ob S^t   A. ROBERTSON.

RC (ViU: TJP); endorsed by TJ as received 1 June 1815 and so recorded in SJL.

To Elizabeth Trist

MY DEAR MADAM   Poplar Forest June 1. 15.

I duly recieved your letter, the date of which I cannot quote because I have it not with me: but I joined you sincerely in the joy

[515]

expressed on the transactions at New Orleans. they were to me infinitely pleasing because they proved that the people there were faithful to the Union, that the place could be defended, & that Kentucky and Tenissee would fly to it's defence. of the maneuvres you suggested for surrendering the place I had not before heard, but they are a key to General Jackson's energetical measures. nobody is more zealous than myself for the supremacy of the law under circumstances which admit appeal to it, and where it's dilatory proceedings may be relied on alone for the public safety. but in the presence of an enemy to propose to take men out of the ranks and even the General from the head of them by a Habeas corpus, is to use the law not for the safety but the destruction of the nation, and merely as a cloak for delivering it up to an enemy. however, all has ended gloriously, and all should now make friends. I confess that this Whorra! with which we closed the war doubled my relish for the peace. but what is next? Bonaparte returned, recieved with open arms, the Bourbons expelled, and the other powers preparing to take from France the right of self government, and to prescribe a ruler to them. I am certainly no friend to Bonaparte. he was an Usurper; but if he becomes the choice of the people, a regard for our own rights dictates respect for theirs, and a wish for their success. our maxim however should be not to intermeddle in the affairs of Europe; to consider ourselves as belonging to an American system, distinct from the European in it's interests and objects, connected with their commerce but not with their quarrels. but whether England will permit us to be clear of their wars is the doubt. governed by common sense she would do it; but governed by her merchants the interests of the nation will be sacrificed to theirs. I shall not wonder therefore to see the orders of council renewed, impressments resumed, and war of course forced upon us. they will force us, as they have forced France to become a nation of souldiers, and themselves will become victims of the might here, as of that they provoked in France. I would rather it should be otherwise, that we should remain in peace, and they continue to be an unit among the balancing powers of Europe. but this is not subject to our will; we must submit to the destinies, & without anticipating evils which perhaps may never happen, let us turn from politics, to our neighbors. your friends mr and mrs Divers are in as good health as usual. I dined with them on peas the 29th of April. here our first peas were the 29th of May. which shews the inattention here to the cheapest, pleasantest, & most wholsome part of comfortable living. the family of Monticello is all well, and cherish your friendship with affection. it is increased by Jefferson's marriage. we have had a deep affliction in the loss of Peter Carr. he was a kind of circulating cement to our neighborhood, and has left a void which can hardly be filled up. be so good as to present me respectfully to mr & mrs Gilmer and to be assured of my constant & affectionate friendship

TH: JEFFERSON

RC (ViU: TJP); addressed: "Mrs Elizabeth Trist at mr Gilmer's near Henry Court House"; franked; postmarked Lynchburg, 7 July. PoC (MHi); endorsed by TJ.

WHORRA!: "hurrah!" TJ's family grew with the MARRIAGE of Thomas Jefferson Randolph to Jane Hollins Nicholas.

From Benjamin Galloway

DEAR SIR.   Hagers Town June 2d 1815.

I was detained some weeks longer in Ann Arundel than I expected, when I wrote the letter to you and which was dated 9th of April last past. On my return homewards; I called at Washington: when I was told by mr Tench Ringgold, that he had forwarded to me at Hagers Town, your letter: supposing that I was still there. It afforded strong presumptive proof that you were in the enjoyment of good health, as you informed me that you should in a few weeks, commence a journey of 90 Miles to the Southward of Monticello. Of the "mens sana" I had before me a plain and positive proof: but, I was rendered doubly happy to learn, that the "in corpore sano" was not wanting: the two choicest blessings, that can attend any person: but more especially One, in So advanced a stage of life, as that, to which, you, Sir, have arrived—

The near approach of that ever-memorable day of the year, July 4th has induced me to postpone my intended visit to you: I now propose to leave home on the 22d or 23d of June: and will probably arrive at your Mansion on the 27th or 28th—I shall not travel more than about 35 miles per day: and as I am informed, that the distance from Hagers Town to Monti Cello is not more than $152\frac{1}{2}$ miles: should the weather not be unfavourable, I shall probably accomplish my Journey in the time above mentioned.

To say, that I was well pleased to hear, that Napoleon had re-ascended the French Throne, would not be making use of language sufficiently strong, to convey an adequate idea of the feelings I experienced, on the receipt of the glorious Tidings.

The United States, were, at that very moment (I so declared my opinion; and I verily thought so) placed in as perilous a situation, as

they had almost ever been at any period of the war of the revolution—
That, Napoleon, is ambitious: that, he may desire to extend his conquests; (tho he is said to have published a declaration in the most[1]
positive terms, counteracting the effects of such a suspicion) may be
All true: but, nevertheless:[2] I still rejoice de die in diem; and am exceeding glad that the Bourbon family have been obliged, once more,
to retreat, pede cito—When peace was established among the european belligerents, I was greatly apprehensive least the Prince Regent
of England, might possess that degree of influence in the French
Councils, as to prevail on Lewis the 18ᵗʰ to assist him with a very formidable body of Land Forces, for the diabolical purpose of trying to
subjugate our beloved Country; and, of re-annexing to the British
Crown: nor, have I particle of doubt on my mind; that such a combined force, would be most cheerfully aided, and assisted, by a considerable body of that description of people among us, who have been
pleased to nick-name themselves "The Friends of Peace."[3] I hope,
and pray, that I may have formed an erroneous judgment: but certain
and very many appearances and notions to the Eastward, and elsewhere, have powerfully strengthened and amply justified a suspicion
at Least;[4] that so abominable, so infamous a line of conduct, would
be pursued by the Hartford[5] Convention Men, and Their Setters On:
that I trust, and believe, it argues no want of charity to think, the
Pickle Herrings and Co; would go all lengths, sooner than not wreck
their vengeance on the now dominant Party. I presume that I shall
pass thro Milton in my way to Monticello? I mean to travel the road
from Hagers Town to Winchester, then to Woodstock where I am instructed that a road will present itself, which leads direct to Monticello, and abounding with good and convenient Stages. General
Ringgold informs me, that he expects Mʳ Geo Hay, the father of Mʳˢ
R at fountain rock in a few days—

I am with great deference, respect and a lively regard
Dear Sir Yrs &   BENJAMIN GALLOWAY

RC (DLC); addressed: "Thomas Jefferson Esquire"; endorsed by TJ as received 14 June 1815 and so recorded in
SJL.

DE DIE IN DIEM: "from day to day"
(*Black's Law Dictionary*). PEDE CITO:
"with swift foot." PICKLE HERRINGS:
"clowns; buffoons" (*OED*). Samuel
RINGGOLD had married George Hay's

daughter Maria A. Hay on 16 Feb. 1813
(*Baltimore Patriot*, 18 Feb. 1813).

[1] Word interlined.
[2] Manuscript: "neverthess."
[3] Omitted closing quotation mark editorially supplied.
[4] Manuscript: "Eeast."
[5] Manuscript: "Harford."

To Pierre Samuel Du Pont de Nemours

DEAR SIR   Monticello June 6. 15.

I am just returned from the journey mentioned in mine of May 15. and find here yours of May 26. I see that you do not despair of your country. but I confess I foresee no definite term to the despotism now reestablished there, and the less as the nation seems to have voluntarily assumed the yoke, and to have made, of an usurper, a legitimate despot. what can we hope from a mind without moral principle, and without that sound wisdom which acts morally, by mere calculation, on the common observation that honesty is the best policy. but come yourself & Correa, & let us talk this over together. we wish alike, but are not equally sanguine in our prospects. and come soon, as your letter gives me to hope; and the more pressingly as within about eight weeks I am to commence an absence of two months from home. you are not unapprised by experience what you are to suffer from the mauvaise cuisinerie of our country. mr Correa had promised me a long visit for this summer. his undertaking a course of lectures in Philadelphia had made me fear it would be retarded by that. but the more a man is master of his subject, the more briefly and densely he is able to present it to others. we shall have other subjects too to grieve over. the desperate ignorance of our country in political economy, and it's limited views of science. but come both of you, and we will settle the affairs of both hemispheres, if not as they shall be, yet as they ought to be. I salute you, and him through you, with sincere affection & respect.   TH: JEFFERSON

RC (DeGH: Pierre Samuel Du Pont de Nemours Papers, Winterthur Manuscripts); at foot of text: "M. Dupont de Nemours." PoC (DLC).

MAUVAISE CUISINERIE: "bad cooking."

To Benjamin Jones

DEAR SIR   Monticello June 6. 15.

The iron announced in yours of Mar. 25. came safely to hand and I have this day, by the mail to Richmond, desired my correspondents Messrs Gibson and Jefferson to remit to you 142. D 76 C the amount of the bill which therefore you may count on some few days after your reciept of this.   Accept the assurance of my esteem & respect
                                    TH: JEFFERSON

PoC (MHi); at foot of text: "Mr Benjamin Jones"; endorsed by TJ.

A missing letter from TJ to Patrick Gibson of THIS DAY is recorded in SJL.

To Joel Yancey

DEAR SIR   Mon[t]ic[ello] June 7. 15.

I omitted among my memorandums to request you to have all the seed of the oat-grass at mr Goodman's saved, in order to make lots near each of the Overseer's houses. it comes a month earlier than any other grass, and is therefore valuable for ewes & lambs, calves, yearlings and poor cows. there should also be good clover lots adjoining, independant of the large clover fields. I have enquired and got good information on the subject of clover sown in the husk. it is to be cut as usual, and laid up in hand-ricks of 3. or 4. feet high to rot to such a degree as to leave the husks separable from the stalk & from one another. whenever it rains the rick should be turned over to prevent it's rotting too much & spoiling the seed at the bottom. when it is sufficiently rotted it must either be beaten to pieces with flails on a plank floor, or passed thro' the threshing machine. the obje[ct] is not to separate the seed from the husk, but merely to separate at their bottom, where they grow together, the numerous husks of which a single clover blossom is composed. 7. bushels of this separated husk is necessary to an acre. the time of sowing is from the middle of February to the 10th of March, and there is no better method than sowing it on snow. the 2^d cutting yields more seed than the 1st & is better, because having been cut all together it starts it's 2^d growth & ripens together. every body agrees that it comes up with much more certainty when sown in the husk. I shall take timely care to procure you 6. tons of plaister which will suffice for 160. acres. in the mean time it will be well to ascertain whether any mill in the neighborhood will grind it for us. it adds immensely to the expence if we are to grind & barrel it belo[w] and makes the transportation higher. accept my best wishes & the assurance of my esteem and respect   TH: JEFFERSON

PoC (MHi); on verso of reused address cover of George P. Stevenson to TJ, 28 Apr. 1815; dateline faint; edge trimmed; at foot of text: "Mr Yancey"; endorsed by TJ.

From Isaac A. Coles

D^R SIR,   Enniscorthy June 9th 1815

After detaining the waggon a whole day I have now the mortification of being compelled to Send it back without the promised Deer.
A Pen had been made on the Park fence which was believed to be
sufficiently secure, and the Deer had been fed in it for Some weeks,
& had become familiarised to it—Yesterday morning the Boy who
keeps them got a fine Spring Doe in and Shut her up, but to our utter
astonishment she in a few moments forced herself through, by breaking one of the Rails, and escaped out of the Park—whether we Shall
ever be able to get her back is uncertain—

The others not being up were not at all[1] frightened by this, and a second was easily Secured in like manner, but the efforts which it made
to escape were beyond any thing that you can conceive—it forced itself out, but fortunately on the Side of the Park, So that we shall not
lose it unless it dies of the bruises which it has received—Hoping
Still if the Pen was taken down and constructed differently that we
might possibly Succeed, I determined to detain the Waggon & to
make Still another attempt—I am just informed by my Boy that after
the fright of yesterday nothing can be done—he has been the whole
morning endeavoring in vain to get them to enter the Pen. They
stand at a distance, and on the least alarm spring off, & hide themselves in the wood. Under these circumstances I deem it unnecessary
to detain the Waggon longer—until some better means of effecting
the object which I have So much at heart, Can be thought of, success
should not be counted on—I cannot Consent however to give it up &
must ask that the frame for carrying them may not be destroyed as I
still hope to have use for it—

Some business carries me to Washington in a few days & nothing
more will be attempted until my return—with Sincere Respectful
attachment

I am very truly y^{rs}   I. A. COLES

RC (DLC); at foot of text: "Thos
Jefferson"; endorsed by TJ as received 9
June 1815 and so recorded in SJL.

[1] Manuscript: "atall."

To John Adams

It is long since we have exchanged a letter, and yet what volumes might have been written on the occurrences even of the last three months. in the first place, Peace, God bless it! has returned to put us all again into a course of lawful and laudable pursuits: a new trial of the Bourbons has proved to the world their incompetence to the functions of the station they have occupied: & the recall of the Usurper has clothed him with the semblance of a legitimate Autocrat. if adversity should have taught him wisdom, of which I have little confidence, he may yet render some service to mankind by teaching the antient dynasties that they can be changed for misrule, and by wearing down the maritime power of England to limitable and safe dimensions. but it is not possible he should love us, and of that our commerce had sufficient proofs during his power. our military atchievements indeed, which he is capable of estimating, may in some degree moderate the effect of his aversions; and he may perhaps fancy that we are to become the natural enemies of England, as England herself has so steadily endeavored to make us and as some of our own over-zealous patriots would be willing to proclaim. and in this view he may admit a cold toleration of some intercourse and commerce between the two nations. he has certainly had time to see the folly of turning the industry of France from the cultures for which nature has so highly endowed her, to those of sugar, cotton, tobacco and others which the same creative power has given to other climates: and on the whole, if he can conquer the passions of his tyrannical soul, if he has understanding enough to pursue, from motives of interest, what no moral motives lead him to, the tranquil happiness and prosperity of his country, rather than a ravenous thirst for human blood, his return may become of more advantage than injury to us. and if again some great man could arise in England, who could see & correct the follies of his nation in their conduct as to us, and by exercising justice and comity towards ours bring both into a state of temperate and useful friendship, it is possible we may thus attain the place we ought to occupy between these two nations without being degraded to the condition of mere partisans of either. a little time will now inform us whether France, within it's proper limits is big enough for it's ruler, on the one hand, and whether, on the other, the allied powers are either wicked or foolish enough to attempt the forcing on the French a ruler and government which they refuse? whether they will risk their own thrones to reestablish that of the Bourbons?   if this is attempted, and the European world again committed to war, will the jealousy of England at the commerce which neutrality will give us, induce her again to add us to the number of her enemies, rather than see us prosper in the pursuits of peace and industry? and have our commercial citizens merited from their country it's encountering another war to protect their gambling enterprises? that the persons of our citizens shall be safe in freely traversing the ocean, that the transportation of our own produce, in our own vessels, to the markets of our choice, and the return to us of the articles we want for our own use shall be unmolested I hold to be fundamental, and that the gauntlet must be for ever hurled at him who questions it. but whether we shall engage in every war of Europe to protect the mere agency of our merchants and ship owners in carrying on the commerce of other nations, even were those merchants and ship owners to take the side of their country in the contest, instead of that of the enemy, is a question of deep and serious consideration, with which however you and I shall have nothing to do; so we will leave it to those whom it will concern.

I thank you for making known to me mr Tickner & mr Gray. they are fine young men indeed, and if Massachusets can raise a few more such, it is probable she would be better counselled as to social rights and social duties. mr Ticknor is particularly the best bibliograph I have[1] met with, and very kindly and opportunely offered me the means of reprocuring some part of the literary treasures which I have ceded to Congress to replace the devastations of British Vandalism at Washington. I cannot live without books; but fewer will suffice where amusement, and not use, is the only future object. I am about sending him a catalogue to which less than his critical knolege of books would hardly be adequate. present my high respects to mrs Adams, and accept yourself the assurances of my affectionate attachment.

Th: Jefferson

RC (MHi: Adams Papers); endorsed by Adams as answered 20 June 1815. PoC (DLC); at foot of first page: "Mr Adams." An image of the last page of the RC is reproduced elsewhere in this volume.

The NEW TRIAL was the return to France of the USURPER Napoleon and his resumption of the French throne, which forced Louis XVIII and his family to flee France. The GREAT MAN who had previously worked to restore a TEMPERATE AND USEFUL FRIENDSHIP between England and America was most likely William Pitt, 1st Earl of Chatham, who advocated repeal of the Stamp Act, denied the authority of the British parliament to levy internal taxes in the colonies, and argued in 1775 for the withdrawal of British troops from Boston (ODNB).

[1] TJ here canceled "known."

From Samuel H. Smith

DEAR SIR   Sidney, June 11. 1815.

I have no doubt of the location of Your Library in Washington[1] being attended with the happiest consequences to the interests of our country. It seems incident to the early Stages of a new country to overlook the benefits of literature, arising, among other causes, from the want of extensive means of information. These being now possessed by our statesmen, we may entertain a hope that the opinions & measures of the metropolis will furnish a model for a free and liberal people, and that the great republic of modern days will soon exhibit in the arts & sciences the same superiority that signalised her predecessors of old, with the brighter glory of extending the conquests of truth instead of the sword. The agency I have had in the translation of the library has been highly agreeable to me, and has been a pleasure instead of a trouble.

It will not now be disputed that Bonaparte is a wonderful man. His reappearance on the political scene is admirably fitted to excite terror as well as hope. If adversity shall have taught him the elements of true grandeur, of wch prudence will ever continue the tutelar genius, he will rise to the pinacle of human greatness. If, on the contrary, lost to moderation, he shall aim more at extending the empire of the sword than the empire of reason, he will deservedly sink, with the abhorrence, if not contempt of mankind.

I thank You for Your kind invitation to Monticello, and m^rs S. sincerely unites with me: but my duties here at present forbid this gratification. Our though[ts, as] ever, are often directed to your dwelling, under whose hospitable roof we hope again to pass some happy hours.

Believe me to be with cordial friendship & constant respect.

SA H SMITH

RC (DLC); mutilated at seal; addressed: "Thomas Jefferson Esquire Monticello Virg^a"; franked; postmarked Washington, 13 June; endorsed by TJ as received 17 June 1815 and so recorded in SJL.

[1] Manuscript: "Washigton."

To William H. Torrance

SIR   Monticello June 11. 15.

I recieved a few days ago your favor of May 5. stating a question on a law of the state of Georgia which suspends judgments for a limited time, and asking my opinion whether it may be valid under the inhibition of our constitution to pass laws impairing the obligations of contracts. it is more than 40. years since I have quitted the practice of the law and been engaged in vocations which furnished little occasion of preserving a familiarity with that science. I am far therefore from being qualified to decide on the problems it presents and certainly not disposed to obtrude in a case where gentlemen have been consulted of the first qualifications, and of actual and daily familiarity with the subject; especially too in a question on the law of another state. we have in this state a law resembling in some degree that you quote, suspending executions until a year after the treaty of peace; but no question under it has been raised before the courts. it is also I believe expected that when this shall expire, in consideration of the absolute impossibility of procuring coin to satisfy judgments, a law will be past, similar to that passed in England on suspending the cash payments of their bank. that provided that on refusal by a party to recieve notes of the bank of England in any case either of past or future contracts, the judgment should be suspended during the continuance of that act, bearing however legal interest. they seemed to consider that it was not this law which changed the conditions of the contract, but the circumstances which had arisen, and had rendered it's literal execution impossible, by the disappearance of the metallic medium stipulated by the contract: that the parties not concurring in a reasonable and just accomodation, it became the duty of the legislature to arbitrate between them, and that, less restrained than the Duke of Venice by 'the letter of the decree' they were free to adjudge to Shyloc a reasonable equivalent. and I believe that in our states this umpirage of the legislatures has been generally interposed in cases where a literal execution of contract has, by a change of circumstances become impossible, or, if enforced, would produce a disproportion[1] between the subject of the contract and it's price which the parties did not contemplate at the time of the contract.

The 2ᵈ question whether the judges are invested with exclusive authority to decide on the constitutionality of a law, has been heretofore a subject of consideration with me in the exercise of official duties. certainly there is not a word in the constitution which has given that power to them more than to the Executive or Legislative branches. questions of property, of character and of crime being ascribed to the judges, through a definite course of legal proceeding, laws involving such questions belong of course to them; and as they decide on them ultimately & without appeal, they of course decide, <u>for themselves</u>, the constitutional validity of the law. on laws again prescribing executive action, & to be administered by that branch ultimately and without appeal, the Executive must decide for <u>themselves</u> also, whether, under the constitution, they are valid or not. so also as to laws governing the proceedings of the legislature, that body must judge <u>for itself</u> the constitutionality of the law, & equally without appeal or controul from it's coordinate branches. and, in general, that branch which is to act ultimately, and without appeal, on any law, is the rightful expositor of the validity of the law, uncontrouled by the opinions of the other coordinate authorities. it may be said that contradictory decisions may arise in such case, and produce inconvenience. this is possible, and is a necessary failing in all human proceedings. yet the prudence of the public functionaries, and authority of public opinion will generally produce accomodation. such an instance of difference occurred between the judges of England (in the time of Ld Holt) and the House of Commons. but the prudence of those bodies prevented inconvenience from it. so in the cases of Duane and of William Smith of S. Carolina, whose characters of citizenship stood precisely on the same ground, the judges in a question of meum and tuum which came before them, decided that Duane was not a citizen; and in a question of membership the House of Representatives under the same words of the same provision[2] adjudged William Smith to be a citizen. yet no inconvenience has ensued these contradictory decisions. this is what I believe myself to be sound. but there is another opinion entertained by some men of such judgment & information as to lessen my confidence in my own. that is, that the legislature alone is the exclusive expounder of the sense of the constitution in every part of it whatever. and they alledge in it's support that this branch has authority, to impeach and punish a member of either of the others acting contrary to it's declaration of the sense of the constitution. it may indeed be answered that an act may still be valid altho' the party is punished for it, right or wrong. however this opinion which ascribes exclusive exposition to the legislature merits respect for it's safety, there being in the body of the nation a controul over them, which, if expressed by rejection on the subsequent exercise of their elective franchise, enlists public opinion against their exposition, and encourages a judge or Executive on a future occasion[3] to adhere to their former opinion. between these two doctrines, every one has a right to chuse; and I know of no third meriting any respect.

I have thus, Sir, frankly, without the honor of your acquaintance, confided to you my opinion; trusting assuredly that no use will be made of it which shall commit me to the contentions of the newspapers. from that field of disquietude my age asks exemption and permission to enjoy the privileged tranquility of a private and unmedling citizen. In this confidence accept the assurance of my respect and consideration.   TH: JEFFERSON

PoC (DLC); at foot of first page: "Mr W. H. Torrance." Tr (MHi); posthumous copy; top of final two pages torn.

William H. Torrance (1792–1837), attorney, was a native of South Carolina who moved with his family in 1811 to Milledgeville, Georgia. He served in the Georgia militia during the War of 1812. Torrance migrated in 1815 to Augusta, Georgia. After an unsuccessful venture in the cotton business, he studied law, opening a practice in 1820 at Milledgeville. In 1825 Torrance served on a state commission appointed to investigate alleged irregularities in recent negotiations with the Creek Indians (Stephen F. Miller, *Bench and Bar of Georgia: Memoirs and Sketches* [1858], 1:296–317; *ASP, Indian Affairs*, 2:820–61; *Report of the Select Committee of the House of Representatives . . . March 3, 1827* [1827; report no. 98]; *Macon Georgia Telegraph*, 30 May 1837). Torrance's 5 May 1815 FAVOR to TJ, not found, is recorded in SJL as received 4 June 1815 from Milledgeville.

The LAW OF THE STATE OF GEORGIA entitled "An Act To authorize the several Courts of Equity in this State to grant remedies in certain cases and to regulate the Courts of Law and Equity in this state, and for affording temporary relief to the Soldiers whilst in the service of this state or of the United States, and for other purposes," 23 Nov. 1814, provided that after a verdict was given in a state court, the party against whom judgment was rendered could give security for the debt and stay execution for a year. It also shielded a soldier's property from seizure while he was in the service of Georgia or of the United States "or on his way to or returning from the place of rendezvous, or within six months after the expiration of the term of service" (*Acts of the General Assembly of the State of Georgia, passed at Milledgeville, At an Annual Session, in October and November, 1814* [Milledgeville, 1814], 3–5). Article 1, section 10, of the United States CONSTITUTION prohibits states from passing any "Law impairing the Obligation of Contracts." The Virginia law RESEMBLING that of Georgia was a 25 Nov. 1814 "Act concerning Executions, and for other purposes," which provided "That the defendant or defendants shall have power to stay any execution upon any judgment or decree for money, . . . by tendering to the Court or Justice of the Peace, by whom the judgment or decree shall have been rendered, bond and sufficient security, payable to the plaintiff or plaintiffs, his, her or their executors, adminstrators or assigns, in double the amount of the demand, conditioned to pay the amount of principal and interest, at the repeal of this Act"; protected the property of those debtors who "shall be ordered into the militia service of this State or of the United States, during the time that such debtor or debtors shall continue in actual military service"; and continued in force until 1 Mar. 1816 (*Acts of Assembly* [1814–15 sess.], 68–75).

The Bank of England suspended CASH PAYMENTS between 1797 and 1819 (Ralph G. Hawtrey, "The Bank Restriction of 1797," *Economic Journal* 28 [1918]: 52). The LETTER OF THE DECREE is derived from William Shakespeare, *The Merchant of Venice*, act 4, scene 1, in which the Duke of Venice presides over a trial at which Shylock insists that the court uphold the literal meaning of the law and award him a pound of flesh. An INSTANCE OF DIFFERENCE occurred in England with the 1702 case of *Ashby v. White*, in which Sir John HOLT, chief justice of the Court of King's Bench, argued that the courts, and not the House of Commons, had the authority to determine the right of an individual to vote in a parliamentary election (*ODNB*; Paul Hamburger, *Law and Judicial Duty* [2008], 227).

Although William Duane was born in the United States nearly eleven years before his family moved to Ireland in about 1771, he did not return to the United States until 1796, having previously resided in London and India. The case in which a court ruled that he was not a citizen on a QUESTION OF MEUM AND TUUM has not been identified. Duane's citizenship was also questioned when he was tried and acquitted in 1799 on federal charges of fomenting a "seditious riot" while obtaining petition signatures against the 25 June 1798 Alien Act (*ANB*; James Morton Smith, *Freedom's Fetters: The Alien and Sedition Laws and American Civil Liberties* [1956], 277–306, 438–40; Francis Wharton, *State Trials of the United States during the Administrations of Washington and Adams* [1849], 345–91).

Like Duane, William Loughton Smith had been born in the United States but spent much of his youth and early adulthood abroad, in Geneva and London. He did not return to the United States until 1783. A political opponent alleged that Smith's election to the United States HOUSE OF REPRESENTATIVES in 1788 was invalid "by reason that he had not been seven years a citizen of the United States" at the time of his election. On 22 May 1789 the House rejected this interpretation of Article 1, section 2, of the Constitution (*ANB*; *First Federal Congress*, 8:542–54, 10:759–79).

[1] Tr: "disapprobation."
[2] Preceding eight words interlined.
[3] Reworked from "a future judge or Executive."

To Mr. Brand

SIR   Monticello June 12. 15.

The bearer comes for 2. flour barrels of lime. the unslacked would be preferred if you have any.

The late mr Bran had a note of mine for a sum of money which I am ready to pay by an order on Richmond: and if wanting in the course of the year I would prefer it's being called for immediately, the season for selling one's crop being the only convenient one for making payments of any size. if the purposes of the family would be better answered by letting it lie in my hands a year longer, it shall[1] be as best suits them, it being perfectly indifferent to me to pay it now or then. but it would be necessary to inform me that I might not keep it lying idle. Accept my best wishes & respects for the family & yourself

TH: JEFFERSON

PoC (MHi); on verso of reused address cover to TJ; at foot of text: "Mr Bran"; endorsed by TJ as a letter to "Bran mr" and so recorded in SJL.

Unslaked (UNSLACKED) lime has not been hydrated (*OED*).

During the preceding twenty years TJ had occasionally bought lime and various agricultural products from Joseph Brand (the LATE MR BRAN), an Albemarle County landowner with nine sons. On 4 Nov. 1811 TJ gave the elder Brand a NOTE for $339.60, which covered some of these purchases and the acquisition for $150 of Brand's share in the Milton warehouses situated near the Rivanna River. TJ had yet to settle this debt with Brand's executors in March 1823 (Woods, *Albemarle*, 149; Mabel Thacher Rose-mary Washburn, *The Virginia Brand-Meriwether Genealogy* [1948], 8–11, 25–6; *MB*, esp. 2:1256, 1270, 1286, 1393–4; *PTJ*, 32:401–2; Craven and Jane Peyton's Conveyance of the Henderson Lands, 22 Aug. 1809; Albemarle Co. Will Book, 5:337–40, 6:62–3).

[1] Manuscript: "shell."

To Joseph Cabell Breckinridge

SIR   Monticello June. 12. 15.

Your favor of May 14. has been duly recieved, and I should willingly contribute to the biography of your estimable father whatever my short acquaintance with him, and still shorter memory would enable me to do. but of historical fact this would be little, and of testimony to his merit only what is known to all who knew him. our acquaintance first arose after my return from Europe. he was so kind as to favor me with a visit and during it's short continuance I had opportunity sufficient to discern the enlarged scope of his mind, the stores of information laid up in it, and the moral direction given to both. his subsequent appointment to Congress renewed my opportunities of estimating his character. he became one of our most valuable bulwarks in stemming the tide which then set so strongly against the republican principles of our government, and labored in it with the zeal and abilities for which he was distinguished. the sense I entertained of his high qualifications and merit was sufficiently proved afterwards by my calling him to our aid in the Cabinet of the government, and confiding to him the important office of Attorney General of the United States; and his death left a chasm in our councils which we sensibly felt and sincerely lamented. in saying this I say no more than was generally known to all, and if my testimony added to theirs can strengthen in any degree the establishment of a character which deserved so well of his country, I give it with pleasure, and in the spirit of the sincere affection I bore him. be so good as, with it, to accept the assurance of my high regard & consideration for his family & for yourself.

Th: Jefferson

RC (CtY: Franklin Collection); addressed: "Joseph Cabell Breckenridge Lexington. Kentucky"; franked; postmarked Charlottesville, 14 June. PoC (DLC); endorsed by TJ.

From Charles Jouett

D SIR   Washington City 12th June 1815

I have this momant laid my letters before the president, and am sorry to say that my prospects of success are doubtful, I was anxious to see Colo Monroe but was disappointed, excuse me if I solicit you once more to interest him in my favour, no man can serve me as effectually as you can, and few indeed are better acquainted with my character,

I could say much to you but delicacy imposes silence, I have been devoted to your political principles, and have always been ready to offer up my life in their defence, If I had been dealt by justly I should be now sleeping in an honorable grave, or be crowned by the honours and approbation of my country. I pray you to excuse me I am extremely agitated, If I go back to Kentucky without employment I shall be ruined

I am with the highest respect Sir Your Obediant Ser^{vt}

C. JOUETT

RC (MoSHi: TJC-BC); endorsed by TJ as received 14 June 1815 and so recorded in SJL. RC (DLC); address cover only; with PoC of TJ to Henry Jackson, 5 July 1815, on verso; addressed: "Thomas Jefferson Esquire Late President of U States Monticello"; franked; postmarked Washington City, 12 June.

Charles Jouett (ca. 1772–1834) was a native of Virginia who practiced law in Charlottesville before becoming a federal Indian agent at Detroit, 1802–05, and Chicago, 1805–11. He was one of the United States commissioners at a treaty signed at Fort Industry (later Toledo, Ohio) on 4 July 1805 with the Wyandot, Ottawa, and other northwestern Indian nations. Jouett moved in 1811 to Mercer County, Kentucky. He received an appointment on 20 June 1815 as Indian agent for the new post at Green Bay, Michigan Territory (now Wisconsin). When it proved impossible to maintain, Jouett returned to his former position at Chicago, 1816–19. In the latter year President James Monroe named him one of three judges of the new Arkansas Territory, but Jouett resigned the post in 1820 and lived thereafter in Trigg County, Kentucky (Henry Higgins Hurlbut, *Chicago Antiquities* [1881], 102–8; Alfred Theodore Andreas, *History of Chicago* [1884–86; repr. 1975], 1:86–7, 89–90; *ASP, Indian Affairs*, 1:695–6, 702–3, 757; *Terr. Papers*, 7:75, 472, 10:94, 575, 16:65–6, 17:190–1, 206–7, 318, 418, 557, 19:37–9, 53–4, 172; TJ to James Madison, 15 June 1815; *JEP*, 3:139, 184, 235 [18 Apr. 1818, 3 Mar. 1819, 23 Jan. 1821]; Josiah H. Shinn, *Pioneers and Makers of Arkansas* [1908], 195–7; DNA: RG 29, CS, Ky., Trigg Co., 1830; Robert Fergus, *Directory of the City of Chicago Illinois, for 1843* [1896], 113).

On 17 Mar. 1815 Jouett wrote President Madison asking for a federal appointment (DNA: RG 59, LAR, 1809–17). No other pertinent LETTERS of this year have been found.

To Thomas Leiper

DEAR SIR   Monticello June 12. 15.

A journey soon after the reciept of your favor of April 17. and an absence from home of some continuance has prevented my earlier acknolegement of it. in that came safely[1] my letter of Jan. 2. 14. in our principles of government we differ not at all, nor in the general object & tenor of political measures. we concur in considering the government of England as totally without morality, insolent beyond bearing, inflated with vanity and ambition, aiming at the exclusive dominion of the sea, lost in corruption, of deep rooted hatred towards us, hostile to liberty wherever it endeavors to shew it's head, and the eternal disturber of the peace of the world. in our estimate of Bonaparte I suspect we differ. I view him as a political engine only and a very wicked one,[2] you I believe as both political & religious, and obeying, as an instrument, an unseen hand. I still deprecate his becoming sole lord of the continent of Europe, which he would have been had he reached in triumph the gates of Petersburg. the establishment, in our day, of another Roman empire, spreading vassalage and depravity over the face of the globe, is not, I hope, within the purposes of heaven. nor does the return of Bonaparte give me pleasure unmixed. I see in his expulsion of the Bourbons a valuable lesson to the world, as shewing that it's antient dynasties may be changed for their misrule. should the allied powers presume to dictate a ruler & government to France, and follow the example he had set of parcelling and usurping to themselves their neighbor nations, I hope he will give them another lesson in vindication of the rights of independance and self government, which himself had heretofore so much abused; and that in this contest he will wear down the maritime power of England to limitable and safe dimensions. so far, good. it cannot be denied on the other hand that his succesful perversion[3] of the force (committed to him for vindicating the rights and liberties of his country) to usurp it's government, and to enchain it under an hereditary despotism, is of baneful effect in encouraging future usurpations, and deterring those under oppression from rising to redress themselves. his restless spirit leaves no hope of peace to the world; and his hatred of us is only a little less than that he bears to England, and England to us. our form of government is odious to him, as a standing contrast between republican and despotic rule; and as much from that hatred, as from ignorance in Political economy, he had excluded intercourse between us and his people, by prohibiting the only articles they wanted from us, that is, cotton and tobacco. whether the war we have had with England, the atchievements of that war, and the hope that we may become his instruments and partisans against that enemy may induce him in future to tolerate our commercial intercourse with his people is still to be seen. for my part I wish that all nations may recover and retain their independance; that those which are over-grown may not advance beyond safe measures of power, that a salutary balance may be ever maintained among nations, and that our peace, commerce and friendship may be sought and cultivated by all. it is our business to manufacture for ourselves whatever we can, to keep all markets open for what we can spare or want, and the less we have to do with the amities or enmities of Europe, the better. not in our day; but at no distant one, we may shake a rod over the heads of all, which may make the stoutest of them tremble. but I hope our wisdom will grow with our power, and teach us that the less we use our power the greater it will be.

The federal misrepresentation of my sentiments which occasioned my former letter to you was gross enough; but that and all others are exceeded by the impudence and falshood of the printed extract you sent me from Ralph's paper. that a continuance of the embargo for two months longer would have prevented our war; that the non-importation law which succeeded it was a wise and powerful measure, I have constantly maintained. my friendship for mr Madison; my confidence in his wisdom and virtue, and my approbation of all his measures, and especially of his taking up at length the gauntlet against England, is known to all with whom I have ever conversed or corresponded on these measures. the word Federal, or it's synonym lie, may therefore be written under every word of mr Ralph's paragraph. I have ransacked my memory to recollect any incident which might have given countenance to any particle of it; but I find none. for if you will except the bringing into power and importance those who were enemies to himself as well as to the principles of republican government, I do not recollect a single measure of the President which I have not approved. of those under him, and of some very near him, there have been many acts of which we have all disapproved, and he more than we. we have at times dissented from the measures and lamented the dilatoriness of Congress. I recollect an instance the first winter of the war, when, from sloth of proceedings, an embargo was permitted to run thro' the winter, while the enemy could not cruise, nor consequently restrain the exportation of our whole produce, and was taken off in the spring, as soon as they could resume their stations. but this procrastination is unavoidable. how can expedition be expected from a body which we have saddled with an hundred lawyers, whose trade is talking?—but lies, to sow divisions among us is so stale an artifice of the federal prints, & are so well understood, that they need neither contradiction nor explanation. as to my self, my confidence in the wisdom and integrity of the administration is so entire, that I scarcely notice what is passing, and have almost ceased to read newspapers. mine remain in our post office a week or 10. days sometimes unasked for. I find more amusement in studies to which I was always more attached, and from which I was dragged by the events of the times in which I have happened to live.

I rejoice exceedingly that our war with England was singlehanded. in that of the revolution we had France, Spain & Holland on our side, and the credit of it's success was given to them. on the late occasion, unprepared and unexpecting war, we were compelled to declare it, and to recieve the attack of England, just issuing from a general war, fully armed and freed from all other enemies, and have not only made her sick of it, but glad to prevent by a peace the capture of her adjacent possessions, which one or two campaigns more would infallibly have made ours. she has found that we can do her more injury than any other enemy on earth, and henceforward will better estimate the value of our peace. but whether her government has power, in opposition to the aristocracy of her navy, to restrain their piracies within the limits of national rights may well be doubted. I pray therefore for peace, as best for all the world, best for us, and best for me who have already lived to see three wars, and now pant for nothing more than to be permitted to depart in peace. that you also who have longer to live may continue to enjoy this blessing with health and prosperity thro' as long a life as you desire, is the prayer of yours affectionately

Th: Jefferson

P.S. June 14. before I had sent my letter to the post office, I recieve the new treaty of the allied powers, declaring that the French nation shall not have Bonaparte, and shall have Louis XVIII. for their ruler. they are all then as great rascals as Bonaparte himself. while he was in the wrong, I wished him exactly as much success as would answer our purposes and no more. now that they are wrong, and he in the right, he shall have all my prayers for success, and that he may dethrone every man of them.

RC (PWacD: Sol Feinstone Collection, on deposit PPAmP). PoC (DLC); at foot of first page: "Mr Lieper." Postscript added separately to RC and PoC.

The LETTER OF JAN. 2. 14. returned previously by Leiper was actually TJ's letter to him of 1 Jan. 1814. The PRINTED EXTRACT from Relf's Philadelphia Gazette was enclosed in Leiper's letter of 17 Apr. 1814. "An Act laying an embargo on all ships and vessels in the ports and harbours of the United States," 17 Dec. 1813, was allowed to RUN THRO' THE WINTER until its repeal on 14 Apr. 1814 (*U.S. Statutes at Large*, 3:88–93, 123). The NEW TREATY was a declaration signed by the representatives of many European nations at the Congress of Vienna on 13 Mar. 1815 that condemned Napoleon's escape from Elba and his return in arms to France, declared him outside of "all civil and social relations," offered support to the French king and the French nation and to any allied government seeking aid, and agreed to make common cause against any disturber of the public tranquility (*New-York Evening Post*, 1 May 1815; *British and Foreign State Papers* 2 [1814/15]: 665–6).

[1] Word interlined.
[2] Preceding five words interlined.
[3] Word interlined in place of "employment."

From John Mason

analostan Island June 13—15—
J Mason presents his respectful compliments, and best Regards to Mr Jefferson, and has the honor to forward him a Packet which he received yesterday under cover from Mr Warden at Paris—

RC (DLC); dateline at foot of text; mistakenly endorsed by TJ as a letter of 3 June received 20 June 1815 and so recorded in SJL. Enclosure: David Bailie Warden to TJ, 7 Feb. 1815, and enclosures.

To Charles Willson Peale

DEAR SIR   Monticello June 13. 15.
In your favor of May 2. you ask my advice on the best mode of selling your Museum, on which however I really am not qualified to advise. this depends entirely on the genius and habits of those among whom you live, with which you are so much better acquainted. I wish first it may be disposed of the most to your advantage, and 2dly that it may not be separated. if profit be regarded, the purchaser must keep it in Philadelphia, where alone the number and taste of the inhabitants can ensure it's maintenance.—it will be yet some time (perhaps a month) before my workmen will be free to make the plough I shall send you. you will be at perfect liberty to use the form of the mould-board, as all the world is, having never thought of monopolising by patent any useful idea which happens to offer itself to me: and the permission to do this is doing a great deal more harm than good.
there is a late instance in this state of a rascal going thro' every part of it, and swindling the mill-owners, under a patent of 2. years old only, out of 20,000.D. for the use of winged-gudgeons which they have had in their mills for 20. years, every one preferring to pay

10.D. unjustly rather than be dragged into a federal court 1. 2. or 300 miles distant.

I think the Cornsheller you describe with two cylinders is exactly the one made in a neighboring county where they are sold at 20.D. I propose to take some opportunity of seeing how it performs. the reason of the derangement of machines with wooden cylinders of any length is the springing of the timber, to which white oak has a peculiar disposition. for that reason we prefer pine as the least apt to spring. you once told me of what wood you made the bars of the pen-frame in the Polygraph, as springing less than any other wood; & I have often wished to recollect it, but cannot. we give up here the cleaning of clover seed, because it comes up so much more certainly when sown in the husk, 7. bushels of which is more easily obtained for the acre than the 3. pints of clean seed[1] which the sowing box requires. we use the machine you describe for crushing corn-cobs, & for which Oliver Evans has obtained a patent, altho' to my knolege the same machine has been made by a smith in George town these 16. years for crushing plaister, and he made one for me 12. years ago, long before Evans's patent. the only difference is that he fixes his horizontally and Evans vertically. yet I chose to pay Evans's patent price for one rather than be involved in a law suit of 2. or 300.D. cost. we are now afraid to use our ploughs, every part of which has been patented, although used ever since the fabulous days of Ceres.—on the subject of the Spinning Jenny, which I so much prefer to the Arkwright machines, for simplicity, ease of repair, cheapness of material and work, your neighbor D[r] Allison of Burlington has made a beautiful improvement by a very simple addition for the preparatory operation of roving. these are much the best machines for family & country use. for fulling in our families we use the simplest thing in the world. we make a bench of the widest plank we can get, say half a yard wide at least, of thick & heavy stuff. we cut notches cross wise of that 2.I. long & 1.I. deep, the perpendicular side of the notch fronting the middle one from both ends, on that we lay a 4.I. board, 6.f. long, with a pin for a handle in each end, and notched as the under one. a board is nailed on each side of the under one, to keep the upper in place as it is shoved backwards & forwards

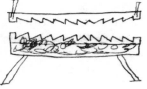

and the cloth properly moistened is laid between them. 2. hands full 20. yards in two hours.[2]

Our threshing machines are universally in England fixed with Dutch fans for winnowing, but not with us, because we

thresh immediately after harvest, to prevent weavil, and were our grain then laid up in bulk without the chaff in it, it would heat & rot.
ever and affectionately yours   TH: JEFFERSON

RC (TxU: Hanley Collection). PoC (MHi); at foot of first page: "C. W. Peale"; endorsed by TJ.

The RASCAL was Michael Withers, of Strasburg, Pennsylvania, who patented an improvement in "the mill gudgeon" on 24 Aug. 1813. Oliver Evans OBTAINED A PATENT on 14 Feb. 1804 for a "screw mill

for breaking and grinding different hard substances" (*List of Patents*, 39–40, 128). The SMITH IN GEORGE TOWN was Thomas Davis, from whom TJ purchased a machine for CRUSHING PLAISTER in 1805 (*MB*, 2:1157).

[1] Preceding three words interlined.
[2] Reworked from "in an hour."

To Joseph Darmsdatt

DEAR SIR   Monticello June 15. 15.

I some time ago desired mr Gibson to pay you 140. Dollars, about one half of which I had scandalously left unpaid for the last year's supply of fish. but really while the war left our produce to rot on our hands, a farmer had not the means of raising a single Dollar, and if it had continued we could have eaten no fish but what we caught ourselves. the balance is for another supply of herrings for the present year, half a dozen barrels to be sent to Lynchburg, and as many with a barrel of shad[1] to Milton as usual. those for Milton to be sent by Wm Johnson's boats; those for Lynchburg to the address of Archibald Robertson merchant there who will pay the freight. we wish to get them by harvest
accept the assurance of my great esteem & respect.
                                    TH: JEFFERSON

PoC (MHi); on verso of reused address cover from Tadeusz Kosciuszko to TJ; at foot of text: "Mr Darmsdadt"; endorsed by TJ.

[1] Preceding two words interlined.

To Charles Jouett

DEAR SIR   Monticello June 15. 15

I recieved yesterday your's of the 12th and have this day written to the President as you requested. I had before spoken to Col^o Monroe who assured me he would cordially do every thing in his power. if you fail, it will not be from the want of good will in the government, but from the difficulties of their situation, which you must be sensible are great at a moment when circumstances oblige them to dismiss so many meritorious officers into poverty. Accept my best wishes for your success & the assurance of my great esteem and respect.

TH: JEFFERSON

PoC (MoSHi: TJC-BC); on verso of reused address cover to TJ; at foot of text: "Mr Jouett"; endorsed by TJ.

To James Madison

DEAR SIR Monticello June 15. 15.

However firm my resolution has been not to torment the government, nor be harrassed my self with sollicitations for office, cases will now and then arise which cannot be denied. Charles Jouett formerly of this neighborhood, was appointed by Genl Dearborne an Indian agent. this was on the sollicitations of W. C. Nicholas, mr Carr & every respectable person of this neighborhood, and indeed from my own knolege of him. he is a man of sound good sense, prudence, perfect integrity and a zealous republican. Dearborne I know considered him, on trial to be the honestest and best agent in the Indian department; and he had great influence over the Indians of his department. he thinks he was shuffled by Eustis into a resignation of his office. he is poor, has married some time ago a French girl as poor as himself, and now sollicits to return again to the same or any other employment which will give him bread. I should not fear answering for his execution of any trust with fidelity and ability, were there an opening for him. but if there be not, without injustice to others, he must submit to it, as his misfortune.—Monroe is with us, and his daughter mrs Hay extremely ill.—Bonaparte, unprincipled as he is, is at length placed in a situation to claim all our prayers against the enterprises meditated on the independance of his nation. ever and affectionately yours TH: JEFFERSON

RC (CtSoP, on deposit CtY); at foot of text: "The President of the US."; endorsed by Madison. PoC (DLC); torn at seal; on verso of reused address cover of John Barnes to TJ, 25 Apr. 1815; endorsed by TJ.

Peter CARR had recommended that Jouett be appointed governor of the new territory of Michigan (Carr to John Wayles Eppes, 8 Feb. 1805 [DNA: RG 59, LAR, 1801–09]).

Jefferson's Letter to
James Maury

EDITORIAL NOTE

In composing a letter to his boyhood friend James Maury, a longtime expatriate serving as United States consul at Liverpool, England, Jefferson included a request that Maury locate an agent who could purchase books for him in Great Britain. The retired statesman was seeking to rebuild his collection after the recent sale of his library to the United States Congress. He intended to supply a list and a sum of money and to repeat the process annually. Jefferson apparently then decided against enlisting Maury in this effort. He canceled the pertinent portion of pages three and four and rewrote the conclusion to what thus became a three-page letter, and he did not broach the subject to Maury thereafter. With its detailed commentary on the types of books Jefferson wanted and how they were to be shipped, the partial draft is of such interest that it and the final version are both printed in full below.

I. Thomas Jefferson to James Maury
(Partial Draft)

[15 June 1815]

both nations.[1] the irritation here is great and general. we percieve the same in the English nation, nourished by the newspapers, that first of all human contrivances for generating war. but it is the office of the rulers on both sides to rise above these vulgar vehicles of passion, to assuage angry[2] feelings, and by examples & expressions of mutual regard and respect, to lead their citizens into good temper with each other. those will be most earnest in this who best know the happiness and prosperity it would bring to both. for myself, I have little personal concern in it. time is drawing her curtain on me. but I should make my bow with more satisfaction, if I had more hope of seeing our countries shake hands together cordially. in this sentiment I am sure you are with me, and this assurance must apologize for my indulging myself in expressing it to you.[3]

I trouble you now with a piece of business. on the destruction of the library of Congress, I thought it a duty to offer them mine. I had been 50. years collecting it, with good opportunities, and it's selection, more than it's number of volumes had peculiarly adapted it to their uses. I must now buy again, for books are the best medecine for the ennui of age. many will not be necessary for the time I have left. having no correspondent in London, I throw myself on your friendship to procure me one, an honest man, who, having the circumstance of price in his own hands, will consider himself as acting for me also, and charge a fair one for both parties. I inclose a catalogue of the wants which I now wish to have supplied. to the prices of 20. years ago, I have added about 25 per cent as the probable growth of price within that period, and supposed the amount would be about 175. Dollars. that sum I have desired my friend John Vaughan of Philadelphia to place at your command, and wherever the fund ends, there also be pleased to let the purchase end, as any remnant of the catalogue may be added to that of the 2ᵈ year with which I may probably trouble you. I like much better the 8ᵛᵒ volume than any other size; because without being too heavy for the hand, it is large enough to lie open on the table according to convenience. you may accordingly observe 8ᵛᵒˢ called for in the catalogue wherever there are good editions of that size. I like good bindings, and handsome, without being over elegant for use. it is of importance that these books should be in time for a summer or autumn passage on account of the damage they almost always suffer from winter weather. Richmond is my most convenient port, and Gibson & Jefferson my correspondents there, to which place I presume you will find abundant opportunities of sending them. accept now the assurance of my great and constant friendship and respect.　　　　　　　　　　　　Th: Jefferson

Dft (DLC: TJ Papers: 204:36315); incomplete, consisting of concluding two pages; undated; endorsed by TJ: "Maury James June 15. 15.　not sent."

¹ The partial Dft begins with these two words. TJ incorporated both pages of the original opening in the final version (see note 3 of the following document).

² TJ here canceled "passions."

³ Remainder of letter canceled with a single diagonal line.

II. Thomas Jefferson to James Maury (Final State)

Monticello June 15. 1815.

I congratulate you, my dear and antient friend, on the return of peace, and the restoration of intercourse between our two countries. what has past may be a lesson to both of the injury which either can do the other. and the peace now opened may shew what would be the value of a cordial friendship: and I hope the first moments of it will be improved to remove the stumbling block which must otherwise keep us eternal enemies. I mean the impressment of our[1] citizens. this was the sole object of the continuance of the late war, which the repeal of the orders of council would otherwise have ended at it's beginning. if, according to our estimate, England impressed into her navy 6000 of our citizens, let her count the cost of the war, and a greater number of men lost in it, and she will find this resource for manning her navy the most expensive she can adopt, each of these men having cost her £30,000. sterling, and a man of her own besides. on that point we have thrown away the scabbard, and the moment an European war brings her back to this practice, adds us again to her enemies. but I hope an arrangement is already made on that subject.   Have you no statesmen who can look forward two or threescore years? it is but 40. years since the battle of Lexington. one third of those now living saw that day when we were but 2. millions of people, and have lived to see this when we are 10. millions. one third of those now living, who see us at 10. millions, will live another 40. years, and see us 40. millions; and looking forward only through such a portion of time as has past since you and I were scanning Virgil together (which I believe is near threescore years) we shall be seen to have a population of 80. millions, and of not more than double the average density of the present. what may not such a people be worth to England as customers, and friends? and what might she not apprehend from such a nation as enemies? now what is the price we ask for our friendship? justice, and the comity usually observed between nation and nation. would there not be more of dignity in this, more character and satisfaction, than in her teazings and harassings, her briberies and intrigues to sow party discord among us, which can never have more effect here than the opposition within herself has there; which can never obstruct the begetting children, the efficient source of growth; and, by nourishing a deadly hatred, will only produce & hasten events which both of us, in moments of sober reflection should deplore & deprecate. one half the attention employed in decent observances towards our government, would be worth more to her than all the[2] duperies played off upon her, at a great expence on her part of money and meanness, and of nourishment to the vices and treacheries of the Henrys and Hulls of both nations. as we never can be at war with any other nation, (for no other can get at us but Spain, & her own people will manage her) the idea may be generated that we are natural enemies, and a calamitous one it will be to both.   I hope in god her government will come to a sense of this, and will see that honesty and interest are as intimately connected in the public, as in the private code of morality. her ministers have been weak enough to believe from the newspapers that mr Madison and myself are personally her enemies. such an idea is unworthy a man of sense; as we should have been unworthy our trusts could we have felt such a motive of public action. no two men in the US. have more sincerely wished for cordial friendship with her; not as her vassals, or dirty partizans, but as members of coequal states, respecting each other, and sensible of the good as well as the harm each is capable of doing the other. on this ground there was never a moment we did not wish to embrace her. but repelled by their aversions, feeling their hatred at every point of contact, and justly indignant at it's supercilious manifestations, that happened which has happened, and that will follow which must follow, in progressive ratio, while such dispositions continue to be indulged. I hope they will see this, and do their part towards healing the minds and cooling the temper of[3] both nations. the irritation here is great and general, because the mode of warfare both on the maritime and inland frontiers has been most exasperating. we percieve the English passions to be high also, nourished by the newspapers, that first of all human contrivances for generating war. but it is the office of the rulers on both sides to rise above these vulgar vehicles of passion; to assuage angry feelings, and by examples and expressions of mutual regard in their public intercourse, to lead their citizens into good temper with each other. no one feels more indignation than myself when reflecting on the insults and injuries of that country to this. but the interests of both require that these should be left to history, and in the mean time be smothered in the living mind. I have indeed little personal concern in it. time is drawing her curtain on me. but I should make my bow with more satisfaction, if I had more hope of seeing our countries shake hands together cordially. in this sentiment I am sure you are with me, and this assurance must apologise for my indulging myself in expressing it to you, with that of my constant & affectionate friendship and respect   TH: JEFFERSON

RC (Jonathan Kasso, Melville, N.Y., 2005); addressed: "James Maury esquire Consul of the US. of America. Liverpool"; endorsed by Maury as received 21 Aug. 1815 and answered 9 Sept. 1815. PoC (DLC). Tr (MHi); posthumous copy.

[1] TJ here canceled "seamen."
[2] TJ here canceled "Yankee." The word is retained in PoC and Tr.
[3] Second page ends here, with text to this point originally part of Dft.

From Jeremiah A. Goodman

DER SIR   June 16 day 1815

I nover new what it was to have my feallings hurt before I ex-
knowledg I was to fast intell you to git a nother man if I Could onley
bin tryed one more year and Also having M^r yancey at the other plase
and then if was not to make as much as he should make I would sur-
mit but my fat I will bare with patience and try to do the best I Can
my daily study has bin for you intrust but Mr Yancey will judge of
this and I trust to god he will give me Justice your good will has bin
all I over ask for

Mr Yancey will Let you know the situation of the Crop my Corn is
very much mended the wheat & owts is too my tobacco is all standing

JEREMIAH A GOODMAN

RC (ViU: TJP-ER); addressed: "Mr Th^{os} Jefferson Albemarle Mounticello"; stamp
canceled; franked; postmarked Lynchburg, 28 June, and Charlottesville, 2 July; endorsed by TJ as received 3 July 1815 and so recorded in SJL.

To James Maury

MY DEAR SIR   Monticello June 16. 1815.

Just as I was about to close my preceding letter, yours of Apr. 29.
is put into my hands, and with it the papers your kindness forwards
to me. I am glad to see in them expressions of regard for our friendship and intercourse from one side of the houses of parliament. but I
would rather have seen them from the other, if not from both. what
comes from the opposition is understood to be the converse of the
sentiments of the government, and we would not there, as they do
here, give up the government for the opposition. the views of the
Prince and his ministers are unfortunately to be taken from the
speech of Earl Bathurst, in one of the papers you sent me. but, what
is incomprehensible to me is that the Marquis of Wellesly, advocating us, on the ground of opposition, says that 'the aggression which
led to the war was from the US. not from England.' is there a person
in the world who, knowing the circumstances, thinks this? the acts
which produced the war were 1. the impressment of our citizens by
their ships of war, and 2. the orders of council forbidding our vessels
to trade with any country but England without going to England
to obtain a special licence. on the 1st subject the British minister declared to our Chargé, mr Russel, that this practice of their ships of
war could not be discontinued, and that no admissible arrangement

[542]

could be proposed: and as to the 2^d the Prince regent by his proclamation of Apr. 21. 1812. declared, in effect, solemnly that he would not revoke the orders of council <u>as to us</u>, on the ground that Bonaparte had revoked his decrees <u>as to us</u>; that on the contrary we should continue under them until Bonaparte should revoke <u>as to all the world</u>. these categorical and definitive answers put an end to negociation, and were a declaration of a continuance of the war in which they had already taken from us 1000. ships and 6000. seamen. we determined then to defend ourselves and to oppose further hostilities by war on our side also. now had we taken 1000. British ships and 6000 of her seamen without any declaration of war, would the M. of Wellesley have considered a declaration of war by Gr. Britain as an aggression on her part? they say we denied their maritime rights. we never denied a single one. it was their taking our citizens, native as well as naturalized, for which we went into war, and because they forbade us to trade with any nation, without entering and paying duties in their ports on both the outward and inward cargo. thus to carry a cargo of cotton from Savanna to St Mary's, and take returns in fruits, for example, our vessel was to go to England, enter and pay a duty on her cottons there, return to St Mary's; then go back to England to enter & pay a duty on her fruits, & then return to Savanna, after crossing the Atlantic four times, and paying tributes on both cargoes to England, instead of the direct passage of a few hours. and the taking ships for not doing this the Marquis says is no aggression. however it is now all over, & I hope for ever over. yet I should have had more confidence in this, had the friendly expressions of the Marquis come from the ministers of the prince. on the contrary we see them scarcely admitting that the war ought to have been ended. Earl Bathurst shuffles together chaotic ideas merely to darken and cover the views of the ministers in protracting the war: the truth being that they expected to give us an exemplary scourging, to separate from us the states East of the Hudson, take for their Indian allies those West of the Ohio, placing 300,000 American citizens under the government of the savages, and to leave the residuum a powerless enemy, if not submissive subjects. I cannot concieve what is the use of your Bedlam, when such men are out of it. and yet that such were their views we have under the hand of their Secretary of state in Henry's case, and of their Commissioners at Ghent. even now they insinuate that the peace in Europe has but suspended the practices which produced the war. I trust[1] however they are speaking a different language to our ministers; and join in the hope you express that the provocations which occasioned the late rupture will not be repeated.   The interruption of our intercourse with England has rendered us one essential service in planting radically and firmly coarse manufactures among us. I make in my family 2000. yds of cloth a year, which I formerly bought from England, and it only employs a few women, children & invalids who could do little in the farm. the state generally does the same, and allowing 10. yds to a person, this amounts to 10. million of yards; and if we are about the medium degree of manufactures in the whole union, as I believe we are, the whole will amount to 100. millions of yards a year, which will soon reimburse us the expences of the war. carding machines in every neighborhood, spinning machines in large families, and wheels in the small are too radically established ever to be relinquished. the finer fabrics perhaps, and even probably, will be sought again in Europe, except broadcloth, which the vast multiplication of Merinos among us, will enable us to make much cheaper than can be done in Europe.

Your practice of the cold bath thrice a week during the winter, and at the age of 70.[2] is a bold one, which I should not, a priori, have pronounced salutary. but all theory must yield to experience, and every constitution has it's own laws. I have for 50. years bathed my feet in cold water every morning (as you mention) and having been remarkably exempted from colds (not having had one in every 7. years of my life on an average) I have supposed it might be ascribed to that practice. when we see two facts accompanying one another for a long time, we are apt to suppose them related as cause and effect.

Our tobacco trade is strangely changed. we no longer know how to fit the plant to the market. differences of from 4. to 21.D. the hundred are now made on qualities appearing to us entirely whimsical. the British orders of council had obliged us to abandon the culture generally. we are now however returning to it; and experience will soon decide what description of lands may continue it to advantage. those which produce the qualities under 7. or 8. Dollars must, I think, relinquish it finally.—your friends here are well as far as I have heard. so I hope you are; and that you may continue so as long as you shall think the continuance of life itself desirable is the prayer of Your's sincerely & affectionately   TH: JEFFERSON

RC (NNGL, on deposit NHi); endorsed by Maury, in part: "recd 24 augt and ansd 9th sepr} 1815   NB should have been 21st augt." PoC (DLC); at foot of first page: "Mr Maury." Tr (MHi); posthumous copy.

TJ believed that the views of the PRINCE Regent, the future George IV, were reflected in the speech given in the British House of Lords on 13 Apr. 1815 by Henry BATHURST, 3d Earl Bathurst, and opposed the same day by

Richard WELLESLEY, Marquess Wellesley (Hansard, *Parliamentary Debates*,
30:587–607). TJ's remarks on former
British SECRETARY OF STATE (and current prime minister) Robert Jenkinson,
Lord Liverpool, came from reading alleged British agent John HENRY's correspondence (James Madison to TJ, [9
Mar. 1812], and note).

[1] Word interlined in place of "hope."
[2] Tr: "72."

From Charles Willson Peale

DEAR SIR   Belfield June 18. 1815.

Since my last to you I have conversed with a few friends on the dis-
posial of the Museum, M[r] Vaughan thinks that by a Tontine it might
be sold most readily, the high interest it would give in a few years he
considers a temptation to subscribers—I never relished the Idea of
gain by the death [of][1] others—And most probably I shall apply to
the Legislature to obtain an act to dispose of it by a Lottery, in a
Scheme of having some few prizes of money sufficient to pay the expence of the undertaking, the Museum being the capital prize. The
question is, whether it would be advisable to debar it from being re-
mooved from Philad[a]?—The Lin-tree, I dont know the classical
Name, is a light, smooth grain, and least liable to warp of any wood,
I am acquainted with. M[r] Hawkins prefered it for the machinery of
the Polly graphs to any other subtance. I admire the simplicity of
fulling Cloath as you have described—but does it not rub rather too
much?—I have the Idea that pounding only should be made use of[2]
in the act of fulling—And the thought came to my mind of the
following plan, perhaps best shewn by a few lines—

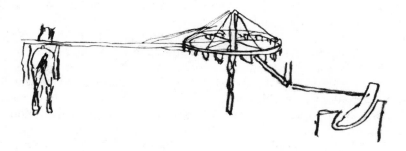

The proportioned parts I do not attend to—the wheel must be
sufficiently high to pass over the fulling stocks &c and they also
within the circumference of the Horses tract. I propose two hammers
to be lifted alternately. If the hammers are not very heavy, the power

will not be overmuch, & I beleive speed by the alternate stroke will be sufficient in the common walking of the Horse. Friction wheels may be put to the tilts of each hammer—The sliding lift may be most agreable, as avoiding sudden strokes in the mooving power—This design is only of a few moments thought, but as the fulling business is much wanted,[3] and the moovement of fulling stocks, by its sudden & racking jolts is very objectionable with other Machinery—(How it would affect your Saw mill as you proposed it in your former letter I am wholly ignorant). perhaps this plan is deserving of mature consideration—But it may be like many other Idea's communicated with fredom in[4] my letters from time to time. If I can give you any amusement I will not think my time ill spent in throwing out my crude Idea's

It gives me concern to know of so many abuses that are practiced under the Patent law. Several Persons have asked me if I did not intend to take a patent for my improvement of the Wind-mill sails, my answer has always been that I wish to give public utility by every aid in my power, and every one may use it. several Persons in the neighbourhood propose erecting wind-mills like mine for various purposses.   In my last letter I mentioned my having put a link to the end of the spring, I now find that the principle of my first invention is the best, and instead of two pins I have put blocks of wood

the block fastened to the outer frame & the spring screwed on the Sail frame—(a) being the joint of the Sail, the point of the spring pressing up the sail to the wind, more wind than is sufficient to the object, the sail yields & the point of the spring sliding on the round part of the block maintains the same power and no more than in the first position of the sail. The round part of the block is the end of the grain, consequently it will be durable; I am told that the spring will be worn out before the wood, a little tallow makes it very smooth. I have just learned the most approved method of making Springs, which I concieve is too important to omit giving you—and I am told it is known only with experienced artisans. first[5] harden as usial; to a white colour, than reduce it to a blue—and with a planishing hammer, hammer it well on one side only, and in this hammering give the Spring its proper sett—being well hammered in closeing the[6] grain of the steel it will become bright—then Blue it a second time. I am told that a Sword tempered in this method may be bent untill the two ends meet, & it will maintain its strait[7] form after being thus bent!—

I feel interested in seeing M[r] Allisons improvements for Domestic spinning, therefore I mean to visit him at Burlington as soon as I can make it convenient. I beleive it is more beneficial to our Country to manufacture with small Machines in families, then by large establishments—where numbers of each Sex are huddled togather to the great derangement of their morals & virtue. The rising generation of Children in small towns near which are Established large Manufactories will receive very little Schooling. In Germanton the Children of all poor families, are imployed in the large manufactories, small children are paid 50 C[ts] ℔ week, when these Children are let loose from their work they are troublesome in many respects, therefore the Inhabitants have formed societies to suppress Vice & Immorality, which I am told has considerably checked the irregularities of such Children. since I began this letter, I have conversed with an intelligent Gentleman of New England (near Boston) he tells me that some very extensive Manufactories in that country have experienced the disadvantage of employing so many hands togather, and that they are now dividing those large establishments into 2 or 3 smaller ones. They do not like to employ foreigheners as <u>foremen</u>, they wish to instruct their Sons and give them the superintendance of their works. He observes that our Women go to market, and do out work, and that with them, the women keep in doors, that they weave and make Straw Bonnets &c.

I have often thought that premiums given for useful inventions, as I beleive was the practice in France, would be much better than granting Patents, the instance you give of swindling of Mill holders out of their money and no one opposing, will incourage such fellows to continue their extorsions throughout the States. It will be difficult to find a remedy, but I foresee that something ought to be done to prevent such practices—Patents are granted in many instancies where the Patentee has had no right of Invention. Triffling alterations of parts and not of the principle ought not to constitute a right of invention, and it is also evident that oaths are violated too frequently—But I always thought that oaths ought not to be administered where the party is interested. Much evil attends the practice.

July 12th The Harvest of Hay & now wheat with some other pressing business made me lay by my pen—and with the hope also, that I might find more interresting matter to treat on. Turning back & considered my hasty thoughts on the Horse-fulling-mill, what strikes me now as a very great objection to it, is the unequal pull, although the alternate stroke might be so adjaused as one hammer would[8] be on the left a little before the other has fallen; yet I apprehend without some regulating power it would still be too much of a jerking draught for a Horse or Horses.   A Gentleman of Baltimore has sent me two small machines for gathering fruit, which I now mean to give a description of.[9] but at the same time I think it very probable that they will not be new to you, as something similar in principle has long been in use with us; That is a ring with points & a net attached to the under side to catch the fruit. However by giveing the exact size & shape, if you have not such it may be useful, as they are simple & easily made:

This is for gathering small fruit such as Nec-turens; Green Gages &c

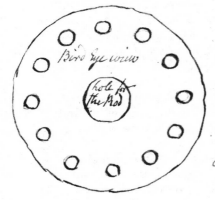

The larger one is turned out of a board $1\frac{1}{2}$ In: thick to make a longer socket for the rod. The diameter is 6 Incches, & the Circle to put the pins $4\frac{3}{4}$ diameter. The Pins nine in number 4 Inches long above the board, made of $\frac{1}{2}$ Inch stuff tapered towards the point—placed a little oblique to the left and gathering in at the points to form a circle of 4 In: diameter. this description with the slight drawing of the smaller machine on the other side will I hope be sufficiently understood.   When I first came to the farm I made a machine like what Doct^r Franklin had to take down Books from an upper shelf which he called his long hand, but instead of flat bills I scooped out and formed them into two spoons, one being a fixture on the long rod & the other spoon on its joint, they were drawn togather by a string comming to the bottom of the long rod. The management of it was not so easey, as in the mode now presented.

I have many calls for my labour at this time, therefore will close this epistle—And will be glad to resume should any thing occur deserving communication—

yours most affectionately   C W PEALE

RC (DLC); edge chipped, with loss supplied from PoC; endorsed by TJ as a letter of 18 June–12 July 1815 received 2[2] July 1815. PoC (PPAmP: Peale Letterbook). Recorded in SJL as received 22 July 1815.

LIN-TREE: basswood, also known as American linden (Albert B. Lyons, *Plant Names Scientific and Popular*, 2d ed. [1907], 462). A PLANISHING HAMMER has polished convex faces and is used to beat a piece of metal flat or to give it a smooth surface (*OED*).

[1] Omitted word editorially supplied.
[2] Manuscript: "off."
[3] Manuscript: "wonted."
[4] Manuscript: "is."
[5] Manuscript: "firt."
[6] Peale here canceled "pours."
[7] Word interlined.
[8] Word interlined in place of "might."
[9] Manuscript: "off."

From George Ticknor

DEAR SIR,   London June 18. 1815.

The great revolution in France, and the war growing out of it, which have changed the face of every thing in Europe, have compelled me, as you may have, perhaps, imagined, to make some change in my plans, of which it may be useful for you to be advised, as you proposed to employ me in purchasing your books in France, It is now no longer possible to go there directly or safe to take the indirect route through the Netherlands, and I have, therefore, concluded to establish myself at Gottingen, until the fall of the year, when I hope the question will be settled either one way or the other & a residence in France will become again both practicable & pleasant.

In the mean time, I have some letters from you to your friends there, which I know not well how to dispose of. They were written during Buonaparte's recess from the throne & may, therefore, contain opinions & expressions which it would not be safe to trust to the ordinary conveyances, under existing circumstances, for the sake of the persons to whom they are addressed. By the advice of your friends, therefore, I shall keep these letters, until the times are a little more settled & I can have an opportunity to deliver them in person. That to the Baron de Moll, Mr. Gallatin thinks it best for me to carry to Germany & put into the post office nearest his residence. If these arrangements should not meet your approbation, I pray you to address a line to me care of Samuel Williams 13 Finsbury Square London, who will forward it to me wherever I may be, and the instructions contained in which I shall exactly observe.

As soon as circumstances will warrant or permit, I shall go to Paris, This I hope and trust will be in the course of the ensuing fall, and there I hope I shall be able to serve you in collecting your Library.

Meanwhile, I pray you to present my respects to Mr. & Mrs. Randolph, and to believe me to be

very respectfully Your most ob^t & very humble ser^t

GEO: TICKNOR.

RC (DLC); endorsed by TJ as received 3 Oct. 1815 and so recorded in SJL.

TJ's letter to Baron Karl von MOLL was dated 31 July 1814 and probably enclosed in TJ to Ticknor, 3 Mar. 1815, for which see note to TJ to Ticknor, 19 Mar. 1815.

From John Adams

DEAR SIR   Quincy June 19. 1815

Education, which you brought into View in one of your Letters; is a Subject So vast, and the Systems of Writers are So various and So contradictory: that human Life is too Short to examine it; and a Man must die before he can learn to bring up his Children. The Phylosophers, Divines, Politicians and Pædagogues, who have published their Theories and Practices, in this department are without number.

Your present Inquiries, I presume, are not confined to early Education; perhaps do not comprehend it. The Constitution of a University is your object, as I understand you. Here also the Subject is infinite. The Science has So long laboured with a Dropsy, that it is a wonder the Patient has not long Since expired. Sciences of all kinds have need of Reform, as much as Religion and Government.

I never know what to write to you; because I consider it, as Sending Coal to Newcastle.

Tallerand Perigord, Soon after his arrival at Philadelphia presented to me his "Rapport Sur l'instruction publique." I presume he presented the Same Work to you, This production has Some fame and may Suggest Some Ideas to you.

The Universities in Protestant Germany have at present the Vogue and the Ton in their favour. There is in Print a "Coup-Dœil Sur les Universités, et le mode D'Instruction Publique de L'Allemagne Protestante; en particulier Du Royaume de Westphalie, Par Charles Villers." Correspondant de l'Institut national de France, de la Societé Royale des Sciences de Gœttingue, etc.

There is also in print "Recueil de recherches Sur l'education; memoire qui a concouru, en l'an XI a la Société des Sciences et Arts de Grenoble, Sur cette question, Quells Sont les moyens de perfectioner l'Education physique et morale des enfans?" Par J. J. Droüin, employé au ministere des relations exterieures.[1]

If I had not reason to presume that you possess these Pamplets I would attempt to give you Some Account of them. They will convince you, that you have a task difficult and perplexed enough.

The War of the Reformation Still continues. The Struggle between different and opposite Systems of Religion and Government has lasted from Huss and Wickliff to Lindsey and Priestly. How many pouder Plotts, Bartholomews days, Irish Massacres, Paris Guillotines, how many Charles'es and Maurices Louis's and Williams, Georges and Napoleons have intervened. And the Philosophers, if we believe Condorcet, have been as arrant Hypocrites as any of them.

I am, as ever,   JOHN ADAMS,

RC (DLC); addressed in an unidentified hand: "Thomas Jefferson—late President of the United States—Monticello"; franked; postmarked Quincy, 19 June; endorsed by TJ as received 30 June 1815 and so recorded in SJL. FC (Lb in MHi: Adams Papers).

The French exile Talleyrand (TALLERAND) arrived in Philadelphia on 28 Apr. 1794 and lived there until he set sail for Europe in June 1796 (John L. Earl III, "Talleyrand in Philadelphia, 1794–1796," *PMHB* 91 [1967]: 282–98). TJ is not known to have owned his *Rapport sur L'Instruction Publique, Fait au Nom du Comité de Constitution a L'Assemblée Nationale, les 10, 11, et 19 Septembre*

1791 (Paris, 1791). POUDER PLOTTS, BARTHOLOMEWS DAYS, IRISH MASSACRES: the Gunpowder Plot was a failed attempt by Roman Catholic conspirators to blow up the English Parliament building on 5 Nov. 1605 and thereby kill James I and the legislators in attendance that day; the Saint Bartholomew's Day massacre of Protestant Huguenots began in Paris on 24 Aug. 1572 and lasted for weeks after spreading to the countryside; and a 1641 rebellion in Ireland that began with the slaughter of many Protestants was soon countered by reprisal killings of Catholics.

[1] Superfluous closing double quotation mark editorially omitted.

From John Adams, with postscript by Abigail Adams

DEAR SIR   Quincy June 20. 1815

The fit of recollection came upon both of Us, So nearly at the same time that I may, Sometime or other, begin to think there is Some thing in Priestleys and Hartleys vibrations. The day before Yesterday I Sent to the Post office a letter to you and last night I received your kind favour of the 10th.

The question before the human race is, Whether the God of nature Shall govern the World by his own laws, or Whether Priests and Kings Shall rule it by fictitious Miracles.? Or, in other Words, whether Authority is originally in the People? or whether it has descended for 1800 Years in a Succession of Popes and Bishops, or brought down from Heaven by the holy Ghost in the form of a Dove, in a Phyal of holy Oil?

Who shall take the side of God and Nature? Brackmans,? Mandarins? Druids? Or Tecumseh and his Brother the Prophet? or Shall We become Disciples of the Phylosophers? And who are the Phylosophers? Frederick? Voltaire? Rousseau? Buffon? Diderot? or Condorcet? These Phylosophers have Shewn them Selves as incapable of governing man kind, as the Bourbons[1] or the Guelphs.

Condorcet has let the Cat out of the Bag. He has made precious confessions. I regret that I have only an English Translation of his "Outlines of an historical View of the progress of the human Mind." But in pages 247. 248 and 249 you will find it frankly acknowledged that the Phylosophers of the 18th Century, adopted all the Maxims and practiced all the Arts of the Pharisees, the ancient Priests of all Countries, the Jesuits, the Machiavillians &c &c to overthrow the Institutions that Such Arts had established. This new Phylosophy, was by his own Account, as insideous, fraudulent hypocritical and cruel, as the old Policy of Priests, Nobles and Kings. When and where were ever found or will be found, Sincerity, Honesty or Veracity in any Sect or Party in Religion Government or Phylosophy? Johnson and Burke were more of Catholicks than Protestants at Heart and Gibbon became an Advocate for the Inquisition. There is no Act of Uniformity in the Church or State phylosophick. As many Sects and Systems among them as among Quakers[2] and Baptists.

Bona. will not revive Inquisitions Jesuits or Slave Trade for which hebetudes, Bourbons have been driven again into Exile.

We Shall get along, with or without War.

I have at last procured the Marquis D'Argens's Ocellus Timæus and Julian. Three Such Volumes I never read. They are a most perfect exemplification of Condorcetts precious Confessions. It is astonishing they have not made more Noise in the World.

Our Athanasians have printed in a Pamphlet in Boston Your Letters and Priestleys from Belshams Lindsey. It will do you no harm. Our Correspondence[3] Shall not again be So long interrupted. Affectionately   JOHN ADAMS

[In Abigail Adams's hand:]

Mrs Adams thanks mr Jefferson for his friendly remembrance of her, and reciprocates to him a thousand good wishes.[4]

[In John Adams's hand:]

P.S. Tickner and Gray were highly delighted with their Visit; charmed with the whole Family.

Have you read Carnot? Is it not afflicting to See a Man of Such large Views So many noble Sentiments and Such exalted integrity, groping in the dark for a Remedy? a ballance or a mediator[5] between Independence and Despotism? How Shall his "Love of Country," his "Honor" and his "national Spirit" be produced.

I cannot write a hundreth part of what I wish to Say to you

J. A.

RC (DLC); endorsed by TJ as received 30 June 1815 and so recorded in SJL. RC (DLC: TJ Papers, ser. 10); address cover only; with PoC of TJ to Patrick Gibson, 28 July 1815, on verso; addressed in an unidentified hand: "Thomas Jefferson late President of the United States Monticello"; franked; postmarked Quincy, 21 June. FC (Lb in MHi: Adams Papers).

Adams's most recent letter to TJ was dated 19 June 1815, not THE DAY BEFORE YESTERDAY. The HOLY GHOST "descended in a bodily shape like a dove" in the Bible (Luke 3.22). BRACKMANS: "brahmans."

Adams's ENGLISH TRANSLATION of Condorcet was *Outlines of An Historical View of the Progress of the Human Mind* (London, 1795). He had PROCURED three volumes translated by Jean Baptiste de Boyer, marquis d'Argens: *Ocellus Lu-*

canus en Grec et en François (Utrecht, 1762); *Timée de Locres en Grec et en François* (Berlin, 1763); and *Defense du Paganisme par L'Empereur Julien, en Grec et en François* (Berlin, 1769). Adams's copies of these works are at MBPLi (Zoltán Haraszti, "John Adams Flays a Philosophe: Annotations on Condorcet's *Progress of the Human Mind,*" *WMQ,* 3d ser., 7 [1950]: 230; Constance B. Schulz, "John Adams on 'The Best of All Worlds,'" *Journal of the History of Ideas* 44 [1983]: 561–77).

The PAMPHLET was Thomas Belsham, *American Unitarianism or a Brief History of "The Progress and Present State of the Unitarian Churches in America"*. . . *Extracted from his "Memoirs of the Life of the Reverend Theophilus Lindsey," printed in London, 1812* (Boston, 1815). Printed on pp. 46–8 are an extract from TJ's letter to Joseph Priestley of 9 Apr. 1803 (DLC) and Priestley's letter to Theophilus Lindsey of 23 Apr. 1803, in the latter of which Priestley wrote that TJ "is generally considered as an unbeliever: if so, however, he cannot be far from us . . . He now attends public worship very regularly, and his moral conduct was never impeached."

[1] RC and FC: "Boubons."
[2] RC: "Quakes." FC: "Quakers."
[3] RC: "Correspondenc." FC: "Correspondence."
[4] In FC, Abigail Adams's postscript follows that of her husband.
[5] Preceding three words interlined.

From Joseph Cabell Breckinridge

DEAR SIR—   Lexington June 20. 1815.

I am sure that no apology will be necessary for troubling you with a letter on a subject which concerns the community at large.

M[r] Baxter, I believe, is now pretty well known in the United States, as an ingenious & successful improver of several machines used in the manufacture of cotton, hemp, & flax. He has invented a machine for spinning cotton—which, by reason of its cheapness, simplicity, and vast saving of labour, is, in this state, rapidly extending into general use. A more recent invention, for the purpose of preparing the cotton for this machine, is the subject of this letter.

After frequent conversations with the inventor, and much reflection, I cannot entertain a doubt of its fitness & utility. If he can succeed to the full extent of his wishes & expectations, the consequent diminution of labour, time & expence, in the manufacture of this important article, will be so great, as probably materially to obviate the difficulties under which our manufacturers of cotton have heretofore laboured, & put them on terms of equality with those countries, in which the immediate interests of a large class of the community is adverse to any further abridgment of manual labour.

M[r] Baxter will send you a rough drawing of this machine, (one of which is now making,) accompanied by explanatory remarks. He wishes your opinion of its practicability—your views, as to the probable extent of its usefulness, should it answer the purpose designed—and any information you may possess on the subject of similar machines (if any there be) in France & England. As a citizen of the Unite[d] States, I feel a deep interest in every improvement of our infant manufactures; and cannot doubt the solicitude of one, whose life has been devoted to establish the independence of his country, and improve the condition of her citizens.

If this machine is to be useful, its utility will be great in other countries; & M[r] Baxter would be glad to procure your advise, how he ought to proceed, in securing the patent right in foreign nations.

American inventions have not unfrequently been in a great measure lost to the individuals who were justly entitled to the wealth & fame attending their publication, by the Superior craft of inferior genius, on the other Side of the water.

I beg you to accept My best wishes for your health & happiness, and the assurances of my very great respect.

JOSEPH CABELL BRECKINRIDGE

RC (DLC); edge chipped; addressed: "Thomas Jefferson Esq' Monticello"; endorsed by TJ as received 5 July 1815 and so recorded in SJL.

To William P. Newby

SIR   Monticello June 21. 15.

Your letter of April 22. was duly recieved, and I should have waited as you requested till August for your final answer, but on going to Bedford in May, I found my affairs there in so total a state of mismanagement as not only to have lost me the last year, but to threaten the loss of the present one. I was therefore obliged to employ a person to take place on the spot, and to put the plantations under his immediate superintendance, which of course will be continued. he therefore will employ the future overseers, and tho' I am sure he would be glad to employ you under the character I should give him of you, yet as this change of superintendance might not be agreeable to you, I have thought it fair to give you timely notice of it. here also I have fo[u]nd it necessary to put my affairs under the direction of my gran[dson] Jefferson Randolph, my activity being too much declined to take care of them myself. had I continued in the care of them myself I should have been glad to have employed you, and should still be glad to see you employed by those now having the charge of them. Accept the assurance of my esteem and respect.

TH: JEFFERSON

PoC (DLC); on verso of reused address cover to TJ; mutilated at seal; at foot of text: "M' Newby"; endorsed by TJ.

Joel Yancey was the new superintendent of TJ's Poplar Forest PLANTATIONS.

From William Short

DEAR SIR   Philadelphia June 21.—15

I had the pleasure of writing to you early in the last month & of informing you of the payment made to me here of the $10500. treasury notes—I sent you at the same time a precise statement of our account up to that time, shewing that this payment left a balance due you of 34\frac{34}{100}$; which conformably with your order I paid to Mr Vaughan, of which he will, no doubt, have informed you. I requested you in my letter, to direct me as to the bonds & the mortgage from you, remaining in my hands; & which are now discharged. I did not venture to send them to you by mail without your authorization—In the mean time I have obliterated the several signatures & shall await your orders. I fear now I shall not be able to comply with them immediately as I shall probably have left the City before I shall hear from you; & these papers will be left among those of mine which cannot be got at during my absence—but on my return here in the fall I will follow the indication of your letter which I hope to receive in the mean time. All letters which arrive here will be taken up & forwarded to me.

The last letter which I have had the pleasure of receiving from you was of the 18th of April—You were then expecting Monroe, & also going to Bedford—I see by the papers that Monroe has gone to Albemarle, but I fear the evil star of the business will have placed that trip during yours—If so, I hope Monroe will name some person to attend for him to the running of this line. I wish it were terminated, as much for your sake as mine; for I really am ashamed of all the trouble I give you.

You know that our new Blackstone financier has been making great efforts to raise public stocks & treasury notes—He has succeeded beyond expectation—6. p^{cts} are now here a little below par—& treasury notes a little above—This varies with every City, in the Union—at New York, they are both below par; at Boston still more so—The price of exchange between this & N. York is now 5. p^{ct}.

Owing to the wise dispositions of our wise Congress in destroying the U.S. Bank, & allowing this hydra head to grow up manifold under the corruption of the State legislatures, there is really now no such thing as an uniform currency in the country—It varies in every State & in every City in the same State as much as in different countries & sovereignties. I see no remedy for this—The only practicable one (that of an U.S. bank established on liberal principles on the condition of paying their notes in specie & obliging others to do the same) will be I fear prevented, first by the administration exacting of such a bank a bonus to an amount that will disable them from paying specie—& secondly by the members of Congress or a majority of them being interested in the multitude of miserable state & county banks, either having brothers as Cashiers or Presidents, or by having borrowed money from them—They will therefore reject an U.S. bank wch would devour this bastard progeny—When you talk to these Gentlemen of a National bank, they have recourse to their pretended republican & constitutional objections, & thus claim a merit for following really a base & corrupt motive, that is, their personal interest in their county banks—Thus there is no uniformity in the value of any thing, or what ought to be the measure of every thing—A short time ago treasury notes were several p^{ct} under par—& I then disposed of them—they are now above par—but as I fortunately vested them in 6. p^{cts} I do not lose by this operation—

Correa is now drawing to a close the course of botanical lectures he is giving us here. He intends in the next month to take Dupont & visit you & Mr Madison with him—You will I am sure derive great pleasure from these two good men & able, so well informed of what is passing in a country[1] that must interest all the world.

I have the mortification to be receiving from time to time old letters from my friends that ought to have been here six & twelve months ago—they speak to me of their situation & of their happiness under the mild administration of L. 18—Poor people! how differently do they now feel whilst I am reading those letters—I rejoice at having not precipitated my return to France; which I certainly should have done, but for my invincible aversion to the sea—I fear if the war in Europe should extend itself as to time, that we shall be again involved—I do not suppose that our administration is mad enough or wicked enough to wish it—but it will grow out of the nature of things—If you have the weight which many insist on attributing to you, & wch I do not believe, pray exert it to ward off this direful event—Adieu to our Republican principles most certainly—& probably to our Republican Government, should a war last here a few years, whether successful or disastrous—God bless you my Dear sir & believe me

ever your friend & servant W Short

RC (MHi); addressed: "Thomas Jefferson mail to <u>Milton</u> V^a"; franked; postmarked Philadelphia, 21 June; endorsed by TJ as received 30 June 1815 and so recorded in SJL.

The NEW BLACKSTONE FINANCIER was Secretary of the Treasury Alexander J. Dallas. L. 18: Louis XVIII of France.

[1] Manuscript: "county."

From John Adams

Quincy June 22^d 15

Can you give me any Information, concerning A. G. Camus? Is he
a Chateaubriand? or a Marquis D'Argens? Does he mean to abolish
Christianity? or to restore the Inquisition, the Jesuits, the Pope and
the Devil?

Within a few days, I have received a thing as unexpected to me as
an Apparition from the dead; "Rapport a L'Institut National, Par
A. G. Camus, imprime par ordre de L'Institut, Pluviose An XI."[1]

In page 55 of this report he Says

"Certain Pieces which I found in the Chamber of Accounts in Brussells gave me useful indications, concerning the grand Collection of
the Bollandists; and conducted me, to make researches into the State
of that Work, unfortunately interrupted at this day. It would add to
the Institut to propose to Government the means of compleating it; as
it has done with Success, for the collection of the historians of France,
of diplomas and ordinances." Permit me, to dwell a few minutes on
this important Work. Note. "The Committee of the Institut, for proposing and Superintending the litterary labours, in the month of
Frimaire an XI. wrote to the Minister of the interiour, requesting him
to give orders, to the Prefect of the Dyle, and to the Prefect of the two
Nethes, to Summon the Citizens, Debue, Fonson, Heylen,[2] and all
others, who had taken any part, in the Sequel of the Work of the Bollandists; to confer with these persons, as well concerning the continuation of this Work, as concerning the cession of the materials destined
for the continuation of it; to promise to the Continuators of the Bollandists, the Support of the french[3] Government, and to render an
Account of their Conferences." End of the Note.

"Almost all the History of Europe, and a part of that of the East, from
the Seven[th] Century, to the thirteenth, is in the Lives of Personages,
to whom have been given the title of <u>Saints</u>. Every one may have remarked, that in reading history, there is no event of any importance,
in civil order, in which, Some Bishop, Some Abby, Some Monk, or
Some Saint, did not take a part. It is therefore, a great Service, rendered by the Jesuits, known under the name of the Bollandists, to
those who would write History, to have formed the immense Collection, extended to Fifty two Volumes in folio, known under the title of
The Acts of the Saints. The Service they have rendered to Litterature,
is considerably augmented, by the insertion in their Acts of the Saints,
a great number of Diplomas and dissertations, the greatest part of
which, are Models of Criticism. There is no man, among the learned,

who does not interest himself, in this great collection. My intension is not to recall to your recollection the original Authors or their first labours. We may easily know them, by turning over the leaves of the Collection, or if We would find the result already written, it is in the historical library of Meusel, T. 1. part. 1. p. 306. or in the Manuel of litterary history by Bouginé. T. 2. p. 641.

I Shall date what I have to Say to you, only from the Epoch of the Suppression of the Society of which the Bollandists were Members.

At that time, three Jesuits were employed in the collection of the Acts of the Saints; to Witt; the Fathers, De Bie, De Bue, and Hubens. The Father Gesquière who had also laboured at the Acts of the Saints, reduced a particular collection intitled Select fragments from belgical Writers, and extracts or Refferences to matters contained in a collection intitled Musæum of Bellarmine. These four Monks inhabited the House of the Jesuits at Antwerp. Independently of the Use of the Library of the Convent, the Bollandists had their particular Library,[4] the most important portion of which was a State of the Lives of the Saints for every day of the Month, with indications[5] of the Books in which were found those which were already printed, and the original Manuscripts, or the copies of Manuscripts, which were not yet printed. They frequently quote this particular Collection in their general Collection. The greatest part of the Copies they had assembled were the fruit of a Journey of the Fathers Papebroch and Henshen made to Rome in 1660; They remained there 'till 1662. Papebroch and his associate brought from Rome, Copies of Seven hundred Lives of Saints in greek or in latin. The Citizen La Serna, has in his Library a Copy taken by himself, from the originals, of the relation of the Journey of Papebroch to Rome, and of the Correspondence of Henshen with his Colleagues. The Relation and the Correspondence are in latin. See Catalogue de La Serna. T. 3. N° 3903.

After the Suppression of the Jesuits, The Commissioners[6] apposed their Seals upon the Library of the Bollandists, as well as on that of the Jesuits of Antwerp. But Mr Girard, then Secretary of the Accademy of Brussells, who is Still living, and who furnished me a part of the documents[7] I use; charged with the Inventory and Sale of the Books, withdrew those of the Bollandists and transported them to Brussells.

The Academy of Brussells, proposed to continue the Acts of the Saints under its own Name, and for this purpose to admit the four Jesuits into the number of its members. The Father Gesquiere alone consented to this Arrangement. The other Jesuits obtained of

Government, through the intervention of the Bishop of Neustadt, the assurance, that they might continue their Collection. In Effect, the Empress Maria Theresa approved, by a decree of the 19th of June 1778 a plan which was presented to her, for the continuation of the Works, both of the Bollandists and of Gesquiere. This plan is in ample detail. It contains twenty Articles, and would be useful to consult, if any Persons Should resume the Acts of the Saints. The establishment of the Jesuits was fixed in the Abby of Caudenberg at Brussells; the library of the Bollandists was transported to that place; one of the Monks of the Abby, was associated with them; and the Father Hubens being dead, was replaced by the Father Berthod, a Benedictin, who died in 1789.

The Abby of Caudenberg, having been Suppressed, the Government Assigned to the Bollandists a place in the ancient Colledge of the Jesuits at Brussells. They there placed their Library and went there to live. There they published the Fifty first Volume of their collection in 1786. the fifth tome of the month of October, printed at Brussells, at the Printing Press, Imperial and Royal, in Types Imperial and Royal. (in Typis Cæsario regiis) They had then two Associates, and they flattered themselves that the Emperor would continue to furnish the expence of their labours. Nevertheless, in 1788, the establishment of the Bollandists was Suppressed, and they even proposed to Sell the Stock of the printed Volumes; But, by an Instruction (Avis) of the 6th December 1788, the Ecclesiastical Commission Superceded the Sale, till the result could be known of a Negotiation which the Father De Bie, had commenced with the Abby of Saint Blaise to establish the Authors and transport[8] the Stock of the Work, as well as the materials for its continuation at Saint-Blaise.

In the mean time, the Abby of Tongerloo, offered the Government, to purchase the Library and the Stock of the Bollandists, and to cause the Work to be continued by the ancient Bollandists with the Monks of Tongerloo associated with them. These propositions were accepted: the Fathers De Bie, De Bue, and Gesquiere removed to Tongerloo; the Monks of Caudenberg refused to follow them, though they had been associated with them. On the Entry of the French Troops into Belgium, the Monks of Tongerloo quitted their Abbay: the Fathers De Bie and Gesquiere retired into Germany where they died; the Father De Bue, retired to the City of Hall, heretofore Province of Hainault, his native Country. He lives, but is very aged. One of the Monks of Tongerloo, who had been associated with them is the Father Heylen: they were not able to inform me, of the place of his residence. Another Monk, associated with the Bollandists of 1780 is the Father Fonson, who resides at Brussells.

In the midst of these troubles, the Bollandists have caused to be printed the fifty Second Volume of the Acts of the Saints, the Sixth Volume of the Month of October. The fifty first volume is not common in commerce; because the Sale of it, has been interrupted, by the continual Changes of the residence of the Bollandists. The fifty Second Volume, or the Sixth of the Same month of October, is much more rare. Few Persons know its Existence.

The Citizen Serna[9] has given me the 296 first pages of the Volume which he believes were printed at Tongerloo. He is persuaded that the Rest of the Volume exists; and he thinks it was at Rome that it was finished. (terminé).

The Citizen D'Herbouville, Préfect of the department of the two Neths at Antwerp, has made, for about 18 months, attempts, with the ancient Bollandists, to engage them, to resume their labours. They have not had Success. Perhaps the present moment, would be the most critical. (opportune). especially if the Government Should consent to[10] give to the Bollandists Assurance of their Safety.

The essential point would be to make Sure of the Existence of the Manuscripts which I have indicated; and which by the relation of the Citizen La Serna, filled a Body of a Library of about three Toises in Length, and two in breadth. If these Manuscripts Still exist, it is easy to terminate, the Acts of the Saints; because We Shall have all the necessary Materials. If these Manuscripts are lost, We must despair to See this Collection compleated.

I have enlarged, a little, in this digression, on the Acts of the Saints, becau[se] it is a Work of great importance; and because these documents, which cannot be obtained with any Exactitude but upon the Spots; Seem to me to be[11] among the principal Objects, which your Travellers, have to collect, and of which they ought to give you an Account."

Now, my Friend Jefferson! I await your Observations on this Morcell. You may think I waste my time and yours. I do not think so. If you will look into the "Nouveau Dictionaire Historique,"[12] under the Words "Bollandus, Heinshemius and Papebrock"[13] you will find more particulars of the Rise and progress of this great Work "The Acts of the Saints."

I shall make only an Observation or two.

1. The Pope never Suppressed the Work, and Maria Theresia established it. It therefore, must be Catholick.

2. Notwithstanding the Professions of the Bollandists, to discriminate the true from the false Miracles and the dubious from both; I Suspect that the false, will be found the fewest, the dubious the next, and the true the most numerous of all.

3. From all that I have read, of the Legends, of the Lives and Writings of the Saints and even of the Fathers, and of Ecclesiastical History in general: I have no doubt that the Acta Sanctorum is the most enormous Mass of Lies Frauds, Hypocracy and Imposture, that ever was heaped together upon this globe. If it were impartially consulted it would do more to open the Eyes of Man kind, than all the Phylosophers of the 18th Century, who were as great Hypocrites as any of the Phylosophers or Theologians of Antiquity.   JOHN ADAMS

RC (DLC); edges chipped and trimmed, with missing text supplied from FC; at foot of text: "President Jefferson"; endorsed by TJ as received 5 July 1815. FC (Lb in MHi: Adams Papers).

Adams's account of the attempt to complete the *Acta Sanctorum*, the GRAND COLLECTION of scholarship on Catholic saints continued by a group of Jesuits known as Bollandists, is a translation of Armand Gaston Camus, *Rapport a L'Institut National, Classe de Littérature et Beaux Arts, D'un voyage fait à la fin de l'an X, dan les départemens du Bas-Rhin, de la rive gauche de ce fleuve, de la Belgique, du Nord, de Pas-de-Calais, et de la Somme* (Paris, 1803), 55–61. An English translation appeared in "The Present State of Brussels. (Translated from Camus)," *Monthly Magazine* 21 (1806): 203–11, but Adams was translating from the original.

In the French Republican calendar FRIMAIRE AN XI corresponded to 22 Nov.–21 Dec. 1802. Jean Antoine Chaptal was the French MINISTER OF THE INTERIOUR, 1800–04. Louis Gustave Doulcet, comte de Pontécoulant, and Charles Joseph Fortuné, marquis d'Herbouville, were the respective prefects in 1802 of the French departments of DYLE and Deux-Nèthes (TWO NETHES) in present-day Belgium (*Dictionnaire des Parlementaires Français ... Depuis le 1er Mai 1789 jusqu'au 1er Mai 1889* [1889–91], 5:18–9; *Galerie Historique des Contemporains ou nouvelle Biographie* [Brussels, 1817–20], 5:304–5). The *Acta Sanctorum* is de-

scribed in Burkhard Gotthelf Struve, Christian Gottlieb Buder, and Johann Georg MEUSEL, *Bibliotheca Historica* (Leipzig, 1782–1804), 1:306–9, and Carl Joseph BOUGINÉ, *Handbuch der allgemeinen Litterargeschichte nach Heumanns Grundriß* (Zurich, 1789–1802), 2:641. The SUPPRESSION OF THE SOCIETY of Jesus (Jesuits) took effect in Belgium on 28 Sept. 1773 (Hippolyte Delehaye, *The Work of the Bollandists through Three Centuries, 1615–1915* [1922], 160).

Joseph Ghesquière directed the publication of a COLLECTION of documents relating to the history of Belgium (Charles De Smedt, "Bollandists," *The Catholic Encyclopedia* [1913–14], 2:635). Daniel PAPEBROCH was accompanied on his journey to Rome by Godfrey Henschen (HENSHEN). Carlos Antonio LA SERNA de Santander listed the diary of their travels as item no. 3903, "Diarium itineris romani anno 1660," in his *Catalogue des Livres de la Bibliotheque de M. C. de la Serna Santander* (Brussels, 1803), 3:69–70.

Heinrich Johann von Kerens was the bishop of Wiener NEUSTADT, Austria, 1775–85 (Charles E. O'Neill and Joaquín M. Domínguez, *Diccionario Histórico de la Compañía de Jesús* [2001], 3:2189–90). Joseph II, EMPEROR of the Holy Roman Empire, supported the decision of the Commission of Ecclesiastical Affairs and Studies to limit imperial support of the Bollandists (Delehaye, *The Work of the Bollandists*, 167–9). The victory of FRENCH TROOPS at the Battle of Fleurus on 26 June 1794 prepared the way for

French rule over Belgium that lasted until the fall of Napoleon in 1814 (Doyle, *French Revolution*, 207, 209).

TOISES are units of a French lineal measure, each of which are roughly equal to 1.949 meters or 6.4 feet (*OED*).

[1] Omitted closing quotation mark editorially supplied.
[2] RC and FC: "Heyten."
[3] Preceding two words interlined.
[4] Preceding nine words not in FC.

[5] RC: "indiations." FC: "indications."
[6] RC and FC: "Commissiones."
[7] RC: "douments." FC: "documents."
[8] RC: "tranport." FC: "transport."
[9] RC and FC: "Lerna."
[10] RC: "to to." FC: "to."
[11] RC: "be be." FC: "be."
[12] Omitted closing quotation mark supplied from FC.
[13] Omitted closing quotation mark supplied from FC.

To Randolph Jefferson

DEAR BROTHER   Monticello June 23. 15

I lent you some years ago the harness of our family gigg, until you could get one made for your own. mrs Marks tells me your gigg is now demolished and out of use. mine has been used with one of our chariot harness. a neighbor asks the loan of it to go a journey, and if we let one of our set of harness go, we shall not be able to use the carriage until his return which will be very distant. under these circumstances I send the bearer to ask the return of the harness I lent you, in order to accomodate my neighbor.

present my respects to my sister and be assured of my best affections

TH: JEFFERSON

PoC (ViU: TJP-CC); on verso of reused address cover to TJ; endorsed by TJ.

TJ LENT the harness more than five years previously (Randolph Jefferson to TJ, 7 Dec. 1809; TJ to Jefferson, 8 Dec.

1809). A 6 June 1815 letter from TJ to his sister Anne Scott MARKS, not found, is recorded in SJL. This day TJ gave 25 cents for travel expenses to his slave Israel Gillette (Jefferson), the BEARER (*MB*, 2:1311). MY SISTER: Mitchie B. Pryor Jefferson.

From Randolph Jefferson

DEAR BROTHER   June 23: 15

I Received yours by the boy the harness in which you were kind enough to lend us was intirely worn out so that they did not scarce las us over to prince Edward and back. mr patteson borrowed our gigg to go over to the springs and had the harness with the gigg and they lasted him as far as stanton on his way to the springs and there he left them and baught a new set in which he gave to us and as our gigg is demolished the harness is of no service to us[1] now and have sent them over by your boy which you are very welcom too your boy informs u[s] of pore mrs Carrs death which I am extr[e]emly sorry to heare of we are very busy at this time in our harvest which I expect will be several days before we shall be able to finish my wife Joins me in love and respect to you and family.—I remain your most affectionately.—

RH; JEFFERSON

RC (ViU: TJP-CC); mutilated at fold; dateline at foot of text; endorsed by TJ as received 25 June 1815 from Snowden but recorded in SJL as received a day earlier.

MRS CARRS DEATH: Eleanor B. Carr, the wife of TJ's nephew Samuel Carr, died on 18 June 1815 (Richmond *Enquirer*, 15 July 1815).

[1] Reworked from "y."

From Andrew C. Mitchell

SIR   New York, June 23ᵈ 1815.

Permit me to invade your Retirement by presenting with the most respectful Sentiments, a Pamphlet entitled the Second Crisis of America, of which I am the author requesting for it the honor of your perusal.

As the Father and Friend to his Country I present this without further apology as however faulty and unworthy the offering may appear the aim of the writer has been devoted to that Cause which has animated your arduous life and ever been the characteristic of your actions—The Welfare of the United States.

I am personally unknown to you, although I have had the honor of being in my early years often in your presence; having been the Schoolfellow and intimate companion of my lamented Friend H. B. Triste

With the highest admiration of your virtues and your talents I am Your Respectful Fellow citizen   ANDREW C MITCHELL

RC (MiU-C); dateline beneath signature; at foot of first page: "Thomas Jefferson"; endorsed by TJ as received 28 June 1815 but recorded in SJL as received a day later. Enclosure: Mitchell, under the pseudonym "A Citizen of Philadelphia," *The Second Crisis of America, or A Cursory View of the Peace lately concluded between Great Britain and the United States* (New York, 1815).

Andrew Caldwell Mitchell (ca. 1778–1826), journalist and clerk, graduated from the University of Pennsylvania in 1793 and operated a tobacco shop in Philadelphia, 1813–14. He was the editor of the Philadelphia *American Democratic Herald, and Commercial Gazette*, 1814–15, and the New York *National Advocate*, 1815–17. Mitchell moved in 1817 to Washington, D.C., where he worked as a clerk in the United States Treasury Department (*University of Pennsylvania: Biographical Catalogue of the Matriculates of the College, 1749–1893* [1894], 36; Madison, *Papers, Pres. Ser.*, 5:635;

John A. Paxton, *The Philadelphia Directory and Register for 1813* [Philadelphia, 1813]; *Kite's Philadelphia Directory for 1814* [Philadelphia, 1814]; Brigham, *American Newspapers*, 1:672, 2:889; New York *National Advocate*, 10 June 1818; *Letter from the Secretary of the Treasury, Transmitting a Statement of the Names of the Clerks in the Treasury Department . . . during the year 1817* [Washington, D.C., 1818], 10; Wesley E. Pippenger, comp., *District of Columbia Probate Records: Will Books 1 through 6*

[1801–1852] and Estate Files [1801–1852] [2003], 134, 398; Washington *Daily National Intelligencer*, 11 May, 3 June 1826).

Hore Browse Trist (TRISTE) (1775–1804), the son of TJ's friend Elizabeth Trist, graduated from the University of Pennsylvania a year ahead of Mitchell (*University of Pennsylvania Biographical Catalogue*, 35; Jane Flaherty Wells, "Thomas Jefferson's Neighbors: Hore Browse Trist of 'Birdwood' and Dr. William Bache of 'Franklin,'" *MACH* 47 [1989]: 1–13).

To Joseph Miller

DEAR CAPTAIN   Monticello June 26. 15.

I recieved in due time the cask of biscuit you were so kind as to send us, and which we found to be of the very best quality. I have deferred acknoleging it until the season is approaching when considerations of health would recommend your leaving Norfolk, and the great heats will suspend the operations of your brewery; and I now take up my pen to assure you you have always a home here, and to invite you to pass the sickly season with us. our brewery of the last autumn is generally good, altho' not as rich as that of the preceding year, the batch we are now using is excellent. that which Peter Hemings did for mr Bankhead was good, and the brewing of corn which he did here after your departure would have been good, but that he spoiled it by over-hopping. a little more experience however will make him a good brewer. my absence in Bedford in the spring prevented our preparing some malt then, which I now regret. mr Bankhead is now with his father, and has unquestionably found great relief both to his body and mind in an entire change of habits and the increased affection of his friends. in hopes of seeing you here in autumn I tender you the assurance of my great esteem & respect.

TH: JEFFERSON

PoC (DLC); on verso of reused address cover of William Short to TJ, 3 May 1815 (see note to TJ to Short, 15 May 1815); at foot of text: "Capt Miller"; endorsed by TJ.

Miller's missing reply to TJ of 24 July 1815 is recorded in SJL both as misdated "Aug (for July) 24" and as received 8 Aug. 1815 from Norfolk.

To Joseph Milligan

DEAR SIR   Monticello June 26. 15.

I wrote to you from Bedford the 1ˢᵗ inst. to which I refer you if you have made a list of the books I forwarded for binding I would thank you for a copy, being at a loss sometimes to recollect whether a particular book was among them. indeed I shall be glad of the books themselves as soon as you can have them bound. I observe there is a mail-tumbrel from Fredsbg weekly to Milton which brings such things. I wish also to know if you have got Tracy's manuscript; how the library got on to Washington? whether it is unpacked, replaced on it's shelves Eᵗc. and whether you expect to print the Catalogue? Accept my best wishes & respects.   TH: JEFFERSON

PoC (DLC); on verso of reused address cover of Nicolas G. Dufief to TJ, 4 May 1815; at foot of text: "Mʳ Millegan"; endorsed by TJ.

To Hezekiah Niles

SIR   Monticello June 26. 15.

Having occasion lately to refresh my memory on the case of Henry the British agent, I was referred by the Index of your 2ᵈ volume to page 45. and turning to that part found the Nº 29, containing it to be missing. this had escaped me when I wrote my letters both of Oct. 29. 13 and March last, and I suppose it escaped me by my having the Supplement of Nº 29. and not observing that it was only the supplement. if therefore you can favor me with the Nº 29. of vol. 2. dated Mar. 21. 1812. I trust my collection will be compleat.
Accept the assurance of my great esteem & respect.

                                            TH: JEFFERSON

RC (MdHi: Vertical Files); addressed: "Mʳ H. Niles Baltimore"; frank clipped; postmarked Charlottesville, 28 June. PoC (DLC); on verso of reused address cover of RC of Tadeusz Kosciuszko to TJ, [14 Mar. 1815]; mutilated at fold; endorsed by TJ.

An entry for the article "John Henry— the British agent" appeared in the INDEX for the Baltimore *Weekly Register* 2 (Mar.–Sept. 1812), referencing p. 45 of issue no. 29, 21 Mar. 1812. For TJ's LETTERS to Niles of 29 Oct. 1813 and 22 Mar. 1815, see note to Niles to TJ, 1 Oct. 1811.

To William Short

DEAR SIR   Monticello June 27. 15.

We are unlucky in our endeavors to procure a settlement of your boundary. immediately on the arrival of Col° Monroe, I proposed to him a settlement. he was as anxious to have it as I was and we appointed the day after the morrow. mr Dawson one of the most probe and respectable men of our neighborhood, and Col° Isaac Coles, who happened to be at Monticello met us as arbitrators, and old mr Price as a witness. we depended on him to shew us the Spanish oak & Dogwood line trees on Dick's branch from which your line proceeds direct up the mountain, and to conduct us up the Southern branch to which Col° M. claims, and the Northern branch which we allege as his limit. we all proceeded up the mountain and the precipices, the bushes & the rocks becoming tremendous, every one sought the best way for himself, and had got far up the mountain before we observed that mr Price was not with us. we halted some time, then hallowed, and hearing no answer, one of the company went back half a mile, & found him on the ground, fallen from his horse, his foot and back too much hurt to proceed. he sate him on his horse, led him back over the difficulties, left him to go on home and returned to us. tho' this misfortune made it impossible that any thing final should be done, yet being so far we determined to examine the grounds as well as we could, & proceeded up the South valley to the top of the mountain, and thence along the top of the mountain Northwardly to your corner on it which we found plainly marked, & 180. yds distant from Col° M's claim. we were then about $\frac{3}{4}$ of a mile as we supposed from the Spanish oak & Dogwood, which would give for the subject of dispute an equilateral triangle of $\frac{3}{4}$ of a mile on a base of 180. yds & consequently of about 24. acres. we then concluded to descend the mountain to the fork of the branch & reascend along the Northern fork, and we proceeded down to the fork. I was then so much exhausted, the heat of the day being excessive (the 21st of June) that I was unable to encounter the precipices, rocks and bushes of another ascent. I was obliged to lie down in the woods and desire my companions to pursue their researches alone, and call at the same place for me on their return. they accordingly proceeded, but at length found the difficulties of the ascent so great that they did not reach the top of the mountain, but descended again to where I was; and we returned re infectâ. however I have got it placed now within my own power. I promised Col° Monroe to take the county surveyor, make him under Price's guidance[1] trace both branches, & your line; and to submit this to the same arbitrators, who being both neighbors, will attend at any time, and on the view of this plat with that they have had of the ground, will decide the question. but this cannot be until the fall of the leaves, these being so thick at present that it would be impossible to take a course of 10. yds with a compass. however as Col° M.'s presence will be no longer requisite, the epoch depends on a natural and fixed limit, at the distance of between 3. & 4 months. on the view[2] of the ground which I have now[3] had, I believe it will be decided in favor of Col° Monroe. the valley to which he claims is evidently the main one which divides his mountain from the Blenheim mountain and leads directly up to the hollow between them, and is that along which mr Carter ought to have conducted us. the other stops considerably short of the top of the mountain, & your line is between the two. still[4] a regular decision is necessary to subject mr Carter to reimbursement to you, and in the mean time I suppose mr Higginbotham must retain about 240.D. of his last payment until decided. however disappointed in this effort, it has so far availed us as to fix an epoch of decision.—I am in the daily hope of seeing M[r] Correa & M. Dupont here. I wish you could think it as good an asylum from the heats of the season, as the shores of Jersey. your presence would aid our speculation on the wonders of Europe, and add much to the happiness of yours affectionately and respectfully.

Th: Jefferson

RC (ViW: TJP); endorsed by Short as received 25 July 1815 at Ballston Spa, N.Y.

probe: French for "upright." re infectâ: "with the matter incomplete" (*OED*). Albemarle county surveyor William Woods did not conduct his survey until 21 Feb. 1816 (enclosure to TJ to Short, 9 Apr. 1816). David higginbotham owed Short a third and final payment of $846.66 on a bond (TJ to Short, 10 Feb. 1813, and enclosure). He had proposed the previous year to make his sec-

ond payment early if Short agreed to a suitable reduction in the interest to be paid (Higginbotham to Short, Milton, 18 July 1814, RC in ViU: Higginbotham Papers; endorsed by Short as received 23 July 1814; docketed by Higginbotham, in part, "$1113⅓ paid").

[1] Preceding three words interlined.
[2] TJ here canceled "however."
[3] Word interlined.
[4] Word interlined in place of "however."

To José Corrêa da Serra

Dear Sir   Monticello June 28. 15
   When I learned that you proposed to give a course of Botanical lectures in Philadelphia, I feared it would retard the promised visit to

Monticello. on my return from Bedford however on the 4th inst. I recieved a letter from M. Dupont flattering me with the prospect
that he and yourself would be with us so soon as my return should
be known. I therefore in the instant wrote him of my return, and
my hope of seeing you both shortly. I am still without that pleasure,
but not without the hope. Europe has been a 2d time turned topsey-
turvey since we were together, and so many strange things have happened there that I have lost my compass. as far as we can judge from
appearances Bonaparte, from being a mere military Usurper, seems
to have become the choice of his nation; and the allies, in their turn,
the usurpers & spoliators of the European world. the right of nations
to self government being my polar star, my partialities are steered by
it, without asking whether it is a Bonaparte or an Alexander towards
whom the helm is directed. believing that England has enough on
her hands without us, and therefore has by this time settled the question of impressment with mr Adams, I look on this new conflict of the
European gladiators, as from the higher forms of the Amphitheatre,
wondering that Man, like the wild beasts of the forest, should permit
himself to be led by his keeper into the Arena, the spectacle and sport
of the lookers on. nor do I see the issue of this tragedy with the sanguine hopes of our friend M. Dupont. I fear, from the experience of
the last 25. years that morals do not, of necessity, advance hand in
hand with the sciences. these however are speculations which may
be adjourned to our meeting at Monticello, where I will continue to
hope that I may recieve you with our[1] friend Dupont, and in the
mean time repeat the assurances of my affectionate friendship and
respect   TH: JEFFERSON

PoC (DLC); at foot of text: "M. Cor-   [1] Tr: "your."
rea." Tr (MHi); posthumous copy.

From Hezekiah Niles

SIR,   Balt. June 30. 1815
    The president['s messa]ge communicating the disclosures of
Henry [was printed in?] no 28, page 19, vol 2, of the Reg. But [I
take?] pleasure to enclose no 29, which is missing [...].
    [With g]reat respect,   H NILES

RC (DLC); mutilated at fold; endorsed
by TJ as received 5 July 1815. Enclosure:
Baltimore *Weekly Register* 2, no. 29 (21
Mar. 1812).   The Baltimore *Weekly Register* 2, no.
28 (14 Mar. 1812), devoted most of its
space to the activities of the alleged
British spy John HENRY. For President

James Madison's 9 Mar. 1812 message to Congress on the subject, which appeared on pp. 19–20, see Madison, *Papers, Pres. Ser.*, 4:235–6.

To James Leitch

July 2. 15.

M[r] Leitch will be pleased to let the two bearers Thrimston & Lovilo fit themselves with woollen hats. TH:J.

RC (MdHi: Vertical Files); dateline beneath signature; written on a small scrap. Not recorded in SJL.

To Stephen Cathalan

MY GOOD AND ANTIENT FRIEND Monticello July 3. 15.

It is so long since I have heard from you that this letter seems almost as if written to the dead: and you have the like grounds for recieving it as from the same region. in truth the eternal wars which our age has witnessed prove it to be literally the <u>iron age</u>, and have suspended all the intercourses of friendship and commerce. scarcely was the temple of Janus closed in our hemisphere by the treaty of Ghent, when it was opened again in your's at all it's doors. such at least we presume to be the case, from the latest informations we have recieved here. your emperor was formerly trying to conquer all nations. all are now trying to conquer him. I was glad he failed: and I hope they also will fail; because I am a friend to the independance of nations. and so the world will remain after 25 years of war, and half as many millions of human beings destroyed, pretty much as it was, with only here & there a change of A. for B. as master. our short war was, in it's beginning, unpropitious, from the want of able & faithful officers. the 2[d] year however began to bring forward those characters which nature had moulded for military purposes, & the tide began with them to turn in our favor; and the 3[d] year saw us every where victorious, and our enemies glad of peace from interest, as we always are from principle, because we believe mankind are happier in peace than in war. during this period of our declared war, and a long preceding one of war de facto, on the part of our enemy, our intercourse with Europe was almost null. now that it is reopened, I resume our old correspondence with a declaration of wants. the fine wines of your region of country are not forgotten, nor the friend thro' whom I used to obtain them. and first the white Hermitage of M. Jourdan of

[570]

Tains, of the quality having 'un peu de la liqueur' as he expressed it, which we call silky, soft, smooth, in contradistinction to the dry, hard or rough. what I had from M. Jourdan of this quality was barely a little sweetish, so as to be sensible and no more; and this is exactly the quality I esteem.   Next comes the red wine of Nice, such as my friend mr Sasserno sent me, which was indeed very fine. that country being now united with France, will render it easier for you I hope to order it to Marseilles.   There is a 3ᵈ kind of wine which I am less able to specify to you with certainty by it's particular name. I used to meet with it at Paris under the general term of Vin rouge de Roussillon; and it was usually drunk after the repast as a vin de liqueur, as were the Pacharetti sec, & Madeire sec: and it was in truth as <u>dry</u> as they were, but a little higher colored. I remember I then thought it would please the American taste, as being dry and tolerably strong. I suppose there may be many kinds of wine of Roussillon; but I never saw any but of that particular quality used at Paris. I am certain it will be greatly esteemed here, being of high flavor, not quite so strong as Pacharetti or Madeire or Xeres, but yet of very good body, sufficient to bear well our climate. there is a name of Rivesalte which runs in my head, and almost identifies itself with the red wine of Rousillon, but without sufficient distinctness or certainty of recollection that it is the same: and should the wine of Rivesalte, from what you know of it, answer the description here given, you may conclude it is that I mean. all this I leave to you. to these I add 50. ℔ of Maccaroni, an article not to be bought in the United states.

Having occasion to place some money in Paris for other purposes, I have added to it 200. Dollars subject there to your orders. Mʳ Girard of Philadelphia is kind enough to give me a credit with his correspondent there. his name I have not learnt, but it will be communicated to you either by mr Girard, or by mr John Vaughan who acts for me in Philadelphia, and negociates this matter with Mʳ Girard; so that on reciept of information from either of them, you may draw on mr Girard's correspondent in Paris. taking from it first the cost of the 50. ℔ of Maccaroni, and reserving enough for all charges till shipped, I would wish about a fifth of the residue to be laid out in Hermitage, and the remaining $\frac{4}{5}$ equally divided between the wines of Nice and Roussillon. I suppose a conveyance may occur direct from your port or it's vicinity; and this would be best; but if not, then the canal of Languedoc & Bordeaux may be adopted. mr Lee, our Consul at the latter place would probably be so kind as to recieve and forward the packages. Richmond is far the most convenient port for me, because on the same river I live on. all ports North of that are equal, and the Collector at any of them will recieve & notify me of their arrival.

I was not inattentive to the wish of my friend mr Sasserno communicated thro' you the summer before I retired from office, respecting the Consulate at Nice. but the decrees of Milan & Berlin & British orders of council having placed us in hot water with both France & England, no appointments could be made to either country. when I went out of office therefore, I left mr Sasserno's appointment in recommendation with the succeeding administration, in case an appointment there should be deemed expedient; and all having been war & interruption since that time, it stands yet I believe on that ground.

Amidst the scenes of war which have environed you, I hope yourself and family have escaped all personal trouble. remember me, if you please respectfully to them, and be assured yourself of my constant friendship & respect   TH: JEFFERSON

PoC (DLC); at foot of first page: "M. Cathalan"; endorsed by TJ; with MS of TJ's Notes on the Cost of French Merchandise, [ca. 3 July 1815], subjoined. Enclosed in TJ to James Monroe, 15 July 1815.

JANUS, the Roman god of doors and gates, is associated with an allegorical gate that opens and closes at the beginning and end of military campaigns. The temple of Janus Geminus in ancient Rome was closed during times of peace (OCD, 793). UN PEU DE LA LIQUEUR: "a little liqueur." VIN DE LIQUEUR is a sweet, fortified wine (Jancis Robinson, ed., *The Oxford Companion of Wine* [1994], 1024). Cathalan informed TJ of the WISH of Victor SASSERNO for an appointment as United States consul at Nice in a letter dated 14 Oct. 1807 (DLC).

Notes on the Cost of French Merchandise

[ca. 3 July 1815]

idea of the produce of 200.D. at old prices, by way of memm.   D

Costs on 200. D worth about $\frac{1}{16}$ or 6. p. cent.   12

50. ℔ Maccaroni @ .20 p^r ℔.   10

42. bottles of wh. hermitage @ $4^{tt}-\frac{1}{2} = 190.^{tt}$

(*excha. $5.^{tt}35 = 1.D$)   36

217. d^o Nice @ $1^{tt}\frac{3}{4}$ (or $.32\frac{1}{2}$) = 380^{tt} 71

284. d^o Roussillon @ .25   71

543. bottles.   200

*it yeilded but $5.^{tt}28 = 1.D,$

MS (DLC: TJ Papers, 204:36341); entirely in TJ's hand; undated; subjoined to PoC of TJ to Stephen Cathalan, 3 July 1815.

From Henry Dearborn

DEAR SIR   Boston July 3ᵈ 1815—
I should not have so long delay'd a reply to your very friendly &
polite letter had circumstancies allowed me to mention the time when
I could probably have the pleasure of seing you at Monticello. I have
Just returned from a visit to my Children in the District of Maine,
and I hope Mrˢ Dearborn & myself shall have the pleasure of seing
you in Septemʳ probably near the end of the month.—
please to accept from Mrˢ D— & myself a tender of the Highest
respect & esteem   H. DEARBORN

RC (NNPM); at foot of text: "Honᵇˡ Thomas Jefferson"; endorsed by TJ as received
15 July 1815 and so recorded in SJL.

To Tadeusz Kosciuszko

MY DEAR GENERAL & FRIEND   Monticello July 3. 15.
I have recently recieved your letter (without date) requesting me to
have the remittance of your annual interest promptly made, adding to
it the principal also, as soon as our peace with England should be
ratified, and 'provided you should not lose much by that.' your distresses from the difficulty and irregularity of remittance, have been
anxiously felt here, and I am confident mr Barnes spared no pains to
make the remittances duly, but so totally were commercial dealings
with the states of Europe suspended by the war that it was very
rarely possible to procure a bill thro' any channel. it was for this reason I endeavored to establish for you a credit with mr Morton of Bordeaux, who might furnish your interest regularly, and recieve his
reimbursement by payments which could be regularly made to a partner or correspondent here. but on the entire interruption of commerce
mr Morton's correspondent here declined giving bills on him. Now
that intercourse with Europe is restored, it is hoped that these irregularities will cease. accordingly on the first revival of intercourse mr
Barnes remitted to messʳˢ Barings of London for your use the draught
of messʳˢ Bowie & Kurtz on William Murdoch of London for 1822
D–22 C which sum he does not doubt messʳˢ Barings have conveyed
to your hands ere this. my preceding letters will have informed you of
the fortunate withdrawal of your 8000.D. from the bank of Pensylva-
nia a little before that, with all the other banks, stopped payment; that
we had reinvested the 8000. in a loan to the US. with a bonus which
raised your capital to 10,000.D. @ 6. per cent, besides a reserve of a

part as interest to be remitted to you; and that the distresses of the treasury having obliged them to allow subsequent lenders to the same loan an additional bonus of 25. per cent, they had in justice extended the same addition to their earlier lenders, in requital of their promptness to aid the government; and this raised your capital again from 10,000. to 12,500.D. @ 6. per cent. my letter of Mar 1. informed you I should deposit the 4500.D. in my hands in the Treasury of the US. in exchange for their notes bearing an interest of $5\frac{2}{3}$ per cent. this was accordingly done. these notes, after remaining at par for some time, are now rising; so also is the stock generally of the US. which has been under par during the war; and could not even now be sold but at a sensible loss. on this consideration and the prospect of their rise to their natural advance above par, I have availed you of the discretionary proviso of your letter, 'pourvu que je ne perd pas beaucoup,' and declined directing a sale of your funds till further orders. their present state is therefore this. instead of your antient[1] capital of 12,500.D. yielding about 8. per cent, & consequently 1000.D. you have now a capital of 17,000 D. yielding $5\frac{2}{3}$ and 6. per cent to the amount of 985.D. annually, as you will see by mr Barnes's accounts now inclosed, with the prospect that on the revival of other monied institutions of higher profits, your enlarged capital, may be invested in them, and produce an enlarged interest of 7. or 8. per cent as before. I have been more confirmed in my doubts as to the remittance of your capital by the clouds which at present overspread the horison of Europe, and threaten it with a general war. I thought it better, on this change of prospect from that under which you wrote, to give you time to consider whether you could place your funds in a situation as safe, and as profitable as their present one. and in the moment you shall communicate to me a confirmation of your wish to change their deposit to Europe, they shall instantly be sold to the best advantage the market may offer, and remitted either to London or Amsterdam, on which places, in time of peace bills are always to be had. perhaps also they may be had on Bordeaux.

It is a matter of great comfort to us that our late war with England was waged single handed. that nation just issuing triumphantly from a general war, freed from all fears of an enemy nearer home, full armed & equipped, suddenly bore down on us, just buckling on our armour, and deserted by the world, with all this mighty force, devoting us to entire destruction. they figured to themselves that they were to take for their own use the province of Maine, to give to their Indian allies the states & territories North of the Ohio, to enable the Yankee states to separate and become their allies, and reduce the poor

residuum to be powerless enemies if not humble subjects. this enemy, the first year, gained some advantages, by bribing the treacherous, & beating the ignorant of our officers. the brave however and the able among these soon becoming prominent, he was defeated at every point on the land and water, leaving it doubtful on which he was most disgraced, and, by a timely peace was glad to save his possessions on our continent, which two campaigns more, if not one, would have certainly made ours.   In the <u>Revolutionary</u> war, we had on our side France, Spain and Holland, and all our successes were ascribed to them. we have now had the battle to ourselves. England has seen that we can do her more injury than any enemy on earth; because no other can get at her; and I trust she will abate in her insults and injuries to us. and the other nations of Europe will, I hope, percieve that we are pacific from principle, but warlike on provocation. we have added about 60. millions to our debt, but shall raise 40. millions by our taxes of this year, without a murmur, so thoroughly had our people begun to devote all their means to the war. Col° Monroe's plan for the army and militia, which would have given full command of every man able to bear arms, was lost by a small majority in one house of Congress, but would have been passed by a great one at their next meeting, every one seeing that that alone would place us above the injuries of the world. I hope, amidst the metamorphoses projected in Europe that something will be done for your country, and that you will live in health and vigor to see it replaced on the map of Europe, and to aid in giving it good laws and a practicable government. this is the sincere prayer of
ever & affectionately yours   TH: JEFFERSON

RC (Uk: Additional Manuscript 39672). PoC (MHi); at foot of first page: "General Kosciusko"; endorsed by TJ. Enclosures: enclosures 1, 2, and 3 to Barnes to TJ, 25 May 1815. Enclosed in TJ to James Monroe, 15 July 1815.

Kosciuszko's LETTER (WITHOUT DATE) is printed above at 14 Mar. 1815.

Secretary of War James MONROE's plan to increase the size of the United States Army and of state militias was contained in a report of 17 Oct. 1814. The Senate approved two bills in response to Monroe's suggestions, but the only one to become law was "An Act making further provision for filling the ranks of the army of the United States," 10 Dec. 1814. The House of Representatives rejected the Senate's militia bill, which called for 80,430 troops from the states and territories. The compromise bill approved 27 Jan. 1815, "An Act to authorize the President of the United States to accept the services of state troops and of volunteers," sanctioned the use of no more than 40,000 militiamen, exclusive of officers (ASP, Military Affairs, 1:514–7; Annals, 13th Cong., 3d sess., 109, 992 [22 Nov., 27 Dec. 1814]; U.S. Statutes at Large, 3:146–7, 193–5; Stagg, Madison's War, 457–68).

YOUR COUNTRY: Poland.

¹ Word interlined.

To Madame de Staël Holstein

DEAR MADAM. Monticello in Virginia. July 3. 15.

I considered your letter of Nov. 10. 12. as an evidence of the interest you were so kind as to take[1] in the welfare of the United states, and I was even flattered by your exhortations to avoid taking any part in the war then raging in Europe, because they were a confirmation of the policy I had my self pursued, and which I thought and still think should be the governing canon of our republic. distance, and difference of pursuits, of interests, of connections and other circumstances prescribe to us a different system, having no object in common with Europe but a peaceable interchange of mutual comforts for mutual wants. but this may not always depend on ourselves; and injuries may be so accumulated by an European power as to pass all bounds of wise forbearance. this was our situation at the date of your letter. a long course of injuries, systematically pursued by England, and finally, formal declarations that she would neither redress nor discontinue their infliction, had fixed the epoch which rendered an appeal to arms unavoidable. in the letter of May 28. 13. which I had the honor of writing you, I entered into such details of these injuries, and of our unremitting endeavors to bring them to a peaceable end, as the narrow limits of a letter permitted. resistance on our part at length brought our enemy to reflect, to calculate, and to meet us in peaceable conferences at Ghent; but the extravagance of the pretensions brought forward by her negotiators there, when first made known in the US. dissipated at once every hope of a just peace, and prepared us for a war of utter extremity. our government, in that state of things, respecting the opinion of the world, thought it a duty to present to it a justification of the course which was likely to be forced upon us; and with this view the pamphlet was prepared which I now inclose. it was already printed, when (instead of their ministers whom they hourly expected from a fruitless negociation) they recieved the treaty of pacification signed at Ghent, and ratified at London. they endeavored to suppress the pamphlet, as now unseasonable. but the proof sheets having been surreptitiously withdrawn, soon made their appearance in the public papers, and in the form now sent. this vindication is so exact in it's facts, so cogent in it's reasonings, so authenticated by the documents to which it appeals, that it cannot fail to bring the world to a single opinion on our case. the concern you manifested on our entrance into this contest assures me you will take the trouble of reading it; which I wish the more earnestly, because it will fully supply the very imperfect views which my letter had presented; and because we cannot be indifferent as to the opinion which yourself personally shall ultimately form of the course we have pursued.

I learned with great pleasure your return to your native country. it is the only one which offers elements of society analogous to the powers of your mind, and sensible of the flattering distinction of possessing them. it is true that the great events which made an opening for your return, have been reversed. but not so, I hope, the circumstances which may admit it's continuance. on these events I shall say nothing. at our distance, we hear too little truth and too much falsehood to form correct judgments concerning them; and they are moreover foreign to our umpirage. we wish the happiness and prosperity of every nation; we did not believe either of these promoted by the former pursuits of the present ruler of France; and hope that his return, if the nation wills it to be permanent, may be marked by those changes which the solid good of his own country, and the peace and well-being of the world may call for. but these things I leave to whom they belong; the object of this letter being only to convey to you a vindication of my own country, and to have the honor of a new occasion of tendering you the homage of my great consideration, and respectful attachment.

Th: Jefferson

PoC (DLC); at foot of first page: "Madane [Madame] la Baronne de Staël-Holstein." Tr (MHi); posthumous copy. Enclosed in TJ to Henry Jackson, 5 July 1815, and TJ to James Monroe, 15 July 1815.

The enclosed PAMPHLET was Dallas, *Exposition.* The PUBLIC PAPERS included the Philadelphia *Aurora General Advertiser*, which printed the pamphlet between 17 and 23 Mar. 1815. YOUR NATIVE COUNTRY: France.

[1] Preceding three words not in Tr.

From William Rush

SIR,   Philadelphia, July 4th, 1815.

I take the freedom to address you on the subject of the immortal Washington; a figure of whom, after much labour and study, I have executed, which gives general satisfaction, more particularly so to those who were intimately acquainted with him; and I am authorized to say, that Judge Washington has given his highest approbation of the work, especially as to the fidelity of the likeness. It is my intention, if liberally encouraged, to furnish Plaister Casts from the original Statue; a description of which, with the terms, are hereto annexed, in the form of a subscription paper.

Should this effort to perpetuate the form of an individual so deservedly beloved, meet your approbation, permit me to solicit your interposition in recommending it to public notice and patronage. In doing so, you will much oblige, Sir,

Your very humble servant,   WM. RUSH.

Printed circular (DLC); at head of text: "CIRCULAR"; addressed in an unidentified hand: "Thomas Jefferson Esqʳ Virginia"; franked; postmarked Philadelphia, 2 Aug.; endorsed by TJ as a "Circular" received 9 Aug. 1815 and so recorded in SJL; on a single sheet folded to form four pages, with letter on p. 1, enclosure on p. 3, and address on p. 4. Enclosure: Rush's Description of his Statue of George Washington and Proposal to Sell Casts of It, undated broadside indicating that the statue depicts Washington "in the act of addressing. The head is uncovered, looking easily to the left. The whole length of the figure is six feet one inch. The upper part of the body is inclining to the right, resting with his right arm on part of the shaft of a column, and a scroll in his right hand. The left arm resting on his hip, which is thrown out considerably, for the support of the figure, which rests upon the left leg. The right foot is advanced. The Costume is mod-ern, and of the civil character, excepting the exterior, which is something of a flowing Grecian Mantle, giving fulness and grace to the outline: it covers his left shoulder and arm. Part of it is taken up by the left hand, the remainder falls on the lower part of the body, left thigh, and leg; it also covers the back of the figure, and part of the pedestal"; offering casts in plaster of paris at a cost of $200, "delivered at Philadelphia"; and stating that production will commence as soon as twenty casts are ordered.

Rush's ORIGINAL STATUE of George Washington, carved in pine, is at Independence National Historical Park, Philadelphia. Rush received only two orders for the full-size casts and instead executed smaller terracotta busts that he exhibited in 1817 (Pennsylvania Academy of the Fine Arts, *William Rush, American Sculptor* [1982], 145–7, 152–4).

To George Ticknor

DEAR SIR   Monticello July 4. 1815.

Availing myself of the kind offer of your aid in replacing some of the literary treasures which I furnished to Congress, I have made out a catalogue which I now inclose. it is confined principally to those books of which the edition adds sensibly to the value of the matter. this, as to translations, notes Eᵗc other accompaniments, chiefly respects the classics: but size and type respect all. I am attached to the 8ᵛᵒ because not too heavy for the hand, and yet large enough to lie open on the table according to convenience. of the Latin classics, their notes add value to particular editions; of the Greek, their notes and especially those of the Scholiasts, their translations & types are circumstances of preference. in some instances I have selected the edition from it's description in the printed catalogues without having

seen it; and as the catalogues cannot exhibit the type, I may sometimes be disappointed in the choice I have hazarded, in the Greek
classics particularly by the obsolete type of that which I have selected,
in the Latin by the Italian letter which is disagreeable to the eye.
sometimes there may be other editions equivalent[1] to the one I name,
in size, translation & notes, and superior in type. in these cases be so
good as to avail me of your better opportunity of comparing for a selection of the best. I like good bindings and handsome, without being
over elegant for use. I should have greatly scrupled to abuse your
kindness by this scrupulous attention to editions were it not for the
circumstance mentioned in my letter of Mar. 3. that having once selected a good bookseller in Paris, he will save you all further trouble
in seeking out any particular edition to be had in Paris, or procuring
them from any part of Europe where they are to be had; giving you
no other trouble than that of recieving & paying. the booksellers of
capital there have their correspondents in every considerable book-
town in Europe, and understand the conveyances by which they may
be forwarded. estimating these books by the prices stated in the catalogues and particularly in Koenig's, a copy of which I inclosed you
and adding about 25. or 30.[2] p.c. as the supposed advance of price
since that date, & for other incidentals, I have deposited with mr Girard of Philadelphia the sum of 350.D. to be answered by his correspondent in Paris, with a request however to answer the amount of
the catalogue, should my reckoning be short, on the assurance of replacing the balance in Philadelphia the moment it is known to me.
the particular details of this part of the business I leave to be communicated by mr Girard to his correspondent, and by my friend John
Vaughan of Philadelphia to yourself, as they shall be arranged between him & mr Girard. and as your first destination was changed
from Paris to London and I am uninformed of the stay you may make
in London, I send a copy of this thro' your father to London, and a
duplicate to Dr Jackson our chargé des affaires at Paris, to be delivered to you if there, or kept until you arrive there. I shall desire mr
Vaughan also to write to you by duplicate for each place, it being important that the books should be shipped so as to arrive before winter on account of the unavoidable damage of a winter passage. indeed
as some of the books will probably be called for by your bookseller
from distant places, which will take time, it would be best to ship
immediately what can be immediately procured, and to reserve the
residue for a second envoi in the Spring. a trunk is the securest package. Richmond is my most convenient port, and Mess[rs] Gibson and

Jefferson my correspondents there. all North of that are equal, and if addressed to the Collector of the port he will give me notice of their arrival. so much for this mass of trouble which your goodness has permitted me to impose on you. I had divided my catalogue between Paris & London, meaning to call for from London those of which the best editions had been printed in England. but a late reciept of a London catalogue, with the present prices, shewed that they had risen there beyond every thing imagined. I have made a little extract from this catalogue (Longman's) which I will subjoin as a specimen, of which perhaps you may profit for yourself, by reserving yourself for the cheaper market of the Continent. I send to my friend mr Maury of Liverpool for English books only.

What is the present state of things in Europe, at this time and what it may be when you recieve this, is unknown to us. their horison seems overspread with clouds, and whether the storm may pass away, or burst on their heads seems uncertain. if the latter, they have long scenes of misery to go through, and not without risk of involving us, and certainty of embarrassing our communications with them. but I hope for peace. I trust that the allied powers will be sensible that they have neither the right nor the power to impose on France a ruler which she rejects, or to displace one who, from being originally an Usurper, seems now to have become a legitimate despot, by the will of the great body of the nation. they have rejected their king Log, and preferred a kite. they have a right to be eaten, if they chuse it. altho' war seems to be one of the obstacles which nature has provided against the too great multiplication of the human species, and therefore can never be expected to be entirely done away, yet there is still room enough in the world for many more than are yet living, and we may therefore, without irreligion, pray for peace, which, while it lengthens the lives of many, gives comfort & prosperity to the general mass.   Whatever we have of great news you will learn thro' our papers, which I presume you recieve, and for small news, that of your own state being alone interesting to you, will be communicated by your friends there. I have only therefore to repeat a thousand apologies for the trouble I propose to you, and add the assurance of my thankfulness, and of my great esteem and respect for you

TH: JEFFERSON

P.S. there is an edition of the Encyclopedie de D'Alembert et Diderot à Lausanne et a Berne, chez les societés Typographiques. 1781. 39. v. 8vo which I bought in Paris for 260. livres. I should be glad to know it's present price, as if still cheap it might make an article in the next year's demand.

RC (MdHi: David Bailie Warden Papers); at foot of first page: "Mr Ticknor"; with MS of enclosure subjoined. PoC (DLC); endorsed by TJ; with PoC of enclosure subjoined. Other enclosure not found. Enclosed in TJ to Henry Jackson and TJ to Elisha Ticknor, both 5 July 1815, and TJ to James Monroe, 15 July 1815.

SCHOLIASTS: those who provide explanatory notes on an author; especially ancient commentators discussing classical writers (*OED*). For TJ's LETTER OF MAR. 3., see note to TJ to Ticknor, 19 Mar. 1815. ENVOI: "parcel; package." The recently received LONDON CATALOGUE was *A General Catalogue of Valuable and Rare Old Books, in the Ancient and Modern Languages, and Various Classes of Literature; which are now on sale at the prices* affixed to each, by Longman, Hurst, Rees, Orme, & Brown, Paternoster-Row, London, 4 parts (London, 1814).

Louis XVIII was the RULER rejected by France, and Napoleon had evidently now BECOME A LEGITIMATE DESPOT. In Aesop's fable of "The Frogs Desiring a King," the frogs asked Zeus to place a monarch over them. He threw them a piece of wood, KING LOG. When they asked for a more energetic ruler, he sent a stork, which promptly gobbled them up. ENCYCLOPEDIE: for TJ's purchase of an edition of Denis Diderot and Jean Le Rond d'Alembert, *Encyclopédie, ou Dictionnaire Raisonné des Sciences, des Arts et des Métiers* (Paris, 1751–72), see *PTJ*, 4:211, 5:15, 311–2; Sowerby, no. 4890.

¹ TJ here canceled "or superior."
² Reworked from "20. or 25."

ENCLOSURE

Notes on London Book Prices

[ca. 4 July 1815]

London prices of books, as a specimen of the present state of that market.

Polybius Gr. Lat. 3. v. 8vo £4–4 or 28/ a vol.   I pd 6^{tt}–10 sous a vol. for the same in Paris

Dion. Hal. Reiskii. 6. v. 8vo Gr. Lat. £5–10. or 18/ a vol.   I pd 13.^{tt} a vol. for the same in Paris.

Catesby's Nat. Hist. £26.   I pd 500^{tt}

Aristophanes Brunckii 46/   I pd 36^{tt}–12 s

Suidas 3. v. fol. £21. or £7. a vol.

Clarendon 6. v. 8vo £5–5. or 17/6 a vol.

Dugdale's Monasticon. 3. v. fol. £42. or £14. a vol.

Dugdale's Baronage 2. v. fol. £21. or 10. guineas a vol.

Hakluyt 3. v. fol. £31–10 or 10. guineas a vol.

Hollingshead. 2. v. fol. £25. or £12–10 a vol.

Hall's Chronicle a single vol. fol. £10–10.

Horsley's Britannia. single vol fol. 15. guineas.

Hume's hist. 9. v. fol. £63. or £7. a vol.

Johnson's dict. 2. v. fol. 8. guineas or 4.G. a vol.

Milton's Poetical works. 3. v. fol. 18. guineas or 6.G. a vol.

Purchas's pilgrimage. 5. v. fol. £48. or £9–12. a vol.

Rapin with Tindal's continuation 7. v. fol. £150. or £21–8–7 a vol.

MS (MdHi: David Bailie Warden Papers); entirely in TJ's hand; undated; subjoined to RC of covering letter. PoC (DLC: TJ Papers, 204:36343); subjoined to PoC of covering letter.

For the source of the LONDON PRICES quoted by TJ, see covering letter. TJ's list included *Dionysii Halicarnassensis Opera Omnia Graece et Latine*, with annotations by Johann Jacob Reiske (REISKII) and others (Leipzig, 1774; TJ's copy at MoSW); Edward Hyde, 1st Earl of CLARENDON, *The History of the Rebellion and Civil Wars in England, Begun in the Year 1641* (Oxford, 1732); Raphael Holinshed (HOLLINGSHEAD), William Harrison, and others, *The First and Second volumes of Chronicles, comprising 1 The description and historie of England, 2 . . . of Ireland, 3 . . . of Scotland* ([London], 1587); and Edward HALL and Richard Grafton, *The Union of the two noble and illustre famelies of Lancastre & Yorke* (London, 1548).

From Patrick Gibson

SIR   Richmond 5th July 1815.

Since my last I have received your favors of the 6th June & 1st July, and shall pay due attention to any drafts you may make—I have remitted Mr Benj: Jones $142.76 & Mr John Vaughan $550 in a dft at 30 $^d/_s$, not having been able to procure one at sight—the amot of Mr Harvie's note is received and at your credit—Since the sale of the 257 bls: flour, I[1] have received only 146 bls: from Shadwell and 13 from Bedford all of which are sold except 2 bls Srf: & 18 fine, that from Bedford was passed there as Srf: but would if reinspected, have been condemn'd here—the bale of Cotton shall be sent up when Johnson comes down Your note for $1000 has not yet been offer'd but so confident am I that it will be done, that you may calculate upon it—

With great respect I am Your obt Servt   PATRICK GIBSON

RC (ViU: TJP-ER); between dateline and salutation: "Thomas Jefferson Esqre"; endorsed by TJ as received 19 July 1815 and so recorded in SJL.

TJ's letter to Gibson of the 1ST JULY is recorded in SJL but has not been found. ^{D}/s: "day's sight." Srf: "superfine."

[1] Reworked from "we."

To Henry Jackson

SIR   Monticello July 5. 15.

Mr Ticknor, a young gentleman of Massachusets, left this country for Europe in March or April last, destined first for London, and, after some stay there, for Paris. having occasion to write him a letter on a subject very interesting to myself, and uncertain at which place it would find him, I have thought it safest to do it by duplicates for both places. that for Paris I have taken the liberty of putting under cover to yourself, with a request to deliver it to him, if at Paris, or to retain it till he arrives there. the urgency of the case and the want of other resource will, I hope, plead my excuse for giving you this trouble; and, with my thankfulness, I pray you to accept the assurance of my great esteem & respect.   TH: JEFFERSON

P.S. I find myself obliged to trespass further on your goodness by inclosing a letter for Madame de Stael also. I do not know whether since the late revolution she remains in Paris.[1] if not I hope you can avail me of some safe conveyance for it, other than through the post office.

PoC (DLC); on verso of reused address cover of Charles Jouett to TJ, 12 June 1815; beneath signature: "Doct^r Henry Jackson"; endorsed by TJ. Enclosures: (1) TJ to Madame de Staël Holstein, 3 July 1815. (2) TJ to George Ticknor, 4 July 1815. Enclosed in TJ to James Monroe, 15 July 1815.

Henry Jackson (1778–1840), educator, emigrated late in the eighteenth century from his native England to Savannah, Georgia. He received a medical degree in 1802 from the University of Pennsylvania. In 1811 Jackson joined the faculty of Franklin College (later the University of Georgia) in Athens, serving as professor of natural philosophy and chemistry, 1811–20 and 1822–23, and professor of natural philosophy and botany, 1823–25 and 1826–27. The gaps in his appointment occurred when he refused to take on certain disciplinary roles required of the faculty. Jackson took a leave in 1813 from his teaching duties to serve as secretary of the American legation under William H. Crawford, the newly appointed United States minister plenipotentiary to France.

When Crawford returned to the United States in 1815, Jackson stayed on as chargé d'affaires until the following year. Jackson resumed teaching at Franklin College in 1819. Crawford recommended him in 1825 for a faculty appointment at the University of Virginia, but no positions were then vacant (Lucian Lamar Knight, *Georgia's Landmarks, Memorials and Legends* [1913–14], 2:368–9; Jackson, *An Inaugural Dissertation on the Efficacy of Certain External Applications* [Philadelphia, 1802]; *Catalogue of the Trustees, Officers, Alumni and Matriculates of the University of Georgia, at Athens, Georgia, from 1785 to 1906* [1906], 5, 10; Trustees' Minutes, University of Georgia [GU]; Chase C. Mooney, *William H. Crawford, 1772–1834* [1974], 52–3; *JEP*, 2:346, 3:39 [27, 28 May 1813, 1, 3 Apr. 1816]; Washington *Daily National Intelligencer*, 4 Jan. 1819; Crawford to TJ, 4 Feb. 1825; TJ to Crawford, 15 Feb. 1825; *Macon Georgia Telegraph*, 5 May 1840).

[1] Word interlined in place of "France."

To Elisha Ticknor

SIR   Monticello July 5. 15.

I had the pleasure of possessing here for a short time your son Mr George Ticknor, a little before his departure for Europe; and expressing my intention of importing some books, he was so kind as to offer his service in looking out for the best editions. his perfect knolege of the subject rendered the offer too advantageous to me not to be accepted thankfully. on his return to Boston he informed me he had changed his purpose of going direct to Paris, and should first go to London; and that there might be no danger of my letter's miscarrying from this circumstance, he recommended to me to put it under cover to yourself, who, he observed, would know his address in London, and would be so good as to forward it to him at that place. on this encouragement from him, I have taken the liberty of inclosing a letter to your address, with the request to forward it to him at London, having sent a duplicate thro' the Secretary of State to be delivered to him in Paris. for presuming to propose this trouble to you, I hope you will find my excuse in the friendship of your son: and I cannot pass over the occasion of congratulating you on the possession of such a son. his talents, his science, and excellent dispositions must be the comfort of his parents, as they are the hope of his friends & country; and to those especially who are retiring from the world & it's business the virtues and talents of those who are coming after them, are a subject of peculiar gratification. Be pleased to accept the assurance of my great respect and consideration.   TH: JEFFERSON

PoC (DLC); at foot of text: "Mʳ Elisha Ticknor Boston"; on verso of reused address cover of William Short to TJ, 9 May 1815 (see note to TJ to Short, 15 May 1815); endorsed by TJ. Enclosure: TJ to George Ticknor, 4 July 1815.

Elisha Ticknor (1757–1821), educator, merchant, and community leader, was born in Lebanon, Connecticut. In 1774 he moved with his parents to New Hampshire. In 1783 Ticknor graduated from Dartmouth College, after which he taught briefly nearby before opening a school in Boston in 1785. He was the principal of a grammar school in that city, 1788–94. Ticknor published a popular textbook, *English Exercises* (Boston, 1792). He became a grocer by 1795, prospered, and retired in 1813. Thereafter Ticknor served as a Boston selectman and justice of the peace, helped found a local savings bank, and strongly supported the creation of free primary schools. After their establishment in 1818, he was active on the Boston Primary School Committee. Although they never met, Ticknor exchanged more than a dozen letters with TJ during the years following his son's stay at Monticello in 1815. He died during a visit to Hanover, New Hampshire (*DAB*; *General Catalogue of Dartmouth College and the Associated Schools, 1769–1925* [1925], 89; Joseph M. Wightman, *Annals of the Boston Primary School Committee* [1860], esp. 18, 63–4; Boston *Columbian Centinel*, 25 July 1795; Boston *Gazette*, 15 July 1813; Boston *Repertory*, 14 Mar. 1815; *Boston Daily Advertiser*, 23 Nov. 1816, 24 Apr. 1818, 25 June 1821; *The Massachusetts Register . . . 1820* [Boston, 1819], 41).

From John Wayles Eppes

DEAR SIR   Mill Brook July 6. 1815.

your letter from Poplar Forrest arrived here while I was absent on a trip to Eppington and Richmond. Any arrangement which you consider calculated to benefit Francis in the course of his education cannot fail to meet my approbation. I have only one fear that Francis amidst the amusements of Monticello will not have resolution enough to pursue steadily the course marked out for him—I had intended removing him from Lynchburg after the vacation so that you have only anticipated my own views by a few weeks—

I shall send for him on the first of August the period at which I should have seen him if he had remained at Lynchburg—He may however return to Monticello after his visit and remain until he has perfected himself in the pronunciation of the French—I have myself experienced the inconvenience of a vicious pronunciation for although I read the language with perfect ease I have always been deterred from making any attempt to speak it—

I finish today my wheat harvest—The quality of the grain in all the country around is excellent, and our prospects for corn superior to any thing I have before witnessed at this season of the year—

Present me to all the family and accept yourself my best wishes.

yours sincerely   JNO: W: EPPES

RC (ViU: TJP-ER); endorsed by TJ as received 10 July 1815 and so recorded in SJL. RC (MHi); address cover only; with PoC of TJ to Mitchie B. Pryor Jefferson, 2 Aug. 1815, on verso; addressed: "Thomas Jefferson Esqʳ Monti-cello near Milton"; stamped; postmarked Raines Tavern, 7 July.

A missing letter from Eppes to TJ of 17 July 1815 is recorded in SJL as received the following day from Mill Brook.

From James T. Austin

SIR,   Boston July 8. 1815

One of the most gratifying circumstances attending the enclosed oration is the renewed opportunity which it allows me of presenting my most profound respects to the author of the declaration of American Independence[1]—   JAMES T AUSTIN

RC (DLC); dateline beneath signature; at foot of text: "Thomas Jefferson Esqʳ"; endorsed by TJ as received 19 July 1815 and so recorded in SJL. Enclosure: Austin, *An Oration, Pronounced at Lexington, Mass. in commemoration of the Independence of the United States of America, and the Restoration of Peace. 4th July,*

1815 (Boston, 1815; Poor, *Jefferson's Library*, 13 [no. 818]; TJ's copy at ViU), praising the patriotic efforts of the statesmen, soldiers, and ordinary citizens who helped obtain American independence; extolling the "patriotism in arms" and the "ardent and generous enthusiasm among the people" during the late war with Great Britain (p. 6); lauding President James Madison for attempting to avoid war, leading the nation to victory once war was deemed unavoidable, and signing the recent peace treaty; blaming the war on "those, who in all preliminary discussions took side with the enemy" (p. 9); calling the Hartford Convention "the most ludicrous and lamentable monument of impotent menace, and party delusion" (p. 13); condemning Great Britain, whose "true character" has been revealed as "vain-glorious, haughty, mean, profligate, unjust; uniting the barbarities of savage life to the more refined cruelties of civilized life" (p. 17); describing Napoleon as "that wonderful Corsican,

who was welcomed by the affections of his people from the rocks of Elba" (p. 19); and concluding that the United States "rises with renovated fame. Its destiny is great" (p. 21).

TJ had his copy of the enclosed speech bound with a group of miscellaneous orations that also included Christopher R. Greene, *An Oration, delivered in St. Michael's Church, Charleston, South-Carolina; on Tuesday, the Fourth of July, 1815; in commemoration of American Independence; by appointment of the South-Carolina State Society of Cincinnati, And published at the Request of that Society; and also of the American Revolution Society* (Charleston, 1815; Poor, *Jefferson's Library*, 13 [no. 818]; TJ's copy at ViU), which is inscribed to the "Hon. Tho. Jefferson From the Author." The date of its receipt and mode of transmission to TJ are unknown.

[1] Manuscript: "Indepence."

From John Vaughan

D SIR   Philad. July 8. 1815

M[r] Patrick Gibson has remitted me on Your acco. a Dft on a good house here for 692$\frac{76}{100}$ at 30 Days (which is acce[d]) out of which I am to pay M Benj. Jones 142[76] & to reserve for your orders 550 which will of Course be complied with—Expecting the pleasure of hearing from you Soon

I remain Your friend & Ser[vt]   J[N] VAUGHAN

RC (MHi); at head of text: "Thomas Jefferson Esq Monticello"; endorsed by TJ as received 15 July 1815 and so recorded in SJL.

To Stephen Girard

SIR   Monticello July[1] 10. 1815.

Having occasion for a remittance to Paris for some books I propose to import from thence, I requested mr Vaughan to inform me through what channel it could be obtained. he wrote me in answer that you would be so kind as to give me a credit with your correspondent there to the necessary amount. the cost of the books I write for, according to Catalogue prices of 20. years ago, would be about 275.D. and I expect that 350.D. would cover the increase of price since that time. this sum therefore I wish to have placed at the order of mr George Ticknor of Boston who proposing to pass some time in that city (Paris)[2] is so kind as to select and forward the books to me. should the augmentation of price be greater than I have allowed for, it can surely be but little, and if answered by your correspondent, the surplus shall be reimbursed to you the moment it is made known to me.   I have also occasion to ask for some wines from my antient friend Stephen Cathalan of Marseilles, and to place at his disposal a further sum of 200.D. if you can conveniently add this to the credit on your correspondent in Paris, it will add to the obligation; and presuming on it, I have desired mr Vaughan to place in your hands the sum of 550.D. which I have directed to be remitted to him from Richmond.

Having long borne high respect for your character as a man and citizen, I embrace with pleasure this first occasion offered of rendering it's just tribute, and, with my thanks for your present kindness, which, from the difficulty of finding a medium of small remittances to Paris, is a real accomodation, I add the assurance of my great esteem & respect.   TH: JEFFERSON

RC (PPGi: Girard Papers [microfilm at PPAmP]); addressed: "Stephen Girard esq. Philadelphia"; franked; postmarked Charlottesville, 19 July; endorsed in a clerk's hand as received 23 July and answered 30 July. PoC (MHi); on verso of reused address cover of Charles Willson Peale to TJ, 2 May 1815; endorsed by TJ.

Stephen Girard (1750–1831), merchant and financier, was born in Bordeaux, France. He joined the crew of a merchant ship owned by his father in 1764 and received a captain's license from the French government in 1773. After living in New York City, 1774–76, he settled permanently in Philadelphia. Girard profited greatly from his involvement in foreign trade, gradually extending his business ventures from the West Indies to Europe and Asia and investing the profits in banks and real estate. After the charter of the first Bank of the United States expired in 1811, he bought the building and all other remaining assets, using them the following year to establish Stephen Girard's Bank, a private, unincorporated enterprise. During the War of 1812 Girard and other businessmen from Philadelphia and New York City united to sell government bonds to investors in order to support the war effort. When the second Bank of the United States was created in 1816, he was one of its five commissioners and a major investor, although he soon withdrew from involvement in the institution. A noted philanthropist throughout his life, Girard left an estate valued in excess of $7 million, the bulk of which he willed in trust to the city of Philadelphia for the education of poor, white, orphaned boys. The resulting institution became Girard College (*ANB*; *DAB*; George Wilson, *Stephen Girard: America's First Tycoon* [1995]; Donald R. Adams Jr., *Finance and Enterprise in Early America: A Study of Stephen Girard's Bank, 1812–1831* [1978]; Harry Emerson Wildes, *Lonely Midas: The Story of*

Stephen Girard [1943]; Girard to TJ, 31 May 1806 [DLC]; Philadelphia *National Gazette and Literary Register*, 29 Dec. 1831; Washington *Daily National Intelligencer*, 29, 30 Dec. 1831).

[1] Reworked from "June."
[2] Word interlined.

From James Monroe

DEAR SIR   washington July 10. 1815.

The intelligence which you communicated to me the evening before I left home, of a vote having been given in the H. of C. against L[d] C. has not been confirmed, and I fear will not be. Little, has been receiv'd of late from Europe, but all accounts concur[1] in the probability of a war, which Engl[d] prompts & leads, that will become general. Nothing can be more unprincipled than such a war, since it strikes at the very foundation of right in every community, not solely as between the sovereign and His people, but assumes a right to a number of sovereigns to interfere in the interior concerns of another country, & to dictate a gov[t] & a King to it. I am strongly under the impression, that the treaty of Vienna, partakes of the quality of that of Pilnitz, and if the parties are successful, against France, that their attention will be directed against this country afterwards, the parent of revolutions, and the imputed source of the misfortunes of the Bourbons. By the vast force said to be collected and collecting, it seems, as if the coalesced powers, intended to risk every thing in a great effort, to accomplish their objects. From our ministers we hear nothing, which may [be][2] owing to their having saild, on their return home, tho' of that, we are uninformd. under these circumstances there seems to be little motive for remaining. The President will not stay long, & I shall soon follow him.

The enclosed is a survey made for me by m[r] Lewis, of the land lying below the old road, comprizing a purchase which I made, of Ch: Carter, after that of John, which bounds on m[r] Shorts, in the point in which we disagree. If m[r] Lewis ever surveyd the tract first purchased, it was at the instance of the m[r] Carters, or some other person after I left the country to whom they sold land, after the Sale to me. By comparing these courses, with those in your possession, you will ascertain whether they are the same, or whether the latter form a survey of my tract first purchasd. If they do, I shall be glad to have a copy of them When I have the pleasure to see you.

It was at Culpeper[3] court house, that I heard for the first time that

M[r] Galloway had arriv'd with you the day I left, Albemarle, or the day before. I regret that I had not the pleasure of seeing him; but as I shall soon get home I hope Still to have that satisfaction.

with respectful & affec[te] regard[4]   JA[s] MONROE

RC (DLC); mistakenly endorsed by TJ as a letter of 8 July received 15 July 1815 and so recorded in SJL. Enclosure: Robert Lewis's 1794 survey of Monroe's 442-acre tract, not found (see *PTJ*, 28:55).

The VOTE in Great Britain's House of Commons AGAINST Lord Castlereagh was actually a division in his favor (TJ to Monroe, 15 July 1815). Far from HAVING SAILD or given up their negotiations, on 3 July 1815 the American envoys John Quincy Adams, Henry Clay, and Albert Gallatin wrote from London enclosing a commercial convention they had negotiated with Great Britain (Clay, *Papers*, 2:54–9). Monroe LEFT THE COUNTRY in 1794 to serve as the United States minister plenipotentiary to France (*ANB*).

[1] Manuscript: "concer."
[2] Omitted word editorially supplied.
[3] Manuscript: "Culpepeper."
[4] Manuscript: "rgard."

To John Vaughan

DEAR SIR   Monticello July 11. 15.

Absences and other avocations have prevented me till now from preparing the catalogue of my wants from France, and the letters they call for. I have now got thro' them, and have desired Mess[rs] Gibson & Jefferson my correspondents at Richmond to remit you the sum of 550.D. to be placed in the hands of mr Girard, as I propose to avail myself of his kind accomodation of a corresponding credit at Paris. 350.D. of this I have to request him to make payable to the order of mr George Ticknor, who will call for it in Paris, and 200.D. to the order of Stephen Cathalan, merchant and Consul for the US. at Marseilles. the former sum is to enable mr Ticknor to procure the books of which I have Sent him a Catalogue; that to mr Cathalan for some wines I have asked of him, from the South of France and I have informed both you will be so good as to drop them a line covering mr Girard's orders on his correspondent. that to Ticknor will require to be by duplicate, the one[1] under cover to mr Adams our minister at Paris, and the other[2] to Dr Henry Jackson, our Chargé des affaires at Paris; it being uncertain at which place a letter will find him. I have addressed him in like manner by duplicates sent to London & Paris, the former through his father, the latter the Secretary of State. with my apologies for this trouble, accept the assurance of my great esteem and respect   TH: JEFFERSON

[589]

RC (PPAmP: Vaughan Papers); at foot of text: "turn over"; addressed: "John Vaughan esq. Philadelphia"; franked; postmarked Charlottesville, 19 July; endorsed in an unidentified hand, with Vaughan's additional notation that it was "received 24—ans[d] 28th" and that he was "to pay Girard 550 of which 350 to G Ticknor 200 to Cathalan remittance of S Girard Bill"; conjoined with RC of TJ to Vaughan, 15 July 1815, and Trs of enclosures to Vaughan to TJ, 31 July 1815.

PoC (DLC); conjoined with PoC of TJ to Vaughan, 15 July 1815; on verso of reused address cover to TJ; endorsed by TJ, in part: "July 11. & 15. 15."

Rather than Paris, TJ presumably intended a duplicate of the money order to be sent to John Quincy ADAMS at his new posting in London.

[1] Preceding two words interlined.
[2] Preceding two words interlined.

From Peter A. Guestier

SIR   Baltimore July 12th 1815—
I have in my possession a Small box Containing Seeds directed to you, this box is from france, I would have forwarded it should I not have been afraid of its having miscaried, please to give me your directions about it, and I Shall make it a duty to follow them
Permit me Sir to Subscribe myself with the Greatest Respect
Your most humble Servant   P. A. GUESTIER

RC (DLC); dateline at foot of text; endorsed by TJ as received 19 July 1815 and so recorded in SJL, which mistakenly describes it as a letter of 5 July 1815. RC (MHi); address cover only; with PoC of TJ to Obadiah Rich, 23 July 1815, on verso; addressed: "Thomas Jefferson Esq[r] late President of the U.S. Monticello"; franked; postmarked Baltimore, 12 July.

Peter August Guestier (1762–1842), merchant, was transacting business in Baltimore by 1795 and resided there from at least 1803. He traded with France and the West Indies and served as an agent for a mercantile firm of his native Bordeaux, perhaps that of Barton et Guestier. A member of the Loge Française l'Aménité, a Philadelphia Masonic lodge, in 1808 Guestier helped oversee a lottery to raise money for the construction of a Masonic hall in Baltimore. In that same year he acquired seeds from European sources for TJ's personal use. Guestier was a founding director of the Patapsco

Insurance Company, 1813–14, and last appeared in a Baltimore directory in 1829 (Paul Butel, *Histoire de la Chambre de Commerce et d'Industrie de Bordeaux des Origines a nos Jours [1705–1985]* [1988], 151; *Federal Intelligencer, and Baltimore Daily Gazette*, 16 Dec. 1795; *Tableau Des F. F. Composant La T. R. Loge Française l'Aménité, No. 73* [Philadelphia, 1802], 11; Cornelius William Stafford, *Baltimore Directory, for 1803* [Baltimore, n.d.], 57; *Report of the Committee of Claims, to Whom was Referred, on the Sixth of December Last, The Petition of Peter A. Guestier* [Washington, 1806]; Michael Stephen Smith, *Emergence of Modern Business Enterprise in France, 1800–1930* [2006], 38; *Laws Made and Passed by the General Assembly of the State of Maryland* [title varies] [1807–08 sess.]: ch. 67 [20 Jan. 1808]; [1813–14 sess.]: ch. 55 [11 Jan. 1814]; Guestier to TJ, 14 Mar. 1808 [DLC]; *MB*, 2:1224; *Baltimore Patriot & Evening Advertiser*, 10 Dec. 1813; *Matchett's Baltimore Directory Corrected Up To June 1829* [1829], 135).

From Benjamin Henry Latrobe

DEAR SIR,   Washington July 12th 1815.

My absence from Washington and the circuitous tour which your letter to me has made, has prevented its reaching my hands before the 6th of this month. For the last 18 months I have resided at Pittsburg, engaged for Mr Fulton in the agency of one of his Steam boat companies, whose object it was to establish a compleat line of boats from thence to New Orleans. But so deficient were the estimates made at New York, that instead of 60.000$, the Louisville & Orleans boats have cost more than 120,000$, & the Pittsburg & Louisville Compy abandoned the undertaking. Thus an establishment which would have been highly advantageous to me proved much the contrary, and when I was invited to resume my labors in this city, it was at a moment, when the pecuniary emolument, was an object of at least equal importance to me, with the testimony thus afforded to the integrity with which I had formerly performed my duties.—

After recieving the invitation of the Commissioners, I left Pittsburg on the 6th of April & staid in Washington till the 10th of May when I returned for my family & arrived on the 22d. I again left Pittsburg on the 2d June & arrived here on the 20th. In the meantime your letter had been returned from hence to Pittsburg, & was sent to me only a few days ago by a private hand.—Mr Nielson[1] arrived here,—(as I understand for the 2d time) a few days ago, and is now in the city. Mr Dinsmore I have not seen.—But the Commissioners have not appointed either of them to any situation, & if you will permit me to state how this has happened, you will, I am sure, approve what they have done.—

Since the commencement of the War, the public buildings have afforded no employment of any importance to building artisans; & all those who had no local ties to the spot left the city. Many of them followed me to Pittsburg, where they found ample employment & good wages. Others however were forced[2] to drag on a miserable existence & remain. They had families, or property in Lots on which they had built, or were detained as Militia men. After the irruption of the British, their case was still more deplorable. The numerous mechanics of the Navy Yard were deprived of bread, and it is almost a miracle that many did not die with hunger & cold[3] during the last winter. The situation of very respectable & once wealthy families has been described to me as inconceivably wretched, from the period of the invasion of the enemy, to that of the appropriation for the repair & rebuilding of the public edifices. Wood was at 25$ ℔ Cord, Coal 1.50$

& 2$ ℔ Bushel, Oats 1.50, & Hay 50$ a Ton; every thing in the same proportion.—The depression of the spirits & exertions of every one during the cold debates of Congress on the subject of removing the seat of Govern. added to the misery of all.—

As soon however as the Law for the restoration of the public buildings was passed the whole face of things was changed, & nothing but the total absence of all building materials prevented the immediate activity of all the Artisans that remained. After the appointment of the Commissioners, all the former agents of the public applied to them for situations in the public works. The principal of these, were Lenox, Meade, Farrell,—Blagden, Harbaugh, Shaw & Birth, and others, who during your administration were engaged at the Capitol & President's house, & many from the Navy Yard who had no immediate prospect of being engaged there again, among them Shadrach Davis, my Clerk of the Works there, Howard, & White, all men of great personal respectability, and the latter three⁴ of whom, had served with great, but useless zeal & courage in the Militia army. They were all wholly out of employ, & in more or less distress. These applications were before the board on my arrival. Mr Hoban having received the charge of the President's house my duties were confined to the Capitol. The names were laid before me, & I nominated to the Commissioners, Shadrach Davis as Clerk of the Works, Harbaugh carpenter, Blagden Stone cutter, Farrell & White bricklayers, Howard overseer, constituting a corps of Mechanics capable of executing any Work of any degree of difficulty or magnitude. The names of Mr Dinsmore & Nielson were then proposed to me supported by your & the Presidents testimonials, & also accompanied by the opinion of the Commissioners, that those who had formerly proved themselves worthy of trust, and who were now on the spot, & suffering in the cause of the city, were entitled (if their merit were only equal) to a preference above others from a distance, & who had not been without employment,—I adhered to my nomination, which was confirmed, & the appointments given. Mr Hoban chose Mr Lenox as his foreman.—

It was not till a few days ago that I received your letter. It came in every respect too late for the object of that part of it which relates to Messrs Dinsmore & Nielson, but I have recommended to Mr Nielson to go to work here, & have promised him as far as lies in my power to promote his interests. I have every reason to believe that I shall be able to start him in a good business before winter, & have already given him recommendations to those persons who can best serve him for the present.

Permit me now to assure you, that the confidence you are pleased to express in me, as to the future conduct of the public Works, from your experience of my former services, is to me by far a more gratifying reward, than I could possibly have received from any emolument, or any other commendation. It is not only because you are certainly the best judge of the merits of an artist in the United States, but because you certainly know me better as an artist and as a man than any other, that your good opinion is valuable[5] to me.—And why should I say so to You, who have forever retired from the seat from which favors are dispensed, & to whom adulation would be an insult, if I were not most sincere in what I express on this subject. You well remember, that if I committed an error in executing the Trust you reposed in me, it was not by blindly yielding my professional[6] opinions to yours, or in executing, without even remonstrance sometimes, what you suggested, in order to win your favor.—My thanks therefore for the kindness with which you express your approbation of what I have formerly done, are offered with sentiments of the Sincerest respect & attachment.—

Some details respecting the state of the ruins of the buildings may perhaps be new, & not unpleasant to be received by You, & may perhaps find you at leisure to read them, as your Library is no longer around you.—

The South wing of the Capitol was set on fire with great difficulty. Of the lower story nothing could be burned but the Sashes & frames, & their Shutters & dressings, & the doors & doorcases. As all these were detached from one another some time & labor was necessary to get thro' the work.—The first thing done was to empty into buckets a quantity of the composition used in the rockets. A man with an axe chopped the wood work, another followed, & brushed on some of the composition & on retiring from each room the third put fire to it. Many of the rooms however were thus, only partially burnt & there is not one in which some wood does not yet remain. In the Clerks office the desks & furniture & the records supplied a more considerable mass of combustible materials than there was else where: & the fire burnt so fiercely that they were obliged to retreat & leave all the rooms on the West side entirely untouched, & they are now as clean & perfect as ever. Two other committee rooms have escaped & the Gallery stairs have none of their wooden dressings injured. Above stairs the Committee room of Ways & Means & accounts is uninjured, & the whole of the Entrance with all the Sculptured Capitals of the Columns has fortunately suffered no injury but in the plaistering, & that from the wet & frost of the Winter. In the house of Representatives the devastation has been dreadful.—There was here no want of materials for conflagration. In 1811, when the number of members of Congress was increased the old platform was left in its place, & another raised over it, giving an additional quantity of dry & loose lumber. All the stages & seats of the Galleries were of timber & yellow pine. The Mahagony furniture, desks, tables & Chairs were in their places. At first they fired Rockets through the Roof. But they did not set fire to it; they sent men on to it, but it was covered with Sheet Iron. At last they made a great pile in the Center of the room of the furniture, & retiring, set fire to a large quantity of Rocket stuff, in the middle. The whole was soon in a blaze & so intense was the flame, that the Glass of the Lights was melted, & I have now lumps weighing many pounds of Glass, run into Mass. The stone, is like most freestone, unable to resist the force of[7] flame. But I believe no known material could have with stood the effects of so sudden & intense a heat. The exterior of the Columns & entablature therefore, expanded far beyond

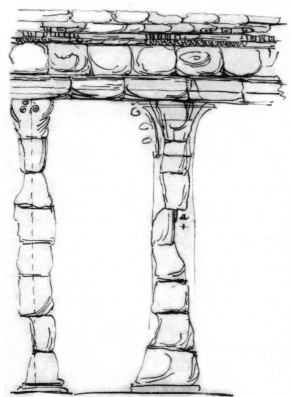

the dimensions of their interior, scaled off & not a vestige of fluting or Sculpture remained Sound. The appearance of the ruin, was awfully grand when I first saw it, and indeed it was terrific for it seemed to threaten immediately to fall, so Slender were the remains of the Columns that carried the Massy entablature. —The sketch below is an exact copy of two Columns, excepting that my paper does not admit of[8] their being of proportionate heighth: but the Blocks stand upon one another in the manner represented, and at $\frac{a}{+}$ the locust pin which I had placed in the center of each block, to keep the next steady while putting into place is bare. If the Colonnade had fallen the Vaulting of the rooms below might have been beaten down; but fortunately there is not a single arch in the whole building which requires to be taken down.—In the North wing the beautiful Doric Columns which surrounded the supreme Court room have shared the fate of the Corinthian Columns of the Hall of Representatives and in the Senate Chamber the Marble polished Columns of 14 feet Shafts in one block are burnt to lime & have fallen down. All but the Vaults is ruined. They stand a most magnificent ruin.

The West side containing the Library which was never Vaulted burnt very fiercely & by the fall of its heavy timbers great injury has been done to the adjoining Walls and arches, & I fear that the freestone is so much injured on the outside that part of the outer wall must be taken down. otherwise the exterior stands firm & sound especially of the south Wing, but of about 20 Windows & doors thro' which the Flames found vent, the Architraves & other dressings are so injured that they must be replaced, All the parapet is gone.—

The most difficult work to be performed was to take down the ruins of the Hall of Representatives. Our Workmen hesitated to touch it. To have erected a Scaffold & to have risked striking the ruins with the heavy poles necessary to be used was not to be thought of. An unlucky blow against the Column I have represented, (& 5 or 6 of them were as dangerously situated) might have brought down 100 ton of the Entablature, & of the heavy brick vault, which rested upon it. It therefore occurred to me to fill up the whole with fascines to the soffit of the Architrave. If any thing then gave way, it could not fall down, the Columns would be confined to their places, & the fascines would furnish the Scaffold. The Commissioners approved the scheme, but as time would be required to cut the fascines from the Commons, Mr Ringgold most fortunately recommended the use of Cord wood, which has been adopted, & most successfully. We have $\frac{4}{5}$th of the Work done, & the remainder is supported, & will be all down in 10. days. The Cordwood will sell for its cost. It required 500 Cord to go half round, which was then shifted to the other side.—I have already nearly completed the vaults of two Stories on[9] the West side of the North wing[10] according to the plan submitted by you with my report to Congress in 1807.—

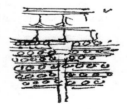

I need not, I hope, apologize to you for this long detail. An alteration is proposed & adopted by the President in the Hall of Representatives,[11] on which I will send you a copy of my report as soon as time will permit.

M[rs] Latrobe joins me in the sincerest wishes that you may long enjoy the repose & happiness at which you are arrived—

With sincere respect & attachment, I am Y[rs]

B HENRY LATROBE

Washington July 18th 1815

RC (DLC); at head of text: "Thomas Jefferson Esq[r]"; endorsed by TJ as received 26 July 1815 and so recorded in SJL. PoC (Lb in MdHi: Latrobe Papers).

Latrobe FORMERLY PERFORMED his duties in Washington as surveyor of public buildings during TJ's presidency (TJ to Latrobe, 6 Mar. 1803 [two letters] [MdHi: Latrobe Papers]; Latrobe to TJ, 13 Mar. 1803 [DLC]). He received the 14 Mar. 1815 INVITATION OF THE COMMISSIONERS of public buildings on 22 Mar. 1815 (Latrobe, *Papers*, 3:634–5). Congress approved an APPROPRIATION of up to $500,000 in "An Act making appropriations for repairing or rebuilding the public buildings within the city of Washington," 13 Feb. 1815 (*U.S. Statutes at Large*, 3:205). Both houses of Congress held extensive DEBATES on removing the national capital to another section of the country, either temporarily or permanently, and changing the location and design of the federal buildings within Washington (*Annals*, 13th Cong., 3d sess., 202–3, 216–22, 311–23, 341–2, 344–76, 387–93, 413–4, 1132, 1134–40 [26 Sept., 3–5, 13, 20 Oct. 1814, 1, 3, 7–8 Feb. 1815]). James Madison decided on John P. Van Ness, Richard Bland Lee, and Tench Ringgold in his APPOINTMENT OF THE COMMISSIONERS of public buildings (Madison to Van Ness, Lee, and Ringgold, 10 Mar. 1815 [DLC: Madison Papers]). The selection of James HOBAN to re-store the President's House was announced in the Washington *Daily National Intelligencer*, 24 May 1815. The NUMBER OF MEMBERS in the United States House of Representatives was increased by "An Act for the apportionment of Representatives among the several States, according to the third enumeration," 21 Dec. 1811 (*U.S. Statutes at Large*, 2:669). Latrobe's REPORT TO CONGRESS of 27 Oct. 1807 was presented to the House on the following day (*ASP, Miscellaneous*, 1:482–3; *Annals*, 10th Cong., 1st sess., 790). Latrobe suggested alterations to the original design of the Hall of Representatives in a 27 Apr. 1815 report concerning the south wing of the Capitol that he made to the commissioners of public buildings (Latrobe, *Papers*, 3:654–60).

[1] Manuscript: "Nelson."
[2] Manuscript: "forcced."
[3] Preceding two words interlined.
[4] Word interlined.
[5] Word interlined in place of "flattering."
[6] Manuscript: "professsional."
[7] Preceding two words interlined.
[8] PoC does not include the following illustration, although space was left for it on the manuscript page. In the RC the text flows inside and around the illustration.
[9] Manuscript: "or."
[10] Manuscript: "Northwing."
[11] Manuscript: "Reprentatives."

From Wilson Cary Nicholas

My Dear Sir   Richmond July 14. 1815

Most unexpectedly to me, my son Robert, writes me from Washington, that he had received such proposals in Baltimore, as induced him to determine to go immediately to Leghorn & to settle at that place. He says "it wou'd add very much to my prospects to be appointed Consul for the U.S. at Leghorn." will you my Dear Sir, add to the obligations that I am under to you by interesting yourself in his favour? The known honor & respectability[1] of my son, his late rank in the army, and his having been brought up to mercantile business by one of the first merchants in America, will I trust justify in the public estimation, his appointment, and I feel great confidence his conduct will be such as to prevent your ever having cause to regret your interposition in his favour if he shou'd be so fortunate as to be again patronised by you.

Robert says "to succeed the application shou'd be made as soon as possible." I owe you an apology for this application, and the trouble I have so frequently given you. I beg you to be assured if from any cause it wou'd be unpleasant to you to interpose in this case, it is sincerely my wish, that you shou'd not do it. I had rather my son shou'd forego any advantage, than to give you a moments trouble.

The accounts from Europe to the first of June are that things were there in the same state that they had been for a considerable time— This delay is most fortunate for the French people—their only danger was from the first shock. I feel a deep interest in their succeeding in resisting the effort of foreigners to impose a government upon them. you my Dear Sir, I am sure will be now as you ever have been, on the side of those who contend for self government, whether you approve of the government of their choice or not.

I am with the greatest respect your affectionate hum. Serv.

W. C. Nicholas

RC (DLC); at foot of text: "Thomas Jefferson Esqr"; endorsed by TJ as received 15 July 1815 and so recorded in SJL.

Robert Carter Nicholas was employed by his uncle Samuel Smith (of Maryland), who was ONE OF THE FIRST MERCHANTS IN AMERICA. On 28 July 1815 the elder Nicholas also wrote to James Madison on his son's behalf (DLC: Madison Papers).

[1] Manuscript: "respactability."

From Samuel Smith (of Maryland)

D^R SIR   Baltimore 14 July 1814 [1815]

Colonel Robert C Nicholas Son of Governor Nicholas will depart[1] for Leghorn in a few days[2] with a View of establishing himself there as a Merchant. he will have the good wishes of the Merchants of Balt^e & their entire confidence—It would tend greatly to his advantage to recieve the appointment of Consul at that port. A Change I am told is to be made, (& Surely it had become necessary.) and I know no person more worthy than Col° N. I write to Solicit your good offices with the President to procure it for him.—If you Should determine to do him that favor you will please to take the earliest Opportunity lest the place should be given to another,—The Choice of Consuls has heretofore been unfortunate. It is time to fill those Posts with Men of honor. With sentiments of the highest Esteem & real Regard I am D^r sir

Your friend & serv^t   S. SMITH

RC (DLC: TJ Papers, 201:35832); misdated; endorsed by TJ as a letter of 14 July 1815 received five days later and so recorded in SJL.

[1] Word interlined in place of "Sail."
[2] Preceding four words interlined.

To James Monroe

DEAR SIR   Monticello July 15. 15.

Your favor of the 10th is this moment recieved. the plat it covers shall be duly examined. you were so kind as to say you would patronise the passage of my letters for France and England. I therefore inclose a packet to you. it is important to me that those to Jackson and Cathalan should have the benefit of the <u>first safe</u> conveyance.

I was soon ashamed of the hasty information I communicated to you. but mr Galloway had just arrived, full of it. he had seen it, he said in a Baltimore paper copied from two N. York papers, the one federal, the other republican. I was soon convinced however he had exactly mistaken the nays on the question for the yeas. he left us on the 7th inst.

I suspect the allies are holding back to see how Bonaparte really stands with his nation, and how the powers of Europe will divide on their enterprize against human rights. my greatest anxiety is to learn that mr Adams has obtained a convention settling the question of impressment, and that this is not made to await the delays of a treaty of commerce, quod deus avertat. if they refuse to settle it, the first

American impressed should be a declaration of war. the depredations on our merchants I would bear with great patience as it is their desire. they make themselves whole by insurances, very much done in England. if the consequently increased price falls on the consumer, it still costs him less than a war, and still operates as a premium to our own manufactures. the other point therefore being settled, I should be slow to wrath on this. affectionately yours　　TH: JEFFERSON

RC (DLC: Monroe Papers); at foot of text: "Col⁰ Monroe." PoC (DLC); on verso of reused address cover to TJ; endorsed by TJ. Enclosures: (1) TJ to Stephen Cathalan, 3 July 1815. (2) TJ to Tadeusz Kosciuszko, 3 July 1815. (3) TJ to Madame de Staël-Holstein, 3 July 1815. (4) TJ to George Ticknor, 4 July 1815. (5) TJ to Henry Jackson, 5 July 1815.

The HASTY INFORMATION concerned a 6 Apr. 1815 message to the British House of Commons from the Prince Regent, later George IV. It announced that, in response to Napoleon's return to power in France, he had given "directions for the augmentation of his Majesty's land and sea forces" and had entered "into communications with his Majesty's allies" to form a coalition that would "effectually provide for the general and permanent security of Europe." Samuel Whitbread ob-

jected to the militant actions being taken by the government and proposed "that an humble Address be presented to his royal highness the Prince Regent, to entreat his Royal Highness that he will be graciously pleased to take such measures as may be necessary to prevent this country being involved in war, on the ground of the executive power in France being vested in any particular person." On 28 Apr. 1815 this motion was soundly defeated, 72 to 273 (Hansard, *Parliamentary Debates*, 30:347–53, 960–97; quotes on pp. 347, 969). Benjamin GALLOWAY may have read the newspaper account of this debate and vote in the *Baltimore Patriot & Evening Advertiser*, 21 June 1815. The debate had been published earlier in the *New-York Courier*, 30, 31 May, 7, 10, 12 June 1815, and the *New-York Evening Post*, 10, 12–14 June 1815.

QUOD DEUS AVERTAT: "which God forbid."

To Wilson Cary Nicholas

DEAR SIR　　　　　　　　　　　　　　Monticello July 15. 15.

Your favor of yesterday is this moment recieved and furnishes me matter of real regret: because there is nothing just & honorable which I would not cheerfully do for yourself or any member of your family. but the case in question stands thus. while I lived in Paris, I became acquainted with Thomas Appleton of Boston, then a young man, and recommended him to the old Congress as Consul for Leghorn, & he was appointed. on the commencement of the new government he was confirmed by Gen¹ W. at my request.[1] he has been now about 30. years in possession of the office, has conducted himself with integrity & diligence and never done an act to incur blame from the government. under these circumstances it would be immoral in me to sollicit his removal.—I recieved a letter from him some months ago asking my aid to get him removed from Leghorn to Paris. I did nothing in it upon my general principle of declining these sollicitations. I know that Fulwar Skipwith was appointed to Paris, & was preparing to go when the return of Bonaparte suspended it; some former transactions having made it doubtful whether Bonaparte would recieve him &[2] whether our government could with propriety propose him. how this has been settled I know not. but in the event of Appleton's removal to Paris there would be an opening at Leghorn. Appleton is not a man who could be put into comparison with your son on any original competition: but 30. years possession & approbation cannot fail to be a weight in his scale.[3] I will chearfully communicate your wishes to the President by our next mail, on the hypothesis that Leghorn may be now vacant; yet I know at the same time that the president's own dispositions to do any thing in his power which would be agreeable to yourself or your family will render my application merely an evidence of my wishes to be useful to you.[4]   While you were living in Albemarle you once proposed that a few of us should join in an enterprize to import our own plaister from Halifax, for the very just reason that we might recieve it clear of the exorbitant profits levied on it by the merchant. I should be glad [to][5] be one in such an adventure to the amount of 15. tons. probably yourself, mr Patterson & Gen[l] Cocke might want what would make up a load for a vessel of 60. or 80. tons: and your present situation might enable you to engage some vessel from Halifax to return here with such a cargo on our account. there is living there as a merchant, a brother of Tho[s] E. Randolph. perhaps we might engage his agency in it. or perhaps you could get some merchant in Richmond to transact the business for us on commission for a reasonable per cent. if any arrangement for this object be practicable I shall be glad to be concerned to the extent I have mentioned, and will concur in any advances requisite for it's execution.   Accept the assurance of my constant esteem & respect   TH: JEFFERSON

RC (MHi); endorsed by Nicholas. PoC (DLC); on reused address cover of Thomas Law to TJ, 8 May 1815; torn at seal; at foot of first page: "Governor Nicholas"; endorsed by TJ. Tr (DLC: James Madison Papers); entirely in TJ's hand; extract in TJ to Madison, 16 July 1815. PoC (DLC).

In a 14 Nov. 1788 letter to John Jay, TJ RECOMMENDED Thomas Appleton for a United States consulship at Rouen, France, not Leghorn (Livorno), Italy. Appleton was CONFIRMED as consul at Leghorn during the administration of John Adams, not George Washington. He remained in this post until his death in 1840 (PTJ, 14:60; JEP, 1:260, 5:290 [7, 8 Feb. 1798, 15 June 1840]). FULWAR SKIPWITH was nominated as consul at Paris on 2 Mar. 1815 and confirmed the following day (JEP, 2:626, 627). President Madison advised Wilson Cary Nicholas on 2 Aug. 1815 that Appleton would not be removed from the Leghorn consulship in favor of Robert Carter Nicholas (RC in MHi; endorsed by Wilson Cary Nicholas).

¹ Sentence interlined. Tr: "on the commencement of the new government he was confirmed by Gen¹ Washington on my recommendation also."

² Tr here adds "perhaps."

³ In Tr this sentence is positioned above, immediately after "sollicit his removal."

⁴ Tr begins after dateline and ends here.

⁵ Omitted word editorially supplied.

From Obadiah Rich

SIR   Georgetown Dist. Colᵃ July 15 1815.

The enclosed letter from my worthy friend the Revᵈ Dʳ Bentley of Salem has been some time in my posession, retained with the hope of delivering it to you personally. I now take the liberty of forwarding it, and of making myself known to you, feeling confident that, having from my youth cultivated the Sciences of Natural history and Botany, Sciences which you have not thought unworthy your attention, you will not consider this as too great an intrusion, nor refuse to accept of the accompanying little work (the production of a few leisure months) and that I may even be permitted to hope you will not consider as impertinent the favor I am about to ask.   Having resided several years in Spain and acquired a knowledge of the language, Commerce &c of that Country, I have been induced to offer myself as a candidate for a Consulate there, and understanding, a native citizen with Suitable recommendations would obtain that of Malaga, I have applied to my friends for their aid in this object.   While I was in Spain my friends in this country volunteered a Strong recommendation in my favor for the consulate of Valencia (copy of which I take the liberty of enclosing) but owing to the State of the country at that time no consular appointments were made for it; and on my return to this country in 1812 I withdrew the application.   I Shall receive the support of all the gentlemen whose Signatures are annexed to that paper, who are Still living, and of many others of equal respectability; but permit me Sir to add, that with none Should I feel So confident of Success, or personally so much gratified, as with the Support your name would give to my application: May I be permitted to Solicit it?

Very respectfully I am Sir Your most obedᵗ — &c   O RICH

RC (DNA: RG 59, LAR, 1809–17); at foot of text: "His Excellency Thomas Jefferson Monticello"; endorsed by TJ as received 19 July 1815 and so recorded in SJL. Enclosures: (1) William Bentley to TJ, 16 Apr. 1812. (2) Rich, *A Synopsis of* the *Genera of American Plants, According to the Latest Improvements on the Linnæn System: With the new Genera of Michaux and others* (Georgetown, 1814). (3) Crowell Hatch and eleven other Boston merchants to James Madison, Sept. 1809, recommending Rich's appointment as United States consul at Valencia in light of his current residence at that place, his "Talent, Integrity, and Love of Country," and his recent efforts on behalf of American fisheries (Tr in DNA: RG 59, LAR, 1809–17; endorsed by Secretary of State James Monroe as "Relating to Mr Rich" and by an unidentified State Department clerk, in part, as "Sundry Merchants of Boston recommend Mr Rich to be Consul at Malaga"). Enclosed in TJ to Madison, 23 July 1815.

Obadiah Rich (1783–1850), merchant, diplomat, and bibliophile, was born at Truro, Massachusetts, but later resided in Boston where, as a young man, he was employed by Hatch. By 1809 Rich was an established merchant in Valencia, Spain. After returning to the United States in 1810, he settled two years later in Georgetown, where he was a founder of the Central Bank of Georgetown and Washington and a commissioner for the Georgetown Importing and Exporting Company. Rich served as the United States consul at Valencia from 1816 until his replacement early in Andrew Jackson's presidency, but he moved to Madrid in 1823 in order to take charge of the archives of the American legation. While there, he collected books and manuscripts relating to the history of Spain and Latin America. Many of his purchases were later sold to American book collectors and libraries, with the bulk of his manuscript collection now housed at the New York Public Library. In 1828 Rich established a home and bookstore in London, where he published a gazetteer, *A General View*

of the *United States of America* [1833; 2d ed., 1836]. He was the purchasing agent in London for the Library of Congress, 1830–50, and served as the United States consul at Port Mahon, on the Spanish island of Minorca, 1834–45. Rich maintained his London bookstore and continued to buy rare books and manuscripts until his death (*ANB*; *DAB*; Norman P. Tucker, "Obadiah Rich [1783–1850]: American in Spain," in Vern G. Williamsen and A. F. Michael Atlee, eds., *Studies in Honor of Ruth Lee Kennedy* [1977], 133–46; Benjamin Homans to James Monroe, 24 July 1815 [DNA: RG 59, LAR, 1809–17]; *Norwich* [Conn.] *Courier*, 25 Oct. 1809; Georgetown *Federal Republican*, 10 Mar. 1815; Washington *Daily National Intelligencer*, 15 July 1815; *JEP*, 3:29, 34, 4:68, 447, 453, 7:6 [14 Feb., 6 Mar. 1816, 12 Mar. 1830, 10, 30 Dec. 1834, 18 Dec. 1845]; Rich, *Bibliotheca Americana Nova; or, A Catalogue of Books in Various Languages, Relating to America, Printed Since the Year 1700* [1835]; Edwin Blake Brownrigg, *Colonial Latin American Manuscripts and Transcripts in the Obadiah Rich Collection: An Inventory and Index* [1978], vii–xv; William Dawson Johnston, *History of the Library of Congress* [1904], 1:226, 246, 350–1; *Athenæum Journal of Literature, Science, and the Fine Arts* [1850]: 102).

GENTLEMEN in Boston and men of EQUAL RESPECTABILITY from Georgetown and Washington signed petitions and wrote letters recommending Rich in 1815. He requested a consular appointment to Málaga in his APPLICATION of 22 July 1815 to Secretary of State James Monroe. Failing to receive a reply, Rich then wrote Monroe on 22 Dec. 1815 and 11 Feb. 1816 asking for an appointment to Valencia instead (all DNA: RG 59, LAR [1809–17]).

To John Vaughan

DEAR SIR   Monticello July 15. 15:

The letter on the preceding page was written at the time of it's date, but was witheld from the post office until I could learn that the remittance therein mentioned was actually made. this I learn from your favor of the 8ᵗʰ this moment recieved. being anxious that the articles desired from France, and especially the books should get in before the bad weather of the winter sets in, I have only to repeat the requests of my letter, and as early an attention to them as is convenient with the assurance of my friendly esteem & respect.

TH: JEFFERSON

RC (PPAmP: Vaughan Papers); on verso of RC of TJ to Vaughan, 11 July 1815, and sharing its address leaf; with Vaughan's notation that it was received 24 July 1815 and answered 28 July 1815; with subjoined Trs of enclosures to Vaughan to TJ, 31 July 1815. PoC (DLC); on verso of PoC of TJ to Vaughan, 11 July 1815; on recto of reused address cover to TJ; endorsed by TJ, in part: "July 11. & 15. 15."

From Hugh Williamson and Samuel L. Mitchill

SIR   New york July 15ᵗʰ 1815

We have the pleasure of informing you that at a meeting of the Literary and Philosophical Society of New york on the 13ᵗʰ instant, you was elected an honorary member.

Be pleased to accept the assurance of the utmost respect

HU WILLIAMSON ⎱ Correspon[ding]
SAMˡ L MITCHILL ⎰ Secretaries

RC (MoSHi: TJC-BC); torn at seal; text and address cover in Mitchill's hand, signed by Williamson and Mitchill; at foot of text in Mitchill's hand: "Thomas Jefferson LL.D. &c"; addressed: "The honᵇˡᵉ Thomas Jefferson Virginia"; franked; postmarked New York, 8 Aug.; endorsed by TJ as received 16 Aug. 1815 and so recorded in SJL.

Hugh Williamson (1735–1819), physician, public official, and author, was a native of West Nottingham, Chester County, Pennsylvania. He studied theology after graduating in 1757 from the College of Philadelphia (later the University of Pennsylvania) and was licensed to preach by the Presbytery of Philadelphia. Williamson soon changed professions. He taught mathematics at his alma mater, 1760–63, studied in London and Edinburgh beginning in 1764, and received an M.D. from the University of Utrecht. Williamson then practiced medicine in Philadelphia before moving in 1777 to Charleston, South Carolina, and shortly thereafter to Edenton, North Carolina, where he kept a medical practice and engaged in trade with the French West Indies. During the Revolutionary War he served as surgeon general for the North Carolina militia, 1780–81. Williamson was a delegate in the North Carolina House of Commons in 1782 and 1785. He represented that state in the Continental Congress, 1782–85 and 1787–88; the 1787 Philadelphia Convention, where he signed the new United States Constitution; and the United States House of Representatives, 1790–93. Already a member of the American Philosophical Society when he moved to New York City in 1793, Williamson became a founder of the Literary and Philosophical Society of New-York and a member of the New-York Historical Society and New York City's Humane Society. He published *Observations on the Climate in Different Parts of America* (New York, 1811), *The History of North Carolina*, 2 vols. (Philadelphia, 1812), and other books and essays on medical, political, and scientific topics. After his death TJ attested to Williamson's erudition and usefulness to the public (*ANB*; *DAB*; David Hosack, *A Biographical Memoir of Hugh Williamson, M.D. LL.D.* [New York, 1820; Poor, *Jefferson's Library*, 5 (no. 165)], esp. 31–2, 67; Louis W. Potts, "Hugh Williamson: The Poor Man's Franklin and the National Domain," *North Carolina Historical Review* 64 [1987]: 371–93; Samuel A. Ashe, ed., *Biographical History of North Carolina* [1906], 5:458–66; Literary and Philosophical Society of New-York, *Transactions* 1 [1815]: v–vii, xv–xvi; APS, Minutes, 2 Feb. 1768 [MS in PPAmP]; *PTJ*, esp. 7:569–70; *New-York Evening Post*, 24 May 1819).

Samuel Latham Mitchill (1764–1831), physician, educator, and public official, was born in Hempstead, New York. After serving a medical apprenticeship in New York City, 1781–83, he enrolled at the University of Edinburgh, receiving an M.D. in 1786. Mitchill was a professor of natural history, chemistry, and agriculture at Columbia College (later University), 1792–1801; professor successively of chemistry, natural history, and materia medica at the College of Physicans and Surgeons (later merged with Columbia University), 1807–26; and vice president of Rutgers Medical College (in New York City), 1826–30. He served three terms in the New York state legislature, 1792, 1798, and 1810, and he represented New York as a Jeffersonian Republican in the United States House of Representatives, 1801–04 and 1810–13, and the United States Senate, 1804–09. A member of the American Philosophical Society, Mitchill was a founder of the Literary and Philosophical Society of New-York, the New-York Institution for the Instruction of the Deaf and Dumb, and the Lyceum of Natural History in the City of New York (later the New York Academy of Sciences), and a president of the Society for the Promotion of Agricultural Arts and Manufactures of New York and the American Mineralogical Society. He was a founder in 1797 and longtime editor of the *Medical Repository*, a pioneering New York medical and scientific journal, and he authored numerous articles, orations, and books on scientific, cultural, and political topics, several of which TJ owned. Mitchill's *A Discourse on the Character and Services of Thomas Jefferson, more especially as a Promoter of Natural and Physical Science* (1826) was based on his 11 Oct. 1826 address to the Lyceum of Natural History (*ANB*; *DAB*; Alan David Aberbach, *In Search of An American Identity: Samuel Latham Mitchill, Jeffersonian Nationalist* [1988]; Mitchill, *Some of the Memorable Events and Occurrences in the Life of Samuel L. Mitchill, of New-York, from the Year 1786 to 1826* [ca. 1828]; "Dr. Mitchill's Letters from Washington: 1801–1813," *Harper's New Monthly Magazine* 58 [1879]: 740–55; APS, Minutes, 21 Jan. 1791 [MS in PPAmP]; Literary and Philosophical Society of New-York, *Transactions* 1 [1815]: v–vii, xv–xvi; Directors of the New-York Institution for the Instruction of the Deaf and Dumb, *Annual Report* 25 [1844]: 13–8; Herman Le Roy Fairchild, *A History of the New York Academy of Sciences, formerly the Lyceum of Natural History* [1887], 52, 57–62; *PTJ*, esp. 32:18–9; Sowerby, nos. 670, 977, 4006; *New-York Spectator*, 9, 13 Sept. 1831).

To John George Baxter

SIR   Monticello July 16. 15.

I have duly recieved your favor explaining to me your improvement on the carding machine; but I am too little acquainted with that now in use to form any opinion of their comparative merits. the only part of your request therefore which I can answer respects the obtaining patent rights in France & England. in France before the revolution (I know not how it is since) no standing law allowed patent rights for inventions. a special law was necessary to be passed in every individual case, and was refused but for great discoveries promising important advantages; nor was it easy under that government to procure attention to a petition for this purpose. in England there is a standing law granting a patent as a matter of right on petition & payment of fees, amounting I believe to about 100. guineas, perhaps more. but the patent is void if for an invention used, before it's date, in any other country. this last circumstance requires your attention.

Mr Breckenridge informs me you have invented a spinning machine which from it's cheapness, simplicity and saving of labor is rapidly getting into general use. I should like to know in what this differs from the old spinning Jenny, or from Arkwright's machines. these last will not answer in the country because they require nice workmen to keep them in repair. I have therefore used the Jenny, because our workmen can make them, and any body can repair them. I have three of these, carrying 24. threads each, in operation in my own family. but if there be any thing yet more simple & of equal effect I should prefer it. Accept the assurance of my respect.   TH: JEFFERSON

PoC (DLC); on verso of reused address cover of Patrick Gibson to TJ, 28 Apr. 1815, for which see note to Gibson to TJ, 3 May 1815; at foot of text: "Mr Baxter"; endorsed by TJ. Enclosed in TJ to Joseph Cabell Breckinridge, 16 July 1815.

John George Baxter (d. 1826), machinist and inventor, emigrated from Dundee, Scotland, to Philadelphia and resided in 1807 in Philadelphia County, where he was working a year later at the Blockley Flax and Hemp Spinning Mill. He had previously been in New York; New London, Connecticut; and Boston. In 1809 Baxter advertised his improved looms and six-spindle machines that spun thread from flax, hemp, cotton, or wool, noting that he had thirty years of background in manufacturing with flax and hemp and considerable experience with cotton. He received a patent in 1811 for a "family cotton spinning machine." Baxter moved about the same time to Lunenburg County, Virginia. His plan to manufacture his various machines there failed, and by 1813 he was in Philadelphia. Two years later Baxter had relocated to Kentucky, and he settled in Frankfort by 1825 (Josiah Stoddard Johnston, ed., *Memorial History of Louisville from its First Settlement to the Year 1896* [1896], 1:623; Baxter to TJ, 1 Apr. 1807 [PHi]; *The Process For Rotting Hemp* [Philadelphia, 1808; broadside in DLC: TJ Papers; content by Thomas Cooper, with Baxter's 21 Apr. 1808 covering letter]; Sag

[605]

Harbor, N.Y., *Suffolk Gazette*, 8 Apr. 1809; *List of Patents*, 99; John S. Ravenscroft to TJ, 21 July 1812; New York *Commercial Advertiser*, 8 Jan. 1814; John A. Paxton, *The Philadelphia Directory and Register, for 1813* [Philadelphia, 1813]; *Kite's Philadelphia Directory for 1814* [Philadelphia, 1814]; Breckinridge to TJ, 20 June 1815; Frankfort *Argus of Western America*, 2 Mar. 1825; Brent Moore, *A Study of the Past, the Present and the Possibilities of the Hemp Industry in Kentucky* [1905], 55; Frankfort *Commentator*, 23 Sept. 1826).

Baxter's undated letter explaining his improvements to the CARDING MACHINE, not found, is recorded in SJL as received 5 July 1815 from Lexington, Kentucky. Although TJ expressed interest in acquiring one of Baxter's carding machines in 1812, he bought a different one instead (TJ to Ravenscroft, 3 July 1812; TJ to Jacob Alrichs, 10 Aug. 1812; *MB*, 2:1287).

To Joseph Cabell Breckinridge

DEAR SIR   Monticello July 16. 15.

I hope that soon after the date of your letter of June 20.[1] you recieved my answer of June 12. to your preceding one of May 14. in compliance with that of June 20. I have writte[n] one to mr Baxter, which I inclose open for your perusal, and will ask the favor of you, after perusal, to have delivered to him. Accept the assurance of my great respect.   TH: JEFFERSON

PoC (MHi); edge trimmed; at foot of text: "Mr Breckenridge"; endorsed by TJ. Enclosure: TJ to John George Baxter, 16 July 1815.

[1] Word added in margin.

To James Madison

D^R SIR   Monticello July 16. 15.

I recieved yesterday from our friend Govr Nicholas a letter stating that very advantageous offers had been made to his son at Baltimore (late a colonel in the army) which would induce him to go and fix himself at Leghorn, and that it would add very much to his prospects to be appointed Consul there, and counting on my knolege of the character of his son, he supposed my testimony of it to you might befriend his views. with respect to the character of the son I should certainly bear honorable and ample testimony, as of a high order: but there is more than that in the case as it respects myself. I suppose the office to be at present full and that there are considerations due to the incumbent from myself. I cannot give you a better view therefore of the footing on which my answer to the governor places it, than by transcribing what related to it, as follows.   'Your favor of yesterday is this moment recieved, and furnishes me matter of real regret; because there is nothing just and honorable which I would not cheerfully do for yourself or any member of your family. but the case in question stands thus. while I lived in Paris I became acquainted with Thomas Appleton of Boston then a young man, and recommended him to the Old Congress as Consul at Leghorn, & he was appointed. on the commencement of the new government he was confirmed by Genl Washington on my recommendation also. he has been now about 30. years in possession of the office, has conducted himself with integrity and diligence, and has never done an act to incur blame from the government. under these circumstances it would be immoral in me to sollicit his removal. he is not a man who could be put into comparison with your son on any original competition; but 30. years of possession &[1] approbation cannot fail to be a weight in his scale.   I recieved a letter from him some months ago asking my aid to get him removed to Paris from Leghorn. I did nothing in it upon my general principle of declining these sollicitations. I know that Fulwar Skipwith was appointed to Paris, and was preparing to go, when the return of Bonaparte suspended it, some former transactions having made it doubtful whether he would recieve him, and perhaps whether our government could with propriety propose him. how this has been settled I know not. but in the event of Appleton's removal to Paris, there would be an opening at Leghorn. on the hypothesis therefore that Leghorn may be now vacant I will chearfully communicate your wishes to the President by our next mail. yet I know at the same time that the President's own dispositions to do any thing in his power which would be agreeable to yourself or your family will render my application merely an evidence of my wishes to be useful to you.'   this extract placing the case fully before you, I will add nothing more to the trouble of reading it but the assurances of my affectionate attachment and respect   Th: Jefferson

RC (DLC: Madison Papers); addressed: "James Madison President of the US at Washington"; franked; postmarked Charlottesville, 19 July; endorsed by Madison. PoC (DLC); on reused address cover to TJ; endorsed by TJ.

TJ's ANSWER to Governor Wilson Cary Nicholas was dated 15 July 1815.

[1] Manuscript: "& and."

To Andrew C. Mitchell

Monticello July 16. 15.

I thank you, Sir, for the pamphlet which you have been so kind as to send me. I have read it with attention & satisfaction. it is replete with sound views, some of which will doubtless be adopted. some may be checked by difficulties. none more likely to be so than the proposition to amend the constitution so as to authorise Congress to tax exports. the provision against this in the framing of that instrument, was a sine qua non with the states of peculiar productions, as rice, indigo, cotton & tobacco, to which may now be added sugar. a jealousy prevailing that to the few states producing these articles, the justice of the others might not be a sufficient protection in opposition to their interest, they moored themselves to this anchor. since the hostile dispositions lately manifested by the Eastern states, they would be less willing than before to place themselves at their mercy: and the rather as the Eastern states have no exports which can be taxed equivalently. it is possible however that this difficulty might be got over: but the subject looking forward beyond my time, I leave it to those to whom it's burthens & benefits will belong adding only my prayers for whatever may be best for our country and assurances to yourself of my great respect. TH: JEFFERSON

PoC (DLC); at foot of text: "Andrew C. Mitchell esq." Tr (MHi); posthumous copy.

On pp. 30–42 of *The Second Crisis of America* (for which see his 23 June 1815 letter to TJ), Mitchell calls for a convention to AMEND THE CONSTITUTION, particularly Article I, section 9, which prohibits Congress from imposing any tax or duty on exports. He argues that an export tax will raise needed revenue; that "when there is not a competitor to undersell in the market abroad," such a duty is "always paid by the consumer" (p. 40); and that it should be placed on a number of products, including tobacco, flaxseed, rice, beef, pork, ginseng, wool, and cotton.

From James Ligon
(for Patrick Gibson)

17ʰ July 1815

Thomas Jefferson Esqᵉ
  To Patrick Gibson Dr
To Cash pᵈ for a Bale Cotton 232ˡᵇ at 22 Cents. $51. 4
  drayᵉ & toll

Harry will deliver Mr Jefferson the above bale of Cotton—Mr Johnson was unloaded at the Locks & I thought it better to send it by the present opportunity than to wait his return
respectfully

PATRICK GIBSON
℥ JAˢ LIGON

RC (ViU: TJP-ER); in Ligon's hand; dateline at foot of text; with unrelated calculations by TJ on verso; endorsed by TJ: "Gibson Patrick."

HARRY worked as a boatman out of Richmond for his owner, Thomas Mann Randolph (George Jefferson to TJ, 23 Aug. 1811; Gibson to TJ, 22 Dec. 1815).

From John Wood

SIR   Petersburg Academy 18ᵗʰ July 1815
I take the liberty of addressing you as the friend of literary establishments, on a subject which may be beneficial to the youth of this state. I received a few days since, a letter from Professor Thomas Cooper of Carlisle College informing me that he quits that seminary in October next, and has yet fixed on no future place of residence and wishes that I might suggest some situation that would suit. It is unnecessary for me to inform you of the acquirements and Talents of Professor Cooper as you are certainly well acquainted with his character as a man of science[1] and general literature. Being confident that any literary establishment of which Professor Cooper was the President, would flourish, I have thought that the situation of Charlottesville would be an eligible one for this purpose; and as you have no seminary of consequence in that neighbourhood I should suppose the Gentlemen of the county would patronise such an institution. Professor Cooper writes me that he would divide his time between Chemical students and Law Students provided he could reasonably expect 2000 Dollars a year. From the unhealthy state of Petersburgh and the bad health which I myself have enjoyed for the last two years, I should also gladly remove to Charlottesville in the event of Mʳ Cooper's coming and with the assistance of a good classical teacher I think a seminary of some importance and utility might be formed, as that village possesses all the local advantages for the education of youth. Professor Cooper's sole motive for leaving Carlisle I believe is the bigotry and the prejudice of the Clergy who I understand usurp the control of the College. I received only yesterday a letter from Professor Blackburn of Columbia College South Carolina late of Williamsburg telling me he has been under the necessity of resigning

his Professorship from the same cause the <u>persecution of the Clergy</u>. It is very remarkable that in this country Clerical influence should prevail in our Colleges much more than in the Seminaries of Europe. I should esteem it a favour if you would as soon as your conveniency permit give me your opinion as to the success of such a seminary. Requesting you will present my respects to Colonel Randolph and Mr Thomas Jefferson Randolph

I remain with sincere esteem your very obedient Servant

JOHN WOOD—

RC (DLC); addressed: "Thomas Jefferson Esqr Monticello by Milton Albemarle"; stamp canceled; franked; postmarked Petersburg, 19 July; endorsed by TJ as received 24 July but recorded in SJL as received 28 July 1815.

COLUMBIA COLLEGE: South Carolina College (now the University of South Carolina) in Columbia, South Carolina.

¹ Manuscript: "sience."

To Joel Yancey

DEAR SIR   Montic[ello] July 18. 15.

I recieved yesterday your favor of the 9th and observe one article in it requiring immediate answer, that which relates to the using our wheat for bread, instead of purchasing corn. the price of last year's flour now at Richmond is 8.D. & of this year's 10.D. which is equal to 8/ and 10/ for wheat; and war in Europe, now I think absolutely certain, will ensure the last price at least, thro' the year. this is equal to 9/ a bushel at Lynchbg. we had certainly then better buy corn at any price it has ever been sold at, & pay for the hauling than eat wheat at 9/. it would be much most convenient to me if it can be bought on credit, till our flour can get to Richmond & be sold. if not, then on a credit of 60. days before which I shall be with you and can meet it. if nothing but the cash will do, then if mr Robertson will advance it, & you immediately advise me of the amount, it shall be placed at his credit in Richmond, within 5. days after I recieve your letter, or shall be ordered up to him at Lynchburg as he chuses.

The toll for crushing and grinding plaister is uniformly one eighth here. I have ground for the neighborhood at my mill & always recieved that, and it is willingly paid. my workmen are engaged in shingling a barn; and the moment that is done they will set out for Poplar forest, & myself the day after them. this will be within three or four weeks. there will be one white, (a brother of mr Goodman) and from 4. to 6. or 7. blacks as I shall find convenient. with respect to the overseers, you know I placed them absolutely at your command. do as you please on that subject without waiting to consult m[e.] if you can rub thro' the year with them (and I expect certainly you ma[y] with one, if not both) it will be better than to be embarrassed with a law suit: for the wages are not the only damages which may be claimed, and costs would probably be high, especially if sued here.

the best overseer I have ever employed leaves this place this year for a fault which perhaps he might not contract at a new place. it has lost him here the respect of those under him. if you should not have a better offer, we may consider, when I come up, whether we may trust him, if he should not get new business in the mean time which he will easily do here.—I am glad you approve my plan of culture, because it will be the more agreeable to you to pursue it. it's general effect is this. one third of the farm (2 fields out of 6.) is in wheat for market & profit. one sixth (that is one field) is in corn for <u>bread</u> for the laborers. the remaining half of the farm, that is to say, one field in peas or oats, one field in clover for cutting, and one in clover for pasture, is for the sustenance of the stock of the farm, aided by 8. acres of pumpkins at each place, which feeds every thing[1] two months in the year & fattens the pork, and as much timothy as our meadow ground can be made to yield, which is very important when the clover crop fails from drought, a frequent occurrence. on this plan I know it to be unnecessary that a single grain of corn should ever[2] be given to any animal, unless a little perhaps to finish the fattening pork; but even for that peas are as good. of these you may certainly count on 10. bushels to the acre, which on 160. acres will be 1600. bushels, or 320. barrels, equal to that much corn, and all fall-fallowing will be saved. to the produce for market my plan adds 80 tobacco hills at each place, as much of it on first year's land as can be cleared. if this plan be fully executed, I will most gladly take all risk of the result to myself, and my own blame. Accept the assurance of my great esteem and respect

Th: Jefferson

PoC (MHi); on reused address cover to TJ; one word faint in dateline; edge trimmed; at foot of first page: "Mr Yancey"; endorsed by TJ.

Yancey's missing FAVOR OF THE 9TH July is not recorded in SJL. William Ballard, the BEST OVERSEER, was employed at Tufton farm (Agreement with Ballard, 18 July 1813; TJ's Account with Ballard, 20 Oct. 1815). EACH PLACE: TJ's Bear Creek and Tomahawk plantations at Poplar Forest.

[1] Preceding two words interlined.
[2] Word interlined.

To Michael Atkinson

[ca. 21 July 1815]

I shall have occasion for 600. feet, running measure of scantling $5\frac{1}{4}$ Inches square, clear of the saw, all of heart poplar, without a speck of sap. when we use it it will be cut into lengths of 2 f 8 I. for ballusters. the stocks therefore must be of such lengths as to cut into these smaller lengths of 2 f 8 I. without waste.
for example a stock of 8.f. will give 3. lengths

10 f. 8 I. will give 4. lengths	
13 f. 4 I.	5 lengths
16 f	6 lengths

to be done immediately so as to be ready on our arrival.

Th: J[e]fferson

PoC (MHi); on verso of reused address cover to TJ; undated; signature faint; subjoined to covering letter; at head of text: "A note for mr Atkinson." Not recorded in SJL. Enclosed in TJ to Joel Yancey, 21 July 1815.

Michael Atkinson operated a sawmill in Campbell County, where he paid tax on six slaves in 1816 and lived until at least 1820. TJ had engaged Atkinson's services for his Poplar Forest estate by 1814. He paid Atkinson a total of $113.89 between 20 May and 29 Sept. 1815 (TJ to Jeremiah A. Goodman, 11 July 1814; *MB*, 2:1309, 1310, 1314; Vi: RG 48, Personal Property Tax Returns, Campbell Co., 1816–20; DNA: RG 29, CS, Campbell Co., 1820).

From Frank Carr

Sir,   Charlottesville July 21st 15

Mr Garrett has just had the misfortune to lose his youngest child. It is the request of Mrs Garrett, many of whose connections have been buried there, that you will permit his remains to be deposited in the burial ground at Monticello. In his affliction Mr Garrett has desired me to present the request to you—
very respectfully y^r ob^t Hb^l Sv^t   Frank Carr

RC (MHi); dateline at foot of text; addressed: "Thomas Jefferson Esqr Monticello"; endorsed by TJ: "Garrett Arch."

No gravestone survives at Monticello for the YOUNGEST CHILD of Alexander Garrett and Evelina Bolling Garrett, who are both buried there. Evelina Bolling Garrett's CONNECTIONS to Monticello came through her grandmother, TJ's sister Mary Jefferson Bolling (Shackelford, *Descendants*, 1:38, 261, 2:217; Wyndham Robertson, *Pocahontas, alias Matoaka, and her Descendants* [1887], 32, 35, 41).

To Joel Yancey

DEAR SIR   Monticello July 21. 15.
In my letter of the 18th I omitted a material article, which was to give the inclosed bill to mr Atkinson & get him to saw it immediately so as to have it ready on the arrival of the carpenters. there are, I imagine, belted poplars in the cleared grounds sufficient to furnish the stocks, for I do not suppose they will take more than 3. or 4. trees. he will need help in pitting, but the shorter he makes the stocks the less help he will need.—in your provision of bread about 3. or 4. barrels must be allowed for the carpenters. Accept the assurances of my esteem & respect   TH: JEFFERSON

PoC (MHi); on verso of reused address cover to TJ; adjacent to signature: "Mr Yancey"; with PoC of enclosure subjoined; endorsed by TJ. Enclosure: TJ to Michael Atkinson, [ca. 21 July 1815].

Yancey's 29 July 1815 reply to TJ, not found, is recorded in SJL as received 11 Aug. 1815 from Bedford.

From William Wardlaw

DEAR SIR   Richmond 22 July 1815
I recd your favour of the 16. currt by the last mail. On enquiry I find that Mr David Michie left this place with his family about the middle or 20th of last month he is no doubt now residing in Albemarle or Louisa.   The Sergt of the City informed me yesterday that he had not been in Richmond since he recd your notices, but that when he returned to town which was expected to be in a short time, that he would attend to it
I return you the blank notices, they will answer if he is in Albemarle. I have procured for you one Doz Lemmon Acid which I will endeavour to place in the care of Mr Opie Norris who goes by tomorrows Stage price $2 50. It will give me much pleasure to render you any service in this place
With much esteem   W WARDLAW

RC (DLC); endorsed by TJ as received 26 July 1815 and so recorded in SJL. Enclosures not found.

TJ's letter to Wardlaw OF THE 16. CURRT and his 14 June 1815 message to the SERGT OF THE CITY of Richmond, William D. Wren, are both recorded in SJL, but neither has been found.

To James T. Austin

SIR   Monticello July 23. 15.

I thank you for the very splendid morsel of eloquence which you have been so kind as to send me. it is a happy and pregnant example to the orators of the 4.th of July, of change from the hackneyed topics of 1776, to those of the current year. I have read it with sensations very different from those which will be felt by our recreant citizens of the East. if theirs be sensations of sorrow 'I shall rejoice; not that[1] they were made sorry; but, in the hope, that they sorrow to repentance.' with wishes that a return of fidelity to their country, and of affection for their fellow citizens, may furnish you with themes for equally eloquent eulogies on the future anniversaries of our independance, accept my salutations and assurances of respect   TH: JEFFERSON

RC (CtY: Franklin Collection); addressed: "Mr James T. Austin Boston"; franked; postmarked Charlottesville, 26 July. PoC (DLC).

I SHALL REJOICE . . . SORROW TO REPENTANCE is from the Bible, 2 Corinthians 7.9.

[1] Manuscript: "that that."

To Samuel Berrian

Monticello July 23. 15.

I thank you, Sir, for the eloquent oration you have been so kind as to send me. it is always matter of comfort to observe the heirs of that independance which has signalised in history the age of their fathers, recalling it to memory, and hallowing it's principles. their own deeds by sea and land are worthy sequels of it, and earnests that they will faithfully maintain it: and we do but justice in offering our prayers to heaven for the maintenance of independance to the friendly nation which aided us in the establishment of our own, and the support of their choice of a ruler, whatever we may have thought of his former enterprises on the peace and freedom of the world. Accept the assurances of my esteem and respect   TH: JEFFERSON

PoC (DLC); at foot of text: "Samuel Berrian esq. New York."

Samuel Berrian (d. 1819), attorney, operated a circulating library in New York City, 1803–08. He received an A.B. degree from Columbia College (later University) in 1809. In 1812 Berrian was admitted to practice law in the New York State Supreme Court. He was a member of New York City's Tammany Society or Columbian Order and the Hibernian Provident Society (Berrian, *A Catalogue, of Samuel Berrian's Increasing and Circu-*

lating Library, No. [20] Chatham-Street [New York, 1803; bracketed number inserted by hand]; Longworth's New York Directory [1804]: 84; [1808]: 76; Milton Halsey Thomas, Columbia University Officers and Alumni 1754–1857 [1936], 125; New York Public Advertiser, 3 July 1811; New York Mercantile Advertiser, 2 Nov. 1812; New York National Advocate, 4 July 1815, 4 Apr. 1817; New-York Evening Post, 13 Nov. 1819).

The ORATION that Berrian sent TJ, one of at least three such efforts that he published, was An Oration, delivered before the Tammany Society, or Columbian Order, Hibernian Provident, Columbian, and Shipwright's Societies, in the City of New-York, on the Fourth Day of July, 1815 (New York, 1815; Poor, Jefferson's Library, 13 [no. 818]; TJ's copy at ViU). France was the FRIENDLY NATION and Napoleon the RULER.

To Peter A. Guestier

SIR   Montic[ello] July 23. 15.

I have to acknolege the reciept of your favor of the 12th and to thank you for your attention to the box of seeds. this is an annual present from the National garden of France to this country the disposal of which is confided to me. I will pray you therefore to forward it to [m]r Bernard McMahon gardener of Philadelphia, who will be most likely to disseminate the useful things the box contains. the stage would be the safest conveyance, if any passenger would so far aid this benevolent work as to take it under his care to Philadelphia. whatever expences you may have incurred by this charge shall be instantly remitted on your being so kind as to inform me of their amount. with my thanks be pleased to accept the assurances of my esteem & respect.   TH: JEFFERSON

PoC (DLC); on verso of reused address cover to TJ; two words faint; at foot of text: "Mr Guestier"; endorsed by TJ.

André Thoüin sent the PRESENT of seeds.

To Bernard McMahon

DEAR SIR   Monticello July 23. 15.

With the return of peace, my old friend Thouin returns to a recollection of me in his annual presents of seeds. a box of them is just arrived at Baltimore to the care of mr P. A Guestier merchant of that place. I have desired him to forward it to you, and if possible by some stage passenger who will take charge of it to Philadelphia. I have taken on myself all charges to Baltimore. Accept assurances of my esteem & respect   TH: JEFFERSON

RC (DGU: Presidential Autograph Collection); addressed: "Mʳ Bernard MᶜMahon Philadelphia"; franked; postmarked Charlottesville, 26 July; endorsed by McMahon. PoC (DLC); on verso of a portion of an unidentified document in an unknown hand, reading in its entirety "Directions for Aggy"; endorsed by TJ.

To James Madison

DEAR SIR   Monticello July 23. 15.

One of those cases now occurs which oblige me to relax from my general wish not to add to your troubles in the disposal of offices. I inclose you the papers which produce the occasion, and they will present to you all the grounds of interest which I can possibly feel in the success of the application. they will have with you exactly the weight they intrinsically merit & no more.   Accept the assurance of my constant friendship and respect   TH: JEFFERSON

RC (DLC: Madison Papers); endorsed by Madison. PoC (MHi); on verso of reused address cover to TJ; at foot of text: "The President of the US."; endorsed by TJ. Enclosures: Obadiah Rich to TJ, 15 July 1815, and third enclosure to that letter.

To Obadiah Rich

SIR   Monticello July 23. 15.

I thank you for the botanical synopsis you have been so kind as to send me. it is a science to which I was formerly much attached; but long abstraction from it by other duties has lessened my familiarity with it. it is too a science peculiarly addressed to the memory, a faculty among the first which suffers decay from years. I still however recieve the synopsis thankfully as a mark of your kind attention, and an evidence of your science in so valuable a branch of knolege

I now write to the President on the subject of your request of the Consulship of Malaga, and forward to him the recommendations recieved with your letter. whether the place be vacant or not, I am not informed. possession of it in another would certainly be an obstacle of weight, as yourself would wish it to be should you recieve the appointment. if vacant the respectability of your recommendations will undoubtedly command attention. with my best wishes for your success, Accept the assurance of my great respect

TH: JEFFERSON

PoC (MHi); on verso of reused address cover of Peter A. Guestier to TJ, 12 July 1815; with most of a line of text repeated due to a malfunction of the polygraph and then canceled by TJ; at foot of text: "Mr Oliver Rich"; endorsed by TJ as a letter to "Rich Oliver" and so recorded in SJL.

To Samuel Smith (of Maryland)

DEAR SIR   Monticello July 23. 15.

Before the reciept of your favor of July 14. I had recieved one from Govr Nicholas on the same subject; had answered it and written to the President. I stated to mr Nicholas, that mr Appleton had been appointed by the old Congress on my sollicitation to the Consulship of Leghorn; had been confirmed by Genl Washington, on my recommendation also, at the commencement of this government; that he had now held the office near 30. years, and had never done any thing within my knolege, incurring blame from the government; and that therefore no principle of morality would permit me to sollicit his removal, however ready I was to do any thing for himself or any member of his family which was just or honorable: that I had learned that mr Appleton had sollicited a removal to another Consulship, in which if he had been succesful, that of Leghorn was of course vacant, and certainly no one more worthy of it than Colo Nicholas; and that on the hypothesis of a vacancy I would write to the President: and I did so. whether the place was vacant or not I have not learnt; but I am sure, if it was, that the president's friendship to Govr Nicholas and his knolege of the merits of the son will ensure him the appointment.   The atrocious & disorganising enterprize of the allied powers against the independance of France has made me at length a sincere votary for success to Bonaparte. he is now engaged in a cause the reverse of that he has heretofore acted in: and if they succeed in carving Europe up into new divisions and regulating their governments we can expect no other favor than that of being last devoured. with my affectionate respects to your brother accept the same for yourself, with an assurance of my gratification with every opportunity of repeating them   TH: JEFFERSON

PoC (DLC); on verso of reused address cover from Patrick Gibson (in James Ligon's hand) to TJ; at foot of text: "Genl Saml Smith"; endorsed by TJ.

In Homer's *Odyssey*, bk. 9, the cyclops Polyphemus offered Ulysses the privilege of BEING LAST DEVOURED.

From Pierre Samuel Du Pont de Nemours

Eleutherian Mill near Wilmington delaware 24 Juillet 1815.

TRÈS CHER ET TRÈS RESPECTABLE AMI,

Nous devions partir demain le bon Corréa et moi pour vous voir à Mounticello. Nous n'avons pu être plus tot prêts l'un et l'autre.

Mais comme il fallait passer à Washington, et nous y arrêter un peu, nous avons craint que le moindre accident arrivé en route ne nous retardât, et ne nous fit nous présenter à votre Porte qu'après votre départ que vous nous avez annoncé pour le 6 august, ou Si près de ce moment que nous vous gênassions ou vous dérangeassions.

Nous remettons ce Voyage, qui nous fera tant de plaisir, jusqu'à votre retour Sur lequel nous comptons du 6 au 10 octobre.

J'ai un extrême désir de vous voir: et j'espere le pouvoir tous les ans, car je ne quitterai plus l'Amérique.

Agréez mon bien respectueux attachement.

DUPONT (DE NEMOURS)

EDITORS' TRANSLATION

Eleutherian Mill near Wilmington delaware 24 July 1815.

VERY DEAR AND VERY RESPECTABLE FRIEND,

The good Corrêa and I were to leave tomorrow to come see you at Monticello. Neither of us were ready any earlier than this.

As we need to pass through Washington and stay there awhile, we feared that the slightest accident on the road would delay us and cause us to present ourselves at your door either after your departure, which you had told us would take place on 6 August, or so close to that time that we would bother or upset you.

We are therefore postponing this trip, which will give us so much pleasure, until your return, which we expect will be between 6 and 10 October.

I want very much to see you, and I hope to be able to do so every year, as I will never leave America again.

Accept my most respectful attachment. DUPONT (DE NEMOURS)

RC (DLC); endorsed by TJ as received 28 July 1815 and so recorded in SJL. RC (MHi); address cover only; with PoC of TJ to Henry Sheaff, 11 Aug. 1815, on verso; addressed: "Th. Jefferson, Esqre late President of the United States, Mounticello"; franked; postmarked Wilmington, Del., 25 July. Tr (DeGH: Henry A. du Pont Papers, Winterthur Manuscripts); posthumous copy. Translation by Dr. Genevieve Moene.

From William Wirt

Dear Sir.   Richmond. July 24. 1815.

Henry's resolutions, as given by Judge Marshall, were copied from Prior Documents. Your conjecture that the 5th resolution was the 5th as offered by Mr Henry, or at all events that which produced "the bloody debate" derives great strength from the resolutions of Rhode Island of which I enclose you a copy. These were obviously copied with a few slight variations from the Resolutions of Virginia, and retain the 5th resolution which was expunged here. But how did this 5th resolution get to Rhode Island, having been expunged from our Journals?—probably by a letter from George Johnston, or some other patriot in our house. I think you are mistaken in supposing that George Johnston wrote the resolutions. Mr Edmund Randolph has left a history of Virginia in which he says that William Fleming wrote them. And Mr Henry, on the back of the resolutions left by him, of which I sent you a copy, expressly says that he wrote them himself on the blank leaf of an old law book, and shewed them only to George Johnston and William Fleming before they were offered to the house. Judge Tyler says on the parol statement of Mr Henry, that they were written by him on the blank leaf of an old Coke upon Littleton. Nor does it seem to me that the style of the resolutions is at all above Mr Henry, but, on the contrary, very much like him. There remain in the office of the clerk of the House of Delegates several of his original letters fully equal to the Resolutions in point of composition.—

It would form a very interesting back ground to the portrait of Henry in exhibiting his resolutions, to give a sketch of the distinguished members who opposed them. I have been attempting some, of whom I write by information, without the aid of any personal knowledge, save the little which I saw of Mr Pendleton and Mr Wythe after they were in ruins. Will you take the trouble to examine these sketches of character and to correct or to enlarge[1] them where they require it.—You have not the journal of '65—I send you a list of the members, and beg you to give me a sketch of any others who may strike you as deserving it. Landon Carter was a writer. I have seen his pamphlet in support of the Two Penny act, and thought it very well—I have been able to learn nothing more of him. Mr Thomas L. Lee is highly spoken of by Mr E. Randolph; but not as a public speaker. I would be obliged to you to mark off those of the members who were considered as composing the aristocracy of the day. and if you could add a statement of the differences between the classes of society and the lines of demarcation which seperated them, you would oblige me very much.

Will you give me leave to found myself on your statements in the following particulars—1st in regard to the project of the loan office and its defeat—2 In regard to Josiah Philips—and 3rdly as to the addresses from congress prepared by Henry & Lee, and superseded by those from Jay & Dickinson?—You may rely upon it that I shall make no use of your name, except so far as you may permit it.—

I do not perceive that Robert C. Nicholas was a member of the House in '65—Edmund Randolph says that he came in, on the death of Peyton Randolph, and, in his place, as the delegate for Wms Burg. The interest which you take in every thing that relates to the history and character of Your country, saves me the necessity of those frequent apologies which I should otherwise feel myself bound to make to you for the[2] trouble I give you.

It has just occurred to me that as you saw Mr Henry in 59–60 it will be in your power to give me a more distinct picture of his mind, information & manners at that period, than any other person who has described him to me—That was three years before his display in the parson's cause—before he had studied the law and before his talent for public speaking is said to have been dreamed of—Will you be so good as to tell me how he struck you at that time.

your much obliged friend & servant   WM WIRT

P.S. The manuscript Journal of '65 is not to be found.—Philips was indicted, tried convicted & executed[3] for Robbery. I have now the original indictment with the names of the witnesses before me and will send you a copy if you desire it.

RC (DLC); addressed: "Mr Jefferson"; endorsed by TJ as received 31 July 1815 and so recorded in SJL. Tr (MdHi: Wirt Papers); misdated 21 July 1815.

Patrick Henry's Stamp Act RESOLUTIONS were given in John Marshall, *The Life of George Washington* (Philadelphia, 1804–07; Sowerby, no. 496), vol. 2, backmatter, pp. 25–7, which copied them from *A Collection of Interesting, Authentic Papers, relative to the Dispute between Great Britain and America* (London, 1777), 6–7. The earlier work was often referred to by its running head, PRIOR DOCUMENTS.

At his death in 1813, Edmund Randolph left a manuscript of his as yet unpublished HISTORY OF VIRGINIA, which Wirt borrowed from the family while writing his biography of Henry (Randolph, *History of Virginia*, ed. Arthur H. Shaffer [1970]; Wirt, *Sketches of the Life and Character of Patrick Henry* [Philadelphia, 1817; Poor, *Jefferson's Library*, 4 (no. 131)]). Wirt enclosed a COPY of Henry's resolutions in a 27 July 1814 letter to TJ. Henry reputedly wrote the resolutions on the BLANK LEAF of a copy of Edward Coke, *The First Part of the Institutes of the Lawes of England: or A Commentary upon Littleton* (4th ed., London, 1639, and other eds.; Sowerby, no. 1781).

TJ's 5 Aug. 1815 reply shows that Wirt enclosed draft SKETCHES OF CHARACTER, not found, of Henry's contemporary burgesses. TJ had relayed anecdotes about the PROJECT OF THE LOAN OFFICE AND ITS DEFEAT and the ADDRESSES FROM CONGRESS in his Notes on Patrick Henry, printed above at 12 Apr. 1812. ROBERT C. NICHOLAS served regularly in the Virginia legislature from 1756 to 1778, except for the 1761–65 General Assembly (Leonard, *General Assembly*). PEYTON RANDOLPH died on 22 Oct. 1775

(*ANB*). Edmund Randolph did not serve as a DELEGATE in the Fourth Virginia Convention, 1 Dec. 1775–20 Jan. 1776, but he did represent Williamsburg in the Fifth Convention, 6 May–5 July 1776 (Leonard, *General Assembly*).

[1] Preceding three words interlined.
[2] Wirt here canceled "frequency."
[3] Preceding two words interlined.

E N C L O S U R E

William Wirt's Notes on Membership in the Virginia House of Burgesses and the Rhode Island Stamp Act Resolves

[ca. 24 July 1815]

On a more attentive persual, I find that the Journal of '64 which you have, contains the names of the members who composed the house of burgesses in '65. So that it becomes unnecessary to send you the list of members promised in my letter. On the first day of May '65 being the first of the session, 4 new writs of election were moved for. 1st for Chesterfield to supply the place of Richard Eppes who had died. 2nd for Amelia, to supply that of Mr Greenhill who had accepted the place of Sheriff. 3rd for Lunenburg, to supply that of Mr Clement Read, appointed coroner. and 4th for Louisa, in the room of William Johnston also appointed coroner. The tradition is that Colo. Johnston vacated his seat for the express purpose of letting in Henry to oppose the Stamp act. The first appearance of a new member on either of those writs is on the 18th May. the name of the member is not given. On monday the 20th another member appeared and then it is added—"Ordered that Mr Ward be added to the committee of claims—and Mr Henry to the courts of justice." Henry's first appearance therefore was on the 18th or 20th of May. Other writs of election had been moved for after the 1st of May, and in the course of the session the new members took their seats from time to time; but no farther[1] notice is taken of names 'till the 30th of May when there is an order that Mr Read, Mr Carrington, Mr William Taylor & Mr Robert Munford should be added to a committee This is all the information which the journal of 65 affords as to the new members.

By the Pennsylvania Gazette of August 29. 1765—Printed by B. Franklin Postmaster, and D. Hall, It appears, that the town of Providence on the 13th of that month instructed their[2] Deputies in General assembly to insist on the exclusive[3] right of the colony to tax itself, and proposed a set of resolutions, which were afterwards adopted, in substance & nearly in words, by the Assembly, as follows—(Resolutions of Rhode I. & P. P. extracted from the P. Gazette of 26. Sept. '65)[4]
1. That the first adventurers, settlers of this his Majesty's Colony and Dominion of Rhode Island and Providence Plantations, brought with them and

transmitted to their Posterity, and all other his Majesty's Subjects, since inhabating in this his Majesty's Colony, all the Privileges and Immunities that have at any time been held, enjoyed and possessed by the People of Great Britain

2. That by a charter, granted by King Charles the Second, in the 15th year of his Reign,[5] the Colony aforesaid is declared intitled to all Privileges and Immunities of natural born Subjects, to all Intents and Purposes, as if they had been abiding and born within the Realm of England.

3. That his majesty's liege people of this Colony have enjoyed the Right of being governed by their own Assembly in the Article of Taxes and internal Police; and that the same have never been forfeited or any other Way yielded up, but have been constantly recognized by the King & People of Great Britain.

4. That therefore[6] the General Assembly of this Colony have in their Representative[7] Capacity, the only exclusive Right to lay Taxes and Imposts upon the Inhabitants of this Colony: and that Every Attempt to vest such Power in any Person or Persons whatever[8] other than the General Assembly aforesaid is unconstitutional, and hath a manifest Tendency to destroy[9] the Liberties of the People of this Colony.

5. That his Majesty's liege People the Inhabitants of this Colony are not bound to yield Obedience to any Law or Ordinance designed to impose any internal Taxation whatsoever upon them other than the Laws or Ordinances of the General Assembly, aforesaid.[10]

6. That all the officers in this colony appointed by the authority thereof be and they are hereby directed to proceed in the execution of their respective offices in the same manner as usual: and that this assembly will indemnify and save harmless all the said officers on account of their conduct agreable to this Resolution.

MS (DLC: TJ Papers, 204:36368–9); in Wirt's hand; undated; endorsed by Wirt: "Members of the house of Burgesses of Virginia in 1765. and Resolutions of R. Island, in the same year."

A 13 Aug. 1765 town meeting in Providence, Rhode Island, INSTRUCTED its representatives to propose a series of resolves on the Stamp Act to the Rhode Island General Assembly (*Providence Gazette*, extraordinary ed., 24 Aug. 1765, repr. in *Pennsylvania Gazette*, 29 Aug. 1765). At its session the following month the legislature passed a set of similar resolutions, which were printed in that year's session laws (*September, 1765. At the General Assembly Of the Governor and Company of the English Colony of Rhode-Island, and Providence Plantations . . . begun and holden [by Adjournment] at East-Greenwich . . .* [Newport, 1765], 59–60) and EXTRACTED with only minor

differences in the *Pennsylvania Gazette*, 26 Sept. 1765, from which Wirt copied. Significant differences between the Providence resolves (as given in the *Providence Gazette*) and those adopted by the Rhode Island General Assembly are noted below.

[1] Word interlined.
[2] Wirt here canceled "Delegates."
[3] Word interlined.
[4] Omitted closing parenthesis editorially supplied.
[5] Providence resolve from this point reads "it is declared and granted unto the Governor and Company of this Colony, and their Successors, that all and every the Subjects of his said Majesty, his Heirs and Successors, which were then planted within the said Colony, or which should thereafter go to inhabit within the said Colony, and all and every of their Children, which had been born there, or

which should afterwards be born there, or on the Sea going thither, or returning from thence, should have and enjoy all Liberties and Immunities of free and natural Subjects within any the Dominions of his said Majesty, his Heirs or Successors; to all Intents, Constructions, and Purposes, whatsoever, as if they and every of them were born within the Realm of *England*."

[6] Providence resolve here adds "his Majesty or his Substitutes, together with."
[7] Wirt here canceled "character."
[8] Providence resolve: "whatsoever."
[9] Providence resolve from this point reads "*British*, as well as *American* Liberty."
[10] Providence resolves end here.

From John M. Carter

RESPECTED SIR,   Georgetown, (D.C.) July 25th 1815.

The favor with which you honored me, in acknowledging the receipt of a copy of Co[l] Taylor's Arator, which I had forwarded by Mail, to you, came duly to hand, and I am grateful for your attention to the liberty I took, inasmuch as I am so far afforded an opportunity to offer you my services as a Printer, if I can be useful to you in the line of my profession.—A report has reached me, that the Hon. Tho[s] M. Randolph is preparing for publication some answer or criticism to Arator, he having taken some personal exceptions at some passages of it.—As I have not the honor of being personally known to this gentleman, may I ask it as a particular favor of you, Sir, (from your convenience to him) to represent me and my profession to him, with a view to serve him in his publication if he should desire it? I feel myself equal or better qualified to this end, than any other person of my profession, that I know of, if I may suppose that M[r] R. should be desirous for his publication to take the same range or distribution that Arator has done, with a view to an equal hearing;—as a knowledge of which rests alone with me,—and I would use every means in my power to publish and circulate the work in question, with the utmost facility.

I would avail this opportunity also, Sir, barely to acquaint you with an intimation I have had, concerning a Correspondence in which you are engaged with the Hon. John Adams of Massachusetts, which, when concluded, may be designed for publication—in which event, I should consider myself highly favored with the execution of it.

I beg you, Sir, to accept my best respects, And am your very ob[t] Serv[t]   JNO. M. CARTER.

RC (MHi); at foot of text: "Hon. Thos. Jefferson Monticello"; endorsed by TJ as received 3 Aug. 1815 and so recorded in SJL.

From John Robertson

SIR   July 27th 1815

Since I saw you I have been informed that m[r] Willson intends continuing his School in milton for another year I do not think that the place could maintain two schools and that there may be no clashing of interest—I must for the present decline accepting the very generous offer You did me the honour to make of your house, offices, &c

Be pleased to accept my hearty thanks, & believe me to be your most Humble & Ob[t] Ser[t]   JOHN ROBERTSON

RC (MHi); dateline beneath signature; addressed: "M[r] Jefferson Monticello"; endorsed by TJ as received 5 Aug. 1815 and so recorded in SJL.

John Robertson (1767–1818), teacher, was born in Govan, near Glasgow, Scotland, and immigrated to the United States about 1791. TJ considered him an excellent teacher of the classics. Robertson kept schools in both Albemarle and Culpeper counties, and at the time of his death he was employed as a tutor at Springfield, the Culpeper County estate of Philip Slaughter. An inventory of Robertson's personal property listed more than 450 volumes in his library and valued them at $1,038.68, more than half of a total value of $1,835.60 that also included two slaves (Lindsay G. Robertson, "Robertsons of Virginia, 1791–1987: John Robertson, Sarah Brand and their Descendants" [1987 typescript in ViCAHi], 1–7; Woods, *Albemarle*, 86, 149; TJ to John Wayles Eppes, 18 Apr. 1813; Raleigh Travers Green, *Genealogical and Historical Notes on Culpeper County, Virginia* [1900], 24; Albemarle Co. Will Book, 7:33–8; *Richmond Enquirer*, 20 Oct. 1818).

To Patrick Gibson

DEAR SIR   Monticello July 28. 15

Your favor of the 5th is recieved and enabled me to send off my letters for Paris through mr Vaughan. I had been assured by the miller at the Shadwell mills that 213. Barrels of flour had been sent off on my account[1] addressed to you. it was in payment of a year's rent of the mills. your letter was the first notice that the whole had not gone to you, and setting me on further enquiry I found that on some sudden necessity, a boatload of it had been changed in it's destination. I was assured it would be replaced as soon as they resume grinding. my grandson being Collector of the federal taxes here, it has been a mutual convenience when I have had occasions to draw on you, to recieve the money from him and give him the draught on you. it saves us both the risk of transmissions by the post. my letter of the 1st instant mentioned such a draught for 167.D. and I have now recieved 230.D. from him for which I have given a draught on you. he will be in Richmond nearly as soon as this letter and will present both. the last is made on the assurance of your letter that my note for 1000 D. will be discounted. the bale of cotton is recieved. Accept the assurances of my esteem and respect   TH: JEFFERSON

PoC (DLC: TJ Papers, ser. 10); on verso of reused address cover of John Adams to TJ, 20 June 1815; mutilated at seal, with missing text supplied by TJ above the line; at foot of text: "Mr Gibson"; endorsed by TJ.

Thomas Mann Randolph and Thomas Eston Randolph owed TJ 213 BARRELS OF FLOUR for the yearly rent due on their lease of TJ's manufacturing mill at Shadwell (TJ to Thomas Eston Randolph, 20 Jan. 1815). TJ's GRANDSON was Thomas Jefferson Randolph.

[1] Preceding three words interlined.

From John Vaughan

D^R SIR   Philad. July 28. 1815
    I recieved your favor of July 11. & shewd your letter to Mr Girard & then enclosed him a Copy, as he proposed given a Credit upon Mr Moreton of Bordeaux or order to him to arrange the business—I wrote him a note requesting that he would furnish me with a Copy of the Credit, which I could multiply & forward agreeably to your Directions, at same time I Sent him the 550$ that no time might be lost; I have not yet recieved any reply from him, as Soon as I do I shall miss no opp^y of forwarding Copies—As soon as the Dft rem^d by M^r P Gibson is paid, ballance payble to B. Jones shall be Sent to him.
    I remain with respect &a   JN VAUGHAN

As I am known to Mr Moreton there will be no difficulty in the Copies I give

RC (MHi); endorsed by TJ as received 3 Aug. 1815 and so recorded in SJL.   REM^D: "remitted."

From John Adams

DEAR SIR   Quincy July 30th 1815
    Who shall write the history of the American revolution? Who can write it? Who will ever be able to write it?
    The most essential documents, the debates & deliberations in Congress from 1774 to 1783 were all in secret, and are now lost forever. Mr Dickinson printed a speech, which he said he made in Congress against the Declaration of Independence; but it appeared to me very

different from that, which you, and I heard. Dr Witherspoon has published speeches which he wrote beforehand, and delivered Memoriter, as he did his Sermons. But these I believe, are the only speeches ever committed to writing. The Orators, while I was in Congress from 1774 to 1778 appeared to me very universally extemporaneous, & I have never heard of any committed to writing before or after delivery.

These questions have been suggested to me, by a Review, in the Analectic Magazine for May 1815, published in Philadelphia, page 385 of the Chevalier Botta's "Storia della Guerra Americana." The Reviewers inform us, that it is the best history of the revolution that ever has been written. This Italian Classick has followed the example, of the Greek and Roman Historians, by composing speeches, for his Generals and Orators. The Reviewers have translated, one of Mr R H Lee, in favour of the declaration of Independence. A splendid morcell of oratory it is; how faithful, you can judge.

I wish to know your sentiments, and opinions of this publication.[1] Some future Miss Porter, may hereafter, make as shining a romance, of what passed in Congress, while in Conclave, as her Scottish Chiefs.

Your friend durante Vita[2]   JOHN ADAMS

Tr (1957 typescript taken from unlocated RC, Adams Papers Editorial Files, MHi); adjacent to signature: "His Excellency Thomas Jefferson"; with editorial note at foot of text: "Signed in JA's hand; text of letter in hand of unidentified amenuensis"; with editorial note that TJ endorsed it as received 9 Aug. 1815. RC (DLC); address cover only; with PoC of TJ to John Graham, 17 Aug. 1815, on verso; addressed in an unidentified hand: "His Excellency Thomas Jefferson Esqre Monticello. Virginia"; franked by Adams; postmarked Quincy, 31 July. FC (Lb in MHi: Adams Papers); at foot of text: "His Excellency Govr McKean"; adjacent to signature, in Adams's hand: "N.B. The same to Jefferson." Recorded in SJL as received 9 Aug. 1815.

John DICKINSON presented his reasons for opposing independence in 1776 in a vindication that appeared in the Philadelphia *Freeman's Journal: or, the North-American Intelligencer,* 1 Jan. 1783. For TJ's contemporaneous summary of the arguments given against independence by Dickinson and others on 8 June 1776, see *PTJ,* 1:309–11. Congressional speeches by John WITHERSPOON were published in John Rodgers, ed., *The Works of the Rev. John Witherspoon,* 2d ed. (Philadelphia, 1802; for 1st ed. see Sowerby, no. 1558), 4:317–57. The TRANSLATED speech of Richard Henry Lee appears in the *Analectic Magazine* 5 (1815): 388–93. Jane PORTER wrote *The Scottish Chiefs, A Romance,* 5 vols. (London, 1810, and other eds.). DURANTE VITA: "during life."

On this date Adams wrote Thomas McKean a letter that varied from the one to TJ only in spelling, punctuation, and capitalization (RC in PHi: McKean Papers; addressed in an unidentified hand: "His Excellency Thomas McKean Philadelphia"; franked; postmarked Quincy, 31 July; endorsed by McKean).

[1] Tr: "publications." FC: "publication."
[2] FC: "vitæ."

From Stephen Girard

SIR   Philad: 30th July 1815.

On the 23^d instant I had the honour to receive your Letter of the 10th Same month, which Shall be attended to, by remitting to Mr John Vaughan a Letter of Credit on Messrs Perregaux Laffitte & Co of Paris for Three Hundred and Fifty Dollars in favour of Mr George Ticknor of Boston, and one for Two Hundred Dollars, in favour of Stephen Cathalan of Marseilles. If an additional Sum is wanted to compleat the purchase of the Books, it will be advanced to Mr Ticknor

Mr John Vaughan has paid me Five Hundred and Fifty Dollars[1] placed to your Credit.

With great Respect Your ob^t Servt.   STEPH^N GIRARD

RC (NNPM); dateline beneath signature; at foot of text: "Th^s Jefferson Esqre"; endorsed by TJ as received 9 Aug. 1815 and so recorded in SJL. RC (ICHi); address cover only; with PoC of TJ to Patrick Gibson, 19 Aug. 1815, on verso; addressed (trimmed) to "Thomas Jeff[erson] Mont[icello]"; postmarked Philadelphia, 1 Aug. FC (Lb in PPGi: Girard Papers [microfilm at PPAmP]).

[1] FC here adds "to be."

To William Wardlaw

DEAR SIR   Monticello July 30. 15.

Your favor of the 22^d is recieved and gave me the first information that mr Michie was in this county. I had yesterday a Notice duly served, so that I have only now to request the further trouble of countermanding that in the hands of the town serjeant; which being for different days from those now served, would produce mischief & confusion. indeed I would wish him to put them under cover to me by mail.

Mr Norris has been in our neighborhood & has left it. I did not see or hear from him while here; but I sent to the stage offices & post offices of Milton & Charlottesville & to mr Norris's lodgings in the latter place, and could learn nothing of the Lemon-acid which your letter expected would come under his charge. I mention this as he may perhaps have left it in the Stage office in Richmond. I salute you with friendship and respect   TH: JEFFERSON

PoC (DLC); on verso of reused address cover to TJ; at foot of text: "Doct^r Wardlaw"; endorsed by TJ.

From Fontaine Maury

Dear Sir   July 31. 1815
My Nephew James Maury of Liverpool having been charged by his Father to give you a call before his return to England, and he being now about to accompany[1] my Sister Matilda to the Springs I avail myself of the opportunity of making them both known to you— with real Esteem I am

Dear Sir Your mo ob   Fontaine Maury

RC (MHi); addressed: "Thomas Jefferson Esq[r]" care of "Master Maury"; endorsed by TJ as received 1 Aug. 1815 and so recorded (adding that it was delivered "by James Maury j[r]") in SJL.

James Sifrein Maury (1797–1864) was born in Liverpool, England, the eldest son of James Maury, longtime United States consul there and TJ's childhood friend. At the time of young Maury's first visit to Virginia, his father described his poor physical condition, and other family letters confirm that he was frail. He went back to England in about 1819, returned to the United States in 1822, and settled near Fredericksburg. In 1825 Maury purchased Ridgemont, a 164½-acre property in Albemarle County. He sold this farm in 1833 (Anne Fontaine Maury, ed., *Intimate Virginiana: A Century of Maury Travels by Land and Sea* [1941], 53–70, 319; James Maury to TJ, 9 Sept. 1815, 24 Sept. 1821, 24 June 1822; James S. Maury correspondence, esp. Maury to James Maury, 30 Apr. 1822, and to Ann Maury, 16 Feb. 1828 [ViU: James Maury Papers]; Albemarle Co. Deed Book, 25:80–1, 27:124–5, 31:33; Woods, *Albemarle*, 269).

The sister was Matilda Hill Maury Eggleston (Maury, *Intimate Virginiana*, 318).

[1] Manuscript: "accopany."

From Joseph Milligan

Dear Sir   Georgetown July 31st 1815
on the 13th instant ℔ steam boat I sent to the care of William Woodford Eqr innkeeper of Fredericksburg two Boxes which I have directed him to have forwarded to you by the mail cart without delay

they Contain Such books as I have had bound for you as ℔ enclosed list of Binding I have also enclosed a list of the Laws of Virginia and the Journals of the Senate which I have to bind for you I do not believe that I shall be able to get the Volumes of the Journal of the Senate that are missing there is in one of the Boxes a copy of Dufiefs Dictionary and one paris in 1802 & 1814 also a Ream of paper Cut down to pattern as ℔ order

I have not yet got Tracys manuscript but have had a letter from Gen[l] Duane on the Subject he is to Send it to M[r] R. C. Weightman of Washington who is to receive $60– from me and deliver it to me he only waits Some private hand to Send it by

The Library arrived in safety in Washington on Monday morning[1] of next week after I left Monticello that is in Six days from the time it was put into the wagons it was safely Laid into the passages of the General post office or Congress hall about three weeks ago I Commenced unpacking it and accomplished it last monday I am happy to inform you that it has not received the Slightest injury by transportation the Room which has been appropriated for it is sufficeently large the Catalogue will be printed as soon as a Suitable paper can be procured to print it on it is the intention to print in Quarto on post paper

I have been very much indisposed through out the whole of the month of June So much So as not to be equil to any business which is the cause that your books were not sent back Sooner or your letters attend to with regularity but I have now so far recovered my health as to attend to my usual business indeed the exertion which it required to set up the library seems to have been of service to me as I[2] gained Strength every day

    With respect yours

JOSEPH MILLIGAN

RC (DLC); endorsed by TJ as received 9 Aug. 1815 and so recorded in SJL.

ONE OF THE BOXES sent by Milligan contained William Shepherd, *Paris, in Eighteen Hundred And Two, and Eighteen Hundred And Fourteen* (Philadelphia, 1815; Poor, *Jefferson's Library*, 7 [no. 323]). The first wagonloads of books from TJ's library ARRIVED IN SAFETY at Washington on Monday, 8 May 1815 (Washington *Daily National Intelligencer*, 9 May 1815). Milligan ACCOMPLISHED the unpacking on Monday, 24 July 1815.

[1] Manuscript: "mornng."
[2] Milligan here canceled "seemed to."

E N C L O S U R E

Joseph Milligan's List of Books Bound and To Be Bound

[ca. 31 July 1815]

A List of Books Bound for Thos Jefferson Esq

prices currant 1812 & 1813 folio Boards	$1 25
1809 & 13 4to	1 00
Universal History La Croze 3 N° folio ½ Bound	1 50
Pamphlets Agricultural 4to Boards	0 37½
Tracts Physics 8 Nos 4to ½ ¹ Bound	1 50
Pamphlets Physics 8 Nos 8v ½ Bound	0 62½
Arts 8vo 28 Nos very Thick	0 75

American Historical Pamphlets 5 N°s 8vo Boards	0	37$\frac{1}{2}$
History 8vo 7^{Nos} Boards	0	37$\frac{1}{2}$
Historical Pamphlets English 3^{Nos} 8vo Boards	0	37$\frac{1}{2}$
Iroquois 8vo 2 N^{os} $\frac{1}{2}$ Bound	0	62$\frac{1}{2}$
Spanish Grammar 12mo 2 N^{os} $\frac{1}{2}$ bound	0	50
Wythes decisions folio $\frac{1}{2}$ Bound	1	00
Pamphlets Medical 8vo 10 N^{os} $\frac{1}{2}$ Bound	0	62$\frac{1}{2}$
Education 5 N°s 8vo $\frac{1}{2}$ Bound	0	62$\frac{1}{2}$
Lysias 2 Vols 8vo full Bound	1	50
Jeffersons Notes 8vo full Bound	0	75
Natural Law 8vo 4^{Nos} $\frac{1}{2}$ Bound	0	62$\frac{1}{2}$
Æsop 8vo full Bound	0	75
Isocrates 3 vols 8vo full Bound	2	25
Aristophanes 18mo 2 vols fancy Binding	1	50
Sagesse de chîarron 12mo 3 vols	1	50
Orations 18mo Red morocco gilt edges	1	25
Gramatica de La lingua plain calf for Miss Randolph	0	62$\frac{1}{2}$
Ideology de Tracy bound to Pattern	1	00
Revised bills 1792 folio $\frac{1}{2}$ Bound	1	00
Revised code 1779^2 folio full Bound	1	25
Religious Pamphlets 12mo 14 N^{os} $\frac{1}{2}$ bound	0	50
Geographical Pamphlets 8vo 7 N^{os} $\frac{1}{2}$ bound	0	62$\frac{1}{2}$
Political Pamphlets 8vo 12 Nos $\frac{1}{2}$ Bound	0	62$\frac{1}{2}$
Sermons 22 Nos 8vo $\frac{1}{2}$ Bound	0	62$\frac{1}{2}$
Pamphlets Agricultural^3 4to 9 N^o $\frac{1}{2}$ Bound	1	00
Fine Arts 14 N°s 8vo	0	62$\frac{1}{2}$
Unitarian 3 Nos 8vo $\frac{1}{2}$ Bound	0	50
Randolphs abridgement 2 N°s 4to $\frac{1}{2}$ Bound	1	00
Zoology 4 Nos 8vo $\frac{1}{2}$ Bound	0	62$\frac{1}{2}$
Pamphlets Ethics 9 N°s 8vo $\frac{1}{2}$ Bound	0	62$\frac{1}{2}$
Education 8vo $\frac{1}{2}$ Bound	0	62$\frac{1}{2}$
Encyclopaedia 8vo 4 N^{os} Boards^4	0	37$\frac{1}{2}$^{5}
prices currant 1796–9 4to Boards	1	00^6
Amount carried over	\$34–25^7	
State papers 1813–1815 8vo Boards	00	37$\frac{1}{2}$
Orations 1810–14 27 N°s 8vo $\frac{1}{2}$ Bound	00	62$\frac{1}{2}$
3 Pamphlets not lettered 12mo $\frac{1}{2}$ Bound	00	50
Politics spanish^8 6 N°s 8vo $\frac{1}{2}$ Bound	00–62$\frac{1}{2}$	
Jays Treaty 12mo $\frac{1}{2}$ Bound	00	37$\frac{1}{2}$
Review of Blackstone 8vo full Bound	00	75
News papers 4to 1795–6 Boards	1	00
Economie Politique 2 vols 8vo bound the Same as Ideology de Tracy (Calf Gilt)	2–00	
Grays Poems 4to bound red morocco	5–00	
Ovedii 18mo		
Reflections Sur la posie 12mo } Fancy bound	\$3 00	
Lucian 2 vols 18mo		
Bellendeni 8vo full bound	0–75	
one Octavo & 1 Duodecimo for Mr Randolph	1–25	
	\$50–50^9	

Journals of the Senate of the U states
2nd Session of the 3 Congress

1st	4th
Ist	5th
Ist	7th
2nd	7th
2nd10	8th
1st	9th
2nd	9th
1st	10th

Journal of the House of Representatives[11] of the United States
First Session of the Fourth[12] Congress

[Remainder of document written perpendicularly to above text:]

Acts of the General Assembly[13] of the State of Virginia
for 1734
6
8
1740
1752
3
9
1760
1
3
4
5 part missing
6
9
1771
2
5
1781
4
5
7 two copies
8
9
1790
1
2
3
4
5
6
9
1800
2
3
4
5

$$6$$
$$7 \text{ passed Jany}$$
Commencing[14] Decembr 7th 1807
$$\underline{8}$$
$$10$$
$$11$$
$$12$$
$$13^{15}$$

MS (DLC: TJ Papers, 204:36420–1); entirely in Milligan's hand; undated; repeated intermediate sum at head of p. 2 omitted; with Milligan's note on p. 4: "Memorandum of Binding and of Books imperfect retainded to be bound when Complete."

The items listed include PRICES CURRANT: *Hope's Philadelphia Price-Current, and Commercial Record* (Poor, *Jefferson's Library*, 12 [no. 713]; TJ's copy at PPL); a UNIVERSAL HISTORY, probably that described in the 1829 sale of TJ's library as "La Croix' Abridgment of Universal History, fol. MS" (Poor, *Jefferson's Library*, 3 [no. 2]); and a work on wisdom (SAGESSE): Pierre Charron, *De la Sagesse* (Paris, 1621; Poor, *Jefferson's Library*, 9 [no. 462]). PATTERN refers to the grain of binding cloths, which came in a variety of designs (Philip Gaskell, *A New Introduction to Bibliography* [1995], 238–47).

TJ also had Milligan bind a work on ECONOMIE POLITIQUE: Jean Baptiste Say, *Traité d'Économie Politique* (2 vols., Paris, 1803, Sowerby, no. 3547; 2 vols., 2d ed., Paris, 1814, Poor, *Jefferson's Library*, 11 [no. 697], TJ's copy at ViU).

[1] Manuscript: "$\frac{1}{2}$ $\frac{1}{2}$."
[2] Reworked from "1799."
[3] Manuscript: "Agricultiral."
[4] Reworked from "$\frac{1}{2}$ Bound."
[5] Reworked from "0 62$\frac{1}{2}$."
[6] Reworked from "0 37$\frac{1}{2}$."
[7] First page ends here.
[8] Word interlined.
[9] Second page ends here.
[10] Manuscript: "2^{n}."
[11] Manuscript: "Representaties."
[12] Manuscript: "Fouth."
[13] Manuscript: "Assenbly."
[14] Manuscript: "Comnencing."
[15] Third page ends here.

From John Vaughan

D SIR   Philad. July 31. 1815

I have received from M Girard a letter for You which I commit to the Mail & two letters of Credit ℔ Duplicate—on Peregaux Lafitte & C° Paris 350$ to Mr Geo Ticknor & to Mr Stephen Catalan 200$—I have Sent them by the Adeline & by the Andrew—former to Bord^x latter to Rochelle—

I remain &c &c   JN VAUGHAN

I shall have Copies made—to go by other opportunities & enclose Copies to you

RC (MHi); endorsed by TJ as received 9 Aug. 1815 and so recorded in SJL. RC (DLC); address cover only; with PoC of TJ to Joseph Milligan, 5 Oct. 1815, on verso; addressed: "Thomas Jefferson Monticello V^a"; franked; postmarked

Philadelphia, 1 Aug. Enclosures: (1) Stephen Girard's letter of credit on Perregaux, Laffitte & Company for George Ticknor, Philadelphia, 30 July 1815, indicating that TJ is "desirous to give a Credit of Three hundred & fifty Dollars, in favour of George Ticknor Esquire of Boston for the purpose of investing the same in Books—I beg that you will pay that sum in conformity, even something more if said sum should be insufficient to complete the purchace alluded to"; and requesting the firm to "place your disbursement & charges for that object to my debit & to forward me your account" (Tr in PPAmP: John Vaughan Papers; at head of text: "Messrs Perregaux Laffitte & Co Paris"; conjoined with RCs of TJ to Vaughan, 11, 15 July 1815, and Tr of following enclosure). (2) Girard's letter of credit on Perregaux, Laffitte & Company for Stephen Cathalan, Philadelphia, 30 July 1815, indicating that TJ, "Our Respectable late President," has "requested

me to pay on his account Two Hundred Dollars to Mr Stephen Cathalan, Merchant and Consul of the United States residing in Marseilles. Be pleased to remit that Sum to that Gentleman, to place the Same and Charges to my Debit, and to forward me your account relative to that transaction" (Dupl in FrM: Cathalan-Samatan Collection, addressed: "Messrs Perregaux Laffitte & Co Paris," at head of text: "2te"; Tr in same, in an unidentified hand, with attestation signed by Vaughan; Tr in PPAmP: Vaughan Papers, conjoined with RCs of TJ to Vaughan, 11, 15 July 1815, and Tr of preceding enclosure).

The schooner ADELINE cleared the port of Philadelphia for Bordeaux on 1 Aug., while the ship *Andrew* cleared the same port for the French city of La ROCHELLE on 31 July (Philadelphia *Poulson's American Daily Advertiser*, 31 July, 1 Aug. 1815).

From Mason L. Weems

SIR.   North Garden. July 31.–15

My Son Jesse Ewell brings you a copy of the Life of Marion which I pray you to accept. It was written for the Moral & Military Services of our Youth among whom it has taken well.

I have a great favor to ask of you, viz your assistance in a little book on a Great Man, to which I believe you can contribute more than any other Gentleman in the U. States. The Great man I allude to is Dr Franklin. I am impress^d with the belief that no American ever led a life better calculated to do good to our youth than did Dr Franklin. And yet I have never seen a Life of him, that I thought likely to please them. I am trying my hand on this great subject—in the size & shape of a School book only. Shou'd it prosper, as some of my little books have done, it may help to multiply the Virtues of Industry, Sobriety, Frugality, Honesty, Patriotism, Devotion to useful Science &c for which Dr Franklin was so illustrious & which you, better than most men, knew to be the only true Gypsum of our young Republican Vine & all its future Interests & Glories. On this account I am led to hope you will lend me your assistance, which you can do more effectually than any other person now living. You were with D. Franklin

[633]

in France, as well as in America, and perhaps in Britain. You have read a thousand Magazines, Museums and all other publications perfum[d] with praises of him by Rousseau, Voltaire, &[c] &[c] also enrich[d] with Bon mots, Anecdotes Stories &c. &[c] All which, if only tolerably "cook[d] up", wou'd make a savoury dish for Juvenile palates. Now All I have to beg of you, Honor[d] Sir, is that you w[d] be so[1] good as tell me where[2] I may find the best collection[3] of these notices. I have Col[o] Duane's book, but that is only for Adults in Philosophy, Politicks[4] &[c] &[c] My Son, on his way back, tomorrow, will do himself the honor to call on you. With highest Respect I am, Honor[d] Sir, yours

M. L. Weems

RC (CSmH: JF-BA); addressed: "Thomas Jefferson Esqr Monticello Virginia"; endorsed by TJ as received 1 Aug. 1815 and so recorded in SJL.

Mason Locke Weems (1759–1825), bookseller, author, and Episcopal clergyman, was a native of Anne Arundel County, Maryland. Having received medical training in London and at the University of Edinburgh prior to the Revolutionary War, he returned to Great Britain after the conflict and was ordained into the Episcopal ministry in 1784. Weems served in two parishes in Maryland, 1784–92, before relocating to Dumfries, Virginia, in the mid-1790s. About that time he became an agent for the prominent Philadelphia publisher Mathew Carey and, as such, spent the rest of his life traveling up and down the East Coast selling books. Following the publication of his famed biography of George Washington in 1800, a later edition of which included the oft-repeated cherry-tree story, Weems wrote biographies of Francis Marion, Benjamin Franklin, and William Penn, as well as a number of moralizing tracts. He died in Beaufort, South Carolina (*ANB*; *DAB*; Paul Leicester Ford and Emily Ellsword Ford Skeel, *Mason Locke Weems*, 3 vols. [1928–29]; Lewis Leary, *The Book-Peddling Parson: An account of the life and works of Mason Locke Weems* [1984]; Weems and Edward Gantt to Benjamin Franklin, 9 July 1784 [PPAmP: Franklin Papers]; Franklin to Weems and Gantt, 18 July 1784 [DLC: Franklin Papers]; *PTJ*, 34:321–2; *Richmond Enquirer*, 1 July 1825).

TJ received at this time a COPY of Peter Horry and Mason L. Weems, *The Life of Gen. Francis Marion*, 3d ed. (Baltimore, 1815; Poor, *Jefferson's Library*, 4 [no. 137]).

[1] Preceding six words centered on own line, possibly to protect against anticipated damage from seal tear.

[2] Preceding five words centered on own line.

[3] Preceding six words centered on own line.

[4] Manuscript: "Politicts."

From John George Baxter

DEAR SIR   Lexington August 1st 1815

Your favour of the 16th ult I have received, you express a wish "to Know in what my machine differs from the old Spining Jenny," my machines requires no engenious attendence, all that it requires is to turn the Handle, which can be done by any person too young or too old for the Labours of the field; when the bobin (spool) is full it is easily lifted off, no fly to screw off, the bobin stands on a dead spindle there is a Band to every two spindles, one band to the Back, or feeding Rollar, and one Band to the front Rollar, or drawing rollar,[1] and a Band to drive the machine, She is very simple and easily Keeped in Repair,

a person may Spin on any machine from The time The[2] Bobin (Spool) is put on, till it is full without even, Looking at it There being no attention at all necessary, the person may read, Talk, or pay their attention to any other Business, I have had a Machine going here for a Number of months & the Thread has never Broke once, there is no education Neccessary, one of your Negro Girles of ten years of age is as good a spiner as I am, The machine of Eight spindles will weigh perhaps 75 pounds, If you will be so obliging as give me leave to Send you one I will esteem it a favour it Can be sent any distanc[e] without any great risk

I am Dear Sir your Obdient & Umbell Servent   JOHN GEO BAXTER

RC (DLC); one word faint; at foot of text: "Thomas Jefferson Esquire Monticello"; endorsed by TJ as received 16 Aug. 1815 and so recorded in SJL.

With this letter Baxter probably enclosed two pieces of supporting material. The first was a blank subscription list for his "Cotton Spinning Machines," offering a six-spindle machine that could "spin, twist and reel at one and the same time" for $150, "ornamented and firnished like the one in Peal's Museum"; as well as six- and twelve-spindle machines for $100 and $150, respectively, "to spin only, and without ornaments, such as those at work in the Female Hospitable Society's Manufactory" (broadside in DLC: TJ Papers, 204:36382; undated; headed by a depiction of such a machine ornamented with an eagle and operated by a girl). The second likely enclosure was an advertisement for an eight-spindle machine capable of spinning "coarse and fine chain and filling," which "Will spin as much cotton as eight women; will last as long as any piece of furniture; and can be spun on by a child of ten years old," at a cost of $75, payable in three equal installments over the course of a year, with a money-back guarantee; offering to make "Throssals upon a new construction, that will spin chain and filling" (a throstle being a continuous-action spinning machine [*OED*]), with a 120-spindle version costing $2 per spindle, warranted against breaking, with carding and roving at an additional $3 per spindle, and with payment expected upon completion; and announcing that "Patent rights, for small and large machines, will be sold at a low price, and on a *liberal* credit" (broadside in DLC: TJ Papers, 204:36383; dated Lexington, Kentucky, 10 June 1815; with same image as in preceding broadside at head, immediately above Baxter's signed, handwritten postscript: "The Machine is a good dale Simplifyed Since this plate was made in 1811," and with an additional illustration of an arch containing the names of the seventeen states belonging to the United States in 1811, plus the District of Columbia and the Louisiana, Mississippi, and Orleans territories surrounding a portion of the printed text).

[1] Word interlined, with insertion mark mistakenly placed after the comma.
[2] Reworked from "she."

To Mitchie B. Pryor Jefferson

DEAR SISTER   Monticello Aug. 2. 15.

your letter of yesterday gave us the first information of my brother's illness. we learn it with great concern mrs Marks would have visited him, but that we have now in our family, both in doors, and out, more sickness than I have ever had since I was a house keeper. Cornelia, Virginia and both of mrs Bankhead's children. all of these are on the recovery except Virginia. without doors two or three are taken of a day, so that all the houses of the negroes are mere hospitals requiring great and constant attendance and care; all of an epidemic dysentery now prevailing thro' the neighborhood. your letter gives us a hope that my brother is mending. we shall be very glad to hear of him by the mail which furnishes a weekly-opportunity.

I return by Squire the harness he was so kind as to lend me. it has answered the only occasion I had for it, and may on some other be useful to yourselves. affectionately Yours   TH: JEFFERSON

PoC (MHi); on verso of reused address cover of John Wayles Eppes to TJ, 6 July 1815; at foot of text: "mrs M. B. Jefferson"; endorsed by TJ.

Mitchie Ballow Pryor Jefferson was the daughter of David Pryor, of Buckingham County, and the second wife of Randolph Jefferson, having married him by 1809. She gave birth on 8 Mar. 1816 to John Randolph Jefferson (d. 1845), whom she later took to Tennessee to live with her brother Nicholas B. Pryor. On 29 Apr. 1819 she married Josiah Johnson, of Williamson County, Tennessee. She died between giving birth to James Monroe Johnson on 2 July 1820 and her husband's remarriage in 1825 (*VMHB* 7 [1900]: 325–6; Bernard Mayo, ed., *Thomas Jefferson and His Unknown Brother* [1942; repr. 1981], 4; note to Randolph Jefferson to TJ, 7 Dec.

1809; gravestone inscription for John Randolph Jefferson, Old City Cemetery, Nashville; T: Williamson Co. Marriages; Albert L. Johnson Jr., *Guardian Records of Williamson County, Tennessee* [2001], 1:iv, 2:234; *Richmond Enquirer*, 15 Dec. 1832).

Jefferson's letters to her brother-in-law TJ OF YESTERDAY, 1 Aug. 1815, and of 10 Aug. 1815, both not found, are recorded in SJL as received from Snowden on the days they were written. The earlier letter was reportedly also addressed to TJ's sister Anne Scott MARKS (TJ's Deposition regarding Randolph Jefferson's Estate, 15 Sept. 1815). Missing letters from TJ to Mrs. Marks of 9 and 16 Aug. 1815 are recorded in SJL. Ann C. Bankhead's CHILDREN at this time were TJ's great-grandchildren John Warner Bankhead, Thomas Mann Randolph Bankhead, and Ellen Monroe Bankhead.

Joseph Milligan's Statement on the Size of Thomas Jefferson's Library

[ca. 2 Aug. 1815]

The following Statement is a recapitulation of the difference of Counting Stated by way of D^r & C^r

over Counted						Lost in Count					
D^r	Chapter	Folio	4to	8vo	12mo	C^{re}	chapter	Folio	4to	8vo	12mo
	12			1	1		2				2
	15		2	8	1		16 §2^1		1		
	16 §I			1			17				1
	17			2			19	2			
	21			1			31			2	
	24			1	3		33			2	
	28			4					2	1	4	3
twice Counted {25 26 27 28}		10	71	134	16						
	30			1							
	36				2						
	37				1						
	39				1						
		10	73	153	25						
Deduct		2	1	4	3						
		8	72	149	22	over counted					

MS (DLC: TJ Papers, 204:36384); entirely in Milligan's hand, with some of the rules in red ink; undated; with Milligan to TJ, 2 Aug. 1815, on verso; endorsed by Milligan: "Statement of difference of Count with Explenations."

^{1} Reworked from "§I." Here and in next line, "§" is a symbol for "section."

[637]

From Joseph Milligan

DEAR SIR   Georgetown August 2nd 1815
    You will please observe that you have over counted   8 folios
                                                          72 Quartos
                                                          149 8^{vos}
                                                          22 12mos

The way that this mistake has happened is, you have Counted chapters 14, 25, 26, 27, & 28 twice over as you will See by a reference[1] to your paper which Contains the Numbers The whole of the Variations are marked with red ink and references[2] So that you will have no difficulty in tracing them.
    The Chapters that are twice Counted are Enclosed in lines thus[3] [   ]
    yours with respect   JOSEPH MILLIGAN

RC (DLC); on verso of Milligan's Statement on the Size of Thomas Jefferson's Library, [ca. 2 Aug. 1815]; endorsed by TJ: "Millegan Joseph."

YOUR PAPER: TJ's Notes on his Library at the Time of Sale, [by 18 Apr. 1815].

[1] Manuscript: "referece."
[2] Manuscript: "referces."
[3] Ensuing box in red ink.

To Mason L. Weems

SIR   Monticello Aug. 2. 15.
    I duly recieved your favor by the hands of your son, and with it the life of General Marion, for which be pleased to accept my thanks. I am sorry it is not in my power to assist you with materials for the life of Doct^r Franklin. I never knew him personally until his arrival from England during the third[1] session of Congress in 1775. and soon after the declaration of Independance he left us for Paris. it was 8. years after this that I met him again in Paris, but he soon after returned to America, and I remained there in his place about half a dozen years. when I returned I past an hour or two with him, while he was confined to his bed by the illness of which he died soon after. so that altho we were engaged in the same line for 14 or 15 years, yet it was so as to have but little personal intercourse. of the incidents of his life therefore I know but little, and that little from hearsay only, as every other person knows it. I recollect nothing within my own knowledge but what the public records & gazettes will furnish with much more exactitude than could be stated from a decaying memory. with my re-

grets at this inability to be useful to you, accept the assurances of my esteem & respect. Th: JEFFERSON

P.S. should you pass thro' our neighborhood, I shall be very happy to see you at Monticello. I am generally out on horseback in the forenoon, but in again before the hour of our dinner which is half after three.

PoC (CSmH: JF-BA); at foot of text: "Mr M. L. Weems"; endorsed by TJ.

Benjamin Franklin arrived at Philadelphia FROM ENGLAND on 5 May 1775. He was selected the following day to represent Pennsylvania in the Second Continental Congress, which first convened on 10 May 1775 (*ANB*; Worthington C.

Ford and others, eds., *Journals of the Continental Congress, 1774–1789* [1904–37], 2:5, 11–2).

Despite TJ's failure to assist him, Weems soon published *The Life of Doctor Benjamin Franklin written chiefly by himself* (Baltimore, 1815).

[1] Word interlined in place of "second."

From Wilson Cary Nicholas

MY DEAR SIR   Warren Aug. 3. 1815

I received your letter of the 15th of July by my[1] messenger. Circumstanced as you were and indeed as Mr Appleton, is, I regret extremely that I gave you the trouble of the application I made. I am sure you will believe I cou'd have had no wish that a deserving man shou'd be removed from office to make way for my son, and that the last thing that I cou'd have expected or wished was that you shou'd have had any agency in doing it. I supposed (and I am sure Robert did too) that the office was vacant, and that it wou'd probably be given to a gent[n] of New York. I have had full proof of your disposition to serve me or any of my family & I beg you to be assured I am incapable of wishing at the expence of your sense of propriety or delicacy. I wou'd have answered your letter sooner but delayed it in the hope of giving you satisfactory information in answer to your enquiries about plaister of Paris. There is no person in Richmond, with whom any arrangement cou'd be made at present upon tolerable terms. I think it best to delay any further effort until the effects of the war upon that article, are done away. If I find an opportunity of making a safe contract the quantity you want shall be included. I beg you to believe that nothing can give me greater pleasure than being useful to you.

I am Dear Sir with the greatest respect your friend & Servant
W. C. NICHOLAS

RC (DLC); endorsed by TJ as received 6 Aug. 1815 and so recorded in SJL.

[1] Nicholas here canceled "servant."

From Peter A. Guestier

SIR   Balt° Augt 4. 1815

Your esteemed favour of July 23 has reached me and I have forwarded the box with seeds agreeable to your directions to Mr Bernard McMahon gardner of Philadelphia Capt Cook has taken charge of it; he will deliver it to Mr Aug^n Bousquet in Philadelphia, who is well acquainted with M^r McMahon and will put it into his hands.

I remain with great respect
Sir Your most obed^t servant   P. A. GUESTIER

P.S.
This box has been left with me by a Gentleman lately arrived from france who requested me to forward it to you in consequence thereof I have no charges against it.

RC (DLC); in a clerk's hand, signed by Guestier; dateline adjacent to closing; at foot of text: "Th^s Jefferson Esqre Monticello"; endorsed by TJ as received 15 Aug. 1815 and so recorded in SJL.

Mark L. Deseaves was the GENTLEMAN (David Bailie Warden to TJ, 9 Apr. 1815).

From Nicolas G. Dufief

MONSIEUR,   A Philadelphie ce 5 d'Août. 1815

Vous me fites l'honneur, il y a déjà du temps, de me demander le cours de mathematiques de la Croix qu'il me fut impossible de vous procurer alors. J'en ai à présent un de rencontre, en 7 vol. 8vo, en bon état, dont le prix est de 15 dollars. Si cet ouvrage vous convient, je m'empresserai de vous l'envoyer aussitôt que J'en aurai reçu l'ordre.

Agréez les vœux que je fais pour votre Santé, & les assurances du profond respect avec lequel Je Suis,
Monsieur votre très-dévoué Serviteur   N. G. DUFIEF

EDITORS' TRANSLATION

SIR,   Philadelphia 5 August. 1815

Some time ago you asked me for the *Cours de Mathematiques à l'usage de l'École Centrale des Quatres-Nations* by Lacroix, but I found it impossible to obtain it at that time. I have now found one in good condition, in 7 octavo volumes, for the price of 15 dollars. If this work suits you, I will lose no time in sending it to you as soon as I receive your order.

Please accept my wishes for your health and the assurances of the deep respect with which I am,

Sir your very devoted servant   N. G. DUFIEF

RC (DLC); endorsed by TJ as received 11 Aug. 1815 and so recorded in SJL. RC (DLC); address cover only; with PoC of TJ to George Watterston, 10 Oct. 1815, on verso; addressed: "Th: Jefferson, Esquire Monticello Virginia"; franked; postmarked Philadelphia, 5 Aug. Translation by Dr. Genevieve Moene.

TJ had ordered a copy of Sylvestre François Lacroix's COURS DE MATHEMATIQUES in his letter to Dufief of 4 Aug. 1811.

From William Wardlaw

DEAR SIR   Richmond 5th Augt 1815

I recd your favr of the 30th ut. The Lemon-acid was sent to Mr Norris' room[1] and left with several articles which Mr Edmond Anderson was about to pack up to go in the same stage with Mr Norris, they were not left & I presume they are in the care of Mr Anderson if you have not recd them. I have sent a note to the Sergents office informing him of your wish with respect to the notices in his hands & I have no doubt but that he will return them by this or the next mail

I am with much respect.   W WARDLAW

RC (DLC); endorsed by TJ as received 9 Aug. 1815, but recorded in SJL as received a day earlier.

[1] Manuscript: "roon."

To William Wirt

DEAR SIR   Monticello Aug. 5. 15.

Your favor of July 24. came to hand on the 31st and I will proceed to answer your enquiries, in the order they are presented, as far as I am able.

I have no doubt that the 5th of the Rhode island resolutions, of which you have sent me a copy, is exactly the one erased from our journals. the mr Lees, and especially Richard Henry, who was industrious, had a close correspondence, I know, with the two Adamses, & probably with others in that and the other Eastern states: and I think it was said at the time that copies were sent off by them to the Northward, the very evening of the day on which they were passed.　　　I can readily enough believe these resolutions were written by mr Henry himself. they bear the stamp of his mind, strong without precision. that they were written by Johnson who seconded them, was only the rumor of the day, and very possibly unfounded. but how Edmund Randolph should have said they were written by William Fleming, and mr Henry should have written that he shewed them to William Fleming, is to me incomprehensible. there was no William Fleming then, but the judge now living, whom nobody will ever suspect of taking the lead in rebellion. I am certain he was not then a member, and I think was never a member until the revolution had made some progress. of this however he will inform us with candor & truth. his eldest brother John Fleming was a member, and a great speaker in debate. to him they may have been shewn. yet I should not have expected this, because he was extremely attached to Robinson, Peyton Randolph E^{t}c and at their beck, and had no independence or boldness of mind. however he was attentive to his own popularity, might have been overruled by views to that, and, with a correction of the Christian name, mr Henry's note is sufficient authority to suppose he took the popular side on that occasion. I remember nothing to the contrary.　　　The opposers of the resolutions were Robinson, Peyton Randolph, Pendleton, Wythe, Bland and all the cyphers of the Aristocracy. no longer possessing the journals, I cannot recollect nominally the others. they opposed them on the ground that the same principles had been expressed in the Petition E^{t}c of the preceding year, to which an answer, not yet recieved, was daily expected, that they were therein expressed in more conciliatory terms, and therefore more likely to have good effect. the resolutions were carried chiefly by the vote of the middle and upper country.　　　to state the differences between the classes of society, and the lines of demarcation which separated them would be difficult. the law, you know, admitted none, except as to the twelve counsellors. yet in a country insulated from the European world, insulated from it's sister colonies with whom there was scarcely any intercourse, little visited by foreigners, & having little matter to act upon within itself, certain families had risen to splendor by wealth and the preservation of it from generation to generation under the law of entails; some had produced a series of men of talents; families in general had remained stationary on the grounds of their forefathers, for there was no emigration to the Westward in those days, the wild Irish who had gotten possession of the valley between the blue ridge and North mountain, forming a barrier over which none ventured to leap, and would still less venture to settle among. in such a state of things, scarcely admitting any change of station, society would settle itself down into several strata, separated by no marked lines, but shading off imperceptibly, from top to bottom, nothing disturbing the order of their repose. there were then, Aristocrats, half breeds, pretenders, a solid independant yeomanry, looking askance at those above, yet not venturing to justle them; and last, and lowest a feculum of beings called Overseers, the most abject, degraded and unprincipled race, always cap in hand to the Dons who employed them, and furnishing materials for the exercise of their pride, insolence & spirit of domination.   Your characters are inimitably & justly drawn. I am not certain if more might not be said of Col° Richard Bland. he was the most learned & logical man of those who took prominent lead in public affairs, profound in Constitutional lore, a most ungraceful speaker (as were Peyton Randolph & Robinson in a remarkable degree) he wrote the first pamphlet on the nature of the connection with Gr. Britain, which had any pretension to accuracy of view on that subject; but it was a singular one. he would set out on sound principles, pursue them logically till he found them leading to the precipice which we had to leap, start back alarmed, then resume his ground, go over it in another direction, be led again by the correctness of his reasoning[1] to the same place, and again tack about, and try other processes to reconcile right and wrong, but finally left his reader & himself bewildered between the steady index of the compass in their hand, and the phantasm to which it seemed to point. still there was more sound matter in his pamphlet than in the celebrated Farmer's letters, which were really but an ignis fatuus, misleading us from true principles.

Landon Carter's measure you may take from the 1st volume of the American Philosophical transactions, where he has one or more long papers on the weavil and perhaps other subjects. his speeches, like his writings were dull, vapid, verbose, egoistical, smooth as the lullaby of the nurse, and commanding, like that, the repose only of the hearer.

You ask if you may quote me 1. for the loan office, 2. Phillips's case, and 3. the addresses prepared for Congress by Henry and Lee. for the two first certainly, because within my own knolege, especially citing the record in Phillips's case which of itself refutes the diatribes published on that subject: but not for the addresses, because I was not present, nor know any thing relative to them but by hearsay from others. my first and principal information on that subject I know I had from Ben. Harrison, on his return from the first session of the old Congress. mr Pendleton also, I am tolerably certain, mentioned it to me: but the transaction is too distant, and my memory too indistinct to hazard as with precision, even what I think I heard from them.　　in this decay of memory mr Edmund Randolph must have suffered at a much earlier period of life than myself. I cannot otherwise account for his saying to you that Rob. Carter Nicholas came into the legislature only on the death of Peyton Randolph, which was in 1776. seven years before that period I went first into the legislature myself, to wit in 1769. and mr Nicholas was then a member, and I think not a new one. I remember it from an impressive circumstance. it was the first assembly which met Lord Botetourt, being called on his arrival. on receiving the Governor's speech, it was usual to move resolutions, as heads for an Address. mr Pendleton asked me to draw the resolutions, which I did. they were accepted by the house, and Pendleton, Nicholas, myself and some others were appointed a Committee to prepare the Address. the Committee desired me to do it; but when presented, it was thought to pursue too strictly the diction of the resolutions, and that their subjects were not sufficiently amplified. mr Nicholas chiefly objected to it, and was desired by the committee to draw one more at large which he did, with amplification enough, and it was accepted. being a young man, as well as a young member, it made on me an impression proportioned to the sensibility of that time of life.

on a similar occasion some years after I had reason to retain a remembrance of his presence while Peyton Randolph was still living. on the reciept of Ld North's propositions, in May or June 1775. Lord Dunmore called the assembly. Peyton Randolph, then President of Congress, and Speaker of the House of Burgesses, left the former body and came home to hold the assembly, leaving in Congress the other delegates, who were the antient leaders of our house. he therefore asked me to prepare the answer to Ld North's propositions, which I did. mr Nicholas, whose mind had as yet acquired no tone for that contest, combated the answer from Alpha to Omega, and succeeded in diluting it in one or two small instances. it was firmly supported however in committee of the whole by Peyton Randolph, who had brought with him the spirit of the body over which he had presided, and it was carried with very little alteration by strong majorities. I was the bearer of it myself to Congress, by whom, as it was the first answer given to those propositions by any legislature, it was recieved with peculiar satisfaction. I am sure that from 1769. if not earlier, to 1775. you will find mr Nicholas's name constantly in the journals, for he was an active member. I think he represented James city county. whether, on the death of Peyton Randolph he succeeded him for Williamsburg, I do not know. if he did, it may account for mr Randolph's error.

You ask some account of mr Henry's mind, information & manners in 59–60. when I first became acquainted with him. we met at Nat. Dandridge's, in Hanover, about the Christmas of that winter, and passed perhaps a fortnight together at the revelries of the neighborhood & season. his manners had something of the coarseness of the society he had frequented: his passion was fiddling, dancing & pleasantry. he excelled in the last, and[2] it attached every one to him. the occasion perhaps, as much as his idle disposition, prevented his engaging in any conversation which might give the measure either of his mind or information. opportunity was not wanting: because mr John Campbell was there, who had married mrs Spotswood, the sister of Col° Dandridge. he was a man of science, & often introduced conversations on scientific subjects. mr Henry had a little before broke up his store, or rather it had broken him up, and within three months after he came to Williamsburg for his license, and told me, I think, he had read law not more than six weeks. I have by this time probably tired you with these old histories, and shall therefore only add the assurance of my great friendship & respect.

TH: JEFFERSON

RC (ViU: TJP); addressed: "William Wirt esq. Richmond." PoC (DLC). Tr (MHi); posthumous copy; incomplete; top edge frayed.

The Virginia House of Burgesses PASSED four resolutions on 30 May 1765. The PETITION E[T]C passed on 18 Dec. 1764 included an address to George III and memorials to the House of Lords and House of Commons (Henry R. McIlwaine and John Pendleton Kennedy, eds., *Journals of the House of Burgesses of Virginia, 1619–1776* [1905–15], 1761–65 vol., pp. 302–4, 359–60). FECULUM is an American variant of "fecula," meaning "dregs" or "lees" (Noah Webster, *An American Dictionary of the English Language* [1828]; *OED*). TJ preferred Richard Bland's PAMPHLET, *An Inquiry* into the *Rights of the British Colonies* (Williamsburg, 1766), to John Dickinson's CELEBRATED *Letters from a Farmer in Pennsylvania, to the Inhabitants of the British Colonies* (Philadelphia, 1768; and other eds., including Sowerby, no. 3076).

The only essay by LANDON CARTER in APS, *Transactions* 1 (1771), is "Observations concerning the Fly-Weevil, that destroys the Wheat" (pp. 205–17). For the May 1769 resolutions welcoming LORD BOTETOURT as written by TJ and as adopted see, respectively, *PTJ*, 1:26–7, and McIlwaine and Kennedy, *Journals*, 1766–69 vol., pp. 199–200. Lord North's PROPOSITIONS of 27 Feb. 1775 proposed that if a colony agreed to adopt provisions for the common defense and the suppport of the civil government and administration of justice in that colony, then the

British government would forbear "to levy any duty, tax, or assessment, or to impose any futher duty, tax, or assessment, except only such duties as it may be expedient to continue to levy or to impose for the regulation of commerce" (Merrill Jensen, *American Colonial Documents to 1776* [1964], 839–40). LORD DUNMORE convened the Virginia General Assembly on 1 June 1775 (McIlwaine and Kennedy, *Journals*, 1773–76 vol., pp. 171–3). For TJ's ANSWER, see *PTJ*, 1:170–4.

[1] Reworked from "reading."
[2] Tr ends here.

To John Wood

SIR   Monticel[lo] Aug. 5. 15.

I have delayed the answer to your favor of July 18. until I could consult on it's subject with neighbors better acquainted than I am with the state of our neighborhood. we had been making an effort the last year to get established here an academy [o]n a more enlarged scale than those established thro' the country, and at one time I hoped from it some success. but my friend Peter Carr, on whom I relied for attending our legislature and getting it placed by them on a proper footing, was prevented from that attendance at the last session by illness, and his death which followed had ended all my hopes. I have now consulted with some of the remaining trustees, and find they do not despair of it but mean at the next session to press their proposition. but when I observe to you that the act is still to be passed the funds to be raised, and the buildings to be erected, you will percieve that it offers no immediate prospect for the employment of talents however eminent & however desired. mr Cooper's qualifications particularly would command every suffrage and none more zealously than mine to whom they have been long known. considering this resource as at some distance, I am not able to say that the neighborhood offers any other worthy of his yours or mr Blackburn's immediate notice. there are in it two grammar schools of from 12. to 20. boys each. but whether these, or others from the country roundabout would, so many of them as might make up reasonable emoluments, engage in the higher branches of science, I am not able to say: indeed you are a better judge of it yourself than I am, from your experience of other parts of the country, and your particular knolege of this. I regret much that it is not in my power to give a more inviting[1] prospect to offers so highly desirable; you know my zeal for the dissemination of knolege among our citizens too well to doubt all it's exertions in any practicable case, and how much value I should set on such an addition to our society. I comfort myself with the hope ho[wever] that altho' delayed, our under taking is not desperate. Accept the assurance of my great esteem & respect.   TH: JEFFERSON

PoC (DLC); on reused address cover to TJ; dateline faint; torn at seal; at foot of first page: "Mr Wood"; endorsed by TJ.

[1] Word interlined in place of "flattering."

From Martha A. C. Lewis Monroe

MY DEAR UNCLE   Salem Kentucky August 6th 1815

Some time has elapsed since we have been favoured with a line from you, or indeed any of our friends, except My Father, Feeling quite anxious to hear from you, And at the same time knowing it to be my duty to write to you as an Uncle I take the liberty of forwarding a few lines by My friend. Yea and a friend to Mankind Mr Woods who has promised to deliver it himself I have written Cousin Martha Randolph three times and have not received a line from you since I have been in Kentucky, it is dear Uncle a moral imposible for me to describe to you the hart rending troubles we have experienced since we left Virginia I dare say you are not unapprised of some of it, However since the 21 of April last I have been some what happier, as on the evining of that day, I maried a Man who has been as Kind to me as you can posibley conceive, we are quite poor but happy Mr Woods can tell you as much or more tha[n] I can write concerning him Mr Woods dear Uncle the last time he was in virginia suggested that you wished to send some money for our benifits, If so you will be so good as to send by Mr Woods My friend as there will be certainty of receiving what you send, A few day before Marage My husband met with a loss to loose all he owned by fire, therefore I cannot shew our surcemstances more planely

With due Respect I remain your affectionate

M A C MONROE[1]

RC (ViU: TJP-ER); edge chipped; at foot of text: "Thomas Jefferson"; endorsed by TJ as received 3 Oct. 1815 and so recorded in SJL.

[1] Reworked from "Lewis."

From Wilson Cary Nicholas

My Dear Sir   Warren Augt 6. 1815
    I have this moment heard that the doctor, who attends your brother left his house last night, under a belief he cou'd not live many hours. It is reported he has lately made a will; by which he has given the whole of his property, except, about six hundred acres of his back land, and eight or ten negroes to his wife in fee simple. I thought I owed it to you to give you this information as it came to me in such a way as to induce me to fear there was some reason to believe both that he is in great danger and that he may have made the disposition of his property I have mentioned. I am sure you will pardon the liberty I have taken
    I am Dear Sir
    yours most respectfully   W. C. Nicholas

RC (ViU: TJP-ER); at foot of text: "T. Jefferson Esqr"; endorsed by TJ as received 6 Aug. 1815 and so recorded in SJL.

From John Holmes

Dear Sir   Alfred D.M. Mass^tts 7th Augt 1815
You will I apprehend deem it evidence of my vanity, that I have ventured to submit the inclosed to your perusal—But I confess that I commit it to your liberality & candour with views somewhat selfish—It is my hope that should you deem it worth the perusal, you will generously point out to me its erroneous sentiments—We who have some trouble in resisting the attacks & preventing the encroachments on republican principles believe that we have some claim on your wisdom & experience—Should you be willing to incur the trouble & waste the time, let me expect the honour of a line from you as a parental monition—
    I hope that I am too discrete to believe that the inclosed is possessed of much merit—It is the production of a day, thrown together without method—The field is new & much too large—To compress correctly all the prominent facts & principles which the times require, is more than an audience on the 4th july could expect or would endure—It is presumed that you will view it, as a mere 4th July production, adapted to the taste of a country audience—In this adaptation, however there is, it is hoped, no sacrifice of principle. I may have treated some classes of our citisens with too much severity.

Living among them as I do I trust that you will charitably suppose that it may arise from a discovery of acts & principles which are not known at a distance—

I could not well deny myself the pleasure of transmitting this imperfect mite to one whose literary & political character are entitled to my profoundest veneration—And permit me, Sir, to congratulate you on the <u>war</u> & the <u>peace</u>—The strength of our constitution could never have been known had it [not been] <u>tried</u>—The experiment of war was necessary to prove its excellency, its efficacy & its <u>stability</u>—To declare war for the sake of the experiment would have been wrong— The injustice of other nations compelled the experiment at a most unfavorable juncture, but it was successful—A stronger or more outrageous foreign & domestic combination is not to be apprehended— I hope & believe that the happy system of our Government will continue—That it will continue so long as the people remain virtuous I have no doubt—Should they become corrupt, our liberties will probably fall—Excuse this intrusion on your time & accept the high consideration & respect of Your friend & very humble Se[rt]

JOHN HOLMES

RC (DLC); mutilated at seal; addressed: "Hon Thomas Jefferson Late President U.S. Monticello Va"; franked; postmarked Kennebunk, 5 Aug.; endorsed by TJ as received 18 Aug. 1815 but recorded in SJL as received a day later.

John Holmes (1773–1843), attorney and public official, was a native of Kingston, Massachusetts. He graduated from the College of Rhode Island (later Brown University) in 1796, studied law, and was admitted to the Massachusetts bar in 1799, the same year that he moved to Alfred, in the District of Maine of that state. Holmes served in the Massachusetts House of Representatives, 1802–03 and 1812–13, shifting his allegiance from the Federalist to the Republican parties between these two terms. He was in the Massachusetts Senate, 1813–16, served as a federal treaty commissioner in 1816, and sat in the United States House of Representatives, 1817–20. Holmes was an active proponent of the separation of Maine from Massachusetts and a leading force behind the adoption of the Missouri Compromise of 1820. On 22 Apr. 1820

TJ wrote him a letter eloquently likening the debate surrounding Missouri statehood to "a fire bell in the night" and indicating that slaveholders precariously held "the wolf by the ear." After Maine became a state, Holmes served in the United States Senate, 1820–27 and 1829–33, and in the Maine House of Representatives, 1836–37. He was appointed United States attorney for Maine in 1841 and held that position until his death (*ANB*; *DAB*; MeHi: Holmes Papers; *The Massachusetts Register . . . 1814* [Boston, 1813], 16–7; *Rules and Orders to be observed in the Senate, of the Commonwealth of Massachusetts* [1815]: 3; [1816]: 3; Ronald F. Banks, *Maine Becomes a State: The Movement to Separate Maine from Massachusetts, 1785–1820* [1970]; *JEP*, 3:23, 24, 5:387, 410, 6:197 [15, 16 Jan. 1816, 17 June, 22 July 1841, 18 Dec. 1843]; Clay, *Papers*, 2:741–2, 746; Charles M. Wiltse and others, eds., *The Papers of Daniel Webster: Correspondence* [1974–86], esp. 1:218; *Washington Daily National Intelligencer*, 27 July 1843).

Holmes INCLOSED *An Oration, Pronounced at Alfred, on the 4th of July, 1815, being the Thirty Ninth Anniversary of American Independence* (Boston, 1815; Poor, *Jefferson's Library*, 13 [no. 818]; TJ's copy at ViU), in which he extolled the decision to declare independence from Great Britain and the subsequent adoption of the United States Constitution; remarked that during the War of 1812 the administration was "assailed with the most outrageous abuse" (p. 6); suggested that among those CLASSES OF OUR CITISENS guilty of such behavior were those in Massachusetts who decided "that the United States had no controul over the militia," despite the fact that the United States Constitution "gave, expressly, to Congress, the power to call forth, organize, arm and discipline the militia, and to employ them in the service of the United States" (pp. 7–8); singled out the "mercantile class of our citizens in the Eastern States," who were "induced to believe that their rights were attacked, and that resistance was essential to *the interests of commerce*," but later decided that "they had been deceived, made their *calcula-*

tions, found that resistance was *unprofitable*, compromised with their consciences, and engaged in the practice of *privateering*, which they had before denounced, as inconsistent with honor, morality and religion" (pp. 9–10); rebuked those in the clergy who, once war was declared, "took their stand in favor of the enemy" and "pronounced him [Great Britain] 'the bulwark of our holy religion'" (p. 12); blamed Massachusetts for devising and promoting a scheme for a "final separation" of the New England states from the Union, a prospect rendered moot by the victory at New Orleans and the subsequent peace treaty (p. 14); and found that the war had had positive effects, in that it demonstrated "the danger of depending too much on foreign luxuries," increased and improved domestic manufactures, and taught "the importance of *agriculture*," which is the "favorite employment of Heaven" and gives the "greatest security to national attachments, prosperity, independence and happiness" (pp. 18–9).

From Elisha Ticknor

SIR, Boston 7ᵗʰ Aug. 1815.

Your letter of the 5ᵗʰ ultimo. reached Boston in due season; but, my absence on a long journey and detention by ill health are my only apology for not replying to it at an earlier period. Your "possessing my son for a short time" was really an honour to him as well as to me, and such an honour too as would gratify the feelings and pride of a parent, who loves and esteems his son. I could not persuade myself to permit him to travel abroad, 'till he had first visited some parts of his own country; and, especially, 'till he had seen and known personally some of the worthies, who have honoured and adorn'd it. I recommend'd to him, therefore, to apply to his and my friends in this town and neighbourhood to furnish him with such letters of introduction, as would not only aid him in his preparations for Europe; but, with such as, <u>out</u> of which, would naturally grow such other credentials as would be extremely useful to him in his absence. On his return to his home, he gave me an account of his journey and of the manner, in which he had been from time to time received by his friends and strangers, and, that no part of his journey gratified <u>him</u>, and by his representation, <u>me</u> so much, as the kindness and attention, with which yourself and family were pleased to shew him, while at Monticello, for which you will please to accept the grateful acknowledgments of his father. Permit me, sir, to add, that, when in the course of conversation, between you and him alone, on his tour to Europe, you were pleas'd to observe to him, that you were now an[1] aged man (I believe seventy years old)—that twenty eight years ago, you had many friends in Europe—that the ravages of time and the devastation of revolutions in that country might have carried away many of the ablest and best of your acquaintance, who could be of any use to him; yet, to the remaining few you would with pleasure give him letters of introduction, provided he would give you a month's notice of his intention to depart. This was an offer so great and so strongly mark'd with attention and kindness to a young stranger, going to a foreign country, and to <u>him</u> and to <u>me</u> <u>invaluable</u>, that to express myself on this occasion as I ought, is not in my power. I leave to you, sir, who are able to imagine what I ought to say and how I ought to feel rather than to attempt to tell to you either of them <u>myself</u>. All I ask is, that he may merit your confidence and approbation and receive your blessing, and transact your business as becomes a wise, judicious and prudent young man.

Your letter shall be immediately forwarded with mine[2] to his address in London; although it is possible he may now be in Holland, making his way to Gottengen, the place of his destination, through the difficulties and threatenings of Europe as fast as he possibly can. His last letter was dated at London, the 30th May, where he was then preparing himself for the Continent. What will be his fate <u>there</u> GOD only knows. I have been extremely solicitous about him ever since the renewal of hostilities; yet, he writes in good spirits and fine health and appears to think there will be no danger, at least to Americans.

Any letter you may please to forward to me for him, shall be immediately transmitted to his address, agreeably to your request: and, also, any business, sir, which you may wish to have done in this part of the country and which can be transacted by me shall be done with the greatest exactness and care.

I am, sir, With the greatest respect and consideration Your much obliged & very humble servant,   ELISHA TICKNOR.

RC (MHi); addressed: "Thomas Jefferson, Esquire, Late President of the United States of America, Monticello, Virginia"; franked; postmarked Boston, 13 Aug.; endorsed by TJ as received 3 Oct. 1815 and so recorded in SJL.

[1] Manuscript: "an an."
[2] Preceding two words interlined.

From Dabney Carr

My Dear Sir,   Winchester. Augt 9th 1815

I rec^d by the last mail your letter of July 30th. The notice now, seems to be perfectly correct—The Deposition shall be taken agreeably to it, & forwarded to you—you were certainly right to leave nothing to Michies honesty—

with respect to the $60. I knew I could get it, at any time; & never finding myself particularly in want of it, did not think it worth while to mention it.

We, of the republican school in this quarter, are like you, praying for the success of France—hers is certainly the cause of self: Government, & ought to interest every American. but alas! we have too many among us, all whose sympathies, are on the other side. There has I see been a great battle fought—Ld Wellington claims the victory, but I question much whether we shall not find, that he has sustained a defeat—the slaughter of Officers is unexampled.

I expect I shall be in Albemarle towards the latter part of this month, or early in Sep; at which time I promise myself the pleasure of seeing you.—

Believe me with the truest respect, & affection yrs &c

                                                        D Carr

RC (ViU: TJP-CC); endorsed by TJ as received 16 Aug. 1815 and so recorded in SJL. RC (DLC); address cover only; with PoC of TJ to Tristram Dalton, 13 Oct. 1815, on verso; addressed: "Thomas Jefferson Esqr Monticello Albemarle" by "mail"; franked; postmarked Winchester, 13 Aug.

TJ's letter to Carr of july 30th, not found, is recorded in SJL. It contained an order on Gibson & Jefferson payable to Carr for $68.10 to settle a 30 May 1813 "assumpsit for Craven Peyton" (*MB*, 2:1289, 1312). British forces under Arthur Wellesley, 1st Duke of wellington, joined with Prussian troops to defeat Napoleon and his army at the Battle of Waterloo on 18 June 1815 (*ODNB*).

To Christopher Hudson

Dear Sir   Monticello Aug. 9. 15.

When I had the pleasure of being with you the day before yesterday, you mentioned your[1] want of a pair of hedge-shears, and that you had to wait till they could be imported from Europe. I knew I had had a pair but it had been so long since I had seen them that I was not sure they could now be found, and therefore said nothing. on my return it was my first object to have them sought for, and I am happy that being found I am enabled to ask your acceptance of them. you will percieve by their having never been used that I have no employment for them. Accept the assurance of my friendly esteem and respect.

Th: Jefferson

PoC (MHi); on verso of reused address cover of a missing letter from Brockholst Livingston to TJ, 8 June 1815, which is addressed in Livingston's hand "Tho⁵ Jefferson Esqʳ Monticello," to be delivered by "Mʳ Bruen," and recorded in SJL as received 1 Aug. 1815 from New York "(by mr Bruen)"; at foot of text: "Capᵗ Hudson"; endorsed by TJ.

Christopher Hudson (1758–1825), planter, lived at Mount Air, his estate near Keene in Albemarle County. He was active in the Virginia militia during the Revolutionary War and warned TJ on 4 June 1781 that British forces were approaching Monticello, thus allowing TJ to escape capture. Hudson helped TJ combat rumors of cowardly behavior as governor with an 1805 deposition describing TJ's composure on this occasion as well as during an earlier British incursion into Virginia in April 1781. Hudson and TJ both held shares in a 400-acre, limestone-bearing tract along the Hardware River in Albemarle County. In 1819 they joined in a lawsuit against two men who claimed ownership of a portion of this land. At his death Hudson left thousands of acres of land as well as personal property valued at about $7,000, including at least twenty-eight slaves ("Bible Record of Hudson, Gilmer, Etc.," *WMQ*, 1st ser., 20 [1912]: 214–5; Woods, *Albemarle*, 86, 98, 231; *CVSP*, 2:533; *PTJ*, 1:664, 668, 4:261, 277–8, 28:570–1; TJ to Mary Stith, 7 Mar. 1811; TJ's List of his Taxable Property in Albemarle County, 14 May 1815; TJ to Robert Anderson, 13 June 1819; Albemarle Co. Will Book, 8:101–3, 115–7, 9:243–4; gravestone inscription in family cemetery at Mount Air).

¹ TJ here canceled "wish for."

To Philip Mazzei

My dear friend   Monticello Aug. 9. 15.

Your letter of Sep. 24. came inclosed to me in one of Octob. 20. from mr Warden, which did not get to my hands until the 15ᵗʰ of the last month. how the present answer will get to you I do not yet know but I shall confide it to the Secretary of State, to be forwarded with his despatches either to Paris or Leghorn.

My letter of Dec. 29. 13. stated to you the circumstances, both here and abroad, which rendered a remittance of the price of your lots impracticable. the money might have been invested in the government loans; but the principal would then have been payable only at the end of a long term of years. it might have been vested in the stock of some of our banks; but besides their daily fluctuations in value the banks had indulged themselves in such extravagant emissions of their paper notes that it was obvious they must be on the verge of bankruptcy; and accordingly, within a very few months every bank in the US. stopt the payment of cash for their own notes, have never since resumed it, and every one is satisfied they never can pay them. so that with all the indulgencies of time which has been given them their insolvency is notorious. there remained then only the resource of placing it on interest in private hands. this the circumstances of the country rendered impracticable but in the usual way of repaiments by annual instalments. we were then under the blockade of the enemy, and an embargo of our own, the sale of produce was as absolutely null, as you remember it in the revolutionary war, and the prospect of peace thought to be distant. under these difficulties therefore I really thought it safest for you to retain the price in my own hands, stating at the same time in my letter of Dec. 19. 13. that the sum being considerable, it's repayment would require a delay of one or two years from the time you should give notice that you preferred placing it there rather than here. the distressing injury which every individual sustained during the war by the entire loss of the produce of their farms for want of a market the expences of the war, and great advance of price on all foreign articles, have left us in so exhausted a state, that immediate paiments are known to be impossible. I am sorry therefore, my dear friend, that the remittances must of necessity be delayed so much beyond your wish; and that you must make up your account to recieve one moiety only the next year, and the other the year after, according to the former advice. this you may count on; and if bills on London will be negociable with you, that mode will be without difficulty. through Paris it would not be so easy. we are ignorant with which of these powers you now have either peace or war.

Our commissioners in London are endeavoring, by a convention with England to put an end to their impressment of our seamen. if they succeed it is probable we may continue in peace. all things here are going on quietly, except that we are[1] in a great crisis as to our circulating medium. a parcel of mushroom banks have set up in every state, have filled the country with their notes, and have thereby banished all our specie. a twelvemonth ago they all declared they could not pay cash for their own notes, and notwithstanding this act of bankruptcy, this trash has of necessity been passing among us, because we have no other medium of exchange, and is still taken and passed from hand to hand, as you remember the old continental money to have been in the revolutionary war; every one getting rid of it as quickly as he can, by laying it out in property of any sort at double, treble, and manifold higher prices. it was this which procured the extravagant price for your lots, and in this paper the payment was made. a general crush is daily expected when this trash will be lost in the hands of the holders. this will take place the moment some specie returns among us, or so soon as the government will issue bills of circulation. the little they have issued is greatly sought after, and a premium given for them which is rising fast.

In Europe you are all at war again. no man more severely condemned Bonaparte than myself during his former career, for his unprincipled enterprizes on the liberty of his own country, and the independance of others. but the allies having now taken up his pursuits, and he arrayed himself on the legitimate side, I also am changed as to him. he is now fighting for the independance of nations, of which his whole life hitherto had been a continued violation; and he has now my prayers as sincerely for success as he had before for his overthrow. he has promised a free government to his own country, and to respect the rights of others; and altho' his former conduct does not inspire entire faith in his promises; yet we had better take the chance of his word for doing right, than the certainty of the wrong which his adversaries avow.   My health continues firm; and I am sorry to learn that yours is not good. but your prudence and temperance may yet give you many years, and that they may be years of health and happiness is the sincere prayer of yours ever affectionately   Th: Jefferson

PoC (DLC); at foot of first page: "Philip Mazzei"; endorsed by TJ. Enclosed in TJ to John Graham, 17 Aug. 1815.

TJ's letter of DEC. 19. 13. was actually dated 29 Dec. 1813. On 3 July 1815 John Quincy Adams, Henry Clay, and Albert Gallatin, the United States COMMISSIONERS, signed a CONVENTION "To regulate the Commerce between the Territories of The United States and of His Britannick Majesty." The convention, however, did not address the issue of impressment (Hunter Miller, ed., *Treaties and other International Acts of the United States of America* [1931–48], 2:595–600).

[1] TJ here canceled "on the eve."

To Wilson Cary Nicholas

DEAR SIR   Monticello. Aug. 9. 15.
I duly recieved your two favors of the 3. & 6th. I was engaged in the moment in preparing some necessary orders before my departure to see my brother, and could not therefore immediately answer them. the circumstances respecting Appleton, and my particular connection with them I knew must be unknown to you & of course could not be under your view in asking my interference. I do not yet know whether he has obtained the change of[1] consulship he desired, but should that have taken place my letter to the President will have

placed before him the considerations which might lead to the appointment of your son.

I learnt on the 6th for the first time the imminent danger in which my brother was, and never till the day before that had any suspicion that he had made any disposition of his estate but by a will in my possession. I put into the hands of one of his sons a paper which if executed might have set all to rights. but they failed to use it. I set out early on the 7th to see him, but at Scott's ferry met the news of his death, and returned. some members of his family had behaved very undutifully to him, and under the impressions from that he must have been led to the act which involves, I fear, the whole in ruin.   I expect to go to the President's with my daughter the day after tomorrow and to return on Monday, within two or three days after which I shall set out for Poplar Forest, and shall have the pleasure of seeing you for a moment on my way, if at home. Accept the assurance of my great esteem and respect.

Th: Jefferson

RC (MHi); at foot of text: "Gov[r] Nicholas"; endorsed by Nicholas. PoC (DLC); on verso of reused address cover to TJ; endorsed by TJ.

[1] Preceding two words interlined in place of "new."

To John Adams

Dear Sir   Monticello Aug. 10. 15.

The simultaneous movements in our correspondence have been really remarkable on several occasions. it would seem as if the state of the air, or state of the times, or some other unknown cause produced a sympathetic effect on our mutual recollections. I had set down to answer your letters of June 19. 20. 22. with pen, ink, and paper before me, when I recieved from our mail that of July 30.   you ask information on the subject of Camus. all I recollect of him is that he was one of the deputies sent to arrest Dumourier at the head of his army, who were however themselves arrested by Dumourier, and long detained as prisoners. I presume therefore he was a Jacobin. you will find his character in the most excellent revolutionary history of Toulongeon: I believe also he may be the same person who has given us a translation of Aristotle's natural history from the Greek into French. of his report to the National Institute on the subject of the Bollandists your letter gives me the first information. I had supposed them defunct with the society of Jesuits, of which they were: and that

their works, altho' above ground, were, from their bulk and insignifi-
cance, as effectually entombed on their shelves, as if in the graves of
their authors. fifty two volumes in folio of the Acta Sanctorum, in
dog-Latin, would be a formidable enterprize to the most laborious
German. I expect, with you, they are the most enormous mass of lies,
frauds, hypocrisy & imposture that ever was heaped together on this
globe. by what chemical process M. Camus supposed that an Extract
of truth could be obtained from such a farrago of falsehood, I must
leave to the Chemists & Moralists of the age to divine.   On the
subject of the history of the American revolution, you ask Who shall
write it? who can write it? and who ever will be able to write it? nobody; except merely it's external facts. all it's councils, designs and
discussions, having been conducted by Congress with closed doors,
and no member, as far as I know, having even made notes of them.
these, which are the life and soul of history must for ever be unknown. Botta, as you observe, has put his own speculations and reasonings into the mouths of persons whom he names, but who, you &
I know, never made such speeches. in this he has followed the example of the antients, who made their great men deliver long speeches,
all of them in the same style, and in that of the author himself. the
work is nevertheless a good one, more judicious, more chaste, more
classical, and more true than the party diatribe of Marshall. it's greatest fault is in having taken too much from him. I possessed the work,
and often recurred to considerable portions of it, altho' I never read it
through. but a very judicious and well informed neighbor of mine
went thro' it with great attention, and spoke very highly of it. I have
said that no member of the old Congress, as far as I knew, made notes
of the discussions. I did not know of the speeches you mention of
Dickinson and Witherspoon. but on the questions of Independance
and on the two articles of Confederation respecting taxes & voting I
took minutes of the heads of the arguments. on the first I threw all
into one mass, without ascribing to the speakers their respective arguments; pretty much in the manner of Hume's summary digests of
the reasonings in parliament for and against a measure. on the last I
stated the heads of arguments used by each speaker. but the whole of
my notes on the question of independance does not occupy more than
5. pages, such as of this letter: and on the other questions two such
sheets. they have never been communicated to any one.   do
you know that there exists in MS. the ablest work of this kind ever
yet executed, of the debates of the Constitutional convention of
Philadelphia in 1788.? the whole of every thing said and done there
was taken down by mr Madison, with a labor and exactness beyond

comprehension.   I presume that our correspondence has been observed at the post offices, and thus has attracted notice. would you believe that a printer has had the effrontery to propose to me the letting him publish it? these people think they have a right to every thing however secret or sacred.   I had not before heard of the Boston pamphlet with Priestly's letters and mine.

At length Bonaparte has got on the right side of a question. from the time of his entering the legislative hall to his retreat to Elba, no man has execrated him more than myself. I will not except even the members of the Essex junto; altho' for very different reasons; I, because he was warring against the liberty of his own country, and independance of others; they, because he was the enemy of England, the Pope, and the Inquisition. but at length, and as far as we can judge, he seems to have become the choice of his nation. at least he is defending the cause of his nation, and that of all mankind, the rights of every people to independance and self-government. he and the allies have now changed sides. they are parcelling out among themselves Poland, Belgium, Saxony, Italy, dictating a ruler and government to France, and looking askance at our republic, the splendid libel on their governments: and he is fighting for the principle of national independance, of which his whole life hitherto has been a continued violation. he has promised a free government to his own country, and to respect the rights of others; and altho' his former conduct inspires little confidence in his promises yet we had better take the chance of his word for doing right, than the certainty of the wrong which his adversaries are doing and avowing. if they succeed, ours is only the boon of the Cyclops to Ulysses, of being the last devoured. present me affectionately and respectfully to mrs Adams, and heaven give you both as much more of life as you wish, and bless it with health and happiness.   TH: JEFFERSON

Aug. 11. P.S. I had finished my letter yesterday, and this morning recieve the news of Bonaparte's second abdication. very well. for him personally I have no feeling but of reprobation. the representatives of the nation have deposed him. they have taken the allies at their word, that they had no object in the war but his removal. the nation is now[1] free to give itself a good government, either with or without a Bourbon; and France unsubdued will still be a bridle on the enterprises of the combined powers, and a bulwark to others.

RC (MHi: Adams Papers); endorsed by Adams as answered 24 Aug. 1815.   PoC (DLC); at foot of first page: "John Adams." Not recorded in SJL.

Armand Gaston Camus published a TRANSLATION of a work by Aristotle in *Histoire des Animaux d'Aristote, Avec la Traduction Françoise*, 2 vols. (Paris, 1783; Poor, *Jefferson's Library*, 5 [no. 170]). DOG-LATIN: "pretended or mongrel Latin" (E. Cobham Brewer, *Dictionary of Phrase and Fable*, rev. ed. [1898], 367). The PARTY DIATRIBE was John Marshall, *The Life of George Washington*, 5 vols. (Philadelphia, 1804–07; Sowerby, no. 496). Louis H. Girardin was probably the WELL INFORMED NEIGHBOR.

For TJ's MINUTES of discussions in the Continental Congress, 7 June–1 Aug. 1776, see *PTJ*, 1:309–29. For the circumstances under which he obtained a copy in 1791 of James Madison's notes on the DEBATES OF THE CONSTITUTIONAL CONVENTION, see *PTJ*, 19:544–52. John M. Carter was the PRINTER. For the BOON OF THE CYCLOPS, see note to TJ to Samuel Smith (of Maryland), 23 July 1815.

¹ Word interlined.

From James Monroe

Augt. 10. 1815.

J. M's best respects to mr Jefferson.

He encloses him a hand bill just receivd which seems to confirm the account of yesterday.

RC (MHi); dateline at foot of text; addressed: "Mr Jefferson Monticello"; endorsed by TJ as received 11 Aug. 1815 and so recorded in SJL. Enclosure not found.

From Mr. Pell

Thursday [10 Aug. 1815]

A Lady & Gentleman from the State of New York, on their return from a Journey through Kentucky & Ohio were reluctant to leave Virginia without offering to pay their Respects at Monticello—

RC (MHi); partially dated at foot of text; endorsed by TJ as received from "Pell mr" on 10 Aug. Recorded in SJL as received 10 Aug. 1815, which was a Thursday.

From George P. Stevenson

DEAR SIR   Baltimore August 10th 1815

Rather more than three months since I sent you the astonishing news of Bonaparte's reascending the throne of France, I now enclose accts of equally surprizing nature—. In addition to the printed account, I have seen letters of respectability from Marseilles stating that the Emperor had been beheaded & both houses of the Legislative body massacred by the populace—What now must be the fate of a once great nation? A people whose feelings and whose conduct have been as changeable as extraordinary scarcely merit our pity—and we are only[1] induced to feel, from the mere fact of such a strong barrier being removed from the views & ambition of our <u>late</u> nay I may safely say our constant enemy, Great Britain—Will the <u>Bourbons</u> return? or will some new claimant such as <u>Wellington</u> assume the throne of France? or will each of the allied powers share a part of a country unfit to be left to it's own control?

With sentiments of high respect

Yr Obed. Servt   GEO: P: STEVENSON

RC (DLC); endorsed by TJ as received 16 Aug. 1815 and so recorded in SJL. RC (DLC); address cover only; with PoC of TJ to Mathew Carey, 13 Oct. 1815, on verso; addressed: "Thomas Jefferson Esqr near Milton Va"; franked; postmarked Baltimore, 10 Aug. Enclosures not found.

The *Baltimore Patriot & Evening Advertiser*, 10 Aug. 1815, contained rumors that Napoleon had been either hanged or BEHEADED and that all members of his family in Paris as well as eight hundred French legislators had been MASSACRED.

[1] Word interlined in place of "almost."

To Joseph Milligan

DEAR SIR   Monticello Aug. 11. 15.

Your letter of July 31. came to hand the day before yesterday only. one of the boxes of books arrived ten days ago. the other is not yet come. the bill in your last letter is of 50½.D. another which came in your letter of May 6. from Fredericksbg was of 41½.D. there have been a few other books furnished of which I have never had a bill, nor know their amount. they were I believe but few; and as I shall set out for Bedford in a few days and shall be absent some weeks, I think it best to send you a draught on Richmond for 92.D. the amount of the two bills above mentioned, and leave the rest to enter into our next account. with the books I requested you to procure for me and not yet forwarded I must ask you to send me Pike's arithmetic, Moore's Greek grammar translated by Ewen, Schrevelius's Lexicon the latest & best edition, and the 8vo abridgment of Ainsworth's dictionary. this last to be bound in two separate volumes, to wit, the Latin & English part in 1. vol. & the English & Latin & other parts in a 2d vol. the books formerly desired and not yet sent, were I believe Garnet's requisite tables, his Nautical Almanac for 1815. and 1816. if published, & the Delphin edition of Virgil with the notes translated lately printed in Philadelphia. other parts of your letter of July 31. shall be attended to at more leisure. in the mean time let the acts of assembly remain unbound. Accept assurances of my esteem & respect.

Th: Jefferson

P.S. since writing the above I have examined my acts of assembly and am satisfied they cannot be digested without your sending back those you have, after which I can return them for binding.

the 2ᵈ box is recieved since writing this letter Aesop Gr. Lat. 8ᵛᵒ not come.

PoC (DLC); on verso of reused address cover to TJ; above first postscript: "Mʳ Millegan"; endorsed by TJ.

The DELPHIN EDITION of classical Latin authors was prepared for the use of the dauphin, the son of French king Louis XIV (*OED*).

To Hardin Perkins

Sir   Monticello Aug. 11. 15.
My brother lately deceased having some years ago made me the depository of his last will and testament, wherein you are named an executor, I think it a duty to put it into your hands, and now therefore inclose it to you. altho' also named an executor, my age disables me from undertaking it,[1] and the pursuits of my life have not been such as to[2] qualify me for any useful interference in the affairs of the estate. the will having been all written with his own hand will need no other proof: but if that could be doubted the witnesses who attested to make it more sure, can all attend when called on. Accept the assurance of my great esteem & respect.

Th: Jefferson

PoC (MHi); on verso of reused address cover to TJ; at foot of text: "Capᵗ Harding Perkins"; endorsed by TJ.

Hardin Perkins (ca. 1773–1821) owned land along the James River in Buckingham County in 1815. Five years later he resided in New Canton in that county. Perkins left an estate that included nineteen slaves valued at $5,270 (William Kearney Hall, *Descendants of Nicholas Perkins* [1957], 26–9, 87–8; Roger G. Ward, *1815 Directory of Virginia Landowners* [1997–2000], 1:51; DNA: RG 29, CS, Buckingham Co., 1820; Perkins's will in *Executors of Littleberry Moon Etc. vs. Administrator of John Perkins Etc.*, case no. 1837-021,

Circuit Superior Court, Albemarle Co. Chancery Court Records).

The enclosed, witnessed version of the May 1808 WILL of Randolph Jefferson has not been found. It presumably corresponded closely to extant versions in which Jefferson directed that all the slaves he owned at his death and those already given to his five sons, Thomas Jefferson (ca. 1783–1876), Robert Lewis Jefferson, Field Jefferson, Isham Randolph Jefferson, and James Lilburne Jefferson, were to be valued and the aggregate brought "into hotchpot," so that each son would receive "only so much as, with those before given, shall make his portion of slaves equal to that of each of his other brothers"; stipulated that "all my lands and other property whatsoever be sold after my death, and the proceeds be equally divided among my said five sons, my son Thomas bringing into hotchpot with those proceeds the sum of one thousand pounds (at which I estimate the advantages I have Given him during my life) and takeing from the proceeds only so much as, being aded to the sd thousand pounds shall make his portion under this bequest equal to that of his other brothers"; and named Perkins, Robert Craig, Randolph Jefferson's son Robert Lewis Jefferson, and TJ as his executors (FC in ViU: TJP-CC, entirely in Randolph Jefferson's hand, dated 28 May 1808, unsigned; Dft in ViU: TJP-CC, entirely in TJ's hand, dated 27 May 1808; endorsed by TJ: "Jefferson Randolph. rough draft of Will"). The 1808 will was presented as evidence in an unsuccessful effort by the five sons therein named to set aside a more recent will favoring their stepmother, Mitchie B. Pryor Jefferson (TJ's Deposition regarding Randolph Jefferson's Estate, 15 Sept. 1815).

[1] TJ here canceled "or."
[2] TJ here canceled "enable."

To Henry Sheaff

DEAR SIR   Monticello Aug. 11. 15.
With the return of peace I return to my old correspondents. I am out of wine and it will be some months before I can recieve what I have written for to Europe. I must request you to fill up the chasm by sending me a quarter cask of either dry Sherry or dry Lisbon, whichever you have, most to be recommended. let it be in a double cask, and sent to Richmond by some vessel going to that place, addressed for me to Mess.rs Gibson & Jefferson of that place who will pay charges and forward it to me. when shipped be so good as to drop me a line of notice with information of the price, and it shall be promptly remitted, say within 90. days from the shipment. I avail myself with pleasure [on t]his occasion of renewing to you the assurance of my esteem and respect.   TH: JEFFERSON

PoC (MHi); on verso of reused address cover of Pierre Samuel Du Pont de Nemours to TJ, 24 July 1815; mutilated at seal; at foot of text: "M.r Henry Sheaff"; endorsed by TJ.

Henry Sheaff (ca. 1751–1820), wine merchant in Philadelphia, sold TJ wine between 1791 and 1804 and also counted George Washington among his customers. His business was at 223 High (or Market) Street in the former year, but he moved to 180 High Street by 1793 and remained there until about 1817. Sheaff suffered a stroke by 1815 and retired. He died in New York City (DNA: RG 29, CS, Pa., Philadelphia, 1790; Clement Biddle, *Philadelphia Directory* [Philadelphia, 1791], 117; *MB*, esp. 2:809, 1141; James Hardie, *Philadelphia Directory and Register* [Philadelphia, 1793], 129; Philadelphia *Dunlap's American Daily Advertiser*, 22 Jan. 1793; *PTJ*, 27:842–5; "Washington's Household Account Book, 1793–1797," *PMHB* 29 [1905]: 398; Philadelphia *Poulson's American Daily Advertiser*, 17 Apr. 1815; J. Sheaff (for Henry Sheaff) to TJ, 16 Oct. 1815; *Robinson's Original Annual Directory for 1817* [Philadelphia, 1817], 390; John Adems Paxton, *Paxton's Annual Philadelphia Directory and Register* [Philadelphia, 1818]; *New-York Daily Advertiser*, 10 Jan. 1820).

From Thomas Paine McMahon

SIR, Washington[1] City Aug[t] 12th 1815
    With feelings of respect and gratitude for your Polite and friendly attention in Answering my letter to you in April[2] 1813 I once more am induced to trouble you with a respectful Solicitation for your interest in having me Continued in the Army of the U. States as I entered it with the intention of making it a Profession; but unfortunately had very little acquaintance with the generals who made the Selection of officers for the Peace Establishment.

    I am fully aware Sir, of the rashness of my addressing You, but would beg you not to attribute it to arrogance; but to Place it to your goodness to me in 1813, and the friendly Sentiments You have expressed towards my father (Bernard M[c]Mahon of Philad[a]).

    Your complying with my request (if consistant) and Answering[3] this letter will be ever gratefully Remembered, by, Sir,
    Very Respectfully Your Obedient Serv[t]

THO[s] P: M[c]MAHON
at M[c]Keowens Hotel.

RC (MoSHi: TJC-BC); endorsed by TJ as received 16 Aug. 1815 and so recorded in SJL. RC (DLC); address cover only; with MS of TJ's Notes on a Conversation with Henry Dearborn and PoC of TJ to Dearborn, both 7 Oct. 1815, on verso; addressed: "Thomas Jefferson Esq[r] Monticello Virginia Per Mail"; franked; postmarked Washington, 12 Aug.

[1] Manuscript: "Wahington."
[2] Manuscript: "Apil."
[3] Manuscript: "Ansswering."

From John Vaughan

D SIR Philad. Aug[t] 12. 1815
    I have this day rec[d] the am[ot] of the note rem[d] by M[r] Gibson $692.[76] & have paid M[r] B. Jones on y/a 142[76/100] for which have taken his receipt M[r] Correa goes on Monday, in commencement of his Journey. I have forwarded the credits of Stephen Girard as directed[1]

    I remain Your ob[t] sev & sincere friend   J[N] VAUGHAN

RC (MHi); endorsed by TJ as received 19 Aug. 1815 and so recorded in SJL. RC (DLC); address cover only; with PoC of TJ to Peter Stephen Chazotte, 15 Oct. 1815, on verso; addressed: "Thomas Jefferson Monticello V[a]"; franked; postmarked Philadelphia, 12 Aug.

REM[D]: "remitted." Y/A: "your account."

[1] Manuscript: "direccted."

From Martha Jefferson Randolph

MY DEAR FATHER   monticello Aug. 13, 1815

The emergency of the occasion must apologise for the liberty I took in opening the enclosed. but as to morrow is Buckingham court and not knowing the danger that might accrue from a dissappointment I ascertained by opening the letter whether it was your self or the witnesses only that were wanting in which latter case they could have been summoned without applying to you but as some thing more seems requisite perhaps you can by writing do the business adieu we are all as you left us the sick mending & no new cases

yours   MR.

RC (ViCMRL, on deposit ViU: TJP); dateline adjacent to signature; endorsed by TJ as received 13 Aug. 1815 and so recorded in SJL. Enclosure: Thomas Jefferson (ca. 1783–1876) to TJ, 12 Aug. 1815, not found, but recorded in SJL as received 13 Aug. 1815.

To Martha Jefferson Randolph

Montpelier Aug 13. '15.

The letter you forwarded, my dear Martha, desiring me to attend the Buckingham court of this month, requires an impossibility because that is tomorrow. I Know also that the trial of the question cannot be at the Same court at which the two wills are presented. Time must be given to Summon witnesses, and I Suppose I shall be Served with a Summons notifying the day I must appear.—We have had a safe journey, shall return to Mr Lindsay's tomorrow night & shall be at home to dinner on Tuesday. Yours with unalterable & tender affection   (Signed) TH: JEFFERSON

Tr (NNPM); in Nicholas P. Trist's hand; at head of text: "(Copy)"; at foot of text: "Mrs Martha Randolph Monticello"; notation dated 23 June 1862 written perpendicularly in left margin by Trist: "The original given to Mr Felton for his daughter." Not recorded in SJL.

Because of a dispute over the validity of his brother's TWO WILLS, on 15 Sept. 1815 TJ gave a Deposition regarding Randolph Jefferson's Estate.

From William Wingate

DEAR SIR,   Haverhill, Mass, August 14. 1815.

I duely received the volume &c you returned to me—I Sincerely
thank you for your candid letter Sent me, on the occasion—I have
Sent the Same volume &c to m^r Maddison, and directed Him to
forward it to Gov. Snyder—Gov. Tompkins and return it to me—I
wrote to General Ripley as He passed on His Tour to the Eastward,
to come and Se me on the Same Subject, but I have not Seen nor
heard from Him Since—I am almost without hope of finding any
person to assist me in carrying the olive Branch into Execution—
America will Soon find it needfull, to ward off the impending
Judgments of God, which has already begun in Europe, and will
Soon Spread over the whole world—God has declared in His Holy
writ, that He will now Send Pestilence, Famine, Earthquakes and
the Sword, and distroy the wicked part of mankind—God tells me
that great distruction is now to take place—God further Says—That
He will now harden the Hearts of the people, as He did in the time
of Pharoah, untill all His Judgments have taken place—Behold
Saith the Lord, I will bring plagues upon the world, the Sword,
Famine death and distruction—For wickedness hath exceedingly
polluted the whole earth—and their hurtfull works are fulfilled—
Therefore Saith the Lord, I will hold my tongue no more as touching their Wickedness, which they profanely commit—neither will I
Suffer them in those things—in which they wickedly exercise themselves—Behold, the Innocent and righteous blood crieth unto me,
and the Souls of the Just complain continually—And therefore Saith
the Lord—I will [surely] avenge them, and receive unto me all the
Innocent blood from [amo]ng them—all this has reference to the
present moment—

[Si]r, here follows a true copy of a letter I wrote to my Brother
Paine Wingate, with whom you are well acquainted, I think this information will have more weight[1] with you, than it Would be to write
otherwise to you—to Wit—

God has revealed to me, and to me only in America, every Important event that has taken place ever Since Napoleon came on the
Stage of Public life—also, every Important event that is to take place
in the world, Between this time and the millineum—it is my Sincere
prayer that God may Suffer me for to reveal all Those Secrets to our
whole Family—and Save them if possiable from being distroyed in
the common distruction of the wicked, that is now begun in Europe,

and will Soon take place throughout the world—God tells me He will harden the Hearts of all the wicked part of mankind, as He did Pharoahs—untill their distruction takes place—if you are one of Those—you will not, nor <u>cannot</u> believe one word I write—Notwithstanding they are all God own words revealed to me—Brother, Remember, if what I State to you is <u>verified</u> in a few days—if you <u>then</u> <u>disbelieve</u> God and me, your distruction and your Families is certain—I am forbid to warn you any further at this time—

God Sent His Angel to Napoleon and told Him all that is to take place—and what to do—God has prepared Napoleon a place on a mountain for His Safety—and where Napoleon can Se both armies—The great Battle is to be <u>in</u> and <u>round</u> the <u>city</u> of <u>Paris</u>—Napoleon has artfully collected Them all there agreeable to God appointment—God <u>has</u> hardened the Hearts of the Allied armies, who feel Sore afraid, yet durst fight—

They <u>cannot</u> <u>avoid</u> <u>refusing</u> to let the French Nation appoint Their own Ruler, which act will bring about their own distruction—

Brother, I will here State to you the manner in which God has promised Napoleon for to distroy all His Enemies—And the city of Paris—which is to be utterly distroyed and burnt all at once—not one will escape as I wrote you before—(I think the city of Paris will be blown up)

Napoleon—neither lift up His Hand, nor held Sword, nor any instrument of War—But only I Saw, that Napoleon Sent out of His mouth, as it had been a blast of fire, and out of His lips a flaming breath, and out of His tongue—Napoleon cast out Sparks and Tempests—And they were all mixt together—the blast of fire, the flaming breath, and the great Tempest—and <u>fell</u> with violence upon the multitude which was prepared to fight—and burnt them up every one, So that upon a Sudden of an innumerable multitude nothing was to be perceived, but only dust and Smell of Smoke—(gun powder)

God interpretation—Behold the days come, when the most High, will <u>begin</u> to <u>deliver</u> <u>them</u> that are upon the earth (Jews) And God will come to the asstonishment of them that dwell on the earth—

Brother, all this will <u>now</u> take place as true as their is a God—if it does—believe your poor disconsolate forsaken Brother—who has no where to lay His Head, <u>even</u> a <u>manger</u>—and has no Friend but God, I ask, nor Seek for no other—I am worth my weight in Gold to the world, my life has been Spared for Some wise purpose—yet

unknown to America and the world—I Shall wait God own time—
to Shew myself, and I hope do good—

y^r Affectionate Brother—   W^M WINGATE
Hon. Paine Wingate—

Sir, you must not reveal this Secret, to defeat God plan—whoever attempts it—God will distroy Him instantly—I warn you for to remember to keep these Secrets as God commanded his Inspired Servants—

Sir, I wrote to m^r Maddison Some time Since, for to appoint me Inspector at Newbury Port—it is now held by a Man who is and always has been, a Malicious Enemy to the Republican cause—which ought not to be Suffered, let their connections be ever So Republican—I have never as yet received a Single line from m^r Maddison—I Still feel myself intitled to that office—if I cannot—rather than not to have any imploy, I would accept at the Post-office, I held under m^r Habersham—I lost all my property for Supporting the Republican cause—is well known—

I remain Your highly Esteemed Friend.

WILLIAM WINGATE

RC (MoSHi: TJC-BC); mutilated at seal; addressed: "Honorable Thomas Jefferson Esquire Monticello Va"; franked; postmarked Haverhill, Mass., 15 Aug.; endorsed by TJ. Recorded in SJL as received 3 Oct. 1815.

In the Bible, Jesus predicted the eventual arrival of PESTILENCE, FAMINE, EARTHQUAKES AND THE SWORD (Matthew 24.6–7; Luke 21.10–1), and God chose to HARDEN the heart of PHAROAH (Exodus, ch. 4, 7–10). BEHOLD, SAITH THE LORD . . . INNOCENT BLOOD FROM AMONG THEM is from the apocryphal scriptures, 2 Esdras 15.5–9. Wingate's BROTHER PAINE WINGATE (1739–1838) was born in Amesbury, Massachusetts, graduated from Harvard College (later University) in 1759, and was ordained in 1763 as pastor to a Congregational church in present-day Hampton Falls, New Hampshire. In 1776 he left the ministry and moved to a farm in Stratham, New Hampshire, where he

resided until his death. Wingate served in the New Hampshire House of Representatives, 1783 and 1795; the Confederation Congress, 1788; the United States Senate, 1789–93; and the United States House of Representatives, 1793–95. He was a judge on the Superior Court of New Hampshire, 1798–1809 (DAB; Sibley's Harvard Graduates, 14:533–48; Charles E. L. Wingate, Life and Letters of Paine Wingate, 2 vols. [1930]; First Federal Congress, esp. 14:654–8 and vols. 15–7; Portsmouth Journal Of Literature & Politics, 10 Mar. 1838).

GOD HAS PREPARED NAPOLEON: William Wingate assigned Napoleon the role and powers of a messenger sent by God in 2 Esdras 13.3–11. BEHOLD THE DAYS COME . . . DWELL ON THE EARTH is from 2 Esdras 13.29–30. William Cross was the INSPECTOR of the revenue at Newburyport, Massachusetts.

¹ Manuscript: "wait."

From Jesse Torrey

Charlottesville, August 15ᵗʰ 1815.

The bearer, and undersigned, of Lebanon Springs, has made choice of this eccentric method of presenting himself to Mʳ Jefferson; as an enthusiastic Student of Physiology and Philosophy.

At an early period of my life, Sir, I contracted a firm belief, that the same permanent laws, which have been ascertained, by Sir Isaac Newton, Benjamin Franklin, Joseph Priestly, and more recently by Sir Humphrey Davy and others; to govern the composition, decomposition and motion of that portion of the Universe, generally termed inanimate matter, the gravitative and repellent properties of the Electric Fluid &c; might with equal certainty and uniformity, be attached to the art, (which ought to be a science,) of producing and subsisting animal bodies, of their preservation and protection from premature destruction, by other causes than casualties.

Except the sustenance required to my young family, the developement of this proposition, has been the favorite object of my labors, studies, reflections and resources, eight years.

I have availed myself of the earliest opportunity that the indigence of my circumstances would admit of, to visit Monticello, where, I have long been impressed with an opinion, (which is not a solitary one,) that I should meet with the greatest accumulation both of original and acquired, Moral, Political, and Physiological Knowledge etc. at least on this side the Atlantic.

If you were to ask, why I do not propose my subject, to the consideration and patronage, of some of our distinguished practical Chemists and Professors of Philosophy and Medicine, who are actually engaged in the advancement of the art which I wish to improve; I should be obliged to enquire of you, Sir, as Monsieur Volney has probably been a personal acquaintance and friend[1] of yours; whether he offered his genuine transcript, of those fundamental laws, which God has imprinted in his constitution (edition) of this Globe in legible characters; for the government and happiness of Mankind; — to the consideration and patronage of a Pope or a Bishop; or whether Thomas Paine solicited the opinion of Monarchs or Princes on the Rights of Man. —

If my sentiments, on the identity of those Laws, which predominate in the organization and disorganization, of Animal, Vegetable, or inanimate bodies; receive your approbation; I will furnish, in a subsequent memorial, some facts in confirmation of the principle; and a proposition for your consideration and encouragement, of a

plan, tending eventually, to a complete developement and establishment of it; by means of collecting the facts in point, which, already,
have existed, and may be selected from the experience on record,
from the time of Hippocrates, of Galen, of Sydenham, of Brown &
Darwin; to some ingenious writers and Practitioners of the present
day; and from the experience, also, of many, not on records of
paper;—and by means, also, of a series of future experiments directly
to the purpose, which will require ample collections and distributions
of the necessary materials; the results of which, can be previously estimated with considerable exactness, provided the Laws mentioned
before, are carefully consulted.

Accept, if you please, Sir, the tribute of my high estimation and
respect, and of my friendly attachment.   JESSE TORREY JN[R]

RC (MHi); at foot of text: "Thomas
Jefferson Esq[r] &c."; addressed: "M[r]
Jefferson present"; endorsed by TJ as re-
ceived 16 Aug. 1815 and so recorded in
SJL.

Jesse Torrey (b. 1787), physician and
reformer, established a free library in
1804 for adolescent residents of his hometown of New Lebanon, Columbia County,
New York. By December 1814 he had established a medical practice in Pittsfield,
Massachusetts. Late in the spring of 1815
Torrey quit this practice and set out on a
journey to promote the creation of public
libraries. He used observations from his
southern tour to write *A Portraiture of
Domestic Slavery, in the United States*
(Philadelphia, 1817). Torrey subsequently wrote books for schoolroom use and *A
Dissertation on the Causes, Preventives,
and Remedies of Plague, Yellow Fever,
Cholera, Dysentery, and Other Pestilential, Epidemic, or Contagious Diseases*
(1832), and he advocated for government
support of free, public education. In 1829
he patented a bookbinding machine, and
the following year he opened an "American Specimen Book Store and Publishers'
Exchange" in Philadelphia. In 1835 Torrey began the short-lived Poughkeepsie
*Herald of Reason and Common Sense, and
Advocate of Equal Rights and Free Discussion*. He was residing in Newburgh three
years later when he petitioned the New
York state legislature to ban the manufacture and sale of strong liquors (Torrey,

*The Intellectual Torch; Developing an
Original, Economical and Expeditious
Plan for the Universal Dissemination of
Knowledge and Virtue; By Means of Free
Public Libraries*, 2d ed. [Ballston Spa,
N.Y., 1817; repr. with biographical intro-
duction by Edward Harmon Virgin,
1912]; *Pittsfield Sun*, 1 Dec. 1814, 8 June
1815; Wilhelmus B. Bryan, "A Fire in An
Old Time F Street Tavern and What It
Revealed," *Records of the Columbia His-
torical Society* 9 [1906]: 204–13; Wash-
ington *Daily National Intelligencer*, 23
Sept. 1829; Torrey to James Madison, 19
Oct. 1829 [DLC: Madison Papers]; *List
of Patents*, 389; Philadelphia *Mechanic's
Free Press*, 27 Feb. 1830; Washington
Daily National Journal, 14 May 1830;
New-York Spectator, 13 July 1835, 26
Feb. 1838).

During Torrey's brief VISIT to Monticello, TJ declined to collaborate with him
in any physiological studies (Torrey to
TJ, 6 Apr. 1816). The GENUINE TRAN-
SCRIPT by the French scholar Constantin
François Chasseboeuf, comte de Volney,
was published in English as *The Law of
Nature, or Principles of Morality, Deduced
from the Physical Constitution of Mankind
and the Universe* (Philadelphia, 1796).
For the original 1793 Paris edition that
Volney sent to TJ and the extensive correspondence that ensued, see *PTJ*, esp.
27:390–1.

[1] Preceding two words interlined.

To Stephen Cathalan

DEAR SIR   Monticello Aug. 16. 15.

I wrote to you, my dear friend, on the 3ᵈ of July, requesting you to send me some wines, and that mr Girard of Philadelphia would place a sum of 200. Dollars at your disposal, in the hands of his correspondents at Paris,[1] then unknown to me. I now inclose to you a copy of his letter to messʳˢ Perrigaux, Lafitte and co. of that place, who will answer your draught of that amount.   We have news from Paris down to the second abdication of Bonaparte. the sequel is too uncertain to be conjectured. I await therefore with the greatest anxiety to hear the fate of a country, for which I feel the deepest interest, and your own especially in a place which seems to have felt the first convulsion. god bless you and conduct you safely thro' the dreadful storm.   TH: JEFFERSON

PoC (DLC); on verso of reused address cover to TJ; at foot of text: "Mʳ Cathalan. to the care of Dʳ Henry Jackson"; endorsed by TJ. Enclosure: second enclosure to John Vaughan to TJ, 31 July 1815. Enclosed in TJ to John Graham, 17 Aug. 1815.

This letter was probably enclosed in a missing and otherwise undocumented letter to Jackson, which Jackson acknowledged on 9 Nov. 1815 as a "note covering the letter for Mʳ Cathalan."

[1] Preceding two words interlined in place of "there."

To Nicolas G. Dufief

DEAR SIR   Monticello Aug. 16. 15.

I wrote you on the 14ᵗʰ from Montpelier (the President's) requesting you to send on La Croix's Course of mathematics, and to procure for me a particular edition of Ovid's metamorphoses, which I am now satisfied is Minellius's. I have now to request that you will add to these Adams's geometrical & graphical essays in 2. v. 8ᵛᵒ and Adams's practical astronomy, 8ᵛᵒ both of which I presume are in the bookstores of Philadelphia. if you recieve this before sending of La Croix, in the way mentioned in my letter, those now asked for may come with them. but if after you shall have sent the others off, these may come volume by volume by the mail. Accept the assurances of my esteem & respect   TH: JEFFERSON

PoC (DLC); on verso of reused address cover to TJ; at foot of text: "Mʳ Dufief"; endorsed by TJ.

The letter TJ wrote Dufief on the 14ᵀᴴ FROM MONTPELIER, not found, is recorded in SJL as being "(for books. no copy kept)."

From George Logan

DEAR SIR   Stenton Augt 16th: 1815

Looking over some private papers a few days since, I found a communication from Dr Priestley to me, respecting the education and character of the Emperor of Russia. I herewith inclose you a copy of this interesting document; from a conviction of its being agreeable, on account of your known attachment to the most virtuous and magnanimous of monarchs

Mrs Logan unites with me in sentiments of respect to yourself and family—

Accept assurances of my friendship   GEO LOGAN

RC (DLC); at foot of text: "Thos Jefferson Esqr"; endorsed by TJ as received 3 Oct. 1815 and so recorded in SJL.

Although Logan described it as a COMMUNICATION from Joseph Priestley to himself, the enclosure seems to have been part of a letter from an unidentified correspondent to Priestley, describing Alexander I as "a sort of Phenomenon in the political world"; acknowledging that the author knows the Russian emperor indirectly through Frédéric César de La Harpe, who educated Alexander "from the Age of eight years, to the time of his marriage" and from whom Alexander received a "thoroughly Republican education"; quoting an undated letter from Alexander to La Harpe in which the em-

peror expresses his desire to reduce "to practice the lessons you have Taught" and become "an instrument of the happiness and liberty of this hitherto ill instructed and ill governed People"; revealing that Alexander has invited La Harpe to return and advise him and that his ukases on liberty of the press and the abolition of slavery show that he has already begun his reforms; and reporting that the author and La Harpe have collaborated to produce a "code to reform as moderate as Republicans could well make" (Tr in DLC: TJ Papers, 208:37017–9; in an unidentified hand; undated; at head of text: "Extract of a Letter from _____ to Dr Priestley, received by him a short time before his Death" [which occurred on 6 Feb. 1804]).

Account with Joseph Milligan

[ca. 16 Aug. 1815]

Thomas Jefferson, Esquire.

To Joseph Milligan		D^r
1812 Feby 4 To 1 British Spy		$1.50
1813 June 30 To 6 Vol^s Ornithology		72.
1814 April 18 To 7th & 8th Vol^s do.		24.
Octo. 10 To 1 Set Heroditus 4 Vol^s	18.	
1 Southey's Life of Nelson	2.	20.
Nov. 17 To Binding & lettering the "Book of Kings."		5.

1815 April 7 To 1 Sampson's Memoirs	2.50		
1 American Gardener	1.		
1 Bracken's Farrier	50		
1 Duane's Hand Book	1.25		
1 Prayer Book	3.		
1 Power of Religion	1.		
1 Harrison's Chancery	9.		
1 Bacaria on Crimes	1.		
1 Burkhard's N. History	1.		
1 young's Farmer's Guide	3.		
1 Hist^y of the French Revolu^n	2.50	25.75	
July 13 To 1 Paris in 1802 & 1814	1.		
1 Dufief's Dictionary. 3V. calf	12.50	13.50	
31 To Binding Sundries—as per Bill Transmitted	50.50		
1 Ream Eng. 4to post, cut down	9.	59.50	
Car^d Over	Doll^s	221.25^1	
To 1 Marshall's Life of Washington	17.50		
1 Cooper's Justinian	6.		
1 Steuart's Philosophy	5.		
1 Walker's Dictionary	3.50		
1 Medical Companion	3.		
1 Criminal Recorder	1.		
1 Priestley's Biography	2.		
1 Porter's Journal	3.		
1 Exposition &c.	1.		
1 Thompson's four Gospels	1.50	43.50	
Dollars	264.75		

MS (DLC: TJ Papers, 204:36273); written in Milligan's hand on both sides of a single sheet; undated; repeated intermediate sum at head of verso omitted; notation by TJ at foot of text: "Aug. 11. by draught on Gibson & Jefferson 92.D." MS (DLC); cover sheet only; with PoC of TJ to Benjamin Waterhouse, 13 Oct. 1815, on recto and verso; reading: "Thos Jefferson Esq in a/c With Joseph Milligan $264.75." Enclosed in a brief covering letter from Milligan to TJ, Georgetown, 16 Aug. 1815, stating that "Agreeably to your instructions I now enclose my account Amount $264.75" (RC in DLC; endorsed by TJ as received 18 Aug. 1815 but recorded in SJL as received a day later).

Milligan's account with TJ includes William Wirt, *The Letters of the British Spy*, 4th ed. (Baltimore, 1811; Leavitt, *Poplar Forest*, 40 [no. 670]); Alexander Wilson, *American Ornithology; or, The Natural History of the Birds of the United States*, 9 vols. (Philadelphia, 1808–14; Sowerby, no. 1022), vols. 1–8; and William Beloe, trans., *The History of Herodotus*, 4 vols. (London, 1791, and later eds.; Poor, *Jefferson's Library*, 3 [no. 6]). For the collection that TJ called the BOOK OF KINGS, see TJ to Milligan, 17

Oct. 1814. The account also included a copy of Cesare Bonesana, Marchese di Beccaria (BACARIA), *An Essay on Crimes & Punishments* (New York, 1809, and other eds.; Sowerby, no. 2349); *An Impartial History of the late Revolution in France* (Philadelphia, 1794; Sowerby, no. 229); a REAM of quarto English letter paper cut to fit TJ's portable polygraph; Dugald Stewart's (STEUART'S) *Elements of the Philosophy of the Human Mind*, 2 vols. (Boston, 1814, and other eds.; Poor, *Jefferson's Library*, 8 [no. 456]); James Ewell, *The Planter's and Mariner's Medical Companion* (Philadelphia, 1807, and later eds.; Sowerby, no. 893; Poor, *Jefferson's Library*, 5 [no. 183]); and Charles Thomson's (THOMPSON'S) *A Synopsis of the Four Evangelists* (Philadelphia, 1815; Poor, *Jefferson's Library*, 9 [no. 509]).

[1] Recto ends here.

To George Ticknor

DEAR SIR   Monticello Aug. 16. 15.

In my letter of July 4. I mentioned that mr Girard of Philadelphia would furnish a credit of 350.D. on his correspondents in Paris, then unknown to me, but of whom mr John Vaughan would give you information. I now inclose you a copy of mr Girard's letter to mess[rs] Perrigaux, Lafitte and co. directing them to pay to you that sum, and more if my catalogue should require more.—I can give you no other, nor better news than that the calm of this country is a delicious contrast to the storms which are shaking the oldest and firmest battlements of Europe. you will [re]ad[1] in that how inestimable is the happy lot of your own country, and the wisdom of it's taking no part in the broils of that Bedlam. ever & affectionately yours

TH: JEFFERSON

PoC (MHi); on verso of reused address cover to TJ; ink stained; at foot of text: "M[r] George Ticknor to the care of Elisha Ticknor esq."; endorsed by TJ. Enclosure: first enclosure to John Vaughan to TJ, 31 July 1815. Enclosed in TJ to Elisha Ticknor, 16 Aug. 1815, not found and not recorded in SJL, but acknowledged in Elisha Ticknor to TJ, 24 Aug. 1815.

[1] Word recopied above the line by TJ but still not fully legible.

To John Graham

[DEAR SIR]   Monticello Aug. 17. 15.

I avail myself as usual of your kindness in asking the benefit of the government channel for the conveyance of the inclosed letters. if there should be a direct conveyance to mr Appleton at Leghorn, that to mr Mazzei would go safest that way, because he is particularly known to mr Appleton. but the choice of conveyance I leave altogether to your discretion & friendship, only observing that it needs a safe, more than a speedy conveyance. I salute you with great friendship & respect

Th: Jefferson

PoC (DLC); on verso of reused address cover of John Adams to TJ, 30 July 1815; salutation faint; at foot of text: "John Graham esq."; endorsed by TJ.

Enclosures: (1) TJ to Philip Mazzei, 9 Aug. 1815. (2) TJ to Stephen Cathalan, 16 Aug. 1815, and covering letter noted there.

To Joseph Milligan

DEAR SIR   Monticello Aug. 17. 15.

I have just sent to Milton for the mail tumbrel a package addressed to the care of mr Gray, portage to Fredericksbg being first paid at Milton as it always will be. and you paying that from Fredericksbg to George town, we may save mr Gray[1] the occasion of ever making any advances of money for what passes between us. the package contains 2. volumes which I wish to be divided the one into two, & the other into 3. vols, as you will see in the directions. I shall be glad to recieve them at my return from Bedford 6. weeks hence.   mr Dufief has procured for me about 10. vols of books, ordered long since & not found till lately. I have desired him to send the package by the stage to Georgetown to your care to be forwarded thro' mr Gray. the portage you will be so good as to place in account between us. Accept my respects & best wishes.   Th: Jefferson

P.S. would it not be better for you to send me the translation of Tracy's work before you begin to print it, that I may revise and correct it & return it to you?

Aug. 18. P.S. I find the transln in the bundle with the original.

RC (ViU: TJP); lacking 18 Aug. postscript. PoC (DLC); on verso of reused address cover to TJ; containing 18 Aug. postscript; adjacent to signature: "Mr Millegan"; endorsed by TJ. Recorded in SJL as a letter of 17 Aug. 1815 with a "P.S. 18."

TJ's PACKAGE contained an English or American edition of the *Tables Requisite to be used with the Nautical Ephemeris for finding the Latitude and Longitude at Sea*

(see note to TJ to Melatiah Nash, 15 Nov. 1811), and Charles Hutton, *Mathematical Tables: containing Common, Hyperbolic, and Logistic Logarithms* (London, 1785; Sowerby, no. 3697; Poor, *Jefferson's Library*, 8 [no. 403]; see also TJ to Milligan, 5 Oct. 1815). The DIRECTIONS enclosed with the package have not been found.

[1] Manuscript: "Grey."

To Hugh Williamson and
Samuel L. Mitchill

GENTLEMEN   Monticello Aug. 17. 15.

I recieved yesterday only your favor of July 15. informing me that the Literary and Philosophical society of New York had been pleased to elect me an honorary member of their body. permit me, through you, to retur[n] them my thanks for this mark of their favorable attention. age, distance, and a relaxation in literary & Philosophical pursuits will, I fear, render me an unprofitable member, but I shall avail myself with great pleasure of any occasion which may arise of being useful to them, and of proving the high respect and consideration with which I have the honor to be their and your

Most obedient servant   TH: JEFFERSON

PoC (MoSHi: TJC-BC); one word faint; at foot of text: "Messʳˢ Williamson & Mitchell"; endorsed by TJ.

From Robert Brent

DEAR SIR   City of Washington Aug. 18ᵗʰ 1815

Mʳ Wᵐ P Rathborne of New York being on a Journey which will take him thro Charlotteville, most probably, is desirous, when in your neighbourhood of paying his respects to you—Being however a Stranger to you personally, I have ventured upon the liberty of giving him this letter of Introduction which I certainly would not presume to do were I not well acquanted with his Character & merit—which entitles him to confidence & respect. he takes with him on his tour his amiable Lady.

I have the honor to be

With every Sentiment of respect & Esteem Dear Sir your Obt Ser

ROBERT BRENT

RC (DLC); endorsed by TJ as received 3 Oct. 1815 and so recorded in SJL. RC (DLC); address cover only; with PoC of TJ to John Glendy, 22 Oct. 1815, on verso; addressed: "The Honble Thomas Jefferson Esq Monticello Virgᵃ" by "Wᵐ P Rathborne Esq."

William P. Rathbone (1784–1862), businessman, was a New York City mer-

chant at the time of this letter. He was the United States Army paymaster in the New York District, 1814–15; an active member of New York's Republican Party; a federal contractor supplying rations for American troops in Ohio and at various posts throughout the northern territories; a New York City alderman, 1825–26; and a member of its Board of Health in 1826. Rathbone later moved to

[675]

New Jersey, representing that state at the Democratic Party's national convention in 1835 and serving as a judge of the court of common pleas for Bergen County in 1838. By 1842 he had purchased land along Burning Springs Run, near Parkersburg, Virginia (later West Virginia), on which he successfully drilled an oil well in 1860 (*Longworth's New York Directory* [1814]: 261; [1816]: 358; Heitman, *U.S. Army*, 1:817; New York *Columbian*, 21 Feb. 1814; New York *National Advocate*, 6 Apr. 1816; *Letter from the Secretary of War, transmitting statements of contracts made in the year 1817* [Washington, 1818]; David T. Valentine, *Manual of the Corporation of the City of New-York for 1852* [1852], 190; *Minutes of the Common Council of the City of New York 1784–1831* [1917], 15:612; Baltimore *Niles' Weekly Register*, 30 May 1835; James M. Van Valen, *History of Bergen County New Jersey* [1900], 45; John T. Harris, ed., *West Virginia Legislative Hand Book and Manual and Official Register* [1917], 590–1; "An Act for the relief of the heirs of William P. Rathbone, deceased," 3 Feb. 1863, in *Acts of the General Assembly, of the State of Virginia* [Wheeling, 1863], 44–7; gravestone inscription in Riverview Cemetery, Parkersburg, W.Va.).

To Patrick Gibson

DEAR SIR   Monticello Aug. 19. 15.

since my last I have drawn on you in favor of Dabney Carr for 68. D 10   L. H. Girardin 25.D.   Joseph Milligan 92.D. and this day in favor of Th: J. Randolph for 275.D.

I set out tomorrow for Bedford, and shall probably be there to the last of the next month.   Not knowing the day when my note of 1000.D. in bank will need renewal, I must ask the favor of you to notify me of it by inclosing a blank directed to me 'at Poplar forest near Lynchburg,' and it shall be attended to. Accept the assurance of my great esteem and respect.   TH: JEFFERSON

PoC (ICHi); on verso of reused address cover of Stephen Girard to TJ, 30 July 1815; at foot of text: "Mʳ Gibson."

TJ had DRAWN on Gibson & Jefferson on 30 July, 2, 11, and 19 Aug., respectively. The payment to Louis H. Girardin covered $19 for books, $2 for plants, and $4 for a year's subscription to the *Daily* *Compiler and Richmond Commercial Register*, probably for the biweekly country edition. The money owed Thomas Jefferson Randolph included $42 for twelve bushels of corn; $14 for "sundry small articles"; $100 toward the salary of Tufton's overseer, William Ballard; and $119 for cash received (*MB*, 2:1312, 1313).

To James L. Jefferson

DEAR LILBURNE   Monticello Aug. 19. 15.

It was at the President's in Orange that I recieved your brother's letter requesting me to be at the next Buckingham court to give evidence on your father's will. it came to hand the Sunday evening & the next day was that of the court. time and distance therefore rendered my attendance impossible. I set out for Bedford tomorrow morning and shall be there to the 1st of October. I do not know that my evidence can be of any importance; but if it be thought so, I could not attend without being subpoenaed; because the testimony of a person volunteering in a cause is not recieved with the same confidence as [wh]en he attends in obedience to a summons. if it be desired therefore a subpoena may be inclosed by mail[1] directed to me 'at Poplar forest near Ly[n]chburg,' and if sent soon I shall recieve it in time. Accept the assurance of my friendship and best wishes.

TH: JEFFERSON

PoC (MoSHi: TJC-BC); on verso of reused address cover to TJ; ink stained; at foot of text: "Mr Lilburne Jefferson"; endorsed by TJ.

James Lilburne Jefferson (d. 1836), who was referred to as Lilburne among family members, was the fifth and youngest-known son of TJ's brother Randolph Jefferson by his first wife, Anna Jefferson Lewis Jefferson. TJ took a special interest in his nephew, offering to design a course of reading for him in 1813. The younger Jefferson apparently never accepted his uncle's repeated offers to live at Monticello, both before and after his father's death. A resident of Columbia in Fluvanna County in 1820, ten years later Jefferson had settled in Lynchburg, where he remained until his death (Bernard Mayo, ed., *Thomas Jefferson and His Unknown Brother* [1942; repr. 1981],

1–9; Malone, *Jefferson*, 6:155–6; TJ to Randolph Jefferson, 25 May 1813; Randolph Jefferson to TJ, 21 June 1813; TJ to James L. Jefferson and James L. Jefferson to TJ, both 18 Feb. 1816; DNA: RG 29, CS, Fluvanna Co., 1820; Campbell Co., 1830; *Lynchburg Virginian*, 11 Oct. 1832; Lynchburg Hustings and Corporation Court Will Book, B:292, 295).

For the 12 Aug. LETTER to TJ from Thomas Jefferson (ca. 1783–1876), see note to Martha Jefferson Randolph to TJ, 13 Aug. 1815. TJ assisted James L. Jefferson and his brothers in an unsuccessful challenge to their FATHER'S WILL, which heavily favored his second wife, Mitchie B. Pryor Jefferson (TJ's Deposition regarding Randolph Jefferson's Estate, 15 Sept. 1815; Mayo, *Unknown Brother*, 9).

[1] Preceding two words interlined.

From Joseph Milligan

DEAR SIR   Georgetown August 20th 1815
Yours of the 11th inst post mark 17th reached me yesterday it covered a draft for ninety two dollars for which please accept my thanks
I wrote you on the 16th enclosing my account amount $264 75 If convenient it is particularly desirable to me to have it Settled as I am settling up all my business to put my stock into better order than I could possibly keep it during the war

The whole of the books ordered shall be got and sent as soon as possible; I trust that you have found Aesop as I feel confident it was included in one of the Boxes, the Smallest Box I think was the last packed it was in the last box that[1] was packed that I put it I packed them in the Bindery from the list that I had made of them when I opened them and as I had no other books of that kind binding it was not easy to make a mistake If it had been left out I would have found it Since, therfore I hope on a review of them you will find it

With Respect & Esteem yours   JOSEPH MILLIGAN

RC (DLC); at foot of text: "Thoˢ Jefferson Esqr monticello milton via [i.e. Virginia]"; endorsed by TJ as received 3 Oct. 1815 and so recorded in SJL.

[1] Milligan here interlined but then partially erased the word "it."

From Tristram Dalton

SIR   Boston Aug 21 1815

I am happy in an opportunity, by favour of my good friend General Dearborn, to tender you my most respectful regards—and to hand two pamphlets, in consequence of a wish expressed by Mʳ Dexter, the introducer of the One on the natural History and Origin of Peat— who is not a little enthusiastical upon the subject—

The Massᵗᵗˢ Agricultural[1] Journal for June gives a partial account of the method practised in this <u>cool</u> & cold Section of the Union—

Allowance must be made in this representation as the Gentlemen composing the Society, and their Correspondents are not generally <u>practical</u> farmers—

Having read,[2] with much satisfaction, the "Rural Socrates," which pamphlet you were so kind as lend me, when in Washington, I did not peruse the copious extracts made in this Number of the Journal—I <u>then</u> formed an opinion that the practise of the Swiss, and his remarks might be peculiarly useful to the Farmers of the Northern States

With high Esteem I am Sir your most obdᵗ Servᵗ

TRISTRAM DALTON

RC (DLC); dateline beneath signature; at foot of text: "The Honorable Thomas Jefferson"; mistakenly endorsed by TJ as a letter of 25 Aug. 1815 received 3 Oct. 1815 and so recorded in SJL.

Tristram Dalton (1738–1817), mer- chant and public official, was a native of Newburyport, Massachusetts. After graduating from Harvard College (later University) in 1755, he read law but went into trade. During the Revolutionary War, Dalton used his business skills and connections to sell prizes, outfit warships, acquire supplies for the Continental army, and manage his own privateers. In 1780 he was a founder of the American Academy of Arts and Sciences. Dalton served in the Massachusetts House of Representatives, 1776, 1782–84 (with service as Speaker, 1783–84), and 1785–86; the Massachusetts Senate, 1784–85 and 1786–89; the Massachusetts ratification convention of 1788, where he supported the new United States Constitution; and the United States Senate, 1789–91. He was treasurer of the United States Mint, 1792–94, but in the latter year he gave up this post, sold most of his property in New England, invested the proceeds in land in the District of Columbia, and became a partner in the mercantile firm of Tobias Lear & Company. Dalton filed for insolvency in 1799. He was appointed agent of the Washington branch of the Bank of the United States in 1800 and then a director in 1801; sat on the federal commission for the District of Columbia from 1801 until the three-member board was abolished the following year; and became postmaster of Georgetown in 1802. President James Madison named Dalton collector of federal direct taxes and internal duties in 1813 for the Ninth Massachusetts District, stationed in Salem. The next year he became federal surveyor of the port and inspector of the revenue for Boston. Dalton served in that position until his death (Eben F. Stone, "A Sketch of Tristram Dalton," Essex Institute, *Historical Collections* 25 [1888]: 1–29; *Sibley's Harvard Graduates*, 13:569–78; American Academy of Arts and Sciences, *Bulletin* 58 [2004]: 115; Merrill Jensen, John P. Kaminski, and others, eds., *The Documentary History of the Ratification of the Constitution* [1976–   ], vols. 4–7; William C. di Giacomantonio, "All the President's Men: George Washington's Federal City Commissioners," *Washington History* 3 [1991]: 70–5; *JEP*; *Votes and Proceedings of the House of Delegates of the State of Maryland. November Session, 1799* [Annapolis, 1800], 30, 32, 46, 54, 111; James O. Wettereau, "The Branches of the First Bank of the United States," *Journal of Economic History* 2 [supplement, Dec. 1942], 79–81; New York *Commercial Advertiser*, 15 Oct. 1801; *PTJ*, 36:312–4; Georgetown *Washington Federalist*, 26 July 1802; *Salem Gazette*, 25 Nov. 1813, 18 Jan. 1814; *The Boston Directory* [Boston, 1816], 92, 233; *Boston Daily Advertiser*, 2 June 1817).

The TWO PAMPHLETS included the June 1815 issue of the *Massachusetts Agricultural Journal*, published by the Massachusetts Society for Promoting Agriculture. Aaron DEXTER, the society's president, supplied a short introduction to an abridged version of a work on PEAT by Robert Rennie published as "Essays on the Natural History and Origin of Peat," *Massachusetts Agricultural Journal* 3 (June 1815): 281–311.

TJ had owned two English translations of the RURAL SOCRATES by Hans Kaspar Hirzel. One appeared as an appendix to Arthur Young, *Rural Oeconomy* (London, 1770; Sowerby, no. 705), and the other, by Benjamin Vaughan, was *The Rural Socrates; or an account of a celebrated Philosophical Farmer, lately living in Switzerland, and known by the name of Kliyogg* (Hallowell, Me., 1800; see *PTJ*, 35:605). Because he had borrowed one of TJ's copies, Dalton decided against reading the EXTRACTS that appeared in the *Massachusetts Agricultural Journal* 3 (June 1815): 354–74.

¹ Manuscript: "Agriculural."
² Manuscript: "reead."

From Louis Philippe Gallot
de Lormerie

Monsieur l'Expresident,   Paris 22 aout 1815.—

Permettés moi de profiter d'une Occasion sure pour avoir L'honneur de Vous presenter L'hommâge de mon respect et de la reconnoissance Eternellé que je vous dois du bonheur que vous m'avés procuré de revoir ma patrie. malgré toutes les agitations politiques Je m'y trouve assés heureux de retrouver parmi mes Amis; et surtout ma fortune tres modifiée par la révolution, mais Encor suffisante pour me procurer Lindèpendance, et le repos.—

> soÿons contens du Nécessaire
> Sans souhaiter jamais des tresors superflus
> il faut les redouter autant que la misére
> comme elle ils chassent les Vertus.
>   florian. fable du Livre 2^e

Jai Lhonneur dEtre votre collégue dans la Soçieté d'Agriculture de la Seine comme membre correspondant; Elle vous a déçerné, a juste titre une Medaille d'or pour votre ingènieuse charrue, il n'est pas d'objêt plus utile.

Jai rappellé a la Societe l'Envoi que jai fait etant dans les E:u— d'un Vegètal qui commence a Etre cultivé en pleine terre et qui n'étoit connu que dans les serres et Chassis. c'est la Patate Sucrée (convolvulus Batatas[1] L) Si commun mais si bon dans votre Patrie— on en récolte dans nos Départem^{ts} du midi et même aux Environs de paris dans les Jardins mais on en obtient difficilement, la Société desireroit qu'on put lui en procurer des Graines c'est au moins le vœu que me tèmoignoit—un de nos membres les plus actif—Si Vous aviés la bonté, Monsieur, de charger quelqun intelligent dans Votre terre ou Environs en Virginie d'en[2] cultiver spécialement 3 ou 4 Plantes pour Graine, de la recueillir bien mure, et de l'Enfermer dans une petite Boïte de fer blanc (tin Box) bien fermante et recouverte de Papier adressée a M Le secrétaire de la Légation americaine a Paris avec lettre d'avis pour me la remettre, Je la présenterois a la Societé de Votre Part, Monsieur, et nous en aurions tous une véritable reconnoissance—

Jai Envoyé aussi—des Graines des E u a M thouin Professeur et adm^r Du Museum d'hist naturelle et il m'a dit que ces Graines lui etoient ainsi parvenues en trés bon Etat.

mille Pardons, de la peine, mais comme cet Objet est Sçientifique et rural Jai cru pouvoir vous en Entretenir, puisque Vous cultivés ces arts & sciences avec autant de Plaisir que de Succés—

M. Crawford avec qui J'ai Eu Lhonneur de Passer des E:u en france Retournant de son Ambassade dans votre intèressante Patrie, et qui m'a Comblé d'honnêteté pendant le Passâge, et depuis icy veut bien Se charger de Vous transmettre la présente. nous le regrettons beaucoup Je suis avec un trés sincere & respectueux attachement Monsieur l'Expresident, Votre trés humble et tres obeïssant serviteur

D LORMERIE

place des vosges

N° 10 a Paris—

EDITORS' TRANSLATION

MR. EX-PRESIDENT,   Paris 22 August 1815.—
Permit me to take advantage of a reliable opportunity to send you a tribute of my respect and the eternal gratitude I owe you for the happiness you brought me by enabling me to see my homeland again. Despite all the political unrest, I am quite happy to find myself once again among my friends and, most of all, my fortune, which, although much altered by the revolution, is still sufficient to give me independence and repose.—

> let us be content with what is necessary
> and never wish for superfluous treasures
> which must be feared as much as poverty
> in that, like it, they chase virtue away.
> Florian. fable from the 2d Book

I have the honor to be your colleague as corresponding member of the Société d'agriculture du département de la Seine; it has deservedly awarded you a gold medal for your ingenious plow. No object is more useful.

I reminded the society that while I was in the United States I had sent it a vegetable that is beginning to be cultivated in the field, having previously been known only in greenhouses and frames. It is the sweet potato (*Convolvulus batatas* L), which is so common and good in your country. Although it is harvested in our southern departments and even in gardens around Paris, it is hard to come by. The society would like to obtain its seeds, or that at least was the wish expressed to me by one of our most active members. If you would be so kind, Sir, as to instruct an intelligent person on your land or nearby in Virginia to <u>cultivate three or four plants specifically for their seeds, harvest them when they are very ripe</u>, enclose them in a <u>little tin box</u> that closes securely, and cover it with a piece of paper addressed <u>to the secretary of the American legation in Paris</u>, with a notice that it is to be delivered to me, I will present it to the society on your behalf, Sir, and we will be most grateful to have it—

I have also sent seeds from the United States to Mr. Thoüin, professor and administrator of the Muséum d'Histoire Naturelle, and he told me that they had reached him in very good condition.

[681]

A thousand apologies for the trouble I am giving you, but since this subject is of a scientific and rural nature, I assumed that I could address it to you, as you cultivate these arts and sciences with as much pleasure as success—

Mr. Crawford, with whom I had the honor of traveling from the United States to France and who was most considerate to me during the passage, has agreed to take charge of this letter to you on his return to your interesting country from his embassy. We miss him greatly. I am with very sincere and respectful attachment

Mr. Ex-President, your very humble and very obedient servant

> D Lormerie
> Place des Vosges
> No. 10, Paris—

RC (DLC: TJ Papers, 203:36237); at foot of first page: "Th⁵ Jefferson Esq Late President of the uS:"; endorsed by TJ as received 3 Oct. 1815 and so recorded in SJL. RC (DLC); address cover only; with PoC of TJ to John Bracken, 23 Oct. 1815, on verso; addressed: "Th⁵ Jefferson Esqʳ Late Président of the U:S: Monticello." Translation by Dr. Genevieve Moene. Enclosed in Albert Gallatin to TJ, 6 Sept. 1815.

The lines by Jean Pierre Claris de FLORIAN are the concluding stanza of "Le bon Homme et le Trésor" ("The Good Man and the Treasure"), the second poem in the second book of his *Fables* (Paris, 1792), 72. CONVOLVULUS BATATAS L (synonym of *Ipomoea batatas* var. *batatas*) is a common variety of sweet potato.

¹ Superfluous closing parenthesis editorially omitted.
² Manuscript: "d'on."

From John Adams

DEAR SIR   Quincy Aug. 24. 15

If I am neither deceived by the little Information I have, or by my Wishes for its truth, I Should Say that France is the most <u>Protestant</u> Country of Europe at this time, though I cannot think it the most <u>reformed</u>. In consequence of these Reveries I have imagined that Camus and the Institute, meant, by the revival and continuance of the Acta Sanctorum, to destroy the Pope and the Catholic Church and Hierarchy, de fonde en comble, or in the language of Frederick, Voltaire, D'Alembert &c "ecraser le miserable," "crush the Wretch." This great Work must contain the most complete History of the corruptions of Christianity, that has ever appeared; Priestleys not excepted. And his History of ancient opinions not excepted.

As to the history of the Revolution, my Ideas may be peculiar, perhaps Singular. What do We mean by the Revolution? The War? That was no part of the Revolution. It was only an Effect and Consequence of it. The Revolution was in the Minds of the People, and this was effected, from 1760 to 1775,¹ in the course of fifteen

Years before a drop of blood was drawn at Lexington. The Records of thirteen Legislatures, the Pamphlets,[2] Newspapers in all the Colonies ought be consulted, during that Period, to ascertain the Steps by which the public opinion was enlightened and informed concerning the Authority of Parliament over the Colonies. The Congress of 1774, resembled in Some respects, tho' I hope not in many, the Counsell of Nice in Ecclesiastical History. It assembled the Priests from the East and the West the North and the South, who compared Notes, engaged in discussions and debates and formed Results, by one Vote and by two Votes, which went out to the World as unanimous.

M[r] Madisons Notes of the Convention of 1787 or 1788 are consistent with his indefatigable Character. I Shall never See them: but I hope Posterity will.

That our correspondence has been observed is no Wonder; for your hand is more universally known than your face. No Printer has asked me for copies: but it is no Surprize that you have been requested. These Gentry will print whatever will Sell: and our Correspondence is thought Such an Oddity by both Parties, that the Printers imagine an Edition would Soon go off and yeild them a Profit. There has however been no tampering with your Letters to me. They have all arrived in good order.

Poor Bonaparte! Poor Devil! What has and what will become of him? Going the Way of King Theodore, Alexander Cæsar, Charles 12th Cromwell,[3] Wat Tyler and Jack Cade; i.e. to a bad End. And What will become of Wellington? Envied, hated despized by all the Barons, Earls, Viscounts Marquis's as an Upstart a Parvenue elevated Over their heads. For these People have no Idea of any Merit, but Birth. Wellington must pass the rest of his days buffetted ridiculed, Scorned and insulted by Factions as Marlborough and his Dutchess did. Military Glory dazzles the Eyes of Mankind, and for a time eclipses all Wisdom all Virtue, all Laws humane[4] and divine; and after this it would be Bathos to descend[5] to Services merely civil or political.

Napoleon has imposed Kings Upon Spain Holland Sweden[6] Westphalia Saxony Naples &c. The combined Emperors and Kings are about to retaliate upon France, by imposing a King upon her. These are all abominable Examples, detestable Precedents. When will the Rights of Mankind the Liberties and Independence of Nations be respected? When the Perfectibility of the human Mind Shall arrive at Perfection. When the Progress of Manillius's _Ratio_ Shall have not only

Eripuit Cælo fulmen, Jovisque fulgores,
but made Mankind rational Creatures

It remains to be Seen whether The Allies were honest in their Declaration that they were at War only with Napoleon.

Can the French ever be cordially reconciled to the Bourbons again? If not, who can they find for a head? The Infant or one of the Generals? Innumerable difficulties will embarrass either Project.

I am as ever   JOHN ADAMS

RC (DLC); addressed in an unidentified hand: "His Excellency Thomas Jefferson Esqre Monticello. Virginia"; franked; postmarked Quincy, 25 Aug.; endorsed by TJ as received 3 Oct. 1815 and so recorded in SJL. FC (Lb in MHi: Adams Papers).

DE FONDE EN COMBLE: "from top to bottom." The ancient Roman author Marcus Manilius (MANILLIUS) wrote *Astronomica*, a poem on astrology in which RATIO, or reason, joins with God to explain life on earth. ERIPUIT CÆLO FULMEN, JOVISQUE FULGORES ("he stole the thunderbolts from heaven and the meteors of Jove") is derived from this poem

(*Astronomica*, 1.104, 2.80–6, in Manilius, *Astronomica with an English Translation*, trans. George P. Goold, Loeb Classical Library [1977], 12–3, 88–9). For the 13 Mar. 1815 DECLARATION issued at the Congress of Vienna, see note to TJ to Thomas Leiper, 12 June 1815. The INFANT was Napoleon's namesake son, Napoleon François Joseph Charles Bonaparte.

[1] Reworked from "1765."
[2] RC: "Pamplets." FC: "pamphlets."
[3] RC: "Crowell." FC: "Cromwell."
[4] FC: "human."
[5] RC: "desend." FC: "descend."
[6] RC: "Sweeden." FC: "Sweden."

From Elisha Ticknor

SIR,   Boston, 24th Aug. 1815.

I have this day received yours dated the 16th ins. at Monticello, covering a letter to my Son. I have not heard a syllable from him since my letter of the 7th ins. to you, which I suppose you must have received before this time — at least I hope it has reach'd you. I have had no opportunity to forward a line to him since your first letter came to hand; but, in about ten days, the Ship New-Packet, which carried him out, I expect will sail from this port to Liverpool, which will give me a fine chance to convey your letters and mine directly to Saml Williams, Esq; his Correspondent, No. 13, Finsbury Square, London. I suppose he is now in Amsterdam. I expect letters from him by the New-Galen,[1] which is and has been hourly looked for in this port for ten or fifteen days. If I get any thing of importance from him, I will forward it to you, sir, immediately.

I am, sir In the highest consideration, your most obedient Servant,
ELISHA TICKNOR.

RC (MHi); at foot of text: "Thomas Jefferson, Esq; Late President of the United States of America"; endorsed by TJ as received 3 Oct. 1815 and so recorded in SJL.

The ship GALEN reached the the the port of Boston from London on 24 Aug. 1815 (*Boston Daily Advertiser*, 25 Aug. 1815).

[1] Reworked from "the Galen."

To Charles Clay

TH:J. TO MR CLAY   Aug. 25. 15. Poplar Forest.

How do you do? and when will you be able to ride thus far? these are my first questions. how you like the changes & chances of the European world may be the subject of conversation. but you must come with your ears stuffed full of cotton to fortify them against the noise of hammers, saws, planes E[t]c which assail us in every direction. affectionate salutations.

RC (ViU: TJP); dateline at foot of text; addressed: "Mr Clay." Not recorded in SJL.

From Nicolas G. Dufief

MONSIEUR,   A Philadelphie ce 25 Août. 1815

J'ai remis, il y a plusieurs Jours à Mr Tom, allant à Fredericksburg, un paquet adressé pour vous d'après vos ordres à Mr Gray, & contenant le cours de la Croix, en 7 vols 8vo. J'espère que vous ne tarderez pas à le recevoir. Je vous envoie par le Courrier de ce matin "Adam's astronomical & Geographical essays" on ne trouve chez aucun libraire de Philad[e] "The Graphical essays" Je pourrai, peut être, dans quelques jours vous en procurer un exemplaire de rencontre. J'ai un livre du même auteur intitulé "An essay on electricity explaining the principles of that useful Science and describing the instruments &c[a] The 5th Edition with corrections & additions by Jones."[1] cet ouvrage vous convient-il?

A l'égard des métamorphoses d'Ovide, je regrette beaucoup de m'être défait d'un exemplaire de l'Edition que vous désiriez, quelques jours avant que de recevoir votre lettre. Je vous adresserai la Semaine prochaine, un ovide complet d'une édition qui je crois répondra à vos vues, à la charge, toutefois, de le reprendre, Si je me trompais. Je vous envoie, puisque vous le demandez notre compte courant

Agreez, je vous prie, les voeux que je fais pour votre Santé & les assurances du profond respect avec lequel Je Suis

Votre très-dévoué Serviteur   N. G. DUFIEF

EDITORS' TRANSLATION

Sir,   Philadelphia 25 August. 1815

Several days ago I delivered to Mr. Tom, who was going to Fredericksburg, a package for you addressed, according to your orders, to Mr. Gray, and containing the *Cours de Mathematiques à l'usage de l'École Centrale des Quatres-Nations* by Lacroix, in 7 octavo volumes. I hope you will receive it soon. I send you by this morning's mail "Adams's astronomical & Geographical essays." "The Graphical essays" cannot be found in any Philadelphia bookstore. In a few days I may be able to procure a copy for you. I have a book by the same author entitled "An essay on electricity explaining the principles of that useful Science and describing the instruments &c[a] The 5th Edition with corrections & additions by Jones." Does this book suit you?

Regarding Ovid's *Metamorphoses*, I am very sorry that I parted with a copy of the edition you wanted a few days before receiving your letter. Next week I will send you a complete edition of Ovid that I think will meet your needs, with the proviso, however, that I will take it back if I am mistaken.

I send you, according to your request, our current account

Please accept my wishes for your health and the assurances of the profound respect with which I am

Your very devoted servant   N. G. Dufief

RC (DLC); endorsed by TJ as received 3 Oct. 1815 and so recorded in SJL. RC (Mrs. T. Wilber Chelf, Mrs. Virginius Dabney, and Mrs. Alexander W. Parker, Richmond, 1944; photocopy in ViU: TJP); address cover only; with PoC of TJ to Patrick Gibson, 20 Oct. 1815, on verso; addressed, in a clerk's hand: "Thomas Jefferson Esq[r] Monticello Virginia"; franked; postmarked Philadelphia, 25 Aug. Translation by Dr. Genevieve Moene.

[1] Omitted closing quotation mark editorially supplied.

ENCLOSURE

Account with Nicolas G. Dufief

Thomas Jefferson Esq[r]
                    in a/c. with N. G. Dufief   D[r]
1815
            To Balance $ 3.43
Aug. 19. To La Croix Mathematicks   15.00
    "   24 To Adam's Geo[l] and Astro[l] essays   3.50
                                               $21.93

MS (DLC: TJ Papers, 204:36413); in a clerk's hand; undated.

From Robert Patterson

SIR   Philadelphia Augt 25th 1815.

It requires an apology that I have not before now sent you the Time-Piece, which has been so long in my custody. The commencement of the late war before the Time-Piece was finished, & the consequent depredations of the enemy on our coast, prevented its being sent before the restoration of peace. When this event had taken place, I perceived that some parts of the veneering were scaling off from the case. I sent it to the maker to have it repaired; & owing to his obstinacy or neglect, notwithstanding repeated applications, he kept it several months in hand. It is now, however, completed, & the clock has been going six or eight weeks, & keeps time remarkably well;— not varying a minute in a whole week.

I have therefore, Sir, now to request, that you would please to inform me by what rout or conveyance I am to send it. Your former letter, containing those instructions, was given to Mr Voigt, & is mislaid

I have the honour to be, Sir, with the greatest respect & esteem, your most obed^t serv^t R^T PATTERSON

RC (MHi); at foot of text: "Thomas Jefferson Monticello"; endorsed by TJ as received 3 Oct. 1815 and so recorded in SJL.

From William Short

DEAR SIR   Ballston Spa Aug: 25—15

Your kind letter of June 27. was in my absence taken up by my agent at Philadelphia & sent after me. I was then on a visit to the beautiful Lake, called by the French le lac du St Sacrament & by their successors Lake George. The French showed their good taste in having chosen this to furnish them their holy water. Nothing can be more pure than it is. The fish there are worthy of being admitted to the rank of Ambrosia—as the water is to that of nectar.   I am ashamed however to have been amusing myself on this picturesque spot, since I have learned that you were at that time laboring for me over precipices rocks & bushes. I hope at length however that this troublesome business is drawing to a close—And although with the prospect of its not being in a way favorable to me, yet I am glad it is to be ended & we are to know what to count on.   The questionable line will be settled, but I little hope to see in my day the consequence of it settled & terminated; that is the re-imbursement to me by Mr Carter. When I saw him at Philad^a a year or two ago, he told me he had found that Co^{lo} Monroe owed him a balance about equal to this sum in question & that he had I think proposed to him to let one go as a set off against the other—but Monroe did not accept it, if he did not absolutely decline it—And it will take some time to put Carter off of this track—Until Monroe shall pay him he will probably not think of paying me—He will as to this payment act I imagine as a friend of mine was advised to act as to marrying—that is not to think of it until he was forty years of age, & then not to marry at all. If the line is decided against me will you be so good as to let me know how I should proceed as to Mr Carter. He will probably offer me an order on Monroe—but I had rather have no claim of the sort against a friend. I suppose Mr Carter will make no difficulty as to this being an arbitration to which he was not a party—for he told me he had written or spoken to you to act altogether for him in this case & of course will or ought to be satisfied with what is done under your eyes— As to M^r H's retaining the sum or his last payment to me, this is a thing of course—& I shall be perfectly satisfied with it. He has made all but his last payment—& that does not accrue until Decr next. Let me once more express to you my real gratitude for all the trouble you have been so good as to take in this business—I feel it as a weight on me—& particularly the fatigue to wch you must have been exposed on the 21^t of June. To me who have become so corporeally indolent this is sensible to an uncommon degree. My weight has a good deal increased, it is true, but in no proportion to my indolence.

I have no doubt that you have long before this had the pleasure of seeing Corea & Dupont—You are persuaded I hope how much pleasure it would have given me to have assisted at your speculations. I have frequently in imagination placed myself among you. Our friend Corea got out of humour with the Allies, the Bourbons &c. insomuch that they have almost reconciled him to Napoleon the 1st—& quite so to Nap. the 2^d. I do not know how Dupont stands, but although dissatisfied evidently with the Bourbons I do not suppose he can ever be brought to be reconciled to any thing of the blood of the Bonapartes. I anticipate much gratification in conversing with Corea after his return to Philad. where I shall be in the beginning of October—My present wish would be to go & pay my respects to you next summer—And as I find mineral waters always useful to my bilious habit I will in that case substitute the Virginia springs to the Ballston spa.

I am too variable to think of deciding absolutely on any thing so far ahead—but this is my present wish & hope.

Bonap: is so rapid in all his actions ascending & descending that he must have got ahead of all speculation—My hope is that he will not arrive in this country; or rather this is my wish—If I were to express my fears & opinions of what he might do I am sure it would be thought an exagerated vision—I therefore shall say nothing—I am one of those who think there is as much coruption in this country as any other, all things considered & under similar circumstances things would pass here much as they do elsewhere—I have long thought so & have long been laughed at for this opinion—some things have happened which have confirmed me in my opinion—& particularly the Baltimore mob & massacre in the prisons—a similar event in Paris has been always considered one of the foulest deeds of the French revolution—that at Baltimore was on a par with it & under much less cause of excitement—Thus give the same excitement in this country & I say you will have to the same degree any thing that has occurred in other countries—This I dare say would not be considered an American sentiment—but I cannot help thinking Americans much like other men. Whatever they may be, better or worse than I believe them, it has no influence on my real respect, gratitude & friendship for you, wch must be ever invariable & would, I can assure you my dear sir, survive our Republican institutions if destined[1] to be overthrown in my day—Yours ever & affectionately   W SHORT

RC (MHi); endorsed by TJ as received 3 Oct. 1815 and so recorded in SJL.

M^R H'S: David Higginbotham's. A BALTIMORE MOB gained entry to the city jail on the evening of 27 July 1812 and attacked Federalist sympathizers who had been given sanctuary there, killing two and maiming several others (Frank A. Cassell, "The Great Baltimore Riot of 1812," *Maryland Historical Magazine* 70 [1975]: 241–59). In a far bloodier incident, PARIS mobs broke into that city's prisons between 2 and 7 Sept. 1792 and killed between 1,100 and 1,400 persons, including half of Paris's prison population and others also deemed to be counterrevolutionaries (Doyle, *French Revolution*, 191–2).

[1] Manuscript: "destoned."

From Thomas Appleton

SIR   Leghorn 26th August 1815.

Early in the present month, I convey'd, by the Brig adeline, Captn Jenkins for Baltimore, a letter to you from Mr Mazzei.—He has now requested me to forward the duplicate, by which you will perceive, he is desirous of Receiving the whole amount for which his house & lot in Richmond was sold, suggesting that a much greater interest can be obtain'd in Tuscany, with the best Security in real estate.—Now the truth is far otherwise, for it is with great difficulty, that money-holders Can find even Six C^t with good Security; and there has been more money plac'd, within the last Year at 5 C^t than at six—this fatal persuasion into which he has been led, is the only & real Cause of all the losses of which he so severely complains, and not arising from any political events as he suggests; for there is always found Some vulnerable part in every contract, however well guarded may be the expressions, if more than the legal interest has been exacted.—The most profound mediations of the usurer, to evade the laws, have in almost every instance I have known, been frustrated; for even the positive acknowledgement of a debt, drawn in every known legal form, has been found unavailing, when circumstantial evidence could be oppos'd, & when Strengthened by the general Reputation of the lender, for usurious contracts—this has been the unfortunate Situation of Mr Mazzei, and in addition to which, his intellectual powers are So totally bewilder'd, that he forgets every event of the day: so that, his family now only Speak to him on Such trivial Subjects, as are not of any importance if remember'd or forgotten.—on politics no one speaks to him, for unhappily there are little remains of what formerly distinguish'd him, but his impetuosity; the consequence is, that almost all his friends have gradually Retir'd, & thus leave him in solitude, to bewail their ingratitude; and Still more, that his miserable existence is prolong'd beyond every moral or physical enjoyment.—In a few words, Sir, his emaciated body is nearly bent to the earth, and his teeth have all fallen, So that he is reduc'd to exist almost intirely on vegetables, and which he never moistens with a Single draught of cheering wine.—an intestinal Rupture has Commenc'd, and his legs are So Swollen, that he with great difficulty moves about his house—under all these evils, which he impatiently bears, he had very lately determin'd to quit alone, this country, and Retire to Virginia.—He made known his determination to all his acquaintance & friends, but their arguments to dissuade him, were either not listen'd to, or forgotten; for he continu'd still making the preparations for his departure—However, I presented to his mind, such a mass of reasons why he should desist from So ill-tim'd a project, that he has finally intirely abandon'd it.—It is with much difficulty that he Can So collect his bewilder'd Senses, as to write a letter; and to Read, is So intirely useless, owing to his instantaneous forgetfulness, that he is now Reduc'd to pass whole days, in Some childish game at Cards, when he Can find any one who has leisure and patience; for he as impatiently bears an unfavorable hand, as though the recompense of a good one, were not a few miserable beans—feeling then as he now does, his own insufficiency to conduct his pecuniary concerns, join'd to the advice of his friends, he has finally consented, that all payments of money shall be made into the hands of his wife & daughter; for otherwise, they had Resolv'd to petition the Grand Duke, to this effect; and agreeably to the usage of Tuscany in similar Cases, the whole management of his affairs would have devolv'd on them.—In addition to all these evils, there is another, which indeed, is of the most distressing kind.—He imagines, as he has often assur'd me, that his wife & daughter are weary of that assistance, which his age & infirmities indispensably Require; and Certainly it is very painful to observe, that there seems Some foundation for his suspicions, for their ennui is not conceal'd under the slightest Veil of affection.—They have then express'd their very earnest desire, that you will not remit the principal as Mr Mazzei has so much rag'd in his letter to you, but that you will forward only the interest as it shall become due: being greatly satisfied, both with the Security & the annual income of six $℔C^t$—They are likewise apprehensive, that if he should get into the possession of so large a Sum, he would conceal it from his family, and it would Soon fall a prey to a number of designing persons; or what I think more probable, it would induce him to abandon his home, and vainly Seek for Contentment & happiness in the U'States.—

I have thought, Sir, this Statement of his present situation, necessary to the forming your own judgment, as to the propriety of adhering to his wishes, or of complying with the Request of his wife & daughter.—It will afford me, Sir, the most Sincere Satisfaction, if I can in any way be useful to you in Italy, as it now does, to beg you will accept the expressions of my very high esteem & respect.—

TH: APPLETON

RC (DLC); at head of text: "Thomas Jefferson Esquire Virginia"; endorsed by TJ as received 25 Oct. 1815 and so recorded in SJL. Enclosure: Dupl, dated 18 Sept. 1814, of Philip Mazzei to TJ, 24 Sept. 1814.

Deposition of Dabney Carr in
Jefferson v. Michie

The deposition of Dabney Carr taken de bene esse at his dwelling house adjoining or near the town of Winchester between the hours of ten in the forenoon and four of the afternoon of Saturday the 26[h] day of August in the year of our Lord 1815, by virtue of a Commission to us directed from the County Court of Albemarle in behalf of Thomas Jefferson in a Certain matter of Controversy (expected) between David Michie and those Claiming under him, and the said, Thomas Jefferson, and those claiming under him touching a Certain piece of real property lying and being in Albemarle. Notice of the time and place of taking said deposition being duly proved before us.—The deponent being first sworn on the holy evangelists deposeth and saith That while he practiced at the Bar there was a suit depending in the High Court of Chancery at Richmond between a Certain John Henderson & Craven Peyton, the subject of which (among other things) was the same piece of real property expected to be in Controversy between the said David Michie and Thomas Jefferson. That during the pendency of that suit he thinks in April or May 1805—he was employed by Craven Peyton to attend as Counsel to the taking depositions (to be read in the suit) at the village of Milton in Albemarle. That M[r] Benjamin Brown attended as Counsel for Henderson. That at the taking these depositions the said David Michie was present, and in the Course of the examination asked some witness a question: that he was immediately interrupted by Peyton who with Considerable warmth[1] and harshness made remarks to him substantially to the following effect. M[r] Michie [you][2] have no interest in this case, nothing to do with the buisiness and therefore no right to open your mouth to the witness. That Michie replied he was an attorney at law and in that Character had a right to appear for Henderson. This Deponent thinks it was then observed, whether by a magistrate or one of the Counsel he does not recollect, that M[r] Michie Certainly had a right to appear and take part in the examination as an attorney. It may be observed here that M[r] Michie was not a practicing lawyer at that time, nor had been for a Considerable time previous, as this deponent thinks. This deponent feels Confident, that this was the sole ground on which Michie rested his Claim to interfere, and that during the whole examination, he did not drop the slightest hint of having any personal interest in the subject of litigation. This deponent would not be understood to speak positively as to the time when this examination took place he finds in his book a charge against Craven Peyton for attending it dated 17ʰ May 1805 and this induces him to believe that it took place some where about that period. & further this deponent saith not. D CARR

Taken and sworn to in due form before us the undersigned Justices of the peace for the County of Frederick and the same persons named in the Commission hereto annexed this 26ʰ Augᵗ 1815 at the dwelling house of said Carr adjoining Winchester and between the hours of 10 in the forenoon & four in the afternoon EDWᴰ MᶜGUIRE

JO TIDBALL

Tr (ViU: TJP-LBJM); entirely in George Carr's hand. Enclosure not found.

DE BENE ESSE: "in anticipation of a future need" (*Black's Law Dictionary*). The COUNTY COURT OF ALBEMARLE issued an order on 4 Nov. 1813 for commissions "to take the despositions . . . of the several witnesses" as requested by TJ in *Thomas Jefferson v. David Michie* (Albemarle Co. Order Book [1813–1815], 267). For the earlier SUIT, see note to Craven Peyton to TJ, 6 Aug. 1809; Decision of Virginia Court of Appeals in *Peyton v. Henderson*, 7 Jan. 1812; and Haggard, "Henderson Heirs," 9–12.

Edward McGuire (ca. 1766–1828), merchant, resided in Winchester and was commissioned a justice of the peace for Frederick County in 1802. He was a proprietor of the McGuire Hotel for a time, secretary of the Jockey Club in 1811, and a commissioner of the Winchester and Berryville Turnpike in 1812 and of the Bank of the Valley in Winchester in 1817, serving as a director of the latter in 1819. McGuire was a founding member of the Charlestown and Winchester Turnpike Company in 1818. He left property appraised at $2,394, including land in Frederick, Hampshire, and Hardy counties (William G. Stanard, *The McGuire Family in Virginia* [1926], 32–3; Frederic Morton, *The Story of Winchester in Virginia* [1925], 274; DNA: RG 29, CS, Frederick Co., 1810; Charles Town, Va. [later W.Va.], *Farmer's Repository*, 4 Oct. 1811; *Acts of Assembly* [1811–12 sess.], 75; [1817–18 sess.], 140; *Alexandria Gazette & Daily Advertiser*, 13 Nov.

1817; *Richmond Enquirer*, 16 Feb. 1819; Frederick Co. Will Book, 15:19–20, 16:230–44, 285–92, 19:255–6; Richmond *Visitor & Telegraph*, 6 Dec. 1828).

Joseph Tidball (d. 1825), merchant and gristmill owner, was a resident of Winchester. He sold military supplies to both the Virginia and federal governments throughout the 1790s, and he received his commission as a justice of the peace in 1804. Tidball was a commissioner in 1817 of the Bank of the Valley in Winchester and a founding member in 1818 of the Charlestown and Winchester Turnpike Company (Frederic Morton, *The Story of Winchester in Virginia* [1925], 118, 275; DNA: RG 29, CS, Frederick Co., 1810, 1820; Warren R. Hofstra and Robert D. Mitchell, "Town and Country in Backcountry Virginia: Winchester and the Shenandoah Valley, 1730–1800," *Journal of Southern History* 59 [1993]: 640; CVSP, 1:44, 74; James McHenry to Charles Lee, 14 May 1799 [MiU-C: McHenry Papers]; Harold C. Syrett and others, eds., *The Papers of Alexander Hamilton* [1961–87], 23:255–7; *Alexandria Gazette & Daily Advertiser*, 13 Nov. 1817; *Acts of Assembly* [1817–18 sess.], 140; Deborah A. Lee and Hofstra, "Race, Memory, and the Death of Robert Berkeley: 'A murder . . . of . . . horrible and savage barbarity,'" *Journal of Southern History* 65 [1999]: 55; Frederick Co. Will Book, 16:293–4; gravestone inscription at Mount Hebron Cemetery, Winchester).

¹ Manuscript: "wamth."
² Manuscript: "who."

From Patrick Gibson

S<small>IR</small>   Richmond 28th August 1815

I have received your favor of the 19th advising sundry drafts on me, which shall be duly attended to—I send you inclosed a note for your signature to renew the one in bank due next month—Our flour market is declining rapidly the present price is 8$ for new wheat 8/.— Tobacco still keeps up notwithstanding the very discouraging accounts from Europe or rather from England as prices on, the Continent are high considering the qualities sent there—

With great respect Your ob^t Servt   P<small>ATRICK</small> G<small>IBSON</small>

RC (ViU: TJP-ER); between dateline and salutation: "Thomas Jefferson Esqre"; endorsed by TJ as received 29 Sept. 1815 and so recorded in SJL. Dupl (ViU: TJP-ER); on verso of RC of Gibson to TJ, 21 Sept. 1815; in a clerk's hand; endorsed by TJ as received 29 Sept. 1815 and so recorded in SJL. Enclosure not found.

From Joseph Milligan

D<small>EAR</small> S<small>IR</small>   George Town August 28th 1815

Permit me to make known to you Mr John Travers of the house of Hutchinson Travers & Co of Lesbon

Who has been for the last eight years under the Care of his Uncle William Riggen esqr many years U.S. Consul at Triest he is now making a tour in the United States partly on business & partly a journey of Recreation previous to taking up his residence at Lesbon

If you have any Commands to Portugal or spain you may Confide in him with the greatest Safety

With Esteem yours   J<small>OSEPH</small> M<small>ILLIGAN</small>

RC (DLC); at foot of text: "Thomas Jefferson Esqr Monticello Milton Via [i.e. Virginia]"; endorsed by TJ as received 5 Oct. 1816 and so recorded in SJL. RC (DLC); address cover only; with PoC of TJ to James Ligon (for Patrick Gibson), 15 Jan. 1817, on verso; addressed: "Thomas Jefferson Esqr Monticello Virginia by Mr Travers." Enclosed in John Travers to TJ, 11 July 1816.

William Riggin (R<small>IGGEN</small>) served as United States consul at Trieste from 1802 until 1815 (*JEP*, 1:406–7, 2:627 [2, 9 Feb. 1802, 2 Mar. 1815]). During his T<small>OUR</small> Travers did not visit Monticello (Travers to TJ, 11 July 1816).

From William Radford

Dear Sir Liberty Bedford [received 29] August 1815
    I have taken the liberty to introduce to you Judge Peter Randolph,
who expressed a desire to call on you as he was passing down the
Country—In doing this I trust that no apology will be necessary on
my part—Accept the assurance of my high consideration

W^M Radford

RC (MHi); partially dated; endorsed by TJ as received 29 Aug. 1815 and so recorded in SJL.

Peter Randolph (d. 1832), attorney and judge, attended the College of William and Mary, was admitted to the Virginia bar by 1809, practiced law in Nottoway County, which he represented in the House of Delegates, 1810–12, and was elected to membership in the Agricultural Society of Virginia in 1818. He served as a judge on the General Court of Virginia with responsibility for the Fifth (Petersburg) Circuit, 1812–21. Randolph sat on a state commission that met at Rockfish Gap in 1818 and recommended that the new University of Virginia be located in Albemarle County, replacing Central College. After resigning his judgeship he moved to Mississippi, where he continued his law practice and his agricultural pursuits. In 1823 President James Monroe appointed Randolph a federal judge for the Mississippi district, a post he held until his death (*William and Mary Provisional List*, 33; DNA: RG 29, CS, Nottoway Co., 1810; Brunswick Co., 1820; Leonard, *General Assembly*, 262, 267; Walter A. Watson, *Notes on Southside Virginia* [1925], 11, 32, 82; *JSV* [1811–12 sess.], 38; *Report of the trials of Capt. Thomas Wells, Before the County Court of Nottoway . . . Charged with feloniously and maliciously shooting, with intent to kill Peter Randolph, Esq. judge of the 5th circuit; and Col. Wm. C. Greenhill* [Petersburg, 1816]; *Richmond Enquirer*, 11 Aug. 1818, 11 Dec. 1821, 1 Mar. 1832; Baltimore *Niles' Weekly Register*, 7 Nov. 1818; Christopher Rankin to William H. Crawford, 26 Apr. 1823, and Randolph to Monroe, 26 Apr. 1823 [DNA: RG 59, LAR, 1817–25]; *JEP*, 3:343, 344, 4:274 [8, 9 Dec. 1823, 13 July 1832]).

From David J. Thompson

Si^R,   Augus 30, 1815
    The timber that was sawed at my Mill for you My Father let Doctr
Steptoe have it, in My absence, While at Norfolk, in the Army But as
I, am in the habit or practice of sawing for the halves you can get as
much more Sawed at any time: or As Soon as you Bring the timber to
the Mill I am Sorry you are Disappointed in the planke I am Yo—

David J Thompson

RC (ViU: TJP-ER); dateline at foot of text; addressed: "Mr Thomas Jefferson"; endorsed by TJ.

David Jones Thompson inherited land in Campbell County in 1830 from his father, John Thompson, including mills on Buffaloe Creek. The younger Thompson possessed at least six slaves in 1820. By 1837 he had emancipated at least one,

Robert Thompson. David J. Thompson first purchased land in Missouri in 1838. Within two years he had moved there, settling in Sugar Tree Bottom in Carroll County (Roger G. Ward, *1815 Directory of Virginia Landowners* [1997–99], 2:16, 47; Campbell Co. Will Book, 6:379–82; DNA: RG 29, CS, Va., Campbell Co., 1810–30; Mo., Carroll Co., 1840; legislative petition of Robert Thompson, 3 Feb. 1837 [Vi: RG 78, Botetourt Co.]; David J. Thompson's land patents in Carroll and Lafayette counties, Mo., dated 7 Sept. 1838 and 1 May 1843 [DNA: RG 49, GRMLO]).

In SAWING FOR THE HALVES one cuts out half the thickness of the end of a piece of lumber so that it will fit flush with a similarly cut piece (*OED*).

From Christopher Clark

DEAR SIR,   Mount Prospect Augt 31ˢᵗ 15

A considerable diversity of opinion, has prevailed and Still continues to prevail about the height[1] of the Peaks of Otter the calculation generally adopted has been taken from your notes on Virginia whether this Standard was the Result of an actual admeasure is not known but I have heard that yourself have had some doubts of its accuraccy and contemplated making a more correct one Perhaps no situation in the immediate Vicinity[2] of the mountain will afford as good ground for the purpose of making the experiment as my plantation and I have long wished the Real[3] elevation ascertained[4] and this to be done under your observation and understanding you will probably Remain some time in Bedford Shall be glad to See you at our house and as this Rout is by far the best to the Natural Bridge If you Should think proper to extend your journey thither will do myself the pleasure to attend you If you can find it convenient to come up will you be so good as to advise me of the time and I will certainly be at home

I avail myself of this opportunity to Renew the assureances of the very high esteem and Regard with which as I am Dear Sir your mo ob set   CHRISTOPHER CLARK

RC (MHi); with twenty-one words copied above the line by TJ for clarity; endorsed by TJ as received "<*Aug.*> Sep. 3. 15." but recorded in SJL as received 31 Aug. 1815.

[1] Manuscript: "heght."
[2] Manuscript: "Visinity." Copied by TJ as "vicinity."
[3] TJ copied this word as "true."
[4] Manuscript: "asertained." Copied by TJ as "ascertained."

To Martha Jefferson Randolph

MY DEAR MARTHA   Poplar Forest Aug. 31. 15.

We all arrived here without accident, myself the day after I left home, having performed the journey in two days, reaching Noah Flood's the 1st day. the story of the neighborhood immediately was that I had brought a croud of workmen to get ready my house in a hurry for Bonaparte. were there such people only as the believers in this, patriotism would be a ridiculous passion. we are suffering from drought terribly at this place. half a crop of wheat, and tobacco, and two thirds a crop of corn are the most we can expect. Cate, with good aid, is busy drying peaches for you. we abound in the luxury of the peach, there being as fine here now as we used to have in Albemarle 30. years ago, and indeed as fine as I ever saw any where. I find the distance from hence to the Natural bridge, by Petit's gap is only 29. miles. I shall therefore go there on horseback; but not until I return from Buckingham court, where I presume I shall meet Jefferson, and hear something from home. indeed it would be a great comfort to me if some one of the family would write to me once a week, were it only to say all is well.

I see no reason to believe we shall finish our work here sooner than the term I had fixed for my return. it is rather evident we must have such another expedition the next year. remember me affectionately to the family & be assured yourself of my warmest and tenderest love my dearest Marth   TH: JEFFERSON

RC (NNPM); at foot of text: "Mrs Randolph." PoC (MHi); endorsed by TJ.

TJ LEFT HOME on 20 Aug. 1815. That evening he reached Noah Flood's ordinary, where he paid $2 for "lodging &c." PETIT'S GAP passes through the Blue Ridge Mountains between Natural Bridge Station, Rockbridge County, and Charlemont, Bedford County. TJ attended the Buckingham County COURT on 12 Sept. 1815 as a witness in a lawsuit between Randolph Jefferson's children and his widow, Mitchie B. Pryor Jefferson (*MB*, 2:1313; TJ to Hardin Perkins, 11 Aug. 1815; TJ's Deposition regarding Randolph Jefferson's Estate, 15 Sept. 1815). TJ there expected to MEET his grandson Thomas Jefferson Randolph.

Appendix

Supplemental List of Documents Not Found

JEFFERSON'S epistolary record and other sources describe a number of documents for which no text is known to survive. The Editors generally account for such material at documents that mention them or at other relevant places. Exceptions are accounted for below.

From James Ross, undated. Recorded in SJL as received 19 Apr. 1815.

From Edward Watkins, 2 July 1815. Recorded in SJL as received from Henrico County on 15 July 1815.

From "Mills," 18 Aug. 1815. Recorded in SJL as received from Charlottesville on 3 Oct. 1815.

INDEX

Abbaye Royale de Panthémont: and education of M. J. Randolph, 513

Abbey (Abby) (TJ's slave; b. *1804*): on Poplar Forest slave lists, 61, 255

Abbott, Thomas Jefferson: letter from, 74; requests assistance from TJ, 74

Abby (TJ's slave; b. *1753*): on Poplar Forest slave lists, 60, 255

Abigail (C. L. Bankhead's slave), 395

Abney, William: federal tax assessor, 257n

Abraham (Old Testament patriarch), 189

An Abridgement of Ainsworth's Dictionary (R. Ainsworth; ed. T. Morell), 660

Abridgment of the Public Permanent Laws of Virginia (E. Randolph), 630

Abridgment of Universal History (La Croix), 629, 632n

An Account of the People called Shakers (T. Brown), 469

Acta Sanctorum (J. de Bolland and others), 558–63, 656–7, 682

An Act authorising William Waller Hening to Publish an Edition of certain Laws of this Commonwealth, and for other purposes (*1808*), 349n

An Act authorizing a Regular Force for the Defence of the Commonwealth (*1815*), 165, 166n

An Act authorizing a subscription for the laws of the United States, and for the distribution thereof (*1814*), 152n

An Act authorizing William Wood of the County of Albemarle, to open and improve the navigation of the Rivannah River, and for other purposes (*1814*), 166, 184

An Act concerning Executions, and for other purposes (*1814*), 46, 525, 527n

An Act concerning the Bank of Virginia and Farmers' Bank of Virginia (*1814*), 35, 36n

An Act fixing the military peace establishment of the United States (*1815*), 443, 444n

An Act for the apportionment of Representatives among the several States, according to the third enumeration (*1811*), 594, 596n

An Act for the assessment and collection of direct taxes and internal duties (*1813*), 126

An Act Imposing Taxes for the support of Government (*1814*), 169, 394n

An Act laying an embargo on all ships and vessels in the ports and harbours of the United States (*1813*), 532–4

An Act making appropriations for repairing or rebuilding the public buildings within the city of Washington (*1815*), 313–5, 591, 592, 596n

An Act making further provision for filling the ranks of the army of the United States (*1814*), 575n

An Act to amend the act, intituled, 'an act to establish an academy in the county of Albemarle, and for other purposes' (*1804*), 93

An Act to authorize a loan for a sum not exceeding three millions of dollars (*1814*), 111n

An act to authorize a loan for a sum not exceeding twenty-five millions of dollars (*1814*), 194, 195n

An act to authorize the issuing of treasury notes for the service of the year one thousand eight hundred and fourteen (*1814*), 302

An Act to authorize the President of the United States to accept the services of state troops and of volunteers (*1815*), 575n

An Act to authorize the purchase of the library of Thomas Jefferson (*1815*), 214, 270, 279–80, 302n, 426

An Act To authorize the several Courts of Equity in this State to grant remedies . . . and for affording temporary relief to the Soldiers whilst in the service of this state or of the United States, and for other purposes (*1814*), 524–5, 527n

An Act to establish an academy in the county of Albemarle, and for other purposes (*1803*), 92, 93, 183

An Act to establish Public Schools (*1796*), 92–3

An Act to provide a library room, and for transporting the library lately purchased (*1815*), 333, 445n

[701]

129, 198–9, 205–6, 663; opinions on standing army, 251n; reduction of, 443, 444n, 536–7; TJ on, 357, 360

Arnaud, Felix: and batture controversy, 64n

Arnold, Benedict: TJ's plan to capture, 423; Va. invasion of, 178, 481, 482n

arsenic: used in manufacture of shot, 98

artichokes, 305

Ashby v. White: TJ references, 526, 527n

asparagus, 78, 305

Astronomica (M. Manilius), 683–4

Astronomical and Geographical Essays . . . and also An Introduction to Practical Astronomy (G. Adams), 670, 685, 686

astronomy: books on, 388, 670, 685, 686; and calculations of Monticello's longitude, 455, 456n

Asturias, Prince of. *See* Ferdinand VII, king of Spain

Atkinson, Michael: identified, 612n; letter to, 612; and millwork for TJ, 63, 71, 612, 613

Auger, Athanase, trans.: works of Lysias, 630

Augustine (Austin) (TJ's slave; b. ca. *1775*): on Poplar Forest slave lists, 61, 255

Augustus (Gaius Octavius; 1st Roman emperor), 505, 508n

Aurora (Philadelphia newspaper): publishes *An Exposition of the Causes and Character of the War* (A. J. Dallas), 381; TJ's subscription to, 435, 436n, 468, 469n, 469

Austin (TJ's slave; b. ca. *1775*). *See* Augustine (Austin) (TJ's slave; b. ca. *1775*)

Austin, Benjamin: as commissioner of loans, 407, 408n; recommends book for TJ, 391

Austin, James Trecothick: identified, 4:38n; letter from, 585–6; letter to, 614; *An Oration, Pronounced at Lexington, Mass.*, 585–6, 614

Austria: relations with France, 138

axes, 23, 222, 313

Bache, Catharine Wistar: family of, 449n; and T. M. Randolph, 448

bacon, 184

Bacon, Edmund: identified, 1:52n; witnesses documents, 396, 398

Bacon, Francis: classification of knowledge, 240, 473, 475n; *Of the Advancement and Proficiencie of Learning: or the Partitions of Sciences*, 473, 475n

Bagwell (TJ's slave): on Monticello slave list, 62n

Ballard, William: identified, 6:304n; as Tufton overseer, 203, 204n, 611, 676n; witnesses documents, 396, 398

balloons, 388

Baltimore, Md.: defense of, 153, 154; *1812* riot in, 689; glass manufactured at, 21, 142; museums in, 462; newspapers, 260, 566, 569–70, 598, 599n, 660n

Baltimore Patriot & Evening Advertiser (newspaper), 598, 599n, 660n

Bankhead, Ann (Anne) Cary Randolph (TJ's granddaughter; Charles Lewis Bankhead's wife): Carlton estate of, 308n; Carlton estate of conveyed to trustees, 394–7; children of, 395, 397n, 398, 636; identified, 2:104n; TJ conveys land to, 278, 397–8

Bankhead, Charles Lewis (Ann Cary Randolph Bankhead's husband): beer for, 565; Carlton estate of, 277, 308n; Carlton estate of conveyed to trustees, 394–7; children of, 395, 397n, 398; debts of, 277, 394; health of, 565; identified, 3:188n; slaves owned by, 395; TJ conveys land to, 277–8, 397–8; TJ on, 277, 278; visits J. Bankhead, 123, 565

Bankhead, Ellen Monroe (TJ's great-granddaughter), 397n, 636

Bankhead, John: family of, 123; health of, 123; identified, 278n; letter from accounted for, 279n; letter to, 277–9; relationship with C. L. Bankhead, 277–8, 565; as trustee of A. C. and C. L. Bankhead, 394–7, 397–8

Bankhead, John Warner (TJ's great-grandson), 397n, 636

Bankhead, Mary Warner Lewis (John Bankhead's wife): relationship with C. L. Bankhead, 277–8; TJ sends greetings to, 278

Bankhead, Thomas Mann Randolph (TJ's great-grandson), 397n, 636

Bankhead, William Stuart (TJ's great-grandson), 397n

Bank of Alexandria: notes issued by, 19, 511

cal work, 486, 487n; publishes *Kentucky Palladium*, 486, 487n
Buchanan, William B.: plans trip to Europe, 421; recommended to TJ by J. Hollins, 421; TJ's letter of introduction for, 432, 436
Buckingham County Court, Va., 664, 676–7, 697
Buckminster, Joseph Stevens: minister of Brattle Street Church, 49, 50n
Buder, Christian Gottlieb: *Bibliotheca Historica*, 559, 562n
buffalo. *See* bison, American (buffalo)
Buffalo, N.Y.: burnt by British forces, 217
Buffalo tract (Bedford Co.), 255
Buffon, Georges Louis Leclerc, comte de: J. Adams on, 552
Buford, Abraham: in Revolutionary War, 494, 495n
building materials: beech, 239; bricks, 86–7, 90n, 252; cement, 130, 166, 168n, 252, 402; cherry, 239; cordwood, 595; ironmongery, 86–7; lime (mineral), 253n, 402; lumber, 613; mahogany, 239; molasses, 253n, 402; pine, xlv–xlvi, 55; plaster, 252; sand, 253n, 402; timber, 86–7, 305; window glass, 21, 142–3, 234–5
Bulletin de la Société d'Encouragement pour l'Industrie Nationale, 421
Burk, John Daly: *The History of Virginia*, 121–2, 140–1, 200, 203, 266, 309, 334–8, 359–60, 384–6, 423, 431, 478, 481, 482n
Burke, Edmund: criticized, 552
Burkhard, Johann Gottlieb: *Elementary or Fundamental Principles of The Philosophy of Natural History*, 388, 672
burnet, 71
Burnside, Samuel McGregore: identified, 7:47–8n; letter from, 207–8; as recording secretary of American Antiquarian Society, 207–8
Burr, Aaron (*1756–1836*): mentioned, 154
Burwell (TJ's slave; b. *1783*). *See* Colbert, Burwell (TJ's slave; b. *1783*)
butter: price of, 307; sent to TJ, 132, 174, 184
Byrd, William (*1674–1744*): library of, 332n; and Westham land, 169
Byrd, William (*1728–77*): and Westham land, 169, 171n

cabbage: seed, 258, 272
Cabell, Joseph Carrington: and Albemarle Academy, 316–7; on banks, 35; books owned by, 429–30; and Central College, 183–4, 316–7; and College of William and Mary, 317; and Destutt de Tracy's writings, 164, 182–3, 317; identified, 2:489–90n; letters from, 35–6, 164–6, 316–8; letters to, 29–30, 182–4; and Rivanna Company, 184; and Rivanna River navigation, 165–6; on J. B. Say's proposed immigration to America, 317; slaves of, 317–8; and TJ's ideas on finance, 29–30, 35, 164, 182; and wartime finance, 164–5
Cabell, William: buys lots in Westham, 171n
Cade, John (Jack) (English rebel): compared to Napoleon, 683
Caesar (TJ's slave; b. *1774*): on Poplar Forest slave lists, 61, 255
Caesar, Julius: mentioned, 683; writings of, 12
Caldwell, Billy (Sauganash): British Indian Department official, 222
Callaway, Richard: land patented by, 255
Campbell, George Washington: identified, 7:354–5n; as secretary of the treasury, 16, 18n, 20n, 126
Campbell, J. (of Baltimore): publisher, 450n
Campbell, John (early acquaintance of TJ), 645
Campbell, John B.: U.S. colonel, 217
Campbell, Mary Dandridge Spotswood (John Campbell's wife), 645
Campbell County, Va.: sawmills in, 612; taxation on property in, 73, 255–6, 256, 351n; TJ's land in, 285. *See also* Ivy Creek (Campbell Co.)
Campbell family, 431
Camus, Armand Gaston: *Histoire des Animaux d'Aristote, Avec la Traduction Françoise*, 656, 659n; leader of the French Revolution, 656; *Rapport a L'Institut National, Classe de Littérature et Beaux Arts, D'un voyage fait à la fin de l'an X*, 558–62, 656–7, 682
Canada: W. Duane on expulsion of British from, 99; Loyal and Patriotic Society of Upper Canada, 225; maps of, 77n; TJ anticipates American conquest of, 133, 575; U.S. atrocities in, 57, 214–9, 221, 222, 224–6; U.S. policy toward, 227n

INDEX

Claytor, John: as Bedford Co. sheriff, 73
clergy: influence of in colleges, 609–10; oppose U.S. government, 175; TJ on, 229, 341–3, 344
Clinton, DeWitt: *Circular Letter of the Literary and Philosophical Society, of New-York*, 409; identified, 348n; *An Introductory Discourse, delivered before the Literary and Philosophical Society of New-York*, 347, 348n; letter from, 409; letters to, 347–8, 456–7; and Literary and Philosophical Society of New-York, 347, 348n, 409
Clinton, George: supporters of, 104n
clocks: R. Jefferson's watch, 173, 258, 272; at Monticello, 393, 485, 486; silver watches, 393, 485; TJ's astronomical case clock, 687
Clopper, Francis C.: patent agent, 15, 135–6, 160, 249, 252
cloth. *See* textiles
clothing: buttons, 234; coats, 74, 234, 241–2, 446; corduroy, 234; cotton, 68, 185; flannel, 234; hats, 446, 449n, 570; homespun, 234, 356, 368; imported, 285; knee breeches, 234; linen, 460; manufacture of, 249, 356, 460; shoes, 234, 241–2; for slaves, 68, 158, 185, 368, 380, 570; smallclothes, 234, 241–2; stockings, 234; velvet, 234; waistcoats, 234, 241–2; wool, 174, 185, 234, 570
clover: as crop, 304, 305, 460, 520; at Poplar Forest, 69, 70, 78, 520, 611; seed, 367, 459–60, 520, 535; threshing of, 459–60, 520
coaches: mentioned, 241; stagecoaches, 232–3, 415, 416. *See also* carriages
Coahuila, Mexico (now part of Tex.): works on, 77n
coal: cost of, 591–2
coats: capes, 74; mentioned, 446; waistcoats, 234, 241–2
Cobb, Mr.: TJ purchases horse from, 174, 497n
Cobbett, William: letters of published, 450n; and War of *1812*, 254
Cochrane, Sir Alexander: British admiral, 218
Cockburn, George: British admiral, 317, 318n
Cocke, John Hartwell: and gypsum, 600; health of, 67; identified, 3:136n; letter from, 66–7; letter to, 41–2; on militia, 66–7; militia service of, 42; TJ purchases horse from, 41, 42n, 47, 66

coffee: at Monticello, xlvii–xlviii, 30–1; pots, 393, 485, 486
Coffee, John: militia service of, 222–3, 264
Coke, Sir Edward: *The First Part of the Institutes of the Lawes of England: or a Commentary upon Littleton*, 619, 620n
Colbert, Burwell (TJ's slave; b. *1783*): and change for TJ, 79; clothing for, 380; identified, 4:496n
Coles, Edward: identified, 2:225–6n; letter from, 99; as J. Madison's secretary, 99
Coles, Isaac A.: court-martial of, 317; and deer for Monticello, 521; and Highland–Indian Camp boundary dispute, 567–8; identified, 1:53–4n; letters from, 21, 521; plans to visit TJ, 21; plans visit to Washington, 521; requests plants from TJ, 21; sends plants to TJ, 21; and War of *1812*, 21
Collateral Bee-Boxes. Or, a New, Easy, and Advantageous Method of Managing Bees (S. White), 388
A Collection of Interesting, Authentic Papers, relative to the Dispute between Great Britain and America, 619, 620n
colleges. *See* schools and colleges
Columbia, S.C.: colleges in, 352–4
Columbus, Christopher: and portrait for J. Delaplaine's *Repository*, 8; portraits of, 239
Colvin, John B.: identified, 1:107n; *Laws of the United States of America, from the 4th of March, 1789, to the 4th of March, 1815*, 151, 152n, 179; letter from, 151–2; letter to, 179; and spelling of Indian tribal names, 151–2, 179
Comœdiæ (Aristophanes; ed. R. F. P. Brunck), 581
Comenius (Comenii), Johann Amos. *See* Komenský (Comenius), Jan Amos
Commentary and Review of Montesquieu's Spirit of Laws (Destutt de Tracy): J. C. Cabell on, 317; and P. S. Du Pont de Nemours, 242; TJ on, 182–3, 236, 242, 294
Condorcet, Marie Jean Antoine Nicolas de Caritat, marquis de: J. Adams on, 551, 552; *Outlines of An Historical View of the Progress of the Human Mind*, 552, 553n; on the philosophes, 551
Congress, U.S.: adjourns, 107, 129n; annual presidential messages to, 252;

cups: Jefferson Cups, 235, 237n; silver, 235, 237n, 393
currants: wine from, 82
currency: amount of in circulation, 16, 27–9, 32, 44; and change for TJ, 79; Continental, 44; exchange of, 248, 377, 382, 488, 497–9, 500, 509–10, 510, 511, 511–2, 556–7, 572; metallic, 16, 17, 27, 28, 32, 306–7; paper, 6, 16–7, 19, 27–9, 32, 35, 36n, 52, 154, 165, 167, 168, 177, 182, 259–60, 306–7, 331–2, 654–5; sent to TJ, 97, 100, 157, 180, 182, 186, 389, 477, 478n; standards for, 556–7; works on, 6
Cutbush, James: *The American Artist's Manual*, 43, 195, 196n; domestic life of, 210–1; and G. Gregory's *Dictionary of Arts and Sciences*, 210; and J. Hall's agricultural improvements, 42–3, 104, 210; health of, 210; identified, 5:633–4n; letters from, 42–3, 210–1; letter to, 104; and J. Sloan's financial reverses, 43, 104
Cuvier, Georges: identified, 6:470n; identifies mastodon, 238; *Leçons d'Anatomie Comparée*, 429

Daily Compiler and Richmond Commercial Register (Richmond newspaper): TJ subscribes to, 676n
Dallas, Alexander James: and appointments, 126–7, 129, 141; *An Exposition of the Causes and Character of the War*, 338–40, 371–2, 381, 471, 472, 576–7, 672; identified, 127n; letters from, 141, 279–80, 451; letters to, 126–7, 426–7; and purchase of TJ's library, 279–80, 426–7; as secretary of the treasury, 18n, 52, 154, 155n, 181, 426, 440, 451, 556, 557n; and TJ's letters on finance, 18, 19n, 32, 154
Dalton, Tristram: identified, 678–9n; letter from, 678–9; sends pamphlets to TJ, 678–9
Dandridge, Nathaniel West: TJ spends Christmas with, 645
Daniel (TJ's slave; b. *1790*): laborer, 185; on Poplar Forest slave lists, 61, 255
Danton, Georges Jacques: leader of French Revolution, 230, 265, 343
Darmsdatt, Joseph: and fish for TJ, 491n, 536; identified, 2:423n; letter to, 536; TJ pays, 491n, 536

Darnell, Mr. *See* Darnil, Nimrod
Darnil (Darnell; Darniel; Darnold), Nimrod: identified, 5:593n; Poplar Forest overseer, 72, 173, 185, 493n; TJ pays, 132
Darwin, Erasmus: medical theories of, 669
Davila, Enrico Caterino: *Istoria delle guerre civili di Francia*, 235, 237n
Davis, Shadrach: clerk of works, 592
Davis, Thomas: as blacksmith, 535, 536n
Davy (C. L. Bankhead's slave), 395
Davy (TJ's slave; b. *1785*): delivers letter, 158n; transports hogs, 158
Davy (TJ's slave; b. *1806*): on Poplar Forest slave lists, 62, 255
Davy, Sir Humphry: scientific theories of, 668
Dawson, Martin: and Highland–Indian Camp boundary dispute, 567–8; identified, 2:281–2n
deafness: and old age, 133
Dearborn, Henry: delivers pamphlets to TJ, 678; family of, 573; identified, 1:280n; and invasion of Canada, 357–8; letters from, 286, 573; letter to, 357–9; on New England politics, 286; plans to visit TJ, 286, 354, 358–9, 573; as secretary of war, 537; and War of *1812*, 216, 227n, 263, 286, 357–8
Dearborn, Sarah Bowdoin (James Bowdoin's widow; Henry Dearborn's third wife): identified, 5:165n; plans to visit TJ, 573; sends greetings to TJ, 286, 573; TJ invites to Monticello, 358–9
debt, public: reduction of, 111n; TJ on, 42, 108–10, 177, 242, 575
De Bue, Jacques, 558, 559, 560
De Bye, Corneille, 559, 560
Decisions Of Cases in Virginia, By the High Court of Chancery (G. Wythe), 630
Declaration of Independence: debate on, 625–6; quoted, 315n
deer: head of mounted, 238; for Monticello, 521
Defense du Paganisme par L'Empereur Julien, en Grec et en François (J. B. Boyer), 553
Defoe, Daniel: *Robinson Crusoe*, 4
Delambre, Jean Baptiste Joseph: writings of, 6
Delaplaine, Joseph: identified, 3:51n; letters from, 8–9, 388–9; letters to,

INDEX

Duane, William (*cont.*)
  Dr. Benjamin Franklin, in Philosophy, Politics, and Morals, 634
Dubos, Jean Baptiste: *Reflexions Critiques sur la Poesie et sur la Peinture*, 630
dueling, 464–5
Dufief, Nicolas Gouin: account with TJ, 435, 469n, 469, 685, 686; bookseller, 640; identified, 3:98n; letters from, 468–9, 640–1, 685–6; letters to, 435–6, 670; letter to accounted for, 670n; makes payments for TJ, 468, 469n; *A New Universal and Pronouncing Dictionary of the French and English Languages*, 469, 514, 628, 672; plans trip to Europe, 468; sends book catalogues, 435, 436n; TJ orders books from, 435–6, 468, 469, 670, 674, 685, 686; TJ pays, 469n
Dugdale, Sir William: *The Baronage of England*, 581; *Monasticon Anglicanum*, 581
Dugnani, Antonio: identified, 328n; letter to, 327–8; TJ introduces B. S. Barton to, 327
Dumouchel, Jean Baptiste: *Narrationes excerptæ ex Latinis scriptoribus servato temporum ordine dispositæ*, 482
Dumouriez, Charles François du Périer: arrests A. G. Camus, 656
Duncan, Abner Lawson: identified, 2:119n; War of *1812* service of, 295–6
Dunmore, John Murray, 4th Earl of: colonial governor of Va., 337, 644, 646n
du Pont, Victor Marie: identified, 5:200–1n; mentioned, 502
Dupont de l'Etang, Pierre: French minister of war, 138, 139n
du Pont de Nemours, Eleuthère Irénée: identified, 3:414n; mentioned, 502
Du Pont de Nemours, Françoise Robin Poivre (Pierre Samuel Du Pont de Nemours's wife): illness of, 505
Du Pont de Nemours, Pierre Samuel: on aging, 502, 504–5; on American financial system, 294; arrives in U.S., 481, 489, 501–2; B. S. Barton's acquaintance with, 325–6; on Cicero, 505; and Destutt de Tracy's commentary on Montesquieu, 242, 294; on European republics, 504; family of, 501, 502, 505; on French affairs, 688; on French Revolution, 504; future

plans, 501–2, 505; identified, 1:201–2n; letter from accounted for, 294n; letters from, 501–8, 618; letters to, 293–4, 489, 519; on marriage, 502; *Mémoire aux républiques équinoxiales*, 503, 508n; on Napoleon, 504, 505; opinion of TJ, 501, 502; plans visit to Monticello, 505, 557, 568, 569, 618, 688; proposed letter of introduction to, 322n; proposed visit with J. Madison, 557; reminiscences of, 502; on representative governments, 503; on South America, 503–4; *Sur l'éducation nationale dans les États-Unis d'Amérique*, 382, 383n, 429; TJ invites to Monticello, 519; TJ on, 490, 569
dysentery: epidemic of at Monticello, 636

East Florida: and War of *1812*, 223–4. *See also* Florida
Edgeworth, Maria: *Moral Tales for young people*, 234
Edinburgh Review, 83, 234
Edmund (TJ's slave; b. *1809*): on Poplar Forest slave lists, 62, 255
education: of Alexander I, 671; books on, 382, 383n, 550–1; bound pamphlets on, 630; classical, 111; T. Cooper on, 12–3, 447, 449n; P. S. Du Pont de Nemours on, 382, 383n, 429; effect of War of *1812* on, 111; elementary, 183; French language, 68, 512–3, 513–4, 585; T. Kosciuszko on, 344–5; Latin, 13, 513, 514; military instruction, 344–5, 388; at Monticello, 240, 585; professional, 135; religious, 7n, 12, 341–2; of TJ, 297; TJ on, 12–3, 90–4, 101, 103, 183–4, 341–2, 386n, 512–3, 513–4, 646–7; C. Wistar on, 243, 445–7. *See also* schools and colleges
education, collegiate: T. Cooper on, 12–3, 447, 449n; curriculum of, 446–7; reform of, 446–7, 449n; in rhetoric, 352–4; TJ on, 12–3, 90–4, 183; at University of Pennsylvania, 445–7, 449n
Edwin, David: engraver, 388, 389; engraving of TJ, 281
Edy (TJ's slave; b. *1787*). *See* Fossett, Édith (Edy) Hern (TJ's slave; b. *1787*)

flour: milling of, 118–9; and New England commerce, 175; from Poplar Forest, 70, 132, 186, 284, 390, 582; price of, 48, 128, 284, 323, 389–90, 477, 492, 610, 694; received as pay, 204–5, 207, 624, 625n; at Richmond, 389–90, 477, 582, 694; sale of, 69, 302, 323, 477, 491, 492, 582; shipment of, 272; transported to Richmond, 70, 157, 186, 284, 492, 624. *See also* Monticello (TJ's estate): flour from

flowers. *See* plants

Fluvanna River. *See* James River

fodder: for hogs, 71, 158; for horses, 32, 71, 109, 126, 129, 158, 163, 268n; for sheep, 71, 158

Fonson, Jean Baptiste, 558, 561

food: artichokes, 305; asparagus, 305; bacon, 184; barley, 439; beef, xlvii–xlviii, 280, 307; biscuits, 79, 97, 100, 565; bread, 613; butter, 132, 174, 184, 307; cherries, 305; eggs, 307; endive, 305; figs, 21, 305; fish, 17, 400, 491n, 536; geese, 307; herring, 536; hominy, 367–8; lettuce, 305; macaroni, 571, 572; mutton, 307; nectarines, 548; peaches, 697; peas, 69, 71, 305, 454, 516, 611; plums, 548; pork, 184–5, 307; preservation of, 697; salt, 63, 67, 68, 72, 95, 105, 109, 132, 174, 184; shad, 536; strawberries, 305; sweet potatoes, 680, 682n; tuckahoes, 232–3; turkeys, 307; turnips, 457. *See also* alcohol; coffee; corn; currants; flour; oil; rice; sugar; tea; wine

Forsyth, Benjamin: U.S. officer, 221

Fort Erie (Upper Canada), 215, 217, 259, 264, 267n

Fort George (Upper Canada), 216, 263, 357

Fort Meigs, Ohio, 227n

Fort Warburton (later Fort Washington), 153

Fossett, Edith (Edy) Hern (TJ's slave; b. *1787*): on Monticello slave list, 62n

fossils: in Ky., 448, 449n; in N.Y., 209; study of, 447–8; TJ's collection of, 447–8, 449n

Foster, Augustus John: British minister to U.S., 220–1

Foulke, Mr.: and window glass for TJ, 21, 142

Fountain Rock (Samuel Ringgold's Md. estate), 518

Fourth of July: orations, 585–6, 614, 615n, 648–50

Fowler, John: identified, 4:285n; introduces T. Smith (ca. *1792–1865*), 509; letter from, 509

Foxall Foundry, 402

France: J. Barnes on, 497–8; Berlin and Milan decrees, 107; Bourbon dynasty restored, 137–8, 151, 263, 449, 476, 477, 489, 504, 508n, 516, 518, 522, 531, 533, 552, 588, 658, 660, 684, 688; and censorship, 294; colonies returned to, 37, 38n; commerce of, 137; Constitution of *1791*, 262; Directory, 292, 331; exchange rate in, 377, 572; expeditions to Africa from, 244; freedom of the press in, 262, 267n; gardens in, 615; and Great Britain, 37, 138, 229–30, 339, 477, 483, 489, 518, 522, 588, 598, 599n; guillotine used in, 551; Louis XVIII's constitutional charter, 263, 267n, 293; manufacturing in, 37–8, 137; ministers of, 137–8, 139n; National Assembly, 262, 263; newspapers of, 449; patent rights in, 605; relations with Austria, 138; religion in, 682; rumored massacre in, 659–60; Saint Bartholomew's Day massacre, 551; seeds from, 590, 615–6, 640; W. Short on, 330–1, 557; taxes in, 137; TJ on, 110, 261–3, 382, 476–7, 482–3, 489, 490, 516, 519, 522, 580, 614, 658, 670; and U.S., 178, 477. *See also* Crawford, William Harris: U.S. minister to France; Gallatin, Albert: U.S. minister to France; Institut de France; Napoleon I, emperor of France

franking privilege: of TJ, 121, 175, 409

Franklin, Benjamin: almanac of, 457, 465n; and diplomatic colleagues, 23; and educational reform, 243, 446, 449n; inventions of, 548; *The Life of Doctor Benjamin Franklin* (M. L. Weems), 633–4, 638, 639n; meeting with R. Howe, 20; and *Pennsylvania Gazette*, 621; portraits of, 239; quoted, 446, 457, 465n; reputation of, 634; science of, 668; TJ's relationship with, 638; M. L. Weems on, 633–4; *The Works of Dr. Benjamin Franklin, in Philosophy, Politics, and Morals* (ed. W. Duane), 634

Frederic (C. L. Bankhead's slave), 395

Frederick II ("the Great"), king of Prussia: mentioned, 552, 682

Frederick Augustus, Duke of York and Albany, 240, 242n

Frederick County, Va., 693

Fredericksburg, Va.: post office at, 566

Frédérique Sophie Wilhelmine, margravine de Bayreuth: *Mémoires de Frédérique Sophie Wilhelmine de Prusse, Margrave de Bareith* (included in Book of Kings compiled by TJ; *see also* Book of Kings), 33, 240

Freeman, James: compared to TJ, 239

freemasonry: negative views of, 150

French language: dictionaries, 236, 237n, 435, 469, 514, 628, 672; letters in, from: N. G. Dufief, 468–9, 640–1, 685–6; P. S. Du Pont de Nemours, 501–5, 618; L. P. G. de Lormerie, 680–2; study of, 68, 512–3, 585; TJ on study of, 513–4; works written in, 5, 164

French Revolution: mentioned, 504, 508n; TJ on, 229–30, 262, 265, 291–2, 293; works on, 291–2, 388, 672, 673n

Frenchtown, Mich. Territory: American army captured at, 259, 263

The Fright of Astyanax (B. West), 136, 137n, 160, 195

Fromentin, Elgius: and congressional Joint Library Committee, 14

Fry, Joshua: buys lots in Westham, 171n; and Viewmont estate, 308n

Fulton, James Forrest: British officer, 221

Fulton, Robert: identified, 2:250–1n; and inland navigation, 591; and steamboats, 591; *A Treatise on the Improvement of Canal Navigation*, 388

furniture: alcove beds, 235; bookcases, xlv–xlvi, 55, 256, 272 (*illus.*), 289–90, 393, 485, 486; chairs, xlvii, 234, 393, 485, 486; chests of drawers, 393, 485, 486; desks, 485, 486; dumbwaiters, xlvii; secretaries, 393; sideboards, xlvii, 393, 485, 486; sofas, 393, 485, 486; of slaves, 71, 132, 158, 186; tables, xlvii, 256, 393, 485, 486; taxes on, 255, 256n, 256, 393, 394n, 485–6

Gabriel (TJ's slave; b. *1814*): on Poplar Forest slave lists, 62, 255

Gaelic language: writings in, 3

Gaines, Edward P.: as brigadier general, 264, 267n, 443

Galen (Greek physician), 669

Galen (ship), 684, 685n

Gallatin, Albert: identified, 1:599n; letters of introduction to, 325, 360–1, 436, 437, 478; letters to, 360–1, 436, 437, 478; mentioned, 372; negotiates convention with Great Britain, 588, 589n, 654, 655n; U.S. minister to France, 360, 361n, 361, 370, 420, 549

Galloway, Benjamin: on aging, 517; on European affairs, 517–8, 598, 599n; identified, 4:37n; letters from, 419–20, 517–8; letter to, 433; political opinions of, 419–20, 518; proposed visit to Highland, 419, 433; proposed visit to Monticello, 419, 420, 433, 517, 518; proposed visit to Washington, 420, 433; sends greetings to Monroes, 420; travels of, 517; visits Monticello, 588–9, 598

games: robin's alive, 182, 184n

gardening: books on, 388, 672; C. W. Peale on, 82. *See also* McMahon, Bernard; seeds

gardens: at Central College/University of Virginia, 87; greenhouse of C. W. Peale, 457; Jardin des Plantes, 325, 615; at Philadelphia, 615, 640. *See also* McMahon, Bernard; Thoüin, André

Gardiner, John: *The American Gardener*, 388, 672

Gardiner, John S. J.: mentioned, 343, 358, 359n

Garland, Mr.: employee of Brown & Robertson, 73

Garland, David S.: and W. Armistead's appointment, 126, 128; letter from accounted for, 127n; political career of, 128

Garland, Samuel: and TJ's debt to B. Griffin, 496

Garnett, John: European travels of, 144, 181; L. H. Girardin sends book to, 309; identified, 144n; letter from, 144–5; letter to, 181; lunar calculations, 144, 181; *Nautical Almanac and Astronomical Ephemeris*, 118, 142, 144, 145n, 181; *Tables Requisite to be used with the Nautical Ephemeris*, 660, 674n; visits Washington, 144–5

Garrett, Alexander: as Albemarle Co. clerk, 308n, 397n, 398n; and burial of child at Monticello, 612; identified, 5:567–8n

Garrett, Evelina Bolling (Alexander Garrett's second wife): and burial of

Grymes, Philip: identified, 2:270n; TJ recommends J. H. Carr to, 124, 125n
Guestier, Peter August: forwards seeds, 590, 615, 640; identified, 590n; letters from, 590, 640; letter to, 615
gunboats, 5
gypsum (plaster of paris): grinding mill for, 535, 536n; ground at TJ's mill, 610; in N.Y., 209n; at Poplar Forest, 520; price of, 610; TJ orders, 421, 600, 639

Habersham, Joseph: as postmaster general, 667
Hackley, Richard Shippey: bankruptcy of, 296n
The Hague: W. Eustis serves as U.S. minister at, 434n. *See also* The Netherlands
Hakluyt, Richard: *The Principal Navigations, Voyages, Traffiques and Discoveries of the English Nation*, 581
Halifax, Nova Scotia: rumored discharge of neutral ships from, 97, 100; TJ on prospects of capturing, 264, 292, 300, 312, 360
Hall (Hal) (TJ's slave; b. *1767*): on Poplar Forest slave lists, 60, 255
Hall, David: and *Pennsylvania Gazette*, 621
Hall, Edward: *The Union of the two noble and illustre famelies of Lancastre & Yorke*, 581, 582n
Hall, James: improved planting technique of, 42–3, 104, 210, 366–7, 369n, 457–8; visits TJ at Washington, 104
Hamilton, Alexander (*1757–1804*): relationship with TJ, 241; supporters of, 152
Hamilton, Paul (*1762–1816*): identified, 2:175–6n; secretary of the navy, 145n
Hammond, Jabez Delano: *Life and Opinions of Julius Melbourn; with sketches of the lives and characters of Thomas Jefferson, John Quincy Adams, John Randolph, and several other eminent American statesmen*, 243n
Hampton, Va.: British attack on, 218, 224
Hampton, Wade: War of *1812* service of, 263
Hanah (TJ's slave): house for, 70
Hanah (TJ's slave; b. *1770*). *See* Hannah (Hanah) (TJ's slave; b. *1770*)

Hanah (TJ's slave; b. *1796*): bed and pot for, 186; and P. Hubbard's dispute with J. A. Goodman, 173, 185; marriage of, 173, 174, 185; on Poplar Forest slave lists, 61, 255
A Hand Book for Infantry (W. Duane), 388, 672
Handbuch der allgemeinen Litterargeschichte nach Heumanns Grundriß (C. J. Bouginé), 559, 562n
Hannah (Hanah) (TJ's slave; b. *1770*): laborer, 186; on Poplar Forest slave lists, 60–1, 62, 255
Harbaugh, Leonard, 592
Hardware River (Albemarle Co.), 392, 485
Harris, Clifton: identified, 7:708–9n; loans money to TJ, 47; and TJ's taxes, 47
Harris, James: *Three Treatises . . . Concerning Art . . . Music Painting and Poetry . . . [and] Happiness*, 388
Harris, John (d. *1832*): identified, 6:482n; and Viewmont estate, 308n
Harris, Richard: purchases patent shares, 15
Harrison, Benjamin: as member of Continental Congress, 644
Harrison, George: Philadelphia naval agent, 490n
Harrison, Joseph: *The Practice of the Court of Chancery*, 388, 672
Harrison, Samuel Jordan: identified, 1:348n; letter sent to TJ through, 49; and TJ's land dispute with S. Scott, 285
Harrison, William (*1535–93*): *The First and Second volumes of Chronicles*, 581, 582n
Harrison, William Henry: identified, 1:575n; War of *1812* service of, 221, 263
Harry (boatman): carries goods from Richmond, 609
Hartford, Conn.: Federalist convention at, 111n, 134–5, 154, 163, 164n, 168, 175, 254, 264, 265, 518
Hartley, David (ca. *1705–57*): J. Adams on, 552
Harvard University: E. Everett's professorship at, 378; S. Williams's professorship at, 283
Harvie, Jacquelin: makes payment to TJ, 142
Harvie, John (*1706–67*): buys lot in Westham, 171n

Hope, Thomas (of Philadelphia): *Hope's Philadelphia Price-Current, and Commercial Record*, 307, 629, 632n
Hope's Philadelphia Price-Current, and Commercial Record (T. Hope), 307, 629, 632n
Horace: quoted by C. A. Rodney, 275, 276n; quoted by W. Short, 52; TJ quotes, 384, 386n
Horrors of Slavery: or, The American Tars in Tripoli (W. Ray), 388
Horry, Peter: *The Life of Gen. Francis Marion*, 633, 634n, 638
horses: books on, 388, 672; cost to hire, 268n; disabled, 390; fodder for, 32, 71, 109, 126, 129, 158, 163, 268n; horseshoes, 313; mentioned, 241; owned by TJ, 390, 392; at Poplar Forest, 10, 70, 71, 174, 520; price of, 307; saddlery, 233; taxes on, 256, 392; TJ purchases, 41, 42n, 47, 66, 71, 78, 79n, 174, 497n, 515n; TJ rides, 236, 639, 697; wartime treatment of, 6
Horsley, John: *Britannia Romana: or the Roman Antiquities of Britain*, 581
Hosack, David: identified, 467–8n; letter to, 467–8; *Observations on the Laws Governing the Communication of Contagious Diseases*, 467, 468n
Hosford, E. & E. (Albany firm), 470n
Houdon, Jean Antoine: bust of TJ, 40, 41n
House, William S.: midshipman, 84, 85n
household articles: artwork, 393, 485, 486; beds, 71, 186; beer jugs, 11, 12; blankets, 68, 132, 158, 186; bottles, 11, 12; candlesticks, 393, 485, 486; coffeepots, 393, 485, 486; corks, 186; cotton cards, 185; cups, 235, 393; curtains, 393, 485, 486; decanters, 393, 485, 486; eyeglasses, 74, 159, 192, 212–3, 246, 279; knives, 222; mirrors, 393, 485, 486; pipes, tobacco, 109; pots, 70–1, 186; razors, 23; sifters, 71; tablecloths, xlvii, 241; teapots, 485, 486; waiters (trays), 241; wax, 81; wool cards, 185. *See also* building materials; clocks; clothing; furniture; tools
House of Representatives, U.S.: clerical salaries in, 115; journals of, 631; number of members in, 594, 596n; and purchase of TJ's library, 26, 36; qualifications for membership in, 526,

528n; and removal of U.S. capital from Washington, 14–5n; Ways and Means Committee, 16, 32, 33n, 155n. *See also* Congress, U.S.
Howard, Thomas, 592
Howe, Richard, Earl Howe: as British admiral, 20
Howe, William: as British general, 20
Howell, Jeremiah Brown, 147
Hubbard, Cate (TJ's slave; b. *1747*): on Poplar Forest slave lists, 60, 61, 62, 255
Hubbard, Jame (TJ's slave; father of James Hubbard): hog for, 72; on Poplar Forest slave lists, 60, 255
Hubbard, Phill (TJ's slave): dispute of with J. A. Goodman, 173–4, 185; laborer, 185–6; marriage of, 173, 174, 185; on Poplar Forest slave list, 61; TJ on, 186
Hubbard, Sally (TJ's slave; b. *1797*): on Poplar Forest slave lists, 61, *255*
Hubbard, Sarah (Sally) (TJ's slave; b. *1788*): hempen bed for, 71; on Poplar Forest slave lists, 61, 62, 255
Hubens, Ignace, 559, 560
Hudson, Christopher: identified, 653n; letter to, 652–3; and Limestone survey, 392, 393n, 485; TJ lends hedge shears to, 652–3
Hughes, Wormley (TJ's slave; b. *1781*): transports TJ's horses, 390
Hull, William: American general, 215, 222, 227n, 540; and surrender of Northwest Army, 215, 219, 259, 263, 357
Humboldt, Friedrich Wilhelm Heinrich Alexander, Baron von: B. S. Barton's acquaintance with, 325–6; identified, 1:24–5n; proposed letter of introduction to, 322n
Hume, David: criticized, 328; *The History of England, from the Invasion of Julius Caesar to the Revolution in 1688*, 235, 581; political opinions of, 328–9; works of, 49, 657
Hunter's ordinary (Campbell Co.; proprietor Robert Hunter), 79
Hus (Huss), Jan (John), 551
Hutchinson, Travers & Company (Lisbon firm), 694
Hutton, Charles: *Mathematical Tables*, 674n
Hyde, Edward, 1st Earl of Clarendon. *See* Clarendon, Edward Hyde, 1st Earl of

INDEX

INDEX

JEFFERSON, THOMAS (*cont.*)
for an Answer to Governor Botetourt's Speech, 644, 645n; solicitations for, 470, 490; Statement of Albemarle County Property Subject to Federal Tax, 485–6; Statement of Bedford and Campbell County Property Subject to Federal Tax, 255–6; Statement of Bedford and Campbell County Property Subject to State Tax, 256; *A Summary View of the Rights of British America*, 175, 231; syllabus of Jesus's doctrines, 149, 212; Virginia Resolutions on Lord North's Conciliatory Proposal, 644–6

Jefferson, Thomas (TJ's nephew; Randolph Jefferson's son): letter from accounted for, 664n; and will of R. Jefferson, 661–2n, 664, 676–7
Jefferson Cups, 235, 237n
Jefferson v. Michie: and depositions, 652, 692–3. *See also* Michie, David
Jeffries, John: *A Narrative of the Two Aerial Voyages*, 388
Jenkins, Capt., 689
Jenkinson, Robert Banks, 2d Earl of Liverpool: correspondence published, 450n
Jenney (C. L. Bankhead's slave), 395
Jenny (TJ's slave; b. *1811*): on Monticello slave list, 62n
Jerry (C. L. Bankhead's slave), 395
Jervey, James: identified, 6:89n; letter from, 315–6; and Seventy-Six Association, 315
Jesse (TJ's slave; b. *1772*): on Poplar Forest slave lists, 60, 255; and purchase of flour, 69n
Jesuits: and *Acta Sanctorum* (J. de Bolland and others), 558–62
Jesus: crucifixion of, 190; doctrines of, 189–90; miracles of, 190; TJ on, 149, 189, 212
Joe (TJ's slave; b. *1806*): on Poplar Forest slave lists, 61, 255
John (TJ's slave; b. *1811*): on Poplar Forest slave lists, 62, 255
John, Prince Regent (later John VI, king of Portugal and Brazil), 503, 508n
John Adams (ship): carries packages, 36
Johnny (TJ's slave; b. *1804*): on Poplar Forest slave lists, 61, 255

Johnson, Mr. (of Germantown, Pa.), 464
Johnson, Benjamin: land transactions with, 255
Johnson, Richard Mentor: identified, 5:586n; War of *1812* service of, 263
Johnson, Samuel: criticized, 552; *A Dictionary of the English Language*, 581
Johnson, William (burgess): and P. Henry, 621
Johnson, William (waterman): carries flour to Richmond, 492; identified, 3:310n; transports goods from Richmond, 97, 100, 536, 582, 609
Johnston, George: and Stamp Act resolutions, 619, 642
Johnston, William. *See* Johnson, William (burgess)
Jones, Benjamin: identified, 4:634n; letter to, 313, 519–20; and nailrod and iron stock for TJ, 313, 380; TJ pays, 519–20, 582, 586, 625, 663
Jones, Enoch: identified, 65–6n; letter from, 65–6; requests assistance from TJ, 65
Jones, Martha Burke. *See* Eppes, Martha Burke Jones (John Wayles Eppes's second wife)
Jones, Skelton: and J. D. Burk's *History of Virginia*, 121, 140, 203; identified, 1:289n
Jones, William (*1753–1822*): as governor of Rhode Island, 444n
Jones, William (*1760–1831*): as secretary of the navy, 5, 205–6
Jones, William (ca. *1762–1831*): *An Essay on Electricity . . . with corrections and additions, by William Jones* (G. Adams), 685
Jones, William R.: engraving by, 8–9n
Jordan (TJ's slave; b. *1810*): on Monticello slave list, 62n
Joseph II, Holy Roman Emperor: and *Acta Sanctorum* (J. de Bolland and others), 560, 562n
Jouett, Charles: identified, 530n; as Indian agent, 537; letter from, 530; letter to, 536–7; seeks appointment, 530, 536–7, 537; TJ recommends, 536–7, 537; wife of, 537
Jourdan, Mr. (French winemaker), 570–1
Journal de physique, 429
Journal of a Cruize made to the Pacific Ocean (D. Porter), 672

Melish, John (*cont.*)
store of, 77n; *Travels in the United States of America*, 77n, 140; works of, 75–8
Mélon, J. B.: witnesses document, 346
A Memoir concerning . . . Various Species of Serpents (B. S. Barton), 422–3
Mémoire aux républiques équinoxiales (P. S. Du Pont de Nemours), 503, 508n
Mémoires de Frédérique Sophie Wilhelmine de Prusse, Margrave de Bareith (Frédérique Sophie Wilhelmine, margravine de Bayreuth; included in Book of Kings compiled by TJ), 33, 240. *See also* Book of Kings
Memoirs (W. Sampson), 388, 672
Memoirs of Bareuth. See Mémoires de Frédérique Sophie Wilhelmine de Prusse, Margrave de Bareith
Memoirs of the Life of David Rittenhouse (W. Barton), 469
Memoirs of the War in the Southern Department of the United States (H. Lee), 178, 179n
Memorial on the Natural, Political, and Civil State of the Province of Cohauila (M. Ramos Arizpe), 77n
mental illness: of George III, 355, 356n; phobias, 332
Mercer, John: owns manuscript of Va. laws, 418
merchants: and bills of exchange, 19, 430, 509; TJ on, 177, 178, 265, 306, 355
mercury: as medicine, 13; used in thermometers, 214, 304
merino sheep: breeding of, 311; TJ on, 311, 544; TJ raises, 234; wool of, 185, 234, 544. *See also* sheep
Metamorphoses (Ovid): J. Minellius's notes on, 670, 685
meteorological observations: by C. W. Peale, 457; by TJ, 366. *See also* weather
Meusel, Johann Georg: *Bibliotheca Historica*, 559, 562n
Mexico: M. Ramos Arizpe's work on, 77n; maps of, 77n
Michaux, François André: and American Philosophical Society, 362; foreign member of American Philosophical Society, 363n; *Histoire des arbres forestiers de l'Amerique septentrionale*, 194, 248, 363; identified, 2:681n; mentioned, 377

Michie, David: and depositions on Henderson lands, 692–3; identified, 5:140n; *Jefferson v. Michie*, 613, 627, 641, 652, 692–3; and *Peyton v. Henderson*, 692–3
Michigan Territory: and War of *1812*, 329n
military: expansion of, 66, 67n, 163, 168, 177, 178, 259, 575; glory of command, 683; in peacetime, 443, 444n; professional education for, 344–5; TJ receives books on, 672; United States Military Philosophical Society, 250; works on, 250, 251n, 388
militia: J. H. Cocke on, 66–7; F. De Masson on, 251n; organization of, 46, 67n, 165, 168, 259, 267; TJ on, 27, 31, 41–2, 177, 260, 293, 357; use of under U.S. Constitution, 442–4; of Virginia, 199n, 233; and War of *1812*, 42n, 64, 111–2, 178, 219, 220, 575
Miller, Joseph: as brewer, 34, 35, 79, 438–9, 565; citizenship of, 35; identified, 6:537n; invests in overseas trade, 79; letter from, 79; letter from accounted for, 565n; letter to, 565; sends biscuits to TJ, 79, 97, 100, 565; TJ intercedes for, 34–5
Miller, Robert (overseer): at Bear Creek plantation, 493n
Miller, William J. (overseer): at Tomahawk plantation, 493n
Milligan, Joseph: account with TJ, 660, 671–3, 674, 676, 677; assists with packing and transportation of TJ's library, 142, 287–8, 288–9, 309, 310n, 366, 369, 373–4, 376, 385, 386–8, 431, 439, 440n, 471, 474–5, 566, 629; binds books for TJ, 33, 566, 629–32, 671–3, 674, 678; carries letter for TJ, 474; and catalogue of TJ's books, 22, 33, 54, 56, 83, 106, 287, 428; and Destutt de Tracy's *Treatise on Political Economy*, 33, 83, 105, 106, 182, 266, 268n, 566, 628–9, 674; health of, 629; identified, 1:37–8n; invoices from, 472, 629–32; letters from, 22–3, 83, 142, 366, 471, 628–9, 638, 672n, 677–8, 694; letters to, 33–4, 54–5, 106, 118, 287–8, 386–8, 514, 566, 660–1, 674; List of Books Bound and To Be Bound, 629–32; mentioned, 423, 473; and sale of TJ's library to Congress, 33, 54, 56, 83, 106, 214, 270; sends books to TJ, 22, 33,

Pennsylvania, University of, 318, 319, 321, 323, 324, 327, 445–7, 449n, 564, 565n

Pennsylvania Gazette (Philadelphia newspaper), 621, 622n

Perceval, Spencer: *"The Book!" or, The Proceedings and Correspondence upon the subject of the Inquiry into the Conduct of Her Royal Highness The Princess of Wales* (included in Book of Kings compiled by TJ; *see also* Book of Kings), 33, 240

Perkins, Benjamin: store of, 79

Perkins, Hardin: as executor of R. Jefferson's will, 661–2; identified, 661n; letter to, 661–2

Perkins, Samuel G., 370, 371n

Perregaux, Laffitte & Company: and TJ's lines of credit in France, 377, 571, 579, 586–7, 589, 627, 632, 633n, 670, 673

Perry, Oliver Hazard: wins battle on Lake Erie, 259, 263

Perry, Reuben: account with, 63; identified, 2:89n; letter to, 63

Persian language: writings in, 6

Persoon, Christiaan Hendrik: *Synopsis Plantarum, seu Enchiridium Botanicum*, 284, 285n, 319, 422

Pestalozzi, Johann Heinrich: work by loaned to TJ, 429

Peter (TJ's slave; b. *1770*). *See* Hemmings, Peter (TJ's slave; b. *1770*)

Peter, Saint: painting of, 238

Peters, Richard: and J. Hall's agricultural improvements, 42

Petersburg, Va.: banks in, 19; unhealthy environment of, 609

Petit's Gap, Va.: on route to Natural Bridge, 697

Peyton, Bernard: and bottles for TJ, 12; identified, 6:51–2n

Peyton, Craven: and Henderson case, 692–3; identified, 1:415n; and lawsuit against I. R. Jefferson, 258; TJ makes payment for, 652n

Peyton v. Henderson: depositions in, 692–3

Philadelphia: *Aurora*, 435, 436n, 468, 469n; construction costs in, 86; *Democratic Press*, 5; and domestic manufactures, 284–5; French merchants in, 430; gardens in, 615, 640; *Hope's Philadelphia Price-Current and Commercial Record*, 307, 629, 632n; merchants in, 19, 430; Museum, 81, 461–2, 465n, 534, 545; newspapers in, 469, 621, 622n; printers in, 210; proposed relocation of U.S. capital to, 104; *Relf's Philadelphia Gazette*, 532, 533n; reservoir and pumping station in, 81, 82n; statehouse in, 461; steam engines in, 81, 82n; water committee of, 81, 82n

Philadelphia Society for Promoting Agriculture: members of, 42, 43n

Philip II, king of Macedon, 265

Philips, Josiah: bill of attainder against, 334–8, 483–4, 620, 643–4

Phill. *See* Hubbard, Phill (TJ's slave)

Phill (TJ's slave; *1742–1810*): on Poplar Forest slave list, 61

Phill (Phil) (TJ's slave; b. *1801*): on Poplar Forest slave lists, 61, 255

Phill (Phil) (TJ's slave; b. *1808*): on Poplar Forest slave lists, 62, 255

Philosophiæ Naturalis Principia Mathematica (I. Newton), 469

Philosophical Essays (J. Ogilvie), 352–4

philosophy: of the philosophes, 551, 552, 562

Philpotts, Oakley: and unpaid tobacco bill, 128, 157, 180

physics: books on, 429; TJ's pamphlets on bound, 629

physiology: study of, 668–9

Pictet, Marc Auguste: identified, 322–3n; letter to, 321–3; proposed immigration to U.S. of, 326, 327n; TJ introduces B. S. Barton to, 321, 326

Pike, Nicolas: *A New and Complete System of Arithmetic*, 660

Pike, Zebulon Montgomery: and War of *1812*, 263

pine trees, 194, 248

pipes, tobacco, 109

Pisa, Italy: TJ on, 326

Pitt. *See* Chatham, William Pitt, 1st Earl of

Pittsburgh, Pa.: and steamboats, 591

Pius VII, pope: and Inquisition, 490, 491n; and Napoleon, 490; TJ on, 490

The Planter's and Mariner's Medical Companion (J. Ewell), 472, 672, 673n

plants: requested from TJ, 21; sent to TJ, 21, 121. *See also* botany; seeds; *specific plant names*

plaster (plaister) of paris. *See* gypsum (plaster of paris)

Robin (Old Robin) (C. L. Bankhead's slave), 395
robin's alive (game), 182, 184n
Robinson, Daniel. *See* Robertson, Daniel
Robinson, John. *See* Robertson (Robinson), John
Robinson, John (*1704–66*): Speaker of Va. House of Burgesses, 642, 643
Robinson Crusoe (D. Defoe): "J. Vonderpuff" mentions, 4
Rochambeau, Jean Baptiste Donatien de Vimeur, comte de: memoir of American Revolution, 266
Rochon, Alexis Marie: identified, 5:302–3n; proposed letter of introduction to, 322n; sends books and pamphlets to TJ, 36, 291
Rockbridge County, Va.: assessor for, 256–7, 257, 281; letter to federal assessor for, 257; taxes in, 257
Roddy, Frederick Y.: and window glass for TJ, 21
Rodgers, John: American naval commander, 220; and D. B. Warden's removal as U.S. consul, 37
Rodgers, John, Rev.: edits *The Works of the Rev. John Witherspoon*, 626n
Rodney, Caesar Augustus: as attorney general, 275; compliments TJ, 275; furniture wrecked, 275–6; identified, 2:191n; legal career of, 275–6; as legislator, 276–7; letter from, 275–7; letter to, 354–6; plans to visit TJ, 276, 354, 358–9; and War of *1812*, 276
Rome, ancient: baths of, 402
Rosewell (J. Page's Gloucester Co. estate), 418
Ross, James: letter from accounted for, 699
Ross, Maria Sabina: War of *1812* diary of, 295–6
Roth, Charles: secretary of the French legation to U.S., 139n
Rousseau, Jean Jacques: J. Adams on, 552; praises B. Franklin, 634
Roussillon, France: wine from, 571, 572
Rumford, Benjamin Thompson, Count: proposed biography of, 283; S. Williams as patron of, 283
Rural Oeconomy: or, Essays on the Practical Parts of Husbandry (A. Young), 679n
The Rural Socrates (H. K. Hirzel), 388, 678, 679n

Rush, Benjamin: identified, 1:185–6n; TJ on, 13
Rush, Richard: as attorney general, 153; identified, 5:79n
Rush, William: identified, 4:357n; letter from, 577–8; sculpture of G. Washington by, 577–8
Russell, Jonathan: U.S. chargé at London, 542–3; writings of, 6
Russia: climate in, 6; Napoleon defeated in, 6, 531; public opinion in, 138. *See also* Alexander I, emperor of Russia
Rutledge, Edward: meets with R. Howe, 20n
Ruyter, Michiel Adriaanszoon de: Dutch admiral, 4, 7n
rye: as crop, 70; seed, 74

Sackets Harbor, N.Y.: British threat to, 18, 44
Saint Bartholomew's Day Massacre, 551
Saint Davids, Upper Canada: burned by U.S. forces, 217
Sainte Marie, Batture. *See* Batture Sainte Marie, controversy over
Sally (C. L. Bankhead's slave), 395
Sally (TJ's slave; b. *1773*). *See* Hemings, Sally (TJ's slave; b. *1773*)
Sally (Sal) (TJ's slave; b. *1777*): on Poplar Forest slave lists, 61, 62, 255
Sally (TJ's slave; b. *1788*). *See* Hubbard, Sarah (Sally) (TJ's slave; b. *1788*)
Sally (TJ's slave; b. *1797*). *See* Hubbard, Sally (TJ's slave; b. *1797*)
Sally (TJ's slave; b. *1812*). *See* Goodman, Sally (TJ's slave; b. *1812*)
Salmon, William: deputy sheriff, 256n
salt: mentioned, 109; mountain of, 5; price of, 63, 105, 109; TJ acquires, 67, 68, 72, 95, 132, 174, 184
Sampson, William: *Memoirs*, 388, 672
sand, 253n, 402
Sandy (TJ's slave; b. *1813*): on Poplar Forest slave lists, 62, 255
Sangster's (Songster's) ordinary (Fairfax Co.), 290
Sanskrit language: writings in, 3
Sarah (C. L. Bankhead's slave), 395
Sargent, Leonard: identified, 60n; letter from, 59–60; requests catalogue of TJ's books, 59–60
Sarjeant, Henry: and water-raising machine, 196n

609–10; president of, 353, 354n; rhetoric class at, 352–4
Southey, Robert: *The Life of Nelson*, 22, 23n, 671
Southwest Mountain tract (Albemarle Co.): J. Harvie pays TJ for, 96–7
Spafford, Elizabeth Clark Hewitt (Horatio G. Spafford's wife): health of, 271; reports weather conditions, 106
Spafford, Horatio Gates: collects minerals, ores, and fossils, 209; editor of *American Magazine*, 470–1, 488; family of, 271; *A Gazetteer of the State of New-York*, 209n, 416; identified, 1:106n; inventions of, 209, 211, 271, 273, 274n, 280–1 (*illus.*), 350, 367, 369n, 414–6, 463, 470, 471n, 488; letters from, 106–7, 208–9, 211, 271, 273–4, 282–3, 413–6, 470–1; letters to, 143, 280–1, 350, 488; and J. Madison, 106; and patents, 209, 271, 273, 274n, 350; proposes biography of Count Rumford, 283; requests memento from TJ, 211; and Society for the Promotion of Useful Arts in the State of New-York, 283; *Some Cursory Observations on the Ordinary Construction of Wheel-Carriages*, 209, 211, 271, 273, 280, 470, 471n; TJ regrets canceled visit of, 143; TJ sends engraving to, 281; visits Washington, 106; and War of *1812*, 271, 283; and S. Williams, 282–3; wishes to visit TJ, 106, 211
Spain: colonies of, 503, 508n; constitution of, 263, 340n; Inquisition in, 490, 491n; politics in, 138, 339, 340n, 630; TJ on, 540; and U.S., 156–7n, 339, 540; U.S. consuls to, 601. *See also* Charles IV, king of Spain; Ferdinand VII, king of Spain; Spanish language
Spanish language: grammar of, 630
Spargella, John Baptiste: and engravings for TJ, 209–10, 254; identified, 210n; letter from, 209–10; letter to, 254
Species Plantarum (K. L. Willdenow), 429, 430n
Spedding, James: and water-raising machine, 196n
Spencer (C. L. Bankhead's slave), 395
spinning jennies, 535, 605
spinning machines: of B. Allison, 547; of J. G. Baxter, 554; described, 634–5; TJ on, 535, 605

Spinoza, Baruch: writings of, 4
spotted fever. *See* typhus
springs: therapeutic, 563, 628, 688–9
Squire (R. Jefferson's slave), 257, 258, 272, 400, 636
Staël Holstein, Anne Louise Germaine Necker, baronne de: identified, 5:452–3n; H. Jackson conveys TJ's letter to, 583; letter to, 576–7; returns to France, 577
Stamp Act (*1765*): resolutions opposing, 619, 620n, 621–3, 641–2, 645n
Stamp Act Crisis: authorship of the Virginia Resolves, 619, 642; memorials and petitions in response to, 641–2, 645n, 646n; Rhode Island Resolves, 619, 621–3
Stansbury, Abraham Ogier: identified, 191n; letter from, 187–92; religious beliefs of, 187–91; and TJ's religious beliefs, 187, 190–1
Stansbury, Tobias: U.S. general, 155
State Department, U.S.: clerical salaries at, 115; clerks at, 495–6; forwards letters, 361, 363, 488, 495–6, 584, 589; papers of, 630; and patents, 408. *See also* Graham, John
State Papers and Publick Documents of the United States (J. Savage): and presidential messages to Congress, 156, 157n; sent to TJ, 156, 252
stationery: letter paper, xlv–xlvi, 514, 628, 672, 673n
The Statutes at Large (W. W. Hening): publication of, 175, 231, 330, 348–9, 398; sources for, 329–30, 348–9, 379, 398–400, 418–9, 424–5, 439–40, 474, 475n
Staunton, Va.: during Revolutionary War, 431
steamboats: for U.S. river navigation, 591
steam engine, 81, 82n
steel: eyeglass frames, 192n; tempering of, 546–7
Stephen (hired hand): as T. M. Randolph's employee, 173, 257–8, 272
Stephen (TJ's slave; b. *1794*): laborer, 185; on Poplar Forest slave lists, 61, 255
Steptoe, William: identified, 7:388n; lumber for, 695
Sterne, Laurence: *Sermons by The late Rev. Mr. Sterne*, 388
Stetson, Benjamin: purchases TJ's tobacco, 492

INDEX

War of *1812* (*cont.*)
259, 263–4; Battle of Fort George,
263, 357; Battle of Frenchtown, 259,
263; Battle of Lundy's Lane, 267n;
Battle of Queenston Heights, 219,
259, 263; Battle of the Thames, 221,
263; Battle of York, 357; British attack on Hampton, Va., 218, 224;
British blockade, 21, 32, 97, 132, 167;
British destruction in Washington,
xlv, xlvi, 5, 11, 13–4, 15, 57, 84, 94,
136, 160–1, 176, 214–5, 216, 218, 224,
226n, 259, 264, 284, 292, 300, 301,
425, 593–5; British liberate slaves
during, 317–8; call for publication justifying U.S. participation in, 94–5;
condition of troops, 233; defense of
Baltimore, 153, 154; defense of New
Orleans, 38–9, 84, 85n, 270, 295–6;
defense of Plattsburgh, N.Y., 112n,
259; defense of Washington, 153,
155n, 178, 264; W. Duane on, 99;
and economy, 109, 126, 301, 536,
544, 591–2, 654; *An Exposition of the
Causes and Character of the War* (A.
J. Dallas), 338–40, 371–2, 381, 471,
472, 576–7, 672; and Indians, 17, 112,
217, 218, 219, 221–4, 227n, 228n,
329n; and Louisiana, 38–9, 64, 295,
357; and military preparations, 105;
militia activity, 27, 31, 42n, 46, 64,
111–2, 178, 219, 220, 442–4, 575; Niagara Campaign, 44, 45n, 84, 254,
259, 264; in Norfolk, 233; opposition
to, 84, 94; orations supporting,
648–50; and peace negotiations, 5, 17,
18–9, 20, 44, 50, 75–7, 112–3, 125,
137, 138, 157, 163, 168, 186–7, 338,
380–1; O. H. Perry's victory on Lake
Erie, 259, 263; and prices, 544; *The
Pride of Britannia Humbled* (T. Branagan), 450–1; prisoners of war,
218–22; privations caused by, 425;
public opinion of, 94–5, 176–7; *A
Scriptural View of the Character,
Causes, and Ends of the Present War*
(A. McLeod), 228, 340–1, 344; W.
Short on, 51–3; J. Strachan on,
214–26; support for, 39; TJ on, 26–7,
31, 41–2, 107–9, 133, 134, 163, 176,
230–1, 241, 253–4, 259–60, 263–5,
292, 300, 303–4, 311–2, 341, 344,
348, 357, 360, 371–2, 533, 542–4,
570, 574–5, 576–7; E. Trist on, 84–5,
295–6; U.S. atrocities in Canada, 57,
214–9, 221, 222, 224–6; U.S. declaration of, 107, 215, 329n; U.S. financing
of, 19–20, 27–9, 32, 33n, 35, 36n, 46,
47, 52–3, 84, 105, 108–11, 125, 126,
154, 155n, 163, 164–6, 168, 169, 177,
254, 257, 259–60, 265, 329n; U.S.
naval victories during, 84, 85n, 177–8,
259, 263, 264, 490; and U.S. privateers, 177–8. *See also* Ghent, Treaty of
(*1814*); Hull, William; New Orleans,
Battle of
Warren, John Collins: compliments G.
Ticknor, 243
Warwick, D. W. & C. (Richmond firm):
purchases TJ's tobacco, 492
Washington (D.C.): banks in, 475, 499;
Blodget's Hotel, 445n; British destruction in, xlv, xlvi, 5, 11, 13–4, 15,
57, 84, 94, 136, 160–1, 176, 214–5,
216, 218, 224, 226n, 259, 264, 284,
285, 292, 300, 301, 593–5; *City of
Washington Gazette*, 5; commissioners
of public buildings in, 591, 592, 595,
596n; defenses of, 153, 155n; government evacuation of, 19n; McKeown
Hotel, 663; mail service to, 172; Navy
Yard, 5; newspapers in, 475; proposed
removal of U.S. capital from, 14–5,
104, 136, 313, 592, 596n; repair of
public buildings in, 313–5, 591–6; as
site for cotton manufactory, 179;
threatened by British forces, 178. *See
also* Capitol, U.S.; *National Intelligencer* (Washington newspaper)
Washington (C. L. Bankhead's slave),
395
Washington (TJ's slave; b. *1810*): on
Monticello slave list, 62n
Washington, Bushrod: and sculpture of
G. Washington, 577
Washington, George: appointments of,
599, 600n; biographies of, 672; divine
inspiration of, 405, 406; Farewell Address, 405, 408n; mentioned, 178,
296, 503; portraits of, xlvii; praised,
405; as president, 607; sculpture of,
161, 162n, 577–8
Wasp, USS (sloop), 84, 85n
watches: R. Jefferson's, 173, 258, 272;
silver, 393, 485
water: for animals, 80; filtration of, 196,
253; machine for raising of, 195–6;
mineral, 688–9; for Philadelphia, 81,
82n; quality of, 402–3, 404–5;
sources of, 457

THE PAPERS OF THOMAS JEFFERSON are composed in Monticello, a font based on the "Pica No. 1" created in the early 1800s by Binny & Ronaldson, the first successful typefounding company in America. The face is considered historically appropriate for The Papers of Thomas Jefferson because it was used extensively in American printing during the last quarter-century of Jefferson's life, and because Jefferson himself expressed cordial approval of Binny & Ronaldson types. It was revived and rechristened Monticello in the late 1940s by the Mergenthaler Linotype Company, under the direction of C. H. Griffith and in close consultation with P. J. Conkwright, specifically for the publication of the Jefferson Papers. The font suffered some losses in its first translation to digital format in the 1980s to accommodate computerized typesetting. Matthew Carter's reinterpretation in 2002 restores the spirit and style of Binny & Ronaldson's original design of two centuries earlier.

✧